# Personality Development and Psychopathology

## A DYNAMIC APPROACH

### Second Edition

NORMAN CAMERON
JOSEPH F. RYCHLAK
*Loyola University of Chicago*

*Houghton Mifflin Company*          *Boston*

Dallas    Geneva, Illinois    Hopewell, New Jersey    Palo Alto

From *The Origins of Psychoanalysis,* by Sigmund Freud. © 1954 by Basic Books, Inc., Publishers. Reprinted by permission of the publisher.

From *Collected Papers,* Vols. 1-5, by Sigmund Freud. © 1959 by Basic Books, Inc., Publishers. Reprinted by permission of the publisher.

Sigmund Freud Copyrights, The Institute of Psycho-Analysis, and The Hogarth Press Ltd for permission to quote from *The Standard Edition of the Complete Psychological Works of Sigmund Freud,* translated and edited by James Strachey.

From *The Ego and the Id* by Sigmund Freud, Translated and Edited by James Strachey, by permission of W. W. Norton & Company, Inc. Copyright © 1960 by James Strachey.

From *Introductory Lectures on Psychoanalysis,* by Sigmund Freud, Translated by James Strachey, by permission of W. W. Norton & Company, Inc. Copyright © 1966 by W. W. Norton & Company, Inc. Copyright © 1965, 1964, 1963 by James Strachey. Copyright 1920, 1935 by Edward L. Bernays.

Quotations from *Beyond the Pleasure Principle* by Sigmund Freud, Translated and Edited by James Strachey, reprinted by permission of W. W. Norton & Company, Inc. Copyright © 1961 by James Strachey.

Quotations from *Group Psychology and the Analysis of the Ego* by Sigmund Freud, Translated and Edited by James Strachey, reprinted by permission of W. W. Norton & Company, Inc. Copyright © 1959 by Sigmund Freud Copyrights Ltd. Copyright © 1959 by James Strachey. Translation & Editorial Matter copyright © 1959, 1922 by the Institute of Psycho-Analysis and Angela Richards.

Printed in the U.S.A.
Library of Congress Catalog Card Number: 84-80710
ISBN: 0-395-34387-9

ABCDEFGHIJ-MP-8987654

# Contents

*Preface*                                                                                          xi

*Preface to the First Edition*                                                                     xv

1  *Basic Terms and Issues in Psychopathology*                                                      1

Dynamic Versus Nondynamic Psychological Explanation      3
Freud as Nativist: Biological Reductionism Versus Naturalism      8
Syndromes of Psychopathology and Problems in Diagnosis      14
Diagnostic and Statistical Manual of Mental Disorders      19
Summary      25

2  *Personality Development: Infancy and Early Childhood*                                          29

Life in the Uterus      31
The Question of Infant Conditioning and Cognitive Abilities      33
Birth and the Newborn      41
Parenting: Mother and Father Roles      43
Psychoanalytical Theory of Child Development      46
The Oral Dependent Phase of the First Year      48
    *Use of Eyes, Ears, and Hands in Early Ego Development*
    *Final Intercoordination of the Perceptual System*
Lack of Functional Boundaries in Early Mental Conditioning      56
Summary of Ego Development and Dissolution of Symbiosis
    with the Mother      57
The Anal Phase of Self-Assertion and Sphincter Control      60
Autoeroticism, Narcissism, Object-Love, and Identification      63
Summary      64

3  *Personality Development: Late Childhood, Latency,
   Adolescence, and Adulthood*                                68

The Phallic Phase and Its Oedipal Conflict    69
Feminine Objections to Freudian Oedipal Theory: Horney    79
The Phase of Latency    81
The Phase of Adolescence    87
The Search for Identity: Erikson    94
Moral Development: Piaget and Kohlberg    97
Adulthood    99
Summary    101


4  *Personality, Motivation, and Defense*                    104

Personality Structure    104
    *Dualism of Mind Versus Body*
    *The Early Mental Structural Constructs: Depth Emphasis*
    *The Final Mental Structural Constructs: Dynamic Emphasis*
Motivation: The Drive Construct in Behavioral Description    111
History of Freud's Instinct Theories    115
Was Freud a Drive Reduction Theorist?    123
The Source of Freudian Dynamics    131
Defense or Dynamic Mechanisms    134
Summary    138


5  *Intrapsychic Dynamics*                                   142

Awareness and the Conscious/Unconscious Dichotomy    142
Fixation and Regression    150
The Three-Stage Compromise Model of Psychopathology    154
Anxiety Theory    158
Dreams and Dreaming    162
Summary    167


6  *Anxiety Disorders*                                       170

Neurotic Anxiety    172
Generalized Anxiety Disorder (Anxiety Neurosis)    173
Panic Disorder    178
Common Dynamics Lying Behind Anxiety Symptoms    180
Phobic Disorder (Phobic Neurosis)    185
Acrophobia: The Fear of Height    188
Claustrophobia: The Fear of Being Closed In    192
Agoraphobia: The Fear of Open Places    194
Zoöphobia: The Fear of Animal Life    196

Counterphobic Measures    198
Comparison of Anxiety and Phobic Disorders    200
Summary    201

7    *Anxiety Disorders Continued:*
     *Obsessive-Compulsive Disorders*    203

Some Background Considerations    203
Regression, Displacement, and Isolation    208
Obsessive-Compulsive Countermeasures    211
Reaction-Formation and Undoing    213
Obsessive Doubt and Rumination    220
Dynamics of Fixation and Regression in Obsessive-Compulsivity    222
DSM-III Viewpoint    228
Summary    228

8    *Somatoform Disorders*    231

Some Background Considerations    231
Somatization Disorder    233
Conversion Disorder    235
Visceral Disturbances as Conversion Disorders    242
Psychogenic Pain Disorder    246
Hypochondriasis    247
Dynamic and Developmental Background    248
    *Conversion Disorder and Behavior Organization*
    *Conversion Symptoms and Meaning*
Fixation, Regression, and Defenses in Conversion Disorders    254
Conversion Disorders and Early Childhood    255
Summary    257

9    *Dissociative Disorders*    260

Normal Dissociation    261
Abnormal Dissociation    262
Estrangement and Depersonalization    263
    *Object Estrangement*
    *Somatic Estrangement*
    *Self-Estrangement or Depersonalization*
Dreamlike Dissociative States    268
    *Sleepwalking or Somnambulism*
    *Somnambulistic Attacks (Hysterical Convulsions)*
    *Trance State (Twilight State)*
    *Psychogenic Stupor*

Massive Amnesias    274
    *Massive Amnesia Without Fugue*
    *Massive Amnesia with Fugue*
    *Dissociated Personality*
    *DSM-III Viewpoint*
Dynamic and Developmental Background    280
    *Dissociative Disorders and Conversion Disorders*
    *Fixation and Regression in Dissociative Disorders*
    *Ego-Splitting in Dissociative Disorders*
    *Defenses in Dissociative Disorders*
    *Childhood Background Factors in Dissociative Disorders*
    *Dissociative Disorders and Psychoses*
Summary    292

**10  *Dysthymic Disorder (Depressive Neurosis)*    295**

Some Background Considerations    295
Clinical Aspects of Neurotic Depressive Disorders    297
    *Precipitating Factors*
    *Onset of Neurotic Depression*
    *Clinical Course of Dysthymia*
Dynamic and Developmental Background    307
    *Neurotic Depressions and Obsessive-Compulsive Disorders*
    *Fixation and Regression in the Dysthymic Disorder*
    *Defenses in the Dysthymic Disorder*
    *Ego and Superego Regression in the Dysthymic Disorder*
    *Childhood Background in the Dysthymic Disorder*
DSM-III Viewpoint    316
Summary    316

**11  *Paranoid Disorders*    319**

Differential Diagnosis: Neurotic Versus Psychotic Symptoms    319
Reaction Sensitivity as a Predisposing Factor    321
Paranoid Disorders Characterized and Defined    322
Varieties of Paranoid Disorders    325
Persecutory Paranoid Disorders    326
    *Personality Background*
Clinical Course    330
    *Early Phases*
    *Finding a Focus: Preliminary Crystallizations*
    *Finding a Focus: The Paranoid Pseudocommunity*
Delusional Paranoid Jealousy    335
Erotic Paranoid Disorder    340
Grandiose Paranoid Disorder    341

Folie à Deux    342
Dynamic and Developmental Background    343
    *Fixation and Regression in Persecutory Paranoid Disorders*
    *Defenses in Persecutory Paranoid Disorders*
    *Ego-Superego Regression in Persecutory Paranoid Disorders*
    *Delusion Formation as Reality Reconstruction*
Childhood Background of Persecutory Paranoid Disorders    351
Summary    353


**12**    *Major Affective Disorders: Depressive Episode*    356

Some Background Considerations    356
Clinical Aspects of Psychotic Depressive Disorders    358
Depressive Delusions    360
Precipitating Factors    362
Onset of the Depression    364
Incubation Period    365
The Depression Deepens    365
Dynamic and Developmental Background    373
    *Mourning and Melancholia*
    *Fixation and Regression in Psychotic Depressions*
Personality Predilections in Major Depressive Episodes    377
Biological Predilections in Major Depressive Episodes    380
Involutional Melancholia    381
    *Biological Factors*
    *Socioeconomic Factors*
    *Personal Factors*
Childhood Background of Major Depressive Episodes    384
DSM-III Viewpoint    388
Summary    389


**13**    *Major Affective Disorders Continued:*
*Manic Episode*    392

Some Background Considerations    392
Clinical Manifestation of Manic Episodes    393
    *Manic Delusions of Grandeur*
    *Precipitating Factors*
    *Onset of Manic Episodes*
    *The Manic Reaction Deepens*
Dynamic and Developmental Background    401
    *Fixation and Regression in Manic Reactions*
    *Defenses in Manic Episodes*
    *Summary of Psychodynamics in Manic Episodes*
Bipolar Disorder: Manic-Depressive Cycles    407

DSM-III Viewpoint    409
Summary    409

## 14  *Schizophrenic Disorders*    411

Some Background Considerations    411
Varieties of Schizophrenic Disorders    418
  *Simple Type*
  *Hebephrenic Type (Disorganized Type)*
  *Catatonic Type*
  *Paranoid Type*
  *Schizoaffective Type*
Clinical Illustrations of Schizophrenic Disorders    424
Thought and Language Disturbances in Schizophrenia    433
Dynamic and Developmental Background    437
  *Fixation and Regression in Schizophrenic Disorders*
  *Defenses in Schizophrenic Disorders*
  *Ego-Superego Regression in Active Schizophrenic Disorders*
Genetic and Biological Theories of Schizophrenia    447
  *Studies of Blood Relationship*
  *Biochemical Studies*
Childhood Background of Schizophrenic Disorders    449
Summary    451

## 15  *Personality and Substance Use Disorders*    455

Personality Disorders: Some General Remarks    456
Varieties of Personality Disorders    458
  *Dramatic and Erratic Personality Disorders*
  *Anxious and Fearful Personality Disorders*
  *Eccentric and Peculiar Personality Disorders*
Factitious Disorders    473
Substance Use Disorders    475
  *Abuse Versus Dependence*
  *Puzzling Aspects of Drug Use*
  *Personality Dynamics and Drug Use*
Summary    483

## 16  *Psychosexual Disorders*    487

Homosexuality    488
The DSM-III Position on Homosexuality: Pros and Cons    489
  *Sigmund Freud and the Question of Homosexuality*
  *The Psychoanalytical Dynamics of Homosexuality*
Gender Identity Disorder: Transsexualism    503

Paraphilias    505
Psychosexual Dysfunctions    511
    *Sexual Dysfunction in the Male*
    *Sexual Dysfunction in the Female*
Summary    514


17  *Psychological Factors Affecting*
    *Physical Condition*                                    517

Emotional Stress and Bodily Illness    518
Psychosomatic Disorders as Adaptations    521
Varieties of Psychosomatic Disorder    523
    *Psychosomatic Disorders and the Gastrointestinal Tract*
    *The Respiratory System*
    *Cardiovascular Disorders on a Psychosomatic Basis*
    *Rheumatoid Arthritis*
    *The Skin*
    *Hyperthyroidism*
    *Diabetes Mellitus*
Dynamic and Developmental Background    535
    *Why Does Anyone Get a Psychosomatic Disorder?*
    *"Choice" of Organ or System*
Summary    541


18  *Organic Brain Syndromes and Mental Disorders*          545

The Organic Brain Syndromes    547
    *Delirium*
    *Dementia*
    *Amnesic Syndrome and Organic Hallucinosis*
    *Organic, Affective, Delusional, and Personality Syndromes*
    *Intoxication and Withdrawal*
Organic Mental Disorders    559
    *Psychopathology in Acute Intoxication*
    *Psychopathology in Head Injury*
    *Psychopathology in General Paresis*
    *Psychopathology in Senile and Arteriosclerotic Brain Degeneration*
Summary    571


19  *Freudian Psychoanalysis*                               574

Some Background Considerations    574
The Basic Theory of Cure in Psychoanalysis    575
    *The Role of Insight*
    *Fundamental Rule of Psychoanalysis: Free Association*

*Resistance and Transference*
*Final Theory of Cure*
*Extent and Permanence of Cure*
*Social Revision as Therapeutic*
Therapeutic Techniques    587
*Evolution of the Relationship*
*View of Therapeutic Change*
*Client Prognosis and Trial Analysis*
*Interpretation Techniques in Dreams and Parapraxes*
*Some Procedural Details*
Summary    593

20    *Biological and Behavioristic Therapies*    596

Biological Therapies    596
*Insulin Coma Therapy*
*Electroconvulsive Therapy*
*Psychosurgery*
*Pharmacological Therapy*
Behavioristic Therapies    602
*Systematic Desensitization*
*Implosive Therapy*
*Operant Conditioning as Shaping Behavior*
*The Role of Teleology in Biological and Behavioristic Therapies*
Summary    617

21    *Psychopathology and the Law*    620

Responsibility in Law and Psychiatry    621
The Insanity Defense    626
Contrasting Psychiatric Views of Punishment    633
Free Will and Freudian Psychology    635
Summary    644

*Glossary*    647

*References*    683

*Name Index*    719

*Subject Index*    729

# *Preface*

My first reading of *Personality Development and Psychopathology: A Dynamic Approach* proved to be a surprise. There was the recognizable Cameron writing style, the biosocial theoretical emphasis, the marvelous case histories, and the thoroughly insightful approach to diagnosis that had graced his earlier works. But this book was essentially Freudian! When I had sat in his classroom as an undergraduate psychology major at the University of Wisconsin in the early 1950s, Norman Cameron was definitely *not* an admirer of Freud. I had been influenced by his critical view of traditional clinical theories such as those of Freud and Jung. I can recall writing a paper for his class in which I castigated Freud in a most sophomoric fashion. I received a grade of A for that paper. Cameron was my first real hero in psychology, and I employed his concepts in my professional work as I went on to become a clinical psychologist.

Cameron's biosocial approach devolved from his teacher, Adolf Meyer. He described this view of human behavior as holistic and analytical rather than atomistic and synthetic. Cameron rejected behaviorism with its reliance on reflexes or instincts as the supposed "building blocks" of personality. He was critical of the concept of psyche as if it existed inside a somatic container to which it could be reduced, preferring to think of people as dynamic organisms, interacting with one another in a social field encompassing both common and contradictory ends. But now here he was, a full-fledged Freudian! Apparently he had been undergoing psychoanalysis at about the same time that I was attending his classes. Doubtless the intensely personal self-examination that analysis entails brought him to an appreciation of Freudian theory.

As I was making my living teaching personality, the responsibility to understand Freud's total effort also fell on my shoulders. When the Strachey translation of Freud's collected works appeared I purchased a set and undertook an in-depth study of Freud, beginning with his earliest writings and carrying on through to his last effort. I enriched this core reading with several books on

Freud's life and his personal correspondence. In time, a picture emerged that was quite in contrast to what Cameron and other professors had taught me about Freud. Indeed, it became clear to me that Freud was *not* the biological reductionist that too many people have made him out to be, and that the underlying thrust of Cameron's writings on human behavior as oriented toward ends could be seen in Freudian psychoanalysis as well.

Though Freud described people as biological organisms with instinctive demands rooted in bodily sources, the psychic energy that arose from these sources was not "used up" in the same way that physical forces are expended. Once set loose in the mind, psychic energy (that is, libido) behaved as an instrumentality enabling psychic identities (id, ego, superego) to behave intentionally. Freud was therefore fundamentally teleological in his view of human behavior, as was Cameron. In time, I came to appreciate that Freud and Cameron were both what I have called in the present volume *biological naturalists*. That is, they refused to be prejudiced by reductive strategies of explanation, took people as they found them, and gave equal weight to psychic and somatic considerations in the description of human behavior. Psychic behavior—including interpersonal behavior—was *not* seen by them as a more complex form of physical behavior. The challenge for both Freud and Cameron was to capture psychic behavior—which is always intentional or purposive—in a way that would not rob it of its uniqueness.

This desire to be true to psychic behavior became the guiding principle of my revision. I have tried to present a picture of Freud's theory of human behavior, justified by detailed reference to his work and frequently in his own words, in which the human being is presented as a purposive, intentional organism. Indeed, thanks to the multiplicity of dynamics afforded by the unconscious aspects of personality, we come to understand the human being as frequently at cross-purposes, intentionally self-deluding and self-defeating! With the rise of cognitive psychological theory in the present I believe that it is important to remove Freudian explanation from the old, drive-reduction style of description that is no longer viable. The basic framework of psychoanalysis can accommodate modern developments in psychological description, as this book now demonstrates. Cameronian explanation is also well suited to modern trends. The reader should appreciate that I felt Cameron's presence throughout the work of revision. His basic views of the psychiatric disorders have been left intact. His relaxed, discursive analyses of the case histories have gone untouched. We read along and think along with Cameron as he instructs us in understanding the complex dynamics of the patients selected for analysis.

Individual psychopathologists of course champion different theorists. I have added sections on Maslow, Horney, Erikson, and Selye. But I have not attempted to make this volume more comprehensive than it was initially. My champions are Sigmund Freud and Norman Cameron. To have attempted a more eclectic treatment would have detracted from the richness and depth of Cameron's initial effort. I did, of course, adapt the book's contents to the DSM-III system of psychiatric classification. When Cameron's views differed from DSM-III, I followed the policy of staying with his views but stating for the reader the DSM-III position and the reasons for departing from it. I added significantly to the contents on human development, substance use disorders, psychosexual disorders, psychoanalytical therapy, and behavioral approaches to therapy. I have updated the empirical research findings in all chapters of the volume. There is a completely new chapter dealing with the insanity plea in courtroom defenses, which I believe is a "first" in texts of this nature. Chapter summaries have been added, as well as a detailed glossary of theoretical terms. References have been placed alphabetically at the back of the book. I have also selected a number of pictures from Freud's life span to enrich the reader's experience.

These are all fairly routine changes. Where I have taken a bolder hand, and must take full responsibility for the consequences, is in the consistently teleological (purposive, intentional) interpretation that I have given to Freudian theory. Here is where I have added to my coauthor's efforts. I trust that he would find this consistent, thoroughly documented interpretation of Freud's theories to his liking. Looking back, from what I recall of him, I feel certain that he would. Norman Cameron was, above all, a humanistic theorist, a student of humanity in all its biological and social richness. It is a distinct honor for me to cement this posthumous partnership with him in a study of the human condition that he above all inspired me to undertake in the first place.

There are some individuals who provided me with significant help at various points along the way in this revision. I would like to thank the following colleagues for this much appreciated assistance: Patrick J. Cavanagh, Robert R. Holt, Ralph W. Hood, Jr., Adelbert H. Jenkins, and Robert V. Kail, Jr. I am grateful for helpful criticisms and suggestions from the following individuals who have reviewed the manuscript: Paul R. Abramson, University of California, Los Angeles; Hal Arkowitz, University of Arizona; Stuart Beasley, Central State University, Oklahoma; Quintin R. DeYoung, Carlsbad, California; Ernest Keen, Bucknell University; Helene Rabinovitz, New York, New York; Jerome Singer, Yale University; Abigail Stewart, Boston University; and J. Richard Woy, Brookline, Massachusetts. I would also like to thank my wife, Lenora, for once again taking on significant responsibilities in the research and editorial production of this volume.

JOSEPH F. RYCHLAK

# *Preface to*
# *the First Edition*

The purpose of this book is to present a picture of the inner life of man, as it interacts with the surroundings, as it is experienced, and as it is expressed in normal behavior and psychopathology. Man's inner life is always a significant source of action; and it arouses in other persons, through its behavioral expression, some of their most important experiences. The dynamic interplay of each person's inner life, his behavioral expressions, and the experiences he arouses in others, are the major forces that constitute society and go to form the culture in which human beings live. Comparisons with the circumstances of animal life, where the environment is much simpler and the reactions to it far less flexible, bring out sharp contrasts as well as some similarities.

The human being is equipped with a few fixed patterns of response, which are necessary for survival and for the development of a human kind of society, but his greatness lies in his incomparable plasticity. We can predict with some accuracy how an infant will behave during the first few months; but even then we have to take into consideration the life patterns of the family into which he is born. Soon prediction, excepting for a limited number of relatively simple variables, becomes inaccurate. The child is father to the man; but he lives out his infancy and childhood among persons who determine the nature of this fatherhood, who provide the influences that stress certain factors and minimize certain others. By the time a child reaches adolescence, his original patterns have been enormously affected by his human environment. Many of them are eliminated entirely. Some of them may even be reversed.

Throughout this book the importance of infancy and early childhood is strongly emphasized. This is in accordance not only with a dynamic approach, but also with the findings of all modern students of psychopathology, to say nothing of those who work with infants and children themselves. Two of the early chapters are devoted to an account of personality development in which the emphasis upon the early years is obvious. Decades of direct clinical experience have influenced this presentation—the experience of the author over a period of thirty years, and the experience of a great community of clinical and experimental workers. The product of this experience is not mere theory, any more than the product of professional experience in other behavioral sciences is.

Of particular importance is the current nationwide study of the nature of fixation and regression in patients with psychopathology as this is related to the observation and testing of normal infants and preschool children. Each of these two fields illuminates the other. The Gesell and the Piaget studies, for example, have had a constructive impact upon our understanding of abnormal behavior or experience in childhood and adolescence, in adulthood and the senium. Often it is the contrast that counts; often it is some remarkable similarity; sometimes it is practically an identity.

Any science that goes beyond a description of what can be directly seen, tasted, heard, smelled or felt, must make use of *constructs* or *intervening variables*. It must make certain assumptions about what goes on when direct observation does not account for what can be observed. Otherwise the descriptive scientist must stop with his description and go no farther. The history of advance in the so-called exact sciences has been a history of such assumptions and their ultimate verification, modification or elimination. The modern physical scientist, for example, often speaks of atoms, electrons, protons and neutrons, as though anyone could buy them in a hardware store. In psychopathology, a similar use is made of such constructs as motive, emotion and memory, of ego-systems, the id, the superego and the ego-ideal, of the unconscious, the preconscious and the conscious. In this book we shall make use of these *constructs* or *intervening variables* in much the same way that physical scientists make use of theirs. It is understood from the start that all such conceptions are provisional, that they may have to be modified or even abandoned as the objective evidence materializes.

There is no advantage in being timid about constructs and intervening variables. They are the tools of scientific logic. Without them we would be lost. It is even widely accepted nowadays in our field that what we call *external reality* is a construct rather than a "given." It is something which each person must evolve for himself, as he grows from infancy through childhood to adulthood, something which he must continually validate through his interactions with other human beings in the same culture.[1] In this book, I have repeatedly emphasized the primitive nonverbal and often illogical undercurrent of everyone's behavior and experience. I have over and over again called attention to the many similarities between neuroses and psychoses, on the one hand, and the universally familiar experiences of dreams and intoxications.

I have also called attention, over and over, to the remarkable effects of *sensory deprivation* or *perceptual isolation* in normal adults, because in many ways they duplicate psychotic experiences. This seems to me one of the major breakthroughs of contemporary psychopathology. It is especially significant be-

[1] Nash, H., "The behavioral world," *J. Psychol.*, 1959, *47*, 277–288.

cause no chemical substances are introduced into the subject, as they are in producing the so-called "model psychoses." The only factors seem to be the isolation of the subject from normal perceptual stimulation and his immobilization. The inferences which one can draw from sensory deprivation experiments are that primitive processes are normally going on all the time, during the day as well as at night, and that they can produce psychotic experiences if a person is prevented from a normal interchange with his surroundings for a prolonged period. It seems to me that it is worth pointing out this comparison between psychopathology and the experimental products of sensory deprivation in normal persons whenever the strangeness of pathological experience or behavior becomes prominent.

This book has a history of its own as well as a purpose. In 1952, John C. Whitehorn appointed a *Special Commission on Psychodynamics* whose purpose it was to prepare and publish a concise account of the psychodynamic principles which were generally accepted at that time. Dr. Whitehorn became chairman of the *Commission* and I became its reporter. The other members were Daniel Blain, Thomas French, Frieda Fromm-Reichmann, Maxwell Gitelson, Theodore Lidz, Sandor Rado and John Romano. There were others appointed to the *Commission;* but they rarely appeared and contributed little or nothing. We met several times during the ensuing year; and I worked on the material between meetings. Everything that was said during the conferences was recorded, typed up, and turned over to me for the final report.

As time went on, it became more and more obvious that we were not likely to achieve our goal. There were many dissident opinions about basic concepts among the members of the *Commission*. Our conferences seemed to result only in repetitions of the disagreements, and in an enormous amount of typed copy which I found impossible to assimilate. Eventually, when our time was nearly up, we managed to work out a report together, going over every item in the tiresome way that is characteristic of most committee meetings. In the end, no one was satisfied with the report. Dr. Fromm-Reichmann said that it had no life in it. Dr. Whitehorn called it unnecessarily wooden, and took it away to revise it. Eventually, however, the report was published essentially unchanged, excepting for a footnote by Dr. Whitehorn in which he expressed his own dissatisfaction. It was only after its publication that we all recognized how inadequate it was. We had forgotten, for example, to include a substantial account of anxiety, even though every one of us knew that anxiety is central to psychodynamics.

Soon after the report had been completed, Frederick C. Redlich invited me to come to Yale to write a fuller account of psychodynamics myself. I accepted the invitation. Unfortunately, my work has been delayed by a series of unavoidable interruptions, each involving long periods away from my manuscript, so that the final account has taken twice as long as I had anticipated. The writing has benefitted, however, by the need I experienced to think things over afresh each time I returned to my work.

At this point, a distinction must be made between a *psychodynamic approach* and *psychoanalysis*. They are not the same. Psychodynamic approaches owe their origin to psychoanalysis, but they have greater latitude. They go beyond the necessarily rigorous practice of psychoanalysis. A psychodynamic approach forms a bridge between psychology and psychoanalysis, as the growing number of dynamically oriented experimental psychologists indicates. Hilgard has recently pointed out, for example, that although Freud's theories have been largely characterized as *affective* or *conative,* they are also *cognitive.*[2] This ties them up with the contemporary trend toward cognitive as well as ontogenetic emphases.

The greatest change in my own outlook has come from a training analysis, from the extended experience of participating in clinical conferences in a dynamic setting, and from listening to my own patients with this background. Much of what my patients say, when they free associate, carries me back to the years at Johns Hopkins where therapists were given freedom to interact with their patients, and the in-patient load was limited to about eight patients for each therapist. The senior staff at Hopkins, including Adolf Meyer, showed little interest in unconscious determinants and no interest whatever in dreams. This is all the more remarkable because our psychotic and borderline-psychotic patients often expressed primitive material quite clearly, and almost all our patients mentioned their dreams. The primary interest of the staff lay in observing and reporting whatever the patients actually said and did.

The advantages of such attitudes are obvious. They fostered accurate observations and reporting. Their disadvantages are also obvious. What patients said or did was treated as though it had no deeper significance. The major emphasis was upon getting the patient symptomatically well as quickly as possible. A patient who was ready to be discharged was considered a well person. This was almost a behavioristic climate.

The trouble with a behavioristic approach in psychopathology is that it leads a person to study human beings almost as though they were computers. It emphasizes information input, it makes mechanistic assumptions about how intervening variables may achieve their immensely complex computing, and it examines the output almost as though it were the output of a machine. Such an approach ignores the inner life of man.

Everyone knows that there are all kinds of private experience going on within him, whether he includes them in what he reveals to others or not. Almost everyone realizes that private experience, often rich and complex, gives character to what a person does, to what he says and what he thinks. Private experience is now generally acknowledged as determining a person's style of life. Whether or not this can all be objectified, quantified, and expressed in measurable units constitutes a completely separate problem.[3] The experience is there all the time. At some level it is always effectual.

This book deals with normal as well as pathological behavior and experience. It focusses upon the inner life of man, with its logical and its magical processes,

[2] Hilgard, E. R., "Impulsive versus realistic thinking," *Psychol. Bull.,* 1962, *59,* 477–488.
[3] Cf. Fowler, W., "Cognitive learning in infancy and early childhood," *Psychol. Bull.,* 1962, *59,* 116–152.

because that is where things go on which are mainly responsible for what a person says and does. It also recognizes that, just as no one has a perfect body with perfect physiology, so no one has a perfect inner life. We are all so organized that we have active infantile and magical processes going on within us, at the same time that we are behaving adequately as mature adults. There is not the slightest possibility of eliminating all these irrational unconscious components; and if there were, we should lose all of our warmth, most of our ideals, and the greater part of our feeling and emotion. We would then be nothing but automatons, with receptors, internal hook-ups, and a fully predictable, measurable output. But we would not be human beings.

The theme is central to this book that we all operate simultaneously at different levels of maturity and rationality. Our learned, adaptive ways of life, and our defensive organization, keep us unaware of these immature and irrational components during most of the daytime. Recent experiments have shown that we all have periods of dreaming every night. Irrational thinking—the so-called *primary process*—appears to reign in dreams. Since everyone indulges in such lapses from realistic logical thinking, we may conclude that some irrationality is essential to mental health. There is, for example, every evidence that what appears in dreams at night has already been at least partially worked out during the day. In short, irrational and often infantile unconscious processes are normal components of everyday behavior and experience.

It is impossible to understand this peculiar split-level thinking without some knowledge of how human personality develops. If we are to ready ourselves for the strange experiences and behavior of persons who suffer from neuroses, psychoses or personality disorders, we must begin with some understanding of the way in which infants appear to develop, as they evolve from biological neonates to biosocial children, adolescents and adults. Fortunately, the past few decades have witnessed many contributions to such an understanding, coming from many different disciplines.

From the work of psychologists, sociologists and psychiatrists, it is clear today that personality development always includes processes of internalization. Infants do not behave like reflex machines. They take into themselves en masse the characteristics of their surroundings, and especially the characteristics of the people who care for them. They develop an inner life which at first seems to be indistinguishable from the realities of their bodies and the external world. Eventually, this inner life becomes a separate existence, or at least an existence which most people can separate from their experiences with their bodies and their surroundings. The inner life of man poses many contradictions for his social behavior. It is basic to the complexity of man's psychopathology, as well as to the richness of his personal experience.

This book could not have been written without long periods of freedom from other tasks, and without the opportunities to learn from living patients, in therapeutic interaction, what they were experiencing and what they had experienced early in their lives. I owe my freedom first of all to Frederick C. Redlich, who has made good the promises originally made to me. Within the past three years, I have owed a large measure of freedom also to Thomas Detre, a talented teacher and clinician, who has carried a great deal of the clinical teaching load which I had earlier accepted as part of my work at Yale. The conception and execution of the manuscript, however, have been mine alone; and I take complete responsibility for the product.

For a critical reading of the manuscript, I wish to express my gratitude to Ingeborg Gross, Ellen Mead and Inez Montgomery, who have been unsparing in their criticism and approval. Most of all I am indebted to my wife and colleague, Eugenia S. Cameron, to whom this book is dedicated. She has followed the growth of the manuscript during the past three years with deep interest and understanding. She has made many suggestions and constructive criticisms, some of which I have incorporated in the finished product. I am also grateful for the suggestions and criticisms of Dr. Leonard Carmichael, who has carefully gone over the manuscript, and to Mr. Richard N. Clark of the Houghton Mifflin Company, who has provided me with advice and encouragement. Finally, I wish to acknowledge the consistent protection from unnecessary interruptions which Mrs. Arthur Gagné has provided while I worked.

NORMAN CAMERON

*Institute of Human Relations*
*Yale University*

# 1

# *Basic Terms and Issues in Psychopathology*

There are four core terms in the title of this volume: *personality, development, psychopathology,* and *dynamic*. Before we can proceed to review the substantial chapters concerned with our subject matter it must be clear what these terms mean and why we feel it necessary to bring them together as a suitable characterization of our study. It is not always easy keeping these terms, or more properly, the meanings subsumed by these terms, separate from each other. To speak of personality is to focus on the *style* that behavior takes on. Ordinarily, we restrict the concept of personality to human beings, but it is obviously true that we also tend to see different styles of behavior in our pets, and we are even tempted to *anthropomorphize* (ascribe human characteristics to) inanimate objects, referring to our sputtering automobile as a "stubborn cuss" and the like. When we stop and consider the matter, it is obvious that in seeing different personalities among other people or other things we are bringing our *own* personalities into the picture as well. To judge others as having one style of personality or another we must make assumptions, use a precedent frame of reference, and contrast their behaviors according to standards of judgment that we our "selves" (personal identity) select and apply.

When we know people long enough, especially from infancy through adulthood, we can see changes taking place in their behavioral styles over time. Surely they change physically, as they mature, acquire secondary sex characteristics at puberty, and then move on into life on an adult basis. There are also some remarkable stabilities that we witness in their behavior. The shy and withdrawn girl rarely grows up to be an outgoing, aggressive woman. But in witnessing both biological and psychological (behavioral) changes in people over time we are dealing with what the present volume considers development. To develop is to unfold through growth, to realize potential, and to acquire different behavior patterns in relation to different life experiences. We like to think of development as taking place smoothly, and pointing always to the more positive potentials of the individual, but of course it is not always this

1

way. When we witness a person developing a behavioral style that is upsetting to his or her family members as well as to friends and even strangers, we begin to think of psychopathology.

The word *pathology* is from the Greek *pathologia,* meaning "study of the emotions." Though its meaning has been greatly expanded to include the effects of all kinds of disease processes on the person, we are thinking along traditional lines when we apply "pathology" to the word *psyche,* which devolves from the Greek term meaning "soul" or "seat of the mind." In other words, psychopathology is a study of the contributions that mental or psychological problems make to the emotional disturbances of behavior, disturbances that may be reflected in physical diseases (psychosomatic illness) or interpersonal relations. It is in this latter interpersonal or social realm that we are first made aware of psychopathology.

Children and adults with a significant degree of psychopathology make up a natural part of our everyday life. There may be someone at the supermarket who is always irritable and short-tempered. The driver of the school bus may be unreasonably permissive with the children in his or her charge but incredibly angry with any adult who happens to step on the bus. Perhaps the little boy next door is being unintentionally trained by his overanxious mother to worry as much over his health as she does. An otherwise effective elementary school teacher may be unable to tolerate the least disorder or disarrangement in the classroom or the slightest change in the curriculum. Self-control for this teacher means absolute control over external circumstances. A child may have a brother who dares not go to sleep for a long time each night because he is afraid that he might stop breathing in his sleep and never wake up again. A sister, otherwise healthy, may lose her voice and go limp whenever she is emotionally upset. In the background there may be an aunt with perpetually frayed nerves or an uncle who is always worried, complains of ulcer pains, and cannot seem to get relief anywhere. Sometimes we find whole families in which every member shows some form of psychopathology, yet none of them is incapacitated.

The impact of such maladaptive, that is, psychopathological, behavior on us is to increase our sense of the behavioral differences that people manifest. In other words, it is not always easy for us to distinguish between a personality difference and a psychopathological difference. Maybe we are being unfair to the irritable, short-tempered person at the supermarket. Maybe rather than being poorly adjusted to the demands of life, the short-tempered shopper is merely exhibiting a simple "personality difference" and no more. Why should everyone be "nice" all or even most of the time? Maybe we are just catching the person at a bad time in his or her life. It would require a longer-term knowledge encompassing developmental considerations in order to make a more just evaluation of this person's style of behavior. Doubts and questions of this type plague the student of abnormal behavior, and we shall be returning to them when we take up the matter of diagnosis later in this chapter.

On the other side of the coin, sometimes there can be no doubt that people are behaving in a psychopathological manner. All children at some time run across people who are said to be insane or "crazy." They read about them in storybooks and see them represented in comic strips and television shows. They occasionally notice someone in the street who seems confused, glances about anxiously, and talks to himself or herself. In many neighborhoods there is an adult whom the children are told to keep away from. They hear their elders discuss this person's maniacal outbursts, or the fact that he or she "talks to people who aren't there." Not a few children are reared with a mixed-up, forgetful grandmother right in the home who, because of a failing brain, calls a child by the name of some relative long dead, wanders about at night, and sometimes tries to prepare breakfast for the family at two in the morning. The average child can have only the haziest idea about the meaning of such disturbances, because his or her elders usually themselves do not understand such behavior. But there can be no doubt that such experiences touch all our lives and impress upon us the reasonable claim that at least *some* behavioral styles are not simply differences in personality to be seen across all people. Some personality organizations are definitely psychopathological. The question remaining is why are these people behaving in this manner, and to answer this we must give detailed consideration to the meaning of the fourth major term in the book title—*dynamic*.

## Dynamic Versus Nondynamic Psychological Explanation

In approaching the study of abnormal behavior we have various alternatives open to us. We can survey and hence sample from a number of different theorists, combining them in an eclectic effort to account for personality differences and psychopathological deviations. We can place our emphasis on the research literature, citing numerous studies—many of which contradict each other—in an effort if not to clarify then at least to cover the field of empirical facts for the reader. Because facts never "speak for themselves," an effort of this sort usually results in a variant form of eclecticism in which the theoretical assumptions guiding the empirical researcher's efforts are lightly touched upon as the observed data are under presentation. It is our feeling that such exhaustive efforts to cover the field eclectically can result in a sense of confusion for teacher and student alike, both of whom come away with the attitude that it is impossible to take a coherent and consistent approach to the study of psychopathological behavior.

Consistent understanding can arise only when we clearly affirm a perspective through which we intend to approach our area of study and thereby to consider the empirical facts that may be emerging in that area. In the present volume, we shall be employing a *dynamic* interpretation of human behavior, drawing on the general tradition of psychoanalysis and focusing specifically on the theoretical suggestions of Sigmund Freud. In discussing his approach to the study of personality and psychopathology Freud had this to say: "We seek not merely to describe and classify phenomena, but to understand them as signs of an interplay of forces in the mind, as a manifestation of purposeful intentions working concurrently or in mutual opposition. We are concerned with a *dynamic view* of mental phenomena" (Freud, 1915-16/1963a, p. 67). This is precisely the view of *dynamic* that we affirm in the present volume.

Note that Freud's concept of dynamic presumes that people behave as agents, that they are intentionally trying to bring about some outcome in their overt behavior. They have a purpose in mind. More correctly, they have *purposes* in mind, which result in oppositional intentions whereby one side of the mind contradicts and/or represses the other. It is in this oppositionality that we find the root source of dynamic mental maneuvers, with one side of the mind expressing a wish or *cathexis* (thesis) and the other countering it with the opposite wish or *countercathexis* (antithesis), resulting in the compromises, symbolisms, parapraxes (slips, misactions), and symptoms (syntheses) that are so familiar to the study of psychoanalysis (see Rychlak, 1981c, Chapter X).

It follows that a nondynamic explanation has no need for some basic, dialectical (oppositional) clash of intentions. In order to appreciate the difference between dynamic and nondynamic explanations of behavior it is necessary to devote a few paragraphs to the nature of causation in scientific description. Sciences like physics and medicine have been dedicated to the description of inanimate and animate structures and processes in terms of what *causes* them to come about, to exist and thereby to change in various ways, including developmental growth. But not all causes are alike. There have been four basic and distinctive meanings of the word *cause* in the history of thought. All four of these meanings were used before Aristotle came on the historical scene, but the names he gave to them have remained to modern times as descriptive tools for our understanding of literally *anything* in our experience (Aristotle, 1952, pp. 267-277). Thus, we can frame theories that emphasize the *material* cause, or the substance that presumably "makes things up" in the sense of a physical matter or a genetically transmitted cell that grows into a physical structure. Another cause of things existing or events occurring is the *efficient* cause, by which is meant the impetus that assembles, builds, moves, thrusts, signals, and so on. Efficient causes are usually what we mean today when we think of "a" cause. Causes have to bring an influence forward from an *antecedent* force or signal, thrusting or cueing a consequent "effect," as when a puff of air causes one's eye to blink or a flashing red light causes one's foot to depress the automobile brake in reflex fashion.

The third cause Aristotle named was called the *formal.* A formal cause is the pattern, shape, outline, order, plan, blueprint, and so forth, that things take on or by which they are assembled. We know that a friend of ours is walking down the street ahead of us "be[formal]-cause" of the familiar pattern of his or her gait. When we speak of personality as a style of behavior we are bringing to bear a formal-cause notion. But formal causation can be seen in the internally consistent arguments of logic or the explicit steps of a mathematical derivation or a proof. The fourth cause gets at the question of purpose and intention, because it refers to the "that [reason, purpose], for the sake of which" something may be said to exist or to take place. Aristotle called this the *final cause.* When a businessman takes a long and dangerous trip "for the sake of" turning an eventual profit, his behavior is said to follow a final-cause style of description (see Socrates' account in Plato, 1952, p. 262). It is this *end* of making a profit that the businessman seeks. The Greek word for "end" is *telos,* and hence it has developed that any theory that makes use of final-cause description is said to be a *teleology* (a study of the ends or reasons for why things exist or events take place).

Teleological or "telic" description was common in ancient scientific theory. Around the seventeenth century, however, the convention arose to avoid using final causes in the accounts of "natural" (literally, "nontelic") science. We cannot go into all of the reasons why this took place, but one of the most notorious historical reasons has to do with Galileo's unfortunate confrontation with the church authorities during the Inquisition. As one of the early scientists, Galileo thought he had found proper evidence supporting the heliocentric theory of the universe, which states that the sun is at the center of our solar system and that the earth and the other planets revolve around it. The church authorities, basing their assumption on biblical scripture, held that the geocentric theory of the universe—with the earth at the center and the sun moving around it—was the ways things "really" were. Biblical accounts are based upon the presumed (teleological) intentions of a God's plan. In effect, science was coming into conflict with religion over a matter of teleological theorizing, and Galileo was placed under arrest until he eventually withdrew his theoretical claims. The upshot was that in the rise of Newtonian science a conscious effort was made to avoid the use of final-cause description altogether. The assumption was made that in accounts of nature *no* final-cause meanings were needed and even formal-cause meanings could be "reduced to" underlying material-cause and efficient-cause meanings (see Rychlak, 1977, Chapter 1).

If we now remind ourselves that the essence of dynamic explanation encompasses intentions and purposes it is clear that a dynamic theory is literally impossible without some way of expressing the final-cause meaning—of "that [reason, purpose], for the sake of which"—*in addition to* any of the other causal meanings we may choose to use in describing behavior. We must appreciate that the causal meanings were never thought by Aristotle to be mutually exclusive categories of description. Indeed, he assumed that the more causes brought to bear in accounting for anything, the *richer* the account. In this spirit, he was not above attributing purposes and intentions even to inanimate natural products like leaves on the branches of trees or rocks as they rolled down a hill.

There is another distinction that we should introduce at this point, having to do with the "slant" any description takes on in causal usage. When we describe events according to final causes we can readily take on the slant of the item under description—as having a reason, purpose, or goal as the "that" for the sake of which it is behaving. If we say that a rock rolling down a hill and a man driving home from the office *both* behave for the sake of a purpose—intending to get down the hill or to arrive home safely—then we are essentially looking at the course of events through the conceptual understanding of the rock and the man. We are taking a first-person, *introspective* theoretical slant in framing our theory of rock and human action (Rychlak, 1981c, p. 27). The rock and the man are said to be *agents,* that is, directing causes, adding to the course of observed action as teleological organisms.

Now, if the theory of the rock and the man holds that these items are *not* behaving according to final causes and that hence they are *not* agents of the actions we see them taking, then it would in all likelihood be written in a third-person or *extraspective* style of description (ibid., p. 27). That is, we would find the theorist accounting for the actions of the rock and the man in an exclusively material- and efficient-cause fashion in which the events take place completely without intention. Early events "cause" later events to happen without self-determination by rock or man. In effect, whereas the introspective theorist is looking "with" the item under description, trying to understand events as "I," "me," or "us," the extraspective theorist is looking "at" the item under description, trying to understand events in terms of "that," "it," or "those."

Returning to our consideration of the history of science, we find that in the seventeenth century the rising natural science was based upon an extraspective, completely material- and efficient-cause style of description. Final causes were no longer to be used in descriptions of nature, where rocks surely do not intend to roll down hills. The question of a man's intention to arrive home was never taken up as a scientific one until the advent of psychoanalysis. Natural science promoted what is now called *reductionism* in descriptive accounts— that is, reducing the causal meanings from four to two in accounting for anything in nature. This is what we mean when we refer to a nondynamic or "mechanistic" account of behavior, where even the formal cause is not held to be a "basic" explanation of anything.

Thus, the form or shape of a tornado funnel that we see swirling in the sky is *itself* an effect of the underlying material and especially the efficient causes of energic thrusts that bring it about quite without intention. There is a mechanism in the "laws of nature" operating through efficient causation that regularizes and frames things into the ways that they will be. We can observe these lawful regularities extraspectively, tracing their influence on events without assuming any form of telic self-direction in strictly natural events. The mechanist believes that the scientist's duty is to trace this extraspective, completely *automatic* (nontelic) process and to avoid postulating reasons, purposes, or intentions in this process. All such teleological conceptions are held to be superfluous.

Of course, this restriction of causal usage by scientists in their formal role did not prevent them from believing in a telic basis for the creation of the universe. For example, Sir Isaac Newton believed that a deity had orchestrated the marvelous coordination to be seen in the mechanisms of heavenly bodies (Burtt, 1955, p. 290). The point of importance here was to keep one's informal beliefs separate and distinct from one's formal role as empirical (observational) scientist. Newton and other scientists also believed that they were as persons subject to natural processes in their biological make-up, but even so, capable of self-direction and personal choice. In other words, the reduction of causes in traditional scientific nature was applied *only* to the empirical description and study of inanimate objects or the strictly biological structures of animals.

This empirical attitude, most fostered by the British, was brought into the study of illness by Thomas Sydenham and others as what is today called the *medical model.* The medical model holds that all illness can be reduced to underlying microorganisms (germs) or biochemical processes having the characteristics of material and/or efficient causes. Sickness per se is not held to be intentional in the medical model. The body is made ill by unfortunate circumstances, as when a foreign substance enters the bloodstream or a genetic predisposition automatically leads to a biological deterioration of some sort (e.g., diabetes). When Freud came on the historical scene at the turn of the twentieth century he began to theorize in ways that went beyond the restriction of the medical model. We shall devote a section to this innovation later in this chapter.

There were also early scientists who were willing to view themselves as identical in every respect to the material- and efficient-cause actions of the universe. "Man the machine," a phrase taken from the writings of La Metrie, was frequently voiced in scientific circles over the eighteenth and nineteenth centuries. When the science of psychology was promulgated in the late nineteenth century and on into the early twentieth century its founders borrowed much from the British empiricists. The assumption was that if psychology was to be truly scientific it would have to be a *natural* science (see J. B. Watson, 1924, p. 8). This meant that every effort be made to *avoid telic theorizing,* and indeed, the tradition of famous psychologists like Thorndike, Watson, Tolman, Hull, Spence, and Skinner is precisely in line with the conscious avoidance of any taint of final causation in the description of human learning. Even though this behavioristic tradition—carried on today in the slightly modified "cognitive" learning theories—did not accept the biological determinism of the medical model, there was a concordance between behaviorism and the medical model in that neither line of theory employed telic description. As applied to the field of psychopathology, medical-model thinkers reduced maladaptive behavior to organic dysfunction and behavioristic-model thinkers reduced behavior to the presumed underlying "stimulus-response (S-R) laws" that supposedly operated in efficient-cause fashion to shape behavior without intentionality.

Thus, even today, we find behavioristic/cognitive psychologists debating with medical-model theorists in psychology or psychiatry over the relative contribution made by innate processes, genetically influenced styles of behavior (personality), as compared with the role of environmental manipulations such as familial training, social pressures to conform, and so forth. Though a legitimate issue is involved here, the debate masks the vast realm of fundamental agreement that these two seemingly antagonistic views have concerning the nature of human behavior. The remarkable fact remains that *neither* of these views captures quite what Freud and other analysts like Adler or Jung had to say about human behavior. When the behaviorists Dollard and Miller

(1950) published their classic work on personality and psychotherapy, they specifically tried to integrate the theories of Freud with those of Pavlov, Thorndike, and Hull (p. ix). Yet anyone who first reads Freud and then comes to this behavioristic effort to subsume psychoanalytical concepts by stimulus-response terminology must be aware of the complete distortion of the human image that is the result (see Rychlak, 1981b, pp. 519-522). Freud's introspective, dynamic image of humanity is completely lost in the translation to the extraspective, nontelic language of behaviorism.

The translation problem stems from the fact that we cannot *in principle* capture the meanings of formal and final causation in an account that relies exclusively on material and efficent causation. This is why Aristotle found it necessary to describe things by way of four causal meanings in the first place. Reductionism changes meaning. Hence, as students of human behavioral style (personality), which sometimes develops into abnormal patterns (psychopathology), we must be fully aware of our basic terminology and the resultant assumptions made in the use of such terms. In the present volume we hold that Freud was caught in a theoretical conflict. He was interested in returning to the full range of Aristotelian causal description, but he also respected and wanted to meet the reductive requirements of the medical model. In the chapters to follow it will be our intent to present Freud in a way precisely *opposite* to that of Dollard and Miller. We shall attempt to show how Freud tried with notable success to pioneer a way of describing people that combined both the biological and social influences on behavior without thereby denying the role of *agency* in the psychic processes of human beings. We begin in the next section with a consideration of Freud's complex attitudes toward reductive explanations of behavior.

## Freud as Nativist: Biological Reductionism Versus Naturalism

In a letter to C. G. Jung dated 27 January 1908, Freud complained about several medical colleagues (Bezzola, Liepmann, and Meyer) who had been criticizing psychoanalytical writings without ever having developed a psychological insight into human behavior based upon the study of dreams. He then observed of these fellow physicians: "I believe that if they were analysed it would turn out that they are still waiting for the discovery of the bacillus or protozoon of hysteria as for the messiah who must after all come some day to all true believers. When that happens a differential diagnosis from Dem. pr. [dementia praecox, i.e., schizophrenia] ought to be a simple matter, since the hysteria parasite will no doubt have only one stiff whiplike appendage, while that of Dem. pr. will regularly show two and also take a different stain. Then we shall be able to leave psychology to the poets!" (McGuire, 1974, pp. 115-116). We see reflected here the frustration that Freud and Jung must have felt in presenting their completely psychological explanations to colleagues who reasoned exclusively along the lines of the medical model. Freud and Jung were framing mental explanations of abnormality in terms of formal and final causation, whereas their medical colleagues could accept only the palpable (material-cause) "reality" of microorganisms that threw the bodily machinery out of kilter in efficient-cause fashion.

But Freud *did* aspire to a reductive explanation of mental functioning in framing his theory of the *libido*. We shall have much to say about libido theory in the chapters to follow, because it is a complex conception that even Freud and Jung could not come to agreement over, leading in some measure to their professional split (there were also personal reasons for the split [Rychlak, 1981c]). Though they feuded over the meaning of libido, neither Freud nor Jung doubted that they needed some such energic construct to explain behavior in a scientific manner. This was the style of scientific explanation during their day. They felt it was necessary to provide a sort of "background" conception, one that attempted to explain the flow of behavior in terms of energic expenditure, even though there might be *additional* factors—other causal meanings—in the explanation. Hereditary biological tendencies, as might be due to hormonal factors that predisposed a person to behave in a certain way, were also "given" factors to take into consideration in the study of behavior. Biological handicaps (e.g., birth disorders) and physical assaults through infections or injuries were also acknowledged as predisposing factors in abnormal behavior. And as for the workings of mind, both men believed that there was benefit in thinking of this as a process that utilized energies of some sort—by analogy to physical explanation if nothing else. Even so, to completely understand the *contents* (thoughts, ideas, wishes, etc.) of a human being's mind Freud and Jung believed that it was necessary to go beyond simply a laboratory study of energies forcing themselves hither and yon without purpose or intention.

Here is where Freud and Jung departed from traditional scientific explanation in their reductive attempts. Rather than viewing mental energy (libido) as capable of accounting for the *meaning* of behaviors to be seen in their patients, the fathers of psychoanalysis used such energy to justify the background workings of mind in both a motivating and an instrumental fashion. Libido is a measure of desire analogous to hunger (Freud) or a creative life principle (Jung), but the ways in which it is used by the psychic organization are *not* fixed within or limited to the concept of an energy per se. Hence, the *patternings* of behavior into meaning (formal-cause conception) are not blindly impelled by the force of libido alone (efficient-cause conception). Libido is an estimate of diffuse motivation or arousal, but the *major* dynamics in personality stem from *psychic identities* or *psychic agents* (id, ego, superego) with purposeful intentions "in mind" that are being put into effect or counteracted *willfully*. Thus, libido is always expended in an instrumental manner to achieve entirely teleological ends (intentions, purposes) (see Chapter 4, p. 127). A psychoanalytical account of the psyche is incomplete without consideration of such telic factors because the instrumental *means* (libido expenditure) never captures the *ends* being sought or the style manifested in achieving such ends.

Even so, Freud's commitment to energic explanations as quasi reductions cannot be denied. This commitment stemmed from his education and early associations in medicine. Freud's beloved professor of physiology, Ernst Brücke, had in his youth formed a pact with colleagues like Hermann von Helmholtz to "fight vitalism" in the description of organic functioning (Boring, 1950, p. 708). *Vitalism* in physiology referred to the Galenic view that living organisms were energized by unobservable forces (*pneumata* or spirits) that mixed with the ebb and flow of blood to stimulate life and nourish the body. As such, these forces could not be studied directly through scientific means and were more helpful conceptions to religion than to medicine. We see here the classic confrontation of a religious teleology and a scientific nonteleology, for what Brücke was to rely on in his future scientific work was the so-called *principle of constancy*. This principle was introduced by Julius Robert Mayer but was greatly popularized as the conservation-of-energy principle by Brücke's fellow pact member, Helmholtz.

The principle of constancy holds that in any isolated (or closed) system, the sum of physical forces at play remains constant—that is, seeks a uniform level of distribution—so that if there is a mobilization of forces at one point there is an immediate and automatic mechanism brought into play that reduces this disparity in pressure points and re-establishes the balance. Helmholtz's refinement was to say that mobilized energy points may be found in such items as wood or coal, which when burned release "so much" heat to boil "so much" water to release "so much" steam to drive a locomotive down the track for precisely "so far," and so on. In a completely closed system the level of potential energy would remain constant, though it can change its *form* of organization (from wood to heat to steam to locomotion). This change in form may appear directed, giving the impression that events are heading intentionally toward some end, but this is merely an illusion based upon an unscientific assessment of what is taking place. The forces of nature are neither divinely inspired (vitalism) nor uniquely directed by the person behaving in this or that way. These forces move blindly along, based upon relative pressure points in the total distribution of energy (efficient causes) or potential energy ("matter" or material causes).

Freud was thoroughly schooled in how to describe events according to the constancy principle. It is clear that he and Josef Breuer, his first collaborator, made use of this concept in their account of how ideas can be "worn away" or mentally dissipated (*abreacted*) along the lines of an energic redistribution (Breuer & Freud, 1955, p. 10). Freud also made use of a constancy explanation as "neuronic inertia" in his unfinished work, the *Project for a Scientific Psychology*. This work was prompted by his close friend and early supporter, Wilhelm Fliess (see Chapter 16 for a more detailed discussion of Freud's relationship with Fliess). Fliess was a physician, a biological reductionist in the true sense of the word, attributing neurotic symptoms to the malfunctions of a kind of biological clock in the bodies of human beings. That is, Fliess's theory held that both men and women behaved according to the physiological influences of *periodic cycles,* which were material- and efficient-cause mechanisms in the body that regulated personal adjustment. If these cycles went out of synchronization, so to speak, the person would suffer in emotional adjustment.

In September 1895, after spending a few days with Fliess in scientific discussion, Freud was inspired to begin work on a completely reductionistic, truly biological explanation of human behavior. By October 1895 he had completed and sent off to Fliess three parts of this projected book. But by November 1895 he wrote to Fliess to say that he was unable to carry the work further and that as a matter of fact he no longer understood the state of mind that prompted him to begin the *Project* in the first place (Freud, 1954, p. 134).

The very first paragraph of the *Project* gives us an impression of Freud's state of mind as he undertook the Fliess-inspired manuscript. Freud wrote: "The intention [of the *Project*] is to furnish a psychology that shall be a natural science: that is, to represent psychical processes as quantitatively determinate states of specifiable material particles, thus making those processes perspicuous and free from contradiction. Two principal ideas are involved: (1) What distinguishes activity from rest is to be regarded as $Q$, subject to the general laws of motion [efficient causation]. (2) The neurones are to be taken as the material particles [material causation]" (Freud, 1895/1966d, p. 295). It seems clear that Freud was sincerely trying to write a strictly biological, reductive explanation of mind. There are scholars who believe that this was his basic interest throughout his career (see, e.g., Sulloway, 1979). It is pointed out by these scholars that some of Freud's basic constructs appear in the *Project* as clearly physical conceptions. For example, *cathexis* is described as occurring when a nerve cell (neuron) is filled or charged with a certain level of $Q$, whereas at other times it will be empty and thus lack a cathexis.

It seems likely that Freud was thinking of $Q$ as electricity, flowing according to neuronic inertia, which is to say that the energy flowed along "automatically." To account for the fact that a collection of neurons might retain this cathected charge rather than allow it to continue flowing, Freud (1895/1966d) postulated a special type of neuron, one that could *resist* expenditure and allow the person to frame a sense of *personal identity* (p. 323). This emphasis on the identity of the person was central to Freud's introspective style of theorizing, even when he was trying to write a conventional natural science. He was always striving to capture the outlook of the person qua identity, to see life through the conceptual eyes of the individual maneuvering within external reality "for the sake of" wishes, fantasies, and the like.

Traditional natural science had no need of identities, for what moves events is not the selection or intention of an identity but the underlying flow of energic forces. Yet Freud quickly had the ego directing the course of further cathexes in a willful manner. A typical excerpt from the *Project* revealing Freud's penchant for such teleological description is as follows: "The education and development of . . . [the] ego takes place in a repetitive state of craving, in *expectation*. It learns first that it must not cathect the motor images, so that discharge results, until certain conditions have been fulfilled from the direction of the perception. It learns further that it must not cathect the wishful idea beyond a certain amount since otherwise it would deceive itself in a hallucinatory manner. If, however, it respects these two barriers and directs its attention to the new perceptions, it has a prospect of attaining the satisfaction it is seeking" (ibid., p. 369).

Freud was obviously striving to find a way of talking about people as agents of their behavior even as he was trying to meet Fliess's urgings to write a "natural" science in the best traditions of the constancy principle. That Freud was unable to complete this task, that he burned his own copy of the work, and that when years later Fliess's draft of the manuscript surfaced Freud tried to have it destroyed are ample testimony to the fact that Freud's heart was just not in this style of description. In postulating an identity within mind Freud was taking an energy conception that was framed in the third-person *extraspective* theories of natural science as material/efficient causation and applying it instrumentally by an ego-identity—that is, an introspectively framed theoretical conception—which holds it back or aims it according to what he said were "purposeful or wishful" maneuvers in thought (ibid., p. 374). Years later (February 1912), when Jung and Freud were feuding (see Chapter 16), we again find Freud saying, "I took myself in hand and quickly turned off my excess libido [in relation to corresponding with Jung]" (McGuire, 1974, p. 488). He also wrote regretfully to Jung, "It would be a severe blow to all of us if you were to draw the libido you require for your work from the [Psycho-Analytical] Association [of which Jung was then president]" (ibid.).

In light of such formal and informal allusions to willful manipulation of libido it is difficult to see how Freud can be characterized as a traditional biological (natural-science) reductionist, trying to find the causes of events totally outside of (final-cause) intentionality. Though he was to return to work on the *Project* after 1895, he also complained to Fliess on several occasions that he could not make sense of the neuroses based solely on the presumptions of an underlying physical-chemical (material/efficient-cause) substrate (Freud, 1954, p. 247).

How then are we to understand Freud? Is there a way of thinking about his theoretical outlook that will help us to grasp what he was trying to accomplish without losing its essentials in the confusing terminology that has been proposed in the rise of natural science? We would like to suggest that Freudian theory can be categorized in a way that gives full credit to the biological basis of behavior without resorting to a reductionism. We must first appreciate that there is a fundamental difference in theories of behavior along the schism of *nativism* versus *environmentalism*.

A nativistic theory is one in which the theorist presumes that there are certain fundamental, *innate* processes and propensities that the organism brings to life and that, *beginning from birth* (or possibly *in utero*), carry forward in some way to influence the organism's learning and behavioral actions. These innate capacities are not themselves learned, but make human learning possible. Indeed, the nativistic theorist may contend that these innate processes make learning unnecessary.

Opposed to nativism, we find the theory of *environmentalism*. The environmentalistic theorist holds that though nature provides the organism with certain crude capacities to behave, these capacities are developed and perfected only because of environmental stimulations and shapings. The latter manipulations are construed extraspectively, in efficient-cause fashion. According to the environmentalist, most of the innate capacities that the nativist attributes to the organism as "given" from birth are actually learned through environmental manipulations and shapings. The father of behaviorism, John B. Watson (1924), reflected an environmentalist position when he said, "*Let us try to think of man as an assembled organic machine ready to run*" (p. 216). Nature made the machine, but what the machine now "becomes" as to a personality is up to the stimulus-response habits that Watson claimed he could manipulate environmentally regardless of the person's heredity or self-selected intentions (ibid., p. 82). As the equally eminent behaviorist B. F. Skinner (1971) said in discussing the causes of behavioral problems such as alcoholism and juvenile delinquency, "It is the environment which is 'responsible' for the objectionable behavior, and it is the environment, not some [nativistic] attribute of the individual, which must be changed" (p. 74).

Looking now more closely at nativistic theories, we can delineate two forms of this position. There is first *biological reductionism*, which holds that the only kind of influence to be seen in behavior is of a material- and efficient-cause variety. All behavior must be understood as due to hereditary forces that make the person what he or she "is" regardless of environmental conditions. We delude ourselves when we think that sociocultural or personality styles have a life of their own. Sociocultural and personality styles are the "effects" of underlying material/efficient causation. A prime example of biological reductionism is Fliess's theory of the *periodic cycles* (see above, p. 10; see also Chapter 3, p. 74). As a biological clock, the person is moved along in good or poor adjustment regardless of what sort of psychodynamics may be active in his or her unique life circumstances. The traditional medical model of Sydenham (see above, p. 7) is also an example of biological reductionism, although in recent times a modification has been taking place in the medical profession to admit of other factors in the explanation of physical illness.

The second form of nativism is *biological naturalism*, which attempts to base explanations on what the organism is biologically, physiologically, and anatomically equipped to do "by nature," without foreclosing on the style of causation to be used in capturing this organismic potential. In other words, the biological naturalist no longer accepts the seventeenth-century prohibitions of natural science. If it seems plausible and consistent with empirical scientific evidence, the biological naturalist is prepared to hypothesize and explain things in terms of formal and final causation. If the human being is indeed an "assembled organic machine ready to run," then is it not possible that the way in which he or she "runs" encompasses teleology (purpose, intention, agency, etc.)? Why must we reduce such explanations to presumed underlying material and efficient causes? Let us focus on the person as we find him or her from birth, proposing theories that further our understanding without limiting bias.

This is how the biological naturalist reasons, lending thereby greater credence to the possible role of the person as an agent of behavior than does the environmentalist. In the environmentalistic viewpoint the person is invariably a manipulated object or process. The naturalist may believe that thanks to certain innate capacities the person is less the manipulated than the manipulator of his or her ongoing life experiences. Unlike the reductionist, the naturalist is willing to assign dynamic qualities to this manipulation of the personal milieu within which a life is being enacted. It is our belief that Sigmund Freud was fundamentally a biological naturalist, even though he did try to meet the canons of biological reductionism (e.g., the constancy principle) in his libido theory. He also acknowledged that certain aspects of human behavior could be attributed to environmental influences, a theme that later psychoanalysts like Karen Horney (see p. 79) and Erik Erikson (see p. 94) were to enlarge upon.

To be more correct, we should look at the distinctions between reductionism, naturalism, and environmentalism as theoretical emphases rather than as either/or approaches to the description of behavior. These are alternative assumptions (premises, models, paradigms, etc.) that any theorist is forced to make in the description of behavior. John Watson's naturalism held that the human being is a nontelic machine. Watson's biological reductionism can be found in his description of the reflex arc and physical drives (see Chapter 4), in which the tissues (material causes) of the body conveyed nervous impulses (efficient causes) and organic satisfactions followed to direct or "run" this machine automatically. But the fundamental emphasis of behaviorism is that the originating source of control and direction is extraindividual and extrabiological, in the environment within which the organism is being shaped (see Chapter 20). We shall in later chapters have occasion to enlarge upon Freud's basic naturalism, as well as the corollary themes in psychoanalysis of biological reductionism and environmental influence.

## Syndromes of Psychopathology and Problems in Diagnosis

Just as normal behavior takes on various styles or personalities, so too does psychopathological behavior take on various styles, which we call *syndromes*. The term *syndrome* comes from the medical model, in which it refers to a "patterned collection of symptoms." Diseases like measles or diabetes have their own unique symptom picture or syndrome. The assumption of the medical model is that if one can accurately diagnose a specific disease syndrome then one can treat the person concerned for the specific malfunction. One does not apply the same therapeutic measures to a diabetic patient that one applies to a patient with measles. However, the diagnosis of psychopathological conditions is not so clear-cut. Though behaviors do seem to fall into psychopathological syndromes, there is usually no specific therapy to be applied to a specific disorder. The same general therapeutic techniques are used for many different behavioral disorders (see Chapters 19 and 20), all of which suggests that drawing a direct parallel between biological and psychopathological disturbances is probably unwarranted.

That is, we know that certain hereditary forms of brain damage (Down syndrome, etc.) and central nervous system infections (paresis, etc.) can have adverse effects on a person's behavioral pattern. But, as Freud lamented concerning his colleagues (see p. 8), to assume that such determinants are the *only* type possible is unwarranted. This debate over the use of medical-model assumptions in psychiatry and psychology has a long history, and we shall not be able to resolve it in the present volume. We have taken Freud's position on the matter, hoping to give equal emphasis to biological and social factors in the behavior of people. The present volume has a *biosocial* emphasis. Also in line with Freud, we fail to see a *qualitative* distinction between normal and abnormal behavior. Our view holds that this is a *quantitative* distinction, meaning that the personality styles of people whom we consider normal are basically the same as those we consider abnormal. Although all people face various adjustment problems, in a person judged to be abnormal these difficulties are considerably more evident in his or her personality style—leading to a diagnosis of some form of psychopathological syndrome.

A few words should be said about what we take to be normal behavior. In the chapters that follow, we shall use three criteria in distinguishing normal from pathological personality functioning. The first criterion is *cultural expectations*. Everyone lives in the presence of cultural expectations. They are internalized from infancy on by way of introjections and identifications, to help construct the ego and superego and to prepare a person for his or her social interactions as a child, as an adolescent, and as an adult. We do not think of this as simply "conformity," of course, because sometimes a person who fails to conform and thereby stands against his or her culture on some issue is advancing the culture in the long run. In recent times we have witnessed civil disobedience through demonstrations and sit-ins by groups of people representing culturally impoverished minorities. We would not wish to call this behavior psychopathological.

Our second criterion is *adequacy of performance* in comparing a person's current level of adequacy with what he or she attained previously, as well as judged against cultural norms in the society for persons of the same sex, age, and social background. Is the person adequately satisfying needs that are essential to human existence, including physiological and social gratifications? We recognize in drawing such comparisons that it is always necessary to have a standard reference point against which to judge the behavior of any one person. There are those in psychiatry (Szasz, 1967) and psychology (Sarbin & Mancuso, 1980) who claim that mental illness is a myth and that by diagnosing the behavior of others as being schizophrenic and the like we are leveling a *moral* judgment, punishing and repressing people who are not so much "sick" as simply "different" in behavioral style.

There is merit to these criticisms of the evaluative process known as *diagnosis*. It is absolutely necessary for the diagnostician to be careful in determining the grounds according to which he or she will render a judgment of abnormality. Even as we look to cultural expectations for our grounding standard of comparison we must be selective and know precisely why we are employing the grounds that we bring to bear. Thus, a person's religious beliefs, dressing habits, and food preferences are to be given less emphasis as grounding diagnostic considerations than the fact that he or she may walk about in a confused state, shout loudly on a street corner in a rambling, incoherent manner, and express a sense of terror over threats from extraterrestrial beings who cannot be identified.

This latter factor, of being personally upset by "people who aren't there," points to the final criterion of normality that we shall employ. Thus, in line with our commitment to psychodynamics, we shall add a criterion of the *internal integrative functions* that manifest themselves introspectively in the personality across levels of consciousness, preconsciousness, and unconsciousness. This internal integration includes the ways in which a person's unique personality organization bears upon personal assessments of his or her body, level of self-acceptance, and sense of well-being in the real and imagined world of other human beings. By adding this third criterion we are not only recognizing the expressed dissatisfactions that people make concerning their lot in life, but we are also accepting the likelihood that some people "look" better adjusted than they are. It is possible to meet the cultural expectations of a society, to perform adequately within its specifications, even to excel at life challenges like a job or forming social contacts, and still to have an impoverished inner life, a sense of frustration, and feelings of being unloved and alone. Sometimes after years of relatively good adjustment a problem surfaces in midlife as a "crisis" in personal identity, in which though nothing dramatic has occurred the person begins to question his or her past choices of marital partner, career, and value system in general (Jaques, 1965).

Classical psychiatric diagnosis is usually traced to the scheme devised by the German neuropsychiatrist Emile Kraepelin (1856-1926). In 1883 Kraepelin took a number of clinical syndromes that had been identified and named by others and, combining these with his own observations, proposed a scheme or *nosology* that has survived in general outline to recent years. Kraepelin modified and perfected his diagnostic scheme several times over the course of his medical career, but he always drew a fundamental distinction between psychoneuroses and psychoses. Kraepelin was biologically oriented in his theories of abnormality, and hence he would have viewed this distinction as a qualitative one. We can, however, align in quantitative degrees of disturbance a dimension of from "normal" behavior on the one extreme through psychoneurotic or "neurotic" disturbances in the middle ranges to "psychotic" behavior at the other extreme. Thus, in traditional diagnostic terminology a neurosis is a decided form of maladjustment but not to the extent of distorting reality through *delusions* (false beliefs) and *hallucinations* (sensory phenomena with no basis in reality), as is typical of psychotic individuals.

Within the neurotic disorders a series of subsyndromes was to be worked and reworked by succeeding generations of diagnosticians, including *hysteria* (malfunctioning sensory or motor processes, dual or multiple personalities, etc.), *hypochondria* (imagined physical illness), *obsessive-compulsivity* (uncontrolled thoughts or actions), *neurasthenia* (extreme fatigue), *anxiety* (apprehensiveness, phobia, etc.), and *depressive reactions* (severe dejection, guilt, etc.). Within the psychotic disorders there were two major branches: (1) the *schizophrenic disorders* (Kraepelin's actual term was *dementia praecox*), falling into four distinctive syndromes as follows: *simple* (distracted, blunted affect, asocial tendencies), *paranoid* (suspiciousness, delusions of persecution, hostility), *catatonic* (rigid and mute, or highly excited and assaultive), and *hebephrenic* ("silly," most bizarre and deteriorated in personality of all subgroups); and (2) the *manic-depressive disorder,* in which a person was either extremely excited and expansive (manic) or extremely retarded emotionally, sorrowful and prone to suicide (depressive), or both.

These classical distinctions were to provide the backbone of psychiatric diagnosis for the greater part of the twentieth century. However, difficulties have plagued psychiatric diagnosis, resulting in repeated calls for the abolishment of the practice altogether (Rogers, 1951; Kanfer & Saslow, 1969). What are some of these problems? A major difficulty stems from the apparent unreliability of the diagnostic process. Studies on the agreement achieved by independent psychiatric diagnosticians of the *same* case have been shown to run in the 50 percent range, particularly for the traditional psychotic/neurotic syndromes presented above (Beck et al., 1962; Spitzer & Fliess, 1974). It is not too difficult agreeing on diagnoses of alcoholism, mental retardation, or organic brain diseases. But the more psychodynamic or *functional* (clearly nonorganic) disorders are quite difficult to agree on.

In a study contrasting national differences in diagnostic practice during a certain period in recent history it was found that New York psychiatrists were much more likely to assign the diagnosis of schizophrenia than were psychiatrists in London (Professional Staff of the U.S.-U.K. Cross-National Project, 1974). Diagnostic biases of a regional nature within the United States exist: it was once found that a diagnosis of manic-depressive disorder was far more likely to be given in Vermont than in North Dakota (Chapman & Chapman, 1973). Similar disparities exist across social-class levels throughout the United States, where it has been found that a hospitalized patient lower in socioeconomic status is more likely to be diagnosed a schizophrenic than a patient who enjoys higher socioeconomic status (Hollingshead & Redlich, 1958). It seems clear that in selecting their grounds for evaluation, diagnosticians have often been unsure of what they should be holding to in common, and as a result they may have allowed irrelevant biases to creep into their evaluative process.

Along with such problems of reliability, critics have pointed to the lack of uniformity to be found among patients all carrying the same diagnosis (Zigler & Phillips, 1961). Patients with quite different personality styles carried identical diagnoses, and there was no consistent relationship to be seen between the behavioral style of a patient and the diagnosis he or she carried. It has also been possible to feign abnormal behavior and obtain a diagnosis of "psychosis" by acting perfectly normal but complaining of the single symptom of "hearing voices" (Rosenhan, 1973). Apparently, in the absence of organic signs or evidence of drug ingestion, these diagnosticians routinely equated "hallucinations" with "psychosis" (usually of a schizophrenic variety). Obviously, as a *syndrome* of disorder psychosis should never be diagnosed on the basis of a *single* symptom, serious though it may appear in and of itself.

As it has been demonstrated that people who are labeled mentally ill have serious problems in being socially accepted by others following their release from the hospital (Lamy, 1966), it is extremely important that diagnosticians be conservative in assigning such labels—especially the more severe labels—to human beings in search of help. The final major argument against diagnosis has already been mentioned above—that is, the diagnostic label applied to a person's disorder often makes little or no difference to the therapy received. If diagnosis is the first step on the road to cure, then it should be tied specifically to a method of curing that "specific" illness (Kanfer & Phillips, 1970).

Given all these shortcomings in the diagnostic process, does it follow that we should dispense with it in psychiatric and psychological practice? This seems a drastic alternative, particularly because it is generally admitted that in broad outline the behaviors witnessed as neurotic and psychotic syndromes *do* recur in human behavior. Doubtless any scheme of typologizing people would suffer from some of the same problems that we see arising in psychiatric diagnosis. If we were to work out a scheme for "diagnosing" Freudian personality types of oral, anal, urethral, and so forth, we would need to examine carefully the grounds on which we make our assignments to one style of behavior or another. Once again, values are basic to this process, and if we did not frame a clear set of principles, based essentially on a professional value system of what we take to be anal-like activities versus oral-like activities, we would run afoul of the very same problems witnessed in the diagnosis of psychopathology.

It seems likely that the reason psychiatric diagnosis persists is that, in spite of its weaknesses, the men and women who work in the helping professions require a common notation system so that they can communicate however awkwardly about their field of common interest. People continue to enact syndromes of disturbance, so that even though there are differences in specific personality there is also an overlay of common symptoms. One person's delusion is far different from another's, but both individuals *do* frame distortions of reality that the term *delusion* properly captures. People do take on obsessive tendencies, with an aggressive personality feeling compelled to think about certain curse words from moment to moment and a passive personality rehearsing a silly phrase designed to ward off some imagined disaster. The level of abstraction at which psychiatric diagnosis is brought to bear may not reflect a one-to-one relationship to the underlying personality style, but there is still a commonality worthy of classification. The theoretical explanation of why such disorders arise may also differ, with resultant therapeutic efforts essentially unrelated to the diagnosis per se. But this does not mean that there is no basis for the syndrome classification chosen in the first place.

We also must not overlook the fact that there are legal requirements of which those in the helping professions must be cognizant in their regular duties.

Hospitals are legally required to keep accurate records of their patients. Insanity continues to be grounds for judgments of "not guilty" in legal cases, and whether we call the qualitative dimension "sane/insane" or "normal/ neurotic-psychotic" the same issues arise. By perfecting the grounding criteria for the sake of which we render diagnostic interpretations, we hope to be able to rectify the injustices of the past. Through public instruction we can help remove the stigma of psychiatric terminology. Suffering through a neurotic episode or having to manage a lifelong tendency to depression must be viewed as no different from suffering through a stroke or having to put up with hypertension for the rest of one's life. We can hardly allow uninformed social stereotyping and prejudice to set the approach we take to the study of psychopathology. By improving our classification system we should add to our understanding of the disorders that people, in their own unique ways, bring to us as manifestations of problems in living. We next turn to the historical development of a diagnostic system that we shall be employing (with some modifications) in the present volume.

## Diagnostic and Statistical Manual of Mental Disorders

In a continuing effort to improve the reliability of diagnosis, the American Psychiatric Association has assembled a *Diagnostic and Statistical Manual* (DSM) to encourage uniform practice among diagnosticians. The Committee on Nomenclature and Statistics of the American Psychiatric Association published the first such manual (DSM-I) in 1952. This committee revised the manual in 1968 (DSM-II) and again in 1980 (DSM-III). We shall employ the latest revision in the present volume to help understand the various syndromes of psychopathology. Dr. Robert L. Spitzer chaired a huge task force consisting of medical epidemiologists, psychiatrists, clinical psychologists, and social workers to effect the vast and even revolutionary changes advanced in DSM-III (American Psychiatric Association, 1980). The manual went through several drafts and was given field trials in order to assure that its contents were applicable to actual practice. It should be noted that the World Health Organization (1978) has sponsored an *International Classification of Diseases* (ICD) that has gone through nine editions as of the present date. The DSM-III presents a more complex diagnostic scheme, with more categories of diagnosis and greater specificity of detail in the description of pathological syndromes, than does the ICD-9.

Due to the consistent theoretical approach we take in the present volume we find ourselves somewhat at odds with the spirit of DSM-III. That is, an effort is made by the authors of DSM-III to divorce the syndrome of psychopathology from the underlying personality dynamics. The approach taken is therefore essentially descriptive, in which a detailed presentation of the total syndrome is made without thereby commenting on an underlying dynamic as of etiological significance. The intent here is admirable, in that every effort is made in DSM-III to avoid entitizing the disease process as reflective of the underlying personality. A person may manifest a schizophrenic syndrome, but this does not thereby make that person "a" schizophrenic. Recall our comments above concerning labeling people in psychiatric terms and the resulting harmful effects that may persist following hospitalization. In the DSM-III approach, the attempt is to divorce the syndrome from the person, who may pass through a psychopathological episode and then return to life as usual without thereby being "judged" according to some personality dynamic that continues on after the illness has passed.

Because of our psychoanalytical examination of etiological factors in the clinical syndromes we shall necessarily be taking a different approach. That is, we shall be attempting to unite psychoanalytical theory with the syndromes of psychopathology, and thus generalizations about personality dynamics will be offered. In such an approach it is impossible to completely divorce the underlying and continuing dynamics of the case, because these are of etiological significance. Actually, DSM-III does not maintain a completely atheoretical, empirical stance, because in those disorders in which there is a well-established etiology these factors are introduced into the definition and description of the resultant syndrome. Thus, it is our position that clinical manifestations of psychopathology may indeed "come and go," but that the underlying personality dynamics associated with these lapses into maladjustment *do* remain. This is not to say that a person who is diagnosed as suffering from a schizophrenic episode remains "a" schizophrenic upon release from the hospital. But if there are delineable reasons for his or her hospitalization in the first place, then it is only good sense to recognize that such reasons may or may *not* be rectified following release from the hospital.

For example, a traditional distinction that has been drawn in psychopathology is that between *organic* and *functional* disorders. The former type of disorder has a known etiology to be noted in the disturbances due to hereditary brain damage, certain infections of the central nervous system, and so forth. The latter (functional) disorders are not clearly tied to an organic malfunction (material causes). Most of the disorders listed in DSM-III are of the functional variety. But surely, if a person enters the mental hospital due to certain infections of the nervous system, which in turn are related to a personality-generated lifestyle in which personal health care is minimized, even after a cure of the organic disorder has taken place, upon release this person might well resume the same style of life, making further hospitalization possible or even likely. Trying to circumscribe underlying dynamics in functional disorders is comparable to this lifestyle characterization. We are trying to frame a generalizable principle of explanation regarding the possible etiological factors underlying the observed clinical syndrome. In neither the organic nor the functional disorder is it necessary to entitize or give independent existence to the clinical picture that results from the precedent personality and lifestyle predilections.

The authors of DSM-III acknowledge that the diagnostic criteria proposed are based on clinical judgment and that every facet of the description has not been empirically validated in well-controlled circumstances. In order to capture a more complete picture of the syndrome in question, DSM-III employs a *multiaxial* system of classification. This consists of five separate dimensions along which each person under diagnostic observation is to be categorized and evaluated. The first three axes constitute the official diagnostic judgment.

*Axis I.* The first axis contains all of the traditional clinical syndromes that we have presented above as the neuroses and psychoses. However, the term *neurosis* has been *dropped* in DSM-III. We can speak of a *neurotic disorder* as a symptom or group of symptoms that merely describes a process including (1) a distressing internal functioning as seen in complaints leveled by the person; (2) diminished effectiveness in overt behavior without organic cause; (3) essentially good contact with reality; and (4) if left untreated, a long-standing maladjustment according to cultural expectations of normality. However, given that we can speak of such a neurotic disorder, it does not follow that we are referring to a specific "neurosis" with some presumed singular course of etiological development or clear-cut diagnostic criteria. Hence, in general we might say that the more seriously disturbed an individual's behavior becomes, departing from culturally defined levels of normality, the more likely it is that he or she will be assigned a diagnostic categorization under axis I.

*Axis II.* The second axis contains personality disorders and specific development disorders (such as reading disabilities). It is often the case that the same person who has experienced a developmental disorder (axis II) *also* acquires a severe behavioral disorder in adulthood (axis I), and hence we would categorize such an individual along *both* axes. In other instances, patients are diagnosed solely on axis I or axis II. Axis II can also be used to indicate specific personality traits when no personality disorder exists. For example, a woman with compulsive personality traits may develop a severe depression. She would be diagnosed on axis I for the depression, and her long-standing compulsivity recorded on axis II. Sometimes the diagnostician assigns a personality disorder to a patient on axis II and then *adds* additional personality traits to round out the clinical picture. Obviously, the implicit tie of psychopathology to personality style is well represented in DSM-III.

*Axis III.* The third axis contains any *current* physical disorder or condition that may be relevant to an understanding of the person. Once again, the same person could be given a diagnosis on axes I, II, and III. The physical illness recorded may have had something to do with the psychopathological state being diagnosed on axes I and/or II, or it may simply be listed on axis III as something for the hospital staff to keep in mind in the care and treatment of the patient. A man who has recently suffered a heart attack would have this fact listed on axis III, since there are obvious precautions that must be taken in prescribing treatment activities, medication, and so forth, in his case.

*Axis IV.* The fourth axis enables the diagnostician to estimate the severity of *psychosocial* stressors revealed by the case history to have brought on developmentally or more acutely (suddenly) the *present* disorder. Here again, the diagnostician relies upon a cultural estimate of how much stress an "average" person would experience given a certain set of life circumstances. The focus is on the content of axes I and II. What happened in the person's life circumstances to stress him or her in a way commensurate with the presenting complaints? In most cases it is assumed that the stressor will have occurred in the year previous to the appearance of the present disorder. However, in some cases the stressor is the anticipation of a future event, such as the forthcoming marriage of an offspring, retirement, or the expected demise of a loved one with a terminal physical illness. Table 1 presents a seven-point scale that the diagnostician follows to code the severity of psychosocial stressors that a person might confront.

Note in Table 1 that each step value (1 through 7) has a descriptive label assigned to it ("none," "minimal," "mild," etc.) and that examples of psychosocial stressors are given for each point on the scale. Both an adult and a child/adolescent example is given. Typical sources of stress include conjugal (marital and nonmarital) relations, parental responsibilities, occupational demands, financial problems, social/interpersonal relations, residential and neighborhood circumstances, involvements with the law (arrests, lawsuits, etc.), physical illness or injury, phases of life transition (puberty, midlife crises), and various other psychological stressors unique to the individual (e.g., fear of flying and having to fly, etc.). Note in Table 1 that a code of 0 is given when there is no information on a person concerning the stress level.

*Axis V.* The fifth axis enables the diagnostician to estimate the highest level of adaptive functioning for at least a few months during the *past year.* Three aspects of the person's life are given precedence in making this judgment: *social relations, occupational performance,* and the *use of leisure time.* The diagnostician wants to know the highest level of adaptation the person has shown off the job (including homemaking responsibilities) and how successfully he or she has been making use of leisure time in the sense of pursuing hobbies. Table 2 presents a seven-point scale that the diagnostician follows to code the person's highest level of adaptive functioning over the past year.

The level of functioning based on Table 2 should be made even though the person under diagnosis may require psychotherapy to maintain it. In other words, the diagnostician tries to assign a score of from 1 to 7 that is descriptive of the person's literal performance, regardless of what it takes to make him or her perform at this level. Once again, if no information is available on the person a code value of 0 (unspecified) is assigned. It goes without saying that in most instances a diagnostician must interview family members as well as the person who is being diagnosed, ensuring that some information on level of performance will be obtained. If the amount of information on the person is inadequate, the diagnostician may (1) defer making a diagnosis or, in more informative circumstances, (2) make a *provisional* diagnosis. It is also possible to render "unspecified" and/or "atypical" diagnoses.

When the information is sufficient for a decision the diagnostician categorizes the person along either the first or the second axis. If the person is to be

TABLE 1

Axis IV: Codes of Psychosocial Levels of Stress

| CODE | TERM | ADULT EXAMPLES | CHILD/ADOLESCENT EXAMPLES |
|------|------|----------------|---------------------------|
| 1 | None | No apparent psychological stressor | No apparent psychological stressor |
| 2 | Minimal | Minor violation of the law; small bank loan | Vacation with family |
| 3 | Mild | Argument with neighbor; change in work hours | Change in schoolteacher; new school year |
| 4 | Moderate | New career; death of close friend; pregnancy | Chronic parental fighting; change to new school; illness of close relative; birth of sibling |
| 5 | Severe | Serious illness in self or family; major financial loss; marital separation; birth of child | Death of peer; divorce of parents; arrest; hospitalization; persistent and harsh parental discipline |
| 6 | Extreme | Death of close relative; divorce | Death of parent or sibling; repeated physical or sexual abuse |
| 7 | Catastrophic | Concentration camp experience; devastating natural disaster | Multiple family deaths |
| 0 | Unspecified | No information, or not applicable | No information, or not applicable |

*Source:* Table 1 is taken from DSM-III, p. 27.

listed under both axis I and axis II, the *principal* diagnosis is taken to be the condition that was chiefly responsible for the current necessity to be diagnosed (the presenting problem). Ordinarily, when a person is given classifications on both axis I and axis II it is assumed that the axis I diagnosis is the principal one, unless there is a notation on axis II indicating otherwise.

Satisfactory diagnosis demands that the diagnostician make an effort to provide any potential therapist with enough information to plan a suitable program for recovery. Thus, after arriving at the decisions required along the five axes, the diagnostician will provide a suitable report of all additional factors in the case history that would be relevant to planning a therapeutic program. It is helpful to give some indication of how well the person being diagnosed relates interpersonally to the diagnostician, the person's level of verbal facility, any signs of unusual thinking patterns, the diagnostician's impressions of family interactions, and the possible role of physical disorders in the future adjustment of the person. Precisely what additional factors will be

TABLE 2

Axis V: Codes of Highest Levels of Adaptive Functioning for Past Year

| LEVELS | ADULT EXAMPLES | CHILD/ADOLESCENT EXAMPLES |
|---|---|---|
| 1. *Superior*—Unusually effective functioning in social relations, occupational functioning, and use of leisure time. | Single parent living in deteriorating neighborhood takes excellent care of children and home, has warm relations with friends, and finds time for pursuit of hobby. | A 12-year-old girl gets superior grades in school, is extremely popular among her peers, and excels in many sports. She does all of this with apparent ease and comfort. |
| 2. *Very good*—Better than average functioning in social relations, occupational functioning, and use of leisure time. | A 65-year-old retired widower does some volunteer work, often sees old friends, and pursues hobbies. | An adolescent boy gets excellent grades, works part-time, has several close friends, and plays banjo in a jazz band. He admits to some distress in "keeping up with everything." |
| 3. *Good*—No more than slight impairment in either social or occupational functioning. | A woman with many friends functions extremely well at a difficult job, but says "the strain is too much." | An 8-year-old boy does well in school, has several friends, but bullies younger children. |
| 4. *Fair*—Moderate impairment in either social relations or occupational functioning, *or* some impairment in both. | A lawyer has trouble carrying through assignments; has several acquaintances, but hardly any close friends. | A 10-year-old girl does poorly in school, but has adequate peer and family relations. |
| 5. *Poor*—Marked impairment in either social relations or occupational functioning, or moderate impairment in both. | A man with one or two friends has trouble keeping a job for more than a few weeks. | A 14-year-old boy almost fails in school and has trouble getting along with his peers. |
| 6. *Very poor*—Marked impairment in both social relations and occupational functioning. | A woman is unable to do any of her housework and has violent outbursts toward family and neighbors. | A 6-year-old girl needs special help in all subjects and has virtually no peer relationships. |
| 7. *Grossly impaired*—Gross impairment in virtually all areas of functioning. | An elderly man needs supervision to maintain minimal personal hygiene and is usually incoherent. | A 4-year-old boy needs constant restraint to avoid hurting himself and is almost totally lacking in skills. |
| 0. *Unspecified.* | No information. | No information. |

*Source:* Table 2 is taken from DSM-III, pp. 29-30.

emphasized depends upon the theoretical orientation of the prospective therapist. Psychodynamic therapists look for factors (e.g., capacity for transference)
that behavioral therapists might find of little use in planning a therapeutic
program. It therefore probably happens that diagnostic reports are elaborated
somewhat differently depending upon the theoretical orientation of the facility
(clinic, hospital) to which a person has been referred. But the fundamental
information along the five axes remains the same no matter who may make use
of the diagnosis rendered.

Although we shall make extensive use of the revised *nosology* (classification system) of DSM-III, it is not our purpose to present an alternative version
of a diagnostic manual. On some occasions we shall disagree with the conclusions of DSM-III, and in such instances our alternative recommendations will
be fully justified. We shall also mention and at times employ psychiatric terminology, even though DSM-III no longer carries these designations. The chapters
concerned with clinical syndromes (6 through 18) are entitled according to
DSM-III, but the chapter contents follow our own style and interests quite
independent of the diagnostic manual. We shall usually refer to DSM-III in a
special chapter section entitled "The DSM-III Viewpoint." As noted above, our
purpose is to provide the reader with what the authors of DSM-III specifically
avoided presenting—that is, a consistent, unified, psychodynamic explanation
of psychopathology in the human being.

SUMMARY

Chapter 1 presents psychopathology as the study of the contributions that
mental or psychological problems make to the emotional disturbances of
behavior, disturbances that may be reflected in physical diseases (psychosomatic illness) or disturbed interpersonal relations. There are both dynamic
and nondynamic approaches to the study of psychopathology. In the present
volume we take our lead from Freudian psychoanalysis, in which a dynamic
analysis is employed. *Dynamic* in this context means the interplay of purposeful intentions working concurrently or in opposition to overt human behavior.
As such, we take a *teleological* view of the human being. Freudian theory is
clearly a telic account of human behavior, although by employing certain
terminology Freud made it appear that he was theorizing according to the
traditional, reductive medical models of his time.

In order to appreciate the factors entering into dynamic theorizing, we
found it necessary to review Aristotle's theory of causation. All of these causal
meanings existed in the writings of predecessors before he appeared on the
historical scene, but Aristotle assigned the names we now use to describe them.
The *material* cause is the substance that presumably constitutes or "makes
things up," such as physical matter. The *efficient* cause is the impetus in events
that presumably gets them moving, thrusting things along in some energic
fashion without regard for the specific direction that they take. The *formal*
cause is the pattern, shape, order, or plan that events and substantial entities

are assembled in terms of. The *final* cause gets at the reason, purpose, or intention in the course of events or the assembly of substantial entities. A teleological theory is one in which the final cause is used, as well as one or more of the other causes.

Due to various historical pressures, stemming in large measure from the repression of Galileo and others during the Inquisition, the practice in the rise of "natural" science became that of limiting explanations to the material and efficient causes. Indeed, the word *cause* has come to mean exclusively an efficient-cause description. This nontelic form of theory was framed from an *extraspective* perspective, that is, a third-person description in which natural events were construed as "that," "it," and the like. An extraspective account of behavior would describe the person as "him" or "her," being acted upon by forces outside of personal (intentional) control. Teleological descriptions shift the locus of explanation to an *introspective* theoretical perspective. In this case, we think of the item under description in first-person terms, as "I" or "me," viewing the person as a self-controlling agent. Natural science had no need of introspective theory, because there was a dichotomy drawn by the early scientists between inanimate and animate natural beings. The formal and final causes were therefore considered acceptable in the description of philosophical or theological accounts of human behavior. But for scientists, who accounted for the inanimate workings of nature, the goal became to reduce the four causes to two—the material and the efficient.

In medicine, this became known as the *medical-model* form of description. Abnormalities of both a physical and a psychological variety were considered explained only when they were tied to presumed underlying biological (i.e., material-cause) shortcomings that were reflected in the malfunctioning (i.e., efficiently caused) processes of the person's total behavioral pattern. There is great misunderstanding of whether or not Freud actually embraced the medical model. In Chapter 1 we learn that he did attempt to conform to traditional medical explanation by way of his libido theory. This style of explanation was an analogy to the *principle of constancy,* but libido theory also departed from such traditional reductive accounts in significant ways.

That is, in psychoanalytical accounts the *basic* explanation does not stem from the efficient-cause expenditure of energy. Behavioral patterns are not impelled by the force of libido alone. Libido is an estimate of diffuse motivation or arousal, but the major dynamics in personality stem from the *intentional* maneuverings and compromises of the psychic identities or psychic agents known as the id, ego, and superego. Freud did attempt to write a completely reductive, biological account of behavior in his *Project for a Scientific Psychology.* This was attempted under the urgings of Wilhelm Fliess, but it was a work never to be finished. Chapter 1 presents the view that Freud is not the biological reductionist that many people make him out to be. This theme will be carried forward into the other chapters of this volume.

A distinction is drawn in Chapter 1 between *nativism* and *environmentalism.* A nativistic theory is one in which the theorist presumes that there are certain fundamental, innate processes and propensities that the organism brings to life and that, beginning from birth (or possibly *in utero*), carry forward in some way to influence the organism's learning and behavioral actions. These innate capacities are not themselves learned, but make human learning possible. The environmentalistic theorist holds that though nature provides the organism with certain crude capacities to behave, these capacities are developed and perfected only because of environmental stimulations and shapings. According to the environmentalist, most of the innate capacities that the nativist attributes to the organism as "given" from birth are actually learned through environmental manipulations, conceived from an extraspective perspective.

Looking more carefully at the nativist, we find two variations on this style of explanation. The *biological reductionist* is a nativistic theorist who presumes that all behavior is reducible to underlying material and efficient causes, construed extraspectively along the lines of the medical model. But we also have nativistic theorists who are *biological naturalists*. In this case, the theorist attempts to base explanations on what the organism is found to be capable of biologically, physiologically, and anatomically, but without limiting the types of causal meanings that may be used to account for total behavior. If human beings seem naturally prone to behave "for the sake of" (final cause) purposeful plans (formal causes), then the biological naturalist does not attempt to "reduce" such behaviors to presumed underlying material and efficient causes. The position taken by the present authors is that Freud was a biological naturalist who took people as he found them, and let other medical colleagues anguish over the ultimate reduction of psychic (i.e., intentional) behaviors to underlying biological factors.

Chapter 1 next reviews some of the problems with classical diagnosis in psychopathology. Freudian theory holds to a qualitative as opposed to a quantitative view of abnormality. The criteria to be followed in distinguishing normal from abnormal personality functioning include cultural expectations, adequacy of performance, and internal integrative functioning. The Kraepelinian diagnostic categories are surveyed, and the distinction between *functional* and *organic* disorders is drawn. Problems of reliability are discussed, as well as the lack of uniformity to be found among patients who carry the same diagnosis. The harmful effects of assigning a label to a person for life are considered.

In reaction to the latter harmful outcomes of labeling, the authors of the third edition of a *Diagnostic and Statistical Manual of Mental Disorders* (DSM-III) have attempted to divorce the 'syndrome of psychopathology from the underlying personality dynamics. The approach taken by DSM-III is therefore essentially descriptive, with detailed criteria given for each of the syndromes included but *no* or very little commentary concerning an underlying personality dynamic of etiological significance. Although the intent here—to avoid entitizing a disease process in calling people schizophrenic, obsessive, and the like—is admirable, it is our position in the present volume that *in fact* there are such underlying dynamics and that it does not do justice to the reality of clinical practice to act as if these dynamics were irrelevant or of secondary importance. Thus, though we decry the tendency to label people as schizo-phrenic or obsessive even as they are discharged from clinics and hospitals as cured, the aim of the present volume is to unite psychoanalytical theory with the syndromes of psychopathology. This necessarily implies that we shall see etiological relationships between certain personality styles and certain syn-dromes of maladjustment.

Chapter 1 ends with a review of the five axes of DSM-III. Axis I contains all of the traditional clinical syndromes, except that the term *neurosis* has been dropped. Axis II contains personality disorders and specific developmental disorders (such as reading disorders). Axis III contains any currently relevant physical disorder that may help the psychopathologist understand a patient's behavior (e.g., a recent heart attack). Axis IV allows for an estimate of the severity of psychosocial stressors that the case history has suggested (e.g., change in jobs, death in the family, divorce, etc.). Axis V permits an estimate to be made of the highest level of adaptive functioning for at least a few months of the patient's life during the past year (from superior to grossly impaired). Axes IV and V are rated on a seven-point scale. Thus, axes I and II contain the major diagnostic classifications. Ordinarily, when a person is given classifications on both axis I and axis II it is assumed that the axis I diagnosis is the principal one, unless there is a notation on axis II indicating otherwise.

# 2

## *Personality Development: Infancy and Early Childhood*

All humans are born into this complex world in such a helpless state that if adults did not immediately take charge of them, meet their daily needs, and protect them, they could not survive. Researchers in child development used to think that the newborn infant was totally lacking in human capabilities at birth, so that such things as perception of the environment or cognitive thought processes were totally beyond the infant's capacities. Research findings in recent decades have served to dispel this view of newborn infants as malleable organisms with poorly developed sensory systems over which they have no control. As we shall see, infants have some capacity to be aware of and to influence their conceptual understanding of experience in the very first days and weeks of life. Such capacities are *innate,* meaning that they do not need to be learned (recall our discussion of naturalism in Chapter 1, p. 13). Their presence immediately following birth suggests that the child is more an active *contructor* (Piaget, 1970, p. 140) or *construer* (G. A. Kelly, 1955, p. 61) of experience than a passively *shaped* product of environmental experience.

Of course, what "happens" to a child in the early days and weeks of life is extremely important. Psychologically considered, infants have difficulty distinguishing precisely between themselves and the persons who care for them, between what is "their" feeling-tone and what is the feeling-tone of the "other." If there is a problem in the relationship between the infant and the mothering person (whether male or female), the infant seems not only capable of sensing the resultant tension but also to use this negative quality as a characterization of self-worth. From the early work of Ribble (1944) to the more recent demonstrations by Bullard and his colleagues (1967), we have continued evidence that infants from a very early age who have been rejected, punished, or ignored fail to thrive in life and tend to *waste away;* indeed, the depression and feeding disorders of these children have even resulted in death. When such rejected offspring mature they are likely to develop into problem children, with hostility, lying, and stealing common manifestations of their underlying negative self-image (Pemberton & Benady, 1973).

Over the long years of infancy, childhood, and adolescence, the human being is transformed from a *biological baby* to a *biosocial adult*. The flow of life is from what the person, as a biological organism with certain innate capacities, brings to the world of "others" and how the person thereby reciprocally interacts with others to form into a *socialized* human being. The *style* of behavior gradually and uniquely developed in this socialization process is termed the *personality* (see Chapter 1, p. 1). In a sense, *personality development* is the name given to the transformation that takes place as one moves from being predominantly a biological organism to a biosocial person. Each child, through reciprocal (two-way) interaction with other human beings in a human environment, comes in time to feel, to think, and to act fundamentally as others in that environment feel and think and act. A personal world of stable experience is constructed by the child, in which persons, things, and causal relations are framed by the same space-time considerations that all people accept as a common assumption about "reality." The real world is therefore a social world, an outer world of commonality and agreement. But there always remains an inner world to which the developing individual is uniquely and introspectively attuned. Much of the skill in attaining a proper adjustment is somehow to bring these two worlds of experience into a reasonable level of compatibility if not perfect agreement. As we shall see, when serious incompatibilities between the developing person's inner and outer worlds arise, the tendency is to deny reality and flee into a realm of pseudoexistence known as the psychotic experience.

The earliest development of personality is in relation to needs and satisfactions that are direct, simple, and concrete. Biological needs for such things as food, air, warmth, and contact are present from the moment of birth. Satisfying these needs is the main task, which is accomplished in infancy and childhood with a great deal of help and later on with much less help. The human society that receives the infant at birth understands his or her needs and is prepared to help in meeting them. Indeed, social organizations are built around basic, animal promptings such as hunger and thirst, the need for warmth, love, shelter, and protection, sexual desire and its many consequences, the human urge to express love and aggression, self-assertion, initiative, pleasure, and anger. Even our most treasured customs, our values, and our highest ideals emerge out of needs that at some time were concrete, biological, and basic to human existence.

During earliest infancy children begin, through the satisfaction of concrete physiological needs, to bind themselves closely to a *mothering figure* who is the immediate source of nearly all early satisfactions. Through this early bond, which is literally vital, the mother first helps her infant develop a *basic trust* in her, and then gradually prepares him or her to enter into family activities and human society. The mother herself, long before she has a child, has already affirmed through her own constructive efforts the values of her society—a process usually called *internalizing* societal norms. As a result, her ways are the ways of her society; her values reflect its values. These ways and values she transmits to her child, through personal example in behavior, through her speech patterns, and through explicit instructions over the years. The mother-child relationship continues through successive phases of weaning or emancipation until the child, now grown to adolescence or adulthood, leaves the home. In what follows we shall escort our human being swiftly through his or her first two decades to see what influences come into play, how the developing personality interacts and adjusts to these influences, and what the resulting dynamic organization is likely to be.

## Life in the Uterus

A human being is created when an errant sperm penetrates a receptive ovum within the mother's oviduct, the tube through which ova travel from ovary to uterus. Sperm and ovum immediately reorganize and fuse to form a unitary cell, the fertilized *ovum*. With this fusion the sex of the child-to-be is determined, and so also is his or her entire biological inheritance. The newly created organism is now launched upon a career of growth and development. It moves down the oviduct and becomes implanted in the uterine wall. Cell divisions begin and multiply with almost explosive rapidity. An organized mass forms, then the ground plan of the embryo appears, and along about the eighth week the developing embryo is termed a *fetus,* or unborn child. Membranes meanwhile develop to form an *amniotic sac* and secrete a fluid in which the fetus floats. A *placenta* organizes and connects the growing fetus with its mother. This placenta acts as a complex digestive and respiratory organ, bringing fetal blood into functional relationship with the mother's blood, but not mixing them together. Eventually this new creation emerges as a newborn baby.

From the moment of conception to the moment of birth the new organism's progress is governed by physiological factors. The relationship between mother and unborn child is mediated through the semipermeable membranes of the placenta, where there is a continuous interchange of chemical substances and gases, day and night. It used to be thought that the placenta provided protection for the fetus against absorbing drugs and microorganisms from the mother's bloodstream, but research has since established that this is incorrect. Indeed, there is concern today over such practices as smoking during pregnancy, because nicotine adversely affects infant body weight and raises the mortality rate (Meredith, 1975). Alcohol consumption by pregnant women in even moderate amounts has been linked to subsequent abnormal behavioral patterns in their offspring (Landesman-Dwyer, Keller, and Streissguth, 1977). The adverse effects of venereal disease (gonorrhea and syphilis) and drug addiction on the fetus are, of course, even more dramatic.

Intrauterine development is moved along by countless biological interactions within the embryo and fetus itself. At first there are no recognizable organs. Then, what appear to begin merely as energy concentrations and energy relations lead to the formation of enduring structures. Tissues and

The Granger Collection

*An 1885 photograph of Freud and his fiancée, Martha
Bernays. He was twenty-nine years old at the time. This
is the year that he spent in Paris, studying under Jean
Charcot at the Salpêtrière hospital. The couple was
married in 1886.*

organs develop, and systems and subsystems emerge and become interrelated.
Given a normal internal milieu and a normal immediate environment, the
growing organism seems to work out biologically its own self-governing plan
and its own timetable of maturational sequences. It is as if a biological clock
were at work within the newly developing organism.

An especially interesting feature of growth and maturation is that embry-
onic and fetal structures form and begin to function before they are actually
needed and before what they do is useful to the organism as a whole. There is,
for example, a well-developed gastrointestinal system, engaged in wavelike
muscular contractions (peristaltic movement) and in secreting digestive juices
and enzymes, long before any food is in prospect. The heart appears and begins

to beat before there are blood vessels and blood to pump. Even breathing movements occur several weeks before birth, although the fetus is immersed in amniotic fluid and cannot benefit from breathing.

What is true of internal organ functioning is also true of external behavior, where we find the rudiments of actions that will be carried on reflexively from the time of birth. Before the sixth month the fetus is already making complex chewing movements and swallowing. Arms and legs move about, hands grasp, and eyelids open and close even though there is no light in which to see. Later, the fetus's head begins making turning movements of a kind that will be useful in the rooting behavior of food seeking. It is clear that when organs and systems and body parts are physiologically ready to function in the fetus, they begin to function, whether or not what they do serves any immediate purpose.

If all goes well with the mother's biological and psychological health, the unborn child has a reasonably tranquil environment in which to develop. There is protection from cold and heat, from bright lights and loud sounds, from blows and sudden stresses. The fetus dwells in a warm, dark chamber, immersed almost weightlessly in a fluid, cushioned by it, and provided through the placenta with continuous nourishment. As long as the unborn child gets from the mother's blood via the placenta what he or she requires to grow, is able to move about a little, and as long as waste products are removed fast enough by the same placental mediation, there are few tensions to adjust to in this most rudimentary of all forms of existence. However, when the mother's emotional state is not satisfactory, it is likely that fetal existence will be upset and thereby adversely affect the child's adjustment following birth. Pregnant women under psychological stress (anxiety, depression, etc.) are more likely to have babies that actively move about *in utero* and that manifest high levels of crying, squirming, diarrhea, eating problems, vomiting, fussiness, and sensitivity to sound following birth (Copans, 1974; Sontag, 1944). We know that hormones in the mother's blood can pass through the placenta, and hence it may be that this is the biological mechanism that triggers such behavioral problems in the offspring of maladjusted mothers.

## The Question of Infant Conditioning and Cognitive Abilities

Before we can proceed to a consideration of birth and early infant experience, an important theoretical issue having to do with how development proceeds must be addressed. We have seen in Chapter 1 that Freud was both teleological (see p. 11) and naturalistic (see p. 13) in theoretical outlook. This means he placed great responsibility on the person for his or her unique psychological development in life. Freud's theories always take the introspective perspective, looking at the world through the understanding of the person who "comes at" life with wishes, purposes, and intentions, even though some of these may be blocked or repressed from consciousness.

Freud's quasi-biological reductionism, which he attempted in addition to naturalism thanks to the promptings of his teachers and colleagues, is reflected in his *libido* theory. We shall have much to say regarding libido theory in Chapter 4 (see p. 117). For now, we simply want to point out that though it is presumably released by the biological sexual instinct, libido is itself *not* a physical construct. Libido is a postulated energy that is said to work completely within the psychic realm; it is a mental and not a physical energy! It can be *cathected* or sent into the image of people or even inanimate things "at will" (at the ego's will; see p. 9). And in his theories of personality development Freud placed great emphasis on the ability of the psyche to cathect and counter-cathect (i.e., repress) desired *objects* (people or things that the person values). All such theoretical speculations suggest an active, self-selecting human intellect, beginning in the first days of life and carrying forward from then on. People are *naturally* like this (see Chapter 1, p. 13).

Critics of psychoanalysis frequently claim that it demands too much of the child, that an infant lacks the self-regulating mental capacities which the theory presumes. American psychologists in the behavioristic tradition have been most outspoken in their condemnation of psychoanalytical suggestions of an "inner" fantasy world having unique dynamic characteristics. Thus, B. F. Skinner (1971) opined, "It would be foolish to deny the existence of [a] . . . private world, but it is also foolish to assert that because it is private it is of a different nature from the world outside" (p. 191).

The going *environmentalistic* assumption (see p. 12) among behaviorists is that whatever is "inside" and hence private to the personality structure has been put there or shaped into existence by external experience. Much lip service is paid to the "interaction" of the person and the environment, but when we come right down to where influence *predominantly* comes from in human behavior, the behaviorists invariably opt for extrapersonal factors. Thus, after suggesting that the person can through conceptualization influence his or her life's course, the behaviorist Albert Bandura (1978) added the deflating proviso that "while it is true that conceptions govern behavior, the conceptions themselves are partly fashioned from direct or mediated transactions with the environment" (p. 348). What we would like to know is, can the conceptions be partly determined by the person "as conceptualizer," or is the person merely a conduit or mediator of early-to-later environmental manipulations? Traditional psychoanalysis clearly places the person *as agent* in the ongoing process of conceptualizing experience, beginning essentially "at birth" (i.e., within the early days of life).

We therefore want to consider two questions: (1) How much evidence is there to suggest that infants are readily "shaped" into behavioral differences by traditional conditioning procedures? and (2) How much evidence is there to suggest that infants are active conceptualizers of their environment in the first year of life? If Freud is to be given any credence we had better find *at least* as much support for his telic interpretation of human behavior as we find for the mechanistic interpretations of the behaviorists Skinner and Bandura.

We shall first consider *classical (Pavlovian) conditioning*. The objective in classical conditioning is to take a natural or reflexively made "response" (e.g., sucking) and see if it is possible to cause it to happen when a "stimulus" that does not naturally bring it about appears in the child's presence. For example, in an early investigation of this type, Marquis (1931), working with infants in the first ten days of life, sounded a buzzer for five seconds and then inserted a milk bottle into the infant's mouth. The buzzer is termed a *conditioned stimulus* and the milk bottle's nipple is termed an *unconditioned stimulus*. Unconditioned stimuli are the observed factors that "naturally" go along with certain observed responses (see Chapter 1, p. 13). Babies naturally open their mouths and such when nipples are placed against their lips. They do *not* do so at the sound of a buzzer. The natural mouth opening and sucking movements are considered *unconditioned responses* when made following nipple insertion—because they occur reflexively in this instance—but when made following just the sounding of the buzzer they would be considered *conditioned responses*. Classical conditioning is therefore a process of taking what the organism does naturally (reflexively) at birth and trying to "attach" or "connect" or "bond" these natural responses to other stimulus cues. This process of rearranging reflexes is what John Watson (1924), the father of behaviorism, termed the *shaping* of behavior. It is believed to be entirely automatic (i.e., nonintentional), with the assumption being that the organism can only respond in a material/efficient-cause manner, on the basis of reflex-arc circuits built into the body. Indeed, the *stimulus-response* (S-R) conception is the sine qua non of efficient causality.

What did Marquis find in her early study? She found that within five days several of her infant subjects were indeed "responding" with mouth opening and sucking movements to the sound of the buzzer, even before the nipple was given to them. The problem with this study, as later researchers were to learn, is that when an unconditioned response is repeatedly being made by an organism (human or lower animal) it is often sensitized in the experimental situation so that literally any kind of fortuitous "stimulus" in that situation will bring it about. Marquis had failed to provide a control group in which some infants were given just the nipple (i.e., without buzzer) as many times as the babies in the experimental group were given buzzer-followed-by-nipple. To round out a proper study there should also have been a control group of infants who were just given the buzzer but no nipple to an equal degree with those infants given buzzer-followed-by-nipple. Subsequent studies by Wenger (1936) and Wickens and Wickens (1940) added such controls. The latter study is especially thorough in its use of controls. Rather than using nipples and sucking responses Wickens and Wickens used a mild shock (S) and foot withdrawal (R) as the unconditioned S-R sequence to modify. Their conditioned stimulus was once again a buzzer.

Wickens and Wickens found that babies who were just given a mild shock *without* first hearing the buzzer did indeed withdraw their foot upon eventually hearing the buzzer in the so-called test trials (i.e., where the experimenter sees if conditioning has taken place). They did so just as frequently as infants who had been given the buzzer-shock sequence. The infants who had just been given the buzzer sound but no shock did *not* withdraw their foot in the test trials. In other words, the conditioned stimulus (buzzer) was irrelevant! Hence, Wickens and Wickens cast doubt on the possibility of classically conditioning a newborn infant. There was no specific association established between the buzzer and the foot withdrawal. At best, a kind of "pseudoconditioning" was said to have taken place, because virtually any stimulus in the situation might "elicit" the response after sensitization had occurred in the initial training or "conditioning" trials.

More recently, the classical conditioning of infants has been tested using highly sophisticated equipment in which heart rate is taken as the unconditioned response to be modified into a conditioned response. We have learned that when a nipple is inserted into an infant's mouth, heart rate *accelerates*. Well, what if one first sounded a tone (conditioned stimulus) and then inserted a nipple (unconditioned stimulus) in the newborn infant's mouth. Could one in time demonstrate that heart rate will accelerate to the sound of tone alone—given the various controls we have already mentioned? Clifton (1974) performed such a well-controlled experiment. In the training or conditioning trials she presented experimental subjects with tone-nipple insertion and recorded heart rate. Control subjects were given a random sequence of nipple-tone and tone-nipple in their training. If conditioning were to come about, we would expect in the test trials to find that the experimental subjects would accelerate heartbeats to the sound of the tone alone, whereas the control subjects who did not get this fixed sequence of events would not reflect a heart-rate increase. What did Clifton find? Control subjects performed as predicted, but the infants in the experimental condition performed *exactly the opposite* of the prediction. When they were given tone *not* followed by nipple insertion their heart rates *decelerated*.

Now, researchers know from studying older human beings that heart rates decelerate when a person is being especially attentive to his or her environment. When one is expecting that something is about to happen, and one very much wants to know what takes place, then the heart is likely to slow down slightly. In line with this knowledge, Clifton interpreted her findings as showing that the infants were reflecting an "orienting reaction" in the presence of an expected event. In other words, the infants were awaiting the onset of the nipple, and hence they were *classically conditioned* in the sense of attaching an expectancy *response* (orienting) to an earlier stimulus (tone) (ibid., p. 19).

Clifton's findings were in effect cross-validated by Stamps and Porges (1975), who argued in the behaviorist tradition that what infants are conditioned to is *not* the conditioned stimulus (tone) per se but rather to the *trace* or connecting association between the conditioned and unconditioned stimuli—between the tone and the nipple insertion. This is termed *stimulus-stimulus learning* in behavioristic theory. Hence, the reason the infants are supposedly expecting the nipple insertion is *not* because they as agents are actively searching their environment, looking for something they expect to happen. Their lowering in heart rate is all part of the S-R sequence—albeit in an S/trace/S-R fashion now—and they as self-determining identities have nothing to do with the observed sequence of events. Sameroff and Cavanagh (1979) have severely criticized the tendency among behavioristic psychologists to "twist" (p. 355) the classical conditioning paradigm in order to accommodate observed relationships of this type. It is clear that the data *fail* to support classical conditioning as originally postulated. It is also clear that a telic interpretation of what the infant "is doing" in these classical conditioning paradigms would *not* do violence to the rigorously recorded observations (see Chapter 1, p. 5).

Incidentally, we have failed to mention the fact that John Watson's famous shaping of "Little Albert's" fear of a white rat was the very first classical conditioning experiment of an infant (of about nine months) (Watson & Raynor, 1920). Watson presented a white rat (conditioned stimulus) to Albert, followed by a loud clanging sound (unconditioned stimulus) made by hitting a steel bar with a hammer whenever the infant touched the rat. Albert responded with fear to the sound of the struck bar, of course. After seven such pairings of rat and noise (in two sessions, one week apart) Albert reacted with crying and avoidance when the rat was presented without the loud noise following.

This experiment has been cited more than any other as supporting evidence for the fact that human behavior is completely automatic and capable of being shaped without a contributing role from the subject under manipulation. And yet recent scholarship has found many weaknesses in the accuracy of reporting in the published account of Little Albert's conditioned fear response. For example, an incidental notation made by Watson and his co-author is that Albert could *stop* his crying and other displays of anxiety by sucking his thumb: "The moment the hand reached the mouth he [Little Albert] became impervious to the stimuli producing fear [the white rat]. Again and again while the motion pictures were being made at the end of the thirty-day period, we had to remove the thumb from his mouth before the conditioned response could be obtained" (from unpublished notes, cited by Cornwell, Hobbs, and Prytula, 1980, p. 216). So the defensive sucking reactions made by Albert *at will* were not even recorded on the filmed "empirical record" that was to circulate the impression that behavior is subject to shaping based on classical conditioning! It goes without saying that the teleologist would take great interest in the fact that the infant "behaved" in this willful manner.

We turn next to what is called *operant (Skinnerian) conditioning* of the newborn infant. Unlike classical conditioning, in which the reinforcement is administered to the subject on every occasion (the child gets the milk *reinforcer* every time), in operant conditioning the reinforcer is not administered to the subject unless a specific behavior is first "emitted." This emitted behavior is termed an *operant response,* and it is supposedly sensed by the organism as literally "operating" on the environment to bring about a reinforcing state of affairs. For example, a bird pecking at a tree branch *operates* on the branch's material structure. If an insect living in the tree bark is stumbled upon through this emission of operant pecking responses, then the bird is rewarded through devouring the "insect-as-reinforcer." Observing this bird, we would see its rate of pecking increase over a certain unit of time.

The bird has reinforced itself, but it would not have been reinforced if it had not initially emitted pecking "responses" or "operants." The contingent state of affairs following pecking is what then determined the subsequent rise in pecking rate for this bird. Though we might be tempted to conceptualize such operant conditioning in a telic manner—as the bird searching, intending, and finding, and so forth—operant conditioners staunchly defend the idea that neither lower animals nor human beings *ever* become initiating sources of control in their lives. Biological and cultural factors are what control people, for as individuals they do not really exist (see Skinner, 1971, pp. 207-208). People are products of control rather than originating sources of control.

The implication in all of this is that virtually any response that a newborn infant makes is subject to operant conditioning, so long as a contingent reinforcer might be forthcoming following the emitted response. Operant conditioners use the word *emitted* because they do not want to speculate on what sort of internal stimulus might have elicited an overt response. Whatever it is that biologically triggers a pecking response in the bird or a sucking response in an infant, the important point is that the resulting reinforcer (insect or milk) would not be forthcoming if the response had not been emitted or carried out to begin with. We can get confused when we refer to something like sucking as an operant response, because we know that this is clearly a reflexive form of behavior, triggered by certain biological structures in the human being's body. If we referred to a child's "looking" at things, the same operant conditioning would hold. A child could not see something of interest unless he or she first looked about. Well, what the child would look at early in life would depend *not* on the child's internal preferences but on the environment's capacity to capture the child's looking responses through some kind of *contingent* (i.e., following) state of affairs. The child looks, brings about an interesting stimulus situation, and the *latter* stimulation is then what continues to control the child's looking behavior. This is how the operant conditioner explains human learning. Once again, there is no agency, no self-determination in the account because the meaning of final causation is *never* employed (see Chapter 1, p. 4).

It is extremely difficult to think of how we might condition a randomly emitted response in the newborn infant. Ideally, we should wait patiently as we did with the bird until an observed response literally creates a reinforcer, which is defined by the fact that the observed operant response rises in emission rate per unit of time, and *then* begin our investigation by manipulating the reinforcers to see if this would influence the level of operant responding in later units of time. Actually, operant conditioning studies on infants have employed the tactic of having the experimenter rather than the infant control the *onset* of reinforcement. A popular "response" here is, once again, infant sucking. In order to capture the operating-on-the-environment feature of operant conditioning, the researchers employ an experimental group in which sucking leads to milk (reinforcer) and a control group in which sucking does not lead to milk (no reinforcer is produced by the sucking response). In a study of this type, infants thirty-five to ninety-four hours following birth were given nipples that fed a dextrose solution through a tube when sucked, and a second (control) group was given the same nipple apparatus without dextrose (Lipsitt, Kaye, & Bosack, 1966). Within fifteen minutes the infants who received dextrose were steadily increasing their rate of sucking, whereas the control subjects were merely sucking intermittently at about a constant rate or dropping off in rate slightly.

Given the remarkable speed with which these newborn infants adapted to the fact that a reward followed their actions, it is not at all certain that we are dealing with the *shaping* of operant behavior. Animal studies in which shaping of totally random operant behavior is attempted take up to several days of repeated trials in which the animal is acclimated to the apparatus and then painstakingly molded to the desired pattern of behavior. These infants seemed "prepared" (Seligman, 1970) by natural endowment to carry out a relevant response in relation to an appropriate set of circumstances—one of which heralded nourishment and one of which did not. In other words, the dextrose solution was not a completely neutral stimulus in relation to the child's reflexive responses. In this connection, Papousek (1967b) was unable to demonstrate operant conditioning to neutral stimuli in the first ten to twenty days of an infant's life. The question then arises: Do infants learn by being *shaped* in a passive sense of having biological and cultural "forces" mold them, or do they possibly "come at" the world from birth as "shapers" of their learning? We have already noted above that Piaget (1970) and others have tended to view the newborn as an active organism, *assimilating* through reflexive processes the environment and then subsequently *accommodating* what is first "known" reflexively to better fit that which is experienced.

Using both classical and operant conditioning procedures, Papousek (1967a) taught infants two and three months old to turn their heads to the right to receive milk when they heard a buzzer. But through careful observation Papousek has rejected the traditional mechanistic explanations of conditioning in favor of the view that the infants were *intending* to learn about their environments. The experimental apparatus may motivate the child to "figure out" what is taking place, but it is surely not "shaping" the child's behavior as traditional learning theories suggest. Papousek found that these very young infants frequently seemed to correct themselves spontaneously as soon as they found they did not receive milk on the side to which they had turned; also, they acted as if they expected the milk when they made the correct response (this reminds us of the heart deceleration phenomenon, above).

Another area of operant conditioning in infants has been the so-called circular reaction, which occurs when an infant achieves eye-to-eye contact with his or her mother, smiles, and makes a vocalization of some type (such as cooing). The mother ordinarily smiles and speaks in turn, prompting a circular reaction as the infant once again smiles, vocalizes, and so on. The question arises, can one influence the rate of such smiling and cooing behavior in the infant by systematically varying the mother's reaction—which is assumed to be a contingent reinforcer? To study this, one would have an experimental group in which mothers *would* contingently reinforce their child's cooing and smiling by talking back to the child and a second group in which mothers *would not* do so. Two studies that have tried to demonstrate such operant conditioning in infants *failed* to find significant differences across experimental (reinforced) and control (nonreinforced) conditions (K. Bloom & Esposito, 1975; Cavanagh & Davidson, 1977).

In drawing out the implications of the findings on infant conditioning, developmental psychologists have begun to believe that infants are far more active in their conceptualizations of experience than was originally believed possible. For example, memory has been shown to be already in operation between two and three months of age (Mussen, 1979). Haith (1980) has argued that infants are not merely reflexive organisms at birth, but that they actively search for relevant or salient contours in their visual field, seeking the corners of geometric figures so as to "conceptualize" what is being seen rather than "storing" an already-made stimulus product. Haith therefore speaks of inborn dispositions or "rules" that the infant follows to actively conceptualize experience and in turn to foster neural development. A vast body of research has been carried out on *infant visual preference* (Berlyne, 1958; Fantz, 1958). In effect, such preferences are studied by presenting two visual stimuli to an infant simultaneously and then recording the total fixation ("looking") time of the infant for one or the other stimulus object. Visual acuity at birth is poor, but rapidly improves over the first few months of life. Numerous experiments have demonstrated that infants generally prefer to look at curved rather than straight lines, colored rather than uncolored pictures, three-dimensional rather than two-dimensional objects, complex rather than simple patterns, and schematic faces rather than featureless faces (L. Cohen, 1979).

Kagan's *discrepancy hypothesis* (1967) suggests that infants prefer to look at moderately novel stimuli and to avoid stimuli that are either too novel or too familiar. When presented with four types of facial pictures—a normal face, two scrambled or incomplete faces, and a blank face—infants past six months of age were found to look most often at the middle two pictures. In a related line of research, Strauss (1978) gave ten-month-old infants varying exposures to facial features of a distorted and/or normal type (e.g., wide, narrow, and normal noses relative to face) and then found that they could not be influenced (shaped) by such "frequency of exposure" to look at just any kind of facial organization. It seemed to Strauss that infants of this age have a capacity to construct (conceptualize) an abstract *prototype* that is an average of what they have been exposed to *regardless* of frequency considerations—where, for example, they may have seen more wide and narrow than normal noses. It is as if even such primitive human reasoners can discount frequently observed extremes and arrive at a kind of "normal" conceptualization on the basis of which they come to know their world.

Now, of course, behavioristically inclined experimenters are likely to view such evidence as we have been reviewing for cognitive activity in the newborn as due to a differential "pull" of some stimuli over others. The claim would be that infants are "wired" to respond mechanically in one direction rather than another (e.g., to attend to colored rather than noncolored pictures). Based on the same empirical evidence, a teleologically inclined experimenter would suggest that the infants are reflecting uniform trends in behavior, but that each of them has *functioned as an individual* in the observed behavioral regularity. It is not the "pull" of the stimulus but the internally adjudged *preferences* that focus an infant's attention on a colored rather than a noncolored picture of something (see Rychlak, 1977, Chapter 9). Color adds a dimension of interest for most observers. This telic interpretation would also account for the fact that in any sample of infants there are always a few who devote as much or more time to looking at the uncolored representations! In short, how we as experimenters *interpret* the observed findings depends upon our precedent (beginning) assumptions or biases.

But surely the honest reviewer of the research on infancy cannot conclude that there is clear evidence for the mechanistic shaping of behavior that traditional learning theory demands. What the evidence *does* suggest is that though an existing (innate) behavioral process which is reflexive can be adapted to new and changing circumstances, the way in which this occurs is hardly mechanical. The reflexive process (sucking, heartbeat, etc.) may readily be explained in material/efficient-cause fashion, but surely the adaptations noted in infant behavior demand that we add formal/final causation if what we observe infants "doing" with such reflexes is to make sense. Though we cannot speak for the newborn infant, we are surely not completely afield to suggest that influences in life may be made known, avoided, furthered, or distorted according to a cognitive capacity that is internally active *from birth,* in shaping as well as being shaped by external experience. Even though we accept such a naturalistic (see p. 13) and teleological (see p. 68) explanation, this does not mean that Freudian theory is correct in its essentials. But we find nothing in the empirical literature to dissuade us from conceptualizing the human being as having the *natural* potential for continually organizing and maintaining the dynamic inner world that psychoanalysis calls for.

## Birth and the Newborn

Birth expels the child from the warm, dark monotony of the uterine waters into a world of everlasting change and infinite space. During the first few weeks of life there are few organized actions to be performed, except during nursing (Kessen, Williams, & Williams, 1961). Most of the time infants appear to be sleeping or dozing. When awake and not hungry, newborns may lie more or less inertly with their heads turned to one side, and perhaps with one arm thrust out, their legs flexed and eyes staring. Except for the symmetry of arm and leg movements, physical activity is rather poorly integrated. Sleeping and waking periods are not clear-cut, lacking the measured rhythm of older children (Gifford, 1960). Occasionally the infant will give a start or a shudder that appears almost convulsive in manner. If the child wakens from a slumber in a state of hunger, he or she is likely to cry violently, turn bright red, flail limbs about, and generally twist and squirm all over. Placed in the position for feeding, the newborn reflexively pushes forward eagerly, clutches ineffectively with his or her hands, roots about for the nipple, seizing it assertively with the lips, and begins to suckle.

Psychoanalysts since Freud have postulated that in sleeping the child establishes a *protective barrier* between himself or herself and the external world. This is not exactly a realm of inactivity, a void in which to retreat. Studies of neonate sleep in which rapid eye movements (REM sleep) are used as a measure of dreaming suggest that there is considerable dreaming going on (Berg & Berg, 1979). But if we can assume that infants actively conceptualize their world early in life (see previous section), then it follows that not only might a child be withdrawing from the hustle and bustle of the world in periods of sleep, but an active psychic (mental) life might also be getting underway in which the child can visualize what he or she would *prefer* to imagine. The capacity to withdraw and thereby to direct thought to an intended end will play an important role in our later discussion of such defense mechanisms as *repression, denial,* and *isolation* (see Chapter 4).

Though infants may show common behavioral tendencies, research has also demonstrated that there is considerable individuality among children immediately following birth. Some children react vigorously to any type of stimulation, such as hearing a soft or loud tone or feeling a cold disk applied to the thigh (Birns, 1965). Others give only mild responses to such stimulations. Some children sleep more than others, and when awake some are more attentive to events in their presence than others (J. L. Brown, 1964). There are even fascinating interpersonal differences to be noted among the newborn. Some children like to be held, kissed, and carried about, whereas others try to avoid such "cuddling" by their parents (Schaffer & Emerson, 1964). Obviously, these innate differences in the seeming need for emotional contact will have an important role to play in the mother's reaction to the child. An expressive baby will have a definite effect on the mother's style of "mothering" that a phlegmatic baby will not. Here we see the beginnings of a complex interaction of the biological organism with the social patternings that will take on increasing importance as development continues.

Psychoanalysis has done much to focus attention on the biological processes involved in swallowing, retaining, or regurgitating food. These are immediate and active mechanisms that the child brings to the world "by nature," along with rooting and sucking tendencies. This is what we now recognize as Freud's biological naturalism (see Chapter 1, p. 13). We should not think of these as merely blind mechanisms, working through material- and efficient-cause biological reductionism. Biological reflexes can also serve as *prototypical actions* in that they form for the child a beginning grounding within which to know things. They are the "that" (given action) "for the sake of which" a child can differentiate, interrelate, and thereby order experiences of both a personal and impersonal variety.

Jean Piaget (1967) has said that for the newborn infant, "the world is essentially a thing to be sucked" (p. 10). He meant that the child begins life with this biological schema (patterned behavior) of "sucking" and brings it to bear as a frame of reference. The child constructs or construes experience based on this precedent activity that nature has provided. Based on this natural frame of reference the child can begin to sense the meaning of things and to extend these meanings into more and more life experience even as changes are made in these meanings.

Thus, the infant moves from the schema of sucking to touching what is sucked, seeing what is sucked, and so on, always beginning in an act of *assimilation* or "taking in" but then *accommodating* or "adjusting" the various schema to fit what is being learned. Sucking will not suffice for everything that can be learned, so new schemata grow out of old schemata. It is important to appreciate that these frames of reference or schemata are *not* filters. They are patterns of meaning that are brought to bear by the child, framing experience and ordering it into increasingly complex levels of meaning. Such meanings can be construed (ordered, conceptualized) in the internal world completely devoid of agreement with external reality.

In like fashion, Freud essentially held that natural acts like swallowing or retaining food could be used as biological schemata through which the primitively forming ego comes to learn things and to imitate the behavior of important people early in life. We shall see how Freud built his constructs of *incorporation, introjection,* and *identification* on a logic of this nature. Regurgitation and vomiting were to form the prototype for the defense of *projection* in Freudian theory. We shall have a great deal to say about these biological processes when we come to our various discussions of ego development, superego formation, and the mechanisms of defense.

## Parenting: Mother and Father Roles

The newborn's parents are also unique individuals. Unlike their offspring, the mother and father enter the familial relationship already equipped with a highly complex personality, the product of many years of social living and of private thinking and feeling. Their personalities have been built upon the biological foundations with which they were born, and their biological foundations may have been different in more than one respect from those of the newborn child. Besides this, the parents have been reared in a particular kind of family, with its own special values, ideals, prejudices, and expectations, its own emotional qualities, and its own variety of subculture. To the mothering situation the mother brings the background of her own childhood experiences of having been mothered. She brings also the background of her lifelong fantasies, her daydreams, and her games of being a mother. She brings whatever realistic experience she may have had with younger babies in her own family and her experiences in baby-sitting or in playing the role of substitute mother for someone else's baby. If she has already been a mother, she will have certain expectations and advantages or disadvantages because of this.

The father also brings to the parenting role a number of attitudes and expectations based upon his earlier experiences. He too has had experience with a father or father-substitute in his earlier life. He might have had younger siblings or served as a leader in community organizations such as the Big Brothers in which he had something to do with looking after a younger person. His fantasies of what it means to "grow up" enter into his understanding of the new role that is unfolding for him. It is likely that the father will have given less lifelong consideration to the fatherly role than the mother will have given to the motherly role. In recent decades the roles of mother and father have been changing, thanks to a liberalization of the female's status in America and elsewhere. The modern family structure seems to be in transition, bringing about less clear-cut distinctions between the roles of father and mother. What this will mean for the future of personality development cannot be stated at present. But insofar as we consider the more traditional family structure, it is probably true that as they come to maturity females will continue to give more thought to parenting than males.

John Bowlby (1969) has shown how infants come to form *attachments* to certain figures in the first year of life, and in most instances this need to be in close proximity to a certain individual focuses on the mother (p. 27). Bowlby considers attachment to be a characteristic of all animals, both human and non-human (ibid., p. 222). It is presumably something that has evolved and is central to the mammalian species. Two-week-old infants will look at a picture of their mother longer than they will look at a picture of a strange female (Carpenter, 1975). Bowlby (1969) and his colleagues have found that an infant of a few weeks will also smile at any visual stimulus that has two black dots placed upon a pale background. By three or four months a real human face is required to bring forth smiling. And by five months an infant requires a *familiar* face before smiling occurs (ibid., p. 149).

Attachment is not said to arise until there is such a strong emotional bond between the child and another person that when this person is removed from the child's proximity there is marked protest (crying, motility, etc.) followed by despair if the separation is prolonged. If this circumstance is not corrected the child is likely to go into a state of *detachment,* which is essentially what we meant above when we spoke about the wasting away of children who sense that they have been rejected (see p. 29). Bowlby suggests that a clear and firm attachment is not seen in infant behavior much before six months of age (ibid., p. 228).

Although there is some disagreement over this six-month figure, research on attachment does support the view that it is *not* evident at birth. Children are dependent upon a parent from birth, but they do not form attachment to *specific* figures (objects) until five or six months later. Some investigators have studied the maternal attachment to the child, promoted apparently in large measure by the smiling and looking behavior of their offspring (see our discussion of the circular reaction above, p. 39; Harlow, 1971). Most authorities believe that a child must first establish a sense of "self/not-self" through discriminating people versus objects before an attachment can be made to "one" person (i.e., the mother). Schaffer and Emerson (1964) were among the first to study attachment to both parents. They found that a high percentage of attachments were formed first with the mother as object. But shortly thereafter, or sometimes concurrently, an attachment was formed with the father. By six months of age over 50 percent of the infants were attached to their fathers as well as their mothers, and by eighteen months of age over 70 percent were attached to both parents. Other studies have found that infants between twelve and twenty-one months of age became attached to *both* parents and, indeed, showed no preference for one parent over the other (Kotelchuck et al., 1975). It appears that children can become attached to parents for different reasons. Thus, mothers are likely to be caretakers, looking after the child's biological needs. Fathers, on the other hand, pick up and hold their offspring in a playful manner, amusing them rather than strictly looking after their needs (Lamb, 1977).

Attachment as a human phenomenon surely attests to the strong emotional ties that human beings generate for each other. In psychoanalytic terms we refer to such phenomena as *object-choices.* The child is seen as *cathecting* the mother (i.e., filling her image in mind) with libido. Mothers also cathect their children. This mutual tie of mother and child has occasionally been called *symbiotic,* a term borrowed from biology suggesting that there is a vital benefit to be gained by two different organisms, one of which lives off the other. In biology we think of a host organism and a parasite organism, each of which is of a different species. But when referring to mother and child the term is analogous rather than exact, in the sense that the child figuratively or literally "lives off" the mother (via milk ingestion, etc.).

Some mothers are eager to have a child, feel comfortable with their offspring right from the start, and find motherhood in every way rewarding. Others who are not eager to have the child find it irresistible when it comes and quickly lose the feeling of unwillingness. Even among accepting mothers many problems arise. There are women who want the baby all through their pregnancy, welcome it when it arrives, and then discover that for them the tasks and restrictions of motherhood outweigh the satisfactions. This circumstance is becoming more evident today than ever before, thanks to the early age at which young women are having children out of wedlock, as high school students, before they have actually had a chance to mature fully themselves. The burdens of motherhood come as a shock to such individuals.

A new baby is usually the center of attention, and some new mothers—as well as fathers—feel pushed to the sidelines when the child arrives. Others are overwhelmed by the added responsibility of caring for an infant, even under the best of circumstances. Studies have shown that when a mother fails to perceive her infant's needs properly the attachment relationship is adversely affected (Ainsworth & Bell, 1974). Some mothers feel uncomfortable with a particular baby (see our discussion of "cuddlers" above, p. 42), or even frightened by it, whereas their previous experiences with babies have been pleasant. We know from research that the more often a child looks, smiles, and vocalizes to the mother, the more likely she is to deeply love the child (Clarke-Stewart, 1973). Considering the wide range of individual differences among the behavior of newborns and among mothers, it is hardly surprising that sometimes the match is not a good one, especially as there is no free choice on either side.

A new baby may pose a special problem if it comes too soon after its nearest sibling. The symbiotic mother-child unit, once it has been formed, takes time to dissolve again, and both mothers and children vary in the amount of time they require to work through their close relationship. If another child arrives before this dissolution is well underway, the mother may be thrown into serious conflict by the demands on her affection made by her second baby at a time when she is deeply involved with the first. Other more obvious problems are posed by prolonged ill health in the mother or child, which may retard or disturb the development of the mother-child unit—as may also, of course, the demands caused by ill health, physical or emotional, in older children or the husband. The tensions of marital discord, as well as interference from the parents' relatives, can seriously disturb early mother-child relationships.

Society's attitudes toward motherhood make maternal rejection or neglect an unforgivable offense. Therefore, rarely does a hostile or indifferent mother put into plain words any socially condemned attitudes that she may have toward her baby (Crandall & Preston, 1961). Furthermore, because of her own moral code, derived during her childhood from her own society, it is unusual for a mother to admit even to herself that she has such attitudes, unless they are merely transient and superficial. As a rule, hostile and indifferent maternal attitudes find subtle, devious, disguised, defensive, and often unconscious expression in what the mother does or fails to do. It has long been known, for example, that overprotective mothers are commonly hostile mothers who restrict their child's freedom and that overprotection by indifferent or rejecting mothers is an exaggerated denial of their indifference and rejection. We call such defensive denial that takes the form of an exaggerated opposite attitude *reaction-formation* (see Chapter 4). Other people are more likely to be aware of what a hostile, indifferent, or rejecting mother is expressing than she herself is. The same can be said for the father, of course.

But whether anyone else recognizes a parent's negative attitudes or not, both clinical experience and empirical investigation (Newsom, 1977) strongly suggest that they can be communicated to the infant at nonverbal or preverbal levels. A mother's accepting, indifferent, or rejecting attitudes, which an infant experiences for years at nonverbal or practically nonverbal levels, significantly influence his or her initial dependency relationships and the later capacity for becoming an independent, self-assured human being. Thus, it is not surprising that two-year-old children who are reluctant to carry out complex exploratory behaviors are also those children who had failed to experience a secure maternal attachment in their first year of life (Main, 1973).

## Psychoanalytical Theory of Child Development

We have to this point in Chapter 2 assured ourselves that newborn infants have remarkable cognitive capacities and that they are not simply being mechanically shaped into their lifelong behavioral patterns. There is also reason to suspect that human beings employ reflexive, sensorimotor bodily actions as "frames of reference" through which they can know experience. It is not beyond comprehension to think of children as framing an inner world, dynamically construing experience according to the primitive biological processes which nature ensures that they have "in place" at birth (à la Freud's biological naturalism; see Chapter 1, p. 13). Suggested interpretations of the empirical data along these lines are quite consistent with psychoanalysis, although Freud was also to propose theoretical constructs based on clinical findings that have never been put to test in empirical research, much less proven. It is difficult to prove Freudian contentions empirically. Much of the difficulty here lies in the fact that we are dealing in the realm of fantasy and infant fantasy to boot! But there is nothing to keep us from adopting Freudian and related psychoanalytical insights concerning empirical regularities that we do know about in human development. Psychoanalysis remains the most thorough and fruitful explanation of human development in the psychological literature.

Dare (1976) has suggested that Freud's view of development includes three basic ideas: (1) phases or stages; (2) growth of thought from primary to secondary processes; and (3) growth of the ego, as arranged within the id versus superego oppositions. Freud and his early colleagues defined the phases of development in terms of the *erogenous* (or *erotogenic*) zones of the body. Erogenous zones are therefore aspects of the physical body through which a pleasurable experience can be had. Sometimes the pleasure comes directly from an activity like sucking; at other times it can come through a sense of mastery, as in the achievement of sphincter control in toilet training.

Psychoanalysis terms the earliest phase of infancy the *oral phase,* since mouth pleasures obviously dominate at first. During the second year of postnatal life, the child first begins to act assertively in achieving bowel control. This has been named the *anal phase.* After a time, when bowel control has become established, interest in it diminishes and interest in genital functions and genital differences holds the center of the stage. This period has been called the *phallic phase.* The final phase of sexual development, the *genital phase,* begins with the onset of puberty and adolescence, when interest in genital function has reached sufficient maturity to make the adolescent aware of his or her approaching adult sex role and of a realistic preoccupation with persons of the opposite sex.

This general scheme has the advantage of being simple and straightforward. In what follows, we shall in general continue in this now traditional sequence. For the sake of greater latitude in dealing with the interactions that take place between a developing person and others around him or her, we shall include these phases in six personality stages. Through these every human being must pass in moving from birth to adulthood. As might be expected in dealing with anything as complex as human development, these stages overlap. They are not always clear-cut and mutually exclusive, but they are always useful and interesting. We shall take them up in Chapters 2 and 3 in the following order:

1. The oral dependent phase (the first year).
2. The anal phase of self-assertion and sphincter control (the second year or so).
3. The phallic phase and its Oedipal conflict (somewhere between the third and fifth years).
4. The phase of latency (from the close of the Oedipal period to about the eleventh or twelfth year).
5. Adolescence.
6. Adulthood.

## The Oral Dependent Phase of the First Year

As we have already suggested above in quoting Piaget (see p. 42), orality in the infant means that initially experience *is* predominantly sucking experience! Oral experiences lay the first foundations for an infant's construction of reality. Psychoanalysis holds that these experiences give to a person's reality and early ego organization an oral stamp that will never be lost. Development builds upon this oral base, so that even as mature adults we still unconsciously utilize a great deal of oral imagery as the grounds for the sake of which we understand experience. Oral allusions appear constantly in everyday speech without our paying any attention to them. We refer to memories as sweet or bitter, admire a person's good taste in clothing, or recoil from the biting sarcasm of a political analyst. There are thousands of such examples of habitual oral imagery in the meaningful expressions of normal adulthood. When we come to psycho-pathology, we shall meet examples of oral imagery that often illuminate other-wise obscure, meaningless symptoms.

*The First Year Is Dependent.* We call the first year *dependent* because infants are helpless. They can do next to nothing for themselves. They cannot even defend themselves in matters of life and death. They can suckle, they can move about and eliminate waste; but even in feeding and eliminating they need adult help to bring food almost to their lips and to keep them clean and healthy. Of course, thanks to this very dependence the infant exists via an unconscious symbiotic relationship with a mothering person, which, as we have seen, evolves into conscious *attachment* by the age of five or six months.

*Oral Experiences in the Earliest Ego Developments.* Oral experiences dominate early ego development because the mouth is the first sensorimotor portion of the body having immediacy and efficiency in drawing the infant's attention. Thus the first *object* to be cathected is an oral one, with the infant having the aim of seeking satisfaction from hunger through the mother's breast (or a related nutritive source). The mouth combines a richly endowed receptor system with an agile motor system, both housed in the same unit. The unit is already integrated at birth with inborn patterns for suckling, engulfing, mouth-ing, tasting, and rejecting. The mouth also has the anatomical advantage of having definite boundaries, the lips, which can be opened to admit things or closed to deny them admission.

Looked at from the (introspective) perspective of the infant, these opposed functions of admitting and excluding provide a beautiful grounds on the basis of which the child can come to understand what *external* (out-of-mouth) versus *internal* (inside-of-mouth) "reality" means. Psychoanalysis thus holds that in the most primitive thought processes the child frames a knowledge of what can be taken in or denied admission, accepted or rejected, in light of the framing sensorimotor system known as the mouth. The meanings encompassed by this already existing activity are, in effect, extended to experience, much as a logician extends premises to inferences and thereby draws conclusions. The importance of orality to early ego development is well symbolized in the fact that psychoanalysts have occasionally called this "first" organization of the personality the *mouth ego* (Hoffer, 1950).

*Oral Discrimination.* The earliest discriminations are made by the mouth. It is a physiological fact that the tip of the tongue yields the finest touch discrimination of the whole body. It is therefore proper to suggest that the first *reality-testing* is actually *reality-tasting,* something that we acknowledge obliquely when we speak of tasting life to the fullest. The hungry mouth turns toward anything that stimulates the face and grasps it with the lips, and if the lips can hold it, the infant begins to suckle. If what is grasped yields milk, the process of suckling, at first imperfectly coordinated with breathing, will go on until the infant is satisfied. If there is no such yield, the suckling stops, and crying or rooting and searching may appear. Freud saw in this differentiation made by the infant a primitive form of *discrimination* between what does and what does not yield pleasurable milk gratification. As such, this oral discrimination was taken as the precursor of ego choice and ego discrimination.

We note here a characteristic of Freudian theorizing that is already presaged in the idea of using existing sensorimotor activities to frame and understand later life activities. That is, Freud took a kind of "primacy" view of development whereby things occurring earlier always serve as prototypes or set patterns through which later things are made known or become possible. The earlier in life something happens, the more relevant it is to the developing personality organization. This theoretical style parallels Piagetian explanations to some extent (see p. 39), and there are psychoanalytical writers who have tried to link Freud and Piaget (see, e.g., Anthony, 1976; A. M. Sandler, 1975; P. H. Wolff, 1960). However, Freudian theory is far more *introspective* in its conceptualization, relying upon intentional fantasy structures that Piaget tends to discount. The ideal for Piaget is for the person to develop beyond unrealistic reliance on his or her infantile fantasies. Freud was impressed by the central role he found for fantasy throughout the human life cycle.

*Pleasure Sucking.* Infants also enjoy sucking when they are not hungry. Sometimes a hungry infant even prefers sucking the thumb or finger to nursing and has to be coaxed or even gently coerced to nurse. Sometimes an infant introduces his or her finger along with the nipple, apparently for double pleasure. It is this pleasure sucking (sometimes called "empty" sucking) that Freud regarded as erotic. This nonnutritive use of sucking is the earliest example of the active self-satisfaction of a need, without the help of someone else, the first example of what one day will become self-sufficiency.

*Oral Anticipation.* The appearance of oral anticipation is another landmark in the development of the ego. After a little experience, the hungry nursling begins to quiet down as he or she is placed in the nursing position, even before sucking commences and food is taken in. Psychoanalysis follows Papousek (1967a, 1967b) in believing that human infants are intentional learners and that such quieting in what is obviously an expectation of food represents oral anticipation. The infant is intending to perform a reflexive act in the immediate future of his or her life. Of course, anticipation introduces delay and often some frustration into the nursing act, a delay between an active approach to the nipple and the moment of orally seizing it with the lips and beginning to suckle.

Delay and moderate frustration are essential to the development of ego organization. They interpolate a period of anticipation between the urge to suckle and the actual beginning of suckling. This period of delay, however brief, can be considered a *phase of desire,* while the moment of grasping the nipple with the lips can be considered the beginning of the *phase of satisfaction.* Such a split in the act of nursing, into desire first and satisfaction later, marks the beginning of the distinction Freud drew between the *pleasure principle* (immediate gratification) and the *reality principle* (putting up with frustration). It heralds the fact that the maturing child continues to make discriminations in experience. The external world, in a sense, *forces* this discrimination, but the way in which it takes place is *not* "stimulus-response" manipulation but rather a kind of internally generated conceptualization made by the child that the external world has demands on the internal world. The child is not verbalizing such discriminations, of course. But the background for later verbal discrimination is being laid down in the oral experience of the feeding situation.

*Oral Imagery and the Internalization of Experience.* As used throughout this book, the term *imagery* means an active central representation, originally based upon perceptual experience. Imagery involves not just a picture, but also emotional or feeling components of the object perceived, recalled, or imagined. Much the same applies to *thinking* and *cognition* (knowing). Neither occurs ordinarily without some contribution from feeling and emotion. The importance of imagery is that, once organized, it can be aroused by the need alone, that is, without the presence of the nipple or the milk. Researchers cannot provide direct empirical evidence that infants retain specific oral imagery, of course, but five-month-old infants have been shown to retain impressions of visual images (e.g., faces) for two weeks after only a few minutes of initial perceptual exposure (Fagan, 1973). Freud merely suggested that, provided the delay between hunger and its realistic satisfaction is not too long, such imaginal capacities can be expected to provide temporary gratification. The assumption is that the child can fill this period of delay with an imagined satisfaction, much as we adults can help ourselves through a day of routine work by imagining the pleasure of the coming evening. With such a beginning, the infant has already begun the process of ego organization, which now includes delays and imagery, as well as the realistic integrations that lead from desire immediately to active satisfaction.

Subsequent experiences consolidate and elaborate the perceptual organizations and their imagery, which now have stable representation in the new functional patterns of the central nervous system. In this way, experiences that originate merely as temporary adaptations to somatic (bodily) and external need can bring about enduring changes in actual psychic organization. It is in some such sense that we speak of the *internalization of experience.* We know that experiences produce lasting changes in the organization of brain function (Sperry, 1977). We speak of the internalization of experience as *incorporation* if it seems to be actually taken into the body in this manner. We call it *introjection* if the taking in is only a *symbolic* taking in. We speak of identification if the *internalization* makes a person feel like that which he or she has internalized. Under certain circumstances, which we shall specify when they arise, the three terms may be used interchangeably. For example, an *introjection* may be a *symbolic incorporation* that is partly experienced as a physical taking in (*actual incorporation*) and makes one *feel like* the person or thing introjected (*identification*). As we shall see, internalization of experience occurs in visual, auditory, and manual forms, as well as in oral forms.

There is no way of finding out when oral symbolization begins in infancy. Symbolization has sometimes been said to begin with the beginning of verbalization, but this is certainly not true. Preverbal imagery and symbolization play an important part in primitive, infantile fantasy, such as we see revived in adult dreams, in psychoses, and in the deep therapy of neuroses. It must be remembered that infants and small children learn to interact in very complex ways with their surroundings long before words have an important place in their thinking. Preverbal interaction at human levels would be impossible without symbolic representation in oral and other forms. It is more in keeping with the facts to assume that symbolization begins around the same time that perceptual organization begins—in other words, soon after birth. Obviously, highly subjective distortions may occur in this early period of psychic living, which Harry Stack Sullivan (1953) referred to as the *prototaxic mode* (p. 38).

*Oral Imagery, Oral Incorporation, and Introjection.* Oral incorporation provides experiences and imagery that are the first models (Piagetian schemata) for the act of symbolic incorporation that we call *introjection.* The assumption is that infant and child are able to imagine swallowing or otherwise taking things in. When children become able to communicate their experiences to some extent, they often express primitive and unrealistic oral incorporations in their playful or fearful fantasies. Symbolic incorporation (introjection) is still more often expressed. We assume that these experiences do not spring suddenly to life with the advent of speech but go back a long way toward the beginning of postnatal life. In the psychotic regressions of adults are sometimes heard introjective wishes or fears expressed primitively in terms of actual incorporation.

> A schizophrenic violinist in her middle twenties brought her violin in its case to the in-patient service with her. She had an unusually possessive attitude toward it, trying to carry it everywhere she went. Twice, when she mislaid it, she became agitated because she felt sure that she had swallowed it. She gave as her only reason the fact that it belonged to her. She seemed to be fusing the notions of possessing, belonging to, and being within her. She was making concrete the feeling she had that it was an inner part of her being, as symbolically it was.

*Oral Refusal as a Prototype for Denial.* We noted above that the mouth has definite anatomical boundaries, the lips, which separate its interior from what will later become external reality. Just as opening the mouth is the earliest form of acceptance, so is closing the lips the earliest form of denying admission of something (Spitz, 1957). This act of closing the mouth, with its attendant imagery, contributes to forms of denial other than the purely oral, as for example the symbolic denial of something that threatens to be painful or dangerous. We shall see later that denial is used as a common defense, by normal as well as by neurotic and psychotic persons. It is a very *primitive* defense mechanism because it begins so early in life.

*Oral Ejection as a Prototype for Projection.* The mouth is also instrumental early in life in active ejections and rejections. The infant can spit out and vomit, sometimes reflexively, sometimes with apparent intent. These acts, with their imagery, become prototypical analogue-models for *projection,* which is a symbolic ejection or rejection. Just as an infant, by spitting out or vomiting, can make something within the bodily locus become something outside the bodily locus, so can the older child and the adult symbolically project something and in doing so make it appear as something that is not a part of him or her (Spitz, 1961). The objectionable qualities and intentions that even normal persons ascribe unjustifiably to others or to "the facts of life" are often projections of their own unacceptable qualities and intentions. The universal use of scapegoats is an example both of denial and projection. There is the *denial* that one has certain impulses or desires, and there is the *projection* of them on to persons considered to be licentious or inferior.

## USE OF THE EYES, EARS, AND HANDS IN EARLY EGO DEVELOPMENT

If the mouth is the infant's first active perceptual focus, the eyes, the ears, and the hands are his or her second group of perceptual foci. Each of these seems to develop and function at first independently of the others, and independent also of oral activity (Piaget, 1956). The organization of the visual system gets a somewhat later start than the oral, and the visual system also matures relatively slowly, over a considerable period. In the beginning it seems to provide a more or less independent perceptual world. For a long time, what infants see they do not bring to their mouths or manipulate. If their own hand appears in this visual field, they merely stare at it, sometimes with apparent surprise, as if it were something emerging out of the void. When it disappears infants promptly lose interest in it, just as they do with regard to other disappearing objects (L. Cohen & Salapatek, 1975).

If visual pursuit and visual searching go on, they do so without reference to oral or manual action. What the hands feel and grasp is not subjected to oral or manual examination. Only the ears seem to be tied up, almost from the start, with optical movements (Wertheimer, 1961). This tie-up is a primitive fore-runner of an orientation in space. It is not until the second month that pursuit movements of the eyes develop that permit them to fixate and hold a moving object with them. A little later, the eyes develop an increased ability to converge upon a visual stimulus and to make spontaneous conjugate movements of both eyes. Such fixating and following movements enable the child to maintain visual contact with things he or she sees. They are visual forms of grasping and holding. By the third month, infants have perfected their coordinated head movements, and these head movements help the eyes to prevent moving things from escaping. Infants have now extended their reality in space and time (Abravanel, 1967). They have begun to gain control over their world.

From the second month on, the infant's hand becomes more and more systematically adaptive. Movements of fingering, touching, scratching, grasping, pulling, and letting go are repeated over and over for long periods. The hands explore each other, the face, the body, and the surroundings. In time, the hand begins searching for things that have escaped it; for a long time, however, searching with the hand seems to be guided solely through manual perception and without any visual aid whatever. Even when infants look directly at their hands while the hand is grasping something, their visual perception seems not to influence what the hand does. Sometimes when the hand loses something, both hand and eyes search for it, but each system searches in accordance with its own biophysical formula. The hand moves around in the general area where it last made contact, but the eyes search inappropriately by turning from side to side, and not by turning toward the hands (Haith, 1980).

*Visual and Auditory Incorporation.* We have said that the eyes and ears "incorporate" experience. This is not a mere metaphor. Whatever the eyes and the ears can take in, and whatever of this the central nervous system is able to assimilate, become true "nutriment" for the visual and auditory organizations of mental life. More than this, the eyes, the ears, and their nervous system representation must have appropriate stimulation if they are ever to develop physiologically along normal lines. Visual and auditory incorporation is thus a biological necessity for normal receptor maturation and for the normal development of the brain as an organ.

*Visual and Auditory Incorporation in Relation to Oral Incorporation.* During the first few weeks, we have said, oral experience is superior to all other kinds of experience, because of the more mature organization of the infant's mouth and of its activities soon after birth. As time passes, however, the superiority of oral functions gives way to visual and auditory experience. The eyes and ears can assimilate or "take in" through conceptualizing things that are distant from the maturing child. Consequently, the eyes and ears are destined to become the major sources of knowledge for the child and adult, both directly in immediate observation and through the medium of language.

The eyes and ears also have special significance for unconscious and preconscious processes. Visual imagery, for example, makes up most of our manifest dreaming. Auditory imagery, although less important in this respect than visual imagery, still contributes more to the "story line" or manifest content of dreams than the remaining senses. Auditory imagery assumes major importance, even surpassing the visual, in the production of hallucinations (Lucas, Sansbury, & Collins, 1962). Oral incorporation remains a primary *source* of imagery in dreams and presumably in the unconscious, even though its *manifestation* in dreams is nearly always visual. Oral incorporation is also a source of symptom formation in neuroses and psychoses, as demonstrated in the description of the schizophrenic violinist given earlier.

*Manual Incorporation.* The fact that the hands also incorporate is still less obvious than visual and auditory incorporation, but it is of great significance in perceptual development and in the construction of reality. Although the hands are of little use at birth, with the passage of time they become more and more adept in exploring whatever comes in contact with them. They touch, feel, pass over, and scratch things very early in life, long before they are integrated with oral, visual, or auditory perception.

The peculiarly flexible form of the human hand makes it possible for it eventually to enclose things, to adapt its own form to the forms it encounters in external reality, including the manipulable realities of its own body. There is an apt metaphor in relation to the use of our hands, for in reaching to grasp and then explore our experience we also *select* and *mold* that which we encounter and come to know. The act of incorporation, whether oral, visual, auditory, or manual, is aptly construed in this metaphor of *engulfing* or *grasping* or *molding* that which is encountered. Incorporation is an active process, one that includes not *only* the Piagetian (1956) *assimilation* or taking in, but also a form of *accommodation* going beyond even adjusting one's schema to form a "better fit" with reality. In psychoanalytical terms, the person molds or creates an inner, subjective reality *in addition to* such fitting of schema to the outer, objective reality.

Manipulation by the hands—including finger exploration and general manual exploration—contributes constantly to an infant's construction of reality. One has only to think of the supreme importance of manual exploration and incorporation for the congenitally blind to realize the potentialities of the hands and the imagery they produce. Ordinary children and adults never give up reality-testing through actual handling. In a sense, the incorporation of manual manipulation supersedes the manipulations made possible by the "grasping" of oral activities such as biting, sucking, and touching with the tongue.

## FINAL INTERCOORDINATION OF THE PERCEPTUAL SYSTEMS

Between the fourth and sixth postnatal months, true eye-hand coordination is established. Both the eyes and the hands can now initiate activity and cooperatively carry it forward to completion of an intended end. The eyes, from their watchtower in the head, gradually gain control over the guidance of visible hand movements. They guide the hands toward things that the eyes can see but cannot reach, toward things that the hands can reach but cannot see. The eyes come to act as scanning and tracking instruments for the originating sources of control in the psyche. They keep the hand "on course" toward what is essentially a visualized end or goal to be attained behaviorally.

With the passage of time, the planes of oral, visual, and manual perception intersect. The hand that is seen goes with uncertain movements toward the mouth, while the hand that has just been mouthed can be held within the visual field and gravely inspected, sometimes with an assist from the other hand. Here again occurs suspended action or delay, which is generally considered essential for the development of an *ego.*

As the functions of the mouth, eyes, ears, and hands become integrated with one another, the evidence of more and different kinds of *anticipation* multiplies. Thus, for example, the eyes and ears as distance receptors can initiate sucking movements, drooling, and hypersecretion while an adult is making preparations for the feeding situation, long before food comes near the mouth itself. It is clear that the eyes and ears can begin imagining the "taking in" of food—or at least, the psyche can be said to begin such anticipatory "incorporation" in phantasy even before the *literal* act of food ingestion takes place. This is actually another way of speaking about the telic capacities of the human being (see Chapter 1, p. 5).

Oral, visual, auditory, and manual incorporation—with the central nervous system changes they induce in perceptual organization, imagery, and cognition—are all prime sources of ego structure. They constitute the models for *symbolic incorporation* or *introjection,* which the human organism uses to build up ego and superego structures, as well as for defensive purposes. It is assumed that such symbolical productions take place cognitively, by a psyche that is not merely shaped through mechanistic conditioning but shaping (molding, conceptualizing) experience through active conceptualizations that grow in complexity and become better integrated as life unfolds. Symbolic incorporation or introjection enters into the most highly integrated "secondary process" thinking, as well as into more primitive, unrealistic thinking, such as we see in the formation of unconscious fantasies, manifest dreams, and symptoms.

Harry Stack Sullivan (1953) outlined this progression of cognitive experience as moving from the primitive *prototaxic* to the *parataxic* mode, in which the various sensory inputs are assembled into fragmentary understanding, and thence as language is attained to a *syntaxic* mode that has the consensually agreed-upon meanings of the culture in general (p. 186). However, Sullivanian theory perceives this progression less as something that the person carries out intentionally than as a sociocultural shaping in the extraspective (see p. 6) style of behavioristic explanations. In traditional psychoanalysis, one always looks introspectively through the perceptive apparatus of the individual, who is "coming at" experience intentionally. This apparatus is innately given (à la biological naturalism; see p. 47), but the way in which it then functions is not to be understood in biological terms alone (i.e., one does not have to embrace biological reductionism; see p. 13). When one does look at the individual in this fashion one is forced to take into account the fact that introjection is dependent upon the level of differentiation that the ego or "identity point" of the personality system has achieved. This takes us to our next section.

## Lack of Functional Boundaries in Early Mental Functioning

The lack of clear differentiation, and particularly the lack of ego boundaries, makes introjection much simpler to carry through in infancy than in later childhood and adulthood. Infants seem at first to lack the functional boundaries that adults take for granted. Among these are the boundaries between external and internal, between fantasy and socially shared reality, between the self and others. It is difficult to imagine what existence must be like totally without such differentiations. We come close to such a phenomenal state in our dreams. One moment a dreamer seems to be watching something that is being done, and the next moment he or she is the one doing it, or, it may be unclear who exactly is doing what is going on. Such "reactive" or distorted contents are quite common in normal dreaming (Rychlak, 1960). The boundaries between *me* and *thee* often fluctuate unstably in a dream, in a way that would be extremely disturbing if one were awake.

Functional boundaries are sometimes inadequate or even lacking when a person, an adult, is awake. The simplest demonstration of this can be made in *intoxications*. A wide range of intoxicating agents, from ordinary alcohol to mescaline and lysergic acid, can dissolve the functional boundaries of most adults. When the intoxication clears up, the boundaries reestablish themselves. The ego organization that depends upon the integrity of such boundaries soon reappears. A demonstration that is more difficult to arrange is that of *sensory deprivation* (Heron, 1957). In this case, subjects are wrapped like mummies or floated in water so that they receive a minimal degree of sensory input. It is not unusual in such an instance for even normal adults to lose their functional boundaries and to hallucinate. Based on such findings, Bruner (1961) has argued that hallucinations (seeing, hearing things, people, etc.) reflect the fact that human beings can and do create their own "realities" when none is presented to them sensorily. Psychoanalysis builds on this telic human capacity. Freud (1913/1955d) never tired of pointing out that neurotics place even more emphasis on "psychical" reality than they do on "factual" reality (p. 159).

Functional boundaries also dissolve in the psychoses, and most strikingly in the schizophrenias (see Chapter 14). Many schizophrenics, without having ingested a drug or having been denied sensory stimulation, nevertheless re-experience the inability to distinguish between themselves and someone else, or between themselves and other things, that they experienced as infants. A schizophrenic young man may complain that he does not know whether it is he or someone else who is doing something—much as dreamers seem to feel. He is often unable to distinguish clearly between his own imaginings and the events that are occurring in the world of external reality or in the reality of his own body (Cameron, 1944a).

Such patients often complain openly that they seem to be "falling apart" or "disappearing," that the world seems to be changing unaccountably, or that something terrible is happening that they cannot put into words. These all seem to be attempts to describe the experience of ego disintegration that occurs in deep *regression* (i.e., returning to earlier life periods mentally). Since in schizophrenic disorders the patient is neither intoxicated nor asleep, nobody can put a halt to this young man's disintegration, or to the regression of his ego functions, by detoxifying him or waking him up. The path back to normality is a difficult one. There are some who never succeed in finding it.

If we remember that external reality and ego orientation are interdependent, that "the world" and "the self" are two aspects of the same unity, it is easy to understand why ego disintegration appears to the regressing person as the disappearance of the world, as well as the disappearance of the self. We have only to remind ourselves that every night both the world of external reality and the self disappear (when we fall asleep) to be able to understand how such a thing is possible. The difference is that, when we fall asleep every night, there is no other world present to confuse and bewilder us, whereas in schizophrenia the world of reality presents itself to the patient as something that does not fit into his or her imaginings.

## Summary of Ego Development and Dissolution of Symbiosis with the Mother

We shall defer further discussion of ego development until we come to Chapter 5 on the intrapsychic dynamics. However, it will facilitate understanding if we now give a summary outline of what we have been driving at to this point in Chapter 2:

*1. Primary identification with the mother.* We have good reason to assume that, during the first few weeks of postnatal life, no human infant is capable of distinguishing between itself and its mother (or mothering one, including the father, surrogate parent, etc.). This state of affairs is known as *primary identification*. It is not an abnormality; it is not a defense. It is simply an incapacity to distinguish objects, a lack of ego organization, and an absence of self-referred feelings. It is an expression of the lack of functional boundaries that characterizes symbiosis in early infancy and that we have compared to the kaleidoscopic shifting of imagery commonly experienced in adult dreaming. Thanks to primary identification, as the infant's level of differentiation grows, and as he or she begins to gain control over personal action, the mother's influence as a model will be noted in helping the offspring to channel behavior along socially acceptable lines (Finney, 1961).

2. *Autonomous ego functions and the conflict-free sphere.* The gradual maturation and development of perceptual, cognitive, and motor functions make it possible for the infant to organize external reality. These functions form the basis of what Heinz Hartmann (1958) has termed *autonomous ego functions.* They are primarily adaptive in character, rather than defensive, and they give rise to a *conflict-free sphere* in ego organization.

3. *Id, ego, and superego conflicts.* Not everything in the psyche is without conflict. Freud believed that psychic life begins in a state typified by domination by the *id,* a completely hedonistic, narcissistic attitude toward the world in which *primary process thinking* predominates. In primary process thinking immediate gratification is expected, and the infant will hallucinate desired (cathected) objects when they are not "really" present. In time, thanks to the infant's incorporation and identification with reality, the *ego* is differentiated from the id. Eventually, a *superego* is differentiated from the ego as well. The matter of delaying gratification in adjusting to reality is important here. The ego is that aspect of the psyche which puts up with frustration, reasoning according to the more mature *secondary process* (reality-oriented) form of thought. However, in order to coordinate the hedonistic promptings of the id, the countering sociocultural mandates of the superego, and the practical demands of reality, the ego must rely upon a series of psychic maneuvers that Freud termed the *defense mechanisms.* These mechanisms function unconsciously, so Freud was to learn that ego and superego aspects of the psyche bridge all levels of awareness, whereas the id portion of the psyche remains throughout life at the unconscious level. We shall take up these defense mechanisms as well as a more detailed review of the id, ego, and superego in Chapter 4.

4. *The defenses and boundary setting.* Early in life the defenses play a leading role in establishing and maintaining functional boundaries between the id, with its primary process, and the ego, with its secondary process form of thought. The defenses also help set functional boundaries between the ego and external reality and between both of these and somatic reality. We shall have opportunities to see what happens if these boundaries begin to dissolve when we come to the clinical chapters on neuroses and psychoses.

5. *Ego introjects.* While perceptual, cognitive, and motor functions are maturing and developing through use, and while the ego is differentiating from

the id, from external and somatic realities, there are also incorporations of certain aspects of maternal behavior taking place. We call the results of such incorporation *ego introjects*. They are actually derived in part from the mothering person's behavior and in part from the simultaneous experiences of the infant. As we have seen, the infant cannot at the time distinguish between the two sources of his or her experience, that which comes from the mothering person and that which comes from himself or herself.

To a lesser degree, but still to a significant extent, the ego introjects also include aspects of the patterns of other persons, particularly those within a child's immediate family (father, siblings, etc.). Although the traditional female role of mother is extremely important, we must never forget that father, siblings, and other significant figures enter somewhat into the *symbiotic* ties of the child at a somewhat lessened level of involvement. Findings cited above on attachment are consistent with this clinically based impression.

6. *Internal objects.* As ego boundaries crystalize, these early ego introjects organize into what we call *internal objects.* The term *object* refers to a person, place, or thing in the external environment that will satisfy a need. The internal objects are particularly likely to represent parental objects. They organize the early fundamentals of personality. They also help the infant to control his or her behavior along the general lines of parental approval and disapproval. In other words, the infant becomes more and more like the parents by introjecting their attitudes and behavioral styles, and these introjections help determine what the infant will do as time goes by. They are therefore precursors of what will later become superego controls. Thus, quite early in life the infant tries to please the *internalized* parents as well as the parents in external reality (resulting in *superego* formation).

7. *The infant as an autonomous individual.* By the time infants can sit up alone and stand, their active relations with what is becoming external reality, and their parallel organization of an ego system within, have progressed to a point at which they can begin to operate as *autonomous individuals.* From the second or third month these abilities, and the corresponding ego elaborations, begin to evolve and their rate of development rapidly accelerates. By the end of the first year the infant has established a separate identity, resolving the symbiotic relationship but continuing to sense attachment to his or her loved ones (parents, siblings, significant others, etc.).

8. *Consequences of abnormal symbiotic relationships.* Two contrasting abnormal symbiotic relationships have been seen clinically. The first is the so-called *autistic child* (Kanner, 1944). Such children do not take an interest in their social world. They do not play with toys. They ignore their parents. Many are mute, and those who do verbalize simply parrot whatever sounds are in earshot. Autistic children remain permanently incapable of forming effective object relationships and of constructing external reality or an effective ego organization. They have, in effect, never gone through the symbiotic relationship preparing them for such an essential personality development in life. It does not appear that autism is caused by "dynamic" factors such as parental

rejection. After considerable research on such infants, most authorities ascribe the condition to some as yet unidentified physiological disorder of the brain (Rutter & Schopler, 1978).

The second abnormal symbiotic relationship results in what has been termed the *symbiotic child*. Such children have entered into a full symbiotic relationship with a mother figure, but then are unable to successfully resolve it. They go on to develop an extremely distorted, dependent relationship with the mother figure. The syndrome is called a *symbiotic childhood psychosis* (Mahler, 1952). The outlook for the symbiotic child is bleak, even though it is not as serious as for the autistic child. Both autistic and symbiotic children are likely to be diagnosed as suffering from *childhood schizophrenia*. However, there are such wide differences between these childhood syndromes and those of adolescent and adult schizophrenia that many experts have raised serious objections to the use of "childhood schizophrenia" as a clinical concept (Ekstein, Bryant, & Friedman, 1958).

As we shall see in the clinical chapters, there are many partial failures to resolve the problems raised by the symbiotic mother-child relationship that result neither in autistic nor in symbiotic childhood disorders. They do give rise to personality structures that are vulnerable to neurotic or psychotic breakdowns later on in childhood, in adolescence, or in adulthood. More often than not, partial failures in dissolving the symbiotic relationship with the mothering person leave the child poorly equipped to develop into an autonomous individual. Some investigators believe that this problem may be caused by a mother who is "overprotective" of her offspring. Thus, it is not uncommon for children who have overprotective mothers to be highly anxious and fearful of even mild life challenges (Jenkins, 1968). This, as we shall see, leaves them poorly equipped to face the rigors of the Oedipal conflict. Let us turn next to the phase of self-assertion and sphincter control.

## The Anal Phase of Self-Assertion and Sphincter Control

The *anal phase* of personality development occupies the second year of postnatal life. It begins with the onset of the dissolving symbiotic mother-child unit and ends with the child's entanglement in the Oedipal conflict of the phallic phase. The "late" anal period is sometimes referred to as the *urethral* period, for the focus of attention shifts slightly from sphincter control of the anus (which usually occurs first) to the sphincter control of the penis or vestibule of the vagina (the urethra is the canal which carries urine from the bladder to the latter two outlets). We shall confine our consideration of sphincter controls to the anal erotogenic zone of the body.

The anal phase of psychosexual development is typified by self-assertion, as the child increasingly demonstrates the ability to stand, walk, and run alone, along with gradual mastery of sphincter controls. The chief pitfalls in this phase are the overdoing of self-assertion, the abuse of freedom in walking, climbing, and running about, and the use of sphincter control to frustrate parents — either by withholding bowel movements when they are asked for or by making them at inappropriate times or places. Children who have been harshly toilet trained have been known to rebel and thereby regress in sphincter controls (Anthony, 1957). The self-assertion in most cases can be easily dealt with by parents, who are readily trained to correct early mistakes (Barrett, 1969). The danger to the child is that if frustrated too much by parents he or she will become either a chronically angry child or a submissive one who lacks normal initiative.

A growing ability to understand speech and to use it is also characteristic of the anal phase of development. Consistent with Piaget and our discussion above regarding active cognitive schemes or prototypes, Nelson (1974) has found that the initial linguistic meanings of the child's first words are based on *action-schemes* that were construed during the first year of life. Hence, a continuing development from reflexive movement to construing actions done reflexively to words that then carry these earlier meanings is accomplished. R. Brown (1973) has also pointed to the rule-governed constructions that children frame and bring to bear in a self-directing and not simply "associative" manner (see also Berko, 1958). Talking and understanding language hasten the child's integration into the family unit as a distinctive individual. It seems likely that, as our review of the attachment research suggested (see above), the father's role in the child's life is growing over this period, facilitated in large measure by language games and jokes, the telling of fairy tales, and so forth.

Language also has its pitfalls. For example, there is the confusion of things with the words that symbolize them, the misunderstanding of what is said because of inexperience and a peculiarly concrete manner of thinking, and the use of speech to tantalize adults, as in the perpetual *why's* of this phase. Sullivan (1953) referred to many of the confusions resulting as *parataxic distortions.* Even as adults, we are still many times confused and trapped by the apparent dichotomy between what we experience in nonverbal ways and what we try to say about such experience — or what others say about similar experiences. Language has its own structure and its own rules, which are not always the same as the structures and the rules of nonverbal experience.

A caution that should be made at this point is that any division of childhood development into separate stages or phases is bound to be somewhat arbitrary and to lead to misunderstanding itself. For example, attempts at self-assertion and even negativism are seen during the symbiotic relationship of the oral phase, and neither self-assertion nor negativism disappears completely when the child enters the phallic phase. Locomotion and general coordination go on increasing in efficiency well into adulthood. The mastery of language and the acquisition of knowledge may not be complete until later maturity. Even sphincter control is not achieved all at once. There may be frequent lapses, especially if a sibling is born soon after sphincter control has been achieved. Obstinacy finds many other channels of expression. The *reaction-formations* (oppositional tendencies; see Chapter 4, p. 137) against soiling, characteristic of this early period, become important maneuvers in self-control that precede formation of the superego.

Normal parents and siblings welcome the child's efforts to become a separate "little person" in the family milieu. The child must attain certain advances before he or she is fully acceptable as an independent family member—in eating habits, in channeling expressions of love and/or rage, in becoming predictable, in gaining self-control, and in achieving sphincter control. During this phase of development it is normal for a child to show special interest in bowel control and in bowel products. Bowel control can be a new and pleasurable accomplishment, a further step toward mastery and maturity, that parents and siblings can appreciate and encourage. Interest in bowel products is also understandable. The child creates them by a voluntary act; they obviously come from his or her own body; they have a recognizable form; and in a sense they are infantile sculptures. Moreover, the child's mother openly values them and expresses her satisfaction to the child. She sees them as evidence of good health and increasing maturity. The great majority of young children lose most of their pride and interest in bowel functions as they mature further and as they find other forms of mastery to awaken their pride and hold their interest.

It is of importance to psychopathology that the childhood problem of bowel control can easily become a call to battle within the family. Children quickly learn that their parents want them to produce bowel movements on schedule and in the right place. They also seem to learn quickly that parents can be readily frustrated by not complying. If a child's noncompliance arouses anger or anxious insistence in the parent, it can become the focus of serious warfare (Sears, Maccoby, & Lavin, 1957). Some mothers react with marked tension and even with rage when their child becomes constipated, especially if it seems to them to be the result of willful negativism. The trouble with such reactions is that they also make the child tense and angry. Tension and anger negate the likelihood of having a bowel movement, and hence a vicious circle in the mother-child relationship develops. As we shall see when we take up disorders such as the obsessive-compulsive neurosis (see Chapter 7), there are any number of influences to be seen on later personality style due to maladaptive toilet-training relationships between the child and his or her mother.

One of the more publicized outcomes involves the so-called *anal personality,* in which an adult may be obstinate, parsimonious, and constricted (Pollak, 1979). Sometimes such tendencies appear in an adult following a life frustration, so that we witness a repetition or re-enactment of childhood sphincter-control problems that have never been resolved. The previously generous person begins hoarding things (food, money, old clothes, etc.) shortly after having been divorced. This tendency for unresolved problems to persist at an unconscious level is known as *fixation* (see Chapter 5, p. 151). Few adults realize that they are reenacting an earlier drama from out of their past, but analytical investigation establishes that this is indeed the case. Sometimes a child is so pressured by the parents during training of sphincter controls that he or she capitulates and becomes overly compliant and manifestly "good" out of a compulsive need to avoid any friction with parents or parental surrogates.

A less common difficulty to be seen in adults who have suffered fixations during their sphincter-control education is *sadomasochism* (obtaining erotic pleasure from inflicting or receiving pain). Psychoanalytical studies of normal as well as neurotic children suggest that emotional ambivalence is experienced by every child during the phase of self-assertion and sphincter control. Love and hate for the same person are readily intermingled. Add to this the fact that pleasurable erotic feelings during this period issue from anal stimulation and we have the potential for sadomasochism if a conflict of wills develops between the child and parent. Thus, sadomasochistic pleasure and anger appear to be related both to infantile self-assertion and to the rage that fills a frustrated child who is able to do so much and yet is subjected to so much control by others (Gero, 1962).

## Autoerotism, Narcissism, Object-Love, and Identification

This is a good point at which to consider a handful of terms that Freud used to describe the course of normal human development as well as to account for various forms of psychopathological illnesses. We have been reviewing the course of oral/anal development without focusing attention on the progression of the sexual instinct per se. According to Freud, there were essentially three levels of libidinal development through which all infants progressed over the phases we have been considering. First of all, the state of libidinal organization in which we all begin life is termed *autoerotism*. By this, Freud (1915/1957i, p. 132) meant that the *organ* (body part, e.g., mouth, anus, penis, vagina, etc.) is of primary importance rather than some kind of *object* toward which that particular organ is biologically oriented to gain satisfaction.

In other words, when the infant is taking pleasure from sucking, for example, or from excretion, there is no emphasis being placed on anything else but the organ itself. There is no "relationship" being formed between the erotogenic (pleasure-producing) zone of the physical organ and "something else" that serves as the object of this pleasurable activity. With development, however, and as the "primacy of the genitals" (Freud, 1913/1959d, p. 188) is established, the state of autoerotism must gradually give way to what is called *object-choice* and/or *object-love*. In sexual life, it is important to direct instinctive promptings and thereby to cathect objects that will be joined in sexual intercourse so that procreation and the survival of the race is ensured (see Chapter 4).

However, there is a "halfway" state between autoerotism and object-love termed *narcissism*, which Freud (1911/1958a) described as follows: "There comes a time in the development of the individual at which he unifies his sexual instincts (which have hitherto been engaged in auto-erotic activities) in order to obtain a love-object; and he begins by taking himself, his own body, as his love-object, and only subsequently proceeds from this to the choice of some person other than himself as his object. This half-way phase between autoerotism and object-love may perhaps be indispensable normally; but it appears that many people linger unusually long in this condition, and that many of its features are carried over by them into the later stage of their development" (pp. 60-61).

Now, as a general rule, if a child *fails* to move smoothly from autoerotism through narcissism to object-love, a groundwork is laid for serious adjustment problems later in life. In certain cases, *regressing* (or going back) *from object-choice to narcissism* means that the person is turning away from interpersonal contact into a self-indulgent form of sexual gratification. As we shall see, Freud was to assign this dynamic to several different disorders, including homosexuality, depression, paranoia, and schizophrenic disturbances of various sorts.

Another aspect of development we might take note of in this context involves the difference between *identification* and *object-choice*. As the promptings of sexual pleasure focus on the genitals, the nature of the relationship between a child and his or her parents changes. We have noted in discussing symbiosis and attachment that the child is framing a primary identification with parents based on the prototype of incorporation. This incorporative psychic maneuver of "taking in" is very primitive. *Identification as a psychological activity is therefore more primitive than object choice!* Identification begins very early, as the child is moving from the autoerotic into the halfway state of narcissism. It therefore happens that problems in development that *fixate* a child in the halfway state of narcissism can adversely affect the child's developing patterns of identification. All manner of personality problems can arise when this dynamic takes place.

There is also the dynamic known as *reverting from object-choice to identification*. We note this when individuals regress from a more adult pattern, become childlike, and symbolically incorporate into their belief systems ideas that they never would have accepted were it not for this regressive reversion to an earlier psychic stage of functioning. For example, a woman may so place her minister on a pedestal that she identifies totally with his highly eccentric and unofficial interpretations of certain biblical passages. Her sexualized attraction (object-choice) to this unstable cleric has reverted to identification (thanks to a predisposing fixation in her psychic organization), and she now is seen to express the most bizarre religious views with an untroubled sense of conviction. The dynamic of reversion from object-choice to identification is found in other personality-related behaviors as well. For example, we shall see it active in the explanations of the Oedipus complex resolution (see Chapter 3, p. 77) and also in the dynamics of paranoia (see Chapter 11, p. 327). We next turn to the phallic stage of psychosexual development with its Oedipal conflict in Chapter 3.

## SUMMARY

Chapter 2 begins a review of the major findings on personality development in infancy and early childhood. Infants today are perceived as much more active in their perceptual and conceptual abilities than used to be the case. Mechanistic theories—those theories that rely upon constructs based upon material-cause and efficient-cause reductionism—have contended that infants are essentially molded or manipulated early in life to behave as they do. Personal agency seems too complex a concept for such theories to take seriously. However, when we look carefully at the experiments that have been specifically designed to test the conditioning of infant behavior we find little support for the mechanistic explanation.

When suitable controls are introduced into experiments on classical conditioning in infants, we learn that there has been a form of pseudoconditioning taking place, because virtually any stimulus in the testing situation might "elicit" the response being assessed after the infant has been sensitized that something is taking place in the so-called conditioning trials. Looked at in terms of a teleological theory, evidence on newborn infants suggests that they are already anticipating or expecting events to occur, rather than "responding" in mechanical fashion to experimental manipulations. Of course, it is possible to adapt such findings to a mechanistic theory, and this is what is typically done. But the evidence per se is *as supportive* of a telic view of infant behavior as it is of a mechanistic view.

Experiments that employ operant conditioning techniques have found infants to be remarkably prepared to adapt their behaviors to their environments. Unlike lower animals, who require days of practice to be "shaped," infants are found to adapt their behavior in minutes. The text follows Piaget and others who view the newborn infant as an active organism, *assimilating* through reflexive processes the environment and then subsequently *accommodating* what is first "known" reflexively to fit better that which is expected. Papousek found infants adapting spontaneously to changing conditions, and he interpreted such behavior as intentional. Other experimenters have been unable to operantly shape infant smiling and cooing by having mothers verbally reinforce such behaviors. Finally, extensive investigation of their visual preference has demonstrated that infants have a clear selective capacity in which they seem to abstract preferential objects to look at. Once again, the mechanistic theorist will frame such findings in terms of material and efficient causation, as if the infant is "wired" to respond to stimuli in certain ways, and so on. But the point made in Chapter 2 is that the telic account is equally if not more suitable to an understanding of these empirical findings.

Chapter 2 continues with an overview of the child's experience following birth. A parallel is drawn between the cognitive theories of Piaget and Freud's biological naturalism. Both these theorists essentially held that natural acts like swallowing or retaining food could be used as biological schemata through which the primitively forming organism could learn things and imitate the behavior of important people early in life. Concepts like *incorporation, introjection,* and *identification* are explained in this manner. Regurgitation and vomiting forms the prototype for the defense of *projection* in Freudian theory. It is as if the child uses the reflexive behavior naturally available to him or her in framing upcoming experience. This process bears the quality of a "that (reflexive pattern) for the sake of which" experience can be known—that is, a final-cause addition to the material- and efficient-cause reflexive action. Patterns are formal causes, of course, so that we have employed the meaning of all four causes in describing "infant behavior" in Chapter 2. Our theoretical slant is introspective, viewing the reflexive capacity of an infant from his or her point of view.

Parenting is discussed next. The roles of both mother and father are considered. Bowlby's concept of *attachment* is given prominent consideration. This need to be in close proximity to a certain individual early in life focuses initially on the mother, but paternal attachments also take place. If the infant is removed from the proximity of a person to whom attachment has been formed, a profound sense of depression termed *detachment* sets in. Bowlby suggests that a clear and firm attachment is rarely seen in infant behavior before six months of age. Other authorities dispute this age level, but all who study this phenomenon agree that attachment is *not* evident at birth. In psychoanalytical terms, attachment relates to object-choice and the cathecting of parents—first the mother and then the father. The mutual tie of mother and child is sometimes referred to as *symbiosis,* a term borrowed from biology suggesting that there is a vital benefit to be gained by two different organisms, one of whom lives off the other. Maternal attitudes are very important as studies demonstrate that a child's adjustment can suffer if there is not a gratifying symbiotic relationship between mother and offspring.

The psychoanalytical theory of development is next to be covered in Chapter 2. The phases in this development are conceptualized in terms of the *erogenous* (or *erotogenic*) zones of the body. We can delineate the phases of *oral, anal (urethral), phallic,* and *genital* psychosexual development. The period of *latency* separates the latter two levels. Chapter 2 next surveys the highly important oral phase in some detail. Reality-testing begins in "reality-tasting." This primitive form of *discrimination* permits the child to begin framing a sense of identity separate and distinct from external reality. Ingestion of milk then begins the process of incorporation and its attendant acts of introjection and eventually identification. Infants in the oral stage are dominated by the *pleasure principle.* We cannot overlook the role of eyes, ears, and hands at this early stage. There is a gradual coordination developed via these various sensory modalities.

A parallel is drawn to H. S. Sullivan's explanation of cognitive experience as moving from the primitive *prototaxic* to the *parataxic* mode, in which various sensory inputs are assembled into fragmentary understanding, and thence as language is attained to a *syntaxic* mode that has the consensually agreed-upon meanings of the culture in general. The tenuous state of functional boundaries in the immature ego is highlighted. Hartmann's "autonomous ego functions," which serve an adaptive and not a defensive role in behavior, are noted, leading to what has been termed a *conflict-free sphere* in ego organization. There are also problems arising due to the *primary process* thinking of the early personality organization. The conflicts between id, ego, and superego are underscored. A severe outcome of unhealthy symbiotic ties is the autistic child, typified by complete disinterest in the social world. It is as if these children are incapable of forming symbiotic ties in life. The *symbiotic child* commits himself or herself to such ties, but then is unable to break them.

Chapter 2 next takes up the anal phase and some of the adjustment problems that arise from the need to achieve sphincter control. A common defense mechanism of this period is *reaction-formation,* in which oppositional tendencies against soiling become important maneuvers in self-control that precede formation of this superego. *Fixations* in psychosexual development at this stage may result in an *anal personality,* typified by parsimony, petulance, and pedantry. *Sadomasochism,* or the obtaining of erotic pleasure from inflicting or receiving pain, is a less common outcome of fixations at the anal level.

Chapter 2 closes with a discussion of some concepts that are essential to an understanding of psychopathology. Every person is viewed psychoanalytically as passing through a period of *autoerotism* in which the bodily organ (e.g., mouth, anus, penis, vagina, etc.) is of primary importance rather than an *object* through which the organ is biologically prepared to gain satisfaction. Infant sucking, for example, is focused on the mouth per se rather than on what might be sucked. With development, such autoerotic behaviors give way to more mature levels of *object-choice* and/or *object-love.* However, there is a "halfway" state between autoerotism and object-love termed *narcissism* (i.e., taking oneself as love-object). If the developing person fails to move smoothly from autoerotism through narcissism to object-love, a groundwork is laid for serious adjustment problems in life. In general, when the person reverts or *regresses from object choice to narcissism* at some later time in life, the personality system is slipping into maladjustment.

The final dynamic we consider in Chapter 2 relates to identification and object-choice. Object-choice is a later activity in life than identification, which is based on the more primitive mechanism of incorporation. It therefore follows that if later in life a person *reverts from object-choice to identification* this too is an indication of burgeoning maladjustment. The person is shrinking from a more mature level of interpersonal relations to a more primitive level. Not infrequently we see the combined dynamics of narcissism and identification in preference to object-choice taking place in the same individual. We shall return to these dynamics in later chapters.

# 3

# Personality Development: Late Childhood, Latency, Adolescence, and Adulthood

The review of personality development that we completed in Chapter 2 was straightforward. We saw that theories that claim infants are shaped into their behavioral patterns through conditioning have no more firm evidence on which to base those claims than theories that view the newborn person as an agent, actively influencing the course of personality development. Freudian theory falls into the latter type of teleological explanation. It focuses on biologically "given" organs and their associated erogenous zones, because it is through these natural structures of the mouth, anus, eyes, and so forth, that the infant is believed to first frame, construe, and conceptualize what William James (1952) called the "blooming, buzzing confusion" of life following birth (p. 318).

But in coming to the next psychosexual phase (or stage) of development—the phallic—we introduce an aspect of psychoanalysis that critics have always attacked as highly objectionable. The word *phallic* is based on the Greek root *phallos,* meaning "penis in erection," and right here we begin to understand the source of this criticism. First of all, a penis is something that only males have as a standard biological endowment. Freud, on the other hand, thought of the female clitoris as in effect a "little penis" that becomes engorged with blood and is a highly pleasurable sexual erogenous zone. Hence, one word for both sexes does not do violence to the theory of a standard phase of development through which both boys and girls pass.

But even though a four-year-old boy's penis or a girl's clitoris may become "erect," surely this cannot be evidence for a *sexual* motive in such young children? This is the question that critics put to Freud. Based upon his personal experience and his work with adults in psychoanalysis he answered, in effect, that just as sucking for pleasure helps the child to know the world, sexualized overtures to an "other" person (object) help the child to know the world. As we noted at the close of Chapter 2, this moves the child from an autoerotic form of gratification to a more mature object-love (by way of a brief period of narcissism; see p. 63). And it is only through such moves to tie ourselves to others in interpersonal relationships that we can become the *human* beings that we are.

It is sometimes thought that Freud's professional colleagues rejected his views because of his infantile sexuality thesis. Recent scholarship has demonstrated rather convincingly that this is *not* true (see Sulloway, 1979). Many of his peers in the medical profession accepted the likelihood of a sexualized relationship between mother and child. It was Freud's elaboration of this widely observed clinical phenomenon, his tying of it to the Sophocles drama, and the way in which he claimed to have seen in the familial Oedipal re-enactment a kind of proof for how primitive society was begun, that provoked criticism and rejection by his contemporaries in medicine. But the idea of a sexualized mother-son relationship has continued to prove repugnant to those nonprofessionals in our culture who have not been subject to a personal psychoanalysis. It is also true that the empirically oriented professionals in psychiatry and psychology clamor for objective evidence supporting the view that *everyone* passes through an Oedipal conflict in late childhood. Evidence substantiating such conflicts in certain family settings is not difficult to find (Sarnoff & Corwin, 1959). But how are we to demonstrate such fantasied aspects of childhood development among *all* human beings? Freud would answer, "Only through submission to a psychoanalysis for all!"

In recent years, a second reason for rejecting Freudian theory concerning the Oedipal resolution stems from the fact that it has presented female development in a negative light. Freud was always challenged on this point, but in recent times with the rise of feminism there has been a particularly hostile reaction to his views. We shall try in our presentation to be loyal to Freud's views on the male and female Oedipal conflict, but also to present the alternative formulations of Karen Horney on the question of female psychology. As anyone familiar with the history of psychoanalysis knows, though there have been some decided splits between outlooks like those of Adler or Jung and Freud's views, there have also been a number of modifications and alternative positions taken within psychoanalysis that did not call for a parting of the ways. As in other branches of science, we can disagree on certain aspects of our outlook without totally invalidating the fundamental point of view. We now turn to a consideration of the phallic stage of psychosexual development.

## The Phallic Phase and Its Oedipal Conflict

*The Legend.* According to an ancient legend, which Sophocles has one of his characters compare to normal incestuous dreams, an infant prince was exposed to die because of a prophecy that he was destined to murder his father. He was rescued by strangers and brought up as a prince in an alien court. When he sought to learn his true origin from an oracle, he was given the kind of confusing information in which oracles seem to specialize. He was simply told to avoid his home because he was destined to kill his father and marry his mother. The prince, whose name was Oedipus, then took to the road as a warrior, thinking that he was indeed leaving his home. In a quarrel on the way, he killed the King of Thebes, who actually was his father, although Oedipus did not know it. He then went on to solve the riddle of the Sphinx, which saved the Thebans from her murderous attacks. The grateful Thebans put Oedipus on the now empty throne and, as was the ancient custom, gave him the slain king's widow as his wife.

The new king, Oedipus Rex, had a long and peaceful reign, during which the queen bore him two sons and two daughters. Then a plague broke out in Thebes. The oracle declared that the murderer of the former king must be driven from the land if the land was to be saved. After an objective but tragically personal searching, which Freud compared to psychoanalysis, Oedipus discovered that the slain king was his father and that he had married his own mother. Before either he or his mother realized the truth, and while Oedipus was beginning to suspect it, his wife and mother tried to reassure and comfort the distraught Oedipus by saying, "Many a man ere now in dreams hath lain with her who bare him" (Freud, 1900/1953a, p. 264). When the truth was finally revealed, the queen committed suicide. Oedipus blinded himself and left his home forever.

Freud used this legend as a kind of metaphor or analogue. That is, he believed that Sophocles' play held such fascination for audiences over many centuries because it dealt with a theme that *everyone* has encountered in his or her life. Thus, in an 1897 letter to his friend Wilhelm Fliess (see Chapters 1 and 16), Freud wrote: "I have found, in my own case too [i.e., in Freud's self-analysis], falling in love with the mother and jealousy of the father, and I now regard it as a universal event of early childhood. . . . If that is so, we can understand the riveting power of *Oedipus Rex* [i.e., the fascination it holds for audiences]" (Freud, 1892-99/1966c, p. 265). In 1900, Freud wound these familial dynamics into *The Interpretation of Dreams,* though he did not formalize the complex as such (Freud, 1900/1953a, pp. 260-261). It was not until 1910 that he specifically referred to "the" Oedipus complex in a paper on object-choice in the male (Freud, 1910/1957d, p. 171).

There are many ramifications to Freud's actual theory of the Oedipus complex, and he was the first to admit that he had never tied together certain loose ends, particularly as regards female psychology. We shall first present the most generally accepted outlines of the male and female Oedipal dynamics and then take up some of the problems associated with this most important conception. We might note at the outset that Freud defined the term *complex* as an ideational content or the meaning involved in a collection of ideas that can influence the person's reactions to stimuli in a selective manner (Freud, 1906/1959b, p. 104).

*The Male Oedipus Complex.* Along about his third year of life, the boy senses pleasurable stimulations from his penis, and he also has some hunch that these pleasant feelings relate to an "other," that is, his mother. Thus, said Freud, "he becomes his mother's lover. He wishes to possess her physically in such ways as he has divined from his observations and intuitions about sexual life" (Freud, 1938/1964f, p. 189). But there is another intuition that the boy senses to the effect that his father objects to such a maternal relationship, and indeed that *castration* can result if the love affair continues (Freud, 1925/1961e, p. 144). With each rise in the level of mother cathexis (the more libido invested in her image as an object-choice), the boy feels a parallel rise in *castration anxiety* as he senses the inevitable punishment (this idea is coming up from unconsciousness to consciousness). The ego is the most intimidated portion of the personality. It is reasoning according to a reality principle, but has the unreasonable, primary process thought of the id to contend with, intent upon joining with the object (mother) in pleasurable sexual union.

When things become threatening for the personality, the ego effects a solution by the mechanism we discussed in Chapter 2 known as *reverting from object-choice to identification* (see p. 64). Thus, rather than continuing to lust after mother (object-choice), the little boy identifies with the father/father's superego, thereby introjecting the standards of the culture. The boy had begun his training in becoming civilized with the toilet-training situation, but now, in identifying with the father's superego, he crystallizes his training definitively. The male conscience ("I believe that to be right and wrong which father believes") is therefore born of fear. "Conform or be castrated" is the civilizing rule. This is why Freud (1923/1961a) said that the superego is the "heir of the Oedipus complex" (p. 36). We shall see in Chapter 11 (see p. 327) that this dynamic of identifying with a potential aggressor functions in the etiology of paranoia as well.

Stated in terms of libido theory, a great wave of *anticathexis* (i.e., repression) accompanies the reversion from object-choice to identification. This usually turns the boy's interest away not only from the mother but also from *all* members of the opposite sex (bringing on the latency phase; see below). Men do not recall their earlier lustful desires (cathexes) for their mothers as objects, because out of castration fear they have succeeded in putting this all down into the darkest regions of their unconscious mind.

*The Female Oedipus Complex.* Jung and others have referred to the female Oedipus complex as the *Electra complex,* basing their analogy on the mythological tale of a slaying of a mother that was instigated and abetted by a revengeful daughter (Electra), but Freud (1931/1961k) specifically rejected this usage and its mythological parallel (p. 229). As we have already noted, Freud was quite uncertain in his theory of female sexuality. He seems to have begun his theorizing in the hopes of drawing a direct parallel between the Oedipal dynamics of males and females, but clinical evidence eventually dispelled this notion (Mächtlinger, 1976).

Freud did not believe that girls experience the great fear of the mother that boys do of the father. The prephallic attachment of a daughter to her mother is far more important in the development of a girl, and it is only much later that hostility and competitiveness with the mother might set in. Put another way, girls do not have a castration fear of the same-sex parent because of course they lack the testicles or penis to fear for. What they do experience is a *penis envy* and as a result a certain sense of inferiority because they assume that they have *already been castrated*—either by nature or by one of their parents (the mother is usually seen as the guilty party after a period of time) (Freud, 1931/1961k, p. 229).

Unlike boys, who revert from object-choice to identification, girls come to shift object-choice from mother to father as the Oedipal dynamic unfolds in their case. The healthiest solution is probably that the little girl find in her father's penis an adequate substitute, cathect it with libido, and thereby come in time to play the feminine, maternal role in her fantasies. This suggests a certain parallel with masculine psychology, because it makes the little girl her father's lover. Many Freudian analysts use this framework today and say that there is a hostile competitiveness between the maturing girl and the mother over who will be the father's genital partner. They surmise that Freud believed this competition set up a comparable level of fear to the boy's castration anxiety and that in this way the anticathexes of latency set in with roughly equivalent force for both sexes. Actually, though Freud *did* feel feminine identification was furthered in the competition with the mother (Freud, 1932-36/1964b, p. 134), he did not propose such a neat parallel with masculine identification.

Freud's theoretical problem was that he did not find this mounting level of anxiety in the female on which to base the final crystallization of the superego. The female's identification with the cultural mandates via fantasying herself in the maternal role (father's lover) seemed to take place more gradually and with less urgency. Freud vacillated about how much trouble this lack of a decided superego crystallization affords the female, noting in one context that it does little harm if she does not fully resolve her Oedipal attitudes (Freud, 1938/1964f, p. 194), but stressing in others that she really has a more difficult Oedipal maturation than the boy (Freud, 1923/1961a, p. 25, 1932-36/1964b, p. 117). Both heterosexual desire and motherly love spring from the root of penis envy. The normal, healthy progression for the girl is thus: castration acceptance *to* penis envy *to* cathect father's penis and thereby take on the feminine role as father's lover (mother identification) *to* desire for a father-substitute's penis (lover/husband) *to* desire for a baby (Freud, 1924/1961c, p. 178).

And what of the type of superego formation to be witnessed in the development of females? Are there noticeable differences from the superego formation of men? It is in response to such questions that Freud can be quoted as saying some things that bring his theory considerable invective from modern feminists. Probably the most notorious of his comments regarding *women* is the following:

> Their super-ego is never so inexorable, so impersonal, so independent of its emotional origins as we require it to be in men. Character-traits which critics of every epoch have brought up against women—that they show less sense of justice than men, that they are less ready to submit to the great exigencies of life, that they are more often influenced in their judgements by feelings of affection or hostility— all these would be amply accounted for by the modification in the formation of their super-ego which we have inferred above. (Freud, 1925/1961f, pp. 257-258)

*The Complexities of the Oedipus Complex.* We noted in Chapter 2 (p. 59) that Freud took a primacy view of life events, in which what comes first or earliest has a *prototypical* influence on all that follows it. In this sense, the familial dynamic known as the Oedipus complex is "the" watershed point of life. How one crosses this developmental point fixes for all time the particular lifestyle that one takes on. Freud wound four major themes into the dynamics of the Oedipus complex in personality development:

1. *The origins of society re-enacted.* It is, of course, very difficult to prove that an infant is *literally* sensing a fear of being castrated. We might agree that sexualized feelings could be directed toward one parent (the mother), but how are we to say that male infants have an intuition of the retribution that will come their way if they persist in such feelings? To buttress his theory at this point, Freud fell back on the Darwinian/Lamarckian theories that were being propounded during his time. The Darwinian zoologist Ernst H. Haeckel had popularized evolutionary theory in Germany and in doing so proposed a "fundamental biogenetic law" suggesting that while *in utero,* organisms essentially re-enact their evolutionary development. Thus, the human fetus at one point in development has gill-like structures, a tail, and so forth, but then gradually changes in the form of an anthropoid. Therefore, Haeckel suggested that *ontogeny recapitulates phylogeny*—that is, development *in utero* proceeds historically, from animals low in the Darwinian alignment of phyla to animals high in this alignment.

Thanks in part to the influence of colleagues like Karl Abraham and Carl G. Jung, in 1913 Freud (1913/1955e) took the position that "the principle that 'ontogeny is a repetition of phylogeny' must be applicable to mental life. . . . This has led to a fresh extension of psycho-analytic interest" (p. 184). He could now suggest that in working their way through the Oedipus complex human beings were, in effect, recapitulating or repeating an historical event which was wound right into their psychic apparatus, just as sucking reflexes are wound into psychic functioning. Following the writings of the evolutionists like Darwin and Atkinson, Freud then proposed an account of how early peoples existed in small hordes, under the domination of a *primal* father who owned all the women and denied his sons heterosexual gratification under threat of castration if they were to violate this prohibition. Accordingly, some of the sons who ran off under the fear of castration banded together, returned in force, and killed their primal father—devouring his remains to obtain his strength (oral incorporation). After dividing their father's women and material possessions amongst them, the sons laid down certain taboos and prohibitions in which women were to be selected in the future from familial groups other than their own (exogamy was initiated). But the ancient concern over castration was never entirely lost to the male psyche (Freud, 1912-13/1955d, p. 132). Here, then, was Freud's justification for the infant's divination of sexual relations and/or castration threats. Children in their phallic phase are re-enacting what actually took place at one point in "their" (i.e., human) history. The biogenetic rule carries forward beyond birth, into the first few years of life!

This rule is no longer generally accepted in the biological sciences, but we should not let this fact dissuade us from an understanding of Freud's theoretical efforts. Here was another example of how he would go to biological explanations in order to justify a more psychological explanation. We invariably find the biological issues coming in *after* Freud has first presented a completely psychological explanation. In such instances, he often took suggestions of colleagues and tried as best he could to combine biological and psychological descriptions to behavior. Thus, his friend and colleague Fliess (see Chapter 1 and Chapter 16) constantly harangued him to underwrite his early speculations with biological explanations. Freud answered one such Fliessian request in an 1898 letter as follows:

> But I am not in the least in disagreement with you, and have no desire at all to leave the psychology hanging in the air with no organic basis. But, beyond a feeling of conviction [that there must be such a basis], I have nothing, either theoretical or therapeutic, to work on, and so I must behave as if I were confronted by psychological factors only. I have no idea yet why I cannot fit it together [i.e., the psychological and the organic]. (Freud, 1954, p. 264)

As we have noted in Chapter 1 (p. 11), this was to be Freud's continuing problem. It is our view that his unique contributions lie on the side of psychological explanations, but we must not overlook his openness to the biological alternative—a factor that became especially important when he considered the influence of bisexuality on the Oedipal conflict (see below).

2. *Superego formation.* In line with what we have been saying about the time when Freud introduced biological themes, it is noteworthy that his beginning ideas on superego formation occurred during his self-analysis, following the examination of his own Oedipal resolution. Thus, in an 1897 letter to Fliess he says, "Another presentiment tells me . . . that I am about to discover the source of morality" (Freud, 1954, p. 206). It was over a decade later that Freud was to bring in his societal-origin theory to justify how it is possible for an infant to intuit sexual intercourse and castration threat. Consider how immensely important this concept of the superego is to human social relations! It is unfortunate that so many critics allow the sexual basis of the Oedipal dynamics to distort their understanding of the sociocultural implications involved. We shall have occasion to consider the psychopathological interpersonal relations that occur due to problems in superego formation.

3. *Bisexuality in identification.* For the major part of his career, Freud focused on the psychological dynamics involved in object-choice and identification. However, he had always accepted the biological fact that organisms have hormonal/glandular similarities and hence that sexual identity is not only something which is learned. Fliess was very much taken with the concept of bisexuality and had built this into a kind of "biological clock" conception in which he argued that both men and women are moved through life according to *periodic cycles* of biological functioning (see Schur, 1972, p. 94; note that this is strictly a biological reductionism as per our discussion in Chapter 1, p.

*Freud and Wilhelm Fliess circa 1893. Freud met Fliess through Joseph Breuer in the mid 1880s, and carried on a singular relationship with him until their eventual breakup in 1900 due to theoretical as well as personal matters.*

13). Women manifest this periodicity in their menstrual cycles, but Fliess had found evidence that men reflect some such cycle in the engorgement of blood vessels in the nasal region (Fliess specialized in nose and throat disorders). During his self-examinations Freud had also found a certain "feminine side" to his nature, and so he informed Fliess (Freud, 1954, p. 318; see also Chapter 16).

There was absolutely no teleology in the theories of Fliess, but as we have demonstrated in Chapter 1 (see p. 12), Freud continually added to his accounts a definite purposive element. This tendency to leave his psychological explanations "hanging in the air" (see above) without a distinctive biological underpinning is what led to the eventual breakup of Freud and Fliess (though there were other reasons as well; see Chapter 16). Fliess tells of his pressing Freud to accept his theory at a get-together in 1900 in Achensee: "I [Fliess] claimed that periodic processes were unquestionably at work in the psyche, as elsewhere; and maintained in particular that they had an effect on those psychopathic phenomena on the analysis of which Freud was engaged for therapeutic purposes. Hence neither sudden deteriorations nor sudden improvements were to be attributed to the analysis and its influence alone" (Freud, 1954, p. 324). Fliess also referred to Freud as a "thought-reader" in this exchange, meaning that the founder of psychoanalysis merely projected his own pet notions onto the client in overlooking the underlying periodic cycles that *really* determined events. Freud's response was, according to Fliess, an attack of personal animosity and violence, one from which the author of the periodic cycles theory never was to recover. The friendship was not to be restored, even though Freud subsequently made efforts in this direction (see Chapter 16).

Despite this vitriolic rejection of a biologically reductive explanation of the cause and cure of neurosis, Freud seems never to have given up his belief in the role of bisexuality in human behavior. And in 1923, when he wrote *The Ego and the Id,* he made a rather provocative suggestion concerning the possible role of bisexuality in the dynamics of identification during the Oedipal conflict. We shall present a key paragraph:

> It would appear . . . that in both sexes the relative strength of the masculine and feminine sexual dispositions is what determines whether the outcome of the Oedipus situation shall be an identification with the father or with the mother. This is one of the ways in which bisexuality takes a hand in the subsequent vicissitudes of the Oedipus complex. The other way is even more important. For one gets an impression that the simple Oedipus complex [i.e., our characterization of it above, p. 69] is by no means its commonest form, but rather represents a simplification or schematization which, to be sure, is often enough justified for practical purposes. Closer study usually discloses the more complete Oedipus complex, which is twofold, *positive* and *negative* [italics added], and is due to the bisexuality originally present in children: that is to say, a boy has not merely an ambivalent attitude towards his father and an affectionate object-choice towards his mother, but at the same time he also behaves like a girl and displays an affectionate feminine attitude to his father and a corresponding jealousy and hostility towards his mother. It is this complicating element introduced by bisexuality that makes it so difficult to obtain a clear view of the facts in connection with the earliest object-choices and identifications, and still more difficult to describe them intelligibly. It may even be that the ambivalence displayed in the relations to the parents should be attributed entirely to bisexuality and that it is not . . . developed out of identification in consequence of rivalry. (Freud, 1923/1961a, p. 33)

This late-born theme in Freudian thought offers a justification for those who would see feminine identification and/or homosexuality as due to biological propensities and not to a certain type of personality development. As we shall see, Freud's more prevalent theory of homosexuality did *not* rely upon an innate "sexual disposition," for indeed, the normal resolution of the Oedipus complex was said to be a heterosexual object-choice (see our discussion of homosexuality in Chapter 16, pp. 488-503). Of course, in this later formulation

Freud is also suggesting that an offspring can take *both* masculine and feminine characteristics from *either* parent by way of identification (see Rychlak & Legerski, 1967). This would form a link between psychoanalysis and the more recent theories suggesting positive benefits from an androgynous identification (Bem, 1975).

More important, in differentiating between a *positive* and a *negative* Oedipus complex Freud actually began to cast doubt on the earlier theories that separated males from females on the question of object-choice. Thus, in the positive Oedipal circumstance the boy would clearly be cathecting the mother and eventually identifying with the father's values. But in the negative Oedipal situation the boy would be investing libido in the father and rivaling for paternal affection with the mother! Possibly Freud was still searching for a *common* explanation of the Oedipal conflict. Bisexuality seemed a way in which he could finally see parallels in object-choice (from mother *to* father) for *both* the developing boy and girl. And once again, in this context he found a biological theoretical construct to be helpful. This is, of course, merely a surmise on our part, but it does have historical plausibility. In any event, the more common dynamic that we see referred to in the psychoanalytical literature is the *positive* Oedipal circumstance for both the boy (mother as object, father as rival) and the girl (father ultimately as object, mother as rival).

The problem with an exclusively biological explanation such as Freud's unelaborated suggestion that ambivalence in the Oedipus complex (i.e., loving and rivaling *both* parents) may be due to bisexuality is that it puts psychoanalysis out of business on the question. This offhand suggestion of Freud's is more a reflection of his open-mindedness than anything else. Taken seriously, it would mean that dozens of other writings by Freud would be invalidated, papers in which thanks to unique psychic maneuverings by a given personality (id, ego, superego) in relationship with a unique set of parents, the Oedipus complex is resolved in some unique fashion. If hormonal (i.e., chemico-biological) factors were *solely* at play then all these papers, including those relating to societal origin, would be made irrelevant. As Freud said to Jung on a related issue, we could then "leave psychology to the poets" (see Chapter 1, p. 8).

4. *Neurosis and Oedipal resolution.* Despite the complexities of the Oedipal dynamics that we have been considering, or possibly because of them, Freud was always to insist that neurotics suffer from poorly resolved Oedipus complexes. As early as 1909 he was referring to the Oedipal situation as the "nuclear" complex of every neurosis (Freud, 1909/1957a, p. 47), and by 1919 he was saying flatly that "the Oedipus complex is the actual nucleus of neuroses, and the infantile sexuality which culminates in this complex is the true determinant of neuroses. What remains of the complex in the unconscious represents the disposition to the later development of neuroses in the adult" (Freud, 1919/1955i, p. 193). There is one proviso here, in that Freud in 1912 distinguished between the *actual* neuroses (neurasthenia, anxiety, and hypochondria) that were presumably due to toxic causes (physical noxa) and therefore *not*

treatable through purely verbal psychoanalysis (Freud, 1912/1958f, pp. 248-249). The remaining disorders were called *psychoneuroses proper,* which included a host of disorders known as the "family" of the hysterias but in fact included syndromes that today we would consider psychotic in nature.

The point seems to be that though Freud recognized how poor Oedipal resolutions might occur in any one person's life, the nature of the symptom suggested that certain disorders were not exclusively "dynamic" in origin. He never solved this question of symptom selection to his satisfaction, and as we know from subsequent developments, even actual neuroses have been submitted to psychoanalytical insights and resultant cures. We shall come up against a similar point of what can or cannot be treated by psychoanalysis when we consider psychoses versus neuroses in the therapeutic relationship (see Chapter 19).

In the main, therefore, the likelihood of having a neurotic problem in adulthood increases as the Oedipal transition is made without suitable resolution. We shall have many examples of how Freud makes use of this inadequate resolution in our consideration of the syndromes of psychopathology in later chapters of this volume. There is an important point to be noted at this juncture, having to do with DSM-III. Recall from Chapter 1 (p. 19) that the aim of DSM-III is to divorce the syndrome of abnormality from the person— that is, the *personality* of the individual—suffering from the disorder. In psychoanalysis this is difficult to accomplish because of the common tie that the Oedipal resolution has both to personality style and the occurrence of neurosis.

There are both positive and negative aspects to this wedding of personality and neurosis in psychoanalysis. On the one hand, a more coherent sense of psychopathology is obtained when personality theory moves directly into the theory of abnormality. Unfortunately, on the other hand one is then committed to the view discussed in Chapter 1 (see p. 18) that episodes of neurotic disorder which appear over a given person's life are not "simply" transitory disorders. Recurring neurotic episodes are therefore *not* analogical to, for example, recurring respiratory infections over a lifetime, infections that are causally unrelated to the fundamental personality system which endures these periods of illness. As dynamic theorists we suspect that if the individual slips back into neurotic states from time to time there is indeed some basic problem that might be solved but is not getting solved or that different aspects of the same problem are not getting solved. This outlook can result in unfortunate social stereotyping regarding mental illness, so that even when the person is not hospitalized for his or her problem others may still harbor negative prejudices against what they consider an "abnormal" person. As we suggested in Chapter 1 (see p. 19), there is probably no easy way out of this likelihood short of better public awareness that we *all* have remnants of our Oedipal resolution in our current personalities and that no one is immune from behavioral idiosyncracies and setbacks. This was Freud's intention, to educate and inform *everyone* rather than to condemn only some to a life of playing "the" abnormal one.

## Feminine Objections to Freudian Oedipal Theory: Horney

Freud's nativism, which we have contrasted to reductive explanation in biological accounts (see Chapter 1, p. 13), led him to base his theoretical explanations on what the human organism has "in place" at birth or physically develops in the first few years thereafter. In this sense, reflexive sucking and reflexive (clitoral or penile) erection can be put in the same theoretical classification, as natural processes through which infants come to know internal and external experience. It follows therefore that the anatomical differences between the sexes might engender different conceptions of such experience. This is the course of theoretical analysis that Freud took in arriving at the phallic phase of psychosexual development.

Although she embraced Freudian theory in the main, Karen Horney was among the first female psychoanalysts to register objections to the interpretation of feminine psychology arising from Oedipal dynamics. Her criticism in *New Ways in Psychoanalysis* (Horney, 1939) takes root from the fact that Freud seemed to insist upon what she felt was a "biologically determined" (p. 79) explanation. Horney challenged this sexual/anatomical argument, citing anthropological evidence to the contrary—namely, that the patterns of interpersonal relations in the family unit vary widely across cultures (p. 85). Furthermore, though she could accept the use of sexuality to relate to others in the family context (including siblings), she did not believe that "the presence of sexual desire [is] strong enough [in the infant] to arouse so much jealousy and fear that they can be dissolved only by repression" (p. 85). She also disliked the repetition-compulsion aspects of Oedipal dynamics whereby Freud continued to press his prototype form of theorizing to say that adults regress (return) to the Oedipal dynamics in working through current behavioral challenges and frustrations. Summing up, Horney observed:

> If we discard the theoretical implications of the theory [i.e., broader implications such as societal origins], what remains is not the Oedipus complex but the highly constructive finding that early relationships *in their totality* mold the character to an extent which can scarcely be overestimated. Later attitudes to others, then, are not repetitions of infantile ones but emanate from the character structure, the basis of which is laid in childhood. (p. 87)

In her examination of feminine psychology vis-à-vis the Oedipal theory Horney deals exclusively with what we now recognize as the "positive" form of this dynamic (refer above). She notes that penis envy may arise in young girls, but this is surely no more significant in feminine personality development than the equally frequent wish "to have a breast" (p. 105). We should not take penis envy at face value, because after subjecting this wish to analytical investigation it is often found that there are other motivations in place than the basic desire to be a man. For example, despair at being physically unattractive may drive the girl to reject her femininity, with the defensive wish to be a man. Since Freud's examination of masculine/feminine is carried on with adults, it is possible that he has either misconstrued the dynamics in some cases or had patients with only one of the multiple dynamics possible.

Horney notes how many of her male psychoanalytical colleagues tended to interpret female behaviors such as competing with men, berating men, envying their success, and striving to achieve in a "man's world" (business, sports, etc.) as signs of penis envy (p. 106). Such women are likely to be called *castrating females.* Yet such easy parallels between adult behavior and anatomical differences in infancy overlook the fact that these women invariably behave this way toward other women and to children as well. Furthermore, identical behaviors are widely found in the patterns of maladjusted men, who also envy their masculine competition in life's reward systems. Citing Alfred Adler's work as a precedent, Horney then points out how certain desirable cultural advantages in Western civilization have been drawn along lines that made it easy for men but *not* women to take advantage of, "such as strength, courage, independence, success, sexual freedom, right to choose a partner" (p. 108). These so-called *masculine* characteristics are obviously not based simply upon anatomical differences between the sexes. Little wonder that women manifest "masculine" tendencies.

The emphasis that Horney then gives to an understanding of feminine psychology is decidedly sociocultural in nature. Cultural instructions and attitudes convey the following: "the greater dependency of woman; the emphasis on woman's weakness and frailty; the ideology that it is in woman's nature to lean on someone and that her life is given content and meaning only through others: family, husband, children" (p. 113). Hence, concludes Horney, "There are no biological reasons but there are significant cultural factors which lead women to overvaluate love and thus to dread losing it" (p. 114). Some of this overvaluation was natural, given the familial organization in Western civilization, which was agrarian and dependent upon many offspring to ensure economic viability. But such divisions in labor are no longer so decided, and as the family size decreases the opportunity for women to gain greater economic and political responsibility increases. Yet the underlying overvaluation of love among many women persists despite a changing sociocultural milieu:

> As long as homemaking was a really big task involving many responsibilities, and as long as the number of children was not restricted, woman had the feeling of being a constructive factor in the economic process; thus she was provided with a sound basis for self-esteem. This basis, however, has gradually vanished, and in its departure woman has lost one foundation for feeling herself valuable. (p. 117)

Written in the late 1930s, these words are remarkably current. We hear similar expressions from modern feminists quite regularly. The point Horney arrived at, then, was that women have been made vulnerable by the changing sociocultural forces related to the modern developments of industrialized society. Their central role in the familial unit has been diminished by economic progress, resulting in a lowering of self-confidence. They see opportunities for countering this low self-esteem by moving outward, into the traditional "man's world." But they unfortunately carry with them an underlying (unconscious?) sense of the importance love has for them as feminine beings—lovers and mothers—despite all such conscious efforts to change their lifestyle. Women are, in essence, caught in a cultural conflict as the society in which they live is changing its familial structure.

Returning to Freud, we must not overlook the fact that he *did* recognize that sociocultural conventions helped to force women into a passive role. Horney cites Freud to this effect in her own writings (p. 118). But Freud's naturalistic tendencies prompted him to base explanations of behavior on the person as an independent unit, looking at the course of this acculturation through the conceptual understanding of the maturing human being. If women are encouraged by their society to be passive, Freud wanted to explain why this encouragement arose in the first place. His reading of history prompted him to make claims regarding the origins of early society in which, thanks to physical domination as well as sexual attraction, men laid down certain familial patterns in wnich the woman's role was pressed upon her. We do not find Freud employing economic arguments, tying the familial structure to agrarian versus industrialized social structures and the like. Freud was a psychologist first and foremost, bringing his level of description down to the most immediate form of interpersonal relationship—that is, the face-to-face encounter of mother/child, man/woman. He found this a sexualized/aggressive encounter and derived sociocultural patterns accordingly.

## The Phase of Latency

Resolution of the Oedipus complex occurs somewhere in the fourth or fifth year of life. While it brings early grief and a massive repression of infantile experience, Oedipal resolution also brings the adaptive internalization of parental standards, parental love, and parental controls, in the form of a highly integrated superego organization. This post-Oedipal superego system, whose conscious part we call *conscience,* always functions in relation to the ego from which it has been differentiated, and always in relation to reality and to the wholly unconscious *id,* out of which the ego has differentiated. The post-Oedipal superego matures along with the maturing ego, often throughout life. Paralleling this superego differentiation is the equally important *separation between ego and id,* enabling the personality system to shift from primary (id) to secondary (ego) process thinking—that is, a more reality-oriented approach to experience. Piaget (1932) demonstrated early in his career that it is not until firm ego boundaries have been established that realistic secondary process thinking can be established and progress can be made toward a mature logic. We shall return to a more detailed consideration of the id, ego, and superego in Chapter 4.

Children in latency are still closely tied to their family contexts. From their family members they can get emotional and physical support. The family home provides them a safe harbor to which they can return whenever frustrations outside are more than they can bear or when others fight or reject them. The major social change in latency is that, while they are still members of a family group, children now go forth alone into the world outside their family, expanding their physical and social horizons, supplementing their family membership with memberships in groups outside of it.

*The Early Neighborhood Group.* The moment a child steps out of the home unaccompanied, he or she loses the status of a protected and privileged son or daughter and becomes merely another child in the neighborhood. The patterns of friendliness, aggression, and defense now encountered are different and less predictable by the child than are those to which he or she has been accustomed at home. It is quite normal for a child to be a bit timid and tentative until he or she has had an opportunity to test this new reality for a time. Other children are apt to be casual and unconcerned about the newcomer once the novelty of his or her arrival on the neighborhood scene has worn off. Sometimes other children are surprisingly critical and even hostile toward the newcomer.

Friendly adults treat a neighborhood child more objectively than his or her own parents do, more as a person, perhaps less approvingly but also less critically, and with different emphases. Differences arising between children are usually settled directly by the contestants and their respective supporters, without adult intervention. When adults do intervene in a squabble between children, it is often to aid their own child against others.

The standards prevailing in the neighborhood are those of the children composing it, each child differing in some respects from the others because he or she comes from a different family background. Sex differences are at first less decisive than age differences. The solitary play and parallel play of infancy gives way to social and cooperative play in which children learn to share objects and activities with other children and prepare to take part in group competitive play (Barnes, 1971). The child's role in active exploration of the neighborhood is not to be overlooked. Preschoolers who actively explore their neighborhood settings are likely to become curious, venturesome, and independent elementary schoolers. Too much restraint in exploration of the world outside the home can foretell a later school adjustment typified by poor social relations and personality problems (Hutt & Bhavnani, 1972).

Some of the earliest participative games involve simple forms of social role taking. The small child must play the baby or the pupil, as directed, so that an older child may play at being mother or teacher. There are also marching games, dancing and running games, and weaving about with other children in structured patterns. The emphasis on rhythmic patterning in childhood play is impressive. Language development is facilitated through such rhythmic "taking turns" of one child proposing something to a second, who then has an opportunity to reply or carry out the implications of the initiating comment. Such rhythmic turn taking flows along into what is often called a "round," as children seem intentionally to be patterning each other's approach to interpersonal contact (Garvey, 1977). The formal/final causal implications of this inter-personal behavior are not difficult to see.

Most experts in child psychology recognize that play is related to the child's current capacities for satisfactory adjustment, as well as prognostic of future adjustment. By entering into the imaginative play of others the child not only gains practice in social discourse and the assumption of social roles but also learns how to meet challenges and the penalties of noncooperation with a minimum of risk. Children who can play imaginatively are usually in better control of themselves, more mature, and more independent (K. H. Rubin, Malone & Hornug, 1976). They smile more, are curious about experience, and express joy in their activities. Age-inappropriate play and deviations in play patterns have been found to be related to anxiety and other emotional problems in young children (J. L. Singer, 1977).

*The Peer Culture.* Children soon separate into groups of their own sex and age with whom they have much more in common than with members of the opposite sex or with older children (Moore, 1967). This pattern persists as the preferred one until puberty. Boys play with boys as soon as they are big enough and skilled enough to enter into the rough-and-tumble competition of boys' games. Their first attempts to join a group of boys may be rudely rebuffed, but eventually they make the grade. Girls play with girls in physically milder games, some of which are highly competitive, and some more on the expressive side. Girls include very small boys in their play if it suits them. It is not unusual for children to rebuke one of their numbers who attempts to play with the opposite sex (Sutton-Smith & Rosenberg, 1970). Of course, parental intervention may play a role, as well as the organized activities of preschool teachers. In recent times, children have been encouraged to play together and to engage in activities customarily thought of as exclusively the province of one sex or the other.

Children can learn both positive and negative things in relating to peers. They can learn to assuage their fears (Bandura, Grusec, & Menlove, 1967) and to resist temptation (Walters & Parke, 1964). But they can also learn to be disobedient, selfish, and aggressive through contact with peers (Hicks, 1965). It is obviously important for parents to consider the child's playmates carefully. Fighting is more common among boys, but here again this probably involves a certain amount of social sanction. The process of identification with what the culture accepts as masculine or feminine behavior continues throughout this process of peer contact. Progressive role differentiation takes place, preparing the child for adolescence and adulthood.

Another vital role played by the group has to do with the child's self-reactions. In comparing himself or herself with others of comparable age, the child comes to form an opinion of self-worth (Pepitone, 1972). If a child is physically attractive and well coordinated, the likelihood of peer acceptance with resultant feelings of self-confidence increases (Dion, 1973; Staffieri, 1967). There is evidence to suggest that a child's physical attractiveness may actually enter into social adjustment in time. Thus, unattractive children have been found to score less well on personality tests, reflect lowered ratings of self-esteem, and do more poorly in their schoolwork (Lerner & Lerner, 1977).

*The School.* Early in latency the child begins going to school. Here he or she enters into new, highly formalized relationships with other children and adults, in which kinship plays no part and there is little regard for previous friendships. The boy or girl is expected to be on time each day and to control personal behavior for several hours—to be quiet and orderly, to suppress many individual impulses, and to engage in supervised work. Racial and social-class differences are likely to be encountered in the school context, if they have not been confronted before. A child can usually identify racial differences at three years of age (Durrett & Davy, 1970; Hraba & Grant, 1970). Although most children prefer friends of their own race, research demonstrates that they also form many cross-race friendships in preschool and elementary school (Shaw, 1974).

Along with family and peer group influences, the school situation has a tremendous influence on the child's learning of sex roles, moral development, and level of aspiration in the work sphere (Bronfenbrenner et al., 1965). Teachers render a more objective evaluation of the child than does the family, although many of the same characteristics making a child attractive to peers function in the teacher's preferential attitudes. An attractive child is at an advantage in life here as well, particularly if he or she is attentive, hard working, or intelligent.

It is important to appreciate that latency does not mean that sexual promptings are totally quiescent. The emotional drives from id functioning are still present and active. They always will be present and active as long as life lasts. The child in latency is viewed by psychoanalysis as highly competitive, because aggressive tendencies are permitted a freer, overt expression. Sexuality is reduced by comparison, even though there is still ample sexual curiosity throughout this period (roughly, age five to puberty). Indeed, there is normally a certain amount of sexual experimentation during the phase of latency.

*The Church and Other Formal Groups.* The church and most other formal groups are dominated one way or another by adults, and unlike the school, they have a high proportion of adults in them. Children tend to look upon such organizations as belonging to adults, and they see their membership in them as extensions of their membership in the family. Churches are organized along lines different from nonsectarian schools. They may increase family and in-group solidarity by representing an extrafamilial source of identification in which the whole family joins.

The church and other similar organizations may represent to the child systems of special belief that demand a high degree of conformity by the participants. They may also provide institutionalized systems of personal guilt, of penitence, and of complex ritual early in the child's life. They often provide systematic group recreational facilities, including in-group social gatherings. When their ideals and demands clash with individual or with family ideals and demands, they may raise conflicts of considerable importance. Political and other social creeds, if they call for unquestioning belief and submission to appointed authority, may operate psychologically in much the same way that strict, authoritarian religions do.

*Stresses Inherent in Latency and Parental Guidance.* Contrary to some popular beliefs, the phase of latency has within it inevitable sources of personal stress for the developing child. To enumerate and discuss them all would require a volume in itself. Here we shall limit ourselves to a brief account of some of the stresses and what they may mean to the child. The major stresses arise from the daily separation from the family, from the necessity for adapting to the peer culture and the school system, and from the increasing demands made upon the child, coming from every direction, to master new skills, exert more and more emotional control, acquire more and more knowledge, and enter into a number of new and often conflicting social roles. Even the most capable, intelligent adult knows how difficult it is to learn entirely new things, to acquire new skills and new forms of control, to move into a new neighborhood or job, and to establish oneself with strangers. Most adults avoid this kind of experience with every resource they have, because they know from their own past experience the rigors of such demands. Even so, the stresses of this phase for the child are often overlooked or minimized by adults, who tend to idealize latency as a period of no responsibility.

The child in the latency period is in need of considerable emotional support and guidance from parents and other adults. In structuring his or her world, the child invariably finds that identification with parents is in itself not enough to ensure a smooth passage through this phase. Children cannot do everything that adults can do. They cannot even foresee and plan as adults can, for they lack the experience in living to do so advantageously. Some of the most serious childhood anxieties come from the failure of parents to set limits to a child's impulsive behavior, providing wise guidance and discipline when these are indicated. A child is not born with self-control; this characterological ability has to be learned through daily interaction with others.

There is much debate over the use of discipline in child rearing and whether it should include physical punishment (spanking, scolding, shaking, etc.) or be limited to intellectual reasoning and argumentation. Research supports the view that at an early age of four or five children may not comprehend all of the nuances that parental reasoning demands (R.V. Burton, Maccoby, & Allinsmith, 1961). At such ages, mild physical punishment seems to be more effective than intellectual reasoning. With age, however, the child can be reasoned with and gradually come to understand the *grounds* on which parental compliance is being requested. Children shown high permissiveness by parents but with little punishment for misdeeds tend to become aggressive, antisocial adolescents (Sears, 1961). Overly indulged children often have diffi-culty facing frustration in life and are unable to project long-term goals (Baumrind, 1971).

On the other side of the coin, children who have been physically punished to excess have been found to develop an aggressive and sometimes antisocial personality (Eron et al., 1974). Parents who vacillate in their standards, punish-ing and then not punishing children for the same behavior, can induce severe conflicts and maladjustment in their offspring (Deur & Parke, 1970). Of course, excesses in punishment do occur, and in recent times we have seen a rise in the apparent incidence of the battered or abused child. Apparently, it is not punishment per se but rather a combination of many factors that lead parents to abuse their children—including low educational level, economic deprivation, unrealistic expectations of the child's capacity to achieve self-control, and an abnormal emotional investment in the child combining parental rejection and a need to extend the symbiotic tie (H. Martin, 1976). It is not unusual for child abuse to "run in families," in that children who have suffered through this relationship with parents grow up to treat their own offspring in the same manner (A. H. Green, Gaines, & Sandgrund, 1976).

It would seem the vital consideration in childhood discipline is that the child not view the physical punishment as a sign or proof of parental rejection. In a family in which the child does indeed represent an economic or emotional threat to either parent, an underlying sense of parental frustration is likely to be sensed by the child. This rejection might even be conveyed interpersonally at an unconscious level. The child is being nurtured as if in a hostile territory— hostile to his or her very existence! Then, when punishment *is* administered, it is taken as a kind of validation of this sensed rejection. Children who are truly loved by the parents and who consequently sense this love in their everyday parental relationship have a totally different experience of what it means to be punished. They are more likely to relate to the *intent* of the punishment than to the punishment per se.

To achieve self-confidence, children need freedom and encouragement to make their own choices and decisions, at least in minor matters, within the restrictions of age, experience, and intelligence. If they are called upon to make important decisions for which they are not prepared, or simply left to make them without judicious adult help, they are likely to become unnecessarily anxious. The situation in the world of the child is not qualitatively very different from that in the adult world. We adults often find ourselves beyond our depth in unfamiliar seas. We feel justified, not humiliated, when we turn for help to relatives, friends, associates, lawyers, or ministers if our own experience seems insufficient to us or our personal resources seem inadequate to meet new or more complex situations.

This is essentially the child's position when faced with complexities that exceed his or her capacities. The major difference is that, whereas mature adults rarely need special support and guidance, and then only in complex situations, children during the latency period need them frequently, and in relatively simple situations. It is self-evident that a child who has been unsuccessful in mastering Oedipal and pre-Oedipal problems will encounter much greater difficulty in mastering the problems of competition, cooperation, and group interaction that characterize the phase of latency.

*Latent into Adolescent.* Whether a child has resolved his Oedipal conflict and developed a satisfactory superego or not, the major part of his or her latency will be absorbed by innumerable tasks and adventures through which efforts are made to gain mastery over self and environment. An essential aspect of this mastery is the development of appropriate social-role behavior, with skills in behaving reciprocally with others of all ages and sexes. The child stores up prodigious quantities of knowledge and develops an ego-superego in accordance with his or her prevailing culture. In time the child becomes a separate person who knows how to behave interdependently with other persons and has at hand a sense of what the attitudinal dispositions of others suggest—whether accepting, rejecting, questioning, and the like. Latency is usually terminated with a brief transitional period of preadolescence marked by emotional disruption without much biological change (Blair & Burton, 1951). Behavior may seem disorganized for a time, even to the point of vagueness and unintelligibility of speech.

Preadolescent children tend to be uncommunicative with their parents, both because they are beginning to feel the need for independence and because sexual fantasies are growing prominent which they try to conceal. Preadolescence must be regarded as an ill-defined period of transition in which the child is making one of the most significant biological/psychological passages of his or her life. Adolescence, the next phase, is ushered in by rapid physiological growth and maturation, especially marked in genital and secondary sex characteristics, both visible and invisible. These are biologically predetermined by the sex of the child at the time of conception. They provide us with some excellent examples of innate growth and behavioral patterns that do not come to full expression for more than a decade and a half of postnatal life.

## The Phase of Adolescence

One of the significant developments in psychoanalysis since Freud's death has been the growing interest taken in the phase of adolescence. His daughter, Anna Freud (1958), once referred to adolescence as a "stepchild" in psychoanalytical theory, meaning that it had not been given the attention and consideration that the oral, anal, and phallic levels of psychosexual development had been afforded. Classical psychoanalytical theory tended to picture adolescence as a time of turbulence and instability, with defensive maneuvers such as regression, sublimation, and repression playing a major role in adolescent behavior. This view hinges upon the fact that with pubescence there is a resurgence of sexual promptings that in turn rekindle Oedipal themes and demand some kind of defensive reaction on the part of the young person.

In discussing the transformations of puberty, Freud returned to his distinction between the autoerotic and object-choice. Before puberty occurs, the pleasure obtained from erotogenic zones of the body are on the side of *fore-pleasure,* meaning they are "the same pleasure that has already been produced, although on a smaller scale, by the infantile sexual instinct [i.e., autoerotic pleasure]" (Freud, 1905/1953e, p. 210). After puberty, the sexualized erotegenic promptings become oriented toward others, resulting in *end-pleasure,* or "the pleasure of satisfaction derived from the sexual act [i.e., an interpersonal act via object-choice]" (ibid.). With the onset of a capacity for end-pleasure and the likelihood of id promptings to find such pleasurable release, the developing ego is put under additional stress, and a number of defensive maneuvers are to be seen in the behavior of adolescents (Blos, 1962). We shall have something to say concerning these problems in this section.

Since Freud's death, a number of psychoanalysts have broadened the conceptualization of adolescence, placing emphasis more on the relation of the ego and ego-ideal or superego, and de-emphasizing thereby the traditional conflict between ego and id. Erik Erikson's influence has been felt in this school of thought, and we shall be considering his theory of ego-identity in a separate section below. But speaking more generally, the revisionists of classical psychoanalytical theory view adolescence as a time when the values taken over from parents are questioned and a working out of a variant, *independent ego-ideal* eventually takes place—thanks in large measure to the support of peers (Kohut, 1971; E. Wolf, Gedo, & Terman, 1972). In effect, the early idealization of parents is thought to be de-idealized and replaced by newly internalized ideals. It is as if each human being must make a search for his or her unique life ideals, arriving at them individually, or else a proper self-image and satisfactory self-confidence will not come about. Sexual values may be included in this individualized search, but they are not the *sole* grounds for adolescent conflicts, as traditional psychoanalytical theory seemed to imply.

Still other psychoanalytical theorists downplay the turmoil that adolescents are supposed to experience during this phase of life (see, e.g., Josselson, 1980; Masterson, 1967). They point to empirical studies that suggest otherwise. Thus, a survey of thousands of adolescent females provided little evidence that they are preoccupied with sexual/hostile drives and their control (Douvan & Adelson, 1966). In longitudinal follow-ups of males through the adolescent period of life no real evidence of great turmoil, ego weakness, or a repudiation of parents was found (Offer & Offer, 1975). It seems likely that whether we characterize adolescence as a period of turmoil or of growth and transition depends in some measure on the perspective from which we come at this field of developmental investigation. One pair of experts in the field beautifully summarized this difference in perspective as follows:

> The picture of the adolescent we construe from a steady reading of *Child Development* [a nonpsychiatric research journal] is of a youngster engaged in implacable expansion of intellectual and moral capacity, whereas the one we will develop from a regular diet of *Adolescent Psychiatry* [a journal devoted to psychopathology] is of

a youngster miraculously holding on to his sanity, but doing so only by undertaking prodigies of defense. In truth we may be observing the same youngster through separate perspectives. Any clinician working with adolescents soon becomes aware that some deeply disturbed youngsters show no signs of difficulty in other realms of functioning, and that the conflict-free sphere of the ego can maintain itself and, indeed, expand during periods of intense personal disorder. (Adelson & Doehrman, 1980, p. 105)

This strikes us as sage advice for the student of developmental psychology. As the present volume is oriented to psychopathology, we shall focus more on the conflict sphere of ego development, keeping in mind that there are aspects of adolescent development that are equally relevant to this phase and yet conflict-free, worthy of study in their own right in another context.

*Adolescent Turbulence and Instability.* Anatomical, physiological, emotional, intellectual, and social factors all enter into the adolescent picture to make it turbulent and unstable. Changes in these various realms do not necessarily coincide in time. Even the rate of change in any one of them is not wholly predictable. As everyone knows, two adolescents of the same chronological age and the same sex may show great differences in physical maturity. Simply reaching puberty does not ensure that a young person will begin manifesting overt sexual activity. Girls in general reach puberty about two years earlier than the average boy (Douvan, 1960; Kestenberg, 1961), but statistics demonstrate that there has been a steadily declining age of puberty among both sexes. Estimates are that children today are reaching pubescence about two years earlier than they were at the outset of the twentieth century (P. Y. Miller & Simon, 1980, p. 387).

The young person's age at pubescence presents some of the first adjustment problems of this period. A precocious boy who acquires the secondary sexual characteristics (facial/genital hair, deeper voice, semen production) before his peers may be looked to as a "mature" leader before he is really equipped to assume such responsibility. Sexual precocity is unevenly correlated with psychological and social precocity, so that through no fault of his own a boy in this circumstance may be under evaluation for capacities his biology suggests are present but his personality system lacks. On the other side of the coin, a boy who is late in acquiring the masculinizing secondary sexual characteristics faces the equally traumatic possibilities of being unjustly considered childlike and sissified. Comparable problems exist in the case of the pubescent girl.

It is, of course, the hormonal changes that define the onset of puberty and thrust the adolescent into that transitional state between childhood and adulthood that has come to be known as adolescence. While still acting in a childish manner, the adolescent feels a demand to be treated as an adult; yet he or she finds the prospects of acting as an adult frightening because of a lack of experience. We witness in their first fumbling attempts the extremes to which adolescents will go to attain some kind of maturity in behavioral style. There is much concern about being embarrassed or suffering a sense of shame. A teenage girl may find herself impulsive and unpredictable, even to herself. She experiences rapid mood changes that she usually cannot fathom and that no one around her seems to understand either. A teenage boy finds himself growing and changing bodily proportions faster than he can adapt to and integrate the developments taking place. At a time when he is extremely sensitive to the opinions of others, his body makes him clumsy and ridiculous. Adolescent orientations, daydreams, and fantasies change progressively as the young man or woman moves anatomically, physiologically, experientially, and socially nearer and nearer to full sexual and social maturity (M. Engel, 1959).

*Developing Male/Female Sexual Attitudes.* A boy's sexual feelings focus upon his prominent, visible external genitalia and upon the obvious changes that they undergo. There is little of the diffuseness that characterizes a girl's sexual feelings. During adolescence the boy's interest in and efforts to actively master the physical world become outstanding. He is likely to be vigorous and boisterous in his competitive play, varied and constructive in his solitary play. He has daydreams of glory and ambition and has a continued interest in power symbols and mechanical things (Lansky et al., 1961). The interests of the pubertal girl are immediately influenced by the onset of menstrual function (*menarche*). It sets the seal upon her femaleness. She can settle down to almost a lifetime of monthly cycles, which make her sex role and its implications now undeniable and which introduce a form of regularity and predictability into her life over which she has no control. Preceding and following the menarche, the girl's body undergoes extensive changes in form. This not only makes her more aware than ever of her body but also gives her direct experience in being an object of sexual attraction.

Because her sexual feelings are relatively diffuse, the girl has a predominantly inward orientation, no matter how practical and worldly she may be. Her external genitalia do not provide her with the kind of objective, thing-like experience that a boy's do. Sexuality concerns the interior of her body. She is much more concerned with secrets than the boy and is less likely to discuss a sexual experience with her friends immediately following its occurrence than a boy (Carns, 1973). The girl is more likely to see life from a subjective point of view. She daydreams a great deal. She is much concerned about the appearance of her body and its adornment and wants to be considered attractive by others.

Sexual mores have been undergoing considerable change in recent times, with the generation of the 1960s and 1970s reflecting the onset of the differences noted. Although precise data for a nationwide or worldwide sampling is never available, most research surveys show that although the level of masturbation and premarital coitus among males has probably remained stable, the number of girls who masturbate and have premarital sex today is significantly higher than it was for their parents (Conger, 1975; Jessor & Jessor, 1975; Kinsey et al., 1948, 1953; Vener & Stewart, 1974). In a study conducted in 1975 it was found that 66 percent of the boys and 33 percent of the girls had masturbated by age thirteen (Conger, 1975). By age nineteen, 85 percent of the boys and 42 percent of the girls reported having masturbated. About 72 percent of these boys had experienced sexual intercourse by age nineteen, whereas 51 percent of the females reported a coital experience by this age. This latter figure more than doubles the findings on premarital sexual intercourse for females in studies conducted in the 1940s and 1950s.

Consistent with their psychosexual development, girls are more likely than boys to believe that partners in advanced forms of petting or intercourse should be in love, engaged, or married (Sorensen, 1973). Girls are therefore more likely to report having their initial sexual experience with a partner whom they were in love with and considered marrying (Simon, Berger, & Gagnon, 1972). The usual pattern for the girls is to keep the sexual union private, possibly revealing it to a special friend much later, after it has been thought about privately and idealistically. The boy, on the other hand, seems more likely to obtain a sense of achievement and mastery through the experience and wants therefore to let his friend or friends know that he is attaining adult stature in life.

Sociopolitical and religious attitudes have been shown to be related to sexual behavior. Politically conservative and religiously active adolescents are less likely to engage in premarital sex than their opposite numbers (Yankelovich, 1974). Among both male and female adolescents, the most widely cited reasons for not engaging in premarital sex are moral objections and the fear of pregnancy (Jessor & Jessor, 1975). Girls are also likely to fear that their reputations will be tarnished or that their parents will learn of the act and reject them. It is not difficult to see that in combination with the other challenges of having to "grow up" to adulthood, the modern trend to greater sexual expression in adolescence has as many threats attached to it as satisfactions. The difficult problems of relating to others, being considered popular or at least accepted, and through it all of achieving a sense of personal identity and integrity are not made easier through greater sexual freedom.

*The Peer Group.* Although adolescents badly need adult guidance, they also fear and sometimes hate their dependent needs as potential blocks to their total emancipation. They are vividly aware of growing up and find it humiliating to be treated as a child. The adolescent boy or girl may overreact to any form of parental intervention with displays of temper followed by long periods of sulking. Adolescence can be a time of great tension in the home, for parents and the adolescent alike. The parents sometimes find themselves treated with indifference, coldness, scorn, or hostility by a child whom they may have always loved unselfishly, and whom they still love. They hear themselves addressed condescendingly and their cherished values rudely challenged. A growing son or daughter may ignore parents, avoid them, or look at them hatefully. If the parents feel sure that their attitudes toward their child have not changed, they are bewildered by this new experience.

When it occurs, adolescent rebellion may appear ungrateful, callous, and senseless to parents. There are unconscious processes at work in this rebellion, but the adolescent does not recognize these feelings, reactivated by Oedipal promptings that have been aggravated by the onset of sexual maturation (Freud, 1922/1955o, p. 246). The resultant change in the adolescent's mood is attributed to external circumstances. The conflict with parents actually serves a positive role in freeing the maturing individual from complete domination by parents. It is not always as stormy as we have presented things to this point, but one way or another there has to be a sense of independence developing, or the adolescent will not fully integrate his or her personality system. Some adolescents never succeed in emancipating themselves from parental influence. They remain as grown-up children in their parents' home or neighborhood community forever. Still others transfer their childlike attachment to a marital partner who may be satisfied with it or find it burdensome.

On the other side of the coin, some adolescents who never break away from parental involvements manifest this tie in the negative sense of a lifelong rebellion—working through the remnants of their Oedipal dynamics but never realizing what they are rebelling against. Failure to find satisfactory love objects outside the home may leave a person vulnerable later in life to one or another form of psychopathology. Most experts who study adolescent rebellion and the less dramatic efforts that young people make to achieve independence from parents are impressed by the fact that a *clique* of four to six close friends of the same sex is often the vehicle by which emancipation is achieved. Actually, it can be shown that friendships become increasingly stable from the ages of five through eighteen years, culminating in the formation of the peer group known as the clique.

There are many benefits to be obtained from association with peers in a clique. Here, adolescents discover that others of their age have the same problems with parents, the same worries over developing sexuality, and the same sense of loneliness and isolation. It was once suggested in psychoanalytical writings that early adolescence reflected a certain "homosexual phase" of life, even though it involves little overt sexual activity. There are strong loyalties in this period of development and strong though often shifting affection for a member of the same sex, and resultant group identifications take place that are significant for later adult group interaction and adult love. If we follow the course of friendship from the ages of eleven to eighteen or so, we find that there is a pattern to it (J. C. Coleman, 1974; Douvan & Adelson, 1966). At age eleven, adolescents are likely to form into cliques around some shared activity like a hobby or social-service group. Conformity to peer pressure seems to reach its zenith at thirteen to fourteen, diminishing gradually thereafter (Costanzo & Shaw, 1966). By age fifteen or thereabouts, the greatest sense of insecurity is shown, as the adolescent looks around for friends with whom to exchange the concerns mentioned above. By age eighteen, the personality and interests of the friend per se are what matter. With the beginnings of heterosexual interest and activity, peers give the adolescent support in this sphere that parents are simply unable to provide due to their "generation" difference.

Researches on teenage friendships have shown that there is likely to be a selective factor in the formation of cliques. That is, the peer group is almost never found to be formed around a value structure totally in opposition to the values of the parents. For example, the adolescent may be in agreement with parental values such as educational plans for the future and yet disagree and find peer support on some other value consideration such as smoking or drinking. As we noted above, many adolescents do not reject their parents' values concerning premarital sex, particularly when this is tied to religious commitment. There is little doubt that parents continue to bear an important influence on their offspring throughout adolescence. Another way in which this fact is demonstrated is that when death or divorce removes the father from the home during adolescence the interpersonal skills of the developing boy or girl in the home are adversely affected (Biller & Bahm, 1971; Hetherington, 1972).

Adolescent girls are usually found to have more turbulent peer relationships than boys. They express more tension, conflict, and jealousy of girlfriends than boys do of boyfriends at all ages across adolescence (Coleman, 1974). The basis for popularity in a clique or in more extensive adolescent groupings (crowds) such as we might find around a high school grounds varies across the sexes. Adolescent boys are usually assured of popularity if they have good athletic ability, and girls are similarly rewarded if they reflect good social skills. Good looks are important for both sexes, as is a pleasant or attractive personality.

There is normally a progressive transition from the like-sex peer groupings to heterosexual groups in later adolescence. Early dating is motivated not so much by conscious sexual desire as by curiosity and the demands of the peer group. There is a curious transitional phase, common among girls but very uncommon among boys, in which two close friends of the same sex share an attraction for an adolescent of the opposite sex. A certain shared learning seems to be the result of these joint "crushes." The common double date has similar protective advantages over single dating. This transitional phase gives the adolescent opportunities for trying out a variety of social roles, including interactions with members of the opposite sex, while he or she remains under the protection of the group. There is still a strong preoccupation with status and a tendency to form cliques in which the adolescent experiences not only a sense of belonging but also practices of censure and approval that may be far stricter than those of parents.

We have not considered the peer-group phenomena to be seen in adolescence resulting in delinquency and other associations such as "families" within communes. These are atypical and even abnormal manifestations of adolescent maturation, and we have been trying to emphasize the more usual course of development. Delinquency is in large measure due to socioeconomic conditions, though it does seem to be extending upward to the middle classes in recent times. Many lower-class youths in urban ghettos join delinquent gangs. These groups have their own mores, often placing more severe demands on the adolescent than anything he or she has experienced at home. It is significant that when studied, delinquents reflect poor self-images. Hostile and destructive, they are also impulsive, deficient in self-control, and lacking in achievement motivation (Gold & Mann, 1972). It is entirely possible that inadequate ego-superego formations have occurred through poor Oedipal resolutions, albeit due indirectly to economic privations leading to parental frustrations and even abandonment by one or more parents.

The youth movement during the 1960s reflected another, essentially socio-cultural and sociopolitical, development in the American culture (Braungart, 1980). In this instance, many of the leading activists were of middle-class backgrounds. Though the total de-emphasis of the so-called Protestant ethic (achievement, hard work, etc.) was not to last, we witness remnants of this important development today in the questions put to government concerning human rights, racial and sexual equality, the arms race, and protection of the natural environment. We have undoubtedly witnessed a social development in recent history—possibly even a social "revolution"—placing human values above impersonal considerations. And much of this change can be attributed to adolescents who, performing in cliques and crowds, effected a re-examination of national purpose. It was out of such humanized utopianism that adolescents and young adults in the 1960s and 1970s began to "return to nature" and establish a communally based style of living.

To the practicing psychoanalyst, all such manifestations of personal adjustment in adolescence reflect the person's continuing need to settle upon a satisfactory resolution of the socializing tendencies begun in the Oedipal dynamic. That is, one side of this adjustment effort has to deal with the proper alignment of id and ego-superego factors in the personality. Here we find problems of aggression and sexuality surfacing. But, there is also another side to adolescent integration having to do more strictly with the ego, its relation to its ideals (superego), and a sense of conscious identity that will reassure the person as he or she comes uniquely and individually forward into adulthood.

## The Search for Identity: Erikson

Erik Erikson (1963, 1968) has focused his attention on that side of human behavior which enters into the interpersonal, the sociocultural, and the conscious sense of continuity that the person senses in referring to "I," "me," "myself." Thus, Erikson (1980) states that a "child who has just found himself able to walk seems not only driven to repeat and to perfect the act of walking by libidinal pleasure . . . [but] he also becomes aware of the new status and stature of 'he who can walk,' with whatever connotation this happens to have in the coordinates of his culture's life plan" (pp. 21-22). Based on the dual perspective of (1) our own recognition of sameness over time and (2) the fact that others recognize us as being the same person we have always been, we are confronted with the necessity of coming to some kind of sense of "being" or of "being somebody." If so, who are we? What are we like? Questions of this sort are especially salient during adolescence, though they follow us throughout life. In answering them we are dealing with our *ego-identities:*

Ego identity, then, in its subjective aspect, is the awareness of the fact that there is a selfsameness and continuity to the ego's synthesizing methods and that these methods are effective in safeguarding the sameness and continuity of one's meaning for others. (Erikson, 1980, p. 22)

We noted in Chapter 1 (p. 11) that Freud's biological naturalism encompassed a reliance upon personal identity in his formulation of the ego construct. This was an essential ingredient in his teleological style of theoretical description. The ego is the agent that directs events following various compromises drawn with the id and superego. We shall have much more to say of Freud's ego conception in Chapter 4. However, for present purposes it is important to realize that Freud's ego-identity is not the same concept as Erikson's ego-identity. Freud was dealing with a most basic characteristic of human behavior, essentially the "point of view" that the individual has on life from his or her perspective as life experience is being encountered daily. The person approaches life from an *introspective* perspective, a first-person ("I," "me," etc.) point of view in which what takes place is always dependent to some extent upon the assumptions, wishes, intentions, choices, and so on, of the identity under description.

Erikson takes this introspective approach to the description of the person, but in speaking of ego identity per se he is adding the ingredient of a kind of conscious self-knowledge, a personal "image" that each person must develop in interpersonal relations or suffer in adjustment accordingly. Healthy personalities not only develop an accurate sense of self but also unify the various aspects of personal behavior in a way that facilitates the further mastery of their environment. Erikson bases his theory on the assumption that in all growth there is an ordered "ground plan" (1980, p. 53) that manifests itself, beginning *in utero* for the human being and carrying forward throughout childhood and on into adolescence and beyond. Although cultural influences may provide variations on this theme of ordered development, there is a proper rate and a proper sequence of developing functions that influence the course of personality.

Personality can be said to develop according to steps predetermined in the human organism's readiness to be driven toward, to be aware of, and to interact with, a widening social radius, beginning with the dim image of a mother and ending with mankind, or at any rate that segment of mankind which "counts" in the particular individual's life. (ibid., p. 54)

Typically, the developing human being confronts life in stages, with a newly emerging capacity for mastery of the environment, and depending upon how well this new capacity is employed to extend the ego's mastery over life crises, acquiring thereby a sense of personal continuity over time, we can speak of "identity" as opposed to "diffusion" taking place. Erikson observed:

The sense of ego identity, then, is the accrued confidence that one's ability to maintain inner sameness and continuity (one's ego in the psychological sense) is matched by the sameness and continuity of one's meaning for others. Thus, self-esteem, confirmed at the end of each major crisis, grows to be a conviction that one is learning effective steps toward a tangible future, that one is developing a defined personality within a social reality which one understands. (ibid., pp. 94-95)

If this identity and its attendant sense of mastery or confidence is not achieved, identity diffusion and confusion occurs—resulting in the "Who am I?" type of self-examination so common to adolescence.

Erikson has paralleled the Freudian psychosexual phases with eight stages of his own. Perhaps it is more correct to say that he has elaborated upon the Freudian phases, because he at no time rejects what Freud has had to say about development. There are certain psychological characteristics that frame each life stage and lend them their unique quality. As with Freudian theory, the earlier stages provide the grounds for later stages, so that there is an inter-related course of personality development through the life cycle. Initially, the psychological emphasis in life is on basic trust, or the sense that we all must have as infants in the trustworthiness of others (*stage of infancy*). The parents must be sensed as reliable and loving, or the child will develop an interpersonal mistrust characterizing all later social relationships. Horney (1939) proposed a similar idea in her construct of *basic anxiety*.

In the second and third years of life, autonomy becomes increasingly important as the child gains a sense of mastery over sphincter control in toilet training (*stage of early childhood*). A certain amount of self-doubt is normal at this time, because it is not easy for any child to meet the growing demands of reality. However, by about the fourth or fifth year the child should have passed through the first two stages and moved into the stage in which initiative is the predominant psychological premise framing consciousness (*stage of play*). If the maturing child is to become a fully integrated adult, then he or she must exhibit the self-determination accomplished through initiative, through meeting the challenges of life, beginning with the explorations of play. The child who does not actively differentiate his or her life experiences in solitary and then interpersonal playfulness comes to sense guilt at having allowed such marvelous opportunities of mastery to pass by.

During the latency phase Erikson emphasizes the role of industry in ego development (*stage of "school age"*). If the child is not willing to meet the challenges of an expanding social world, to partake in the organizations and activities of peers at this age level, it is always due to the underlying sense of inferiority that has begun early in life—initially as mistrust, moving into shame and doubt, and thence through a sense of guilt into the self-doubts of inferiority feelings. It is in the *stage of adolescence* that identity per se takes on great importance, because now for the first time the person begins sensing the need for distinctive self-characterization. Development to this point must have eventuated in "something," an identity that stamps the person as distinctively who he or she "is." If this ego identity does not take place, then *diffusion* and *role confusion,* a sense of aimlessness, an underlying anxiety, and all of those manifestations familiar to the psychopathologist take place. Erikson refers to this as an *identity crisis* (1980, p. 111). Once again, a certain amount of such diffusion is natural during adolescence, as the young person confronts the dramatic changes taking place in his or her biological capacities.

We might mention briefly in passing that Erikson carries this succession of psychological life premises forward to adulthood, where intimacy with another is required in order to escape a sense of isolation (*stage of young adulthood*). Erikson also stresses what he calls *generativity* or the capacity to avoid stagnation by creating new experiences, challenges, and interests quite intentionally (*stage of adulthood "proper"*). Too many adults fall into defensive habits, using *distantiation* or the repudiation of other people or challenging possibilities that provide a threat to the integrity of the person's self-image. (ibid., p. 101). Better to avoid threats than to put one's ego at risk. Alfred Adler (1968) proposed a similar concept in *distance,* or the disparity between where one is in life and the possibility of a beckoning but challenging goal (p. 167). People are too ready to widen this distance, but they do so at the cost of a declining level of confidence.

Gradually, as the person comes to full maturity, he or she realizes that "identity" is not simply the sameness of competent mastery over a lifetime; it also includes a fundamental *sharing* of one's essence and life experiences with others (Erikson, 1980, p. 129). This interpersonal sharing transcends the personal bonds of parental- or marital-familial commitments to reach out for a tie to humanity in general (*stage of maturity*). Those who fail to attain such basic human integrity are likely to live out their final years in a sense of disgust and despair.

Some psychoanalysts have criticized Erikson for the reliance made on consciousness in his theory of ego-identity. Though he recognizes that he is dealing in relatively conscious experience (see ibid., p. 127), he also stresses that ego-identity is something that is earned, appearing as a by-product of our actively living out our lives. Indeed, we are often surprised by our emerging identity, particularly in adolescence. We acquire a reputation among peers when we have not set out to do so. We accomplish something and then realize: "Gee, I can really do that 'grown-up' thing." Researches on self-identity typically support the Eriksonian suggestion that the higher and better ego-identified an adolescent or young adult is, the better his or her adjustment is likely to be (Marcia, 1980).

## Moral Development: Piaget and Kohlberg

Closely related to the development of ego-identity is the question of moral development in adolescence. Research on morality has been based predominantly on the work of Piaget (1965) and Kohlberg (1976), both of whom emphasize that early in life children take a very literal view of "do's" and "don'ts" so that they obey rules without fully grasping the grounding reasons for doing so. Piaget termed this *moral realism*. Gradually, children come to appreciate that there are reasons for behavior. They also discover that it is possible to feel that an action is wrong or "bad" without knowing why this is the case, and they also find that occasionally a harmful outcome can result from the best of intentions.

Kohlberg argues in line with Eriksonian theory that moral growth results from exposure to levels of moral reasoning that are moderately higher than the person's current level. As a result, the maturing child senses a certain cognitive conflict or disequilibrium that challenges him or her to find a solution, to make sense out of what may seem a contradiction. As maturation continues, such experiences help build personal mastery along with developing a sense of mature judgment in ethical and moral matters. There have been a number of empirical demonstrations of the positive relationship between high ego-identity and advanced levels of moral reasoning and ethical behavior in adolescence and young adulthood (Marcia, 1980, pp. 163-164).

Religious beliefs and practices have reflected some complex changes in recent decades. Some authorities believe that there has been a form of polarization taking place, with declining religious beliefs on the one hand and a revivalistic fundamentalism on the other. A review of recent history and the research literature would seem to support this belief. Most young people aged twelve to eighteen continue to express a general belief in God, but their formal religious views become more abstract and less based upon obeying dogmatic rules (Conger, 1977; Gallup, 1977). There is evidence to suggest that interest and participation in formal religious denominations have declined in the 1970s, as compared with the level observed in the 1940s and 1950s (Yankelovich, 1974).

Most experts interpret the declining emphasis on formal religion to be due to the changing values on sexuality that we discussed above, ranging from liberalization in premarital activity and use of contraceptive devices to women's rights for abortion on demand. Traditional religious denominations cannot embrace such changes. There is little difference on other interpersonal dimensions than the sexual between adolescents and traditional denominations. Thus, adolescents emphasize *love* and *friendship* as the two most important values in life (ibid.). A possible exception to this agreement is the growing sociopolitical cynicism to be seen among adolescents in recent decades, who have called into question the wisdom, altruism, and sometimes even the honesty of government, big business, big labor, and the military establishment.

Even as formal religion may be suffering, today's adolescent places more emphasis than his or her predecessor on *personalized* religious views (Bengston & Starr, 1975). Undoubtedly, sociocultural factors come into play here in that we have witnessed in the post–World War II years a trend to emphasize personal decisions and personal values rather than relying on traditional institutions. Even so, we must not forget that there has also been the opposing swing to charismatic movements and/or a revived fundamentalism in the traditional religious denominations (Catholic, Protestant, Hebraic). We have also to take account of the attraction that adolescents have shown to the more atypical in the American culture such as the Children of God, Hare Krishna, and the Unification Church.

Whether personal or institutional, liberal or conservative, clear or unclear, the valuations that developing human beings affirm in their lives are fundamental to their eventual psychological adjustment and to the style of psychopathology that they may manifest. Freud may have devoted more time to unconscious than conscious processes in the establishment of the superego and its subsequent role in the personality. But he most certainly did not underrate this most human of all tendencies—to moralize, to evaluate, to judge the behavior of self and others according to a frame of reference. This is the sine qua non of teleological activity, the factor that most distinguishes higher from lower animals. As Freudians, we can accept a possible change in the way that moral evaluations will take place in the future. But the basic personality that Freud so early delineated will not be affected by this sociocultural change.

## Adulthood

What are the psychological criteria of adulthood? Most experts would probably agree that they are the disappearance of the turmoil, uncertainty, and conflict of adolescence, the appearance of emotional control and general predictability, the establishment of self-confidence and self-respect (via ego attainment or ego-identity), a willingness to accept adult responsibilities, and a self-assertive independence of thinking and judgment. These are the marks of emotional maturity, of the channeling of sexual and aggressive emotions, of adult ego integration, of the stabilization of superego functioning—in providing both self-criticism and self-esteem—and of a realistic construction of a person's external and internal worlds. A brief discussion of maturity and the normal adult at this juncture will prepare us to consider in more detail the organization of experience and behavior and its disturbances.

Maturity is always relative. It is justifiable to speak of an infant, a child, or an adolescent as mature for his or her age. It is also justifiable to look upon maturity as something that comes only with middle age or old age, if indeed it comes at all. Many adults, as we shall see, marry and have children without ever becoming themselves psychologically mature. On the other hand, some who choose a life of celibacy, in the pursuit of some ideal, show a degree of mature responsibility and predictability greater than that of many of their married adult peers (Allport, 1961). Many adults who seem wild and irresponsible in their twenties or thirties, and even in their forties, develop personal and social responsibility in middle or late life. Some of these become models of maturity, and a few become recognized hero figures and/or saints. Many of the criteria proposed by experts for *normal personality* are not to be found among the millions whose socioeconomic status and family background do not provide them with realistic material material security.

In what follows we shall use the term *maturity* to designate a post-adolescent equilibrium that allows a person to pursue the life he or she chooses or is given, with a minimum of stress and strain but with a capacity for frustration tolerance when conflicts arise. Regressive behavioral setbacks should be rare in a mature personality structure. The postadolescent equilibrium of which we speak is mainly *internal,* as we shall see in the chapters following this one, but it demands a vast amount of *external experience* for its development and for its maintenance. The equilibrium changes in character as a person grows older and his or her physiological and social functioning changes. It can be seriously impaired and even destroyed by adult catastrophe; the less firm its infantile childhood and adolescent foundations are, the more vulnerable it will be to adult impairment or destruction.

Adult normality, like maturity, is always relative. The normal adult man of twenty-five would be abnormal at fifty if he remained the same. On the other hand, he would be abnormal at twenty-five if he thought and acted like a man of fifty. In recent years we have witnessed the changing role of women in our society. Women now seek careers outside the home and quite often arrange marriages in which their husbands share the duties of homemaking and child rearing. Every woman who now leaves her home to take up a career is not necessarily better off psychologically, even as her opposite number who remains in the home setting is not necessarily a well-adjusted human being. In recent years there has been growing interest in the so-called *midlife crisis,* in which essentially normal middle-aged men and women experience acute anxiety thanks to the fact that they either finally accept their mortality or seek to deny it further, and thereby make sweeping lifestyle changes in reaction to this acceptance or denial (Jaques, 1965).

When it comes to the achievement of adult equilibrium, we are faced with innumerable normal patterns. Their components will be discussed in some detail as we pass on to the psychodynamics of human behavior and experience. Here it is enough to say that adult normality requires a person to achieve and to maintain a reasonably effective psychodynamic balance within and reasonably effective interpersonal relationships without. For this, a person must be able to control and channel emotions, maintain initiative and zest, use inhibitions sparingly, and avoid distortions of character. There must be satisfactory ego development (mastery, identity, ability to compromise, etc.), so that the individual can cope with unavoidable external and internal (including physical) distresses and be able to enjoy social interactions as well as sexual experiences. Finally, the normal person's superego should be able to represent ethical and moral standards in the absence of other persons, or even in opposition to their opinions, and provide a kind of balance wheel that is neither too permissive nor too punitive.

In actual life we do not meet paragons of perfection. There are always regrettable flaws and lapses. In fact, adult life cannot be considered normal unless it shows some defects, at some level, in some area. Those who treat the psychopathologically disturbed or deal with character distortions know that even grave imperfections can be compensated for, or masked, by defensive and adaptive structures. We can go even further than this and say that, just as absolute perfection of physique and physiology are rare rather than normal, so perfection of adult equilibrium in behavior and experience is rare rather than normal. We expect to find minor imperfections in normal bodily function and in normal mental function. We often find reasonably normal bodily function in persons who suffer from a serious defect that they have learned to master, and we find poor bodily or mental function in persons with a mild defect who have not learned to master it.

This concludes our survey of development, begun in Chapter 2 with the fetus and carried now through adulthood. In Chapters 4 and 5 we shall look more specifically at the personality system that is moving in psychodynamic fashion through the stages of life, under various forms of motivation and employing various defenses in order to retain some semblance of integrity.

## SUMMARY

Chapter 3 continues with a review of personality development to late childhood, latency, adolescence, and adulthood. The phallic stage of psychosexual development, with its *Oedipal conflict,* is taken up first. Problems arise because of the contrasting Oedipal dynamics of males and females. In the male, the case for a firm superego is readily made based upon the *castration anxiety* sensed by the boy who lusts after his mother. Due to this anxiety, the boy reverts from object-choice (lusting mother) to identification (with father's value system). In the female Oedipus complex (sometimes called the *Electra complex*) there is no motivating force of castration to assist in the dynamics. The little girl in this situation experiences *penis envy*.

Unlike boys, who revert from object-choice to identification, girls come to shift object-choice from mother to father. The father's penis is sought as a substitute for the lack of a personal penis. In time, the little girl comes to play the feminine maternal role in her fantasies. Gradually, the desire for a child serves as a substitute for the lack of a penis. Because of the lack of crystallization by way of anxiety, Freud suggested that the female superego is never as independent of emotional factors as is the case in the male. The resultant picture of female personality has been severely criticized by feminists.

Drawing an analogy to Haeckel's biogenetic rule that *ontogeny recapitulates phylogeny,* Freud suggested that in the familial Oedipal dynamic we witness a repetition or re-enactment of the origins of society. The father takes the role of *primal* father, who literally castrated his sons for sexual conduct with the women of the primal horde. This literal history of an Oedipal dynamic is what accounts for the child's divination of the paternal castration threat.

Thanks to an influence from Fliess, Freud also discussed the possible role of *bisexuality* in the Oedipus complex. Here we have a biological (material- and efficient-cause) theme in Freudian theory. Both sexes have masculine and feminine biological dispositions. If one or the other of these biological tendencies was strongest, then the outcome of the Oedipal dynamic could be effected.

Indeed, there is a *positive* and a *negative* feature to every Oedipal conflict. A little boy, for example, is not merely ambivalent toward his father and affectionate toward his mother; at the same time, he behaves like a girl and displays an affectionate feminine attitude to his father and a corresponding jealousy and hostility toward his mother. It is therefore possible to have an Oedipal dynamic go "in reverse," negating the customary positive outcome. This theme is not prominent in Freud's writings, but it has attracted advocates who would like to trace certain dynamics, such as homosexuality, to an innate sexual disposition. The *positive* Oedipal dynamic, in which the boy takes mother as object and the girl takes father, is by far the one we see discussed most in Freud's writings.

The Oedipus complex is the "nuclear" complex of *every* neurosis. All neurotics have poorly resolved Oedipus complexes. That is, all neurotics suffering from the *psychoneuroses proper* have such poor resolution. This includes the broad family of the hysterias. Freud suggested that the *actual* neuroses (i.e., neurasthenia, anxiety, and hypochondria) resulted from toxic causes. Today, *all* forms of psychopathology are likely to be traced to poorly resolved Oedipus complexes.

There have been vigorous and insightful objections leveled against Freud's conceptualization of female psychology. Chapter 3 takes up Karen Horney's counter to the Freudian claims. Horney noted that so-called penis envy is no more prominent in young girls than the desire to have breasts. Psychoanalysts are too ready to overlook the fact that so-called *castrating females* are just as competitive and demanding in their relations with other females as they are with men. Horney underscored the cultural advantages enjoyed by anyone who behaved "masculinely"—male or female. To bring such sociocultural factors down to biology or a repetition of the societal origins seemed an unnecessary stretch of imagination to Horney. Her interpretation of female psychology stressed current sociocultural influences. Women are instructed by their culture to overvalue love and consequently they dread losing it. Freud's naturalism prevented him from ascribing differences between the sexes to supraindividual cultural influence alone.

The next psychosexual phase discussed in Chapter 3 is *latency*. Neighborhood and peer influences are important during this period of life. Sexual modeling of like-sex playmates becomes important. Latency is not a worry-free period of life. There are definite stresses that arise, and the young person during this period requires considerable emotional support. The phase of *adolescence* follows as the child passes through pubescence. Anna Freud has contributed to a growing interest among psychoanalysts in the phase of adolescence. Empirical data on the changing sexual patterns of adolescents is reviewed. The importance of peer pressures is highlighted.

Erik Erikson's theory of development and the search for identity is next reviewed. Erikson views *ego-identity* as the awareness of a selfsameness and continuity in the ego's synthesizing methods, which allow for a sameness and continuity of the person's meaning for others. Not only do healthy personalities develop an accurate sense of self, but they also unify the various aspects of personal behavior in a way that facilitates the further mastery of their environment. Typically, the developing human being confronts life in stages, with a newly emerging capacity for mastery of the environment. To the extent that the ego's mastery over life crises is successful, acquiring thereby a sense of personal continuity over time, an *identity* is being fashioned in the personality rather than *diffusion*. Such diffusion in personal identity is fairly common in adolescence.

Erikson has elaborated on the Freudian psychosexual phases, suggesting eight distinctive stages: *infancy, early childhood, play, school age, adolescence, young adulthood, adulthood "proper,"* and *maturity.* When the adolescent is experiencing serious diffusion and role confusion, he or she is said to be suffering from an *identity crisis.* In adulthood it is important to avoid stagnation of the personality by promoting *generativity,* or the creation of new experiences, challenges, and interests. Too many adults employ *distantiation* in repudiating challenges in life and putting themselves free of such risks. In order to attain a healthy maturity it is necessary for the adult to *share* his or her personal essence and life experiences with others.

Chapter 3 next reviews the findings on moral development in maturing children. Both Piaget and Kohlberg found that young children function according to a *moral realism* in which a very literal view of "do's" and "don'ts" is taken. Gradually, children learn to appreciate that there are reasons for moral decisions, grounding assumptions regarding what is right and what is wrong about various behaviors. Several investigations have found a positive relationship between ego-identity in the Eriksonian sense and advanced levels of moral reasoning. The final topic discussed in Chapter 3 is adulthood. Maturity is viewed as a postadolescent adjustment pattern in which the person pursues life with a capacity for frustration tolerance and a minimum level of stress. The phenomenon of the *midlife crisis* is noted, in which essentially normal middle-age men and women sometimes experience anxiety thanks to the fact that they finally accept their mortality or that they seek to deny it altogether. Sweeping lifestyle changes occur in reaction to this acceptance or denial.

# 4

# *Personality, Motivation, and Defense*

We have to this point presented Freudian developmental theory without clearly describing the finished product—a psychodynamic system known as the "personality." In Chapter 4 it will be our aim to pull several loose ends together by first going through a description of the structural constructs of personality proposed by Freud, following with a discussion of the very complicated issue of motivation, and closing with a review of all the defense mechanisms except fixation and regression. The latter mechanisms, which take us back to the developmental phases (oral, anal, phallic, and so forth), will be considered in Chapter 5, where we shall get into the complexities of both normal and abnormal personal adjustment.

## *Personality Structure*

### DUALISM OF MIND VERSUS BODY

Freudian psychology is a *dualism,* meaning that it builds on the assumption that there are two interacting spheres of behavior—the *psyche* (mind) and the *soma* (body). As we shall see when we consider the brain disorders (Chapter 18), when the physiological activities of the central nervous system disintegrate, the psychic capacities of the individual also disintegrate. Had Freud committed himself totally to biological reductionism (see Chapter 1, p. 13), he would have framed a *monism,* that is, a theory in which there is only one realm of explanation. His teacher Ernst Brücke and his colleagues Josef Breuer and Wilhelm Fliess favored such monistic explanations. The *Project* was Freud's abortive effort to write a monistic psychology (see Chapter 1, p. 10).

When we speak about the "personality" in psychoanalysis we are referring to the psychodynamic system encompassed by the psyche. The resultant problems of description and understanding in psychoanalysis are legion. What is the relationship between the psychodynamic system and the body? Where is the psychodynamic system located physically—in the brain alone, or elsewhere as well? We know that the psychodynamic system can disintegrate while the central nervous system continues to function normally at physiological levels. This is most obvious in panic states, in mania, and in the depressions as well as the schizophrenias. Even the lesser, neurotic disturbances can reflect such deterioration of the personality without organic disturbance.

We cannot say where the ego or the id are located biologically. Nor can we trace the physiological mechanisms through which body and mind interact. We are certain that the physical is primary, that mind flows from the biological mechanisms of body. But Freud's genius lay in his appreciation of the strictly mental, psychodynamic factors in human behavior. He never rejected the hypothesis that someday the psychic structure might be taken over by traditional biological reductionism (see Chapter 1, p. 9). We shall have some of his comments on this possibility later in this chapter. But he also never gave up on his strictly naturalistic interests in finding that the psyche per se had a structure of its own that exerted direct influence on behavior. Here is where he placed greatest emphasis in his theoretical explanations.

## THE EARLY MENTAL STRUCTURAL CONSTRUCTS: DEPTH EMPHASIS

Though he had always used the term *ego* in his writings, Freud's technical descriptions of the psyche at first emphasized the *depth* at which various psychic contents (wishes, ideas) might be situated. There were three regions to consider: *conscious, unconscious,* and *preconscious.* Freud defined consciousness as a "sense organ for the apprehension of psychical qualities" (Freud, 1900-01/1953b, p. 574), through which the individual is aware of sensory input (seeing, smelling, thinking about things seen, etc.) and also of pleasurable or painful experiences. Consciousness does *not* rule mind in Freudian psychology. It does not even retain memories, which are kept down below the level of conscious awareness. Freud considered mental contents to be in consciousness only if one is *presently* aware of them (Freud, 1912/1958g, p. 260). Thoughts do *not* originate in consciousness. For centuries, philosophers had identified ideas in awareness with thought, but Freud broadened the concept of mind when he said that "every psychical act begins as an unconscious one, and it may either remain so or go on developing into consciousness, according as it meets with resistance or not" (ibid., p. 264).

Freud found in his early cases that a *censorship* often functioned in the mind, keeping certain ideas or certain aspects of an idea out of consciousness. He was soon aware that if he were ever to understand what he later called the "true psychic reality" he would have to look into the deeper depths of mind— that is, into the unconscious (Freud, 1900-01/1953b, p. 613). Freud considered the unconscious a much larger aspect of mind than consciousness. The analogy to an iceberg is often made. The portion of the iceberg seen above the water line is merely the tip of this icy mass; the vast majority of an iceberg is below the surface of the water. Consciousness is like the tip of the iceberg, and

*An 1897 photograph of Joseph Breuer, who collaborated with Freud on the*
Studies on Hysteria *in the early 1890s. Freud's psychodynamic under-*
*standing of mental disorder distinguished him from Breuer's traditional*
*medical explanations and the collaboration was to dissolve accordingly.*

unconsciousness is the vast area below. Belief in the unconscious is what
prompts us to speak of a "dynamic" approach to the study of behavior, for in
contradistinction to behaviorists like Skinner (see Chapter 1, p. 13) who claim
that there is no difference between internal and external experience, Freud
(1915-16/1963a) had this to say: "The unconscious is a particular realm of the
mind with its own wishful impulses, its own mode of expression and its peculiar
mental mechanisms which are not in force elsewhere" (p. 212). We can get in
touch with the unconscious only by interpreting what it seems to be indicating
in our dreams, waking fantasies, *parapraxes* (slips of the tongue, misactions),
and so forth (Freud, 1932-36/1964b, p. 70).

To account for that region of unawareness over which we often *do* have some control, Freud proposed the term *preconscious.* The preconscious region of the psyche is made up of contributions from *both* the conscious and the unconscious, and it is the area of mind where *censorship* (repression) takes place (Freud, 1915/1957k, p. 187). The conscious and unconscious never communicate directly, but only by way of this intermediate level of preconsciousness. When we forget something like the telephone number of a friend only to recall it after an effort of concentration, we have dealt exclusively with a preconscious content. Truly unconscious contents (like a death wish) would not be recovered this directly.

## THE FINAL MENTAL STRUCTURAL CONSTRUCTS: DYNAMIC EMPHASIS

The depth model is all right for describing interactions *across* levels of mind, as between unconscious and preconscious contents, but what about those mental interactions that seem to go on *within* as well as across levels? To accommodate such dynamics Freud modified the depth model by combining it with what he called a *topographical* model. Topography is the science of graphing or mapping a region that is capable of being divided into different kinds of terrain. In 1923 Freud added to his ego terminology the constructs of id and superego, rounding out the now well-known tripartite aspects of the psychodynamic system. Unconscious and/or preconscious mind no longer opposed conscious mind, but *three identities* (i.e., introspectively conceived mental outlooks) opposed one another within or across these levels of psychic depth. This clash-and-compromise model fixed once and for all the *dynamic* quality of Freudian psychology. We shall take up each of these psychic identities in the order that they are seen to be active in the personality.

*The Id.* At birth, the child enters the world with a psyche that is completely unconscious and totally *id* in nature. Some psychoanalysts reject this progression of development from id to ego, contending that these identities have separate origins and independent lines of development (see, e.g., Hartmann, 1958, 1964). According to Freud, the id never leaves the unconscious realm of mind during the person's lifetime, and as we shall see when we discuss motivational aspects of the personality, the id is the identity point at which instinctual promptings that begin in the bodily sphere first make contact with mind. The id seeks satisfaction in all things, being in essence greedy, envious, and thoroughly selfish. This hedonistic prompting is what Freud meant by the *pleasure principle.* As Freud (1932/1964c) poetically defined the id, "we call it a chaos, a cauldron full of seething excitations" (p. 73).

The id is not concerned with realistic evaluations of the demands of society, much less of logic. It reasons according to a primitive logic that Freud termed *primary process* thought (see Chapter 2, p. 58). Thus, it might lust after and want to kill the same person (Freud, 1932/1964c, p. 73). The id is full of such contradictions and never bothers to iron out inconsistency. The id is not concerned with the passage of time or of changes that may take place; but it never forgets because it never forgoes anything it wants (ibid., p. 74). The fact that human beings carry forward into adulthood wishes that they have framed as infants stems from this timeless aspect of the id's desires. The id never becomes socialized (it remains "unshaped" by environmental pressures). Since the id continues to bear an influence on the personality throughout life, we can say that every human adult is in one sense still a "psychic infant" as well as a more-or-less mature individual.

Primary process thinking occurs throughout life as the primitive, rock-bottom activities, the raw strivings and strange unconscious maneuverings, of the human mind. It includes prelogical archaic symbolism, a peculiar interchange of expressive vehicles, a tendency to condense mental contents into one symbolical image, and an absence of such logical necessities as negation, denial, resolution or inconsistency, and recognition of time and spatial relations. This form of mentation is responsible for much of the weird experiences that we have in dreaming and that occur in delirium, intoxications, psychotic symptomatology, and sensory deprivation.

*The Ego.* Out of the unorganized, self-serving heritage from nature (i.e., the id) there develops a portion of mind devoted to reason, the realistic evaluations of external conditions, and "the" self-identity point of the personality system. It does not exist at birth, but as conscious awareness progresses over the first few months of life, the *ego* begins to be differentiated and identified as an unchanging permanent component of the personality structure (Freud, 1937/1964e, p. 240). The ego is what the developing child comes to think of as "I," "me," "myself," and so on. The role of muscular sensations in this developmental process is important, as the newborn child begins to identify a difference between "over here" (selfhood) in the movements of the body and the external world "over there." Although the ego has contact across all three levels of mind, its sphere is predominantly that of consciousness (Freud, 1923/1961a, p. 18).

The ego has a commitment to the external world, but it is also directly tied to the id. In fact, since it develops out of the id, Freud (1926/1959g) once referred to the ego as the "organized portion of the id" (p. 97). It is in this organization and order that the ego becomes useful, because the id is totally lacking in these qualities. The ego begins to function coherently, according to *secondary process* thinking (Freud, 1900-01/1953b, pp. 601-603) (see Chapter 2, p. 58). This involves adapting to the demands of reality—also known as living according to the *reality principle*—rather than distortions and imagined gratifications of the id. But we must never forget that the ego wants to get the *same* pleasurable things out of life that the id wants. These two sides of the same personality system differ only over the means to the ends sought. As Freud (1932-36/1964b) said, "The ego stands for reason and good sense while the id stands for the untamed passions" (p. 76).

In our review of personality development in Chapters 2 and 3 it was the ego portion of the psychodynamic system that entered into the socialization process, not as a "shaped" outcome of environmental manipulation but as a mediator between id promptings (intentions) and restrictions of the culture in which the child is being reared. The superego rounds out this process (see below). Freud held that the ego is capable of organizing experience and behavior in ways that are rational, precise, practical, and appropriate to the human environment. In developing higher-level cognitive abilities the personality system is reflecting ego functions. It is the ego that brings to bear native capacities such as sucking to explore and organize experience. In doing so, consciousness is being furthered. So, though the ego begins to contact reality from the unconscious realm, it gradually construes a conscious sense of what reality "is." Between these two levels of consciousness and unconsciousness we have that gray area known as the preconscious. Much of the dynamic maneuvering that we shall be taking up in Chapter 5 is thought to take place at the point where the preconscious and unconscious levels of mind merge. It is here where ego can, in effect, negotiate compromises with the id concerning some wished-for pleasure. However, there is a third part to such negotiations, the superego.

*The Superego.* Freud (1914/1957h) initially referred to internal judgments on the basis of which we sense a pang of conscience as due to the *ego-ideal,* which defines how we ought to behave (pp. 93-94). These internal judgments are the values which the child incorporates following resolution of the Oedipus complex (see Chapter 3, p. 69). When he later (in 1923) introduced the id construct, Freud referred to the ego-ideal as the *superego.* He did not draw involved distinctions between the ego-ideal and superego, and in fact sometimes referred to the superego as simply the ego (Freud, 1923/1961a, p. 28). The main point is that, as the id is organizing into the ego, a portion of this ego organization is forming into a superego—that is, an identity point in mind that is ego but is also beyond or above it as a built-in ideal.

Since the superego has developed from the same mental beginnings as the ego, it too is basically a product of the id (ibid., p. 36). The id portion of the personality wishes to take something even if it is stealing. The superego wishes that the id would be punished for thinking such thoughts or for bringing them about if the person actually does steal. Rather than confronting the id directly, the superego makes its wishes known to the ego. As a result, the ego is said to serve as intermediary between *three* masters—id, superego, and the demands of external reality (Freud, 1932-36/1964b, p. 78).

The superego is just as unbending and unreasonable as the id. It has, like the id, ties to the past. The id is tied to the historical past via organic evolution (which is where we found the rationale for re-enactment of society in Oedipal dynamics; see Chapter 3, p. 73); the superego is tied to the sociocultural past in the fact that it has affirmed traditional ethico-moral principles like the Ten Commandments. The superego sticks to these principles rigidly and can never see exceptions to the rule. The id's inheritance from the past is physical and hedonistic, and the superego's is sociocultural and moralistic, but both of these identities in mind try to dictate to the ego. The superego dictates in a dual sense, for it not only tells the ego what it "ought to be like," but also tells the ego what it "may not be like" (Freud, 1923/1961a, p. 34). The seat of reason, common sense, and good judgment in changing circumstances are thus found only in the ego.

Many analysts hold that the superego which differentiates itself from the ego during the resolution of the Oedipal conflict is by no means the first sign of internal moral control. The earliest precursors of the superego are most likely included in very early *ego introjects* and *ego identifications* that are taken from attitudes and behaviors of either parent (Ritvo & Solnit, 1960). Studies of many kinds of regressive states all suggest that at first these ego introjects and identifications are experienced neither as internal nor as external (Loewald, 1962). This implies that in early infancy, ego boundaries have not yet been established that make it possible to distinguish between inside and outside, between ego and object.

It is generally believed that infants experience good and evil in some such direct way as soon as they can distinguish the *good mother* from the *bad mother* that they have internalized. We know that small children, when they have learned to speak a little, report such experiences. It is most unlikely that the acquisition of speech introduces a child for the first time to feelings of what is good and what is bad. For the very young infant, the good is the pleasurable, and the bad is the unpleasurable. Later on, the child adopts the prevailing attitudes of family members as to what is good and what is bad. Invariably, these attitudes encompass the values of the child's society and culture as well.

As the superego differentiates from the ego following Oedipal resolution, it takes on many controlling and evaluative functions besides those arising directly from Oedipal conflicts. Eventually, it comes to include many systems and many hierarchies of goodness or cleanliness and superiority, or badness or dirtiness and inferiority. It is finally organized as an internal overseer, the judge of thoughts, words, and things, and the internal source of love and self-esteem for good behavior and of hatred and self-condemnation for bad.

Since it is situated within the psychodynamic system, the superego cannot be escaped. It can exercise a constant surveillance over everything that goes on within the system, including even unconscious impulses and conflicts. Its range of influence extends across all three levels of mind, which is why we noted above that it enters into any negotiations that the ego and id may be motivated to conduct. Superegos can be defective, of course, depending upon the success with which the person resolved his or her Oedipal conflict. Defective superegos can produce a severely inhibited or distorted personality system, as in certain personality disorders, or a person who has no sense of remorse for antisocial acts whatsoever, as in the case of certain criminals.

We must never forget that the ego begins its life experience as that of a small child, who is in direct relationship with nonverbal and early verbal reality but is full of misinterpretations as well as accurate understandings of reality. The preconscious ego systems evolve over a period of years before the massive repression that gives final form to the post-Oedipal superego. Successive childhood organizations, precursors of the superego, may all persist in the unconscious side by side, as it were, with all their conflicts, infantile perspectives, and primary process derivatives. When an adult regresses, as in sleeping or experiencing a psychotic episode, some of these early organizations from oral, anal, and phallic phases of development are reactivated.

Some of the precursors of the post-Oedipal superego that result in striking examples of adult superego pathology arise during the pre-Oedipal, sado-masochistic phase of development, the anal phase of self-assertion and sphincter control. The cruelties of a small child's sadism may be preserved into adult-hood as primitive superego structures that interact with reciprocal masochistic tendencies in a repressed unconscious ego. It is this pre-Oedipal organization that we shall see revived with special clarity in compulsive disorders, in which patients sometimes actually punish themselves sadistically, are often incredibly preoccupied with conflicts over cleanliness and dirt, and occasionally show open concern with fecal contamination and sexual fantasy. When regression leads to a psychotic depressive illness, as we have mentioned earlier, there is danger that the sadistic superego may drive the masochistic ego to actual suicide. Sometimes, obsessive-compulsive symptoms appear when a depression clears up, suggesting that there may be a fundamental relationship between depression and compulsion, since in both there is the same overwhelming sense of guilt.

## Motivation: The Drive Construct in Behavioral Description

In Chapter 1 we defined *personality* as the *style of behavior* taken on by an individual (see p. 1). *Motivation* is that aspect of a personality theory which attempts to account for such variations in behavioral style. We have seen in the final personality constructs of id, ego, and superego what makes people pretty much alike. Now, we want to know what makes them so different, including the differences we have characterized as psychopathological disturbance. Unfortunately, there is no more controversial aspect of psychoanalysis than the libido theory, which deals directly with this matter of motivation. Many psychoanalysts believe that libido as a mental energy is directly comparable to physical energy, so that it serves as "the" motivating *drive* in the personality structure. Other psychoanalysts believe that there are enough differences between libido and biological drives to weaken if not destroy the analogy between them altogether.

In the present volume, we lean in the latter direction, believing that though Freud did try to apply the principle of constancy to his descriptions of behavior (see Chapter 1, p. 10), his teleological interests continually interfered so that the biological reductionism called for was never achieved. We shall first get clearly in mind what drive theory has entailed in psychological theories that have used them properly and then move on to a consideration of Freud's efforts and the problems he encountered.

It hardly seems necessary to point out that we human beings have certain needs that must be satisfied if we are to survive or even to live comfortably. There are numerous physical needs—for warmth, food, water, sex, and so on—

that press upon us at times and therefore must be dealt with in some way. There are also psychological needs for affection from others and for self-acceptance. But how are we to think of these various needs? Are they all alike? Can we explain the psychological needs by tracing or reducing them to the biological needs? If we follow traditional natural science explanation, in which material and efficient causes are said to explain *everything* in experience, then we would indeed expect to find the psychological nestling in and reducible to the biological (see Chapter 1, pp. 7-8).

It is not difficult to show that psychological explanations that embraced a drive construct did indeed follow natural science description. That is, they sought to explain the patterning of behavior without invoking teleological terminology such as intention or purpose. The concept of *reinforcement* in behavioristic theory suggests that when an antecedent stimulus occurs in close proximity to a consequent response, there is likely to be a linkage or connection formed between the two. In classical conditioning (see Chapter 2, p. 34), the theory issued from such important psychologists as Edward L. Thorndike, John B. Watson, and Clark L. Hull was that the stimulus-response (S-R) habit formed because the linking of antecedent to consequent was followed by a biological satisfaction or positive hedonic tone (Rychlak, 1981b, pp. 378-383). This pleasurable physical experience was termed a *positive* reinforcement.

Though the various classical conditioning theorists differed in suggesting precisely how positive reinforcements come about, they all tried to limit their explanations to physical conceptions like the reflex arc of the central nervous system, and they interpreted "behavior" as an automatic sequence of antecedent events impelling consequent events *without* choice or self-direction. As we have suggested, though the basic mechanisms of conditioning relied upon biological reductionism, it is in the environmentalism of behaviorism that we find the real source of individual differences (see Chapter 1, p. 12). It would not be incorrect to suggest that all behaviorists are social psychologists, because it is from the social milieu that they find their shapings of behavior.

As one aspect of the theory suggesting that stimuli and responses become attached into habitual sequences, the behaviorists proposed that the organism had first to be experiencing an elevation in some biological drive, like hunger, which in turn was satisfied with the response made to the stimulus in question. This *drive reduction* explanation thus suggests that a dog in the conditioning apparatus learns to salivate to a flashing light or sounding bell because, when the food powder is blown into its mouth, a drive reduction or satiation of a drive results (see Chapter 2, p. 35). Because it takes time for the complete drive to be satiated via ingestion, digestion, and absorption of foodstuffs, Hull (1943) later modified the explanation to suggest that merely the so-called *drive stimulus* has to be modified in order for a cementing of stimulus-to-response to take place.

Hull was suggesting that a partial reduction in the stimulations that herald a drive's presence and not the "total" drive elimination might be all that an organism needs to learn S-R habits. For example, once food is in the mouth of an organism, the stimulus value of a drive—in this case, *taste*—may be said to reduce the drive due to previous learning that the taste of food in the mouth is followed by total satisfaction of the hunger drive. This theoretical maneuver removed the criticism that an S-R habit could not wait on full and complete drive reduction in order to be reliably conditioned. But the point of importance for present considerations is that in no case is a stimulus-response habit said to arise out of the *intentions* of the behaving organism. The entire process is automatic, shaped by an interaction of *nature* (drives) and *nurture* (sociocultural circumstances).

It is also possible for certain sociocultural items to acquire *secondary* drive characteristics. For example, money can be a secondary drive, and when its motivating properties impel a person to work, the receipt of a financial payment (salary) is presumed to work as a drive reduction analogically to the reduction of primary drives like hunger and thirst. There are many such cultural secondary drives, which is why people are so widely influenced by their social milieu. Even language encompasses such secondary drive characteristics, so that the "power of the word" serves to shape people's behavior via encouragements, flattery, promises of future rewards, and certificates of achievement in which there is a printed reinforcement embodied (diplomas, awards, licenses, military discharge papers, etc.). The assumption is that people have a drive to be recognized or appreciated, and hence such signs of merit or recognition can reduce their drive levels and result in a conditioned stimulus-response habit of some sort.

In the case of operant conditioning, an effort is made to describe the shaping of behavior without recourse to drives or their reduction (see Chapter 2, p. 37). This is due to Skinner's desire to remain completely empirical in the description of behavior (1974). Operant theory is the most rabidly environmentalistic position in the behavioristic tradition. The operant conditioner will take whatever is found by empirical observation to "work" as a *reinforcer* of behavior to be just that, without speculating on whether or not there is a drive being reduced. Just so long as the behavior under observation is seen to increase its rate of emission when followed by the reinforcer, the operant theorist claims that conditioning is taking place. Skinner can therefore opine, "As far as I'm concerned, if a baby is reinforced by the sound made by a rattle, the sound is just as useful as a reinforcer in accounting for behavior as food in the baby's mouth" (R. I. Evans, 1968, p. 10). Surely babies do not possess innate drives to shake their rattles! Skinner does not deny that there are "inside-the-organism" processes taking place (ibid., p. 95). He just does not see the merit of postulating a drive for every bit of behavior that psychologists take an interest in. The environment is what shapes the person, and this is what attracts Skinner's interest as a behavioral scientist.

Even so, it would not be wrong to suggest that many if not most psychologists lump together the constructs of "reinforcer" in operant conditioning with "drive reducer" in classical conditioning. There is a practical necessity to account for the habitual regularity of behavior without invoking a telic native endowment in which the person is conceived as an agent, having what is commonly known as the free will to select a "that" (reason, purpose) for the sake of which behavior will be intended (see our discussion of causation, Chapter 1, pp. 4-5). An exception to this rule is the "third force" psychology of Abraham Maslow—which postulates a force in addition to behaviorism and psychoanalysis. Maslow is a naturalist/nativist in the style we have attributed to Freud (see Chapter 1, p. 13). He views the human being as having an inner, essential nature that brings about growth from within rather than shaping from without (Maslow, 1970, p. 341). This inner nature prompts *self-actualization* tendencies in all people, based on a hierarchy of need satisfactions that begin in the organic factors of existence but soon transcend them.

Maslow therefore distinguishes between basic needs and overriding or "metaneeds," which are quite distinctive. *Basic needs* include motives such as hunger, sex, security, and so forth. *Metaneeds* build upon these basic requirements of life but emerge as distinctive motivations for beauty, justice, and order in life. The need to grow and self-actualize is a major metaneed of the human being. The point of importance in Maslowian theory is that we cannot find the meaning of the higher-level metaneeds by reducing them to the lower-level, physiologically derived needs (in the style of biological reductionism). In addition, it is clear that the higher needs of humanity are all teleological in nature. Maslow's image of humanity demands that we think of behavior as moved by formal/final causes in addition to the material/efficient causes of traditional scientific explanation.

This does not mean that Maslow (1968) dismissed biological considerations in his broader theory. He, like Freud, found much of merit in the Darwinian theory of evolution. He felt there was a "growing tip" to the evolutionary advance of all organismic life and that if psychologists want to get a sense of the higher life that evolution is making possible, they should study *not* abnormal personalities but the more self-actualized individuals of our time. Maslow did just that, isolating what he thought were the important factors in the lives of self-actualized people such as Lincoln, Einstein, and Eleanor Roosevelt. He also studied what he termed *peak experiences,* which occur in the lives of everyone but are of special significance in the lives of self-actualized individuals. A peak experience is an incident in one's life that is exceedingly wonderful, submerging everything else in life by comparison.

Maslow claimed that self-actualized individuals see life more clearly than other people. They are more decisive and can take a stand with greater confidence, for they are prepared to name what is right and what is wrong about life. They have a childlike simplicity and usually admit their lack of knowledge in an area of what is clearly their expertise. In other words, they are not defensive. Indeed, though very confident they are humble and more open in their general approach to others than the average person. They identify with humanity and have humanistic values, but they are also independent and have a strong need for privacy. Self-actualized people have their share of peak experiences, which are not necessarily spiritual but somehow pull things together for them so that they are convinced that the well-integrated outlook on life which they enjoy has validity.

Without exception, self-actualized individuals have some worthy task to which they commit themselves completely—a career, duty, or vocation that presses on them, fascinates them, and gives them a sense of fulfillment even though it is not always easy or pleasurable to accomplish. They are, above all, spontaneous and creative in their behavior, willing to "be themselves" without pretense. Maslow coined the term *Eupsychian* to describe the society which a group of self-actualized individuals would form if left to their own devices—say, on a secluded island or some such. Presumably the society would reflect their common tendencies: a biological utopia of our very best people, the "growing tip" clipped off and transplanted to flower as all utopias do—apart and unmolested by the common foliage.

Of course, Freud was more concerned than Maslow with meeting the expectations of medical colleagues. The problems Freud faced in his explanation of behavior emanated from the traditions of medicine, epitomized in the *constancy principle* (see Chapter 1, p. 10). Biological processes unquestionably follow some such homeostatic, balancing, redistribution of energies throughout a system without selective choice or freedom to direct the course of events. The internal organs "work" in concert not out of a collective will but simply out of the organic tissues (material causes) and energic discharges (material/efficient causes) of anabolism/catabolism in the ongoing process of physical metabolism. But Freud was a dualist, recognizing needs of a purely psychological nature in addition to the biological needs. If the somatic realm is driven by biological deficit then Freud must find a way of describing how the psychic realm is driven by purely psychological characteristics. It is this integrity of description that literally forced Freud to be teleological in his accounts, because it is flatly impossible to capture the psychological maneuverings of human thought without some use of final causation. We shall next trace his instinct theories and try to get a better understanding of what he meant by libido.

## History of Freud's Instinct Theories

*Instinct and Energy.* Freud did not make much use of an instinct construct in his earliest writings. It was not until about 1905, following his major work on dreams, that he began employing the instincts as an important theoretical tool (Freud, 1915/1957i, p. 113). By that time Freud was beginning to attract colleagues and students who met with him weekly at his home, a group that in 1906 became the Vienna Psycho-Analytic Society (Nunberg & Federn, 1962). These discussions with colleagues had brought up the question of the relation between mind (*psyche*) and body (*soma*). Freud found that the *instinct* construct could help him here, and he eventually made three definite points concerning instincts: (1) they are based on a stimulation taking place within the body and not in the external world; (2) they provide a *constant* level of stimulation that cannot be run away from as one can run away from pressing stimulations like cold or heat in the external environment; and (3) they seem always to function "on the frontier between the mental and the somatic" (Freud, 1915/1957i, pp. 121-122).

Instincts therefore act like bridges between mind and body. They are also Freud's answer to the environmentalist, for as points (1) and (2) make clear, the handling of instincts is an *intrapersonal* matter, one that is not subject to modification through external manipulations. The instinct conceptualization, based as it is in the biological substrate of the human being's native equipment, provides Freud with the theoretical justification for his dynamic approach to the description of behavior. Only the person, working inwardly, can confront and deal with instinctive promptings that have been wound into a certain psychic structure. This places doctor and patient on an equal footing, for there is nothing the doctor can accomplish to which the patient will not be a party.

Each instinct is said to have the *aim* of satisfaction, or removing the *pressure* (extent of stimulation) from its *source* (the point in the internal body area from which it originates). If one has a great need for something, a given instinctual stimulus is exerting great pressure on the person with the aim of achieving satisfaction, and the particular nature of the instinct (let us say it is to eat when hungry) determines just how one acts (one looks for something to eat). Now, the thing in regard to which the instinct is able to achieve its aim is the *object* (ibid., p. 122). As we have already seen in earlier chapters, this term is a widely used technical construct in psychoanalysis that can refer to a person, an item of food, or an imagined set of circumstances. It can even refer to one's own person, as in the case of narcissism, which will be discussed later in this chapter. Literally *anything* that might conceivably lead to the satisfaction of an instinct is an object. But it is also possible for the person to "switch" objects and strive for satisfaction of an instinctive prompting in some other way, or to deny an object-choice altogether (see the discussion of substitution and sublimation below, p. 136).

Freudian instinct theory is essentially an alternative way of talking about *hedonism.* Pleasure consists in removing the pressure of an instinctive prompting in the body. But how do we explain this homeostatic balancing of tensions in the body so that the individual no longer feels hunger, thirst, sexual lust, and so on? Here is where we see the influence of the constancy principle on Freud's thought (see Chapter 1, p. 10). When Freud and Breuer were collaborating on the *Studies on Hysteria,* they made use of the constancy principle idea in what they called the *principle of neuronic inertia,* as follows: "If a person experiences a psychical impression, something in his nervous system which we will for the moment call the sum of excitation is increased. Now in every individual there exists a tendency to diminish this sum of excitation once more, in order to preserve his health" (Freud, 1893, 1962a, p. 36). The manner in which the mind succeeds—however effectively—in ridding itself of these states of heightened excitation is called the *vicissitudes* of the instincts (Freud, 1915/1957i, p. 126). A vicissitude is a regular or irregular state of change in something (like the weather!), and this is the pattern of change we see in our instinctive promptings as we get hungry and eat, only to get hungry again and eat once more. Sexual instincts are somewhat more difficult to satisfy.

It would not be wrong to identify the constancy principle with the pleasure principle as a homeostatic mechanism in mind seeking an even keel (Freud, 1920/1955k, p. 9). As Freud (1916-17/1963b) said, "It seems as though our total mental activity is directed towards achieving pleasure and avoiding unpleasure—that it is automatically regulated by the *pleasure principle*" (p. 356). Freud did not believe that human beings have an instinct to feel pain. At best, pain is a pseudoinstinct that has as its aim "simply the cessation of the change in the organ and of the unpleasure accompanying it" (Freud, 1915/1957j, p. 146). Pain is thus merely another way of saying "loss of pleasure," and Freud assigned the role of pleasure seeker (balancer) to the instinct construct. How many instincts with related "needs" do human beings have? Before we can speak of Freud's theory of instincts as a whole, we must consider the *one* instinct and need he could never forgo in his view of the human being.

*The Sexual Instinct.* Interpreters of Freudian theory have had no little difficulty trying to keep the concept of "sex" and the concept of "pleasure" separate and distinct. Over the years, Freud was to use these concepts interchangeably, as when he once suggested that in "man the sexual instinct does not originally serve the purposes of reproduction at all, but has as its aim the gaining of particular kinds of pleasure" (Freud, 1908/1959d, p. 188). Recall that Freud referred to a region of the body that gives rise to *autoerotic pleasure* as an *erogenous* or *erotogenic zone* (see Chapter 2, p. 47). Literally *any* part of the skin can become an erotogenic zone, stimulating the person to seek pleasure in some way. It can be the mouth area (pleasure in sucking) or the anal area (pleasure in defecation); even the eye can serve as a sexual stimulant (pleasure in pornographic viewing) (Freud 1910/1957f). In line with his view that there are a number of erogenous zones, Freud made perfectly clear that he believed there are *many* sexual instincts, each contributing its components to the overall state we think of as "sexual excitation" (ibid, p. 187). There are also other than sexual instincts in the body, a theoretical view that Freud was never to reject.

We come now to the complicating features of Freud's libido theory. The point we must always keep in mind is that the concept of instinct is a *bridge construct*. Although somatically based and hence stemming from material/efficient causes, the instincts were said to set loose energy in the psychic region. The question that we now put to Freud's view of psychic energy is: *How compatible is such mental energy to physical energies functioning according to the principle of constancy?* As we shall see, the parallel between mental and physical energy is nothing like that we have seen in the drive reduction theories of behaviorism.

Despite the multiplicity of instincts suggested by Freud, he actually named only *one* of the energies in mind, so that whenever he described a patient's behavior based on the psychodynamic system of id, ego, and superego, he would frame the description exclusively in terms of this single mental energy. This energy was, of course, named *libido,* and Freud defined it variously as *"psychical desire"* (Freud, 1894/1962c, p. 107), all of the person's "erotic tendencies" (Freud, 1917/1955g, p. 139), "sexual desire in the broadest sense" (Freud, 1910/1957b, p. 101), and "the motive force of sexual life" (Freud, 1932-36/1964b, p. 131). But probably the most complete statement of libido in his writings, one that also gives us a good picture of Freud's use of *love,* may be found in the following quotation:

> Libido is an expression taken from the theory of the emotions. We call by that name the energy, regarded as a quantitative magnitude (though not at present actually measurable), of those instincts which have to do with all that may be comprised under the word "love." The nucleus of what we mean by love naturally consists (and this is what is commonly called love, and what the poets sing of) in sexual love with sexual union as its aim. But we do not separate from this—what in any case has a share in the name "love"—on the one hand, self-love, and on the other, love for parents and children, friendship and love for humanity in general, and also devotion to concrete objects and to abstract ideas. (Freud, 1921/1955m, p. 90)

The fact that Freud places libido in his "theory of emotions" is important, for as we shall see below, it is not at all clear that emotions per se act as drives in the personality. The pleasure principle is not simply and only a principle of "seeking good feelings" in the sense of emotional release. There is a pleasure to be found in the homeostatic quiescence of a life devoted to humanitarian ideals, self-denial, or the love of abstract ideas. We should therefore be cautious about equating the rise of libido with the rise of emotion or the lowering of libido with an emotional release. Drive theories tend to rely upon emotions in this fashion, but psychoanalysis does not.

How are we to think of libido "working" in mind? Freud needed a term to describe how this psychic energy oriented the person vis-à-vis some desired object. The term he settled on was *cathexis.* Freud first used this term in the *Project* (see Chapter 1, p. 10) as a strictly physical construct, suggesting that neurons (cells of the nervous system) were *cathected* when they were filled with a certain quantum of physical energy (*not* libido!) (Freud, 1895/1966d, p. 298). This style of theorizing was related to the principle of neuronic inertia, because what happens when a "sum of excitation" is increased is that a neuron "fills up" with physical energy.

Later in his theoretical development, Freud was to use the concept of cathexis in a purely psychological fashion—as a sort of investment in or an affection for some desired object. Indeed, the libidinal cathexis of an object is what makes it desirable. Thus, if a man were to fall in love with a woman, he would mentally "fill" her image in his mind's eye with libido (Freud, 1911/1958a, p. 74). His libido would "occupy" her image and hold fast, orienting his psychodynamic system toward her in either a conscious or unconscious manner (Freud, 1915/1957l, p. 234). We must never forget that unconscious thought orients the person through cathexes just as certainly as does conscious thought.

Motives are therefore concerned with the libidinal cathexis of this or that object (person, place, thing, idea, etc.). The next step is to attain the cathected object (in our example, for the man to win the woman's love in return).

However, simply cathecting an object does not mean the individual will always seek to attain it in the external world (that is, external to the contents of mind). For example, if the id lusts for some object—let us assume it is a parent during the Oedipal dynamic—then the ego can *anticathect* this investment of libido in the image of the parent by opposing its own supply of libido to the id's cathexis (Freud, 1900-01/1953b, p. 605). Here again, the constancy principle begins to break down because there is definitely a suggestion of intentionality entering into this account. We see here a description of the ego *repressing* id impulses by using libido instrumentally, just as in Chapter 1 (p. 12) we saw Freud telling Jung that he (Freud) was removing libido from their interpersonal relationship "at will." Physical energies do not "work" this way, of course. We shall return to this discussion below, after we first trace the history of Freud's changing instinct theories.

*Freud's Changing Instinct Theories.* Now that we have an understanding of some basic terms, let us review the history of Freud's thinking on the role of instincts in human behavior. The first question that arises is, just how many different instincts are there in the human animal? Freud believed that this was unknown and that the only way the question could be answered was to study the problem empirically by tracing each instinct in turn to its ultimate *source* in the body (Freud, 1915/1957i, p. 123). The problem here, Freud noted, was that one is tempted to think up too many instincts to describe behavior. For example, to explain *playfulness,* we might propose that human beings have an instinct to play. Yet if we were to break this activity down into its components, we might find that an underlying instinct entered into this activity in combination with one or possibly two other *more basic* instincts, so that playfulness was not a true instinct at all. Freud therefore suggested that we probably need think of only a small number of underlying instincts to explain all kinds of behavior at more complex levels.

Freud called these underlying instincts *primal instincts,* and the instincts made up of these he called *compound instincts.* Now, it is very important to keep in mind that, as a general theoretical strategy, *Freud was always to base psychoanalytical theory on the interplay of two dialectically opposed primal instincts, even though he implied that more than two were in effect.* He changed the names of these primal instincts over the years, but the fundamental opposition of two basic "forces" in the personality remains constant in Freudian thought. In fact, Freud maintained that instincts occurred in pairs of opposites, usually taking an active and a passive dialectical opposition (Freud, 1909/1957a, p. 44).

Freud's first opposition of instincts was that of the *self-preservative instincts* (or *ego instincts*) and the *sexual instincts* (or *object instincts*) (Freud, 1917/1955g, p. 137; 1929/1961i, p. 117). Recall that the ego was seen as the seat of reason in the personality. Whereas the id was guided initially by the pleasure principle, the ego's negotiations with external reality brought about its reliance upon a "reality principle." Freud (1920/1955k) stated: "This latter [reality] principle does not abandon the intention of ultimately obtaining pleasure, but it nevertheless demands and carries into effect the postponement of satisfaction, the abandonment of a number of possibilities of gaining satisfaction and the temporary toleration of unpleasure as a step on the long indirect road to pleasure" (p. 10).

Libido was said to be the energy of the sexual (or object) instincts, but Freud never coined a term naming the energy of the self-preservative (or ego) instincts. He continually spoke of *energies* at work in the psychodynamic system, entering into cathexes and/or anticathexes (repressions), but in specifying the dynamics of a case history Freud always ended up stressing the role of libido. With further clinical experience and some challenges on certain points from his critics, Freud was eventually to change his theory of instincts. In place of self-preservation, he introduced the construct of a *death instinct.* This addition was part of a masterful piece of theorizing, and the way in which he accomplished it was to base the death instinct theory on two preliminary ideas: *narcissism* and the *repetition compulsion.* We shall work our way into this change by way of these preliminary constructs.

In Greek mythology, Narcissus, the beautiful son of the river-god Cephissus, was supposedly the embodiment of self-conceit. Many nymphs wanted to be his lover, but he rejected their flirtations. One such rejected maiden prayed to the deity that Narcissus might know what it meant to love and not be loved in return. A curse was put on his head, so that one day, leaning over a river bank for a drink of water, Narcissus was doomed to fall in love with his own reflection. He talked to it, tried to embrace it, lusted after it, and pined away until he died without ever achieving satisfaction. Freud was to take this theme of self-love and use it to alter his instinct theory.

At about this period in his theoretical development, problems were mounting for Freud. Some of his colleagues, like Alfred Adler, had wanted Freud to give a more central role in the personality to conscious, reasonable ego functions. Such arguments took the spotlight off of the object instincts (sex/ libido) and focused it on the ego instincts (self-preservation). Others, like Carl Jung, felt that he was redefining the meaning of libido, making it into an *élan vital,* a general life force subsuming sexuality and many other (including telic) functions as well (Freud, 1929/1961i, p. 118). What Freud felt compelled to do was to explain functions (self-preservation) as a special case of the sexual instincts, yet to avoid making the sexual instinct the *only* primal instinct of his theory. In short, he deliberately set out to remove self-preservation from the list of primal instincts and to replace it with some other opposing forces in the personality.

His first step was accomplished through his use of *narcissism,* a term that had been used by Paul Näcke and Havelock Ellis to describe a person who treats his or her own body as if it were a sexual object (Freud, 1914/1957h, p. 73.) Rather than saying that the ego looks after self-preservation because of a *primal* (basic, underlying) instinct of this nature, Freud now claimed that the *ego is itself cathected* with libido from the outset. Thus, in developing out of the id, the ego takes over its share of libido in the psychodynamic system and to that extent has invested this "in itself"—a narcissistic form of (self-) love. We can now draw a parallel between autoerotism (see Chapter 2, p. 63) and narcissism because they both refer to gaining sexual pleasure from an investment of libido in our own bodies. In the case of autoerotism the investment is confined to the organ per se, so that, for example, the pleasure obtained by a male infant from masturbation would be confined to the penis in an autoerotic state, but then when moving to narcissism the child would cathect his "person," which is tantamount to the developing ego. Ideally, the child will move through narcissism to object-choice before long and enter thereby into the Oedipal conflict (where mother becomes the first "unnarcissistic" object). Freud referred to the libido invested in the ego as *ego libido* or as *narcissistic libido* and the libido eventually sent outward to others as *object libido*.

Freud had now successfully done away with self-preservation as a *primal* instinct, even though the same kinds of self-preservative actions that the ego carries on continue as a secondary (component) instinctual pattern. The person looks out for himself or herself, avoiding injury whenever possible. Self-care is self-love. But what do we now oppose to the sexual instinct and its pleasure principle? At this point, Freud (1920/1955k) in *Beyond the Pleasure Principle* introduced one of his most controversial theoretical constructs as opponent to pleasure—the *death instinct*! Not until roughly 1920 did Freud decide to drop the pleasure principle as a major concept and to substitute in its place an entirely new concept of mental functioning, that is, the *repetition compulsion*. He had been observing for decades that neurotics in psychoanalysis seemed to have a compulsion to repeat the dynamics of their past life in therapy, bringing him as therapist into their conflicts as if he were their parent in the re-enactment. Recall that he related Haeckel's biogenetic principle of recapitulation to this repetitive tendency in the Oedipal theory (see Chapter 3, p. 73). He was also struck by the fact that children are ever willing to repeat the same game or to hear the same fairy tale over and over again. It was as if they were working through some anxious concern that preoccupied them—like the mystery of birth—in their hide-and-go-seek amusements. There are repetitive dreams and repetitive fantasies that everyone experiences occasionally, and even historians have noted that history tends to repeat itself.

Basing his argument on such points, Freud then concluded that in addition to the pleasure principle, "there really does exist in the mind a compulsion to repeat" (ibid., p. 22). Note that this is a mental principle, whereas Fliess's repetitive periodic cycle theory had suggested something of the sort in the biological realm (see Chapter 1, p. 10). Freud then brought his two final primal principles together by a stroke of genius that ties them both back to the constancy principle. He observed that "*an instinct is an urge inherent in organic life to restore an earlier state of things* which the living entity has been obliged to abandon under the pressure of external disturbing forces; that is, it is a kind of organic elasticity, or, to put it another way, the expression of the inertia inherent in organic life" (ibid., p. 36). Instincts do not make new things happen so much as they cause things happening to return to an earlier state (the conservative nature of instincts). As in the case of the pleasure principle, a state of quiescence is achieved through sexual activity, thereby returning the organism to its even, homeostatic level. Life is a rhythm—expressed initially by Freud in the construct of vicissitudes of the instincts. But the ultimate state of quiescence is death itself!

If we consider the issue biologically, even physical matter has a way of returning to a common inorganic state, as the biblical reference of "dust to dust" reminds us. Thus, Freud can say, in a biological manner of speaking, "*the aim of all life is death*" (ibid., p. 38). This now permits us to oppose our two instincts and view life as a vacillating rhythm of self-destruction (death) and self-perpetuation (life). He called the life-propelling instincts *eros*, which then took over the role of the older sexual instincts, including self-preservation by way of narcissism. Eros ensures that the final quiescence (death) will not come about too quickly. We love ourselves, so we look out for ourselves and try to extend our stay on this planet. Eros also ensures that there will be offspring to perpetuate the race as a by-product of pleasurable copulation between the sexes (ibid., p. 56). Opposed to eros is another collection of instincts that have as their *aim* the restoration of living human beings to the inorganic state from which they presumably had sprung during centuries past. This collective name is the *death instinct* (Freud did not like the term *Thanatos,* which some psychoanalysts have used since). Grisly though they may be, the aims of death are the satisfactions of the grave—repose, rest, and organic constancy.

As when he seemed to be identifying libido with "pleasure in general," Freud here again seemed to be identifying death with "general satisfaction" or the ultimate pleasure! He referred to this final reduction in tension into the quiescence of death as the *nirvana principle,* a phrase taken from Barbara Low (ibid., pp. 55-56). But for all practical purposes, as a theoretical device the nirvana principle is nothing more than a rephrasal of the constancy principle and identical to the pleasure principle. Thus, in his final theory of instincts, Freud had *eros* and *death* as the two *primary instincts* entering together into all kinds of *secondary* or *compound instincts* found in the personality (that is, the interactions of id, ego, and superego). This was sometimes called a *fusion of instincts* (Freud, 1923/1961a, p. 41). For example, sadism (receiving pleasure from inflicting pain) would be termed a compound instinct in which there has been a fusion of hostility (death) and sex (eros) (Freud, 1920/1955k, p. 53). Even something as simple as looking out for oneself, being willing to fight if necessary to retain one's integrity as a person, could be seen as a fusion of self-love (eros) and hostility (death). In fact, Freud once said that the life and death instincts hardly ever appear in their pure form in human behavior; there is almost always some fusion of the two (Freud, 1929/1961i, p. 138).

We might now ask, because Freud named libido as the energy of eros in this final formulation of his instinct theory, did he ever name an energy in opposition to it? No, this was never to be the case. Even though he said that the death instinct can turn into a destructive instinct during wartime and thus send out its hostile influence toward objects in the external world, Freud never named an energy to account for such hostile forms of cathexis (Freud, 1932/1964c, p. 211). Some psychoanalysts call this energy *mordido* today. In his analysis of President Woodrow Wilson, published after Freud's death, Freud and his coauthor (Bullitt) actually refer to the mixture of life and death energies without naming one of them, as follows: "and the charge [ that is, quantum] of mingled libido and Death Instinct was again without outlet and remained repressed" (Freud & Bullitt, 1967, p. 279). It seems certain that he *did* have an energy in mind for the death instinct, and his theory surely called for it, but Freud was not moved to raise other energies into the prominence he had assigned to libido.

Why was this the case? We can only surmise that in his clinical practice he found the Oedipal dynamic and its attendant sexual components so central to *all* behavior—normal and neurotic alike—that he wanted to keep this emphasis in the forefront. As we shall see, the lion's share of clinical dynamics are framed in terms of pre-Oedipal, Oedipal, and post-Oedipal dynamics, and the theoretical requirement here is more in the direction of eros than of the death instinct. We shall enter into the dynamics of the personality in Chapter 5. For now, a more important issue must be settled having to do with whether or not Freud was a drive reduction theorist in the sense we have discussed above.

## *Was Freud a Drive Reduction Theorist?*

It is clear that drive reduction theories are de facto biological reductionisms in that the formation of habits depend upon a postulated underlying physico-chemical process of some kind. Mental direction may enter into the succession of events, but only *after* there has been an initial etching upon the *tabula rasa* (smoothed tablet) mind at birth, recorded passively as an "input" from the environment and then subsequently working as a mediational aid to direct behavior in efficient-cause fashion. This passive etching reflects the environmentalism in such theories, where no credence is given to human agency. Thus, the behaviorist would suggest that the infant learns language by hearing a word like *mama* in contiguous relation to a certain person's visage (i.e., the infant's mother). Under a security drive, or generalizing the effects of a basic hunger drive, the infant automatically—that is, unintentionally!—associates the word *mama* to the physical mother because of the reduction in mounting insecurity or mounting hunger whenever this physical "other" is present (contiguous tie of word to visual image). Repetition or frequency of contact plays a role in strengthening the association as well. The biological drive reduction cements the word as "response" to the physical person as "stimulus."

Later, when the child wants mother to appear, he or she can call out *mama* as a mediational aid and be rewarded once again with the mother's appearance. By *mediational* we mean that the child's mental processes are always working "between" current stimuli and responses, using old responses (*mama*) that are already learned to further the ongoing succession of antecedents (stimuli) impelling consequents (responses) in efficient-cause fashion. This succession is *not* intentional. Ideas are *not* being freely expressed. An automatic or mechanistic sequence is simply being moved along thanks to mediating cues like *mama*. In fact, the behavioristic theory of Dollard and Miller (1950) refers to language terms like *mama* as *cue-producing responses*. Note that this style of theorizing is completely *extraspective* (see Chapter 1, p. 6), for there is no effort made to understand behavior from the point of view of the child's reasoning processes. What determines behavior is all of the previous reinforcements that have cemented certain stimuli to certain responses by way of mediating cues. One can look at the history of these reinforcements and predict from what has been input, stored in mediating processes, and then output to behavior without taking the child's viewpoint, purpose, or choice into consideration. The child is a conduit of past antecedents impelling current consequences in a lawful manner.

The question posed by this section is whether we can see any trace of such theoretical descriptions in Freudian theory. Is libido a drive that works comparably to the drives of hunger, thirst, and the various emotions like sex or anxiety? The constancy principle that Brücke taught Freud would be entirely consistent with such a drive reduction theory, for this is precisely what occurs when an organism under the tension of drive elevation is given satisfaction. The "satisfaction" is a return to biological quiescence. How well does such theorizing mesh with Freud's explanations of behavior? We have already argued that Freud was not a biological reductionist (see Chapter 1, p. 13; it follows that drive reduction explanations would not mesh well with his theoretical preferences. There are several reasons why the traditional "constancy" way of thinking about drives is not applicable to Freudian explanations of the psyche. There are four points to be made in this regard, and we now turn to these arguments before locating the basic source of Freudian dynamics in the section to follow.

1. *Instincts and emotions are never unconscious.* If we are to believe that something like a drive impels the human being's personality dynamics, then surely it should be true that *both* conscious and unconscious levels of behavior should be affected by this drive's force. Because, as we have seen, all human mentation (thinking, wishing, etc.) begins in unconsciousness and then develops into consciousness, the unconscious should be *especially* vulnerable to instinctual promptings. Yet Freud's dualism negated this very implication. As he expressed it:

I am in fact of the opinion that the *antithesis* [italics added] of conscious and unconscious is not applicable to instincts. An instinct can never become an object of consciousness—only the idea that represents the instinct can. Even in the unconscious, moreover, an instinct cannot be represented otherwise than by an idea. If the instinct did not attach itself to an idea or manifest itself as an affective state, we could know nothing about it. When we nevertheless speak of an unconscious instinctual impulse or of a repressed instinctual impulse, the looseness of phraseology is a harmless one. We can only mean an instinctual impulse the ideational representative of which is unconscious, for nothing else comes into consideration. (Freud, 1957k, p. 177)

Terms like *unconscious* and *repression* refer to ideations and related mentations, *not* to instincts! We have italicized the word *antithesis* in the above quote for a reason that will be made clear in the section to follow. It is common for even psychoanalysts to forget the important distinction between psyche and soma, and the concomitant fact that libido is an energic force *only* in the former realm. As a result, they are prone to speak of "repressed emotions" or "unconscious emotions" which supposedly enter into the dynamics of the personality structure. Surely libido enters into repression, for it is in the cathexis/ countercathexis confrontations of the psyche that a repression is said to take place. Yet Freud was quite clear on the matter of unconscious affects or emotions:

> Strictly speaking . . . and although no fault can be found with the linguistic usage, *there are no unconscious affects* [italics added] as there are unconscious ideas. But there may very well be in the system *Ucs.* [unconscious] affective structures which, like others, become conscious. The whole difference arises from the fact that ideas are cathexes—basically of memory-traces—whilst affects and emotions correspond to processes of discharge, the final manifestations of which are perceived as feelings. (ibid., p. 178)

It is clear that "libido" and "emotion[s]" are *not* the same thing! In saying that ideas are cathexes, Freud spelled out for us that ideas are compounds of libidinal energies, occupying desired objects and orienting the psychic apparatus to further or attain these conceptualized ends. Note also in the above quotation that Freud thought of emotions as on the side of *discharges* ending in the actual feeling tones that we experience. The person who blurts out "I hate you" with a flush of hostility is experiencing an emotion. But the sense of relief in expressing (discharging) the emotion is *not* a drive reduction of the energy of the death instinct. The person who experiences orgiastic relief in sexual intercourse is *not* sensing the actual reduction in the drive of libido! Libido and mordido are involved in the *ideas* that frame the emotional experiences of sexual lust or hatred. That is what Freud meant by the unconscious "affective structure" that may enter into consciousness. But psychic energies have their role to play in the *strictly ideational* understanding of experience. And as we shall see below, ideas do *not* follow the lines of a constancy principle, smoothing out the high-pressure points in mind without purpose or intention. More important, sexual intercourse may give physical release, but *not necessarily* libidinal satisfaction (see point 4, below).

2. *The emotion of anxiety is limited to ego consciousness.* When Freud advanced his topographical model of mind (see p. 107) he made it even clearer that a drive reduction account could not suffice to explain human behavior. He did so by clarifying his theory of anxiety, a topic which we will review in some detail in Chapter 5 (see pp. 158-162). For now, suffice to say that he came to the

position that "the ego is the sole seat of anxiety—that the ego alone can produce and feel anxiety" (Freud, 1932-36/1964b, p. 85). Anxiety is, of course, an emotion, and therefore like all emotions it is experienced by a person consciously. Freud was adding the idea that only the conscious portion of the ego senses the discharge of physical feeling known as anxiety. The id and superego do not even "feel" anxiety and hence are in no way motivated by this emotional release or discharge. What role does anxiety play in Freud's final formulation of behavior, and how does this compare with the role of anxiety in traditional drive-reduction theories?

In Hull's drive reduction theory (1943), anxiety is taken as a drive, and the reduction of this drive can serve to cement stimulus-response bonds in the typical fashion of any drive, such as hunger. For example, if a woman is made anxious by a mild automobile accident, she may find herself getting increasingly tense each time she contemplates or actually sets out to drive her car following the accident. This mounting anxiety can be eased by avoiding the task of having to drive her car. Each time she makes an excuse not to drive her mounting anxiety is reduced. Each time she "stops thought" concerning driving, the anxiety drive is reduced. This "stamps in" her avoidant response to the car stimulus. But then, with each avoidance the anxiety is likely to be greater because she is not meeting the challenge of learning to overcome her fright. A kind of snowballing or hothouse effect can occur in such anxiety, which feeds on itself. This is the way in which Dollard and Miller (1950) explain the learning of neurotic behaviors like the acquisition of a phobia (p. 214).

In Freud's final theory of anxiety, however, this emotional discharge is a kind of instrumental reaction that signals danger or threat to the personality system. Sometimes this signal is automatic, but at other times it can be brought on intentionally. Thus, Freud theorized as follows in suggesting possible ways in which anxiety might have arisen in the life experience of anyone:

> One [way of anxiety generation] was involuntary, automatic and always justified on economic grounds, and arose whenever a dangerous situation analogous to birth had established itself. The other [way of anxiety generation] was produced by the ego as soon as a situation of this kind merely threatened to occur, in order to call for its avoidance. In the second case the ego subjects itself to anxiety as a sort of inoculation, submitting to a slight attack of the illness in order to escape its full strength. It vividly imagines [at an unconscious level] the dangerous situation, as it were, with an unmistakable purpose of restricting that distressing experience to a mere indication, a signal. (Freud, 1926/1959g, p. 162)

As we shall see in Chapter 5 (p. 161), Freud termed the automatic type of anxiety *realistic* and the latter, ego-induced anxiety either *moral* or *neurotic* in character. But the point of importance here is that, unlike the drive reductionists, Freud did *not* base behavioral dynamics on anxiety reduction! Anxiety is a "reaction to a dangerous situation," but some dangers can be completely psychological, based on belief systems or past actions that are "better forgotten." Freud therefore tied the above dynamic, of the ego inoculating itself, into his theory of repression and defense (ibid., p. 163). Rather than anxiety reduction following the repression of a fearful idea (like the driving of a car following an accident), requirements of maintaining repression forced the personality to *induce* anxiety, and thereby raise the level of conscious discomfort. In this sense, Freud was a *drive induction* theorist—the very antithesis of behavioristic explanations!

Freud would argue that to say that neurotics are motivated to "avoid anxiety" by repressing some distressing thought is like saying that we would be exclusively motivated by anxiety as we stood on a railroad track with a freight train bearing down on us, roaring and whistling our imminent destruction. We would surely be anxious in this situation. But why exactly would we jump off the track bed? Would we jump because we wanted to remove the signs of emotional discharge in anxiety, including heart palpitation, rapid breath, and the knotting up of our stomach? If we could take a pill that instantly removed these uncomfortable physical discharges (symptoms), would we go on standing the track bed and watching, knowing that in a second or two the train would most surely crunch our bodies into a lifeless pulp of flesh and bone? Obviously, Freud would argue, we would jump off because of the latter, purely *psychological* reason. The biological discharge known as anxiety helps us assess our life circumstance, and it surely influences our behavior. But so would falling rain or hot sunshine provide us with a biological warning that we should do something about our physical state by finding shelter from such elements.

More to the point of psychological motivation, what the conscious ego is "sensing" as anxiety is *not* this warning sign but the underlying *meaning* of the repressed content that is bearing down on the personality system as a whole. Some despised, unacceptable "something" is perfectly known at the unconscious level, and it is bearing down on consciousness like the train with whistle ablast and warning lights flashing. We must never forget that in the realm of mind, the unconscious always *knows* what the conscious presumes it does *not* know. Freud liked to refer to that "strange state of mind in which one knows and does not know a thing at the same time" (Breuer & Freud, 1955, p. 117). Even when it comes to understanding the meaning of dreams, people know full well what their dreams mean. As Freud (1915-16/1963a) said, "For I can assure you that it is quite possible, and highly probable indeed, that the dreamer *does* know what his dream means: *only he does not know that he knows it and for that reason thinks he does not know it*" (p. 101). The concepts of both knowing and not knowing, knowing versus admitting what is known, or knowing that one already knows are hardly deducible from a principle of constancy. We are going far beyond the matter of drives in speaking about such machinations of the personality. We are involved here in meaning, purpose, and intention.

3. *The concepts of libido, cathexis, and mental ideas share an intentional theoretical meaning.* Even though it is set loose by an instinct rooted in the body, libido is *not* itself an instinct, nor is it an affect or emotion. Libido is psychic energy embodied in conscious or unconscious ideas that cathect items relating to external experience. Ideas get things psychically underway, and once the end being sought or intended is achieved in behavior, the accompanying biological/physiological discharge of a physical energy is termed

emotion. Libido theory is essentially a reflection of Freud's teleological bent (see Chapter 1, p. 11), translating the *meaningful content* of an idea into energic *mental activity.* This mental energy does indeed interact with physical energy so that at some point libido influences or is "transformed" (as Freud once referred to it; see Chapter 5, p. 160) into emotional discharges like anxiety. The mind and body interact and influence each other. But we should not reduce libido to emotion anymore than we should reduce id to instinct.

There can be no doubt that Freud's use of the term *cathexis* has served to confound the issue. If we return to his speculations on the nature of psychic *attention* (alert to the external world) in the *Project,* we find the following statements: "I find it hard to give a mechanical (automatic) explanation of its [i.e., attention's] origin . . . . Tension due to craving prevails in the ego, as a consequence of which the idea of the loved object (the *wishful* idea) is cathected" (Freud, 1895/1966d, pp. 360-361). This clearly demonstrates that even when he was trying to write a reductive explanation of behavior, Freud had wishes obtaining as ideas in the brain process. Freud could not begin his account by using automatic, material/efficient causes. He had to begin with the concept of a *wish,* which is a hoped-for end or an intention. Later, he spoke of this wishful intentionality as the *libidinal anticipatory idea* (Freud, 1911/1958b, p. 100). It is these ideas and the cathexes that they embody that are countered in the repressive process known as anticathexis. This repressive process too is not automatic. As Freud said of hysteria:

> Before hysteria can be acquired for the first time one essential condition must be fulfilled: an idea must be *intentionally repressed from consciousness* and excluded from associative modification. In my view this intentional represion is also the basis for the conversion, whether total or partial, of the sum of excitation. (Breuer & Freud, 1955, p. 116)

Now, if repression or the opposition of one idea (cathexis) by another idea (anticathexis) were completely successful, there would be no problems of psychopathology because there would be no or very few differences in personality style across people. But the intentionally framed ideas that have been repressed do not simply "stay put" in the unconscious or preconscious. They find ways of making their meaning known, for after all, that is what ideas do—they express meanings! These repressed ideas are most frequently reflected in dreams, albeit in a disguised fashion. Thus, Freud (1913/1955e) could say, "Psycho-analysis raises the status of dreams into that of psychical acts possessing meaning and purpose, and having a place in the subject's mental life, and thus disregards their strangeness, incoherence and absurdity" (p. 169). Another common manifestation of repressed ideas is in the *parapraxes* (misactions, slips of the tongue, etc.) that we all make in life. Parapraxes are not due to chance mishaps, but rather suggest a "will striving for a definite aim" (Freud, 1901/1960a, p. 238). There is also a *counterwill* (see p. 131) involved in parapraxes, for as Freud (1915-16/1963a) once defined these errant actions, "Parapraxes are psychical acts and arise from mutual interference between two intentions" (p. 60).

The more serious forms of repression result in symptoms of maladjustment. Such symptoms are not simply happenstance malfunctions of the body. Freud's mind-body interaction is never more clear than when he speaks of the malfunctions of abnormality: "We have comprised two things as the 'sense' of a symptom: its 'whence' and its 'whither' or 'what for'—that is, the impressions and experiences from which it arose and the intention which it serves" (Freud, 1916-17/1963b, p. 284). It is possible to interpret symptoms in the same way that we interpret dreams. Indeed, as we shall see in Chapter 5, every symptom always reflects *two* ideas or wishes—cathecting and anticathecting—now compromised and deflected (converted) into a disorder of some type. But the disorder symbolizes in some way the *meanings* involved in the mental compromise. In short, mental illness is intentional! As Freud (1909/1955b) said while discussing his case of the Rat Man: "The chief result of his illness was an obstinate incapacity for work, which allowed him to postpone the completion of his education for years. But the results of such an illness are never unintentional; what appears to be the *consequence* of the illness is in reality the *cause* or *motive* of falling ill" (p. 199).

We could cite many other examples of Freud's use of intention. No one who reads Freud's work can help but be impressed by the teleological view of human behavior that he embraced. As we shall see in Chapter 5, he made every effort to account for mental disorders based upon biological malfunctioning. But in the end, he was to frame an introspective psychology relying upon formal and final causation *as well as* on material and efficient causation. This is not to say that he particularly welcomed the role that fate had seemed to sketch for him to play. He once apologized for making teleological arguments (Freud, 1912/1958f, p. 247) and seems to have believed that by making certain concessions to biology he was free to proceed at his own level of description. The libido theory was his conceptual tie to the reductive sciences, and he did seem to rely more and more on this concept in later years.

4. *Libido is a theoretical construct without a methodological justification.* The most obvious difficulty with the concept of libido is that it is a theoretical construct without a methodological justification. In the related natural sciences, energy is defined in terms of measurable, mathematically calculable units of force that can be observed in experimental situations to bring about some kind of motion or work. Freud had no way of calculating the force of libido, nor could he design experiments to prove methodologically that libido does "function" in the mind. His concept is really no more than an analogy, sounding like the energic forces of physical science yet actually gaining its explanatory power from another level (see the next section). Freud was cognizant of the difficulties involved in explaining mental events through biological terminology, as his comments to Fliess over how to account for human behavior make clear (see Chapter 1, p. 11). Indeed, as late as 1914 he had the following to say about his libido theory:

We must recollect that all our provisional ideas in psychology will presumably some day be based on an organic substructure. This makes it probable that it is special substances and chemical processes which perform the operations of sexuality and provide for the extension of individual life into that of the species. We are taking this probability into account in replacing the special chemical substances by special psychical forces.... I should like at this point expressly to admit that the hypothesis of separate ego-instincts and sexual-instincts (that is to say, the libido theory) rests scarcely at all upon a psychological basis, but derives its principal support from biology.... It may turn out that, most basically and on the longest view, sexual energy—libido—is only the product of a differentiation in the energy at work generally in mind. But such an assertion has no relevance.... Let us face the possibility of error; but do not let us be deterred from pursuing the logical implications of the hypothesis we first adopted of an *antithesis* [italics added] between ego-instincts and sexual instincts. (Freud, 1914/1957h, pp. 78-79)

Note that we have again italicized the word *antithesis* in the above quotation. The reason for doing so will be made evident in the next section. Another interesting attitude we find in Freud's writing concerns the fact that as a *psychic* energy, libido cannot be expended and result in sexual gratification through just "any" copulatory act: "Only in a minority of cases can the pathogenic situation of frustration and the subsequent damming-up of libido be brought to an end by the sort of sexual intercourse that can be procured without much trouble" (Freud, 1916-17, 1963b, pp. 434-435). It is no use for the physician to prescribe sexual intercourse with just anyone, given that the libidinal cathexis concerned involves a *certain* person and a *wished for* love relationship bearing a *specific* meaning for the patient concerned. One does not always satisfy intention A by substituting intention B, even though such defensive maneuvers are common enough.

It is widely known that Freud and Jung had a running dispute over the nature of libido, even though they both accepted the necessity of having to account for mentation by way of some kind of energy. In the *Freud/Jung Letters* (McGuire, 1974) we can trace their interesting points of disagreement. In a letter of 1910 Jung defended the construct of libido, which had recently come under attack by Adler (ibid., p. 382). Jung tried over the next several months of 1911 to bring libido into his studies of the zodiac and other mythological motifs (ibid., pp. 408, 421, 427). The explanations of these conceptions continued to reflect Jung's basic commitment to dialectical oppositionality, and the libido for Jung had to fit in here in some way. Jung hoped to bring libido under an oppositional umbrella, relating it as an energic process to both ends of a contradiction, or a negation. Thus, if a man were to affirm dominant behavior into his conscious personality pattern (his ego), behaving dominantly in overt ways, Jung would want to say that the opposite possibility of passive behavior would be incorporated in his unconscious attitude (alter ego or "shadow"). Libido would be involved in both directions, in the framing of both personality tendencies. Sexuality is merely one of the manifestations of this *élan vital*.

However, in November 1911 Freud nailed libido down to a single energic source, as one of at least two basic life drives—the "power behind the sexual drive" (ibid., p. 469). The following month Jung told Freud that he (i.e., Jung) was trying to conceptualize libido in a global sense, one that would transcend the more "recent-sexual libido" in the course of life to base the psyche as a whole on this vital (i.e., telic) principle (ibid., p. 471). Freud and Jung's relationship was very strained at this point, and the disagreement over libido was wound into the supposed motives that each man had for agreeing or not agreeing with the other. Freud believed that Jung was desexualizing the libido construct to curry favor with the detractors of psychoanalysis. As we noted in Chapter 1 (p. 12), by February 1912 Freud could speak of "turning off" his excess of libido in relation to Jung. The irony here is that, though both men were indulging in telic theorizing, they found something very basic to disagree about (ibid., p. 488).

From his point of view, Jung was trying to raise the libido construct to a higher level—subsuming not only sexuality but *all* aspects of the personality system. In his hands, libido lost its analogical relation to a physical energy à la the constancy principle. It became the *desired value of a person's intention,* reflecting the worth of a goal for the sake of which (final causation) the person behaves (Jung, 1961, p. 111). Libido is said to be experienced as conation and desire, very much as in Schopenhauer's concept of *Will* (Jung, 1964, p. 147). And most important of all, libido is always brought about through a dialectical oppositionality, beginning in the first efforts of mental differentiation and carried on throughout life according to what Jung now called the *principle of opposition.* This principle supplants constancy in Jungian psychology. Thus, by the late 1920s Jung (1961) was saying, "I see in all that happens the play of opposites, and derive from this conception my idea of psychic energy" (p. 337). In one of those fascinating parallels of history, Freud too had begun his career by seeing the play of opposites. Indeed, it is our contention that he always looked at behavioral dynamics in this dialectical light.

## The Source of Freudian Dynamics

If, as we contend, Freud was *not* a biological or drive reductionist, and if the analytical personality system is *not* driven along on the basis of instinctive thrusts of a bio-emotional nature but rather on the basis of meaningful ideas encompassing conflicting intentions, then just how did Freud arrive at his dynamic explanations of human behavior? To understand the father of psychoanalysis properly we must return to 1892—the year preceding publication of Breuer and Freud's preliminary communication of their *Studies on Hysteria* (1955)—when Freud advanced an explanation of hysteria that presaged the Jungian explanations which he later found objectionable. In this *very first* theoretical effort by Freud (1892/1966b) we find an explanation of hysteria entirely at the level of ideas.

Thus, Freud suggested that *all* people behaved on the basis of intentional ideas carried out willfully, but also on the basis of the dialectically opposite ideas prompted by a *counterwill* in the personality. Human beings, Freud said, hold certain expectations concerning the likelihood that they can actually put their intentions (willful ends, goals, etc.) into effect. There is always a subjective uncertainty in behavior, and with many, if not all, intentions we human beings immediately think of counterintentions as *antithetical ideas* to those intentions we really want to affirm and thereby have reach "motoric action" in our behavior. We think "I will do that," and immediately the dialectical meaning "I can't do that" is suggested through oppositionality. At certain low points in life, whether through fatigue or extended mental conflict, these antithetical ideas can take over and manifest themselves in various types of counterwilled symptoms so that people actually do what they have no intention of doing! In the case Freud reported on, Frau von N. made noisy ticlike exclamations by clacking her tongue, stammering, and occasionally calling out, "Don't say anything." Freud explained her symptoms as follows:

> Our hysterical patient [Frau von N.], exhausted by worry and long hours of watching by the bedside of her sick child which had at last fallen asleep, said to herself: "Now you must be perfectly still so as not to awaken the child." This intention probably gave rise to an antithetic idea in the form of a fear that she might make a noise all the same that would wake the child from the sleep which she had so long hoped for. Similar antithetic ideas arise in us in a marked manner when we feel uncertain whether we can carry out some important intention. . . . It appears that a conflict had occurred between her intention and the antithetic idea (the counter-will) and that this gave the *tic* its discontinuous character and confined the antithetic idea to paths other than the habitual ones for innervating the muscular apparatus of speech. (Breuer & Freud, 1955, pp. 92-93)

This kernel theory of *completely psychological* intentions encompassed as ideas and having to confront opposite or antithetical ideas in mind was *never* to leave Freud's style of explanation. This is why we italicized the term *antithesis* in the quotations in the previous section. The dialectical notion of a given idea (thesis), its opposite meaning (antithesis), and some defensive maneuver into compromise, repression, sublimation, projection, and so forth, is what stamps Freudian explanation as unique and different from traditional explanations of the medical model. Jung merely built upon this bedrock.

It was Breuer and not Freud who wrote constancy principle types of explanation into the *Studies on Hysteria* (Breuer & Freud, 1955, pp. 196-200). Breuer began by stressing the fact that all cases of hysteria arise from "an abnormal excitability of the nervous system," whether or not this stems from a psychological conflict of opposing intentions (ibid., p. 191). He went on to suggest that there is in a human organism an innate *"tendency to keep intracerebral excitation constant"* (ibid., p. 197). If such abnormal excitations are not *abreacted*—worked over and released via "living them through" in imagination—hysterical symptoms can result. How does this come about? After a period of time, said Breuer, the "idea" (memory of the reason that abnormal emotions arose in the first place) becomes split off from the rest of the psyche and functions at a subconscious level (ibid., p. 226). Why does this splitting of the psyche take place? Because of an innate hereditary disposition to what

Breuer called the *hypnoid state* (ibid., pp. 235-236). Some people are born with this tendency to split, and so they may in time clack their tongues when they would not will to do so but are unable to counteract this innate tendency for an idea to become split off in this fashion. Pierre Janet (1920) would later complain that Breuer and Freud had simply adapted his concept of the *fixed idea* to this hypnoid state explanation of hysteria.

Of course, in actuality it was only Breuer's traditional medical model that "accounted for" hysteria in a way similar to Janet's theory. Both Janet and Breuer favored biological (i.e., material/efficient-cause) reductionism (see Chapter 1, p. 13). Freud, on the other hand, departed from this traditional reductive explanation to assert, "I was repeatedly able to show that *the splitting of the content of consciousness is the result of an act of will on the part of the patient;* that is to say, it is initiated by an effort of will whose *motive* [italics added] can be specified" (Freud, 1894/1962b, p. 46). Freud called this splitting of consciousness *defense hysteria* in contrast to Breuer's *hypnoid hysteria*. Rather than material/efficient causal meanings, Freud was continuing in his formal/final causal explanations as embodied in his concepts of ideas, wills, intentions, and the like. Later Freud drafted his unfinished work, *Project for a Scientific Psychology* (see Chapter 1, p. 10). In the *Project,* Freud postulated two types of neurons: one that allowed energy to be expended and one that allowed it to be held back—to be "bound" or "repressed," as the case might be. Though scholars are likely to think of the *Project* as reflecting Freud's biological theoretical propensities (see Chapter 1, p. 11), it is equally plausible that the antithetical-ideas paper of 1892 was a purely psychological precedent for the misfired biological reductionism of the *Project.* Freud's theoretical strategy was always more on the side of a dialectical clash of intentions than the blind working out of pressure point levels in a closed system. We have to know the person's conflicting intentions to really "know" the person.

As for Breuer's hypnoid state theory, Freud succeeded in dismissing it through a series of brief theoretical references in papers on related topics. In 1895 he stated that though hypnoid hysteria is an important hypothesis, every hysteria he treated had "turned into a defence hysteria" (Breuer & Freud, 1955, p. 286). In 1896 he noted that "there are often no grounds whatever for presupposing the presence of such hypnoid states" (Freud, 1896/1962d, p. 195). He then added that if the analyst would only search deeper into the psyche of the patient, he or she would find a repressed defense in time. This is in effect a reverse reductionism, in which underlying psychic ramifications of what appear to be purely physical symptoms can in time be discovered. Rather than formal/final causes reducing to material/efficient causes, the reverse is true. Finally, in 1908 Freud dismissed the phenomenon of a hypnoid state as supposedly due to the physiological sensation of a protracted pause following a climax of intense sexual release (Freud, 1908/1959e, p. 233). As such, it plays no role in the etiology of neurosis!

We therefore conclude that Freudian dynamics, though based upon instinctive promptings of a sexual and/or hostile type, not to mention the myriad other biophysical needs of the body for hunger, thirst, and so on, are uniquely arrived at by examining the purely mental ideas of human beings. Ideas encompass ends. They always deal with "that for the sake of which" a line of action is to be carried out. But some lines of action are totally unacceptable, both to the society in which the person lives and to the person's sense of self-identity per se. We all have intentions that we know at one level but do not know—or that we fail to admit—at another level. We are therefore forced to deceive ourselves lest we admit to being the kind of person we consciously abhor. There are memories that we all have stored up thanks to our development through infancy and childhood, with special relevance to the Oedipal conflict. *All* neurotic individuals have poorly resolved Oedipal conflicts (Freud, 1909/ 1957a, p. 47). Furthermore, *all* individuals employ various psychic maneuvers in dealing with their known and unknown (unadmitted) wishes or intentions. These dynamic mechanisms are what give us that array of behavior known as "personality differences" in psychoanalytical theory. We next turn to these interesting maneuvers, many of which have already been mentioned in previous chapters.

## Defense or Dynamic Mechanisms

The choice of *mechanism* as descriptive of the dynamic maneuvers of this section is perhaps unfortunate. These are mechanisms in the same sense that logical deduction and induction are "mechanisms" of thought. What Freud meant by the term *mechanism* is that there are certain discernible patterns of thought which people manifest in seeking to adapt their internal (psychic) reality to the external (factual) reality of their experience. We do well to think of these as logical devices, including the often contradictory form of dialectical logic that occurs when the person both knows and does not know something at the same time (see Rychlak, 1981a, Chapter IX). Because Freud was in most instances describing abnormal behavior when he pointed to these mechanisms, we have come to think of them as *defense* mechanisms. These are the ways in which people delude themselves, satisfy id promptings, punish themselves via superego wishes, and through it all achieve compromises thanks to the inter-cession of the ego. However, as the extension was made to normal individuals by way of what Freud called the "psychopathology of everyday life," we have come to think of them as simply *adjustment* or *mental* mechanisms. A suitably abstract designation would be *dynamic* mechanisms. As we have already seen, each of the mechanisms can be given an energic definition or a purely psychological definition.

*Repression* (and *Denial*). As Freud (1914/1957g) said, "Repression is the corner-stone on which the whole structure of psycho-analysis rests" (p. 16). We can define *repression* in two ways: (1) it is a countering of one cathexis by an anticathexis, or (2) it is the opposing of one idea in mind by an opposing idea. These are two ways of saying the same thing. We really cannot understand why one energy cathexis is opposed by a countercathexis (synonymous with anticathexis) unless we know the meaningful content of the ideas involved on either end of the conflict. The ideas are the embodiments of *intentions,* preparations for motor action that come into conflict with one another (Freud, 1901/1953c, p. 55).

Though it is common today for a person to say "I have repressed that" in referring to something that is annoying to think about, actually this is a misuse of the term. If we *know* that we have put something out of mind because it is threatening or annoying, then we have not repressed but *suppressed* a mental content or meaning. It is possible to suppress and remove mental contents from consciousness to the preconscious—as when we "think about something else" rather than go on worrying about a forthcoming job interview or school examination. We have to get worries off our mind, at least for a time, and suppression is the dynamic mechanism by which we achieve this peace of mind. However, true repression is *always* maintained unconsciously. We are unaware of our repressed ideas consciously, though we know them full well unconsciously.

Despite its cornerstone role in Freudian theory, repression is not without precedent in the personality system. The defense mechanism of *denial* is generally thought to be a primitive manifestation of the very same dynamic that takes place in repression. Repression is said to occur when there has developed a certain distinction between the levels of consciousness (*unconscious, preconscious,* and *conscious*). But even before this development in layers of consciousness occurs, the infant with a tenuous sense of consciousness is said to be capable of denial. In denial, the person contradicts reality. Something that is perceived is treated as if it did not exist, rather than pushing its cognizance into another layer of mind as in the case of repression. Denial eventually takes a back seat to repression in the developing personality system, but it is never lost to the personality system, and we shall have occasion to discuss its role in certain psychopathological disorders (see Chapter 9, p. 285).

There are actually two stages in the defense or mental mechanism of repression. The first, *primal repression,* takes place during the time of the original conflict between ideas. This results in what Freud called a *fixation,* a mental mechanism that we shall put off for discussion in Chapter 5 (see p. 150) because it relates to *regression* (another mechanism that we shall put off), which in turn helps us understand not only personality differences but also the psychopathological process. Following the primal repression, we invariably find that the meanings that are pushed far from consciousness tend to make themselves known indirectly or symbolically—as *derivatives* of the repressed contents. These derivatives are what slip by the censoring agency of primal repression and show up in dreams and parapraxes. It is at this point that the psyche carries on the second stage, called *repression proper,* which is a kind of continuing effort to hold things out of mind. This shows that repression is not a "onetime" thing, like closing a trap door. Repression calls on the person to expend libidinal effort continually, holding down meanings that are threatening to the personality system. A person who is overly repressed is therefore vulnerable to a kind of mental exhaustion, with increasing derivatives and a diminishing grasp on his or her repressed contents.

*Displacement.* Freud introduced *displacement* to describe how it is possible to fool the *censoring agency* (e.g., the superego) and in a dream formulation to displace the true meaning of a dream content onto an unrelated event or happening (Freud, 1900/1953a, pp. 307-308). For example, if a hypothetical individual, John, has an unconscious hatred for his brother Robert, he might displace this hatred in his dream onto a bobcat, which he tracks down and kills after a satisfying hunt. John never actually realizes *consciously* that his victim is Bob, which is a shortened version of his brother's name. Unconsciously John has killed a sibling, but consciously only an unconscious derivative symbolized by a game animal has been done in. The term *displacement* has come to be used more generally than for dream analysis alone. Anytime a person redirects a concern from one realm to another in life, displacement is taking place. For example, a person who is angry at a superior may displace this hostility onto a subordinate, redirecting the flow of hostility down the chain of authority rather than upward, where it makes more sense.

*Substitution.* Humans can often find alternate objects in life. We can redirect our interests, for example, and find a new libidinal object if we are blocked from getting our first sexual preference. Freud (1892-99/1966c, p. 209) suggested that when an aging unmarried woman dotes over a pet dog, or when an old bachelor collects snuff boxes, the woman has found a substitute for the marital partner she never acquired, and the man has substituted a series of pretty boxes for the succession of beautiful women he never conquered. Substitution thus specifically refers to the replacing of one object by another.

*Sublimation.* Freud (1922/1955o) defined sublimation as follows: "The most important vicissitude which an instinct can undergo seems to be *sublimation*; here both object and aim are changed, so that what was originally a sexual instinct finds satisfaction in some achievement which is no longer sexual but has a higher social or ethical valuation" (p. 256). Sublimation thus goes beyond substitution, to change *both* the object and the aim of the instinct. For example, a young woman who considers her sexual promptings to be "dirty" (due to severe superego formation) might turn to art and sublimate her sexual instinct's aim (to be satisfied "as" sex) *and* object (i.e., directing her libido into the cathexes of her paintings rather than the image of a lover). Actually, most of the instances that Freud used to demonstrate sublimation deal with sex or eros, but it seems clear that he meant *any* (primal or component) instinct could be sublimated—including the death instinct. If we can speak of a mordido, then it too can be sublimated—as when rather than shooting a gun to kill, the marksman shoots plastic discs to demonstrate his skill as a potential killer.

*Projection.* Freud repeatedly found that his patients—particularly those with paranoiac tendencies (extremely suspicious)—would behave like a dreamer and attribute internal fantasies to the external world. For example, the id might prompt the patient to feel hostility toward another person, but the superego would negate any expression of this anger in overt behavior. At this point, the patient could *project* his or her own hostility onto the disliked person and say, "I'm not hostile to her, but she is very irritated with me." Notice that the *nature* of the projected instinct remains the same—it is still hostility (Freud, 1911/1958a, p. 66). Freud believed that the capacity to project internal perceptions (including wishes, fantasied beliefs, etc.) outward was a fundamental characteristic of thought. In fact, he went so far as to suggest that projection "normally plays a very large part in determining the form taken by our external world" (Freud, 1912-13/1955c, p. 64).

*Reaction-Formation.* Freud introduced the construct of reaction-formation to account for those instances in which people seem to be arguing or favoring some action, point of view, or intention in diametrical opposition to what they *really* wish would occur. There is no clearer example of dialectical reasoning in psychoanalysis. The pregnant young woman who unconsciously wishes that her forthcoming child would miscarry may profess consciously that she wants the child "very, very much" (Freud, 1913/1958i, p. 299).

*Rationalization.* Freud's student and biographer, Ernest Jones, introduced the term *rationalization,* which refers to the fact that a person often finds an acceptable (plausible, rational) reason to justify some action that is really prompted by a completely different (usually irrational, emotional) motive (Freud, 1911/1958a, p. 49). Thus, an otherwise gracious and friendly woman who unconsciously dislikes another woman in her circle of friends may find all manner of reasons for avoiding contact with this particular person. Her real reason is unconscious hatred (death-instinct components), but her consciously stated reasons (rationalizations) may include that she is too busy to call the woman on the telephone, she is never free when this woman has a party, she was sick on the occasion when they were to travel together, and so on.

*Isolation.* A disturbed person may sometimes be able to keep a rather horrible or frightening idea in mind. In order to account for this feature of mental life, Freud (1894/1962b) introduced the construct of *isolation,* by which he meant separating an idea from its emotional ties—that is, the normal discharge that would occur if the idea was entertained without isolation (p. 58). Thus, a psychotic man might have a delusional belief that his stomach had turned into a huge snake and that it was eating him alive, or some such. The normal person would be horrified, but this psychotic individual might continue to think about the delusion without showing a sign of emotion. Normal individuals might occasionally isolate, such as in times of war when killing is required, or when a parent tries to remove a child's badly mangled finger from a wire fencing where it has become impaled while playing. We cannot always let our emotions get the better of us and must sometimes carry out a difficult task with a cool head even though it may appear unnatural to others.

We have already given considerable attention to the constructs of *intro-jection* and *identification* (see Chapter 2, p. 64) in our coverage of the developmental stages. We shall add the concept of *fixation* and *regression* to these developmental conceptions in Chapter 5, in which we move to the more complex intrapsychic dynamics of both normal and abnormal personalities. We shall also take up some dynamic mechanisms involved in dream formation.

## SUMMARY

Chapter 4 takes up the specifics of Freudian personality theory, which is based fundamentally on the *dualism* of a *psyche* (mind) and a *soma* (body). Freud's first or *depth* model of mind framed the *conscious, unconscious,* and *preconscious* levels of mentation. Defensive maneuvers on this model stressed *censorship,* which in time became the concept of *repression.* In his second or *topographical* model Freud extended the dynamics possible in the human psyche by elucidating the relationship between the *id, ego,* and *superego.* In general, human development follows the course of moving from *primary process* thought based on the *pleasure principle* to *secondary process* thinking based on the *reality principle.* The earlier phases are id dominated, and the later phases begin to reflect the influence of the ego and superego. Both ego and superego seek to gratify id wishes, but in a more acceptable and rational fashion than would be the case if the id were left to its own devices. The superego or *ego-ideal,* we may recall from Chapter 3, is heir to the Oedipus complex.

Personality or the *style of behavior* is thus the sum total of the interactions occurring both within and across levels of consciousness. The id, ego, and superego have conflicting intentions, and many of the unacceptable wishes of the id are simply *not admitted* to conscious awareness. Unconscious means unadmitted rather than unknown, for the person *always* knows unconsciously what he or she does not know consciously. When we take an interest in the behavioral differences among personality styles, we are dealing in the *motivation* prompting such differences. Chapter 4 takes up this question of motivation in light of *drive* theory and the concept of *reinforcement. Drive reduction* theories in *classical conditioning* (Pavlovian) models are discussed. These are nontelic, completely mechanistic formulations in which behavioral patterns are "stamped in" without intention or purpose being manifested on the part of the behaving organism.

The same is true of the *operant* conditioning (Skinnerian) style of explanation, in which it is assumed that even though we can never know if "a" drive is being reduced or not, the regularities to be traced in behaviors are all that matter. Just so long as an organism's level of doing something brings about a contingent reinforcer, defined as whatever it is that increases the rate of response emission, it is assumed that behavior is being shaped without intention. Most psychologists lump together the constructs of "reinforcer" in operant conditioning with "drive reducer" in classical conditioning.

An exception to this rule is Maslow's "third force" psychology, in which a telic principle of *self-actualization* is employed. Maslow distinguishes between *basic needs,* such as hunger, sex, security, and *metaneeds* that build upon such basics to form higher motivations for beauty, justice, and order in life. The need to self-actualize is a major metaneed of the human being. Self-actualized people often report *peak experiences,* which are exceedingly wonderful occurrences that submerge all else by comparison. Self-actualized persons live life more fully and clearly than other people. They also commit themselves to some worthy task, such as a career, civic duty, or vocation that presses on them and aids their self-fulfillment. This entire theoretical development is heavily teleological, even though it rests upon a biological basis. Maslow is a biological naturalist because he does not attempt to explain the metaneeds by reducing them to the basic needs.

Chapter 4 next takes up Freud's developing *instinct* theories. The instinct is viewed as originating in the body rather than in the external world, and it releases energy into the psyche. Each instinct is said to have the *aim* of satisfaction, or removing the *pressure* (extent of stimulation) from its *source* (the point in the internal body area from which it originates). The *object* is that person or thing in terms of which the instinct is able to achieve its aim. Literally anything that might conceivably lead to the satisfaction of an instinct is an object. The *vicissitudes* of the instincts refer to the fluctuating levels of instinctive promptings. It would therefore appear that Freud may have been proposing a drive reduction theory in his instinct conception. The concept of *libido* or "psychical desire" as an energic force is drawn on the analogy of the constancy principle. This mental energy can be *cathected* or sent into the image of an object, orienting the personality toward this potential satisfier of the instinct in question. But it is also possible to *anticathect* or block the cathexis of one side of mind (id) by using libido apportioned to another (ego). Such countering measures (repression) obviously go beyond the traditional accounts of the constancy principle.

Freud viewed instincts as capable of combining into complexities. Thus, *primal instincts* could be brought into a *compound* of instincts. Freud was to base psychoanalytical theory on the interplay of two dialectically opposed primal instincts, even though he implied that more than two were in effect. His first opposition of instincts was that of the *self-preservative* (or *ego*) *instincts* and the *sexual* (or *object*) *instincts.* In time, he accounted for the self-preservative instincts as a special case of *eros* or the *life instinct* and its attendant *narcissism.* Self-preservation was based on self-love (ego cathexes). Freud referred to the libido invested in the ego as *ego libido* or *narcissistic libido* and the libido eventually sent out to others as *object libido.*

In opposition to the life instinct Freud then proposed the *death instinct,* which in effect draws upon the *repetition compulsion* to account for the fact that there is a general urge inherent in organic life to restore an earlier state of things. Thus, instincts do not impel so much as they cause things happening to return to an earlier state. Sexual rises seek quiescence in the vicissitudes of libido (eros). And life too seeks the quiescence of the inert state; hence, said

Freud, "the aim of all life is death." Instincts are thus conservative in their functioning.

The question remains: Was Freud a drive reduction theorist? Chapter 4 answers no to this question. This conclusion is based on the following facts regarding Freudian explanation. The unconscious is crucial in psychoanalytical accounts, yet technically speaking, instincts and emotions are never unconscious. Anxiety cannot be thought of as a drive, since it is "inflicted" intentionally by unconscious compromises and is experienced *only* in ego consciousness as a kind of warning sign. Freud's distinction between *realistic, moral,* and *neurotic* anxiety is based on a purely instrumental role for the emotion of anxiety. If anything, Freudian theory is a "drive induction" formulation. Finally, as we make clear throughout this volume, the concepts of libido, cathexis, and mental ideas share an intentional theoretical meaning. As such they are heavily laden with final-cause meanings, as when Freud spoke of *libidinal anticipatory ideas.* Repression is an intentional "mechanism," which amounts to a virtual contradiction in terms.

Chapter 4 next traces the source of Freudian dynamics to the clash of completely psychological intentions, framed in terms of a dialectical style of explanation. Freud's *very first* theoretical account of *antithetical ideas* and a *counterwill* is offered in evidence that he first thought of the psyche as a telic organization of intentions and then secondarily introduced psychic energies to "account for" his explanations in a pseudoreductive effort to placate colleagues. Of course, there were helpful insights gleaned from energic explanations as well. But the fascinating thing about Freud is that we can see in his supposedly biological effort known as the *Project* purely psychological precedents drawn from his *even earlier* theory of antithetical ideas. Freud's theoretical strategy is always more on the side of a dialectical clash of intentions than the blind working out of pressure points in a closed system (the constancy principle).

Chapter 4 closes with a survey of Freudian *defense mechanisms.* As already suggested, the term *mechanism* is misleading. What Freud meant by the term is that there are certain discernible patterns of thought that people manifest in seeking to adapt their internal (psychic) reality to the external (factual) reality of their experience. These thought patterns were initially conceived as *defense* mechanisms but are often referred to as *adjustment* or *dynamic* mechanisms today. The mechanism of *denial* is viewed as a primitive manifestation of the same dynamic we have referred to above as *repression.* Consciously striving to keep things out of mind is *suppression,* whereas repression and the other mechanisms occur without such conscious intention. *Primal repressions* take place during the time of the original conflict (e.g., during the Oedipal situation), and *repression proper* is then carried on throughout life.

Other defense mechanisms presented in Chapter 4 include *displacement,* in which concerns from one realm of life are placed on another realm. *Substitution* is a related mechanism in which alternative objects are cathected. In *sublimation* both the object and the aim of the instinctive prompting are changed in the direction of a higher social or ethical outcome. *Projection* involves the attribution of a personally held attitude, desire, sense of hostility, and so forth, onto another person or group of persons. *Reaction-formation* permits the individual to pretend that the very opposite of what is unconsciously intended is being enacted in behavior. *Rationalization* involves the finding of an acceptable (plausible, rational) reason to justify some action that is really prompted by a completely different (usually irrational or emotional) motive. Finally, *isolation* involves the separation of an idea from its emotional implications.

# 5

# *Intrapsychic Dynamics*

We have to this point reviewed the essentials of Freudian theory. It remains for us now to begin putting all of these basics together into a coherent picture of both normal and abnormal behavior. The chapters to follow this one will take up specific clinical syndromes in terms of psychoanalytical terminology. Chapter 5 will prepare the reader for this in-depth survey by taking up such relevant issues as conscious versus unconscious awareness, fixation and regression, the compromise model of mental illness, and dream interpretation. All of these issues are reflective of the complexities of what in Chapter 1 we quoted Freud as calling the *"dynamic view* of mental phenomena" (p. 3). We begin with a most interesting question concerning the role of awareness in human behavior.

## *Awareness and the Conscious/Unconscious Dichotomy*

One of the more deceptively confusing aspects of Freudian theory is the question of conscious versus unconscious mentation and what this can mean to the description of behavior as either self-determined or "blindly" determined. Is an organism that is being directed by unconscious factors tantamount to a controlled mechanism? There are many psychologists who would equate unconscious behavior with blind determinism. Dollard and Miller (1950) interpret unconscious behavior as "unverbalized" or "unlabeled" behavior, meaning that there are no mediating cue-producing responses occurring between the input stimuli and the output responses (pp. 136, 198). Thus, a woman who has an abnormal fear (*phobia*) of dogs might have been frightened as an infant by a shaggy toy in the shape of a dog. Unable to verbalize the (mediating) connection between this early experience and current stimuli, she therefore "unconsciously" responds with anxiety to dogs (stimuli) that she now encounters.

As we shall see, this type of explanation has no relevance for psychoanalysis. In essence, it has whatever is "out of consciousness" (the connecting link between dog [stimulus] and anxiety [response]) as essentially "out of mind." Freud's explanations placed the "out-of-consciousness" or *unconscious* factors at the very *center* of mentation (mental thought). Freud looked introspectively through the conceptual eyes of his clients and saw them having both visual and verbal conceptions of things yet "not knowing" that they had such conceptions (i.e., repression). Fundamental to the Freudian explanation is the assumption that human beings must be somehow aware of that which they are confronting in life, even though they may not admit this awareness to themselves. Framed teleologically, we could say that Freud has the person intending ends that go unacknowledged. In light of such theorizing, what have the findings been on awareness in the behavioristic experiments on conditioning? The mounting evidence provides fascinating support for a teleological interpretation of human behavior—evidence to which we now turn.

*Awareness in Conditioning Experiments.* The classical and operant conditioning procedures were described in Chapter 2 (pp. 34-38). Most of what we know about conditioning stems from experiments on lower animals, and insofar as human conditioning is concerned, the preponderance of this research has been conducted on people beyond their infancy. As we learned in Chapter 2 (pp. 33-41), the evidence for either classical or operant conditioning on infants is hardly convincing. In recent decades, a development in the conditioning research literature has had immense implications for the description of behavior—particularly human behavior.

We can best appreciate what has occurred by retracing our steps to the historically important operant conditioning experiment conducted by Greenspoon (1955). In the 1950s and 1960s this experiment was held up as an example of how it is possible to manipulate human verbal behavior and, by extension, human reasoning itself. The basic design of the Greenspoon experiment calls for a period of time in which the subject (a college student) is asked to "emit" (say aloud) verbal "responses," with no limitation placed on the class of responses (that is, nouns, verbs, adjectives, and so on, are all equally acceptable). For example, the subject sits with his or her back to the experimenter and says aloud all the words (single words, not sentences) that come to mind spontaneously. It is possible after a period of time (let us say ten minutes) to get a *base-rate estimate* of the classes of responses the subject typically emits. Of all words voiced by the subject, what proportion are nouns, adjectives, singular or plural references, and so forth? Electrical sound recording of a subject's responses makes this analysis a simple matter.

In the next ten-minute phase of the experiment, the experimenter selects a class of verbal responses and operantly reinforces *only* those words which fall into this classification. Greenspoon reinforced plural nouns during this second ten-minute period. The reinforcer used was *mmm-hmm,* but since Greenspoon's initial study the word *good* has been used quite often. Thus, in phase two, each time the subject says a word from the classification selected—let us say plural nouns (books, trees, clouds, etc.)—the experimenter follows by saying *mmm-hmm* or *good.* Finally, a closing ten-minute phase is electronically recorded in which the subject relies again on his or her own devices, "emitting" words without the reinforcer being given by the experimenter.

What did Greenspoon find? The verbal class of plural nouns showed a significant increase in operant level between the first and third phases of the study. Greenspoon took this as evidence that he had manipulated the subjects' verbal behavior. Moreover, he claimed to have accomplished this manipulation without the subjects' being aware that it was taking place! In fact, Greenspoon could find no differences in verbal behavior between those subjects who had discovered the relationship between the emitted nouns and the contingent *mmm-hmm* reinforcers and those who had not. Conditioning took place even when a subject did not state clearly in a postexperimental interview, "Every time I said a plural noun you [the experimenter] said *mmm-hmm*." Greenspoon concluded that there *was* operant conditioning and hence "shaping" of verbal behavior without awareness on the part of a subject. Rather than an intentional form of expression, in which certain meanings were being expressed rather than others, language appeared to be a manipulated sequence of words, strung together based upon the reinforcing circumstances that they brought about *unintentionally*!

As later events were to establish, Greenspoon's postexperimental interview was just not sophisticated enough. For example, he overlooked the possibility that a subject may have been verbalizing *intentionally* according to a premise or assumption that called for plural nouns quite incidentally. Assume that a subject had heard *mmm-hmm* after saying *books* and then after saying *pencils*. He or she might well have jumped to the conclusion (and framed thereby a premise) that the experimenter was looking for "things in a school building" and gone on reciting words like *blackboards, chairs, students,* and so on, without really discovering the specific intent of Greenspoon's experimental format. The experimental findings might show that this subject had been operantly conditioned to emit plural nouns without awareness—that is, he or she could not state the relationship between plural nouns and the *mmm-hmm* reinforcer—when in fact there *was* an awareness of sorts in that an inappropriate premise or incorrect hypothesis "worked" quite by accident. Other subjects who failed to reflect conditioning sometimes knew the relationship between the so-called operant response (plural noun) and the contingent reinforcer (*mmm-hmm*). Greenspoon took this as evidence that awareness was irrelevant, but a more detailed questioning could have established that these subjects *willfully* (intentionally) chose not to "go along with" the experimental design (see below). Surely this is not good evidence for conditioning without awareness!

In order to get such nuances in the operant conditioning format, a number of psychologists subsequently worked out a more sophisticated interview procedure (DeNike, 1964; Dulany, 1962; Spielberger, Berger, & Howard, 1963). Based on this extensive follow-up research it gradually became evident that the reason operant conditioning works on human beings is that those subjects who catch on to—are aware of—the connection between the operant response (plural noun) and the contingent reinforcer (*mmm-hmm*) make the graphed lines supposedly reflecting "conditioning" in the Greenspoon experiment rise and fall across the three ten-minute phases. If these subjects are removed from the study, leaving only those who are unaware of the connection, there is *no conditioning effect at all*!

Occasional studies appearing in the research literature claim to have achieved operant conditioning without subject awareness. The vast majority of evidence (approximately 90 percent of all experiments run) is that operant conditioning *without* some form of awareness either does not occur or produces only a limited and nonverbal response, such as a minute thumb contraction (Hefferline & Keenan, 1963; Hefferline, Keenan, & Harford, 1959). Furthermore, as we have already implied above, there is no assurance that a subject who is aware of the operant-response/contingent-reinforcer relationship will comply with experimental instructions. Experiments have been conducted to demonstrate that subjects can be aware and uncooperative *by intention* (Page, 1972). Some subjects know what is expected of them, but out of a sense of hostility or simply humorous mischievousness, they negate what the experimenter would have them do in "getting conditioned."

Another line of research casting doubt on operant manipulation of behavior involves having all subjects reinforced according to a certain *schedule* (patterned order of reinforcers) while leading them to believe that they are on a different schedule (A. Kaufman, Baron, & Kopp, 1966). The crank-turning experiment is an example. Subjects are asked to perform a manual task like turning a crank, for which they are contingently reinforced with money (a coin of some denomination) *approximately* once every minute (variable-interval schedule). Only some of the subjects are told the truth about how often their responses will be rewarded; others are told that their behavior is being reinforced *exactly* once each minute (fixed-interval schedule) or after they have performed "about" fifty turns of the crank (variable-ratio schedule), no matter how long this takes. Operant conditioners find that the rate of crank turning varies as a function of the kind of schedule that is used to reinforce the behaving organism. What would we find in this type of study, in which we contrast what is *really* taking place with what the subject *thinks* is taking place in his or her reinforcement schedule? We would find that it is more important what the subject thinks is happening than what is really happening! The kind of learning curve that results is *not* shaped without the subject's conscious premises about what is supposedly taking place. This is readily viewed as a form of awareness, a behavior "for the sake of" a premise which is enacted in unfolding behavior with foresight and intentionality.

Turning to Pavlovian or classical conditioning, we find a similar reliance on cognitive awareness taking place when human beings are studied (Brewer, 1974; Page, 1974). Subjects in classical conditioning experiments do not have to be aware of the particular response being studied (though often they are), because in some cases this is totally reflexive in nature. For example, the *galvanic skin response* (GSR) is a measure of the resistance to electrical conductance in the skin brought on by autonomic nervous system reactions (that is, it is completely automatic in a material/efficient-cause sense). It is noticeable during states of emotion and can be induced by shocking a subject electrically. In such a conditioning experiment, the unconditioned stimulus would be an electroshock, the conditioned stimulus might be a light (which would flash just before shocking a subject), and the response to be conditioned would be the GSR (which in time would occur when the light flashed even before the shock was administered.

The results of numerous studies of GSR and awareness have made it abundantly clear that only those subjects who became aware of the relationship between the conditioned and unconditioned stimuli—who personally realized, "Every time that light flashes I get shocked!"—actually conditioned their GSR to the light. Subjects who did not grasp this (formal-cause) pattern did not get conditioned. As in operant conditioning, it is not necessary for a subject to have the precise relationship between a conditioned and an unconditioned stimulus in mind. The wrong hypothesis may be employed as premise, but so long as it is close to what the experimenter is trying to accomplish, the desired experimental effects will come about.

When the response to be conditioned is motoric rather than autonomic, the subject can easily prevent its taking place following conditioning. For example, another experiment might  condition a subject's finger-withdrawal response (motoric) to a light by using shock. The subject rests a finger on an electrified stand. Once he or she knows that the light (which occurs first) and the shock bear a meaningful relationship, the subject will be seen quickly removing the finger from the stand before the stand is electrified—using the flashing light as the conditioned stimulus. However, assuming that the shock is not extremely painful, the subject can also *stop* removing his or her finger at any time, given the suggestion to do so by the experimenter. Undoubtedly, subjects could do so at will, even without this suggestion. It is somewhat more difficult to prevent the conditioned response when the unconditioned stimulus is a puff of air aimed at the eye, causing it to blink following the flashing of a light (the conditioned stimulus). However, even in this case, many subjects can willfully keep their eyes open after classical conditioning has been established and suffer the puff of air blown into their eye. Finally, on the other side of the coin, subjects who are told from the outset exactly what the unconditioned and conditioned stimuli are can begin showing this conditioning immediately. They do not need any shaping trials to get them fixed into an automatic pattern of cause and effect. Simply knowing what the experiment is aiming at is enough to fix the classical conditioning response.

Putting all of the findings on awareness in conditioning together, we can reasonably conclude that the experimental subject is much more of an agent in the process of "manipulation" or "shaping" than traditional theories of classical or operant conditioning have led us to believe. This body of research lends further support to the arguments made in Chapter 2 (p. 34) concerning the great responsibility that psychoanalysis places on the individual to direct his or her life by way of an inner, dynamic psychic perspective. Another important theoretical issue has to do with the cementing of awareness to conscious experience. This is what we have seen taking place in the reasearches on conditioning. To be aware is to be conscious of the relationship between the operant response and contingent reinforcer or between the conditioned and unconditioned stimuli. But what about the other side of the coin? Would the subject who does *not* grasp these relations and hence is consciously unaware *also* be considered "unconsciously aware"? Would such unconscious awareness be possible *in principle*? The answer of a behaviorist to both of these questions would be no, but a psychoanalyst would answer "sometimes" to the first question and yes to the second.

*Awareness and Levels of Consciousness in Psychoanalysis.* One of the most difficult things to understand about Freudian theory is its claim that awareness, or the recognition of what is going on in one's life, is *not* limited to consciousness. As Freud (1900-01/1953b) said in most unambiguous language: "*The most complicated achievements of thought are possible without the assistance of consciousness*" (p. 593). To grasp intrapsychic dynamics completely we must think of "awareness" on the one hand and "conscious/unconscious" on the other. How is it possible to do so? By making clear what is meant by *psychic determinism* in human behavior. Since the behaviorists do not accept final causation, there is no room in their account for a determinism issuing from this quarter. The truth is, we can modify the term *determinism* by all four of the causal meanings (see Chapter 1, p. 4).

Thus, there exists *material-cause determinism,* as in the fact that a statue made of marble has a different life expectancy than a statue made of wood or ice. *Efficient-cause determinisms* flow from energic concepts such as the principle of constancy (see Chapter 1, p. 10), so that when air is blown into a balloon the pressure distributes itself without aim into every aspect of the confined space. *Formal-cause determinisms* are to be seen in logic and mathematics, in which the framing assumptions (theorems, premises) limit what can be proved or deduced. When we now add the possibility of a final cause, it becomes possible to speak of a reasoning intelligence actually *framing* these assumptions, accepting or rejecting what is "given" or how a mathematical value is to be defined. Thus, a *final-cause determinism* literally directs what the "that" (reason, premise, assumption, hypothesis, etc.) will be even before the formal-cause determinism can operate to suggest a conclusion.

We can now see why it is true that formal- and final-cause conceptions tend to go together in descriptions of behavior. The formal cause encompasses patterns, and patterns are what meanings always come down to. Something "means" what it is patterned in relation to. The word *mother* means a certain parental tie, but it also suggests unique experiences and images of a positive or negative nature *in relation to* our own mother. Whether we actually think about our mother or not is up to us. As a psychic determinist, Freud held that we take on this (formal-cause) meaning and behave for its sake (final-cause) *or not.* We can always dialectically dismiss the intent of a meaning. There is another dialectical maneuver—a kind of reverse of the antithetical-ideas concept which Freud proposed (see Chapter 4, p. 132)—in which we can behave for the sake of a meaning and at the same time refuse to admit (deny, repress) the fact that we are doing so, even to ourselves! This is where we begin to see the possibility of an aware, intended albeit unconscious, form of behavior. But the important point here is that psychic determinism is a formal/final-causal determinism. The formal cause is a necessary but not sufficient ingredient of psychic determinism. We need the patternings (*mother*), but we also need to say that an *identity* (the person) reasoning about such patternings will opt to further them or to repress them, deny them, and so forth. This capacity to choose what will or will not take place in mind is what Freud's psychic determinism is all about.

Freud was a strict or *hard determinist* in the psychic sphere. Nothing humans say or do is without meaning: "Psycho-analysts are marked by a particularly strict belief in the determination of mental life. For them there is nothing trivial, nothing arbitrary or haphazard. They expect in every case to find sufficient motives where, as a rule, no such expectation is raised" (Freud, 1909/1957a, p. 38). Once a compromise has been struck within unconsciousness, there is *no* manifestation within consciousness that is without a meaning tying back to this unconsciously *intended* line of action. Even the parapraxis is dialectically tied to the unconscious compromises under intentional direction by the psyche. The new bride says to her mother-in-law, "Please fall, *er . . . please call me tomorrow,*" and the psychoanalyst assumes there is a definite reason why this "slip" of the tongue has come to light. The slip is 100 percent determined (hard determinism) by the unconscious reasonings (wishes, etc.) of the young woman, who probably has a hostile regard for her mother-in-law that is totally hidden to her consciousness.

But now, is this the same kind of hard determinism embodied in the behavioristic explanations of human personality? No, the mechanisms of behaviorism rest *exclusively* upon efficient-cause determination. It is possible to believe in a hard determinism in the mental sphere, yet hold to a *soft determinism* in the physical sphere of everyday life. This is, in effect, what Freud did. Soft determinisms admit of some indeterminism in events, and Freud was always ready to acknowledge that *chance* played a role in our lives (Freud, 1910/1957b, pp. 136-137). Moreover, the emphasis he gave to the psychic, as being more important than reality in neurosis, as requiring insight to rectify the harmful effects of repression, and so on, all testify to Freud's commitment to a self-determining human organism, maneuvering within the onslaughts of life to arrange the best personal advantage.

What then is "awareness" in Freudian theory? To a certain extent, the problem is semantic in nature. If we wish to equate *awareness* with *conscious,* then we shall need to introduce another term—such as *known*—to account for Freudian explanations. In this case, we would say that conscious behavior is aware behavior, and that there are certain things we know about in this psychic state. But there are *other* things that we know about unconsciously and that we are therefore unaware of. Alternatively, we might not want to introduce new terminology, preferring to simply think of awareness as referring to the "breadth" of our intentions. We are never simply "aware" but always "aware of" something or other. To be fully aware we must know all of the facts, all of the alternatives, all of the possibilities open to us. In this usage, *unconscious awareness* might refer to a broader range of knowledge about what is taking place. Alternatively, *conscious awareness* has a narrower scope. The woman who let slip her hostility toward her mother-in-law was behaving consciously within a psychic realm that does not have "all of the facts" about her intentions. There are meanings that she affirmed unconsciously—and that she was aware of unconsciously—but she did not participate in their intended ends consciously.

Why do people avoid certain intentions (wishes, etc.) like this? To understand this repressive process we must recall Freud's dialectical theory of the antithetical ideas and counterwill (see Chapter 4, p. 132). There is always more than one line of intentional thought going on in the mind. There is the basic confrontation of id with superego, each of which has intentions in view, and the compromising ego, which has its intended aims as well. When the line of thought is somehow unacceptable to the ego—as morally reprehensible, self-demeaning, highly challenging, extremely demanding, and so on—then the ego as executive of the personality system can delimit what it will admit or acknowledge. This act of repression (denial, censorship, etc.) that goes on in the mind is what Freudian psychoanalysis opposes, based ultimately on the view that *meanings will out* one way or another. Psychoanalysis teaches us how to read the human acts of self-deception. After years of such study, Freud (1901/1960a) could thus say of himself: "Perhaps . . . my being scarcely able to tell lies any more is a consequence of my occupation with psycho-analysis. As often as I try to distort something I succumb to an error or some other parapraxis that betrays my insincerity" (p. 221).

*Awareness* is therefore a term that the psychoanalyst uses to refer to the level of self-admission that the person arranges through dialectical maneuverings in thought. And in a way that is diametrically opposite to the theories of behaviorism, the "out-of-consciousness" levels of awareness are *greater* than the "in-consciousness" levels of awareness. We are more aware of things at our unconscious than our conscious levels of thought. This is why we suggested above that a psychoanalyst might say that any one subject in a conditioning experiment might be *intentionally* unaware of the operant-response-to-contingent-reinforcer pattern unfolding in the experiment. For example, assume that a subject unconsciously equated plural usages (plural nouns) with possessing "many" things. This subject as a child was deprived and did not have much in life. Stating things in the plural might well arouse mental dynamics provoking anxiety or hostility for this past deprivation. Hence, rather than risk the possibility of furthering a negative mood, the subject could be unconsciously aware that plural nouns are called for in the experiment, yet intentionally avoid such conscious admission through the defense mechanism of repression. Behavioristic theories find such explanations superfluous because they do not admit psychic determinism a role in their accounts. Psychoanalysis entertains such explanations because it does indeed add a psychic to the physical/mechanistic determinisms of the body.

Before we leave this topic of awareness, it should be noted that experiments on hypnotism conducted by Ernest R. Hilgard (1977) lend support to the idea that there is more awareness to be found in the unconscious than the conscious state of mind. Hilgard found that a portion of the psyche of a hypnotized subject observed what was taking place during a hypnotic trance in which pain was inflicted by inserting a pin in the flesh of the subject. This "hidden observer" later commented on the hypnotic procedure and actually experienced the pain, which was *never* felt by the "primary" identity of the hypnotized subject. Hilgard dislikes the psychoanalytical reference to a "depth" in consciousness, preferring to speak of a "divided" consciousness. But the effect of his research is to support the view that—as in cases of multiple personality (see Chapter 9)—it is always the identity in the "secondary" (un-)consciousness that knows more about what is occurring than the identity in the "primary" consciousness. Hilgard's subject had a portion of the psyche "standing aside," knowing what was taking place during the hypnotic trance and yet not directly entering into the course of the trance to disrupt the suggestions being enacted. The support for dialectical reasoning here is obvious. Freud's antithetical-ideas theory has survived, and his views on conscious/unconscious psychic processes flow readily from this early assumption about human thought.

## Fixation and Regression

Unconscious dynamics are frequently involved in the personality mechanisms that we earlier put off to be considered in this chapter. These constructs are related to the psychosexual stages that we reviewed in Chapters 2 and 3, including (following birth): the oral stage, the anal (urethral) stage, the phallic stage, latency, adolescence, and adulthood. Freud based his explanations of personality differences and mental illness on the various ways in which people pass through these psychosexual stages. By "pass through" we mean in the psychic realm—a realm that never loses any of the impressions formed in life. The libido construct plays an important role in Freud's theory of fixation and regression. Though libido is frequently analogized to a flow of electricity, in the passages on fixation and regression Freud tended to analogize libido to a stream of water or a riverbed, giving this energic concept a hydraulic property (Freud, 1905/1953e, p. 170). He was fond of using the phrase "psychical damming-up," which he took from Lipps (Freud, 1905/1960b, p. 118). When Freud used *libido* in this hydraulic sense he usually referred to this usage as the *quantitative factors* of mental energy. By this he meant that any one person has just so much libido available to the total personality at any given point in time.

Since all aspects of the personality—id, ego, and superego—require libido to function properly, it follows that the portion commanding the largest supply of this precious mental energy will exert the greatest influence on the personality dynamics (Freud, 1929/1961i, pp. 103-104). For example, a person whose superego has a large portion of the libido available to the personality would be likely to behave in a socially proper, perhaps morally correct manner. The superego would have a commanding role in the id, ego, superego confrontations at the unconscious level. Based on a similar logic, if for some reason the progression of libido were halted or dammed up at one psychosexual stage, then the personality "as a whole" would begin taking on the characteristics of this earlier phase. This is another manifestation of the "primacy" view of development that Freud always favored (see Chapter 2, p. 49). An oral personality development, in which the infant child, adolescent, and then adult is prone to indulge in oral activities (sucking, gum chewing, overeating, smoking, etc.) reflects this influence of a stage having more than its share of "pocketed" libido.

This psychic trapping or pocketing of libido during any given state of psychosexual development is what Freud meant by the mechanism of *fixation*. Freud noted that the pathway to adulthood is never without its share of problems or frustrations, and it is these negative developments that lead to the damming up of libido (Freud, 1905/1953e, p. 235). Such fixations can take place at any time in psychosexual development, and they can occur repeatedly —although usually one phase takes on the predominant influence as major fixation point. Why does a person fixate? Freud did not rule out the possibility that there were hereditary or constitutional factors predisposing some people to fixate more readily than others (ibid., p. 236). But in the main, fixations occur because of various problems in the relationship with parents (Freud, 1896/1962d, p. 163). Of course, it is sometimes true that even when parents are especially loving and caring of their children, a fixation may occur because the child does not want to mature further. Having to move from the oral to the anal level, where toilet training demands are made, can prove a frustration to certain children who fixate libido at the oral level accordingly.

What is the dynamic behind fixation? That is, of what possible benefit can it be to the personality to shunt off or hold back libido in this fashion? Basically, this is a maneuver through which the personality system attempts to correct past wrongdoings, rectifying the situation that necessitated a fixation. In 1896, before he had concocted his libido theory, Freud referred to this process as a *fuero* (Freud, 1892-99/1966c, p. 235). A fuero is an ancient Spanish law or decree made by a ruler that is given to a province for some reason and can at some later date be exercised or used. For example, a king might give a province exemption from paying taxes or the right to avoid contributing manpower to the military forces. A fuero is thus a claim on the head of state for privileges.

In like fashion, said Freud, we have personal fueros that dictate to us from out of our own past (recall that the unconscious is timeless!). The infant who wishes not to leave the pleasures of orality for the demands of anality may have a fuero of the following sort: "But I did not wish to leave this nice life. Let me once again have the pleasures of sucking to enjoy." A person suffering from obesity for psychological reasons is presumably attempting to "cash in" or "put into effect" a personal fuero of this sort, if the world about him or her would only comply. Now, rephrasing this prelibidinal theory (which was obviously telic in nature), we would say that the fixated person's libido "colored" later development. We could also bring the repetition compulsion into our account at this point (see Chapter 4, p. 121), because a fuero claim or fixated pocket of libido is essentially trying to bring the personality system "back" to the earlier time when a frustration and fixation took place.

Photograph by Edmund Engelman

*The exterior of Freud's apartment house at Berggasse 19, taken in 1938 as Freud was preparing to emigrate to England "to die in freedom" rather than under the Nazi regime. Freud took up residence in the building in northern Vienna in 1891. It was here that psychoanalysis per se was created.*

To round out this theory Freud suggested that there are times when the personality system does indeed revert to the earlier time. This is *regression,* or the return to an earlier stage of development at which a fixation or partial fixation had taken place (Freud, 1915/1957n, p. 269). It is most likely to happen when the maturing personality—possibly in adulthood—receives additional frustrations. For example, the orally fixated adult might be fired from a job or confront an unhappy love affair. At such frustrating points in life, said Freud (1901/1953c), as when a "stream of water . . . meets with an obstacle in the river-bed" (p. 51), there is a redirecting taking place of the flow back into old channels.

When this happens, all of the fuero complaints and claims may be enacted in behavior. The orally fixated man may go off on a drinking or eating binge, which regressively re-creates the preoccupation of this stage (i.e., taking in passively). A woman who cries easily and needs constant reassurance from her friends may be regressing to oral passive dependencies on a regular basis. The slightest life challenge may send her into one of her crying spells. The teenage "tough guy" who has a reputation for hotheadedness and is ready to fight at the drop of a hat may in fact be regressing in the face of social frustrations. Being easily intimidated and basically afraid of relating to people, this young man is essentially re-enacting the hostility he feels toward parents who frustrated him when he should have been learning the first lessons of social propriety (toilet-training requirements); now, instead of feeling at ease socially, he is constantly on edge and ready to fight at the slightest provocation. His conscious reasons for fighting are foolish, but unconsciously there is a serious battle being waged—a fuero claim is being settled, again and again, as he tries to get back at his parents (repetition compulsion).

Freud was fond of using as an analogy to mind the stratified levels of Rome, the "eternal city," which is constructed of layer upon layer, city ruin upon city ruin, open to all manner of archaeological excavation (Freud, 1929/1961i, p. 69). So too with the psyche. No matter when something has taken place in the past, it is open to study today because "the primitive mind is, in the fullest meaning of the word, imperishable" (Freud, 1915/1957o, p. 286). Freud used the term *topographical* for these spatial layers of the psyche (recall his models of mind, Chapter 4, pp. 105-111), and he spoke of *topographical regression* whenever he meant the return of libido across these levels. If an adult returns completely to an earlier psychical state and becomes infantile as a whole person, the descriptive term would be *temporal regression*. And if only certain primitive behavior styles replace the more mature styles in the person's current behavior, the descriptive term for this limited form of regression would be *formal regression*. A psychotic person who literally becomes babylike in total behavior would be experiencing a temporal regression, whereas an occasional reversion to childishness by an otherwise mature adult would be formal regression.

Because everyone experiences some degree of fixation at one or more of the psychosexual stages, it is correct to say that the adult personality system is colored by these early points of libidinal storage or originating sources of the fuero claims. Freud made it clear that *all* personality styles are analyzable in terms of the particular fixation levels and the defense (dynamic) mechanisms employed by people to deal with their past life experience (Freud, 1913/1955e, p. 184). Hence, by *personality* Freud meant the working out of conflicts among the id, superego, and ego (Freud & Bullitt, 1967, p. 43), involving the repressions, sublimations, and reaction-formations of instinctual pressures (Freud, 1908/1959c, p. 175) and the resultant compromises that can be worked out across the topographical levels of mind. It is for this reason that we can point to oral, anal, and phallic personality "types." In the same way that Freud used the reflexive apparatus of the sucking reflex as a *prototype* conception through which the child comes to know reality (see Chapter 2, p. 42), so too do the predominant characteristics of each of these phases serve as prototypes for the conceptualizing of reality, given only that a person has been fixated during its ascendancy in development. We next turn to Freud's compromise model of psychopathology, which rests on the fixation/regression dynamic.

## The Three-Stage Compromise Model of Psychopathology

The antithetical-ideas theory that we reviewed in Chapter 4 (see p. 132) must be seen as an early effort on Freud's part to account for psychopathological conditions. Since antithetical ideas are *reverse intentions,* that is, intentions that we *do not* wish to carry out, they must bear some meaningful import in opposition to what we consider proper or acceptable behavior. They must be at odds with our conscious ego structure. Freud was to find in his clinical work that invariably a sexual experience was somehow involved in the mental dynamics of antithetical reasoning. Two of his earliest sexual theories of illness are of historical interest because they were efforts to account for psychopathology based upon a biological reductionism. Freud was obviously searching about for a straightforward physical explanation of the possible relationship between the sexualized memories his patients were recalling and the nature of the neurotic illnesses that had prompted them to seek treatment.

*Coitus Interruptus.* One of the complaints Freud often heard, especially from patients suffering from what was then termed an anxiety neurosis, was that they could not obtain gratification in sexual intercourse. Late in 1893 he told Fliess of a female patient who could not achieve climax because she feared having children. There was also a male patient who became hysterically ill during a period when his wife was physically ill and sexual intercourse had to be suspended (Freud, 1892-99/1966c, p. 185). Freud tentatively suggested a theoretical hypothesis of *coitus interruptus* (interrupted sexual intercourse) based on such clinical findings, implying that a kind of *sexual noxa* (harmful physical substance) was physiologically generated in the body during the time when a pressing sexual need was not being gratified (he did not speak of instincts at this time).

Freud did not try to trace the dynamic psychic factors that might have led to an inability on the part of some people to copulate successfully. Just *any* interruption was taken as a potentially harmful event, and he thought of this process in a reductive sense. In fact, he also suggested that there may have been a predisposing hereditary factor involved in such cases. This style of theorizing is an obvious remnant of the medical model in Freud's theorizing (ibid., p. 183). As we have seen in his rejection of Breuer's hypnoid state theory (see Chapter 4, p. 133), Freud was not to rest with such explanations for much longer. But the coitus interruptus hypothesis was not the last reductionistic explanation that Freud was to entertain.

*Childhood Molestation ("Seduction" Theory).* A few years later, in 1896, Freud was to propose his second reductive theory, based on the belief that neurotics had been molested or seduced into sexual activity before their physical apparatus had matured (Freud, 1896/1962e, p. 203). He again had a series of patients who could recall an early childhood experience of having been either raped or at least sexually fondled by a parent, a sibling, a relative (an uncle or aunt), or a household servant (Freud, 1905/1953f, p. 274). Accepting these memories as factual, Freud felt that the premature introduction to sexuality might well have acted like a precipitator of the maladjustment he was then observing in coitus interruptus. Here again, the weight of explanation was on what had happened to the individual in the past. It was just an unhappy accident that the neurotic was molested as a very young child, and his or her present disturbance was therefore in large measure free of any *personal* responsibility. Something had happened to the neurotic, who was not in any way at fault.

Freud found that he was unable to sustain his belief in the molestation or seduction theory. Based on his personal analysis, which was begun in 1897, Freud (1912-13/1955c) came to appreciate the important role that personally created fantasy plays in the generation of neurotic illness: "What characterizes neurotics is that they prefer psychical to factual reality and react just as seriously to thoughts as normal people do to realities" (p. 159). In his reformulation, the individual was no longer conceptualized as an innocent bystander in life's sexual misfortunes. Freud now claimed that recollections of seduction scenes are not always copies of past reality but rather the memories of *fantasies* indulged in during what we now call the early phallic phase (Freud, 1905/1953f, pp. 274-276). While masturbating at this stage, the child had fantasied the sexual rape or molestation and then had repressed the entire affair following the Oedipal resolution. The memory of a fantasy is subsequently recovered while the patient is in treatment and taken as fact. Of course, Freud was fully aware that sometimes this experience is indeed a factual recollection. The difference between fantasy and fact in the memory of patients is always difficult to distinguish (Freud, 1896/1962d, p. 168), but the confusion makes no difference because psychical reality is what takes precedence.

*The Final Model.* Freud's mature theoretical formulation encompassed what we shall call a *three-stage compromise model* of psychopathology. In this formulation he retained the kernel ideas of both coitus interruptus and the seduction-to-fantasy theory, added them to the original theory of antithetical ideas, and then proposed a *deflection* concept that could account for how psychopathological symptoms might arise. The libido theory was also being worked out at this time, and we shall see Freud using this conception to help us picture how the deflection is accomplished.

The coitus interruptus theory gradually evolved into what Freud called the *actual neuroses*—which were in turn then opposed to the *psychoneuroses proper.* The actual neuroses (neurasthenia, anxiety, and hypochondria) were presumed to be caused by a somatic (bodily) toxic factor, a *physical noxa* much like the one he had attributed to frustrated copulation (Freud, 1908/1959d, p. 185). The psychoneuroses proper were those disorders (hysterias) that were due to purely psychological causes. Because they were due to a physical toxic factor, Freud said that the actual neuroses could not be treated by purely verbal psychoanalysis; the physician had to prescribe definite changes in sexual routine in order to cure them (Freud, 1912/1958f, pp. 248-249). Of course, since that time numerous psychoanalysts have treated fatigue (neurasthenia), anxiety, and hypochondria through psychoanalytical treatment.

The major difference between the original seduction theory and the fantasy-recollection theory was that the abnormal person moved from the role of an innocent victim to that of a central and willing actor in the re-enactment of the Oedipal situation (see Chapter 3, p. 69). Freud was emphatic in calling the Oedipus complex the nuclear complex of every neurosis (Freud, 1909/1957a, p. 47). *All neurotics have unresolved Oedipus complexes.* In their ongoing psychopathological conditions the neurotics are re-enacting family situations that have never been properly resolved and are now very difficult to restrain from consciousness. Recall that Freud referred to the initial stage of repression as *primal* (see Chapter 4, p. 135). Later, the individual is forced to keep repressed material back from consciousness through a continuing repression proper (sometimes called *after-repression* by psychoanalysts). Since people cannot always repress, countercathect, or sublimate successfully, there is an alternative that permits a kind of "expression" of the repressed contents "out in the open" without thereby making them meaningfully known to the individuals concerned. It is possible to *create* a symptom of neurosis.

To grasp this dynamic we have to think in terms of three stages of personality development and adjustment. The *first stage* occurs during a pregenital stage of development, as during the resolution of the Oedipus complex. Let us assume that a teenage boy had at five years of age repressed sexual desires for his mother (eros) and hostile "death wishes" (death instinct) for his father. The *primal repression* at this time set these thoughts out of consciousness, but let us assume that the resolution was not very successful. There is much that was not worked through and accepted by this young man. Put in libido terms, this would mean that a fixation of considerable libido existed at the phallic phase of development. Of course, there may have been sizable fixations of libido even earlier, in the oral and anal phases as well. Now, it is highly likely that a boy with this much libido fixated would have difficulty in adjustment at the close of latency, brought on by the quantitative increase of libido following pubescence (Freud, 1912/1958e, p. 236). With the surge of new libido into the psyche following pubescence this young man's repressed wishes (cathexes) begin to press forward to expression in consciousness. He is in danger of expressing openly his lust for mother and death wishes for father— possibly feeling moved to enact either or both of these implications.

This represents the *second stage* of the compromise model, because now the entire personality system is threatened by what Freud (1896/1962d) called the *"return of the repressed memories"* (p. 169). Desperate efforts are made at this point to keep up a repression proper, but without real success. A more drastic dynamic is called for if the personality is to continue the self-deception (i.e., the idea that this boy loves his father and is not at all sexually attracted to his mother). Freud's brilliant theoretical suggestion at this point was to say that the boy, like all human beings, can express psychological meanings physically! There are always two sides to any repression—a wish to attain some cathected object and a wish not to attain the cathected object. But what if the intentions of *both* wishes could be expressed openly? Would that not be at least a middle-ground solution to the mental conflict, a step in the direction of the person having to confront a *concrete* problem that is at least in the open now for consideration and resolution?

Based on a logic of this type the psyche moves to the *third stage,* in which the id, ego, and superego reach a compromise that deflects the competing wishes into a physical manifestation. That is, a *symptom* of psychopathological disorder arises. Symptoms are always both *compromises* and *wish fulfillments* (Freud, 1892-99/1966c, p. 256). And as we have seen above in our considera-tion of awareness, the neurotic's unconscious mind always knows what such symptoms mean even though his or her conscious mind does not. The teenage boy might develop any of a number of clinical syndromes. As we suggested, even the so-called actual neuroses have been explained in this fashion. We shall be devoting most of the remaining chapters of this volume to a study of the various clinical manifestations of such compromise processes (as well as other etiological processes). Let us say for didactic purposes that the teenage boy like the Oedipus of legend is struck with a serious loss in vision. This hysterical (nonorganic) symptom came on the boy shortly after he had "accidentally" walked into a room in which his mother was dressing, so that he viewed her seminude body. The hysterical symptom expresses the lustful id wish that *actually* directed the boy's "misstep" that day, but it also expresses the superego wish to be punished for visually lusting after one parent and hoping to see the death of the other.

Freud called this process of compromise and deflection *conversion,* which he defined on one occasion as "the translation of a purely psychical excitation into physical terms" (Freud, 1901/1953c, p. 53). As our example demonstrates, neuroses actually begin in early childhood, but they do not show themselves until the second wave of libido comes on at pubescence or possibly after years of failing repression efforts (Freud, 1938/1964f, p. 184). Freud's definition of the *neurotic symptom* is as follows: "A symptom is a sign of, and a substitute for, an instinctual satisfaction which has remained in abeyance; it is a conse-quence of the process of repression" (1926/1959g, p. 91). We shall have more to say on the various origins and manifestations of symptoms in the later chapters of this volume. Basically, the symptom of a disorder expresses a meaning. It captures the intentions of the wishes involved. Freud (1915/1957k) even re-ferred to the *organ speech* of a symptom (p. 199).

Freud held to a quantitative as opposed to a qualitative view of mental illness (see Chapter 1, p. 15). He therefore did not draw a hard and fast line between normal and abnormal or between neurosis and psychosis within the abnormal disorders (Freud, 1923/1961b, p. 204). Some people fall ill from the same frustrations that other people bear up under (Freud, 1909/1957a, p. 50). What makes the former more vulnerable than the latter? It was in his attempt to answer this question that Freud fell back on his fixation-regression model. The nature of the illness will be colored by (1) the initial developmental level at which fixation took place, (2) the amount of libido fixated, and (3) the extent of libido that is later regressed once this process is underway in a clinical disorder (Nunberg & Federn, 1962, pp. 100-101).

Thus, someone who as an adult is behaviorally abnormal enough to be considered psychotic would therefore have repressively fixated a large amount of libido at one of the pregenital levels or a moderate amount very early in the oral stage (weakening the developing personality accordingly because at this point more libido was not available for proper psychic growth). Neurotic fixations are not so libidinously profound, nor do they ordinarily occur so early in life as the psychotic fixations. As we have already noted in discussing the developing personality system, everyone must confront frustrations in life. Everyone also regresses occasionally, reflecting in the childlike tendencies the fixation points of a past life experience. But the difference between normal and abnormal regression centers on what the person is trying to accomplish in the process.

Freud believed that the neurotic individual does not reject reality or try to change reality as he or she understands it to be; the neurotic merely exhibits a *flight into illness* through regressive symptom formation (Freud, 1901/1953c, p. 43). The psychotic individual, on the other hand, *rejects* commonsense reality in the regressive process and then seeks to reconstruct it along fantasied lines. Though both psychotics and neurotics are heavily involved in fantasy, the former manufacture delusions and hallucinations to deny reality, and the latter keep on reasonably good terms with the external demands of their life circumstances. Freud (1924/1961d) once suggested that a normal personality combines the best of both clinical syndromes in adapting to life: "We call behaviour 'normal' or 'healthy,' if it combines certain features of both [clinical] reactions—if it disavows the reality as little as does the neurosis, but if it then exerts itself, as does a psychosis, to effect an alteration of that reality" (p. 185). In short, the normal person fights to keep in contact and to effect a constructive outcome, a change in the frustrating state of things in external (non-fantasied) reality. Normal individuals neither run away from a challenge nor settle for a dream-world solution, even though they might regress and act childlike from time to time.

## Anxiety Theory

We have already referred to Freud's final theory of anxiety in our discussion of the motivational factors in the personality system (see Chapter 4, p. 125). We want now to review in greater detail his developing thoughts on anxiety, because no other single dynamic is more relevant to psychopathology. Misunderstandings abound concerning anxiety partly because Freud—as with his attempts to explain the origins of neurosis—began his speculations with a biological emphasis and then gradually modified this to a more psychological explanation in which anxiety plays merely an instrumental role.

Freud's first theory of anxiety was based on a daring analogy between the similarities in bodily responses during an acute anxiety attack and those to be seen during sexual intercourse (palpitation, heavy breathing, etc.). This theory was advanced around 1894 as an offshoot of his coitus interruptus theory mentioned earlier in this chapter. The libido theory had not yet been formulated. Freud described anxiety as a physical-release mechanism, in which the individual uses primarily the breathing apparatus of the body to rid the self of physical stimuli that cannot themselves be worked over mentally. By "working over mentally" Freud meant a kind of releasing à la the constancy principle, or what he was then calling the principle of neuronic inertia, in which a mounting energy dissipates itself by being carried throughout the nervous system and, by extension, throughout the mind.

For example, if because of her prudish attitudes a woman cannot gain full sexual release in copulation, then there will be a mounting sexual tension generated in her physical (bodily) apparatus. She will be experiencing *biological emotions* that she is *psychologically* unprepared to accept. Were she able to accept the meanings involved in sexual intercourse, then even if her climax in sexual release were not always attained, she could at least take some satisfaction in the foreplay and the mental understanding of what such romantic displays from her lover signify in their relationship. She could *work over* the experience mentally and thereby allow the sexual energy—viewed now more as physical than mental energy—to be dissipated.

But she cannot mentally confront the meanings of sex, and since she also cannot gain release in the sexual act, there is no place for the rising sexual tension—the physical *emotion* of sex in her bodily apparatus—to go. In such a case, an anxiety neurosis is likely to show itself in this woman's behavior (the fixation point would probably be the phallic, reflecting poor Oedipal conflict resolution). As Freud (1892-99/1966c) put it, "*Anxiety* has arisen by *transformation* out of accumulated sexual tension" (p. 191). Thus, in an anxiety attack, this neurotic woman would show the clinical appearance of sexual intercourse— heavy breathing, shortness of breath, heart palpitation—because she is draining off her physical sexual tension through a common autonomic nervous system pathway in the body (ibid., pp. 192-193). It is all due to a kind of short circuiting, in which a *physical* sexual tension is released through a *physical* display of anxiety!

An indirect release is therefore attained solely at a physical level without any intervention of mind at all. Freud said very clearly that, whereas hysterics convert a psychical excitation (e.g., fellatio fantasy) into a physical symptom (a cough or sore throat), anxiety neurotics convert one physical excitation (sexual emotion) into another physical manifestation (an anxiety attack) (ibid., p. 193). Of course, we are referring now to anxiety in the actual neurosis. It is also possible to suffer anxiety hysteria (psychoneurosis proper); in this case the patient would be said to transform or, as Freud later referred to this process, *convert* a strictly mental excitation (cathected libido) into a physical manifestation (symptom) along the lines of the compromise model.

It was this latter use of anxiety that Freud turned to and began using exclusively. He dropped the solely physical interpretation of anxiety as a short circuiting within the autonomic nervous system after about three years, and then for the next thirty years referred to anxiety simply as *transformed libido* (ibid., p. 257). Freud was thinking here in terms of the compromise/conversion model (mentioned above). A person represses libidinal cathexes made by the id via anticathexes put up by the ego-superego, and then in time this combined libido is reflective of a compromise worked out among the three parties. In a manner of speaking, the id presents a fuero claim (thesis), the superego demands that it be disregarded (antithesis), and the ego represents the spirit of good sense to strike a compromise that might satisfy *both* id and superego to some extent (synthesis). The clinical manifestation of this compromise is a symptom of some sort, or possibly a dream (Freud, 1906/1959a, pp. 60-61). Framed now in libido terms, this would mean that the combined libido of id, superego, and ego is transformed or converted into the symptom picture or dream theme.

This second theory of anxiety as transformed libido presented a few theoretical problems, which Freud eventually had to deal with. First of all, it was difficult to explain the type of *traumatic neurosis* (sometimes called *shell shock*) that developed in many soldiers following World War I as being due supposedly to transformed libido (Freud, 1919/1955j, p. 210). Such veterans often had repetitive nightmares regarding the battlefield from which they awakened in a state of absolute panic. The construct of repetition compulsion (see Chapter 4, p. 120) as a need to repeat a traumatic situation out of the past as part of the striving to master it seemed a more accurate description of what took place in these war neuroses than did an explanation based on libidinal factors alone.

Second, and more important, a theoretical conflict arose because of the tendency to substitute anxiety for libido in explanations of behavior. Freud had a number of colleagues—of whom Otto Rank (1968) was the foremost example—who seemed too ready to consider anxiety the prime motivator of the personality. Recall from Chapter 4 (p. 125) that Freud was always clear on the distinction between libido—a psychic energy—and emotion. Emotions were physical discharges of physical energy, the end state of a process which began mentally in the expenditure of psychic energy (libido). Hence, emotions were more "effects" than "causes" of the dynamics of personality in psychoanalysis. The person can, of course, recall mentally the circumstances surrounding past emotional experiences, and these memories—even unconscious memories— can enter into the dynamics of behavior. But, strictly speaking, it is the *idea* in memory that motivates the person today and *not* the emotion per se (see our discussion of this motivational process in Chapter 4, p. 127).

In order to clear up such theoretical problems, in 1925, some thirty-odd years after proposing his first (entirely physical) theory of anxiety to Fliess in their correspondence, Freud (1926/1959g) settled on a more general definition of *anxiety* as simply "a reaction to a situation of danger" (p. 128). Anxiety symptoms occurring at the third stage of the compromise model are the means whereby the individual can avoid facing up to the return of the repressed. The prudish woman has her Oedipal memories wound into sexual intercourse with a lover, and by having attacks of anxiety each time she contemplates anything sexual she can defend against the haunting memory of an earlier time when such lustful preoccupations were fixed upon her father. In this reformulated theory, anxiety, rather than being a major motivator, is a mere *signal* or *instrumentality* of the real danger to the integrity of the personality—the repressed memories of past fantasies!

It was in this context that Freud (ibid.) referred to the *self-inflicted* use of anxiety by the unconscious portions of the ego against the conscious portions: "The ego subjects itself to anxiety as a sort of inoculation, submitting to a slight attack of the illness in order to escape its full strength. It vividly imagines the danger-situation, as it were, with the unmistakable purpose of restricting that distressing experience to a mere indication, a signal" (p. 162). In speaking of the ego subjecting itself to anxiety, Freud meant that the unconscious portion of the ego, which knows what the "danger-situation" is, submits its conscious portion to anxiety, thereby offsetting a complete confrontation of the Oedipal themes that are bringing on the danger.

Thus, as we have already noted in Chapter 4 (p. 126), in his final theory Freud spoke of three forms of anxiety paralleling what he had earlier called the "three tyrannical masters" of the ego, namely "the external world, the super-ego, and the id" (Freud, 1932-36/1964b, p. 77). But all three of these sources of anxiety functioned identically—that is, to signal the ego of an impending situation of danger (Freud, 1926/1959g, p. 144). Freud did not always draw a hard and fast distinction between anxiety and fear. The convention today is to suggest that people are anxious when their worry is uncertain or unclear, but fearful when the point of the worry is clear. A woman may be anxious about going to the dentist because she may have a cavity or may not, but once the diagnosis is made and the dentist prepares to drill her infected tooth, she becomes fearful. Freud's first form of anxiety probably always touches on the emotion of fear at some point. He called this *realistic* anxiety, because it points to a factual challenge in the external world (the first of the three tyrannical masters). Realistic anxiety is experienced by a young man who knows that he is to go into battle tomorrow; he is safe for the night, but what of tomorrow? It is this kind of fear that many of the traumatic neurotics (shell-shocked) have, for any of a number of reasons, failed to master. Freud said that the very first (prototypical) form of this anxiety occurs at birth, which is the first traumatic situation we all face (ibid., p. 93). Simply growing up and taking leave of one's parents can also be seen as involving realistic anxieties in living (ibid., p. 130).

The second form of anxiety is the type that issues from the compromise model, and it was termed *neurotic* anxiety. If a maturing girl had an inadequately resolved Oedipus complex, then the id wishes (fueros) that have not been properly defended against (repressed, sublimated, react formated, etc.)

would threaten to return to consciousness following her puberty. The thought "I wish mother were dead" might come dangerously close to conscious aware-ness, and thanks to the compromise worked out, instead of actually thinking this thought she would experience a recurring sense of dreaded anxiety, cul-minating possibly in a fainting spell. As a result, we find her in the teenage years completely preoccupied with her fainting spells (conversion) and no longer in danger of confronting what these spells signify or symbolize.

Freud termed the final type of anxiety *moral,* tying it to the superego of the personality. Recall from our discussion of the Oedipus complex (Chapter 3, p. 71) that in the ideal case the superego should be formed out of fear. In the father's castration threat to the son, there is a form of anxiety that serves as the initial pattern (prototype) of the conscience the boy later forms. Freud said that castration anxiety develops into moral or *social anxiety* (ibid., p. 139). Hence, all of the moralistic teachings that are introjected by the child in framing the superego (the heir of the Oedipus complex!) can later serve as grounds for calling down the ego as acting sinfully (Freud, 1932-36/1964b, p. 62). This is actually what is meant by *guilt;* as Freud (1929/1961i) put it, "The sense of guilt is at bottom nothing else but a topographical variety of anxiety; in its later phases it coincides completely with *fear of the super-ego*" (p. 135). Note here again that it is the ego that is always made to feel moral anxiety or its derivative, guilt. The id and the superego are often extreme in their demands because they do not have to suffer these biologically based feelings—feelings that are intentionally stimulated by and suffered by the compromising ego under its three harsh masters.

## Dreams and Dreaming

The final topic we shall consider in Chapter 5 is extremely important to an understanding of Freudian dynamics. It was in the act of dreaming that Freud was to learn most of what he came to teach us about human nature. He always considered *The Interpretation of Dreams* (Freud, 1900/1953a, 1900-01/1953b) his finest psychoanalytical publication. Freud once said that he based the entire science of psychoanalysis on the cornerstone of dream interpretation (Freud, 1913/1955e, p. 170). As totally mental phenomena, dreams express a meaning, they say something, and though we think we do not know what their content is getting at, in the unconscious regions of mind *we know full well* (Freud, 1915-16/1963a, p. 101). Dreams have a *manifest* (apparent, evident, overt) content or story line that often appears foreign and even odd to us because we do not understand its meaning. For example, one might dream that one is walking upside down on the ceiling and that one's hair is falling out but is moving upward to the ceiling instead of dropping to the floor below. Each of these dream concepts would be taken as a potential content for hidden meaning.

Freud's technique of dream analysis was aimed at translating this manifest content into what he called the *latent* (hidden, potential, covert) content, which gets at the real meaning of the dream (Freud, 1900/1953a, p. 135). We can use the compromise model to understand this dynamic, because the latent content is what gets converted (or transformed) into the manifest content. At this point it would be helpful if we present and partially analyze a nonsensical manifest dream reported during therapy by an intelligent patient.

*The patient.* A thirty-four-year-old married businessman had been in analytic treatment for about a year when he reported the dream that follows. He was suffering from a personality disorder, with chronic dissatisfaction over his work, diffidence in social contacts, and timidity in the presence of women other than his wife. He had three children. His own personal history was not remarkable, except that his mother had always dominated the home, while his father was passive and shy. The patient had only one sibling, an older sister. She and his mother had always seemed strong and self-assured; they had treated him and his father as though they were of no importance.

*The manifest dream.* There were two very large naked women in a forest, half-turned away from him. They looked like Greek goddesses in a Renaissance painting. One of them gave him a bow and arrow to shoot her with. It seemed she had done something of the kind herself before. She was confident and contemptuous. He seemed to have shot at her and missed, although he could not remember this happening in the dream. One of the women had disappeared, but the one who had given him the bow and arrow said something about making herself so big that he could not miss. She swooped past him and he shot her in the abdomen with an arrow or a javelin. She had not turned toward him, and he could not recall actually doing this, but somehow he knew he had. Then there was a man facing him at a distance, partly doubled up ("like a martyr") and moving sideways, with a javelin in his mid-abdomen and blood flowing from the wound. It seemed that a woman had done it to him. The man clawed at what looked like a windowsill, as high as the patient's head, leaving blood marks followed by a message in the wood of the sill, in the form of dots and dashes.

The patient felt guilty about the man's death (although the dying appeared in the dream as something that had already happened). He became furtive and watchful. He went around trying to wipe the blood from things, but without success. Then he was in a mixed group and a woman was offering drinks. He asked for milk because that would make him seem incapable of killing someone.

Then he was in a house with the widow of the killed man, and he felt uncomfortable about her husband's death. But now it seemed that it was her son who had been killed, and she was a widow, with only a daughter left. The patient's guilt disappeared. The son who had been killed seemed to be himself. There was now a "sort of architect" present who knew all about the widow's house and seemed to have built it. This man said, "Isn't it beautiful" and asked if the patient had seen the barn. The patient said he hadn't, and at that moment he was back in the widow's house squeezing through a narrow passage toward a disarranged kitchen. He awoke with palpitation and colicky pain.

*Some of the patient's associations.* A manifest dream as long as this and as complex cannot be thoroughly explored in forty minutes, or even in as many hours. There are a few signs of childhood remembrances which the patient did not himself contribute. These were the enormous size of the women—as adults appear to little children—their being naked, the childish bow and arrow, the patient's being the only person to get milk from a woman, and his finding the windowsill at the level of his head. His own associations follow.

Both of the women seemed to be his mother. If so, this would illustrate a characteristic of primary process thinking—to emphasize a point by *duplicating* it. His mother had always treated him with good-natured condescension, as though she and his sister were superior beings. He had owned a bow and some rubber-tipped arrows in childhood, and had gotten into trouble for shooting at other children. He felt "there was something sexy in the atmosphere" of the dream.

Because of the abdominal pain, he felt that the house which the "sort of architect" seemed to have built was his own body, and that the architect was his father, who, in the dream, seemed to know all about it. (The architect might also have been himself, although he did not say so, because he was meticulous about his appearance and vain.) The disarranged kitchen made him think of menstruation and his mother again, or perhaps, he said, his sister. His sister had worked in a telegraph office.

The theme of being alone in the house with the widow of a man he had killed needed little translation. This woman also seemed to be his mother, and she had a son and a daughter, as his mother had. The victim seemed to be the patient's father, and since the guilt faded to mere sympathy as soon as the son seemed to have been killed, it must have been the patient who killed the father, or at least wished him dead. There is primary process maneuvering here. The primary process cannot express negation, and it can tolerate dialectical contradictions. It was a woman who killed the man, and therefore it was not the patient, even though it was he who a moment earlier had held the arrow or a javelin. Furthermore, even though the widow's son—who the patient felt was himself—had been killed and the widow was left with a daughter, it was he himself who was left with the widow in the dream.

Later therapeutic work with this patient threw more light on the primary process displacement and condensation in the dream. To *condense* is to press several different concerns or several different people into one dream image; to *displace* is to remove the resultant combination into a seemingly unrelated activity or an irrelevant social context (Freud, 1900/1953a, p. 279). This patient had envied his sister in childhood because she seemed self-assured and because she was openly preferred by their mother. Toward the end of this dream, "the widow with only a daughter left" meant what it depicted: his mother widowed and left alone with him in the preferred position that his sister always had. The wounded, dying man seems also to have represented his sister (dialectically defined in the dream image), since she was the only person he knew who could make messages in dots and dashes with her "claws" (telegraphy).

A further reference came out still later in therapy. The patient had a repressed childhood belief, still unresolved, that birth took place through a "cut in the abdomen," or through the umbilicus, he was not sure which. He retained this belief in spite of knowing the facts about childbirth. This retention of two contradictory interpretations, without either affecting the other, is another characteristic of the dialectical nature of primary process thinking. Here we see a common childhood fantasy coexisting with adult knowledge, as though both were components of the primary process and had once been part of an original ideation framed by the infantile (id) psychic reasoning process.

There is also confusion of sex role in the manifest dream. A huge arrogant naked woman gives the dreaming patient the means for shooting her in the abdomen, as if he were Dan Cupid himself. It is somehow implied in the dream that she has done something like the shooting herself. Then she swoops near him avowedly to make a target of herself that he cannot miss, since it is implied that he has previously missed. Yet what next appears in the manifest dream is a dying *man* with a bleeding wound where the patient's childhood fantasy placed childbirth. The primary process confusion is compounded by the patient's sex identity confusion, of which, up to the time of the dream, he seemed not to have been aware.

The confusions multiply. The man dying of a javelin wound was killed by a woman, but it is the patient who is furtive and guilty. The guilt disappears as soon as it seems to be not the husband but the son who has been killed. Yet the patient felt that he was the son; and in contradiction to all this, the dream leaves the woman a widow (in reality no one in the family had died), and cancels out the death wish expressed against the father by a death wish against the son. But as only the primary process can do, it allows the original fantasy of possessing the mother alone to triumph, at least until the "architect" appears. Nothing more childish can be imagined than this dream solution of the Oedipal conflict, or than its representation of the inverted Oedipus complex at the same time—for the dying man seems to have represented the patient himself, as well as his sister and his father.

Nothing so far has been said about the symbolism in the dream. A stable translation, one that invariably means the same thing no matter who dreams it, is what Freud (1915-16/1963a, p. 150) meant by a *symbol*. Thus, in general, elongated objects are taken to be masculine (penis symbols) and enclosed objects are likely to be more feminine (vaginal or uterine symbols). The bow and arrow of the present dream has been used for millennia as a symbol of sexual love (cathecting an image as well as actual penetration of intercourse). The javelin is an obvious phallic symbol. A bleeding wound of the kind depicted by the patient usually means the female genitalia. The house could be a woman's womb, or as is suggested in the present instance, it could signify the integrity of the patient's own body (with father as "sort of" architect).

We might wonder where a patient like this gets the initial ideas to prompt a dream creation on any one night. Do these ideas pop up from the unconscious, or are they related to the ongoing life experience? Actually, both aspects of psychic experience are involved. A dream is put together by the unconscious mind from *day residues,* which are scraps and pieces of experience during the sleep day (i.e., the day before the night of the dream) on which we have probably not fixed our conscious attention though we can usually recall these items if we try (Freud, 1900/1953a, p. 228). Our patient may have seen from out of the corner of his eye on the sleep day a child playing with a bow and arrow or a fleeting exposure of a Renaissance painting in a book through which he was rapidly paging to find a certain passage. It does not take much.

The dream is prompted by a wish fulfillment, but we must keep in mind that this can be a lustful wish of the id, or it can be the self-punishing wish of the superego. We must not make the error of assuming that by claiming every dream is a wish fulfillment Freud necessarily referred to a pleasurable outcome (Freud, 1932-36/1964b, p. 27). Freud relented on the early idea he entertained that all dreams have to have a sexual content, but his wish-fulfillment construct was retained to the end. We regularly see the wishes of the superego represented in a dream, a fine example of which now follows:

A patient near the beginning of her analysis expressed anxiety concerning what might be brought to light. That night she had the following manifest dream:

She was with her analyst in a deep hole dug in the ground. Somebody had a spade and they had just struck an iron lid that was covering what lay beneath. Then there was a woman up above, on the edge of the hole, all dressed in white (purity?). She was pointing upward and calling down a warning not to dig any further. The patient felt uneasy when she awoke.

The patient's associations showed that the dream had more than one meaning for her (condensation). What mystified her most was the fact that the woman in white, who called down the warning, seemed to be herself, even though she was somehow also involved in digging at the bottom of the hole. She also felt when she awoke that there was something very dangerous under the iron lid, which she described as like the hinged doors that covered the farmhouse cellar in the house where she was born. To her analyst the woman in white seemed to represent her superego, which was more aware of what further digging might release, especially if the iron lid of her defenses were to be forcibly raised. It was some time before she was able to reduce her anxiety sufficiently to go deeper with her analysis. The superego wish was not easily overcome.

In this dream the superego plays a defensive role, trying to protect the self-deluding image of the personality that "all is well enough" and hence exploration into the past is not called for. Do not raise that iron lid! But in some cases the superego wish is more punitive than anything else. Dreams in which the person suffers through a terrifying experience are often prompted by superego demands that the person *suffer* for some misdeed. It is also true that sometimes this punishment is brought to bear following a period of dreaming in which the person is allowed to express sexual lust or murderous hostility. Thus, following a visualization in which the male patient above may have actually fantasied sexual copulation with his mother, he could have punished himself by being struck by the arrow—which is the only portion of the Oedipal theme recalled. The compromise struck is for the id to be gratified, but then a superego wish for punishment in the form of injury must also be effected.

The creation of a theme encompassing such wish fulfillments is what Freud referred to as *dream work*. We do not dream in ideas (words, sentences), but in images, so that dreaming is like "thinking in pictures." Freud (1900/1953a) put it well when he observed that "a dream is a picture-puzzle" (p. 278). Dreaming also bears a psychological tie to the process of hallucination in psychosis (Freud, 1915-16/1963a, p. 129). In fact, Freud (1938/1964f) was to say that "a dream . . . is a psychosis, with all the absurdities, delusions, and illusions of a psychosis" (p. 172). Thanks to the dialectical logic of primary process thinking, in which condensations occur with regularity, it is possible for *one* dream to express *several* (even contradictory) themes at once. Freud referred to this as *overdetermination,* because any one wish or intention could have accounted for the dream by itself, but now we find more (psychically) determining promptings than are really necessary (Breuer & Freud, 1955, p. 263). It is for this reason that dreams so readily suggest more than just one interpretation. The truth is, more than one latent meaning may be involved in any single manifest dream content (Freud, 1925/1961e, p. 130). We shall return to the interpretation of dreams when we take up the practice of Freudian psycho-analysis in Chapter 19.

## Summary

Chapter 5 crystallizes a number of themes relating to the dynamic view of personality that the text is based upon. The first theme deals with the distinct-ion between conscious and unconscious behavior. It is stressed that "out of consciousness" is *not* "out of mind." Behavioristic explanations of behavior stress the supposed mechanical or automatic—that is, materially and efficiently caused—nature of behavior. However, recent research has demonstrated that there is more to conditioning than meets the unsophisticated eye. If we ask subjects in conditioning experiments what is taking place, we soon learn that *only* when a subject in an operant conditioning experiment knows the relation-ship between his or her "emitted" response and the contingent reinforcer to follow, *and* when he or she conforms to what is expected or implied in this cue, does "conditioning" occur. Similarly, in a classical conditioning format, *only* those subjects who know the relationship between the conditioned and uncon-ditioned stimuli, *and* who thereby comply with what is suggested, find them-selves being "conditioned."

The fact of the matter is that a subject's *awareness* and *voluntary com-pliance* are crucial aspects of so-called automatic (i.e., nontelic) conditioning. Ninety percent of the empirical studies addressing this issue have supported this conclusion. It is highly likely that the experimental subject in a condition-ing experiment is more of an agent in the process of "manipulation" or "shaping" than the theories underwriting these experiments would suggest. This essentially teleological summation of the research evidence is in line with the thinking of Freud on human behavior. That is, it is essential in psycho-analytical explanations that awareness and volition *not* be thought of as limited to consciousness. We shall return to this point in Chapter 21.

To facilitate understanding of "awareness" on the one hand and "conscious versus unconscious" on the other, Chapter 5 discusses the concept of *deter-minism* in light of the four causes. To determine is to limit the range of alternatives regarding anything. But it is possible to think of material-, efficient-, formal-, and final-cause determinisms in events. *Psychic determinism,* which is the sort of determinism that Freud employed to account for behavior, is clearly on the side of a formal- and final-cause account. Thanks to our dialectical reasoning capacity we human beings can transcend the dictates of "reality" and set a course based upon purely internal intentions. Freud was a *hard deter-minist* in the psychic sphere, but this is underwritten by the formal- and final-cause meaning of determinism. Behaviorists are entirely dependent upon material- and efficient-cause determination to account for behavior. As such, they are hard determinists in the physical sphere who base little or none of their explanations on the psychic sphere. Indeed, to be "psychic" means to behave for the sake of intentions, wishes, purposes, and the like.

Thus, in psychoanalysis it is not a contradiction in terms to speak of both *unconscious* and *conscious awareness*. The latter has a narrower scope. In a true sense, awareness in psychoanalysis refers to the degree of self-admission or self-revelation that a person is prepared to live with. Repressive maneuvers continually act against admitting certain unacceptable wishes and impulses. Psychoanalysis helps us understand what these unadmitted contents are and how they might be dealt with to the person's advantage. Recent work on hypnotism has found a *hidden observer* taking note of the entire procedure and actually experiencing the pain that was never felt by the primary identity of the hypnotized subject. This "feeling and not feeling" at the same time is a beautiful reflection of the dialectical style of explanation used by Freud to describe how people both know and do not know something at the same time.

The next intrapsychic dynamic discussed in Chapter 5 is *fixation* and *regression*. These constructs are also considered defense mechanisms (see Chapter 4). The explanation of fixation, or a halting in development, is usually framed in terms of the libido theory—that is, as a psychic trapping or pocketing of an amount of libido during any given stage of psychosexual development. But even before he had elaborated on the libido theory, Freud drew an analogy to the ancient Spanish practice of offering *fueros* or special considerations to certain provinces for services rendered. A *psychic fuero* would thus be a claim made on the personality because of past concessions made to progress to higher levels even though there was no desire to do so, and so on. The concept of *regression* encompasses the *repetition-compulsion* idea of Freud's changing instinct theories (see Chapter 4), because a fuero claim or fixated pocket of libido is in effect seeking to bring the personality system "back" to an earlier time in which a frustration and primal repression took place. Regression is therefore a return to an earlier stage of development to rectify a previous fixation or partial fixation. Freud distinguished between *topographical, temporal,* and *formal* regression. Temporal regression is the most serious form of defensive maneuver, because the entire personality becomes infantile.

If we now put all of our dynamics together we can define *personality* in the Freudian vein as the working out of conflicts among the id, superego, and ego, involving the repressions, sublimations, and reaction-formations of instinctual pressures on the personality with the resultant compromises that can be worked out across the topographical and depth levels of mind. A *three-stage compromise* model of psychopathology is next presented, based upon Freud's developing thoughts on this question. His early theories of *coitus interruptus* and *seduction* (childhood molestation) were eventually modified into the three-stage model. The initial attempts he made to describe neurosis on the basis of a *physical noxa* evolved into the *actual neuroses* (i.e., nondynamic abnormalities). In the *psychoneuroses proper* (i.e., dynamic abnormalities) we expect to find the three-stage compromises taking place.

The first stage of the compromise model occurs during the pregenital level of development, in resolving the Oedipal conflict and the *primal repression* flowing from this effort. If this resolution is not satsifactory, following pubescence, in which a new wave of libido is brought about, the second stage of the *"return of the repressed memories"* occurs. There are always two sides to any repression—a wish to attain some cathected object and a wish *not* to attain this object. Due to this ambivalence the third stage is accomplished, in which a *compromise* is struck between id, ego, and superego. The resultant *symptom* of neurosis is thus always dual in meaning, representing both the wishes of the repressed contents (id) and the wishes of the repressing contents (ego and superego). Freud called the process of compromise and deflection of a psychic conflict into what is often a physical manifestation a *conversion*. Freud's theory of mental illness is a quantitative rather than a qualitative one. Neurotics have a *flight into illness* without intentionally seeking to change reality. Psychotics try to change reality, distorting it in their delusions and hallucinations to meet what they wish to believe.

Chapter 5 next discusses Freud's changing views on anxiety. His first theory had anxiety a kind of physical short circuiting in which accumulated sexual tension was transformed into anxiety release. Later he referred to anxiety as *transformed libido*. In his final formulation, anxiety was viewed as a "reaction to a situation of danger" that can have *realistic, neurotic,* or *moral* aspects (see Chapter 4 on this point). Moral anxiety can be termed *social anxiety,* for it is based on religious or ethical instruction, and this sense of fear for violating sociocultural tenets results in what we call *guilt.* Guilt is tantamount to a fear of the superego.

The final intrapsychic dynamic considered in Chapter 5 is dreaming. Dreams have a *manifest* and a *latent* content, with the former masking the latter meaning. Dreams can *condense* several meanings or images into one content. They can also *displace* the content of a dream from one area of life to another. Dreams are always wish fulfillments, but this does not mean they are always pleasant. We must recall that the superego has wishes to fulfill as well, and that in this case there can be punishing dreams, reflective of a sense of guilt over id promptings. Dreams, like neurotic symptoms, always have the repressing and repressed mental contents wound into their manifestation. Dreams are concocted from *day residues,* which are scraps and pieces of experience during the day before the night of the dream. Freud referred to the creation of a dream sequence as the *dream work*—work which includes *condensation* and *displacement*. It is also possible for one dream to express several (even contradictory) meanings at once. This capacity to write several meanings into the same dream scenario is called *overdetermination*.

# 6

# *Anxiety Disorders*

We have now completed our review of the personality system as framed in Freudian psychoanalysis, including at points those like Horney and Erikson who have enlarged upon the traditional viewpoint to some extent. We have also reviewed the course of personality development and presented evidence from researches on human beings that generally support the telic view of behavior that we have seen Freud's biological naturalism encompassing. Beginning with Chapter 6 and running through to Chapter 18 we shall survey the major syndromes of psychopathology in light of our dynamic approach, relying upon actual case histories to bring the material to life. Chapters 6 through 18 are titled in compliance with the terminology of the *Diagnostic and Statistical Manual,* Third Edition (DSM-III). However, in keeping with the more traditional language that Freud and psychoanalysts since his time have continued to use, we shall not avoid use of the term *neurosis* as is true of DSM-III (see our discussion of neurosis versus psychosis in Chapter 1, pp. 16-17).

It is not our intention to present a manual of diagnosis in surveying the syndromes of psychopathology. We are trying to provide the reader with a theoretical understanding of the dynamic patterns that underlie such clinical manifestations. But as it seems advisable for didactic purposes to relate our presentation to the current thinking in psychiatric diagnosis, we will make every effort to present the "DSM-III Viewpoint" in separate paragraphs headed by this title, or simply in a sentence or two during our regular discussion. Chapter 6 picks up where Chapter 5 ended, taking us into the anxiety disorders one is likely to find in clinical practice. Chapter 7 continues the anxiety disorders with a consideration of the obsessive-compulsive syndrome, a diagnosis that used to be listed separately but is now combined with psychopathological anxiety manifestations.

As might be suspected from Freud's three-stage compromise model (see Chapter 5, p. 154), anxiety plays a leading role in every neurosis; but we reserve the term *anxiety disorder* for those cases in which diffuse emotional tension and free anxiety clearly dominate the clinical picture, while other symptoms are merely incidental. To suffer from an anxiety reaction is to feel continually apprehensive and to have no idea what the danger is or from where it comes. Most of the *symptoms* in anxiety reactions represent the patient's efforts to rid himself or herself of excessive tension by direct discharge, in voluntary (skeletal) muscle action or in autonomic activity. The rest of the symptoms reflect the disturbing effects that the tension has upon ego function (sometimes called *secondary anxiety*). Here are four brief clinical examples that will serve as an introduction:

A young man complained of feeling that something terrible was about to happen to him. For several months he had been continually fatigued. He had had pains in his head, his back, and his legs. He suffered from frequent nightmares. Every once in a while he had sudden attacks of cardiac palpitation, in which he thought he was dying. During the course of psychotherapy it soon came out that he hated working for his aggressive, domineering father, but that he felt too afraid and too guilty to face up to the situation and quit his job. When psychotherapy brought this state of affairs out, the young man was soon able to face his father with the fact that he wanted another job and was determined to look for it. It goes without saying that the situation was complicated; but the psychotherapeutic help removed the young man from it, and his anxiety reactions disappeared.

A young woman whose fiancé had postponed their wedding for the third time began having bad dreams from which she would awaken frightened and sometimes crying. During the day she felt tense, angry, and preoccupied. Her hands and feet became chronically cold and clammy. She developed a noticeable tremor in her fingers. Her menstrual periods became irregular. When, with the aid of psychotherapy, she recognized that her fiancé was afraid of marrying her for his own personal reasons, she was able to handle the situation successfully.

A middle-aged businessman whose profit margins were progressively narrowing found himself under pressure to work harder and harder and to take on more and more responsibility. He grew short-tempered with his family and with his employees. At times he felt as though he would "explode." He found that he could not enjoy recreation. He could not even relax after work. Sometimes he felt that he wavered unsteadily as he walked. He had attacks of dizziness, especially at the telephone, and he could not seem to concentrate or to think clearly. At times he felt as though a "steel band" were compressing his head. He slept poorly, lost his appetite, and became relatively impotent. It was interesting that he had never related these symptoms to the increase of responsibility or to his own deep dependency needs. Psychotherapy helped him to make these connections himself, without interpretations by the therapist.

A married woman whose life was complicated by her mother's living in the home complained that she felt tense and irritable most of the time. She was apprehensive lest something happen to her mother, her husband, her children, or herself. She had no definite idea what it was that she feared might happen. She suffered from occasional attacks in which her heart pounded and was irregular and she could not seem to get her breath. Often she broke out in a profuse perspiration. Her mouth always seemed dry, even though she drank a great deal of water, and because of this and her diffuse anxiety, she had micturition.

All four of these individuals believed themselves to be the victims of some organic disease, so gripping was their physiological reaction in the anxious state. It is hard to believe that a purely psychological problem could bring on such dramatic physical discomfort. Yet all four made good recoveries through insights gained from psychotherapy. They had not suffered from realistic or even moral anxiety (see Chapter 5, p. 161). They had suffered through a period of neurotic anxiety.

## Neurotic Anxiety

A certain amount of emotional tension and anxiety can serve useful functions. The moderately anxious person makes a vigilant, attentive watcher who is alert to relatively slight stimulation and prepared for prompt and vigorous action. Moderate anxiety often increases the pleasures of anticipation. It is a common source of laughter and a common ingredient of many forms of entertainment. Even intense anxiety can be helpful when it increases one's strength, speed, courage, and endurance in an emergency (*realistic anxiety*). In such situations it is important for the person to feel competent enough to cope with the emergency, in which case effective behavior can be sustained even under rather high levels of anxiety (Lazarus & Launier, 1979; Seligman, 1975).

However, the advantages of moderate anxiety disappear when emotional tension grows too great, lasts too long, or underlies much of one's behavior. At such points we begin to suspect the deterioration of efforts to repress something that needs to be confronted before relief will be forthcoming. This is when we begin thinking of *neurotic anxiety* in a person's behavior. The point is finally reached at which tension and anxiety so narrow a person's focus of concern that even routine matters put him or her under tremendous strain. Almost anything in a daily routine can arouse the person's anxiety (D. H. Kelly & Walters, 1968). Sometimes a clinical picture of neurotic anxiety begins with prolonged or acutely experienced realistic anxiety, as in the *post-traumatic stress disorders* (formerly "traumatic neuroses") of excombat soldiers or civilians who have lived through terrifying disasters such as a tornado or airline crash (Grinker & Spiegel, 1945a; Janis, 1958). In such cases, anxiety persists following the traumatic situation with or without a neurotic factor complicating the clinical picture (R. May, 1950; Zetzel, 1955). In the present context, we are primarily concerned with those persons who are experiencing the imminent threat of an upsurge of unconscious impulses and conflicts.

We might define *anxiety* as experienced by the person as follows: *a state of apprehension, without an apparent object, in which attempts are made to discharge internally generated tension and to reduce physiological discomfort through increased bodily activity.* Anxiety, like all emotion, is on the side of a biological discharge, experienced as feeling tones of a decidedly negative sort. The person's skeletal muscles are characteristically tense and his or her autonomic nervous system is overactive. Habitual rhythms of living, including the physiological functioning of bodily viscera, may be seriously disturbed. The anxious individual is predisposed to give exaggerated and inappropriate responses upon slight provocation.

Of course, not everyone is incapacitated by anxiety. Researchers have demonstrated that there are those who live under what is tantamount to a *trait* of anxiety-laden activity, which contrasts with a transitory *state* of increased tension and apprehension (Spielberger, 1972). Freud's realistic anxiety would probably come under the rubric of a state anxiety, for it referred to a provoking situation in the person's life that called for an adaptation of some sort to meet and remove it. Neurotic and moral anxiety would probably be on the side of a trait anxiety. And as we have suggested, some people get along remarkably well even though they suffer through a life of fluctuating levels of moderately high to high anxiety. Some of these individuals succeed in discharging tensions through continual overactivity in everything they do. Among these are many of the indefatigable workers, tireless enthusiasts, unofficial vigilantes, and high-strung critics of daily life. These persons are not so much led to action as *driven* to action, driven by an urgent need to master their own anxiety. It is when such devices fail, or when circumstances push tension up to unmanageable levels, that these basically pathologically anxious persons seek help, though usually what they seek is only help to combat their *symptoms*. Many of these types are candidates for drug abuse.

## Generalized Anxiety Disorder (Anxiety Neurosis)

This is by far the most common form of anxiety neurosis the practicing clinician is likely to encounter. The patient with a *generalized anxiety disorder* suffers from an unstructured fear, so that he or she cannot point to what is bringing on the chronic anxiety. The DSM-III suggests that this state of anxiety be sensed by the person for over one month. It is not uncommon for the person to say that he or she is "waiting for something terrible to happen." Signs of fatigue are beginning to surface, as the person makes the continual effort to get rid of tensions and tremors that persist no matter what is attempted. Alcoholic and related drug indulgences complicate the picture in many instances.

A man complains openly of his tension, of feeling strained, apprehensive, and fatigued. He cannot relax. Almost any unexpected stimulation startles him—the doorbell and the telephone, the noise of an auto horn or something dropped, someone suddenly speaking to him or entering the room unnoticed. He may approach every new task, every little crisis or decision, with misgivings—a minor change in work, the prospect of buying something, or employing or letting someone go, of having guests come, or even of going out in the evening. He may grow anxious about such trivial everyday matters as making a right turn in traffic, entering his office or factory, facing his fellow workers, and so on.

A woman suffering from a generalized anxiety disorder finds even the routine tasks of the day filled with unreasonable dread. How will breakfast go?

Will she be able to get the children off to school on time? Can she really be a mother and career person at the same time? What should she do about lunch? Are the children safe in school? Is her husband really safe on his job? Why does she insist on working? Why is she so frightened to remain at home? Can she really keep up her efficiency on her own job? How can she possibly do the housekeeping as well?

Usually the anxious person *looks* and *acts* strained—in posture, gait, facial expression, movements, gestures, and the way in which he or she talks. Such muscular signs of tension are supplemented with complaints of headache, of a tight sensation around the head, and of aching in the neck, back, and legs. There are often tremors in the fingers, tongue, eyelids, and sometimes the lips of chronically anxious patients. They find it hard to think clearly, and they are too restless and on edge to stick to any one activity long. They may start reading something and then give up halfway through it. They may switch channels on the television nervously, unable to take an interest in any one show. Poor recall, inability to concentrate, and unclear thinking are common direct effects of any excessive tension and anxiety, even in persons who are only temporarily disturbed.

These effects are intensified further by the patient's preoccupation with internal threats and conflicts, coming from the margins of preconscious and unconscious activity, which now begin to interrupt or to invade his or her thinking. The neurotically anxious person often engages in fantasies about things feared and dreaded—past, present, and future. Sometimes a conscious daydream is so frightening that is is enough to precipitate a sudden *anxiety attack*. The anxiety attack may then be so alarming in itself that it blots out all memory of the daydream that precipitated it. The attack seems to the patient to come from nowhere and to be a sure sign that he or she has some terrible organic illness or is going insane. *Anxiety attacks are acute episodes of emotional decompensation usually appearing in a setting of chronic anxiety, and exhibiting to an exaggerated degree the characteristics of normal fright.* The fright usually comes from within, from a sudden upsurge of unconscious material that threatens to disrupt the personality's integration. The anxiety attack often climaxes a long period of mounting tension to which the anxious person has been progressively adapting, but with ever-increasing difficulty. It represents an overwhelming discharge, a sudden physical release.

Dreaming at night can become another fruitful source of frightening fantasies. Anxiety dreams and nightmares form part of a general sleep disturbance in anxiety disorders. Often a manifest dream theme, as the patient remembers it, seems to have started off well, perhaps depicting the frank fulfillment of a forbidden wish. But matters soon get out of hand. Frightening figures appear—such as the police officers who appear in real life when one is breaking the law—or there is some transformation in the manifest dream that makes the whole situation seem suddenly horrible, fearful, weird, or disgraceful. If the intensity of such developments is great enough the dreamer awakens with all the classical signs of an acute anxiety attack. Here is an example:

A male patient dreamed that he was walking through a suburb with an unknown companion. Suddenly he was alone, facing a cemetery, while people were fleeing to his right down a highway away from an atomic explosion which filled the sky. He began running, too, but he ran toward his left and into the atomic blast. He tried to yell. He awoke perspiring and acutely anxious. The situation in the dream included part of the setting of his therapist's office. In approaching it, one actually went toward a cemetary and turned off to the left. The atomic blast in the dream was a symbol representing the still unconscious dangers which the patient was running into, when he came for his therapeutic hours.

Sleep disorders are almost universal in anxiety reactions; the frightening dream is only the most dramatic complaint. Nearly all anxious patients complain that they cannot fall asleep, and when they eventually do drop off, the slightest noise awakens them. To fall asleep again may be as difficult as it was the first time, and for the same reasons—bodily tensions, fearful anticipations, fantasies, and a dread of letting go that amounts to a dread of losing control. Thus day and night the anxious person's body seems to be alerted for some danger that never materializes and never disappears.

Manifestations of this constant strain and apprehension can be found in almost any organ or system of the body (D. H. Kelly & Walters, 1968). The heart may thump, accelerate, and skip beats. Breathing is often shallow and irregular, interrupted every now and then by sighing. Appetite suffers. The anxious person may feel queasy, finding it hard to eat and to keep food down. An occasional patient experiences emptiness, and instead of losing taste for food, he or she eats voraciously. The diarrhea of fear and the constipation of tension are both common, well-known symptoms. Glands of internal and external secretion participate in the general emotional disorder. Sexual functions are almost always involved. Relative impotence in the male and menstrual irregularities and frigidity in the female are the most obvious sexual manifestations.

The social life of perpetually anxious people suffers in the same ways that their more strictly physiological and personal life does. If recreation involves highly coordinated movement, for example, the movement loses its fluid character and becomes effortful or awkward. When the anxious woman drives her car, she holds the wheel in a tight grip, she is vigilant and apprehensive, and she develops aching muscles and tired eyes during what used to be a relaxing experience. If she goes dancing, she holds her partner tightly, makes mistakes, and moves with little grace. If she plays golf she cannot swing freely or maintain a good stance; she tries too hard and is intolerant of her own bad plays. In social conversation she becomes abrupt, and either too self-assertive or too silent, with a general tendency to make irritated and disparaging comments.

In trying to avoid whatever increases their anxiety, those who suffer from this maladjustment tend to make self-protection their main concern in life, subordinating everything else to this desperate goal. This seriously impoverishes their lives by cutting them off from many avenues of self-expression, social interchange, and pleasure. Even though they may not restrict their activities and contacts as *rigidly* as those who suffer a *phobic* disorder, people with generalized anxiety disorders can develop restrictions on their activities covering so much territory that their interpersonal relationships are even more seriously curtailed. A case of anxiety disorder will illustrate the operation of many of the factors that we have been discussing.

### Case of Walter A.: Generalized Anxiety Disorder

Walter A., an American oil geologist, aged thirty-two, who had been living abroad for many years, came for diagnosis because of symptoms that he feared might mean that he was going insane. For five or six years he had been having attacks of dizziness, blurred vision, weakness, and unsteady gait. For three years he had been suffering from constant "nervous tension," irritability, fatigue, increased sex pace with incomplete satisfaction, inability to relax, poor sleep, and frequent nightmares. For a year his restlessness had grown so marked that he could scarcely stand still, sit, or lie still. He felt driven to overactivity so that he wore out everyone who worked with him and himself also. He was drinking liquor during the day, to "steady" himself, and taking barbiturates at night to sleep.

Soon he began having frequent anxiety attacks. The first came on suddenly while he was dressing to go out for the evening. Something seemed to snap in his head, everything looked unnatural, and he felt he was fainting. He lay down for a long time, his heart pounding, his breathing labored, and with the recurring thought, "I'm dying, I'm dying." Other attacks came later. They consisted of "queer head sensations," weakness, sweating, coarse tremor, palpitation, and a conviction that something terrible was happening to him. It was his fear of these attacks and of what they might mean that drove him to seek and accept help.

From the nature of the complaints, and the outcome of thorough diagnostic studies, it was clear that we were dealing with chronic anxiety of long standing. In the course of psychotherapy, in which the patient was seen three times a week for two months, a great many factors emerged to account for the development and perpetuation of his anxiety disorder. On several occasions a great deal of free anxiety appeared during therapeutic sessions in relation to confidential material. When this happened, Walter always leaned forward on the arm of the chair and performed rhythmic mouth movements that gave an immediate impression of energetic infant nursing. This maneuver, he explained spontaneously, was one that he had discovered as an emergency measure in reducing tension. Twice during therapeutic sessions he had full-blown anxiety attacks. During the first attack he became furious because the therapist did not share his alarm and call in a heart specialist.

*Discussion.* A brief life history, extracted from the initial interviews and from the therapeutic hours, will give the background of this man's illness. Walter was the youngest of five children, brought up strictly in great fear of committing sin. He was taught to search his conscience every night for "unworthy" thoughts or acts during the day, which might need forgiveness. He suffered from night terrors as a child, and remembered one in which he was being carried off to hell fire. He saw the flames of hell so clearly in this dream that it frightened him even to think of it afterward.

In his home the sinfulness of sex and the sanctity of marriage were held up as first principles. It came, therefore, as a shock when at fifteen he was told by his mother that she was divorcing his father. He remained with his mother after the separation, but he found he could forgive neither parent for the divorce. He felt that they had swindled him with their fine talk about marriage. His self-righteous mother seemed to him both a sinner and a hypocrite. He concluded that all women were untrustworthy.

After two years at home with his mother this disillusioned young man went off to college. During his first year there, he felt lonely and in continual conflict over the moral and ethical discussions that he heard there. A summer session then threw him in with rebellious adolescent companions, whose talk and conduct led him to adopt a new philosophy of life. Everything was now directed toward success and self-aggrandizement. He chose new friends, wangled a good income out of his divorced parents, bought a car, drank heavily, and enjoyed sexual relations with the young women he dated when such were possible. He behaved in a sinful fashion, according to his earlier superego demands, but was no longer willing to dwell on such negative evaluations of his behavior. At the same time, he could not help but despise himself for what he was doing; at times he hated his male friends, and he always felt contempt for the women he dated. After a year of graduate study in geology, and two more in American oil fields, he accepted a lucrative position abroad.

Walter found his new work taxing, the climate hot, the standard of living luxurious, and the social life full of intrigue. The Americans and the Europeans formed a small community in which everyone knew everyone else and saw a great deal of one another. As an unmarried man who was not without charm, he soon found himself entangled in a succession of minor affairs with the bored wives of other men. One of these affairs became serious. To escape it Walter asked for a six-month leave, but when he returned he found himself involved with the same woman. This period coincides with the increase in symptoms listed at the beginning of the case history. After three years had passed he sought professional help.

It was quite clear that Walter did not at the time see any connection between his personal difficulties and his symptoms. Psychotherapy, however, brought out multiple relationships. His simplest conflict arose from the fact that his mistress was the wife of a close friend. At first he told this with the kind of contempt that he had felt toward his "dates" in college. As he became freer to experience other emotional attitudes, his feeling changed to anger, first at his therapist and later at the woman. He now said that she had reinforced his distrust of women, pushed a normal marriage further from his grasp, and spoiled his friendship with her husband. The limitations of time and psychological understanding prevented an exploration of this triangular situation, beyond the fact that it was related to his own adolescent experiences at home. There were obvious Oedipal themes at play.

The first acute anxiety attack began a few weeks after Walter found out that others knew the details of his affair. He now had reason to fear exposure and retaliation. His basically strong sense of guilt, reinforced now by a realistic sense of anxiety, redoubled his tensions and led to his second flight from the situation. This time, however, he fled as a sick man who *knew* that he was sick.

The outcome of therapy, which was of relatively short duration, included a beginning understanding of his own personality limitations and susceptibilities, and some ability to relate his symptoms to their current and their childhood origins. He lost his anxiety attacks completely, and he considerably reduced his chronic level of tension. Four years later he wrote that his anxiety symptoms had disappeared, but his distrust of women persisted. After another six years he sent a message to his therapist on a Christmas card saying that he had married and felt confident that he had chosen well. Apparently the process of personality maturation, initiated by his therapy, had continued for several years.

In this case the patient was clearly aware of his intense anxiety and of his urgent desire to escape from it. He was *not* prepared to confront the ambivalent feelings directed toward his mother (hate but *also* lust), and though he advanced somewhat in the direction of letting the past *be* the past, we could not say that Walter had completely resolved his neurosis. His bodily symptoms—which were his main concern at first—his overactivity, his nightmares, and his anxiety attacks—all pointed to the burdensome efforts his repressions demanded. There is also the suggestion in his affair with the married woman that he had been enacting one aspect of the Oedipal situation which called for a *punishment.* Re-enacting the Oedipal situation with other "married/maternal" figures, he must then be punished in some way. The superego's vengeance may be surmised in the internally directed sense of disgust, guilt, and eventual death wishes, which were symbolized in his fear of dying or going insane. The interesting rhythmic movements of the mouth during highly anxious periods suggest regression to an oral level, with the possible maneuver of reverting from object-choice to identification (see Chapter 2, p. 64). It could well be that his psychic organization was striving to reaffirm his more traditional values, incorporated in youth and set aside with mixed success in his adolescence. In any case, it appeared that he had come to a position on "the" woman for him after years of working through his unique Oedipal dynamic, of which we have only a sketchy understanding.

## Panic Disorder

The *panic disorder* is an extension of the generalized anxiety disorder in which the patient experiences recurring anxiety attacks, some of which are so extreme as to threaten complete decomposition of the personality. The panic may be a prelude to violent aggression, headlong flight, loss of ego control, or suicide. The clinical picture is one of uncontrollable fear. Psychoticlike manifestations, in which the patient may even misinterpret his or her environment, suffer from delusions of persecution, and experience auditory hallucinations of a threatening, taunting, or reviling character, are not uncommon. The duration of panic may be brief, lasting for a few hours or days, or it may persist for months, during which the intensity of the panic fluctuates within wide limits.

The eventual outcome of a panic reaction is difficult to predict, especially when the episode is prolonged or if it recurs. If the patient is given adequate protection and support, in a situation which allows him or her some degree of seclusion without forcing such isolation, a recovery may be effected. Sedation may be called for as well. However, even in those who are recovering, delusions often persist for weeks after panic has subsided, and suspicion may persist for months. In prolonged excessive fright there is always the possibility that some permanent damage to personality organization will result. Sometimes impulses, fears, and conflicts which escape repression and become conscious during acute emotional decompensation, cannot be repressed once again after the acute phase subsides. The sequel to panic is sometimes a chronic paranoid disorder (see Chapter 11) or a schizophrenic disorganization (see Chapter 14), as the following case demonstrates:

> Edgar R., a clerk aged twenty-eight years, was listening at the office to a discussion of homosexuality and sadomasochistic sexual perversions. One of his fellow workers suddenly noticed that Edgar was blushing and accused him laughingly of "being one of those people." His reaction to the accusation was so exaggerated that he became the target of bantering and obscene epithets over a period of about three weeks. The first change his wife noticed was that he seemed preoccupied and uncommunicative. Then he developed insomnia, lost his appetite, and began harping tensely upon the persecution that he was experiencing at work. Finally he ended up with personality deterioration in a violent outburst of shouting and threatening which necessitated his immediate hospitalization.
>
> In the hospital, Edgar actively hallucinated voices which accused him of various sexual perversions. He believed that his reputation was ruined and his life in danger. He accused attendants of planning to assault him. At one point in a climax of fear, he pulled his cot to pieces and barricaded himself in a corner of the room, threatening to brain anyone who approached him. The psychiatrist in charge treated this episode as the last-ditch stand of a terrified man, and saw to it that no one entered the room without obtaining the patient's permission. Through careful handling the panic eventually subsided, but Edgar remained in a state of chronic schizophrenic disorganization. As is so often the case in repression, where others are able to sense what the person does not consciously admit, the office force had come close to the truth. Their merciless teasing had led previously repressed impulses, fantasies, and conflicts to break through the patient's inadequate defenses and to become an irrepressible part of his conscious experience.

This panic reaction gives a dramatic picture of the strength of infantile urges, fantasies, and conflicts in a person who had remained partially fixated at a primitive level and was therefore susceptible to a sweeping regression. For more than twenty years the defensive organization of Edgar R. had succeeded in containing or repressing his primitive infantile forces. The fellow worker who noticed that Edgar was blushing inferred correctly that a secret had been uncovered—a secret that at the moment might not have been more than a conscious fear because of the defensive efforts of the unconscious portion of the ego (see Chapter 4, p. 126). The malicious teasing that followed, however, had the double effect of further stimulating id promptings while at the same time furthering superego retributions in the form of self-condemnation. Under the combined effect of accusations from fellow workers, increasingly irresistible urges from within, and assaults of a primitive superego, this man's precarious equilibrium disintegrated. His personality organization suffered a sweeping regression in which *denial* and *projection* reached psychotic proportions. He denied his own impulses and projected them to the outside, where they joined forces with the malicious teasing of his fellow workers. The ego's "three harsh masters" (id, superego, external reality) had totally defeated its defensive efforts.

*DSM-III Viewpoint.* As in the case of Edgar R., the diagnostician must decide whether a case is limited to a panic disorder or whether it is simply an acute onset of a more serious disorder such as schizophrenia. If the diagnostician opts for the latter diagnosis, the developmental aspects of the underlying personality may be recorded on axis II (see Chapter 1, p. 21). It is important to rule out certain physical disorders, such as hypoglycemia, which can cause similar symptoms. Patients in withdrawal from drugs such as barbiturates also present symptoms of a panic disorder for purely organic reasons.

## Common Dynamics Lying Behind Anxiety Symptoms

As with other syndromes of psychopathology, there are many ways in which to arrive at that point in maladaptive behavior calling for a diagnosis. We cannot cite "one" dynamic for each clinical syndrome. We are relying upon the insights of psychoanalysis to afford us a certain "oneness" in approach to the understanding of the dynamics that lie behind anxiety symptoms. In the present section we shall review some common dynamics. We shall see that for Walter A., the oil geologist, current life situations revived and intensified certain basic conflicts around which his childhood and adolescent personality was organized.

*Fixation.* Adults who develop anxiety reactions always harbor unconscious conflict systems that are powerfully cathected (valued) and easily reactivated. This is because the conflicts had never been successfully worked through during infancy, childhood, or adolescence. In other words, they are examples of arrested development, of prematurely interrupted learning, of *fixation.*

Fixation early in life, at an immature level of functioning, can result from a variety of experiences. At one extreme, we find that an infantile wish has been repeatedly aroused but consistently *frustrated* (blocked from attaining the end wished for). It has been denied satisfaction or the child has been threatened with reprisal. At the other extreme, an infantile wish might have been completely realized for so long a time that it cannot be given up as development to a higher level proceeds. Walter's rhythmic movements of the mouth may reflect the extreme satisfaction which he obtained in the oral phase, and which he could not forgo as maturity progressed. In addition to these extremes, fixations at pre-Oedipal levels may result from threatening Oedipal experiences that make the child retreat from confronting the resolution of this conflict in a suitable manner. Finally, fixation in an infantile mode can result from a fear of regressing into the symbiotic mother-child relationship, in which the child had no genuine independent existence as a person. The person in this last situation is like someone who has narrowly escaped falling into a canyon but is still too frightened to go away from it.

In all of these cases the product is essentially the same. A powerful, undying infantile *fuero* (see p. 151) pushes forward continually toward preconscious and conscious expression; but an adult living in an adult environment can never fully answer such a claim. Nevertheless, even though they may be infantile in organization and goal, these psychic desires have a strength and tenacity of purpose that cannot be overestimated. We see something like them only occasionally in adults who have conscious longings for an impossible display of love from others. The demands they place on others for signs of affection and loyalty are impossible to fulfill.

*Defective Ego Boundaries.*  Some analysts believe that during maturation a defective separation of conscious and unconscious portions of the ego identity occurs in those with chronic anxiety. This is sometimes expressed by saying that the chronically anxious person "lives too close to his or her unconscious." In other words, the functional boundaries between conscious and unconscious are too permeable, permitting unconscious contents to intrude on the person's everyday activities more readily than normal. Reasons for this permeability are to be found in the developing personality system or, as some analysts believe, in a biological predisposition of some as yet undetermined sort.

*Split-Level Functioning.  Split-Level functioning* refers to a phenomenon that is common to everyone but that enters centrally into the likelihood of exhibiting overt displays of anxiety of the sort we are considering. During our daytime routines we are engaged in split-level functioning (Isakower, 1938). At one level we are dealing with realities, as reasonable, logical adults. At other levels we are operating simultaneously in unconscious, primitive, and even primary process modes. Sometimes, when fully awake and while experiencing ourselves as responsible adults living in a realistic world, we are also surreptitiously trying to resolve unconscious infantile conflicts. When we fall asleep, when external reality seems to vanish and the boundaries between preconscious and unconscious grow vague, our previously unconscious fantasies become our preconscious realities, and primary process maneuvers rule the night (C. Fisher, 1957). In short, what had been going on surreptitiously during the day may come out into the open when we are asleep.

Such unconscious conflicts can also come out in a panic state, overwhelming the personality organization as in the case of Edgar R. Especially when ego boundaries are defective, there is always the chance that some ongoing adult circumstance will arouse infantile conflicts and long-standing fantasies, including dream contents. This is what happened to Edgar. It is common to find in both manifest dream themes and neurotic symptoms the reactivation of childhood and infantile impulses, fantasies, conflicts, and frustrations, which are much more successful in invading preconscious levels than normal consciousness—such as in a normal adult who is awake. Split-level functioning is not limited to anxiety reactions. It may occur in any of the syndromes of psychopathology.

*Symptom Formation in Anxiety Reactions.*  In anxiety reactions the infantile and childhood versions do not *themselves* appear in conscious experience. The defensive organization succeeds in repressing the infantile impulses, conflicts, fantasies, and frustrations, that is, in keeping them unconscious. When they do break through into conscious or preconscious experience, they are usually limited to frightening dreams, irrational impulses, inexplicable inhibitions, apprehensions, or anxiety attacks.

The *indirect derivatives* of the unconscious processes, however, including derivatives of the *unconscious defenses* and the *superego,* do get through. Some of these constitute the neurotic symptom. For one thing, as we have seen, patients with anxiety disorders are fully aware of being vigilant and exhausted, of being constantly alert for something that they cannot identify and do not understand. The vigilant alertness is a derivative of the high pitch at which the patient's defensive forces are operating; it is also a measure of the pressures being exerted by unconscious ego, id, and superego dynamics. The patient feels exhausted because of this defensive effort of having to put up with wave after wave of emotional release in the discharging anxiety. The alternative to this defensive physical exertion would be that of experiencing a living nightmare, such as Edgar R. experienced in his panic reaction.

The necessity for being alert and vigilant is itself disturbing to ego integration. Even at normal levels, tension and anxiety tend to narrow one's range of perception and cognition, and to restrict or suspend action. Patients with anxiety disorders are also vividly aware of their somatic discharge processes. They usually interpret these as signs of organic disease or of beginning insanity. And, finally, the simultaneous occurrence of adult experience, along with derivatives (residuals, re-enactments) of infantile or childhood experiences, is likely to confuse the patient and to make a good deal of what he does seem mixed up and irrational—as, in fact, it often is (primary process cognitions).

Walter A., the oil geologist patient, was painfully aware of his exhausting vigilance, of his frightening somatic symptoms, and of his seeming to be irrational and mixed up. He was aware that he could not relax or even sit still, and that every so often he would have attacks in which something terrible seemed about to happen. He knew that he was at times overwhelmed by vague but intense fears of some catastrophe—that he would die, lose control, or go insane. His anxiety attacks, which were massive somatic discharges of an infantile character, always occurred during states of consciousness, just as clearly as those of a nonneurotic person who faces environmental danger. He was fully aware of their actual violence and of the fright they gave him.

Yet this otherwise intelligent and capable man remained completely unaware, until therapy was well underway, that any of this was related to his mode of living or to his childhood traumas. His defensive efforts did not prevent his attempting to act out his childhood conflicts. They did not protect him against experiencing excessive tension and anxiety directly. They did succeed in keeping repressed the Oedipal dynamics that generated the tension in the first place. Thus his ego defenses kept him in ignorance of the *sources* of the urges that confused and frightened him and of his superego attempts to oppose and punish these re-enactments of mother lust in the liaisons with married women. All of this remained unconscious, inaccessible to him. He looked upon it as a sign that he was suffering from some mysterious disease for which he was in no way responsible.

A specific emotional trauma in adolescence, such as Walter A. suffered, is by no means the necessary antecedent of an adult anxiety reaction. Adolescence is frequently a critical phase of maturation, during which unresolved Oedipal and pre-Oedipal conflicts may be revived and worked through afresh as preparation for assuming a fully adult role. If a severe adolescent trauma is experienced, the intensity and duration of its effect will depend upon the total situation at the time and upon how well Oedipal and pre-Oedipal conflicts had been resolved earlier in life.

The pattern of Walter A.'s neurotic behavior is also not the standard pattern for all anxiety disorders. It is only one example in which the basic symptomatology of apprehension and somatic discharge was exceptionally clear. In a great many cases of anxiety disorder there appears to have been a reasonably well-worked-through adolescence and a satisfactory marital relationship. What seems to be a common factor in all cases is a hypersensitivity to tension-provoking stimulation and a kind of snowballing, reactive sensitization to respond with diffuse apprehension and somatic discharge. We develop a *reaction sensitivity* when we develop selective attitudes that focus our attention on some one item of our experience rather than another. A common example is the increasing sensitivity to an "itch" that we effect once we have indeed concluded that "I have an itching nose." Sometimes, it is possible to induce such sensitivity by observing someone else scratching himself or herself. We sensitize ourselves to physical stimulations based on a precedent expectation or attitudinal disposition. Research employing the galvanic skin response (GSR), which is often used as a measure of tension or anxiety, finds that patients suffering from anxiety disorders show a higher skin conductance at both rest and in reaction to auditory stimulation than do normal individuals and those with other clinical syndromes (Lader & Wing, 1966). The possibility of a genetic component in sensitization to anxiety-provoking stimuli cannot be overlooked (Slater & Shields, 1969).

Some sources of neurotic anxiety are more regressive, more infantile, than those we have been discussing. These sources may not involve guilt because they present reactivations of developmental phases even before a primitive superego precursor had been differentiated from the ego. The anxiety seems to come from fears of becoming completely helpless, of being abandoned, or even of ceasing to exist. Such dangers arise when regression moves back toward the symbiotic mother-child relationship (see Chapter 2, p. 45), in which the child has not yet become a separate individual. If this unconscious fear is revived in anxiety reactions, it is only incidental and momentary, because the neurotic defense structure of these patients is strong enough to protect them from profound regression. It may play a leading role, however, in certain of the psychoses, in which patients sometimes express the fear clearly and consistently.

*Self-Defeating Intentions.* At first glance it seems as though neurotic patients get into anxiety-provoking situations wholly by accident. A careful study of the life situations of the patient, however, and where possible a study of his or her dreams, daydreams, and fantasies, reveal quite a different picture.

Chance does play a part, of course, as it does in the mishaps of everyone. But in addition we find that certain conflictual situations attract these individuals, possess a special fascination for them of which they are nearly always (consciously) unaware. They are unconsciously preoccupied with unresolved conflicts and fuero claims, and this preoccupation pushes them into situations that allow their conflicts some degree of overt expression. In fact, they themselves often help to create such situations out of whatever interpersonal relationships present themselves, as in the case of Walter A. In many cases such a propensity becomes a major therapeutic problem.

Sometimes anxious patients say openly that they know what they are doing and where it will lead, but they still cannot avoid the impulse to repeat their self-destructive or at least anxiety-laden behavioral pattern, again and again. The repetition compulsion has taken hold of their lives (see Chapter 4, p. 121). Careful study of dreams, daydreams, and actual life events can reveal to the psychotherapist the kind of adult circumstance that parallels the childhood circumstance which is being repeated and worked through. The patient will be seen unconsciously assuming an infantile role and yearning for a reciprocal role behavior from certain others in his or her adult orbit. Freud (1912/1958e) referred to these yearnings as *libidinal anticipatory ideas* (p. 100). Such yearning is foredoomed to be frustrated, since the adult is rare who can derive any satisfaction from meeting infantile needs in another adult. The inevitable frustration of the patient leads to the tensions of infantile rage, and the rage, with its primitive fantasies of revenge, leads to overwhelming guilt and the fear of retaliation.

*Childhood Experiences with Parental Models.* We cannot overlook the fact that children adopt patterns of behavior through identification with anxious parents, resulting in what is tantamount to a training in being anxious themselves. In the following clinical illustration we see an anxious, insecure girl grow to womanhood, encounter serious difficulties, and react to them with an anxiety pattern that she had witnessed all her life in her mother.

> The patient, a woman of thirty, had seemed nervous and apprehensive as a child. She had slept poorly and cried easily. As far back as she could remember she had lived in daily dread of her mother's sudden death and the loss of her home. The mother, from the time of the patient's birth, had suffered from "heart attacks" and shortness of breath, cause unknown. When upset the mother would often say that one day she would be found dead, "just like your grandmother was." The grandmother's death had made a profound impression upon the patient; her mother's threat never failed to disturb her. This was the specific pattern of insecurity in which she grew up.
>
> At twenty-two she married a stable and responsible older man. He died four years later, a year after they had lost their only child through tuberculous meningitis. Following this the patient nursed her brother through a year of pulmonary tuberculosis until he recovered. During this period she learned of the dangers of contact infection and suspected that her child had died because of exposure to her brother's illness. She found herself thinking that the brother could have kept away

from home, or died himself, instead of being the cause of her only child's death. She began hating the sight of her brother, while she was still looking after him, and blaming herself as well as him for letting her child die. In this setting of marked ambivalence and guilt she began having "heart attacks" and shortness of breath. She was now afraid that she would die just as she had feared in childhood that her mother would. She realized that her attacks duplicated those of her mother.

Children can be trained to be tense and anxious by parents who are not themselves especially anxious persons. An overprotective parent, for example, may train a small child to be habitually apprehensive by making sudden protective lunges and by giving continual warnings of danger. Adults who, for cultural or personal reasons, are especially alert to strange noises and strange people, or who are too dramatic about the ordinary precautions, such as crossing the street when there is traffic, may instill chronic anxiety in a child long before he or she is able to identify the specific danger that is involved. Some parents teach their children to ferret out in imagination every hidden danger that might conceivably lurk in an apparently innocent situation. They learn to think always in terms of the future but never to have confidence in it, to cross bridges before coming to them, and to imagine each bridge collapsing the moment they give it their full weight.

Parental standards and attitudes enter into anxiety training as well. Anxiety disorders have been found to develop in families in which parents place high expectations on their children but then fail to acknowledge or even disparage their offspring's accomplishments as substandard (Jenkins, 1968). If a daughter is trained to strive always beyond and above what is possible for her to attain, and to feel satisfied with nothing short of perfection and completeness, it is obvious that she has been schooled in how to live a life of dissatisfaction. On the other side of the coin, overpermissive parents can inadvertently instruct their children in anxious behavior. This is because children need a stable framework within which to develop their behavior. Children often actively seek out the limits within which they may act freely. They feel freer and more secure with parents who set limits for them, who in effect function as their ego substitutes. Self-control has to be learned, just as the control of one's movements have to be learned. The child who finds out where reasonable boundaries exist can afford to act and think freely within these limits. If a child is allowed to do anything in the world that he or she can "possibly" do, then the world becomes dangerous because there are so many threatening alternatives for action and imagination.

## *Phobic Disorder (Phobic Neurosis)*

*Phobias* are specific pathological fears. They sometimes begin with an anxiety attack; but once this has been mastered, the patient crystallizes his or her anxiety around some external object or situation, which is then avoided at all costs. The target of phobic anxiety can be almost anything, but we commonly hear of the fear of height, enclosed places and open spaces, animal life, sharp pointed things, darkness, wind and lightning, and literally hundreds of special, personal fears. It has been demonstrated empirically that when they are exposed to these targets, phobic individuals show increased physiological activity (rapid pulse, GSR changes, heavy breathing, etc.) (J. R. May, 1977). The phobic usually does not complain of aches, pains, visceral disturbances, or confusion of thinking (Greenson, 1959). This suggests that tension is minimal so long as the feared objects are avoided. Phobic symptoms fall into two general groups: techniques of avoiding whatever seems to provoke anxiety, and attacks of anxiety whenever these avoidant maneuvers fail and a confrontation with the feared object results.

Logical reasoning rarely helps phobics to overcome their fears; reassurance does them no permanent good. Even a clear, objective demonstration that a fear is groundless seldom alleviates it; often it only increases the phobia's intensity. For although phobias are usually irrational, they are never actually groundless. Something is really threatening the patient, something from within of which he or she is unaware. This may not be objectively demonstrable, but neither is a toothache or a feeling of distrust. Phobias are common in childhood. At one time or another almost every little child develops an irrational, more or less specific fear, which persists awhile and then disappears. These are normal variations of the clinical disorder, but research suggests that even serious phobias seem to make their peak appearance in adolescence, falling off to roughly age thirty, when they once again show a rise in incidence (Marks & Gelder, 1966).

It is frequently possible to account for the small child's selection of what frightens him or her, based on some incident or accident (Monsour, 1969; Rachman & Costello, 1961). Often, however, this is not possible. Even when it is, the intensity and the persistence of the fear are difficult to explain, as, for example, due to accidental or unintentional behavioral conditioning (see Marks, 1977). We are justified in assuming that other factors, other fears, internally generated and externally projected, must be at work—as we know they are in adult phobias. A great many otherwise normal adults retain some small remnant of an irrational childhood fear: for example, a mild uneasiness while crossing a wide street, or when shut in a small room; some discomfort while looking down from a height even when there is a strong protective railing to lean on; some tendency to pull back from strangers or strange animals; and so on. Seldom can such fears be dismissed as innate protective devices; they nearly always have a personal history (see K. Lorenz, 1952, 1957, for a discussion of innate factors in fear responses).

The line is difficult to draw between normal, persistent fears, or between the insignificant remnants in adults of their infantile fears, and the definitely *phobic fear*. There are undoubtedly thousands of adults living in relative peace in spite of one or two minor phobias. Women tend to report more phobias than men, but this may be due to greater social acceptance of such "weakness" in women than in men (Marks & Gelder, 1966). A minor phobia may restrict a woman's freedom somewhat, since she has to avoid whatever seems to be "off limits" for her (airplanes, elevators, etc.); but what she has to give up appears to her trifling in comparison with the anxieties she avoids. She is like a person with a specific food allergy who keeps comfortable and well by eliminating something from her diet. It is only when the protective devices in a phobia fail, when fear generalizes and feared things multiply, or when a feared situation for some reason has to be faced, that a person with a minor phobia or a phobic remnant comes for therapeutic help.

*Definition:* A phobic disorder is a persistent and irrational fear of a specific object, activity, or situation that results in a compelling desire to avoid the dreaded object, activity or situation (DSM-III, p. 225). Phobias persist because they are adaptive; they achieve something, even though what they achieve is neurotic. Common defensive maneuvers in the phobic disorder are displacement, projection, and avoidance. The displacement and projection take the form of an irrational fear of some external object, activity, or situation, and the avoidance follows. Most authorities agree that in focusing his or her fear on a specific object, activity, or situation, the phobic is trying to avoid having an anxiety attack (Arieti, 1961). Something concrete is now focused upon, and that vague apprehension of the generalized anxiety disorder is now pinpointed and manageable. The phobic has managed to effect some kind of control over his or her fears.

*Varieties of Phobias.* Phobias have been typically named by coining Greek or Greco-Latin terms that designate the target object, activity, or situation which the person is avoiding. Estimates are that we are approaching two hundred such terms, and it would seem that the list is endless (English & English, 1958, p. 388). Table 3 will give the reader a sampling of such terms and their attendant target fears.

For all practical purposes, anything in a person's experience can become the focus of a phobia. Chance may play some part in the selection of a target, but chance is never the whole story. Phobias are always overdetermined (see Chapter 5, p. 166). The *dynamic organization* of all phobias, regardless of their different targets, is basically the same. We may summarize this process in light of four points: (1) In the background there is always the *danger* that repressed materials may come to consciousness, resulting in the disintegration of the personality. (2) Contributing to this danger is a *defective defense system,* which is incapable of preventing intrusions from unconscious ego, id, and superego compromises. (3) These intrusions are crystallized in the form of *fearful fantasies,* by the same mechanisms and in the same general way that manifest dreams are constructed (see Chapter 5, p. 162; Lewin, 1952). (4) Finally, these fantasies, usually unconscious and often infantile, are *symbolized* as something external, something that serves as an equivalent for the internal danger—a threatening animal, the brink of a cliff, a storm, mobs, dangerous wide-open or shut-in places. This final displacement and projection completes the phobic symptom formation and gives the patient something tangible that he or she can avoid.

TABLE 3

Typical Phobias

| Phobia | Fear Of |
| --- | --- |
| Acrophobia | Heights |
| Agoraphobia | Open spaces |
| Algophobia | Pain |
| Arachnophobia | Spiders |
| Aviophobia | Airplanes |
| Brontophobia | Thunder |
| Claustrophobia | Closed spaces |
| Hematophobia | Blood |
| Microphobia | Germs |
| Nyctophobia | Dark places |
| Ocholophobia | Crowds |
| Pyrophobia | Fire |
| Xenophobia | Strangers |
| Zoöphobia | Animal or animals |

We next turn to a more detailed description of four representative phobias —fear of height, fear of open spaces, fear of closed places, and fear of animals —in each of which we shall include case illustrations as concrete examples. We shall discuss what is feared and why; and then we shall mention the gratifications involved in each phobia. This separation into the *fear* and the *gratification* will remind us of Freud's insight that all neurotic symptoms are the result of compromises, and hence they reflect the intentions of *two* sides of the personality (id, superego) as united by a third (ego) (see Chapter 5, p. 154).

## Acrophobia: The Fear of Height

An acrophobic person experiences irrational fear whenever he or she finds it necessary to be on a high place. Anxiety may be generated just by thinking about such a necessity. The anxiety experienced varies from a typical anxiety attack to a feeling of nausea and vertigo, or merely to a mild level of uneasiness. The acrophobic person avoids going up to high places whenever possible. So long as the target situation provoking anxiety can be avoided, the acrophobic is usually as free from anxiety as the nonphobic person.

*The Fear.* Human beings are not born with an instinctive fear of height. If they were, parents would have an easier time guarding their small children from danger. Nevertheless, almost everyone acquires some fear of height. Children learn through innumerable falls and endless warnings to be somewhat wary of height and to be attentive to their footing. In other words, the pathological fear of high places is related to a realistic danger; hence realistic anxiety is hardly an abnormal reaction. As Freud, (1910/1957e) said, "A person suffering from anxiety is not for that reason necessarily suffering from anxiety neurosis; such a diagnosis of it cannot be based on the name [of the symptom]" (p. 224).

If there were no more to the fear of height than direct learning in concrete situations, fear of height would probably remain a reasonable caution. No pathological acrophobia would develop. But another factor besides that of concrete learning must be considered—the factor of symbolization. Falling in self-esteem and in the esteem of others is also related symbolically with an actual tumble. A child may equate falling on a cement sidewalk with falling, for example, in a beloved parent's favor. The fall in favor is no less painful to the child than a physical fall, and is portrayed psychically no less vividly. With the development of an increasingly mature superego, children may find a fall in favor or in self-esteem harder to bear than a fall from a swing onto the hard ground. The fact that the latter is a shared social episode, and arouses sympathetic responses in others, helps the child to endure it.

While each of us is learning directly, early in childhood, to avoid the pain and fright of bad falls, we are also learning indirectly about symbolic painful and destructive falls from high places. These the child at first symbolizes and represents to himself or herself as being similar or even identical, in somewhat the manner that adults symbolize falling from grace or power in their allegorical speech and writing, in poetry, and in caricature. Humpty Dumpty had a great fall and no one could put him together again. People tumble from high places—a worker is demoted, the grocer falls in favor, a police officer is broken, an official drops in everyone's estimation, a pillar of the church slips, and so on.

It seems to the child that nobody wants to pick these people up. Adults often seem pleased with another person's disaster; they even gloat over it. The child hears of men and women tumbling out of windows, or in front of subway trains, and learns that they are killed in a terrifying manner. He hears that a neighbor woman has fallen in the eyes of others who say they look down on her. Such phraseology is not labeled as metaphorical. It seems to mean literally what it says. Grownup talk makes it plain that bad people fall and deserve their fate. We know that, during the early years, children picture such adult conceptualizations quite concretely. It is in part this primitive concrete imagery—the imagery of allegory, poetry, and caricature—which makes up primary process thinking and leads to neurotic symptom formation, as we shall soon see.

*Gratifications.* So far we have stressed only the painful, destructive side of acrophobia, but psychoanalysis teaches us that there is also something positive about every neurotic symptom, something gratifying and attractive. Under certain conditions all normal children enjoy falling and jumping from a height. Little children love to be thrown into the air and caught, dropped suddenly from one's knee and safely caught again, put up on a chair to jump anxiously into daddy's or mommy's arms. Children have endless jumping and falling games when they are small, including wrestling, tackling, and sliding games. The same child who cries bitterly when he falls accidentally on the way to school will fling himself down on the playground with glee and abandon, if this is the game and he does it of his own accord. Children learn, of course, to limit the distances they jump and fall in accordance with the hurts they receive and the degree of excitation they can tolerate and enjoy. In all of this we see unmistakable evidence of excitement and gratification—giggling, laughing and screaming, insistence upon more and more—increased tolerance for his or her anxiety going hand in hand with the child's intense pleasure.

For adults there is also a thrill in falling and sailing through the air that imparts a sense of power and abandon. Normal healthy men and women travel long distances for the chance to dive into water over and over, or to make dangerous ski jumps. Millions who cannot do these things delight in watching others do them on television and movie screens. We need these reminders of the fascination in jumping and falling if we are to understand part of the impulse that seizes many phobic persons as they stand on a high place, part of the impulse that frightens them. For they may be impelled toward a destructive jump, not alone by archaic, irrational superego pressures, but also by irrational, unconscious fantasies about the powerful pleasures of flight and abandon. It is for this reason that Freud (1909/1955a) once said, "Theoretical considerations require that what is to-day the object of a phobia must at one time in the past have been the source of a high degree of pleasure" (p. 59). Such "flight-and-abandon" fantasies in phobias use the same imagery that motivates high-divers, parachutists, and ski jumpers; but they may also be linked with perilous masochistic wishes for self-destruction and the end of everything. A clinical case will illustrate many of these cross-currents as they actually appear in a phobic patient.

### Case of Agnes W.: Acrophobia

Agnes W., an unmarried woman of thirty, had been unable to go higher than the second or third floor of any building for a year. Whenever she tried to overcome her fear of height she only succeeded in provoking intolerable anxiety. She remembered when it all began. One evening she was working alone at the office when she was suddenly seized with terror lest she jump or fall out of the open eighth-story window. So frightened was Agnes by her impulse that she crouched behind a steel file for some time before she could trust herself to gather up her things and make for the street. She reached ground level acutely anxious, perspiring freely, her heart pounding and her breathing rapid.

After this the patient found that as soon as she reached the office each day her anxiety over height made it impossible to attend properly to her work. At the end of two months she gave up her position. For a while she tried unsuccessfully to accustom herself directly to high places. Finally her need for income drove her to take whatever she could get within the limitations imposed by her phobia. The result was that she was downgraded from a confident, well-paid secretary to an unhappy, poorly paid salesperson in a store. This was her situation when she came for treatment.

In therapy it soon came out that Agnes had been deeply involved in an affair of long standing with a married man who could not, for religious reasons, get a divorce. She found herself caught in a severe conflict, guilty over her own conduct, too much in love to break off the liaison, and unable to give up a belief that one day she and her lover would marry. The crisis came when she was informed that she was pregnant. Rejecting all thoughts of abortion, she told the man that he would have to get a quick divorce and marry her. When he refused she threatened to expose him. A few days before her acute anxiety attack, and the onset of the phobia, she received a farewell letter from him and discovered that he had left town with his wife and family.

Agnes had felt humiliated and angered at having to beg and threaten her lover. His desertion was the final disillusionment. It overwhelmed her with helplessness and hatred. She now concluded that she was no better than a prostitute, and suicide seemed to her the only solution. It was in this setting of shame, fury, and abandonment that she became acutely frightened and phobic. She was terrified by her own sudden impulse to leap out of a hopeless situation to her death. When she displaced and projected this fear of suicide to a fear of height she replaced a reasonable fear with an irrational phobia.

The motivation for suicide was multiple. Agnes was prompted to kill herself by a wild desire to avenge herself upon her faithless lover, to punish herself for her sins, perhaps to act out concretely the drama of the fallen woman, and certainly to escape from intolerable anxiety (some of which was of a realistic nature!). Instead of giving in to this formidable array of self-destructive impulses, Agnes was able, as we have seen, to mobilize enough realistic ego functioning to flee from the perilous situation to the street. But each time she returned to the office, her intense anxiety also returned. The only way that she was able to avoid it was to stay near ground level. It is noteworthy that she no longer connected her fear of height with her fear of suicide. We saw that in anxiety attacks the patient tends to focus on the symptoms and to ignore what originally aroused the acute anxiety. We now see that in phobias the patient focuses on the fear and ignores what started it. In both cases there is a defensive inability to relate cause and effect.

Phobias are neurotic compromises that partially disable a person but make acute anxiety manageable through the technique of avoidance. By keeping away from heights Agnes kept away from intolerable anxiety and the risk of suicide. She *projected* the danger from her own uncontrollable impulses of self-destruction, of which she was half-aware, onto the impersonal and controllable fear of situations like the one in which she had originally experienced the self-destructive impulse. She *displaced* the upsurge of vengeful hatred toward her lover, which also alarmed her by its force, to a feeling of abhorrence for high places. This feeling of abhorrence, as her therapy eventually brought out, was a mixture of anger and hate, together with an irrational but terrifying fear of superego retaliation.

Phobias have the advantage that, however irrational they may sound, one can admit having them to oneself and to others. This is not true of the impulses, the attitudes, and the fears that they conceal. Agnes, for example, could acknowledge her fear of height with only a little embarrassment and perplexity. She could not admit to herself or to others the intensity of her hatred of her lover or her own need for self-punishment. Neither could she accept the fact that she wanted to kill herself, to say nothing of killing the unborn child that she believed she carried. It is not surprising that when she discovered she was not actually pregnant, the discovery did not change her phobic state. The phobia, as we have seen, represented far more than her fear of pregnancy. It represented also her suicidal and homicidal impulses, her feelings—based on early moralistic attitudes—of being "a fallen woman," despicable and abandoned, her ambivalent (superego) prompting for punishment and her dread of it.

When Agnes learned to recognize and express her ambivalent love and resentment toward her lover, she brought out earlier resentful loving toward other men who, one after the other, had failed her in some way. She shifted her attention from a narrow neurotic symptom and found behind it a broad neurotic pattern of living. It dawned upon her that for more than a decade she had been unable to establish a lasting relationship with any man, even though opportunities had not been lacking. Her curiosity over this personal failing led Agnes quickly into a reconsideration of her life at home.

At home this woman of thirty had been living in the shadow of elderly parents who treated her as an adolescent girl. They expected conformity. When her conduct and opinion met with their rigidly conventional outlooks they gave her warmth and praise; when they disapproved they gave her cold formality and silence. They welcomed the men she brought to the house with courteous hospitality. After a man had come a few times, however, they began pointing out his shortcomings in a gentle, humorous, mocking way, when he had left. Soon Agnes would find herself uncomfortable with him and even ashamed of him. Whatever lovemaking went on she viewed through her parents' eyes, not through her own. Discomfort and shame soon gave way to a feeling of contempt, and the relationship soon terminated, an outcome that she now began to suspect her parents had always wanted.

Agnes had found that she could avoid this whole pattern, which was really a prolongation of her adolescent conflicts, by seeking the company of men whom she did not have to bring home. She could develop strong and enjoyable attachments as long as her parents were kept in ignorance of them. But now the furtive character of these affairs revived some of her unresolved infantile conflicts and made her feel guilty and afraid. The guilt and fear at the time were fully conscious, but their infantile sources were not. If we add this troubled background of infantile and adolescent conflict to the realities of her supposed pregnancy and her real desertion, we can easily understand why she came close to being swept out of the office window to her death. We can understand also how a childish defense like her phobia, with its multiplicity of meanings, could rescue her from facing such a fate.

We have given this case in some detail to illustrate the ways in which phobias speak a symbolic language, just as dreams do. Some of the symbolism the patient understood directly, without interpretation, as her neurotic fears and inhibitions subsided. We do not know for certain why Agnes hit upon acrophobia unless it was because its meaning best symbolized her prevailing fantasies. Had she developed one of the other phobias instead, the dynamic organization behind the symptom would have been much the same.

## Claustrophobia: The Fear of Being Closed In

The claustrophobic person experiences irrational anxiety whenever he or she must enter an enclosed or narrow place. Usually, there is the thought that escape will be impossible. In such circumstances the claustrophobic grows restless, tense, and uneasy, reflecting the gradual onset of a typical anxiety attack. Sometimes the person becomes desperate to escape into the open, and flees in a state of panic. By avoiding enclosed or narrow places this type of individual can often avoid acute anxiety completely.

*The Fear.* Claustrophobia is another pathologically acquired fear which, like the fear of height, is related to common realistic dangers. Here the phobic person fears being shut in, trapped, cut off from help, and perhaps left to die of hunger and neglect. The claustrophobic may have conscious albeit fleeting daydreams of being buried alive, caught in an elevator stuck between floors, or trapped underwater in an automobile, an airplane, or an ocean liner. Childhood experiences and stories give form and substance to such fears, while the tales carried by newspapers, illustrated magazines, radio, and television reinforce them. A bus plunges into the river, a train into the bay, and an airplane into the sea. Everyone on board is drowned. Children are trapped by cave-ins; coal miners are suffocated in mine accidents. People are cornered and mugged in narrow alleyways, apartment vestibules, or hotel rooms and corridors.

*Gratifications.* Solitude, which is so much used as punishment, can also be a highly valued privilege, a condition of freedom from outside interference, an opportunity to be alone with one's fantasies. Some of the most mature and meaningful experiences of adult life depend upon limiting the impact of one's human surroundings to one's own solitary behavior or to that of a chosen companion. Children, as well as adults, like to be able to shut themselves in a room, where they can be free to follow their own impulses without supervision or hindrance. Every normal child invents games in which he or she is secluded in a small place—a closet, a tent, a cave, or simply an enclosure made of furniture.

Many claustrophobic fears originate in situations of infantile and childhood gratifications, situations that may overwhelm a child with excitement and lead to adult discovery and punishment. A child alone, or with another child or two, may be tempted to sexual adventures in the seclusion of a hiding place—under the covers, in closets, bathrooms, basements, attics, cloakrooms, corridors, and alleyways. Touching, looking, exhibiting, tussling, and sex play are common incidents in such settings. Moreover, children are almost universally punished by being shut in or locked in bedrooms and small closets. Here they may ease their pain and loneliness by erotic play, but at the same time perhaps increase their sense of guilt. For these and many other reasons the small enclosed place is especially well suited to serve as the symbol for the pleasures of taboo activity, for fears of the intensity of one's own impulses, for the dangers of seduction and the threat of punishment. In the following case some of these symbolic meanings emerge with great clarity, as products largely of the patient's own unaided efforts.

### Case of Kenneth E.: Claustrophobia with Other Symptoms

Kenneth E., twenty-two years of age, could not stay in theaters because they made him feel suffocated and afraid that he would not be able to get out in case of illness or a fire. His fear generalized to elevators, busses, and downtown city streets.

He sought therapeutic help because his fears were restricting his life without reducing his overall anxiety. In therapy he concentrated at first upon his most recent symptoms and gained his first insight into his phobias.

At the beginning of therapy Kenneth said that whenever he was in downtown streets he felt he might fall ill or be injured in an accident. Since he would be among strangers he might not get the help he needed in time to save his life. There was nothing objective to justify such fears. Later on Kenneth realized that fears of accident and illness were secondary. What he primarily feared was that if he were to "fall in a fit," or be injured, he might lose control of himself and shout something, or talk without realizing what he was saying. Obviously there was something he must hide, something that at the same time he had an impulse to proclaim. This discovery of an impulse to give himself away in public led ultimately to the origin of his phobia.

The onset of his claustrophobic symptoms followed an acute anxiety attack in a theater. The play contained a homosexual theme to which Kenneth was doubly sensitized, by his own trends and by a recent threat to expose them. The anxiety attack was his response to the total stress. When this occurred he became still more frightened that people around him in the theater would notice his agitation and guess its cause. As soon as the curtain fell for the intermission he staggered out, feeling weak, tremulous, and nauseated. After this, he could go to the theater only if he sat near an exit, and even then he felt so anxious that he lost all pleasure in being there. The phobia generalized to places where he was thrown with strangers under crowded conditions.

Kenneth's experience in the theater had merely dramatized his current conflict and made him for the moment vividly aware of it. His phobias appeared as defensive devices that moved his conflict over homosexuality from the center of the stage and put a group of expanding fears in its place. What Kenneth feared was not theaters, elevators, busses, or downtown streets, but rather his own homosexual promptings, which if enacted would give him away publicly as something that he was striving to deny. His phobias shielded him from situations which aroused this prompting, offering him the neurotic compromise of freedom from anxiety in return for restricted activity. When the restrictions became too great, he was forced to seek help.

## Agoraphobia: *The Fear of Open Places*

The person suffering from agoraphobia becomes irrationally frightened whenever he or she must confront an open area, such as a park, plaza, field, or beach. The term is also used to include neurotic anxiety due to crossing a wide street, and even fears of being in the street. The anxiety that develops varies from an acute discharge to mere alertness and discomfort.

*The Fear.* Like acrophobia and claustrophobia, the fear of open places is derived from realistic dangers. This time the danger is that of being exposed in the open without protection or shelter. It is an exaggeration of normal prudence. The prudent person, when entering dangerous territory, does not expose himself or herself in an open area. Living in a high crime area, one does not walk the streets if he or she can avoid it. To the agoraphobic person fields, plazas, and beaches seem filled with danger, a danger that is no less threatening because of its inexplicableness.

Kenneth E., discussed in the preceding section, suffered from a typical street phobia with typical fears of exposure and desertion. He pictured himself lying helpless in the open with a crowd looking on which might be indifferent to the possibility that he was dying. Another patient, a woman, saw herself hurrying along the street frightened, with men staring at her ominously and women looking haughty and aloof. She combined a temptation to go for a walk on the streets with a fear of it, just as Kenneth did. Such people experience in anticipation the fright of helpless exposure; they try to avoid streets and open public places as though these were radioactive. Some agoraphobics can go about in relative comfort if someone accompanies them, someone to whom they can cling if necessary. This is especially interesting because it repeats the early childhood situation in which to be left alone in public was to feel helpless and abandoned in a universe of unknown dangers, while to have an adult to cling to was to feel safe.

*Gratifications.* Much of what has been said about gratification in relation to claustrophobia and acrophobia could be repeated here. To be left alone in the open means not only to be abandoned and in danger; it may also mean to be free from being watched and restricted, free to have one's fling. Thus, along with fears of loneliness, desertion, and attack, the agoraphobic may experience a promise of excitement and freedom from restraint. To walk the streets and plazas, to be in parks or at the beach, means to have opportunities to satisfy libidinous and aggressive wishes that are never met indoors at home. Thus gratifications, many of them taboo and most of them unconscious, are mingled with the dread of being alone and unprotected, the fear of what one may feel impelled to do. The agoraphobic symptom serves the double (antithetical, dialectical) purpose of providing severe restraint while preserving the excitement of the temptation.

### Case of Ethel H.: Agoraphobia

Ethel H., a married woman of twenty-six, had suffered her first acute anxiety attack two years before she began therapy. She was arriving alone by plane from England after visiting her parents there. As she entered the high-ceilinged terminal, where no one met her, she suddenly felt terrified at the huge empty spaciousness. She began "shaking like a leaf"; she could not get her bags through customs without constant help; she had an impulse to tell everyone around who she was in case she went mad. A porter, sensing her anxiety, expressed his concern over her openly and this comforted her. She managed the rest of the trip by train without mishap, but reached home exhausted and unnerved, certain that something awful was happening to her. She told her husband of this when he returned from a business trip because she was afraid of expressing her resentment at not having been met.

During the ensuing two years Ethel felt nervous a great deal of the time, uneasy about driving on parkways and highways, and lonely when walking along strange streets. Then she made another trip to England, intending to stay three months with her parents. As time went on, however, she heard from her husband less and less frequently, while his letters seemed more and more impersonal, until she began to fear that she would lose him. Her fear was confirmed when he finally wrote that he wanted a divorce. Her immediate reaction was to become depressed, to weep bitterly, lose sleep and appetite, and declare that she was alone in the world.

The day after this letter arrived, Ethel was crossing a moor toward dusk when she was suddenly struck by the desolate surroundings. She felt isolated from the world and terribly frightened. She told herself that she might as well be exiled to Siberia as stranded here. Then she became afraid that she would step into a bog and disappear. Her legs were so weak that she could scarcely walk on to the house. Following this experience Ethel could not cross large open spaces anywhere without acute anxiety, unless someone whom she knew accompanied her. She avoided concerts because of the "emptiness" of concert halls. On the advice of a physician friend she returned at once to the United States. At the air terminal she repeated her experience of two years earlier, even though this time her sister was there to meet her.

Because of the impending divorce Ethel moved to another city, terminating therapy, which she believed would be unnecessary once the divorce was finalized. During the brief period of treatment, certain matters of dynamic interest surfaced. Ethel ascribed her feeling of desolation, which now permeated all her thinking, not only to her husband's desertion but also to her lifelong neglect by her father. She had always wanted to be close to him but he had never shown a genuine interest in the family. We learned of earlier phobias that reflected her frustrated unconscious wishes for a father's love. Around pubescence she often dreamed that burglars had broken into her bedroom. She would wake up with the feeling that someone was in the room; she was too frightened then to move, turn over in bed, or even to breathe, for fear of disclosing her position. She was afraid that somebody was hiding behind the door when she entered a room. She would push the door hard against the wall to make sure before going in. When she was a little girl, Ethel was often frightened that something was in bed with her and was creeping toward her. Whenever this happened, she would run to her parents' room for comfort and insist upon sleeping with them the rest of the night. The Oedipal implications here are obvious.

## Zoöphobia: The Fear of Animal Life

The zoöphobic person is irrationally afraid, sometimes to the point of helplessness, when he or she is in the proximity of certain forms of animal life. The fear is usually limited to one or another kind of living being. Horses, wolves, lions, and tigers have always been favorite zoöphobic targets; so also are spiders, insects, and vermin. Sometimes the fear is quite specific. Cats are frightening for some people while dogs are not; snakes may be frightening but not frogs or turtles. Zoöphobic children often scream and cringe or run away when the excitant appears. Adults are usually more controlled, but not always; sometimes they too become acutely anxious in the presence of the feared animal.

*The Fear.* Fears of animal life can easily appear reasonable since they involve something that might conceivably attack. Children often learn to be afraid through actual experiences of hurt or fright—being barked at or growled at loudly, falling over an animal that jumps up, or being scratched, bitten, or knocked down. Children also acquire fears through visiting farms and zoos, and especially from the frightening warnings that other children and adults give. Picture books, fairy tales, magazines, stories, moving pictures, and television may all add to a child's anxieties about animals. But this sort of thing accounts at most for reasonable caution and the moderate fears which, in most children, soon disappear. It does not explain the persistence or the intensity of animal phobias in the relatively few.

Animals become the focus of phobias, especially for the child, because they are unpredictable, violent, and sexually uninhibited. They can therefore easily be made into symbols of frightening primitivity around which infantile fantasies cluster. Domestic animals commit crimes of violence without hesitation, including theft, assault, and murder. Dogs and cats kill and eat small, helpless animals while the child's parents encourage and reward them. They mate with their own offspring and siblings without regard to the most relentless human taboos. Yet they prosper and are loved. Sometimes pet dogs eat their pups, and cats their kittens. Parents are likely to be shocked by such cannibalism, but they seldom punish the offending animals. All of these considerations make it easier to understand the existence of incestuous, murderous, and cannibalistic fears and fantasies among small children.

*Gratifications.* It is obvious from what we have been saying that the animal fantasies included in zoöphobia allow a person to symbolize all manner of erotic wishes and destructive promptings. Everyone young or old has witnessed the unbridled violence of animal aggression and the unrestrained indulgence of animal sexuality. Animals breed and care for their young openly in every intimate detail. They express the most uninhibited interest in feeding, grooming, and elimination. Almost everything that can arouse human excitement, envy, shame, and disgust is at some time witnessed or heard about as animal activity. Thus everyone is provided with unlimited symbols of "animalistic" gratification that can be worked into the structure of an animal phobia.

### Case of Little Hans: Childhood Zoöphobia

The most famous case of zoöphobia is also the first one ever to be studied dynamically by Freud (1909/1955a) in collaboration with the father of "Little Hans." This boy of five years refused to go out into the street because he was afraid of horses and actually feared being bitten by them. In the course of therapy it turned out that the horses symbolized the hated and feared aspect of his father. The little patient harbored hostile aggression against his only male rival for his mother's love, but at the same time he also loved his father dearly.

Reduced to its simplest terms the phobic solution was about as follows. The love this boy bore his mother was repressed; it disappeared. The love for his father was retained, while the hatred for him was displaced on the horses. This had the added advantage that the horse could easily be avoidèd, whereas his father could not. The castration anxiety in the Oedipal resolution was thus projected onto horses. The selection of a horse to symbolize the Oedipal resolution was accounted for by Freud (ibid.) as follows: "For Hans horses had always typified pleasure in movement ('I'm a young horse,' he had said as he jumped about); but since this pleasure in movement included the impulse to copulate, the neurosis imposed a restriction on it and exalted the horse into an emblem [symbol] of terror" (p. 139).

The whole displacement in the case of Little Hans was made easy by certain other partial identities: (a) the father had often played "horsie" with Hans; (b) the horses' bridles reminded Hans fearfully of his father's dark moustache; (c) therapy also brought out his wishes that his father might fall and hurt himself, as the boy had seen horses fall, and as his playmate with whom he also played "horsie" had fallen and hurt himself. As a result of therapy this patient recovered from his phobia. It is interesting that, years later when Hans chanced upon the account of his illness and its treatment, all memory of the once vivid phobia had been *completely repressed*. Some of the incidental comments about his parents made him wonder if he could have been this famous little patient, and led him to visit Freud from whom he found out that he was.

## Counterphobic Measures

There is an especially interesting derivative of phobias that merits our attention before we go on. This is the so-called *counterphobia* or *counterphobic measure*. Children show it most clearly when they act out in play something frightening that has happened to them in reality. A child, for example, acts out a visit to the doctor, a painful injection, or a surgical procedure to which he or she has just been subjected. Often he or she does this over and over (repetition compulsion). In the play situation the child is active, willing, and in control of the situation, instead of being acted upon, unwilling, and helpless. Adults who have been the victims of traumatic anxiety in combat situations do the same kind of thing when they repeat their terrifying experiences under narcosis and hypnosis or in dreams (see Chapter 5, p. 160).

In all such normal instances the child or adult connects his or her counterphobic acting out with the originally frightening experience. This is an important condition for successfully mastering the original anxiety. Most neurotic counterphobic attempts do not operate with this advantage. The sources of phobic anxiety are usually hidden from the phobic person by his or her own defenses. Thus, the phobic individual seems drawn or driven to dangerous situations without consciously knowing why.

The most common form of counterphobia is *reactive courage*. The phobic person deliberately seeks out situations of which he or she is afraid because of an unconscious drive to master a specific anxiety. There are also, of course, the contributing factors of excitement and pleasure in the anxiety of phobics and in its relief, which we have already described. Innumerable examples of counterphobic tendencies occur in ordinary life. The most dramatic examples are to be found among acrophobic persons who choose such hobbies as mountain

*Photograph by Edmund Engelman*

*Freud's study at Berggasse 19. The windows looked out into a central courtyard. Note the many antiquities that he had collected over the years. Freud liked to read at his desk by draping his left leg over the left arm of his chair, nestling the book on his elevated thigh.*

climbing or such professions as tightrope walking and aviation. There are also actors with chronic severe stage fright who need to be pushed onto the stage, but who still actively seek out public performances, experiencing pleasure and relief in each appearance but never mastering their anxiety.

Daredevils are by no means all counterphobic. Some of them have always enjoyed doing what other people fear. Some have at one time been phobic but have overcome their neurotic fear and now enjoy repeating the dangerous feat with a sense of mastery, just as normal children also do. The counterphobic character of an activity is shown by the appearance of unusual tension, anxiety, symptomatic acts, and anxiety dreams related to the phobia that is being defended against. Counterphobic repetitions of feared situations do not usually lead to mastery of the phobic anxiety because the patient's defenses make him or her unaware of the neurotic fear that is in the process of being surmounted.

*DSM-III Viewpoint.* The many different phobias have been combined into three groupings: (1) *agoraphobia,* in which there is a marked fear of being alone, or being in a public place where escape would be difficult in the case of a sudden incapacitation; this includes fear of crowded streets, bridges, stores, elevators, or a public conveyance; (2) *social phobia,* in which the fear is primarily that of being seen, assessed, or scrutinized by others, whether in a group or in individual contact; this includes fears of eating in restaurants, using public lavatories, speaking before groups, or even having to write something in the presence of another person; and (3) *simple phobia:* any persistent, irrational fear of and compelling desire to avoid an object or situation not covered by the other two categories. This latter diagnosis thus acts as a residual classification in which we would place acrophobia, claustrophobia, and zoöphobia. The most obvious change here is that agoraphobia, which has traditionally meant what the dictionary defines it as being—that is, fear of crossing or being in open places—has been redefined as being without a feeling of close *personal* contact. Hence, "open" means something akin to "impersonal" and "without support" in the DSM-III redefinition of agoraphobia.

## Comparison of Anxiety and Phobic Disorders

Phobias have a more mature structure than anxiety disorders, no matter how absurd or childish their form appears to be. They are successful most of the time in eclipsing the anxiety. This is achieved through a regression, not to the early primitive and distorted levels of personality development, but to a level where there are perceptual and cognitive structures—images, memories, fantasies, and daydreams—capable of absorbing and utilizing large amounts of energy. The dynamic succession of events in phobias may be summarized as follows: (1) an upsurge of emotional discharge as anxiety; (2) beginnings of ego disintegration (i.e., loss of countercathectic control); (3) automatic partial regression to more primitive levels; and (4) ego reintegration at the lower levels, as the fixated memories, fantasies, and daydreams are relied upon to focus the source of threat on some external target.

In thus organizing and focusing his or her irrational fears on the target, the phobic patient gains mastery over the upsurge of anxiety. With the more amorphous ambiance of a generalized anxiety disorder, in which the cognitive factors are not so focused, a much more serious anxiety attack is the result, and a deeper regression is also more probable. The generalized anxiety-disorder patient must remain continually vigilant because he or she feels the constant threat of catastrophe from some unknown source within the realm of consciousness. Phobic defenses, by contrast, provide an escape by furnishing fearful (symbolized) targets for the anxiety against which the person can maneuver to find relative security via avoidance—until, of course, the phobic targets multiply and the person is finally overwhelmed.

The dominant fantasies, memories, and daydreams appearing in phobic symptoms do not necessarily indicate the *origin* of the phobic defense. Instead, they point to the most severe and often the latest childhood crisis in which displacement and projection have been employed. Thus, the Oedipal child (aged four or five) probably is likely to use a phobic defense because the defensive mechanisms of displacement and projection have been the most well-developed mechanisms at that age. Phobic adults have evidently experienced such childhood phobias at this psychosexual level more severely than the average, since they do exhibit such strongly fixated, fearful perceptual organizations. As a result, the childhood phobia, which has been more successful than the archaic discharge of an acute anxiety attack to regain a proper level of repression (countercathexis of ego) (see Chapter 5, p. 156), remains as a possible corrective later in life. Just as a soldier who runs out of ammunition may use his carbine as a club, so the adult who has handled Oedipal threats in the past with a phobia is likely to do so again. This regressive maneuver is obviously not so extreme as the person in an anxiety attack, who is seen regressing to crude, archaic discharges of emotion reminiscent of an infant's yelling and thrashing about in a temper tantrum.

## Summary

Chapter 6 begins our survey of the diagnostic categories with a review of the anxiety disorders. We reserve the term *anxiety disorder* for those cases in which diffuse emotional tension and free anxiety clearly dominate the clinical picture, while other symptoms are merely incidental. Most of the symptoms of anxiety represent the patient's efforts to discharge the tension of anxiety in voluntary muscle action or in autonomic activity. Other symptoms, sometimes called *secondary anxiety,* reflect the disturbing effects that tension has upon the functioning of the ego. When the emotional tension of anxiety grows too great, lasts too long, or underlies much of the person's behavior, we begin to suspect that *neurotic anxiety* is underway. Anxiety may be defined as a *state of apprehension,* without apparent object, in which attempts are made to discharge internally generated tension and to reduce physiological discomfort through increased bodily activity.

The most common form of disturbance seen in clinical practice is the *generalized anxiety disorder,* in which an unstructured fear haunts the person for over one month. Signs of fatigue are common as the person finds it difficult bearing up under a sense of impending doom. An occasional *anxiety attack* may punctuate the clinical picture. Anxiety attacks are acute episodes of emotional decompensation usually appearing in a setting of chronic anxiety, and exhibiting to an exaggerated degree the characteristics of normal fright.

The *panic disorder* is an extension of the generalized anxiety disorder in which the patient experiences recurring anxiety attacks, some of which result in personality decomposition. The panic is a state of uncontrollable fear that may be a prelude to violent aggression, headlong flight, loss of ego controls, and even suicide. The diagnostician must decide whether a case is limited to a panic disorder, or whether it is an acute onset of a more serious disorder such as schizophrenia.

Among the common dynamics lying behind anxiety symptoms Chapter 6 mentions fixation, defective ego boundaries, and split-level functioning. The *split-level functioning* dynamic refers to the fact that ongoing unconscious conflicts may be reflected in dreams or in abnormal states like anxiety attacks or panic reactions. In the main, the anxiety patient's defensive system is successful in keeping infantile impulses, fantasies, and frustrations from appearing in consciousness. When these characteristics do break through into conscious or preconscious experience, they are usually limited to frightening dreams, irrational impulses, inexplicable inhibitions, apprehensions, or anxiety attacks. Indirect derivatives of infantile unconscious processes do show themselves. The vigilant alertness that often fatigues the patient is a derivative of the high pitch at which the anxiety patient's defenses are working. The patient feels exhausted because of this defensive effort of having to put up with wave after wave of emotional release in the discharging of anxiety.

The dynamic of *reaction sensitivity* is commonly observed in the anxiety disorders. This refers to the fact that the patient can develop selective attitudes that focus his or her attention on some one area of concern rather than on another. In this manner, anxiety can feed on itself because the person expects its occurrence relative to certain life areas and totally disregards the fact that other life areas could readily be anxiety provoking. Not infrequently the anxiety patient is found to literally create the conflict situations that germinate the fear so dreaded. On other occasions he or she may be seen to model the anxiety behaviors of parental figures.

*Phobic disorders* arise when the person has fixed his or her anxiety onto some external object, activity, or situation, which is then avoided at all costs. The feared item's presence results in heightened physiological activity in the patient, with rapid pulse, heavy breathing, and a feeling of faintness as prominent symptoms. Common defensive maneuvers in the phobic disorder are displacement, projection, and avoidance. Chapter 6 lists a series of phobic disorders, such as *acrophobia* or the fear of heights, *claustrophobia* or the fear of closed spaces, *agoraphobia* or the fear of open places, and *zoöphobia* or the fear of animal life. Actually, anything in a person's experience can become the focus of a phobia. The dynamic organization of all phobias involves dangerous repressed contents, a defective defensive system, and fearful fantasies that are symbolized as something external rather than as a threat from within the psyche. This final displacement and projection completes the phobic symptom formation and gives the patient something tangible that he or she can avoid.

A derivative of phobic disorders is the so-called *counterphobia* or *counterphobic measure* that some people manifest. In children this can take the form of simply acting out fearful situations, such as going to the doctor or the dentist. But in the neurotic adult we often witness *reactive courage,* in which the basically phobic individual deliberately seeks out situations that bring on fear in order to master the phobic symptoms. Thus, the acrophobic person may choose mountain climbing as a hobby. In the DSM-III system, there are but three types of phobia recognized: (1) a broadened interpretation of *agoraphobia,* as a fear of being alone or in a public place; (2) *social phobia,* in which the fear is that of being seen, assessed, or scrutinized by others; and (3) *simple phobia,* in which there is a persistent, irrational fear of objects, actions or situations that are not covered by the other two categories. Finally, it should be noted that phobias have a more mature structure than anxiety disorders. They are usually successful in eclipsing the anxiety or at least bringing it under partial control.

# 7

## Anxiety Disorders Continued: Obsessive-Compulsive Disorders

### Some Background Considerations

Kraepelin considered obsessive-compulsive neurosis to be an independent diagnostic category (see Chapter 1, p. 16), but DSM-III groups it within the family of anxiety disorders. Unconscious conflicts are expressed openly by the obsessive-compulsive patient in apparently senseless repetitive acts, words, or thoughts, in rituals and ceremonials, in endless doubting and ruminating. The major conflicts deal with problems of love and hate, right and wrong, cleanliness and dirt, orderliness and disorder. Sadism and masochism find free expression, and as we might expect, strong feelings of guilt appear, sometimes rivaling the overwhelming guilt in psychotic depressions. Magical thinking and superstition appear more clearly than in the manifest symptoms of any other neurosis. And finally, the patient usually is conscious of being in conflict, even though he or she may not understand what the conflict is about. A few brief clinical examples will illustrate the wide range of this disorder:

A boy of twelve years suffered from sudden impulses to call his parents obscene names. He managed to control these impulses by saying to himself out loud, "Stop it! Stop it!" Sometimes he swore at himself for having such impulses.

A man with irresistible impulses to utter blasphemies actually taped up his mouth at times, both to control and to punish himself.

A middle-aged woman occasionally had so strong an impulse to choke her husband while he slept that she would have to get up and leave the bedroom.

A young woman, in conflict over erotic fantasies, developed the need to think of a different person with each separate act she performed in her daily routine. If, for example, she thought of the same person twice while walking along the same street, she felt sure that something terrible would happen.

A senior engineering student was afraid that if he just looked at people they might die. He was a modern example of the superstitious belief in the "evil eye." He knew rationally that if someone at whom he had looked should happen to die, this would be pure coincidence; but he could not get rid of the feeling that he had a deadly power in his eyes, or of the awful guilt that went with this feeling.

We shall have more to say about the boy of twelve and the young woman later in the chapter.

As these cases demonstrate, the symptoms of this disorder do not result in feelings of pleasure, but serve only to remove a mounting level of anxiety. DSM-III refers to the obsession (thought) or compulsion (act) as being *ego-dystonic,* that is, as involuntary and carried out by conscious aspects of the ego even though they are senseless and sometimes repugnant. Research demonstrates that performing a compulsive act usually brings a feeling of reduced tension from the mounting anxiety, but this is relatively short-lived, and if the person should try to resist thinking or doing something the level of anxiety quickly rises once again (Carr, 1971; Hodgson & Rachman, 1972). Obsessive-compulsive disorders are rarely totally disabling (Grimshaw, 1965). Signs of this disturbance begin appearing before the person reaches the age of fifteen, and they are not likely to develop in someone past the age of twenty-five (Pollitt, 1960).

*The Normal Counterparts of Obsessive-Compulsive Symptoms.* Obsessive-compulsive symptoms are exaggerations and often caricatures of normal human trends. This does not make them normal, but it does make them more intelligible and acceptable. It is not always recognized that repetition and ritual, magic and superstition, enter into our everyday living in a great many ways. Some of these are basic to our most highly prized customs and social institutions.

If we examine compulsive ritual dispassionately, we find that it springs from the same roots as do the rituals which have given rise to the evolution of modern society—the rituals of the practical skills, of science, politics, social customs, art, religion. Unless we recognize that the relationships between normal and abnormal in this area are more than superficial resemblances, that both go deep into human nature, we cannot begin to understand the obsessive-compulsive disorder. We shall not recognize neurotic devotion to exact repetition, rigid uniformity, strict taboo, and severe self-punishment as pathological variants of universal human trends.

These trends are clearly expressed in children's games. Anyone who watches a group of children playing a game such as hopscotch will be immediately struck by the insistence upon inflexible rules of procedure, exact repetition, fixed formula, and precise ceremonial, down to the most minute detail. Piaget (1965) has studied this phenomenon in children's games, noting that a rule is like a sacred reality to very young children (p. 102). It is true, of course, that the patterns and rules of such play are transmitted culturally from older to younger children. But this fact in itself cannot account for the intense moral indignation that sweeps the group if one child inadvertently changes or omits a step in the traditionally fixed sequence of how to play the game. The child who is playing actively at the moment is being watched closely by every other child in the game to see that he or she conforms rigorously to the established patterns. It is clearly not only the outcome that counts but also the precise repetition of every step in the ritual.

When children improvise new games among themselves, they show the same intense concern over repetition, rule, formula, and ceremonial. Nor are these attitudes confined to play. Children also insist upon hearing a familiar story read or told by an adult without a change. Here, too, they may greet the most trivial omission or alteration with passionate and irritated outcries. Innovations or gaps in the recital of a story seem to interrupt the expected, familiar sequences. This frustrates the child because it cheats him or her out of the anticipated experience of closure, that is, the experience of having the story fulfill his or her expectations as a rounded out, familiar whole. This seems to be a reflection of the teleological mentality under maturation. Children are frustrated when a story loses predictability because they lose control, fail to experience what they *intend* experiencing.

The normal adult also shows a passionate insistence upon maintaining inflexible, arbitrary rules. Ritualistic practices are jealously preserved for centuries after their direct relevance has passed. One has only to look at the archaic language of contemporary law to realize the power of ritual for ritual's sake in human affairs. Thousands of contracts worded in a jargon belonging to an ancient language that hardly anyone today can understand are executed between ordinary persons every day. The same is true of rituals and ceremonials in other areas. Some special virtue attaches to uniformity, exact repetition, uncompromising procedure, and unvarying sequence. These are among the most primitive forms of mastery, and they are also basic to the most advanced forms of scientific inquiry and practical skill.

In courts of law any person capable of raising his or her right hand, in swearing to tell the truth, would be discredited and possibly held in contempt of court if the left were raised instead. Why? Suppose a man has the signing of his will witnessed by two persons, not knowing that in his state the law is exceptional and calls for three. The will may be declared invalid even though no one doubts that it represents the true intent of the deceased. Ritualistic practices obviously come to serve as frustrating "means" that then can block the very "ends" they were designed to promote.

In politics and in custom it is the same. If a woman hopes to achieve a certain thing in the public interest, she must proceed meticulously, step by step, in accordance with established expectations. No matter how urgent the need for speedy action, she must not omit a single station, or someone will make her start her pilgrimage all over again. This compulsive trend helps to build bureaucracies that only the bold genius can circumvent, and even she not often or for long. Scientific, artistic, and ethical advances have always depended upon the repetition of successful techniques, upon preserving their continuity and building them through cultural transmission into a lasting tradition, a human heritage.

In the course of transmitting cultural traditions it has happened over and over that human beings have concocted techniques of control and prediction long before they were able to understand thoroughly what they were doing, or what they were observing take place. Nevertheless human beings demand explanations and cannot resist giving them. The result has been that plausible hypotheses about prediction and control have again and again been adopted in which the superficial, accidental, and irrelevant have not been properly distinguished from the essential. Many discredited hypotheses still flourish in the form of magical practice and superstitious folklore in the culture at large, and they also persist as scientific mythologies (see our discussion of the nature of experimental conditioning in Chapter 5, p. 143).

Obsessive-compulsive procedures often appear to be caricatures of normal practices, such as the use of lucky charms, stylized statements, and meaningless words used to influence the roll of dice, or magic formulas like tossing the spilled salt over one's shoulder. Most of us at some point in our childhood have avoided stepping on a crack so that we would not break our mother's back. Obsessive-compulsive mechanisms have comparable goals, those of retaining control and avoiding disaster. Sometimes they express a belief that misdeeds can be undone and freedom from guilt can be gained through private rituals and self-imposed penalties. Obsessive-compulsive disorders thus take their place beside other neurotic behavior as exaggerations, distortions, and inappropriate uses of ordinary human trends. Behind the symptoms, as we shall see, there lie the familiar unresolved conflicts with their threat of disrupting ego integration.

*Definition. Obsessive-compulsive disorders consist of apparently useless but irresistible repetitious acts, words, or thoughts whose aim is to reduce tension and anxiety (1) by indulging in something forbidden, (2) by denying such indulgence or guarding against it, or (3) by punishing oneself for having had the impulse to indulge.* All three aims, no matter how contradictory they may be, are often included together in the symptomatology of the same obsessive-compulsive disorder (we shall see a comparable multiplicity and overdetermination in the symptoms of the somatoform disorder; see Chapter 8).

Obsessive-compulsive symptoms vary in complexity from ordinary trivial little acts—such as tapping, counting, snapping the fingers, saying a set word or phrase over and over, imagining some prescribed sound or scene—to complex ceremonials carried out in fixed, unvarying sequences. Some symptoms seem superficially absurd or ridiculous; some seem humiliating, horrifying, or disgusting; some appear to be dangerous; some are limited to abstract doubting, ruminating, or speculating, in which there is no feeling. Although DSM-III continues the tradition of calling irresistible thoughts *obsessions,* and irresistible impulses to act out *compulsions,* some modern authorities use these words interchangeably. Thus, obsessions are sometimes called *compulsive thoughts.*

What makes the obsessive-compulsive disorder especially illuminating is that in it one can often witness the elements or the direct derivatives of an unconscious conflict being acted out as manifest symptoms in plain view. Hostile or erotic impulses may appear openly upon the stage of consciousness, with the meanings and origins thinly veiled. Sometimes countermeasures against unconscious or preconscious wishes emerge among the visible symptoms with little or no disguise. Self-punishment, carried out under the influence of an archaic, retaliative superego, may be so obvious that a person would have to be functionally blind to miss its meaning. Sometimes, especially in obsessive doubt and rumination, all feeling seems to be replaced by a cold intellectual detachment (isolation).

*Adaptive Function.* Obsessive-compulsive patients vary greatly in the degree to which their maneuvers actually reduce emotional tension and anxiety. Some are tense and anxious only when there is interference with their indulgence or with a countermeasure. Some show little anxiety and seem mainly perplexed and ashamed of their symptoms. Some seem to lose all tension and anxiety; they appear to look upon their manifest symptoms as an objective scientist is supposed to look at factual data.

Incidental unimportant obsessions and compulsions are common. We run across them clinically by accident. From this fact it is fair to assume that a great many people succeed in reducing their tension to manageable proportions by the use of minor obsessive-compulsive defenses—repetitious little acts, rituals, penances, and ceremonials—without attracting particular attention and without significantly distorting their general life pattern.

Some persons utilize obsessive-compulsive trends to make their work or their play more effective and enjoyable. Among these may be mentioned the activities of some librarians, bookkeepers, statisticians, chartists, theoreticians, and systematizers, as well as a host of hobbyists, for example, collectors and classifiers, chess players, amateur designers, organizers, and architects. Obsessive-compulsive trends may enter into almost any activity that involves meticulous detail, extreme orderliness or disorder, exact repetition or systematic doubting, rumination, speculation, or superstition. This is not to say, of course, that all such interests indicate an obsessive-compulsive neurosis, any more than it is true that all test pilots or stunt men or women are counterphobic. Such normal trends of obsessive-compulsivity actually promote efficiency in the task at hand and are tantamount to strengths rather than weaknesses. It is worth mentioning here that work involving arbitrary demands that others conform to one's will in every detail also attracts persons with irresistible compulsive wishes to control themselves. This they in part realize by controlling others, whether children or dependent adults.

For the average obsessive-compulsive patient an indulgence in his or her symptom brings only temporary relief. The tension and anxiety, coming as they do from internal instability, soon become intolerable again. It is then necessary to repeat the symptom to regain relief. With the passage of time obsessions and compulsions often tend to generalize. They may grow into more or less stereotyped methods of meeting all emotional tension and anxiety, whether internally or externally generated and whether related to the original conflicts or not.

*Compulsions and Phobias.* Compulsions often appear combined with phobias. Some obsessive-compulsive persons displace and project in such a way as to make over fear of an internal conflict into a fear of some external object or situation. This means the development of a phobia, allowing such patients to focus on ever-present dangers just as all phobics do. Clinicians have usually found that the obsessive-compulsive who is also phobic suffers more from conscious guilt than does the typical phobic patient (see the case of Erika M., below).

*Varieties of Obsessive-Compulsive Disorders.* In the clinical material that follows in Chapter 7 we have not attempted to create a strict classification of the varieties of obsessive-compulsive symptoms. Instead, we have formed three clinical groups that represent an ascending scale of complexity. Each group will highlight a different facet of the obsessive-compulsive disorder. At the end we have added obsessive doubt and rumination, which does not fit into this arrangement. The groups are as follows:

1. Attempts to handle tension and anxiety through *regression, displacement,* and *isolation.* These are unconscious defensive techniques that we have discussed in Chapters 4 (pp. 134-137) and 5 (p. 153).
2. The overt use of one neurotic maneuver as a *countermeasure* in an attempt to offset the effects of some other neurotic maneuver. This technique is present to some extent in most obsessive-compulsive disorders.
3. The use of *reaction-formation* (see Chapter 4, p. 137), ritualistic *undoing,* and openly *sadomasochistic self-punishment.*
4. *Obsessive doubt and rumination.* Here a great deal of the emotional aspect of obsessive-compulsive disorders has been repressed. The result is what we have called caricatures of magic, scientific, artistic, and religious practice. Obsessive doubt and rumination may almost paralyze a person by suspending all decision and by replacing action with speculation.

## Regression, Displacement, and Isolation

Regression, displacement, and isolation are all intentional evasions. In obsessive-compulsive disorders, *regression* replaces a current sexual or aggressive conflict with problems belonging to a pre-Oedipal level, at which the patient may feel stronger or more at home. *Displacement* is used throughout obsessive-compulsive disorders to shift the focus from current conflicts to infantile problems, or from a dramatic struggle to a colorless action—a chess game in place of a battle. *Isolation* is also used to separate opposing aspects of a conflict or to eliminate emotional components from compulsive symptoms. Freud (1926/1959g) noted that in an obsessional neurosis, rather than seek to repress every unconscious wish pressing to consciousness, a special isolation is effected:

"In obsessional neurosis . . . the [traumatic] experience is not forgotten, but, instead, it is deprived of its affect, and its associative connections [memories] are suppressed or interrupted so that it remains as though isolated and is not reproduced in the ordinary processes of thought" (p. 120). The effect of this isolation is the same as the effect of repression with amnesia. If successful, isolation can also prevent the confrontation of opposing psychic attitudes. In this sense, its effects are similar to those achieved in dissociative disorders by denial and ego-splitting (see Chapter 9).

All three maneuvers are employed when repression begins to break down, of course. They are defensive in that they make it possible for a patient to escape further ego disintegration. It is assumed by most clinicians that through the use of these maneuvers the obsessive-compulsive patient avoids the deeper regression possible to a psychotic level. Freud (ibid.) suggested that the regression in obsessive-compulsive neurosis is tied to fixations in the phallic level, with its Oedipal involvements, but that due to the ego's enfeebled efforts for some reason (including constitutional weakness), there is a further regression back to the "earlier sadistic-anal level" (p. 113). Problems associated with anality, such as self-control, meeting schedules, resistance, frustration, and open hostility are therefore likely to be seen persisting as the "fuero claims" intruding upon the obsessive compulsive's behavioral pattern.

Jason N., aged twelve and an only child, is the boy to whom we earlier referred as having impulses to call his parents obscene names. He controlled himself by saying out loud, "Stop it! Stop it!" At the beginning of his adolescence, in the face of increasing emotional tension, he had reacted by regressing to a level of ego/ superego development similar to that at which he had tried to resolve the same general problem in childhood. By this maneuver he was able to displace his disturbance over his own adolescent sexuality onto the sexuality of his parents— without in the least recognizing what he was doing. His obscenities were early adolescent expressions of the angry resentment that a child of two or three years might feel with regard to parental intimacy and his own sense of frustration over being excluded, particularly during the period of toilet training, when he was likely to be reprimanded for inadequate self-control.

This case is especially instructive because at twelve Jason felt no resentment or anger toward his parents, but only anxiety and humiliation because of his obsessive symptoms. This switch is clearly the work of his unconscious ego defenses. The obscenities seemed to Jason to be automatic intrusions, without feeling, which he could not begin to understand. He had not only *displaced* his own rising tide of sexuality onto his parents; he had also *isolated* all emotional tone from the obscenities that emerged against his (conscious) will.

When Jason said, "Stop it! Stop it!" to himself, he was repeating actual parental commands that he had heard in his own childhood during periods of misbehavior— issuing quite often from problems of self-control in both a physical (sphincter control) and psychological (temper tantrums) sense. This exclamation was, in other words, an attempt to control his own thinking by the use of parental injunctions, which he had internalized early in his life—the precursors of his own superego.

A further instructive aspect of this case is that, in swearing at himself for wanting to say obscene things, Jason was giving a classical example of the way in which forbidden impulses often come through into consciousness as part of the defense. Jason was like a police officer who must use violence to preserve the peace. The unconscious impulse to say forbidden things gained its expression in his obscene self-reproach.

Our second case is that of Cheryl I., a young mother who sought help because of what seemed to her a senseless, dangerous impulse of brutality toward her infant daughter. The impulse seemed to well up within her suddenly every so often without any apparent provocation. She said, "I'm looking at my little baby, so sweet and precious, and then I get the feeling I might choke her or drown her!" Aside from these isolated sadistic impulses she felt nothing but love for her child.

In the course of therapy no hatred toward the baby came to light. But this young mother had a younger sister, born when Cheryl was four years old. Cheryl reacted to the birth of her sister, as many little children do, by persistently soiling and wetting (note the anal fixation suggested here). For this she was severely punished. She loved her baby sister as a living doll, a baby such as she herself wanted; and she hated her as a rival for her mother's love, and probably as a constant reminder that her mother could have babies while she herself could not. She never succeeded in resolving this early childhood conflict. The best she had been able to do as a child was to buttress her inadequate repression with a reactive oversolicitude toward her sister (reaction-formation).

The sister grew up to be prettier and more popular than Cheryl. She was married sooner and already had two sons before Cheryl had her first child. Cheryl wanted a boy. When she gave birth to a girl the whole bitter competition with her younger sister was rekindled. She unconsciously cast her baby daughter in the role of her sister as a baby. The hatred that welled up toward her daughter expressed unconscious resentment at two levels: the old hatred for the baby rival of her childhood and the current bitter envy over this same rival sister having two boys, while she was given a girl. As therapy progressed, the irrational hatred for her sister emerged from behind her exaggerated solicitude for her. As this was worked through the homicidal fantasies of killing her own baby disappeared.

Our third case is that of Roger E., an unmarried man aged forty-two, whose widowed mother was slowly dying at home. He was shocked when he experienced sudden waves of hatred toward her and had the conscious wish that she would hurry up and die. These experiences repeated themselves at intervals without warning, sometimes when they had been gazing tenderly at each other. The rest of the time he felt himself to be, as he had felt all his life, her devoted and self-effacing son. These sudden symptoms were not only distressing but they seemed to Roger to make no sense at all.

Roger was the unwelcome child of his mother's middle age and by far the youngest of the four children she bore. She fastened him to her with a domineering, possessive love. Throughout his childhood she infantilized him in one or another way. Roger, for his part, loved his mother when he was a child as the source of all good and all affection; and he hated her because she was self-willed and frustrating. The only serious rebellion that he could recall took place during his toilet training. They would sometimes spend an hour or more in a contest of wills while she tried to compel Roger to move his bowels. Eventually she always won because if he did not give in she gave him an enema which both excited and infuriated him.

Now on her deathbed she was weak and helpless. Sometimes she soiled. Her approaching death loomed as the final frustration for Roger. She was about to leave him alone in the world, with no one to depend on, after she had monopolized his affection all his life. Following her death he developed a severe depression for which he had to be hospitalized.

In all three of these cases we see sadistic-anal manifestations coming into consciousness, which isolation suggested in the behavior of Jason and Cheryl, but not in Roger's conscious feelings of hatred toward his mother. It is clinically plausible to suspect that this failure to complete a full obsessive-compulsive dynamic in Roger's case is what accounted for the subsequent depression (Gero & Rubenfine, 1955).

## Obsessive-Compulsive Countermeasures

In many cases of obsessive-compulsivity we can witness *countermeasures* taking place, by which is meant to oppose the expression of unconscious wishes through a calculated scheme aimed at stopping the thoughts or acts that are offensive to the person. In a sense, the countermeasure is to consciousness what repression or "countercathexis" is to the unconscious realm of mind. Sometimes the countermeasure results in a full-dress public performance. The first case to be given sounds childlike and simple; the second case mingles phobias and compulsions together in a complex and desperate struggle.

> Karen P. was an unmarried computer analyst, aged twenty-four. She was trying to control erotic fantasies that she could not repress. Her countermeasures put into practice, in a compulsive way, the advice often given to adolescents who are struggling with sexual temptations, "Think of something else!" Walking to work was an activity that permitted erotic fantasies to emerge easily. So each time Karen stepped on or off the curb at a corner she made herself think of a different person. This kept her mind busy preparing for the next intersection. If she ran out of persons she allowed herself to change streets and start the list over again.
> This obsessive countermeasure cost Karen time and effort, which is one of the first points we look for in judging precisely when a normal obsession or compulsion is reaching neurotic proportions. Does it invade on the person's efficiency in living? As Karen's obsession became entrenched, it made her shun company to avoid having to explain her preoccupation and her zigzag course as she changed streets. She needed to concentrate upon the task of having names ready in time for the next block. The device failed, however, to eliminate all her erotic fantasies, it tended to sustain rather than to reduce her anxiety, and it kept her from the benefits and pleasures of sharing in the company of others.
> In time the countermeasure generalized to other activities. As Karen dressed and undressed she found that she had to think of a different person with each article of clothing that she put on or took off. Later this became necessary for each mouthful of food, and for each act in doing her laundry or in housecleaning. It began creeping into her work in programming the computer and compiling reports. She had to assign names to each of the steps she took in her calculations and assembling of data. The symptoms became so bad that she could not perform her duties and was forced to seek a leave of absence as she sought professional assistance.

Karen had a passive, defeated attitude toward her symptom. She said, "For a long time I couldn't break it; and now it just seems easier to go on." She was speaking as much of her drift into uncontrollable erotic fantasy as of the generalization of her tyrannical countermeasures. Her outlook for recovery was considered guarded.

The next case is far more complex and more dramatic. It consists of the interweaving of apparently senseless fears with strict obsessive-compulsive countermeasures to ward off what was feared. The momentary flash of a murderous impulse is the most important clue that we have to the meaning of whole systems of compulsive safeguards against killing others. Without this clue the woman's symptoms might have remained as unintelligible to us as they were at first to her and to her intended victims. The patient herself knew of the occurrence of this impulse before entering therapy, but she had never connected it with her neurotic illness. She had kept the knowledge isolated.

Erika M. was the forty-two-year-old wife of a Minnesota businessman and the mother of three children. Her symptoms appeared suddenly. She was serving the family dinner one evening when she dropped a dish on the table and smashed it. The accident appalled her. While clearing up the fragments she was seized with an unreasonable fear that bits of glass might get into her husband's food and kill him. She would not allow the meal to proceed until she had removed everything and reset the table with fresh linen and clean dishes. After this her fears, instead of subsiding, reached out to include intense anxiety over the possibility that she herself and her children might be killed by bits of glass.

The patient's fears and defensive rituals did not stop with this. Erika developed an irresistible need to examine minutely every piece of glassware that she handled. If anything had the slightest chip in it she threw it away; and she had to carry it to the trash can herself to make sure that it went out of the house. Then she would hunt for the missing chip which, of course, she could rarely find. She had read somewhere that copper pots and aluminum pots were not safe for certain kinds of cooking. Her worries now included their use. She remembered that her wedding ring had some copper in it as well as gold. First she took it off whenever she cooked or washed dishes; then she lost it.

Meanwhile she heard about other things which raised new fears and touched off further compulsive countermeasures. These included the danger of a spread of virus disease from toilet to kitchen, the dangers of lye and pesticides, and of the chemical and organic fertilizers used on the lawn. Eventually all potential poisons of every kind had to be isolated from cooking utensils and dishes by storing them in the garage—even the cleaning fluids and scouring powders needed for everyday washing and cleaning.

These endless precautionary rituals drove the family almost frantic. Yet they brought Erika no lasting peace. Her list of potential dangers kept growing until she simply did not have enough attention to bestow upon them all. If she was not certain that she had or had not done something in a certain way, she would have to rehearse her steps to make sure, or else begin all over again.

One of the hardest things for her to endure was that she could not control what the others did or convince them that her precautions were essential. She tried to make someone stay beside her to help keep track of every move she made; but when they did they proved to be not nearly as meticulous or concerned as she was. She found herself watching her husband and her children furtively for signs of ill health. In the end the whole situation became too much for her and the family to handle. Erika had to give up housekeeping and seek full-time therapeutic help.

What was the meaning of this network of fears and precautions? In due course, psychoanalysis established that Erika was protecting everybody from herself. Eventually she recognized the source of her dangerous hostility. Some time before breaking the glass dish she had discovered what she considered to be certain evidence that her husband was having an affair. This humiliated and angered her, but she said nothing about it. What appalled Erika when she smashed the dish was the momentary conscious hope that he would eat glass and die, a homicidal wish that her carelessness would kill him (id wish). She immediately denied and repressed the wish (ego/superego antithetic wish). But from that moment all her obsessive-compulsive countermeasures were directed against the possibility of some new accident in which she might inadvertently carry out her unconscious wish. At the same time, overt evidence mounted of her wanting to end all signs of the marital union (lost ring, children's possible illness and death, etc.). The fear for her own safety is suggestive of a superego wish for punishment, given the murderous intentions of the id. Once again, anal involvements are clearly suggested in the preoccupation with contamination and cleanliness.

## Reaction-Formation and Undoing

In addition to the mechanisms and countermeasures discussed thus far, Freud (1926/1959g) has noted the frequent use of *reaction-formation* (p. 115) and *undoing* (p. 119) in the obsessive-compulsive disorders. Reaction-formation was discussed in Chapter 4 (see p. 137). Reaction-formation becomes pathological when a person has unusually strong sadistic impulses that he or she can neither express nor repress. If the threatening impulse is to soil, directly or symbolically, the person may insist upon being so meticulously neat and clean that even friends and associates suspect his or her behavior of being a defense against something feared. Infantile aggression associated with the anal level is closely allied with impulses to soil.

The other mechanism to be stressed in this section, *undoing,* is an example of magical thinking that all of us use normally in one form or another. When, for example, a small child falls and hurts himself, his mother may kiss the hurt place and say, "Now that will make it all better again!" She uses the magic of her love to undo the pain. If her magic works the hurt child's crying is modulated to a whimper. Apologies among adults often follow similar principles. We say that we did not mean something when sometimes the truth is otherwise. Nevertheless, our disavowal may magically undo the hurt or the insult of our action. Undoing also appears in the practice of sending a conciliatory gift. A person tries to *undo* a quarrel by an offering of flowers or a present—anything that symbolizes his humility and esteem in the wake of some meanness or anger.

We all use *symbolization* in our practice of undoing. What is more, we often symbolize both guilt and innocence in the same fantasy, the same word, action, or symbolic object. The cross, for example, signifies to Christians both the burden of their sins and their redemption from their sins, their inevitable guilt and their eventual innocence. When they gaze religiously upon the cross, their fantasies may be a blending of sin and forgiveness or an alternation between the two.

For a billion and more human beings, of many different creeds, washing rituals have the same symbolic elements. They are an acknowledgement of sinfulness, of having been an unclean transgressor; at the same time they are a statement of newly acquired cleanliness or innocence. The contamination of dirty thoughts, of evil deeds and bad intentions, is ritualistically washed away by a symbolic act.

No believer tries to justify such thinking through an appeal to verbal logic. No one thinks of asking for a scientific study of the cleansed person and the cleansing agent. Religious behavior belongs to a different realm of experience. For thousands of years the public ablution has been used as a visible, tangible ritual to serve notice upon others and upon oneself that sins have been committed and are now in the process of being undone. The act is literal and physical, but its target is symbolic and spiritual. What the evil thought or intention has been may never be revealed to another person. Yet washing can still signify the desire to regain innocence or to reassure oneself of being guiltless.

Obsessive-compulsives often use undoing in forms that seem more primitive, more childlike and magical, than normal rituals. This is in part because the obsessive-compulsive ritual is likely to be personal, inventive, and unfamiliar to others. It is also in part because the patient regresses, and in regressing he or she reactivates and releases unconscious fantasies or their derivatives. These belong to an immature age and account for the often childlike nature of this symptom picture. The more sadistic side of superego admonitions may be encompassed here, as they were initially put down in the anal psychosexual stage. A whole system of unconscious thinking, never lost to the psyche and always to some extent present in adult behavior, now comes forward to dominate the neurotic situation. This system of thought is especially clear in matters of love and hate, cleanliness and dirt, moral right and wrong.

The case of Sally J., which we are about to present, forms an interesting contrast to our previous one. Sally was at least the intellectual equal of Erika M. Culturally and educationally she was superior. Yet her hostility was crudely expressed in frank physiological symbols, and her handwashing ritual followed a monotonous, primitive pattern. Her preoccupation with soiling showed little of the defensive displacement through which Erika was able to focus upon chipped glassware, lye, cleaning fluids, and scouring powders. And whereas Erika tried to head off her unconscious hostile impulses by means of elaborate protective devices, Sally openly expressed her hostility, and only afterward turned to her magical washing ritual to undo the evil and punish herself.

*Case of Sally J.: Obsessive-Compulsive Handwashing*

Sally J. was an attractive unmarried state employee in her twenty-seventh year. She came for help because her symptoms had forced her to break off an engagement of three years' standing. She complained of ungovernable outbursts of rage against her fiancé, of continual thoughts about contaminating others, and of irresistible impulses to wash her hands over and over. Once again we find here a familiar obsessive-compulsive trio: *intense emotional ambivalence* (hating a loved one), *preoccupation with contamination,* and the use of *defensive countermeasures* (handwashing against soiling).

*Childhood background.* Sally's childhood throws a great deal of light upon her neurotic illness. She was an angry child. As an infant she had frequent breath-holding spells in which she would go purple with rage. Temper tantrums continued right through childhood into adulthood. Sally grew into a demanding, willful little girl with a strong Oedipal attachment to her father. She made such a terrible fuss over his leaving her that sometimes he had to sneak out of a side window to get to work. Her father never spanked her, but her mother did and Sally never forgave her for it. She remembered sitting alone in a corner on the floor as a child, weeping over her mother's treatment of her.

Great difficulties over bowel function seem to have begun in infancy and to have extended into adolescence. The mother, a practical nurse, was most exacting. Sally appeared always to be getting constipated; and to this challenge her mother responded by giving the child enemas, just as the mother of Roger E., mentioned earlier in this chapter, did. Sally remembered watching the preparations in helpless rage. The contest of wills often ended with Sally messing up the bathroom, which, in later years, she had to help her mother clean. She recalled how peaceful it seemed when the storm was over and everything had been put away.

Sally had a vivid memory of sitting on a log in the backyard with her father, waiting for something. She was then three and a half years old. The something was her baby brother's birth. She had known for some time that her mother was "going to be sick." Sally had said then that she could look after herself; but after Billy was born everything got worse. He was clearly the favorite of her father no less than of her mother. All through the rest of her childhood she felt herself compared unfavorably with him. At first she used to say to her father, "Put him down! Take your *own* baby!" She remembered brooding over this preference for her brother, feeling terribly jealous and resentful toward her parents.

In time, however, Sally gave up expressing hatred toward Billy. She adopted instead a protective attitude toward him of tender loving care. This change was a product of *reaction-formation.* The hate was still there not far from the surface; for whenever Billy teased her, she responded with violent temper outbursts. Sally also used reaction-formation in her attempts to handle her conflicts over bowel function and soiling. Around the age of five years she became fastidious in the extreme. Her own person had to be meticulously clean, her hair smoothed out, and her dresses without a crease or a speck of dirt. She always sat down carefully, like a woman in a party dress, smoothing her skirt and watching to make sure that it did not wrinkle. There was a big row over an expensive coat that Sally wanted when she was only six. She got it.

She identified with her mother in an ambivalent admiring, hating way. According to Sally, her mother had been a beautiful woman who devoted much silent attention to her own appearance. Sally boasted about her mother to her little friends, but at home she always treated her mother with disdain. She went on trying to win back her place as her father's favorite without success.

As long as she could remember, Sally had suffered from an absurdly guilty conscience. Almost anything could arouse it. If something at home was missing she felt that she was suspected of having made away with it. Even when she was sick in bed she felt that she was only pretending. Her parents impressed upon her a strict sense of moral responsibility from the very start. She never lost a fascination for unpardonable sin and the fate of sinners. Her childhood dreams sometimes turned into nightmares; but when they did it was to her mother, not to her father, that she went for comforting when she awoke.

Another thing that went back to early childhood was an insatiable curiosity about sex. Her baby brother's genitals caught Sally by surprise, but her parents would not allow her to speak about them. She decided that there was "a surface way of living and a hidden life." Later on she discovered that it was safe to discuss such things with her girlfriends. Between the ages of ten and twelve Sally had occasional episodes of mutual masturbation with other girls. She felt wicked at the time but developed no serious manifest conflict. She was quite shy with boys, preferring during her adolescent years to "hero-worship" a boy from afar rather than date him. Indeed, she did not have a clear-cut date—as opposed to group get-togethers in which both sexes were present—until she was twenty years old.

*Adolescent symptoms.* The first frankly obsessive-compulsive symptoms appeared when Sally was twelve or thirteen, well after she had given up her exaggerated neatness and cleanliness. For several months, in early adolescence, she found herself continually counting parked automobiles and passing automobiles in groups of seven. She had to keep the count of parked cars completely separate from the count of passing cars. Otherwise something terrible would happen—she was not sure what. The parked cars, she said, seemed to her more like girls and the passing cars like boys. At this time she was also haunted by abstract uncertainties over right and wrong. She engaged in anxious rumination about God's will, and how she could ever be sure what it was.

In high school, in business school, and at work Sally developed a variety of obsessive-compulsive doubts, repetitions, and rituals concerning numbers, equations, balancing accounts, filing systems, indexing, and the like. These seemed to rise and fall with the rise and fall of difficulties over interpersonal relationships. At home she grew generally more and more irritable, she slept poorly, and she had temper outbursts and occasional crying spells. This gives us a sketchy picture of the tense, uneasy situation in which Sally developed her acute illness.

*Guilt and mild depression.* When she was twenty Sally began dating and going steady with a dignified, reserved man of thirty-five. Her parents disapproved of him on religious grounds. She found herself getting more and more tense with him as time went on. Finally, after nearly two years, she flew into a rage one evening and told the man she never wanted to see him again. She never did.

Her second serious interest in a man, six months later, ended disastrously for her. One evening her escort unexpectedly began sex play. Sally reacted with a violent upsurge of anxiety and guilt, returned home at once, and went immediately to her mother for comfort, just as she had done after her childhood nightmares.

This episode of essentially normal sex play brought out into the open a long struggle with sex and hostility that Sally had been trying to wage secretly and alone. She made a series of abject confessions to her mother, passing quickly from the evening's petting to focus upon her sex play with other girls in preadolescence, and upon her solitary masturbation before that. She told her mother in a spirit of self-abasement that she had sinned against God and that her hands were unclean. No handwashing occurred at this time.

In the weeks that followed Sally talked a great deal to her mother about right and wrong, about being sinful and unworthy, about being different from others because of all that she had done. There is reason to believe that Sally's mother was just as infantile about morality as her daughter, failing completely to differentiate between natural biological urges and the intentional furthering of immoral behavior as defined by religious prescriptions. Sally explained that for years she had been troubled by what she called "sensual sensations." These occurred especially when she was sexually aroused, when she was constipated or had a full bladder, and whenever she indulged in "evil thoughts." She thus tied together her sexual, bowel, and urinary functions with evil thinking.

Her trouble with men, Sally said, was that they stirred up these "sensual sensations" until she could not stand it. Then she would have a violent temper outburst and feel relieved; but with the outburst she often had orgasm, and this led to a new build-up of guilt and tension. We see here the confusion of love and hate in an adult, and the linking of this sexual-aggressive (eros/death instincts) experience with bowel function, which was to precipitate a classical handwashing compulsion.

For several months Sally remained subdued and mildly depressed. She managed to stay at work, but she ate and slept poorly. She went out with no one, and there were no temper outbursts. Then she took advantage of her summer vacation to obtain a ninety-day sick leave. She spent this period resting on a Western ranch that took paying guests and that had only one lavatory which everyone used. It was here that Sally replaced her mild depression with an obsessive-compulsive disorder.

*The handwashing compulsion.* In using a communal toilet, with towels that everyone shared, Sally found herself worrying about—not *being* infected but—infecting others! She obsessed over the possibility of causing someone else's death by infecting them with some unknown disease. This obsession was a combination of guilt, hostility, and an infantile overvaluation of the powers of her excreta (anal fixation). The only way that Sally could relieve the tension of this obsession was to wash her hands—a particularly irrational, magical remedy, since it did not change the fact that there was only one toilet for everyone to use. Nevertheless, each time she thought of contaminating others she had to scrub her hands. She began using a harsh, yellow soap and a nail brush, and she scrubbed her arms up to the elbows. Sometimes she added Lysol, which was available on the ranch.

Sally returned home in relatively good spirits but with a fully developed handwashing compulsion, which did not go away. She soon had an ugly, painful dermatitis. Her hands and forearms became red, tender, and swollen; sometimes there was a crack in the skin that oozed serum. But ugly and painful or not, the hands and forearms had to be scrubbed every time Sally went to the toilet, and every time she had a "sensual sensation" or thought about contamination. If she resisted the impulse to wash and scrub she had an anxiety attack. Her heart would pound, and she would break out in a sweat and feel panicky and breathless—"as if something were pressing the life out of me," she said.

Obsessive thoughts behave as all assumptions and inferences; that is, they extend to more and more aspects of the patient's life. Thus, before long Sally began thinking that she was contaminating everything she touched. Towels and under-clothes had to be laundered after a single use; dresses had to be cleaned after one wearing. Her bureau drawer became filled with discarded brushes, combs, gloves, and handbags which, she felt, might contaminate others. They were dangerous to use and too dangerous to throw away. A streak of omnipotence, an unconscious fantasy of being the foul fiend, lurked behind this primitive, regressive belief. At the same time, as might be expected, there was a marked increase in orderliness at work (reaction-formation). Sally was more than ever repetitious, uncertain, and ritualistic at the office.

When she was twenty-four Sally fell in love with a man of whom her family approved. She soon became engaged, but all the old difficulties arose again and new ones appeared. Just being in her fiancé's company gave Sally "sensual sensa-tions." This made her feel guilty and resentful, and at the same time frustrated, neglected, and unappreciated, much as she had felt in early childhood. Every so often the situation would get beyond her control and a violent temper tantrum would erupt, something like her childhood response to her brother's teasing.

Two new elements entered the situation: actual soiling and penitential sado-masochism. Sally's temper outbursts now culminated in the physiological act of passing traces of urine, gas, or feces, which to her meant a deadly assault upon the man she loved. She had to change her clothes immediately and scrub her hands and forearms. Sally began to feel pleasure in hurting herself. While she was using the nailbrush, and wincing, she would tell herself under her breath that she had it coming to her. Something in her seemed to gloat when the pain made her wince and whimper. Her remorse over her now open hostility toward her fiancé added fuel to this sadistic attack upon herself. When the ritual was over she felt relaxed and gratified. In therapy, it reminded her of the peace that had always followed after her mother had given her enemas as punishment in childhood.

A homoerotic component also appeared in the clinical picture, but only in Sally's manifest dreams. One dream she related as follows: "I was kissing a person. I can't remember—maybe it was a girl. I can't remember. Maybe one of the girls at work or one I know in the neighborhood. At least the girl had that girl's dress on." In another dream that she had repeatedly she seemed to be walking down the street with another woman, each of them with an arm around the other's waist. The pressure of the other woman's arm would begin to squeeze her—an awful feeling as if something were closing in upon her, as though she could not bear it, as though her breath were being taken away. She associated this repetitive dream with her mother, and also with the anxiety that came whenever she resisted handwashing, "as if something were pressing the life out" of her. In this dream, with its associa-tions, Sally's childhood love, her fear, and the "sensual sensations" were brought together.

The now well-established cycle—hostile and erotic thoughts, token soiling, scrubbing, and final relaxation—generalized further to all kinds of situations. Whenever Sally heard somebody else praised and her old inadequacy feelings came back, like the ones she had experienced in relation to her little brother, this was enough to start off the cycle. The same thing happened when she compared herself with anyone she admired, and whenever she felt neglected or unfairly treated. Any erotic, jealous, or angry rumination was enough to do it. Even standing in line, when she could not move forward fast enough, started off the cycle—angry thoughts, token contamination, handwashing, and then peace. In spite of her tensions and rituals, the engagement with her fiancé lasted two and a half years. Then there was a temper outburst, the engagement was broken, and Sally sought psychotherapeutic help.

Therapy began, as usual, with what the patient herself first provided. Broadening and deepening of this material developed slowly as the interviews progressed. What has just been told as a consecutive, unfolding story actually emerged in a more or less scattered order. The fragments emerging were themselves a product and a part of the treatment. Sometimes things seemed to emerge out of context, as things often do in dreams; but they were not really out of context with Sally's focal conflicts and fantasies. Some fantasies and conflicts appeared consciously in the form of ritual and magical thinking. Improvement came with the new insights and perspectives which Sally was able to work out. Her tolerance for anxiety increased, so that she could face things which she had formerly repressed, and her obsessive-compulsive behavior became much less tyrannical. She was still far from a complete recovery when she terminated her treatment. It was learned a few years later that she had married and borne a child.

*Discussion.* This case has been presented in some detail because it expresses openly many characteristics that often can only be inferred in obsessive-compulsives. While it is still fresh in our memory we shall discuss some of its dynamic and developmental background, even though this anticipates the general discussion of obsessive-compulsives at the end of the chapter.

Perhaps the most striking pathological characteristic that Sally showed was her *ambivalence.* As a small child she hated her little brother, although she grew to love him. She hated her mother but admired her and turned to her for comfort and forgiveness. She bitterly resented her father's desertion in favor of her brother, but she never gave up trying to win him back. She was meticulously clean and neat at the same time that—during a decade of childhood struggling with her mother for independence—she was messing things up with her excretions. As an adult she was an attractive, well-dressed, laydlike young woman; yet she was using soiling, flatus, and wetting whenever she became tense or angry. And whenever she began to love a man she flew into violent temper tantrums.

This ambivalence itself rested upon defective repression. One of the signs that repression is chronically defective is the overuse of reaction-formation as a defense. The child who becomes too good, too clean, or too obedient is usually a child who has not been able to come to terms with his or her unconscious impulses in the dialectically opposite direction. As we have seen, Sally's extensive use of reaction-formation was not enough to enable repression to hold hostile and erotic impulses within normal bounds.

The regressive nature of Sally's behavior appears in many ways. Openly hating loved ones, messing while being clean, liking pretty things and soiling them, expressing love and hate through bowel and bladder functions—all these belong more to a two-year-old level than to adult maturity. So also, of course, does the use of reaction-formation to buttress the defenses when repression is still underdeveloped.

Sally's magical thinking was also regressive. It expressed childlike omnipotence clearly. She was frightened that her excreta might kill, and she dared not throw away things that she had used for fear of what they might do to other people. Even her thoughts about contamination seemed potentially dangerous to Sally. This is not the logical reasoning of a sophisticated adult, which in other respects the patient was, but the prelogical, primary process thinking of a confused little child.

Much of the same can be said of the purifying handwashing ritual as the patient used it. Handwashing might have been in part a return to the reactive cleanliness that Sally abandoned when she was twelve; but, if so, its use in adulthood was also in her case a return to ritual magic. Her fear, as we have seen, was that she might harm others through her thoughts of soiling. Yet it was her own hands and forearms that she scrubbed. In this symptomatology Sally neither distinguished clearly between herself and others nor recognized the everyday logic of cause and effect. Her attempt to undo her magical harm to others by washing herself was on the same general level as the ritual practice of rattling dry beans in a gourd to make the rains come. Sally's purification ritual, like her fear of exercising omnipotent evil, belongs to prelogical, primary process thought.

Outstanding in the clinical picture is also an archaic precursor of the superego, a sadistic monitor and punisher. This superego precursor goes far beyond her mother's sadism by carrying retaliatory self-punishment to cruel extremes. Sally's mother used enemas to subdue and punish her in childhood. Sally, as an adult, used laundry soap and water on her hands and forearms. She scrubbed them with a nailbrush and sometimes added Lysol. All this she did, not only to undo magically her dangerous contaminations, but also to give herself savage punishment.

Sally gloated vindictively as she gave herself pain. Her own words were, "A part of me seems to gloat." At the same time she sometimes whimpered out loud like a cruelly treated child. Thus she brought to light her immature superego identifications, which belonged to a period when parental punishment is experienced as torture and the parent as a relentless tormentor. These superego identifications Sally used immaturely, as an archaic superego struggling with a partially regressed ego. Instead of an interaction between two aspects of a unitary personality, we witness here a punitive mother image and a suffering daughter image, both viewed from the perspective of a confused, sadomasochistic little child.

We shall turn next to forms of obsessive-compulsive neurosis that contrast sharply with the vivid drama present in the case of Sally J. These forms have similar dynamic roots, but in spite of this the life seems to have gone out of the struggle. What remains of it seems to operate entirely upon an intellectual plane.

## Obsessive Doubt and Rumination

Doubt and rumination are among the commonest obsessive-compulsive symptoms. Some of the patients whom we have been discussing were beset by continual uncertainty and concern over what they had or had not done, or over the efficacy of their countermeasures and rituals. There are also cases, however, in which doubt and rumination are the chief and even the only manifest symptoms. The French had a name for this. They spoke of *la folie de doute,* "the madness of doubt." Obsessive doubt can literally be maddening.

Obsessive doubts and ruminations have been, as a rule, unconsciously *displaced,* from something forbidden or highly conflictual onto something apparently senseless, harmless, or merely intellectual. The feelings that originally belonged to the forbidden and the conflictual have been isolated, as per Freud's comments mentioned above (see p. 209). The result is that whatever doubts or ruminations appear in consciousness as symptoms seem to be nothing more than meaningless preoccupations or speculations about reality, existence, or morality. These preoccupations may seem unrelated to anything else, or, as in the case that follows, they may seem directly related to some practical aspect of what the patient is about to do.

Scott H., a college student, went to a telephone booth to call up a wealthy young woman whom he had met recently, to ask her for a date. He spent an hour there, anxious and indecisive, unable to put the coin in the slot and unable to give up and go home. Each time his hand approached the telephone he anxiously withdrew it because he felt that telephoning her might ruin his chances with her. Each time he withdrew his hand he seemed to be throwing away a golden opportunity. Every positive argument for telephoning her he matched with a negative argument for not doing so, reminding us of Freud's antithetical-ideas theory (see Chapter 4, p. 132). He went into all the ramifications of his ambivalent motivations. He imagined to himself what the girl and the members of her family—whom he scarcely knew—might think of his attentions to her; and then he had to picture himself what they would think if he neglected her!

His whole future seemed to Scott to hang on the outcome of this little act. Had he any right to put his coin in? If he did so would the girl respond favorably? If she did, what would happen next? Such telic projections into the future pressed on him relentlessly. Scott was hopelessly caught in an obsessive dilemma, as he had been caught before hundreds of times. The more he tried to be sure of what he did, the more things he imagined going wrong, any one of which might ruin everything. In the end he gave up the anxious debate and went home, exasperated and worn out. Later he became convinced that in not making the call at that particular time he had missed the chance of a lifetime for winning security and happiness.

This absurd little episode sounds like the mere exaggeration of a shy suitor's hesitancy, but it was much more than this. It was a considered symbolic expression of an intensely ambivalent personality, one that was volatile, impulsive, and unpredictable. Almost every enterprise upon which Scott had embarked since early adolescence had involved similar obsessive rumination. Into each decision he funneled all of his ambivalent conflicts—conscious, preconscious, and unconscious —and then he found himself unable to follow through to a decision. The same thing unfortunately happened in his search for therapeutic help. He began with despair, switched quickly to great optimism, and then got bogged down in endless doubting and rumination over whether to continue. In the end he withdrew from therapy without ever becoming really involved in it.

Obsessive doubting such as this often turns from indecision over some specific action to a more general fruitless, abstract speculation. The patient may ruminate about the same problems that have occupied some of the greatest thinkers. *What is time? What is space? What is eternity? What is man? What is God? Where are we all going? What is justice? What are right and wrong? What is the meaning of life?* No matter how sophisticated and intellectual obsessive rumination may sound, it is actually primitive and pseudointellectual. It represents an extreme of displacement and isolation, in which logical processes are carried out in the service of magical, primary process fantasy—just as they are in fairy tales, myths, and dreams. We next look into the problems of fixation and regression in obsessive-compulsivity, with a special interest in what we have called the archaic superego.

## Dynamics of Fixation and Regression in Obsessive-Compulsivity

*Pre-Oedipal Regression.* The single most revealing thing about obsessive-compulsive symptoms is that they represent a regression to pre-Oedipal levels of fixation, particularly to the anal level. This regression reactivates the angry frustrations (fuero claims) of a small child who has not yet succeeded in establishing a personal identity, who has not resolved the conflict between dependency on parents and a developing sense of self-assertion. The struggle revived in obsessive-compulsive adults is an infantile power struggle. It was originally carried on in an atmosphere of toilet training, at a time when bowel products and bowel control were among the child's paramount interests. Because of unusual difficulties during this phase of development the child remained partially fixated at this level. The characteristics reappearing in adult obsessive-compulsive patients, as we have already seen, reflect derivatives of the anal fixation.

The child in the phase of toilet training is normally aggressive, often stubborn and even rebellious. Ambivalence toward parents is common. When a small child courts love, approval, and cleanliness—trying to be a "good" child—he or she feels drawn toward the conformity that the parents desire. Clinical findings in psychoanalysis suggest that this sense of conformity can be threatening to a child who has had some difficulty breaking away from the dependency of the symbiotic relationship (see Chapter 2, p. 45). In a symbolic way this child may sense a loss of identity, a slipping back into a state of nothingness.

When a small child hates, messes, and asserts a nonconforming course—indulging in the distinction of being a "bad" child—he or she can actually gain in independence through this negative avenue. We have known patients whose regressive dreams re-enacting this struggle over negativism suggest that it has taken on life-and-death proportions, so far as the child's personal identity is concerned. That is, when a child is struggling to preserve identity and gain independence, firmness or willfulness on the part of a parent can be experienced as harsh, sadistic treatment. The merely insistent parent seems a relentless persecutor. A determined parental face, seen by a small child who is filled with fury and frustration, may be seen in the adult's re-enactment dream as the cruel face of a monster. Undoubtedly, the image here is contributed to by the projected hostility of the child. But it is also true in some of our cases that the parental contribution to this characterization was decisive.

The adult who develops obsessive-compulsive symptoms under stress has in his or her make-up focal conflicts whose major points of fixation are at these levels. Though Oedipal themes do occur (see Freud's comments above, p. 209), it is also true that a major feature of the obsessive-compulsive profile is the regression to these pre-Oedipal fixations and the conflicts that they have never completely settled. We see the adult trying to work through the resultant fuero claims in imagination and overt behavior. To regress in this sense does not, of course, mean to become once again a child. The adult neurotic utilizes adult patterns of behavior in the regression, carrying these back to the earlier period for the re-enactment. Part of the forcefulness often seen in obsessive-compulsive behavior comes from the expression of powerful infantile wishes and counter-measures by a powerful adult.

*Ego Regression and Archaic Superego.* Obsessive-compulsive disorders are sometimes called *guilt neuroses* because the anxiety most openly expressed by the patient is concerned with being good or bad. However, as we shall now demonstrate, this is a misnomer in that the superego formation is not yet crystallized. This does not occur until the phallic stage, of course, and given that obsessive-compulsive neurosis implies *by definition* that there is a poorly resolved Oedipal conflict (see Chapter 5, p. 156), it follows that the sort of anxiety experienced in this disorder is *not* moral anxiety (see Chapter 5, p. 161). Of course, as we have seen, the topics of good and evil, right and wrong, helping and harming, cleanliness and contamination, seem to preoccupy every obsessive-compulsive patient in one form or another. Proper dynamic understanding of these cases suggests that such conflicts are really more between "approval and disapproval" than between "guilt and innocence." That is, moral imperatives have very little to do with such preoccupations, which are in effect analogized to the cleanliness-versus-contamination struggles of toilet training.

Although not proven to everyone's satisfaction at this point, it would be our view—in line with Freud's suggestions (see above, p. 209)—that regression in obsessive-compulsive disorders reactivates an early version, an early precursor of the ultimate superego. For the sake of discussion we shall call this the *archaic superego,* even though many psychoanalysts object to using the term *superego* for anything but a post-Oedipal differentiation of the developing ego (e.g., see P. Weissman, 1954, 1959). The archaic superego is the remnant of some of the earliest attempts made by the infant to gain self-control (ego control). This remnant persists to some extent in all of us; but in most of us its expression is confined to dreams and to whatever preconscious fantasies manage to escape repression during intoxication or febrile illness. Otherwise it remains deeply repressed.

Because of fixations at pre-Oedipal levels these remnants of archaic super-ego function seem to be better preserved in persons subject to obsessive-compulsive neuroses. They probably lie closer to the preconscious than in other persons; their derivatives play a more important role in adult superego functioning; and when regression occurs they are expressed *sadistically* as superego attacks. At the same time, reciprocal areas of ego functioning are also regressed to the same levels, and these contribute the reciprocal *masochism* that we saw so vividly expressed in the symptomatology of Sally J. This is, in effect, a revival of the primitive pre-Oedipal ego-superego relationship in which precursors of the mature superego were already instituting punitive, controlling directions in relation to precursors of the mature ego. Thus, we could speak of an *archaic ego* in this instance as well. As we noted in Chapter 4 (p. 109), Freud did not really draw a hard and fast distinction between ego and superego. It was the predominant function of these different aspects of the same personality identity which he wanted to call attention to. The appearance of *sadomasochism* in obsessive-compulsive neuroses is therefore a reflection of this early working out of the relationship between ego and superego functions, with the latter reflecting very primitive incorporations of parental pressures bordering on hostility as well as projections of hostility onto parental figures.

We have seen that Sally J. repeatedly flew into a rage with each of her suitors in turn, as her sexual tension and frustration grew to be more than she could bear. This always ended in her driving her suitors away, which, as far as she was concerned, meant destroying them. According to her own account, she tormented some of them with a capricious willfulness as long as they and she could endure it. This might have been a repetition of her capricious, willful behavior as a frustrated little pre-Oedipal and Oedipal girl who, it will be recalled, created such a furor over her father's going to work that he sometimes had to crawl out of a window to escape her. In her handwashing compulsion, Sally obviously identified with a sadistic rendering of her mother (including a certain amount of fantasied imagery!), as well as with herself as a whimpering, helpless little child. Our other cases showed similar identifications, but less clearly.

In most obsessive-compulsive reactions the patient is fully aware that he or she is in active conflict, even though the form taken by the conflict may be defensively obscure. Jason N. experienced consciously his struggle against conscious impulses to call his parents obscene names, and he used his infantile cries of "Stop it! Stop it!" with conscious intent (Hollander, 1960). Cheryl I. was consciously battling a conscious urge to choke or drown her own child. Roger E. knew about his death wishes, and he paid for them later with a psychotic depression that put his life in danger. Erika M. was taking deliberate precaution against involuntary manslaughter; she even remembered the flash of a conscious death wish that started off her neurosis. Sally J. was fully aware that her soiling was hostile and that she was fighting contamination through compulsive handwashing. Scott H. had an acute experience of conflict as he sat in the telephone booth, even though he was not fully aware of its sources. All of these patients were openly waging a regressive war in which they were both victim and persecutor.

We have said that even though obsessive-compulsives regress partially to the level of little children and become preoccupied with problems of good and evil at the level of toilet training, they are still actually adults. They all use adult language, not baby talk, and they employ adult secondary process logic in addition to their infantile symbolism and acting out. The rituals, countings, groupings, symmetries, equations, and even complex systems that appear in their symptomatology are far beyond the capacities of a small child. Obsessive doubts and ruminations sometimes rival the complexities of professional philosophical speculations.

These are examples of the use of secondary process forms in the interest of primary process aims. Artistic creativity has been discussed as regression in the service of the ego by Kris (1950). We can similarly formulate obsessive-compulsive symptoms as regressive thinking in the service of maintaining a neurotic equilibrium. This thinking is in reality being used by the patient prelogically, in a way described by Piaget (Piaget & Inhelder, 1967) as *syncretic* (p. 343). Very young children think syncretically, which means they jumble items together into an ill-conceived whole so that the elements of knowledge are not properly related to each other in a more operational fashion. The adult uses complexities in regressive maneuverings during obsessive-compulsivity, but these global assumptions lose their intricate meaning and fail to organize or interrelate in the way they should.

That is, in adulthood counting orders events and hence suggests a course of action or progression leading to a solution. Cleansing and setting straight a messy situation eventuates in a task completed. Practicing a ritual of prayer or sacrifice lends a sense of union and totality with one's creator that is satisfying and uplifting. But in the obsessive-compulsive neurosis counting, cleansing, ritualistic behaviors *fail* to advance solutions, lend a sense of completeness, or raise the person to a higher level of experience in life's way. The teleological organizers of adulthood are brought to bear as globalities on an infantile problem, and hence, as when children pretend at being adults, they are mere caricatures of what is really taking place in the personality system. These organizers fail to organize, for they are isolated from the dynamic elements that they are supposedly handling (see Freud's comments above, p. 209).

*Parental Figures and the Archaic Superego.* The *archaic superego,* precursor of the mature superego, as we see it in operation in obsessive-compulsive patients, is clearly a neurotic rendering of parental figures from the patient's own pre-Oedipal childhood. It is, we have said, a reproduction of the way the patient experienced his or her parents when he or she was two or three years old. If we were to assume that the patient's experiences reflect objectively what actually went on during this phase of development, we would have to conclude that the parents were indeed overdemanding, relentless, and sadistic. We would have to conclude that they threw their irresistible will into a power struggle over conformity, cleanliness, and obedience and that they actually enjoyed wielding unrestrained power and seeing their child coerced into an anxious, resentful obedience. How much truth is there in such a portrayal of parental attitudes and actions as the foundation for adult obsessive-compulsive disorders?

There are no statistical data to point to in answering such a question. We know that infants and children who are abused by their parents grow into adults who have severe problems in handling aggression and often sadistically abuse their own offspring (Spinetta & Rigler, 1972). Based on clinical experience, we would suggest the following breakdown as a first approximation to the truth. A minority of obsessive-compulsive patients have had at least one sadistic parent who could enjoy coercing a child and witnessing his or her outbursts of helpless rage. A much larger number seem to have had parents who were not consciously sadistic, who would have preferred to avoid the outbursts of rage, but who simply could not themselves tolerate a normal degree of soiling in their child or could not endure the headstrong negativism of infant self-assertion. This latter group of parents is pushed into a battle of wills with their children because of their own uncontrollable anxiety and counteraggression. Clinicians encounter both types of parents often enough— during periods when battles over self-assertion and bowel control are actually being waged in the home—to indicate that such parent-child relationships are not unusual (Littin, Giffin, & Johnson, 1956).

Such parents are often themselves compulsively clean, conforming, and perfectionistic (Adams, 1972). They may be demanding no more of the child than they demand of themselves. On this point, it is interesting to note that obsessive-compulsive personality tendencies tend to go along with increasing scores on IQ tests and measures of social status (Adams, 1972; Pollitt, 1960). Even so, such parents are adults with adult resources and adult pleasures, whereas the child is still an infant with limited resources and primitive infantile pleasures. The demands made upon the infant to curb certain self-satisfactions and related self-assertions may be at least premature. The child is often physiologically incapable of genuine bowel control. Added to this, the child may not yet be psychologically ready to give up the anal privileges of soiling whenever and wherever the biological prompting presents itself. Such a child needs not only to understand and accept parental demands for punctuality, orderliness, and cleanliness, but he or she must also have other resources and pleasures that can be turned to in compensation for the perceived loss.

It takes time for a child to acquire these resources, to gain an understanding and genuine acceptance of parental demands. It depends upon a certain degree of maturing, upon crystallizing the personal freedom to assert oneself along socially acceptable lines. A tolerant, loving parent will encourage the negativistic child—when the child is not being negativistic—to acquire more mature forms of self-assertion as the child's inner resources and his or her mastery of the environment grow. No major battle lines will be drawn by this parent at the level of negativism and sphincter control.

May an obsessive-compulsive adult have had parents in his or her childhood who were not themselves unusually coercive, hostile, or compulsive? It is certainly possible. There are at least four other factors in childhood development to consider.

1.  In the first place, there may be inherent characteristics of the child as a person that favor fixation during the phase of dawning self-assertion and bowel

control. This is a period in which children are normally obstinate, negativistic, anally oriented, and aggressive. Whatever individual differences tend to accentuate this phase of development might favor the development of an archaic superego with strong pathogenic potentialities. In that case, regression under stress in adulthood might lead to obsessive-compulsive reactions independently of pathogenic parental influences. We would have to add the effects of early illnesses, suffered before the beginning of the anal psychosexual stage, as possible early sources of obsessive-compulsive predisposition, particularly those involving bowel function.

2. Children with only moderate fixation in their pre-Oedipal phase may be driven back upon it because their later Oedipal experiences are too frightening. They fail to work out Oedipal conflicts at Oedipal levels, and they retreat or regress while still little children to try working Oedipal conflicts out at pre-Oedipal levels. Such children, grown to adulthood, are likely to do the same kind of thing again. An adult sexual or aggressive crisis reawakens their poorly repressed, unresolved Oedipal conflicts, and they regress as adults to pre-Oedipal levels carrying their conflicts with them. In some of these cases— Scott, in the telephone booth, is an example—the primitive sexual or aggressive character of the regressive processes is kept under repression. Only abstract, pseudointellectual doubt or rumination appears on the surface.

3. It is well known that fixations may develop during any phase of development because of overemphasis rather than frustration. Parents who overemphasize bowel control, cleanliness, and punctuality—because of competition with other parents or because of unwise advice—may lend an exaggerated importance to these things that they had not consciously intended. Thus, for example, parents who overemphasize self-control when a child is still only able to be negativistic may influence their offspring to develop some dialectically framed pattern of oppositionality rather than a genuine sense of independence and self-direction. Such children feel a sense of identity only when they are in an oppositional, negativistic, hence hostile stance with others. They go through life seeking the opponent against whom they must maneuver and somehow keep at bay through obsessive-compulsive tendencies.

4. Finally, a child who develops an obsessive-compulsive disorder later in life may have received too little patience and affection during the anal phase because his or her parents were preoccupied with other problems. Whenever children have to endure weaning of any kind, a determining factor in the outcome is always the compensation they get in the form of loving encouragement from their parents. Even adults who are called upon to suffer temporary loss of privilege in order to learn something new will do it more gladly and with less pain if they are treated with patience and affection. The small child is in the special situation of extreme dependency and uncertainty even as he or she is being coerced to accept weaning and the further demands of bowel control. It is therefore essential that children have a reasonable degree of patient understanding and affection from parents if they are to avoid harmful fixations of hate and resistance.

## DSM-III Viewpoint

As noted in Chapter 7, DSM-III retains the distinction between (1) *obsessions* as ideas, thoughts, images, or impulses and (2) *compulsions* as repetitive, stereotyped behaviors or overt actions. The essential point is that in each instance these ideas or actions are ego-dysotonic (see p. 204), and *not* pleasurable. Tension reduction and anxiety reduction may occur temporarily as a result of performing the ritualized obsession or compulsion, but this cannot be considered the result of pleasure seeking on the part of the person. It is for this reason that DSM-III rejects the common tendency in recent times to refer to compulsive eating, drinking, gambling, or sexual activity. In the latter activities the person *does* derive pleasure from the so-called compulsion.

There is a related point having to do with the excessive rumination that we have mentioned above, in the form of "What-is-life?" examinations of a (*pseudo-*)philosophical nature. From the DSM-III point of view, such ruminations would not be ego-dystonic because the person would regard such ideation as meaningful and therefore not be seeking to resist its occurrence. Hence, though possibly excessive and usually annoying to others, such ruminations would not be considered true obsessions.

It is our belief that this line of reasoning is open to question. For example, Scott's ruminations concerning his telephone call meet the criteria of being meaningful and ego-relevant. Yet they were true obsessions that made his behavior less effective. The criteria of ego-dystonic contents and a sense of displeasure make good sense, but they do not cover every aspect of this disorder. We must add the criterion of how adequately a person performs (see Chapter 1, p. 15), how efficiently he or she actually advances on life to attain those goals that are being intended. In this latter sense, meaningful and ego-relevant but nevertheless self-frustrating ruminations are well named as neurotic obsessions.

### SUMMARY

In the Kraepelinian diagnostic system the obsessive-compulsive disorders were given separate status from the anxiety disorders. However, as Chapter 7 makes clear, the DSM-III system considers obsessive-compulsivity to be a variant form of anxiety disorder. *Obsessive-compulsive disorders* consist of apparently useless but irresistible repetitious acts, words, or thoughts whose aim is to reduce tension and anxiety by indulging in something forbidden, by denying such indulgence or guarding against it, or by punishing oneself for having had the impulse to indulge. Although DSM-III continues the tradition of calling irresistible thoughts *obsessions* and irresistible impulses to act out *compulsions,* some modern authorities use these words interchangeably. Thus, obsessions are sometimes called "compulsive thoughts." Obsessive-compulsive dynamics are fairly common in even normal populations, where people employ repetitious acts and rituals "for luck" or to ward off possible disaster. Compulsions often appear in behavior combined with phobias.

In obsessive-compulsive disorders, *regression* replaces a current sexual aggressive conflict with problems belonging to a pre-Oedipal level, where the patient may feel more in command of things. *Displacement* is used throughout such disorders to shift the focus from current conflicts to infantile problems (often of an anal character), or from a dramatic struggle to a colorless action. *Isolation* is also used to separate opposing aspects of a conflict or to eliminate emotional components from compulsive symptoms. In many cases we witness *countermeasures,* by which is meant to oppose the expression of unconscious wishes through a calculated scheme aimed at stopping the thought or acts that prove to be offensive to the person.

Other defensive maneuvers in obsessive-compulsive disorders include *reaction-formation* and *undoing.* Reaction-formations appear when the person has unusually strong anal-sadistic impulses that can no longer be repressed. The person may compulsively insist upon being so meticulously neat that his or her behavior takes on obvious pathological overtones. In the defense of undoing we witness magical thinking of one sort or another. The compulsively self-critical and apologetic individual may also be employing undoing defensiveness. Obsessive fantasies often *symbolize* both guilt and innocence. In general, the undoing actions of obsessive-compulsives are more primitive and childlike than the normal rites of undoing as practiced in religious services.

The obsessive-compulsive neurotic presents us with a picture of great *ambivalence* in every facet of life. This leads to obsessive *doubt* and *rumination* because this type of individual cannot align his or her attitudes properly. Obsessive doubts and ruminations have usually been unconsciously *displaced* from something forbidden or highly conflictual onto something apparently senseless, harmless, or intellectual rather than emotional. The result is that whatever doubts or ruminations appear in consciousness as symptoms seem to be nothing more than meaningless preoccupations or speculations about reality, existence, or morality.

The regressive aspects of obsessive-compulsivity clearly suggest a pre-Oedipal regression, particularly to the anal level. This regression reactivates the angry frustrations (fuero claims) of a small child who has not yet succeeded in establishing a personal identity, that is, who has not resolved the conflict between dependency on parents and a sense of self-assertion. Chapter 7 discusses the quasi guilt implied in obsessive-compulsive ruminations as not due to moral anxiety—because the superego is not yet crystallized in the anal phase—but as reflective of conflicts between "approval and disapproval." The regression in obsessive-compulsive disorders is presented as reactivating an *archaic superego,* that is, a precursor of the superego that will be formed in the Oedipal resolution. The archaic superego is the remnant of some of the earliest attempts made by the infant to gain self-control (ego-control). Because of fixation at pre-Oedipal levels these remnants of the archaic superego seem to be better preserved in persons subject to obsessive-compulsive neuroses. When regression occurs, the *derivatives* of the archaic superego are expressed *sadistically*. At the same time, reciprocal areas of ego functioning have regressed to comparable levels and present a *masochistic* countermeasure to the sadism. The appearance of *sadomasochism* in obsessive-compulsive neuroses is therefore a reflection of this early working out of the relationship between ego and superego functions, with the latter reflecting very primitive incorporations of parental pressures bordering on hostility as well as *projections* of hostility onto parental figures. The archaic superego is essentially a neurotic rendering of parental figures from the patient's pre-Oedipal childhood.

The DSM-III system stresses that obsessive and/or compulsive behaviors in the abnormal person must be *ego-dystonic,* or *not* pleasurable. Tension reduction and anxiety reduction may occur temporarily as a result of performing the ritualized obsession or compulsion, but this cannot be considered the result of pleasure seeking on the part of the person. Also, in DSM-III it is suggested that ruminations that are meaningful to the person and ego-relevant (i.e., not trivial) should not be considered true obsessions. The text challenges this position on the grounds that if such meaningful and ego-relevant ruminations adversely affect the person's level of performance, a genuine neurotic obsession is underway.

# 8

## *Somatoform Disorders*

### *Some Background Considerations*

In the somatoform disorder we witness an expression of anxiety through changes in some specific bodily function or an overconcern with the possibilty that such changes may occur. Physical symptoms come to express psychological problems thanks to unconscious *intentions*. Freud (1901/1953c) referred to "the translation of a purely psychical excitation into physical terms" (p. 53) as a *conversion* and for some period of time the somatoform disorders were known as the family of conversion disorders. In DSM-III a considerably delimited role is given to the conversion-disorder phrase per se, and we shall follow this revision in Chapter 8, where four subtypes of the somatoform disorders will be discussed.

Practicing clinicians refer to the unconscious conflicts that are symbolized in the symptoms of a somatoform disorder as *body language*. Freud (1915/ 1957k) had called this symbolic expression of unconscious compromises "organ speech" (p. 198) and Alfred Adler (1964a) had termed it "organ dialect, or organ jargon" (p. 156). The essential point is that the person speaks out through physical means to express an unconscious dynamic that is no longer capable of being repressed. Rather than fixing anxiety on an object in experience that must then be avoided, as the phobic does, a patient using the somatoform defense actually "speaks out" and tells the world something through a physical manifestation or overconcern in the physical sphere. Of course, the patient does not consciously know what is being symbolized in the physical manifestation, so that we have that interesting dialectical state of mind that Freud spoke of as knowing and *not* knowing at the same time (see Chapter 5, p. 149). Here are some brief clinical examples of what we are driving at:

> A soldier who had recently killed an enemy in combat found that his right arm was paralyzed. It was neurophysiologically normal and the soldier had suffered no injuries.

An adolescent girl, after being chased through the streets by a strange boy, developed terrifying dreams in which her legs seemed to be paralyzed. The dreams were premonitory. Following a week in bed with the "flu," she actually developed paralysis of her legs, but there was no sign of nervous system involvement. She first expressed her unconscious fear in preconscious dreams, and then brought them out overtly in the form of a conversion disorder.

A college student went numb in his hands and arms after failing in his examinations. This cleared up when he found work, but it returned when he took entrance examinations later in another college, and again just before his graduation. The numbness did not correspond in distribution to that of sensory nerves.

A middle-aged woman lost her voice following a long-distance call from her mother, during which she learned that her father was dying. All medical examinations, including bronchoscopy, were negative. She recovered her voice spontaneously after a period of mourning.

At the age of eighteen, a young man was struck in the eye by a snowball. He was experiencing a general unpopularity among his classmates when this happened. He now found that he could not see and therefore could not study or remain in school. Whenever he sought work, over a period of four years, he would become functionally blind. He mixed well with his friends who were working and, although jobless himself, he seemed contented with his lot. As long as he did not try to work or to study, his vision remained normal.

The use of body language symbolization, no matter how primitive it may seem, is by no means necessarily abnormal. It occurs in normal behavior as well. Thus, a woman who wants to speak out but who either does not dare to or feels it would be useless averts her head and shrugs her shoulders. This nonverbal body language clearly symbolizes turning away from something and not caring, even though not a word has been said. A man who cannot bear to see something that he knows is about to happen covers his face and shuts his eyes as if to deny its happening in advance. People try to avoid hearing bad news by putting their hands over their ears; or they may resist its impact by pulling themselves up straight and refusing to respond overtly at all. Children whose feelings have been hurt stand and look as though they had been struck by someone's hand. We are all familiar with such body language expressions as the flushed face and erect posture of courage or triumph, the stance and strut of arrogance, the bent passive waiting posture of humility, and the drooped body, loose gait, and lined face of defeat. All of these are examples of symbolic body language and all of them are normal.

Symbolizing something in body language becomes abnormal when its expressive, defensive, or self-punitive function is lost through repression, and the patient mistakes his or her symbol for a sign of disability or bodily illness. For example, it may not be abnormal to vomit as a direct, primitive expression of the refusal to accept a repulsive situation. But to go on expressing rejection by chronically vomiting and to mistake this expression of disgust for a sign of gastrointestinal disease are without question abnormal. In the conversion disorder, abnormality is all the more apparent if the patient accepts his or her disability with indifference instead of being troubled by it. Such an unnatural reaction to a loss of physical function, still called by its French name, *la belle indifférence,* has been recognized for nearly a century as a common attitude in conversion disorders (see, e.g., Grinker & Spiegel, 1945a; Mucha & Reinhardt, 1970).

*Definition. A somatoform disorder is a process whereby an unconscious conflict is linked with or transformed into a body symptom that reduces or accounts for anxiety by expressing the conflict symbolically.* Unlike phobias, which often end in mere avoidance, and unlike anxiety reactions, which are often mere discharge, the conversion reaction means a dedication and a sacrifice. The function of some body part is dedicated and sacrificed to the expression of a forbidden impulse, or as a defense against such an impulse or a denial of it, or as self-punishment for having such an impulse. All of these meanings may be combined in a single symbol. For example a paralyzed arm may express the fact that it is an arm that was killed, an arm that can no longer kill, and the self-punishment (superego wish) or paralysis for having killed. It is guilty, innocent, and punished at the same time. If, in addition, the paralyzed arm also expressed childhood sin, denial, and penance, as usually it does, then the paralysis is further reinforced by forgotten fantasies, which like forgotten and repressed happenings are influential without becoming conscious. Under such circumstances, to begin using such an arm again would also be to rekindle old fires of early superego self-punishment.

There is another factor that, although present to some degree in other neuroses as well, is nowhere else as plainly evident as in conversions. Freud (1916-17/1963b) termed this factor the *secondary gain* of mental illness (p. 384). The *primary gain* of any mental illness is the fact that it is a "convenient solution" (Freud, 1901/1953c, p. 43) to a vexing personal problem. This *flight into illness* is essentially *internal,* resulting from the three-stage compromise that we reviewed in Chapter 5 (p. 154). However, there is an *external* advantage to be had from falling into illness, and that is the fact that the patient gains concessions in interpersonal relations with others. The patient can use the illness qua illness to curry favor, extract favors, make excuses, and otherwise dominate the lives of others in some way. It is this latter, external advantage that we mean when we speak of secondary gains of illness. Sometimes these secondary gains are so useful to the person that they stand in the way of therapeutic progress. The person's symptom picture becomes, in effect, a way of life.

## Somatization Disorder

Long-term somatoform disorders beginning before the age of thirty and lasting with varying levels of intensity are considered somatization disorders of DSM-III. Complaints may involve almost any organ system, and although they are often crystallized into a specific loss—such as paralysis or blindness—sometimes they are presented in a vague albeit dramatic and exaggerated manner.

These patients frequently seek out and obtain medical attention from several physicians, sometimes simultaneously.

### Case of Linda F.: Abdominal and Back Somatizations

Linda F., a married woman of thirty-four and mother of a twelve-year-old girl, came to the clinic because, in spite of her complaints of abdominal pain and of digestive disturbances, her husband threatened to leave her if she had another operation. During the previous seven years she had undergone five abdominal and pelvic operations, none of which had been justified by the findings. The loss in finances and the emotional drain on the family had simply become too much to bear, but Linda persisted in her complaints. Her first operation had merely been exploratory, and the second was done to remove some "possible" postoperative adhesions. Each of the succeeding three operations was performed by a different surgeon after months of "clinical shopping" by Linda in which her vivid complaints had been supplemented by accusations of heartlessness and incompetence against those who withstood her insistence. She expressed open resentment and resistance when referred for psychiatric examination.

In taking the patient's medical history the psychiatrist found, as without doubt her surgeons had found in years past, that for practically every organ and system he mentioned she had one or more complaints. She showed by her use and misuse of medical terms that she was quick to appropriate anything she heard as a corroboration of her own conclusions. Physical examination was complicated by the patient's reporting tenderness almost everywhere. Some of her complaints pointed to one possibility, some to others, and all had to be explored with the aid of consultations and technical procedures. In the end only a small group of symptoms remained to suggest organ and system pathology. These pointed in the direction of possible gall bladder disease and a gall bladder series gave unmistakable support for this group of the patient's complaints. Linda's husband required some high-powered assurances before he consented to her sixth operation—which nevertheless turned out to be highly necessary. A follow-up one year later revealed that Linda experienced the same galaxy of complaints, substantially unaltered, and that she had no less aversion to psychiatric treatment than she had shown before her sixth operation.

This case dramatizes the danger of possibly overlooking a real physical disease because of the patient's history of somatoforming her psychological problems. Linda was in the position of the little boy in the fable who had cried "wolf" so many times insincerely that when he really meant to convey a warning no one would believe him. Obviously, diagnosticians must exercise considerable patience and approach such patients with routine physical evaluations even though the total picture implies rather strongly that no positive signs will emerge (see, e.g., Slater & Gilthero, 1965).

Education and sophistication enter into the etiology of conversion reactions because a patient must be personally convinced that the symptom is a sign of organic illness or disability if he or she is to maintain it. Linda's lifelong pattern was that of a hypochondriac (refer below), worrying since childhood about every little ache and pain which she suffered, aided and abetted in this endeavor by a highly indulgent mother. Physical illnesses are concrete demonstrations of a shortcoming or handicap, whereas the neurotic patient is subject to the charge of being a *malingerer* (faker) or a "head case." Given these likelihoods, better to express personal conflicts physiologically than psychologically. Individuals who are more sophisticated and who have received a higher education are less likely to be intimidated by the admission that they may be suffering from a neurotic illness. As a result, they are more open to the suggestion that Linda simply would not entertain.

## Conversion Disorder

There is no fundamental difference in the psychodynamics of the somatizing patient and the patient with a conversion disorder. DSM-III merely includes here the types of disturbance that are likely to focus on a *single* symptom through which the person is achieving a sense of secondary gain as well as handling the primary factor of internal psychopathology. When we see the myriad disorders suggested as in Linda's case (above), or when the complaint is exclusively pain or exclusively a sexual disturbance, then we are not likely to place it under this designation. The "classic" conversion symptoms suggested neurological diseases of various sorts, including paralysis, aphonia (loss of voice), dyskenesia (involuntary tics, spasms), blindness, tunnel vision, anosmia (loss of smell), and anesthesia (loss of sensation). We shall include a few disorders which DSM-III does not place here but which have the classical signs and can be included. We shall note differences between our presentation and DSM-III in the proper context.

Clinicians have long noted that paralyses and anesthesias are likely to persist much longer than conversion symptoms such as tics or spasms, vomiting, or tunnel vision. We next turn to a case history in which there is a long-standing symptom of paralysis, but which is restrictive enough so that we would not wish to place it in a somatization designation. It is, indeed, a classic conversion disorder with secondary gain very prominent.

### Case of Sue Ellen: Paralysis as a Conversion Disorder

Sue Ellen A. was the daughter of a Rocky Mountain rancher whose means and education were extremely limited. She was in her early adolescence when she lost the use of both her legs. At the time there was an alarming epidemic of paralysis among ranch animals, and it was generally assumed that Sue Ellen was a human victim of the epidemic. This explanation was welcomed by the girl's parents although they knew originally that this was not true.

What actually happened was that Sue Ellen was alone in the ranch house one afternoon when a male relative came in and, after embracing her, attempted to rape her. She screamed for help, her legs gave way, and she slipped to the floor. Here she was found unharmed a few moments later by her mother, who had just returned from visiting a neighbor. Sue Ellen could not get up, so she was carried to her bed and waited upon for several days with unaccustomed devotion. Whenever attempts were made to get her up, she seemed frightened, her legs buckled under her, and she could not stand unsupported. The family physician correctly ascribed her reaction to fright, but he unwisely recommended that she stay in bed until her legs grew strong again.

When it became evident that the girl was not recovering, she was allowed to displace her father in the parental bedroom, which opened into the living room. Here she spent her days in sewing, talking, reading, and napping. Neighbors brought her homemade things to eat or to wear. They discussed her disability over and over. As an invalid and a victim she received the best of food and attention. Her mother continued waiting upon her hand and foot, massaged her legs morning and evening, and slept with her at night. Attempts to get Sue Ellen to stand and walk were finally abandoned because the effort required to encourage her and physically hold her up proved too much for the hard-worked family. She never lost the ability to move her legs in bed or to pull things she needed toward her with her toes.

Sue Ellen might never have come to the attention of neurologists and psychiatrists had it not been for the intervention of a newcomer in the neighborhood ten years later. The newcomer recognized that the paralysis might be psychological in origin and raised hopes of a miraculous cure among family members and their friends. Money was collected, arrangements were made, and the girl with her parents journeyed several hundred miles to a general hospital. As soon as they arrived it was obvious that the parents expected something to be done immediately to make their daughter well. It was obvious also that she herself resented the whole move and felt that the examinations and the questions asked were really accusations of dishonesty.

After the preliminary examinations, consultations, and laboratory work had been completed, and after a recital of her illness, its onset, and its course, Sue Ellen came to the end of her willingness to cooperate. She and her parents gave the same story of the epidemic and insisted that her illness was "like infantile paralysis." That was all. Her mother summed up parental feeling when she declared, "It's you and not her that's supposed to do the curing." In the face of Sue Ellen's sullen resentment and noncooperation, the parents' secrecy, and the powerful background of primary and secondary gain, therapy could not succeed. In a month's time the patient left for home unimproved. It was only later, by chance, that the traumatic onset of Sue Ellen's illness as given above was disclosed by another member of the family.

Sue Ellen's conversion disorder began in the setting of a threatened sexual assault that terrified her. She faced the problem of a betrayal of a close relative toward whom she had strongly ambivalent feelings. Her solution followed the suggestion given her by her own immediate reaction to the fright, paralysis of her legs. This symptom proved capable of expressing in regressive symbolism her ambivalent unconscious impulses, her defense against a lustful cathexis, and her self-punishment for having such promptings (in the typical sense of conflicting wishes; see Chapter 5, p. 147).

Early adolescence is often a turbulent phase of development. In it emotional conflicts that have long lain dormant may be reawakened with startling intensity. Both boys and girls, as they stand on the threshold of adulthood, are likely to be plagued by ambivalent fantasies—conscious, preconscious, and unconscious—in relation to father and mother, brothers and sisters, chums and rivals. In these one can find admixtures of fear and fascination, love and hate, hostile aggression and sexual desire. We know that Sue Ellen expressed strongly ambivalent attitudes toward her would-be aggressor after she developed her symptom, and we assume that she had similar attitudes toward him before this.

The paralysis of Sue Ellen's legs made them the center of attention and therefore a convenient unconscious symbol of erotic display, to which meaning her mother's devotion may have contributed. At a still further regressed level, Sue Ellen was able to enjoy being waited upon and cared for as a baby. The invalidism also expressed vengeful feelings, since it kept alive her family's resentment, as well as her own, over what had precipitated it. Within the family group she appeared as the innocent victim of assault; but the invalidism also punished Sue Ellen by denying her all of the pleasure and freedom of an active life.

Sue Ellen was both a victim and a beneficiary of the conspiracy of silence. She was a victim in that she was forced by it to occupy the role of a helpless invalid; she could not escape from this role with honor. She was its beneficiary in that her invalidism saved her from the drudgery of life on a marginal ranch, both as the daughter of a poor man and as the prospective wife of some other poor man. As it was, Sue Ellen became a community institution, a much discussed wonder, someone who worked neither in the kitchen nor in the fields. Her *primary gain* had been escape from intolerable anxiety and conflict. Her *secondary gain* was the freedom from want and drudgery. She developed her conversion disorder to achieve the first; her family and neighbors presented her with the second because everyone gained by it. Long before she came to the hospital she had become firmly established in the privileged role of a highly respected invalid. It was to this role that she finally returned.

Conversion disorders used to be called *hysterias,* along with certain of the dissociative disorders that we shall be taking up in Chapter 9. The term *hysteria* is of great antiquity. It is derived from the Greek word for uterus (hystera), just as is *hysterectomy,* the surgical term for removal of the uterus. Judging from their writings, the ancients evidently recognized that sexual problems often play a leading part in maladaptive behavior of this type. However, in theorizing about what caused the loss of function we have seen an example of in the case of Sue Ellen, the Greeks suggested that the uterus had become dislodged and roamed about the body like an animal within an animal, producing the local disturbances in question. On the basis of this theory a therapeutic procedure was developed that apparently was successful in curing patients. Since the wandering uterus was feminine, it might be likely to be repelled by bad odors and attracted by fragrance. Accordingly, fragrant oils were applied to the patient's genitals and foul-smelling substances placed under her nose in order to coax the uterus back where it belonged and end the "hysterical" disorder (Whitwell, 1936, pp. 76-77).

It obviously followed and for centuries it was naturally assumed that only women could suffer from conversion disorders (hysterias). Tradition has it that Freud was among the first physicians to present a clear-cut, male hysteric to his medical colleagues, but the evidence that he did so is not indisputable. More certain is the fact that a case of hysteria is probably what got the body of theory and practice known as psychoanalysis started in the first place. We refer here to the famous "Case of Anna O." (Breuer & Freud, 1955, pp. 38-39). Anna suffered from many different losses, such as an inability to understand her native tongue of German though she *could* understand English, but her central symptom, like Sue Ellen's, was a paralysis. Anna was twenty-one years old at the time she sought help from Breuer for a paralyzed right arm. Through the use of hypnosis, Breuer was able to pinpoint the exact onset of this symptom. Anna recalled sitting in a chair next to the bed of her father, who was terminally ill (he died shortly thereafter). Her mother was out of the house and the servants were dismissed for the evening, so doubtlessly Anna felt frightened at the responsibility of looking after someone so close to death.

Suffering from fatigue and prone to what she called *absences* (momentary blackouts like sleepwalking), Anna seems to have had what Breuer called a *waking dream*—which we recognize today as projected derivatives of the unconscious. She "saw" a black snake coming from the wall next to her father's bed, ready to bite the dying man. Anna tried to fend the snake off, moving her right arm from the back of her chair where it had been positioned. Apparently it had become slightly numb due to the lack of proper blood circulation, for when she tried to move it, she could not. Glancing at her hand, Anna was further appalled to see that her fingers had turned into little snakes, with her fingernails appearing to be like "death's heads."

Though she was unable to scream or otherwise express the terror she felt at the time—Breuer and Freud later called this the *pathognomic situation*—Anna *did* vent her emotions under hypnosis. She relived the horrible experience in tears and shrieks of horror. The choking-off of emotional expression was termed *strangulated affect.* After several such relivings of the pathognomic situation (hypnotically induced), Anna's right arm returned to normal. Breuer and Freud were later to call this *mental* reliving of a situation out of the past an *abreaction.* The physical expression of emotion was called *catharsis.* These terms have since been used interchangeably by psychoanalysts, but strictly speaking there is a mind (abreaction) versus body (catharsis) issue involved here. As we have seen in Chapter 4 (p. 133), it was in the explanation of how hysterical symptoms arose—how the personality was dissociated or divided— that Freud and Breuer began to disagree. The complete dynamics of this case were never worked out, for Breuer ended therapy when signs of Anna's transference surfaced. It is significant to note that all of Anna's hysterical symptoms were traced back via hypnosis to interactions with her father. Wittels (1924) later commented on Breuer's inability to see the dynamics of Anna's illness, as follows: "Breuer, in the record of his case, has nothing to tell us of the young woman's fixation upon her father, not a word about the transference of affect upon the physician, not a word about sexual symbolism [snakes, etc.]. It was inevitable that the dynamic of repression would elude him, seeing that he practiced hypnotism. The whole 'conflict' was left in the dark" (p. 42).

Many people have found themselves unable to speak during a period of great trauma. "I was too scared to talk" is a common exclamation. There are many everyday situations in which this happens without surprising anyone—a child facing an audience from a platform for the first time, an adolescent boy being introduced to an attractive adolescent girl, a clerk standing before a stern executive, a private being suddenly addressed by a reviewing officer. Almost anyone can be struck speechless by good news or bad news, by intense anger or intense love, by extremes of anxiety, fright, conflict, injury, or disappointment. The normal disability is usually short-lived and incomplete, and it does not bring with it a relief from anxiety. Loss of speech as a conversion symptom is usually both more complete and more long-lasting—although it seldom lasts longer than a few days—and it often bestows upon its victim a welcome relief from anxiety.

Sudden mutism, a loss of the ability to speak, can be an eloquent symptom. It represents a public renunciation of the person's most important means of social communication. It proclaims dramatically to everyone, "I cannot say anything!" or "I must not utter a word!" or "I am afraid to speak!" It expresses a disability with maximal display so that nobody can possibly miss it. In a less dramatic manner, stammering, stuttering, and the inability to speak above a whisper carry similar symbolic meanings. A brief clinical example of mutism will illustrate the drama of the symptom as well as the use made of it for secondary gain.

### Case of John P.: Mutism as a Conversion Disorder

John P., a small-town businessman of good repute, found himself suddenly facing prosecution for a major fraud of which he was completely innocent. His business associates, without informing him, had carried through some illegal deals that threatened members of the community with financial ruin. As a member of the board of directors of the firm he was technically guilty. The prosecuting attorney persuaded him to turn state's evidence in return for immunity from prosecution. To his initial intense anxiety over the situation was now added a terrible guilt over betraying close friends. He made his decision to do this because that was the only way he could save himself from unmerited imprisonment and his family from poverty and disgrace.

One day he was accosted in the street by two of his indicted friends, out on bail, who accused him loudly of throwing them to the wolves in order to save his own skin. They next tried to give him a beating. Bystanders intervened and separated them. John P. then discovered that he could not utter a sound. Medical examination showed him to be physically normal. He was referred to a psychiatric clinic, where he remained mute and unresponsive to therapy, although apparently in good spirits, until some time after the date of trial. Then he recovered suddenly and went home.

Such a mode of escape from anxiety and from the awful choice between betraying one's friends and betraying one's family may seem childlike and contrived. Yet it was genuine and it was successful. John P. appeared to himself and to the world as the silent, innocent victim of an undeserved assault by guilty men. The forbidden impulse to speak out, to accuse the men publicly who had sullied his reputation, was clearly expressed in his loss of speech, which called everybody's attention to itself. At the same time, his mutism defended him against actually having to betray his friends by word of mouth. The patient retained his immunity from prosecution because he had already agreed to turn state's witness. His muteness appeared immediately following an attack upon him as state's witness;

Photograph by Edmund Engelman

*Freud's consulting room at Berggasse 19. He sat in the armchair at the left of the room. His patients reclined on the couch, looking away from him. Freud once remarked that he could not bear to be looked at for a full day of psychoanalytical work.*

and apparently the prosecution did not wish to press him further given that his illness was diagnosed as genuine. That is, he was not consciously faking the symptom, which would then make him a *malingerer.* The physicians believed that he was not malingering, and indeed, that if further pressure were applied John might well develop other conversion symptoms. It should also be noted that in striking himself dumb, John punished himself. As in all neurotic symptoms, we find *at least* two wishes (intentions) being expressed.

The final example we shall give of a conversion reaction has to do with an involved tic, one that mimicked the symptom of a central nervous system disease. *Tics* are forms of unconscious gesture language. They appear to be useless, involuntary coordinated movements that keep recurring intermittently. In normal persons they are usually called mannerisms—little meaningless movements of hands, shoulders, fingers, or feet or grimacing, sniffing, throat clearing, eye blinking, head nodding, and the like. Normal mannerisms are often the remnants of a forgotten repetitious gesture that at one time expressed something specific—an identification with someone having a similar mannerism or an organic defect or with someone who had a conversion disorder, an attitude of disdain, indifference, apology, or compliance. Tics continue as an habitual act even though they no longer express anything but a piece of one's past.

As conversion symptoms, tics can be much more versatile than tremors or spasms in expressing conflict. Sometimes they look to an observer like the sign language people in trains make through a closed window to people they are leaving on the platform—gestures full of an earnest meaning that seldom succeeds in getting communicated. In conversion reactions the unconscious meaning of the tic is a mystery to the patient as well as to other people; it is like the fragment of a sentence from some story that he or she cannot recall. Some patients make a display of their tic but regard it as a meaningless twitch. Others look upon the tic with some concern, seeing it as the possible sign of an organic disturbance but not, of course, as a symbol of conflict. This was the interpretation given his tic by a young physician whose case we shall next consider.

### Case of George D.: Tic as a Conversion Disorder

George D. was serving his medical residency when his tic appeared. It took the well-known form of *spasmodic torticollis,* a recurrent rotation of the head to one side while the chin is sharply raised. This movement looks like a reaction of aversion and disdain, but it is usually a result of central nervous system disease. George had good reason to know about its nervous system origin, as we shall see, but in his case there was no organic pathology. The source lay in George's past. His father was an easygoing general practitioner whom George's mother despised. To her he seemed a man without dignity, self-respect, prestige, or culture. She herself had come from a family that placed its highest values on appearances, pride, and prestige. It had more than one distinguished member.

Under the mother's influence George felt ashamed of having such a father and turned away from his affectionate approaches as coming from an outsider. Until he was eleven or twelve years old he was a mama's boy, shy and withdrawn. Then his family moved to a new neighborhood, where circumstances forced him to leave his mother's side and play freely with other boys. Their teasing and bullying led him to turn against his mother, who had encouraged both his dependence upon her and his attitude of arrogant superiority. Although he got along well for many years, his internal equilibrium was not stable. For he had turned away from his mother without in the least working out his deep attachment to her; and he had identified, not with his actual father, but with an ideal, imaginary physician who bore his father's name. His choice of profession grew out of this fantasied identification, and into it he carried his still unresolved childhood problems.

The crisis came years later. After getting his medical degree, George took a residency in a strange city. Here he worked under a chief who appeared amiable but who treated him with constant teasing behind which there was an obvious attitude of mild contempt. George found himself in a serious predicament. He could not endure being teased and depreciated; but he could not quit without jeopardizing his career. In this setting he saw a clinical demonstration of spasmodic torticollis by his chief who behaved toward the patient in a friendly but amused, condescending way. Soon afterward George developed his spasmodic tic. Since it looked like the patient's symptom George assumed that it must have the same organic sources. After diagnostic procedures had shown that it was a conversion disorder, he agreed reluctantly to enter psychotherapy.

George's major problem was a still unresolved identity conflict. His official role was that of an amiable, easygoing physician. This he had modeled according to an idealized version of his father, for whom in real life he felt neither respect nor affection. Behind this official facade there was an entirely different personality, proud and disdainful like his mother, which had no legitimate outlet.

Goaded by the teasing condescension of his chief, George identified pathologically with the patient and adopted the torticollis gesture as a tic. Now he was able to show disdain and aversion in the grand manner, as his mother might have done. He expressed publicly what he deeply felt, and at the same time he preserved his official role of the amiable physician. As long as he regarded his tic as a sign of neurological disease, and therefore not his personal responsibility, he did not have to face the contradiction in his fundamental attitudes. Therapy soon revealed to George his identity conflict and gave him opportunities to work out his problems to a more mature and realistic solution.

## Visceral Disturbances as Conversion Disorders

We now depart from the DSM-III array of somatoform disorders to take up two unique visceral disturbances that, according to the dynamic approach we are following, strike us as related to the conversion disorder. In the DSM-III scheme these disturbances are labeled "eating disorders of adolescence" and hence are considered in a different chapter from the conversion disorders.

Not all visceral disturbances that have an emotional basis are conversion disorders. If a visceral disturbance is only part of an emotional discharge, without clear evidence of having a symbolic function also, it belongs under the *anxiety disorders* (Chapter 6) or *psychosomatic disorders* (Chapter 17). This is the case when, for example, vomiting or diarrhea simply represents a direct, primitive expression of anxiety or fright (see Chapter 17 for further discussion of this point). If, on the other hand, vomiting or diarrhea symbolizes a conflict over acceptance and rejection, if it represents in body language an unconscious sexual or aggressive drive, or if it expresses ego defenses or identifications, then we call it a *conversion disorder*. Visceral disturbances of all kinds can be employed to express unconscious conflicts in a nonverbal body metaphor. They can reduce emotional tension and anxiety just as conversions in skeletal muscle and sense organs can. Disturbances of visceral function in these cases result from the use of the internal organ to say something, to express something that is not its primary function. Such an exploitation has effects upon internal organs similar to those it has upon skeletal muscles and sense organs.

Practically all of the viscera, we have said, can take part in symbolic activities. We shall limit ourselves to two important disturbances of appetite. That is, what evidence we have suggests that these eating disorders seem to be on the increase in recent times (Bemis, 1978). Eating and drinking always mean more to human beings than mere food intake. From the earliest weeks of life we all experience love and closeness in feeding situations. All through childhood and adolescence we eat and drink in the company of persons whom we usually love and sometimes hate. To be given food and drink lovingly is to be given love; to be denied food and sent from the table is to be denied love and excommunicated. As adults we often eat or drink with others to restate acceptance and affection; we sometimes eat or drink alone to express solace and self-love. To refuse to eat or drink with someone is apt to be interpreted as a personal rejection. Add to such considerations the fact that food adds weight to a person and, conversely, the avoidance or regurgitation of food takes weight off, and we have a highly complex dynamic wound into the management of food. That is, in recent times the ideal of sexual attractiveness has emphasized increasingly the "slim" over the "voluptuous." Here is an entirely different realm of meaning that can be symbolized in the eating or not eating of food.

In what follows we shall discuss both loss of appetite and excessive appetite in cases that obviously express through body language deep unconscious conflict over sex and aggression with their related fantasies.

*Anorexia Nervosa.* Anorexia means the loss of appetite. It can signify many different things. Here we shall be concerned with loss of appetite that expresses an unconscious conflict in body metaphor. In the clinical case that we have chosen to illustrate anorexia nervosa, the function of eating has more than one meaning for the patient. The refusal to eat is carried so far that finally the patient becomes unable to retain anything that she manages to get down. This combination of refusal and ejection is not rare, and it has a rich symbolic yield.

### Case of Betty S.: Anorexia Nervosa as a Conversion Disorder

Betty S. was the immature daughter of domineering, overprotective parents. At puberty she found herself suddenly facing the approach of an adulthood she did not want. She rebelled against her developing womanhood and especially against the prospect of her adult sex role. Her parents had always told her that children must eat if they want to grow up. Therefore she launched her rebellion by sharply reducing her food intake. This engaged her at once in a battle with her parents, who insisted that she go on eating as before.

Betty now had two reasons for losing her appetite—her aversion to becoming an adult woman, with the prospective role of wife and mother, and her resentment at having the parental demands forced down her throat (to use an apt metaphor). In earlier years she had done what many children do when they are required to eat more than they want. She had concealed food at the table and later disposed of it. Now she went further. She not only revived this practice but also began vomiting much of what she had swallowed. The battle went on without a decisive trend for almost two years. Then the situation got out of hand. To her growing loss of appetite she added nausea and a positive disgust for food. She could scarcely eat anything without feeling full, and she could no longer keep down what she managed to eat. Eventually Betty had to be hospitalized for vomiting and semistarvation. Psychiatric cooperation was then enlisted.

Once she had learned to trust her therapist she was able to put into words, and to experience clearly, both her aversion to adulthood and her anger over parental domination. As psychotherapy progressed the nausea, vomiting, and aversion to food gradually disappeared. Betty's parents, however, reacted to her improvement in a most interesting fashion. They insisted that she give up therapy. Thus the chance to work through her problems slipped from her grasp. She left treatment with great symptomatic improvement and a better understanding of her conflicts. Her fundamental problem centered on a wish to be a mother in conflict with a wish to deny this eventuality. In the vomiting of food Betty was symbolizing both sides to this conflict.

There can be several different motives prompting an anorexic pattern, of course. The disorder continues to be most prevalent among adolescent females, many of whom have been overweight at some period in their life (Maxmen, Silberfarb, & Ferrell, 1974). In rejecting her corpulence the anorexic girl comes to view the other extreme—emaciation—as an acceptable alternative. Indeed, although she may look like a refugee from a World War II concentration camp, when she looks at herself in a mirror she does not find her image objectionable. She may in fact see a fantasied image of her earlier obesity. The likelihood here is great that unconscious wishes to be thin have combined with wishes to be punished for some reason, and the resultant compromise has pushed the anorexic over the bounds of reasonable weight loss. When they are assessed for personality style, anorexic patients are likely to be described as introverted, anxious, and dependent individuals (Smart, Beumont, & George, 1976).

*Bulimia (overeating).* People overeat for a great many reasons other than enjoying food. A person is likely to eat well when he or she is with friends, but also when alone and feeling lonely or depressed. In the former instance eating is an accompaniment of affection; in the latter instance it is a substitute for affection. Eating can also have direct aggressive or sexual meaning. When we say a man attacks his meal we sometimes mean it literally; sometimes it appears that he has just killed the juicy steak he is "tearing into." The best places to witness aggressive eating are at picnics and on camping trips, when no one is concerned about appearances. Adults in love speak of wanting to eat each other up, like the praying mantis. Parents may say to a child, affectionately, "I could eat you up!" There are obviously ample meanings here for symbolization in a most concrete manner through eating disorders.

Fantasies of eating and being eaten are among the most primitive of all. Myths, rituals, fairy tales, and adult dreams do not hesitate to express oral destructiveness and even cannibalism. Adults undergoing intensive psychotherapy sometimes experience waking fantasies of devouring or being devoured. Sexuality as eating is usually expressed less openly in more indirect symbolism, but it can still be recognized. Some children's fairy tales of sudden growth through eating a magical food belong in this category, as does the common childhood belief that mother is growing large (in pregnancy) because of something she has eaten. Such fantasy was probably central in Betty's case of anorexia. It is clearly focal in the following case, in which excessive eating (*bulimia*) expresses an unconscious conflict in the language of body symbolism.

### Case of Mary G.: Bulimia as a Conversion Disorder

Mary G. was a high school science teacher aged twenty-five. Her parents seemed always to have preferred her younger brother and her older sister and to have treated Mary as a child of little worth. The brother was born when Mary was three. He replaced her in the parents' bedroom and held first place in their hearts. She could always gain praise and attention by eating well, especially from her father, who was a food faddist. She recalled no particular difficulties during latency except that she seemed always hungry. Before meals she sometimes felt lonely and deserted; after them she felt heavy and contented (note the oral-fixation implications!). In high school she took to cooking "like a duck to water," and around this activity she shaped her major satisfactions. She became an excellent cook.

Mary entered adolescence as a fat girl. When she found herself passed up by the boys she tried going on a diet. This went against the grain with her; but what made it doubly difficult was that her father acted as though her refusal of food were a mortal sin. He had not treated her older sister this way. After a heavy meal Mary sometimes induced vomiting secretly in the woods near home, but this made her feel as if she "had broken all Ten Commandments." By the time she got to college she had achieved some loss of weight. But when she went on dates a new symptom appeared: she could not eat in the presence of her escort.

This was her confused and inconclusive situation when Mary was graduated from college and went to spend the long summer vacation with her now married older sister. The sister was near the end of her first pregnancy. Mary at once felt intensely jealous and unexpectedly attracted to her sister's husband. When a baby boy was born she disliked him from the start. She moved back to live with her parents as soon as she began her new job in her home town. She tried dating, but found herself angry and bitter toward men and still unable to eat in their company. When her parents went off on a trip, Mary regaled herself with enormous meals that she cooked and ate alone, feeling completely satisfied. She also became alarmed over her mental state because she found herself also devouring enormous amounts of "junk food" like potato chips, candy bars, cookies, and ice cream. When her parents returned from their trip, Mary decided to seek professional help.

Therapy provided Mary with the first experience in her life of talking in the presence of someone who was interested in her but not inclined to sit in judgment. Most of what has just been related had never before crystallized for her into anything meaningful: the compound meanings of her food indulgences and her guilt over vomiting; her father's demand that she eat and be fat as the price for his interest in her; her inability to eat in the company of a male escort and her bitterness toward men; her surprising upsurge of jealousies, affection, and dislike in her sister's home where—as in her own early childhood—a baby boy was born; her regression to the point where she felt unloved and could not love, and where she ate enormously when alone. These interwoven themes she succeeded in working through in relation to her current living as well as in relation to her past. After two years of therapy Mary seemed to have good prospects of realizing the combined goals of a career in teaching and marriage to a fellow high school instructor.

Often the same person will combine anorexic and bulimic dynamics in an effort to (1) become or remain thin even as (2) eating binges are indulged. A young woman struggling to become a high-fashion model may slip into an anorexic pattern and then at some point find herself on an eating binge in which she consumes truly *huge amounts* of junk food, forcing herself to vomit between such massive engorgements. This cycle of "binge and purge" can become compelling, aided by physiological processes such as the massive swings in blood-sugar level.

The dynamics can appear to be compulsive in nature, but on closer examination we are likely to find oral (rather than anal) fixations/regressions, and this plus the fact that the eating binges are pleasurable (not ego-dystonic; see p. 204) leads us to believe that we are dealing here with a conversion of psychological meaning into a physical manifestation. Clinical experience suggests that an unconscious wish on the part of the anorexic/bulimic patient both to be *gratified* and *punished* is in operation. Some of these patients also symbolize an "I am in control" attitude in their cyclical pattern, because they *do* in fact emaciate their bodies even as they take in thousands upon thousands of calories on a regular basis. Unfortunately, the means by which they achieve this questionable control is not only likely to destroy their health, it can actually bring about their death. It seems likely that visceral disturbances of the type now under consideration will become increasingly prevalent in the practice of psychiatrists and psychologists in the future, due in large measure to the cultural prescriptions regarding what is or is not beauty in the form of a woman or man—especially of a woman (Bliss & Branch, 1960; Bruch, 1957; S. Fisher & Cleveland, 1958).

## Psychogenic Pain Disorder

We return now to the DSM-III format for somatoform disorders. The psychogenic pain disorder is typified by *complaints of pain* that cannot be related to physical causes and that give evidence of a psychological origin. The pain symptom either is inconsistent with the anatomic distribution of the nervous system or, if it mimics a known disease entity (as in angina or sciatica), cannot be adequately accounted for based exclusively on organic principles.

### Case of Leonard M.: Psychogenic Pain Disorder

Leonard M., a black male, married, aged thirty-two, was admitted to the medical service of a metropolitan hospital because of cardiovascular complaints. Examinations, however, failed to yield evidence of systematic pathology, but there were indications that cardiac illness in others and incautious comments made to the patient might both be important factors. Leonard's major symptom was a "stabbing pain, deep in my breast-bone," which occasionally radiated down his left arm. It was relatively easy to establish a temporal relationship between the patient's pain symptom and an event in his life—an important factor in diagnosing this disorder.

When Leonard was twenty-eight his father had the first of a series of heart attacks that terminated two years later in death. A few weeks after his father's heart symptoms began, Leonard began sensing cardiac palpitation and pain at the end of a strenuous weekend in the country. Although denying that he was frightened, he became shaky, felt "all in," and noticed that his head, ears, hands, and knees were throbbing. "I just became conscious of my heartbeat," he said. "I never knew I had it before but I've noticed it ever since. I think I strained my heart, and I might have been suffering a nervous shock," that is, from his father's illness. The day after this episode the patient visited a physician who he said, told him that he had angina and high blood-pressure—"A hundred and seventy high and a hundred and twenty low," as he expressed it. The druggist who filled his prescription said, smilingly, "These aren't for you, I hope!" and informed the patient that one was for morphine and the other for nitroglycerin. Leonard already knew that the latter was used in cardiovascular disease.

There were numerous similar incidents of cardiac pain and palpitation during the four years before the patient was finally admitted to the hospital for study. These were particularly apt to occur when he hurried, but they sometimes came when he was resting. Leonard watched over his heart constantly, counted his pulse, noticed that his suspended foot moved with each heartbeat when he crossed his legs and that his throat, buttocks, feet and fingers often seemed to pulsate. He spared himself in every possible way to prolong his life. At the time of his admission he was seriously considering retirement from a lucrative but tension-provoking position to a part-time job that would make fewer demands on him (secondary gain). Leonard agreed to psychiatric examination, but he would not seriously contemplate a course of therapy.

The results of psychiatric examination suggested that the patient was considerably ambivalent concerning his father, with whom he never felt really close but yet admired "from afar." His father was a very competent small businessman who devoted many hours to his work. Leonard was expected to follow in his father's footsteps and to take over the family business—but he did not do so. Professing a lack of interest—which he admitted was more a fear of failure than a lack of interest—Leonard went on to be successful in another line of work. It seemed likely that his anginal identifications with his father's illness related somehow to the realm of "hostility-love-guilt" that touched upon the father-son relationship as perceived by Leonard. However, he was not willing to seek psychotherapy and instead gradually overcame his somatoform disorder through the assistance of a family physician who was not easily stampeded by dramatic symptoms.

## Hypochondriasis

Hypochondriacal disorders are characterized by habitual preoccupation with a supposed disease or defect in an organ or body part that is actually functioning within normal limits, or by habitually exaggerated concern over organs or body parts that are defective or diseased. The unrealistic fear or belief of having a disease or the exaggerated concern over a minor illness persists despite medical reassurances that there is nothing really to be worried about. Occupational and social impairments usually flow from the hypochondriacal concern. The varieties of body overconcern are endless, and more than one organ may be involved at the same time. In the case we present below the concerns are predominantly of a gastrointestinal nature.

### Case of Carlos Z.: Gastrointestinal Hypochondriasis

Carlos Z., a married man of thirty-nine, came to the clinic complaining, "I have trouble in my bowels and then it gets me in my head. My bowels just spasm on me, I get constipated, and then my head must get toxic. It seems to poison my system." The patient's complaints dated back twelve years to an attack of "acute indigestion" in which he seemed to bloat up and pains developed in his abdomen and spread in several directions. He traced some of these pathways with his finger as he spoke. Carlos spent a month in bed at this time and then, based on an interpretation of something the doctor said, rested for another two months before working again. Words of reassurance from his doctor failed to take effect. He felt "sick, worried, and scared," fearing that he really would never get well again.

For three or four years after this attack he took enemas, three a day at first, reducing gradually to one a day. For eight or nine years he had taken laxatives and devoted constant attention to his diet. He described variations in residue with enough detail to indicate conscientious watching of his bowel movements. Four months before coming to the clinic he was discharged from his job as a clerk in a paper mill because of too much sick leave and an unwillingness to do anything he considered outside of his duties. Since that time he has lived with his wife's relatives.

Of his childhood, Carlos said: "My folks brought me up to feel I wasn't strong and husky, that I was not like other boys. I was always an obedient, good child." He had night terrors throughout childhood, bit his fingernails, had temper tantrums, and was very "choosy" about food. He preferred watching television to playing actively with other children. He always disliked his one sibling, a sister four years younger than he, because his parents seemed to give in to her too easily. He missed a good deal of school because of his own "weakness" and the frequent sicknesses that this supposedly brought on. Carlos was fourteen when his father died, and his mother followed suit a few years later. After dropping out of high school, Carlos began to work full time at the age of sixteen. He has never really enjoyed his work.

Carlos became very dependent upon the woman he married when he was twenty-two years old. He left most of the decisions to her and showed little interest in sexual relations. His wife was several years older than he and did not seem to mind his totally passive approach to life. His attack of "acute indigestion" followed her death, five years after marriage, by three months during which he had felt lost and hopeless. In time, he moved to a rural area and remarried. His second wife proved less willing to assume major responsibilities for him than the first, and she made sexual demands upon him that he felt unable to meet. He became more and more preoccupied with his gastrointestinal welfare until he finally lost his position in the home. In the complete absence of community facilities for psychological assistance where he lived, prognosis for recovery from chronic partially disabling hypochondria was deemed poor.

## Dynamic and Developmental Background

Most of the theory and research conducted on the somatoform disorders has been done on the conversion disorder. In order to simplify the presentation of dynamic and developmental factors we shall confine our comments to this disorder, with only an occasional reference to the other subgroupings (i.e., somatization, pain, and hypochondria). It is a relatively easy matter to extend the points we shall make to all manifestations of a somatoform neurosis.

## CONVERSION DISORDER AND BEHAVIOR ORGANIZATION

*Exclusion and Inclusion in Normal Behavior.* It is a truism that in both the learning and the performance of skilled acts as much depends upon what is excluded from the act as upon what is included in the premise that frames the action. This holds true whether we consider manual skill, close attention, problem solving, consecutive speech, logical thinking, or comprehensive understanding. To be optimally effective, it is essential that one exclude competing and contradictory premise affirmations from the course of action.

Merely to sit and read, for example, means intentionally to inactivate innumerable promptings from both internal and external sources of potential concern and/or interest. The sense organs to whose activity one does not respond are normal, the corresponding nerves are certainly intact, and there is no question of central nervous system damage or muscular impairment. Yet, as far as the man or woman intent upon reading is concerned, there might just as well be no stimulation whatever beyond that which falls within the narrow range of the reading matter focused upon. The reading person has learned to become, in effect, deaf and selectively blind, insensitive to the irrelevant and competing stimulation that still assails his or her sense organs. Even distracting fantasies and the recall of things undone must be kept out of mind by design. If the reading has a strong enough personal appeal, its organization may even exclude the smell of something burning, the discomfort of heat or cold, the demands of hunger, and the call to dinner. The comparison of such normal exclusion with what happens in conversion reactions is too obvious to merit further exposition. We shall see its operation in still more striking examples when we take up the dissociative reactions (Chapter 9).

*Behavior Organization and Conversion Symptoms.* There was a time when clinicians believed that the only conceivable explanation of conversion symptoms lay in some undiscovered lesion of the nervous system, and as a matter of empirical fact, follow-ups of such patients reveal that a fair number of them actually do develop central nervous system disorders (Slater & Gilthero, 1965). Even so, the far more typical findings on these patients is that they are highly suggestible—sometimes referred to as having "histrionic personalities"—shallow in emotional responsiveness, and particularly adept at ignoring, denying, and repressing experiences that they find unacceptable; they also tend to exaggerate and are quite manipulative in interpersonal relations (Alacron, 1973; Chodoff, 1974; Slavney & McHugh, 1974). Such findings support the clinical impression of a person conveying meaning through unconsciously concocted physical symptoms.

From a strictly anatomical or physiological standpoint conversion symptoms make no sense. They are irrational and unintelligible. The patient who displays them seems to be pretending to be sick or disabled (malingering). From the standpoint of symbolization, however, these patients are neither irrational nor unintelligible. They merely use an idiom that is different from the idiom of anatomy and physiology. It is the idiom of words and names, of the perceptual and conceptual things in terms of which we all live our everyday lives.

The hand that becomes insensitive or paralyzed under stress is therefore not the anatomical hand but the social hand. It is the hand which the patient has normally used as a tool, in working and playing, in loving and fighting, in eating and drinking, in creating and sinning. It is the hand to which the patient can also react as he or she does to other social objects, in much the same way that others have reacted to it. The same is true of all inactivation in the conversion reactions. Speaking, for example, grows out of social interaction in childhood. It remains always one of the most effective means of social communication.

Eyes and ears help us to build our worlds of internal and external reality from the earliest phases of infancy. They come to participate in human interaction to a degree rivaled only by hand and tongue. Eating and swallowing, regurgitation and elimination, the comforts of body contact and human warmth, the multiple meanings of movement and posture—all these have influences upon personality development and personal functioning that leave their anatomy and physiology as irrelevant to what they symbolize as is the chemistry of the materials used to create a painting. The anatomy and physiology must be understood, taken into account and allowed for, but they cannot be made central to an understanding of the final product, the meaning conveyed. As Freud was to learn (see Chapter 1, p. 11), such reductive explanations of conversion hysteria never capture what is centrally involved. Formal/final-cause meanings convey something completely different from material/efficient-cause meanings.

Conversion symptoms, as we have seen in our case material, are unconscious concoctions, as misunderstood by the patient who creates them as by the layperson who merely sees them. This process of symptom formation may be likened to the process of forming normal manifest dreams—something that all of us engage in during normal sleep, when we often express in dream symbols and primitive fantasies what we cannot put into words when we wake up. *Displacement* and *projection* are often as obvious in manifest dream imagery as they are in phobias and in conversion symptoms. In dreaming, such primitive processes seem natural and acceptable because we are out of contact with external reality and because our perceptual and cognitive organization is normally much regressed. Thus what we are dreaming appears at the time as if projected upon a screen. Here the similarities between symptoms and manifest dreams end. The final product in *phobias* is a projected fear, isolated upon an object or situation that now *is* discernible to the unconscious portions of the ego. The final product in *conversion* is a change in the function of some body part that has a symbolic meaning.

The fascinating thing about a conversion disorder is that the clearer the bodily manifestation seems to express the conflict under repression, the lower the person's level of anxiety. Anxiety is not always escaped by the conversion patient (Lader & Sartorius, 1968). But when the irrational symptom is most clearly conveying what the problem is, what might be solved if the "sickness" were only genuine (secondary gain), then we are likely to witness less discharge of anxiety and a manifestation of the classical *la belle indifférence*. In a study of fifty-six naval cadets who were learning to become pilots and suffered conversion symptoms such as blurred vision, blind spots, diplopia (double vision), paralysis of arms or legs, and loss of hearing, *every one* of these patients exhibited such indifference about the long-range effects of his disorder (Mucha & Reinhardt, 1970). It is almost as if once the person has really clarified the message being conveyed in a symptom—in this case, a message like "Look, I cannot fly a plane because my vision is blurred"—the resultant need for anxiety manifestation diminishes. An inner problem has been solved, and the "next move" is up to the external world.

*Somatic Compliance in Conversion Disorder.* The body part selected for metaphorical expression in body language is well suited to represent the focal conflicts involved. We call the body part that lends itself to such unconscious exploitation *compliant,* and we call the process one of *somatic compliance,* that is, compliance with unconscious wishes and compromises. Unconscious selection such as this appears to us as mysterious. In part this is because our explanations of it are as yet inadequate, in part because it does not operate in terms of our familiar logical thinking. We must assume a more dialectical logical perspective, being able to see how gains occur in losses, and how intended punishments can be unknown to the one who is inflicting the punishment. Above all, we must assume that the organism creating these symptoms *is* a teleological organism, doing what we have shown everyone does "physically" to an exaggerated extent.

Freud was struck by this telic capacity as he observed Charcot placing hysterical conversion patients under hypnosis, offering them alternative premises—that they *could* see and *could* use their legs—and, as if by magic, these new intentions were put into immediate effect (Wittels, 1924). He learned from the French what his Germanic professors refused to entertain seriously—that is, the body/mind interaction was a two-way street! We have plenty of evidence that primative wishes, infantile imagery, fantasies, and dreams arise in the daytime activities of normal adults. Normal repression is sufficient to take care that these influences do not disrupt adult thinking and lead to ego disintegration and regression. Only enough escapes normal repression to brighten up the otherwise austure and calculating nature of adult reason, to give it lightness and let it play, to spill over into nonsense and laughter, to allow empathy and feelings that may be quite unreasonable, and let us grieve and mourn when we know what has happened cannot be helped. We owe it to the influence of unconscious processes within us that we can have fanciful daydreams as well as reason, that we can celebrate feasts which can be rationalized but not logically explained, and that we have poetry, drama, decoration, and the beautiful, irrational arts.

## CONVERSION SYMPTOMS AND MEANING

To call something irrational is not to deprive it of its meaning. On the contrary, some of the most meaningful experiences in life are irrational in the sense that they cannot be fully expressed in traditional, nondialectical terms having internal consistency and the like. The form of any neurotic pattern is simply an expression of a person's preferred way of handling intolerable tension and anxiety. Some hit upon the method of massive emotional discharge, as if giving in to the inevitable or allowing a culmination to take place. Such persons develop what we then call *anxiety disorders.* Others displace their revived infantile conflicts, with all their passion, to something impersonal that has a perceptual structure. This concrete structure they drive out, or project, as a symbolic fear that they can then avoid. This, we have seen, is the general pattern of the *phobic disorder.* A third neurotic "style," which we have been discussing in this chapter, is the *conversion disorder.* The anxiety and guilt of the phobic seem to have disappeared in the conversion process, once a clear meaning has been framed and conveyed in body language. In dialectical opposition to the avoidance behavior of a phobic, we have a marked *display* of the conversion neurotic. Understanding this process is like trying to understand why some people are dominant in personality and others are passive.

The selection of a body part as the site of the symptom poses the interesting question of whether the body language symbol says what it says and nothing more, or whether is is *overdetermined* and hence fraught with several meanings, as we find in the case of dream symbolism. Most clinicians take the latter view, seeing in the conversion symptom a reflection of the same primary process thinking that enters into the translation of latent into manifest dream content. The translation of manifest dream or neurotic symptom must remain vague and tentative unless a great deal is known about its context and its origins from other sources.

It is at first only possible to say that this or that fantasy seems primarily sexual or aggressive in character, that it seems to reflect early infantile dependency needs, or that it expresses Oedipal wishes, fears, and conflicts. Certainty and precision of translation, if they come at all, must come from the knowledge and emphatic understanding of what has produced the symptom in each individual case, of what defenses have been used and are now being used, and of what the most pressing emotional discharges are likely to be. In short, the translation of body language into verbal language requires insight into the chief strains within the psychodynamic system of the individual conversion patient, including those produced by his or her superego wishes. The complex meaning of body symbolization, and its relation to childhood feeling and symbolic play, are especially clear in the following case.

### Case of Debbie W.: Symbolic Expression of a Symptom

Debbie W., a married woman aged twenty-three, complained that whenever she tried to typewrite her forearms became rigid in a half-raised position and her hands became clenched. She had been obliged to give up a position as a secretary a few weeks previously because of this symptom. A general medical and neurological examination revealed no organic pathology to account for the disability, which appeared only in relation to typewriting and not in relation to other activities, even when the same muscles were used. Her only other relevant complaint was that for some years she had been dreaming of little boys lying in the street mangled, apparently having been run over by an automobile or a truck. In the rest of the case abstract we shall limit discussion to just three events forming part of the context of the conversion symptom.

When Debbie was four years of age a brother was born, the first boy in the family. She and an older sister were sent to stay with relatives on a farm just before the brother's birth. She remembered taking a violent dislike to the new baby because of the fuss everyone made over his being a boy. She did not recall any aggressive fantasies about him; but the current dreams of mangled little boys suggest strongly that she had had them as a little girl.

Debbie recalled that, after the brother's birth, she and her older sister played in secret at being boys by putting some object between their legs so that it protruded. She remembered that this play was accompanied by much giggling and excitement, and that she and her sister openly ridiculed the brother's genitals which they secretly resented. The patient apparently solved her conflict over the brother's birth by attaching herself passionately to her older sister and ignoring her brother's existence as much as possible. This maneuver was so successful that even after several months of intensive psychotherapy no early memories or fantasies about her brother returned from repression.

This young woman had the misfortune to marry an ineffectual husband. Their low income and her own restlessness and dissatisfaction drove her to seek a job even though her husband seemed highly threatened by her actions. She enrolled in a secretarial school while still feeling that if she were allowed to do what her husband was doing for a living she could certainly "do it better." Her subsequent frustration of learning to type was heightened by the teacher's pressure to work harder. She eventually completed the course with great effort, doing a creditable job. Not long afterward she secured a reasonably good position as a secretary. Yet at work she found that she quickly resented having to do what she was doing, and she often lived out her working day in a spirit of sullen anger. It was in this setting that her conversion symptom appeared. It repeated in a different mode her resentful, envious childhood play with her sister after her brother's birth, it expressed doubly her masculine protest, and in the form of clenched fists it symbolized both her general aggressive hatred and her specific unconscious refusal to do work that she was never genuinely motivated to perform. Here, then, is an example of a conversion symptom that was clearly overdetermined (i.e., expressing more than one meaning).

Freud was quite explicit in his recognition of the importance of meaningful expression in the somatic compliance of an hysterical symptom. Here is what he had to say on the matter:

> As far as I can see, every hysterical symptom involves the participation of *both* sides [i.e., psychic and somatic factors]. It cannot occur without the presence of a certain degree of *somatic compliance* offered by some normal or pathological process in or connected with one of the bodily organs. And it cannot occur more

than once—and the capacity for repeating itself is one of the characteristics of a hysterical symptom—unless it has a psychical significance, a *meaning*. The hysterical symptom does not carry this meaning with it, but the meaning is lent to it, soldered to it, as it were; and in every instance the meaning can be a different one, according to the nature of the suppressed thoughts which are struggling for expression. (Freud, 1901/1953c, pp. 40-41)

## Fixation, Regression, and Defenses in Conversion Disorders

In most of the cases that we have used to illustrate conversion, the *regression* has developed suddenly and often dramatically, in response to identifiable external and internal stresses. But suddenness and drama are not necessary to produce such regression. The external stress may be relatively slight and difficult to identify. The rise in internal stress may be gradual or in widely spaced steps. The only essential conditions are that emotional tension and conscious recognition of mounting anxiety rise to such a level as to exceed a person's normal defensive capacities—that is, the level at which all of us succeed in retaining our force of countercathexes. There is probably also a second essential factor, in the sense of the person's selection of a conversion type or "style" of manifesting symptoms of neurosis. As we have noted above, this is very much up to the person's unique lifestyle (see the last section of this chapter for some likely childhood precursors).

It is not that the rise in emotional tension or anxiety discharge "causes" the regression in the sense of a mechanical cause-effect action. We must recall that such emotional displays are calculated instrumentalities of the unconscious portions of the ego, literally arranged to take place as an aid to repression (see Chapter 4, p. 126). But when this maneuver fails and the personality is threatened by a massive return of the repressed contents, the only recourse is for the total personality system to regress in "service of the ego," to hopefully re-enact and work through the long-standing fuero claims. Put in energic terms, the fixated libido is sought as additional "fuel" to rectify the weak spots in the personality. With the regression, primitive fantasies are reactivated, leading to a frequently overdetermined bodily symbolism in the symptom that expresses unconscious aims in compromise fashion.

Conversion symptoms originate in the stresses emanating from the Oedipal conflict (see Freud, 1926/1959g, p. 113), but clinical experience suggests that the fixation points in this disorder are multiple (see, e.g., F. Deutsch, 1959; Rangell, 1959). We find both pregenital and genital fantasies arising in the regressive maneuverings of this type of patient. Such fantasies freely express oral and anal conflicts as well as phallic ones. The instinctive promptings are usually more likely to be libidinal than aggressive in nature. There is probably a larger relative fixation in the oral level of psychosexual development than the other levels, rendering the kind of personality style we noted above (i.e., suggestible, gullible, etc.).

If the fixations in conversion reactions are often multiple and go back to different phases of development, so also are the defense mechanisms that help determine the form of the body symbol. We have already mentioned *displacement* and *projection* in relation to the formation of the symptom. *Repression,* we have said, is both exaggerated and defective. In some cases it seems to dispose of the focal conflict completely, although repression in conversion reactions can achieve this only through the aid of displacement and projection to a body part. Repression is responsible also for the failure of sexual and aggressive elements to appear openly in the symptoms when sex and aggression are focal in the pathogenic conflicts. Repression helps account for the absence of anxiety in many cases in which the disability would otherwise be distressing or even frightening. In some respects conversion disorders are essentially severe emotional repressions. They go much further than the repression in anxiety disorders, in which the source of anxiety is hidden but not the anxiety itself (see Geleerd, Hacker, & Rapaport, 1945).

Another defensive maneuver we are likely to see in conversion disorders is *internalization*. Recall from Chapter 2 (p. 51) that this is a primitive symbolic *introjection,* as a taking in through the mouth, and we can see it occurring quite clearly in the case of Mary G., the woman with bulimia. She introjected love when she orally incorporated her food. She also expressed the same meaning of introjection, that is, the meaning of a physical incorporation of love, when she was unable to take in food in the presence of male escorts other than her father. Mary's bulimia pointed to the same kind of refusal to incorporate that Betty S., the anorexic girl, exhibited. Internalization often takes the form of identification through imitation. The *imitative identification,* although somewhat more mature than introjection, is still childlike. We see an example of such identification in the case of Leonard M., who out of guilt and fear acquired his father's symptoms.

## Conversion Disorders and Early Childhood

Because the conversion symptom represents a body change, it is better suited than any of the other neurotic symptoms to symbolize concretely the focal conflicts of the Oedipal phase of development. It is possible to find a combination of factors lacking apparent dynamic significance and still related to somatoform disorders. For example, research suggests that hypochondria is more prevalent in families who have suffered considerable physical illness, upon whom unnecessary operations have been performed, and in whom considerable life frustrations are encountered (Bianchi, 1973). Such global experimental findings rarely do a focal study of the personality predilections of the parents in relation to the child who may be prone to body language symbolization. Clinical experience suggests that two childhood factors seem of special importance in the backgrounds of conversion disorder patients. One is the presence of a narcissistic, histrionic parent. The other is the effect of pre-Oedipal fantasies.

*The Narcissistic, Histrionic Parent.* A special role in preparing a child for a later conversion disorder is played by the narcissistic, histrionic parent, usually the mother. A narcissistic, histrionic woman calls attention to herself, her body, and the moody exhibition of her feelings. She provides her child with a dramatic model for identification; but she suppresses similar behavior in the child, both because it seems insincere to her and because it calls attention away from herself. The frustration that the child then experiences is almost sure to arouse the anger of the narcissistic parent.

The effect of this double suppression is to drive the needy, frustrated child into dramatic fantasies and daydreams. These express the child's infantile fury over the frustration, and they give rise to furious fantasies about the retaliation that he or she may anticipate. Both the child's fury and the danger of fantasied retaliation prove frightening. The pre-Oedipal fantasies stimulated in such circumstances are likely to include those of swallowing up, of engulfing and being engulfed, of biting and being bitten, of attacking, soiling, destroying, and killing. Along with these go also the forbidden gratifications, which take the form of attention-getting fantasies and daydreams, including those of exhibitionistic display, such as the narcissistic parent indulges in but does not countenance in the child.

*Masochistic Fantasies.* A further source of failure to solve Oedipal conflicts is to be found in the pre-Oedipal overdevelopment of pleasurable masochistic fantasies. These often arise through identification with sick or injured persons, who lead the child to feel that it is necessary to suffer if one is to be loved. Pleasurable masochistic fantasies are also encouraged by unusually punitive parents. It may seem to the child that parents "take notice" only when he or she is "being bad" or being punished. The result is that such a life premise encourages the seeking of punishment as a form of love. Following a parental spanking the child may have experienced some of the most tender feelings in relation to the punisher—who, feeling slightly remorseful over a loss of temper, tries to right the scales a bit in the family setting. The upshot is that the infliction of punishment can be eroticized. It is then but a short step for the child to equate love with injury and to symbolize an expression of love through some sign that he or she is suffering. In effect, the body symbol becomes a symbol of this deep-seated wish to be loved.

Of course, we must be careful not to oversimplify the direct effects of the parent on the child. The influence of parental defect upon a child's development need not be as decisive as it sounds. Not every child exposed to parental defects succumbs to them. Some children with poor parental models (Kadushin, 1967) and even with psychotic parents (M. Bleuler, 1974) manage to grow up as reasonably well-adjusted individuals. A child is an energetic, active human organism, with all the potentialities for normal growth and development inherent in human organisms. As a telic organism, the child is capable of seeking and finding much of what he or she requires in the way of psychological nourishment, even in an emotionally unfavorable climate. If there are two parents in the home, one may be able to compensate for what the other lacks. Siblings and relatives also enter the picture to provide alternative avenues of affection and identification.

### SUMMARY

Chapter 8 takes up the *somatoform disorders,* in which an unconscious conflict is linked or transformed into a bodily symptom that reduces or accounts for anxiety by expressing the conflict symbolically. Freud referred to the translation or transformation of a purely psychical excitation into physical terms as a *conversion.* Hence, somatoform disorders are occasionally referred to as conversion disorders. The bodily symptoms in somatoform disorders express certain intentions. The *symbolical* aspect is always an intentional expression of both the repressed and repressing wishes. The resultant *body language* or *organ speech* tells us a great deal about the conflicts that the patient is attempting to master. Symbolizing something in body language becomes abnormal when its expressive, defensive, or self-punitive function is lost through repression and the patient mistakes his or her symbol for a sign of disability or bodily illness.

It is not unusual for persons with severe bodily malfunctions to reflect an attitude of indifference toward their symptoms. The French referred to this as *la belle indifférence.* Patients who are ill usually gain concessions in life, so that symptoms can be used as excuses and the like. This is referred to as *secondary gain,* and we note its presence rather prominently in the somatoform disorders. Freud referred to the *primary gain* of illness as an internal problem solution in which the person flees into illness and thereby gains a certain clarity in his or her situation. Secondary gain is a more external outcome, through which sympathy and reassurance from other people is forthcoming. The *somatization disorder* begins before age thirty and lasts with varying levels of intensity for long periods of time. Complaints may involve almost any organ system, and although they are often focused on one specific loss—such as paralysis or blindness—sometimes they are presented in a vague albeit dramatic and exaggerated manner. It is these latter histronics as well as the patently childlike nature of the complaints that lead to charges of *malingering* or conscious faking being leveled against such patients. In a *conversion disorder* the patient focuses attention on a *single* symptom. The classic conversion symptoms suggested neurological diseases of various sorts, such as aphonia (loss of voice), dyskinesia (involuntary tics, spasms), blindness, tunnel vision, anosmia (loss of smell), and anesthesia (loss of sensation).

Conversion disorders used to be called *hysterias,* along with certain of the dissociative disorders that are presented in Chapter 9. The ancient Greeks thought of hysterical disturbances as limited to female behavior, in which the uterus (*hystera*) had supposedly become dislodged from its normal location in the body and "wandered" about to bring on the problems observed. For several centuries it was assumed that only women suffered from hysteria. Chapter 8 reviews the famous case of "Anna O.," which can be viewed as "the" case that initiated the style of thought we now identify with psychoanalysis. Anna was Josef Breuer's patient, but the explanations introduced by Breuer and Freud to account for her symptom picture grew into psychoanalytical theory. Concepts like the *pathognomic situation* (in combination with the fuero analogue) presaged fixation theory. *Abreaction* presages Freud's later thoughts on working through and even the repetition compulsion. The choking off of emotional expression known as *strangulated affect* presages Freud's censorship and repression concepts. And the emotional release of *cartharsis* presages the idea of recovery through emotional discharge with appropriate insight.

Chapter 8 next takes up two unique visceral disturbances that are considered conversion disorders in the text but "eating orders of adolescence" in DSM-III. It is important to appreciate that only when visceral disturbances have a symbolized expression are they to be considered a somatoform or conversion disorder. Thus, vomiting or diarrhea as a direct expression of fright occurs in both the anxiety and the psychosomatic disorders. *Anorexia nervosa* is a severe loss of appetite that expresses an unconscious conflict in body metaphor. This disorder is most prominent among adolescent females, many of whom have passed through a period of life in which they were overweight. *Bulimia* is a somatoform disorder in which excessive overeating is employed as a symbolic expression of some unconscious conflict. The dynamics of bulimia can appear to be compulsive in nature, but on closer examination we are likely to find oral (rather than anal) fixations and regressions. Also, the eating binges that bulimics engage in are considered pleasurable (i.e., *not* ego-dystonic as is true of compulsive actions). Both anorexic and bulimic patterns can be seen in the same patient, who often seems to be seeking both *gratification* and *punishment* for some unconscious conflict.

The next somatoform disorder taken up is the *psychogenic pain* disorder, in which complaints of pain cannot be related to physical causes but there is evidence of a psychological reason for the symptom picture. The pain symptom either is inconsistent with the anatomic distribution of the nervous system or it mimics a known disease entity (e.g., angina) and cannot be adequately accounted for based exclusively on organic principles. Another disorder considered in Chapter 8 is *hypochondriasis,* or a habitual preoccupation with a supposed disease or defect in an organ or body part that is actually functioning within normal limits. Exaggerated concern over organ functions or bodily integrity is also a reflection of hypochondriasis. Here again, the organ or body part selected for concern symbolizes an unconscious conflict.

Chapter 8 next looks at the dynamic likelihoods to be found in the conversion disorder—that is, where some single symptom is focused upon symbolically. All human beings are capable of *excluding* certain considerations of behavior from consideration lest behavior become entangled in irrelevance. Certain items of concern must be *included* for smoothly functioning behavior to occur, but other items may be excluded. It is in some such capacity that a conversion disorder finds its roots, for people can willfully albeit unconsciously *intend* to bring about inactivations and loss of functions through exclusion—by simply acting as if the organ or body part were inoperative. *Displacement* and *projection* are often obvious in conversion symptoms. Anxiety is often reduced with the onset of the symptom, but this is not true in every case. The success of anxiety reduction seems related to the success of the symptom in solving the life problem that precipitated the psychopathological process.

The body part that lends itself to symptom formation is said to be *compliant,* and the process of conversion is said to occur by way of *somatic compliance* —that is, compliance with various unconscious wishes and compromises. Most clinicians accept the likelihood that the meaning being expressed in body language via somatic compliance can be *overdetermined.* Just as dreams can express more than one meaning in the same dream theme, so too can the symptoms of a conversion disorder have multiple meanings. *Repression* in the conversion disorders is exaggerated and defective. Oral fixations are prominent, and by way of such incorporations we witness primitive *internalization* and *introjection.* The dynamic of reverting from object-choice to identification is not uncommon (see Chapter 2), so that through *imitative identification* the conversion patient can take over symptoms from significant persons in his or her early life (e.g., parents, siblings, or playmates).

# 9

## *Dissociative Disorders*

Dissociative disorders consist of the separation of one or more components of the personality system from the rest. This separation begins as an *ego defense,* as an attempt to isolate something that arouses anxiety, to gain distance from it. But the psychological separation ends up as an *ego defect,* a disturbance in object relations.

In the mildest forms of dissociation the patient suffers from feelings that familiar places and events and even the self (conscious aspects of the ego) have somehow become unfamiliar. In more serious forms, the external world becomes so strange that the patient feels himself or herself in a dream world. Sometimes painful experiences are blotted out on such a widespread scale that the patient forgets his or her own past and may even lose personal identity altogether.

The strangeness and dramatic possibilities in some dissociative disorders have made them favorites in fiction and on the stage, as well as in semipopular accounts of actual cases. The most famous fictional example is Stevenson's *Doctor Jekyll and Mr. Hyde.* The most famous case history from real life is probably Ms. Beauchamp (Prince, 1906), although in recent times the cases of Eve (Thigpen & Cleckley, 1951) and Sybil (Schreiber, 1973) have received considerable notoriety. Here are some clinical examples that will serve to orient the reader:

A young woman had episodes of acute anxiety which were followed by an uncomfortable feeling that people's voices seemed far away and that people and things no longer seemed real. At times she also felt unreal herself and as though it were not she who was thinking her thoughts. Although the acute anxiety that preceded the onset of the dissociation meanwhile disappeared, this patient experienced the strangeness and unreality feelings even worse than the original anxiety.

A senior medical student, living in a dormitory, walked in his sleep almost every night, apparently searching for something he could never find. He entered the rooms of other students and rummaged about in their closets, desks, and book-shelves, sometimes mumbling to himself. When spoken to while in this state, he would stare vacantly and grope for words like a drunken person, and then go back to bed. In the morning he had at most only fleeting memories of the sleepwalking; often he remembered nothing of it at all.

A young married woman, chronically unhappy and in conflict over her marriage, occasionally wandered from her home in the daytime and got lost, much as unhappy little children do. She would suddenly "come to" far from home with no memory of having left it. None of these three persons was psychotic; none gave evidence of nervous system abnormalities.

Until recent times it was customary to group dissociative disorders with the conversions under the common name *hysterical disorders* or *conversion hysterias* (see our discussion of the term *hysteria* in Chapter 8, p. 237). Today the DSM-III classification separates conversion disorders from dissociative disorders, and there is a theoretical rationale for doing so in the dynamics of these two types of hysteria. In *conversion disorders* the unconscious conflicts are typically expressed in symbolic form by some specific body part. The symptom, thus constructed, is displayed publicly by the patient, as evidence that he or she is ill or disabled. In *dissociative disorders,* as we shall see, the patient tries to escape from conflicts, not to display them, even if the escape maneuvers separate him or her from the immediate surroundings or recollections of the past. The rare cases of public display that do occur take place when the patient is in a dreamlike state and out of contact with the actual persons around him or her. Another point worth making here, which will become more apparent as we go into the case material, is that the separation technique used by dissociative patients resembles the ego defense of *isolation,* which is characteristic of obsessive-compulsive neuroses. Moreover, under test conditions, some dissociative patients reveal a personality organization closer to that of obsessive-compulsives than to that of the conversion patient (Geleerd, Hacker, & Rapaport, 1945).

## Normal Dissociation

Mild and temporary dissociation, sometimes hard to distinguish from repression and isolation, is a relatively common normal device used to escape from severe emotional tension and anxiety. Episodes of transient *estrangement* and *depersonalization* are often experienced by entirely normal people when they first feel the impact of bad news or a catastrophe. Everything suddenly looks strange and different; things seem unnatural, distant, indistinct, and foggy or too distinct and clear. Often the person feels that he or she is "not real." It is not he or she who is hearing, witnessing, or feeling what is going on. Examples of normal estrangement and depersonalization can be found at the scene of a terrible accident or at a time when dreadful news arrives. Sometimes even so commonplace an experience as a long trip by plane leaves a person with transient feelings of strangeness and unreality, in his or her own home as well as in a foreign land.

The *dreamlike states* and the *massive amnesias* of dissociative disorders also have their normal counterparts. Sudden anxiety can make a man feel dazed or stunned; he may behave as though he were walking in a dream or in another world. He seems deeply preoccupied; we say he is "not himself." He may also be unable to remember anything about an accident which has just happened, even though he himself is not injured. Soon afterward he may give a reasonably accurate account of it, showing that during the accident he had been wide awake. Even psychogenic fugues or flights, which seem at first glance so strange, turn out to have something in common with the flights from daily life that many responsible businesspeople take each year when they go off on vacation into the wilderness. Their purpose, so they say, is to get away and forget everything. This is exactly the purpose of psychogenic fugue. The businessperson does not succeed in forgetting everything when "away from the grind." He or she can tell you all about the vacation when returning from it. But the person who flees in a fugue succeeds only too well in forgetting everything that took place during this abnormal state. As we shall soon see, when the person emerges from it he or she can tell next to nothing about what went on while the fugue lasted.

## Abnormal Dissociation

Dissociation becomes abnormal when the once mild or transient expedient becomes too intense, lasts too long, or escapes from a person's control. It becomes abnormal whenever it leads to a separation from a person's surroundings that seriously disturbs object relations. Feelings of estrangement and depersonalization, we have indicated, develop as a defense against anxiety, as an attempt to put unacceptable or catastrophic events at a distance, or as an attempt to deny their reality. Their weakness is that they may lead to a form of separation anxiety that turns out to be worse than the original anxiety from which the patient has managed to escape. The patient now feels strangely detached from the world of objects and persons that made up the familiar background of his or her personal behavior in the normal state. There is also the sense of being detached from the past and even from one's present identity.

Dreamlike states carry the apparent separation further. They create a situation similar to that which can be artificially induced in normal persons by extremes of sensory deprivation (Solomon, et al., 1961). Massive amnesia, with or without fugue, separates a person from his or her own past. If the amnesia is complete there may be no anxiety manifested at all. As a rule, however, the patient seems deeply preoccupied and troubled without being able to tell why.

*Definition. Dissociative disorders are attempts to escape from excessive tension and anxiety by separating some parts of personality function from the rest.* As we have already seen, this may take several forms: (1) a state in which familiar objects, places, persons, or the self become strange and unfamiliar (*estrangement* and *depersonalization*); (2) an apparent withdrawal from the external world into a world of fantasy (*dreamlike states*); (3) a sweeping amnesia in which most or all of the past seems to be forgotten (*massive amnesias, fugues, multiple personalities*).

*Adaptive Functions.* It will be obvious in the case material that dissociative disorders in their fully developed forms are not adaptive in the sense of preserving ego integration and keeping the "emotionally disturbed" person in effective contact with present surroundings and past life events. Nevertheless, this miscarriage of an attempt at adaptation, which often disables a patient as seriously as do the worst conversion disorders, must not blind us to the essentially adaptive character of its beginning. Dissociation is an attempt to preserve ego integration by reducing ego span, that is, by eliminating some ego functions in order to bring emotional tension within manageable limits. The process is a pathological form of the common demand of many a normal harassed person who exclaims tensely, "One thing at a time, please!"

In *estrangement* and *depersonalization* the adaptive attempt miscarries when the strange or artificial appearance assumed by objects, places, persons, or even the sense of selfhood, exposes the patient to a "distancing" or an unreality experience that precipitates him or her secondarily into a kind of separation anxiety. It is impossible even for a stable person to feel secure and confident while seemingly living in a mockup world with an artificial self. Adaptation miscarries in *dreamlike states* because the familiar external world seems to be replaced by an unstable fantasy world, with all the unpredictable and unintelligible characteristics of a dream. In *massive amnesias* the attempt at adaptation miscarries because, although emotional tension and anxiety may almost disappear, the loss of memory and of personal identity make it impossible for patients to maintain their previous level of ego integration. They become people without pasts, who do not even know their names.

We shall organize Chapter 9 in slight variance from the official diagnostic categories of DSM-III. However, the basic fundamentals of the dissociative disorders are contained in our presentation, so that it is quite easy to draw parallels to the official manual. We shall take up three varieties of dissociative disorders: (1) estrangement, which also includes depersonalization, (2) dreamlike states, and (3) massive amnesias.

## Estrangement and Depersonalization

Estrangement is one manifestation of the dissociative attempt to escape from excessive emotional tension and anxiety by creating a separation within the personality system. It fails because it results in a feeling of strangeness and detachment from once-familiar experiences that patients find difficult to endure. It merely exchanges one evil for another. Before the dissociation the patient is frightened by feeling too close to familiar anxiety-provoking things;

after the dissociation the patient is frightened by their unnatural distance or their weird unfamiliarity.

If estrangement develops in relation to objects, people, events, or situations, we speak of *object estrangement*. If it develops in relation to one's own body, body part, or body image, we speak of *somatic estrangement*. If it develops in relation to one's self or self-image, we speak of *self-estrangement* or more commonly, *depersonalization*. Some patients suffer from one of these forms of estrangement, some suffer from two, and many suffer from all three at once.

## OBJECT ESTRANGEMENT

In object estrangement the once-familiar world of ordinary objects—by which we mean things, persons, places, events, and situations—seems to have undergone a disturbing and often indescribable change (Bird, 1957). What once seemed lively and interesting now appears colorless, lifeless, and artificial; it may seem unnatural, unreal, and too far away or too distinct and sharply defined like stage scenery.

In attempting to alleviate their anxiety by making the objective world seem unfamiliar, some patients succeed in impairing one of their most important ego functions, that of maintaining *object constancy*. They may, for example, perceive round tables seen from one side as oval tables, and square tables as diamond shaped. Such perception corresponds to the retinal image perceived; it represents objects as artists learn to represent them, but it fails to correct automatically for the distortions in images upon which object constancy depends.

Estrangement is likely to introduce another source of anxiety secondarily. When patients try to describe to someone else what they are experiencing, they discover that no one seems to understand them. To the barrier set up by the experience of strange detachments is now added the barrier of being unable to communicate. This further isolates the dissociative patient; it disturbs his or her object relations in their own right.

### Case of Joanne K.: Object Estrangement

Joanne K., a married woman aged thirty-four, entered the clinic because she could not get through an ordinary day's routine without continual guidance. Her dominant complaint was that everything seemed strange and different. She said: "I can't understand it. Things don't seem like they used to. On the way here it was like a foreign country. Is this really Wisconsin? Will I be able to find out why things are so different? Things look out of shape. That table—I know it's straight, but it looks all crooked on the top." (Her gesture showed that she meant to say that there were unexpected angles, i.e., the right angles did not look like right angles from where she sat.) "And the signs on the highway weren't the same. The arrows pointed to places we didn't want to go to."

On the ward Joanne conversed normally with other patients, but afterward she would ask if they really were patients. People, she said, seemed to change their personality in the clinic from day to day. When relatives visited her they sometimes looked so different to her that she wondered if they were who they claimed to be. These feelings, of course, represented fluctuations in her own degree of object estrangement from time to time.

When Joanne went for walks outside, the shops and houses looked strange and unreal. People walked as if they were robots. One day she exclaimed: "Look at that little boy! He isn't running the way a little boy would!" She thought that the statue on the university campus could not be one of Lincoln, which it was, because "people just don't sit that way."

As she improved this patient grew more and more skeptical of her earlier mis-interpretations, which she remembered well. She said, for example, "Was this all my imagination? I don't feel the way I did [before] at all." When she was trans-ferred to an open ward, she exclaimed with pleasure, "These look like *real* patients!" Later on she commented, "Everything looks normal to me now but I'm scared because it does." That is, Joanne was afraid that the change to normality might not in itself be real or might not last. After she had recovered she expressed astonishment that she could ever have thought things had all changed.

All the way through this dissociative illness, which had been precipitated by a real personal tragedy, Joanne groped her way about in a make-believe world of distorted shapes, peopled by what seemed imitations of human beings. She accepted her distorted perception as direct evidence that the world of objects, and not her own feelings, had undergone drastic change. This is obviously a poor way of handling intolerable stress, both because it is incapacitating and because it only substitutes one awful anxiety for another. To understand such a development it is necessary to bear in mind constantly that people do not choose such a solution consciously, that they do not know where it will lead them.

We assume that persons who easily develop severe object estrangement are persons who, for one reason or another, have always been somewhat defective in their object relationships. We assume that their hold on external reality and its objects has always been somewhat tenuous, or that object relationships have always aroused more than an average degree of anxiety. Expressed in another way, these seem to be persons who have experienced more than average difficulty in maintaining object constancy under stress. It should be added that, because they succeed in weathering their dissociative reaction without regressing into a psychosis, we can also assume that their overall ego integration is more stable than that of a psychotic person.

## SOMATIC ESTRANGEMENT

In somatic estrangement it is the body as a whole, some part of the body, or the body image that seems to have become unfamiliar or unreal. A woman may look with anxiety or bewilderment at her hands, her face, or her body con-formation. What she sees or feels no longer appears to be the same as it used to be. It may even seem no longer to be her own. For example, one male patient complained, "My legs move, but it feels like someone else's legs moving; my arm moves from the table to my lap, and it feels like another's arm moving and doing what mine actually does." Another patient, a young woman of twenty-two, felt that she looked old and different, although objectively she had not changed in appearance. Another middle-aged woman felt that her body had become as light as straw and that the wind might pick it up and whirl it away.

*Somatic Estrangement and Body Image.* Often somatic estrangement concerns the patient's body image, that is, the conception a person has of what his or her body is like, how it appears and how it feels. A brief digression is needed at this point to indicate in what way the body image is involved. Even normally the image that one has of one's body is never "true" or an objective representation of actual bodily conformation. One's body image is significantly influenced by a great many things that do not enter into the making of a photograph or even into another person's conception of what one's body is like. We all have personal experiences with different parts of our body and their interaction, and even with our body as a whole, that no one else can share. These experiences are of great importance in forming and maintaining a body image (Lerner & Lerner, 1977). Every person sees himself or herself differently from the way that others do. One has only to observe the embarrassment that most people express when they see themselves in a moving picture to realize how different their body image must be from the camera's image.

The body image is distorted one way or another by infantile, latency, and adolescent experiences, including those of the growth, maturation, and functioning of body parts, which assume a different importance at different times (S. Fisher & Cleveland, 1958). It is also influenced by adult emotional experiences, by anxiety and narcissism, by a person's particular mechanisms of defense, by the effects of illness, injury, and aging, and, in women, by experiences with pregnancy and childbirth. Even the ordinary daily experiences of falling asleep and of waking up often leave strange imprints of apparent body conformation that may definitely affect the body image (Federn, 1951).

Anyone who suffers severe regression while awake may experience a frightening or bewildering somatic estrangement. We see this commonly in febrile illnesses, in intoxications, in hypnosis, and in such special states as those induced by sensory deprivation. Some individuals seem to be especially vulnerable to this kind of regressive change. Whenever they pass beyond the limits of their tolerance for emotional tension and anxiety they develop somatic estrangement. A particularly interesting facet of the *denial of bodily change* is to be found in the phenomenon of the *phantom limb.* In this case we see the dialectically opposite form of denial of a bodily circumstance. Thus, a male patient who has lost part or all of his arm ignores the loss, or even denies that it has taken place. Sometimes he speaks and acts as though no loss had occurred, even complaining that the missing hand pains him (see S. Fisher & Cleveland, 1958). Once again, the denial of bodily change may be seen in everyday normal behavior, as when an adolescent fails to acknowledge the development of secondary sex characteristics or an aging person denies the graying of the hair and the wrinkling of the skin.

## SELF-ESTRANGEMENT OR DEPERSONALIZATION

In self-estrangement, or as it is usually called, *depersonalization,* the patient seems no longer to be the same person that he or she was. The depersonalized individual feels somehow changed, unfamiliar as a person, or even detached and unreal. Reactions to such an awareness vary all the way from uneasiness and perplexity to extreme distress and fright. Object estrangement and somatic estrangement often accompany depersonalization, but sometimes it occurs alone. The depersonalization in neurotic dissociations is only partial, not the full dynamic process that occurs in psychotic dissociations. The neurotic patient recognizes that he or she is, in fact, the same person—only feeling quite different about self-identity or self-image.

*Depersonalization and the Self-Image.* In depersonalization there is a basic disturbance in the internal frame of reference used to define the "self," by which we usually mean the conscious aspects of the ego/superego. Various terms are used to describe this premise that the person holds toward himself or herself, but in the main we can think of this as the *self-image.* In depersonalization there is a loss of self-constancy or self-consistency. A few words need to be said at this point about the self-image. In normal as well as in neurotic persons the self-image is more inclusive than the *body image.* The self-image is a product of an infinite number of interactions with other human beings, in which the person is likely to see identities and dialectical opposites between himself and herself and other people (Lemon & Warren, 1974). These inter-actions have in the past led, and go on leading, to internalizations of the experiences of interaction as *ego identifications* and as *superego identifications.*

We sometimes forget that identifications can be fashioned out of the *opposite* to what the identification figure "is." However formed, the identifica-tions modified or transformed by the ego or superego organization into which they enter also interact with each other within the personality system. The resultant self-image represents one's status as an organism, as a unit in a series of social systems (family group, neighborhood group, school, religious and work groups), as a person toward whom, within the different social systems mentioned, other people have many different and conflicting attitudes, and vice versa. The child, as he or she matures biologically and socially, comes to know with great assurance what kind of person he or she is. Recall Erikson's discussion of *ego-identity*—in effect, what we have been calling self-image or self-identity—in Chapter 3 (pp. 94-97). There are pitfalls and crises in coming to maturity, but most of us make it reasonably well and acquire a "sense of selfhood" that gives our lives continuity.

The self-image is indispensable for everyday living, but it is by no means invulnerable. As we all know, alcohol or drug intoxication and head injury can seriously disrupt it. The police are continually running across drunken individ-uals who are still able to navigate fairly well but who have no clear idea of who they are, what they do, and where they belong. Patients suffering from head injury often pass through a phase during which they cannot identify themselves or recall their status as individuals or as members of social groups. As the intoxication and the effects of head injury clear up the self-image usually re-establishes itself much as it had been before. It is evident from centuries of clinical and experimental evidence that emotional stress can have similar effects (Jacobson, 1959; Peto, 1955). One patient, who experienced deperson-alization most acutely when she awakened in the morning, expressed it as follows: "I don't know who I am when I wake up in the morning. I seem to need someone to help me get things straight. My mind seems to be on a sort of precipice, and I'm not sure which way it's going."

Severe emotional stress in vulnerable people can disrupt their self-image almost completely, leaving them disoriented in a world they cannot fathom. They may wander about aimlessly in familiar territory as though they were lost in a jungle. Combat soldiers who are stunned not by shell fire but by a close companion's death sometimes stumble around fearlessly because they no longer have any conception of who they are, where they are, and that there is imminent danger that they may be killed (Bloch, 1969; Grinker & Spiegel, 1945b). As we turn to a discussion of dreamlike states, we shall witness the disorientative effects of still more severe disruptions of the self-image. Later on, when we come to the section on massive amnesias, we shall deal finally with the dissociation of personality that Freud (1936/1964d) called the extreme of depersonalization.

## Dreamlike Dissociative States

As in estrangement, in *dreamlike dissociative states* there are certain common forms with which we are all familiar and others that occur with relative infrequency. Sleepwalking or *somnambulism* is something we have all seen and some of us have experienced, at least as children. Somnambulistic attacks and psychogenic trances and stupors, on the other hand, are uncommon and strike everyone at once as pathological. Yet the familiar and the unusual forms have many things in common. In all of them the person typically has open eyes and reflects an ability to avoid obstacles but is clearly not in normal contact with the environment. This lack of contact can get the person into dangerous situations, as we shall see below. Sleepwalkers, upon wakening, can sometimes tell something about what it was that they were trying to do while they were walking in their sleep, though often they remember nothing about it at all. Patients who have been in a psychogenic trance or stupor usually cannot give a spontaneous account of the dreamlike experiences, although in exceptional cases they can, with or without the help of narcosis (Grinker & Spiegel, 1945b). But it is reasonably certain that experiences in trance and stupor resemble those in ordinary sleepwalking.

### SLEEPWALKING OR SOMNAMBULISM

Ordinary dreams, without sleepwalking, are dissociative experiences in which the dreamer has already withdrawn from his or her surroundings and regressed into sleep. They characteristically express conflicts in some form, often a forbidden wish (id) distorted beyond recognition by countering wishes (super-ego). Experimental studies on the phenomenon known as rapid eye movement establish that everyone dreams every night (Dement & Kleitman, 1957). If subjects with electrodes attached to the area of the eyes are awakened when their closed eyes begin moving about jerkily, it will be found that they have been dreaming. Although most of these dreams are not recalled, some are, and as a person becomes familiar with dream interpretation it is likely that he or she will recall more and more of the dreams actually *expressed* in sleep.

The person who gets up and walks about while asleep, the somnambulist, is exhibiting a special kind of dreaming. The somnambulist's motility is more or less at the service of the dream fantasies concerned, so that he or she moves about with open eyes and carries out complex tasks before returning to bed. Walking about with eyes open does not happen in ordinary dreaming.

Sleepwalkers, without awakening, go in search of something about which they have been fantasizing in the dream, or they try to work out a conflict, or they attempt to escape from something they have been imagining. The wishes, conflicts, and fears expressed are often related to daytime matters of the present—as in the famous sleepwalking of Lady Macbeth—but they also represent in some form a revival of childhood fantasies.

Although sleepwalking is commonest in childhood, it is by no means rare in adults. A somnambulistic woman may get up without wholly waking, her eyes open and her movements reasonably well coordinated. She rummages about, sometimes asking incoherent questions or giving strange answers to what an awakened person asks her. She may dress and go out, or go out half-dressed as she is, walking down corridors, down flights of stairs, into other rooms, or into the street. Eventually, something awakens her or she just goes back and continues sleeping. In either case she may remember nothing coherent when she wakes or she may recall a manifest dream in which some of the events from her sleepwalking episode can be identified.

Performances such as this, as we have said, can lead a person into danger. Sleepwalking soldiers in wartime service have more than once been fired upon for not responding to a sentry's challenge (S. Sandler, 1945). Sleepwalkers have been known to climb out of windows and seriously injure themselves in the process. Somnambulistic children and adults get out on ledges and roofs, walk in front of moving vehicles, or fall down stairs. Sometimes they break into a run when they are dreaming of a fearful object or situation, and this can also prove to be risky activity. Here are three clinical examples of somnambulism:

> A girl aged four years began walking in her sleep at a time when serious marital discord between her parents was smouldering near the surface of their life and she herself was in the Oedipal phase of development. One night she was walking along the upstairs hall, in a somnambulistic state, when a ghost seemed suddenly to come out of her parents' bedroom. She rushed to the stairs, ran down them at top speed, and near the bottom tried to jump the rest of the way. Fortunately her parents, who were still downstairs, heard her, and her father was able to catch her as she jumped.

Back in bed she asked openly that her mother go away, and she persuaded her father to stay with her until she fell asleep again. According to her mother, the child remembered the whole episode, including the ghost, as something that had really happened. There were other related dreams that need not detain us here.

An adult male in therapy recalled that when he was seven years old he found himself out on the fire escape one night, with one leg over the railing, five stories above the street. He had been dreaming that the apartment was ablaze and that he was fleeing from it in panic. The vividness of the dream, and the settings in which he again and again recalled it during therapy, suggested that he had been trying to escape from the fires of an early childhood conflict, in which passion, hatred, and the fear of retaliation each played a part.

Another adult in therapy awoke one night to find himself running downstairs in the hotel where he was staying during a business trip. All that he could remember was that somebody was terribly in need of help and that he was running to the rescue. At one point he ran into a fire extinguisher and badly bruised his shoulder. Similar dreams without sleepwalking soon made it clear that the "somebody" needing help was himself.

Chronic sleepwalkers seem less able than the average person to keep their dream life and waking life apart. The boundaries between sleep and waking seem to be somewhat blurred. Perhaps sleepwalking is commoner in childhood than in adulthood because the functional boundaries separating fantasy from objective reality are much less clearly marked early in life than they are later on. It should be noted, however, that even though sleepwalking places perceptual, cognitive, and motor systems at the dream's disposal, it can be found among adults who otherwise show no signs of personality dissociation. It gives us, therefore, a more or less normal foundation from which to understand the definitely pathological somnambulistic attacks, the trances and stupors, the fugues and dissociated personalities.

## SOMNAMBULISTIC ATTACKS (HYSTERICAL CONVULSIONS)

The somnambulistic attack, which used to be called an hysterical fit or hysterical convulsion, is actually not one of the convulsive disorders. This has been recognized for over a century. It is a little drama, as we shall see, in which a person becomes suddenly oblivious to the immediate surroundings and acts out some fantasy that up to then he or she had been repressing. During the attack, the socially shared world exists as little for the patient as it does for an ordinary sleepwalker. When the person comes out of the somnambulistic attack, there is no memory of what has taken place. Sometimes he or she will behave as though nothing out of the way has happened at all. There may be a slight disorientation for a short time. At other times, the patient may go into a passive dreamlike trance state after the attack, as the following case demonstrates.

*Case of Marla D.: Somnambulistic Attack*

Marla D., an unmarried woman aged twenty-three, was brought to a psychiatric inpatient service on a stretcher by the police. The admitting officer stated that she seemed to be having a generalized atypical convulsion. The day after admission she appeared normally alert and willing to talk about herself. Everything went well until she told of a sexual assault she had suffered, which, she said, had led her mother to drive her out of her home. As she spoke about this, Marla's account grew vaguer and vaguer. She seemed preoccupied and confused, like a person going into a stupor. Suddenly she slid from the chair to the floor, let out a scream, and began her somnambulistic drama.

Her behavior was clearly not that of someone in a generalized convulsion at all. It was a melodramatic piece of unconscious acting out in which she gave a vivid pantomime of a woman being raped. Marla seemed to be engaged in a violent struggle with an invisible assailant who appeared finally to subdue her. She screamed at the beginning as if in fright, she struggled and fought throughout her fantasied rape, she screamed in outrage when she finally gave up the struggle, and she sobbed afterward without shedding tears. The solitary drama she repeated over and over, each performance separated from the next by a period of rest. While resting, Marla rolled her head from side to side, breathed heavily, knit her brows, and sobbed occasionally in what might have been only a discharge of tension, but which had the sound of outrage.

The somnambulistic attack just described came as an immediate sequel to the verbal description of a rape. It was as if Marla had said, "Let me show you what happened!" But the act was not really intended as a communication. It was a sudden dissociation in which a previously half-suppressed memory returned to dominate her behavior completely, even to the exclusion of her human environment. When Marla slipped onto the floor she slipped into her fantasy world. She slipped out of the shared realistic world to which her verbal description up to that moment had belonged. She was to repeat this performance many times during the ensuing weeks. Whenever she recalled or reconstructed this past event she lost her hold on contemporary social reality and regressed to a traumatic memory, which she was then compelled to act through again and again. Here we have a fantasy, based upon a memory, that is being played out overtly before our eyes instead of remaining in partial repression.

What is the repressed and what is merely the suppressed in this case? Although Marla's assailant was never identified, there were intimations enough to lead us to believe that a personal family member was involved. If not the father or one of three brothers, then an uncle seemed a prime candidate as the rapist. In any case, the deeply repressed material that threatened Marla's consciousness was her *own* sexual wishes for the person of the rapist. She did not consciously desire this person, of course, and as we see in her disorder, the countercathecting injunctions of her superego wishes definitely punished her for lusting after a family member. She in no way enjoyed the conscious experience of the rape. It disgusted and depressed her. She tried to put it out of mind through suppression, but the Oedipal conflict (which can be displaced onto siblings or uncles!) was too close to consciousness, and hence we witness her clinically interesting behavior.

Marla ended each series of attacks, which sometimes lasted many hours, by going into a deeply preoccupied trance state that lasted as much as a day and a half. Although we shall not discuss trance states until the next section, it will be useful to describe what Marla did in hers at this point. Her trance behavior, in contrast to what went on in the attacks, was passive and subdued. She stood or sat wherever she was placed. She went wherever she was led. At the same time, she avoided obstacles normally, went upstairs and downstairs without stumbling and without help, and waited for doors to be opened for her. She took food and drink only when it was put to her lips; she chewed and swallowed like a stunned, grief-stricken person. Her facial expression was sorrowful and perplexed. Occasionally she shook her head slowly from side to side, as if to say, "I can't believe it." But she neither spoke a word spontaneously nor responded verbally to anybody's speech. Although she seemed to be in a dream she lacked entirely the initiative of a sleepwalker. Once the trance state had terminated, Marla appeared normal again, but she could recall nothing of what she had so recently acted out and nothing about her trance state.

Marla turned out to be unresponsive to psychotherapy. For one thing, she was poorly educated and of limited intelligence; for another, she was in trouble with the police whose presence for some time in the background was evident. An additional factor was that the somnambulistic attacks were a form of unconscious display that must have brought her gratification in itself. They also brought her secondary gain. When she was lonely, especially in the evening when things were quiet, she would sometimes let out a startling scream and begin another series of attacks. Other patients crowded sympathetically around her, openly expressing their concern. For a day and a half after the attacks ended Marla received special attention from nurses and attendants, since she was helpless in the trance state. Although there is no reason to doubt the genuineness of these attacks, it is interesting that they decreased in frequency when the patients were instructed not to get near her when she had them, on the grounds that excitement made her worse.

Therapeutic sessions eventually had to be abandoned, since they invariably precipitated a somnambulistic attack followed by another trance state. Instead, Marla was given a program of light housework and allowed ground privileges on condition that she had no attacks. Within four months after her admission she was discharged symptom-free. Two years later, under similar circumstances, she was readmitted with similar somnambulistic attacks and again discharged after symptomatic recovery.

Rare cases such as this give us equally rare insights into the dynamics of dreamlike states. Marla could be precipitated into a dissociative attack almost at will, by a set of circumstances that could be predicted. The form of the fantasy acted out had obvious meaning; it referred to a life experience that was known. Finally, and perhaps most important, once Marla entered into her dreamlike state she could not leave it until she had acted through her melodrama many times. Neither could she cut short the protracted trance state that followed the attacks, in which she seemed to be a helpless, grieving child. In other words, this was not a conscious play-acting, put on to gain sympathy and escape punishment. It was an unusual process of dissociation, occurring automatically when the patient was frightened, lonely, or in the midst of recounting her traumatic memories. It was a regression into an individualistic pattern of fantasies, which the human environment could encourage or discourage but which, once begun, followed an undeviating course controlled by unconscious processes.

The patterns of somnambulistic attack are highly individualistic from patient to patient, varying greatly in complexity, duration, and repetitiousness. Often they give the superficial impression of deliberate theatrical display, as in the case of Marla D. They differ from mere display, however, in becoming uncontrollable once they have started, and in the fact that patients are usually amnesic for the period of the attacks, as well as for the trance state, if there is one.

## TRANCE STATE (TWILIGHT STATE)

Trance states have also been called twilight states. Trance patients seem to be living in a kind of half-light, between clear reality and dark fantasy, like a person who is stunned or lovesick. They move about in an objective environment where there are other human beings, but they remain deeply immersed in regressive preoccupations that they cannot express in words or share with others (as in the case of Marla D., just discussed).

It is unfortunate that most persons who experience a trance cannot tell about it at the time or recall it afterwards. Nevertheless, the trance state is as genuine as the everyday dream and usually much better structured. We know something of this from direct evidence. Occasionally patients are able to talk about what they are experiencing while in a trance or to describe it after it is over. We also have indirect evidence of the power of unconscious or partially unconscious processes in determining mood and action from the study of dreams and fantasies in normal, neurotic, and psychotic persons.

What is the relationship between the trance and sleepwalking, which we have just discussed, and what is the relationship between the trance and the massive amnesias, to which we shall soon turn? In both instances the relationship is a close one, and the dynamic differences between them are relatively minor.

Sleepwalkers are easily awakened—although they should not be—whereas people in dissociative trances are not. Both may follow instructions in a dreamy way and even answer questions in more or less incoherent phrases, although the latter is unusual in trance states. The person in a trance or twilight state is as a rule more withdrawn than sleepwalkers are. The person in a trance is not asleep: he or she is held in bondage by fantasies that are normally unconscious.

Amnesic patients, as we shall see, are less dazed than is the patient in a trance state, less passive, and more able to navigate without help. Amnesic patients maintain a surface integrity of behavior by almost completely repressing their otherwise disruptive fantasies. The trance patient's behavior is poorly integrated because his or her repression is less complete. The patient in a trance state seems not to be quite of this world; the amnesic patient seems to be of this world whereas actually he or she is not. Both trance states and amnesias result from the use of archaic defense mechanisms. The regression in both is deep; but whereas repression in trance states is insufficient, in the massive amnesias it is excessive.

## PSYCHOGENIC STUPOR

*Psychogenic stupor* looks at first like an attempt to escape from the anxious confusion of a trance state by flight into apathy and inaction. Stuporous patients sit motionless, except for an occasional shift in position, or they lie with eyes closed as if in a deep coma, without overt response. If they do respond it is only because their stuporous fantasy has been interrupted by some insistent outside stimulus or by some powerful inner urge.

It takes little clinical experience to discover that patients in psychogenic stupor are neither as apathetic nor as inactive as they look. They may perceive a great many things going on around them that they are able to recall and talk about once the stupor has lifted. Like patients in a trance, stuporous patients have become deeply preoccupied with previously unconscious fantasies that have become conscious or preconscious because of their regression. This we also learn about from the occasional patient who is able to give us a retrospective account, either spontaneously or under narcosis. Psychogenic stupor, in short, utilizes wholesale repression in massively inhibiting expressive and adaptive behavior. It is much less successful, however, than it may seem. Like the trance state, the stupor experience has a nightmarish quality in which anxiety is often painfully felt.

## Massive Amnesias

The *dreamlike states,* which we have just been discussing, form a bridge between the more limited dissociative states seen in *estrangement* and the more sweeping dissociation characteristic of the *massive amnesias.* We shall distinguish three main varieties of massive amnesia: (1) *massive amnesia without fugue;* (2) *massive amnesia with fugue;* and (3) *dissociated personality.*

### MASSIVE AMNESIA WITHOUT FUGUE

When massive amnesia enables a person to escape bodily from a situation and to forget all about it we call the flight a *fugue.* This we shall discuss in the next section. Massive amnesias also occur without an actual flight from the situation; patients simply wander aimlessly about because they have forgotten who they are and where they belong. It is not unusual for such an amnesia to clear up suddenly, after lasting two or three days, as we shall see in the following clinical case:

#### Case of John Doe: Massive Amnesia Without Fugue

A young man, dressed in working clothes, appeared at the main entrance of a general hospital one Saturday morning with the complaint that he did not know who he was. He seemed dazed. There was nothing on his person by which he could be identified. In the emergency service he was found not to be intoxicated by any drug, there was no evidence of bodily injury, and he was not medically ill. He was admitted to the psychiatric inpatient service under the name of John Doe.

There was nothing evasive about this man. He kept asking earnestly, though laconically, for help. He could remember nothing about himself—who he was, where he lived, what work he did, and who his relatives and friends were. Most of the time he sat staring at the floor with his head in his hands, as though deeply preoccupied. Every now and then he raised his head and shook it slowly and sadly, or he looked up at someone and said, "Can't you help me?" Hypnosis was tried with no effect. Narcosis only put the man to sleep. To avoid the publicity that such cases as this arouse no alarm was sent out about him; the staff heard nothing about a missing man over the radio. He spent Saturday and Sunday on a closed ward, going about the usual routines without any noticeable change in his clinical picture.

On Monday morning John Doe awoke in great distress. He demanded to know why he was in a hospital. He told the nurse who he was. He insisted that he must leave at once in order to appear at a coroner's inquest. Here is his story:

At dawn on Saturday morning the patient was driving his produce to the vegetable market. On the outskirts of the city an elderly man stepped from between two parked cars directly in his path. There was no time to put on the brakes. The truck ran over the man and killed him. The police who arrived at the scene seemed convinced that John Doe was not responsible. They released him on condition that he send a report of the accident at once to the Commissioner of Motor Vehicles and appear at the coroner's inquest the following Monday.

Much shaken, John went to the home of friends in town, where he filled out a form for reporting accidents that the police had given him. His friends succeeded in alarming him. They appeared to think that he would be found to blame and might go to prison for committing manslaughter. They finally left for work, and John went out alone to send off his report, leaving his wallet in his friends' home. The last thing he remembered was the act of dropping the report into the mailbox. It was learned later that a stranger, who probably saw how dazed he was, led him to the door of the hospital and then departed.

The precipitating factors in the case are obvious—the terrible accident at dawn, the police, the shadow of the coroner's inquest, the frightening friends, and also probably the haunting sense of guilt in feeling that "just maybe" he might have indeed been at fault. The moment at the mailbox was crucial. John Doe had signed a report that amounted to a confession of manslaughter, as his friends had pointed out, and he had mailed it. There was something irrevocable about dropping the letter into the box. Given the proper personality predilections, a solution to the intolerable prospects of what would now occur was achieved through repression and a massive amnesia. He literally set aside the premise that he as a given identity was involved in the incident. He made no attempt at flight. All that the amnesia gave him—and it was quite a lot—was two days of freedom from a clear recognition that he had killed someone and might be held responsible for it.

This kind of reaction is common in what are sometimes called the *traumatic neuroses,* as when soldiers suffering from extreme combat fatigue simply block out everything (Bloch, 1969) or civilians who have lived through a tornado find it difficult getting their thoughts straight (Schanche, 1974). People who live through such catastrophic circumstances as war or natural disasters frequently recall trivial incidents and not the main current of events, The selective recall of trivial incidents, with amnesia for the major trauma, is probably related to the trivial recall that is characteristic of screen memories and manifest dreams.

## MASSIVE AMNESIA WITH FUGUE

As we noted in the previous section, an amnesic flight by a patient who tries to escape from some intolerable set of circumstances by forgetting everything and running away is referred to as a *fugue*—the name under which it was originally described by the French. The patient carries out in literal action what anyone who is extremely harassed expresses verbally in the oft-heard exclamation: "I'd like to get away from it all, just go away and forget everything!" The fugue is the kind of literal acting out that our sleepwalker exhibited when he tried to get help for his inner turmoil by going out of his hotel room toward the street. Instead of simply wandering about in a daze, as John Doe did, the person in a fugue takes to the road or "drops out of the picture." The following is a case illustration.

### Case of Juan S.: Massive Amnesia with Fugue

Juan S., an impoverished graduate student living far from home, was invited to dinner at the home of an instructor whom he had known when they were socioeconomic equals in another town. He accepted the invitation because he was lonely and hungry, but he regretted it almost at once because his clothes were much out of fashion and getting threadbare. He thought, in retrospect, that the instructor had seemed condescending. That evening he left his rooming house in plenty of time for the dinner, but he failed to show up at the instructor's home. Two days later he was picked up by the police in a neighboring state. He could remember vaguely having ridden a freight train, talking with strangers and sharing their food; but he had no idea who he was, where he had come from, or where he was going. The contents of his pockets identified him and he was taken home by relatives.

Later on, Juan was able to remember the events leading up to the fugue and something of what went on during it. He had started for the instructor's house while still in strong conflict over going there. He was ashamed of his appearance, resentful over the condescension, and afraid to express what he felt and call the dinner off. On his way he was held up at a grade crossing by a slowly moving freight train. He had a sudden impulse to board the train and get away. When he acted on this impulse he apparently became amnesic. He retained enough ego integration, however, to be able to carry through complex coordinations, to converse with others, and to get food. Nonetheless, Juan was much less in contact with people than anyone suspected until the police began to question him.

This is almost all that we know for certain about our fleeing graduate student. But from studies of others like him we can assume that throughout his dissociative flight Juan was deeply preoccupied, caught in a web of conflictual fantasy (see, e.g., C. Fisher, 1945). Before his encounter with the patronizing instructor an emotional turmoil had probably been seething beneath the surface. The dinner engagement was only a precipitating factor that increased the turmoil and brought its components into sharper focus. This then made flight irresistible once the impulse to flee clearly emerged. Flight under such circumstances, however, is a turning away from realities—from social responsibility, job, and future. This kind of turning away, and the regression that makes it effective, can also seriously disturb an already unstable inner equilibrium and awaken dormant conflicts to new life (Easton, 1959; Berrington, Liddell, & Foulds, 1956).

## DISSOCIATED PERSONALITY

The dissociated personality is the star performer among the dissociative reactions, the most dramatic, the favorite of stage, screen, television, and the newspapers. It is a rare disorder. Estimates based upon literature reviews suggest that there have been about two hundred documented cases as of the mid-1960s (Abse, 1966). These reports have been appearing for well over a century. Freud regarded this clinical state as an extreme form of depersonalization. We have found it convenient from a dynamic standpoint to distinguish two main varieties: (1) *alternating personality* and (2) *double* or *multiple personality.*

*Alternating Personality.* This variety consists of two or more ego/superego organizations that have become more or less completely dissociated from one another. One such system dominates all conscious perception, thinking, and action for a time to the virtual exclusion of its rival or rivals. Such organizations may *alternate* in dominating the situation as often as several times a day or as seldom as once in several years. The alternating personalities are actually incomplete organizations; each one suffers from massive amnesia for characteristics of the others.

Sometimes these ego-superego organizations contrast with one another strongly. In one personality, for example, a person may seem shy, timid, and overconscientious, while in the other he or she is bold, enterprising, and even unscrupulous. As mentioned earlier, a fictional account of this kind of contrast, exaggerated for dramatic purposes, is given in the famous *Doctor Jekyll and Mr. Hyde.*

Real alternations of personality seem themselves to be exaggerations of the normal differences that we see every day in the attitudes and behavior of ordinary persons as they turn from one to another of their social roles. There is, for example, the hard-boiled businessman driving a bargain, who shows little or no consideration for the feelings of others, and the same man at home, an easy mark for everyone in the family. He may keep these two roles separated so strictly that he has little or no recall for his prevailing behavior in one while he is in the other. Unlike the victim of personality dissociation, however, the businessman can make himself remember both roles if it becomes essential. Most alternating personalities can be seen to have developed out of a dialectical confrontation of this type.

Indeed, the alternation in personality is often akin to a dialectical parting of the ways, a kind of logical extension of the fact that one value system is inconsistent with a second. If two value systems do not synthesize, logic would dictate that we divide the person holding to both of them. For example, in one case that we felt would have developed into an alternating personality, a young woman of twenty-one who had been brought up in a very strict home, with "black and white" distinctions between good and evil based upon fundamentalist religious principles, left her folks to attend college. There she fell in love with a young man who returned her love and eventually convinced her to have sexual relations. Undoubtedly, she very much wanted such a relationship at the unconscious level even though consciously she resisted premarital sex for a long time.

Shortly after she began having sexual relations this young woman found herself dissociating into a "different person" while alone in her room at night. She would put on heavy make-up, arrange her hair in what she took to be a seductive fashion, and attire herself in scanty, sexually stimulating clothes. Following this, she would call her lover—often bringing him out of a sleep in the early morning hours—and speak to him in a most salacious fashion. The young man was especially worried because her voice "didn't sound like her—it was kind of throaty and sexy." The young woman could not always recall everything she said over the telephone, but she did recall her urges to change her appearance and the beginning stages of the transformation.

Therapy in this instance was aimed at offsetting the crystallization of the personality in dialectical opposition to the conscious personality. This young woman had to grasp that "going all the way" sexually did not mean that she had to "go all the way" toward becoming a "whore," which was the kind of parallel frequently drawn by her parents. In their belief one was either totally good or totally bad; there was no in-between state. Conflicts with the parents were discussed, and superego problems relating to the Oedipal situation did in fact surface. With the help of her lover, whom she eventually married, a successful conclusion to the case was achieved. A follow-up some two years later revealed that the symptoms had never returned.

Occasionally an alternating personality begins with a fugue that does not clear up for years. Suppose the graduate student who ran away and lost his memory on the way to dinner had failed to recall his preamnesic life, had carried no identification, and had escaped detection as a vagrant. His massive amnesia robbed him of his present identity and of his personal history. Without these a person cannot hold a job for long, which means that he or she cannot pay for food and shelter. What can such a person without a present or a past do?

The solution that people with lasting massive amnesia hit upon is that of inventing a past and of building it up as they go on living in a community through more and more inventions. In time they believe their own confabulations, just as many of us think we recall a childhood that is actually quite different from the childhood we really lived. Sometimes the name a person chooses, to attain some form of identity, reveals an identification with some adult belonging to his or her forgotten life. Men have invented a past under such circumstances, settled down in a new kind of work, married, and reared children. Then one day somebody comes along who recognizes them, or they see a picture in a newspaper, and the real past comes back to eclipse the fictional one—and usually to ruin both. If there is another wife and other children in the background, the man is lucky who is not indicted for bigamy. Even if he escapes indictment, he still must deal with the fact of bigamy and illegitimacy, usually in an atmosphere heavy with suspicion of fraud.

*Double or Multiple Personality.* In this variety of dissociation there is no real alternation. One comparatively mature and realistic ego-superego organization dominates nearly all the time, while one or several other relatively circumscribed and sometimes incompetent organizations may occasionally take over (Rapaport, 1942, pp. 197-224). The dominant personality in double or multiple personality is as a rule completely amnesic for the subordinate one or ones, or there may be partial amnesia in relation to the subordinate organizations. Sometimes it is the case that the order of appearance dictates the level of awareness, so that the first personality is amnesic of the second, which is amnesic of the third. But this last personality is quite aware of the other personalities.

The number and variation of these personality systems is apparently quite open. Ms. Beauchamp had three personality systems: the saint, the devil, and the woman (Prince, 1906). The case of Eve began with three faces—Eve White, Eve Black, and Jane—but in subsequent years Evelyn replaced Jane (Thigpen & Cleckley, 1951). In the case of Sybil, sixteen different personalities were fashioned, although three personalities were predominant (Schreiber, 1973). As the case of the conflict-laden college woman discussed in the previous section suggests, it is entirely possible that by in essence validating the various personalities as they appear, a therapist may unwittingly encourage their crystallization and the continuation of a creative line of new personalities. This is not to say that the patient is *consciously* striving to please the therapist. But the dissociative maneuver as all defensive maneuvers can be unconsciously furthered *or not.* And therapists must be sensitive to the possibility that their own attitude can serve the neurotic defensive process.

A final observation: one is struck by the close resemblance of such rare cases of dissociation, with their open warfare between partial personalities, to the common struggles in normal conflict and ambivalence and to the less obvious relationship between unconscious motivation and conscious knowledge. They also resemble in some ways the open warfare that goes on in some cases of obsessive-compulsive neurosis (see Chapter 7).

## DSM-III VIEWPOINT

Although we have not followed DSM-III exactly, the review of terms and concepts completed to this point in Chapter 9 meshes nicely with this manual. DSM-III distinguishes four subsyndromes within the dissociative disorders: *psychogenic amnesia, psychogenic fugue, multiple personality,* and *depersonalization disorder.* Sleepwalking disorders are classified among the disorders that are usually first evident in infancy, childhood, or adolescence. The distinction we drew between alternating and double or multiple personalities is not made in DSM-III. Both of these types of dissociated personality would fall under the multiple personality designation. As with many of the clinical syndromes, there is an "atypical" category for cases that are difficult to place into the four designations listed above.

## Dynamic and Developmental Background

Earlier in the chapter, when we were stressing the adaptive achievements of dissociative disorders, we said that an attempt was made in dissociation to preserve the overall ego integration by reducing the total ego span, that is, by eliminating some ego functions. This elimination varies all the way from denying the reality or familiarity of something perceived to the splitting off of large segments of socially integrated personality functions, as for example in the dissociation of a personality.

As we have also pointed out, all the dissociated states have their normal counterparts. This does not make them normal, of course. It only makes them acceptable as variants within the repertory of human behavior. It gives us a basis for understanding them as pathological exaggerations and ineffectual uses of defense mechanisms that every human being has in his or her unconscious ego organization. We shall discuss in a moment what defense mechanisms are most characteristic of dissociative reactions. Before doing so, it will be helpful to re-examine some of the basic similarities and differences between the conversions and the dissociations.

### DISSOCIATIVE DISORDERS AND CONVERSION DISORDERS

*Similarities.* The most obvious similarity between conversions and dissociations is their exaggerated and pathological use of processes of *exclusion*. It will be recalled that in our discussion of the dynamic and developmental background of conversion disorders we began with a section on *exclusion* and *inclusion* (see p. 249). We said there that the learning and the performance of skilled acts depend upon excluding all competing and contradictory tendencies from participation in the act. This is an *intentional* effort on the part of a conceptualizing intelligence. We cannot place every possible alternative into our premise as we come at the world to behave if we are to retain a certain level of efficiency. It is possible to *overinclude* meaningful affirmations in our ongoing mental activity.

The other side of the coin, of course, is *overexclusion*. This occurs when too much is kept out from our premises. Overinclusion and overexclusion are related to the repressive processes to be noted in the conversion and the dissociative disorders. Both of these disorders have their origins in a grossly defective repressive function which fails to prevent eruptions of unconscious derivatives into preconscious and conscious personality organizations when the patient is made vulnerable to external circumstances. The inevitable regression to more primitive levels, common to all the neuroses, leads both the conversion patient and the patient who dissociates to exaggerated and pathological processes of exclusion (i.e., overexclusion). Some segment of reality, internal or external, gets separated from the rest of the personality organization.

*Differences.* The dynamic differences between dissociative disorders and conversion disorders become obvious in the form taken by the manifest symptoms that follow the overexclusion. In conversions the patient unconsciously creates the symbol of a conflict and then treats the symbol as a sign of illness or disability. In dissociations the patient does not create symbols in this way but instead pathologically denies the reality or the familiarity of something that is already present in the preconscious or conscious personality organization. We shall restate these differences in a little more detail.

In conversion disorders, as we have seen, a circumscribed disturbance or loss of function appears in some body part, the part used for symbolic expression. This disturbance or loss may go as far as paralysis or anesthesia. The rest of the personality—which is to say nearly all of it—remains little affected by the functional change. In some instances the patient even seems to be satisfied at being ill or disabled (*la belle indifférence*). The conversion symptom itself gives unconscious symbolic expression to more than one facet of the focal conflict that may have been involved in precipitating the neurosis. This expressive function of the symptom can have the value for the patient of a creative act.

In dissociative disorders it is only in experiences of estrangement that the presenting symptom is restricted to some object or to some body part, for example, to something that now seems unreal or unfamiliar. And even when there is such restriction the act of overexclusion in dissociative reactions does not dispose of the anxiety, as conversions often appear to do, but tends rather to increase it even to the point of extreme fright.

With this exception, in certain cases of estrangement, the dissociative disorder typically involves large segments of external or internal reality. Often, as we have seen, the estrangement or depersonalization is sweeping; the patient reports that everything seems strange or that he or she is no longer the same person as before. In dreamlike states the dissociation leaves the person so ineffectual that he or she stands in need of constant protection. In massive amnesias, especially in fugue states and in dissociated personality, the patient may deal with external reality in a remarkably effective way—considering the extent of dissociation—but he or she does so at the cost of losing touch with whole areas of experience identifying the person as a unique human being.

## FIXATION AND REGRESSION IN DISSOCIATIVE DISORDERS

The process of symptom formation in dissociative disorders follows the same general pattern as that in other neuroses. Increased internal or external stress brings about a decompensation in the ego defense system, which can no longer dissuade unconscious id and superego wishes from reaching consciousness. An upsurge of derivatives of these wishes threatens to destroy the

Freud in 1906, at fifty years of age. He had by this time published his works
on the Interpretation of Dreams (1900-1901) and The Psychopathology of
Everyday Life (1901). The weekly meetings with colleagues that grew into the
Vienna Psycho-Analytic Society began in 1902. In April of 1906 Freud began
to correspond with Carl Jung.

conscious ego's rational sense of psychic unity, and hence the unconscious ego
raises the level of anxiety to an intolerable level (see Chapter 4, p. 126). A
partial regression then occurs which makes it possible for an ego integration
(conscious and unconscious portions in their usual alignment) to take place.
There is a major difference between the outcome of this regression and that
which characterizes phobias and conversions. This difference can be summed
up by saying that in dissociations the regression reactivates earlier and more
primitive ego organizations than in phobias and conversions. It revives processes
of primitive denial and ego-splitting that were used in infancy before mature
repression had developed.

The major fixation points in dissociative disorders toward which regression leads are multiple fixation points belonging to more than one phase of personality development. In *somatic estrangement,* for example, the patient undergoes a partial regression that revives archaic problems related to formation of the *body image.* Patients who complain that some body part has become unreal or has changed in some way often stare at it as though it were not a part of themselves. This reaction is not found elsewhere in the neuroses; but it does occur in toxic psychoses, in schizophrenia, and occasionally in experimentally induced sensory deprivation (P. Solomon et al., 1961). It also seems to repeat early infantile experiences that occur before the body image has been constructed and used.

In *object estrangement* and in *depersonalization* the regression revives archaic problems related to the distinction between a conscious ego (*self*) and external reality (*not-self*), between one's sense of identity and one's sense of the separate existence of other things and persons. Sometimes it seems to be the *self-image* (definition known to conscious ego) that is chiefly affected; sometimes it seems to be the object world, while the self appears relatively whole; most often both self and object world are involved in the estrangement, since self and object are actually dialectically defined, reciprocal constructs (see Piaget, 1954, pp. 75-127).

Estrangement and depersonalization form a bridge between the relatively stable, symbolic conversion symptom and the dreamlike or amnesic dissociations. In mild estrangement and depersonalization patients are far from being overwhelmed by their symptoms. The strangeness of their experience may make them uneasy or anxious at the moment, but the estrangement or depersonalization may provide a separation from something traumatic that adaptively lessens its immediate impact. On the other hand, in severe estrangement or severe depersonalization, as in dreamlike states and massive amnesias, the patient is often overwhelmed by the resultant symptoms, thrown into a world of weird unreality, engulfed by a world of fantasy, or cut off from large segments of his or her own personality organization. In these states the patient does not gain control over the situation, as is often true in conversion disorders, but tends to lose control of events as well as to lose self-control.

## EGO-SPLITTING IN DISSOCIATIVE DISORDERS

In all the varieties of dissociative disorders we find examples of pathologically sharp or pathologically exclusive cleavages in the personality organization. That is to say, the dissociations are not diffuse or haphazard but involve more or less orderly separations into suborganizations that may or may not interact with one another. Such cleavages illustrate a process that may be termed *ego-splitting,* that is, separation of the ego organization into two or more autonomous parts.

The universal normal form that ego-splitting takes is the division into an *observing* and an *observed* personality process, made possible by the fact that human beings can reason according to a dialectical logic that allows for transcendence in thought, self-reflexivity, and "knowing that we know" things. We all discover this innate capacity during early childhood, as we look upon our own thoughts and feelings in the same way we look upon the acts of other people. It is this capacity for self-examination that probably gives rise to our conscious self-image, an image which never has all of the information available to it regarding the total personality system.

The most significant permanent splitting of the ego occurs in the process of forming a mature superego, which then functions in such a way as to approve and love or to disapprove and punish the rest of the ego organization (see Chapter 4). Striking exaggerations of this split into ego and superego occur in the obsessive-compulsive neuroses and in depressions. Exaggerations also occur in the dissociative disorders, as for example in the apparent loss of superego control in the behavior of Juan S., who went off in a fugue instead of facing a dinner engagement, and in Marla D., who slipped into her rape fantasy and acted it out in public without shame.

Most of the ego-splitting in the dissociative disorders is not simply an ego-superego split. In estrangement and depersonalization the splitting seems to be motivated chiefly by an attempt to gain psychological distance from something traumatic or from something that demands too abrupt an adaptation. In dreamlike states the chief split seems to be between orientation with respect to one's fantasy life and orientation with respect to one's surroundings. It is obvious in all dreamlike states, from ordinary sleepwalking to psychogenic stupor, that the fantasy orientation prevails and that orientation to external reality is maintained only to the extent that it is necessary for acting out the fantasy. In massive amnesias the ego-splitting develops along other lines. To a large extent the orientation to external reality remains fairly adequate, especially in fugues and dissociated personalities. The split seems to separate the present-day personality from its past identity. It is obvious that such highly developed skills as one's communication—the use and understanding of language—are unimpaired in most cases. (Our case of the amnesic John Doe is an exception; it was part amnesic, part dreamlike.) Other skills and a general understanding of one's complex culture are not lost in even the most severe massive amnesia.

The reason that dissociative disorders lead to ego-splitting and not to ego diffusion is that ego development does not begin with combinations of reflexes or of sensory or perceptual elements. The most elementary grouping, which seems to be that described by Piaget as mouth, hand, and eye organizations, still embraces in its earliest form an exceedingly complex integration. The interaction of mouth, eye, and hand organizations leads very early to a stable and unitary ego organization that becomes incapable of breaking down into its components without a general disintegration. What we are witnessing in dissociative disorders is not a disintegration but the forcible separation of functions, a separation which makes such heavy demands upon the defensive system that it cannot as a rule be long sustained.

## DEFENSES IN DISSOCIATIVE DISORDERS

The regression and ego-splitting already discussed belong among the chief defensive maneuvers in dissociative states. It is significant that Freud's view of hysterical dissociative processes (1894/1962b) was predicated on a teleological assumption, as follows: "*The splitting of the content of consciousness is the result of an act of will on the part of the patient;* that is to say, it is initiated by an effort of will whose motive can be specified. By this I do not, of course, mean that the patient intends to bring about a splitting of his consciousness. His intention is a different one; but, instead of attaining its aim, it produces a splitting of consciousness" (pp. 46-47). To understand the phenomena peculiar to the dissociations it is essential to understand the role played by denial and repression in them.

*Denial as a Defense.* Denial as a defense is older than repression (see Lewin, 1950; also Chapter 4, p. 135). It operates early in childhood, before functional boundaries have been firmly established between ego and id, between ego and external reality, and of course long before there is a recognizable, autonomous mature superego. Denial operates before there is adequate distinction between what will become unconscious and what will become preconscious and conscious. It consists originally, perhaps, as a separation from the rest of the emerging personality organization of that which hurts or is unpleasant or heightens anxiety.

Denial is the antecedent of repression, the model for the development of repression, and ultimately a relatively minor auxiliary defense that is never given up (Jacobson, 1957). *Normal adults use denial chiefly as a defense against something that they perceive, something that has already gained access to the preconscious but may not yet have become conscious.* It is possible to avoid a great deal of anxiety through denying the possibility, the approach, and even the immediate presence of danger (Janis, 1958). But, of course, denial is apt to leave the denyer exposed to harm that he or she could have avoided. It is the mythical ostrich sticking its head into the sand when danger threatens. Denial is a contradiction of something known or perceived. In the young child the reality that is contradicted or split off from the rest of the personality organization is perceptual reality. Something actually *perceived* is treated as though it *did not exist.* In a very primitive dialectical maneuver the child "sees" and "knows" but fails to affirm what is seen and known into his or her life premises.

This is quite different from mature repression. In denying something that is known or has been perceived, a person is actually admitting its existence; he or she only denies its effectiveness. In repressing something perceived or known, a person eliminates it from all consideration. It becomes to all intents and purposes as though it did not exist and never had existed. Where denial only splits something off, repressing seems to destroy it, to push it out of the known and perceived world and keep it out (of course, *derivatives* of the repressed material continue to press a fuero claim in symbolic form!).

*Denial and Repression in Dissociative Disorders.* In the dissociative disorders it is denial that comes to the rescue when repression fails. It supplements the inadequate repression and, especially in the amnesias, it provides large areas of preconscious functions for a secondary act of repression. In what follows we shall touch upon the regressive uses of denial and repression in each of the major varieties of dissociative disorders, and indicate where possible the role they play in the ego-splitting that develops.

*Estrangement and depersonalization.* Even in the mildest case of estrangement and depersonalization there is an obvious disturbance in object relations. Something that a person certainly perceives is experienced as strange or unreal. He or she stares at it as a child stares at what arouses uncertainty or anxiety. No cognizance is given to the estranged object, either perceptually or intellectually.

The same is true if what is perceived is part of one's own body or one's self. The first step in separation is that of experiencing the body part or the self as strange or unreal. The ultimate step is that of denying it completely, even to the point of losing one's identity; however, this comes only in massive amnesia. In object estrangement, somatic estrangement, and depersonalization, what has actually undergone distortion is the patient's feeling, perception, and cognition of something; but patients usually *project* this distortion, so that it is the object, the body, or the self-image that seems distorted.

The distortion—the splitting off of something as *ego alien*—is introduced in the first place as a primitive defense, as a regressive attempt to reinforce an insufficient repression. It is a revival of a device successfully used in early childhood before repression was well developed. As we have pointed out, things that could not be handled by the weak repression of childhood were simply denied admission to the dominant ego organization of the moment. They were then perceived as alien; often their emotional aspects were eliminated, much as an obsessive-compulsive eliminates emotional aspects of his or her experience by isolation (see Chapter 7, p. 208).

The weakness of this maneuver, as we have said, is that it leads to a form of separation anxiety that sometimes frightens an adult patient more than whatever gave rise to the defense in the first place. The small child who uses such means can turn to a parent for the renewal of his or her confidence. The adult who uses it must stand alone. Once again, the *choice* of this logical strategy in handling meanings that are pressing to consciousness is up to the person. Just as there are myriad ways in which to approach and understand any life situation, so too are there many ways in which to defend against unconscious wishes and characterizations of experience. We are merely studying the logical and mentalistic maneuverings that people are seen to employ, and that any one of us could have used in our own lives—but due to unique circumstances in our unique lives—did or did not choose to do.

*Dreamlike dissociative states.* The dreamlike dissociative states, it will be recalled, include sleepwalking, somnambulistic attacks, trance or twilight states, and psychogenic stupor. In all of these the split is between fantasy and external reality. The fantasy life in all of them has become dominant; it has escaped repression; it is not denied. The person acts out fantasies with as little regard as possible to external reality or else passively experiences his or her fantasies with so much denial of external reality that extreme protective measures are called for if self-destruction is to be avoided.

The somnambulistic attacks of Marla D. give us the most clear-cut and at the same time the most pathological example of the denial of external reality and the acting out of a personal fantasy. Each time this patient came to a traumatic memory she regressed to the point at which she excluded her surroundings almost completely and slipped into her fantasy of rape, which had much that she desired as well as feared. This is the epitome of neurotic acting out instead of remembering and verbalizing. Marla was overwhelmed by her fantasy material; the best she could do was to deny her surroundings so that she could give way to it.

The much more common and less pathological sleepwalking has some of the same defensive and adaptive properties. The sleepwalker has already regressed normally in going off to sleep. But while sleeping some of his or her previously unconscious conflicts emerge and create their own active ego organization by invading the preconscious and activating part of its organization. The attempt is then made to act out or to find a solution to the conflict while remaining asleep. It should be stressed that such an activity as sleepwalking could not be carried on without denial and exclusion of the actual environment of the sleepwalker. Neither could it be carried on if the sleepwalker were unable to perceive anything in the environment, for then he or she would simply bang into something or fall over something and awaken. Sleepwalkers accept the unconscious fantasies, which have now gained access to the preconscious because of their regression into sleep, and they deny whatever in the perceived environment contradicts their fantasies, that is, the totality of the environment and the fact that they are sleeping. There are many points of similarity between the state of sleepwalking and the state of partial intoxication. In trance or twilight states and in psychogenic stupors the patient gives the impression of being either like the sleepwalker, able to make use of the surroundings as long as they do not interfere with ongoing fantasies, or almost entirely out of contact with what goes on around him or her. Even in the latter case, as clinical evidence repeatedly shows, the denial of the environment does not prevent patients from perceiving a great deal of what is going on, and in some cases does not prevent their recalling it after the trance or stupor has passed.

The general impression that all dreamlike dissociative states give is one of being swamped by fantasy material that would normally be repressed. The patient tries to handle what might be a chaotic situation by denying what he or she cannot afford to face. Because of the depth of regression in dreamlike states this means denying much of external reality and experiencing the intrusive fantasies with as little general disorganization as possible.

*Massive amnesias.* The regressive development of massive amnesia has its counterpart in normal childhood. It has often been pointed out that all of us have massive amnesia for events of the Oedipal and pre-Oedipal phases of development, even though these phases include experiences of great vividness and emotional involvement. A part of this amnesia can be accounted for by the fact that a child's poverty of verbal expression hinders both the registration of early events and their adult recall. Nevertheless, there still remains the fact that all of us do remember much that is trivial and unemotional from our childhood, while we cannot remember the vivid and significant events in which we took part during those same years. This massive amnesia for the events of early childhood seems to be a necessary result of the development of repression through which functional ego boundaries are formed and maintained. In intensive psychotherapy and psychoanalysis, for example, it has been found that the ability to recall Oedipal and pre-Oedipal events and fantasies with great ease and emotional fullness is often not a sign of good ego integration in an adult, but rather a sign of poor ego boundaries.

The pathological massive amnesias of dissociated adults point to a similar insufficiency of ego boundaries that quickly shows up during regression. The patient is at first overwhelmed by the upsurge of unconscious derivatives of id and superego activity and of unconscious conflictual fantasies. If this state of affairs persists, the result will be what we witnessed in our John Doe case, in which involuntary manslaughter was the event precipitating dissociation. This patient continued his massive amnesia without making much use of his environment but without going into a dreamlike state. He remained dazed and stunned as if by grief but with no memory for what had happened and for who he was. This is a sweeping denial of the tragedy and of his own participation in it. It is probably also a sweeping repression of all that had been denied. The denial takes place first, with respect to material already preconscious or conscious; and the repression follows it, making inaccessible and unconscious all that has been denied.

In cases of fugue and in many dissociations of personality the patient retains or regains mastery over the environment to the extent that is necessary to prolong massive amnesia. Our graduate student, Juan S., who went off like a vagrant, certainly had to execute complex coordinations to ride hundreds of miles on freight trains, which must usually be boarded and left while the train is in motion to escape the notice of railroad personnel. He engaged in conversations with strangers and obtained food without money. In other words, the denial of reality that characterizes dreamlike states and estrangement seems not to play a leading role in fugues and dissociated personality. It is rather the selective denial of one's identity and one's personal past. It is easy to see how this denial and repression are maintained. By denial the patient has dissociated or split off all that connects him with what cannot be tolerated. By subsequent repression he has made all of this unconscious. In this way he loses every clue to his own identity, every clue to the fact that he is the person who had or was having the intolerable experience.

Denial of responsibility and the repression of one's identity must involve dissociation of much that we attribute to superego function. Nevertheless, even in massive amnesia there does not seem to be complete loss of superego function, but rather a split in the superego between areas denied and repressed and areas that go on operating more or less normally. Our case of John Doe showed deep preoccupation with trouble, in spite of the fact that everything connected with it had been denied and repressed. The denial and repression in dissociated states seem to be maintained because to accept and remember means to the patient to bring back the flood of intolerable feelings that initiated the regression and the massive amnesia. While the great majority of massive amnesias clear up spontaneously within a few days, some last for weeks, months, or years. We have no ready explanation for this difference, although often we can see factors in the patient's life that suggest the termination is intentional. Thus, in John Doe's case, the requirement of having to attend a coroner's hearing was apparently the primary reason for his return to normalcy.

## Childhood Background Factors in Dissociative Disorders

*Mild* and *transient* experiences of *estrangement* and *depersonalization* are so common that, as we have indicated earlier, they can be regarded as modes of defense available to almost everyone in the face of stress. Most adults who report that they were sleepwalkers as children suffer no psychopathology as adults whatsoever (Bixler et al., 1979). Sleepwalking in childhood seems related to developmental factors, whereas when it occurs in adulthood we find it related to psychological problems. We have pointed out that *denial,* which is responsible for feelings of estrangement and depersonalization, is one of the earliest ego defenses to develop. It is also a defense that practically all adults utilize to some extent when they face unpleasant, dangerous or anxiety-provoking situations—situations which have already become preconscious or conscious. The denial results in *ego-splitting* because part of the ego organization, something actually perceived, is treated by the rest of the ego organization as something alien to it.

*Severe estrangement* and *depersonalization, dreamlike states,* and *massive amnesias* are not modes of defense available to everyone. They are available only to those who readily dissociate when they deeply regress. They, too, may protect a person from being overwhelmed by immediate intolerable stress, but they involve a degree of dissociation that becomes in itself in the end overwhelming. The dissociation results from an extensive utilization of denial in a primitive form. This happens because the repressive defenses have been inadequately developed and denial has been overdeveloped.

The excessive use of primitive denial in adulthood, when repression fails and a deep partial regression occurs, points to *an excessive use of denial before repression had developed into the key defense.* This in turn implies that *early in childhood* (oral level) the person who later dissociates readily must not have been sufficiently protected by others at a time when his or her ego had not reached sufficient maturity to provide itself with protection. The person must have been exposed repeatedly to unpleasant, dangerous, and anxiety-provoking situations that demanded immediate effective defense at a time when *denial* was the best means for providing it.

Before *repression* has matured and before firm functional boundaries have been established between ego and id, unconscious and preconscious, internal reality and external reality, *denial* of what cannot be kept out of preconscious ego function is a major defense. It is, as we have said, the forerunner of repression and the model upon which repression is built. The small child, for example, uses *denial in fantasy* to a far greater extent than does the average adult, and far more successfully. When children feel unprotected and faced by more danger than they can otherwise handle, they may fantasy themselves as under the protection of powerful friends or even mythological animals of some sort.

One reason why the small child is able to utilize denial in fantasy successfully as a defense is that as yet he or she has not made a clear-cut distinction between external reality and imagination. The child is in the same state much of the time that we occasionally experience when we are not sure whether something we recall was a dream, a waking fantasy, or something that really happened. This difficulty in distinguishing imagination from reality in early childhood is itself also the product of inadequate ego boundaries and of inadequate boundaries between unconscious and preconscious mentation. The child experiences imaginary dangers as real and defends against them by creating imaginary defenses. It follows that when the child must defend against threatening situations in external reality or quasi reality, the same use of fantasy will be employed.

We assume that the overuse of fantasy as an escape from danger, unpleasantness and anxiety makes it more difficult for a child to arrive at a normal distinction between fantasy and external reality than its moderate use. We assume also that such overuse leaves a person, after maturing to adulthood, more vulnerable to regression into fantasy and to denial of reality than the ordinary person. In other words, the child who overuses denial and does not distinguish between imagination and external reality as early or as fully as possible is the child who will be relatively vulnerable to dissociative disorders in adulthood.

A disturbance in object relations is obvious in all dissociative disorders. When these disturbances are severe or prolonged they imply a defective ego integration in the same sense that the overuse of denial does. Since a major source of early ego integration lies in the development of identifications with significant persons in a child's surroundings, a failure to develop strong ego integration means *a failure to establish strong early identifications*. Actually, of course, object relations and identifications early in life are in a reciprocal relationship with one another. In order to be able to identify strongly with a parent, for example, a child must be able to establish that parent as a safe internal object. This demands, in turn, that the child be able to experience the parent as a safe, protecting external object.

There is thus an interaction between external and internal objects that goes on for years before external and internal become distinct realms for the child. If all goes reasonably well with the interaction, strong, secure identifications are constructed within internal reality; at the same time, strong, stable, secure *object relations* are established with respect to external reality. An integrated person interacts with an integrated world. We assume that adults who dissociate readily under stress have not been successful in setting up effective, stable identifications and object relations in early childhood.

## DISSOCIATIVE DISORDERS AND PSYCHOSES

Major disturbances in object relations and the overuse of denial are characteristic of psychoses. Why, then, should not the dissociative disorder be grouped with them rather than with the neuroses? The answer to this question gives more weight to tradition and convenience than to basic psychodynamics. The dissociative disorders have until recent times always been grouped with conversion disorders as hysterical neuroses or as conversion hysteria; and no one doubts that conversion disorders should usually be included among the neuroses. Occasionally a conversion disorder borders on the psychotic or develops into a psychosis, which is most often a schizophrenic disorder. Often a dissociative disorder borders upon the psychotic, and in many cases of dreamlike states it is doubtful if the distinction between neurosis and psychosis can be maintained. Moreover, experiences of estrangement and depersonalization are common components of psychotic reactions of all kinds.

In mild or moderate estrangement and depersonalization there need be no sign of delusion formation or hallucination, two of the chief forms of so-called *restitutive processes* whereby the psychotic person tries to reconstruct reality in fantasy rather than to adjust to or change reality as it is actually taking place. The same is true of most massive amnesias; they do not involve delusional or hallucinatory restitutional processes. In fugues and personality dissociation the patient usually retains enough ego function to invent a plausible past to replace the past that he or she lost through denial and repression. As a result, this kind of patient can meet the demands made by others to elaborate a past and present identity. The fact that the account he or she gives of such identities is a confabulation does not thereby make the dissociating person a psychotic.

The delusional and hallucinatory processes invented by psychotic persons are not confabulations made in response to the demands of other persons, and they rarely vanish spontaneously as dissociations so often do. The psychotic is building a realm of fantasy quite independently of the demands of the interpersonal environment. Delusions and hallucinations appear and persist in spite of the determined resistance to them that this interpersonal (human, social) environment puts up. They are distortions of reality that become essential to the psychotic person because of the distorting pressure of unconscious derivatives. Hence, though the psychotic can tell you who he or she is, the hallucinatory and delusional content cannot be done without in the psychodynamics of this type of mental disorder.

Severe estrangement and severe depersonalization may be looked upon as transitional states between neuroses and psychoses, the issue depending upon how far the falsification of reality is carried (see Blank, 1954). We have already said that dreamlike dissociative states are also transitional. Sleepwalking, for example, hardly deserves to be called psychotic, even though object relations are ludicrously distorted and external reality denied. On the other hand, the somnambulistic attacks of Marla D. hardly deserve to be called neurotic; they might as well be characterized as schizophrenic episodes. The same is true of many trance or twilight states and psychogenic stupors. Some of these similarities and differences will become clearer when we discuss the psychoses in more detail.

## SUMMARY

Chapter 9 takes up the *dissociative disorders,* which are attempts to escape from excessive tension and anxiety by separating off some parts of personality function from the rest. Until recent times it was customary to group dissociative disorders with the conversion (somatoform) disorders, under the common name *hysterical disorders* or *conversion hysterias.* As we noted in Chapter 8, conversion disorders symbolize the unconscious conflicts by way of some specific bodily symptom. In dissociative disorders, the patient tries to escape from conflicts by disengaging the personality from the immediate surroundings and recollections of the past. *Dissociation* is an attempt to preserve ego integration by eliminating some ego functions in order to bring emotional tension within manageable limits. Dissociation becomes abnormal when the once mild or transient expedient becomes too intense, lasts too long, or escapes from a person's control.

*Estrangement* is one manifestation of the dissociative attempt to escape from excessive emotional tension and anxiety by creating a separation within the personality system. In *object estrangement* familiar objects take on a lifeless artificial quality, seeming to the patient to be unreal, too far away, or too distinct and sharply defined like stage scenery. In *somatic estrangement* it is the body as a whole, or some part of it, that seems to have become unfamiliar or unreal. The person's *body image* may become distorted, so that he or she observes dramatic changes in physical appearance that no one else can recognize. A dialectical reversal of this phenomenon is the *phantom limb,* in which case the person denies the loss of a limb and complains of a pain in the nonexistent arm or leg.

*Self-estrangement* or *depersonalization* is an even more complex form of self-reaction in that the patient seems no longer to be the same person that he or she once was. The depersonalized individual feels somehow changed, unfamiliar as a person, or even detached and unreal. We are dealing here with a more inclusive sense of self-understanding than the body image. We are concerned here with the *self-image,* a concept embracing an understanding of one's psychological being as well as one's physical being. In the main, a self-image conception relates to the *ego* and *superego identifications* of the personality. This is akin to Erikson's ego-identity conception (see Chapter 2).

Chapter 9 next considers the *dreamlike dissociative states.* Ordinary dreams, without sleepwalking, are dissociative experiences in which the dreamer withdraws from his or her surroundings and regresses psychologically. The sleepwalker or *somnambulist* is exhibiting a special kind of dreaming. Although sleepwalking is commonest in childhood, it is by no means rare among adults. Chronic sleepwalkers seem less able to keep their dream life and waking life apart than the average person can. Even so, they often show no signs of personality dissociation. The *somnambulistic attack* is a more serious condition mimicking a convulsion in which some repressed fantasy is acted out. There is no memory for the attack once it is over.

In the *trance state* or *twilight state* patients are seen to live in a kind of half-light between clear reality and dark fantasy. They remain immersed in regressive preoccupations that are inexpressible in words. Most are amnesic of the state once it has ended. Some can describe it rather vaguely afterward. In *psychogenic stupor* the patient sits motionless, except for an occasional shift in position, or lies prone with closed eyes as if in a deep coma. Even so, stuporous patients are neither as apathetic nor as stuporous as they look. They often recall many things that went on around them during their stupor. Like patients in a trance, stuporous patients have become deeply preoccupied with previously unconscious fantasies. Often in both trance and stuporous conditions anxiety is prominent so that a nightmarish quality is lent to the dissociative experience.

Chapter 9 next discusses three types of *massive amnesias*. The first is *massive amnesia without fugue*. A *fugue* occurs when the patient flees a life situation and literally forgets about his or her earlier experiences entirely. In a massive amnesia without fugue the person wanders aimlessly about because he or she has literally forgotten everything. Such patients do not know who they are or where they belong. After two or three days of such amnesia it is not unusual for the condition to suddenly clear up. This condition is sometimes termed a *traumatic neurosis,* as when soldiers under great battle stress or civilians suffering through a natural disaster (tornado, fire, etc.) simply block out everything. In *massive amnesia with fugue* the patient flees a life situation entirely, usually showing up in another city or state.

The most dramatic of the massive amnesias is the *dissociated personality,* a categorization that can in turn be divided into two subcategories. In the *alternating personality* we witness two or more ego-superego organizations taking turns dominating all conscious perception, thinking, and action. The alternating personalities are actually incomplete organizations, with massive amnesia for the attitudes and characteristics of the other. Sometimes an alternating personality begins with a fugue that does not clear up for years. In such cases a past life history may be invented. In other cases, a value clash may lead to "two persons" emerging within the same personality so that when one value system is in ascendance "the person" representing that outlook "takes over" direction of behavior for a period of time.

In *double personality* or *multiple personality* there is no real alternation. One comparatively mature and realistic ego-superego organization dominates nearly all of the time, while one or several other relatively circumscribed and sometimes incompetent organizations may occasionally take over. The dominant personality in double or multiple personalities is as a rule completely amnesic for the subordinate ones, although there may be partial amnesia in relation to the subordinate organizations. In the DSM-III system, only four subsyndromes are recognized within the dissociative disorders: *psychogenic amnesia, psychogenic fugue, multiple personality,* and *depersonalization disorder.* Sleepwalking disorders are classified among disorders that are first evident in infancy, childhood, and adolescence. The distinction we drew between alternating and double or multiple personalities is not made in DSM-III.

As with conversion (somatoform) disorders, dissociative disorders rely heavily on *overexclusion.* Too much is intentionally kept out of premises regarding the self and life in general. At the same time there is defective repression prominent in the clinical picture, so that unconscious *derivatives* emerge into the preconscious and conscious levels of mind. Rather than create a physical disorder symbolizing such derivatives, the dissociative patient denies the reality of something that is already expressing a meaning at the preconscious or conscious levels. The resultant estrangement and/or depersonalization may be sweeping in the dissociative patient.

The fixation points in dissociative disorders are dispersed across several levels of psychosexual development. Archaic problems between one's identity as a self-unit versus other people—as is typical of early oral experience—are evident in such case histories. Some analysts speak of *ego-splitting* in the dissociative patient, whereby an *observer* and an *observed* aspect of the total ego-identity is differentiated. This can be exacerbated during the restrictive admonitions of the anal period (toilet training, etc.), at which time an opposition between ego and superego may set in that is far beyond the normal pattern of conscience formulation. Ego-splitting may also occur in the sense of the patient's fantasy life being separated from his or her lived reality. Dissociations are willfully created separations. *Denial* is a prominent defense mechanism in this process. Denial is a primitive defense, operating before clear functional boundaries have been formed between ego and id, not to mention superego and id. Denial works closer to consciousness, enabling the person to dismiss what is dimly known by consciousness. Denial merely separates a mental content off, whereas the more mature act of repression destroys the content entirely (except for derivatives, which can always arise). In the dissociative disorders it is denial that comes to the rescue when repression fails. Denial makes certain things *ego alien* by splitting them off but still enabling them to live a life of their own.

# 10

## Dysthymic Disorder
## (Depressive Neurosis)

### Some Background Considerations

The Greek word *thymos* refers to the mind, soul, or spirit, and the root meaning of the prefix *dys-* is "bad" or "difficult." Hence, when we speak of a *dysthymic disorder* we are referring to a negative mood disturbance in which the person complains of feeling sad, blue, or "down in the dumps." The depression in this case is of neurotic proportions. We shall move in Chapter 11 to depressions of psychotic proportions. Neurotic depression appears to be a reaction to loss or threatened loss, to failure, discouragement, or disillusionment. The basic symptoms are self-depreciation, dejection, and appeals for reassurance. The neurotically depressed person loses initiative in life and takes no interest in people, things, or activities. There is not a complete withdrawal from effective interaction with the environment. Though regressive tendencies are evident, ego integration remains intact. In short, the neurotically depressed patient maintains the greater part of his or her hold on object relationships. For this reason the neurotically depressed person does not become psychotic.

Neurotic depressive disorders are among the easiest to understand. Rises and falls in mood without apparent cause are normal and common. We all have happy days and unhappy days, days that seem interesting and worthwhile and others that seem dull and purposeless. Some nights we go to bed feeling pleased with life and with ourselves. Other nights we go to bed feeling that life is a bit empty or futile and sleep seems a welcome escape. When morning comes the mood may have shifted again. Although we seldom make a systematic effort to find reasons for the shift, if a systematic effort is made we can often find them.

In addition to such apparently spontaneous rises and falls in mood, nearly everyone gets discouraged, dejected, or disillusioned from time to time on the basis of identifiable, objective conditions. When things go wrong, almost anyone may feel like a failure and suspect that he or she may not be much good. When this happens a temporary indulgence in gloomy, self-depreciatory daydreams and even in some mildly depressive complaints still falls within the range of normal behavior.

If a loss is heavy and irreparable, as in the loss of a loved one, a depressive disorder may go fairly deep and last a long time, without incapacitating the grieving person. In such a case, we speak of *normal mourning*. Mourning is a process that a grieving person must usually go through before he or she can reach a new stable equilibrium.

Gloomy self-depreciation becomes a dysthymic disorder when a person grows chronically preoccupied with complaints of unworthiness, failure, or hopelessness, remaining dejected in spite of everything; loses initiative and interest; and lapses into repetitive expressions of futility that his or her actual situation, objectively considered, does not justify. Somatic symptoms may appear that are very much like those we described as *anxiety disorders*. The mood, however, is not merely one of apprehension but one of despair.

*Definition. Dysthymic disorders are mood disturbances in which tension and anxiety are expressed in the form of dejection and self-depreciation, somatic disturbance, and repetitive complaints of feeling inferior, hopeless, and worthless.* Guilt plays a prominent role in neurotic depressions, just as it does also in obsessive-compulsive disorders. There is, however, a fundamental difference in the way that guilt is handled in the two neuroses. The obsessive-compulsive uses displacement, isolation, reaction-formation, undoing, and various countermeasures in attempting to deny guilt or magically to counteract it. The dysthymic person, on the other hand, *expresses* guilt thinly disguised as inferiority, hopelessness, and worthlessness. These insistent complaints coincide with his or her mood, but they also are adaptive in the sense that they call forth assurances of support from other persons.

*Adaptive Functions.* Neurotic depressions are adaptive in the sense that they keep a person in effective contact with the external environment, thereby preventing an even deeper regression from occurring. They are also adaptive in that they provide outside aid in the struggle against his or her destructive superego attacks. Through incessant complaining, the neurotic depressive patient prompts relatives and friends to counterbalance his or her feelings of inferiority, unworthiness, and hopelessness by providing "morale-boosting" reassurances to the contrary.

This process of nagging others to reassure and protest is the neurotic depressive's chief defensive maneuver against the internal assaults of superego evaluations. The patient is not consciously aware either of the superego attacks nor of his or her use of self-complaints to combat them. As in other neuroses, the symptoms appear to the patient as signs of illness. He or she does not single out some of them, as we do, and call them defenses.

*Maladaptive Outcomes.* Unfortunately, the reassurances and protests of friends and relatives, which the patient unconsciously seeks and urgently needs, can bring at best only partial and temporary relief. This is because he or she has suffered partial ego-superego regression. An infantile ego—even more infantile than that of obsessive-compulsives—is now under attack by an archaic superego, something that we shall see still more clearly when we come to psychotic depressions (Chapter 12).

The dysthymic patient, feeling the superego attack unclearly as a sense of gloom and worthlessness, reaffirms his or her dejection and self-depreciation, which in turn encourages others to try more reassurance and counterclaims. But the superego attacks continue, the patient continues to complain, and in due time his or her comforters lose patience and begin to upbraid or flatly reject the dysthymic individual. Empirical research has demonstrated that normal subjects who have been asked to relate to depressed individuals, as well as to those with other clinical syndromes, find the depressed patients least desirable as co-participants in social relations (Coyne, 1976). The final rejection of the dysthymic patient by others acts as a confirmation of what he or she has been claiming all along! No one likes or cares about him or her. There is no hope for improvement. All is lost. It is at a point like this that patients are usually moved to seek therapy or are pushed into it by others. Let us turn now to a clinical discussion of neurotic depressions.

## Clinical Aspects of Neurotic Depressive Disorders

Neurotic depressions appear in many forms, depending in part upon the many different ways in which depressed persons communicate their feelings of dejection and futility, in part upon the character of the somatic involvement, and in part upon the intensity of the reaction. In the following discussion we shall take for granted the many variations in the pattern of neurotic depressions, even though we do not always spell them out. All the varieties have certain symptoms in common—dejection and self-depreciation, loss of interest and initiative, somatic disturbances, and repetitive complaints of inferiority, unworthiness, and hopelessness. They also have certain common precipitating factors that, while often present in other neuroses, are especially characteristic of neurotic depressions.

### PRECIPITATING FACTORS

A dysthymic disorder is precipitated by deprivations and frustrations that exceed the limits of individual tolerance. Depressive persons are especially vulnerable to anything that destroys or seriously threatens the satisfaction of their deep dependent needs and to anything that lessens their self-esteem. The commonest precipitating factors are: (1) loss of love or emotional support; (2) personal or economic failures; and (3) new responsibilities or the threat of new responsibilities. To such factors the patient reacts with a partial regression; this regression reactivates infantile conflicts, infantile ego attitudes and defenses, and an archaic superego.

*Loss of Love or Emotional Support.* The adult who becomes neurotically depressed is one who has always needed a great deal of emotional support to shore up a chronically low sense of self-esteem. To lose love, or even be threatened with its loss, is for this person to experience an attack upon the most vulnerable part of his or her personality organization.

The death of a loved one is a potentially dangerous form of such loss because the dysthymic person, like the obsessive-compulsive, forms ambivalent love relationships. On the one hand, the dysthymic may irrationally resent being deserted through death, actually hating the deceased person for this desertion. On the other hand, the dysthymic is likely to identify with the deceased as a loved object. At one level or another—conscious, preconscious, or unconscious—the person suffering neurotic depression will therefore be experiencing love, hatred, resentment, self-condemnation, and identification with the deceased.

Love can be lost, of course, without a death. A patient may have been scorned, deserted, or divorced. A leader may lose his or her followers. A loved one may go away emotionally without leaving physically. Some married couples, for example, scarcely speak to one another over a period of years. For a chronically dependent, self-disparaging adult such experiences as these can become completely demoralizing. So also may disillusionment with respect to a loved one; weakness appears where the patient had expected strength, failure where success had been counted on, and irresponsibility where integrity had been indicated. These losses, desertions, and disillusionments profoundly disturb a dependent person's internal equilibrium. They arouse in him or her feelings of dejection, hostility, and guilt.

*Personal and Economic Failure.* Failure strikes at the heart of the security systems with which dependent persons try to surround themselves. Losses in power, prestige, property, or money may cut a person off from important sources of moral and material support. The same is true of waning strength, health, youth, or beauty. Many potential depressives cannot get along without these sources of support to counterbalance the internal weakness and hunger of their personality organization.

*New Responsibilities.* New responsibilities, or even their prospect, can set off neurotic depression. In some persons the success of being advanced in position itself arouses unconscious guilt; it represents to the neurotic some forbidden triumph related to his or her early childhood.

This last is particularly true of many so-called *promotion depressions.* A businessman sees his efforts finally crowned with an important advancement. He is consciously proud and delighted, but he becomes depressed. One explanation for such a strange contradiction is that the competitive victory unconsciously represents a triumph over a father figure or a sibling figure whom the patient is supplanting. Another is that the prospect of increased responsibility pushes away further than ever the fulfillment of an unconscious longing to be dependent, loved, and protected.

From what has just been said it should be obvious that not all potentially depressive persons are overtly weak, passive, or dependent. Many of them actually reach and sustain high levels of attainment. As long as they are well they may show exceptional courage and initiative. Their exceptional dependence upon approval and success does not become apparent unless they lose their emotional support. We read in the newspapers every now and then of a sudden and sometimes tragic depression that has overtaken a strong public figure when he or she has lost power or prestige.

## ONSET OF NEUROTIC DEPRESSION

Neurotic depressive disorders are provoked more often than not by something that would upset anyone. They were once referred to as *reactive depressions,* meaning that they occurred in reaction to an objectively discernible incident, of the sort we have just reviewed in the previous section. In contrast, psychotic depressions were said to be *retarded,* meaning they were excessive manifestations of the same general symptoms noted in the neurotic disorder, and also suggesting that they were more likely to develop insidiously. Though the overt incident triggering a neurotic depression can be the same as that which triggers a psychotic depression—death of a loved one, for example—in many instances we are hard-pressed to point to a specific reason for the onset of a psychotic depression. There is also an *agitated* form of psychotic depression; we shall review these more profound affective disorders in Chapter 12.

The onset of a neurotic depression is sometimes in the form of a *sudden decompensation.* Up to a certain point the patient has preserved a personality organization that, although internally in precarious equilibrium, has appeared superficially adequate. The balance of internal wishes (id, superego, ego) is not stable enough to withstand a severe external stress. Neither is the defensive organization (countercathexes). With the occurrence of sudden loss or failure, and the frustration of dependent needs, the patient develops a deep partial regression, and his or her depressive illness appears.

The more usual onset is *gradual,* with a steady building up of tension and anxiety over a long period of life setbacks that anyone could point to—that is, these are usually not fantasied failures. The precipitating factor is therefore the last push that starts the landslide. During the period of incubation, which usually precedes the appearance of an outspoken depressive picture, we find many of the familiar products of rising tension and anxiety. The patient complains of headaches and backaches, of diffuse aches and pains in the legs, of chronic fatigue (*neurasthenia*) and poor sleep. There are changes in appetite and in gastrointestinal functioning; and there are sexual disturbances that range from impotence, or frigidity and menstrual irregularities, to increased sex pace without lasting satisfaction. Often there are angry outbursts, periods of bitter sulking, gloomy daydreams, and nightmares. Suicidal fantasies are nearly always a part of the depressive picture; sometimes open threats of suicide are made.

## CLINICAL COURSE OF DYSTHYMIA

Signs of deepening preoccupation now appear. The patient may begin expressing more and more openly various worries and misgivings about his or her health and personal competence. The loss of interest and initiative in life pick up momentum. Nothing is pleasurable anymore—neither work, home, nor recreational pursuits. The patient begins to withdraw, becomes irritable, lonely, and short-tempered. There may be a demand made that he or she be given fewer burdens and more consideration generally. This suggests that a regression toward infantile dependency is underway.

Closely related to the preoccupation with the negative aspects of life and the partial withdrawal are the common complaints of being unable to concentrate, to remember, to understand what is said, to think clearly. Patients also complain of mild experiences of estrangement and depersonalization ("unreality"), as in the dissociative disorders (see Chapter 9). All of these complaints have some basis in fact. Anyone who is deeply preoccupied, worried, and anxious, whether depressed or not, will suffer a reduction in general efficiency and in the effectiveness of contact with the world, that is, his or her object relations.

Many patients focus their attention, at least for a time, almost exclusively upon overconcern with their bodies. Some insist that all their difficulties stem from a hidden physical illness. They may refuse to consider any other possibility and demand that their physical symptoms be given direct treatment. The physical health of most of these patients is reasonably good. What their complaints express is in part the loss of a sense of well-being, an intensification of what everyone feels when he or she is downhearted, and in part an increased sense of personal inadequacy. The patient translates this feeling of inferiority—based as we shall see upon unconscious guilt—into a belief that his or her body is inferior. "I am no good" becomes "My body is no good." Having made this translation unconsciously, the patient then accepts this somewhat infantile metaphor in its literal adult meaning. The bodily metaphor lends a kind of rational basis to his or her irrational complaints. This also accounts for the determined resistance to an alternative explanation because a physical sickness has "nothing to do" with a psychological "cause."

Self-depreciation is the neurotically depressed person's most striking symptom, as well as dynamically the most important. Self-accusations of being no good, a failure, of not being able to "take it" anymore, fill his thoughts and overt speech. These statements, apparently so simple, are irrational products of deep unconscious conflicts, of ego defense and ego adaptation, of superego pressure and appeals for outside aid. The original sources of depressive self-depreciation, the sources that defeat all attempts by other persons to reassure and to reason, lie in a state of ego-superego tension that is called *unconscious guilt*. As we shall see in Chapter 12, a psychotically depressed person expresses this guilt openly, often with savage insistence.

In essence, the neurotically depressed person hates himself but does not know it. This is all the more ironic because what he or she says in a self-deprecatory manner surely conveys this self-hatred. As Freud has taught us, people do know and not know at the same time, if we but keep in mind the levels of consciousness. A part of the dysthymic patient is looking down upon another part, as if the two parts were two persons. For convenience of description we say that an *archaic superego* is looking down upon—rejecting, despising, attacking—an *infantile, regressed ego*. But this terminology is only a system of notation, a technical shorthand. What it describes is a process by which the patient rejects, despises, and looks down upon himself or herself. Clinically, we find such self-reactions patterned upon the way that the patient felt the parents had once reacted to his or her being a "bad" child in some way. There is often considerable fantasy in such patterned self-reactions, because children do not always assess parental attitudes correctly.

However it is acquired, the neurotically depressed adult revives this mood of self-hatred in relation to other adults. There is a working-through attempt, a fuero claim aimed at resolving the fixated dynamic. All of this occurs in the context of a regression, of course. Since these patients unconsciously hate themselves, they are justified in saying that they feel unloved and unlovable. They also realize that they do not feel the love for others that they used to feel. Neurotically depressed persons usually go further than this; they behave cruelly to those whom they would like to love and go on loving. If, as a result, they suffer from remorse, the remorse is fully justified. Each curt answer or sharp protest, each temper outburst, each quarrel, leads to an increase in realistic guilt; and each increase in realistic guilt brings an increase in the hostility of the archaic superego.

The neurotically depressed individual's anger and sadism result in an isolation from the very people needed to counter his or her self-hatred. This isolation leads to further feelings of loneliness, desertion, and hopelessness. One reason for the anger and sadism is the regressive nature of the dysthymic process; another is the infinite amount of reassurance and support that the person requires. Nobody can give this to an adult. It is given only to babies. When the patient tries resentfully to *force* people to provide support, the sadism that colors such pressures defeats his or her intentions. People are driven away rather than attracted to the dysthymic individual. This self-defeating cycle will be seen in the following case history.

### Case of Ernest F.: Dysthymic Disorder

Ernest F. was a thirty-year-old married bus driver, the father of two small children. Chief among his complaints were the following. He felt tired, discouraged, and unfit for work all the time. He slept badly and spent part of each night roaming around the house downstairs. His legs and ankles ached. He had backaches, especially at work. His head ached and his eyes smarted; sometimes while driving the bus everything would blur. He had no appetite, he was constipated, sexual desire was infrequent, and part of the time he was impotent. He took no pleasure in anything anymore.

What worried Ernest most was his incompetence on the job. He had always been a dependable, steady worker who prided himself on leaving and coming back from each bus trip on the dot. Now he was having difficulty in remembering schedules. Whenever he was shifted to a different route he would skip some of the stops. Once, to the passengers' consternation, he went the wrong way. He was now growing irritable with passengers and with vehicles that blocked his way. He made angry jerking stops and starts. To the passengers' protests he gave angry retorts. They reported him to the company. When the starter (i.e., the foreman) told Ernest about the complaints, the best Ernest could do was to say he guessed he was no good and had better quit. The starter would then tell him that he was the best driver they had ever had, that he ought to take it easy and not let those so-and-so's get him down.

At home Ernest felt lonely, irritable, and aloof. He lost his temper with his children and quarreled with his wife. Each time this happened he hated himself for it and called himself all kinds of humiliating things. He was a no-good, run-down bastard, he said, and a failure in life. He was getting too old to be a good bus driver, and soon he would have to give up work. Then they could all go and live with their in-laws, who were so much better than he was.

Ernest had entertained suicidal thoughts—his wife and children knew it—but he said that he did not have the guts to do anything to himself. No one understood him, he said, and nobody sympathized with him. His wife lost patience with him, and every time he tried to say anything to the children they began to cry. The in-laws sneered at his illness and ridiculed him to his face. Everyone appeared to agree on one point, even the patient himself, that if he were a man he would snap out of it.

*Childhood.* Ernest had a long history of unsatisfied dependent yearnings. He was the third of four children. A brother was ten years his senior, a sister eight years, and another sister two years his junior. The two older siblings always treated him as a know-nothing and a weakling. His younger sister was the family pet. His mother gave him a mocking kind of affection that made him feel ridiculous and left him hungry for the tender love his sister got. He had wet his bed until he was six years old, bitten his nails until he was fourteen, had frequent nightmares, and was noted for his fits of angry sulking. Ernest's mother encouraged him to tell her about his troubles, his failures, and his longings. She would give him a little hugging and then push him away, telling him what a big boy he was and that he was acting like a baby.

Ernest's father was energetic, brusque, and hard. His one affectionate interest was his auto repair shop. He treated his children, with the exception of the youngest, as nuisances. The older brother was allowed to do some tinkering in the shop in his early adolescence; when he graduated from high school he went to work permanently with his father. Ernest was never welcome in the shop. Whenever he tried to hang around the place his father or his brother told him bluntly to go home, which he remembered doing sometimes in tears.

In spite of the frustrating character of his life at home Ernest disliked leaving it. He often helped his mother with her housework on Saturdays instead of going out to play. She paid him for this choice, but she also laughed at him publicly for being "a better daughter" to her than his younger sister. He made few close friends. Usually he had a chum older and stronger than himself who extracted a certain amount of subservience from him in return for a patronizing kind of protection. In high school he got on the school paper in a minor capacity. Whenever he was chosen as an officer in anything it was always as secretary, which meant to him that he got the work without the real glory.

*Work.* Upon graduation from high school, after a short, intensive course in automobile mechanics, Ernest also went to work for his father. He was eager to please his father, he said, and to show his brother, who had never had any formal training, what he could do. But all he ever seemed to get was criticism. They took tools out of his hands and finished jobs that he felt he could do better than they could. (Even depressed as he was he told his therapist that he was a better mechanic than his brother ever would be.) Whenever he tried to show either of them something that he had learned at the trade school he was jeered and called "our little Einstein."

Ernest finally gave up hope and apparently went into a mild neurotic depression. He became sullen, resentful, and unhappy, he slept and ate poorly, and he felt himself to be a total failure. He confided in his mother that he felt useless and unwanted. She comforted him enough to whet his appetite for affection and then spiritually dropped him on the floor, saying that he was old enough to stand on his own feet and not to go around whining all the time.

*Leaving home and marrying.* Military service gave Ernest his chance to break away from home and to recover from his mild depression. There was a shortage of auto mechanics, and he was assigned to repair work that he liked and could do well. While in the service he read in a magazine about life in a western town. He persuaded a buddy to go there with him to live when they were discharged. His friend opened a garage and filling station and tried to talk Ernest into joining him as a junior partner. Instead, he took a job on a milk route. Soon afterward he met his future wife and, he said, "married her in the teeth of her family's objections."

The father-in-law had a managerial position with the local bus company. He persuaded Ernest to take a job as a bus driver. The pay was not quite as good, but the hours were much better. Four relatively peaceful years followed during which two children were born. The in-laws were critical of Ernest's lack of ambition and publicly compared him unfavorably with another daughter's husband. He saw a great deal of Buck, his army buddy, now also married, and whenever he did, Buck asked him when he was going to join him at the filling station, which was always in need of extra help. Ernest was reluctant to give up a job in which it seemed so easy to please people.

*Precipitating factors.* Two crises upset everything. Ernest's family had to move and then Ernest lost all his teeth. He was strongly attached to the home they had to give up. He had put in a lot of work on it after hours. But the street was being integrated into a truck highway and this made it too dangerous for the small children. They moved into a larger house next door to his wife's parents who owned it and let him have it at a nominal rent. It had modern kitchen conveniences that delighted Ernest's wife. The secret clause in this apparently generous arrangement was that the in-laws were going to supervise their daughter's home life and billet friends and relatives with them, sometimes practically without notice.

The flow of house "guests" was a serious nuisance to a man who loved his home and liked a schedule that he could count on. But much worse was the interference with his private affairs—amounting at times to quarrels as to who had jurisdiction over his own children—so that he became exasperated beyond words. He grew angrier and angrier, but there was little he could do about things because his wife was torn between him and her domineering parents. When he tried to vent his anger against them she became upset and began defending them. He felt alone, as he had in his childhood, surrounded by critical people, with no one to comfort him and take his part.

The climax came when Ernest lost his teeth. It was a painful experience but, as he soon discovered, one that brought him little genuine sympathy. He found himself the target of a sadistic kind of humor from his in-laws. They called him "grandpa," made jokes about his food, and mimicked his defective speech—all supposedly in "good fun," of course. Ernest had no difficulty seeing the cruel humiliation intended. His wife, he said, protested against their teasing him; but she did it laughingly. At work he met a more benign form of the same teasing, which spoiled the beginnings and ends of his bus runs. His new teeth hurt him, made him gag, and dulled his sense of taste.

*The depression.* Ernest thought he could have weathered the dental crisis if his home life had not turned so sour. As it was, he no longer looked forward to going home. Some of his days off he spent at the station with Buck, who gave him profane advice that he did not have the courage to follow until some time later. Meanwhile the depressive symptoms began to show up—dejection, insomnia, headaches, backaches, aching legs and ankles, eyestrain and blurred vision, constipation, no appetite, and no sexual desire. He was tense and irritable; and the terrible loneliness of his childhood returned. He lost pleasure in everything and felt that he had no love and no future. His work became almost more than he could face, especially now that complaints were coming in about him. Each time he turned in the fare money he thought with anger that this was helping pay the manager, his father-in-law.

Ernest's in-laws saw that he was slipping. They told him so, and they told him that he was making a big fuss over nothing. If he were a man, they said, he would snap out of it. Ernest began harping on his physical decline, telling his wife over and over that he was growing old before his time and everybody knew it. He called himself "a dental cripple" and wished out loud that he were dead. It might be easier for her and the children. She could find another husband any day who was better than he was, and the children would have a decent father. Then he opened up on his own worthlessness as a person. His father-in-law was right, he said, he never would amount to anything, he had always known that he was really no good. What could he do? A bus driver all his life, and now not even good enough for that! He could hardly stand himself. And so on, over and over, on and on.

For a long time his wife tried to combat his endless complaints and self-depreciation with endless reassurances. She reasoned with him. She took issue with him over his unrealistic self-condemnation, meeting argument with counterargument, over and over, on and on, sometimes far into the night. But it was useless. In the morning he would be as gloomy and sullen as ever, and in the evening the whole thing would start over again. She tried to keep her parents out of the home, get the children to bed early, and have the place quiet and peaceful for him.

Nothing worked. The endless repetitions finally wore her down and made her break into fits of exasperation. They quarreled. She told him to straighten up for his children's sake even if he cared nothing for her. Sometimes she agreed angrily with his self-accusations. Then he would say, "See? That's what I've been trying to tell you! It's true!"

The payoff came at the funeral of the wife's grandmother. Ernest had a crying spell that he could not stop. After everything was over there was a solemn family dinner at which the father-in-law made a caustic remark to someone in the patient's presence about his tears. Ernest astonished everyone by flying into a rage and telling the whole crowd exactly what he thought of them. Some of the language he used came from Buck and his military service. The in-laws were speechless. His wife told the therapist that at the time she had been secretly proud. Ernest left the place for Buck's shop, had another crying spell, and took Buck's advice to go the next day for therapeutic help.

*Therapy: anger.* In the initial interview Ernest was gloomy and tearful. He said grimly that he had messed up his life for good. There was a mix-up in his next appointment. The social worker said that he had looked angry; he only said that it didn't matter and apologized for giving her so much trouble. A medical checkup was arranged for the same afternoon. It gave essentially negative results.

Ernest broke the next appointment and came to the third with a sheepish grin and further apologies. He had trouble in talking. He frequently interrupted a silence to ask, "Where are we getting?" or "What good is this doing?" The next time he talked about his failure in life and hopeless future as a bus driver. They used him more as a "jumper" than they did anyone else, that is, he was put on fill-in runs during rushes or when other drivers failed to show up. He often felt pushed around. He would get to work and have to wait around for a bus. They couldn't get away with this with the other drivers, he said. He got paid for his time all right; but he was treated as if he was always the one they could push around. At home it was the same. He could come home from work and there would be guests—the in-laws' relatives or friends—supper an hour late, and his wife too rushed to notice him.

The therapist said that it must have made him angry to come to the clinic and have to wait around for nothing. He said, no, that it hadn't at all, that he was glad to get the medical checkup. They would probably find out what was wrong with him. "That woman [social worker] will tell you I wasn't mad," he said. After awhile he remembered that, yes, he had been angry; but he knew it wasn't the woman's fault. Everybody treated him fine here. He had no right to be mad. At the end of the hour he asked irritably, "Where is this getting us?"

*Resentment.* There were other opportunities for working on this angry man's resentment. When he had to wait an hour on another occasion he had meanwhile gained enough confidence and insight to be openly hostile. He asked the secretary who we thought he was and said he couldn't wait. He did wait, however, because he wanted to tell off the therapist, which he proceeded to do.

This led him into new paths. In his childhood everybody else came first. His mother was too busy with the baby sister. The older sister and the brother, being much older than he, freely exercised their rights to superior strength and know-how. The father let it be known that he was supporting the whole show and that nobody had better bother him. Ernest had always felt like the proverbial "odd man out."

This theme came up once again, later in the therapy series. It surfaced in relation to Ernest's feelings that after their first child was born, nothing that he wanted mattered until after the baby's wants were all satisfied. It was not as bad with the second child's arrival, because Ernest had learned that he did not count when there was a baby around, and besides now the older one had to wait too. At this point he stopped his tirade suddenly to say, "I felt like taking the bottle out of the baby's mouth. Some father, huh? Some damned bastard."

*Need and guilt.* It cost Ernest a great deal of work to bring out and recognize how much he needed to feel preferred above everybody else. To be loved, for him, meant to be first in line for handouts. He had to find out he was chronically angry because these demands were never really gratified, and that they never could be as long as they were pitched so high. Ernest was doomed to frustration by his own demands. He had to find out, too, that his guilt over his suppressed fury made him give up the ordinary rights he should have had—like his bus schedule and the privacy of his home, which he now called his father-in-law's "motel."

*Improvement.* As therapy progressed, Ernest became for a while more aggressive and less angry. The bodily symptoms waxed and waned. They appeared often enough in relation to home and work situations to make him suspect their dynamic origin without admitting it. In time they became negligible. The self-depreciation also had its ups and downs. Sometimes a phase of self-assertion was followed by further self-disparagement—"no good," "a screw-up," "no guts," "no future." But in the absence of reassurance or condemnation, self-assertion finally gained the upper hand and held it most of the time.

On the job Ernest's irritability gradually disappeared. But he could not seem to regain the pleasure he once had in greeting the passengers, in serving them, and in making model runs. He himself attributed his indifference to the complaints the passengers had formerly made about him, but it is probable that the effects of his therapeutic work were responsible. He no longer needed to be incessantly courting everybody's favor, being paid in advance by them for everything he did, being the Number One Person on the bus, or earning a pat on the head from the starter, which resulted in fewer shifts for him but a cooler and less friendly relationship.

His angry outbursts against the in-laws after the funeral made it easy for Ernest to bring the discussion of them into therapy, once his guilt and self-disparagement had weakened. In the process he ventilated a lot of resentment against his wife; this, in its turn, allowed him to take the initiative in insisting that they move out of his father-in-law's house. He had a rough time of it; but when it was over, and they were settled two miles away, his wife found herself as relieved as Ernest was. It was like starting life over again in their own home.

Ernest gave up his driver's job and went to work for Buck even though it was not clear exactly what his status there was to be. He still had some important things to work out about himself. He needed and received further therapy. But he was no longer clinically depressed.

What this case has shown us is a pattern of life that is made up of infantile pleasures, smothered angry resentment, demands upon the human environment that cannot be satisfied, and the practice of self-depreciation. On the positive side, we see a person who is capable of loving others, who reaches out for affection, enjoys being kind, and is conscientious. The patterns of loving needed to become more maturely masculine, so that the patient could enjoy caring for his family as a husband and father, could enjoy being kind without having to be rewarded with the kind of approval a little child craves, and perhaps could restructure his conscientiousness so that it was motivated by a more mature pride. The strength that burst forth under the stress of the sadistic treatment that Ernest endured from the in-laws gave the patient a good prognosis, since this was done without the support of a therapist and in the teeth of what seemed to Ernest overwhelming, unanimous opposition to him.

It is essential that one understand the smothered anger and resentment that lead to depression if one is to understand both the cruelty that depressed persons show to others and the much more dangerous sadism they exhibit toward themselves. The depressed person, we have said, is often an angry person as well as a sad one. The sadness relates depression to normal mourning; the anger relates it to compulsions. As we turn now to discuss the dynamic and developmental background of neurotic depressions, we shall make these relationships clear.

## Dynamic and Developmental Background

The neurotic depressive reaction forms a natural bridge that connects the neuroses with the psychoses. It involves only a partial regression, so that the neurotically depressed person is nearly always able to continue with his or her daily work, just as most obsessive-compulsives are. The partial regression, however, goes very deep—deeper than that of any other neurosis. This is why a great deal of what we shall have to say about the dynamic and developmental background of neurotic depressives will be found to apply also to the more disabling and potentially dangerous psychotic depressions. An understanding of the relatively circumscribed neurotic depression, in which the patient retains good contact and can effectively communicate with other persons, will provide us with an easy transition to the more sweeping psychotic disorders, in which object relationships are distorted and communication becomes difficult or impossible. Let us begin with a review of the similarities and differences between neurotic depressions and obsessive-compulsive neuroses so as to describe one span of the bridge.

### NEUROTIC DEPRESSIONS AND OBSESSIVE-COMPULSIVE DISORDERS

Neurotic depressives and obsessive-compulsives both regress to pre-Oedipal levels at which the focus is upon being good or being bad. In both there is an infantile ego facing an archaic punitive superego. Attempts are made in both disorders to meet the conflicts by resorting to overt behavior in the form of active symptoms. Both are *guilt neuroses,* although the expressions of guilt in the two take very different forms.

We have already said that there are many differences between neurotic depressions and obsessive-compulsive reactions. The most obvious one is that the neurotic depressive seems dejected; the obsessive-compulsive does not. The obsessive-compulsive is also action centered, using primitive defenses and magic but trying to "go it alone." There are obviously anal characteristics wound into the dynamics of obsessive-compulsivity. The neurotic depressive turns outward, looking to other people for reassurance and support. The oral characteristics of a deeper regression are evident here. Whereas obsessive-compulsives, with the exception of the withdrawn doubters and ruminators, are typically self-assertive, neurotic depressives do not wish to assert themselves. They want to be taken care of like a helpless baby. They are both seeking oral dependency and fearful of what this might entail.

Obsessive-compulsive patients are notoriously obstinate, negativistic, and at least superficially self-sufficient (see Chapter 7). They even try to force others to conform to their ways, to obey them, to do as they direct. Neurotic depressive patients, by contrast, seem to be clinging, compliant persons who are sometimes almost parasitic. They do not demand conformity or obedience; they do not try to direct what others do. Rather, they demand special privileges and affection; they reproach others for not giving them enough (oral dependency and gratification).

The obsessive-compulsive usually reveals unconscious guilt through his or her ritualistic precautions and penitential self-punishment. This type of patient is often aware of feeling guilty and may express this feeling openly. Neurotic depressives sometimes express guilt feelings also, but usually they are unconscious of their guilt. They express it in such disguised forms as feelings of inferiority, of worthlessness and hopelessness, of feeling that they are unloved and unlovable. There is a great deal of hostile aggression (oral sadism) behind these disguises, of hatred and frustration as well as a longing to be loved.

## FIXATION AND REGRESSION IN THE DYSTHYMIC DISORDER

The regression in neurotic depressions reactivates fantasies and conflicts that tell us that the fixation and attendant fuero claims involved are at the oral level. The fantasies and acting out we see taking place in dysthymic disorders are expressive of oral dependency. All infants eventually are weaned from their phase of oral dependence—gradually if they are fortunate, abruptly if they are not. They are usually allowed to be somewhat oral and somewhat dependent, but they learn to derive great pleasures from normal modes of experience and they learn pleasure in doing things for themselves. Even normal adults still take pleasure in their orality and in their relative dependence upon other people. They enjoy eating and drinking, mouthing, chewing, kissing, talking, singing, and whistling.

During the period of being weaned from the pleasures of suckling and of being almost completely dependent, young children experience many complex difficulties in addition to those of simple adaptation. They often feel an unwillingness or a fear of going forward. A sense of separate identity is often difficult to distinguish from sheer loneliness and even desertion. There are also fears of slipping back or being drawn back into their former state of helplessness. Sometimes a small child feels strongly tempted to give up his or her dawning independence. Rankian (1968) and Rogerian (1951) explanations of behavior rely almost exclusively on the dynamics of becoming an independent, self-directing human being through maturation, *or not*. It is in this state of mind that primitive oral fantasies are probably formed, full of longing, fear, and conflict, which in subsequent childhood undergo repression.

It is necessary at this point to make a preliminary distinction between neurotic and psychotic depression because they are in fact closely related (see our discussion of neurotic versus psychotic disorders in Chapter 11, pp. 319-321). The major distinction is that neurotic regression is only partial, whereas psychotic regression is complete. The neurotically depressed person manages to keep hold of external reality almost completely, to restructure the world in regressive terms of desertion and impending disaster. He or she can seldom go on with daily work, due to excessive apprehension, retarded mentation, and the constant threat of suicide. The neurotically depressed person, in spite of the depth of regression, has preserved most of his or her defensive organization intact.

## DEFENSES IN THE DYSTHYMIC DISORDER

Recall that in Chapter 2 (p. 63) we introduced the maneuver of reverting from object-love to narcissism. If this regressive maneuver is complete, the person turns away totally from interpersonal contact into a self-indulgent form of libidinal gratification. This dynamic is to be seen taking place in depressions, but since it is a more completely fulfilled maneuver in the psychotic depressions, we shall put off to Chapter 12 a more detailed discussion of the process concerned. By that time we shall also have taken up in more detail the basic differences between neurotic and psychotic symptomatology (see pp. 319-321). Even so, it is important to realize at this juncture that the oral dependency and narcissism we shall be discussing in the present section rest on the assumption that a regression and reversion from the level of object-choice to narcissism has taken place in the dynamics of the depressed individual. From our perspective, the three most important constituents of neurotic depressive defense are *repression, projection,* and the use of continual complaining to extort from others the *narcissistic supplies* (self-indulgent, oral-based demands for reassurance, praise, and esteem).

*Defective Repression.* We have seen in the other neurotic disorders that defective repression seems to be a precondition to their development. The same is true for neurotic depressions. Neurotic depressives owe their escape from a psychotic depression to their ability to maintain repressive defenses at a reasonable level of effectiveness. This is accomplished, as we shall see below, by the use of projection and by complaining in such a way that allies are gained in the struggle against internal assaults upon a poorly framed self-esteem.

The repression in neurotic depressions is aimed in two directions and is defective in both. It is aimed at the control of id impulses, in whose derivatives there are oral dependent longings for love mingled with hostile resentment because these longings are not fulfilled. Repression is also aimed at the control of attacks by the archaic superego. This latter is the most significant repression in neurotic depressions. When superego aggression is dominant a sense of guilt threatens to become conscious. It usually does not become conscious, partly because repression is intensified, partly because projection is also introduced, and partly because the complaining brings to the patient increased narcissistic supplies. What does emerge is chiefly a feeling of inferiority, worthlessness, self-disparagement, and hopelessness—chief among the cardinal depressive symptoms.

Neither of these repressions is successful; some derivatives of each appear as symptoms. The unconscious guilt emerges, not only as inferiority feelings and self-disparagement, but also as a vague sense of feeling responsible for something or ashamed of something. The referent, the "something," is often displaced, and its intensity is always diminished. The oral dependent longings emerge in derivative form as demands for narcissistic supplies and as passive-dependent acting out. The hostility appears in the form of insistent complaining, accusations of neglect, and threats of suicide or physical disability. In all of these derivatives, which we call "symptoms," we see the participation of other defense mechanisms. Among these we shall pay particular attention to the characteristically depressive use of complaints to gain needed narcissistic supplies.

*The Defensive Use of Complaints.* The manifest complaints of neurotic depressives give us the key to an understanding of the whole defensive structure. These are the continual complaints—often exasperating to relatives and close friends who continually hear them—of being inferior, unworthy, unlovable, and so on. To some extent these complaints are actual discharge processes; they provide an emotional expression for the hostile superego attitudes and wishes with which the patient's ego is bombarded. They are also urgent appeals for help from outsiders against the sadistic attacks of the archaic superego. Because the regression to narcissism is not complete, and object relations are consequently rather intact, the neurotic depressive is able to utilize the reassurances, protests, and contradictions of other people as narcissistic supplies and in this way to offset superego sadism. The complaints thus represent attempts to restore an internal equilibrium, by expressive discharge and by stimulating others to give narcissistic supplies, and to make good the loss that originally precipitated the neurosis.

Two factors render these attempts unsuccessful. One is that other people eventually weary of having to give constant reassurance; the other is that the unconscious archaic superego attacks continue indefinitely. When, as in the case of Ernest F., everyone eventually becomes exasperated with the patient and gives up reassuring, he or she must either find other sources of emotional support or sink deeper into a psychotic depression. Ernest F. found emotional support of a different kind when he turned to Buck and to his therapist. We shall next discuss the use of complaints further under four headings: (1) maintaining good object relationships, (2) ensuring narcissistic supplies, (3) discharging superego aggression, and (4) discharging ego aggression or id aggression.

*Maintaining good object relationships.* Neurotic depressive complaints, for all their seeming ineffectuality, do help materially to keep the patient functioning at a realistic level in a realistic field of interpersonal relations. The dysthymic individual does not slip into the abyss of psychotic depression. Even though the patient unknowingly plays an unrealistic game—in stimulating others to contradict the archaic unconscious superego—he or she plays the game in deadly earnest and manages to recruit the aid of real persons. The archaic unconscious superego of the neurotically depressed person represents an originally introjected parental figure, which was experienced in early childhood as dangerous and destructive. The reassuring other person in adulthood, in the case of Ernest F. his wife, takes the role of a kindly supporting parent who battles without knowing it against the introjected parental figure. If people turn their backs, leaving the patient deserted and alone to face the archaic superego, he or she may eventually lose hold on external reality and regress further to psychotic levels. We shall see how much more dangerous such a regression can be when we come to discussions of the psychoses.

*Ensuring narcissistic supplies.* It must be clear now that neurotic depressives are seriously lacking in wholesome pride and self-esteem while they are sick or even when they are not overtly depressed. Some experts have pointed to a so-called depressed personality type, in which the person is vulnerable to rejection and disappointment and prone to deny feelings of anger and hostility (Laughlin, 1965). In less dynamic explanations of dysthymic disorders it is common to hear of "learned helplessness" (Seligman, 1975). Such people have learned that they cannot function on their own. Harking back to our review of development in Chapter 2 (p. 44), some experts view the neurotically depressed individual as sensing an underlying loss of attachment to a loved one—sometimes due to death, but also due to a kind of emotional estrangement (Akiskal & McKinney, 1975). This dynamic of loss is especially relevant to the psychotic depression, and we shall return to a more complete discussion of it in Chapter 12.

The complaining of depressed adults is like the crying of a hungry baby. It is an expression of urgent need and a means of stimulating someone to meet it. Narcissistic supplies, like food, can have only a temporary effect; the need for more comes back. But without them survival may become impossible. The neurotic depressive is repeatedly overwhelmed by the tensions of unconscious guilt. Anything that reinforces self-esteem will tend to decrease guilt, and hence there is this incessant pursuit of support from others.

*Discharging superego aggression.* Everyone recognizes the insistent self-depreciation of neurotic depressives as a value judgment passed by the patients upon themselves or, as we find it more convenient to say, passed by their superegos upon their egos. When patients give voice to this judgment—reflecting, incidentally, their teleological nature—they not only challenge others to contradict it but also discharge guilt tension at the same time by externalizing their superego condemnation. One could say metaphorically that some of the superego hate is funneled out through the expression of verbal symbols.

The repeated self-accusations are symbolic equivalents of a continued superego offensive. They relieve internal stress in the same way that public confession often does, in the same way that confessions to a loved and trusted person do. They temporarily satisfy the need to accept a little self-punishment in exchange for a little self-forgiveness. Each self-depreciatory repetition acts as a rebuttal to the case being presented. As the superego builds up its evaluative case self-accusation counters with the other side of the coin. It is a dialectical clash reminiscent at this point of Freud's early theory of antithetical ideas (see Chapter 4, p. 132). In typical Freudian dialectical style, the complaints express both the superego harangue and the countering defensive maneuver.

*Discharging ego and id aggression.* The unconscious hostility that creates the intolerable tensions of guilt in neurotic depression comes as much from unconscious ego and id sources as from superego sources. Oral dependent persons, in particular, are forever being frustrated by people around them. They can never be fed enough, taken care of, comforted, and protected enough. Their experiences of frustration go deep and generate violent archaic hostility. This archaic hostility is basic to the tensions of depressive guilt because it stimulates superego counteraggression. Hence, if some of this hostility can gain direct expression there will be a corresponding decrease in superego attack.

Because the patient makes inordinate demands upon loved ones, they are most apt to be his or her frustrators. This is why we find the dysthymic person leveling complaints, regrets, threats of suicide, and the like in the direction of loved ones. In effect, these verbal expressions thinly veil the underlying complaint of feeling unloved, unwanted, and even despised by the loved ones. Such discharges of id and ego aggression (death instinct involvement) serve the same dynamic purpose as the superego discharge. The aggressive display lowers for the time being the overall tension of depressive guilt.

*Projection.* A further important defense in dysthymic disorders consists of the *projection* of superego aggression onto external reality, that is, the ascription of one's own superego attitudes to other persons. Loved ones are insistently accused of holding the patient in contempt, a maneuver that has two advantages for dysthymic patients. First, it permits them to protest openly, as they may have done in childhood, that they are unloved. Second, it enables them to enlist the aid of these superego figures against their own attacking superego. Eventually these important figures find they cannot keep the process up and may actually affirm the viewpoint that the patient has been projecting on them. They take the patient's self-depreciation as capturing the reality of the situation.

It is interesting that, even when neurotic depressives have turned people against them in this manner, they may be better off dynamically, even though they are worse off socially. When loved ones become hostile, the patient can keep on projecting his or her superego hostility onto them with less guilt. The now more realistic bad treatment that the patient experiences may provide the opportunity to discharge further ego and id aggression in hating and resenting those who have now obviously turned away. This is what we saw in the case of Ernest F. After he had goaded others into expressing genuine contempt, he was able to burst out with righteous indignation and then to accept the help of a neutral therapist in reaching a more stable equilibrium. The now reasonable complaint, "I hate them because they hold me in contempt!" replaced and

*A 1909 photograph taken in the United States during Freud's visit to Clark University. Front row: Freud, his host, G. Stanley Hall, and Carl Jung. Back row: A. A. Brill, Ernest Jones, and Sandor Ferenczi. It was on this trip that serious problems arose in Freud's relationship with Jung.*

obliterated the original irrational complaint, "I am no good! I hate myself!"— the last being unconscious superego aggression.

### Ego and Superego Regression in the Dysthymic Disorder

Ego and superego functioning are for the most part normal in neurotic depressions, just as they are in other neuroses. This is what enables neurotic persons to keep in effective contact with their surroundings. The partial regression, however, revives infantile processes that the patient cannot control. In each neurosis regression leads to a different pattern. The infantile pattern reactivated in neurotic depressions reflects some of the earliest desires, fears, and conflicts that human beings experience—those involving helpless dependence. Infants can enjoy helpless dependence as long as their needs are dependably met. When an adult partially regresses to infantile dependence no one can meet his or her unreasonable needs. This is what happens in neurotic depression.

The regressive superego in neurotic depressions is at least as archaic as the superego in obsessive-compulsives, but apparently regression and projection are more effective, since patients are able to use their complaints in such a way as to keep the archaic superego activities unconscious. As we shall see in Chapter 12, in psychotic depressions the archaic superego activities are more nearly preconscious and conscious. Nevertheless, the archaic superego hostility succeeds in making the patient feel irrationally inferior, deserted, and unloved. The partially regressed ego is incapable of resisting the archaic superego attack, just as was true when the patient was an infant. This is why, as we have seen, the patient turns to others for reinforcement (narcissistic supplies).

## CHILDHOOD BACKGROUND IN THE DYSTHYMIC DISORDER

The unique characteristics of the personality matrix in neurotic depression, those which distinguish it from all other neuroses and psychoses, are deep oral dependence, self-depreciation and unconscious guilt, and through it all, good object relationships. We shall take these points up in order.

*Deep Oral Dependence.* It is generally assumed, on the basis of clinical and research evidence (see Chapter 2), that an oral orientation is the dominant *prototype* or meaningful assumption made by the infant in the early months of life (see p. 42). The suckling experiences the world primarily in terms of passively receiving food, which he or she then actively takes in or rejects. If we group with these experiences the related ones of body care, of being held, warmed, moved about, comforted, and lovingly watched over, we have most of the overt contributions to an infant's well-being which we call the *narcissistic supplies.*

This sense of love and well-being forms the grounds for the infant's judgment of self, for what we have been calling self-esteem. To be free to love oneself normally, to have self-esteem, it is necessary to have had infantile experiences of being fully loved. Not to have had this experience consistently in infancy and early childhood is to lack the foundations of normal self-esteem (see Chapters 2 and 3). Once basic trust or basic confidence has been established, the child is free to go on building up the foundations for self-esteem and resultant confidence in interpersonal relations.

Fixation at the level of deep oral dependence is always pathological. It implies one of two opposite conditions. Either the patient as a child enjoyed excessively deep gratifications from early nursing experiences—including what we have called the narcissistic supplies—or else there was a denial of adequate oral and related gratifications. In one case the fixation is the result of extravagant indulgence; in the other it arises from the frustration experienced. It is not illogical to suggest that opposite circumstances may result in an identical fixation, any more than it is illogical to suggest that a man became avaricious because he once was poor *or* because he once was very rich. In either case the fixation paves the way for the enjoyment of dependent, submissive, subordinate roles, as well as for periodic rebellion against being dependent, submissive, and subordinate. It may also lay the foundation for later adult declarations of being helpless, unworthy, and inferior and even for a lifelong desire to be treated like a baby.

*Self-Depreciation and Unconscious Guilt.* Self-depreciation is not only the expression of a lack of normal self-esteem but also the product of archaic superego attack. This means that during the pre-Oedipal phases of development the child has introjected his or her experiences of severity or neglect in the form of enduring sadistic internal objects. And it is, of course, such internal introjects (*prototypes, imagos*) that go to make up the precursors of the later mature superego, the precursors that we have been calling the *archaic superego*. We must keep in mind that fantasy plays a role in the archaic superego, so that though we do believe actual parental attitudes have been detrimental, there is always a modicum of the child's *interpretation* and *understanding* to be considered. Since the ego is quite primitive and fraught with fantasied distortion and exaggeration, the archaic superego is similarly subject to the drawbacks of such initial organization in the developing personality system.

Much of what is experienced during infancy becomes later unconscious when repression develops functional boundaries that differentiate experience into conscious, preconscious, and unconscious. The archaic superego, with its good and bad internal objects, is among the early experiences that undergo a sweeping repression. This does not mean that it ceases to exist, of course. It may, however, have no appreciable effect upon adult behavior and experience. It is when the archaic introjects persist unconsciously in an unusually active state, and when repression is inadequate, that they produce in conscious and preconscious experience a persistent feeling of being inferior, unworthy, and unloved. This result is especially likely if during the rest of a child's development the life experiences prove to run consistent with the early introjects.

*Good Object Relationships.* Why is it that neurotic depressives, in spite of deep oral dependence, self-depreciation, and unconscious guilt, still manage to maintain good object relationships—often better than those in other neuroses? The responsibility for this redeeming quality, which protects the patient from becoming psychotic, rests partly with the parents and partly with the patient as a child.

Parents who demand submission to an unusual degree may give the child a great deal in return for his or her submission. Within the frame of a powerfully dominant-submissive relationship there can be many opportunities for free-wheeling expression and for identification with parental characteristics that build good object relationships. A domineering father or mother presents the child with a strong model for identification if he or she can find channels for expression that do not go counter to the domineering parent's will. It is better, for example, to have a colorful domineering parent than a wishy-washy permissive parent as far as the development of internal richness is concerned. Parents who encourage infantile dependence are often themselves able to give and receive a great deal of affection without breaking down the ego boundaries of their dependent child. A child growing up under these conditions should be well equipped to maintain good object relationships in spite of becoming depressed.

The child's contribution to maintaining good object relationships comes from his or her capacity to be flexible and creative within the framework of dependence that defines the broader life outlook. Instead of fighting off encroachment, as obsessive-compulsives do, the child of domineering parents may learn to exploit parental domination in such a way as to get more than average attention, solicitude, and opportunity. We are all familiar with exploitative persons who, in spite of having infantile oral trends, manage to attract and to gratify others who enjoy acting as patrons and protectors. These represent extremes of the kind of reciprocal behavior with which orally dependent adults are equipped to contribute to interpersonal relationships.

## DSM-III Viewpoint

In DSM-III the dysthymic disorder is lumped together with all of the other *affective disorders,* including the major affective disorders that we shall cover in Chapters 12 and 13. Distinctions are made, of course, between the psychotic and neurotic manifestation of depression. There are no hallucinations or delusions in the dysthymic manifestation. The diagnosis of a depressive neurosis is to be made only if there is a chronically depressed mood, with only intermittent periods of normal mood. The diagnosis of dysthymic disorder should *not* be made if depression is interrupted by a period of normal mood lasting more than a few months.

### SUMMARY

Chapter 10 takes up the *dysthymic disorders,* which are mood disturbances in which tension and anxiety are expressed in the form of dejection and self-depreciation, somatic disturbance, and repetitive complaints of feeling inferior, hopeless, and worthless. In previous diagnostic schemes this disorder was known as a *depressive neurosis,* and the psychopathologist is still likely to hear this label employed. Guilt plays a prominent role in dysthymic disorders, expressed in the self-depreciations of those afflicted with this disturbance. Under severe superego attack, the dysthymic individual seeks reassurances from others concerning his or her worth, but these supports rarely help for long. The patient continues to complain, and in due time his or her comforters lose patience and begin to upbraid or flatly reject the dysthymic individual.

Common precipitating factors in neurotic depressions include loss of love or emotional support, as in a divorce or the death of a loved one. Economic failures may be involved in the onset of depression. New responsibilities on the job or in the family setting may precipitate the symptom picture. Clinicians have long noted a *promotion depression* that springs up at a time in life when the person should be most happy. Any of a number of such challenging life circumstances may precipitate a dysthymic disorder.

It was once accepted practice to refer to dysthymic disorders as *reactive depressions,* because they were seen to be reactions to objectively discernible losses or challenges. In contrast, a psychotic depression (see Chapter 12) was said to be a *retarded depression* because it developed insidiously in the context of a generally retarded personality development. When anxiety complicated the clinical picture an *agitated depression* was referred to as a special variant of psychotic depression (see Chapter 12).

The onset of the dysthymic disorder can be gradual or sudden. The *sudden decompensation* of a tenuously balanced personality following some loss in life is dramatic. But just as often the person seems to be in a state of shock for some time following the loss, and eventually in a relatively gradual manner begins to slip into a depressed state. Related complaints during the gradual onset include headaches, backaches, inability to sleep, and chronic fatigue. Life begins to lose its pleasurable aspects altogether. A patient may begin to withdraw, become irritable, and complain of feeling lonely all of the time. Evidence suggests that a regression toward infantile dependency is underway. Soon the patient is unable to concentrate or to remember things.

Preoccupation with bodily illness may enter the picture. Feelings of unreality approximating a dissociative disorder (see Chapter 9) may appear. But it is *self-depreciation* that is the neurotically depressed person's most striking symptom, as well as being dynamically the most important. There is a heavy component of *unconscious guilt* in the self-deprecatory statements made by this person, who actually hates himself or herself but does not know this consciously. In a manner of speaking, the archaic superego is rejecting, castigating, and despising the infantile, regressed ego. The dysthymic patient gradually loses the capacity to love others in a way that was possible previously. It is not unusual for the neurotically depressed person to treat loved ones in a cruel manner. This trace of sadism isolates the patient from precisely those people who might aid in recovery.

The neurotic depression forms a natural bridge to the psychotic depression, stopping short of the greater involvement thanks to a less severe regression. As with the obsessive-compulsive disorder, the dysthymic disorder is a form of *guilt neurosis,* with superego involvements prominent in both the former and the latter. One has the distinct clinical picture of an oral fixation in the depressive neurosis, whereas the obsessive-compulsive patient shows us more of an anal fixation. In the main, the fantasies and acting out that take place in dysthymic disorders are expressive of *oral dependency.* We find the dynamic of reverting from object-choice to narcissism (see Chapter 2) in the dysthymic disorder, but to a somewhat lesser extent than in the psychotic depression (see Chapter 12). The three most important dynamics in neurotic depression are *defective repression, projection,* and the use of complaint to extort *narcissistic supplies* from others.

The repression in dysthymic disorders is aimed in two directions and is defective in both. It is aimed at the control of id impulses, in whose derivatives there are oral dependent longings for love mingled with hostile resentment because these longings are not fulfilled. Repression is also aimed at the control of attacks by the archaic superego, which germinate feelings of unconscious guilt. The complaints of the dysthymic patient actually help to maintain contact with reality. Hence, *good object relationships* occur, at least early in the disorder. Reassurances from others about personal worth act as narcissistic supplies, which in time can germinate further regression to where object-choices are no longer retained as the person slips into narcissism. Projection enters the dynamics of this disorder when the patient begins to assign his or her superego recriminations to other people.

It is through such projection as well as the inability of others to satisfy the narcissism, resulting in continual frustration, that the dysthymic person begins to discharge aggressive impulses from the id and ego portions of the personality as well. The dysthymic person begins to level threats at loved ones, mistreat them, and imply that if a suicide results it will be their fault. Although there is still better reality contact here than in psychotic depression, it is clear that the regression is complete when this phase of the illness is entered upon. Even so, the hostility that the depressive patient engenders in others through such maneuvers acts as a grounds for projecting unconscious superego condemnations onto others. The now more realistic bad treatment received from others can provide opportunity for discharge of further ego and id aggression onto others, rather than turning it inward in an act of suicide.

# 11

## Paranoid Disorders

Chapters 11 through 14 will carry us through the psychotic manifestations of personal adjustment. We have already at various points in the present volume taken up aspects of psychotic behavior. Before turning to the paranoid disorders, we should now like to crystallize things a bit more by considering in greater detail precisely how Freud looked at the distinction between a neurotic and a psychotic disorder. We shall then discuss our concept of reaction sensitivity before moving on to a full treatment of the paranoid disorders.

### Differential Diagnosis: Neurotic Versus Psychotic Symptoms

Differential diagnosis was a challenging problem to Freud, one which he never entirely solved to his satisfaction. He has given us many excellent leads, however. We have in the preceding chapters been prepared to understand all mental illness in terms of his three-stage compromise model (see Chapter 5, p. 154). We have outlined in the intervening chapters the ways in which fixation and regression play a role in the choice of a particular symptom. We have contrasted the symptoms to be noted in disorders stemming from pre-Oedipal fixations with those stemming from later fixation points—as in contrasting dysthymia with obsessive-compulsivity. We have seen the contributions of both *primary gain* (flight into illness) and *secondary gain* (excuse making) to the psychopathological process.

When he specifically defined the term *symptom,* Freud (1926/1959g) used such phrases as "a function [that] has undergone some unusual change" (p. 87) or, more thoroughly, "A symptom is a sign of, and a substitute for, an instinctual satisfaction which has remained in abeyance; it is a consequence of the process of repression" (p. 91). A phenomenal aspect of the symptom-making process is evident, as in the following: "Symptoms—and of course we are dealing now with psychical (or psychogenic) symptoms and psychical illness—

are acts detrimental, or at least useless, to the subject's life as a whole, often complained of by him as unwelcome and bringing unpleasure or suffering to him" (Freud, 1916-17/1963b, p. 358). The dialectical (compromise) features of the symptom were always made clear by Freud, as in the following: "Thus the symptom emerges as a many-times-distorted derivative of the unconscious libidinal wish-fulfilment, an ingeniously chosen piece of ambiguity with two meanings in complete contradiction" (ibid., p. 360). Finally, the telic nature of symptom manifestation is readily identifiable, as when Freud (1892-99/1966c) noted: "Thus symptoms, like dreams, are *the fulfilment of a wish*" (p. 256). To be more precise, we should say *two* antithetical wishes in dialectical opposition are always involved in any symptom manifestation (see Freud's early theory of antithetical ideas, Chapter 4, p. 132).

As we have noted in previous discussions, Freud embraced a quantitative as opposed to a qualitative view of mental illness. He did not draw a hard and fast line between normal and abnormal or between neurosis and psychosis within the abnormal disorders (Freud, 1923/1961b, p. 204). Not infrequently, people fall ill from the same frustrations that others bear up under (Freud, 1909/1957a, p. 50). In trying to understand the types of symptoms that enter into a syndrome, we have to consider the factors already mentioned in this section *plus* the "way in which the repressed ideas return" (Freud, 1892-99/ 1966c, p. 223). In other words, just as people take on personality dynamics in common via the expression of their intentional wishes, so too do people take on styles of symptom manifestation as their repressed contents come forward intentionally to express themselves overtly. We must therefore always think in terms of (1) the point of fixation; (2) the unique contents of the fixation (specific fueros, etc.); (3) the extensiveness of psychic commitment to point of fixation (i.e., amount of libido committed); and (4) the *style* in which (1), (2), and (3) are manifested when a return of the repressed contents threatens conscious recognition/admission (resulting in the syndrome picture). Compromises are effected when there is a return of the repressed ideas in neurosis, and when the ego is completely overwhelmed by the return we can begin speaking of the manifestations of a psychotic disorder (ibid., p. 228).

Everyone is subject to regression in life. We all have our setbacks, and we all return in our psychical orientation to earlier fixation points of one sort or another. But the difference between normal and abnormal regression centers on what the person is trying to accomplish in the process. Freud believed that the *neurotic* does *not reject* reality or try to change reality as he or she understands it to be phenomenally; the neurotic merely flees into illness through a regressive symptom formation (primary gain). The *psychotic,* on the other hand, *rejects* perceived reality in the regressive process and then seeks to reconstruct it in fantasy according to how he or she would prefer (wish, intend) reality to be. Thus, psychotics concoct *delusions* (unrealistically false beliefs) and *hallucinations* (seeing, hearing, etc., things or people that do not truly exist), whereas neurotics retain a better contact with perceived reality. Freud then suggested that the *normal* personality combines the best, most constructive features of both syndromes of abnormality:

We call behaviour "normal" or "healthy," if it combines certain features of both reactions—if it disavows the reality as little as does a neurosis, but if it then exerts itself, as does a psychosis, to effect an alteration of that reality. (Freud, 1924/1961d, p. 185)

In short, the normal person fights to keep in contact and to effect a constructive outcome, a change in the external state of things. Normal individuals neither run away from a challenge nor settle for a dream-world solution—a pseudocommunity (see p. 332) of imagined occurrences and fancied achievements—even though they might regress and even act childlike from time to time.

## Reaction Sensitivity as a Predisposing Factor

It is our view that there is an element in all forms of maladjustive behavior that can be traced to the fact that people become sensitized in the initial reactions they make to certain life challenges and traumata. In other words, once a person experiences anxiety in relation to certain circumstances (e.g., closed-in surroundings), or once a person senses depression in relation to certain circumstances (e.g., rejection by a loved one), there is a readiness to react in the same emotional direction even more rapidly the "next" time that these relevant circumstances are encountered. In fact, it is possible in time to begin sensing anxiety or depression in relation to circumstances that have little actual (objective) grounds to call forth such negative emotions. We witness a kind of snowballing effect, in which the level of anxiety or depression increases, as well as the circumstances in which an anxiety-provoking or a depression-provoking *interpretation* is advanced by the person involved.

Consistent with our biosocial approach, we presume that some of this hypersensitivity to the circumstances of life, both positive and negative, stems from congenital sources. Some people, as biological organisms, probably do sense feelings of fear, defeat, and loss more intensely than others. The course of living in certain home environments undoubtedly makes it probable that some children will be sensitized to negative or positive emotional expressions (see Chapters 2 and 3). Even so, it is important to stress that we view reaction sensitivities to be a reflection of the basically telic nature of human behavior. The person who is "under stimulation" by the environment is never simply a pawn to pressures from without. There is an attitude, a set, a *phenomenal point of view* that enters into such physical sensations and lends them "stimulus power" far beyond what the objective circumstances would dictate.

Given this tendency to reaction sensitizations in life, it is but a short step to begin selecting certain targets for overconcern, certain interpersonal situations to avoid, certain people to be suspicious of when the emotional discharges take on a negative coloring. Countermeasures must then be taken if personal integrity is to be maintained, and the more one is sensitized to life threats, the more difficult it is to adapt in conventional ways. Extreme measures are soon called for. Since people can settle on only a handful of alternative maneuvers—that is, we are all pretty much alike as human beings—we find the *patterns* of avoidance and countermeasures taken falling into recognizable syndromes of maladjustment. Thus, symptom-pictures are like personality-pictures, but with greater ranges of deviation and, ultimately, deterioration in interpersonal effectiveness. Precisely when the person moves from normalcy through mere eccentricity to neurosis and psychosis is a matter of judgment—a judgment rendered by others based upon competent principles. The present volume is devoted to a thorough examination of this judgment process.

## Paranoid Disorders Characterized and Defined

Paranoid disorders are grouped with the psychoses. Their chief characteristic is the presence of persistent organized delusions, which are usually persecutory but are sometimes jealous, grandiose, or erotic. The prevailing mood is in keeping with the dominant delusions, being hostile in delusions of persecution and of jealousy, erotic in erotic delusions, and exalted in delusions of grandeur. There is no general personality disorganization in the paranoid disorder such as we see in schizophrenia (see Chapter 14). Paranoid persons usually remain in relatively good contact with their environment, much better than most schizophrenics do, and better than most manics and psychotic depressives. Because of this good contact, the paranoid disorder forms a bridge between the *neuroses* and the *psychoses*.

*Normal Thinking and Delusional Thinking.* Paranoid disorders also form a bridge between *normal* and *delusional thinking*. It is common knowledge that attitudes of belief, confidence, and expectation—or their reverse—are a part of the context of every normal person's thinking, just as they are in paranoid reactions. We are all continually acting in accordance with such attitudes, even in such simple matters as approaching a door to open it, waiting for the evening paper to arrive, or driving to work. We take a lot for granted in all such ordinary matters. We assume that the door will open, that the evening paper has been composed and printed, and that we are among those destined to receive it. We assume that when we drive to work the place will still be there and that our services will still be in demand. None of these assumptions is absolutely trustworthy. In short, we act most of the time upon telic anticipations that are based upon incomplete information.

In perception it is the same. We usually see only parts of things, the mere beginnings of some complex series, or only its end product. From such fragments we continually make assumptions that enable us to act confidently, as though the whole thing or every step were there in front of us to see. We seldom have either the opportunity or the patience to wait until all the evidence is in before we act. All cognition involves inductive leaps, often based upon dialectical reasoning that transcends the demonstratively "given facts" and places a new interpretation on them. Children take it for granted that they understand things even when they do not. Adults use classical Aristotelian (i.e., demonstrative) logic only when they need to, and when it suits them. Often they use sound logical reasoning in a defensive manner, in the service of an intuitive or irrational conclusion after it has been drawn. Even rigorous scientists make bold, intuitive leaps in theorizing before putting the fruits of these hunches to test via the scientific method (see Rychlak, 1977). In other words, to make inferences on the basis of incomplete evidence, and even to lead to conclusions that may turn out to have been unwarranted, are not necessarily abnormal procedures. It is only when the inferences and the conclusions become fixed, adamant, inflexible, and untouched by contrary evidence that we begin to speak of delusional thinking.

A great deal of ordinary communication also has this fragmentary character. We say, or hear, only parts of a sentence. We assume the rest either from the context or on the grounds of general familiarity. We know in what sense to understand something that is said, or how to communicate something potentially ambiguous, by the inflection of certain words, by using emphasis, by facial expression, and by gesture. A mere word or a sound may be enough to convey complex meanings and start off a program of action, or to stop one. Something left on a table, or something missing from it, may indicate some conscious or unconscious intention of communicating not otherwise expressed. When it comes to personal interaction, all of these factors are normally taken into account, usually at preconscious or unconscious levels.

In whatever we do, whether it is an anticipation, a response to some fragmentary stimulus, an intuitive induction, or an attempt to communicate, we all depend heavily upon hidden meanings, special significance, and intuitively experienced evidence (Maddi, 1961). Our daily activities are almost all based upon probabilities, upon attitudes of belief and confidence, or of disbelief and distrust. We see a shadow near a corner where there has recently been a holdup, and immediately we perceive a threatening figure who is actually harmless. We look out of the window and see a brilliant star, but even the most superficial follow-up shows it to be only a street lamp. We pass a group of strangers just as everyone in it bursts out laughing. The laughter has nothing whatever to do with us, but there are times when for a moment we are unsure. We see and hear many things that we want to see and hear, even though they are absent. We miss seeing and hearing many things that we do not want to see and hear, even though they are visible and audible.

Recall has many of the same characteristics. What we remember is rarely a simple repetition of what we have experienced (Neisser, 1967). It has nearly always been edited. Everyone who has gathered testimony from eyewitnesses knows this. Each witness, no matter how honestly and intelligently he or she reports, will give an account of the same happening that differs in some respect from the account of every other witness. In short, to remember is not simply to recall. It is rather to reconstruct, even sometimes to create, to express oneself through the medium of telling something (Bartlett, 1932, 1958).

We must not forget the feeling or emotional discharge which is related to that which we are thinking about or trying to recall. If our feelings were not related to our ideas, the use of anxiety as a mechanism of defense would not be possible (see Chapter 5, p. 160). If we are frightened in a situation, we experience that situation differently from the way we experience it when we are serene. When we are in love, the whole world seems a more lovable place than ever before, including even the landscape and the city streets. When we are filled with hate, the whole world seems to be filled with hatred. When we feel jealous, we can find all kinds of things to be jealous about, things that before had not seemed significant. When we grow suspicious, we are more apt to notice things that justify our suspicions than when we are trustful.

All of this leads to the question of distinguishing between *delusional* and *nondelusional thinking.* The way we all have of acting on the basis of fragmentary information, of interpreting signs and signals, of depending heavily upon hidden meanings and intuitions, of reconstructing what we "recall," and of always being subject to shifting emotional influences, makes a clear distinction exceedingly difficult to formulate. At the same time, such examples help us to recognize that delusional thinking has normal counterparts, and that paranoid disorders can best be understood if we bear this fact in mind.

*Definition. Paranoid disorders are attempts to escape from the return of repressed ideations, and the anxiety/tension with which they are associated, through processes of denial and projection that result in more or less systematized delusions. A delusion is a fixed belief that persists even though social reality contradicts it.*

Delusions are characteristic of paranoid disorders, but they are found in other psychoses also. As we shall see in Chapters 12 and 13, it is the delusions from which psychotically depressed and manic persons suffer that render them socially incompetent. The schizophrenias (see Chapter 14) are also delusional disorders; but schizophrenic delusions are as a rule *poorly systematized* (i.e., inconsistent, fragmented), and often they are extremely bizarre. We sometimes hear of delusions among normal persons. The full acceptance of a belief, and its indefinite persistence, even though it contradicts all the objective evidence, is not uncommon in ordinary life. When this is true, however, the belief is one that is shared by others in the same culture. It is a belief that depends, not upon objective evidence, but upon group identification and/or shared values.

*Paranoid Disorders and Phobias.* Phobic and paranoid patients are alike in denying and projecting their internally generated tension and anxiety in order to get rid of them. Yet the symptomatic style of the two disorders is very different. The phobic patient regards the projected fear as something unreasonable, peculiar, or even absurd. It is *ego-dystonic* or *ego alien,* and something to be gotten rid of. The paranoid patient does not consider the delusion ego alien, but accepts it and sees nothing unreasonable, peculiar, or absurd about it. The delusion is what Freud (1932-36/1964b, p. 19) called *ego-syntonic,* that is, in conformity with the reality outlook of the conscious ego. Paranoid persons often try to convince others of the objective reality of their delusions, and sometimes they succeed. If they fail, they are likely to suspect a skeptical person of being a possible party to the "conspiracy." They appeal to a therapist, not to get rid of their symptoms but to help ward off the persons who seem to be threatening them.

Another outstanding difference between phobias and paranoid disorders is a difference between impersonal and personal involvement in the symptomatology. Phobic patients typically focus their fear upon animals, upon things and situations, or upon people in general, as in the fear of crowds (Arieti, 1961). Paranoid patients, in striking contrast, focus upon persons and interpersonal relationships. They do not feel threatened primarily by dogs, insects, closed rooms, or height, but by the hatred of some person or the "plot" of some pseudocommunity. It is fairly certain that paranoid persons are suffering primarily from a disturbance of personal interrelationships, a defect in understanding and trusting other people, while the phobic person is not.

## Varieties of Paranoid Disorders

In what follows we shall recognize four varieties of paranoid disorders: (1) *paranoid delusions of persecution,* (2) *paranoid delusions of jealousy,* (3) *paranoid erotic delusions,* and (4) *paranoid delusions of grandeur.* To these four clinical varieties we shall add brief discussions of *classical paranoia,* an extreme form of delusional systematization, and of *folie à deux,* a special situation in which a suggestible person takes over the delusions of a dominant paranoid person.

It should be said at the outset that, just as a pure neurosis is rare, so pure paranoid disorders are rare. Almost all paranoid disorders include some neurotic symptoms. Indeed, it could be argued that paranoid disorders are a combination of neurosis and psychosis (see Cameron, 1959b). The psychotic element appears in the fixed, inflexible delusional development and in the distortion of social reality, the formation of a pseudocommunity, to rationalize the delusion. The neurotic element appears in the good residual object relations that, in many cases, allow the patient to carry on a comparatively normal life as a business person, as a professional person, or as a wife and mother, in spite of the delusions.

Some paranoid persons are mildly depressed or mildly elated, but we call them paranoid because the delusional aspect is more striking than the mood. A great deal of what we shall have to say about the emotional discharge, the ego defenses, the ego adaptations, and the delusional reconstruction of reality will be found to apply also to cases of psychotic depression, mania, and schizophrenia. Paranoid disorders are more often adaptively successful than the latter psychotic disorders. Paranoid manifestations lack the desocialization and disorganization of schizophrenia, and they do not show the profound mood changes that are seen in psychotic depressions and in manias. It is generally agreed that paranoid delusional psychoses without deterioration appear most often in middle or later life. It is rare to find either delusions or hallucinations in the psychotic disorders of childhood (Elkind & Weiner, 1978). In adult paranoia, the most common type of socially distorted, fixed belief encountered is the delusion of persecution (Meissner, 1978; Swanson, Bohnert, & Smith, 1970). We shall therefore devote most of our discussion to this variety, treating the others as relatively minor variants.

## Persecutory Paranoid Disorders

Even normal people, when they are acutely anxious, badly frightened, or shocked, cannot reason well at first about a suspicion or a fear. Their greatest need under these conditions is to be able to check the validity of their observations, to be able to look at the situation from more than one angle, and to question their own conclusions. For these vital procedures three things are necessary: (1) *trust in others,* an ability to put faith in someone else even when one is frightened and suspicious; (2) *tolerance for suspense,* an ability to stem the tide of emotional reasoning so as not to be swept away by it into premature action; and (3) *skill in shifting perspectives,* an ability to take the role of a detached observer for a few moments under stress, even to take the role of the feared or suspected person. In these borrowed roles, and with final judgment suspended, a person can reconsider his or her situation from different angles and perhaps arrive at different interpretations.

An ability to tolerate suspense and shift perspectives is the product of mature ego-superego development. In an emotional crisis this ability may be lost even by a maturely organized adult. When such a loss occurs, a person's only salvation lies in his or her continuing ability to share personal fears and suspicions with somebody who is less emotionally involved and can be trusted. The shocked or frightened adult can then treat a trusted confidant as his or her temporary *substitute ego-superego,* making use of the confidant's reality-testing, social skills, and detached perspectives. Through some such maneuver we experience the enormous comfort of sharing our anxiety with someone who is concerned but does not get upset. We gain the advantage of seeing things from cooler, more objective points of view.

### PERSONALITY BACKGROUND

Trust in others, a readiness to tolerate suspense, and skill in shifting role perspectives under stress are exactly what paranoid personalities lack. As children, most individuals who later develop a paranoid disorder are found to be aloof, suspicious, seclusive, stubborn, and resentful (Sarvis, 1962; D. A. Schwartz, 1963). It is as if they had never mastered their primal fears due to some lack in the family context that failed to protect the infant from excessive tension and anxiety early in life. Paranoids have not been able to build the conception of a stable, friendly, dependable world. In short, they lack the behavioral foundations and the ego-superego organization for making safe, close interpersonal relationships.

The paranoid person is equipped with a chronic expectation that others will treat him or her badly, which in turn generates a readiness to react aggressively to any hint of maltreatment from others. In many cases, the patient has actually been treated sadistically during infancy or early childhood, with the result that he or she has internalized these attitudes and framed life in terms of them. Recall in Chapter 2 (p. 64) that we spoke of *reverting from object-choice to identification,* and that this dynamic is at the heart of the Oedipal resolution discussed in Chapter 3 (see p. 71). Because the father is seen as an aggressor in the dynamics of the Oedipal resolution for the male, a phenomenon known as *identification with the aggressor* has been alluded to in the psychoanalytical literature. As this relates to paranoia, the assumption is that such individuals have through personal terror incorporated the very terror that interactions in infancy with parents and a terrifying home environment generated and/or never succeeded in allaying. The resultant sadistic identifications make the paranoid exquisitely sensitive to the smallest traces of hostility, contempt, criticism, or accusation in the attitudes of other people.

*Paranoid Hypersensitivity to the Unconscious Attitudes of Others.* The trouble with this hypersensitivity is that it always finds something on which to feed. All of us harbor minute traces of hostility even in some of our most favorable attitudes toward others. Most of us at times feel indifferent toward everyone, especially when we are preoccupied. These traces are usually unconscious and the periods of indifference unimportant. Sometimes they are momentarily conscious—a passing resentment toward a good friend, a temporary annoyance with someone whom we love, an occasional feeling of aloofness that we may not always recognize. Nearly all of us manage to get along, without suffering serious disturbance, in a social atmosphere that has its negative components and negative moments in its overall friendliness.

Not so the paranoid personality. This individual detects our contradictory traces clearly and consciously, even when we are totally unaware of them ourselves (Bychowski, 1956, 1958; Jacobson, 1954). Sensitive to dialectical nuances in mood, the paranoid experiences our negative inclinations as though they were conscious, dominant, and completely intentional in our thinking and feeling. Because of a hypersensitivity to slight, resentment, or rejection, the paranoid greatly magnifies what he or she picks up from our attitude. Half-truths or quarter-truths are made the whole truth. Molehills are made into mountains. Transitory irritation in our manner becomes a seething, total animosity and hatred for the paranoid as a person. Because of their intolerance for suspense and their inability to imagine the roles of other people, paranoid patients take it immediately for granted that the minute traces of hostility or indifference that they detect are clear, dominant, and conscious in the thoughts and feelings of others. Due to this reaction sensitivity, paranoids will even pick up hostility meant for others and attribute it to themselves.

*Paranoid Insensitivity to His or Her Own Attitudes.* There is still another disturbing factor in the paranoid personality. Along with this exquisite sensitivity to the unconscious trends in others goes an equally striking unawareness of the hostile, contemptuous, critical, and accusing attitudes that the paranoid personally embraces. This unawareness is unfeigned. It is an important product of denial and projection, which operate at wholly unconscious levels. One trouble with these unrecognized attitudes is that they stimulate avoidance and dislike in others; this seems to the paranoid person objective evidence that his or her expectation of being discriminated against was justified.

Such is the background that a paranoid personality brings to an emotional crisis. This person is acutely sensitive to traces of hostility, contempt, criticism, and accusation in others but blind to their presence in himself or herself. Although constantly questioning the motives of others, the paranoid never questions his or her own motivations. Always ready to look behind the friendly or neutral appearances of others, the paranoid lives in the constant expectation of sadistic treatment from others. There is a long-standing fuero claim of this nature in the psychic history of the fixated and regressing paranoid personality. People can never be trusted, for they all hate and despise the person of the paranoid personality.

*Paranoid Disorders and Sexuality.* As a rule, paranoid personalities feel secretly inferior in their sexual development, whether or not such a feeling is justified by their performance. The inferiority has its roots in poorly repressed sexual identity confusions from their early life, in the conflicting fears and wishes of a childhood that they never succeeded in working through. Sometimes a low level of overt sex drive adds objective evidence of relative sexual inadequacy, as one of the following cases will demonstrate. Sometimes homoerotic and pregenital trends are present in the preconscious and are denied and projected with great difficulty as well as incompletely. Occasionally, homoerotic trends are openly expressed and made the basis for a homosexual way of life. The question of homosexuality and mental abnormality will be discussed at length in Chapter 16.

Even when a paranoid personality manages to reach an adult heterosexual level, he or she may have difficulty in maintaining mature genitality. Many respond to heterosexual invitation as though it were a challenge to prove themselves. Many approach sexual relationships with an expectation of being rebuffed, disparaged, and rejected. The expectation of rejection probably comes from experiences in early childhood of being belittled and rejected when they were longing for love. Now, as adults, their feelings of love revive the infantile expectations of unkind, depreciatory treatment, which are poorly repressed and vividly reactivated. The result is that they approach the heterosexual situation not only with these expectations, but also poised to retaliate with behavior that is certain to provoke rebuff. Failure in sexual relations is all but certain under such conditions, and failure is one thing that the paranoid personality cannot tolerate.

Some paranoid personalities are selectively hypersensitive to traces of unconscious homoeroticism and other pregenital trends in persons around them, reacting as though these traces were major, conscious attitudes (Klaf, 1961a, 1961b). This is the same kind of reaction as that which we have discussed in relation to hostility. Such a response becomes especially serious when a social isolate is pushed into close contact with others, as, for example, in military barracks. The minimal unconscious and sublimated homoerotic expressions of other people seem to the frightened paranoid person to be actual threats of seduction or assault. Such a presumed threat may precipitate a psychotic episode.

It is noteworthy that, even in frank delusional developments, the paranoid patient can defend against deviant erotic trends through vigorous denial and projection. Paranoid patients seem normal to themselves, but feel surrounded by perverse persons who make outrageous insinuations about their sexual practices and preferences. Paranoids remain angrily innocent.

*Lack of Self-Esteem.* Though paranoids rarely recognize this fact, they suffer seriously from a lack of healthy self-esteem. Basically, they do not even trust themselves to meet life challenges effectively. This lack of self-esteem is easy to understand if the patient lacked *basic trust* during early infancy and if he or she made hostile or untrustworthy ego and superego identifications. For the same infantile reasons, there is a powerful undercurrent of unconscious guilt in the paranoid personality, handled inadequately through ineffective denial and projection. The paranoid person usually holds grudges like the proverbial elephant, never forgetting an injury and always taking it for granted that others know how he or she feels about them and why. It is a relatively small step from such ingrained attitudes to the development of frank delusions.

*Onset.* When adult life frustrations exceed the limits of what the paranoid personality can phenomenally tolerate, he or she turns away from the frustrating situation and turns inward to solitary rumination. We may witness at this point a deep and massive regression with serious ego disintegration. Unconscious fantasies and conflicts are now reactivated at infantile levels. They escape repression and press toward preconscious and conscious expression. The mature repressive defense structure crumbles, while projection and denial —always overactive in persons vulnerable to paranoid disorders—now take over repression's major defensive functions.

The symptoms that emerge bear the distinct imprint of paranoid conflicts, fantasies, sensitivities, and primitive defenses. They are wish oriented rather than reality oriented. The patient then tries to deal with the environment in true psychotic fashion—that is, by reconstructing reality so as to make it correspond with his or her reactivated fantasies. This is the restitutive attempt that results in the organization of a paranoid pseudocommunity.

We can distinguish three clinical types of onset in the paranoid disorders, as follows:

1. *The onset is sudden and dramatic.* The patient meets with sudden internal or external crises that overwhelm his or her adaptive and defensive systems. Alternatively, there is a prolonged period of steadily increasing stress, until the adaptive and defensive systems abruptly decompensate. In either case, there is a sudden upsurge of primary process material from unconscious

sources into preconscious and conscious organizations. By vigorous denial and projective disowning the patient succeeds in preserving some ego integration, but the result is a delusional system which contradicts reality. The DSM-III characterization for this sudden and dramatic onset is *acute paranoid disorder.*

2. *The onset is preceded by a well-marked period of incubation, terminating in sudden clarification.* The patient reacts to stress at first by partial or complete withdrawal and regressive fantasying. Through private effort, the patient tries to figure things out and thereby frame a unifying "explanation" that will serve as a focus for aggression. Due to the fact that the paranoid person suffers from defective reality-testing, this solution/explanation will usually be a premature and inaccurate crystallization of partial truth with excessive projection. The "sudden clarification" is an erroneous insight, solving a problem that is mere fantasy through actions which will bring on some real problems for the paranoid individual in due time. This type of onset would also fall in the *acute paranoid disorder* designation of DSM-III.

3. *The onset is gradual and insidious, without a sudden crystallization.* The patient progresses slowly from being a paranoid personality to becoming a paranoid psychotic over a period of many months or years. The paranoid may cross and recross the vague boundary line before finally taking up a definitely delusional position. The progressive "adaptations" of the paranoid include more and more deviation from realistic solutions. Social reality is gradually replaced in his or her thinking by delusional reconstructions. In DSM-III, this form of onset would be linked to the diagnosis of *paranoia.* Highly systematized delusions are likely in these cases, with reasonably clear and orderly thinking making the delusional arguments virtually unshakable. In the history of psychiatry, these cases were referred to as the "true" paranoiacs, meaning that they were in no way related to the more bizarre forms of paranoia seen in certain types of schizophrenia. These disorders emerge when the person is more mature—thirty, forty, or fifty years of age—and therefore has a background on which to draw in framing delusional beliefs.

## Clinical Course

Paranoid patients are constantly vigilant, even when they are not actively psychotic at the time. They live uneasily in a dangerous world, a disparaging hostile world, in which it may seem wise to keep one's distance from others. The personality of such a person is in a chronic state of precariously held, unstable equilibrium. Paranoids walk through life on a tightrope.

### EARLY PHASES

Whenever the paranoid's unstable equilibrium is threatened, his or her immediate reaction is to heighten vigilance and to increase psychological distance from others. Hostility is prominent in the clinical picture, usually wound into fantasies aimed at "explaining" the situation to which heightened tension is attached. Paranoid persons rarely feel secure with others; they cannot put their full trust in anyone. Therefore, in an emotional crisis they are thrown upon their own inept resources to keep afloat as best they can alone. They may at first share their suspicions with another person, but their basic defects nearly always trip them up. When they are emotionally aroused, they can assert convictions and pile up evidence, but they cannot endure doubt or disagreement, they cannot tolerate suspense. Once started they must go on. Another person's doubt or disagreement seems only an obstruction to the patient's forward thrust. It is experienced as frustration, and the frustrater becomes an opponent and is classified with other opponents as another enemy.

Now the patient faces the emotional crisis alone. Like someone wanted by the police, he or she watches everything and suspects everyone. The more the paranoid watches, listens, and ponders, the more his or her suspicions grow. Hypotheses framed on flimsy grounds are put to test inadequately, leading to conclusions that could have been predicted beforehand. Besides, if the paranoid finds there is no evidence for his or her delusional belief, he dismisses the counterevidence that all is going along satisfactorily. Paranoids find what they are looking for, one way or another. The same inflexible, inept frame of reference is pressed onto life again and again, leading to the sort of evidence the paranoid *intends* to find—and finds!

When paranoid persons make an inference it becomes for them an unchangeable fact. They build up chains of inference, usually interspersed with actual observations. But they do not make clear distinctions between what they see and hear and what they merely think. They recall selected incidents from the past, reshaping them to fit their present concerns (retrospective falsification); thus they use distorted memories to buttress their unsound beliefs.

To a normal listener, who does not know which things have been actually observed and which only inferred, the chains of logic may sound irrefutable. This is why an intelligent and earnest paranoid person sometimes convinces relatives and friends, and occasionally even juries and the public, that his or her delusional convictions are social fact.

It is not the force of reasoning that determines this inexorable march from fear or suspicion to delusion. Paranoid reasoning is sick; its logic is faulted by the questionable premises under affirmation; but its onward press is impressive. The force of this irresistible forward movement comes from id wishes. Delusional reasoning is propelled forward by libidinal and aggressive pressures. Its directions are determined by previously unconscious motivation that has come to take charge of thinking.

## FINDING A FOCUS: PRELIMINARY CRYSTALLIZATIONS

We must not forget that, for all its social ineptness, delusion formation is a serious attempt at *restitution*—an attempt to *reconstruct reality* so as to bring it into harmony with previously unconscious fantasies. In persecutory paranoid restitution the patient tries to reconstruct the environment in such a way that it serves his or her intention to *act out* in a hostile manner. In early life, the person who is to experience paranoid persecutions as an adult is dominated by an expectation of sadistic treatment and by a readiness to meet such treatment with counterattack. It is this infantile pattern that the paranoid psychotic reactivates during regression, and it is this pattern that is projected onto the adult world in which he or she lives.

The frightened solitary patient, who lacks the basic skills needed for reality-testing, is like an unskilled and inexperienced man who gets lost in a jungle at night. He appears suddenly to become the focus of a hostile, living environment, obscure and unintelligible. Now everything he sees and hears seems to threaten him personally. It is his own vigilant anxiety that binds together trivial and unrelated things going on around him into a great net from which he can see no escape. His projected fears become predatory animals, and he becomes their prey. His tension may eventually become so intolerable that he must take action even though action threatens to kill him (Davitz, 1959). Sometimes it seems easier to go out to meet death than to sit and wait for it to come, knowing that it is near.

We have seen how the paranoid person is and always has been intolerant of suspense, even before taking ill. Now that we see this person regress and become psychotic he or she seems irresistibly motivated to take violent action. The real source of danger is the paranoid's own pent-up hostility. The paranoid hungers after clarification, something on which to focus this hostility so that it might be destroyed before it destroys him or her.

## FINDING A FOCUS: THE PARANOID PSEUDOCOMMUNITY

It is this irresistible necessity for a tangible target that quite literally forces the psychotic paranoid person to find culprits and to uncover plots. A paranoid woman begins by attributing a malicious intent to the actions of real persons in her environment and of other persons whom she merely infers. The actions themselves may be trivial and unrelated. She begins to organize these real and imagined persons into a community of plotters. All of their supposed activities seem unified against her in one grand, hostile purpose—to control and eventually do her in. In short, this woman has organized a *pseudocommunity* with which to bind together her projected fears and wishes, to justify her own hostile aggression, and to give it a tangible target.

*The paranoid pseudocommunity is a reconstruction of reality. It organizes the observed and the inferred behavior of real and imagined persons into a conspiracy, with the patient at its focus.* This organization of a hostile pseudocommunity will not comfort or reassure our paranoid woman, but it will satisfy her psychological desire to frame a clarifying reason "why" she senses the hostility and fear that she is discharging emotionally. She now finds out "what it is all about." She believes that now she has some idea of what may be expected to take place "next." She now knows whom to watch and why, and what countermeasures to take. The formation of a pseudocommunity may even increase a patient's fright, but at least the obscurity has gone. The fright is no longer a nameless, formless terror. Now it is organized and has a focus.

In most paranoid disorders the pseudocommunity has a principal person or two. Patients do not choose their pseudocommunity leaders at random. The significant person is usually well suited for some special reason to act as the symbol of a patient's major conflicts. This person might be a stranger—someone in authority or someone prominent in public life—a politician, an actor, an industrialist, a scientist, or a criminal. Sometimes the significant person is an unsuspecting friend, a neighbor, or a fellow worker who happens to have characteristics or connections that fit him or her for the imaginary role of chief watcher, slanderer, and persecutor—the embodiment of a patient's projected hostility and guilt. Sometimes the significant person is close to the patient, and the reasons for his or her selection are obvious.

As a reconstruction of reality the pseudocommunity may have an initial benefit for the psychotic person. At least now the preoccupations of the psychopathological process are focused, and a plan of action has been affirmed in relation to the actors within the pseudocommunity. However, pseudo-communities, like real communities, tend to expand and to include new persons, new actions, and new dangers. If this expansion continues, a point may finally be reached at which the patient can no longer tolerate the growing threat. The patient is likely then to burst out into violent action and thus to run afoul of reality—the real social community. Such action then brings about actual intervention or actual counteraggression. It is true that intervention may save a patient's life and make it possible for a cure to be effected. But the patient is fortunate who gets expert help promptly and is able to profit by it.

Intervention sometimes makes matters worse instead of better. If it includes counteraggression—a violent struggle or police action—the immediate effect is always bad. But even under the most favorable conditions some paranoid psychotic persons never recover fully. Some of them remain permanent patients, inside or outside the hospital. They may live in the community as suspicious, aloof, angry eccentrics. Some are able to return to relatively normal living, although they still have active, even though concealed, delusions. Among this group belong the litigious paranoid persons who continually seek reaffirmations of their injured rights and proof of their innocence in courts of law. It goes without saying that no court of law can absolve a paranoid person's unconscious guilt that he or she is projecting onto others. Let us turn now to a clinical case of persecutory paranoid disorder.

### Case of Charles G.: Persecutory Paranoid Disorder

Charles G., a bachelor of forty-nine, became involved in a furious quarrel with some illegal racehorse bookmakers. They insisted that he had not put money on a certain horse that had unexpectedly won, and he insisted that he had. He was superficially a pleasant, reserved person, but on this occasion he worked himself into a towering rage. Fortifying himself with a few drinks at a nearby tavern, he returned to the bookmakers, demanding the payoff, shouting threats and insults at them, and inviting them into the street to fight. When he found that this was ineffective, he returned to the hotel where he lived, still furious.

Later on, as he pondered over the injustice and his rage, Charles began to worry over the possibility of retaliation against him. He recalled that some book-makers are "mob connected," and he had seen enough movies on the Mafia and other gangster activities to begin ruminating on the danger his outburst might have put him in. With these thoughts his fury changed to fright and his recklessness changed to vigilance. The next day he noticed strangers loitering about the hotel lobby. They seemed to be watching him and making little signs which referred to him. An automobile full of men stopped in front of the hotel entrance. He now felt sure that he would be kidnapped, "taken for a ride," and killed. He barricaded himself in his room and arranged by telephone with a relative to flee the city the next morning. His relative accepted the patient's fears as reflecting factual reality.

As Charles thought over his plan that evening, he suddenly "realized" that the telephone wire had probably been tapped by the Mafia. They would undoubtedly force his relative to betray him. So he fled alone in his car during the night, to outwit the imagined pseudocommunity. We shall see this sequence of confiding and then anticipating betrayal again in his behavior pattern. We know from other evidence that this sequence had been repeated over and over by Charles in the past. It was probably basic in his personality organization and had its roots in his early childhood.

In his long flight across the country he kept seeing signs that he was being followed. He could not possibly doubt these signs. He decided that he would never be caught alive. When he reached the home of relatives a thousand miles away they at first believed his story. When, however, they found poison and a straight razor concealed in his clothing, and he admitted that he was planning suicide, they brought him to a psychiatric hospital to preserve his life.

Charles was courteous and pleasant to the hospital staff, but he always chose solitude when he could. Although he obviously wanted to confide in his therapist, and several times started to do so, he could never bring himself to talk about anything but trivialities and the plot. He persuaded a local pastor to visit him in the clinic. He then arranged a later meeting which was to be kept secret from the clinic. There was something in his past, he said, that he wanted to confess. As soon as the pastor had gone, however, Charles "realized" that he had made a terrible mistake. The pastor was dark-complected. Hence, he must be a foreigner and a gangster in disguise. Charles made a suicide attempt, and when this was unsuc-cessful, he insisted upon transfer to a Veterans Hospital, for which he was eligible. He thought that he would be safer in a solidly "American" hospital.

*Discussion.* An outburst of frustrated rage marked the onset of this psy-chosis. Charles could neither endure his furious hostility nor adequately dis-charge it. When he turned from reality to fantasy he turned suddenly from an angry aggressor into a frightened victim, a dialectical maneuver commonly seen in paranoid delusional formation. The underlying dynamic here involved denial and projection of a self-directed hostility, the sense of guilt that drove him to ask for a priest while in the hospital. It is unlikely that the real "sin" motivating Charles' request to see a confessor was known to him consciously (he knew full well unconsciously!). Just as there are manifest dream contents masking latent themes, so too are there sins being admitted that are far removed from the actual transgressions. Oedipal wishes are particularly repre-hensible and rarely acknowledged consciously.

We can surmise from the fact that Charles was a bachelor and never married that he had experienced a rather difficult Oedipal resolution. Scanty background material in this case suggested that his father was indeed a threatening figure and that he probably became the prototype for the gangsters in Charles's delusional system. Charles had actually lived as if a hunted man all his life, moving from city to city, living in cheap hotels, and doing various types of sales work. This pattern has long been noted among male paranoid patients (Bak, 1946). It is as if they live under a heavy burden of guilt, which they seek to escape by superficial interpersonal contacts and easy mobility in place of residence. As we shall see later in this chapter, there is the suggestion here of an archaic superego involvement. We next move to an interesting case of paranoid jealousy.

## Delusional Paranoid Jealousy

Jealousy is never wholly rational. Even when it deserves to be called normal, it arouses unconscious and preconscious fantasies that are not in the service of the conscious ego and that usually make the jealousy seem disproportionate to the objective situation in which it originates. Jealousy is most commonly precipitated by a fear of the loss of love or loss of status, by hostility toward both the rival and the loved one, or toward the origin of the loss, together with a painful blow to one's narcissism that takes the form of a severe loss in superego self-esteem.

Delusional jealousy is not just an exaggeration of normal jealousy. It is a psychotic reconstruction of reality that falsifies and invents "facts" in order to be able to rationalize the feeling being discharged. It shows the typical paranoid characteristics of inflexibility, of the exclusion of everything that might contradict the delusion, and of the inclusion of trivialities and distortions that seem to support it. Primitive defensive forms of denial and projection dominate the dynamic picture. Delusional jealousy has the same tendency to expand, to feed upon itself, that persecutory delusions have. Let us begin with a clinical case that brings these and other characteristics of paranoia to light.

### Case of Alan K.: Delusional Paranoid Jealousy

*Infancy and early childhood.* Alan K. was the youngest child in a mother-dominated household. He had two sisters, one six years older and one eight years older than he. His mother was a strong-minded, independently wealthy woman who was used to giving orders and doing things her way. The father played a subordinate role, moderately successful in business but an insignificant figure in the home. "She treated him like a servant," Alan said of his mother and father. "She enjoyed humiliating him in front of us."

Alan felt that his father's attitude toward him was one of amused detachment tinged with mild contempt. He in turn looked down upon his father as a passive, ineffectual person. Toward his mother he had always felt a passionate mixture of loving admiration and exasperated hate. "I'm devoted to her," he said as an adult, "because she's a great woman; but I can't stand being near her."

Alan's mother told him that he had been a fearful and stubborn baby from the very start. He never felt relaxed in her arms as the two girls had. He stiffened and cried when she held him. He was afraid of the dark, of being alone, and particularly of strangers and of animals. His mother was determined to make him into a manly man, she said, "not like your father." To this end she avoided "coddling" him and ridiculed his fears. He was plagued by nightmares from which he often woke up screaming. Fits of rage also plagued Alan. Everybody teased him, most of all his mother. He felt that she enjoyed seeing his fury and encouraged his attack as a show of masculinity.

Alan was not directly punished for his angry outbursts. If they got out of bounds he was shut in a room alone to cool off; but he was not forced to suppress all his rage and adopt a passive, compliant attitude in this kind of situation. It is probable that his freedom to be furious when he was teased and frustrated is what allowed him to grow into an angry paranoid adult instead of a compliant schizophrenic.

There was much ambivalence in Alan's attitudes toward his two sisters, just as there was toward his mother. They also teased him when he was small by mischievously hiding his things and following him about as he tried to find them. According to Alan they enjoyed taking care of him as a baby, treating him as a living doll, feeding and diapering him, dressing and undressing him, and fussing over him so much that his mother often had to intervene to protect him. All this must have given him extensive experience with dependent gratifications, erotic stimulation, and frustrating restraint.

Alan described his sisters as haughty and superior. He secretly envied them their self-assurance and their pride in their appearance. He felt "shabby and small" beside them. There is a parallel between his feelings of insignificance in relation to his sisters and his father's shabby unimportance in relation to his mother. Such feelings help to form patterns that may determine a child's later conception of himself.

*Childhood and adolescence.* As he grew up, Alan had his friends and chums, but he was unpopular and he was often excluded from group games. He recalled having been a stickler for rules, penalties, fairness, and equal rights. Sometimes when he lost an argument over a decision he would shun everyone for several days, indulging in vengeful fantasies that kept him feeling "hot all over." Alan was always fascinated by accounts of murder, torture, imprisonment, and execution.

In first talking about himself to his therapist Alan said that during latency and adolescence he had little interest in sex. When he had gained more confidence he modified this statement significantly. He was actually much attracted to girls, he said, because they seemed worldly, self-assured, and "all together." When he was in their presence he became tongue-tied and timid. He felt that they looked down upon him. During his junior year in engineering college he had a blowup with his fraternity brothers when they teased him about never going on dates. He moved out of his fraternity house and experienced great relief at being alone. Alan defended himself by saying that his studies "left no time for girls." He said that he "fought off" masturbation by regular workouts in the gymnasium. Whenever he gave in he felt "weak and degraded" following manual stimulation to ejaculation.

*Career.* Alan had his heart set on becoming an architect, but his mother persuaded him to follow a career in engineering because it would give him more security. He graduated with honors and obtained a fine position. Though he made a good start he did not progress as expected, evidently because he was a serious personnel problem. He criticized his fellow workers and showed overt contempt for his superiors. He welcomed newcomers on the job as friends, but soon grew jealous of them. Thus he was forever making and losing friends. Each new boss was "a great relief" from the previous one; but then difficulties would soon accumulate and the old tension would return. After one particularly hostile outburst with a superior, Alan was asked to see the company physician for a thorough examination. When this physician referred him to a psychiatrist, Alan began to suspect that the company was trying to frame him in some way by claiming he was a "head case." At the first opportunity he changed jobs.

*Marriage and parenthood.* When he was twenty-nine the patient married on impulse after a brief courtship a registered nurse of twenty-five. Alan found his wife, Betsy, to be a shy person who readily deferred to his lead. There were sexual difficulties in the marital union from the outset. Although Alan had by this time in life experienced sexual relations with other women, he was reassured that Betsy was not the sort of woman who "slept around" with just anyone. They did have premarital sex, but on a limited basis. Within the first month of their marriage Alan began feeling increasingly anxious and even embarrassed in the sexual situation. He felt that Betsy was almost too interested in sex. She initiated most of their foreplay, and took more satisfaction in intercourse than Alan did. As time went on, and his passivity seemed to increase, Betsy changed from "a meek little thing" into a decisive woman who gradually took charge, as Alan's mother had done in his childhood home.

The couple had two boys and then a girl. Alan was jealous of their first baby when it came, but he soon discovered that he enjoyed looking after it. He liked it when Betsy went out of an evening and left them alone. During his wife's third pregnancy he began an affair with a woman in the neighborhood that played a part in his later delusions of jealousy. When a girl was born to Betsy he was disappointed. He could not fully accept his new daughter. "I'm just the opposite of my father," he said. "He always liked my sisters better than me."

*Psychotic disorder.* When the patient was thirty-nine his wife became actively interested in community affairs. It was this that led indirectly to his developing delusional jealousy. Betsy was put on a welfare committee with one of Alan's factory superiors, Todd D., whom Alan described as "an attractive bachelor." The committee met weekly in rotation at the various members' homes. Each time it met at Betsy's house, Alan would retire upstairs with the children when the members arrived—"like a nursemaid," he said. This situation made him feel publicly humiliated before his wife and before his factory superior. A teasing cliché, something about Alan's being "a good mother," which one member repeated each time, made the patient furious.

One evening he telephoned the home where the committee was supposedly meeting only to be told that it was not there. He drove at once to Todd's apartment. The lights were on there, but no one responded to his ringing and knocking. Betsy came home late and explained that the meeting had been held at a roadside inn so that they could discuss a member in his absence. Alan was beside himself with rage. He accused her bluntly of infidelity, and she retaliated with counteraccusations, citing his diminished potency as evidence. He felt doubly injured, first by her attack on his virility and second by her accusations. It did not help matters that both were based upon fact. From this point on the two were estranged and the children sided with their mother.

Soon after this the firm asked Alan to work evenings while they did some redesigning and renovation. When he saw Todd leaving at the usual time Alan felt sure that he was being "shelved" by this boss so that the affair with Betsy would have "smooth sailing." He began a systematic campaign of spying on his wife and Todd, often leaving work suddenly to check on their movements. He discovered nothing. This did not make him doubt his convictions; it only made him more certain and more angry. Obviously, he felt, someone at the factory was tipping them off when he left. The more he brooded over the situation the clearer the picture seemed to become, and the more things he could recall from the past that fitted into the plot. He saw himself as the stupid victim of a transparent conspiracy that was making him ridiculous in everybody's eyes.

In the meantime, Alan continued with his affair. While he was with his lover his suspiciousness multiplied so that he began noticing noises over the telephone and in the wall. These he interpreted at once as signs of wiretapping and of hidden dictaphones. Now apparently people were spying on him. He complained to the telephone company and got polite reassurances. This sounded to him like complicity. He began tapping the walls until he located solid places where he felt sure the dictaphones must be. He could not persuade his mistress to let him crack open the plaster in her apartment and disclose them. She insisted that the sounds came from steam pipes that had always been there. Her obstinacy and apparent anxiety — she was probably getting alarmed at his delusions — convinced him that she also was a party to the plot. He left her abruptly without a word, too frightened even to start a quarrel.

The climax came when Alan half awoke one night to "see" (dream/hallucinate) his wife standing at his bedside with a syringe in her hand. He struggled hard to awaken fully but only went back to sleep. He decided afterward that he must already have been given an injection. In the morning when he awoke he found small brown specks on his arm that he was sure were the marks of previous injections. He flew into a rage, accusing his wife of trying to kill him and threatening to kill her and Todd instead. Betsy told him that he must be having a nervous breakdown and that he should consider entering a hospital. He was frightened enough to agree to enter a hospital, but he did so on the express condition that no one else whom he knew should come into contact with the psychiatric staff. He was openly afraid of further conspiracy against him.

*Therapy and recovery.* In the clinic Alan was suspicious of everyone he saw, even of the maintenance men. He was especially vigilant during visiting hours and on walks outside. Progress in therapy began when he recognized that he had had serious problems long before the supposed plot of Betsy and Todd. At first he would talk of nothing but the plot. He was preoccupied with vengeful fantasies of killing the pair and himself. A change came when he admitted to himself that his vision of his wife with a syringe at his bedside, ready to kill him, might have been a dream. His therapist had early expressed this possibility casually when he said that it sounded like a dream. Although the immediate effect of this comment had been to make Alan distrust the whole clinic, it succeeded in penetrating his delusional armor, and it helped provoke the change.

Alan now narrowed down the blame to Todd. He said, "If I could just go and kill that bastard I'd be so relieved I wouldn't care what they did to me. At least I'd be able to sleep again. To keep from doing it all the time uses up my strength. It gives me an actual all-gone weakness."

On several occasions Alan quarreled with another patient over trivial matters, a patient who had strong but well-defined latent homosexual trends. He was alarmed at having fantasies of killing this man also. He saw spontaneously a connection between these fantasies and his thoughts about Todd, although he said nothing about the connection until much later.

Alan remarked one day that he guessed we all thought that he was "a homosexual," adding, "and I guess subconsciously I am." He went on to tell something he had not mentioned before: a fascination with the male body. He said that in his college days his favorite recreations were those of exercising in the gymnasium, watching others exercise, and attending boxing and wrestling matches. He had come to the conclusion that this fascination might somehow be related to perversion, which he abhorred. The mere possibility frightened him, he said. Having verbalized and met this fear, and finding himself none the worse for it, he went on to talk about the meaning of homosexuality to him, and to speak with greater frankness about his own sex worries.

In early adolescence the patient had tried mutual masturbation twice with chums. He had enjoyed the close contact, but afterward he had been overwhelmed with guilt and shame. The fact that his own level of sexual desire had never seemed powerful to him made him feel inferior and incomplete. He was puzzled by the strength of his erotic fantasies that seemed to contradict what he said. His marital life had been marred by his inability to measure up to his wife's sex needs, which he regarded as unreasonably demanding. Interestingly, in his extramarital affair he spent "less time in the sack than you might think." Apparently, he found a sexual partner more demure and passive than Betsy, and this reassured him in some way about his own biological promptings.

Although nothing dramatic came out of these discussions, their effect was to ease up noticeably the patient's tension and suspiciousness. The quarreling on the ward stopped and the therapeutic atmosphere was freer. Alan used his first chance to go out alone as an opportunity to make a surprise visit to his home. He said afterward that he had done it to check up on his wife. The reception that his wife gave him convinced him that she was through with him. After he had digested this experience, with therapeutic help, he took the initiative in getting himself transferred to another of the company's plants.

Alan left the clinic still suspecting that there might have been something between his wife and Todd, but no longer afraid that anyone was plotting against him. He expected his wife to divorce him and marry the other man. It is unknown whether this prediction was justified or not because the clinical staff never heard from Alan again.

The therapeutic result achieved was recovery from a paranoid psychotic episode, with some improvement in a basically paranoid personality and with increased tolerance for latent homosexual trends. If such an improvement is consolidated the likelihood of further psychotic reactions is correspondingly reduced. In the discussion of paranoid disorders that follows we shall have more to say about the dynamics of this case.

## Erotic Paranoid Disorder

In erotic paranoid disorders the patient has the delusional belief that someone loves him or her but dares not make an open avowal because of other commitments or because of embarrassment. With the paranoid person's hypersensitivity to unconscious attitudes and the tendency we noted of selecting whatever supports his or her delusional system, it is not difficult to interpret irrelevant actions of others as disguised signals of love. Clinical experience suggests that the erotic paranoid disorder is most common among women and among passive men. The delusions usually focus upon a prominent public figure of the opposite sex. Many persons with such delusions act upon them. They approach their supposed lover in private or in public, or send letters urging that the love between them be acknowledged before the world. Their victims are likely to appeal to the police for protection from possible scandal.

One of our patients was an unmarried woman of thirty-six who had been attending a series of popular lectures on the history of art. She became more and more attracted to the lecturer and then began to notice all kinds of little signals that he was emitting to let her know that he loved her. Assigning meaning like this to inadvertent, meaningless events is termed *ideas of reference* — that is, the delusional paranoid is referring things to himself or herself that have no basis in fact. The situation came to a head when the woman approached the lecturer after one of his presentations, and insisted that he declare publicly the love she felt sure he felt for her. He was wise enough to call for a conference, which included the patient, himself, members of her family, and a psychiatrist, so that she was able to get help without police intervention. She did not succeed in giving up her delusion, but she at least renounced her original goal of having the lecturer declare his love.

The love expressed in erotic paranoid disorders is usually a narcissistic love projected onto another person; that is, the other person is not really an *object-choice* because of the regressive psychotic process. The other person is a kind of stand-in for the patient's own identity. When this dynamic occurs the sex of the supposed delusional lover is not really important (Fenichel, 1945, pp. 432-433). Sometimes the delusion is a defensive maneuver that dialectically substitutes a heterosexual attachment for a denied or repressed homosexual one. In Freud's formulation for a male (1922/1955n), we would phrase this dialectical logic as follows: "I don't love *him*; I love *her* because she loves me." For women this would become, "I don't love *her*; I love *him* because he loves me."

Some patients with erotic paranoid reactions feel themselves to be persecuted by love and make indignant protests. Others treat the situation with a narcissistic pleasure similar to the normal pleasure felt over being loved, except that it is delusional and goes unsatisfied. Erotic paranoid reactions that elicit pleasure in the patient are generally considered to be very difficult to treat, if not untreatable. If, on the other hand, the patient feels persecuted by love, the situation is similar to that in other persecutory paranoid disorders and calls for similar therapy.

Mary Evans Picture Library/Sigmund Freud Copyrights

*Freud in 1916, at sixty years of age. He had by this time written* The Case of Schreber *(1911) and* Totem and Taboo *(1912-1913). His approach was established enough to allow him to write a history of the psychoanalytical movement in 1914. The International Psycho-Analytic Association was founded in 1910, with Jung as its first president. Jung resigned from this position in 1914, following a lengthy debate in correspondence with Freud over various theoretical and personal matters.*

## Grandiose Paranoid Disorder

Delusions of grandeur are also much less frequent in paranoid disorders than are the common delusions of persecution. They are more common in severe cases than in mild ones, probably because a more primitive, transparent denial is required to sustain them. As in the case of persecutory delusions, the most prevalent themes are derived from the surrounding culture, including its folklore and popular stories. Patients may picture themselves as immensely talented or irresistibly attractive, as of noble birth or of rich heritage, a powerful leader, an inspired genius, a saint, a prophet, or even a god. They may feel that they have secret knowledge or that they have been chosen to perform a great mission.

We shall see similar grandiose delusions in schizophrenia, but in schizophrenia they are poorly organized, vague, mystical, and shifty. Grandeur also characterizes mania, but the manic expresses his or her delusions garrulously and can be easily distracted. It is only in the paranoid psychoses that delusions seem stable, persistent, earnest, and well organized. These characteristics give further evidence that paranoid persons preserve and use complex secondary processes of thinking in the service of the id.

Complex secondary process thinking appears in the grandiose delusions of paranoid "inventors," "scientists," and "mathematicians." Some of these have specific plans—often worked out in minute detail—for solving industrial problems, overcoming natural barriers, transforming one substance or force into another, changing the calendar, or setting up new systems of numbers and symbols. Some plans are conceived on a huge scale, involving schemes for saving or destroying the world and for manipulating planetary systems. With the rapid advance today of scientific systems for destroying the world and for interplanetary travel the problem of distinguishing between paranoid and scientific planning becomes more and more difficult. It is not rare, for example, to find that a paranoid patient has already taken out a patent for some fantastic delusional idea. From a dynamic standpoint, it seems highly likely that a preoccupation with inventive, scientific, or mathematical logic or pseudologic may defend many a paranoid person from ego disintegration.

In both political and religious fields one is likely to meet paranoid persons who believe themselves to have been chosen to perform a great mission, usually to save others, sometimes to destroy them. The origins of such "missions" lie in a tremendous necessity that the patient senses to save himself or herself or to discharge hostile aggression in a relatively acceptable manner (destroying evil beings, etc.). Inspired paranoids have been known to crystallize their delusions into a belief that they are a modern Messiah, Joan of Arc, or Napoleon, someone who can bring universal peace or universal destruction to the world.

## Folie à Deux

In DSM-III the disorder of *folie à deux* is referred to as *shared paranoid disorder. Folie à deux* presents the interesting picture of two persons sharing the same delusional beliefs. One of the two is usually a dominant paranoid person with more or less fixed delusions. The other is likely to be a suggestible, dependent person who takes over the dominant one's delusions intact but gives them up easily when separated from the dominant person and given therapeutic help. When three or more persons are involved in a shared delusion such terms as *folie à trois,* and so on, are sometimes employed, but the principle of explanation remains the same—a dominant paranoid person providing the framing delusional beliefs which are then affirmed by others (Pulver & Brunt, 1961).

Most of the delusions reported in *folie à deux* have been persecutory, as we might expect from the general prevalence of persecutory delusions in paranoid reactions (Gralnick, 1942). Often the people involved are related, such as two sisters, husband and wife, two brothers, mother and child, or father and child. The participants do not always verbalize the dominant/passive relationship involved in the shared delusion. Some analysts consider the assumption by the more dependent person of the dominant one's delusions to be an attempt by the dependent person to recover a lost object through identification (reversion from object-choice to identification). This identification may be with the dominant person or only with his or her delusional system (H. Deutsch, 1938). Any two persons living in close communication are likely to have unconscious bonds between them. A shared delusion may be an expression of such bonds. In the final reconstruction of reality, which constitutes the *folie à deux,* the two participants will share a common pseudocommunity. The dominant paranoid person is its major architect, while the dependent person does little more than agree with the delusional reconstruction.

## Dynamic and Developmental Background

Paranoid thinking does not succeed in becoming objective where it should. It tends to treat impersonal things and events as though they were personal (ideas of reference). These defects come from a lack of development of *basic trust* in other human beings, and from defects in the paranoid's defensive system (Finney, 1961). When paranoid persons believe that they can identify the persons and activities "responsible" for what they are experiencing, they act as though their inferences and suspicions were established fact. Because of their lack of basic trust, paranoids cannot share their suspicions with others. Above all, they seem to lack the capacity to place themselves in another person's shoes. They cannot see life from other people's perspectives. In personal crises, they are left to their own ineffectual, distorted, and poorly tested devices.

### FIXATION AND REGRESSION IN PERSECUTORY PARANOID DISORDERS

We have noted at the outset of this chapter that psychotics tend to regress more completely than neurotics and that they attempt to alter or to reconstruct the nature of their reality in framing delusional systems. We would now like to emphasize the vital importance of the developmental dynamics first discussed in Chapter 2 (p. 63) and touched upon at various points in both the present and other chapters. We refer to the movement from autoerotism through narcissism to object-choice in development, and the fact that this can be *reversed* in the regressive maneuvers of psychopathology. As a general rule, we find that Freud assigns the most serious forms of disorder to a reversion to *narcissism*. This is the time of life in which a fixation can prove devastating to the developing personality, and paranoia is our first clear example of the Freudian explanation.

The crucial factor in the dynamics we are now considering relates to the turning away from, reverting from, or regressing from (all of these phrasings have been used) object-choice "to" something else—narcissism and/or identification, as the case may be. It is clear that Freud and other psychoanalysts have observed a close relationship in their clients' dynamics between narcissism and identification. This is the period of life in which the developing child is beginning to identify with others even as he or she is taking on a personal identity as the "first" object of the sexual instinct (i.e., narcissistic libidinal investment). Of course, technically, a narcissistic investment is not an object-choice. Narcissism is a stage slightly advanced beyond primitive autoerotism, but it has not yet met the inevitable human need to form interpersonal ties through a legitimate object-choice.

When the (male) child finally gives up the mother cathexis, reverts from choosing her as object, and identifies with the father's superego standards (supplanting the archaic superego), there is a standard resolution of the Oedipus complex (see Chapter 3). We can call this dynamic process an "identification with the aggressor" (see above, p. 327) if we like, because the father is perceived by the boy as a physical threat (castration anxiety). A dynamic of this type was seen taking place in the concentration camps of World War II, where Jewish internees slated for death actually identified with and took on the values of their Nazi exterminators (Frankl, 1959). So-called brainwashing techniques used during the Korean War can be interpreted in the same fashion (Farber, Harlow, & West, 1956).

Now, in order to understand paranoia we must add another relevant defense mechanism—that of *projection*—to the intertwined factors of narcissistic regression and identification. In discussing the origins of a persecutory delusion, Freud framed a kind of dialectical syllogism, in which the paranoid's logic runs as follows:

> The proposition "I (a man) love him" is contradicted by: . . .
> Delusions of *persecution*; for they loudly assert:
> "I do not *love* him—I *hate* him."
> This contradiction, which must have run thus in the unconscious . . . cannot, however, become conscious to a paranoic in this form. The mechanism of symptom-formation in paranoia requires that internal perceptions—feelings—shall be replaced by external perceptions. Consequently the proposition "I love him" becomes transformed by *projection* onto another one: "*He hates* (persecutes) *me,* which will justify me in hating him." (Freud, 1911/1958a, p. 63)

We have already seen an alternative form of this kind of reasoning in the erotic paranoid disorder (see above, p. 340), where we noted that sometimes the logic would run (for the male): "I don't love him; I love *her* because she loves me." The essential feature here is that in a paranoid disorder there is likely to be a *homosexual* dynamic involved. Freud suggested that this might invariably be true of paranoia (ibid., p. 77). And the reason we have such a tie of paranoia to homosexuality—suggested or at least readily implied in both the cases of Charles G. and Alan K.—is that in Freudian theory homosexuality is at heart a narcissistic disorder. As we shall see when we take up homosexuality in Chapter 16, the (male) homosexual is in effect projecting his own identity onto the persons of other males. The "other" in this sexual contact is therefore *not* an object but a self-projection. Hence, homosexuality is a variant type of narcissistic disorder. There are, of course, modern views in opposition to this Freudian explanation and we by no means intend to ignore such alternative points of view when we go into the question of homosexuality in detail.

Now, it would be a serious mistake to conclude that as paranoids are likely to have a homosexual involvement the reverse is true—that is, that homosexuals are likely to be paranoiacs. This is *not* what Freud is suggesting, and surely this erroneous conclusion should not be drawn based on anything we have said to this point. Our purpose here is simply to clarify the frequently misunderstood psychodynamics of Freudian theory. This theory suggests that paranoia is a *psychotic* disorder and that homosexuality is a *personality* disorder (see Chapter 16, p. 325).

It is clear from vast clinical experience that the paranoid person is not as severely or totally regressed as individuals suffering from the other psychotic disorders. We noted as much in our introductory comments to this chapter (see p. 000), where we suggested that there was almost a neurotic aspect to the paranoid disorder. Paranoids might be said to have both a neurotic and a psychotic fixation. Practically speaking, this means that the paranoid psychotic has reasonably good contact with reality. Delusions of persecution begin with a focus on real persons and real situations. Paranoid psychotic episodes occur later in life than other psychotic episodes. Paranoid delusions distort social reality, and they often lead to tragic results, but the object relations that the paranoid patient maintains are superior to those of any equally ill manic, depressed, or schizophrenic patient. Even so, there is a psychotic deficit in the ego defenses of the paranoid patient, and we next turn to a discussion of these adjustive handicaps.

## DEFENSES IN PERSECUTORY PARANOID DISORDERS

*Defective Repression.* The paranoid person is one who has had to compensate throughout life for defective repression. This compensation includes the overdevelopment and overuse of denial and projection. It is probable that the overdevelopment and overuse of denial and projection in the beginning actually interfered with the development of normal repression. That is to say, primitive denial and projection were called into action to such a degree (because of excessive tension and anxiety early in life) that they became established as major forms of defense before repression took over as the keystone of the defensive organization.

Repression cannot operate effectively unless there is a relatively mature ego organization. During psychotic regression, with its ego disintegration, there is a progressive weakening of repressive defenses. The functional barrier that has "contained" the unconscious system begins to disappear. Previously unconscious processes now invade the preconscious and conscious organizations on an increasing scale. This invasion itself has the effect of rapidly weakening the barrier, much as waters rushing through defects in a dam hasten the dam's destruction. This invasion also further disintegrates the preconscious and conscious systems and thus prevents restoration of the repressive defenses, in somewhat the same way that flood waters destroy a community that might have been able to restore the dam. By the time regression is halted in paranoid disorders and reorganization at more primitive levels has begun, repression has become so defective that only the overuse of denial and repression can save the patient from deep ego disintegration.

*Denial and Projection in Paranoid Disorders.* We noted in Chapter 9, in discussing dissociative disorders, that denial as a defense is older than repression (see p. 285). Denial operates early in childhood before ego boundaries have been established and much before a mature superego has materialized. Denial operates before there is a clear separation of unconscious from preconscious and conscious organizations. It is, in effect, a defense against something that is perceived or felt, something that has not been repressed or has escaped repression. Denial is overdeveloped in paranoid persons. When, therefore, the defective repression allows a breakthrough of primary process material in a paranoid disorder, it is denial that defends the psychotic person from having to admit potentially disintegrated trends (e.g., homosexual impulses) as coming from himself or herself.

Denial can be successfully used by normal and neurotic persons to ward off anxieties from sources that cannot be avoided or repressed. Denial alone is not sufficient, however, to dispose of threatening disintegrating forces in paranoid disorders. The fears, suspicions, and accusations that erupt in persecutory paranoid disorders have to be disposed of in some way if the patient is to escape further disintegration. Since repression is inadequate to dispose of them, the patient is forced to supplement denial with projection. Paranoids not only deny but also disown; they not only disown, but also attribute what they deny to someone else.

The person who develops a persecutory paranoid reaction is basically a hostile person who feels surrounded by hostility and whose major ego and superego identifications have been sadistic. When such a person regresses under stress he or she becomes overwhelmed by sadistic impulses (discharges of hostility, death-instinct promptings, etc.) and by corresponding fears (discharges of anxiety). The sadistic impulses are denied and projected upon others, who can then be viewed as the source of the fear as well (see the case of Charles G.).

At this point the paranoid person begins framing the pseudocommunity and the drama being enacted there. The paranoid is the central character of this drama, fighting against terrible odds to maintain personal dignity. The patient's persecutors, pursuers, tempters, and slanderers are the embodiment of his or her projected fantasies. Real and imagined persons are now selected to play the role called for, based upon internal perceptions of fear and hostility. Projection is obviously self-defeating, for the patient gets more of what has been projected in the long run—more fear, more sense of hostility, more desperation, until the only way out of the predicament seems to be either murder or suicide.

The obvious question is: If these defenses and all this laborious work to frame a delusional system get patients nowhere, why do they keep it up? There are three answers. The first is an old familiar one: this is the best solution of which paranoids are capable without expert help. The second is that, by means of their delusional activities, patients remain in contact with some semblance of reality—a restitutive or reconstructed reality that does connect with their everyday world. They do not give up on external reality completely, so that the road for further contact is kept open. The third answer is that all this activity—including even the senseless violence—contains the hostility by focusing it on targets other than the personality system. At least, this activity redirects the hostility up to a point. The result is that a complete deterioration in the personality is offset, at least until such time as the desperation of the patient reaches intolerable bounds. As we know, in such extremes nothing can help and the only solution seems to be suicide. The paranoid may then barricade himself or herself in a room, or take captives, and with the use of firearms invite a horrible self-destruction through a shoot-out with the police.

To a large extent paranoid symptomatology is an expression of the methods used in disposing of excess aggressive/hostile discharges in overt or covert behavior. Some of these methods are: (1) to form elaborate new preconscious fantasy systems, which are extremely hostile, by an intensive use of secondary process thinking; (2) to increase perceptual vigilance, muscular tension, and strenuous activity—watching, checking, investigating, gathering "evidence," taking elaborate precautions; (3) greatly to increase primitive defenses, especially denial and projection, and to keep up an incessant, aggressive projective discharge (distrusting others, etc.); and (4) to burst out into hostile talk and violent action. We see these various maneuvers in normal behavior, and the paranoid individual takes them to their logical—and distorted—extremes.

*Reactivation and Reorganization at Infantile Levels.* In paranoid psychoses, regression comes to a halt when fixation points are reached that correspond roughly to revived experiences of the second and third years of life. This general level is indicated by the dynamic structure of the paranoid pseudocommunity that adult patients organize—with its fears of external persecutors and accusers, its primitive defenses, the prominence of sadism and pregenital elements, and the way guilt is denied and projected. The child of two or three is still subject to more or less arbitrary parental control in matters of right and wrong. The child's superego is rudimentary and diffuse. Primitive defenses such as denial and projection are active, while repression remains weak, and pregenital, sadistic interests prevail.

Regression stops at this general level, of course, because it is here that nuclear unconscious structures are fixated and stable—preserved almost unchanged from early childhood. Around these reactivated stable nuclei a new ego organization begins to crystallize. In this new ego organization the previously repressed urges, fears, fantasies, and conflicts will escape repression and remain dominant as long as the psychosis lasts.

*Return of the Repressed and the Formation of Symptoms.* Paranoid regression goes deep, but it does not sweep everything away. An ego defensive structure still remains in which projection and denial play leading roles. There is still an ego adaptive organization, with many of its perceptual and coordinative skills intact. There are even active secondary process operations. They show damage but they are by no means ineffectual. Charles G., for example, could still telephone, drive a car along strange roads, get meals and lodging, and converse normally. Alan K. could walk alone to a psychiatric clinic, arrange his own admission, and conduct himself on the ward with at least surface normality. In other words, the unconscious conflicts and fantasies pressing forward toward expression meet a residual ego organization that is still capable of molding infantile material and directing hostile impulse discharges into a pseudocommunity. In short, the return of the repressed in paranoid psychoses may be an eruption, but it is rarely an explosion.

Nevertheless, when this eruption merely threatens, the paranoid patient experiences tremendous anxiety. When the unconscious breakthrough actually comes, the paranoid's preconscious and conscious organizations are flooded with discharges of both anxiety and hostility. The immediate result is intense confusion and a sense of impending destruction. This the patient experiences as the danger of external assault and death, but we recognize it as the danger of internal personality disintegration and death of the self. It is now impossible for the paranoid to distinguish clearly between private fantasy and social fact. And, as we have seen, a paranoid person is unable to trust anybody else so that assistance in reality-testing is never attained.

Even so, paranoid psychotics keep in contact with their surroundings. In their emergency they automatically increase projection and denial. As a matter of clinical observation, we routinely see patients beginning to increase projection even before their regression comes to a halt. The same projective operation that makes danger seem to threaten from the outside also makes them turn to the outside to meet it directly or outmaneuver it in some way. In doing so, paranoids re-establish contact with their environment, piece by piece, almost as quickly as they lose it. The new contact, of course, is on a delusional basis, since perception and interpretation are now dominated by the revived infantile fantasies and conflicts. The replacement is thus a replacement of realistic interpersonal relationships by unrealistic ones.

## EGO-SUPEREGO REGRESSION IN PERSECUTORY PARANOID DISORDERS

The ego-superego regression is not merely *partial* in paranoid reactions, as it is in neuroses, but *subtotal.* This means that the greater part of ego-superego function operates at a more or less infantile level. This statement must be enlarged upon. In spite of the delusional distortion present, good object relations are retained in paranoid disorders, much better than in comparatively severe manic, depressive, and schizophrenic disorders. This, we have already pointed out, indicates that a neurotic regression is involved as well as a psychotic regression. The dynamic picture in paranoid reactions therefore has three characteristics: (1) preservation of more of the mature ego-superego organization than in other psychoses; (2) regression to neurotic fixation levels at which, for example, one also often finds sadomasochistic relations with other persons; and (3) deep psychotic regression that necessitates delusion formation if object relations are to be preserved. In other words, the mature ego-superego that persists in this psychosis allows relatively well-organized ego adaptation — the patient handles his or her environment well — but at the same time there is a deeper regression that compels delusion formation. If we recall the social character of the pseudocommunity, its concern with other persons, and its organization, we shall see at once that both in perception and in action the patient is not nearly as desocialized as are other psychotic persons.

The psychotic regression seems to rest upon a lack of basic trust or confidence. Adults who are especially vulnerable to paranoid psychoses have not been adequately protected from excessive tension and anxiety in early infancy. Such protection requires that a mother figure furnish the buffering action which later on will be furnished by the child's own maturing ego. Without such a *substitute ego,* in the form of a protective and providing mother figure, a child must somehow develop an ego of his or her own, with whatever primitive defenses and coping behavior may be available at the time.

This is the task facing paranoid persons in their infancy. They meet it by crystallizing a precocious ego organization at a time when denial and projection are available as defenses, but mature repression is not. The infant who in adulthood will develop a persecutory paranoid disorder is an overstimulated, angry, aggressive baby whose parents allow displays of anger. This freedom to express rage is not the result of permissiveness on the part of the parents. It is the result either of indifference toward the baby's fury or of actual enjoyment of the fury. There is clinical evidence to indicate that the paranoid patient must have experienced sadistic treatment in infancy and that he or she must have reacted to this with ungovernable sadistic rage.

The precocious crystallization of ego organization distorts all later ego maturation sequences. Repression matures late and imperfectly because its early functions are already being performed by the overdeveloped denial and projection. It never reaches the level of supremacy that normal and neurotic repression reach. Thus a normally strong repressive barrier that will contain unconscious processes does not develop. A weak repressive barrier allows unconscious fantasies and conflicts to invade preconscious and conscious organizations. It permits primary process contamination of logical thought and perception. These influences are obvious in the perceptual hypersensitivities and misinterpretations of paranoid persons.

In all of this one sees a deeply regressed superego that is destructive and highly personalized, but at the same time diffuse. The paranoid superego suffers the same regressive fate as the paranoid ego. This is hardly surprising in view of the fact that the superego originated in childhood as a differentiation within the ego and that the superego always operates in close relation to the ego. The level to which the paranoid superego regresses is doubly interesting. On the one hand, it reflects some of the basic defects of paranoid personality integration; on the other hand, it accounts for some of the outstanding paranoid symptoms.

Paranoid regression carries the superego organization to a level just preceding the transfer of moral control from outside agents (parents and others), to moral control by an internalized, unified, self-regulating set of values, the post-Oedipal superego. This transfer is never a complete one, even in the most independent, mature adult. Moral self-control is always responsive to the reactions of other people. But paranoid personalities suffer from an arrest of development that interferes both with their realistic responses to others and with their ability to exercise mature self-regulation. The ease with which such persons project their own self-criticism, even when they are not psychotic, makes it look as if *superego control* and *control by outside agents* were still interchangeable, that is, still fixated at a level of unstable equilibrium. It looks as if the paranoid superego were not freed from the primitive, personalized images of childhood, and for this reason not freed from interchange with and confusion with external objects.

What paranoid psychotic regression does is to intensify a weakness that has always been present. A diffusely organized superego is reactivated, in its primitive form, with personalized sadistic images. It is this diffuse, primitive organization which the psychotic paranoid person projects as a pseudocommunity of enemies, critics, and slanderers. But even in this, the patient is only intensifying a lifelong tendency to blame failures on others, to feel discriminated against, belittled, and disliked. As children, paranoid persons were no match for their seemingly sadistic parents. When they regress as adults, their infantile ego is no match for its sadistic superego; and even when they project their superego onto others, they find themselves no match for their delusional sadistic enemies (Hesselbach, 1962).

## Delusion Formation as Reality Reconstruction

Regression stops when a new ego-superego organization is crystallized around the nuclear conflicts and fantasies of the major levels of fixation. A place in this organization must be found for the reactivated fantasies and conflicts. Since those reactivated in persecutory paranoid patients cannot be accepted as their own, and since they can no longer be kept in repression, it becomes necessary to deny them and project them. This also requires a reconstruction of one's perception of external reality, in order to give them an intelligible place. When such a reality reconstruction is carried out in a well-organized way, a paranoid delusion exists. The delusion, like the neurotic symptom, is a compromise, but the distortion of external reality that is required is much greater than that in the neurotic symptom.

Delusions are not only evidence of illness, but also signs of an attempt to work out a spontaneous cure. They are the best the patient can do at the moment in the way of adapting to a situation that places his or her fantasies on an equal footing with objective reality. The only alternative to such reconstruction under the circumstances would be to withdraw from the confusion into a stupor. It is sometimes of the greatest importance to recognize the appearance of delusions as heralding a new attempt to cope with reality.

## Childhood Background of Persecutory Paranoid Disorders

When a person decompensates under stress in adult life and develops a persecutory paranoid psychosis, it can be assumed that he or she has suffered throughout life from the following personality defects: (1) a distorted defense structure, with inadequate repression and strong tendencies to use denial and projection; (2) vulnerability to traumatic anxiety; (3) powerful fixations in early infantile conflicts; (4) incompetent reality-testing; and (5) a poorly integrated, sadistic superego system.

Some of these defects are usually apparent during adulthood, even before the psychosis surfaces. Paranoids are often tense, insecure persons who easily become anxious even though they hide these emotions behind a facade. They find it difficult getting close to other people, and cannot trust others or "open up" in relationships with them. Often paranoids are solitary ruminators, but highly inept at understanding the motivations of others. They deny responsibility for their failures, and assign blame to others or make excuses for their shortcomings. They turn everything in their life orbit into a personal reference of some sort, and tend to hold a grudge when they think they have been crossed (Sarvis, 1962; D. A. Schwartz, 1963).

What factors in childhood development are responsible for such an adult personality style? Many answers have been given to this question, not all of them in agreement. It is a difficult matter to reconstruct an adult patient's probable childhood, and different factors can often contribute to the same end result. There are few areas of general agreement (Meissner, 1978; Swanson, Bohnert, & Smith, 1970).

It is generally believed, on the basis of several decades of clinical study, that paranoid persons have not been adequately protected from excessive tension and anxiety during the first two years. Consequently, they have not been able to develop a *basic trust* in childhood. They have not had an adequate *substitute ego* at a time when they were already using denial and projection but had not yet developed adequate repression. On the other hand, they had been allowed to *express* their tension and anger openly (recall the case of Alan K.). In many instances the paranoid patient seems to have identified with whichever parent appeared to him or her the more hostile one—which results in cross-sex identification entering into the homosexuality dynamic, which we will be taking up in Chapter 16.

Often what is called sadistic treatment of a small child turns out to have been only maternal indifference, coldness, teasing, or belittling. These can *seem* cruel to the child's phenomenal understanding. Just as often, however, a parent has been actually cruel. A sadistic mother, for example, may deliberately provoke and encourage her child to become furious because she enjoys the helpless violence of the rage expressed. This seems to have been true of Alan K.'s mother. In such situations, the infant or small child is overstimulated, angry, and aggressive. Though the expression of feelings overtly may protect the child from the futility that leads to a schizophrenic personality organization, it does not allow the child to work through love-hate ambivalence in a normal way. Sometimes a parent behaves toward a child in ways that *anyone* would call cruel. Later on, persistent interference with a child's freedom of action, through parental domination and control, creates further problems. So does a home atmosphere of watchfulness, suspicion, and chronic disapproval.

The period of self-assertion and toilet training, which we described in Chapter 2, is especially important in producing a basically hostile, distrustful person. This is the period of rapid increase in muscular strength and skill, of negativistic self-assertion and independence. At this time a child can easily be pushed into hatred and temper outbursts by a teasing or domineering parent. Normally, parental love and patience soften a child's resentment at being controlled, and lead to the internalization of parental controls in the formation of his or her own superego.

The superego of paranoid persons seems to have remained fixated at a period when they were still under parental control. They develop a post-Oedipal superego also, but this remains tenuously unstable. In regressing, the patient returns to the older patterns of childhood. Outside agents, which are the paranoid's own projections, seem again to be controlling, criticizing, and threatening him or her, as they did in childhood.

Some paranoid adults clearly give evidence of sexual cross-identification. This is more common among men than women, and the pattern emerges because of a dominant, aggressive mother and a passive, relatively ineffectual father. We find paranoid patients recalling childhood fantasies in which they assumed the identity of the opposite sex, or greatly admired the opposite sex and identified with opposite-sex attitudes. There are also cases like that of Alan K., in which out of this admiration for the competence of the female, and the fear of the female, choice of a love object proved threatening and dangerous in its own right. It is probable that sex identity confusion is more likely in the child of parents who themselves show contradictions in their sex roles. We shall return to this complex issue in Chapter 16, when we take up the dynamics of homosexuality.

## Summary

Chapter 11 takes up the *paranoid disorders,* which are attempts to escape from the return of repressed ideations, and the anxiety/tension with which they are associated, through processes of denial and projection that result in more or less systematized delusions. In an opening discussion it is stressed that to understand the dynamics of both neurotic and psychotic disturbances we must give as much consideration to the return of the repressed ideas as to the initial act of primal repression. That is, there are different styles of manifesting this return of unconscious materials. In the case of the *neurotic* person, symptomatology does not reflect an intention to reject or distort reality. In the case of the *psychotic,* there are clear symptoms suggesting a turning away from and an effort to rewrite reality. *Delusions* (unrealistically false beliefs) and *hallucinations* (false and imagined sensory experiences) are the hallmarks of this distortion of reality in trying to deal with the return of the repressed mental contents. *Normal* persons attempt to change reality, but not through distortion and denial.

The paranoid disorder is therefore a psychotic reaction, in which the delusional thinking of the patient is somewhat more *systematized* than is true of schizophrenia (see Chapter 14). The delusional system of the paranoid is *ego-syntonic,* that is, in conformity with the reality outlook of the conscious ego. Thus, though the paranoid *projects* internally generated anxiety outward, unlike the phobic who considers the projected fears unreasonable and even absurd (ego alien), the paranoid is ready to make sense of the threatening circumstance by way of delusional formulations. Chapter 11 takes up four varieties of the paranoid disorder.

The first form is typified by *paranoid delusions of persecution.* The dynamic of *reverting from object-choice to identification* (see Chapter 2) is apparent in the persecutory form of the paranoid disorder. The result is an *identification with the aggressor* (e.g., a boy in fear of castration identifies with his father, rejecting mother as object). The resultant sadistic identification makes the "future paranoid" sensitive to the smallest traces of hostility, contempt, criticism, or accusation in the attitudes of other people. When the regressive process sets in later in life, the paranoid "solution" is inevitable.

Sexual problems are prominent in paranoia. In Chapter 16 we take up the specific theoretical ties of paranoia to poorly handled homosexual tendencies. In the main, homoerotic and other deviant sexual tendencies are dealt with through *denial* and *projection.* The DSM-III classification distinguishes between *acute paranoid disorder,* in which the onset of disturbed behavior is sudden, and *paranoia,* in which the onset is more gradual and insidious. The more insidious form of disorder is characterized by the most systematized and well-defended delusional system. In the early history of psychiatry such cases were termed "true" paranoiacs. It is not always easy establishing that such patients are delusional, as opposed to being highly individual, rigid, and eccentric in manner.

The background to paranoia is vigilance and suspicion. Nothing is to be taken at face value, nor are people to be trusted. Evidence running counter to the delusional theme is dismissed. Paranoids have a knack of finding what they intend to find, which is trouble. We refer to the cementing of a delusional belief system as a *crystallization*. From early life there is an expectation that the world is the source of sadistic attack, and the paranoid is prepared to counterattack. At some point, things fall in line, supporting his or her expectations. There is a crystallization of lifelong expectations in a delusional drama of some sort.

In time, a *pseudocommunity* is formed. This is a reflection of that psychotic tendency we noted in which an effort is made to reconstruct reality. The pseudocommunity organizes the observed and the inferred behavior of real and imagined people into a conspiracy, with the patient at its focus. In most cases, there are one or two persons who form the initial crux of the pseudo-community and with whom the patient enters into a dramatic albeit totally fantasied relationship. In time, the number of fantasied participants grows, as do the threats from more and more sources. It is when the threat mounts to what the patient views as an insurmountable level of persecution from others that countermeasures may be taken. It is at this point that some regrettable act of aggression may occur, in which the paranoid individual actually harms or even kills an assumed persecutor.

The second type of paranoid disorder considered in Chapter 11 is *delusional paranoid jealousy*. Along with the typical dynamics noted thus far, we see a blow to the person's narcissism in this disorder. This psychotic reconstruction of reality can expand just as readily as persecutory paranoia. Jealousies feed upon themselves and expand geometrically. The third form of the paranoid disorder considered is the *erotic paranoid disorder*, in which the patient believes erroneously that someone loves him or her but dares not make an open avowal because of other commitments or personal embarrassment. This paranoid individual can blatantly misinterpret simple acts of kindness from another person as clear signs of erotic commitment. *Ideas of reference*, in which the patient turns irrelevant, inadvertent, or meaningless signs or statements into highly personal references, abound in the clinical picture. The love expressed in erotic paranoid disorders is of a narcissistic quality, so that true object-choice is not achieved (see Chapter 16).

The last type of paranoid disorder discussed in Chapter 11 is the *grandiose paranoid disorder*. Delusions of grandeur are less frequent in paranoid disorders than are delusions of persecution. Delusions of grandeur occur in schizophrenia and mania, but in the latter disorders the delusions are not as stable, persistent, and well organized. It is probable in most of these cases that the preoccupation with grandiose plans, inventions, or self-origins helps to keep the narcissistic paranoid personality from disintegrating. It is as if the person fixes so on these expansive ideas that they afford a stability that is not otherwise available to the person concerned.

The DSM-III recognizes a *shared paranoid disorder*, which in earlier times was known as *folie à deux*. As the name suggests, this occurs when two people share the same delusional belief system. When more than two share these beliefs it is possible to speak of *folie à trois,* and so forth. Most of the delusions in *folie à deux* are persecutory.

*Regression to narcissism* and *identification with an aggressor* constitute the primary Freudian explanations of paranoia. We add to this the defense mechanism of *projection,* seen so prominently in paranoia, and we can frame an explanation of such cases. We shall leave the detailed explanation in light of homosexuality for Chapter 16. The important point to appreciate is that though paranoid patients may have homosexual involvements it does not follow that all homosexuals are paranoids. Paranoids are not so severely regressed as other psychotic patients, such as the schizophrenics. Practically speaking, this means that the paranoid psychotic has reasonably good contact with reality.

Prominent defense mechanisms in paranoia include defective repression, denial and projection. The ego-superego regression in the paranoid disorder is said to be subtotal, which means that the greater part of ego-superego functioning operates at an infantile level. Even so, the mature ego-superego that persists in the paranoid disorder is capable of maintaining an effective relationship with the environment, thanks in part to the pseudocommunity and the framing ideas of reference. In a sense, paranoid regressions have the character of both a psychotic and a neurotic regression. They are on the border region, because though there is an effort to reconstruct reality this is done more along the lines of commonly accepted "interpersonal" relations (via pseudocommunity reformulations). The psychotic aspects of the regression seem to rest upon a lack of basic trust or confidence. Paranoids seem to lack the internalized controls that a secure superego affords. Their post-Oedipal superego formation seems incapable of distinguishing between internal control and control by outside agents.

Paranoid persons seem not to have been adequately protected from excessive tension and anxiety during the first two years of life. Consequently, they have never developed *basic trust* in childhood. They have not had an adequate *substitute ego* (protective mothering one) at a time when they were already using denial and projection, but lacked adequate repressive capacities. On the other hand, they had been allowed to express their tensions and angers openly. In many instances paranoids seem to have identified with whichever parent appeared to be the most hostile, resulting in identification with the aggressor and certain cross-sex identifications resulting in homosexuality by way of narcissistic sexual proclivities.

# 12

# *Major Affective Disorders: Depressive Episode*

## *Some Background Considerations*

In Chapter 10 we presented the symptoms and likely dynamics of the *dysthymic disorder,* or depressive neurosis. We noted at the close of Chapter 10 (see p. 316) that DSM-III treats the dysthymic disorder as one of the *affective disorders.* The dysthymic disorder is, in effect, a milder form of affective disorder. The more serious manifestations of the latter clinical syndrome are called the *major affective disorders.* Traditionally, affective psychoses (major affective disorders) have included *retarded depressions* (see Chapter 10, p. 299), *manic disorders* (including manic-depressive cycles), and *involutional melancholia.* In DSM-III the manic and depressive features of a major affective disorder are termed *episodes.* Hence, there is no longer a specific category for "manic disorder" or "manic-depressive disorder" in the DSM-III system.

We therefore have two broad categories of the *major affective disorder:* a *manic episode* and a *depressive episode.* The discarded diagnoses of retarded and involutional depressions would now fall under the latter designation, that is, "major depressive episodes." If a person suffers a series of manic episodes, with or without a history of experiencing the major depressive episode, he or she would be assigned the diagnosis of *bipolar disorder.* The latter designation effectively replaces the older diagnosis of a manic-depressive disorder.

In effect, we have the historic clinical distinction being drawn here between neurotic (dysthymic, reactive, "minor") depressions and mood disorders reaching psychotic proportions (i.e., major depressive or manic episode, bipolar disorder). We shall treat psychotic manifestations of mood disorder in two chapters. In the present chapter, we shall discuss the major depressive episode (psychotic depression) as well as the depressions of the involutional period of life. In Chapter 13, we shall consider the manic episode of the major affective disorder as well as the bipolar disorder. The reader should appreciate that

DSM-III combines the material in Chapters 10, 12, and 13 in *one* section, under the single rubric of "affective disorders."

Major depressive episodes are mood disorders in which dejection, guilt, and organized delusions of self-depreciation dominate a person's thinking. The prevailing delusions are in keeping with the dejected and often apprehensive mood (termed *mood-congruent* in DSM-III). They are usually exaggerations and distortions of what any normal adult might feel after personal failure or serious loss. Psychotic depressives lose effective contact with their human environment to a much greater degree than do comparably ill paranoid psychotics. They do not, however, suffer general personality disintegration such as we commonly see in schizophrenics. Hallucinations occur but are not common in the typical psychotic depressive picture.

When a person develops a severe psychotic depression, he or she shuts out as much of the environment as possible and withdraws into deep preoccupation. The patient may do this suddenly or gradually, reflecting in the process an overwhelming absorption in some conflict over guilt and unworthiness to the virtual exclusion of everything else. When delusional self-accusations and self-debasements surface, it becomes obvious to everyone that the patient is ill. Rarely do relatives and friends take a severely depressed person's delusional statements at face value, as they so often do with paranoid psychotics (see Chapter 11). The commonest and most dangerous mistake they make is to underrate the murderous self-hate in depressions, and so to let suicide take them by surprise. Estimates are that three out of four people who commit suicide are depressed at the time of their self-destructive act (Leonard, 1974; Zung & Green, 1974). Anger and hostility are frequently cited complicating emotions in the suicidal individual (Gottschalk & Gleser, 1960; M. M. Weissman, Fox, & Klerman, 1973). The older the patient is, the more likely that a successful suicide will be carried out (Schneidman & Farberow, 1970). Suicide attempts are common in the age range of twenty-four to forty-four, but successful self-destruction seems to peak in the age range of fifty-five to sixty-five.

It is not as easy to understand psychotic depressions as it is to understand neurotic depressions. This is because of the deep regression and the loss of interest in almost everything in the environment. Discouragement, dejection, and disillusionment are not only deeper in psychotic depressions, but are also much more fixed and rigid than in neurotic depressions. Complaints are not made to stimulate others to contradict superego attacks; they are made as statements of fact. Attempts at reassurance are met with stubborn and often angry rejection. Depression has reached a delusional level; it has replaced external reality with an overwhelming internal reality. We shall have more to say about this when we come to the dynamic and developmental background of the major depressive episode.

*Definition. Major depressive episodes or psychotic depressions are mood disorders in which dejection, self-depreciation, and self-condemnation reach delusional proportions*. The sense of worthlessness and guilt persists in spite of what anyone else says or does. In fact, when other people attempt to contradict and reassure the patient, they may deepen the depression rather than lessen it. This contrasts sharply with the neurotic depression, in which patients stimulate others to contradict and reassure them so as to ward off their own superego attacks. The psychotic depressive is moved by contradictions and reassurances to heap up further self-depreciation and self-recrimination, which are more and more delusional. The deep-seated guilt relates psychotic depressions also to obsessive-compulsive neuroses, but the guilt in psychotic depressions is acutely conscious and the depressed patient is interested in almost nothing else. Moreover, he or she is usually actively suicidal in personal fantasies, which is not true of obsessive-compulsives and much less true of neurotic depressives.

*Adaptation*. There is little of adaptive value in psychotic depressions. They involve such deep regression that patients can make little use of their environment and, unlike paranoids, they do not project their internal hate and fear; or if they do, they consider any punishment received from external sources to be well-deserved. The only sense in which the term *adaptive* can be used in psychotic depression is that the patient manages somehow to escape the fragmentation and the abyss of schizophrenia. This is probably related to a better organized personality in the premorbid state.

## Clinical Aspects of Psychotic Depressive Disorders

In discussing dysthymic disorders in Chapter 10, we said that when a depression becomes acute and severe, the patient loses grip on external reality and regresses to infantile levels almost totally, but not quite (see p. 313). There is a deep but subtotal regression requiring hospitalization to protect the patient from his or her suicidal superego impulses. Under such circumstances we are no longer dealing with a neurotic depression but with a psychotic one. There are the same numerous varieties of psychotic depressions as there are of neurotic ones. Even the precipitating factors may be closely similar—at least on initial examination. But the difference in level of and totality of regression is a clearly differentiating characteristic separating neurotic from psychotic depression. We attribute the vulnerability to deep, subtotal regression in adult psychotic depressives—who may begin their illness in a neurotically depressed state—to personality defects that go back to early childhood (J. R. Hilgard & Newman, 1961), though genetic factors cannot be ruled out (Kallmann, 1958).

We have made it appear to this point that all acute, severe psychotic depressions are retarded in nature (see Chapter 10, p. 299; also, above, p. 356). Actually, clinicians have long distinguished between *agitated* and *retarded* forms of psychotic depression (Kelly & Walters, 1969; Lader, 1975). Even so, these two manifestations of psychotic depression are not so much different in fundamental pattern or in psychodynamics as they are in degree of overt activity manifested by the patient. The same patient may be agitated at first, and later on become slowed up, or retarded. Another may begin by slowing up, and only later become agitated.

*Agitated Depressions.* Many patients begin by developing more and more anxious overactivity until they grow so restless and tense that they cannot sit still or lie down for more than a few minutes at a time. They may talk incessantly about their despair and their fears, or they may limit their talk to desperate exclamations or expressions of self-hate. Many of these patients are extremely apprehensive. They seem to expect some disaster to descend upon them at any moment, often without being able to say what kind of disaster they expect. Patients pace back and forth, moan and cry, rub and pick at their body, wring their hands, and rock from side to side as if suffering a constant level of pain. Some patients anticipate severe punishment for their misdeeds; some, like the agitated patient we shall present below, demand that they be punished cruelly, and even regard punishment as inevitable in the end. There is often bitterness and resentment about being cruelly punished, even though the patient demands it. We assume that it is the archaic superego that demands it, and that it is the suffering ego that resents it with bitterness.

*Retarded Depressions.* Patients in a deep retarded depression look stunned by grief, with backs bent, arms limp, eyes fixed to the ground, brows furrowed, and faces immobile. A patient with retarded depression is the picture of a person who has lost everything in life. When he or she sits down there is a slumping of the body, a lowering of the head, and a kind of immobility that permeates the immediate environment. The patient may simply stare at the floor, head in hands. Movements are slow and leaden. The patient has enormous difficulty in initiating activity and in keeping it up. Talk is slow, repetitious, and monotonously uninflected. The patient cannot enter into a conversation. The best he or she can do is to answer questions briefly, often almost inaudibly. Sentences often trail off unfinished, as if the effort were not worthwhile.

By the time a patient has reached this degree of depression, hospitalization has become inevitable. The patient has lost his or her appetite and is usually constipated. Sleep may have decreased to as little as two or three hours nightly. The patient loses weight and looks careworn, haggard, and unmistakably ill. Retarded depressed men usually become impotent. Retarded depressed women become frigid, and their menses grow irregular or stop entirely.

Extreme cases of retarded psychotic depression are sometimes called *depressive stupor.* In these patients all spontaneous activity stops. The patient becomes almost completely unresponsive and apparently oblivious to the immediate environment. This person sits motionless, as if in a daze or a state of shock. His or her face is fixed in tense anxiety or else is without expression and immobile. In appearance the stuporous depressed patient may be indistinguishable from a stuporous schizophrenic. It is often necessary to care for the stuporous depressed patient like a helpless baby, including tube feeding, if life is to be preserved. We learn after such a patient recovers that he or she was lost during this stuporous period in fantasies of abandonment and despair.

## Depressive Delusions

In this section we shall review some of the most common forms of delusion we are likely to see in the major depressive episode.

*Delusional Self-Depreciation and Self-Accusation.* Patients who begin by calling themselves no good, worthless, a failure, and a burden now say that they are beyond all hope, outside the pale, unfit for decent human company. They are absolutely sure that they will never recover, never be able to work again, never be able to face people. Some accuse themselves of unpardonable sins, say they are degraded and despicable, call themselves fool, thief, liar, hypocrite, degenerate, and murderer. Many also project their self-depreciation and self-accusation, insisting that others secretly hate and despise them. *Ideas of reference* creep in to support the projection. To the patient, people seem to look at him or her with pity, aversion, and disgust.

Actual misdeeds, often trivial, are dredged up from the past and their importance greatly magnified. One middle-aged depressed woman, dressed in black from head to foot, including quite inappropriate black gloves, harped continually upon the fact that she had stolen a plum when she was a little girl. Such a complaint usually symbolizes childhood sin and functions like a screen memory by representing more serious sinning in a trivial act. Often less trivial misdeeds, which may have caused only temporary conflict at the time, are now recalled with crushing remorse. Still other events are given a delusional reinterpretation and then paraded as further evidence that the patient is really vile. We shall see in both our case illustrations below how self-accusation is used sadistically to punish other people as well as the patient (Buss, 1961; Fromm-Reichmann, 1959b).

In all of this, the patient is finding explanations for his or her overwhelming sense of guilt. Based on analytical theory, we suspect that the immediate source of this guilt is in superego aggression, that its origin is infantile and its intensity irrational. We also suspect that in a great many instances the self-accusations are taken over directly from the patient's own previous accusations directed against an ambivalently loved person, now reversed and turned against the self. We shall see a clear example of this in the case of Sharon R., who began accusing herself of the irresponsibility that had actually been the behavior of her brothers. Nevertheless, the patient is unable to grasp such dynamics and insists that his or her delusional beliefs are monstrous facts.

Depressive self-accusations are sometimes grandiose, so that the patient calls himself or herself the *world's greatest sinner or criminal,* a *colossal failure,* the *cause of widespread suffering and disaster.* Such delusions are really infantile fantasies of hate and destruction. They are *omnipotent* in the same sense that a small child's imaginings are. A depressed person who pictures himself or herself as the cause of ten thousand deaths by infection—as one of our patients did—is certainly far from humble. Such a patient is committing mass murder in fantasy. Hatred and resentment are suggested here, as well as a regression to a level at which the patient can no longer differentiate between the self and others, as targets of the venom needing release. Suicidal acts also express this generalized hostility, as when a depressed patient tries to take others with him or her to the grave.

*Delusional Expectation of Punishment.* Many clinicians have noted what amounts to a general law of human behavior in the fact that people who experience guilt must somehow be expiated of that burden (Rado, 1959). Many depressed persons wait in a spirit of hopeless resignation to be punished—often to be killed—feeling that they deserve it. The delusion that they are destined to be punished terribly makes some patients desperate. Some demand that the terrible suspense of waiting for the inevitable be ended—as we shall see in the case of Sharon R.—that they be put on trial, that they be imprisoned, executed, or lynched. Some psychotic depressives ask to be beaten, starved, degraded, or mutilated. Some visit punishment on themselves. It is the unbearable suspense, the frightening expectation, and the absolute conviction of terrible guilt that drive many depressed people to suicide.

*Delusions of Unreality and Estrangement.* All depressed persons experience disturbing changes in their own emotional responsiveness. On the basis of their own feelings many of them develop delusions that the world around them is changing or that they themselves are undergoing a transformation. It is not uncommon for a psychotically depressed person to believe that the nurses on his or her ward are not really nurses at all, but only women dressed up to look like nurses, that the other patients are not patients at all, and that visiting relatives are fraudulent impersonators. The whole ward, some insist, is not real. The surroundings appear to be as artificial as a stage set. All such beliefs are expressions of the patient's own altered feelings, of his or her own *estrangement.* They are exaggerations of normal projections, such as those which make it possible for us to speak of a "gloomy landscape" or a "lonely landscape." Most normal individuals have fleeting sensations of unreality at various times in their lives.

*Nihilistic Delusions.* Anxious and agitated depressed patients are especially apt to feel that some terrible catastrophe hangs over them, that a desolate loneliness is coming and the end of everything (*nihilism*) is near. In psychotic depressions these delusions are especially common in the middle-aged and the elderly.

> An elderly woman felt sure that the end of the world was at hand. She went about the house at night, heaping blankets and woolens upon her sleeping relatives to preserve them from the cold. Nothing could symbolize more vividly her own depressive loss of warmth and the impending danger of losing reality, which actually threatened her. (Fromm-Reichmann, 1959b)

> Another depressed middle-aged woman talked endlessly, in a weary monotone, of being condemned to wander over the face of the earth forever. She wanted a

steel identification band riveted on her wrist so that future generations would know who she was.

A wealthy man was certain over a period of a year that he was penniless and would starve to death. His accountant and his banker brought him certified statements of his real financial situation; but he called the statements "fakes," and he angrily tossed them aside. His lawyer also tried his hand at demonstrating the patient's financial solvency, but he finally gave up. The patient and his advisers seemed to be talking about the same thing, but actually they were not. He was talking about his bankrupt personality without knowing it, and this personality bankruptcy was a fact that no amount of reassurance or contradiction by accountant, banker, or lawyer could actually deny. When this man recovered, he remembered his nihilistic delusions clearly. He dismissed them as "just crazy ideas."

*Somatic Delusions.* A conviction that something is the matter with one's body often develops out of an earlier phase of bodily overconcern. The regressed, psychotically depressed person who has been worrying about personal health without good reason is now convinced that he or she is physically deteriorating or dying from a fatal disease.

Another source of somatic delusions is the regressed psychotic patient's experience with estrangement. Actual physiological changes, such as decreased gastrointestinal motility and secretion, may lead the patient to symbolize them in concrete terms. For example, the patient complains that his or her stomach and intestines have "gone" or that they have turned to wood. One of our male patients complained that his head was full of granite, a woman said that her bowels had become stone, and a man thought that his hands were now shaped like claws and were turning black.

Guilt itself gives rise to some somatic delusions. A guilty, depressed psychotic looks in the mirror, sees a heavily lined, haggard face, with dark rings of sleeplessness and suffering around the eyes, and interprets his or her appearance *not* as that of a sick person but as that of an evil, depraved person.

## Precipitating Factors

People who are vulnerable to psychotic depressions do not have normal personality organizations, no matter how "normally" they may live when they are well. They always have to work against certain odds. They are fundamentally deficient in self-esteem because their superego condemns readily and supports reluctantly. They need constant reassurance, appreciation, encouragement, and approval from others—the so-called narcissistic supplies—to help make up for their standing personality deficit and to offset their personal feelings of worthlessness and guilt.

An adult vulnerable to psychotic depression is not likely to admit or even to recognize this need for *narcissistic supplies* as long as he or she remains well. But the patient's way of living usually reveals it. However mature the patient may appear in other ways, there is a marked dependency on others for the maintenance of his or her equilibrium (R. W. Gibson, Cohen, & Cohen, 1959). Losses and failures for such a person—or even the mere threat of loss or failure—may prove dangerously disturbing, and sometimes catastrophic. The danger arises because, after a certain point has been reached, the depressive personality gets only a momentary lift from the love and reassurance that others can provide. Regression may grow irresistible, and unconscious conflicts may begin to emerge into preconscious and conscious thinking. Once this happens, love and reassurance from the outside are likely to lose their effectiveness.

Clinical experience suggests that there are three kinds of losses that make someone with a depressive personality vulnerable to the development of a major depressive episode (see A. T. Beck, 1972, for a comparable discussion): *loss of love, loss of personal security,* and *loss of self-esteem.* We shall take up each of these precipitating factors in turn:

*Loss of Love.* Loss of love may come in the form of a death (Abraham, 1949; Freud, 1915/1957m; Ostow, 1960; Rochlin, 1959). It may also come through separation, divorce, desertion, disillusionment, severe disappointment, rebuff, humiliation, or neglect (Briscoe et al., 1973; Paykel, 1973). Personal failure or a decline in health, status or attractiveness that threatens the loss of another person's love can also precipitate a psychotic depression. Likewise, when forbidden impulses emerge that—if acted out—would threaten loss of love, their emergence alone may be enough to precipitate depression.

*Loss of Personal Security.* Almost everyone finds deep satisfaction in having friends, possessions, prestige, and a good reputation. These afford emotional support and reassurance in times of trouble. For most people a home, familiar surroundings, and habitual ways of living also have the same significance. The loss or threatened loss of such resources is enough to sadden or discourage anybody. For a depressive personality such losses are equivalent to a loss of love. It is interesting to note that some evidence has been advanced suggesting that the incidence of psychotic depression may be higher in upper than lower socioeconomic classes (Bagley, 1973).

Despite this latter finding, we must never forget that what represents a loss to the individual depends upon his or her phenomenal assessment and the value system on which such judgments are based. Psychotic depressions can be set off by what looks to others like a minor threat or loss in status. The prompting circumstances may even look like a gain, as in the depressions that follow a job promotion. In such cases we can take it for granted that the situation has for some reason stirred up deep unconscious dangers. It symbolizes something traumatic in the patient's past, and he or she reacts as if what it symbolized has actually happened again or is about to happen.

*Loss of Self-Esteem.* We have said that depressive personalities are dependent upon love, approval, reassurance, and support from outside sources because they seriously lack self-esteem (A. T. Beck, 1972). It is nonetheless true that they need all the self-esteem that they can muster. This they derive from the same experiences that contribute to normal self-esteem—the feeling that one has lived up to one's expectations, has acted with integrity and competence, has achieved something in whatever is personally important, that is, happiness, friendliness, a respectable or an enviable status, success, power over others or service to others, and so on.

It is failure in such areas that lowers or destroys the depressive person's self-esteem. Once more we see the depressive reacting to losses and threats that might trouble anyone, but his or her way of reacting is exaggerated and long-standing. Failure to live up to personal expectations, for example, disturbs the depressed individual at a point earlier than it would a normal person, and he or she seems to view this shortcoming as if it were a serious crime.

One of our depressed patients, a small-town banker, failed to lay in a stock of currency in preparation for a town celebration. When he discovered his lapse he was powerless to remedy it; he then developed delusional fears that the townspeople might lynch him when they found money was not available. Another patient, a rather prudish young woman, committed a minor indiscretion during her vacation. Although she was criticized by few people, she withdrew from work and from her friends, called herself a "slut," and expected to be beaten and thrown into the streets.

## Onset of the Depression

Psychotic depressive reactions typically occur in the form of an attack. Patients may seem stable and well for many years before illness surfaces; after recovery they may again seem well and stable. This appearance of stability is deceptive. That is, patients manage to develop adaptive and defensive systems that work reasonably well as long as there is no exposure to certain personal losses or threats of such loss. Under ordinary circumstances they are able to maintain an effective balance of internal stresses, but if their stress tolerance is exceeded they may suddenly lose their actually tenuous grasp on an unstable personal equilibrium. At this point, we witness through the person's regression into a primitive delusional state the basic weakness of his or her personality organization.

As we have already noted, in the retarded depression we frequently see an insidious, long-term development of the disorder occurring. However, sometimes the onset of illness can be quite sudden. Everything seems to have been going along reasonably well until some personal catastrophe plunges the person into a full-blown depression within a few days. But usually we expect a gradual onset—for more than one reason. In the first place, the stressful situation may itself be slow in developing. But even when there is a sudden blow, the patient may give little immediate evidence that he or she is heading into a major depressive episode. This preliminary phase we shall call the period of incubation.

## Incubation Period

There is usually a period of incubation, lasting a few weeks or months, before the depression becomes unmistakable. During this phase many signs of rising tension and anxiety make their appearance. Patients complain of fatigue and headache, of tightness in the head and neck, of aching limbs and tired eyes. They cannot relax or get refreshing sleep. Their appetite falls off, and they may develop indigestion with constipation or diarrhea. These individuals now begin to look as tired as they feel. They suffer an overall slowing down in activity, even though they are at the same time restless, irritable, and indecisive. They lose interest in conversation, in going places, and in doing things. They are dissatisfied, discouraged, gloomy, and preoccupied.

It is not unusual for depressed persons to try to overcome their weariness and gloom by sheer effort, urged on by their relatives and friends. This seldom works. Instead, they become even more preoccupied with their life dissatisfactions. Many patients focus their major attention upon bodily overconcern. Some insist that all their difficulties stem from physical illness. They seek repeated medical examinations and resort to all kinds of medication. Their somatic complaints are intensifications of the ones already mentioned—aches and pains, fatigue and poor sleep, inability to relax, changes in appetite and in gastrointestinal functioning, and finally, a decline in sexual desire and potency. In women, menstruation usually becomes irregular or stops altogether.

## The Depression Deepens

Life now seems to have lost meaning and purpose. Things the patient used to undertake with pleasure now leave him or her unmoved or even filled with a sense of aversion. Not only does the patient lose personal emotional resonance, but a sense of empathy with other people's joys and sorrows no longer takes place. The same is true of what is read in the newspapers or seen on television and in the movies. At this point, everything in life becomes a burden—including eating and looking after personal needs.

Meanwhile, thinking difficulties arise to complicate matters. Patients find they cannot concentrate without great effort, and that they cannot think clearly or remember. They may not even be able to understand what they hear. Now and then they have fleeting feelings of estrangement—things and people look different or seem far away. All this can be frightening. Patients fear that they are losing their minds and wonder what is happening to them.

It is true that anyone as anxious, worried and preoccupied as this might have thinking difficulties, whether depressed or not. But the depressed person is justified in worrying about the growing incompetence. Something negative is actually taking place. The everyday world of people and things is losing its meaning because unconscious processes, belonging to another world, are on the verge of breaking through. When they do break through, the patient's world of social reality will largely be replaced by an unrealistic delusional world (pseudocommunity). The patient will then be in regression to infantile conflicts and memories of long-past feelings, and a sense of hatred will rule his or her life.

In reaction to the increasing incompetence the patient now complains of being no good, a failure, worthless, a burden to everyone, and so forth. In such depressive complaints there are both self-accusation and an indictment of others. If a loved one now offers reassurance, the patient simply repeats the complaints, often focusing them around the relationship with the loved one. The depressed person's voice is full of vengeance, not of meekness.

The patient takes his or her lost emotional responsiveness as a sign that love can no longer be given to others or expected from them. This, too, is a mingling of an attack upon the loved one and upon the self. If we listen dispassionately to such a patient, the hostile note comes through every time. We see the depressed person telling a loved one a negative tale, again and again, and there is little doubt that both individuals are suffering the pain involved, even though it is the patient who is supposedly the target of the hostility being expressed.

### Case of Sharon R.: Agitated Psychotic Depression

Sharon R., a single woman aged forty-eight, found herself facing heavy expenditures to help her two brothers. They had for years been a constant financial drain upon her. She had never received from them either appreciation or repayment in return for her sacrificing her own security and pleasure. Now it became clear that, even though her previous sacrifices had been in vain, she would have to make still further ones.

Sharon became more and more tense with time, more anxious and more irritable. In the daytime she could not concentrate; at night she could neither relax nor sleep. Her angry resentment grew until she considered killing herself so that her brothers would be left to shift for themselves. Eventually the dreaded family conferences came. When they were over Sharon found herself a thousand dollars poorer. There was no prospect of an end to the demands upon her purse. During a vacation in the country she set out three times to drown herself, but each time she could not take the final step.

In the end Sharon went to her old family physician. To him she poured out her angry complaints against her brothers, her own feelings of misery and hopelessness, and even her suicidal plans. He advised her to go to a hospital at once, which was good, but he also added his opinion that, in her own way, she was just as bad as her brothers. The latter comment proved to be the turning point. She was looking desperately for sympathy and love, but what she got was a harsh rebuke. She now turned away from the realistic crisis that faced her and began attacking herself with accusations which soon reached delusional proportions. It was then that relatives took her to a psychiatric hospital.

Hospitalization brought no improvement. Sharon sat staring in front of her, silent, tearful, and dejected, wringing her hands, rubbing her forehead, and picking at her skin. She was the picture of a woman in profound grief. She rarely spoke. When she did she said that she had no feeling and no thoughts, that she was like a statue, a vegetable, lifeless. To an experienced eye it was obvious that she was deeply preoccupied and in an emotional turmoil. Before long both the preoccupation and the inner turmoil came to light.

Sharon began to grow less withdrawn and more aware of her surroundings. As she re-established contact with the hospital environment, her quiet grief gave way to restless agitation, and in place of brooding there were outspoken self-accusations and insistent demands that she be punished. It became clear that she was no longer living in terms of social reality, but rather in terms of a delusional world of her own. The whole hospital, with its patients and personnel, grew to be a stage on which she acted out her fantastic drama of self-degradation and hate.

Now Sharon denounced herself venomously as a person steeped in sin, a liar, a hypocrite, and a cheat. These were all accusations that she had previously leveled at her two brothers. She confessed publicly an affair she had had with a married man many years earlier. She demanded repeatedly, angrily, tormentingly, that she be brought to trial for her supposedly terrible crimes, that she be imprisoned for life, that she be beaten and thrown naked into the street. She continually harped on the refrain, "Get it over with!" meaning, "Bring me to trial and punishment!"

Sharon's delusions spread. She said that autos were painted yellow and sent past the hospital to advertise that she was a dirty, yellow dog. When a door on one of the nearby houses was painted red, she told everyone that this was to show the world that she was a "whore" (*ideas of reference;* formation of a *pseudocommunity*). She kept demanding that she be debased and made to scrub floors and do menial work. Her angry insistence, and her way of following nurses and doctors about with her noisy self-accusations and demands, made everyone dread seeing her. She seemed bristling with hostility. Eventually, Sharon was able to work through her depression, recover her composure, and return to her previous work.

*Discussion.* Here we see the psychotic reaction of a woman frustrated by a final disillusionment in her emotional life. She had never been able to establish a stable love relationship with a man outside her family. All her life she remained attached to her brothers, loving them enough to rescue them over and over from personal disaster, hating them for always failing her and neglecting her callously when they were not in desperate need. Eventually she reached a point where she could no longer blind herself to the futility of her sacrifices and the certainty that she could expect nothing whatever in return. When she was so full of unbearable hate that she made plans to kill herself so as to spite her brothers, the last person to whom she appealed for help told her bluntly that she was as bad as her worthless brothers. This was the final frustration that tipped the scales. It focused all her violent hatred upon her already guilty, ambivalent self.

As we have seen, Sharon at first reacted to this final blow by withdrawing into what looked like deep grief. She was stunned. Because of her personality defects, however, the withdrawal led to a deep regression and to hateful self-accusations. In her delusions she now accused herself of her brothers' faults, which were not really her own, and she raised the ghost of an old sin—her long-buried love affair with a married man—to bear witness against her. She attacked herself sadistically, demanding outrageous punishments and making everyone around her dread the sight of her.

Can any sense be made of such delusional, self-defeating behavior? Psychotic behavior always makes sense if we understand the meanings being affirmed by the personality system concerned. Under the stress of her frustration, and given her personality defects, Sharon suffered a sweeping disintegration and regression. This psychic process reactivated an early phase of her development when the psychodynamic balance was quite different. In this regressive phase her ego integrations were relatively weak, and they were dominated by an abnormally severe, archaic superego. As we shall see later in the chapter, such an interpretation helps to make the otherwise absurd but terribly dangerous behavior of depressed delusional patients intelligible. In this particular case there is also a certain grandiosity—all the world is interested in her sins—which serves to link it with the paranoid disorders (Chapter 11) and with manic disorders (Chapter 13) as well.

### Case of Gary W.: Retarded Psychotic Depression

Gary W., a businessman aged forty-three, father of four children, was brought to a psychiatric clinic by his wife. She said that he was deeply depressed and could not work, that he felt he was a disgrace to his name and ought to die. He had made no suicidal move; but she was frightened because she knew that if he once made up his mind to kill himself she could do nothing to stop him. His own complaints were as follows: "I've 'had it.' I've failed everybody. I'm no damned good. I'll never be able to face anyone again. I feel numb but I'm frantic inside. This is worse than being dead."

Gary sat slumped in the chair, his chin sunk on his chest, his eyes fixed on the floor, the picture of dejection and despair. He looked more like a sick man of sixty than a man of forty-three. After his first statements he spoke only when spoken to, his answers were brief, and his voice was monotonous and sometimes inaudible. His face was masklike, but his eyes were troubled and his brow was furrowed. Occasionally he spoke with disgust about himself, and when he did he looked bitter and he almost snarled. He agreed to hospitalization with only a nod. He got up heavily and moved off like a man being led to prison.

*Immediate background of the depression.* Gary's wife said that he had never recovered from his mother's death five months earlier. When she was found to have incurable cancer Gary was stunned. Why hadn't it been discovered earlier? He blamed the doctors first and then himself. If he had paid more attention to her, he said, and made her get more frequent medical checkups, this would never have happened. "She was always so uncomplaining—a saint if there ever was one." He kept repeating, "I shouldn't have let this happen. I shouldn't have let it happen." Sometimes he said, "How could she *do* this to me!"

When the will was read, it was discovered there was a codicil leaving Gary a larger share of his mother's equities than his siblings got. They were polite but cool. One of them remarked that of course he had stayed close to his mother in recent years. This was true but unjust, since he had always been close to her, and they all knew it.

*Mourning becomes melancholia.* After the funeral Gary remained quiet, sad, and silent. He ate poorly, toyed with his food, spoke little at meals, and was unresponsive to his family, which had never been true before. He seemed always tired. He would throw himself into a chair immediately after dinner. He went to bed early, but his sleep grew worse and worse, until he was reading half the night and getting up for coffee at four or five o'clock. Interest in sex disappeared. Gary's wife accepted all this as the not unnatural mourning of a favorite son. She tried to comfort him but he pushed her away. She persuaded him to get a medical checkup. He was still able to put up a good front away from home, so he got a clean bill of health.

As time went on Gary did not get better. He got worse. He could hardly drag himself to work. He confessed one evening to his wife that someone at the office had told him he was slipping. He could not remember things or concentrate on his work. Everything worried him. It was as if he were "holding things off." He checked and rechecked his work, but his mistakes were increasing. He said, "I guess I'm getting old before my time." He began calling himself a lazy bum, a "has-been," and an "also ran."

His growing silence at the table threw a pall over every meal. Gary began excusing himself and leaving soon after the meal started. His wife now felt that he was carrying his grief too far. She told him in private how upsetting his behavior was to the children. He was surly at first and then apologetic. He could not help it, he said, and he was beginning to realize the kind of man he was and trying to face it. He said that he had always been selfish and demanding, that he was neglecting the children just as he had neglected his mother and let her die. He added, "I've lived as if the world revolved around me. I realize now what life must have been like for you and the children all these years."

Following this Gary seemed to come out of his shell a bit, but he was also more disturbed. He sat through meals and tried to converse, but his talk was forced and everybody felt uncomfortable. Meanwhile his wife noticed that he was getting hesitant and indecisive, even about little things like choosing a tie or a sweater to wear for the day. Sometimes he seemed lost in thought, motionless, right in the middle of dressing. Sentences were left unfinished. Gary sighed a great deal. On the next trip to his physician he failed to conceal his despondency. A prescription raised his spirits for awhile, but it also made him more restless and sleepless than before.

*The acute onset.* One evening at dinner Gary put down his knife and fork and left the house. His wife followed him and brought him back. They went upstairs together and he told her that he had reached the end of the road, that he could not go on. Now he knew how hateful he was. Look at what he was doing to everyone. His brothers and sisters were right—he was as good as a murderer. How could he face his own children with this on his conscience? If they knew what he was like they would not stay in the same room with him. He could not go on pretending that he was a decent, responsible man when he had broken every trust he had ever been given. He went on to tell her about a premarital affair. When Gary's wife told him that she did not care what he had done before marriage he stared at her as though she had struck him. It was then that she called in their doctor and arranged for his admission to a psychiatric clinic.

*Behavior in the clinic.* Gary gave a general impression of indifferent submissiveness. He took no initiative, he went where he was led, and he accepted hospital restrictions without a word. Most of the time he sat or stood alone. When he walked he moved slowly and heavily, with head bowed and body stooped. He ate only when coaxed. Sometimes he had to be reminded to chew the food he had in his mouth. If he was prodded he sometimes became nasty. He slept only two or three hours a night, and he never wanted to get up to face another day. He rarely spoke unless spoken to, but he often moaned, muttered, and sighed. When asked what he was saying he only stared and said, "Nothing, nothing."

During therapeutic sessions Gary was formal, grave, and uncommunicative. He complained that everything was an effort and useless, that his head was "in a vise," that he could remember nothing and concentrate on nothing. "I'm just going downhill," he would say, "and you know it as well as I do." He spoke briefly in a monotone of his failures and guilt. He was utterly convinced that everything was his own fault. "You'll tell me this is an illness," he would say, "but there's no excuse for being like this. It's just the final failure." His whole life now seemed nothing but "failure and broken trust." He had failed his mother, his wife, and his children. He had never really loved anybody in his life and he was unfit to be loved. He paraded all his mistakes. He wished he had a broken leg or a real illness to justify the way he felt. His wife and children seemed to be a thousand miles away. At times he could not picture them at all.

*Further delusional development.* Gary's most bitter self-reproach now was that he had left his wife to care for their four children alone, that he was selfish, irresponsible, and "a hell of a figure of a man." When his wife visited him, Gary would at first simply stare at her, or look away and say that it was no use, that she had better forget him. As he began to regain contact with his surroundings he grew more cruel. He used self-condemnation and contempt in such a way as to undermine every ideal his wife had ever had of him. He repeated statements that had hurt and frightened her before he was hospitalized. Sometimes he told her to take the children somewhere and start a new life without him. Other times he told her to bring the children with her so that they could see the kind of father they had. After some of these visits the wife needed therapeutic help herself.

Gary developed a few delusions of reference. He knew that everybody hated him from the way they looked at him and walked away from him. The patients must know all about him from the doctors. The nurses looked pityingly at him. One of them seemed sad and disappointed when she was with him. If they knew the kind of life he had lived they would despise him. He insisted that he was not sick, but only a "gutless quitter." His mother had always said, "No W's are ever quitters!" It was a good thing she was in her grave and was spared the disgrace of seeing him mindless and a quitter.

There was something else that he had been hiding. He had been turning in "dishonest reports" at the office. Gary expected to be prosecuted for this and sent to prison. He knew it would be found out sooner or later. He suspected that the hospital staff was holding him until his company could work up a case against him and put him into the penitentiary. He would rather face it now, he had no defense. "I've led a Dr. Jekyll-Mr. Hyde life. I've always known about Mr. Hyde, and now everybody else will know." He wrote a letter to his firm, admitting his wrongdoing and offering his resignation, which the firm refused. (There actually had been serious mistakes and omissions in his reports after his mother's death.) Gary also brought up an old income tax error that had long since been straightened out. He had been expecting every day for weeks, he said, that the IRS would come and claim him.

*Signs of improvement.* The ideas of self-reference were actually signs of improvement. They represented an attempted return to reality relationships by way of *delusional reconstruction (restitution).* The fact that Gary could talk about them and write a letter, even a delusional letter, was a further sign of a return toward a lost reality. He had spent many weeks in a fog of psychotic unreality, wrestling with imagined crimes and conflicts belonging to a forgotten childhood. Now he was getting a little paranoid on his way back toward health. Besides, his expressions of guilt and worthlessness had less finality and doom about them than earlier.

There were other signs. Sleep and eating were noticeably better. Constipation, as characteristic of depressions as insomnia, was disappearing. Gary was talking more and smiling sometimes. Once he even laughed during a television show, and then looked startled, as if he had been caught laughing at a funeral. He was able to sit and read a bit, and eventually to play cards in a group. Like most depressives, he could not admit improvement until long after everyone else had seen it.

*Therapy and recovery.* Early in any severe depression treatment is aimed primarily at keeping the patient alive and keeping him free from the demands of a normal environment, which are more than he can possibly meet. Electroconvulsive treatments are administered in many cases to cut short the more acute phase and bring the patient back into effective contact. Typically, the patient is given an anesthetic and an intravenous injection of a muscle relaxant to prevent injury when the convulsions induced by the electroshock occur. A typical course of treatment is six to twelve induced convulsions given at the rate of three per week. More treatments than this are rarely called for because most patients who do in fact respond to electroconvulsive therapy do so within this range of administrations (see Chapter 20; Mendels, 1970).

Once a reasonable contact with reality has been re-established, the insight form of therapy can be introduced. While Gary was in the clinic he gained considerable insight into his own personality problems and their childhood origins. Some of his dynamics we shall include in the discussion of his family background, but first we shall mention a few specific things about his more immediate past.

Toward the end of his stay in the clinic, Gary recalled much of his delusional material spontaneously. He now found it absurd; he could not understand how he had ever believed it. He seemed to himself at the time, he said, to be standing before the world as an utterly worthless failure, a man devoid of love, responsible for his mother's death and his family's ruin, with even his name disgraced by dishonesty at work.

He remembered that when his mother's will was read he had felt a glow of pride over her preference for him. This was at once followed by guilt, which received a boost from his sibling's remark, as we have seen. He was angry over the remark, but as usual he was not able to retort. This reminded him that he had never been able to get angry unless he lost control. Whenever his sister had teased him beyond endurance in childhood, for example, instead of fighting back he would go out to the back porch and spit. He remembered also that when his mother lay dying he had wished her dead for her own sake, instead of praying for a miraculous cure. This had made him wonder how much his love for his mother might have been motivated by secret hopes of profit.

After his mother died Gary felt angry as well as sad. He found himself making comparisons between his mother and his wife in which his mother came out much the better of the two. His loyalties had always been divided between them, and he had felt double guilt because the two women obviously disliked each other. He recalled slighting things that his wife had said about his mother, which now seemed sacrilegious, and his mother's poor opinion of his wife. He wondered what his mother would have said if she had known about their premarital sexual relationships. Perhaps now that she was dead she knew. Gary was obviously identifying with his mother. He began to hate his wife and the children she had given birth to.

It was with this background of feeling that Gary confessed his premarital affairs to his wife. It was a typical depressive confession, always two-edged and usually sadistic. His stunned confusion over what his wife replied—that she did not care what he had done before their marriage—had two sources. Here was a mother substitute saying something that would have outraged his dead mother; and here was his wife in effect sanctioning their own premarital behavior when he had always been consciously guilty about it. Though he had feigned a liberal outlook on premarital sex, living together before marriage, and other aspects of the "sexual revolution" taking place during his adulthood, the truth was quite otherwise. Due to personality predilections and a strong religious orientation—fostered, of course, by his mother but also by his father—Gary had never quite resigned himself to such sinful violations of a religious moral code. He tried to be "modern," but this was only an act.

When Gary got well enough to go out walking with his wife, his children came to see him. He spent a few weekends and paid one visit to his place of business before he was discharged. Afterward he went with his wife on a vacation, during which he became mildly elated and then mildly depressed, before he settled down to a normal pattern. In turning now to an account of the patient's childhood we shall be dealing with a composite picture derived from accounts given by Gary himself and by his wife and sister, neither of whom shared his admiration for his mother.

*Remote background of the depression.* Gary was the youngest of four children. His sister was four years older than he, his brothers six and eight years older. To his mother he seemed "the flower of the flock." His father was seventeen years older than his mother—an austere, pious, silent man who rarely needed to do more than speak to the children to make them behave. When he punished them he was severe but never angry. He was an antivivisectionist and opposed to the use of alcoholic beverages on religious grounds. It goes without saying that sexual promiscuity was a mortal sin in the father's eyes. Gary was always frightened of his father. In fact, he pictured God as his father's father. His father died when Gary was twenty.

The description of Gary's mother came from three sources. Gary had admired her all his life; his sister had mixed feelings about her; his wife disliked and resented her. Their accounts were not much at variance, but their emphases and interpretations were. She seems to have been as piously strong-minded as her husband, but affectionate, accessible, and talkative. She kept herself the emotional center of the family, while at the same time deferring to her husband, whom she revered.

Gary's sister called her mother straitlaced and idealistic, a woman who never allowed her children to criticize anyone but who gave her own judgments freely to guide them. She ran things in the home without seeming to do so. She treated her children with affection as long as they conformed to her wishes. She disapproved of all her sons' girlfriends, but once marriage became inevitable she allowed herself to be won over. Gary's struggle for independence was the hardest of all.

Gary's wife called his mother self-righteous, a holy martyr, shrewd and posses-sive, a woman who gave moral opinions with her chin held high. You either agreed with her or you had no standards, she was always in the right, a puritanical snob. Gary at his very worst was like her. He never got free from her influence. The mother liked to say, "Love conquers all!" but what she meant was her love. She threw a shadow over their lives which could not be "run out from under."

During therapy Gary modified his idealistic conception of his mother consider-ably, but she still came out rather well. He said at first that he owed all that was best in him to her—his tastes, his feelings, his moral outlook, and desire to do his best. He treasured the knowledge that he had always been her pet, and it took him some time to see that he had paid a price for this advantage. As long as he could remember he had placed her approval before everything else. She had seldom punished him, but whenever he erred she became silent, solemn, hurt, and with-drawn. This he could never endure. He always gave in, even when he felt angry and exasperated. She usually referred to herself in the third person—"Mother doesn't like you to do that"—which made her seem more a sacred principle than a flesh-and-blood woman. Three things she could never forgive: irresponsibility, dishonesty, and immorality. Another thing was Gary's choice of a wife. She gave up open opposition when she realized that she was going to lose, but she never became reconciled to her youngest son's marriage.

With the suffering, hate, and penitence of a depression now behind him, with his mother dead and his wife at home with the children, Gary had a chance to look at his life through different eyes. He could begin to give up his dead mother and turn his affection toward his living wife and children. The shadow of his mother's displeasure was still there and so were his infantile conflicts, but the shadow was lighter and the conflicts less intense. When he was nearly well, Gary seemed remarkably independent, self-reliant, considerate, and kind. His wife said that these were his normal traits. He had evidently regained his previous adult personality structure with a good deal of insight into what lay beneath it.

## Dynamic and Developmental Background

Psychotic depressions are common and usually easy to recognize clinically. Analysts generally agree that they involve profound regressions in persons who are more than ordinarily dependent and oral in their personality orientation. Analysts tend also to agree that psychotic depressions always include delusions of guilt, self-depreciation, and self-condemnation. There are still controversies regarding the relation of psychotic depressions to neurotic depressions. We shall follow the prevailing trend, already set forth in the chapter on dysthymic disorders, according to which the milder forms are called neurotic and the more severe and sweeping forms psychotic.

Denial and distortion of external reality may occur to some extent in neurotic depression, in order to make external reality seem to conform to internally generated fantasies and conflicts. But whenever such denial and distortion reaches delusional proportions, we are dealing with a psychotic disorder—that is, a depressive episode of a major affective disorder. This holds true whether or not the patient is able to compensate for defective reality-testing and to conceal his or her delusional thinking. The same point can be made in relation to psychotic paranoid reactions, as we have seen, and to psychotic schizophrenic disorders, as we shall demonstrate in Chapter 14. There are always some patients who, in spite of psychotic delusions, somehow manage to maintain object relations sufficiently to hide the fact that they are at the time psychotic. These last are the patients who seem psychotic to their therapist but to no one else, sometimes not even to themselves. For the majority, however, the psychotic regression renders the patient incompetent to deal with his or her everyday object relations. It is with the majority that we are here concerned.

## MOURNING AND MELANCHOLIA

The basic psychoanalytical explanation of mourning and melancholia is as follows. While in childhood, the person who eventually becomes depressed has experienced a strongly ambivalent attitude toward a love-object with sadistic tendencies. This relationship is formed very early in life, in the oral stage of psychosexual development. We can say that the person has framed a fixation around this ambivalent tie to a sadistic love-object. In addition, there is early identification or (oral) "incorporation" of this love-object's behavior into the rudimentary ego and *especially* the primitive or archaic superego. The psychopathological aspects of this dynamic arise when the ambivalent love-object is *lost* through death, desertion, or related separations of a traumatic nature. (F. Brown, 1961; R. W. Gibson, Cohen & Cohen, 1959; Klein, 1950).

Thanks to the primitive identification, the sadism and hatred that the love-object has overtly modeled is taken in by the developing personality of the eventual patient—along with more positive kinds of attitudes and outlooks that the love-object has displayed toward the eventual patient. Freud suggested that when the sadistic side of the love-object is activated by directing these hostile behaviors toward others and the self as well, we witness the regressive behavior of the psychotically depressed individual (Freud, 1915/1957m, p. 249). Freud suggested that not infrequently the sadism (hostility toward others) and masochism (hostility toward self) to be seen in a depression can actually be pleasurable (combination here of life and death instincts) (ibid.). However, there is clearly a wretched side to the depression experienced by the regressing individual. Freud (1921/1955m) once said that the melancholic suffers from an "ego divided" (p. 109) in which one side side (*archaic superego*) rages against the other side (*primitive ego*).

So the depressed person who regresses to a psychotic degree enlivens fixated material relating to ambivalence, oral incorporation (primitive identification), and the resultant sadistic infliction of mental anguish and pain by way of acting out the lost love-object's sadistic tendencies. The direction of this sadistic hostility is both outward, toward others, and also inward via the archaic superego incorporations, resulting in a form of masochism as well as serious personal deterioration that can result in suicide. We did not have enough clinical data on which to assess the lost love-object of Sharon R.'s case, but Gary W.'s lost love-object was almost surely his mother. Note the additional dynamic in the fact that, by enacting her sadistic side toward his wife, Gary was literally aggressing against his mother's enemy. Through identification Gary was keeping his mother's sadism alive!

Identification can be seen in both normal and abnormal forms of melancholia (Rochlin, 1959). The mourner tends to take over some of the characteristics of the lost love-object, acting, speaking, looking, or living as he or she did. It is as though the mourner were saying to the world, "My loved one lives again in me!" This is usually done without awareness; it is rarely a conscious mimicry. Friends and relatives notice it before the mourner does. Nevertheless, it seems to be a normal defense against crushing loss, a process of taking into oneself parts of the behavior and appearance of the lost person, so that they are in a sense preserved alive.

There are differences, however, between normal individuals in mourning and a psychotic slipping into severe depression. Psychotic depression may begin with identification and acting out that we see in normal mourning; but the sweeping regression that soon develops transforms the clinical picture into a life-and-death struggle between a sadistic superego and a cringing but also sadistic primitive or infantile ego. The situation is often compared with that in severe compulsive reactions, like those we have discussed in Chapter 7. There, too, we witnessed the struggle between an archaic superego and a cringing infantile ego. But the level of regression in compulsives is neurotic. The patient may act out a drama of ritual self-punishment, but these fantasies and conflicts do not swallow up the realistic world as they do in psychotic depressions. We next look at the character of fixation and regression in psychotic depressions.

### FIXATION AND REGRESSION IN PSYCHOTIC DEPRESSIONS

In psychotic depressions there is regression to the earliest levels, just as in neurotic depressions. The regression reactivates conflicts and fantasies belonging to phases of development much earlier than those seen in (anal) obsessive-compulsive disorders, to phases of oral-dependent relationship in which the frustration of dependent wishes provoke savagery. The patient who regresses to psychotic levels when he or she grows depressed loses the relatively good object relationships that the neurotic depressive manages to retain.

This *loss of object relations*—ties to other people, a sense of real actions and real things taking place external to fantasy—makes the whole clinical picture different from that of neurotic depressives. In normal and neurotic life it is the meaningful relationship with external reality that helps keep a person free from being overwhelmed by his or her internal reality, with all of its primitive fantasies and conflicts, with its primary processes and its lack of stable objects. The mechanism of projection is used very little in psychotic depression, so that when the patient slipping into the latter disorder senses an upsurge of hostility, he or she is overwhelmed by it and cannot direct it onto others in the style of a paranoid. It is as though a primitive sadistic hostility had escaped from repression with an irresistible rush, disintegrating ego-superego organizations and reducing defenses to infantile levels.

The manifest products of such a regression seem to represent a split into two more or less reciprocal organizations, one of which has been historically equated with the sadistic archaic precursor of the superego, and the other with the archaic infantile (primitive) ego. Actually the clinical picture is not as distinct as this. What we find is a person who hates, abuses, and abominates himself or herself, but who also can be hateful and abusive to others as well. This hatred of others is more realistic by far than the self-directed hatred. It is true, as we have pointed out above, that psychotically depressed people are capable of killing loved ones as well as themselves, and it is true that this seems an extension of self-hatred to these others. But psychotically depressed persons do not typically call for the cruel, inhuman punishments for others that they commonly do for themselves.

Instead of a mere increase in unconscious guilt, such as neurotic depressives show through their complaints of inferiority, worthlessness, and hopelessness, the psychotic depressive experiences overwhelming conscious guilt. Instead of merely feeling unloved and unlovable the psychotic feels personally vile, hateful, and utterly despicable. The violence of self-hatred exceeds anything seen in neurotic depression, and the psychotic's actual inaccessibility to objective reality comes out clearly the moment anyone tries to provide support, assistance, or reassurance.

To validate the overwhelming self-hatred that he or she is experiencing, the psychotic depressive develops unmistakable delusions. In this sense the delusions are adaptive, even though maladaptive. Through them patients reconstruct their world in such a way that they can find a place in it. Admittedly, this reconstruction of reality contradicts facts, and all too often puts the depressed person in jeopardy (e.g., suicide). The alternative would be to disintegrate still further, to become acutely schizophrenic and run the risk of nonrecovery. It is probably for this reason that about 80 percent of patients suffering a major depressive disorder recover, whereas the figures are much lower for schizophrenics (Baastrup & Schou, 1967; Becker, 1977). Of course about a third of those who recover from such a serious depression reflect serious social impairment, especially if they have not been given supportive psychotherapy (i.e., the recovery occurs through spontaneous remission without insight therapy as a follow-up).

If we bear in mind the obvious fact that, no matter how deeply a person regresses in a depression, he or she never literally acts like an infant or sounds like an infant, we shall find it convenient to characterize the life-and-death struggle of the psychotic depressive as a fundamentally infantile one. It is a struggle between the revived derivative of a sadistic superego, a product of the internalization of the sadistic love-objects in infancy, and a sadomasochistic ego, a product of reciprocally developed reactions to the introjected love-objects of infancy. The regressive psychotic state is not like anything in normal infancy. Instead it represents the pathological *adult products* of early infantile interaction between the patient as an orally dependent infant and the others around him or her, as the patient experienced them at that early life period.

## Personality Predilections in Major Depressive Episodes

There is considerable agreement among practicing clinicians that psychotic depressions appear in certain kinds of adult personalities and not among others. In the present section we shall review some of the clinically observed personality tendencies often seen in such patients, and then discuss a purely biological-genetic explanation of psychotic depression that has many advocates today.

*Deficiency in Self-Esteem.* Depressive personalities are deficient in their capacity for maintaining a normal, stable level of self-esteem. They can never generate enough to meet their own personality demands. As a result, they may appear merely humble and chronically self-disparaging. They belittle themselves, are apologetic, and compare themselves unfavorably with others (Arieti, 1959; R. W. Gibson, Cohen, & Cohen, 1959). They may ingratiate themselves with their associates by deferring to them or by playing the ignoramus or even the clown. They may seek to overcome their negative self-assessments by trying to achieve or be successful in order that they will be praised by others. When praise comes, depressive personalities tend to have difficulty accepting it. They become anxious instead.

*Dependence upon Others.* It is because the depressed person cannot deal with evidence of his or her personal worth that we witness a constant search for support from others. Depressive personalities are therefore often said to be dependent. This in itself says nothing. Everyone is dependent upon someone else. The critical point is that when depressive personalities have their external sources of support threatened, they deteriorate rapidly and lose contact with reality. They are unable to defend themselves against their own inner hostility. Narcissistic supplies to the depressive person are as essential as insulin is to the severely diabetic individual.

*Reality Adaptation.* In their patterns of reality adaptation depressive personalities give many signs of the infantile needs and anxieties from which they have suffered and which they have tried to master. The stern lesson that they overlearned in early childhood was that any failure to comply with parental wishes meant an immediate loss of love and care, the desolate experience of loneliness and emptiness. The child who is given the alternative between love and desertion is hardly likely to express an independent pattern in order to run the risk of desertion. Under constant threat of desertion by the parents, this child is likely to smother his or her frustrations, give up all efforts to achieve

*Freud and his "inner circle" of closest supporters circal 1920. Front row: Freud, Sandor Ferenczi, and Hanns Sachs. Back row: Otto Rank, Karl Abraham, Max Eitingon, and Ernest Jones.*

independence, and frame a reality in which some semblance of conscious self-worth is achieved by allowing others to counter the raging self-hatred going on unconsciously.

As an adult, the depressive personality must adapt to external reality in such a way as to ensure the narcissistic supplies that are by now fundamental to life itself. For a *cautious* adult this means making certain at all times that he or she does not forfeit the approval and support of others. For a more *enterprising* adult it means always striving for achievement and attractiveness, so as to stimulate expressions of love, admiration, or envy, the outward signs that one is worthy and esteemed. Many retirement depressions of elderly achievers arise because of the loss of the source of such continual expressions.

A realistic conception of the external world is beyond the reach of such persons. In their childhood they construct a world dominated by infantile attempts at mastering threats of desertion. Their reality-testing is continually distorted by an anxious emphasis upon securing narcissistic supplies. In adulthood the basic unconscious orientation is still that of an insecure, helpless child in a world of powerful adults, who give love and care only when they are pleased, and without whose love and care even survival becomes impossible. Depressives act as if the significant people in their lives were parents, not contemporaries, and as if they were called upon continually to demonstrate that they are innocent, compliant, and worthy.

*Social Interaction.* It is clear enough that, like paranoid personalities, the depressive lacks *realistic role representations* (Cameron, 1947; Cameron & Magaret, 1951). There is a basic difference between these two disorders, however. Paranoid persons expect others to attack them. They themselves feel innocent, and they stand on the offensive, ready to retaliate for the expected attack. Depressive persons expect to be deserted, rebuffed, or belittled. They stand ready to do whatever they can to appease others and win their approval. Depressed patients feel guilty and expect punishment as expiation. They have one great advantage over paranoids: as long as they remain clinically well, they are able to accept closeness and to respond with pleasure to signs of affection and approval. Their difficulty is that they can never get enough or be sure of a future supply.

A depressive personality can manage to live in reasonable comfort and security if a situation can be found that repeats in some form the one in which he or she grew up. Some adults actually go on living with their parents indefinitely and perpetuate a childlike emotional relationship. A depressive man may marry a woman who treats him much as his mother did; a depressive woman may find a husband who is willing to be a second father to her. Even in business and professional careers such persons may find it possible to play a childlike role successfully. They may subordinate themselves to the dictates of parental figures or arouse continual expressions of admiration such as a dependent small child seeks from his or her mother.

Not every depressive personality is as fortunate as this; even those who are may discover that human relationships are subject to change without notice. Husbands grow less attentive and indulgent; wives get tired of always giving protection and getting none in return; the patterns of employers and of fellow workers are seldom stable; and one's competence and attractiveness may begin to wane. People grow tired of someone who is constantly self-disparaging. One day the depressive personality may do something that cannot escape severe criticism. If this sensitiveness to hurt and rebuff forces everyone to be overcareful, it can lead eventually to resentment, to the very rejection that the depressive personality cannot tolerate.

*Hostility.* Depressive personalities, like paranoid personalities, face the same basic problem of excessive internalized hostility (Fromm-Reichmann, 1959a). But whereas in frank paranoid personalities the hostility is obvious, even when they are not psychotic, in depressives it usually is not. The difference is to some extent a difference in target, to some extent a difference in technique. Paranoid personalities, with their denial and projection, turn their hostility upon the environment and suffer from exaggerated innocence. Depressive personalities rely instead upon introjection. They turn their hostility upon themselves and suffer from exaggerated guilt.

Clinical experience leads us to believe that there are large numbers of well-compensated depressive personalities who have mastered the techniques of ensuring the stream of narcissistic supplies that they must have. These people show no unusual signs of hostility unless the equilibrium they have established is seriously disturbed (Rado, 1956a). In less well-compensated depressive personalities there is an unmistakable undercurrent of hate. Many are emotionally ambivalent toward everyone whom they love. Such ambivalence has its roots in early childhood, when love and care were made contingent upon compliance and expressions of hate were suppressed.

*Oral Traits and Oral Defensive Maneuvers.* Oral traits are present in every human being, some symbolic and some direct, but in depressive personalities these are exaggerated in degree and primitive in function. When a depressive person develops a frank psychotic depression it is obvious that repression has failed and that introjection has become a dominant defense. What is not always obvious is that depressive personalities suffer from defective repression all their adult lives, and that a lifelong overuse of introjection is responsible for their characteristically *oral orientation.* In other words, introjection is itself patterned on *oral incorporation.*

In seeking narcissistic supplies, and speaking now metaphorically, the adult depressive personality behaves toward others on the prototype (fuero claim) of an infant suckling. Depressive personalities seem to "swallow up" a marital partner, an employer, or an associate, to make this other person as much a part of themselves as were their own mothers. The oral maneuver is rarely completely effective, because dependent ties of this nature invariably arouse frustration and hostility in the depressed person's personality structure. Not infrequently, he or she consciously or unconsciously hates the very people from whom narcissistic supplies are being sought.

*The Depressive Superego.* The depressive superego has peculiarities quite different from those of the paranoid (Rosenfeld, 1959). The depressive superego is certainly infantile, but it is a unified system of moral self-control that seems much better integrated than the paranoid superego. Perhaps because denial and projection are minimal, while introjection is prominent, the depressive feels that the chief danger is coming from within himself or herself. Such an individual appeases others because they threaten to stir up self-hatred, either by denying the needed support or by encouraging and supporting aggressive attacks by the superego. Because such guilt-prone individuals tend to blame themselves easily and to belittle themselves, they are less of a threat to others than the paranoid personalities. Therefore, they stand a better chance of being acceptable to others, of having close friends and confidants.

## Biological Predilections in Major Depressive Episodes

In recent decades, an increasingly popular theory of both mania and depression has been advanced that relies upon a reductionistic explanation. Referred to as the *catecholamine hypothesis,* it is based upon the actions of various biogenic amines (catecholamines) synthesized and active in the brain. As background to this hypothesis we should remind ourselves that repeated empirical studies have demonstrated that the closer the familial tie to a psychotically depressed or manic individual, the greater the likelihood that any one member of that family context will manifest the same disorder. First-degree relatives have been found to be at least ten times more likely than the general population to be diagnosed as having an affective disorder (Rosenthal, 1970).

A growing number of researchers have therefore been working on the assumption that genetic factors may influence the production of catecholamines found at specific sites in the brain. These substances have been shown to act as neurotransmitters or modulators that influence the transmission of nerve impulses across the synapse (connecting point) from one neuron to the next. One catecholamine substance, *norepinephrine,* has been studied extensively as playing a central role in the biochemistry of the major affective disorders. This neurotransmitter is believed to mediate between active motor behavior and the emotions. *The catecholamine hypothesis suggests that depression is caused by a deficit of norepinephrine and that mania is the result of an oversupply of this neurotransmitter at the synaptic connections of the brain's neural tissues* (Becker, 1974; Bunney et al., 1979; Schildkraut, 1965; Weiss, Glazer, & Pohorecky, 1975).

Of course, as with all such efforts, the evidence has not always supported the catecholamine hypothesis. There have been no demonstrable differences reported in mood when patients have been administered drugs known to influence the levels of their cerebral norepinephrine (Akiskal & McKinney, 1975; Shopsin et al., 1974). It is clear that no one at the present time can (1) conclude that the catecholamine hypothesis has been confirmed, but even more important, that (2) given its validity, this would invalidate the personality predilections we have been considering in the previous section.

As we have argued in earlier chapters, the *biosocial* approach that we favor recognizes and expects to find such biological (material and efficient) causes at play in the behavior of human beings. But this does not mean that the more dynamic types of (formal and final) causes are irrelevant to a full understanding of the resultant psychopathology. Hence, so long as we do have clinical observations of personality differences to take note of, and so long as we treat these as dynamic *hypotheses,* we need have no fear of alternative biogenic hypotheses (which are not all-inclusive in any case).

## Involutional Melancholia

Practitioners no longer use the diagnostic category of *involutional melancholia,* but it does have historical importance, and we should take it up for this if no other reason. We sometimes hear the phrase *involutional psychotic disorder,* meaning either a depression or a manic episode occurring later in life. But the main syndrome referred to is *involutional melancholia,* which is for all practical matters an agitated depression occurring predominantly in older women. This disorder was supposed to be a direct, metabolic product of glandular changes in the menopause (*climacterium* or "change of life"). As recently as the 1920s this kind of classification, centering on female reproductive functions, was taken for granted. When, in the relatively recent past, there was talk of a *male climacterium,* thought to be the equivalent of the female menopause, the concept of involutional melancholia gained a new lease on life. If men also experienced a change of life, then perhaps this was the explanation of middle life and late middle life depressions in the male.

Since the 1950s we have seen the demise of the involutional melancholia diagnosis, although occasional references to the involutional psychotic disorder persisted. DSM-III does not single out either of these diagnostic syndromes, having subsumed the differential diagnosis as simply a matter of the age at onset. There is no problem with this solution, except of course when a diagnostician is attempting to assign some kind of reductive explanation to the onset of an illness in terms of the presumed influence of biochemical changes taking place during the climacterium.

Thus, if a woman grows depressed at the age of forty, sometimes even as early as thirty-five, and her depression includes bitterness, inflexibility, and a tendency to remain chronic, she is often said to be "approaching the menopause." Her depression is then considered to be the direct result of the hormonal imbalance of an early involution, in other words, *involutional melancholia.* If another woman has her first depression at age sixty, she may be said to be suffering from "a delayed effect of the menopause," actually long past, and therefore she too is called *involutional.* This elastic age range actually covers the period of most depressions occurring before senility. When it comes to the male, no one seems to be quite sure that he really goes through anything that can be called a climacterium or change of life. Those clinicians who think he does vary in their opinion as to when the change occurs, placing it anywhere between age forty and sixty-five.

All in all, the concept of involutional melancholia proved not to be justified, and the substitution of an *involutional psychotic disorder* seems no more than a nod to the history we have just alluded to. It should be given up because it is confusing and unreliable as well as useless. Aging raises difficulties for most people. It must be considered as one factor leading to dissatisfaction in some persons, neuroses in others, psychoses in still others, and psychosomatic disorders or personality disorders in persons vulnerable for some reason to these. We shall review biological, socioeconomic, and personal factors associated with later life that frequently enter into the development of affective disorders.

## BIOLOGICAL FACTORS

In almost everyone, the autonomous ego functions of motor coordination, perceptual grasp, and new learning show impairment as one moves into the forties and fifties. In most persons, sensory acuity and sensory adaptation also diminish. The need for reading glasses seems to some middle-aged persons a personal affront of a narcissistic wound. Impairment of hearing, which many escape, can lead in those who experience it to all kinds of adaptive difficulty. Physical attractiveness also declines, as the hair grows sparse with age and the skin gradually loses its elasticity and becomes wrinkled, dry, and discolored. Obviously, such changes can lead to a sense of depression in individuals who do not have the fundamental depressive personality to which we already alluded (see above).

People in their forties and fifties find that they tire more easily than they used to and that they recover from exertion slowly. There are also involutional changes in the viscera that, although invisible in themselves, may appear as physiological disturbances in visceral function. Gastrointestinal, urinary, and genital disturbances are among the most common. The blood vessels, like the skin, lose their elasticity with age. They cannot respond as well as they could in youth to sudden or prolonged strain. Hormonal changes, which are most dramatic in the menopause, occur also at other times and in other systems, both in men and in women. To all these we must finally add the residuals of accidents and illnesses, which leave behind them their scars and their reduced effectiveness.

We all know the signs of aging are much less marked in some individuals than in others of the same chronological age. There are also individual differences in the kind of function most affected by the aging process. Early cardiac aging, for example, is more threatening and disabling for most persons than gastrointestinal aging. The loss of sensory acuity or early aging of the skin may require greater adaptive effort in persons whose security and prestige depend upon sensory acuity or youthful appearance than in those with cardiac impairment.

## SOCIOECONOMIC FACTORS

It is inevitable that one generation will one day supersede the previous generation in the active control and direction of affairs. It is not until middle and late middle life that this socioeconomic threat begins to materialize for most persons. What will happen? Must the middle-aged person give up established patterns of living and adapt unwillingly to patterns that are strange and uncongenial? Will he or she become a person of no significance and even a burden to others?

The threat of becoming a helpless dependent may arouse anxiety, tension, fatigue, dejection, and resentment in middle life, long before there is any immediate prospect of being helpless and dependent. The fear of dependency here includes the sense of becoming a burden to offspring and other family relations, which in turn detracts from the person's self-esteem. It is therefore not surprising that the hypersensitivity of middle-aged people to their dwindling independence and significance leaves them wide open to the development of depressive disorders and delusions of abandonment.

## PERSONAL FACTORS

Many persons treat a reduction in physical strength or attractiveness as nothing short of a disaster. This is especially likely when the change comes suddenly, following an illness or an accident, or in the wake of the loss of a loved one through death, separation, or desertion. To a minority such losses may lead to a collapse of defensive and adaptive systems. The regression that ensues will then light up long-buried anxieties, conflicts, fantasies, and guilt. Depressive or paranoid psychoses may then develop, but when they do they are no different from other depressions and paranoid reactions in persons who feel hopeless, anxious, guilty, and unloved. The delusions by means of which such regressed persons may attempt to reconstruct their external reality are the delusions with which we are already familiar.

Some persons in their forties and fifties, finding that increased effort and overcompensation are not enough to maintain them or to reinstate them in a position of prestige, give up and become depressed at once. Those who have good object relations will be neurotically depressed; those with poor object relations will regress subtotally and become psychotically depressed. Other persons in the same life situation wear themselves down by continued effort, grow anxious, sleepless, and irritable, and eventually arrive by a different route at an agitated depression. Once more, the depressions are not essentially different from depressions at other times or from depressions developing in patients who have been depressed before in life.

In conclusion, we may accept the fact that middle and late middle life pose special problems, just as adolescence and senility do. There are "mid-life crises" (Jaques, 1965), just as there are "early" and "late" life crises. The psychotic disorders that emerge during middle and late middle life, however, are in no way distinctive in the sense of being directly attributable to the metabolic changes taking place. These disorders are products of subtotal regression in the face of frustration, conflict, guilt, and fantasy. They belong with the other psychopathological disorders of the present volume. We next return to childhood background of the psychotically depressed patient.

## Childhood Background of Major Depressive Episodes

We shall begin with a condensation of what has already been said on this subject, and then discuss it further. As a result of early childhood trauma, the depressive personality suffers from the following lifelong defects:

1. *An unstable ego organization,* which disintegrates if narcissistic supplies are cut off, either through actual loss or through the patient's own withdrawal.
2. *A powerful archaic superego system,* which is basically sadistic, gives rise to feelings of inferiority and worthlessness, and drives a person to

constantly seek relationships that yield love or support in order to offset his or her own superego aggression.

3. A *distorted defensive structure,* in which *repression* is chronically inadequate and *introjection* is overdeveloped and overused.

4. *Vulnerability to traumatic anxiety* whenever dependent demands are not met and narcissistic supplies endangered, with a resultant intolerance for rejection because of the threat of his or her own superego attack.

5. *Powerful fixations in infantile conflicts* that center on love and hate, right and wrong, sin and forgiveness. Because repression is ineffectual, these conflicts penetrate into preconscious thinking and distort interpersonal relationships.

6. *Distorted reality-testing,* which, while more competent in health than preparanoid reality-testing, is deflected by an excessive need to be reassured and dependent, by a hypersensitivity to signs of rejection or rebuff (even in old age), and by an overuse of introjection.

*Infantile Experiences.* The infant who will develop a depressive personality is one who gets full protection from excessive primal anxiety by complying fully with his or her mother's (mothering one's) wishes. It is important not only that the mother be present but also that she be pleased. If the infant fails to meet the mother's expectations, he or she loses support and love in a most distinctive and direct manner. The demand made upon such a child is that he or she submit to severe restrictions of freedom, including the freedom to express rage, in return for security and love. The depressive person's pathology comes from a parental demand that is too severe and comes too early. Even when the mother or mother substitute is physically present, a child may be left hopeless, a prey to anxiety and loneliness, because she disapproves and withholds her love.

Throughout this long period of learning, the infant has no way of reliably anticipating the mother's sudden withdrawals of support and love. To the infant, her behavior must seem as startling and capricious as the behavior of some strange and powerful society seems to a man who is in its power, but who understands neither its intentions nor its language. The only way an infant can meet the situation is to choose behavior that ensures love and support. This means, in effect, to adopt a *dependent, submissive role* and at the same time *to introject the mother* (oral incorporation) as a frame of reference for playing such a role.

Even normal demands for compliance require a selective process on the child's part. This is a part of the process by which every infant and child constructs a realistic world in which he or she lives more or less realistically. Normal adaptation and mastery depend upon a certain amount of compliance. Of course, during infancy and early childhood the adaptive and defensive methods available are primitive. These work well enough under ordinary circumstances at first. They are normally superseded by more effective means of adaptation and defense as infant and child mature.

If, however, parental demands for compliance are *too sweeping and inflexible* during early infancy—for example, the child must be "perfectly still," no frustrated crying is allowed, and so on—excessive use must be made by the developing personality system of primitive adaptive and defensive methods. This excessive use of crudely adapted mechanisms does three things: (1) it gives the primitive methods a fixed and elaborate form in the developing organism; (2) it distorts the later developmental sequences; and (3) it induces structural changes in the personality system, such as we see in the ego-superego interactions of depressives.

The depressive adult, we have said, is a person who has had to meet implacable demands for compliance during infancy by the *overuse of introjection. Introjection* is a *symbolic engulfing,* a perceptual taking in, the primitive forerunner of social role organization (Cameron, 1947, p. 97). It is modeled upon the physical act of taking in food (oral incorporation). Instead of internalizing merely the social roles enacted by the mother as prototype to socialization, the depressive personality internalizes the entire *frightening image* of the mother (including mother-father, mother surrogates of either sex, etc.). This primitive *imago* (image of the object involved in a psychic dynamic) then serves to control the depressive personality's behavior.

This introjective maneuver not only enables the infant to survive, but also enables the person to evolve an adult personality which is more effective and socially acceptable than that of most paranoid and schizophrenic persons. This is mainly because the depressive personality is more compliant and conforming than the paranoid or schizophrenic. It is nevertheless true that the presence of a threatening internal object like this also hastens a precocious ego development in depressive personalities. A depressive ego organization is early committed to a lifelong overuse of introjective defenses and introjective adaptation. Repression is invariably poor, and there is an eternal need for outside help against internal hostility. The ego is guilt-ridden and ruled by superego threat and faces the world with feelings of inadequacy and weakness.

*Advantages of Depressive Personalities.* How is it that depressive personalities, with such a handicapped start, operate reasonably well unless they suffer an actual psychotic break? Why does the depressive in health give a much better impression as a social person than either the paranoid or the schizoid personality? Why is it that the person who develops a depressive psychosis usually makes an excellent recovery? We shall single out two reasons here for these superiorities.

1. *Consistent treatment during infancy.* Hard as it must be to learn strict compliance and submission, it is at least *possible* to do so if the mother provides consistent treatment. Consistency is a necessary condition for developing anticipation, and telic organisms must have some sense of what is unfolding in their immediate (and more distant) futures if they are to adapt successfully. The internal object (*imago*) that a consistently treated infant introjects is a

*predictable one,* a *well-integrated one.* It permits *well-integrated reciprocal behavior* to develop in relation to it; and this lays the foundation for fairly *realistic role organizations* that always predicate interpersonal relations. The infant who can count upon consistent severity, even though he or she suffers from much suppressed rage, is better off than one who never knows what to expect. The latter seems to be the plight of preschizophrenic infants, for example, who are offered no stable, consistent object to introject. They cannot, therefore, organize well-integrated role behavior early in life, and they cannot construct for themselves a realistic world. The depressive, on the other hand, has managed to develop reasonably good object relations and reasonably good personality organization as a result. The depressive's vulnerability lies in the fact that he or she places too much reliance on the interpersonal for dependent, narcissistic supplies to offset the raging hostility from within.

2. *Emotional acceptance and closeness.* In return for strict compliance and submission, the depressive person is rewarded in infancy with *emotional acceptance* and *closeness.* The preparanoid infant, by contrast, is sadistically frustrated and rejected. Even though the preparanoid individual is allowed to react with infant rage (crying, screaming, thrashing about), the major lesson this infant learns is that he or she will be sadistically treated and rebuffed. The mothering of the preschizophrenic is even worse. It is not only inconsistent and unpredictable, but is also lacking in emotional acceptance and closeness. From this the characteristic feelings of futility develop. The preschizophrenic child finds that nothing he or she does seems to be right.

An infant who is consistently rewarded with closeness and affection can go ahead and construct a fairly realistic object world (Fairbairn, 1954). Since object organization and ego integration are independent, this means that he or she will develop a fairly well-integrated ego, one that includes close dependent emotional relationships.

This is the depressive personality's situation. His or her life will always be overshadowed by the effect of having introjected *sadistic internal objects;* but these objects, and the superego that evolves from them, are at least *predictable.* They are at least experienced as *a part of one's own personality;* they are neither denied nor projected. The depressive thus develops more effective *self-boundaries* than do paranoid and schizoid personalities. It is only when he or she suffers a sweeping regression that the depressive person's personality organization is threatened with disorganization and deterioration. Even so, we find clinically that depressive patients re-establish personality integration quite nicely as they recover from an acute episode.

*Identification.* In spite of their bad start, and in spite of a strong residual oral dependence—indeed, possibly because of it!—depressives seem to develop a reasonably good capacity for identification. They give the impression of having made a good initial recovery from their early traumatic experiences of frustration, of having mastered the art of suppressing forbidden reactions.

They seem to have enjoyed a considerable period of freedom from excessive anxiety during early childhood, a period during which they were able to participate in the power and personal qualities of their parents. The chief source of a child's self-esteem lies in identification with the strength and virtues of his or her parent figures. In a manner of speaking, children who are likely to become depressed have participated in the power of their parents as if there were no differences in their own behavior and the behavior of their parents.

The opposite side of the coin is that the hostile, demanding, and rejecting attitudes of the parents are *also* identified with and taken as personal attitudes by the depressive personality. Hence, in due course, as life's subsequent challenges and the failures that result thereby to everyone come about, the depressive personality begins to manifest this darker side of his or her parents' behavior. The result, as we have seen, is the development of a major depressive episode (Jacobson, 1954).

## *DSM-III Viewpoint*

Before closing this chapter and moving on to a consideration of the manic episode in the chapter to follow, we might review the core diagnostic criteria that DSM-III suggests must be present before a major depressive episode is diagnosed. At least four of the following symptoms should be noted in the patient's behavior for fourteen consecutive days previous to the day on which a diagnosis is assigned (children under six should display at least three of these symptoms).

1. Poor appetite or a significant weight loss (when not dieting) or increased appetite or significant weight gain; in children under six, failure to make expected weight gains should be considered as a "loss."
2. Insomnia or hypersomnia.
3. Psychomotor agitation or retardation that can be seen by others; that is, subjective complaints of being slowed down, tired, or restless per se are not enough.
4. Loss of interest or pleasure in usual activities, or decrease in sexual drive not limited to a period when the patient is delusional or hallucinating; in children under six, apathy is the major indicant.
5. Loss of energy; noticeable fatigue, including complaints (see number 3).
6. Expressed feelings of worthlessness, self-reproach, or excessive inappropriate guilt (either may be delusional).
7. Complaints or evidence of diminished ability to think or concentrate, such as slowed thinking, or indecisiveness not associated with marked loosening of associations or incoherence.
8. Recurrent thoughts of death, suicidal ideation, wishes to be dead, or an actual suicide attempt made by the patient.

## SUMMARY

Chapter 12 begins by noting that the DSM-III scheme recognizes two broad categories of the *major affective disorders:* a *manic episode* and a *depressive episode.* If a person suffers a series of manic episodes, with or without a history of experiencing the major depressive episode, he or she would be assigned the diagnosis of *bipolar disorder.* The latter designation replaces the older diagnosis of *manic-depressive disorder.* The dysthymic disorder, which we reviewed in Chapter 10, is viewed by DSM-III as a milder form of the affective disorder. Chapter 12 takes up the *major depressive episode,* or, as we have referred to it, the *psychotic depression.* Major depressive episodes or psychotic depressions are mood disorders in which dejection, self-depreciation, and self-condemnation reach delusional proportions. The prevailing delusions are in keeping with the dejected and often apprehensive mood (termed *mood-congruent* in DSM-III).

The psychotically depressed individual experiences a deeper and more total regression than the neurotically depressed (dysthymic) individual. Both genetic factors and personality dynamics are probably involved. Often, the psychopathology begins as a dysthymic disorder and extends to the major depressive episode. Chapter 12 takes up the long-standing distinction between *agitated* depressive states, in which anxiety, restlessness, and overt tension dominate the picture, and *retarded* depression, in which the patient is limp with grief. Extreme cases of retarded psychotic depression are sometimes called *depressive stupor.* The psychodynamics of both clinical types are not that much different, and the same person may reflect both symptom patterns over a long period of psychotic depression.

Chapter 12 next considers the major forms of depressive delusions, including delusions of self-depreciation, self-accusation, expectation of punishment, unreality, estrangement, nihilism, and somatic complaints. Trivial acts may be recalled and blown out of proportion as wretched misdeeds. This dynamic reflects a form of *screen memory* (akin to manifest dream memories), in which the more serious "sin" is screened by recollection of an insignificant indiscretion. Nihilistic delusions herald the "end of everything" in the patient's life or in the world at large. As in the case of dysthymic disorders (see Chapter 10), the source of such delusions is a superego formation in which there is reluctance to support the ego's achievements and a readiness to condemn its (real or imagined) failures. The demand for *narcissistic supplies* is ever present, reflected in a marked dependency on others. If this support is lost, particularly during a period of life challenge, regression can become complete and the psychotic symptoms begin to appear. Thus, loss of love and support, personal insecurity, and a flagging self-esteem are common precipitating factors.

The onset of depression can be insidious and long-term, or sudden. There is usually a period of incubation, lasting a few weeks or months, before the depression becomes unmistakable. As the disorder progresses, thinking difficulties arise to complicate matters. Concentration becomes difficult. In reaction to the increasing incompetence the patient complains of being no good, a failure, worthless, a burden to everyone, and so forth. As with the dysthymic disorders, the person suffering from a major depressive disorder is ordinarily dependent and fixated predominantly at the oral level of psychosexual development. The difference between the neurotic and psychotic disturbance is therefore a question of degree. We follow here a *quantitative* rather than a *qualitative* theory of mental illness.

Chapter 12 next takes up the classical relationship between *mourning* and *melancholia* (depression). The basic theory holds that the person who eventually becomes depressed has experienced a strong ambivalent attitude toward a love-object with sadistic tendencies. This relationship is formed very early in life, during the oral stage of psychosexual development. Later in life, the ambivalent love-object is *lost* through death, desertion, or related separations of a traumatic nature. Thanks to the primitive identification with the sadistic love-object, the developing personality takes on these characteristics. When regression sets in following the loss of the love-object, there is an internal clash between the archaic superego and the primitive ego. The result is that the depressed person who regresses to a psychotic degree enlivens fixated material relating to ambivalence, oral incorporation (primitive identification), and the resulting sadistic inflation of mental anguish and pain by way of acting out the lost love-object's sadistic tendencies. Hostility can be sent outward or inward. When excessive hostility is sent inward, *suicide* can be the result.

The psychotically depressed patient seems unable to project hostility in a consistently satisfactory manner, as does the paranoiac. This is why in time there is a *loss of object relations,* as the person cannot relate to others on even a satisfactory level of suspicion and animosity. Such self-destructive behaviors are invariably sent inward, leading to a disintegration of ego-superego organization and reducing defenses to infantile levels. The psychotically depressed person comes to feel absolutely vile, hateful, and utterly despicable. To provide a framework justifying such feelings the patient frames delusional beliefs. This effort at restitution—regaining some grip on reality—is termed a *delusional reconstruction.* Such efforts probably prevent a schizophrenic disorganization from developing.

Chapter 12 next takes up some of the personality predilections to be seen in the major depressive episode. We find evidence of low self-esteem, heavy dependence on others, and many signs of infantile needs and anxieties in such patients. Narcissistic supplies become fundamental requirements to life itself. Psychotic depressives lack *realistic role representations.* They continually feel guilty and expect punishment as expiation. They consequently attach themselves to another person in whom they place utter reliance and from whom they expect total caretaking. Psychotic depressives reflect this *oral orientation* in almost every aspect of their behavior.

Chapter 12 next takes up the *catecholamine hypothesis,* which suggests that depression is caused by a deficit of *norepinephrine* and that mania is the result of an oversupply of this neurotransmitter at the synaptic connections of the brain's neural tissues. The evidence for this hypothesis is contradictory at this point in time. The long-standing diagnosis of *involutional melancholia* is not singled out in DSM-III. In effect, this refers to an agitated depression occurring in later life. Traditionally, this was thought to occur in women during their climacterium, brought on by some kind of hormonal imbalance. Eventually, this disturbance was attributed to men as well. The phrase may still be seen in clinical evaluations, bearing the meanings of old age and hormonal imbalance in relation to an agitated depression.

Chapter 12 next delineates childhood background factors in the development of a personality suitable to the formation of a psychotic depression. These factors include an unstable ego organization, a powerful archaic superego system, a distorted defensive structure in which repression is inadequate and introjection is overused, oral fixations, vulnerability to traumatic anxiety, and distorted reality-testing.

# 13

## Major Affective Disorders
## Continued: Manic Episode

### Some Background Considerations

The *manic episode* is a major affective disorder contrasting in type of mood disturbance with the depressive episode. Whereas the depressed person is "down," the manic person is decidedly "up" in mood. Manic episodes are exaggerations and distortions of normal elation or self-assertion that attain psychotic proportions accompanied by delusions. They are often mistaken at first for happiness. They resemble the changes that come over many people after they have had an alcoholic drink or two, but the manic reaction lasts for weeks or months, not hours, and no sign of intoxication is present.

Manic patients seem at first glance to be in good contact with their human environment, and their talk, though rambling, seems to spread freely over a wide range of topics. A closer examination, however, always reveals that both impressions are mistaken. The manic patient's contact with others is shallow and fleeting; his or her talk is limited in scope as compared with that of the normal happy person (M. Lorenz, 1953; M. Lorenz & Cobb, 1952). Mania is deeply regressive. Manic patients use their environment in the service of fantasies and conflicts that are still more primitive than those of paranoid persons. Their defenses, as we shall see, relate them to major depressive episodes, in spite of the prevailing opposite mood. In these patients there is no general disintegration, such as one finds in a high proportion of schizophrenics, and there are no hallucinations in typical cases.

*Definition. Manic episodes are psychotic excitements characterized by overactivity and by delusional elation or self-assertion, but without disorganization.* The behavior of the manic patient is a caricature of joy, optimism, or self-assurance, often a childish caricature. The patient makes no secret of the power he or she feels, telling others everything that comes to mind, evaluating the actions of others, and showing no reservations about what is expressed.

Relatives and other associates easily recognize well-developed cases of mania as abnormal. They usually call for outside help more quickly than in the case of comparably ill depressives because they feel more threatened themselves. They can no more control the manic's excesses than the patient can himself or herself. There are real dangers in mania, including the danger of self-injury, the danger of starvation and physical exhaustion, of financial and erotic adventures, and strange to say, even of suicide. The pervasive sense of aggressive self-assertion or seeming joy is dampened little or not at all by what other people say or do (Lichtenberg, 1959). If there is any change because of attempts at outside control it is most likely to be a change to irritability and increased self-assertion. Genuine communication is next to impossible (M. Cohen, 1954). The manic patient's overactivity is self-propelled. Thoughts seem to press on the person and "run away" with him or her as topics flit quickly and irrationally from one thing to another. This is referred to as a *flight of ideas*. The manic's speech is full of puns, sounds that rhyme (*clang associations*), and wit, the sure signs of primary process thinking, but there is no general disorganization, such as we often find in schizophrenics.

*Adaptation.* There is little of adaptive value in mania. Regression is too deep, reality-testing too severely impaired. Manic patients are like overexcited children who are unable to quiet down and unable to make use of their environment in adult ways. They behave as though there were every reason for their being madly playful and aggressively, insistently self-assertive. Their expansive and often silly talk, their often dangerous lack of consideration for others, their inability to run their own lives and cope with their own daily needs—all these seem to manic patients to be right and normal.

The only sense in which mania can be considered adaptive is that it does *deny a reality* that is too painful to be faced, a reality that would justify a psychotic depression in anyone with such a personality organization. In this sense the manic reaction can be considered as a defense against psychotic depression, as a refusal or inability to accept the intolerably painful truths of a reality situation. There are many cases on record, for instance, in which a personal loss such as the death of someone has precipitated mania where one would ordinarily expect profound grief or a depression. There is also the fact, recognized for centuries, that mania and psychotic depression sometimes follow one another in the same person. We shall take up the latter *bipolar disorder* later in the chapter and illustrate it clinically, after discussing the clinical manifestations and dynamic background of manic episodes.

## Clinical Manifestations of Manic Episodes

There is no designation for a "mild" manic episode in the sense of a neurotic mania to match the dysthymic disorder. It would be logical to make a place, not only for neurotic manic reactions, but also for neurotic paranoid reactions and neurotic schizophrenic reactions. In outpatient clinics and in office practice one certainly sees patients who merit such designations, that is, *manic, paranoid,* and *schizophrenic* patients whose hold on reality enables them to work reasonably well and to make use of their environment in ways that are quite out of the reach of fully psychotic persons. We have already stressed a neurotic component in paranoid disorders (see Chapter 11). In Chapters 10 and 12 we have emphasized the close relationship of dysthymic disorders and major depressive episodes, not only in the symptomatology, but also in the precipitating factors and in the personality background.

Here we shall follow custom, for the sake of clarity and convenience, and distinguish between mild and severe manic disorders without calling one neurotic and the other psychotic. As usual, it is the severe disorder that demonstrates both the symptomatology and the dynamics best. Minor, slight manic episodes, usually called *hypomania,* are too much like the mild elations and reactions of self-assertion that a majority of adults at some time experience to make them convincing illustrations of psychopathology. Indeed, some persons appear to remain in a more or less constant mild manic state, and to perform a prodigious amount of work or play because of this. It should be noted that the DSM-III nosology does include the diagnosis of *cyclothymic disorder,* which in a sense parallels the dysthymic disorder. In the cyclothymic disorder there are symptoms characteristic of *both* depressive and manic syndromes, but these manifestations are not of the severity and duration in time to meet the criteria for major depressive or manic episodes.

## Manic Delusions of Grandeur

The grandiose delusions of mania stand in contrast to the delusions of psychotic depression. They are often little more than mere exaggerations of ordinary self-assertive pride, boastfulness, optimism, and self-aggrandizement. When this is the case, what makes them pathological is that the circumstances under which the delusions arise seem to the observer to call rather for sadness, discouragement, disappointment, or even self-depreciation.

Manic delusions often go much further than this. As in the cases we shall describe, patients make extravagant and impossible claims. They say that they are enormously wealthy, immensely powerful or clever, have unlimited talent, are irresistibly attractive, and have the right to do or say anything they feel like. They may boast of their great achievements, great conquests, the importance of their social and personal connections, of their potency and fruitfulness. The very exaggeration and the self-assertive, expansive manner of these patients give us valuable hints that all of this is a rather childlike defense against admitting failure or inadequacy (D. A. Schwartz, 1961). In keeping with their delusions manic patients often behave like vulgar clowns or become pompous, arrogant, and provocative. They make it necessary for those who are caring for them to remind themselves that such behavior and such attitudes are the products of a regressive illness, that they arise from an *absolute necessity to deny things* of which the patient has already had some awareness, at least at preconscious levels. In short, manic delusions should be looked upon as "holding actions," as defensive denials that give the patient time and opportunity to work through something he or she is at the same time denying. They may also be, and in our two cases actually were, acts of vengeance (see below).

## PRECIPITATING FACTORS

The precipitating factors for a manic episode seem in most cases to be no different from those that are effective in precipitating psychotic depressions, especially a loss of *love, personal security,* and *self-esteem.* These we have described in detail in Chapter 12 (see pp. 377-380). In some cases there is a brief depressive reaction just before the manic episode (M. Cohen, 1954). In others, there seems to be no depressive reaction to usher in the manic attack. Nevertheless, the ease with which sadness or self-depreciation can be demonstrated in most manic episodes suggests that they are usually attempts, and often successful attempts, at staving off a psychotic depression.

The person who develops a manic episode seems to differ from the one who develops a major depressive episode chiefly in his or her sweeping use of *denial,* and the *reconstructing of reality* by means of *grandiose delusions.* Manics behave in a hopelessly irresponsible, uncontrollably expansive manner. It is as if they thought no one else mattered in the world but themselves, as though they were capable of doing anything they wanted, and as though any efforts directed at controlling them or depriving them of what they wanted would be intolerable injustices. These attitudes, of course, are childlike and unrealistic. They represent a serious loss of social perspective.

Manic patients develop pseudocommunities that are quite different from the actual interpersonal relationships existing around them. With the development of their delusions of grandeur, manics place themselves at the center of this imaginary world, as someone of great importance. Once this personal elevation is achieved, the role enacted is literally the *dialectical opposite* of sadness, dejection, and self-depreciation. Unable to confront the increasingly intolerable anxiety, manics deny reality, deny the attacks of their own superego, and flee to the opposite mood disposition that such negative factors would ordinarily call for in overt behavior.

## ONSET OF MANIC EPISODES

It is important to recognize the fact that manic episodes always begin after a phase of increased tension and anxiety, even though they sometimes have an abrupt onset and seem to be precipitated by a single incident. The patient, who has usually been suffering from an unhappy ambivalent conflict, finds himself or herself in an acutely anxiety-provoking situation. The setting is thus one of unrelieved stress and strain. Usually the patient goes through a phase in which he or she attempts to meet the challenge that the situation presents, in terms primarily of the social community. That is, the manic-prone individual is at first oriented in relation to the functionally integrated group of which he or she is a member. It is only after this attempt fails that such an individual develops a grandiose delusional pseudocommunity.

> One of our patients, Amy H., developed a full-fledged manic attack within a few hours of the death of her husband, to whom she had been unhappily married for ten years. Lest this be mistaken for excessive joy, let it be said that this patient became psychotically depressed after she had recovered from her manic attack.
>
> Another patient, Kevin L., an unmarried farmer aged twenty-five, who had been greatly overworked by his father, burst into tears when his father harshly criticized him. He tried to get a gun and kill himself. Later the same day Kevin was found excited, sobbing, and distressed over his failure to complete his work. The very next day he developed a full-fledged manic attack, in which he was tremendously overactive and elated, with plans that were delusional and grandiose.

In both of these cases there was reason to assume a basically ambivalent and somewhat infantile attitude toward a loved person, and in both we see a sweeping regression that seems to make both external reality and the critical functions of the superego ineffectual. Both Amy and Kevin seemed to escape a depression by the use of denial once they had regressed and were in the process of reconstructing reality in terms of their primary process, wish-fulfilling cognitions (H. Deutsch, 1937).

In cases of gradual onset, patients go through a more obvious preliminary phase of tension and anxiety. They become overactive, restless, irritable, excited, and self-assertive. They are characteristically intolerant of criticism or restraint; but they are also usually critical of others, domineering, impatient, and outspoken. They easily become angry and combative when interfered with, or even when remonstrated with. They are in open rebellion; at the same time, they have regressed to a point at which they can no longer take into account the consequences of what they do and say, nor can they exert normal self-scrutiny and self-control. The manic patient may show a striking increase in initiative with, at the same time, an elementary want of adult judgment. One male patient, near the beginning of an acute attack that led to hospitalization, tried to hire a fleet of trucks for a grandiose business enterprise, and actually did engage an internationally famous vocalist and an orchestra to entertain his friends, even though he did not have the money to pay for the planned extravaganza.

### THE MANIC REACTION DEEPENS

As the manic reaction deepens the patient becomes more and more excited, elated, and aggressive. At the same time, unlike either the paranoid psychotic or the psychotic depressive, the manic patient becomes exceedingly distractible. It becomes difficult to remain at any one thing for long. Manic patients shift quickly from one thing to another, without having become really engaged in doing anything; if they do stick at anything for awhile, they work feverishly and with little regard for consequences. Nowhere is the superficiality and distract-

*Freud in 1922 at age sixty-six. He is pictured here at the height of his career, a world-renowned figure. The* Introductory Lectures on Psycho-Analysis *(1915-1917) and* Beyond the Pleasure Principle *(1920) had been published by this time. He was at work on the* Ego and the Id *when this photograph was taken. The latter work appeared in 1923, a fateful year for Freud in that the first signs of his cancer of the mouth and jaw were manifested that February.*

ability more obvious than in the continuous flow of manic talk, which, without becoming incoherent or bizarre, shifts without pause from one topic to another (*flight of ideas* or *topical flight*). If elation dominates the clinical picture, the talk is interspersed with quips, puns, rhymes, witticisms, and personal references, some of which may be vulgar or obscene (Katan, 1953). If aggressive self-assertion is dominant, the talk has less wit and more anger, boasting and threat.

In extreme manic instances manic patients sing and shout themselves hoarse, dress in colorful attire or strip themselves naked, go through calisthenic exercises, walk in circles, tease others, play pranks, and generally play the fool. They may have neither time nor attention for the ordinary routines of eating, eliminating, and resting. They sometimes sleep only half an hour in twenty-four. A prevalent belief that manic patients are generally hungry and will gobble food is not supported by clinical experience. Unless the patient is carefully looked after, he or she is likely to become starved and dehydrated because, like an overexcited child, the manic individual cannot take time to eat and drink. Gastrointestinal motility seems actually to be slowed during manic attacks. In spite of all the overactivity and excitement, the acutely manic patient does not show the kind of ego disintegration that an excited schizophrenic patient does.

### Case of Arnold B.: An Aggressive, Self-Assertive Manic Episode

Arnold B., a married man of fifty-eight, worked at a small racetrack. His income depended upon the racetrack's prosperity. Both had been steadily declining due to a shift in the population density of the area, so that fewer people were attending the races. It hurt Arnold's pride when he had to move his family to a poor neighborhood; but even this move did not save him from finally coming to the end of his financial resources. He was the only child of an aged father, whom he still referred to in childlike language ("pops," "daddy"), and of whom he was still afraid. The father had inherited a large income late in life on which he was living in comfortable idleness. He was said to be squandering large amounts of money on horses and horse racing, on friends, and on women, apparently on everything but the patient and his family.

When Arnold had nowhere else to turn for money he appealed to his father. The father, however, refused over and over to help him. Instead he criticized Arnold harshly, calling him stupid, no good, and a "loser." Arnold felt humiliated, angry, and at his wit's end. For a month he seemed to his wife tense and discouraged. He appeared to be brooding constantly and he could not sleep.

One day Arnold showed up at a racing event a changed man. He was garrulous, excited, argumentative, and belligerent. This surprised his friends, for he had always been known as an even-tempered man, somewhat overconscientious but generally cheerful. At home he now became extremely critical and hard to please. Things went on like this for another month. Arnold's financial situation grew worse and worse. His father showed no signs of relenting.

Arnold owned two mediocre racehorses, and it was when he entered them both in an upcoming important racing event that his illness deepened. His high hopes that this victory would solve all his financial problems seem to have sparked his smoldering manic tendencies into a conflagration of delusional grandeur. Arnold suddenly became excited, jovial, and expansive. He could scarcely sleep at all. He wrote letters incessantly; he telephoned friends all over the country about horses and racing, even in the middle of the night; he also began sending telegrams offering to buy expensive racehorses. Finally, he bought three thousand dollars worth of gear for his horses, which was unnecessary and entirely beyond his means. At this point Arnold was hospitalized.

In the hospital Arnold indulged in childlike boasting, in loud self-assertion, and in unrealistic optimism. He talked excitedly, telling everyone that he was going to make a fortune on his horses. Every patient was to get a television set, the nurses were to have mink coats, and he would donate a million dollars to the hospital. He promised his own nurse $100,000 and told her he wanted to marry her, ignoring the fact that he himself was already married. He said he never felt better in his life. He liked the hospital, he said, even if it was like a jail—"No, worse than a jail because you sometimes get out of a jail."

Not far beneath the surface there was sadistic aggression, as irresponsible as his boasts and promises. Arnold made cruel anti-Semitic tirades in front of a confused and frightened schizophrenic Jewish youth. These could be ended only by taking Arnold to his room and keeping him there until he had quieted down. He told an agitated, depressed clergyman that he had heard the doctors making plans to castrate him. For a few weeks Arnold continued aggressive, loud, self-assertive, erotic, and grandiose. Then the attack subsided, he made his peace with his father—who had been footing the bills—and he went home almost well.

*Discussion.* As in the case of the agitated depressed woman, Sharon R., described in Chapter 12 (see p. 366), we see here someone faced with disillusionment in relation to an ambivalently loved person and subjected to harsh criticism. Yet the result is not a clear-cut depression but a clear-cut manic excitement. Arnold could certainly have felt himself to be a hopeless failure, unsuccessful, unlucky, and unloved. He even went through an initial period of preoccupation, as Sharon did. Then for some reason there came a sweeping denial of his intolerable frustration, a period of hopelessly unrealistic self-assertion, boasting, and aggression. This is clearly a dialectical maneuver (see Chapter 4, p. 135), the manifestation of an unconscious thrust in the direction opposite to that taken by Sharon.

By means of his expansive, grandiose delusions, Arnold reconstructed his world, building a pseudocommunity that made him appear to himself as a wealthy spendthrift. He played the irresponsible child in his boasts, his promises, and his love. There is the suggestion of an identification with his father in this dynamic, for the father was pictured by Arnold in this irresponsible role—and not without some justification. Arnold therefore acquired boundless wealth in his delusional scenario. He squandered money on horses and horse racing; and he would squander more on his friends, the patients, the nurses, and the hospital. He seldom so much as mentioned his wife and children. It was as though he were young again and could marry his nurse.

There were also hostility and vengeance in the picture. Arnold's noisy, pushing behavior on the ward was as aggressive as the insistent demands of the depressed woman, Sharon R. He spoke cruelly to frightened patients. He made his father pay handsomely for his manic illness and said so. In the end, his illness brought him the help from the father that he needed.

### Case of Leslie S.: Elated Manic Reaction

Leslie S., a childless married woman aged thirty-four, had been living for the ten years of her married life with her husband's parents, in spite of her repeated insistence upon having a home of her own. For three months she had been working at a summer resort in upper Michigan, after telling her husband before she left that she would leave him if he did not provide her a separate home. Two weeks before she left Michigan for home a visiting relative found her downcast, irritable, and in tears about her husband's having done nothing about moving. The day before she left she was hurt and humiliated because her husband did not drive up to get her from the southern part of Michigan, as he had promised. She arrived home the next day alone and went to her husband's place of business, kissed him, and gave him a severe scolding for neglecting her. This was a week before her admission to the clinic.

During the next five days Leslie was uncommunicative and unfriendly to her husband and his family. She herself was away from home most of the time because she was helping her lodge to prepare for a forthcoming town celebration. Even when she was at home she seemed to be engrossed in memorizing the part she was supposed to play in the festivities. Two days before her admission to the clinic Leslie suddenly appeared at her husband's lodge to see if he was really attending a meeting there; when she found that he was, she merely left with a smile. This visit seems to have been the beginning of her excitement.

When Leslie left her husband's lodge she did not go home but went instead to the local hotel in the small community where all of this took place, and made the proprietor—an old friend—play cards with her until one in the morning. Then she insisted that he and a guest at the hotel drive her around the small town looking for her husband. She laughed and sang as they went through the streets in the middle of the night. Leslie arrived home around one-thirty to find her husband already in bed, asleep. She undressed but could not settle down. She was overactive and overtalkative, jumping from one topic to another, reciting the piece she had been memorizing, singing, laughing, and making up rhymes. Her husband, now awakened, tried as best he could to settle her down after he determined that she had not been drinking. At two-fifteen the town fire siren sounded and Leslie immediately dashed out of the house in pajamas, bedroom slippers, and a coat. Her husband found her in another building, hiding behind a door. It took him an hour to get her home, and then in a few minutes she was out again. She walked up and down the streets, laughing and singing, stole a banana from a truck, and sat on the hotel steps with her perplexed husband for two hours. She finally got home and went to bed at six in the morning, but half an hour later she was up again.

All the next day Leslie talked, laughed, and sang. She swore at her father-in-law, made various domestic scenes come about, and in one of these latter incidents actually slapped her husband's face. She had never expressed such overt hostility before. To everyone around her she kept saying, "I told you this would happen!" On the day following she was taken to the city, where she and her husband stayed at a friend's home. When they were out driving she threatened playfully to jump out of the car. All the next night she stayed up, working around the house with a dust mop, talking, singing, and praying. She entered the hospital the next morning at the urging of her husband and in-laws.

In the hospital Leslie continued much as she had been before entering it. She was not disoriented, intoxicated, or disorganized. There was no evidence of physical illness. When her husband left her the next day to return home, she became agitated and wept for a short period; then she brightened up and resumed her previous overactive and overtalkative behavior. The following sample of talk shows flight of ideas, rhyming (*clang associations*), punning and distractibility: note also the play of dialectical oppositionality in the verbalizations:

"You go out and stand pat—pat, you hear? Who was Pat? What does he wear when he's in Ireland? . . . See this pillow [raising it behind her head]? Now is it even or odd? Even or odd, by God. I take it even, by God. By God we live: by God we die. And that's my allegiance to these United States. See my little eagle [a bedsheet wrapped around her feet and stretched taut ]? These are my wings. No. I have wings of a girl." At this point Leslie broke out into a chorus of the *Prisoner's Song,* making flying movements with her arms to accompany the lines, "Oh, I wish I had the wings of an angel. Over these prison walls I would fly." Then she sang, "One little Indian, two little Indians," and shouted, "Heap big Indian chief! I'm not afraid. I got a heart right here. I've got a key to my heart. . . ."

In her outpouring of talk during the first week following her admission to the hospital, Leslie revealed her chief concerns, her ambivalent attitudes toward her husband and herself, and her underlying anxiety and unhappiness. She said she was going to have a baby, said she would someday conduct an orchestra, and boasted about her bridge playing and her evening dresses. Within a week after admission she had quieted down to an almost normal level of general activity and talk. She was irritable and had occasional temper outbursts.

Five weeks after admission Leslie went with her husband to spend the night at her mother's house. There she quarreled with him because he had stopped her charge accounts and destroyed her charge cards. She returned to the hospital the next day tense, overactive, and overtalkative. At first she was fearful, irritable, and sleepless. She spoke of fears that both she and her husband would die. Within four more days she was again elated. She laughed and sang, rhymed, punned, swore, and said she would divorce her husband. She told everyone of her desire for children. Her recovery after this was slow. There were episodes of irritability, resentment, and angry crying, but no sadness. Four months after admission she was discharged as recovered.

*Discussion.* As in the preceding case, there is a background that might have been expected to precipitate a depression—a married woman's desperation over not having a home and family of her own after ten years of marriage. Leslie's three-month separation from her husband and her ultimatum to him had produced no results whatsoever. She felt deserted and unloved. Yet the clinical picture that we see is full of singing, laughter, rhyming, punning, and swearing. All of this seems to be denial of her underlying hopelessness and despair. The anxiety, fear, and anger managed to penetrate the defense and appear in Leslie's general behavior and her talk. Nevertheless, she did not actually become depressed, unless we choose to call her brief episodes of crying depressions, and she recovered from her whole illness without special treatment within four months.

## Dynamic and Developmental Background

It is not enough to depict mania as simple denial, in defense against the development of a depression. Mania is probably always some such maneuver, even when depression is not present, but it is also dynamically more than simple denial (R. W. Gibson, Cohen, & Cohen, 1959; Lewin, 1950, 1959; D. A. Schwartz, 1961). The history of mania and the depressions is one that repeatedly, almost continuously, has emphasized that however opposite their mood and activity may seem they are closely interrelated. This relationship was specifically stated in the first century A.D., given the name of *manic-depressive insanity* in the seventeenth century, and called *circular insanity* by Falret in 1851 (Cameron, 1944b). Kraepelin incorporated it in his classification late in the nineteenth century (see Chapter 1, p. 17).

We shall present mania here as a substitute method of working through problems that threaten to precipitate a depression. The reasons for doing this are both clinical and theoretical. Clinically, it has long been recognized that mania may follow or precede depression. Both of our major cases had been brooding over trouble for some time before their manic attacks supervened. Both had been more or less realistically struggling with genuine external situations that they could not resolve, Arnold with the reality of poverty and an unjust refusal of help, Leslie with an unjust refusal to provide her with a home of her own. Their final manic attacks came, not as an excess of joy or triumph, but as an overwhelming aggression that plunged them both into deep regressions.

We propose that the *latent content* in both these cases, and in other manias, is profoundly *depressive* and *pathologically dependent;* while it is the *manifest content* that appears to be the opposite of this thanks to the person's dialectical reasoning capacities. The person can enact superficially what he or she is *not* actually intending to convey meaningfully (see Chapter 4, p. 131). Arnold was almost successful in defending against his underlying depression, but he bristled with hostility, which happy people do not, and occasionally made dejected references to the bad treatment he had received from his "daddy." Leslie, in spite of showing more elation than Arnold, was much less successful in keeping her latent depression under cover. She gave abundant evidence of fear, anxiety, and suicidal wishes, sometimes disguised as "playful," sometimes openly expressed along with agony, dread, and depletion. Both patients were furiously angry.

The ancient linking of mania with depressions seems to be justified, not only by their clinical descriptive aspects and their close association often in the same patient, but also by their dynamic characteristics. Both occur in fundamentally oral dependent persons; both represent a deep oral regression (Lewin, 1950, 1959), and both are unable to make use of external reality relationships because of superego and ego defects. Let us turn to the dynamic aspects of mania.

## FIXATION AND REGRESSION IN MANIC REACTIONS

Freud's explanations of mania followed his general approach to the depressions (see Chapter 12, p. 374). Recall that the essential dynamic in depression is that of an "ego divided," in the sense of the archaic (pre-Oedipal) superego being arrayed against the primitive ego. The sadistic hostility of the love-object is carried by the superego via identification (oral incorporation), and this attitude is directed toward the ego. Well, Freud (1921/1955m) was to find in certain of his cases that sometimes a *fusion* of the ego and superego (also called the *ego-ideal* in early Freudian writings) took place, resulting in a mood of triumph, self-satisfaction, and a loss of inhibition (p. 132). This was the manic episode, and it could be sustained for varying periods of time, either alternating with a period of depression or not.

Another way in which this fusion of ego and superego might take place is after an actual period of melancholic disturbance following the loss of the loved object. Recall that the depressive personality is highly ambivalent regarding the lost object. Occasionally, as the person is working through the positive (manic) and/or negative (depressive) moods in relation to the (ambivalently) loved object, the former succeed in taking control of the personality system. In a sense, the ego triumphs over the superego (which represents the lost love-object) (Freud, 1915/1957m, p. 249). The hostility witnessed in the behavior of manics is thus a continuing reflection of the underlying ambivalence, which does not simply go away. It is clumsily sublimated into vulgar humor and overly frank evaluations of other people.

In this context, it is interesting to note that Freud considered humor an act of psychological rebellion, a "triumph of narcissism, the victorious assertion of the ego's invulnerability. The ego refuses to be distressed by the provocations of reality, to let itself be compelled to suffer" (Freud, 1927/1961h, p. 162). Of course, in the case of a manic episode, the elation is merely a smokescreen, ineffective because it is not based upon genuine grounds for the manifest expansiveness. The manic is pretending that the very opposite of his or her reality is taking place. Despite this charade, the manic, like the depressive, is in much better contact with external reality than is the schizophrenic. The effort to use humor is a reflection of this relatively more integrated contact with the external world, because a "sense of humor" is in fact an excellent weapon in the person's continuing battle to maintain his or her mental health.

In manic episodes the regression seems to be at least as deep as it is in depressive episodes. In some respects it seems to be even deeper. The principal fixation levels represent orally dependent relationships. The orientation that manic regression reactivates depends upon very early severe oral frustration. This frustration is responsible for the aggression that appears in some form as an outstanding characteristic of manic patients. Rage is held in check by most manic patients with difficulty. Slight frustrations during the illness itself provoke violent outbursts which, however, are likely to vanish quickly if the provocation can be eliminated or the patient distracted. In this respect, the manic patient resembles the small child and is very different from an angry paranoid or schizophrenic person.

The situation with regard to object relations seems to be quite different from that in psychotic depressives and different from that in paranoid disorders also. In perhaps a majority of manic attacks, possibly in all of them, there is an initial withdrawal into brooding and silent preoccupation. This phase may be depressive in character; it is certainly not the vigilant, suspicious aloofness of the paranoid reaction. In the manic attack proper, however, the patient gives the impression of being outgoing and in contact with his or her surroundings in an overactive, greedy way. This impression is belied by the fleeting, kaleidoscopic, rapid shifting of the focus of the manic patient's attention. It is soon apparent that this person is incapable of maintaining genuine adult object relations, that he or she is as distractible and impulsive as a small child (Rochlin, 1953).

Manic patients are often described as greedy, as hungry for new objects and new topics. This is true, but manics are also insatiable. Their attempts to satisfy their originally orally dependent needs are not characteristically made through actual eating—they are too busy to concentrate on eating—but through all kinds of other "taking in," such as visual, auditory, and tactile sensations. The reason that manics cannot satisfy their oral needs is that they have regressed too deeply to be able to use the new objects or people in a meaningful adult manner.

### DEFENSES IN MANIC EPISODES

The *regression* that occurs in manic reactions cannot be considered a merely defensive maneuver. It is the irresistible outcome of a massive breakthrough of unconscious material, in which aggression and derivatives of the primary process are dominant (Katan, 1953). The manic episode is a sign that subtotal psychotic regression has already occurred, a regression so sweeping and so deep that the patient can no longer deal with his or her environment effectually. It is also a sign that certain defenses have failed and that certain others have taken their place.

*Defective Repression.* It is obvious from the manifest symptomatology that repression has grossly failed in manic reactions. Conscious and preconscious secondary process thinking is everywhere contaminated by primary process derivatives. Unbridled aggression wells up upon the least provocation. The derivatives appear in the unabashed clowning, the cruel teasing, the silly rhyming, punning, singing, and laughing, even in the otherwise unaccountable overactivity. Manic patients are often compared to persons intoxicated by alcohol, and the comparison in many ways is apt. One of the major differences is that whereas the manic patients tend to be well coordinated, even when outrageously overactive, intoxicated persons tend to become poorly coordinated and disoriented. We have seen straitjacketed manic patients sitting on a ward and yet marvelously in touch with what is taking place there. Though uncontrollably hyperactive, they were sensitive to the activities and moods of other patients.

*Denial.* It is denial that seems to transform what might have been a psychotic depression into a manic episode (Lewin, 1954). Denial in mania works in more than one direction. In the first place, the circumstances that would justify at least some depression are denied. This was most obvious in the case of Arnold B., who, in spite of being hopelessly bankrupt and without prospects, declared himself on the verge of becoming enormously wealthy. Certainly his lifetime experiences working at a racetrack would ordinarily have made him realize the tremendous odds against his becoming wealthy through his already manic investment in two undistinguished horses. In the case of Leslie S., denial of the sources of her unhappiness was less blatant. Nevertheless, she did proclaim to everyone that she was going to have a baby, something she had always longed for, and that she was going to conduct an orchestra.

Denial also extends to the patient's predicament. Here, again, Arnold was more successful in making merry, even though he was confined to a hospital, where liberty is inevitably limited and one is separated from one's relatives and friends. It is true that he called the place worse than a jail, but unlike a depressive, he did not behave in accordance with this complaint. Leslie S. also denied her predicament, as well as her poor outlook, when she sang and laughed, punned, rhymed, and shouted. Every now and then, however, the denial failed her, and she more realistically reacted with anxiety and fear, and even for short periods with weeping.

*Reaction-Formation.* We propose that the overactive, garrulous, superficially outgoing, laughing, teasing, singing, manic patient is striving to reinforce denial and repression through the dialectical machination known as reaction-formation. Thus, the manic person not only denies the depression and its causes, but also brings to bear in exaggerated form the apparent opposite of depression. In effect, manics shout, boast, and laugh down the depressive promptings that threaten from within. This is what some cultures try to achieve by having professional clowns perform at all public funerals. The grim reality of a present death is denied and subjected to reaction-formation by culturally demanded laughter and celebration. Among our own subcultures this is achieved by the "wake," when it leads to heavy drinking, brawling, and laughter among the mourners.

*Identification.* Identification may be prominent among manic defenses; when it is, however, it does not lead to such primitive introjection as appears in psychotic depression, or at least not openly. In the case of Arnold B. the identification was extensive, clear, and obviously delusional. It was his spendthrift father with whom Arnold was identifying in his manic enactment—wealthy, irresponsible, and erotic. He was no longer the even-tempered, somewhat overconscientious man whom his associates had known. Identification entered into the clinical picture of Leslie's manic attack also. She suspected her husband of infidelity and, since she was declared to be fertile by her physicians, she blamed his failure to give her a child upon his supposed infidelity. Her manic attack began with definite erotic moves and with attempts to expose herself half-dressed around the town. This behavior was completely foreign to her normal conduct, but it probably represented an acting out of what she believed her husband to be doing. One gets the impression in all manic episodes that the patient is playing a role that is not his or her own. The manic role seems to be a variety of reaction-formation, which buttresses the patient's denial of an underlying depression.

## SUMMARY OF PSYCHODYNAMICS IN MANIC EPISODES

The manic attack appears to be a substitute method of working through problems that threaten to precipitate a psychotic depression. The *latent content* in mania is deeply depressive; but the *manifest content* is superficially playful, boastful, aggressive, and overactive. The general personality of the manic, like that of the depressive, is pathologically oral dependent; and manic regression, like that of the psychotically depressive, leaves the patient unfit to handle external reality in effectual adult ways. Adult frustration seems likewise to arouse regressively deep oral frustrations belonging to infancy.

Mania often, perhaps always, begins with preoccupation, but it soon becomes an apparently outgoing overactivity. Object relations, although numerous, are fleeting, superficial, ineffectual, and unsatisfying. For this reason the manic's hunger for objects cannot be gratified in his or her adult surroundings; it is hunger for early oral satisfaction.

Because repression is grossly defective in manic personalities, unconscious material threatens to break through and contaminate the conscious and preconscious organizations. In a *manic attack,* this threat is realized. Primitive fantasies and primary process material appear in the symptoms of the manifest mania. Denial, reinforced by reaction-formation, transforms what might have been a depression into an elation that, although superficially the opposite of depression, is actually "forced" and has many signs of depression near the surface. Identifications may be prominent, especially if these support the defense or provide outlets for the excessive aggression.

Though Freud's original suggestions concerning a fusion of ego and superego (or ego-ideal) and the resulting mania have been widely supported, there are also psychoanalytical views departing from this formulation. Thus, some analysts have suggested that in the depth of regression to be seen in mania, there is literally an enlivening of the so-called purified pleasure ego (Klein, 1948), which exists even before any superego formation is underway. In this state, only that which is pleasurable is psychologically acknowledged; all that is negative is rejected through primitive denial. The result is a manic episode, emphasizing the pleasurable, uninhibited, and expansive aspects of life. Whatever the case may be, psychoanalysts tend to agree that the regression in mania is deep but not as disorganized as that to be seen in schizophrenia.

As we noted in our consideration of the major depressive episode, it appears likely that the oral tendencies of this personality system help to keep its contact with reality on a firmer footing. It is almost as if the manic's symptom picture is patterned after the current environment, as both a denial of aspects of it but also as a direct copy of it. Thus, both Arnold in his claims to wealth and Leslie in her claims to pregnancy denied reality even as they copied other aspects of that reality in their respective enactments of irresponsibility and infidelity. In schizophrenia, we do not find this thread of contact with reality, which has become completely disorganized and hence confusing to the patient who is trying to restructure it in bizarre fashion. Doubtless this thread of contact with ongoing reality is what makes the depressive and manic episodes have a better prognosis than we find in the other psychoses.

## Bipolar Disorder: Manic-Depressive Cycles

The final major affective disorder we shall consider is the *bipolar disorder,* in which there may be a full symptomatic picture of both manic and major depressive episodes, intermixed or rapidly alternating every few days. This is what we have referred to above as the classic *manic-depressive cycle (psychosis,* etc.). In DSM-III, the manic episode is what matters in this diagnosis. That is, if a patient were to have a *series* of manic episodes without intervening depressions, he or she would be assigned the diagnostic category of *bipolar disorder, manic.* If a patient were brought in suffering from depression, but the case history revealed that once before he or she had been in a manic state, the diagnosis would be *bipolar disorder, depressed.* This would imply that a "cycle" of mood alterations may be involved, but that at the present moment the individual is depressed with no immediate signs of elation. Finally, if the patient does reflect *both* manic and depressive mood swings daily (Jenner et al., 1967) or with several days intervening, the diagnosis would be *bipolar disorder, mixed.*

Empirical studies have found age differences in the onset of bipolar as opposed to unipolar affective disorders. It appears that bipolar patients experience their first breakdown in the twenty-five- to thirty-year age range, whereas the unipolar disorders are more likely to occur in the twenty-five- to forty-five-year age range (Research Task Force of the National Institute of Mental Health, 1975; Winokur, Clayton, & Reich, 1969). Evidence has also been presented suggesting that the relatives of patients with bipolar disorders have an increased incidence of manic disorders when compared with relatives of patients with unipolar disorders. Some investigators take this as suggestive of a genetic difference between unipolar and bipolar illness, particularly since it appears that the drug *lithium carbonate* has no effect on unipolar depressives, but does have a positive effect on bipolar patients (Fieve, 1975; F. Goodwin, 1974). The average length of a manic reaction in a bipolar disorder is from two to four months, and that of a depressive reaction is from four to nine months (Beck, 1967; Pugatch, 1971).

Theory in manic-depressive psychosis has been heavily influenced by biological speculations, crystallized by Kraepelin in the hypothesis that was long maintained that it was an *endogenous* as opposed to an *exogenous* disorder. Thus, an endogenous depression would presumably be due to bodily factors, such as heredity, biochemistry, and neurological disease. Exogenous depression would therefore present the opposite case, of a mood swing due to external events such as divorce, death of a loved one, or failure in a career development. DSM-III has dropped this distinction, but some clinicians are still likely to think of mania and depression as contrasting swings in mood due to an endogenous disturbance of some type.

We have seen, particularly in the case of Leslie S., sudden changes from boisterous elation to brief episodes of anxiety, fear, and outspoken bitter unhappiness and back again to boisterous elation. The sameness of precipitating factors —death may bring on a manic attack instead of the expected depression—

the ambivalence seen in both, and the common prodromal period of tension and anxiety, all emphasize the close relationship between manic excitements and psychotic depressions. We come back again to the conception of the manic reaction as a coordinate substitute for depression that not only defends the patient from having a psychotic depression, but also seems able in some way to work through the same general unconscious problems. It is in this sense that we must understand the dynamics of the relatively rare *manic-depressive cycle.* Here a full-fledged manic attack leads directly into a full-fledged depression, or a full-fledged psychotic depression leads directly into a full-fledged manic attack (Cameron, 1942).

What seems to happen in the first case is that the manic defenses of denial and reaction-formation for some reason fail. The underlying depression then appears in the manifest clinical picture. In the second case, after a period of manifest depression, the defenses of denial and reaction-formation dominate the manifest scene, and boisterous gaiety or aggression take the place of despair. The earlier onset of bipolar disorders would be consistent with this theoretical view of failing defensive measures calling for the dialectically opposite manifestation in the clinical picture. Once the swing in mood takes place it is likely to continue. Let us return to the case of Amy H., mentioned above (p. 396), to illustrate such a succession:

Amy H., a thirty-year-old widow, developed a manic attack immediately after her husband's death. She had not fully recovered from this manic attack, which had all the classical symptoms of self-assertion, forced gaiety, boastfulness, overactivity, and insomnia, when she went into a deep depression, which lasted more than a year. After this she had two more manic attacks, separated by periods of apparently good health.

In all of these illnesses, manic as well as depressive, Amy complained of loneliness and of her need for close affection. She was obviously an orally dependent person who had never achieved emotional maturity. Even as an adolescent Amy had been known as a person who concealed her shyness, timidity, and dependence behind a mask of witty, happy-go-lucky sociability.

When she married, Amy exchanged a stern, domineering father for a similar husband (ambivalent love-object). In this way, she continued living the life of an habitually dependent, dominated, dissatisfied woman. There were no children in the marriage, so Amy literally had no need to assume a more adult pattern in interpersonal relations. Her husband's sudden death in an industrial accident seemed to promise Amy the freedom that she had always claimed that she wanted. But her own emotional immaturity made his death a disaster, since she no longer had a dominant person upon whom to depend.

Amy denied this need, and she denied the critical attacks of her superego through the countering dynamics of a manic reaction. When the first of these subsided, however, the basic depression appeared and plunged her into pathological mourning. This was in turn succeeded by another manic attack, which was apparently more successful than the first, since it was not followed by a depression. It should be noted in passing that the psychiatrist in whose care Amy was placed during her first two manic attacks witnessed clear episodes of crying and despair, sometimes lasting only a few minutes, but impressive for their marked contrast to the then prevailing boisterous gaiety and self-assertion.

## DSM-III Viewpoint

As we did with the major depressive episode in Chapter 12, we shall end our consideration of the manic episode of the major affective disorders with the core diagnostic criteria listed in DSM-III. If for the period of one week a patient reflects three of the following criteria for an expansive mania or four of these criteria for an irritated mania, then the diagnosis to be assigned is *manic episode, major affective disorder.*

1. Increase in activity (either socially, at work, or sexually) or physical restlessness.
2. Increased talkativeness or pressure to keep talking.
3. Flight of ideas or statements by patient suggesting that his or her ideas are racing along.
4. Inflated self-esteem (grandiosity, which may be delusional).
5. Decreased need for sleep.
6. Distractibility; that is, attention is too easily drawn to unimportant or irrelevant external stimuli.
7. Excessive involvement in activities that have a high potential for painful consequences which is not recognized by the patient; for example, buying sprees, sexual indiscretions, foolish business investments, reckless driving.

### Summary

Chapter 13 continues with the major affective disorders, taking up the *manic episode,* in which there is a psychotic level of excitement characterized by overactivity and delusional elations or self-assertion without disorganization. The manic patient's overactivity is self-propelled, with *flight of ideas* and a speech pattern filled with puns, *clang associations,* and wit. There is a profound denial of reality in the regressive pattern known as a manic episode. It is not unusual for a mania to take root following the loss of a loved one or some other personal tragedy in the life of a patient. A minor or slight manic episode is termed *hypomania.* DSM-III recognizes the diagnosis of a *cyclothymic disorder,* in which there are symptoms characteristic of *both* depressive and manic disorders, but lacking in the severity and duration to be diagnosed as the latter syndromes.

The most common delusion in manic episodes is that of *grandeur.* A manic is likely to boast of great achievements, important social or financial connections, or the possession of immense wealth. The underlying denial of reality prompts these—often ridiculous—claims to be made. As with depressive episodes, the prompting factors in the manic episode center on losses in the realms of love, personal security, and self-esteem. The person who develops a manic episode seems to differ from the one who develops a major depressive episode chiefly in his or her sweeping use of denial, and the reconstructing of reality by means of grandiose delusions. Manics behave in a hopelessly irresponsible, uncontrollably expansive manner, in which no one else in the world seems to matter but themselves.

It has been traditional in the history of psychopathology to refer to manic-depressive insanity, or circular insanity, because of the frequent manifestations of depressive and manic episodes in the same patient (see Chapter 12 summary). The text views mania as a substitute method of working through problems that threatened a depression. The latent content of a manic episode is therefore profoundly depressive and pathologically dependent, but the manifest content is opposite in tone. Oral dependency is characteristic of both the manic and the depressed patient.

Freud traced the manic episode to a fusion of the ego and superego during the conflict between the archaic superego and the primitive ego. It is also possible for the manic episode to arise from the ambivalence felt toward a lost love-object. Depression flows from the hostility felt toward this love-object, but the more positive feelings of love can also manifest themselves in a patient's behavior as a manic episode. Of course, there is considerable hostility in the "humor" and elation of such manic conditions, which merely reflects the negative affect directed toward the lost love-object. Regression in a manic episode matches the depth of regression in a depressive episode (to the oral level). The manic episode is a sign that subtotal psychotic regression has already occurred in the patient's behavior, a regression so sweeping and so deep that the patient can no longer deal with his or her environment effectually.

In addition to defective regression, manic episodes reflect the clear functioning of denial. Denial is what turns what might have been a depressive episode following regression into a manic episode. Reaction-formation is also typical of the manic patient. In effect, manics shout, boast, and laugh down the depressive promptings that threaten from within. Identification with others is also noted in the fact that manics begin to play a role, taking over attitudes and privileges of others whom they choose as examples of grandiose lifestyles.

Chapter 13 closes with a discussion of the *bipolar disorder,* that is, a manic-depressive cycle to be seen in the same patient. According to DSM-III, if a patient has a series of manic episodes without depressive periods his or her illness would be diagnosed as *bipolar disorder, manic.* If a patient is known to have had a manic episode previously, but is now suffering a depression, the diagnosis would be *bipolar disorder, depressed.* If a patient has actual swings (daily, weekly, etc.) in mood the diagnosis would be *bipolar disorder, mixed.* Bipolar cases manifest their abnormal patterns at an earlier age than the unipolar disturbances. Theory in manic-depressive psychosis has been heavily influenced by biological speculations. An *endogenous* depression would presumably be due to biological factors such as heredity or neurological disease. *Exogenous* mania would presumably be due to some traumatic life experience. DSM-III no longer makes the endogenous/exogenous distinction, but some clinicians still view things in this manner.

# 14

## *Schizophrenic Disorders*

### *Some Background Considerations*

Schizophrenic disorders are the most fascinating in all behavior pathology. They show a bewildering wealth of symptoms, some of which seem on the surface to be quite contradictory, although, as we shall see, they really are not. DSM-III has modified the classical Kraepelinian subtypes (see Chapter 1, p. 16) by dropping the *simple* diagnosis and renaming the *hebephrenic* diagnosis, but we can still see the outlines of Kraepelin's logic in the scheme that is retained. It is our position, based upon clinical experience, that a great many patients, perhaps a majority, can be diagnosed in more than one of these schizophrenic subtypes. We can no longer regard the Kraepelinian subtypes as anything but overlapping and changeable collections of symptoms reflecting a common psychopathological disorder.

It is our feeling that the best way to approach schizophrenic disorders is to recognize that all of the symptoms are signs of a breakthrough from primary processes in the unconscious. There is nothing in schizophrenia that cannot be traced to the instrusion of primary process material that should have been kept out of secondary process conscious and preconscious organizations. The intrusion occurs along a wide front, and it comes from several different levels simultaneously or in quick succession. This multiplicity of origins contributes to the appearance of disorganization that characterizes schizophrenia.

During recent years schizophrenia has taken its place beside the dream as a royal road to the unconscious. This is not to say that schizophrenic reactions and dreams are the same, although such a claim has been made more than once in the past. Unlike the dreamer, the schizophrenic patient is awake and usually responsive to the immediate surroundings, however strange his or her responses may seem. If one lives among schizophrenic persons, after dark as well as during the day, during quiet periods as well as during excitements, one gets an impression very different from the impressions derived from indirect reports and from occasional, formal contacts. Many of the classical descriptions of schizophrenia have come from persons who derived their information largely from formal clinical sessions and tests. These are misleading.

Schizophrenia seems destined to become not only a royal road to the unconscious, to the nature of primary processes, but also a royal road to basic information about normal infancy and early childhood. Many of the most fruitful hypotheses concerning early infantile object relations and early ego differentiation were originally derived from the study of deeply regressed schizophrenic adults. The recognition of early autism in children has led to the direct study of childhood schizophrenia, and such study is throwing a new and unexpected light upon normal infancy, as well as upon adult schizophrenia (Kanner, 1943; Stewart & Gath, 1978).

The extent and permanence of cure in schizophrenia is debatable. As we shall see below, there are many experts who believe that this disorder is genetically and biologically determined. It follows that only some type of physical therapy can rectify the condition. Empirical evidence suggests that even when schizophrenia is in remission, there is a continuing deficit in the person's ability to sustain attention (Wohlberg & Kornetsky, 1973).

DSM-III acknowledges that though there is always a possibility of full remission or recovery, the actual frequency of such positive outcomes in schizophrenia is unknown. The more common course is a series of acute phases of the disorder, with increasing personality deterioration between such episodes. Though Freud's projection for a cure of schizophrenia was quite negative (see below, p. 439), psychoanalysts have since reported successful treatments in such cases (Bullard, 1959; Bychowski, 1952). It is wisest simply to conclude that schizophrenia is one of the most serious and disabling disorders in behavior pathology and that, especially if it has developed insidiously or has remained untreated for long, the outlook for substantial improvement is poor (T. Freeman, Cameron & McGhie, 1958; Topping & O'Connor, 1960).

Instead of beginning our study in the conventional way, with an account of each official *type* or symptom group and a recital of how such types originated historically, we shall begin with the account of an actual clinical case (see Cameron, 1947, Chapter 15, for an historical overview). The case we shall begin with has the merit of being a response to a situation that everyone can understand. It is, therefore, much more intelligible than schizophrenic episodes that develop because of weird ways of thinking, some of them lifelong, or because of unknown situations.

The schizophrenic disorder we are about to describe begins and ends rapidly. The sudden onset we can safely ascribe to the personally catastrophic nature of the situation. Precipitating stresses in the lives of schizophrenic patients are not difficult to find (G. W. Brown, 1972; Forgus & DeWolfe, 1974). The quick recovery of the patient has at least two explanations. One is that she had a basically strong, though defective, defensive and adaptive system. Research has shown that interpersonal competence before the onset of a schizophrenic episode predicts the likelihood of successful outcome following hospitalization and treatment (R. A. Knight et al., 1979). A second reason for her quick recovery was the calm but expert understanding of her therapists. This patient, as we shall see, was originally a surgical patient; and it was from the surgical staff, particularly from the nurses, that we obtained the early information that enabled us to proceed intelligently. Because of the patient's fear of hospital personnel she received little psychotherapy. She also received no medication. Yet she was able not only to recover promptly but to return to a home environment that was essentially unchanged.

### Case of Rita T.: Sudden Onset and Quick Recovery from Schizophrenic Disorder

Rita T., a single woman aged thirty, owned and operated a small dress shop. As long as she could remember she had been terribly afraid of hospitals. She would even cross the street to avoid passing near one. Whenever a relative or a friend was hospitalized she could not make herself go to the hospital. She always sent flowers and an apology.

Two weeks before her own sudden hospitalization Rita developed recurrent abdominal pains and vomiting. Her family physician diagnosed appendicitis and advised surgery. For two weeks Rita rejected the advice. One night, however, she became so frightened by an attack that she allowed herself to be taken to the hospital, where she was almost immediately operated upon. The appendix, when removed, showed only chronic inflammation, and recovery from surgery was uneventful.

The surgeons requested psychiatric consultation soon after the operation because Rita was behaving strangely. She seemed in a daze. She spoke vaguely about having cancer, about dying, about giving birth to a baby, and about seeing angels and flowers. When the psychiatric consultant saw her, Rita was lying almost motionless in bed. Most of the time her eyes were closed and her eyeballs rolled upwards, and a faint but serene smile would light up her face.

It was difficult to communicate with Rita in her semistuporous state. Most of the time she was unresponsive. When she did speak, her talk was fragmentary and often appeared irrelevant. She spoke slowly and disconnectedly of angels and music, of "the garden," of cancer and of dying. Several times she said, "All the beautiful flowers." Once she remarked that she might have been baptized a Baptist or have gone to a Methodist kindergarten. (Actually, she had had a Catholic upbringing in a Spanish-American family.)

After she had finished speaking she would stare at the ceiling with a tranquil look and a faint smile. Then she would close her eyes again. Rita was well oriented, as she might not have been had she been suffering from a severe systemic intoxication. She missed the date by only two days; she got the month and the year right; she named the hospital she was in and the city; she knew that the persons around her were nurses, doctors, and patients.

With the surgeons' blessing Rita was transferred to the psychiatric service, kept out of bed, and given a full regimen of planned activity under the close supervision of a resident and the head nurse. She required constant pressure during the day to prevent her from lapsing into deep preoccupation and immobility. When left alone for a few minutes she would slump in her chair and sometimes slip down onto the floor. It is worth pointing out that at this juncture in her regression Rita was obviously trying to escape her frightening reality by taking refuge in complete inaction and unresponsiveness. If she had been neglected she would almost certainly have slipped into a stupor. She would then have probably been diagnosed as a case of *catatonic schizophrenia,* and it is quite possible that her unresponsiveness might have become chronic. We shall need to recall this when we come to identify the classical schizophrenic types. As it was, she was kept active enough to prevent a flight into stupor.

Rita refused to eat or drink spontaneously. Because of her terrible fear of hospitals and of medical procedures, she was not given intravenous feeding. With great patience and kind persistence, the nurses spoon-fed and cup-fed her like a baby. Enemas were discontinued entirely when they were found to be making her acutely anxious. She complained that snakes were being put into her body, and that they would gnaw her insides.

Within a week after her transfer to the psychiatric service, Rita was able to give a retrospective account of the development of her psychiatric illness on the surgical ward. The objective facts in it were checked against observations made by the surgeons, the surgical nurses, and the family. This retrospective account revealed more than one source of intense anxiety, some of them unknown to the staff and the family.

When Rita went under the general anesthetic she was dominated by two fears: one that she would die, and the other that she would reveal to everyone an adolescent misdeed that was on her conscience. When she came out of the anesthetic she was frightened at being on a surgical service. She thought she was dying, and she kept saying, "Take care of father and mother." The day after her operation a doctor brought some nurses to her bedside and discussed her case. She could not understand all that he said, but in her frightened state she gathered that something terrible was the matter with her. She asked about her appendix and was told that it had not been found acutely inflamed.

This last information might have reassured Rita if it had not been for an unnoticed visit from another patient who was resentful over what had been done to her surgically. This patient heightened Rita's already intense anxiety about herself by advising her never to trust the doctors and nurses. She also had been told, she said to Rita, that she had had appendicitis, but what she really had was cancer and they had been lying to fool her. "Now look what they've done to me," she said, and she showed Rita her colostomy wound under the surgical dressings. Although this ghoulish visitor did not actually say so, the implication was clear to Rita that she, too, had been fooled by this talk about appendicitis.

In her helpless anxiety Rita came to the following frightening conclusions: there was a conspiracy to keep the truth from her; even more terrible things would happen to her in the hospital; she was dying; the nurses and doctors were against her; she must have made her secret public under the anesthetic and everyone would now disown her; she had cancer or a "disease"; she had given birth to a baby; something crooked was going on around her; she was being killed by a "dry gas"; her blood was gone or it was bad.

If these ideas had been communicated to anyone at the time, Rita would undoubtedly have been diagnosed as a case of *paranoid schizophrenia.* This changeability emphasizes the important fact that the so-called types are only groups of symptoms that fluctuate from time to time even in the same patient. They reveal the psychotic regression and some of the defenses active at the time. As this case demonstrates, neither the regression nor the psychotic defenses need become fixed, especially if the patient is protected by an understanding environment and given adequate normal stimulation.

The day after Rita had been visited by the colostomy patient, with her resentment and her strange wound, Rita's family was upset to hear her say that they must get her out of the place, that the nurses would give her no attention and were trying to get rid of her. She asked her sister to pray for her soul and said that she had cancer or "a disease." These complaints were all the more surprising because Rita had never before confided in anyone and had rarely criticized anyone.

During the night that followed Rita heard her mother's voice saying, "Do the best you can for her. No use taking her home now." Another voice spoke of killing her sister and of throwing a rock through the window. These voices might have been parts of dreams, but Rita accepted them as real happenings outside her own psychic identity. The next day she was openly suspicious of everyone and refused all food and fluids.

Then Rita began seeing and hearing angels in the daytime. They were in the air above her, and they kept saying, "Come up into the garden," which meant to die. There were beautiful flowers and there was music. Rita said to the nurses, "I feel like I'm going up and away." This all sounds like experiences of death, resurrection, and ascension, during which the patient was apparently in a partial trance. The belief that she was dying or was already dead, about which more will be said later, represented products of her unmanageable fears. The angels and the "garden" sound like delusional and hallucinatory reconstructions which served a defensive or reassuring function. The flowers and the music could certainly have belonged to a funeral; but Rita's almost ecstatic reaction to them made them also a refuge from the external reality that was frightening to her.

Later on, Rita described her experiences further. "I would just start to wander up in the air, rise and leap, then find I was in bed. . . . I was dreamy all the time, from morning to night, just dreamy. I couldn't wake myself up. I've been dreaming for two days. (*Are you coming out of it?*) I hope so. (*Did you enjoy it?*) Oh, no! I had everybody in my dreams—angels, flowers all around. They thought I ought to come up there. I thought I was. I thought I had cancer. (*Before the operation?*) No, after that."

The instability of Rita's organization at this time comes out clearly. She was asked when she had had her operation; and she replied correctly, "Monday." But, probably because this brought her fears to the fore again, she immediately closed her eyes and went limp, in what might have become a catatonic episode. When aroused she at once asked, "Why did my blood go out? I'm waiting for the gas to go through and touch my heart. When it fills up it'll put me to sleep. They'll put me in the morgue. I'm not afraid to die now." The content was quite different now from the angels and the beautiful flowers, and the level of communication was definitely lower than in the preceding talk.

On the psychiatric service, two days after Rita had become practically symptom-free, she suffered another sudden regression and both delusions and hallucinations reappeared. Fortunately they did not last long. They began when a fellow patient, who assumed that Rita was married, asked her how many children she had at home. She became greatly disturbed. Soon after she told the resident that she now believed that all her fears about revealing her secret under the anesthetic had been well founded. That evening she heard the radio broadcasting the news about her, and she insisted that a "special announcement" had been made on television concerning her past life. She interpreted crying on the ward as a sign that others knew she was doomed. She seemed fearful, suspicious and bewildered. She said, "I'm drawing my last breath. I beg you to send me home so they can put me in the graveyard. . . . It's too late now to think anything." Later she said, "I guess I'm only a spirit now and these are angels around me, the nurses. It's all too good to be true. I know they are real. I'll be dead and you can throw me in a furnace." It is not difficult to see that these experiences, while certainly delusional, expressed much more uncertainty about death and the angels than the earlier ones.

The next day Rita seemed much improved. She said, "I don't know if it was all a nightmare or what," which clearly expressed an ability now to tolerate doubt. There were no further episodes of fear and confusion. She was finally discharged, clinically well, three weeks after her operation. Because of her fear of hospitals Rita did not return for a follow-up. A relative, who saw her often, reported during the ensuing two years that she seemed to have recovered completely. After this, the hospital lost track of her.

*Discussion.* Even though we know little about Rita's childhood, we have chosen her case as a beginning because it seemed to have understandable precipitating factors, clear-cut schizophrenic symptomatology, and an uncomplicated recovery. A fear of hospitals is still widespread today in spite of their being far more often the road to recovery than the "last stop" in life. The fear that one will disclose secrets under a general anesthetic is not only widespread but quite justified. Anxiety before and after surgery may also be counted as a normal reaction, though not in the extreme form that Rita showed. Indeed, careful psychological studies of surgical patients indicate that moderate preoperative anxiety helps prepare a person for the inevitable physiological shock of the operation and its immediate consequences (Janis, 1958). The complaint that one is not getting enough attention after surgery is often only an expression of dependency needs that the emergency and the helplessness have brought to the surface.

Nonetheless, Rita reacted to stress with frankly psychotic symptoms. Her delusions and her hallucinations do not fall within normal limits as postoperative reactions. Neither does her tendency to fall into a stupor that could not be justified on physiological grounds. Taken together these symptoms constitute a schizophrenic episode. Even so, if we were to assign a diagnosis to Rita based on DSM-III, it would *not* be that of a schizophrenic disorder. This is so because of the convention adopted in DSM-III that the delusions, hallucinations, and thinking disruptions she manifested be present for a period of *six months*. Rita would be diagnosed as suffering from a *schizophreniform* disorder, meaning that it is a brief manifestation of schizophreniclike symptoms. Another convention adopted in DSM-III is that the onset of schizophrenia must be seen occurring before forty-five years of age. Rita met this criterion. If she had persisted in her psychopathology for six months, we would then have had grounds for assigning a diagnosis of schizophrenia.

Rita denied the simple realities of her situation, because of her fright and her regression, and she replaced them with experiences that lie outside those of a normal or neurotic person who is awake. Rita projected her fears of death in the form of delusions that she was already dead or was being deliberately killed. She projected her fear of betraying a secret in the form of delusions and hallucinations that everyone knew about her and that her secret was being made public through the radio and press. She also projected her wishes and fears regarding death and resurrection in her experiences of having angels hovering over her and of rising toward heaven or "the garden"; but she also projected them in her belief that she was dying, that all the blood had run out of her, and that she would be sent to a morgue or thrown into a furnace.

The attacks of extreme lassitude, in which Rita slumped in her chair and slipped onto the floor, may have represented her own death to herself. They might, like the earlier trance states, represent only a flight from the frightening situation into immobility and unresponsiveness. We have no way of knowing which of these possibilities her catatonic symptoms of immobility and unresponsiveness expressed, but we have an enormous amount of information from other patients that either of these meanings may have dominated.

We cannot call Rita's psychotic episode either mania or a psychotic depression. What little ecstasy she experienced was strictly in the service of a defense against the delusion that she was dying or dead. She had childlike visions of angels and flowers without genuine elation or aggression. What depressive experiences she had were of a macabre character, mingled with fears that she had cancer, that she had given birth to a baby, and that she was being gassed. These assorted delusions have in them the themes of birth and death, but strangely unorganized, as though each delusion appeared without relation to the others. There was no sign of a persecuting superego such as occurs in the major affective disorders.

We cannot call Rita's psychotic episode a paranoid disorder because the delusions were poorly organized, vague, unfocused, shifting, and dreamlike. Moreover, Rita had outspoken hallucinations, which do not appear in paranoid disorders, and she intermittently lost effective contact with external reality. Indeed, she would have abandoned external reality and sought to flee into a catatonic stupor if she had been left alone.

*Definition. Schizophrenic disorders are regressive attempts to escape tension and anxiety by abandoning realistic interpersonal object relations and constructing delusions and hallucinations.* As we said at the beginning of the chapter, schizophrenic disorders show a bewildering array of symptoms. Some of them seem to be the opposite of others, but all of them result from the breaking through of primary process material along a wide front. The manifest symptoms of schizophrenia are thus as varied and complex as manifest dreams. Some of these reach a depth of regression unequaled in the rest of psychopathology (Pious, 1961). When profound regression overwhelms a patient, as it almost overwhelmed Rita, we may witness the relatively simple external picture of a psychogenic stupor. But this outcome is relatively rare. As a rule the schizophrenic patient regresses gradually; as this regressive process continues, the person tries to regain the lost contact with objective reality, at various psychosexual levels and for varying periods of time.

The clinical results of such oscillations are bewildering both to the patient and to those who try to understand him or her. The manifest behavior in schizophrenia is often a conglomeration of regressive products, of reconstructive attempts to recover reality contacts, and of whatever residuals of normal behavior and experience the patient is still capable. Even such frankly pathological symptoms as delusions and hallucinations may express not only regression but also a renewed attempt to deal constructively with the shared social environment. In this sense they can be signs of improvement as well as signs of illness. We shall leave a description of schizophrenic symptomatology for a later section.

*Adaptation.* Schizophrenic reactions can be considered adaptive in the limited sense that regression and withdrawal may protect a person from a frightening social reality. Withdrawal has the virtue of reducing the complexity and the pressure of external reality, but it leaves the patient helpless. Delusions and hallucinations are adaptive if they provide satisfactory substitutes for whatever the patient has lost in his or her object relations. The advantages of such adaptive attempts are lost if schizophrenic patients, when they regress and withdraw into fantasy, either find themselves in an objectless world, which is in itself frightening, or encounter the kinds of primitive experiences that normal adults meet in dreams. Since the schizophrenic person is not asleep he or she cannot escape from desolate or frightening fantasies by waking up. Moreover, as we shall see later, the instability of ego-superego organization in the potentially schizophrenic person makes regression and withdrawal perilous. Such maneuvers may lead to disaster instead of adaptation.

## Varieties of Schizophrenic Disorders

Recall from Chapter 1 (see p. 19) that the World Health Organization has proposed an *International Classification of Diseases* that is now in its ninth revision—hence, ICD-9. We have not alluded to this scheme in the intervening chapters because our focus has been that of the DSM-III scheme. However, we come now to some basic changes in DSM-III that alter its course from that of ICD-9 sufficiently to call for comment. Thus, DSM-III has dropped all reference to *latent* and *borderline* schizophrenia, whereas ICD-9 continues to use these designations. More important, as we noted above, DSM-III has dropped the classical Kraepelinian diagnosis of *simple* schizophrenia. The ICD-9 scheme continues to use the diagnosis of simple schizophrenia, and thus it is still not entirely inappropriate to go on doing so (a fact recognized by DSM-III, incidentally).

The motivation behind these changes in DSM-III is, of course, to downplay the idea that mental illness is a *continuing* process that goes on even though the person involved is past an actual episode of the disorder (see our discussion to this effect in Chapter 1, p. 19). Hence, to speak of latent, borderline or even simple manifestations of schizophrenia in which there would be no actual signs of delusions, hallucinations, or thought disturbance would be to violate the general thrust of DSM-III. There is a concern being expressed here about entitizing psychopathological disorders.

Another change to be seen in DSM-III is the removal of the *schizoaffective disorder* from the chapter dealing with schizophrenic disorders, and placing it in a special chapter entitled "Psychotic Disorders Not Elsewhere Classified." This is also where we would find the *schizophreniform disorder* that Rita would be said to have experienced. We shall consider the schizoaffective disorder in the present section—as a variety of schizophrenic disturbance—even though we recognize and agree with the grounds for removing it from a clear-cut, schizophrenic diagnosis. DSM-III does recognize an *undifferentiated* and a *residual* type of schizophrenic disorder. The latter terms are, quite frankly, convenient labels for clinical cases that are difficult to classify.

As we noted in Chapter 1 (p. 16), the bringing together of the four classical types of psychopathology into a common disorder we owe to the classificatory genius of Kraepelin. The truth is, these basic clinical manifestations have changed very little since his initial collation, no matter how we may rearrange the terminology in the present (Klaf & Hamilton, 1961). Before Kraepelin's contribution, each of these four varieties was regarded as a more or less independent disease. One of them, *catatonia,* was even considered to be a neurological syndrome, comparable in specificity with general paresis. On the basis of his extensive clinical experience and his gift for organization, Kraepelin was able to recognize that these apparently diverse symptom pictures belong together. In line with existing prejudice about the alleged incurability of these psychoses, he conceptualized them as variations of early deterioration. He therefore applied to them all a term that was already current, *dementia praecox,* setting them in opposition to *dementia senilis. Dementia praecox* was first looked upon as a dementia that occurs precociously, in young people. Actually there need be no *dementia* at all.

The Kraepelinian types have been under fire ever since they were first formulated. In a voluminous and classical monograph, E. Bleuler (1950) helped to get rid of the misleading term *dementia praecox,* which was an advance, because the illness that Kraepelin had described is neither necessarily a dementia nor precocious. Bleuler coined the term *schizophrenia* to emphasize the fragmentation which is evident even on a descriptive level. He also made extensive reinterpretations of the symptomatology along psychodynamic lines, for at the time he was under the influence of Freud and of Freud's disciples, as he clearly indicates in his preface. In the end, however, even though he openly expressed his reluctance, Bleuler retained the Kraepelinian types because he did not know how to improve upon them.

It is probably correct to say that few clinicians are completely satisfied with the Kraepelinian types, in part because they are purely descriptive, in part because actual living schizophrenic persons too often exhibit symptoms that belong to more than one type, as the case of Rita T. has shown, and as other cases which we shall describe below will also demonstrate. Nevertheless, schizophrenic symptoms are so numerous and complex that we need some kind of subdivision if we are merely to be able to hold on to them and talk about them

(Cameron, 1944b). The current situation is that we still have the Kraepelinian types with us, albeit more clearly in ICD-9 than in DSM-III. Let us now review the four Kraepelinian types, as well as the schizoaffective type, in more detail.

## SIMPLE TYPE

What we call the *simple type* conforms closely to the old concept of dementia praecox. This form was recognized and described over three hundred years ago by Willis, who is also noted for his description of the basic arterial arrangements in the brain (*circle of Willis*). In 1674 he wrote of "young persons, lively and spirited, and at times even brilliant in their childhood, who passed into obtuseness and hebetude during adolescence." In the simple type we emphasize today a slow, insidious onset and an undramatic downhill course. The whole process looks like a slow fading of the promise of childhood, a gradual arrest of personality growth, followed by a monotonous, inexorable decline. It should be noted, however, that in many of these cases the patient has never been particularly lively, spirited, or brilliant. It is interesting, and it may be of some dynamic significance, that in the simple type neither delusions nor hallucinations seem to play a part. Delusions and hallucinations are often active attempts to regain lost object relations and hold on to them.

After a steady downward course, the decline may come to a halt at some relatively low level of adaptation. Here the patient often lives an idle, ineffectual, and apparently meaningless life. If the level of adaptation is very low or if behavior is too unpredictable, the person may require permanent institutional care. If not, he or she may lounge about the house or the neighborhood as an irresponsible idler or wander aimlessly from place to place as a vagrant. Some patients in this group are able and willing to hold temporary jobs that are, however, far below the level of their original promise. They can easily be distinguished from mentally retarded persons, if they will cooperate, by their often surprisingly good score on intelligence tests. In short, what looks like simple deterioration is actually something much more complex. A general reduction in adaptive level is not always inconsistent with a high level of creativity in some special field; that is, sometimes a person who is unable or unwilling to maintain ordinary social relationships may show exceptional talent in some creative work of his or her own.

## HEBEPHRENIC TYPE (DISORGANIZED TYPE)

DSM-III refers to this as the *disorganized type*. Hebephrenic schizophrenia is a caricature of early normal adolescence, which it often replaces. The term *hebephrenia* means literally "mind of youth." The onset may be slow and insidious, but it may also be sudden, following quickly upon a personal loss or failure. Silly, disorganized behavior is common. Giggling, smiling, and laughter that seem empty and irrelevant to the observer occur. If, on the other hand, there is sadness it seems shallow, and if there is weeping it may appear inexplicable. There may be outbursts of anger. Studies suggest that this diagnosis is rare, accounting for only about 5 percent of schizophrenic categorizations (Guggenheim & Babigian, 1974).

A young woman, for example, newly admitted to a hospital, spent several days sobbing, crying real tears and seeming to be in terrible distress. Yet she could not account for her weeping even to herself. All she could say was that she had lost something. As it turned out, she had lost the world of object relations, and she never succeeded in reorganizing so as to get it back.

With these emotional expressions go also gestures, postures, and mannerisms that appear to be symbolic, but are usually strange, more or less fragmentary, and often bizarre. Speech becomes manneristic also, even to the point of being incoherent (*word salad*) and including made-up words (*neologisms*). The delusions that develop are also likely to be bizarre and incoherent, often including weird notions of body change. Hallucinations are usually prominent, although if the patient is uncommunicative they may have to be inferred from his or her behavior.

With time, hebephrenics often withdraw more and more into preoccupation with private fantasy until they become almost completely desocialized and inaccessible. They may even wet and soil like a baby. They may sleep in the fetal position. They may have to be helped to eat, or they may eat greedily like a starved person. Occasionally a hebephrenic patient who has regressed almost to a vegetative level manages to reorganize and regain his or her lost object relations, with the help of an undaunted and gifted psychotherapist. As a rule, however, there is no complete return.

## CATATONIC TYPE

About 8 percent of all schizophrenics are classified as catatonic (Guggenheim & Babigian, 1974). The stress in this subtype of schizophrenia is laid upon motor disturbances. At one extreme a patient may be in a disorganized excitement; at the other extreme he or she may be mute and motionless, as though in a stupor. In a study of 250 patients diagnosed as catatonic schizophrenics, 110 were judged predominantly withdrawn, 67 were predominantly excited, and the remaining 73 were said to be "mixed" (Morrison, 1973). The latter designation is consistent with our claim that various manifestations of the schizophrenic regression can be found in the same individual.

In catatonic excitement there may be the same degree of incessant activity that one sees in mania, the same inability to sleep, and the same unwillingness to eat or drink. It differs from mania, however, in seeming weird, unrealistic, and incoherent. In catatonic stupor the behavior seems constricted, sometimes negativistic and sometimes overcompliant. The patient may lie rigidly, eyes closed and with a masklike face, as though he or she were dramatizing a personal death. Or the patient may sit or stand and stare blankly ahead or at the floor for hours at a time. It is sometimes possible to move such a patient's arms about in various positions—such as extending them from his or her sides—and observe a very slow return of the arms to the sides of the body. This slow malleability has been termed *waxy flexibility,* and the symptom was once quite prevalent, although modern medications have made it less likely to appear in catatonic behavior. Sometimes a patient comes abruptly out of such a stupor, revealing that he or she was in better contact with the surrounding environment than we might have expected. For example, one of our male catatonic patients once broke a stuporous silence of over two years in protest to the demand we were making on him to attend a group therapy session.

In both the excited and the immobile catatonic patient there are delusions, persecutory in character or mystical and miraculous. There are nearly always hallucinations also. These consist predominantly of terrifying visions, unintelligible apparitions, religious visitations, or voices and other sounds having fearsome or mysterious meanings. One can often learn something about the character of these delusions and hallucinations during relatively clear phases of the illness, but the chief source of information is the retrospective account that many patients are willing and able to give after partial recovery. Catatonic schizophrenia is more likely than the other types to come on suddenly and to clear up suddenly. This statement must, however, be tempered by the realization that pure types seldom appear.

## PARANOID TYPE

This is the largest subgroup, holding 50 percent or more of the patients diagnosed as schizophrenic (Nathan et al., 1969). Delusions hold the spotlight in this type of schizophrenia. The paranoid schizophrenic patient has usually had serious interpersonal difficulties for many years before he or she actually develops "the" illness leading to hospitalization. These patients are characteristically tense, uneasy, and distrustful, with a tendency to read hostile and belittling meanings into other people's comments and to apply these to themselves. They may have tried to compensate for their mistrust by keeping a watchful, suspicious eye on whatever goes on around them, so as to be ready if anything untoward occurs. They may, instead, have remained for many years defensively aloof, asocial, and withdrawn, so that nothing can touch them. Their lifelong custom is to mull things over alone, looking for explanations that seem plausible to them. Naturally, the paranoid's personal fears, needs, wishes, and uncertainties play a large part in such lonely brooding.

The onset of paranoid schizophrenia comes when the person begins to lose grip on reality, substitutes personal misinterpretations and fantasies for the realities of shared social operations, and acts upon these delusional beliefs as though they were publicly accepted fact. When this happens, the paranoid schizophrenic person regresses more quickly and further than the person with a paranoid disorder (see Chapter 11). The paranoid schizophrenic's delusions are likely to be vague, bizarre, and unconvincing. Their structure varies all the way from a mere succession of disjointed fragments to the most florid, imaginative jungles. Some are full of contradictions, of condensations and displacements, and of archaic symbolism such as in ordinary dreaming. Persecutory delusions are common, as are also delusions of influence and of grandeur, with ideas of reference (Lucas, Sansbury, & Collins, 1962). There are mixtures of the magical, mystical, religious, and sexual, often in weird combination. Somatic delusions are characteristically bizarre. One finds sometimes vivid delusions of catastrophe, world destruction, salvation, and world reconstruction.

Hallucinations are nearly always present, and in greater profusion than in any other major syndrome, with the possible exception of toxic and infectious states. The hallucinations usually support and enrich delusional beliefs. Auditory hallucinations are the most common; visual the next most common (Sartorius, Shapiro, & Jablensky, 1974). Hallucinations of smell, taste, bodily equilibrium, and skin sensation may also appear as important expressions of the patient's dynamics.

Emotional involvement is usual in paranoid schizophrenia, at least while the illness is active. The persecuted patient is terrified, indignant, and belligerent and may go into a whirlwind of furious retaliation or plan revenge relentlessly for an imagined wrong. Even when the patient's response is submissive and compliant, he or she usually shows emotional feeling appropriately. Likewise, grandiose schizophrenic patients look grandiose; delusions of royalty make a person look proud and lofty; the transfigured patient usually looks as he or she feels. It is still true, however, that more schizophrenic patients exhibit emotional incongruities than other patients do, and we are still not certain why. It is interesting to note that studies reveal that high emotional expressiveness in the schizophrenic's home makes the chances of (nine-month) relapse rise to 55 percent, as compared with the 16 percent relapse probability found in homes with low emotional expressiveness (G. W. Brown, Birley, & Wing, 1972).

Recovery from paranoid schizophrenia is most likely to occur during the first year or two of frank psychosis. Such recovery does not mean that the patient will necessarily create a new personality. The goal of helping a decompensated patient back to as good an equilibrium as was experienced before the psychotic break is a realistic one. It is sometimes possible to guard against a second break by helping the patient to understand the areas of vulnerability, so that he or she can try to avoid the kind of situation that helped precipitate the first. The experience of having been able to confide in a therapist can be a new and strengthening one to which the patient may return in times of later stress.

If the paranoid schizophrenic patient does not get well, he or she is likely to undergo some further disorganization. Delusions grow more and more vague and unintelligible, or they become fixed and stereotyped. The patient gives up trying to account for them. Speech may also grow less organized and become limited in scope, stereotyped, and jumbled. Mannerisms become established. Emotional responses lose their flexibility and may become unpredictable. In the end, patients who remain ill tend, as in the other subtypes, to live a greatly impoverished, desocialized life. If not made angry, they may lead an aimless, detached life of surly, silent defiance. It is not unusual for catatonic or hebephrenic characteristics to appear or for the person to suffer a general decline like that of the simple type.

## SCHIZOAFFECTIVE TYPE

As noted above, DSM-III refers to the schizoaffective type as the schizoaffective disorder, places it in a separate chapter, and holds out no real hope that it will be a lasting diagnostic category. We shall refer to it as a "type" of schizophrenia, to retain a certain consistency with our section headings. The schizoaffective type is exactly what the name implies, a mixture of schizophrenic symptoms with manic or depressive ones. This type is the rarest of all schizophrenic diagnoses, accounting for not much more than about 1 percent of all such patients.

Many clinicians view this diagnosis as a necessary convenience in classification, although it may have dynamic implications. The clinical picture is essentially that of an elation or a depression in which delusions are more weird, vaguer, and less well organized than usual. Hallucinations are common, whereas they are not in mania and depression (Dempsey et al., 1975). Estrangement, depersonalization, and bizarre somatic delusions are common. On the other hand, the elated or depressive component is more stable, better organized, and deeper than in most other schizophrenic illnesses. The mode of onset, course, and outcome are as variable as in other types, but the chances for recovery are perhaps better. If there are recurrences after recovery, the schizophrenic features grow more prominent and the chances for recovery grow poorer. It should be noted that some clinicians hold out the possibility that this disorder is what it actually suggests—the consecutive occurrence of two forms of psycho-pathological disease in one person at the same time (Carson & Adams, 1979). In the same way that a person might suffer from heart disease and tuberculosis at the same time, a seriously disturbed person might have both psychotic depression and schizophrenia at the same time.

## Clinical Illustrations of Schizophrenic Disorders

Having now described the classical subtypes of the schizophrenic disorder, we shall give in some detail an account of two cases that will illustrate many of the typical symptoms. It will be seen that characteristics of more than one so-called type enter into each case, as is true of most schizophrenic patients in real life. For example, the high school girl exhibited almost typical paranoid delusions, went through weird, semimagical rituals, and at times suddenly became catatonic. The man suffered from weird somatic delusions and later on seemed to deteriorate and become hebephrenic as well as mute. Both patients heard voices. Neither of them recovered. Both of them lost an important person through death, a person who had probably been helping to hold together a basically defective maladaptive personality in the patient. The girl was mixed up in a confusing Oedipal conflict for three years before hospitalization. The man was so strongly attached to his mother that he could not marry. He also showed signs of serious confusions regarding his sexual identity.

*Case of Joan R.: A Schizophrenic Disorder in Adolescence*

Joan R., a Kansas City high school girl, was admitted to a psychiatric clinic after she had attempted suicide by drinking iodine. We shall begin with her childhood. She had suffered the loss through death of two important mother figures, one when she was two years old, the other when she was fourteen. These are critical ages in personality development, ages when a mother figure often plays her most significant role. Joan's mother had been ill for some time before her death, so that the little girl lacked the ego support that should have been available to her for the structuring of her early personality. At fourteen, when an adolescent normally lives through in altered form the Oedipal conflicts of early childhood, Joan's foster mother died, and Joan was again left with no one to help her build her adolescent personality. To further complicate matters for Joan, her foster mother was her father's sister, a domineering widow with a daughter of her own. It will be simplest if we briefly present the patient's life history.

As we have said, Joan was two years old when her mother died. Her father's sister moved at once into the home, taking Joan's mother's place, and bringing with her Stephanie, an eight-year-old daughter. We shall see how Joan tried to repeat what her foster mother had done as soon as death left her place vacant. Stephanie's mother was an anxious, probably superstitious woman who encouraged Joan to be overdependent. The two girls apparently hated each other. When Stephanie's mother died, Joan was fourteen and Stephanie was a grown woman of twenty. The household now consisted of Joan, Stephanie, and Joan's father, a mathematician with little psychological understanding.

To her father's surprise Joan showed no sorrow over the death of her foster mother. Instead, she tried at once to take her place in the home, just as her foster mother had immediately taken her own mother's place. She became self-assertive, arrogant, and demanding. The home, she said, was now hers, and Stephanie could henceforth obey her orders. Joan's father spent the next two years trying unsuccessfully to keep the peace between these two women, rivals for control of the home.

Without a mother figure and without a stable personality of her own, Joan soon got out of control. She continued for the time being to be affectionate to her father, but she also behaved toward him as a nagging wife rather than as a young adolescent daughter. She openly criticized his appearance and his ways, even in front of guests. She demanded that he give her more attention and more money. She reminded her father that her foster mother, her father's sister, had been afraid in the house, often saying that there was a curse upon the place. She protested violently against his going out in the evening and leaving the key under the mat, where thieves and rapists might find it. As we shall see, Joan was already beginning to develop delusional fears in relation to this evening situation—which was obviously a source of realistic anxiety as well. Toward Stephanie, her grownup cousin, she remained relentlessly hostile. Once, during a quarrel over the selection of a television program for viewing, Joan bit Stephanie, giving her a wound that took two weeks to heal. From other evidence it is clear that Joan's emotional problems, with which no one helped her, were precipitating a general personality disorganization.

When Joan was sixteen her cousin married. This removed her rival from the home, but it also left Joan, in a state of emotional turmoil, alone in the house with her father. Her attitude toward him abruptly changed. She no longer gave or accepted tokens of affection. The hate that she had visited upon her cousin she now directed toward her father. She behaved insolently toward him, accusing him even before visitors of mistreating her. These accusations, which completely mystified her father, were actually the product of delusional experiences that she was having, experiences in which weird primary process fears and wishes had escaped repression and were mingling with preconscious and conscious mental contents. What these were we shall soon see.

Whenever Joan had frightening dreams she would make her father join her in bed, as her aunt had always done, but later she would rail against him for having done this and accuse him of mistreatment. He was greatly disconcerted by all this contradiction and confusion, but he did not know what to do about it. He thought she would outgrow it. One night he came home late to find his daughter thrashing about the room with a cane—killing snakes, she said. She used to keep her light on all night long because she was having "scary dreams," which were probably delusional and hallucinatory experiences rather than dreams.

As might be expected, after the aunt's death, when Joan was fourteen, her schoolwork grew poorer and poorer. She seemed bored, inattentive, and irritable. By the time she was fifteen and a half she needed a tutor to keep her from being dropped from school. Eventually even this help was not enough. When she was sixteen, Joan was dropped from school, and her father was told to consult a psychiatrist. The psychiatrist recommended immediate treatment, but his recommendation was not followed. Joan simply stayed at home.

Joan showed a corresponding decline in her social relationships. Undoubtedly because of her personality defects, and because she was overdependent upon her foster mother, Joan had never reached an adequate level of social skills. She frightened and repelled the neighborhood children with her temper tantrums and uncompromising demands. As an adolescent she was far too much involved in the rivalry with her cousin for domination in the home, in her own revived Oedipal conflicts, and her preoccupations with frightening experiences to be able to interact normally with her peers, the boys and girls around her.

The climax came when Joan was sixteen, a year before she came to the hospital. She bought a new dress for a high school dance, but when her escort arrived she refused at first to see him. After considerable persuasion she finally consented to go with him; half an hour later she returned home without her escort. Perhaps she knew that her father had arranged to have her escorted when he found that nobody had invited her to the dance. At any rate, this was her last social engagement. Following Joan's withdrawl from school, her father arranged little parties for her, "to help get her well," but she would shut herself in her room until the guests left the house. The best he could do about the situation was to engage a housekeeper.

During the months between leaving school and entering the hospital Joan was living in a nightmare. She was afraid to sleep at night because of all that seemed to be going on. During the day she lay around the house, preoccupied, worn out, and doing next to nothing. Her behavior became obviously strange, reflecting the hopeless confusion of her thinking. For example, her father gave her eighty dollars to buy some clothes, and she spent it all on history books that she never read. On another occasion she spent thirty dollars on cosmetics, but a few days later she destroyed the lot. She got up early one morning, collected all the playing cards in the house and burned them, saying that they were sinful. She began talking about religion, the church, sin, charity, and the hereafter. She gave the housekeeper ten dollars because she had to be charitable "to get to heaven."

Joan said that all her troubles came from masturbation. At fifteen she concluded without telling anyone that this was driving her crazy. Her conclusion increased her already intolerable guilt, anxiety, and confusion and contributed to her belief that she would burn in hell for her sins and that her hands were diseased. "I have leprosy!" she said at the hospital, "look at my hands. But that's not punishment enough for all my evil. Faust, yes, he gave himself to the devil. That's what I've done. Don't touch me! You'll be sorry, you'll get leprosy too!"

Joan's unconscious material, which ultimately emerged and overwhelmed her, seems to have appeared first as anxiety dreams and frightening nighttime fantasies — of snakes, assault, strangers in the house, and murder. "I used to read stories and things," she said, "and then I'd go to bed and lie awake and think about them. I'd be scared silly to be in the room by myself. That house is so spooky." The last statement repeats what her foster mother had always said. When Joan closed her eyes and tried to sleep, she would have horrible visions, and see faces that seemed to grow enormous (a phenomenon that is noted in normal individuals who are falling asleep; see Isakower, 1938). She thought men were walking on the roofs, which were flat and connected with one another, and that they were climbing in the window. Eventually a man across the street seemed to control the house, and she began hearing voices. Finally a man's voice dominated, telling her to do whatever she was told.

Joan now used weird delusions to reconstruct the reality that she had lost in her steady regression and disorganization, delusions that would help explain her previously unconscious fantasies, now fully conscious. Her home, she told herself, was now the headquarters of a dope ring. Her father had been murdered and an imposter put in his place. "My father wouldn't treat me the way this man has treated me," she said. "My father and I were friends. This man will get into bed with me. I've been love-starved and forsaken; and I thought someone was bringing in heroin or opium or something." In her fantasies, which Joan considered real, people seemed to beat her and tie her up. They seemed able to read her mind, to control her by reading her thoughts. She tried to keep back her thoughts, but the effort hurt the back of her head.

Joan began having horrible dreams and fantasies of killing her father and other people, of cutting them up and chewing their flesh, of being God, and of being murdered as a sacrifice. She felt at times that she was someone else, that her body was changing, that she might be going to have a baby, that she had a brain tumor and was going crazy.

In the hospital, where people listened to her when she spoke, some of her sadomasochistic fantasies became obvious. Joan said that her suicide attempt was an act of self-punishment. She was going to hell for her sins, she thought, and the quicker she got there the better. "I thought it would make me suffer. If I hadn't become so hardened it would have hurt terribly." At times she was sure she would be executed for her crimes, which seemed real to her, or that she would get life imprisonment. She wished that she would "get black smallpox or something." She said, "I got hyped-up on the subject of Christianity. I thought I should torture myself. . . . I try to figure out ways of torturing people. It seems I have been in so much pain; and I want other people to have the same thing."

Joan had many outbursts of rage. One night a nurse found her trembling and wringing her hands. "I think I'm pushing people's eyes in. I'm totally freaked-out and deadly. . . . It's those awful thoughts that go through my head." Once in the daytime she cried to a group of patients, "If I had the strength of Christ I would kill every one of you! Yes, I would kill you all because a more horrible doom awaits you than death." There is a sign of confusion between herself and the others in this histrionic statement. Another day Joan became angry and struck an inoffensive depressed patient. "That's nothing in comparison with what I'm going to do," she cried, "I'm going to chop off your heads, every goddam one of you. . . . You're not going to keep me here and make me bear children!" In the more permissive atmosphere of the hospital, Joan was giving vent to the violent aggression that she had felt for years at home. After expressing it, she excused herself on the grounds that she would be saving the patients from something worse by killing them.

There were grandiose delusions also. Joan said that she felt she had a powerful influence over people and was responsible for everything that happened. She thought that she might get superhuman ideas, "such as how Christ turned water into wine—I had to find out how it was done." As God, she thought, she must suffer to help others, and because of her sins she ought to kill herself. But the attempt failed. "So," she said, "I came to the conclusion that I would have to forget. As time goes on, I'll forget all my troubles, my experiences and so forth." This was just what Joan seemed to be achieving. She expressed, in well-organized secondary process speech, the disintegration that she was experiencing, and to which she was resigned.

There were two definite catatonic episodes. One day, while telling her therapist that she liked dreamy states, Joan slipped into a stupor. Her eyes closed, her eyeballs rolled upward, and her limbs went limp. Her eyelids resisted opening, however, and her jaws and limbs grew stiffer as they were manipulated. When she was left alone she soon recovered. Another day Joan was lying on her side on her bed, just before lunch, when there was a sudden loud clap of thunder close by. Joan instantly became so rigid that the nurses could pick her up and place her in a sitting position with no more change in her posture than if she had been a statue. Then the lunch trays arrived, and an experienced nurse began coaxing her gently and spoon-feeding her. After about ten minutes of this, Joan suddenly got up, rubbed her eyes as though she had just awakened, and ate her lunch with the others as if nothing had happened.

Therapy was unsuccessful with Joan. She slept well at night without medication, in spite of occasional disturbing dreams. In the daytime she spent most of her time daydreaming. She became less and less communicative, her talk developed more and more disorganization. She was frequently observed talking excitedly to herself. Sometimes she smiled and laughed as though she were hallucinating. Often she stood straight against the wall with her hands high above her head, but she would give no explanation of this posturing. Her father decided to place Joan in a state hospital near her home. Her prognosis for social recovery was very poor.

*Discussion.* In this case we see the progressive disorganization of an adolescent girl during a period of over three years. Joan suffered two severely traumatic losses. Her mother fell ill and died when Joan was only two, before she had time to establish her own childhood personality. Her foster mother confused the child by immediately taking the dead mother's place and by introducing a rival girl into the home. The fact that the woman who took the place of Joan's mother in the house was the sister of Joan's father must have added to the confusion, although we have no information about this. What we do know, however, is that neither girl seems to have been adequately protected from the hostility of the other, at least after the foster mother died. The death of her domineering foster mother when Joan was only fourteen was the second severe trauma. It was compounded by the father's ineptness in handling emotional situations.

The affectional situation was suddenly complicated when the foster mother died. If Joan had been four years older or younger, she might have weathered it, in spite of having always been overdependent and overprotected. We have seen how unskillfully Joan tried to identify with her dead foster mother and take over the household immediately, as her foster mother had done. Her growing confusion can in part be attributed to the conflicts and contradictions, the tumult of early adolescent love and hate, which Joan's ineffectual attempts must have stimulated. A fourteen-year-old girl with such a background could hardly take the role of a domineering mother toward her twenty-year-old cousin; neither could she transform her dependent daughter role into that of the woman of the house in relation to her father. She had been reared an anxious, socially immature child without adequate opportunity to develop a mature ego-superego organization. As such, she was left alone to work out her multiple conflicts, including her clearly expressed guilt over sex and hostility, in a household with a man who did not understand her and a woman whom she hated.

Another important factor in promoting Joan's disorganization was the progressive intrusion of primary process fantasy into her nighttime and daytime thinking, once she had been abandoned to the complex home situation by the death of her aunt. Long before her aunt's death, probably throughout her life, Joan had found difficulty in distinguishing between dream and daydream. She had utilized fantasy freely in satisfying personal wishes, and she had also experienced terrifying dreams and hypnagogic visions that drove her to seek the protection of her aunt's bed. We have seen how she carried her conflicts, her wishes, fears, and furies, over into her waking and sleeping fantasy life after her aunt was dead.

This procedure settled nothing. On the contrary, the confusion of fantasy and fact only increased Joan's anxiety and complicated her problems. There was now no adult to whom she could flee for comforting in the night, no adult who could act as substitute ego in support of her own inadequate one. The childhood fantasies came tumbling out of repression, through the defective defensive boundaries, and into Joan's daytime thinking. She was able to halt her regression by constructing fantastic delusions, which sounded like murder mystery stories, but this halt did not last. Even before she was admitted to the hospital Joan had regressed into the jungles of primary process thinking. Therapy did not succeed in rescuing her. She continued regressing into an autistic world of fantasy where she ignored her surroundings as much as she could.

*Case of Mark J.: A Schizophrenic Disorder in Young Adulthood*

Mark J., an unmarried man aged thirty, had been trained as an electrical engineer. In part because of adverse business conditions, in part because of his own awkwardness and immaturity, he had never succeeded in establishing himself in his profession. Instead, he had been in succession a draftsman, an amateur inventor, and a mechanic's assistant. His early life throws light upon his failure in ego development.

Mark's mother died a few days after he was born. He had always felt in some way responsible for this. He was almost immediately placed with a childless couple and separated from his siblings. His foster parents were unusually indulgent, his foster mother was domineering and possessive, and Mark had no children to play with at all until he began school at the late age of eight years. He said that he had always been happy playing imaginative, solitary games. He regarded his foster mother as perfect, an opinion that was not shared by his relatives, who described her as demanding, nagging, and short-tempered.

When Mark was fourteen he began to masturbate, and he developed great concern and guilt about it. By the time he was fifteen he had developed what may have been an adolescent schizophrenic flurry. He was extremely anxious. He imagined terrible things happening to him because of his sin, among them the feeling that his blood had been turned into a snake that whirled about in his body. This illness lasted about six months, but it never kept him from school for more than a few weeks at a time. He had two similar episodes in engineering college, of short duration, each developing in a setting of stress, fatigue, and failure in examinations. At the age of twenty-two Mark was graduated from engineering college, obtained employment as a draftsman whose task it was to devise and test electrical circuits, and returned to live with his foster mother, who had meantime been widowed.

Although Mark spoke of this phase of his life as "the happy days," it must also have been difficult for him. His foster mother was soon paralyzed by a stroke and became, according to relatives, a terrible old lady, cantankerous, an "impossible" invalid. Mark had to run the house and the finances and look after his foster mother at the same time that he was holding down an exacting job. In spite of all this he managed to devise and patent a new kind of wheelchair in his spare time.

During this period Mark fell in love with a girl and asked her to marry him. She accepted his proposal on condition that he give up his mother. He decided to stay with his mother and give up the girl. When he was twenty-eight Mark lost his job and, failing to get another, he began making and selling his patented wheelchairs. This brought him only a few thousand dollars a year. Then he came down with influenza and gave it to his foster mother, so he said, and she suddenly died. He had to get out of a sickbed to make the funeral arrangements and attend her burial. It reminded him of his feeling that he was responsible for his mother's death.

When it was all over, and he had sold the home and gone to live with acquaintances, he still felt ill and sad. He had made few close friends while his foster mother lived, and now he felt life to be lonely and empty. He tried hard to establish himself in the affections of his siblings, behaving as though he had been brought up with them. They were cool to him, and their failure to accept him hurt his feelings and bewildered him. His only consolation was the friendship of a girl whose acquaintance he had made at this time. He did not propose to her until later, but he took it for granted that when he did so the girl would accept him.

A year after his foster mother's death, and eight months prior to his admission to the clinic, Mark succeeded in getting a job as a mechanic's assistant in another city. Here he worked with a gang of good-natured but earthy men. As an awkward, socially inexperienced person he quickly became the butt of his fellow workers' witticisms. He admitted one day that he had never had sexual intercourse, and from then on he was called "the virgin" by his workmates. His virginity, with its possible implications (i.e., homosexuality), was repeatedly discussed and hilariously commented upon in his presence. Since teasing of this kind often includes ambiguous references to the sex of the person being teased, it is highly probable that this banter contributed to Mark's confusion about his sex identity, which came out clearly as soon as he fell ill.

For recreation Mark spent weekends in his home city, where he visited acquaintances and his girlfriend. During the week he occasionally went to bars with fellow workers, one of whom coaxed him into frequenting a local "massage parlor" in hopes of ending his virgin status. Mark did engage in masturbatory sexual play with a woman at the parlor, and later noted a slight abrasion on his penis. A few days later a rash appeared on his body, and he leaped to the conclusion that he had developed syphilis. This he regarded as punishment for his sex play, but he did nothing about it except to worry.

Two months before admission to the clinic Mark developed back pains after changing to harder work. At about the same time his girlfriend told him that she was in love with someone else and not interested in him. The pains then became worse and spread to his abdomen and his groin. His fears about syphilis finally drove Mark to seek medical help. In the course of diagnostic investigation he was cystoscoped (visual examination of the bladder). This was not only painful, it also resulted in genital paresthesias and heightened his already intense anxiety about himself.

According to Mark, he was told that he had a kidney infection, given a bottle of medicine, and told not to worry because the kidneys had been washed out. Unfortunately he believed in the folklore that tampering with the kidneys may change a man's sexual powers. He said later: "It all started after I had my kidneys cleaned out. . . . The medicines cleaned me out front and back; and I was practically hollow there." He returned to work, but "everything seemed like a dream," his eyesight was dim, and he saw spots before his eyes. He returned to his physician twice, "to see what it was all about," but the medicines prescribed made him feel more upset than ever. With this focus Mark quickly developed bizarre somatic delusions, some of which he experienced as dreams, some as waking experiences.

It seemed to Mark that his two sides were no longer working together. The right seemed to be stronger than the left. One night he awakened to find that he seemed to have grown a female breast on the left, and to have acquired a boy's genitals that were not a part of himself. He believed that he could choose which of these three persons he might become—the man, the woman, or the child. But the medicines, he said, made the boy win out. His voice seemed to grow boyish, his hands became soft, his heart felt weak, only one side of his intestines was working, and a hernia that had been corrected in boyhood seemed to come back. At one time Mark was sure that he had three hearts, one on the right, one on the left, and one in his genitals. He thought that his father's blood was in the right side and his mother's in the left. The blood rushed back and forth between these two sides.

Mark heard a voice telling him to drink much more milk and this would make him well. He was not sure whether it was God's voice or the devil's. At night he had horrifying dreams. In the daytime he began walking the streets alone, feeling that terrible things were happening to him. He dreamed, for example, that he was giving birth to a litter of kittens, all chewing and scratching. Another time, after an anxiety dream, he turned the light on to find his body had turned "milk-white." One night he dreamed that his body had shriveled up, and he awoke expecting death. In his fright he made a will and sat down in a chair to die. His body seemed to go stiff and then he knew he was dead, but after a while he felt better and went out for something to eat. The next morning he was so weak that he could scarely walk. His food fell through him like a stone, and then he realized that there was a snake in him.

Of this last episode he said: "I've been bothered by seeing myself in all kinds of shapes after I'd taken that medicine. . . . My body was shrinking up, and I felt death creeping up on me, and I ate sour fruit. Next morning the snake was in my belly and then in my back; and it's been traveling around in me ever since. . . . When I walk, I walk like a snake." Mark said that his blood rushed around his body "like a wriggling snake." This is the same complaint that he made in adolescence when he was worried about masturbating.

Mark went in desperation to his home city for help. His old family physician advised him to go to a psychiatric clinic. His friends told him he was getting on their nerves. He telephoned his former girlfriend, but she only said, "You must paddle your own canoe." To himself he said, "There's no one in the world to help me now." Back in the city where he worked he at first wandered about indecisively; but he eventually appeared at the outpatient psychiatric clinic. Here he complained that a snake was in his belly, and that he was three persons in one—a man, a woman, and a child. He was admitted to the inpatient service at once.

After a few days of confusion Mark appeared to improve rapidly. He dismissed his former complaints as "crazy stuff," saying that he "must have been nuts." At the end of four weeks, since he was in the hospital on a voluntary basis, he was discharged at his own request to return to work. Arrangements were made for him to report to the outpatient clinic for further psychotherapy.

Mark disappeared for eleven days. He was readmitted to the inpatient service, dirty and disheveled, agitated, suspicious, and confused. He could not say where he had been. His complaint now was that he was "falling to pieces," a complaint which seemed justified by his behavior. In the ensuing five months he improved only superficially. Then he was taken by relatives to a hospital near his home. According to a report received a year later from that hospital efforts at therapy had been fruitless. Mark had become mute and withdrawn. He spent his time sitting alone, smirking and giggling, and apparently hallucinating. He was evidently living in a world of fantasied things, people, and situations, at a greatly regressed level.

*Discussion.* We have presented this case because of the fantastic somatic delusions it illustrates and because of the frantic but inept attempts the patient made to establish object relations with other people after his foster mother died. The symptoms are exceedingly bizarre, showing an invasion of thinking by concrete primary process interpretations. As in the case of Joan R., the patient was unable to distinguish clearly between dream, fantasy, and fact once he became seriously upset. This kind of confusion, appearing in a person who is not toxic, indicates serious defects in ego organization, ego defense, and ego adaptation. It indicates that normal boundaries between ego, id, superego, somatic reality, and external reality had never been firmly established.

If we look at his early childhood, we find that Mark was denied the ordinary opportunities for interacting with other children, or for that matter with anyone but his tyrannical foster mother and perhaps his foster father, until he was eight years old. He seems to have lived almost all of his life in bondage to a person who demanded obedience and affection but gave nothing in return. His play was confined to solitary imagining. There is no hint in his life story of anything approaching normal independence of action or thinking. Even his invention of a wheelchair was prompted by his desire to look after his foster mother following her stroke.

Mark weathered three illnesses during his adolescence in which somatic symptoms of a bizarre character appeared. It is probable that he weathered them because he could rely upon the strength of his tyrannical foster mother. During his adolescence, he had a strong mother figure in the background who could provide ego support at times when he was on the point of "falling to pieces." When he finally did fall ill, it was only after his foster mother had died, when he tried turning in all directions to find someone to save him from disintegrating.

We do not know the childhood origin of Mark's confusion of sex identity, a symptom not uncommon among schizophrenic patients. We do know that the teasing by his fellow workers, with all the implied ambiguity, seemed to bring it out clearly in his bizarre somatic complaints. Added to all the other anxiety-provoking confusions was also Mark's feeling that he had killed his own mother at the time of his birth and his foster mother through infecting her with influenza.

## Thought and Language Disturbances in Schizophrenia

As we have seen, schizophrenics manifest severe regression with the attendant hallucinations and delusions springing from primary process fantasies to equal and surpass all other syndromes of psychopathology. They have severe disturbances in object relations, emotional control, and defensive functions, as is more or less true of the other disorders of this volume. But what stamps the schizophrenic disorder as unique in the family of mental disorders is the unique thought and language disturbances that patients diagnosed as schizophrenic reflect. A major finding of subjective reports of such patients after they have passed through a schizophrenic episode is that they simply could not focus their attention and concentrate on anything (Freedman, 1974). The slightest distraction threw their line of thought off course.

Schizophrenic patients report that if someone to whom they are talking scratches himself or herself, they lose their trend of thought in the conversation. While reading a book, if something comes up in the story that is especially interesting, the possible outcomes and associated details begin to intrude on their thoughts so that the schizophrenic patients literally begin to depart from what they are reading, get confused, and end up putting down the book with a sense of fear and anxiety. It appears that with the onset of the schizophrenic episode these kinds of thought disturbances and distractions multiply. In conveying what is taking place the schizophrenic patient then begins to reflect increasingly alarming signs that his or her language usage is losing its relatedness to reality. Some of the first signs of the actual "schism" in reality relations occurs in the schizophrenic's peculiar use of language.

At the outset, a schizophrenic patient's talking and thinking may show no greater change than an indefinable vagueness, with perhaps complaints of being unable to think clearly. A schoolteacher, for example, said: "I just exactly can't talk as clearly. I'd give a pretty dime to talk like I like or place my words in talking with people noticing." Of her thinking this schizophrenic young woman said, "It slips because you go on and talk and have imaginations and try for others and seems just to come back to you." A high school boy of sixteen, in a psychological test situation, completed the phrase *My hair is fair because* with the statement, "Because of something else, it's on my head, it comes from my mother." After partial recovery he completed the same phrase with, "Because I inherited it from my parents." To the test phrase *The wind blows because* he replied while he was ill, "Just cosmic dust," but after partial recovery from the schizophrenic episode his answer became, "Because of atmospheric air currents changing." We must keep in mind that such language distortion reflects underlying problems of thinking, whether the latter be in "words" alone or in "images *and* words" (Cameron, 1938, 1944b).

As the schizophrenic disorientation continues, the patient may reach a level of verbal discontinuity at which his or her talk becomes useless as an instrument of communication. Conventional sequences of words and the use of appropriate connectives disappear, and the flow of talk becomes disjointed. The result is not the same as aphasic speech, but it can be just as socially disabling to the patient. Early in a schizophrenic illness this verbal discontinuity, usually called *scatter,* may be evident only in relation to personal conflicts, much as one finds it in an embarrassed adolescent. If the illness goes on, however, it may include everything but a few stereotyped replies to stereotyped questions. Neologisms appear in the talk of some patients. Sometimes these are *condensations* typical of the primary process; sometimes they represent the development of a highly individualized idiom that communicates little to others (Gottschalk et al., 1961; Lothrop, 1961).

Related to the latter is the development in schizophrenia of a mode of language that uses words and phrases with approximately their common meaning, but with enough imprecision to confuse the average listener in the same way that an imperfectly known foreign language confuses him or her. The private idiom that some patients develop and use as speech may be unintelligible until it has been translated. To be able to make the translation one must usually study the patient's speech in relation to his or her personal history, including difficulties in adjustment, delusions, and lifelong verbal habits (Chapman & Chapman, 1973). An example of a personalized idiom follows:

A patient states that he is alive, "Because you really live physically because you have menu three times a day. That's the physical." (*What else is there besides the physical?*) "Then you're alive mostly to serve a work from the standpoint of methodical business." A knowledge of the patient's habitual idiom and his preoccupation with serving the world makes this translation possible: "You live physically because you have three meals a day and you live to perform a service in your daily routines." The use of such personal idiom, even without other disorganization, is in effect to cut the patient off from the interpersonal relations that he needs to regain contact with reality. Neither his family nor the other patients were willing to make the constant effort that was necessary to communicate with this man. He himself gave the impression of not caring whether he communicated with anyone or not. He had been hospitalized for several years.

*Mutism in Schizophrenia.* Mutism is not uncommon in schizophrenic disorders. Its most distinctive characteristics are the abruptness with which it may begin and end and its often obvious relationship to the rest of the patient's behavior. The abruptness of onset and ending may be related to the fluctuation in fixation level that defines schizophrenia. It may also be a direct product of the situation. There is extensive empirical evidence supporting the view that schizophrenic symptoms of all sorts come or go or are otherwise modified depending on the situational demands facing the patient at the time (Levy, 1976; Shimkunas, 1972). Here are some examples of mutism:

One schizophrenic patient was put under too much pressure by her therapist to tell her troubles. After having done so she said, "I've talked too much," and she remained mute for almost a year. Another patient, mute for several months, awakened one night and asked to see her therapist. When he came she conversed with him for over an hour. Her manner was somewhat dreamy and her sentences sometimes trailed off without a finish, but the general form of her talk was otherwise normally relevant and coherent. She spoke as one who had been in another world and had just returned—which was one of her beliefs—asking questions about the hospital, the nurses and the attendants, the other patients, and her family. Finally she said she wanted to go back to bed. The next morning she was mute as ever. A month later she began to speak in the daytime, and eventually she make a social recovery. A third patient, mute even before admission, received an unexpected visit from her relatives. She jumped up from her chair at once to greet them and conversed freely and naturally. When her therapist appeared she became mute, but resumed speaking as soon as he left. As soon as her visitors left she stopped talking. Some months later she also recovered. None of these mute patients explained their long silences when they recovered. In each the reason may have been different.

*Overinclusion in Schizophrenia.* It is obvious that ego organization in perceptual and cognitive mental operations, as well as in autonomous functions, depends as much upon what is kept out as upon what is included. There are advantages, of course, in allowing a certain amount of instability and inclusiveness in unstructured, developing situations. For then ego organization is flexible enough to be able to adapt to unforeseen changes in the field. When it comes to structured situations, when one needs precision in close-knit sequential mental steps, there must be a stable ego organization that *excludes* competing and contradictory lines of thought. Since human beings reason dialectically, it is always possible to see alternative directions in thought, to allow one line of meaning to suggest its opposite, concoct a middle position between these extremes, or to bring the whole complex of alternatives into question with the "possible" aim of denying its validity.

It is the failure to exclude such dialectically generated competing, contradictory, and even irrelevant impulses that characterizes overinclusion. This failure is obviously related to defects in defensive as well as in adaptive functions. It appears most clearly in schizophrenic disorders in which defective ego boundaries permit both perceptual confusion and the invasion of cognitive organizations by primary process material.

We may define *overinclusion* as *the result of unstable ego organization which fails to limit the number and kind of simultaneously effective excitants to a relatively few coherent ones.* The concept of overinclusion was first developed operationally in studies of sorting according to classes by schizophrenic patients (Cameron, 1939). Since then its use has been expanded to include a wide range of behavior disorganization, but it is in schizophrenic disorders that one sees it most clearly (Payne, 1961; Payne, Mattussek, & George, 1959). This may be related to the fact that schizophrenic patients attempt to interact with their environment in terms of their private fantasies (Arieti, 1955).

The following verbatim statements illustrate the confusion that a regressive disorganization can bring. They were made by a patient while he was engaged in the task of sorting colored blocks of several shapes into a specified number of groups. Throughout the task this schizophrenic young man was earnest and cooperative. He showed, as will be seen, an irresistible tendency to include in the task all kinds of actually irrelevant objects—the desk blotter, parts of the room, things he pulled from his pockets, racial problems, a man outside, and even the experimenter himself. Here are some of this patient's comments, which illustrate the disorganizing effects of overinclusion:

> "I've got to pick it out of the whole room. I can't confine myself to the game. . . . Three blues—now, how about that green blotter? Put it in there too. (Green) peas you eat, you can't eat them unless you write on it (the green blotter). (Patient had just come from a meal at which he had eaten green peas.) Like that wristwatch (experimenter's). I don't see any three meals coming off that watch. . . . White and blue (blocks) is Duke's Mixture. This (pulling out cigarette paper) is white. All this wood and Japan (pulling out matchbox). There's a man out there with a white tie; that's got something to do with white suits. . . . To do this trick *you'd* have to be made of wood. You've got a white shirt on, and the white blocks, you have to have them cut out of *you!* You've got a white shirt on. This (white block) will hold you and never let you go. I've got a blue shirt on; but it can't be a blue shirt and still go together. And the room's got to be the same." Contemplating a

grouping of similar white and yellow blocks, he asked, "Are there any Chinese working here? (*No*). Only white ones, then you can't put *them* together."

The overinclusion to be seen in a schizophrenic's line of thought is often due to the apparently uncontrollable rhyming of words. Such *clang associations* can almost give the patient's expressions a lilting quality. In the following example of a severely regressed young male adult, we see some excellent examples of dialectical divisioning, overinclusion, and clang associations, all wound into a personal delusional system reflecting moral and sexual-identity preoccupations. To the question *Why are you in the hospital?* this schizophrenic young man replied:

> I'm a cut donator, donated by double sacrifice. I get two days for every one. That's known as double sacrifice; in other words, standard cut donator. You know, we considered it. He couldn't have anything for the cut, or for these patients. All of them are double sacrifice because it's unlawful for it to be donated any more. (*Well, what do you do here?*) I do what is known as the double criminal treatment. Something that he badly wanted, he gets that, and seven days criminal protection. That's all he gets, and the rest I do for my friend. (*Who is the other person that gets all this?*) That's the way the asylum cut is donated. (*But who is the other person?*)
>
> He's a criminal. He gets so much. He gets twenty years' criminal treatment, would make forty years; and he gets seven days' criminal protection and that makes fourteen days. That's all he gets. (*And what are you?*) What is known as cut donator Christ. None of them couldn't be able to have anything; so it has to be true works or prove true to have anything, too. He gets two days, and that twenty years makes forty years. He loses by causing. He's what is known as a murder. He causes that. He's a murder by cause because he causes that. He can't *get* anything else. A double sacrifice is what is known as where murder turns, turns the friend into a cut donator and that's what makes a daughter-son. (*A daughter-son?*) Effeminate. A turned Christ. The criminal is a birth murder because he makes him a double. He gets two days' work for every day's work. . . . (*What is a "birth murder"?*) A birth murder is a murder that turns a cut donator Christ into a double daughter-son. He's turned effeminate and weak. He makes him a double by making him weak. He gets two days' work for every one day's work because after he's made a double, he gets twice as much as it is. He's considered worth twice that much more. He has to be sacrificed to be a double.

## Dynamic and Developmental Background

We said at the beginning of this chapter that schizophrenic reactions show a bewildering wealth of symptoms and that all of them can be traced to the massive intrusion of primary process material. This intrusion, we said, comes from different levels of early fixation, the various levels finding expression either simultaneously or in quick succession. The distinctive appearance of disorganization in schizophrenia is in part a product of this multiplicity of origins. In part it also reflects the presence of primary process function along with residuals of normal secondary process function. In some patients the primary processes are considerably modified by ego defenses that are still operating, although usually at primitive levels. In other patients there is little defensive modification. In still others, the degree and even the kind of ego defensive action fluctuate through wide ranges.

The clinical picture that a given schizophrenic patient presents at any time will depend, of course, upon what defenses are being used and how effective they are in protecting preconscious and conscious organizations from primary process invasion. In office practice one meets many basically schizophrenic persons who are able to function reasonably well in a normal, competitive human environment—some of them exceptionally well even in comparison to their normal associates—in spite of persistent regressive tendencies that occasionally may lead to delusions and hallucinations. Only a few persons, sometimes only the therapist and the patient, know about the psychotic trends. To the rest of the world the person appears normal or at most neurotic.

At least since the time of Bleuler's original monograph on the subject, there has been a general recognition that schizophrenia consists of many manifest illnesses. More recently, some researchers who take a genetic view of the origins of schizophrenia have referred to the *schizophrenia spectrum* in order to capture the range of disturbance from classical manifestations through the mixed and less frequent but acute episodes of distortion, on to the schizothymic personality types and related neuroticlike thought disruptions (Kety, 1967; Rosenthal, 1970). As we have seen in our clinical cases, schizophrenic patients seldom correspond to a single Kraepelinian type and frequently shift from one type to another. Joan R., for example, began as a paranoid schizophrenic, but soon after hospitalization she developed clear-cut catatonic episodes. It was difficult at first to assign Mark J. to any of the Kraepelinian subtypes, but in time he presented a clinical picture that could be definitely called hebephrenic or disorganized. As many as a third of all schizophrenic patients seem to go in and out of the different types or never fall clearly within any of them (Jacobson, 1954; Nathan et al., 1969). Hence the presence in the official classification of undifferentiated and residual subclasses for the otherwise unclassifiable patient.

The great variability of the manifest clinical form of schizophrenic disorders makes the task of describing their dynamic and developmental background extremely difficult. To take into account all of the common variations would be to present an almost unintelligible complexity of exposition. What we shall do instead is to focus upon certain core characteristics of the schizophrenic and preschizophrenic personality, characteristics that describe the defects of those who are or have been seriously ill with deep regression and with delusional and hallucinatory episodes. Such a core group can be easily distinguished from neurotic persons and from those with organized paranoid psychotic disorders, or with psychotic depression, mania, or toxic psychosis. It will include patients who never get well and patients who, in spite of deep regression, eventually recover and return to their previous level.

### FIXATION AND REGRESSION IN SCHIZOPHRENIC DISORDERS

In schizophrenic disorders the adult regresses to fixation points that are deeper and more widely dispersed than in any other form of behavior pathology. Object cathexes in the person's external environment are no longer taking place, as the narcissistic process assumes full sway in the personality system. As Freud (1915/1957k) said: "In the case of schizophrenia . . . we have been driven to the assumption that after the process of repression the libido that has been withdrawn does not seek a new object, but retreats into the ego; that is to say, that here the object-cathexes are given up and a primitive objectless condition of narcissism is re-established" (pp. 196-197).

As he or she regresses, the schizophrenic patient revives fears, wishes, conflicts, and fantasies belonging to the earliest phases of personality development, phases in which no genuine object relationships exist (i.e., *primary narcissism*). The patient may then live in a sort of dream world where personal awareness and the people and things around him or her seem to lose their identity and appear to merge. What is happening outside the patient's identity seems to happen inside, and what is going on only within his or her thinking seems to be happening outside it. Most of us have experienced this kind of perplexing, kaleidoscopic change in our manifest dreams. One moment we are watching something going on; the next moment we are doing it or it is being done to us.

We have said that fixation points to which regression carries a person in schizophrenic disorders are widely dispersed as well as deep. This dispersion adds to the patient's confusion. The effect of this situation is that the schizophrenic fluctuates from one level to another, even within a single hour. One moment regression carries a patient to a level at which reality contact is lost, and the next moment it may be regained either partially or fully. Normally the process called *reality-testing* helps us to establish and to maintain a differentiation between *fantasy-oriented* and *reality-oriented* experience and behavior. It helps us distinguish between what is contributed to perception and cognition from internal need, wish, fantasy, or emotional drive. We all know that these distinctions are rarely absolute, even in the most normal person. There is always some contribution of internal wish or fear, of fantasy or emotional drive, to modify realistic perception and cognition; and external reality is always modifying our private fantasies, even in our dreaming at night.

Nevertheless, the distinctions that we ordinarily make are complete enough for the practical business of coping realistically with our external, socially organized environment and for the pleasurable or anxiety-provoking business of make-believe, story, or daydream. We may enter into the make-believe fantasy of a play wholeheartedly, even to the point at which we feel ourselves to be a part of it; but this does not prevent our switching to reality during the intermission, and again after the last curtain falls. A great deal of the emotional enjoyment—the warmth, depth, and devotion of life—is made possible by our ability to fuse fantasy with reality when we want to and to use primary processes in the service of the grownup self.

*Failure of Reality-Testing Mixes Fantasy with Fact.*  Most of us are able to return to a clear distinction between fantasy and fact when circumstances call for it. A minority of persons cannot achieve this distinction. Included in this minority are those persons who, like Joan R., have always relied upon fantasy to a much greater degree than do normal persons. Under conditions of stress, such persons are likely to develop a schizophrenic illness.

A basic source of confusion between reality and fantasy in schizophrenic regression is a defect in the development of a clear *self-image,* that is, an image of the *self* as a distinctive *identity* that is distinct from the *surroundings.* We have reason to believe that this defect in reality-testing has its deepest roots in failures to resolve the early symbiotic relationship between mother and infant (see Chapter 2). Because of such failure, the child never succeeds in establishing a separate identity, remaining more or less fixated at an undifferentiated level. Later in life, when the person regresses he or she begins to lose the unstable differentiations of *self* from *not-self,* or *self* from *others.*

At these deep levels of regression, as we shall see in a moment, *repression* grows incompetent. The dominant defenses and methods of coping are once more the infantile ones: *primary identification, introjection,* and *projection.* There is no longer a clear separation between what has been preconscious and what has been unconscious. What has been unconscious now becomes easily accessible. Primitive modes of thinking again dominate preconscious and conscious thinking. Representations of the self comingle with representations of other people. They now pass easily across the boundaries that should separate them because the boundaries have become vague and pathologically permeable. They fuse and they interchange positions, just as they do in everyone's nightly dreaming. In deep schizophrenic regression, the contributions of primitive, archaic fantasy and of primary processes to perception and cognition become great, while the contributions of external reality become correspondingly small.

*Attempts to Re-establish Reality Contacts.*  When a regressed schizophrenic patient attempts to re-establish relations with external reality, it is understandable that he or she may experience intense *estrangement* and *depersonalization* (see Chapter 9, pp. 263-264 for a discussion of these concepts). Such experiences often generate enough anxiety to drive a person back into deep regression and isolation once more. Anxiety is heightened all the more as previously unconscious material of a primitive nature pours into the preconscious and conscious realms of mind. Strange things are happening to the person. As Harry Stack Sullivan (1962, p. 149, 243) liked to point out, the schizophrenic person is like a sleepwalker or a person who has just awakened from a horrible nightmare and is trying to understand what is going on. Unfortunately, the schizophrenic cannot hope to benefit from further waking up, because he is already fully awake.

The successions of deep regression and attempts at regaining effective relations with external reality give us clues as to what is going on during the fluctuations in level of regression, which we observe in clinically active schizophrenic patients. When patients give up trying to regain effective contact with external reality, they can escape the anxiety that their primitive experiences tend to arouse only by becoming apathetic or by allowing themselves to live their lives of primitive fantasy, without letting external reality penetrate into their thinking.

This last is what we see clinically in the so-called *deteriorated* or *vegetative* schizophrenic patient. Mark J. presented such a clinical picture after he had given up; and so did Joan R. The "deterioration" that then develops is a defensive maneuver, a way of keeping out whatever the patient cannot handle. However hopeless it may appear, we have the fact that many "deteriorated" schizophrenic patients can be rehabilitated after years of withdrawal, so that they are willing and able to lead a fairly normal life.

*Constructive Functions of Delusions and Hallucinations.* We have indicated earlier in this volume (e.g., see Chapter 11) that delusions and hallucinations are not only signs of illness; they are also often signs that a patient is actively trying to cope with the regressive illness from which he or she suffers. A major challenge presents itself in the necessity of having to incorporate the bizarre eruptions from the unconscious into the ongoing conscious experience. Psychotic patients can no more ignore these intrusions than dreamers can ignore their dreams. The delusion and the hallucination often represent attempts to synthesize these products of previously unconscious wishes, fears, conflicts, and fantasies with the external reality which the patient is trying to handle (Cameron, 1943, 1959c).

Because of the greater regression in schizophrenia, and because schizophrenic patients tend to fluctuate from one level of fixation to another, their delusions are usually less well organized and less realistic than the delusions of paranoid patients. In fact, within the subtypes of the schizophrenias, the paranoid schizophrenic is most likely to report delusions that are reasonably systematized and organized along plausible lines (Hamlin & Lorr, 1971; Zigler, Levine, & Zigler, 1977). But the reason we find greater deterioration in the schizophrenias generally is because there is greater penetration of primary process material in the delusional material advanced by such patients.

Sometimes florid schizophrenic delusions and hallucinations suddenly disappear for no apparent reason. The patient has somehow managed suddenly to re-establish effective repression, to shut down the hatch, and once more to "contain" the primitive unconscious processes, the fueros of an earlier time of life. Even those of us who have witnessed such an extraordinary change have not been able to understand how it was achieved. Apparently, even the patient does not understand it, or at any rate declines to discuss it. We have to remind ourselves that repression is itself an unconscious defense that operates without a person's being consciously aware of it, although there *is* an unconscious intention being enacted in the process.

Hallucinations are more of a mystery than delusions, perhaps because they

Mary Evans Picture Library/Sigmund Freud Copyrights

*Freud and his daughter Anna, photographed in 1929, the year in which he completed* Civilization and Its Discontents. *Freud bravely continued to work despite his cancer of the mouth and jaw. He was to sustain thirty-three operations before his death.*

occur during states of deep regression. Patients who are able and willing to communicate while they are hallucinating assert that their hallucinatory experiences are as vivid and as real as their perceptions of socially shared reality.

## DEFENSES IN SCHIZOPHRENIC DISORDERS

The wide dispersal of fixation points in schizophrenic disorders, and the often rapid fluctuation from one level to another in the regressions of active cases, make it difficult to say anything definite about schizophrenic defensive maneuvers that will hold for all cases, or even for a single case over a long period of time. When regression is relatively slight and does not lead to isolation of the patient from his or her surroundings, it may serve defensive functions in simplifying a schizophrenic patient's world by reducing the number and complexity of effective stimulations. The patient becomes less effectual but does not disintegrate. At the other extreme, when a patient withdraws and becomes stuporous, he or she may also preserve some ego-superego integration by shutting out the confusion of external stimulation almost completely. These two extremes are not the most common results of schizophrenic regression. No matter how important they may be for successful therapy, they are best eliminated from our discussion of schizophrenic defenses, so that we may consider the core of schizophrenic cases that make up the great majority, the middle ground.

Within the middle ground, we find the majority of psychotic schizophrenic disorders, those in whom regression varies from slight to subtotal and in whom regression often reaches depths not reached in mania, depression, or paranoid disorders. Such regression, with its unpredictable fluctuations and its abysmal depths, can only be called defensive in a very limited sense, in the sense that it may protect the patient from "falling to pieces," as schizophrenic patients themselves spontaneously describe their experience. What happens in deep schizophrenic regression is the greatest loss of differentiation of personality or psychic structure so far seen, a loss of differentiation that allows self-images and object images to merge and separate again and then merge once more, which replaces even the archaic superego by early infantile introjected objects —usually "bad objects." The struggles of an infantile regressive ego against such introjected objects is often aided by projection, as we shall see, which at least allows the patient to battle against them as outside persecutors. When schizophrenic regression occurs in a person who has managed to get along reasonably well up to the time of the onset of illness, it occurs because of the failure of repression.

*Defective Repressions.* In persons who react to stress with a schizophrenic regression there has apparently always been an inadequacy of repression. This is probably related to the multiple fixation points in preschizophrenic personalities. Their multiplicity indicates that almost from the beginning of life the patient has been exposed to real or imagined tension and anxiety, that he or she has never received adequate protection from unavoidable internal and external stress. The clinical evidence points to sadomasochistic experiences in relation to the patient's mother or mother substitute. In short, persons who are especially vulnerable to schizophrenic disorders are persons who have never had the opportunity to establish *basic trust.* It is immaterial whether this is the "fault" of the mother or of the infant. For our present purposes it is enough to recognize that the adult who develops schizophrenia has very probably had such experiences in early life. Laing (1969) has suggested that, in response to the destructive experiences early in life, the preschizophrenic person divides his or her self, relating to others on the basis of a false external self that accepts the stigmatization of being insane to escape the expected contemptuous rejection from other people.

We therefore take it as granted, as we also did in relation to paranoid reactions, that the person vulnerable to schizophrenic regression had matured as an ego defense. The mother or mother figure of such a person was unsuccessful in providing him or her with a substitute ego at a critical time of life, when the ego was still poorly differentiated. This accounts for the overdevelopment of denial and projection regularly seen in schizophrenic disorders; as we have seen, such an overdevelopment early in life interferes with the normal development of a defensive organization in which a strong repressive barrier is the keystone.

In schizophrenic disorders, however, we find also some of the most primitive forms of identification, introjection, and incorporation. Patients themselves, without foreknowledge of psychoanalytical theory, complain of their archaic incorporation fantasies. Joan R. is by no means unique in her experiences of chewing people up and eating them. Such fantasies, undoubtedly derived from early nursing experiences and from such common adult remarks as "You look good enough to eat!" appear in a large percentage of schizophrenic experiences. We may take them as evidence of fixation at early phases when identification was still equated with taking a person in through the mouth. Here, as in psychotic depression, there is evidence that introjection had to be used too much and too early, before repression had matured, and while introjection still was conceived or experienced as incorporation. Such early uses and overdevelopment of introjection (and archaic identification) would interfere with the growth of a normal defensive system in which there was mature repression as the keystone.

The failure of schizophrenic adults to develop adequate repressive defenses in early childhood leaves them always susceptible to invasions by primary process material, unconscious fantasies, and the like. They are therefore defective in their subordination of primitive drives and needs to the demands of social reality. They are subject to interferences with attempts at realistic, logical thinking. They are less tolerant of ambiguity than normal persons because of their inability to control and channel their emotional drives. They have serious difficulties in evolving reciprocal role behavior and in structuring a coherent self that will resist intrusions from external reality.

*Denial and Projection.*  Schizophrenic patients depend heavily upon primitive forms of denial and projection. Although denial is used first of all against parts of external reality that have managed to break through into preconscious and conscious infantile perception, it is eventually used also against primary process intrusions from unconscious internal reality (Jacobson, 1957). When schizophrenic patients suffer severe regression, and when their always inadequate repression fails them almost completely, they utilize denial and projection to get rid of the primary process material and the unconscious fantasies which threaten to overwhelm them. Since they are threatened mainly by upsurges of primitive aggressive drives, what they deny and project is chiefly aggressive and hostile in character, although not exclusively so.

Denial and projection in schizophrenia lead to delusions and hallucinations in which the patient's own irrepressible and uncontrollable emotions and fantasy productions seem to him or her to be embodied in outside existences. The degree of ego-superego regression that has occurred will usually determine the degree of communicability and intelligibility of the delusions and hallucinations, as well as their primitive character. Occasionally we find a patient with deeply regressive, archaic experiences who is willing and able to communicate them. From such persons we get clinical insights that enable us to understand and interpret the much more common weird and fragmentary communication of archaic material.

It is worth repeating at this point, because it is so often overlooked, that delusions and hallucinations may not only be symptoms of a deep pathological regression, and therefore signs of illness, but also attempts by the patient to understand what is going on, and therefore signs of recovery. The recovery may fail because a patient cannot get the primary process material and unconscious fantasies under repression again. But the delusion and the hallucination are attempts to reconstruct reality in such a way as to include the parts of internal reality that have to be dealt with somehow because they have escaped repression.

In some schizophrenic patients, regression revives situations in which there are virtually no ego or self boundaries. When this is so, projection is a very primitive process, and the delusions and hallucinations that develop succeed only in confusing external and internal reality, in much the same way that manifest dreams do. Things and events that should be experienced as internal seem to be external, or fluctuate between seeming internal and external. At the same time, because of fluctuating and permeable boundaries, parts of the external world seem to be internal, and parts of the self seem to be outside the self. It is probable that in patients who regress deeply and do not improve, representatives of the self and of the external world, including somatic parts, swim in an almost undifferentiated objectless dream world.

*Introjection and Identification.* We have already discussed introjection and incorporation under repression because they antedate the maturation of repression and are overused in primitive forms by persons who have been exposed in infancy to excessive tension and anxiety. Here it is only necessary to add a few words. Introjection is a symbolic incorporation, that is to say, it is a symbolic act that is modeled upon the prototype act of swallowing. Drinking in through the eyes and ears, tasting goodness and evil, chewing one's cud in relation to some decision, swallowing bait, propaganda, and one's pride, engulfing with one's arms—these are only a few samples of thousands of introjective expressions, with incorporative implications, that are current in everyday speech. In schizophrenic regression, fantasies of introjection appear with openly archaic incorporation expressed.

A schizophrenic girl, who expressed many other incorporative fantasies, became frightened when her violin case was mislaid. She was immediately sure that she had swallowed it and persisted in this belief until the violin case was found, in spite of the nurses' attempts to tell her that swallowing it was impossible. To her this probably sounded as irrelevant as telling someone who was drinking in scenery that scenery cannot be swallowed.

Identification may also be derived from introjection as well as from imitation. This is especially obvious in processes of normal mourning and in psychotic depression. In schizophrenic regression identification may become imitative and introjective, but in childlike archaic forms. A patient may imitate the behavior of someone else, not playfully or ambitiously, but merely to increase self-control or to have within his or her behavioral sphere the powers that other people seem to possess. This is actually a form of sympathetic magic. Sometimes schizophrenic patients identify with others in order to "fuse" with them fantastically—to become as one with them. This is probably a return to primary identification, that is, to phases of childhood development in which self-images and object-images lacked clear boundaries and could be experienced as merging, separating and merging again.

*Other Defenses.* During fluctuations of regression, while a person is beginning to disintegrate, and when he or she is returning again toward health, most of the other ego defenses commonly used reappear in schizophrenic disorders. Thus, for example, the defenses most characteristic of obsessive-compulsive disorders—reaction-formation, undoing, displacement, and isolation (see Chapter 7)—are common precursors of a schizophrenic breakthrough. Without question many persons escape a schizophrenic illness by rigidly adhering to obsessive-compulsive defenses. We can readily see the similarity of obsessive doubting to schizophrenic disorders; indeed, one may lead over into the other. A relationship between hysterical disorders—that is, conversion and dissociative reactions—has long been recognized. The somatic disturbances in both may look alike. This isolation or split in the ego that characterizes dissociation also appears in schizophrenic reactions. Finally, we know that schizophrenia usually involves severe anxiety at some phase and that phobic defenses may be a vulnerable person's chief defenses against a schizophrenic psychosis.

It is an old story among therapists that one should always look behind a *neurotic facade* to see, if possible, whether or not it hides *psychotic trends.* Likewise, though this is not as often commented upon, in treating a schizophrenic person one looks for signs that neurotic defenses are being constructed. It is a triumph to be able to help a psychotic schizophrenic person to become neurotic instead, even though he or she cannot progress beyond becoming neurotic. A neurotic personality is less in danger of disintegration than a psychotic one. A regressing schizophrenic person is in danger of the deepest of all disintegrations short of intoxication and brain damage.

EGO-SUPEREGO REGRESSION IN ACTIVE SCHIZOPHRENIC DISORDERS

By "active" schizophrenic disorders we mean simply reactions in which the patient is actively trying to find a solution, and has neither given up nor retreated into a persistent withdrawn state. As in the other psychoses, ego-superego regression in schizophrenia is *subtotal.* It is not merely partial, as in the neuroses. Much of the time, the greater part of ego-superego function operates at infantile levels, sometimes at regressive levels so deep that distinctions between the *self* (i.e., personality system as an identity) and others are lost. Moreover, the *proportion* of the ego-superego organization involved in schizophrenic regression fluctuates widely, varying from total psychotic withdrawal, such as one sees in catatonic stupors, to minimal loss of contact, that is, to minimal disturbance of ego-superego organization (Moriarty, 1961).

These wide fluctuations have double significance. They help us to understand the sudden changes in adaptive capacity and in the ability to communicate and interact effectually with other people. A suddenly increased involvement of the ego-superego organization would account for the sudden massive withdrawals that we witness clinically. A suddenly decreased involvement would account for the sudden good contact that we also witness. A knowledge of these wide fluctuations helps the psychotherapist to be prepared for sudden increased cooperativeness on the part of the patient and to be ready to take advantage of it. The therapist can likewise be reconciled to sudden unexpected regressions and can console himself or herself with the expectation that they may suddenly end.

## Genetic and Biological Theories of Schizophrenia

As in the case of psychotic depression (see Chapter 12, p. 380), there have always been and continue to be theories of schizophrenia based upon material- and efficient-cause reductions of one sort or another. Indeed, there has been greater effort expended to establish genetic linkage and/or biochemical agents in the family of the schizophrenias than in any other diagnostic grouping of psychopathology. We shall take a brief look at some of these major nondynamic theories—that is, theories that propose additional factors to the dynamic factors upon which we focus in the present volume.

### STUDIES OF BLOOD RELATIONSHIP

Kallmann (1953) conducted some of the earliest and most convincing investigations on the relationship of heredity to mental disorder. He found that, statistically speaking, the chances of becoming schizophrenic are positively related to the closeness of blood relationship to a schizophrenic patient. These statistical relationships do not follow a simple Mendelian ratio of transmission. Some investigators have suggested that schizophrenia may follow a complex Mendelian distribution in which a modified dominant gene exerts major influence (Karlssom, 1968); others have suggested that a polygenetic explanation is called for in which several genes uniquely combine to bring about the disorder (Shields, 1967).

We referred to the *schizophrenia spectrum* above (see p. 438). Those who hold to this view believe that there are both *hard* and *soft* aspects of this spectrum. The "hard spectrum" disorders are those in which a substantial proportion of the relatives of schizophrenic patients also develop schizophrenic disorders, even when they may not have had direct social contact with the patient. The "soft spectrum" disorders are those in which there is substantially less schizophreniclike behavior among the relatives of patients (Kety, 1967; Rosenthal, 1970).

Kallmann's research strategy (1953) encompassed such variables as the comparison of monozygotic (one egg) and dizygotic (two eggs) twin pairs, the incidence of illness in the offspring of patients, and the similarity or difference of place of residence for those compared. It is immediately apparent in studies of blood relationship that there is a social-influence factor to consider. Is the likelihood of schizophrenia among relatives due to a genetic linkage or to the social linkage of a family milieu holding to common values, attitudes, and behavioral styles that dramatically increases the likelihood of abnormality? We can also add the many problems in psychiatric diagnosis discussed in Chapter 1 (see pp. 15-19); undoubtedly, a psychiatrist working on a genetic assumption is going to take special account of the fact that relatives of the patient now under study have been diagnosed as schizophrenic. All such factors must be taken into consideration in conducting studies of blood relationship, and they *have* been experimentally evaluated over the years. Consistent but not entirely conclusive results have issued from this line of research.

The general strategy in these studies is to find the *concordance* rate between twins. This refers to the likelihood that if one twin is diagnosed as a schizophrenic the second will also be diagnosed as having a disorder in this spectrum. Though the studies have found broad ranges of concordance rates, it is now generally believed that monozygotic twins fall somewhere between 25 and 40 percent and dizygotic twins fall in the 5 to 10 percent range of concordance (Gottesman & Shields, 1972; Kringlen, 1967; Research Task Force of the National Institute of Mental Health, 1975; Shields, 1968). When studies are made of children who are the offspring of schizophrenic parents but have been adopted away from these parents and reared in different homes, the likelihood of such children one day being diagnosed as suffering from a schizophrenic disorder is significantly greater than adopted children whose parents have never experienced a schizophrenic episode (Heston, 1966).

Hence, we are left with the impression that a genetic linkage may indeed contribute to the schizophrenic disorder within a population of people, but we are unable to predict this course for specific individuals, and there is considerable variance in such data that cannot be accounted for in any case.

## BIOCHEMICAL STUDIES

We noted in Chapter 12 (p. 380) that psychotic depressions have been linked to various biogenic amines or *catecholamines* that are synthesized in the functioning of the brain. A comparable line of research has been conducted in the study of schizophrenia, with many different biochemical substances targeted for study. An early candidate was *taraxein,* a ceruloplasm that was said to be found in the blood of schizophrenics but not in normals (Heath, 1960; Heath, Guschwan, & Coffey, 1970; Heath & Krupp, 1967). According to the theory, taraxein helps to produce a foreign substance in the septal region of the brain.

Antibodies are then formed to defend against this biological action, and the antibodies attack neurohumors that are essential for normal brain functioning. The result is a bizarre behavioral pattern known as schizophrenia. Though researches initially found that taraxein injected into the bloodstream of nonschizophrenic volunteers produced schizophrenic symptoms in these volunteers, subsequent studies have been unable to replicate these findings (Levit, 1972; Siegel et al., 1959).

In recent times, the *dopamine hypothesis* has been advanced to account for schizophrenic symptoms (Snyder, 1974, 1976). Dopamine is one of the catecholamines, a chemical forerunner of norepinephrine. Dopamine is a neurotransmitter involved in the chemical transmission of nerve impulses from one neuron to another. Evidence from various directions supports the hypothesis that schizophrenia may be due to an excess of dopamine at the synaptic sites of the schizophrenic patient's central nervous system. For example, schizophrenic symptoms have been found to be exacerbated by the administration of *methylphenidate,* a drug believed to increase the functional supply of body dopamine (Van Kammen, 1977). On the other side of the coin, *phenothiazine drugs* block the reception of dopamine in a receptor neuron, and it is well documented that schizophrenic symptoms decline when phenothiazine is administered to such patients (Carlsson, 1978).

It is, of course, entirely possible that biological mechanisms in which taraxein and dopamine play a role are the instrumentalities of psychopathology rather than "the" cause of the disturbance in a strictly biological sense. We all know that in a state of emotion our bodies release hormones that dramatically affect our behavior and that can in time injure our physical and psychological well-being (see Chapter 17 on the psychosomatic disorders). Hence, precisely what is "the" cause and/or "the" effect in such biochemical studies remains open to question. Once again, we reaffirm our *biosocial* approach to the study of psychopathological disorders. As psychodynamic theorists, we must continue to make sense of our clinical observations even as we applaud the efforts of those colleagues who would pursue a purely reductive explanation of mental illness.

## Childhood Background of Schizophrenic Disorders

There has been a good deal of research conducted on the family background of schizophrenic patients, spurred in large measure by the pioneering work of R. W. Lidz and Lidz (1949). The latter line of investigation eventually found that families that produced schizophrenic patients lacked integration (T. Lidz, 1978; T. Lidz, Fleck, & Cornelison, 1965). In one common familial style there existed a *marital schism,* so that parents were seen to undermine each other's values and actions. If the child identified with one parent in some way he or she was disparaged and shunned by the other parent. Another common pattern was termed *marital skew,* for in this case the bizarre actions and ideas of one parent (e.g., an unstable father) dominated the family ambience. In either home environment the child destined to manifest schizophrenic symptoms was obviously being psychologically prepared to play this regressive role in life.

It is not uncommon to find that the parents of schizophrenic patients are themselves maladjusted. There is the suggestion that mothers on sum may be the more disturbed parent, employing psychoticlike defenses in their adaptation to life (I. Kaufman et al., 1960; Tsuang et al., 1974). Often a decided emotional distance can be discerned in the parental union, so that even when the partners try to convey love to each other or to their offspring, the effect is one of pretense and insincerity (Bowen, 1960; Waring & Ricks, 1965). It is some such schism between the outer appearance and the inner psychic truth that Laing (1969) suggests is at the heart of the schizophrenic's "divided self." Indeed, Laing suggests that some schizophrenics take on the "mask of insanity" quite intentionally, as a way of coping with the inconsistencies of life.

An important familial dynamic that has received considerable research attention is Bateson's *double-bind hypothesis* (1959, 1960, 1972). According to this hypothesis, schizophrenic behavior is often the result of the fact that a person is reared in a home that has placed him or her in a chronic "double bind," having to struggle with the implications of contradictory communications from parents. This is, in essence, a dialectical dilemma. The offspring caught up in this conflict hears a parent saying one thing but in behavioral display implying quite the opposite intention. Thus, the mother mildly scolds her son for not being more self-sufficient as she stirs his morning coffee and lightly passes her hand through his hair. The father complains that his daughter does not love him as he does her, but whenever she comes close he tenses up and finds some excuse to remove himself from her presence.

After several years of this sort of interpersonal relationship the child is incapable of interpreting anyone's intentions accurately. He or she constantly misreads other people, and then must fall back in social contact to assume a passive and confused role in what is going on, or he or she must counterattack and fight imaginary battles over interpersonal slights and manipulations that were never intended by others. Much research evidence testing the double-bind hypothesis has been supportive of the dynamics it advances (Bateson et al., 1956; Jacobs, 1975; Sojit, 1976). However, there have been difficulties with this explanation as one that is supposedly limited to the dynamics of schizophrenia. That is, other, less disturbed patients such as those reflecting a personality disorder have family backgrounds in which double-bind communication is prominent (A. Berger, 1965). More critically, the reliability of the double-bind construct as well as the research designs that purport to test it have been brought into question (Broen, 1968; Fontana, 1966; Ringuette & Kennedy, 1966). Even so, this realm of investigation remains a highly interesting one and it will undoubtedly continue to promote future researches on the schizophregenic family.

Of course, it is much too simple to think of family influences like this in blanket or one-way fashion. That is, we have the problem of having to explain why it is that only *certain* of the children in a family actually do go on to develop schizophrenic (or other) disorders. We know from empirical research that children coming from homes with undesirable parental role models do grow up to be successful and well-adjusted adults (A. Kadushin, 1967). Even in the worst of circumstances, half to three-quarters of the children being reared by a parent with a history of psychotic episodes remain entirely normal (M. Bleuler, 1974). And on the other side of the coin, we know that often the observed family disruption and emotional deterioration is initiated or at least exacerbated by the child who is sinking into a schizophrenic disorder. In attempting to deal with their offspring's disorder the parents begin themselves to manifest the unhealthy interpersonal patterns that we have mentioned above (Liem, 1974; Mishler & Waxler, 1968).

Thus, it could be that in certain families a given offspring is targeted to be the "sick one." This might begin with an unwanted pregnancy or at birth during a period when one or both parents are striving to deal with a problem through regressive maneuvers of one sort or another. The selection process may occur later, when a child is unconsciously selected as a scapegoat so that the other members of the family might be protected from becoming overly psychotic themselves. It is difficult to see how such nuances will ever be capable of "on-the-spot" empirical investigation. Though it has serious drawbacks, and we must always follow up on its retrospective findings with additional research when possible, there is at present no substitute for the clinical method. It is our view that, used properly, with balanced judgment and a sensitivity to nuances, the clinical investigation of personality and psychopathology can continue to move us toward a better understanding of personality and psychopathology.

## SUMMARY

Chapter 14 takes up the schizophrenic disorders, which are regressive attempts to escape tension and anxiety by abandoning realistic interpersonal object relations and constructing delusions and hallucinations. DSM-III has made several basic changes in the diagnosis of this disorder, some of which conflict with the International Classification of Diseases (ICD-9). First of all, DSM-III has dropped the Kraepelinian subtypes of *simple* and *hebephrenic* schizophrenia. The distinction between *latent* and *borderline* schizophrenia has also been dropped. The convention has been adopted in DSM-III that before the diagnosis of schizophrenia is assigned, the patient concerned should have displayed symptoms of delusions, hallucinations, and thinking disruptions for *at least six months*. Anything less than this results in a diagnosis of *schizophreniform disorder*. Another change to be seen in DSM-III is the removal of the *schizoaffective disorder* from the chapter dealing with schizophrenic disorders and its placement in a special chapter entitled "Psychotic Disorders Not Elsewhere Classified." DSM-III does recognize an *undifferentiated* and a *residual* type of schizophrenic disorder.

The term *schizophrenia* was coined by Bleuler, who sought to capture the *fragmentation* of this disorder and to remove the implications of Kraepelin's *dementia praecox* designation. Chapter 14 takes up the classical Kraepelinian types of schizophrenia (see Chapter 1) because they are still in use both formally (e.g., in ICD-9) and informally by many clinicians. The *simple* type of schizophrenia has a slow, insidious onset and an undramatic downhill course. Neither delusions nor hallucinations seem to play a part in the course of the disorder. Simple schizophrenics appear superficially to be mentally retarded, but intelligence testing proves otherwise.

*Hebephrenic schizophrenia* is referred to as the *disorganized type* of schizophrenia in DSM-III. *Hebephrenia* means "mind of youth," which in a sense captures the silly, disorganized behavior of the person afflicted, who may be seen smiling, smirking, and giggling to irrelevant cues. There may be outbursts of anger. Speech becomes manneristic, even to the point of being incoherent (*word salad*) and employing made-up words (*neologisms*). Weird delusions and various hallucinations are prominent in the clinical picture. In the *catatonic* form of schizophrenia we witness the extremes of a dimension of motor disturbance. At one extreme the patient may be in a state of disorganized excitement. At the other, the patient may be motionless or malleable (*waxy flexibility*). Delusions and hallucinations occur at both extremes. Sudden remissions have been noted in the catatonic form of schizophrenia.

Most schizophrenic patients are placed in the *paranoid type* designation. Delusions hold the spotlight in this disorder. After a life pattern of aloofness and suspiciousness, this patient begins to lose grip on reality and to substitute personal misinterpretation and fantasy for common sense. There is a much quicker regression at this point than we see in the paranoid disorder (Chapter 11). The paranoid schizophrenic's delusions are not as systematized as the patient suffering from a paranoid disorder. *Persecutory delusions* are common in paranoid schizophrenia, along with *delusions of influence* and *grandeur*. *Ideas of reference* are common. Hallucinations are nearly always present, with auditory the most common and visual the next most common.

Chapter 14 next takes up the *schizoaffective type* of disorder, which as we noted above is removed from primary consideration in DSM-III. This is a rare form of schizophrenia that combines the symptoms we have noted above with manic or depressive symptoms. The clinical picture is that of an elation or a depression in which delusions are more disorganized and weird than is typical of the affective disorders. Hallucinations are common, whereas they are not in mania or depression. Some clinicians believe that we witness two disorders in the same patient when this label is employed.

In no other psychopathological disorder do we witness so directly the manifestation of primary process thought and fantasy as we do in the schizophrenic disturbance. It is the *thought disorder* reflected among schizophrenics that stamps their illness as unique. Thoughts run together even though irrelevant. Confusion runs rampant. It is impossible to focus attention or to concentrate when the regression is at its lowest ebb. Many clinicians have noted that the first signs of the "schism" in reality relations occurs in the patient's peculiar use of language. Neologisms that cannot be understood by others intrude. A verbal discontinuity termed *scatter* is evident. Many times there is an obvious *condensation* of meanings so that the same word conveys several intentions, some of which are at variance with what the patient seems to be grappling with in personal expression. When things get unmanageable, it would appear that the only alternative is to become *mute.*

Condensing meanings and becoming confused over the mass of information that enters consciousness occurs because schizophrenics are prone to over-include. *Overinclusion* is the result of an unstable ego organization that fails to limit the number and kind of simultaneously effective excitants to a relatively few coherent ones at any point in time. Private fantasies intrude with reality contact. We see this occurring in other disorders, but schizophrenia reflects the most pronounced tendency to overinclusion. Many times rhyming leads to overinclusion, so that the schizophrenic patient's speech is full of *clang associations.*

The disorganization in schizophrenia reflects the deep and extensive nature of the fixations involved. The consequent range and variety of symptoms to be seen in this disorder have led some experts to refer to the *schizophrenia spectrum.* In clinical practice patients rarely conform to one Kraepelinian category with perfection, and often show signs of two or more such distur-bances. This strongly suggests that there is a common basis to the disorder. There is a heavy component of narcissism in schizophrenia, as cathexes from the external world are withdrawn and focused upon the self. Patients regress to *primary narcissism* levels of psychosexual functioning. The patient lives in a kind of dream world where *reality-testing* is foregone altogether. There is a lack of clear self-definition in the development of such individuals. They are distracted by irrelevances in the environment because they have not successfully distinguished themselves from their surroundings. The "schism" is a late-born maneuver to attain personal identity.

When efforts are made to regain reality contact we witness symptoms of *estrangement* and *depersonalization* (see Chapter 9). Anxiety rises as more of the unconscious material intrudes on preconscious and conscious levels. If this road back to reality is not traversed, the patient is able to escape the total confusion only by becoming mute and apathetic, turning inward to a life of primitive fantasy without allowing external reality to penetrate whatsoever. This results in what is often called the *deteriorated* or *vegetative* schizophrenic patient. In addition to defective repression, denial, projection, and introjection of parental attitudes, the defense of employing neurotic symptoms as a facade hiding psychotic symptoms is sometimes said to occur in schizophrenia. As in other psychoses, ego-superego regression in schizophrenia is *subtotal.* Much of the time, the greater part of ego-superego function operates at infantile levels, sometimes at regressive levels so deep that distinctions between self and others is lost.

Chapter 14 next considers certain genetic and biological theories of schizo-phrenia. Statistical studies have found that the chances of becoming schizo-phrenic are positively related to the closeness of blood relationship to a schizophrenic patient. Both Mendelian and polygenetic theories have been advanced to account for these findings. Monozygotic twins have higher rates of concordance in being diagnosed schizophrenic than do dizygotic twins. The major biochemical explanations of schizophrenia have stressed *taraxein,* a ceruloplasm that is believed to produce a foreign substance in the septal region of the brain, and *dopamine,* which is a neurotransmitter involved in the chemical transmission of nerve impulses from one neuron to another. Excessive dopamine at synaptic sites has been suggested as the cause of the deteriorating thought processes in the schizophrenic individual.

There are also several theories of schizophrenia that stress the pathogenic familial patterns in the background of such patients. One theory stresses *marital schism,* or lack of integration. Children identifying with one parent in such a family were rejected by the other. Another pathogenic familial pattern is termed *marital skew,* by which is meant a family under domination by the bizarre actions and ideas of one of the parents. In either home environment the child is bound to feel confused and torn apart from reality and the experience of sound interpersonal relations. The *double-bind hypothesis* traces the dissociation of experience in preschizophrenic children to the language patterns of their parents. Communication is contradictory in such homes, binding children in two directions at once and making it virtually impossible to achieve a sincere relationship with loved ones.

# 15

## *Personality and Substance Use Disorders*

In Chapter 1 we outlined the five DSM-III axes along which a patient is to be diagnosed (see pp. 21-25). We noted in that context that axis II codings involve personality disorders and specific developmental disorders such as reading disabilities. In the present chapter we shall review the ten or eleven personality disorders that have been delineated in DSM-III as well as the addictions or substance use disorders that frequently combine with these maladjusted behaviors. Recall that we defined personality as the *style* that behavior takes on (see Chapter 1, p. 1). DSM-III refers to this identifiable pattern of behavior as a *trait,* a term we are reluctant to use because of its history. That it, traits have been used to designate a collection of presumed "givens" that enter "more or less" into the behaviors of human beings. It is our feeling that this form of theorizing sometimes lost the person in the collection of traits presumed to "make up" personality "systems."

Actually, both the terms *trait* and *style* take their meaning from the formal cause (see Chapter 1, p. 4), and we shall presume that the essential idea being expressed here is that we can see identifiable patterns in the behavior of people. According to DSM-III, when such behavioral patterns (styles, traits) become somehow inflexible and maladaptive, when they lead thereby to significant impairment in social or occupational efficiency, as well as to subjective distress (anxiety, depression, etc.), then we are justified in speaking of a *personality disorder.* Recall that in Chapter 1 we outlined the factors of cultural expectations, adequacy of performance, and internal integrative functions as criteria for the assessment of *all* psychopathology.

Some interesting theoretical problems arise thanks to the clinical observation of personality disorders. Perhaps the most perplexing of these has to do with whether or not these disorders follow the same developmental course in the personality as the neuroses and psychoses. Honest differences of opinion exist on this question. Some clinicians believe that personality disorders have, in effect, a unique course of development separate and distinct from the neurotic and psychotic forms of maladjustment, which they supposedly imitate but are not directly rooted in. Others believe that there is a common etiology, and that whether one calls something a personality disorder, a neurosis, or a psychosis depends on the nuances of a common developmental course within the personality leading to different levels of maladjustment. Although we follow the latter style of theorizing, we do not dismiss lightly the alternative possibility. The student of psychopathology must be cognizant of the fact that important theoretical work is continuing in this most interesting area of clinical practice, and that it is probable that through future analyses of these cases we shall witness important breakthroughs in our understanding of psychopathology and human behavior in general.

The problems associated with drug addiction in modern times are staggering. Considering the sociocultural, political, legal, and economic ramifications of this realm of behavior, we cannot think of it as the exclusive or even primary domain of the psychopathologist. Drugs of various types and levels of experiential distortion are today being ingested by people in all walks of life, with vastly different personalities and levels of personal adjustment. Though we may not be likely to cite a routine dynamic in these often harmful practices, there are always personological considerations in the habitual abuse of drugs. Consequently, the present chapter seemed a reasonable context within which to take up the DSM-III diagnostic criteria concerning those individuals who become addicted. We shall also take a brief look at the so-called *factitious disorder* in the present chapter.

## Personality Disorders: Some General Remarks

*A personality disorder arises when some distortion of the personality develops early in life and persists as a person's style, as the characteristic way in which he or she copes with the environment and defends against real or imagined threats to personal competence and integrity.* A personality disorder may never be experienced as something abnormal or intrusive and may therefore never give rise to anxiety once it becomes established. It is the bent twig of childhood that distorts the form of the personality and gives rise to compensatory changes to offset the distortion. The end result may be an adult who seems always inhibited in certain areas of function, who shows exaggerations of certain personality characteristics, or who rushes impetuously into every quickening stream that passes nearby. If such adults and those who are close to them accept such peculiarities as simply "natural," they are not likely to be changed. As a matter of fact, such eccentricities may be taken by those who manifest them as signs of individuality.

It is only when a person with a personality disorder realizes that a lifelong pattern of interpersonal tension and interpersonal conflict is ego alien or ego-dystonic that a possibility arises that change may occur. The realization often comes with repeated failures and dissatisfactions that a person can no longer explain away. It may come because new circumstances force a person to compare himself or herself with others, and the comparison raises self-doubt, dissatisfaction, and perhaps anxiety. The person may even recognize that at least some of what he or she has regarded as a special virtue or mark of individuality may be in fact a pathological need, fear, or incapacity. For example, a woman discovers that her vaunted firmness rests upon a rigidity that keeps her from changing even when a change is necessary, or a man begins to realize that his widely known affability is actually a fear of displeasing anyone, repeatedly robbing him of the opportunity to be his own person in life. We find in clinical practice that a person with a personality disorder seeks therapeutic help because of some such growing dissatisfaction with what has been to that point an ongoing pattern of adjusting to life.

If it is true that personality disorders are developmentally related to neuroses and psychoses, then what constitutes the major differences between these various syndromes of psychopathology? Personality disorders differ from the more severe disturbances in that they are distorted strategies in living that enable the person to achieve a stable level of functioning with this distortion included. For example, a compulsive personality is so organized that the person having it can operate—as an overconscientious, inhibited, rigid individual—without developing symptoms of an acute conflict, such as we saw in the cases described under obsessive-compulsive disorders (see Chapter 7). There is a distortion of personality style that more or less permanently alleviates anxiety, but leaves a person with less flexibility, less maneuverability than normal.

Under stress, such a distorted personality organization may develop its own characteristic peculiarities to the point at which a neurotic or psychotic or psychosomatic illness appears, with symptoms that are only exaggerations of the distortion. For example, an overconscientious, inhibited, rigid person may develop typical obsessive-compulsive symptoms, thereby becoming frankly neurotic. There is also the possibility, repeatedly seen in practice, that such a person may regress under stress and develop a psychotic disorder.

This possibility is of more than theoretical interest. In entering upon the treatment of personality disorders one must bear in mind the risk that a psychotic regression may result from therapeutic disturbance of the pathological equilibrium. Effective psychotherapy and psychoanalysis often involves risk, just as surgical interference does. The therapist who takes such inevitable risks into account is not to be blamed if, in spite of all reasonable precaution, they materialize in the course of therapy. The therapist must be ready to change the approach and even to taper off therapy if the dissolution of a personality disorder seems to be leading toward psychotic regression or has actually precipitated one. No surgeon makes an incision without thereby endangering his or her patient's health; without this danger there can be no surgery. No psychotherapist or psychoanalyst opens up the old conflicts crystallized in personality distortion without endangering his or her patient's equilibrium; without this danger there can be no effective psychotherapy or psychoanalysis.

## *Varieties of Personality Disorders*

The personality disorders are conceptualized as ancillary and even multiplex designations. Thus, a patient diagnosed as schizophrenic on axis I (see p. 21) might be given a diagnosis of personality disorder on axis II. If this or *any* patient were to meet the criteria of *more than one* personality disorder, it would be appropriate to list those designations that apply. Hence, these are not mutually exclusive descriptive categories on axis II. DSM-III groups the personality disorders into three broad categories, and we shall follow this organization in presenting the varieties of this psychopathology.

### DRAMATIC AND ERRATIC PERSONALITY DISORDERS

*Histrionic Personality Disorder.* The *histrionic personality disorder* used to be referred to as the *hysterical personality,* for we see in this behavioral style many of the underlying behavioral tendencies of the somatoform and dissociative disorders (Chapters 8 and 9). This person is characterized by a lifelong flair for a dramatic, exhibitionistic, and egocentric behavioral pattern. We have here the woman who is constantly drawing attention to herself, has a lively, theatrical interpersonal style, and tends to exaggerate every incident that takes place in life. We have the man who is easily bored with a normal life routine, craves novelty and excitement, and is prone to excessive displays of emotion, including uncalled for elation and irrational displays of anger.

Through it all we sense in such individuals a shallowness in emotional commitment, a lack of sincerity and genuineness that makes us realize that they are playing a shaky dramatic role in life, enacting an effort-laden pretense. Though they can be quite charming and are quick to form friendships, they always take more than they give in the relationship. Once a friend is acquired, the demands on his or her understanding and loyalty may be too much for anyone to bear. Those with histrionic personalities are demanding, egocentric, and inconsiderate individuals who expect to be showered with affection from others. Freud (1931/1961j, p. 218) referred to them as *erotic libidinal types,* because they are dominated by fear that others will withhold or withdraw love. As a result, constant reassurance is demanded from others that the histrionic personality is appreciated, loved, even adored. This need for concrete signs of affection from others is often wound into a sexually seductive pattern (Reich, 1949). It is not unusual for the histrionic person to oversexualize life and to be continually falling in and out of emotionally charged love affairs (Fenichel, 1945).

There are some histrionic trends in most normal persons, just as there are compulsive trends. Without some tendency to be dramatic, boastful, or frivolous on occasion a normal personality would seem dull, solemn, and emotionally uninvolved. The person who can be the "life of the party" is often a person with normal dramatic or frivolous trends. A self-centered, boastful enthusiasm over what one is doing can be entertaining to others and lift their morale. The origins of such behavior are in the normal "showing off" and silliness of little children who have been allowed a limited, healthy expression by parents who understand a child's need to be childishly happy. Its normal adult product is sometimes the artist of screen, stage, or television, the scientist, the politician, or the writer—those who remain stable and develop their talents as their profession.

We speak of a histrionic personality only when the self-centered, exhibitionistic display continues into adulthood almost as it appeared in childhood and when criticism of display or interference with it provokes unreasonable anger, sullenness, or self-depreciation. In mild instances, the "life of the party" soon becomes a public nuisance. In more pronounced cases, the person with a histrionic personality seems never to have grown up. The woman referred to above seems always to have been an actor who insists upon being "on stage" in the interpersonal context. She does things to shock, amuse, or impress people, not so much because she needs self-expression—everybody needs self-expression —but because of a pathological egocentricity, a consuming need to be noticed (loved), to be admired, but always to be conspicuous. When she frames enemies, they too must "take notice" of her flair for the dramatic in her hostile displays. The impression of instability, insincerity, and superficiality in such a woman's behavioral style is also a consequence of an orientation that places attention getting at the top of the motivational hierarchy.

Many psychoanalysts link the histrionic personality to fixations at the phallic level of personality. The so-called phallic personality is closely aligned with the histrionic personality in that phallic types are likely to be highly self-indulgent, sexually seductive, and constantly in search of the "center stage" in life. However, a phallic personality type is more likely to be aggressive and interpersonally independent than is the histrionic personality, who tends to be dependent or to withdraw in the face of interpersonal pressure. The decompensation of a histrionic personality may lead to one of several regressions. Among these is, of course, the development of an outspoken conversion or dissociative reaction. Here the person's dramatic tendencies take the form of a disabling symptom that, even though unconsciously concocted, serves the purpose of forcing people to pay continual attention to the patient. Another likely possibility is that the patient's constant need for affection makes him or her especially vulnerable to depression when such demands are not met by others.

*Narcissistic Personality Disorder.* The *narcissistic personality disorder* is a new diagnostic category, one that was not included in DSM-II. It seems to be emerging as an important characterization of abnormal behavior in recent years. Some clinicians believe that the rise in the philosophies of self-indulgence and self-improvement so popular in the post–World War II years may be providing a social background compatible with narcissism. Whatever the case, there seems to be a rising number of narcissistic personality disorders being seen in clinical practice today. The essential features of this disorder are an exaggerated sense of self-importance, self-centeredness, and self-absorption without any appreciation of the impact that such attitudes and behaviors have on other people. The narcissistic individual merely assumes that he or she is someone special and is therefore entitled to considerations and privileges that other people only hope for.

Here we find the man who never admits to failure or shortcomings of any sort, rationalizing his errors and missteps by assigning blame to others or to circumstances beyond his control. Here we have the woman whose fantasies know no bounds, so that she is aghast and humiliated when local financial institutions fail to provide the funds for one of her poorly reasoned "million-dollar" business propositions. If we looked into the life history of this man and woman we would find a long-standing pattern of exhibitionism, interpersonal exploitativeness, and a lack of empathy for the feelings and viewpoints of others.

A preoccupation with success is frequent in such disorders, so that unrealistic goals are set. Expectations for support and admiration from others also color the picture. This is not quite the same thing as the erotic motivation of the histrionic personality, who is not concerned with the power considerations of the narcissist. Narcissistic persons want affection from others, but this is more in the sense of admiration and acknowledgement for their presumed superior capacities—intellectual, physical, moral, and so forth. Of course, there is considerable overcompensation in the narcissist's claims on self-worth, so that even though he or she rationalizes failure, the astute clinician can perceive the underlying sense of rage, shame, and flagging self-esteem that takes place when things go wrong. Usually, friendships or romantic involvements begin with a period of intense commitment, followed by a sudden and even explosive breakup. Naturally, the narcissistic person never takes blame for the breakup.

Interestingly, Freud (1931/1961j, p. 218) drew a picture of the narcissistic libidinal type that is quite consistent with DSM-III. He noted that these individuals had not clearly differentiated their ego and superego, allowing them to live out their ego-ideals (superego aspirations) as if this were an accomplished reality. This gives the narcissist's behavior a more independent style than that of the erotic or histrionic type. Narcissists are fairly aggressive, and in love relationships they like to be adored but also to assume the more active role, in line with their power needs. Freud noted that such people are well suited to take a leadership role and to attack the established social order.

Recall from Chapter 2 that the infant moves in libidinal development from autoerotism through narcissism to object-choice (p. 63). Narcissistic personalities would presumably have fixated at least partially during the narcissistic phase of this transition. Freud's suggestion of a poorly differentiated ego/ superego implies that, in addition to the secondary fixations at the phallic level (unresolved Oedipus complex; see Chapter 5, p. 156), there is also a "late [sadistic] oral" to an "early anal" fixation involved in the narcissistic personality disorder. Some analysts (e.g., Reich, 1949) would assign the primary fixation to the phallic stage, seeing the pattern of self-idealization as an effort to compensate for the castration fear or penis envy typical of this developmental stage. Karen Horney's theory of self-idealization (1939) in reaction to the basic anxiety of the earliest months of life would be consistent with a prephallic level explanation. Recent psychoanalytical theory on narcissism has introduced significant deviations from the traditional account (e.g., Kernberg, 1970). Some theorists even picture an independent developmental line for narcissistic libido, rejecting the traditional intermediate phase explanation that places it between autoerotism and object-choice (e.g., Kohut, 1966). The suggestion here is that this independent developmental course of narcissistic libido can eventuate in healthy behaviors such as humor or creativity, or it may through unfortunate familial and other interpersonal dynamics result in unhealthy behaviors such as hypochondriasis, feelings of emptiness, and lowered self-esteem.

*Antisocial Personality Disorder.* The *antisocial personality disorder* has a long history, having been referred to in times past as *psychopathic inferiority* (psychopathy, psychopathic personality, etc.) (Koch, 1891), *sociopathic personality* (Birnbaum, 1914), and *semantic dementia* (Cleckley, 1941). All such terms have tried to capture the clinical picture of an individual who over a lifetime (beginning before age fifteen) has consistently violated the rights of others, said one thing and then done another, and generally behaved in a manner that brought him or her before the authorities in school, on the job, and in the community. Here we have the young boy known for his lying, stealing, fighting, and truancy. In adolescence he drinks excessively on a regular basis, takes illicit drugs, and belittles authority in any context. This attitude and his unreliable, irresponsible manner in general result in a history of going from one job to another, constantly being let go for missing work, fighting on the job, or failing to carry out assignments.

One might suspect that a diagnosis of "antisocial" refers not to a personality style per se but an evaluation of this pattern of behavior in light of accepted social standards. Some clinicians have been critical of the designation for precisely this reason (see Millon, 1981, p. 181). However, it is the lifelong pattern of deceit, manipulation, self-indulgence, and lack of consideration for others that the term *antisocial* is signifying, rather than the record of arrests which the person may compile. There are delinquents and criminals who violate the law but still do not habitually lie to, steal from, and consistently antagonize their partners in crime. It is also true that not every antisocial personality becomes a criminal. Occupations of a seasonal, piecework, or high-risk nature may actually attract the antisocial personality due to their unconventional nature. These people are sometimes seen as "loners" and as such they can even carry on a small business enterprise in which they take pride in being their "own boss."

Thus, one of our patients, a woman of twenty-six years, was able to support herself and two children from two previous marriages by doing seamstress work in her own home. During her early teens she had learned this skill in a foster home where she was placed after having been sexually abused in her natural home. This woman was impulsive in behavior, was essentially a pathological liar, and bore a hair-trigger temper. One had to treat her with kid gloves and not expect the work commissioned with her to be finished on time. However, she did excellent work at a good price and was fiendishly proud of her product—as if her creations were a mark of her independence. For dynamic reasons relating to an earlier competition with her mother (Oedipal derivatives), she was able to sublimate hostility into the creation and repair of wearing apparel. In a sense, the resulting skill kept her in reasonable contact with others, because she never ceased receiving praise from customers who did not mind putting up with her shortcomings in character.

Psychoanalytical explanations of the antisocial personality—actually, the "psychopath"—have taken their lead from a paper by Freud (1916/1957p) in which he pointed out that some people manifest their poorly resolved Oedipus complexes by carrying throughout life a certain burden of guilt (p. 333). As a result, they behave in a way so as to make certain that conflict with authority will occur, and most interesting of all, that they will eventually be punished in some way. In other words, there is a repetition compulsion in such cases to re-enact the Oedipal dynamics, to create a situation in which the person can feel unjustifiably imposed upon, but also in which a punishment of some type *is* conveyed. Interpersonally this might simply be an argument with someone who represents to the patient a parental figure from out of the past (termed an *imago;* see Chapter 19). If a greater burden of unconscious guilt is involved, the antisocial personality might actually commit a crime in order to en-sure that a punishment (imprisonment, etc.) takes place (Alexander, 1930, pp. 14-15).

Another theme that has emerged more recently in analytical writings is that the antisocial type is seeking to manipulate others in order to bolster his or her own weakened sense of self-esteem (Bursten, 1972, p. 319). It is as if, having rejected the parental superego standards on which self-esteem is usually built, the antisocial personality must aspire to a substitute standard of action that will lend some semblance of personal mastery in life. The resultant ego-ideal of the antisocial personality is one of manipulation, "putting something over" on others, and continually rejecting the grounds on the basis of which other people behave. Whatever the case, it is probably correct to say that a phallic fixation is primary in the dynamics of the antisocial personality. We also cannot fail to take note of the clearly teleological formulation here, in which the person intentionally seeks punishment and aspires to enact a personally affirmed value system.

*Borderline Personality Disorder.* The *borderline personality disorder* is one of the more disputed diagnostic categories in DSM-III, since it really has no distinctive stylistic features about it (Perry & Klerman, 1978). The key descriptive word seems to be *instability* in a number of different behavioral spheres, such as mood, interpersonal behavior, and self-image. A classical designation that seems to fit here and that is not elsewhere accounted for in DSM-III is the so-called *cyclothymic personality* (Kahlbaum, 1882; Kraepelin, 1921). In effect, this dynamic was conceived of as a personality system either prone to or actually suffering from a mild case of the manic-depressive disorder. Fluctuations in mood were observed in certain people that bore no real tie to their external life circumstances, so that they were "up" one day and "down" the next. Based on such clinical observations, Kraepelin and others concluded that the cyclothymic (or cycloid) personality was due to underlying biological factors, hereditarily transmitted.

But the borderline diagnostic category involves more than just an unstable or fluctuating mood picture. There may be a loss of identity suggested, or a confusion over precisely what the person values and is seeking in life. Here we find the woman who settles upon a new work career, pulls up stakes, and moves to a new location full of seeming enthusiasm. Within a few weeks she is completely disillusioned about her altered status, angry with herself and others, and repeatedly asking herself, "What am I doing here? Where am I going? Who am I, really?" Such questions are not new for her. She has been raising them all her life, and when she feels she has an answer for them things look very hopeful. She has impulsively arrived at plans to carry forward some aspiration or other. But then, as in the past, nothing goes as initially projected, bringing her down from the clouds in a confused state. In her low period she as all borderline personalities represents a serious threat to life, because the impulsivity typifying such patients often includes self-destructive attempts at suicide.

The dysphoric (ego-alien) mood rarely lasts more than a few days. Interestingly, it can sometimes pass in the course of a few hours. Here we have the man who devotes much time to body building, lifting weights, and looking after his nutrition. One day, for no apparent reason he becomes totally upset with his muscular physique and inflicts a severe gash in one of his pectoral muscles as an act of self-disgust. A few hours later, after being rushed to the hospital for surgical repairs, he is normal once again and asking, "What came over me? I don't understand myself anymore." Some clinicians view the borderline disorder as an advanced state of the less severe dependent, histrionic, compulsive, and passive-aggressive personality disorders (e.g., see Millon, 1981, p. 332). Others consider this illness to be a variant of the so-called *schizo-affective psychosis* in that it involves serious symptoms of thought and mood disturbance.

Psychoanalytical writers have framed the borderline personality disorder as either a stage between neurotic and psychotic disorders or as a kind of amalgam of neurotic, psychotic, and even psychopathic disorders (Schmideberg, 1947). The level of fixation is essentially distributed across all psychosexual stages, with the severity of the illness dependent upon the extent to which the personality system is libidinally invested at one point or another. Some analysts have found the instability in behavioral pattern to be due to a general approach to life in which a sort of *vicious circle* is generated (Wolberg, 1952). It is as if the borderline patient has been caught betwixt and between in life, never really having committed himself or herself to anything. As a result, there is a constantly shifting grounds for judging what is taking place, how one ought to behave, and how successful one has actually been in life. Another theme found in this literature is the suggestion that borderline patients are those who employ a neuroticlike defense in order to avoid becoming psychotic (R. P. Knight, 1953).

The recurring identity problems among borderline patients have prompted some psychoanalytical writers to focus on maturation of the ego as an etiological factor (Cary, 1972; Kernberg, 1975). There is just enough reality-testing available to the borderline personality to retain a foothold in the external world, but the ego relies on primitive defenses like denial rather than repression and more advanced defense mechanisms. In particular, there is a tendency to avoid integrating contradictory emotional displays into a single sense of "self(ego)-hood." Another characteristic of these patients is a poor differentiation between the self-identity of the person and external objects that have been or are likely to be cathected. This poor differentiation injures the patient's sense of identity and makes it probable that external losses or failures in expectations will be taken as direct assaults on the integrity of the personality (Jacobson, 1953b). Surely, the borderline personality disorder—along with the paranoid, schizoid, and schizotypical disorders (see below)—must be judged among the most serious of the disturbances now under consideration. We next move to a series of disorders that have anxiety and fear as prominent features.

## ANXIOUS AND FEARFUL PERSONALITY DISORDERS

*Avoidant Personality Disorder.* The *avoidant personality disorder* is a new diagnostic category and may be contrasted with the schizoid personality disorder (see below) on the basis of how social relationships are averted. Thus, whereas schizoids are perceptually insensitive to their surroundings and therefore passively detach themselves from the relationship of others, avoidants are oversensitive to the moods and evaluations of others and *actively* seek to avoid social contact as a type of defense (Millon, 1969). Here we have the college woman who lives alone, refuses to join any sorority or organization on campus, studies by herself at the library, and will not mix with others unless she is absolutely certain that the contact will not focus on her as a person. At the same time, she is very desirous of having friends and longs for the affection of others. She is alert to any signs of acceptance, even from strangers whom she passes on the street. By the same token, any sign of rejection or indifference from others—even a brusque manner from a merchant or a waitress—leaves her feeling humiliated and more unworthy than before.

Patients with this disorder are able to verbalize their distress, and they also make many statements reflecting low self-esteem. They present themselves as shy and apprehensive individuals, and invariably their timidity and uncertainty in social contacts bring on the very thing they are trying to avoid. The interpersonal tension rises thanks to the discomfort obviously being felt by the avoidant personality, leading in turn to a poor social contact all around. Sometimes people will make friendly jokes about the shyness and uncertainty being displayed, but this fails to break the ice because the avoidant person is humorless and unable to participate comfortably in such give-and-take. The speech of avoidants tends to be slow and serious in content, and overt emotional displays are kept to a minimum.

The avoidant will go to some lengths in order to feel socially active and yet retain the sense of distance from others that his or her dynamic demands.

Going to movies is one mechanism that seems to work. This is better than sitting at home, alone, watching television. People laugh and shudder in common at the movies. One patient we knew attended baseball games for the same reason. He became quite knowledgeable concerning baseball, and found that he could occasionally add to the conversation of fans sitting nearby when it was a matter of some factual information about his team favorites. This afforded him an amount of acceptance from these strangers without great risk. He never argued the merits of a ballplayer or a decision made by an umpire or the team manager. Even so, when the game ended and he returned home his feelings of wanting personal contact were stronger than ever.

Psychoanalytical theories of relevance to this disorder have typically been framed in terms of a *phobic* problem, in which the person is irrationally fearful of rejection from others (Fenichel, 1945; MacKinnon & Michels, 1971; Rado, 1969). The patient seems to have introjected a conflict between strong libidinal needs for affection and an expectation of depreciation if not rejection from the loved object. Anal fixations are usually implied here, with the likelihood that parental demands on the person in toilet training either actually were or were interpreted as unusually harsh and demeaning. The resultant avoidance, inhibition, and apprehension anxiety of the patient become characterological defenses. Horney (1945) traced the interpersonal style of "moving away from people" to the person's reaction to a basic anxiety that presumably obtained from early in life thanks to parental attitudes toward the infant.

*Dependent Personality Disorder.* In sharp contrast to avoidants, patients with *dependent personality disorders* gravitate to others and allow them to assume responsibility for major decisions in their lives. Dependents assume a passive role in social contact and follow the lead of others uncritically. They can make no demands on others, for they lack the self-confidence this requires. The dependent personality is often good-natured, easygoing, and thought to be very considerate of others. This consideration is based in large measure on the fear that others will reject anyone who is not constantly deferent, self-demeaning, and willing to be of help no matter how inconvenient the circumstances. Here we have the man who is a lifelong follower of others, who describes himself as "not very bright," and who responds to the most outlandish demands on his time from others without complaint. He is vulnerable to the aggressive salesperson. He takes the advice of people whom he has only recently met. He is like a child in the world of adults.

Although dependent personalities usually present a good front, an underlying unhappiness and sense of insecurity breaks through regularly. These patients will be seen to detract from their abilities, criticize their physical attractiveness, or admit to wanting more from life than they express openly. Depression is fairly common among these patients. Their typical lack of ambitiousness and lowered aspirations in life often mask a fantasy realm in which dependents gain immediate success and are instantly accepted by everyone for strong points in character.

Dependents tend to be self-indulgent when depression comes on, and they are always likely targets for obesity and alcoholism. Here we have the woman who, unlike her sisters, never married. She still lives with her parents. She was always a "bit on the plump side" as a child and adolescent, but since reaching adulthood she has steadily put on weight to what is now an alarming degree. Her jovial manner and willingness to play "Helpful Hannah" to everyone has made her reasonably popular in her very limited social orbit. But there is something pathetic in her Pollyannish acceptance of familial demands and her sweetness to others. Friends are growing alarmed about her physical health, but her parents seem unconcerned over the weight gain.

We witness definite oral involvements as primary fixations in the dependent personality disorder (Abraham, 1927; Fenichel, 1945). One has the sense in these disorders of a person who continues to function primarily on the basis of the pleasure principle, substituting pretense for reality whenever possible. The notion of obtaining oral gratification from others is contained in Fromm's *receptive orientation* (1947). From literal food ingestion the oral or receptive personality extends behavior to satisfactions of all sorts, trading off personal independence and integrity for the passive-dependent role in life. Though he departed from traditional psychoanalytical theory, Adler (1964b, p. 129) was also to find a discernible group of behavioral characteristics in children that he typified as *passive,* including timidity, anxiety, obedience, and laziness.

*Compulsive Personality Disorder.* We find some of the same tendencies in the *compulsive personality disorder* as we have already considered in Chapter 7 when we reviewed the obsessive-compulsive neurosis. Compulsive personalities are typified by inflexibility, a cheerless outlook on life, inability to express warm and tender emotions, and a fanatic preoccupation with order, rules, organization, and efficiency. Here we find the woman who is so caught up in her need to do things a certain way that she actually loses efficiency in the long run. Over shorter periods of time she seems to be well organized and efficient. But her inability to see the woods for the trees, getting her lost in trivial details that must be accomplished precisely or she cannot go forward, interferes with the fluid completion of tasks. Since she has such rigid steps to the attainment of a goal, time is always running out on her and she begins missing deadlines and target dates.

Work and productivity are prized by the compulsive personality to the exclusion of taking relaxed pleasures along life's way. It takes time to cultivate friends, so the compulsive forgoes such interpersonal commitments. One sometimes suspects that these individuals do not much care whether or not an ultimate achievement takes place in their work. They are not aiming toward eventual promotion, financial reward, or even the recognition of others per se. They seem to work for work's sake. The routine of work is what orders their existence and allays their underlying sense of anxiety. Many people have this attitude toward work, but one of the marks of the compulsive person is that he or she begins to shy away from decision making, which is vital to the effective accomplishments in the work sphere. Here we find the man who works his way into a responsible position in some job, one calling for setting policy in his company. But now he finds himself putting off making such decisions. He seems unable to commit himself to a course of action, due in part to the fact that he sees so many alternatives opening up, as well as his fear that any slight error would be a disaster to his entire career. He ruminates and procrastinates, bluffs, and waits for other executives and subordinates to influence company policy. Even as he does so he sees possible weaknesses in the recommendations of others.

Compulsives can be very insensitive to the feelings of others. In a less demanding work environment they are reasonably effective supervisors, insisting on the carrying out of routinized procedures without variation. If a subordinate on the job (or an offspring in the home) violates their detailed instructions, compulsives can be quite heartless in overreacting to minor failings. When people do well the compulsive finds it almost impossible to express genuine pleasure with the performance. As a parent, the compulsive never really relates to his or her children in an openly loving manner. Compulsives advance on life as if they were drill sergeants in the military. Problems with morality are common, thanks to the compulsive personality's tendency to scrupulosity. Everything seems to be a sinful transgression. When things begin falling to pieces for these individuals outbursts of hostility or bouts with depression are common.

Traditional analytical explanations of compulsivity are framed in terms of the *anal personality* (Abraham, 1927; Freud, 1908/1959c; E. Jones, 1938; Reich, 1949; Sadger, 1910). Compulsive personality dynamics are traced to anal-sadism, with fixations usually linked to struggles with parents over bowel control. The triad of basic traits for the anal personality includes parsimony, pedantry, and petulance. There is a negativistic outlook and a lifelong struggle for independence and self-sufficiency manifested in this triad, in compensation for severe feelings of self-doubt and ambivalence concerning authority figures. The dynamics of anality relate to our discussion in Chapter 7, but the symptoms are not so extreme or acute as in the obsessive-compulsive neurosis. The great majority of compulsive personality disorders never break down into an acute neurosis or psychosis. These patients remain inhibited, rigid, obstinate, excessively orderly, and overconscientious, or they mix some of these compulsive characteristics with their opposites to form a contradictory picture. Thus, compulsive disorderliness and dirtiness may coexist with inhibitions, rigidity, and obstinacy. The same person may be compulsively stingy and a compulsive spendthrift.

*Passive-Aggressive Personality Disorder.* The *passive-aggressive personality disorder* is one of the least reliable diagnoses among the personality disorders (Millon, 1981, p. 247), due in part we think to some terminological confusions. Thus, the terms *passive, aggressive, hostile,* and *assertive* are widely employed in the literature of psychopathology, but not always with uniform meaning. Some clinicians reserve the term *hostility* for the case in which a person is behaving aggressively with harmful intent. For example, a young man playing aggressively in a football game would not be considered hostile even if his aggressiveness resulted in an injury to an opponent. If this young man begins to play "dirty," inflicting pain on an opponent intentionally, then we would be witnessing an act of hostility. Other clinicians would say that vigorous play without an intent to injure is *assertive behavior,* but that intentionally trying to injure opponents is *aggression.* DSM-III adopts the latter usage, so that aggressive behavior refers to an intentional form of negativism or resistance in interpersonal relations.

Assertion bears the meaning of a positive commitment, a clear position or claim advanced and enacted by the person openly. The problem with referring to nonaggressive behavior as assertive is that frequently very unassertive or *passive* people behave in a negativistic or resistive manner. DSM-III resolves this seeming inconsistency by suggesting that individuals who passively engage in negativistic or resistive behavior are asserting *covert* aggression! Thus, in the passive-aggressive personality disorder we find the person who has habitually been a resister, a negator, or an obfuscator. Here we find the stubborn man who cannot be pushed. On the job he is inefficient and forgetful, tends to ask meaningless questions of superiors, and treats each admonition to improve his performance as an unreasonable demand put upon a union worker by management. Even when he can easily innovate and improve his efficiency on the job, this man will find some way in which to complicate procedures and make matters worse.

Though this portrait is clear enough, it is not always easy determining whether or not a passive person's continual procrastination and dawdling are really a covert manipulation reflecting aggression (hostility). *Passive-dependent* people are prone to behave in this way out of their need to be looked after, directed, and constantly reassured. However, a passive-aggressive individual is less likely to be assuaged by such direction and reassurance. He or she reacts with irritation and dissatisfaction even when given good advice. The passive-aggressive person tends to be envious of others, so even after receiving direct assistance there is a lingering feeling of resentment. We witness a sulking, critical person carrying out the sensible ideas of others, but doing so in such a way as to *reduce* their chances for effectiveness.

Here we find the woman whose husband must constantly make familial plans, yet who cannot seem to carry them out as initially framed and supposedly agreed upon. Budgets are never maintained. Important bills are misplaced. Projected vacations are disrupted through subsequent scheduling errors. Even the daily household routine is chronically out of orderly control. If her husband complains, this woman may either burst into tears or vent considerable rage, blaming circumstances, other people, and even her husband for the disorientation in their lives. She then closes herself in a bedroom and sulks for hours. Passive-aggressive individuals rarely voice personal complaints of inefficiency. They envy others for their supposedly "easy" lives, and complain bitterly about how difficult their lives have been.

The psychoanalytical literature has generally placed the fixation point for this disorder as late oral, getting into what Abraham (1927) referred to as *oral-sadistic* behavioral tendencies (see Menninger, 1940). There may also be secondary fixations in the anal stage, accounting for certain of the negativistic aspects of the syndrome. Reich (1949) emphasized the masochistic aspects of sadomasochism. Passive-aggressive persons go through life in a constant state of turmoil, but in doing so they implicate others as their sadistic maltreaters. There is an underlying spitefulness, a desire to retaliate against those who would constantly inflict pain (parental imagos). The oral sadomasochistic behavioral style is reflected in the finding that these individuals rarely inflict physical pain on others (Small et al., 1970). As children, they were not likely to be active participants, much less winners, in a physical tussle or a fistfight. But verbal abuse toward others is prominent in the clinical picture. Passive-aggressive personalities go through life constantly being pummeled by circumstances that they claim are beyond their control but that in fact are unconsciously orchestrated.

We next move to the final subgrouping of the personality disorders, those that are most eccentric and peculiar in nature and therefore likely to be reflective of the greatest personal maladjustment (with the possible exception of the borderline personality disorder).

## Eccentric and Peculiar Personality Disorders

*Paranoid Personality Disorder.* In Chapter 11 we discussed the nature of paranoia in some detail, and what was mentioned there has relevance for the present diagnostic category. The *paranoid personality disorder* is found in people who are constantly suspicious and mistrustful of others, hypersensitive to criticism or seemingly "personal" questions directed to them, and highly controlled in emotional expressiveness or spontaneity. Here we have the man who has a history of avoiding blame for any little thing, who is argumentative and willing to make mountains out of molehills. He prides himself on being objective, rational, and unemotional but comes across to others as a "cold fish" who does not know how to take a joke or when it is worthwhile making an issue of something and when it is not. He is particularly likely to see meaning in events when there is none, and his tendency to question the motives of everyone makes him a difficult person to get close to, much less keep as a long-time friend. As the years go by these tendencies worsen and he becomes the "odd duck" of the neighborhood.

Many clinicians view the key problem in a paranoid personality as the basic *lack of trust* he or she senses in relations with others. Through constant sensitivity to nuances in social relations the paranoid person can sometimes actually acquire a facility for interpreting unconscious attitudes and wishes in others. These unconscious traces are selective and magnified by the paranoid personality into issues of prime importance. That is, only the negative inclinations of others are focused upon. Here we have the woman who is quick to see any hints of boredom, irritation, or envy in the manner of others. She never senses the unconscious promptings of empathy, good humor, and support that concerned friends send her way. Her lack of basic trust hampers her reality-testing operations. She magnifies the negative aspects and overlooks the positive. Also, she assumes that everyone is as clear on what is supposedly "taking place" as she is. Hence, there are all sorts of secretive maneuverings with tricky questions, framed by her in order to signal others that she knows how little they think of her, or how they are trying to "put her down." Such maneuverings simply confuse her associates and make her appear increasingly odd in social relations. She cannot keep friends and rapidly turns into an isolate.

One unconscious tendency that a paranoid seems to pick up in other people's behavior is homosexual interest. In Freud's broader theory (1911/ 1958a, p. 77) there is a technical reason for tying paranoiac sensitivity to homosexuality. We shall take up the question of homosexuality in some detail in Chapter 16, and therefore shall simply observe in the present context that the question of a necessary tie between homosexuality and paranoia is still a moot one. Indeed, the question of whether homosexuality constitutes psychopathology has in recent years become a moot one. We shall return to this complex matter in Chapter 16.

Although Freud's tie of paranoia to homosexuality arises in the phallic psychosexual stage, there have been psychoanalytical explanations of paranoia tracing it to anal fixations, with anal eroticism and anal expulsive tendencies highlighted (Abraham, 1927; Menninger, 1940). Thus, the dynamics associated with poor resolution of the Oedipus complex in paranoia seem to be underwritten by fueros stemming from the anal level, in which the patient dismissed personal failures in sphincter control as due to others, was jealous of the mastery achieved by siblings, and introjected sadistic behavioral patterns from the actual or perceived sadistic treatment afforded by parents in the toilet-training situation. Thus, there is a strong undercurrent of sadism and hostility (aggression) in the paranoid personality that must be dealt with in some way. We noted in Chapter 11 that one of the major ways in which to deal with paranoid problems was to begin relating to others in a realm based in large measure on fantasy (i.e., the pseudocommunity) where interpersonal relations are in effect "made to order." The paranoid personality keeps this pseudocommunity just close enough to everyone's experience of reality to avoid slipping into a full-blown paranoid disorder.

Of course, it is to be expected that at times in life when the paranoid personality is confronting unusual stress ideas of reference begin to appear, and a near-psychotic period of adjustment is lived through. However, thanks to the minimally effective level of reality contact there is rarely a flagrant delusional system to be noted, and hallucinations are uncommon and of brief duration when they do occur. Often, the pseudocommunity of paranoid personalities is idealized into a "new vision" for humanity, either in this world or the "next." Paranoid personalities are therefore seen gravitating to and even becoming leaders in esoteric religions, extreme political groups, or quasi-scientific organizations. Intelligence plays a role here, of course. Since paranoid personalities tend to exaggerate their importance and they easily threaten others in interpersonal contact, it is not difficult to understand how it is that the more intelligent among them emerge as leaders in such fringe groups. Of course, as the rise of Nazism in Germany demonstrated, sometimes a fringe group can become a leading force in the culture as a whole.

*Schizoid Personality Disorder and Schizotypal Personality Disorder.* The *schizoid personality disorder* and the *schizotypal personality disorder* are new diagnostic categories. Previously, both of these manifestations would have been diagnosed as a schizoid personality disorder. However, due to growing evidence from both clinical sources and empirical research, a distinction was drawn that separated those patients with problems exclusively in interpersonal relations from those who seem to have eccentricities in communication and odd behaviors in addition to such interpersonal adjustment difficulties. These two categories are obviously variations on the common theme of schizophrenia, which we reviewed in detail in Chapter 14. Thus, what was stated there has relevance for present considerations.

Recall from Chapter 14 (p. 420) that we included the traditional diagnostic category of *simple schizophrenia* in our overview. This clinical picture is essentially what the *schizoid personality disorder* points toward. Schizoid personalities are characterized by a fundamental inability to form social relationships due to a lack of emotional stability and spontaneity. Here we have the seemingly shy adolescent who slinks along the corridors of his or her high school, dodging others and making no efforts to enter into the usual banter. In classes this person never speaks up, never laughs when others do, or does so haltingly and after the natural point at which laughter is called for. If he or she is pushed into conversation a bland and indifferent kind of interaction ensues. It is as if this person is just not actively engaged in life. School grades are mediocre to poor. Almost nothing seems interesting. Friends are few and far between. Everyone agrees that this person is humorless, dull, and aloof.

Kraepelin (1919) referred to such individuals as *autistic personalities* and Bleuler (1922) was the first to use the term schizoid (*schizoidie*). Kretschmer (1925) subsequently refined the concept and gave it modern form. One has the impression that schizoid personalities are mentally retarded, but their IQ test scores belie this fact. Furthermore, if we review their early history we often learn that they were achieving at a perfectly normal level in elementary school, though their personality might still have been considered a bit on the shy and withdrawn side. There is a range of adjustment in this personality disorder, moving from the fairly well-adjusted individuals who are simply "loners" and prone to go along in the shadows of life's opportunities to the obviously inadequate individuals who are for all practical purposes living out a life of simple schizophrenia inside or outside the confines of a mental hospital, prison, or related protected environment.

If a person of this sort begins to use speech in an unusual way, or if there are eccentricities in his or her thoughts and behaviors, the diagnosis of *schizotypal personality disorder* is assigned. This alternative is further strengthened if a history of schizophrenia is found in the person's family. Clinically, we would look for such things as magical thinking ("I never try to do a math problem until I hum this little tune to myself"), frequent depersonalization without accompanying anxiety ("I feel like I'm really not 'here' most of the time"), ideas of reference ("Why is everyone so interested in what I am doing?"), and loosening of associations ("I know what I'm supposed to say. My sister knows things too"). Neologisms, clang associations, or stilted and confused sentence structures would also be evidence of a serious thought disorder, and lead the clinician to begin thinking about a frankly schizophrenic diagnosis. Delusional or hallucinatory experience not related to drugs would also confirm a more serious diagnosis.

The question of a range of (mal-)adjustment is even more relevant to the schizotypal than to the schizoid disorders. Many clinicians view a schizotypal person as actually suffering from a mild form of schizophrenia, or at least being on the verge of a schizophrenic deterioration. Various labels have been applied to these individuals along this line in the past, such as *latent schizophrenics* (E. Bleuler, 1922; Bychowski, 1953; Federn, 1947), *ambulatory schizophrenics* (Zilboorg, 1941), and *preschizophrenics* (Rapaport et al., 1968). When Rado (1956b) coined the term *schizotypal,* he did so on the theoretical assumption that there was an underlying hereditary predisposition (genotype) being reflected in such personality styles. This line of reasoning, supported by the research evidence of familial predisposition that we discussed in Chapter 14 (see p. 449), has obviously been influential in the present DSM-III separation of schizotypal from schizoid personality tendencies.

We find ourselves in the same situation as we were in concerning the etiology of schizophrenia. There may well be biological factors stemming from hereditary influences in these schizophreniclike personality disorders. From the psychodynamic perspective, however, these disorders are presumed to originate from the same lack of trust in the symbiotic mother-child relationship that typified paranoid disturbances, though with less of an emphasis on anal tendencies. There are stronger oral features in the picture, suggesting an even earlier problem in adjustment than paranoid personalities, with a satisfactory sense of self-identity never having been achieved. Paranoids have the advantage of feeling pulled together into a person taken advantage of by others. Schizoid and schizotypal personalities find it impossible to commit emotionally to a self which is really "not there," and hence continue to mature in a kind of artificial existence that is not genuinely their own. Such individuals grow to adulthood feeling detached not only from others but also from themselves. They are aloof because they do not know where or when or *whom* to commit to life.

Whether or not such a person will regress into a full-blown schizophrenic disorder depends upon the life frustrations sustained. In an uncomplicated environment, such as a rural setting or a close-knit familial context with mutual support, these individuals can acquire a level of adjustment that allows them to pass through life without psychotic episodes. However, the more likely outcome is not good. Since they do not fight back (as does the paranoid), such individuals can be vulnerable to tensions others might be able to offset. They also can be manipulated into drug habits and other forms of petty criminal behavior. Holding a job becomes a major problem. The chances are obviously high that schizoid and schizotypal personalities will experience serious adjustment problems at some point in their life.

## Factitious Disorders

Most of us have had the experience of feigning illness in order to gain some advantage in life, such as "playing hooky" from school, being excused from demanding work, or avoiding an embarrassing confrontation with someone. Many of us can also look back and appreciate that certain illnesses we suffered through in the past were at least partially brought on or made worse by our attitude at the time. Still others would never realize that a physical illness was actually serving an intention in their lives at the time of its occurrence. There are surely varying levels of complexity and insight reflected in the fact known by many physicians that people can make themselves ill in order to bring about certain ends (sympathy, revenge, etc.).

The disorder we are considering in the present section is concerned with a dynamically motivated, unconscious intention to appear mentally or physically ill to the external world. *A factitious disorder is one that is not genuine, but that seeks to give the appearance of mental or physical illness through voluntary albeit unconscious efforts on the part of the person.* We can sometimes discern how being ill might prove beneficial to the person concerned. For example, a man arrested for attempted bank robbery may begin showing signs of mental illness following incarceration, but these "symptoms" are so unnatural and excesive as to appear a caricature of the real thing. He may look at a clock displaying the time of one and claim that it is now four-thirty. He may put the lighted end of a cigarette into his mouth and persist in blowing smoke out of the opposite end, acting all the time as if these were the signs of "crazy" behavior, while his viewers perceive this as a burlesque performance.

This man may claim memory loss for all events surrounding the bank robbery, complain of hearing voices that direct his behavior, grimace and possibly giggle while appearing lost in thought, and request treatment for sundry physical pains. There is nothing in the patient's record indicating that he has gone through an episode of this sort before. But there is little doubt that he has some form of acute disturbance in the present; indeed, he readily takes on new symptoms as the diagnosing clinician asks questions of him. This disorder was once diagnosed as *Ganser syndrome,* as well as *pseudopsychosis* or *pseudodementia.*

Another form of the factitious disorder, occurring in a more chronic fashion, was formerly termed the *Munchausen syndrome.* Here we find the woman who for years has gone from one doctor to another, seeking to be hospitalized for various physical problems such as lower back pains, nausea, and vertigo. She complains of developing skin irritations easily, of having frequent gastrointestinal problems, and of suffering from recurring headaches. When questioned in detail she is vague and inconsistent in her delineation of symptoms. In fact, she tells outright lies about her medical history. However, the woman does not demonstrate the bizarre signs of pseudopsychosis noted in the prisoner. If this woman succeeds in being hospitalized she proves a burden for the staff, because she constantly seeks attention and refuses to obey rules and regulations. If her original symptoms are found to be of no real consequence in the tests that follow, the woman will promptly concoct another series of complaints. If discharged from the hospital she almost immediately seeks admission to another.

The prisoner would be diagnosed as having a *factitious disorder with psychological symptoms,* whereas the "sickly" woman would be given the diagnosis of a *factitious disorder with physical symptoms.* Both of these individuals seem to be trying to play the role of a "patient," seeking we surmise a kind of secondary gain through mental and/or physical illness that almost never fools anyone because of the transparency of their behavior. In the past, these disorders were related to the family of the hysterias. However, today we recognize a greater affinity to the personality disorders. Thus, factitious disorders are seen as compounding aspects of underlying personality disorders such as the histrionic, narcissistic, avoidant, dependent, and passive-aggressive. It is not always apparent on the face of things why the patient is seeking to play the patient role. In the prisoner's circumstance we could readily understand why, but the sickly woman's motivation is not directly evident. Of course, if we looked into the case more deeply we could find plenty of clues as to why she needed such attention.

A ticklish problem facing the diagnostician is to differentiate between a factitious disorder and outright *malingering.* To malinger is to pretend at being mentally or physically ill in order to gain advantage, but in this instance the voluntary manipulation is completely conscious. The assumption clinicians make in the factitious disorder is that the person is under so much present threat or is so psychically unprepared to face life that an unconscious decision is made to adopt the role of patient—however crudely this enactment is accomplished. A malingerer, on the other hand, need not have such deep-seated personality deficits. When we do find a personality disorder associated with habitual malingering it is likely to be the psychopathic or antisocial personality. But the point is that malingerers are consciously seeking to obtain a goal that illness will afford them. A malingerer can actually do a better job of faking illness, because in laying plans for the goal he or she sometimes studies the illness to be enacted and thereby carries off the subterfuge to better effect than does the factitious patient.

What we look for in the factitious patient is some intrapsychic dynamic wound into unconscious motivations and prompting the person to take on the role of patient. We suspect malingering when there is no such inner dynamic and when the diagnostic circumstances are directly tied to an outcome that the person is clearly trying to bring about. For example, when a person is referred for mental or physical evaluation by an attorney, and the outcome bears on a legal case being brought in the court, we are likely to suspect malingering if the symptoms are exaggerated and inconsistent. Malingering is also to be suspected if the person's claims of disability far outweigh the objective clinical evidence. Malingerers do not so readily concoct "on-the-spot" additions to their clinical complaint. They exaggerate and insist upon the clinical picture that they brought to the diagnostician—and more of the same! Malingerers are also notoriously unwilling to carry out a treatment program once a diagnosis has been settled on. In the final analysis, it is up to the clinical judgment of the diagnostician to decide whether the voluntary pursuit of the "sick" or "injured" patient role is conscious or unconscious. This is not always easy, but with skillful interviewing it can be determined in most instances.

## Substance Use Disorders

### ABUSE VERSUS DEPENDENCE

It is beyond the scope of the present volume to consider the ramifications of *substance use disorders* or, as these were formerly referred to, *drug addictions.* Undoubtedly, both terms will continue to be used. There are so many sociological, legal, economic, political, moral, and simply recreational aspects associated with substance use disorders that it would require a separate volume to do the subject justice. We shall present an overview of relevant DSM-III terminology, consider some puzzling aspects of drug use, and then take up the known personality dynamics of problem drug users.

We can get a reasonably good overview of the physiological reactions that drugs induce by dividing them into three broad categories, although there is no assurance that a particular drug effect will be limited to only one of these categories. Drugs can induce (1) feelings of relaxation and comfort, (2) feelings of enthusiasm, endurance and excitement, and (3) cognitive experiences of "mind expansion" through the hallucinatory distortion of everyday perception. Human beings seek all three of these kinds of experience through the ingestion of drugs. Occasional recreational uses—even excessive uses—of substances providing these psychological states are not considered abnormal, though they may be illegal. *A substance use disorder is diagnosed when the person takes a substance affecting the central nervous system (CNS) on a regular basis, leading to undesirable developments in his or her experience.* Undesirable outcomes of drug taking would include such things as impaired social relations, serious loss of concentration in school or on the job, inability to get through the day without (usually increasing amounts of) the drug being ingested, and physical sickness when the drug is taken in smaller amounts or discontinued entirely.

DSM-III distinguishes between *substance abuse* and *substance dependence.* There is a "level of severity" estimate involved in this distinction between two kinds of problem drug abuse, but in point of fact both of these patterns can be highly detrimental to the life adjustment of the person involved. The reader will find in some cases that what we are here referring to as substance abuse is considered "psychological dependence" by others (see, e.g., Snyder, 1971, p. 86). There are psychological as well as physiological aspects to the distinction between substance abuse and substance dependence.

*Substance abuse* refers to the fact that a person can no longer get through the day without ingestion of the crucial substance. Here we find the man who is a covert tippler, but in recent weeks seems to be losing control. He normally has an "eye opener" shortly after arising in the morning; throughout the day he takes unobtrusive drinks from a hidden bottle. In recent weeks he has begun heavy binge drinking followed by blackouts. This has frightened him, so that now he tries to hold off taking his first drink of alcohol until right after work. But this makes him ill at ease all day long. He is distractive, argumentative, and prone to bouts of depression. His boss is beginning to keep an eye on him because his work effectiveness is deteriorating. At home, he is experiencing frequent fights with his wife over his drunkenness and late hours. DSM-III requires that a clear pattern of this sort exist for *at least one month* before assigning the diagnosis of *alcohol abuse.*

*Substance dependence* is diagnosed when the pattern of abuse is made worse by increasing physiological needs for the substance, so that it is no longer a question of "getting high" but one of "getting by" in a relatively decent manner. Physiological dependence is diagnosed based upon two symptoms: (1) *tolerance,* or the ability of the addict's central nervous system to absorb the initial dosage and function without generating the desired effect ("high"), thereby requiring that a larger dose of the substance must be ingested; and (2) *withdrawal,* or feelings of illness when the drug level is reduced or discontinued.

As tolerance rises so do the chances of experiencing withdrawal symptoms, which range from nervousness, mild anxiety, and slight nausea to severe reactions like fever, tachycardia, perspiration, chills, diarrhea, insomnia, and a sense of panic over the need for additional drug ingestion. Since drugs are expensive, particularly illegal narcotic drugs, the addict living at a high tolerance level is likely to spend all of his or her savings, sell anything, or do anything to procure the necessary funds to support a habit. It is out of such misery and personal urgency that modern social violence often takes root—including mugging, prostitution, burglary, and robbery, not to mention the constant likelihood of physical injury or murder in connection with such crimes.

All drugs can enter into a pattern of abuse, but not all of them have been proven to induce physiological dependence. DSM-III recognizes the following five types of drugs as resulting in *both* abuse and dependence (i.e., reflecting tolerance and/or withdrawal) [the drug effect is given in brackets]: (1) alcohol [CNS depressant; euphoria]; (2) barbiturates or similarly acting sedatives or hypnotics (e.g., amytal, nembutal, seconal) [CNS depressants; relaxation and sleep]; (3) opiods (e.g., heroin, morphine) [CNS depressants; pain relief, relaxation]; (4) amphetamines or similarly acting sympathomimetics (e.g., benzedrine, dexedrine, methedrine) [CNS energizer; elation]; and (5) cannabis (marijuana, hashish) [mild hallucinogenic, euphoria].

Due to the lack of clear evidence for physiological dependence when they are used, the following three classes of drugs are listed in DSM-III as leading *only* to substance abuse: (1) cocaine [CNS energizer; elevated endurance and sexual urge]; (2) phencyclidine (PCP) or similarly acting arlcyclohexylamines [severe hallucinogenic, stupor]; (3) hallucinogens (mescaline, LSD, psilocybin) [perceptual distortions, "mind expansions"]. Finally, DSM-III classifies nicotine [CNS energizer, relaxant] as a substance associated only with dependence, since heavy use of tobacco per se is not indicative of social or occupational maladjustment (though its use may provoke aversive reactions in others).

Therefore, depending upon the substance employed and the kind of disorder it generates in the patient concerned, the specific problem would be diagnosed as alcohol abuse, alcohol dependence, opiod dependence, cocaine abuse, hallucinogen abuse, and so on.

## PUZZLING ASPECTS OF DRUG USE

Since there are socially acceptable substances like tobacco and alcohol that many people in all countries on earth regularly ingest, the problem of drug usage becomes one of explaining why it is that some people can use such substances in moderation or occasional abuse, while others become psychologically or physiologically habituated to the point of losing self-control. The link of cancer to smoking has not dissuaded everyone from smoking by any means, nor has it stopped young people from adopting the habit. Marijuana impairs lung function to a greater extent than tobacco cigarettes do, and it has 70 percent more of a cancer-producing chemical (benzopyrene) than does tobacco smoke (Petersen, 1980, p. 3). Yet findings of this sort have only slight impact in dissuading potential users when aligned against the myriad factors that prompt drug use in the first instance.

Most experts acknowledge that the motivations for using drugs are varied, complex, and often obscure (Solomon, 1977). No single explanation will suffice, though we can find some common influences. A good place to begin is in the fact that drug usage is involved in both physical health care and recreational/social activities. Chemicals have a vital role to play in the treatment and prevention of disease. Children are reared in households where parents administer medicines to them, take aspirin and prescription drugs, and imbibe alcohol in varying amounts depending upon the situation. It is therefore not surprising to find that a drug abuse like alcoholism tends to run in families. Between 20 and 30 percent of the offspring of alcoholics become alcoholics themselves upon reaching maturity (Research Task Force of the National Institute of Mental Health, 1975). This naturally suggests a possible genetic link (P. M. Miller, 1976), but adoptees raised by alcoholic parents are just as likely to become alcoholics as children who are reared by their alcoholic biological parents (D. W. Goodwin et al., 1974). Fraternal (dizygotic) twins have the same rates of concordance in alcoholism as identical (monozygotic) twins (Rosenthal, 1971).

There is a period of time in the development of young people when they are particularly vulnerable to modeling the behavior of others—peers, admired musicians, cinema stars, or any celebrity appearing to be socially adept and "modern." One aspect of this period of youth obviously entails what has been called *sensation seeking* (Kilpatrick, Sutker, & Smith, 1976). This is a period in which most teenagers and young adults will try to "have a good time," and this intention often includes the ingestion of some kind of intoxicating substance. A drug abuser will rarely stay with one substance, such as alcohol. Studies show that abusers tend to widen their indulgences to virtually any drug that is available (Kohn, Barnes & Hoffman, 1979).

Sensation seeking is an active, moving-toward type of behavior. But there are many individuals who indulge in drugs as a form of passive withdrawal, an effort to relieve anxiety and psychological or physical pain by retreating from life. Sometimes this retreat is very understandable. For example, here we have the soldier in a foreign land, facing danger in actual combat and often hostile rejection from elements of the population during lulls in the fighting. Estimates are that over 40 percent of the U.S. soldiers in Vietnam used some form of narcotic drug (opiods), and about half of this number considered themselves addicted (Harris, 1973). It is also found that the chances of becoming a heroin addict relate to such situational factors as living in an impoverished urban neighborhood and being a member of a minority group (Braucht et al., 1973). We know that there are criminal suppliers or "pushers" of drugs in such neighborhoods, but no doubt the demoralization and tension level in a milieu of this type adds to the likelihood of seeking escape through the sedating effect of narcotic drugs like morphine or heroin. On the other side of the coin, advantaged middle-class and upper-class individuals are likely to seek sensations through use of the hallucinogenic (psychedelic) drugs like LSD.

We cannot overlook the person in the matter of drug usage. Biological predispositions to drug addiction have not yet been convincingly established. Some people obviously do "get hooked" more easily than others; after becoming addicted some people are able to get off and stay off drugs more permanently than others. This is a fascinating problem for the psychopathologist, and one that surely relates to personality dynamics. However, before we turn to the question of personality it would be helpful to consider some interesting aspects of the problem of drug management.

One of the continuing puzzles is just how much the experience of being affected by a drug is due to the chemical action of the drug per se as compared with the psychological expectations and understandings of the drug ingestor. Some investigators believe that certain people absorb alcohol into their system very rapidly, triggering a physiological impulse to take in even more until intoxication is achieved. Yet experiments in which the taste of alcohol was masked by being mixed in tonic water failed to provide evidence for this biological explanation of alcoholism. Thus, alcoholics drank more liquid than nonalcoholics—whether it contained alcohol or not!—so that a learning explanation would seem to fit the facts better than one based upon biological predisposition (Marlatt, Demming, & Reid, 1973).

Drive reduction explanations of drug ingestion are common in the literature of alcoholism. However, extensive study of the alcoholic shows that though a transitory relief in anxiety is experienced, prolonged drinking is often associated with *increased* anxiety and depression (McNamee, Mellow, & Mendelson, 1968). Alcohol acts on the physical apparatus of the body and can be shown to relax the person's musculature. However, alcoholics continue to report high levels of tension and distress even though in actuality their muscle tonus is significantly relaxed during their state of inebriation (Steffan, Nathan, & Taylor, 1974). Obviously, there are psychological factors entering into the total experience of chronic alcoholic intoxication.

Intentional contributions to the drug experience show up in empirical studies that look for this factor. For example, marijuana ingestion is known to adversely affect time estimation as well as memory recall of learned items. Yet in a study that gave experienced marijuana smokers either a marijuana cigarette (*reefer*) or placebo cigarette to smoke, it was found that subjects *could* intentionally improve their time-estimation scores when urged to do so while under the effects of the drug (Cappell & Pliner, 1973). However, memory recall could not be improved "at will" in this fashion. The conclusion would seem to be that at least part of the mind distortion in hallucinogenic drug absorption is dependent upon the person's willingness to allow the experience to take hold ("go with the flow," as some drug users term this process).

Along this line, there is some evidence that having a negative attitude toward convention and a willingness to reject conforming behavior in the social milieu goes along with both use of drugs and a successful effect ("high") once the indulgence occurs (Gorsuch & Butler, 1976). Socially conforming adolescents are less likely to find the drug experience totally satisfying, and even if they have a pleasant experience they are not thereby so ready to reindulge or to expand their sphere of experimentation in drugs. Multiple-drug users are likely to be individuals who have had discipline problems in both the home and school, leading to school dropout and truancy, as well as a history of legal infractions taking them into the police stations and courts of their communities (Halikas & Rimmer, 1974).

A final point we should consider is the facility with which certain individuals have to become cured of drug dependence. Some experts claim that withdrawal symptoms are no worse than a bad case of the flu (see Ausubel, 1961). If this is true, then obviously certain individuals suffer through withdrawal with exaggerated feelings of discomfort. Some depictions of withdrawal are literally a living hell. We do know that many of the servicemen mentioned above, who had formed addictions to narcotic drugs in Vietnam, returned home to live in areas where hard drugs of this sort were not easy to obtain. Using alternative supporting drugs like alcohol or nonprescription narcotics like codeine (found in cough medicines), these men managed to cure themselves of drug dependence.

Of course, just as many seem to have continued on with their habits, or finding drugs unavailable, admitted themselves to hospitals and treatment clinics in the wretched throes of withdrawal. Similar differences exist in the adaptation to problem drinking. Some individuals can sense when the problem is acute and take steps to avoid the complete personal deterioration that engulfs others. A growing trend in recent decades is to provide addicts with a support system including halfway houses, communal living arrangements, and organizations like Alcoholics Anonymous and Synanon, in which former addicts lend their collective will to the conquering of substance use disorders.

## PERSONALITY DYNAMICS AND DRUG USE

Although no single type of "drug personality" is associated with abuse or dependence, there is empirical evidence of several personality disorders in studies done on addicted individuals. Here again, we must keep in mind factors discussed in the previous section such as social class, minority status, and type of drug experience being sought by the addict in question. We have already noted that drug abusers are likely to pass through an adolescent period in which they reject conventional social mores and behave delinquently. Their need for money to purchase drugs often gets them involved in criminal acts of various types. Given this scenario, it is not surprising to find in studies on this type of drug abuser that *antisocial personality disorders* begin showing up as a major diagnostic category (Salmon & Salmon, 1977; Sviland, 1972).

Almost all of the studies on heavy drug users report serious maturational fixations, so that these individuals are likely to be described as immature, shy, lacking in self-discipline, and irresponsible. The social ineptness of these individuals makes them highly vulnerable to influences from others. There is a clear suggestion here of the *dependent personality disorder* (Ausubel, 1961). Here we can think of the type of drug abuser who may be rejecting of social convention, but is greatly influenced by others with similar attitudes. In a true sense, this individual may be led into drug abuse through dependent ties to others, and then one day be kept off drugs through close association with others in organizations bringing former addicts together. Dependency underwrites both the initial addiction and the eventual cure from addiction.

Another frequent finding on the personality of drug addicts is that they cannot deal with the aggression (hostility) springing from life's frustrations. There is some evidence that a young person who abuses alcohol may be relatively aggressive and impulsive (Braucht et al., 1973). This young person is likely to engage in gang-type activities, and we would probably place him or her in the antisocial diagnostic category. But the more typical solitary alcoholic is rarely able to express aggression overtly (McClelland et al., 1972). Studies done on users of narcotic drugs tend to find these individuals to be passive, socially inept, and unwilling or unable to deal with interpersonal aggression (Haertzen, Hill, & Belleville, 1963; L. Kadushin & Kadushin, 1969). If such a person has a core of hostility and negativism, we are likely to see it manifested in terms of a *passive-aggressive personality disorder.*

A reasonable question at this point involves the possible source of the personality tendencies we have been considering. Are there "befores" or "afters" in the sequence of living that eventuate in drug addiction? Possibly drugs bring about antisocial tendencies and the passivity and dependency that we witness in such individuals. Several of the studies we cite in the present section have dealt with this very question, and in the main, they suggest that the tendencies we are considering occur *before* drug abuse and drug dependence come about in the person's life. Even so, we must be properly cautious in this regard and accept the possibility that drug ingestion may reinforce the personality patterns we are considering.

When drug abusers are given tests of personal adjustment, they invariably reflect a profound sense of *low self-esteem* (R. C. Knight & Prout, 1951; Laskowitz, 1962). This ties into much of what we have already noted. It seems that in the drug experience, where reality may be escaped and a new realm of visual distortion substituted, the problem drug user is putting aside his or her feelings of inadequacy at almost any cost. We can find traces of an *avoidant personality disorder* in this kind of person. Many clinicians and researchers have noted that drug addicts tend to live for the present (Stephens & Levine, 1971). Their entire focus is on the drug which they require in order to get through "today." By avoiding responsibility for tomorrow, in which successful attainment and a satisfying life is to be earned, the drug addict is totally unable to devise a suitable plan (formal cause) *for the sake of which* (final cause) he or she might counter the wretchedness that life has become. Thus, we can see a teleological cause of the deteriorating lifestyle of drug addicts, even though it may appear that material and efficient causes are solely at fault.

Another theme we note in the findings on chronic users may be suggestive of an underlying *narcissistic personality disorder.* Thus, addicts are notoriously self-centered, caring little for others except as sources of personal needs (Braucht et al., 1973). Everything in the addict's life is geared toward personal satisfaction in light of the drug dependence. Chronic alcoholism and heroin addiction reduce sexual drive. A mature relationship in which there is the give-and-take of equality is virtually precluded by these self-centered tendencies. It is probable that withdrawal symptoms are exaggerated by a person with such narcissistic tendencies.

If we follow the sanctioned practice of DSM-III and combine several of the personality disorder tendencies like dependency, narcissism, and the inability to deal with hostility into an overall dynamic, we can understand why some experts speak of a *sadomasochistic* interpersonal style in drug addiction (Guttman, 1965). The demeaning relationship that drug-dependent individuals form with their pushers is a prime example of sadomasochism in human affairs.

The final personality disorder that one is likely to see referred to in this literature is the *schizoid* (Sviland, 1972). Schizoid personalities are among those individuals whom we find at the fringes of social convention. They drift into contact with the drug culture or the skid row culture and seem to melt into this pattern as a natural extension of their shiftless and indifferent style of life. Alcohol and narcotic drugs seem to complement their autistic tendencies. We should also be aware that *schizoid* and *schizotypal* symptoms might well appear in a sample of drug addicts following prolonged physiological deterioration and physical injury. Drugs can have deleterious effects on the body (including brain damage), and people who are intoxicated fall down and strike their heads a good deal (or have others deliberately strike it in acts of mugging or "rolling").

Such physical insults can eventually result in disorientation and impaired ability to recall events or maintain concentration. Peculiar language expressions often accompany such deteriorations in performance. The "acid head" (LSD user) is likely to be considered schizotypal at some point in his or her life.

The dynamics of the addictive personalities that we have presented (i.e., antisocial, dependent, passive-aggressive, avoidant, narcissistic, and schizoid) would of course be comparable to those we discussed under these headings earlier in Chapter 15. Freud was of the opinion that drug addicts were poor prospects for psychoanalysis because at every setback or challenging point in the therapy series they are likely to select the drug experience over working through to insight (Freud, 1974, p. xix). It is well known that Freud during the period from 1884 to 1887 experimented with cocaine in hopes of finding therapeutic uses for it in the anesthetizing of the stomach and the treatment of seasickness, diabetes, and other disorders (E. Jones, 1953, Chapter VI). A colleague (Carl Koller) followed Freud's lead and successfully employed cocaine as an anesthetic in eye surgery.

Freud's experiments on the drug did not bear fruit. In one instance, although he helped get a much admired friend (Ernst von Fleischl-Marxow) off morphine by substituting cocaine (akin to *methadone* substitutions of today), the unhappy result was that his friend became a severe cocaine abuser. In another instance a patient died through an overdose of cocaine prescribed by Freud (ibid., p. 94). Though he took cocaine himself and also gave it as an energizer to his sister and his fiancée, Freud never felt any sense of growing dependency on the drug, and for some time he argued with colleagues that it was *not* addictive. He was correct as regards withdrawal symptoms, but following his later experiences as well as reports from colleagues all over the world he had to admit the addictive (abusive) properties of cocaine. In the end, he seems to have believed that oral dosage would not result in addiction, but that subcutaneous injections of cocaine might indeed result in addiction (ibid., p. 96). Freud's later writings on psychoanalysis are generally free of discussions of the psychodynamics of the drug abuser.

We might now close this chapter with a consideration of the psychodynamics of drug ingestion per se. Psychoanalytic explanations of the drug experience have emphasized the regressive properties of the drug's effect during relaxation, euphoria, or even stupor. For example, the elation and sense of total mastery under a drug like heroin may be seen as a re-enactment of the *oceanic feeling* that the infant experiences via the uninhibited manifestation of the pleasure principle. Some analysts add the fact that primitive denial occurs in this regressive experience, so that the addict is denying that there will be any loss of primal love for the mothering one (Lehman, 1963). Others emphasize the orgiastic pleasure sensed in drug ingestion, and suggest that this pleasure is akin to the infant's experience of total satisfaction following breast feeding (Chessick, 1960; Rado, 1933; Winkler & Rasor, 1953). Orality is focused upon in these explanations and it has been frequently noted that alcoholics are orally dependent individuals (Blane, 1968; Fenichel, 1945).

Hence, the narcotic drug experience is a deeply regressive interlude in which the addict is seeking to regain the sense of mastery once enjoyed in the early oral stage. Sensation seeking and hallucinatory experiences can be viewed similarly, for the drug-induced feeling of personal power, expanding vision, and oceanic omnipotence that stimulants and hallucinogens bring on are passively acquired in the mode of early orality. Personality dynamics are tied to other fixation points (see the various sections on personality disorders above), but the drug experience per se is a "magical" re-enactment of life's very beginnings. Unfortunately, this is not a genuine "new beginning" or rebirth, but a chemically induced shell of the sense of mastery and totality that teleological organisms naturally strive toward.

## SUMMARY

Chapter 15 begins with a consideration of the *personality disorder,* which arises when some distortion of the personality develops early in life and persists as the characteristic way in which the person copes with the environment and defends against real or imagined threats to personal competence and integrity. A personality disorder may never generate anxiety in the personality system. Usually, through repeated failures interpersonally the individual begins to recognize *ego-dystonic* aspects of his or her behavior. The distorted strategies in living often enable the person to achieve a stable level of adjustment, one that prevents more serious regressions into neurosis or psychosis. Even so, the person with this disturbance has less flexibility and maneuverability than a normal person.

A number of personality disorders are surveyed in Chapter 15. Not infrequently, these diagnoses occur on axis II of the DSM-III system (see Chapter 1). The *histrionic personality disorder* (formerly known as the *hysterical personality*) reflects a lifelong flair for the dramatic, exhibitionistic, and egocentric forms of behavior. There is a basic shallowness in emotional commitment, and a lack of sincerity and genuineness in this type. Freud termed these *erotic libidinal types.* Many psychoanalysts link histrionic personality types to a fixation at the phallic level, but there are oral features in the dynamic as well.

The *narcissistic personality disorder* reflects an exaggerated sense of self-importance, self-centeredness, and self-absorption without any appreciation of the impact that such attitudes and behaviors have on other people. Narcissistic persons interpret affection from others as admiration and a sign of personal superiority. Freud believed that the narcissistic libido types have failed to clearly differentiate their ego from their superego, enabling them to live out their ego-ideals. The *antisocial personality disorder* has a long history, having been referred to in times past as the *psychopathic personality* and *sociopathic personality.* This diagnosis is to be assigned to someone who for a lifetime, beginning before age fifteen, continually violates the rights of others, says one thing and does another, and generally runs afoul of authorities in the school setting, community, and job location. Alcoholism may complicate the picture in time. Freud traced the dynamics of the antisocial person to a residual guilt following resolution of the Oedipal, ensuring that a continual repetition of the conflict with authority will take place and punishment will be meted out (repetition compulsion).

The *borderline personality disorder* is a disputed category in which the key descriptive word is *instability* in various behavioral spheres such as mood, interpersonal behavior, and self-image. The now discarded *cyclothymic personality* (mood swings) would have been placed here. Occasionally there is a loss of identity or confusion over precisely what the person values and is seeking in life. Some clinicians place the *schizoaffective* psychosis here (see Chapter 14). Psychoanalysts have traced this disorder to a broad range of fixations, resulting in a symptom picture combining neurotic, psychotic, and even psychopathic tendencies. The person with an *avoidant personality disorder* tries to avoid social contact as a form of defense. The avoidant personality complains of low self-esteem. Shyness, timidity, and uncertainty in social relations typify his or her behavior. Traditional psychoanalytical explanations of this disorder stress *phobic* tendencies, in which the person is irrationally fearful of others. Anal fixations are suggested, with great ambivalence over the need for affection and the expectation of rejection. The individual with a *dependent personality disorder* gravitates to others and allows others to assume the major direction of his or her life. No demands can be placed on others by this person. The dependent personality is often good-natured, easygoing, and thought to be considerate of others. There is a strong underlying insecurity in such people, with depressions popping up regularly. Fixations are clearly oral in nature. Fromm's *receptive orientation* typifies this kind of person.

The *compulsive personality disorder* is typified by inflexibility, cheerlessness, and a dearth of warm, tender emotions. Friends are forsaken for work. Rumination and procrastination color the clinical picture. Compulsives can be very insensitive to the feelings of others. Traditional analytical theory traces this disorder to fixations at the anal level. In referring to a *passive-aggressive disorder* the DSM-III system identifies the person who is intentionally negative and resistive in interpersonal relations. Thus, individuals who passively engage in such behaviors are viewed as asserting *covert* aggression. The psychoanalytical literature traces such personality dynamics to oral-sadistic tendencies, possibly with secondary fixations at the anal stage.

The *paranoid personality disorder* is found in people who are constantly suspicious and mistrustful of others, hypersensitive to criticism, and highly controlled in emotional expressiveness or spontaneity. There is a lack of basic trust in such individuals. Freudian speculations would suggest fixations in the phallic stage, with homosexual ramifications (see Chapter 16), but other psychoanalysts have traced paranoia to anal fixations, with anal eroticism and expulsive tendencies highlighted. The *schizoid personality disorder* captures what used to be termed *simple schizophrenia* (see Chapter 14); thus, the patient with this disorder is unable to form social relationships due to a lack of emotional stability and spontaneity. Kraepelin referred to such individuals as having *autistic personalities.*

If the person with a schizoid personality begins to use speech in an unusual way, or if thought disorders begin to emerge, we assign the diagnosis of *schizotypal personality disorder.* Many clinicians would refer to the patient diagnosed with the latter designation as suffering from a mild form of schizophrenia. Traditional labels used in the past for this kind of diagnosis have been *latent schizophrenia, ambulatory schizophrenia,* and *preschizophrenia.* Genetic, biochemical, and psychodynamic explanations of the schizoid and schizotypal disorders are to be found in the literature. Psychoanalysis emphasizes the extensive regression to both oral and anal levels in which a satisfactory sense of self was never achieved (ego-identity).

Chapter 15 next considers the *factitious disorder,* which is an ingenuine enactment of abnormality in which the person seeks to give the appearance of mental or physical illness. This is *not* an instance of *malingering.* The "symptoms" of a factitious disorder are so unnatural and excessive as to appear a caricature of the real thing. This disorder was once referred to as the *Ganser syndrome,* as well as *pseudopsychosis* or *pseudodementia.* A more chronic form of the factitious disorder is the *Munchausen syndrome,* in which physical symptoms are constantly being created unconsciously to place the person under the care of a physician.

Chapter 15 next turns to the *substance use disorders.* These were once termed *drug addictions.* A substance use disorder is diagnosed when the person takes a substance affecting the central nervous system on a regular basis, leading to undesirable developments in his or her experience. The DSM-III approach distinguishes between *substance abuse* and *substance dependence.* Substance abuse refers to the fact that a person can no longer get through the day without ingestion of the crucial substance (e.g., alcohol). DSM-III requires that a clear pattern of this sort exist for at least one month before assigning the diagnosis of (e.g., alcohol) *abuse.*

Substance dependence is diagnosed when the pattern of abuse is made worse by increasing physiological needs for the substance (as in the abuse of heroin). Physiological dependence is based upon *tolerance,* or the ability of the addict's nervous system to absorb the initial dosage and function without generating the desired effect, thereby calling for a larger dosage; and *withdrawal,* or feelings of illness when the drug level is reduced or discontinued. DSM-III recognizes the following drugs as resulting in *both* abuse and dependence: alcohol, barbiturates or similarly acting sedatives or hypnotics, opioids, amphetamines or similarly acting sympathomimetics, and cannabis. Due to the lack of clear evidence for physiological (*not* psychological) dependence when they are used, the following drugs are listed in DSM-III as leading *only* to substance abuse: cocaine, phencyclidine (PCP) or similarly acting arlcyclo-hexylamines, and hallucinogens.

Many young people try drugs as part of a general pattern of *sensation seeking.* There may be biological reasons why some people become addicted more readily than others. There is no single personality type involved in drug abuse or dependency. Antisocial personality types are frequently seen in this context of the "drug culture." Low self-esteem is typical of drug abusers, which is consistent with dependent and avoidant personality types. Passive-aggressive and narcissistic personality types are not uncommon. Schizoid and schizotypal personalities may drift into the pattern of abuse as well. Psychoanalytical explanations of the drug experience have emphasized the regressive properties of the drug's effect during relaxation, euphoria, or even stupor—reminiscent of the *oceanic feeling* of infancy. Oral fixations are frequently cited in the cases of alcoholism. Hence, the narcotic drug experience is viewed as a deeply regressive interlude in which the addict is seeking to regain the sense of mastery once enjoyed in the early oral stage.

# 16

## *Psychosexual Disorders*

We come now to an area of psychopathology in which there is considerble disagreement among the experts, particularly concerning the status of homosexuality as an abnormal pattern of behavior. Today, it is possible for a person to be permanently and exclusively homosexual in behavior and yet *not* be considered psychopathological in any way. Not every psychodiagnostician agrees with this modern practice. We shall want to look into the various arguments of this ongoing debate in psychiatry.

As the name implies, *psychosexual disorders* are those in which, due to psychological factors in development, the individual finds it impossible to function sexually in ways that are indicated as normal for his or her sex. Disorders of sexual functioning that are due to physical injury or disease, even though they may have psychological consequences, are not to be diagnosed as psychosexual disorders. For example, impotence due to nerve damage or disease would be listed on axis III (see Chapter 1, p. 21), and coordinate psychological difficulties necessitating a diagnosis (e.g., depression) would be listed on axis I.

DSM-III depicts the sexual cycle as falling into four distinctive stages: (1) *appetitive,* in which the person begins to fantasize about sexual activity and cultivate thereby a desire for such activity; (2) *excitement,* in which physiological changes occur (penile tumescence in the male, vaginal lubrication in the female, etc.); (3) *orgasm,* or the peak of sexual pleasure in a sense of release, with rhythmic contraction of the perineal muscles and pelvic reproductive organs, and ejaculation of semen by the male; (4) *resolution,* or the sense of relaxation and well-being that follows orgasmic release. During this phase men are physiologically incapable of further erection and orgasm for a period of time; women may be able to respond to additional sexual stimulation almost immediately.

Psychosexual disorders may occur in relation to any one of the four stages of the sexual cycle, but it is probably in the first stage that the greatest array of potential difficulties occurs. The psychological mood, tone, or ambience created by this initiating, appetitive stage carries on throughout the other three stages, lending sexual experience its unique meaning for the person concerned. What sort of *object* does the person's fantasy bring into play in raising the desire for sexual activity? Are there fantasized acts of a seemingly nonloving nature (hostility?) that enhance this sexual appetite? Are there items of clothing or inanimate items of any sort that although not biologically called for are considered essential by the person if excitement and orgasm are to be achieved? The sexual cycle is essentially a biological pattern of excitement and release, but it seems clear that in psychosexual disorders we are concerned primarily with the framing set of circumstances "for the sake of which" this cycle is put in motion and allowed to run its course. As psychodiagnosticians, we are involved in the teleological aspects of this psychobiological process.

## Homosexuality

Here are three cases taken from our files which help set the stage for our discussion of homosexuality:

>   Martin, a twenty-three-year-old graduate student, was seen in therapy for developing homosexual tendencies that he felt were pleasurable but wrong. One night, when both he and the young man with whom he shared a small apartment were quite intoxicated, they began "acting silly" and found themselves kissing. This rapidly escalated into mutual masturbation and the pattern continued in the following days and weeks until Martin sought psychotherapy. He reported that though he enjoyed the sexual experience with his roommate, this was always followed by extreme guilt and some personal revulsion at what he seemed to be "turning into." Even so, he was unable to resist the temptation when his roommate began to "act flirtatiously" in his presence. Through insight therapy, supplemented by techniques such as masturbation while viewing pictures of nude females, Martin eventually parted company with his roommate and began dating young women—as he had done in the past. Within several months he had completely revised his sexual pattern. Another year found him married, and some five years later he contacted the therapist to say that he was still happily married, had fathered a child, and had experienced no recurrence of his homosexual behavior.

>   Stuart, a twenty-year-old undergraduate student, entered psychotherapy because he was not certain whether he was or was not homosexual. He found himself attracted to both men and women, but in recent months he was more excited by the prospect of a homosexual experience with a seemingly willing male associate than by his usual heterosexual contacts. Stuart was not threatened by his homosexual tendencies. As a budding novelist he felt that the range of sexual interest he displayed reflected a certain strength rather than a weakness. But he sensed that he had a preference and wanted to find out "one way or the other" what his basic sexual preference really was. During the course of one year in therapy Stuart was given insight into his personality development, and an examination was made of the heterosexual and eventually the homosexual activities in which he engaged (over this year's time). At the end of this period, Stuart decided that he really was a

homosexual and that he would continue in this lifestyle because it was more gratifying. He took the developmental evidence of therapeutic insight as helpful background material, but since he was more at ease with male than female lovers he simply opted in this direction and terminated therapy with complete satisfaction.

Rodney, a twenty-five-year-old black male, was working as a waiter in a restaurant after having dropped out of a predominantly black college in the southern United States to take a job in a metropolitan area of the north. Lonely and trusting, he said that he had been essentially "seduced" into homosexual behavior by a white male patron of the restaurant. Following this seduction, Rodney said that he was "hooked" by the homosexual subculture of the city. Interestingly, he only engaged in homosexual affairs with white men. He referred to homosexuality as his "white castle." But Rodney was not pleased with the course his life had taken, and entered therapy with the aim of breaking the spell he seemed to be under. He was immensely excited by the "game" of picking up male partners (cruising), but often depressed by the impersonalism and lack of a continuing relationship once the sexual act had been completed. Though he gained some insight from therapy, he decided to return to college in the South, where he would have predominantly black friends and where he had found that there was immense negative sanction against homosexuality in any case. He thus broke off therapy after four months in order to regain his "straight" status even as he completed his education.

These three cases highlight points of disagreement over the nature of homosexuality. If we are prone to think of homosexuality as a developmentally learned variation in lifestyle we can view the varying levels of success noted in these cases as evidence for our view. Martin and Rodney wanted to change; Stuart did not. On the other hand, if we think of homosexuality as an innate biological propensity, then we can say that Martin was not a genuine homosexual but that Stuart and Rodney were. Rodney was simply putting off the inevitable date on which he would "come out" as a full-fledged homosexual, with black partners as well as white. And even if we accept a learning explanation of homosexuality, we can still argue that all three of these young men were *opting* for the lifestyle they preferred, and that it is patently incorrect and even malicious to say that the one (Stuart) who opted for a homosexual lifestyle is "sick" whereas the others who did not are "normal." Attitudes such as these are prevalent, and they lie at the heart of the arguments for or against the DSM-III position on homosexuality.

## The DSM-III Position on Homosexuality: Pros and Cons

We have noted in other chapters the distinction between *ego-syntonic* and *ego-dystonic* behavioral tendencies (see Chapter 7, p. 204; Chapter 15, p. 456). *Ego-syntonic behaviors* are those that the individual accepts as natural for him or her. Stuart's acceptance of homosexuality reflects an ego-syntonic behavioral manifestation. According to DSM-III, so long as he had no distress over the fact that homosexual contacts were attractive to him from the outset, and that once completed he did not suffer a feeling of depression (like Rodney) or guilt (like Martin) for having behaved in this way, Stuart's homosexuality per se was perfectly normal and psychologically healthy. There is *no* diagnostic category in DSM-III for ego-syntonic homosexuality.

*Ego-dystonic homosexuality* is to be diagnosed only when the person engaged in homosexual relations is distressed by this fact and wishes in some way to increase his or her heterosexual feelings so that a genuine change in sexual lifestyle might be effected. This desire to reject a homosexual pattern must be a consistent motivation on the part of the individual. It is not unusual for a homosexual person to feel some anxiety at the point of realizing that he or she is "in fact" homosexual. According to DSM-III, it would be wrong to take this relatively fleeting alarm as evidence for ego-dystonic homosexuality.

We have already noted that not all psychiatrists, psychoanalysts, or psychologists agree that homosexuality per se can be thought of as a normal form of sexual expression. Several distinctive arguments have been leveled on both sides of this question. Before turning to these arguments, it shoud be noted that precisely "when" the person may be said to be engaged in a homosexual behavioral pattern or lifestyle is not easy to decide. We do not ordinarily label as criminal a person who has performed one or two antisocial *acts* (e.g., thievery) in a lifetime. The act per se is a necessary but not sufficient factor in the diagnosis of an antisocial or criminal lifestyle. In like fashion, Kinsey, Pomeroy, and Martin's finding (1948) that 37 percent of white American males had at least one homosexual experience leading to orgasm between adolescence and old age tells us something about an *act* and very little about a personality style of behavior. Four percent of the sample in their study adopted an exclusively homosexual lifestyle from age sixteen through fifty-five. It is obvious that the meaning of homosexuality shifts dramatically if we think of it as either (a) an act or (b) a lifestyle. Arguments for or against the proposition that homosexuality is normal have actually encompassed this distinction. We shall review three predominant realms of argument on the question of homosexuality.

*Biological Arguments.* One of the major points of disagreement over the classification of homosexuality as normal or abnormal stems from the sexual act per se. Those who claim that homosexuality is normal like to cite the fact that bisexual behavior has been noted in more than a dozen mammalian species (Beach, 1950, p. 276). It would seem, therefore, that human beings are simply carrying out an alternative form of sexual expression that is biologically based. On the other hand, those who are opposed to the normalcy thesis stress that mounting behavior among, for example, all-male monkey groups is not true sexual behavior in that orgasm is rarely or never achieved. It has not yet been authenticated that lower animals actually form homosexual preferences, and indeed, the predominant evidence suggests the contrary (Karlen, 1971, p. 309).

A related argument has to do with the evolutionary implications of homosexuality. The critic of DSM-III argues that heterosexuality has biological (as well as social) usefulness, in that it organizes human beings into primary groups around the production of offspring (Socarides, 1978b, p. 423). Indeed, if the homosexual pattern were followed completely, there would be no offspring and hence biological termination of the species would take place. The response to this argument is that homosexuality does have evolutionary advantages, because it reduces the level of hostility among males and thereby helps the gene pool to survive because there is less killing off of enemies and opponents (W. Paul, 1981).

The final biological argument we might take note of is not focused on the act but on the supposed inheritance of homosexuality. Many homosexuals as well as those who agree with the DSM-III position on homosexuality hold to the theoretical view that this is an innate condition. People are homosexuals because they are born that way, and there is nothing they or therapists attempting to change their orientation can do about this fact. Although there has been some suggestion that genetic factors may play a role in homosexuality (Kallmann, 1952), the preponderance of the findings on this question have failed to support an inheritance thesis (Rosenthal, 1970). One popular theory in the study of homosexuality was that homosexual men might have relatively lower levels of male sex hormones and higher levels of female sex hormones, and vice versa for lesbians. Although some studies have supported this biological hypothesis (R. B. Evans, 1970; Gartell, Loriaux, & Chase, 1977) other data collections have disconfirmed it (Doerr et al., 1973). At the present time, neither the genetic-transmission nor the hormonal-imbalance theories can be taken as having been satisfactorily validated.

*Sociocultural Arguments.* Our second realm of argument gets at some of the basic issues in psychiatric diagnosis, because what we find the experts doing here is questioning the very *grounds* "for the sake of which" a diagnosis is rendered. If we cannot find grounds for a judgment of normalcy or abnormalcy in the act per se, then it is the attitude fostered in the sociocultural milieu that matters. Those who would accept homosexuality as a normal pattern of behavior point out that more than half of the myriad societies studied over history have concurred in this view (Beach, 1950). Ancient Greece is often cited as an example of a high form of civilization that also accepted homosexual behavior between older men and youths (Marmor, 1973, p. 1209).

Continuing in this vein, the argument runs that simply because people deviate on a dimension of sexual preference that brings them condemnation and repression within their culture is no reason to ascribe psychiatric illness to them (Gonsiorek, 1977, pp. 37-38; Saghir & Robins, 1973, p. 317). Psychiatry places itself in an unnecessary adversarial relationship with the homosexual community by accepting the social conventions of its time (Spitzer, 1973, p. 1214). Some have gone so far as to suggest that it is unethical for therapists to offer therapy to homosexuals with the aim of changing their preferential patterns of sexual expression (Davison, 1977). Better to help the homosexual adjust to what is presumably a biologically based condition than to offer false hopes of a cure that is only occasionally realized (Saghir & Robins, 1973, p. 317).

Those on the other side of the question like to point out that it is always possible to find some aspect of other cultures that, when viewed from a narrow perspective, seems to support a favored position (Karlen, 1971). For example, to hold up ancient Greece as a model for interpersonal relations is to hold up a society in which slavery was also considered natural and hence was incorporated as an institutionalized practice. More to the point, it is argued that the grounds for judging people as well adjusted or poorly adjusted *must* be framed in terms of sociocultural mores, beliefs, and attitudes. Critics of DSM-III contend that what is taking place in the decision to drop homosexuality per se from the mental disorders is a politically motivated maneuver, which in turn makes it a sociocultural maneuver to change the assumptive mores of the present historical period (Bayer, 1981). For example, it is noted in recent years that homosexual organizations such as the Gay Activist Alliance, the Mattachine Society, and the Daughters of Bilitis have actively lobbied before the Nomenclature Committee of the American Psychiatric Association that finalized DSM-III (see Socarides, 1978b, p. 419).

This is perfectly proper in a free society, of course, but in responding to such political pressure the critics of DSM-III believe that the Nomenclature Committee has performed a disservice to the profession of psychiatry and to those homosexuals who seek assistance to rectify their lifestyle. Many if not all of the sociocultural arguments advanced for the changed attitude toward homosexuality are valid for other sexual disorders (e.g., voyeurism, bestiality). Are we not possibly relieving one group of a social stigma only to imprint it all the more firmly on another? Out of a well-motivated, humanitarian effort to protect the homosexual person from legal and social repression, the Nomenclature Committee has cast doubt on the entire procedure of psychiatric diagnosis—a doubt that has already been voiced by supporters of the homosexual decision who would be willing to "scrap" the current diagnostic system altogether (see Stoller, 1973, p. 1208). The final point made by critics of DSM-III is that to date the World Health Organization's diagnostic scheme has not followed the lead of the American Psychiatric Association regarding homosexuality (Socarides, 1978b, p. 420).

*Personal Adjustment Arguments.* The final realm of argument, which must touch upon issues involved in the previous two sections, has to do with the actual adjustment of homosexuals, bisexuals, and heterosexuals. Can we find discernible differences in the adjustment of the individuals with such diverse sexual preferences, and if so, are these differences indicative of maladjustment (as defined through the sociocultural influences of medicine, psychoanalysis, psychiatry, and psychology)? One line of empirical research on the question has involved contrasting groups of homosexuals and heterosexuals on various tests of personality and/or personal adjustment (Clark, 1975; R. B. Evans, 1970; Hooker, 1957; Manosevitz, 1970; Thompson, McCandless, & Strickland, 1971). In the main, these studies have failed to distinguish homosexuals from heterosexuals, and in opposition to the traditional expectation, they also failed to turn up empirical evidence that homosexuals are demonstrably maladjusted. Advocates of the DSM-III position on homosexuality are therefore likely to advance such evidence in support of their view.

On the other side of the coin, those who view homosexuality as a disorder are likely to cite investigations in which therapy has been used successfully to alter patterns of sexual preference. The cure rate is not exceptional, however, and a fair generalization would be that somewhere between 35 and 50 percent of patients in treatment for homosexuality have become *significantly more* or *exclusively* heterosexual after therapy (Acosta, 1975; Birk, 1974; Feldman et al., 1969; Hadden, 1966; Henrichsen & Katahn, 1975; Masters & Johnson, 1979; Mayerson & Lief, 1965). The best results seem to occur when the patient is engaged in bisexual contacts. Exclusively homosexual patients are particularly recalcitrant to psychotherapy, and some experts contend that they are incapable of changing their sexual preference (Bell, Weinberg, & Kiefer-Hammersmith, 1981).

Even so, the fact that partially homosexual (i.e., bisexual) patterns can be altered by psychotherapy challenges the view that homosexuality is an irreversible outcome of development. It may be that at some crucial period in the homosexual person's development his or her sexual identity might have gone another way, given only that a proper support system, pattern of fantasy, and satisfying heterosexual contacts had been possible. Critics of DSM-III point out that homosexuals *are* capable of heterosexual *physical* contact, and that all claims to the contrary, there is evidence to suggest that a remnant heterosexual interest remains. Thus, using a device that measured the degree of penile tumescence as a sign of sexual arousal, investigators have shown that male homosexuals may voice disgust at the verbal description of heterosexual intercourse, but they nevertheless reflect increased penile volume while listening to such accounts (Freund et al., 1973). Similarly, though they have more penile tumescence while observing slides depicting sexual relations between same-sex partners than between opposite-sex partners, homosexuals *do* reflect more sexual arousal while watching the slides of heterosexual relations than while watching completely nonsexual slides (Langevin, Stanford, & Block, 1975).

This latter finding of a disparity between what is voiced by the homosexual and what his or her actual physiological reactions may be to heterosexual stimuli provides some support to those who claim that simply taking frequency counts of empirical tests of personality and adjustment cannot possibly get at the introspective, unconscious, hidden motivations of the individual's behavior (Socarides, 1978b, p. 417). The psychoanalytical tradition has consistently placed the person's private world over the overt, empirical world of interpersonal relations. According to this view, a sexual perversion may serve as a substitute mechanism for ego-dystonic feelings of—for example, heterosexual—anxiety (ibid., p. 423). And the only way in which to study this inner dynamic with validity is through a typically long-term psychoanalysis, which alone can meet with the unknown (to the person) dynamics that motivate the personality from beneath conscious awareness.

There are two major, widely cited investigations in the literature of homosexuality that highlight the strengths and weaknesses of the two schools of thought we have been considering. The first study was conducted by Irving Bieber and his associates, in which 107 male homosexuals were studied during 150 to 350 hours of psychoanalysis (Bieber et al., 1962). Once again, as to actual outcome in therapy the bisexuals were most improved, approximating the 50 percent figure that we cited above. More important, however, a consensus was reached concerning the basic developmental difficulties of these homosexual clients, who were reared in family contexts in which pathological relationships existed between parents and male offspring. Bieber summarized the clinical picture as follows:

> Typically, mothers of homosexuals are inappropriately close, binding, often seductive, and tend to inhibit boyish aggressiveness. The fathers are overtly or covertly hostile; this is expressed in detachment, streaks of cruelty, or frank brutality. The relationship between the parents is generally poor; often the husband is held in contempt by a wife who prefers her son. The pre-homosexual child may be exposed to rejection and hostility from other significant males, such as brothers and peer mates. Defective masculine relationships deprive such a boy of needed masculine figures for identification and modeling that are ultimately sought, in part, in homosexuality. It then becomes a substitutive adaptation replacing the heterosexuality that is made inadequate or unavailable by a network of induced fears about heterosexual behavior. Within a substitutive adaptation, attempts are made to acquire missing sexual and romantic gratification. Through various homosexual maneuvers and activities, reparative attempts are made to strengthen masculine self-esteem and to alleviate profound feelings of rejection from men. Through homosexuality, reassurance and acceptance are sought from other men. Contrary to popular notions, homosexuality is not an adaptation of choice; it is brought about by fears that inhibit satisfactory heterosexual functioning. (Bieber, 1973, p. 1210)

Bieber's summary of the parental dynamics, which are consistent with Freud's original speculations (discussed in the following section), have not gone unchallenged. It is pointed out by critics of psychoanalysis that some homosexuals are far from being emotionally removed from fathers. Indeed, sometimes they have overidealized their male parent (Marmor, 1971). Another criticism of the Bieber report is that all of the psychoanalysts involved in this project were members of the same psychoanalytical society, and hence they probably were biased in a uniform way so that more unanimity was achieved than was probably deserved in the case material (Gonsiorek, 1977). Finally, criticisms regarding representativeness of the sample of patients have been leveled, as well as the resultant problems which have been experienced in attempts to cross-validate Bieber's findings (Churchill, 1967; Siegelman, 1974). Bieber (1976), on the other hand, has continued gathering data on homosexuals and insists that the above-cited familial context has general validity.

The other major study was conducted by Alan Bell and Martin Weinberg (1978) in the San Francisco gay community, where a random sample of 979 homosexual men and women were individually interviewed for a period of three to four hours. The contents of these interviews were contrasted with the contents of interviews conducted with 477 heterosexual men and women who had been matched on major socioeconomic variables with the comparison group of homosexuals. According to the results of this in-depth survey, only about 13 percent of the male and 5 percent of the female homosexuals were clearly distressed in personal adjustment. Twenty percent of the homosexual men had attempted suicide at some time in their life. One homosexual in four believed that his or her sexual preference was a sign of an emotional disorder. This could be a social stereotype, of course, accepted by the homosexual person uncritically. Bell and Weinberg classified fully 60 percent of the homosexuals as relatively well-adjusted.

About 33 percent of the lesbians and less than 20 percent of the gay men had been married. Lesbians were less active sexually than gay men. The majority of lesbians had fewer than ten partners throughout their lives, whereas the typical gay man had many more, and sometimes hundreds of sexual partners. Bell and Weinberg found that some homosexual partners lived together in a closed relationship with fidelity to each other, much as "happily married" heterosexual couples do. Others formed open relationships, in which they lived together but did not limit their sphere of sexual activity to the primary partner. The so-called *functional* homosexual, who formed freewheeling liaisons with many different lovers, was the least conflict-laden member of the sample. On the other hand, there were *dysfunctional* (ego-dystonic) homosexuals, who were quite tormented over their situation in life. There were also *asexuals* in the sample, and they seemed the most secretive and withdrawn of all, indulging in less sex than other members of the sample. Asexual lesbians were most likely to report thoughts of suicide.

It seems clear that if the psychoanalysts from whom Bieber drew data were turned loose on the sample which Bell and Weinberg studied, we would have quite a different picture of the supposedly good adjustment of the homosexuals. It is surely an interesting time in the history of diagnosis, and the student of psychopathology must expect a continuation of the arguments we have been surveying. The issues we have addressed are not going to go away, and psychopathologists of the future will be sorely tested to refine their views and make clear precisely what the process of diagnosing mental illness entails. The present volume is written within the psychoanalytical tradition. Hence, it is our responsibility to clarify for the reader why it is that Freud conceptualized homosexuality as an *abnormal* form of personal adjustment. As we shall see, this question touched his life in a most personal way.

## SIGMUND FREUD AND THE QUESTION OF HOMOSEXUALITY

It is ironic that Freudian psychoanalysis should be pictured today as an unprogressive theory, too willing to assign labels of maladjustment to a minority of individuals whose only demonstrable problem is that they happen to cathect objects within their sex rather than cross-sexually. Yet, not only did Freud constantly preach acceptance and understanding of conditions like overt homosexuality (see his letter to the mother of a male homosexual [1935];

Freud, 1951), but he more than anyone else has brought to light the underlying role of latent homosexual feelings in *all* human relations. The decision to see homosexuality as an undesirable solution to the human being's need for intimate interpersonal contact is not based on the sexual act itself (refer above) but rather on the developmental dynamics of individuals who employ this manner of libidinal cathexis, as well as the coordinate difficulties (such as paranoia) that are seen arising from these dynamics.

As a biological naturalist (see Chapter 1, p. 13), Freud was most assuredly no defender of the cultural status quo. If he had found evidence to support the view that homosexuality was a normal variation on human sexuality he would most certainly have expressed this professional opinion. The fact that he did not do so stemmed from his analyses of cases and, a fact of equal importance, his *personal* involvements with Fliess. We are naturally reluctant to bring Freud's personal dynamics and interpersonal relations into a textbook discussion, but believe that the modern furor generated by the question of homosexuality demands that we review the historical record, allowing Freud to speak for himself whenever possible.

To understand the succession of events we must recall from previous discussions (see Chapter 1, p. 10, and Chapter 3, p. 75) that Freud had a very close emotional tie to Fliess for over ten years, before they had their falling out in 1900 at Achensee over the utility of Fliess's "biological clock" theory with its attendant *bisexual* features (i.e., both men and women functioned emotionally according to "periodic cycles"). Though Freud was undoubtedly influenced by this Fliessian theory, which we saw reflected in his discussion of a *positive* versus a *negative* form of Oedipal resolution (see Chapter 3, p. 76), he was predominantly drawn to the *psychological* possibilities of bisexuality. That is, he did *not* accept Fliess's biological reduction of both masculine and feminine tendencies to an underlying periodic cycle. Freud's father died in October 1896 and this seems to have precipitated Freud's self-analysis, begun in 1897.

What were the findings of Freud's self-analysis? It seems unquestionable that, among other findings, Freud had through self-analysis come to see that he and Fliess had formed a close bond of friendship based on latent homosexuality (via normal bisexuality), that this kind of union among members of the same sex is probably a lot more common than people realize, and that it can be sublimated into a mature bond of loyalty if used properly or can be detrimental if allowed to detract from the integrity of the individual person through domination of one person by another. We know from Freud and Fliess's correspondence that in May 1900, some three months before their meeting in Achensee, Freud (1954) wrote to Fliess that "there can be no substitute for the close contact with a friend which a particular—almost a feminine—side of me calls for" (p. 318). We also know that the two colleagues did discuss bisexuality at Achensee, and in a letter to Fliess *after* this meeting Freud said to his (now "former") friend:

> If as soon as an interpretation of mine makes you feel uncomfortable you are ready to conclude that the "thought-reader" [Fliess's appelation of Freud] perceives

nothing in others but merely projects his own thoughts into them, you really are no longer my audience, and you must regard the whole technique as just as worthless as the others do.

I do not understand your answer about bisexuality. It is obviously very difficult to understand one another. I certainly had no intention of doing anything but get to grips, as my contribution to the theory of bisexuality, with the thesis that repression and the neuroses, and thus the independence of the unconscious, presuppose bisexuality. (Freud, 1954, p. 337)

The reference to interpretations making Fliess feel uncomfortable suggests that Freud had done some analytical work during their Achensee discussions. Freud tried to salvage the relationship following these stormy exchanges, but except for an acrimonious incident in 1904 when Fliess accused Freud of releasing unauthorized information on bisexuality for publication, there was no Fliess-induced contact after 1900. We can find independent evidence concerning the Freud/Fliess relationship in the writings of Max Schur (1972), Freud's personal physician, who treated the father of psychoanalysis for various maladies including heart difficulties and a long bout with oral cancer. According to Schur, after the pain was becoming intense and further excisions of cancerous tissue were no longer possible, Freud was put to death at his own wish. Schur administered two centigrams of morphine to Freud on two occasions, with approximately twelve hours intervening, and death occurred several hours after the second hypodermic injection (ibid., p. 529). Schur reflects exceptional insight concerning Freud's personality and the dynamics of latent homosexuality in the Fliess relationship:

Freud had alluded in his letter of May 7, 1900 . . . to the feminine quality of his need for a friend [refer above]. Now he had recognized and was stating openly that intimacy and friendship between men could be the highly adaptive outcome of sublimated "androphile" [bisexual] tendencies in men or, to put it more simply, of the ubiquitous latent male homosexuality. The ability to recognize this specific aspect fully, resulted from self-analysis which, as seen from his correspondence, he continued at least until 1912. . . . What made it so painful and guilt-producing was the fact that Freud was actually telling Fliess, although he was speaking about Breuer: "You, too, have contempt for this type of friendship. Therefore you, too, will be left by the wayside." Here we see at work the incredible feat of Freud's self-analysis, for one of the most difficult accomplishments of a regular analysis is to show the analysand both the existence of latent homosexuality and its adaptive possibilities. Fliess, in turn, was doomed to come to grief over it. (Schur, 1972, p. 217)

Schur goes on to point out that the Fliess dynamic, of a close male confidant with an eventual breakup, was operative in Freud's relationship with others in his life—especially with Jung!—albeit in a mitigated way. A careful study of the correspondence between Freud and Jung, which began in January 1907 and carried to the same month in 1913, provides ample evidence that Schur was correct. But in this case, Jung was more accepting of latent homo-

sexuality in men than Fliess (see McGuire, 1974, pp. 297-298). Freud could joke
that he lacked the homosexuality to take an interest in a passively feminine
man of his acquaintance (ibid., p. 353). Jung analyzed the unrecognized homosexual feelings that Bleuler held toward him (ibid., p. 371). In fact, the corre-
spondents equated "social motives" with "homosexual motives" in discussing the
interpersonal relations of men (ibid., p. 393). Even so, there are two dramatic
incidents in which Freud *fainted* in Jung's presence, and which seem to have
been somehow related to the homosexual cathexes that Freud had once affixed
to Fliess!

The first fainting spell occurred in a restaurant in Bremen on 20 August
1909, the day before Freud set sail with Jung and Sandor Ferenczi for America,
where they were to address psychological colleagues at Clark University. It was
on this voyage that Freud refused to go on analyzing his dreams in Jung's
presence, saying that he would lose his authority in their relationship were he to
continue (ibid., p. 526). The following year, in a letter to Ferenczi dated 6
October 1910, Freud made the following observation concerning his mental
state in that period of life: "You not only noticed, but understood, that I *no
longer* have any need to uncover my personality completely, and you correctly
traced this back to the traumatic reason for it. Since Fliess's case, with the
overcoming of which you recently saw me occupied, that need has been
extinguished. A part of homosexual cathexis has been withdrawn and made use
of to enlarge my own ego. I have succeeded where the paranoiac fails" (E.
Jones, 1955, p. 83). This passage is extremely interesting, for not only does it
presage Freud's eventual explanation of how psychoanalysis works as therapy
(see Chapter 19), but it also brings in the theory of paranoia—an essential
ingredient to any discussion of Freudian homosexuality theory. We shall return
to this latter point shortly.

The second fainting spell occurred in a dining room at the Park Hotel in
Munich on 24 November 1912. By this time the relationship between Freud and
Jung had become quite strained, and it was soon to end altogether. In a letter to
Ernest Jones dated 8 December 1912, Freud commented on this second
fainting as follows: "I cannot forget that six and four years ago I suffered from
very similar though not such intense symptoms in the *same* room of the Park
Hotel. I saw Munich first when I visited Fliess during his illness and this town
seems to have acquired a strong connection with my relation to that man.
There is some piece of unruly homosexual feeling at the root of the matter"
(E. Jones, 1953, p. 317).

So it is clear that Freud was cognizant of a continuing problem in his
working through of the Fliess involvement. But what of Fliess? Did he recipro-
cate by affixing a homosexual cathexis to Freud? Freud seems to have believed
that he did, for in a letter to Jung dated 17 February 1908 he remarked, "My onetime friend Fliess developed a dreadful case of paranoia after throwing off his
affection for me, which was undoubtedly considerable" (McGuire, 1974, p.
121). Once again we have the allusion to paranoia. Both Fliess and the
theoretical problem of paranoia come up repeatedly in the correspondence as
Freud is convinced of the "enormous significance of homosexuality for para-

noia" (ibid., p. 369). The famous case of Schreber was analyzed and recorded during this period of Freud's life, and there can be no doubt that he ascribed the dynamics of Schreber to Fliess as well. A key paragraph from the Schreber case is the following:

> But in paranoia the clinical evidence goes to show that the libido, after it has been withdrawn from the object, is put to a special use. It will be remembered that the majority of cases of paranoia exhibit traces of megalomania, and that megalomania can by itself constitute a paranoia. From this it may be concluded that in paranoia the liberated libido becomes attached to the ego. . . . A return is thus made to the stage of narcissism (known to us from the development of the libido), in which a person's only sexual object is his own ego. On the basis of this clinical evidence we can suppose that paranoics have brought along with them a *fixation at the stage of narcissism,* and we can assert that the length of *the step back from sublimated homosexuality to narcissism* is a measure of the amount of *regression* characteristic of paranoia. (Freud, 1911/1958a, p. 72)

In other words, Fliess's paranoia stemmed from the fact that, instead of removing the cathexis that he had affixed to Freud and using the free libido to build his own ego through insight and understanding, Fliess rejected such insight and allowed another dynamic to take place. Having earlier in life fixated at that transitional period of narcissism, which falls between autoerotism and object-love (see Chapter 2, p. 63), Fliess like Schreber allowed a regression to take place (by refusing to acknowledge the homosexual relationship) and *took his own ego as object!* We have the familiar dynamic of regression from object-choice to narcissism taking place (see Chapter 2, p. 63). Narcissism is the "libidinal complement of egoism" (Freud, 1915/1957l, p. 223). The paranoiac is now above reproach, and projects onto others all of the blame for problems arising in life; indeed, a profound distrust of others becomes typical of the paranoiac (Freud, 1896/1962d, p. 184). If a persecution arises in the behavior of a paranoiac, we can expect to find that the person who was formerly loved has become the persecutor (Freud, 1923/1961a, p. 43). There can be no doubt that Freud's interpretation of Fliess's behavior in the 1904 incident mentioned above was as a manifestation of such unwarranted assertions of persecution by a formerly loved (cathected) object.

It is therefore the *narcissistic* aspects of the homosexual pattern that forced Freud to conclude that homosexuality is an abnormal pattern of sexual development—an *inversion* as he called it (Freud, 1916-17/1963b, p. 307). We can surmise from this brief overview that he had come directly into contact with the problems posed by homosexuality, both in his own personality dynamics and those of important associates. He took it as given that every human being is bisexual and that, throughout life, we all vacillate between homosexual and heterosexual inclinations (Freud, 1911/1958a, p. 46). But an overt homosexual lifestyle is not simply a choice among alternatives in the normal psychosexual path of development. It is a narcissistic resolution of a problem in living, one that is difficult and often impossible to rectify.

Freudian psychoanalysis is surely no enemy to a personality dynamic that it claims *everyone* may be subject to in its latent form and a complication of which its founder traced to his personal neurosis. Freud believed that Fliess's paranoia developed *following* his unwillingness to confront a perfectly natural homosexual prompting. Every homosexual prompting does not result in paranoia. There is no evidence that Freud ever considered himself an overt homosexual, nor did he engage in homosexual acts at any time. He bravely looked inward and acknowledged human tendencies that we all are subject to and to which we all must admit frankly and openly once they begin to affect our level of adjustment. To deny the neurotic element in homosexuality would be for Freud just as harmful as the individual's defensive denial of latent homosexuality à la Fliess (see Freud, 1916-17/1963b, pp. 307-308). Neurotics can be objectively successful in life, adjusting to the external world in a reasonably satisfactory albeit nonoptimal fashion. So too can homosexuals. Psychoanalysis is no more an enemy to the homosexual than it is to the neurotic. It would be a distortion of history and a heartless disregard of Freud's personal integrity to make it appear somehow that psychoanalysis has singled out the homosexual for condemnation. We next turn to the explanations of homosexuality as worked out in classical analytical theory.

### The Psychoanalytical Dynamics of Homosexuality

We must set aside the question of paranoia at this point. It would be a gross error to think that every homosexual develops paranoia. Though Freud was always judicious in allowing for the possibility of biological factors in neurotic conditions (Freud, 1922/1955n, p. 230), he did not believe that there was any justification for distinguishing a special homosexual instinct (Freud, 1909/1955a, p. 109). Freud's initial explanation of homosexuality relied upon two psychological dynamics, one of which we have already focused upon in the previous section: (1) regressing from object-choice to narcissism, and in the process, (2) reverting from object-choice to identification (see Chapter 2, p. 64). Thus, given a developmental history of fixation at the transitional period of narcissism (which comes between autoerotism and object-choice), and given a certain familial dynamic in which the Oedipus complex is handled in a certain way, the person adopts a homosexual pattern in hopes of retaining a self-indulgence enjoyed to that point in life. The picture was clearest for Freud in describing male homosexuality. Here is a good summary of his essential theory:

> The genesis of male homosexuality in a large class of cases is as follows. A young man has been unusually long and intensely fixated upon his mother in the sense of the Oedipus complex. But at last, after the end of puberty, the time comes for exchanging his mother for some other sexual object. Things take a sudden turn: the young man does not abandon his mother, but identifies himself with her; he transforms himself into her and now looks about for objects which can replace his ego for him, and on which he can bestow such love and care as he has experienced from his mother .... A striking thing about this identification is its ample scale; it

remoulds the ego in one of its important features—in its sexual character—upon the model of what has hitherto been the object. In this process the object itself is renounced . . . (Freud, 1921/1955m, pp. 108-109).

Naturally, this "transforming into mother" and "looking for objects to replace the ego" encompass the regressive move to identification and the narcissistic investment of libido into the homosexual's own identity (ego). Homosexuals are, in one sense, making love to themselves by seeking like-sexed partners. Freud subsequently added another reason for the development of male homosexuality. He found that homosexual men seemed to place an inordinate value upon the penis per se, so that the cathecting of this organ— probably during masturbation in early pubescence—conflicted with later neces-sities to cathect a person who *lacked* this valued organ—that is, a woman (Freud, 1922/1955n, pp. 230-231). This *idealization of the penis* is greatly furthered by fantasy. Homosexually prone men indulge in narcissistic fantasies of "their" penis, which eventually becomes "the" or "any" penis as a love-object. Therapeutic procedures aimed at changing the homosexual object-choice through use of appropriate heterosexual fantasy during masturbation have met with some success (J. N. Marquis, 1970; Marshall, 1973). Recall that we used this technique successfully with Martin (refer above). Another motive lying behind homosexuality seems to be fear of the father. That is to say, if *castration anxiety* is overly intense in the Oedipal conflict, the male offspring may renounce all women as in the sense of the original tribal prohibitions (see Chapter 3, p. 71). Finally, Freud proposed a source of homosexuality in the *jealousies* of a male against siblings, as follows:

> Observation has directed my attention to several cases in which during early childhood impulses of jealousy, derived from the mother-complex [i.e., cathected object] and of very great intensity, arose [in a boy] against rivals, usually older brothers. This jealousy led to an exceedingly hostile and aggressive attitude towards these brothers which might sometimes reach the pitch of actual death-wishes, but which could not maintain themselves in the face of the subject's further develop-ment. Under the influences of upbringing—and certainly not uninfluenced also by their own continuing powerlessness—these impulses yielded to repression and underwent a transformation, so that the rivals of the earlier period became the first homosexual love-objects. (Freud, 1922/1955n, p. 231)

It is, of course, possible to think of these various dynamics occurring together in a given case history. For example, the tendency to seek a narcissistic object-choice might make the pubescent male more vulnerable to homo-sexuality when keen jealousy is stimulated by the mother's praise of an older sibling. Preoccupation with the male organ adds further to this dynamic. Castration anxiety from a brutal father adds yet another factor. All or some combination of these factors would be expected in the dynamics of a homo-sexual male. As we noted above, Bieber's characterization of the typical clinical picture of male homosexuality matches rather well the dynamics that Freud had observed in his clinical practice. There are, of course, other themes

Freud photographed in his study at Berggasse 19, shortly before leaving Nazi-occupied Austria in June 1938. He had completed the New Introductory Lectures on Psycho-Analysis (1932) by this time, and was at work on Moses and Monotheism.

that various psychoanalysts have developed over the years, including such factors as pre-Oedipal inability of the male to differentiate himself from the symbiotic ties to his mother's identity, an inordinate fear of male aggression (projected castration fears), and a yearning for male acceptance and affection stemming from an underlying sense of masculine inadequacy (emasculation) (Socarides, 1978a).

Unfortunately, the explanation of female homosexuality has not been so uniform or internally consistent—not the least of the reasons being that the female Oedipal dynamic has presented special theoretical problems (recall our presentation of Horney in Chapter 3, p. 79). In discussing female homosexuality Freud (1901/1953c, p. 60) tended to emphasize the *aim-inhibited* period of intrasexual allegiances and "crushes" that are seen developing between pubescent girls, sometimes accompanied by hugs, kisses, and vows of eternal allegiance. When later in life something comes up to threaten heterosexual possibilities such a history of emotional satisfaction in a like-sex commitment makes it likely that a girl will take this course as a permanent lifestyle. In one of his cases, Freud traced a pubescent girl's homosexuality to the fact that her mother had just given birth to a child. At precisely that period (pubescence) when the girl's Oedipal fantasies were enlivened, and she was the one desirous of bearing her father's child, the "rival" in the situation gained ascendance. This in turn led her to forswear her womanhood, with the outcome being a reversion to narcissism, masturbatory activities, and eventual homosexuality (Freud, 1920/1955l, pp. 156-157). This theme of women—in contradistinction to men—framing a "primary homosexual attachment" that can be revived if normal heterosexuality is blocked recurs in the literature of psychoanalysis (see e.g., H. Deutsch, 1932). Logic would demand that the female homosexual be pictured in some way reverting from object-choice to identification, as in the dynamics of the male. And so we do find this suggestion of identification with the father and a narcissistic mirroring of the self in other women, including the mother (E. Jones, 1927). The reason for doing so is usually said to be a frustration during pubescence, when the Oedipal conflict is revived and re-enacted, either in the home or in some deflected context as the school building, where teachers are brought into the re-enactment as parental surrogates.

Karen Horney (1925) suggested that Oedipal fantasies and the ensuing fear of being injured internally during vaginal penetration play an important role in presaging homosexuality in the female. Here again, the important role of fantasy in preparing the person for homosexuality is recognized. Horney noted that the young male can inspect his genitals to see whether any consequences of masturbation are taking place. Unable to do so, the girl in Oedipal fantasies during masturbation may alleviate the attendant anxiety and guilt by identifying with her father. The wish to be a man supplants the earlier wish to be the father's lover. The course of homosexuality from this point on hinges upon the elaboration of this wish in fantasy (including taking the mother as a projected self-object) and interpersonal contacts with other women of the same general persuasion. Psychoanalysts have always appreciated that femininity in the male or masculinity in the female does not necessarily mean that the person is homosexual (Fenichel, 1953). The final point we should make is that the dynamics of the *positive* versus *negative* Oedipus complex (see Chapter 3, p. 76) greatly compounds the picture on homosexuality, and it would take a volume to unravel these implications. We have attempted to cover the topic sufficiently to give the reader an understanding of both the modern disagreements over homosexuality and the reasons that psychoanalysis takes the view that we are dealing here with a disorder in psychosexual development.

## Gender Identity Disorder: Transsexualism

According to DSM-III, *gender identity* is knowing what sex one belongs to, in the sense of "I am a man" or "I am a woman." This is a private experience, which may not be reflected in overt behavior or *gender role*. The common gender roles include masculine and feminine patterns of behavior, as recognized and approved by cultural standards. It is expected that a person with anatomical structures of the male sex will behave masculinely, and a person with anatomical structures of the female sex will behave femininely. Ideally, gender roles are congruent with gender identities. However, sometimes it happens that a person's gender identity is *incongruent* with his or her anatomical sex. When this occurs, we speak of a *gender identity disorder*. There are gender identity disorders of childhood, but we shall consider only the major adult disturbance, known as *transsexualism.*

*Transsexuals are individuals who believe that they have somehow been placed in the wrong physical body.* A twenty-four-year-old man comes to the clinic asking for a sex-change operation, because he has never really felt that he was a man. Since he was a boy his interests have always gravitated to feminine activities. He was considered a "sissy" by his boyhood playmates. He despised rugged activities, avoided sports, and took an interest in playing girls' games, dressing dolls, and the like. He forced himself to have dates with girls in his adolescent years, but never felt "right" in the role of the boy. He just knew that something had gone wrong when he was conceived and that he should have been a female. He is attracted to other men, but not as a homosexual. In fact, he finds the male sexual organ rather disgusting. He would like to be rid of his own penis, and then perhaps he would one day be emotionally attracted to a man in the role of a woman.

Case studies of male transsexuals find that they come from families in which feminine behavior was encouraged and that in all probability there was a confusion generated in the identification patterns of the boy involved. The family constellation is related to the homosexual pattern as noted in the previous section, with an overprotective mother and a missing or weak father figure (R. Green, 1968). However, we do not find the element of castration anxiety. Indeed, the transsexual male seems to have gained a certain love from his mother for cross-dressing and behaving in a feminine manner. Transsexuals usually avoid homosexual partners. As our case suggests, they would rather relate to the male as a woman than as a homosexual partner. They do fall in love with men, however, which is one of the prompting motives for seeking a sex-change operation (Benjamin, 1967).

There is some disagreement over the kinds of people who seek a sex-change operation (R. Green & Money, 1969). Some experts suggest that candidates for sex reassignment are often maladjusted individuals, such as certain homosexuals, schizophrenics, and even some transvestites (Newman & Stoller, 1974). It is therefore extremely important to provide preoperative counseling and detailed diagnostic assessment before the operation is allowed. Some studies have found that the postoperative suicide rate for transsexuals is higher than that for the general population (Herschkowitz & Dickes, 1978). Other studies report that 85 percent of the postoperative adjustments of patients with sex reassignment have been perfectly satisfactory (Gagnon, 1977; Roback et al., 1976).

DSM-III cautions against assigning the transsexualism diagnosis to people who may be going through a stressful period in life, one that might be corrected if they were but of the opposite sex. A *homosexual panic* may precipitate a young woman to seek a sex reassignment, but in due time it is clear to her that she really does not think of herself as a man. She is simply and suddenly becoming aware of her homosexuality, and rather than confront this period of traumatic life change, she seeks to rectify her plight biologically. Transsexualism is a profoundly psychological experience, one that persists over long periods of time. In fact, DSM-III stipulates that the disturbance must be *continuous*—that is, not simply appearing during times of stress—for a period of at least *two years* before the diagnosis is made.

# Paraphilias

The descriptive label of *paraphilia* was cointed in the DSM-III revision to capture the fact that a deviation (*para*) in sexual practice is what attracts (*philia*) the individual. *The paraphilias are therefore psychosexual disorders in which the person either carries out or in some cases merely fantasies unusual acts, or utilizes atypical objects in order to become sexually aroused.* Employing these unusual practices merely to *enhance* sexual excitement would not be considered a paraphiliac disorder. For example, a woman who finds that imagining herself bound and humiliated during sexual intercourse increases her excitement and orgasmic satisfaction does *not* have a paraphiliac disorder. But if she could *only* contemplate sex (*appetitive stage*) and become aroused (*excitement stage*) in the context of such fantasy or, more profoundly, when literally bound and humiliated in some (masochistic) fashion by her sexual partner, she would be said to have a paraphiliac disorder. More than one form of such disorder can be had by the same person, and we often see these paraphilias as compounding factors in personality disorders and the schizophrenias. We shall now review the major forms of the paraphiliac disorders.

*Fetishism.* This disorder involves the use of inanimate objects (fetishes) as a repeatedly preferred or exclusive ingredient in the person's sexual arousal and orgasmic release. The diagnosis is not made when the inanimate objects are limited to female garments used in cross-sex dressing (transvestism). Nor is it made when the object is made as a tool for sexual stimulation (e.g., a vibrator). The point of a fetish is that it has taken on a kind of *symbolic* power, so that the meaning of sexual arousal (*appetitive stage*) for the person concerned is encompassed in this unique object—a woman's shoe, a man's necktie, and so on. Sometimes the fetish is valued for its olfactory significance, such as the smell of rubber, tar, or fingernail polish. Tactile sensations are important, so that the feel of velvet is a common type of fetish. Virtually anything can become a fetish thanks to the unique ability of human beings to fantasize.

That is, clinical practice and empirical surveys of fetishes have found them to be products of fantasies engaged in by the person during pubescence, and having decidedly Oedipal overtones. The object focused upon is frequently something associated with parents and teachers (parental surrogates) who have been especially nurturant to the individual (Caprico, 1973). In other cases, the fetish may be a fragment of some highly exciting sexual experience— heterosexual, masturbatory, or even homosexual—engaged in at some critical point in early adolescence. The location of this experience may provide odors, and the fumblings and gropings of excited sexuality provide ample opportunities for some item of clothing or object in the environment to take on a symbolical significance that will be used again in recalling the incident, getting excited once again, and so forth. Freud (1927/1961g, p. 155) noted that the shoe probably owes its preferred status as a fetish to the fact that the pubescent boy has either viewed or thinks of the woman's (i.e., mother's) genitals from below. Black velvet conjures pubic hair, and so on.

Any person can find his or her sexual appetite enhanced by the feel of velvet or silk, the odors of certain perfumes or incense, and even the thought of some item of clothing such as a brassiere or an athletic supporter. However, what is abnormal about the fetishist is that these items begin to be abstracted from the *interpersonal* context and begin serving as substitutes for actual human contact (Freud, 1901/1953c, p. 154). It has been shown that men with certain fetishes will begin selecting sexual partners based on their possession of the item in question. It is the kind of shoes that the woman is wearing, *not* the woman, which attracts such a patient (K. L. Jones, Shainberg, & Byer, 1977). In time, the male fetishist may have a collection of favorite items (bras, panties, stockings, shoes, etc.). He may steal these from family members or from friends. He may then want his sexual partner to wear these particular items. If a woman is not available, the fetishist can become sexually aroused and masturbate while fondling the preferred items. Studies have shown that men with serious disorders of this type have few female companions, and few friends in general (Gebhard et al., 1965). They have removed their cathexes from people and affixed libido predominantly to inanimate objects. Fetishism appears to be more prevalent among men than women.

*Transvestism.*    The term *transvestism* literally means *cross-dressing.* In this deviation, gratification is obtained, or identification with the opposite sex is symbolized, by wearing the clothes of the opposite sex. DSM-III assigns this diagnosis *only* to men, because of some unique features of cross-dressing. Like fetishism, transvestism is a disorder confined largely to men. Moreover, although some homosexual males do cross-dress, three out of four transvestites are exclusively heterosexual (Benjamin, 1967). Almost that many have fathered children. On the other hand, clinical findings suggest that a woman who dresses completely like a man (i.e., not simply in masculinelike women's fashions) is likely to be a homosexual.

There are degrees of cross-dressing, ranging from occasional solitary wearing of a few female undergarments to wearing completely feminine attire while mixing socially with other transvestites in organizations devoted to this activity. Some men appear sufficiently feminine to move about in the community unrecognized, particularly in the evening. Transvestite men often say that the period of cross-dressing helps them to relax, and it is not uncommon for a wife to support her husband in this relaxing interlude. That is, some wives help in the cross-dressing, and even go out with their transvestite husbands on shopping trips and the like (Buckner, 1970). Other wives are extremely upset when they discover transvestite tendencies in their husbands, and frequently the strain on the marriage is too great, resulting in separation and divorce.

About one-fifth of the wives of transvestites never learn of their husband's cross-dressing, which is confined to underclothing.

Psychoanalytical interpretations of transvestism have tended to emphasize the role of castration anxiety during the Oedipal resolution. The young boy, fearing paternal retribution for cathecting mother, identifies with her through external attire even as he turns his attention to other female sexual objects (Freud, 1919/1955i; Jucovy, 1976; Lorand, 1930). In this way he submits in part to the paternal punishment—becoming himself a quasi female (castrated!)—and yet also retains a close identity with his mother through her attire. Whenever his (castration) anxiety mounts, he becomes a woman for a period in symbolically re-enacting his Oedipal fixations. Empirical findings on transvestites suggest that at least some of them experience a sense of inadequacy in the masculine role (Bentler, 1976). They tend to be inhibited, dependent personality types (Bentler & Prince, 1969). Marriage is sometimes seen as a refuge and source of support, but it rarely eliminates the need for such men to continue their cross-dressing during periods of tension and anxiety, or to achieve a proper level of sexual excitement.

*Zoöphilia.* This is a rare disorder in which the person either fantasizes or actually engages in sexual relations with a lower animal as a repeatedly preferred or exclusive method of gaining sexual release. Actual copulation may be achieved, or rubbing and licking of the genitalia by the animal may be the method of release. Household pets and farm animals are the most frequent sources of sexual arousal and release. It is hypothesized that such perversions arise from early (pre-Oedipal) fantasies accompanying genital manipulation and then resorted to during pubescence as a reasonably "safe" form of sexual release—given only that the opportunity presents itself. Once again, the diagnosis is made only when this becomes the *preferred* alternative. Occasional sexual play with animals is not evidence of a zoöphiliac disorder.

*Pedophilia.* In this disorder, the person either fantasizes or actually engages in sexual relations with prepubertal children as a repeatedly preferred or exclusive method of achieving sexual excitement and release. DSM-III sets the arbitrary age disparity between the prepubertal child and the adult at ten years. For late adolescents with this attraction the clinician must exercise judgment as to whether there is a case of pedophilia involved or simply an immature adolescent unable to confront the threat of adult sexuality. This disorder often shows up in midlife, and the sex of the prepubertal sexual object is just as often the same as that of the patient as it is of the opposite sex. The legal problems for the pedophiliac are, of course, immense. A compounding factor here is that of incest with parents or adult relatives (Boekelheide, 1978).

The psychoanalytical explanation of pedophiliac behavior stresses the immaturity factor. Such adults are found to have fixated their sexual relations at pre-Oedipal levels, and it can usually be shown clinically that even their adult heterosexual or homosexual relations have been dominated by the early stages of the sexual cycle in which they took primary pleasure in the fantasies and acts of disrobing, looking, touching, and related foreplay activities. Homosexually oriented pedophilia is especially chronic, and the recidivism rate for such individuals is second only to that of exhibitionism. Obviously, very serious mental disorders can be related to pedophilia, including the severest forms of schizophrenia.

*Exhibitionism.* Genital exhibitionism is almost exclusively confined to men. It is a postpubertal and usually a postmarital phenomenon. There is a compulsive quality to the exhibiting act so that, as we noted above, offenders show the highest rate of recidivism of all sex offenders and account for one-third of all arrests for sex crimes (Abel, Levis, & Clancy, 1970). Exposure usually takes place outdoors in parks and other public areas. Sometimes the exhibitionist frequents parking lots, where he pulls his car up alongside a woman, gets her attention, and then exposes his genitals. This facilitates a quick retreat from the area, before police arrive. Exposures are often repeated several times in a day, and usually there is a sense of anxiety *following* each of these exposures (Christoffel, 1956). Popular portrayals of the nude man in a raincoat acting as a "flasher" tend to do an injustice to the clinical state of such men, who are anything but lighthearted tricksters.

Probably the reason exhibitionism is taken lightly stems from the fact that is is rarely associated with further sexual contact, such as rape. In fact, DSM-III has written this prescription into the definition of exhibitionism—that is, there must be no attempt made for further sexual contact with the woman to whom exposure is directed. In one study of thirty exhibitionists who had been repeatedly convicted of this offense, only five of several hundred arrests included an assault charge; all five of these assaults were limited to an effort to touch the woman's breast or genital area (Rooth, 1973). Naturally, there is always the danger of a more hostile assault, and women are properly wary of such behavior in men. The exposure is humiliating to most women, and interestingly enough, the very disgust that they show to exhibiting men can become a motivation for further exhibiting (Katchadourian & Lunde, 1975). It is almost as if there is an element of masochism in some cases, where the man wants to be shown disgust and hostility. Others seem to need reassurance that their penis is large, even "shockingly" large, or otherwise attractive to the woman involved. Fantasies about being watched and admired by female observers are common among exhibitionists (Hackett, 1975).

Most exhibitionists are socially inhibited and timid. They report few close companions in childhood, and there is a definite lack of association with members of the opposite sex in their background. They feel inadequate as adults, and their married lives are typified by sexual insecurity and an inability to enjoy sexual intercourse with their wives (Gebhard et al., 1965). Some of these men have an unexplained tendency to spy upon and betray other exhibitionists, a tendency that may have its origins in narcissistic rivalry and sadistic enmity.

The psychodynamics of exhibitionism are probably multiplex. Castration anxiety and narcissism are the factors most often cited in the analytical literature. Unlike the transvestite, who resolves the Oedipal threat by identifying with motherly attire and relates to members of the opposite sex outside of the family context, the exhibitionist withdraws from feminine contact "in general." Indeed, his personality appears to have been successfully emasculated even as he continues a narcissistic pattern in which his masturbatory fantasies include "showing" his penis to mother-substitutes "from afar." He will show but avoid actually copulating with mother[-substitutes] as per the Oedipal demands of the father. However, this symbolical re-enactment seems not to be satisfactory, as the exhibitionist re-experiences (castration) anxiety following the exposure. A sadistic element may be seen in the motivation to humiliate women (mother-substitutes). Possibly there is in such cases a remnant hostility for the mother, who must be put to shame for allowing the father to take the exhibitionist's place in her complete affections.

*Voyeurism.* A voyeur is a person who repeatedly achieves sexual excitement and obtains release by observing unsuspecting people, usually strangers, disrobe, perform sexually, or simply be naked (as in taking a bath). As with fetishism and exhibitionism, voyeurism is an act committed predominantly by men. Only a small number of women are arrested for "peeping," as it is called. The average voyeur is a male in his mid-twenties and unmarried when first arrested. Nine out of ten peeping incidents are premeditated. The peeper will walk through alleys, climb over fences, and stand on ledges to engage in his disordered sexual activity (Gebhard et al., 1965). Observation alone produces sexual excitement, but masturbatory self-stimulation is usually indulged in to reach ejaculation (Katchadourian & Lunde, 1975). Although voyeurs do not always present a threat to the woman they are watching, a small number of them do increase their excitement by entering a building or home to observe—and to call attention to the fact that they are watching (Yalom, 1960). In the main, however, voyeurs are not likely to have severe personality problems.

Psychodynamically considered, the voyeur like the exhibitionist is fixated at an infantile level. As Freud early noted, sexual looking in childhood is a normal extension of the sexual curiosity of small children. Sexual looking is also a normal aspect of the preparatory, appetitive stages of the sexual cycle in adulthood. But the voyeur replaces this preparatory act of sexual looking for the entire process of sexual union and shared pleasure with another person (Freud, 1905/1953e, p. 157). The fact that the voyeur cannot find this pleasure in looking at his female lovers (wife, prostitutes, etc.) gives us our first clue that there must be something thrillingly forbidden about the looking or peeping situation; that is, we are dealing with *Oedipal survivals.* Castration anxiety seems less important to the voyeuristic dynamic than it is to transvestism or exhibitionism. But clearly, the regressive need to do something sexually forbidden—symbolically, to see mother, sister(s), and so on, in the nude, or to catch parents in a sexual embrace (primal scene)—is what provides the desired level of sexual excitement for the voyeur because it is a neurotic re-enactment (repetition) of his past Oedipal dynamics.

*Sexual Sadism/Sexual Masochism, and Sadomasochism. Sadism* means sexual pleasure in inflicting pain, including psychological suffering and humiliation. *Masochism* means sexual pleasure in suffering such injuries and indignities. The term *sadomasochism* combines these two forms of psychosexual disorder. DSM-III makes it possible to diagnose a patient as exclusively sadistic or masochistic. Freud (1919/1955i) thought that sadism and masochism are opposite sides of the same coin and, indeed, that masochism "originates from sadism which has been turned round upon the self" (p. 194). Empirical study of hundreds of men with this psychosexual disorder supports the Freudian view (Spengler, 1976). On the other hand, if sadism is primary one might expect that this would be the most frequent manifestation of the disorder. But masochism is the more frequent manifestation. It is very rare to find sadistic women.

There is some reason to believe that sadomasochism is practiced in mitigated form by normal sex partners and that it may be commonly employed in fantasy during sexual relations in a more extreme sense. Thus, roughly half of the men and women sampled by Kinsey (et al., 1948, 1953) said they would like to be bitten during sexual intercourse. Oral infliction of minor bruising through biting or sucking a sexual partner's face or neck (a hickey) is an acceptable form of sadistic treatment. Fantasies during masturbation as well as sexual intercourse in which there are themes of sexual abuse, rejection, and forced sex are commonly employed by college students of both sexes (Sue, 1979). In the more overt practices, lovers are tied up, whipped or slapped about, cursed at, and generally humiliated. The resultant tension heightens sexual excitement and release for both partners, who often exchange roles during the same encounter. Even when the psychosexual disorder becomes this extreme, only 15 percent of the individuals concerned seem to confine themselves to such overt displays in their ongoing sexual life (Spengler, 1976).

The dangers of sadism are obvious enough. Occasionally, during the height of sexual stimulation the sadist seriously injures and even kills the masochistic recipient. It is also true that sadistic tendencies in a man can be brought to light in a sexual encounter with a nonmasochistic woman. The partner does not have to be consenting in order for the sadist to experience sexual stimulation. Rape is a crime that sometimes results from a sadistic motivation, although there are dynamics in the rapist's case that may be quite different from sadism. Some rapists are dissuaded by the injury of a victim, the sight of blood, and so on. Sadistic sexual abuse of a child is an especially heinous crime.

Freud (1901/1953c) viewed sadomasochism as the active manifestation of a single instinctual prompting that takes either the sadistic or masochistic form of expression. He tried to relate this dynamic to the theory of bisexuality, with sadism considered the masculine and masochism the feminine reflection of sadomasochism. This also relates to his view of sadomasochism as due to the mingling of libido (life instinct) and the energy of the death instinct. A Darwinian rationale was also employed, since sexual pursuit and subjugation are common manifestations of animal life (ibid., p. 159). This masculine component (sadism) of the sexual act has its complement in the vulnerable, capitulative aspects of the feminine component (masochism).

How then does sadomasochism arise? A common explanation found suitable to many analyzed cases is that the pre-Oedipal child *misinterprets* signs of vigorous, flirtatious sexual play between parents—such as poking, slapping, tickling, wrestling about on a couch, and so on—as signs of fighting or attack, particularly by the father. If the child happens to witness the primal scene, this too can be misinterpreted as a brutal subjugation and humiliation of the mother by the father. Mothers who complain openly about their husband's sexual demands add to this misinterpretation, of course. It follows that as the child moves into the Oedipal dynamic during the phallic stage the fantasied enactment of sexual relations will have considerable aggressivity about it. The little girl will picture her role in sex as essentially demeaning, passively being used by the father, and so on. The focus in sadomasochism is therefore on the father's behavior, for he is viewed as the initiator and aggressor. Since he is also the "punisher" in the family, the one who is most likely to administer spankings and set limitations on freedom, the scene is set for a thoroughgoing misconceptualization in the psychosexual development of a sadomasochist.

The fact that more men are sadistic than women is accounted for by some analysts on the basis of castration anxiety. Picturing the father as hostile and fearing castration during the Oedipal conflict, the boy does "identify with the aggressor" (see Chapter 3, p. 71) but in this case it is a sadistically hostile aggressor. We must recognize that in some families the father is precisely as perceived. In others, the child has built his image of father and sexuality on misperception embellished by fantasy. But, in taking father's role the maturing boy is more likely to assume a sadistic pattern than the girl, who identifies with her mother. And the greater the castration anxiety generated in the family context, the more likely it is that the maturing boy will evolve into a sadist if other circumstances are as described above.

## Psychosexual Dysfunctions

The final disorder we will consider is the *psychosexual dysfunction,* in which the person's appetitive or psychophysiological changes that characterize the complete sexual response cycle are somehow inhibited. The diagnosis is not made if the sexual dysfunction is due to organic disease or if it is merely one aspect of a broader clinical picture falling within the definitional boundaries of some other clinical syndrome. Psychosexual dysfunctions are to be found at any one of the four stages of the sexual cycle. The person may find that he or she no longer desires sex, and rarely thinks about it (*appetitive stage*). A man may find that although he would like to have sexual intercourse he is unable to achieve penile erection (termed *impotence* in the *excitement stage*). A woman may be unable to achieve orgasm, or she may have involuntary spasms of the musculature of the outer third of the vagina that interferes with penile penetration (termed *vaginismus* in the *excitement stage*). A man may prematurely ejaculate, bringing the coital experience to an end before his partner has achieved release (*orgasm stage*). A woman may complete the first three stages of the sexual cycle only to feel somehow unsatisfied, dirty, or guilty (*resolution stage*). All such problems are to be considered as psychosexual dysfunctions, and they have unique diagnostic labels depending upon the symptoms involved.

## SEXUAL DYSFUNCTION IN THE MALE

Impotence and premature and retarded ejaculation are among the commonest forms of sexual dysfunction in the male. These malfunctions are only rarely signs of physiological pathology; they are almost always the result of psychodynamic factors (Hogan, 1978), but possible biological causes should not be overlooked in diagnosis (Spark, White, & Connolly, 1980). It is true that potency and male sex performance depend upon complex physiological coordinations and sequences, but these proceed more or less automatically when conditions are favorable and the man is normal. Difficulties arise because anything that stimulates anxiety, guilt, or fear may interfere with masculine sex functions; so also may conflicts about sexuality, emotional ambivalence toward the woman, or a feminine identification. Such interfering factors may be not only irrational but also unconscious. The symptoms then appear not to involve the personality at all, and this in itself may increase a man's anxiety and his fear of a hidden illness.

Both maternal overindulgence and maternal domination can leave a male at pregenital levels, either because he has remained sexually infantile or because the female seems dangerous to him when he experiences mature sexual impulses. Perhaps a fear of engulfment and the loss of identity still lingers from failure to resolve the symbiotic attachment to the mother. For example, a man may be timid and inhibited when he faces the genital engulfment that is normal to adult sex experience. Perhaps Oedipal fears are still dominant in the unconscious of this man.

Sometimes a strict superego makes sexual activity seem sinful, dangerous, and even unthinkable with a "respected" or "idealized" woman. In this group belong males who are pathologically guilty over masturbation and a special group of men who have learned to idealize "good" women as somehow above base sex and find satisfaction only with "bad" women like prostitutes (*split imago*). This is a pathological exaggeration of the Oedipal resolution that represses a child's sexual impulses toward his mother, but leaves his tender, almost asexual love for her intact in his preconscious and conscious life.

Still other unconscious determinants of male sexual dysfunction are the pre-Oedipal childhood fears of untamed rage and hostility in relation to a mother's suppression or coercion. In adulthood these reactions may be rearoused by sexual intimacies with an eligible woman. It should be noted, however, that the aggression aroused by anger sometimes leads to effective male functioning. Thus, for example, sexual relations immediately following an angry quarrel are successful in some males who find a willing, passive, or receptive sex partner unattractive. The sadistic component here is obvious.

Unconscious resentment toward women, or even an infantile envy of their reproductive role, may interfere with male sexual function. Unresolved Oedipal fears of a father figure who seemed sadistically dangerous in early childhood sometimes result in an irrational ability to fulfill the male sexual role adequately in adulthood. Whether or not such interferences with male performance should be treated as distinctively psychosexual disorders or as components of a broader neurosis is still the subject of much controversy in analytical circles.

Finally, we cannot minimize the factor of sexual technique. It is possible for the satisfaction of partners in sexual intercourse to suffer or be inhibited completely due to ignorance of the opposite sex and poor practices in the actual mechanics of copulation. Sex therapists today can improve a man's performance in the sexual act, affording more pleasure to his partner, which in turn raises his level of self-esteem. Such improvement can in itself rectify problems of impotence or premature ejaculation (Kaplan, 1974; Masters & Johnson, 1966). Deep-seated problems will not respond to such coaching, of course, but then not every sexual dysfunction stems from serious personality difficulties. Sometimes one bad experience presages another, and then the man is reaction sensitized enough to inhibit his own intentions out of needless anxiety over the "next" try to achieve and maintain an erection. Sex therapists today are remarkably successful in breaking this vicious cycle.

## SEXUAL DYSFUNCTION IN THE FEMALE

Most of what we have said concerning sexual dysfunctions in men applies equally to women. Inhibited sexual excitement in women is commonly referred to as *frigidity*, and it is the psychodynamic equivalent of impotence in men. There is no unique personality style to be noted among women who suffer from sexual dysfunctions. The only difference to be noted is an understandably higher incidence of depression among women with such disorders (Munjack & Staples, 1977). A woman who is frigid or suffers from genital pain during sexual intercourse (*dyspareunia*) or has involuntary spasms of the vaginal musculature (*vaginismus*) that interfere with coitus can usually be found to have discernible reasons for reacting in this way.

Often there are early life problems connected with such disorders, including incest and rape. Many women have misconceptions about sex and know very little about their own physiology, much less that of a man. There is a fear of the unknown and an expectation of pain from the outset. If they have experienced any of the familial dynamics related to sadomasochism it is understandable how a fear of sexuality might have arisen even though they did not develop this more profound sexual disturbance. Many women have been reared in homes where the mother, either for a great commitment to religious orthodoxy or for personal reasons, has prepared her daughters sexually "for the worst." Even more dynamic factors of unconscious homosexuality, a fear of losing control, guilt over symbolically copulating with a father figure (husband), or a sense of anger or envy concerning men may also be at play. Women are more likely than men to allow marital frictions of any type to be reflected in their attraction to and enjoyment of sexual intercourse. Finally, we must mention the factor of technical skills involved in carrying out a satisfying sexual experience. Both husband and wife can be aided in this regard through straightforward coaching.

## SUMMARY

Chapter 16 takes up the *psychosexual disorders,* in which the individual finds it impossible to function sexually in ways that are indicated as normal for his or her sex. The sexual cycle falls into four stages: *appetitive, excitement, orgasm,* and *resolution.* Disorders can occur in one or more of these phases. *Homosexuality* is the first disorder discussed. DSM-III does not recognize *ego-syntonic* (self-accepting) homosexuality as a disorder. It does recognize *ego-dystonic* homosexuality as a disorder; in the latter instance the person engaged in homosexual behaviors is distressed by this fact and wishes to effect a change in heterosexual behavior. There is considerable disagreement among psychopathologists over whether homosexuality is simply a matter of sexual preference or reflects a basic abnormality in personal adjustment. There are biological arguments supporting the view that homosexuality is innate. There are sociocultural arguments that view the homosexual as under repression for deviations from a norm which is, in the final analysis, arbitrary.

In looking at the personal adjustment of homosexuals, sincere and well-meaning authorities on both sides of the question continue to debate the issue. Freudian theory holds that homosexuality as a final life solution to the question of sexual adjustment is *not* the best solution, even though latent homosexual feelings may be seen in all human relations. In order to clarify and help in the understanding of Freud's views, his personal relations with Fliess are discussed in some detail. Fliess's views on *bisexuality* were more biologically than psychologically based, but they influenced Freud in his conceptualization of the psyche. The latent homosexual attraction in Freud and Fliess's relationship proved difficult to resolve. Freud ascribed the same dynamics to Fliess that he had ascribed to the famous case of Schreber.

The basic dynamic in homosexuality is thus a fixation at the transitional period of narcissism. Later in life, a regression takes place in which the homosexual person takes his or her own ego as object (see Chapter 2). Thus, in seeking relations with like-sex partners the homosexual is actually self-indulgent. Freud noted that narcissism is the libidinal complement of egoism. Paranoiac symptoms enter because the person believes himself or herself to be above reproach and thus projects onto others all manner of shortcomings. It is therefore the *narcissistic* aspects of the homosexual pattern that forced Freud to conclude that homosexuality is an abnormal pattern of sexual development — an *inversion,* as he called it. Of course, not all homosexuals develop paranoia.

In addition to regressing from object-choice to narcissism, the homosexual is prone to revert from object-choice to identification (see Chapter 2). This usually means that the child identifies with the parent of the opposite sex, accounting for the feminized male and masculinized female homosexuals.

The next psychosexual disorder to be considered in Chapter 16 is *transsexualism,* a gender disorder in which the person believes that he or she has somehow been placed in the wrong physical body. This is not the same as *transvestism,* in which the person takes satisfaction in cross-sex dressing. The transsexual must be seen as someone who has for many years experienced feelings of being out of *gender role*—that is, a man living in a woman's body or vice versa. These individuals seek and often obtain sex-change operations. DSM-III assigns the diagnosis of transvestite *only* to men. Women who dress solely like men are likely to be homosexuals. Psychoanalytical interpretations of transvestism have emphasized the role of *castration anxiety* during the Oedipal resolution. The son can assume a castrated role (feminine attire), identify with mother (reverting from object-choice to identification), and thus deal with the Oedipal demands placed upon him. Transsexuals have far deeper fixations and, of course, may actually be biologically influenced to seek sex changes.

The *paraphilias* are next considered, in which the person either carries out or in some cases merely fantasizes unusual acts or utilizes atypical objects in order to become sexually aroused. In *fetishism* there is the use of inanimate objects (fetishes) as a repeatedly preferred or exclusive ingredient in the person's sexual arousal and orgasmic release. The point of a fetish is that it has taken on a kind of symbolic power, so that the meaning of sexual arousal (appetitive stage) for the person concerned is encompassed in this unique object—a woman's shoe, a man's necktie, and so on. Fetishes have been found to be products of fantasies engaged in by the person during pubescence and having decidedly Oedipal overtones. Fetishes are within normal limits until the items concerned are abstracted from the interpersonal context and begin serving as substitutes for actual human contact.

*Zoöphilia,* in which the person either fantasizes or actually engages in sexual relations with a lower animal, is a rare disorder. The diagnosis is made only when this becomes the person's preferred sexual alternative. *Pedophilia,* in which the person either fantasizes or actually engages in sexual relations with prepubertal children as a preferred alternative, is more common than zoophilia. Pedophilia shows up in midlife, and the patient may select children of the same or opposite sex to his or her own. Psychoanalytical explanations of pedophilia stress the immature, pre-Oedipal fixations of such patients. More men than women tend to have this disorder.

*Exhibitionism,* in which the person compulsively displays the sexual organs, is almost exclusively confined to men. DSM-III assigns this category only when there is no effort made for further sexual contact. Most exhibitionists are socially inhibited and timid, suffering from feelings of inadequacy as adults. Castration anxiety leading to reaction-formation and counterphobic measures are cited in the psychoanalytical literature. A sadistic element may be seen in the motivation of many exhibitionists who seek to humiliate the women they take as targets for their symptomatic acts.

We speak of *voyeurism* when a person repeatedly achieves sexual excitement and obtains release by observing unsuspecting people, usually strangers, disrobe, perform sexually, or simply be naked. Here again, the disorder is found primarily in men. Psychodynamically, the voyeur (peeper) is fixated at an infantile level. The immature personality that manifests voyeurism has replaced the preparatory act of sexual looking to obtain excitement for the entire process of sexual union and shared pleasure with another person. This is viewed as an Oedipal survival, as the sort of forbidden "peeping" done in relation to the mother.

*Sadism* means sexual pleasure in inflicting pain, including psychological suffering and humiliation. *Masochism* means sexual pleasure in suffering such injuries and indignities. The term *sadomasochism* combines these two forms of psychosexual disorder. Though Freud viewed sadism and masochism as opposite sides of the same coin, DSM-III allows for a diagnosis on exclusively one end or the other of this sadomasochistic dimension. Empirical research tends to support Freud. Psychoanalysis views sadism as the masculine and masochism as the feminine manifestation of sadomasochism. The disorders we are now considering arise when the pre-Oedipal child misinterprets vigorous, flirtatious sexual play between parents as signs of fighting or attack.

Chapter 16 closes with a discussion of *psychosexual dysfunction* in men and women. In a psychosexual dysfunction, the person's appetitive or psychophysiological changes that characterize the complete sexual response cycle are somehow inhibited. This can include a loss of interest in sex or an inability to achieve penile erection (*impotence*) or to reach climax. Some women have involuntary spasms of the musculature of the outer third of the vagina that interfere with penile penetration (*vaginismus*). Some men suffer from *premature ejaculation.* Some women have *frigidity,* or an inhibited sense of arousal. Others suffer vaginal pain during sexual relations (termed *dyspareunia*).

Problems of this sort in the male are traced dynamically to such behaviors as holding to a *split imago,* in which the man cannot perform sexually with a "good" woman (i.e., sex is "bad" and hence he needs a "bad" woman). This is an Oedipal survival. Often, in both men and women there is an unconscious hatred of the opposite sex, traced to Oedipal fixations, that inhibits satisfactory sexual union. Adults who have been sexually molested as children can develop psychosexual dysfunctions. It should be emphasized that if a person has some biological or anatomical problem leading to symptoms of the sort we are considering, the diagnosis of psychosexual dysfunction would not be made.

# 17

## *Psychological Factors Affecting Physical Condition*

Chapter 17 is entitled according to DSM-III terminology, but the disorders we shall be considering in its pages have been traditionally referred to as *psychosomatic disorders,* and that is how we shall refer to them in what follows. *In a psychosomatic disorder the patient reacts to stress, tension, and anxiety with direct physiological malfunction, which may lead to irreversible organ or tissue damage.* Unlike the neuroses, these disorders ordinarily do not involve symbolic expressions of conflict; if they do, the expression is incidental. There is no significant distortion of reality such as we see in the psychoses. A brief comparison with some of the neuroses and the psychoses will help to clarify the position of the psychosomatic disorders in the family of abnormal adjustment patterns.

Neurotic *anxiety disorders,* for example, are dominated by an apprehension that stems from the threatened emergence of unconscious conflicts and fantasies. The patient attempts to discharge his or her tension and reduce a sense of anxiety by increasing bodily activity, especially the activity of the general (skeletal) musculature. The *psychosomatic* patient need not be apprehensive at all, and his or her discharge takes the form of autonomic and vegetative malfunction. In *conversion disorders,* which were most often confused with psychosomatic disorders in the past, unconscious conflicts are expressed symbolically by some change in a body part—usually in a sense organ or in the skeletal musculature—and this symbolic change can be translated into language without doing violence to the symptom. Any damage to organs or tissues is only secondary, through disuse. The general impression given by a conversion symptom, while it is also primitive and regressive, is that of a more sophisticated use of the body part involved. While, as in any other field, one often sees intermediate clinical syndromes, a well-defined *neurosis* can easily be differentiated from a well-defined *psychosomatic disorder.*

A striking feature of the *psychoses* is the distortion of reality through delusions, and sometimes hallucinations, both of which may be spontaneous attempts at self-cure but tend to incapacitate the patient interpersonally. Without going into further detail, it is only necessary to say that delusions and hallucinations are not essential characteristics of *psychosomatic disorders*. In fact, on rare occasions a psychosomatic patient may develop a psychotic episode when his or her physiological disruption is corrected. This helps to point up the differentiation. Here are two brief case excerpts to illustrate psychosomatic illnesses:

> A businessman, aged thirty-five, had been working hard under great pressure to build up his advertising agency. He was a typical "achiever" or "go-getter," full of energy, initiative, and push, never able to relax, and driving himself to the limit. When one of his close associates left the firm to establish a rival agency, the patient developed a peptic ulcer. To a psychiatric consultant he at first presented a bland picture of indifference; but after reaching the point where he was able to express angry resentment over what he considered a betrayal by his former associate, his medical course showed marked improvement.

> A woman, aged thirty-two, who was rising steadily in a highly competitive law firm seemed on the surface to be stable and matter-of-fact. Nevertheless, whenever she felt that her husband or parents were not sufficiently appreciative of her performance, or responsive to her needs for affection, she developed attacks of bronchial asthma and episodes of dermatitis. At other times she was symptom-free.

A realization that emotional disturbances are tied up with physiological overactivity, which can lead to illness and even to death, is not new. It is confined neither to our times nor to our culture. The ancients wrote about it, and what they wrote has been confirmed and expanded through the ages. During the nineteenth and twentieth centuries, the rapid advances in knowledge about infectious diseases, metabolic disorders, and surgical intervention, however, focused attention upon laboratory and surgical techniques, with a corresponding decrease of interest in the patient as a person (T. Lidz, 1959).

During the modern era of medicine an interest in the patient as a person has been revived (Dunbar, 1943, 1946). Physicians recognized that certain illnesses were often influenced significantly by emotional disturbances, physiologists contributed information about this relationship, more and more psychiatrists turned their attention to various aspects of the problem, and both experimental and clinical psychologists entered the field. Psychosomatic medicine and the study of emotional problems in relation to illness express the convergence of this interest in all directions. It is now recognized that susceptibility to any illness may be influenced by emotional disturbance, either directly or through unconscious neglect and exposure (Janis, 1958).

## Emotional Stress and Bodily Illness

In all normal activity there is involvement of the internal organs and tissues, even though most of the time we are not aware of it. The heart varies in beat and in blood volume, the lungs expand and contract, the genitourinary systems change in pace and pattern, and the gastrointestinal system undergoes muscular and glandular changes—all as parts of ordinary everyday living. Even the skin, which both separates a person from his or her environment and makes important contacts with it, shows vascular and glandular changes that are not under voluntary control. It flushes and blanches in much the same way that mucous membranes flush and blanch.

With increased general activity, all of these systems may change their functioning to meet the extra demand. In emotional experience and behavior, even when these fall within normal limits, the visceral (or internal organ) involvement becomes marked. The heart beats faster and harder, a person may gasp or pant, the genitourinary systems may change their pattern, and the gastrointestinal system increases or decreases its activity. The skin of an emotionally aroused person may turn pale or blush deeply; we know that his or her gastric mucosa also turns pale or becomes engorged.

When a person is exposed to unusual stress, whether the stress is internally or externally generated, he or she is likely to become physiologically alerted, to show a readiness for fight or flight. Such preparation was found to be mediated through the adrenal glands and the autonomic or vegetative nervous system (Cannon, 1932). Since the autonomic nervous system also functions in such a way as to regulate the equilibrium of the internal organs throughout the body, and the skin as well, these become inevitably involved in the preparation for emergencies. The autonomic or vegetative nervous system has widespread, diffuse effects because of its anatomical distribution and its physiological mode of operation.

If overt action is possible, if anger can be aggressively expressed or if fear leads to immediate flight, the energy mobilized in the visceral reactions is dissipated and used up. If, however, there is no possible outlet, if no overt expression or action can occur, the visceral changes are likely to persist. Visceral tension, unrelieved by action, may include a wide range of physiological alteration. It is when this kind of thing becomes chronic, or recurs repeatedly, that visceral changes apparently go beyond normal limits, become pathological, and lead to a *psychosomatic disorder*. Such an origin is currently ascribed to many cases of peptic ulcer, bronchial asthma, ulcerative colitis, hypertension, migraine, and arthritis (Alexander, 1950; G. W. Brown, 1972; H. Robinson et al., 1972).

Precisely how such physical disorders arise has been the subject of a line of research dating back to at least 1833, when patients with open wounds (fistulas) in the stomach wall enabled investigators to observe the mucous membrane of the stomach directly (Beaumont, 1833; S. Wolf & Wolff, 1943). The visible changes in this membrane during times of psychological stress for the patient provided some of the first evidence of a link between mental and physical disturbance. It is often forgotten that Ivan Pavlov's work (1927) leading up to the discovery of conditioning was concerned with demonstrating the ways in which internal organs and the skin come to respond to stimulation that had not previously elicited such a reaction. Research by medical specialists over the present century has added to our understanding of physiological and psychodynamic interrelations with respect to the *central nervous system,* the *autonomic nervous system,* the *hypothalamus,* the *reticular* and *limbic systems,* and the various *metabolic* and *hormonal* changes—all with their aftereffects and feedback.

The work of Hans Selye (1976) is of particular importance in this line of research. Beginning with the hypothesis of a generalized (nonspecific) defense system in the body capable of warding off any form of stress to which the tissues and organ systems might be subjected, Selye eventually established a triadic syndrome that functioned in this manner. He named this generalized process the *general adaptation syndrome* (GAS). Selye noted that the physical body also has a *local adaptation syndrome* (LAS), which comes into play at the region of injury or infection. A good example of the LAS is the fact that inflammation occurs where microbes enter the body. This action was taken by Selye as a defensive maneuver on the part of the body to keep the infected area isolated from the rest of the bodily tissues (incidentally, Selye openly espouses the use of *teleological* descriptive terminology; see ibid., pp. 359-361).

The LAS also sends out chemical alarm signals to the centers of coordination in the nervous system and thereby to the endocrine glands, especially the pituitary and the adrenals. The adrenal glands produce adaptive hormones to combat wear and tear in the body. This broader action is conceived as the action of the GAS. Roughly considered, the adaptive hormones fall into two classifications: the *anti-inflammatory hormones* (ACTH, cortisone, cortisol), which inhibit excessive defensive reactions, and the *pro-inflammatory hormones* (STY, aldosterone, DOC), which stimulate them. Collectively these hormones are called *syntoxic* because they facilitate coexistence with a pathogen, either by diminishing sensitivity to it or by encapsulating it within a barricade of inflammatory tissue. They are to be distinguished from the *catatoxic* hormones, which enhance the destruction of potential pathogens, mostly through the induction of poison-metabolizing enzymes in the liver (ibid., pp. 55-56).

The GAS consists of three stages: (1) the *alarm reaction,* in which the nonspecific process is activated as a "call to arms of the defensive forces in the organism" (ibid., p. 36); (2) *resistance,* in which the countermeasures of the hormonal, autonomic nervous system, and related immunological mechanisms (not all of which are fully understood) come into play to confine the stress to the smallest area of the body possible (ibid., p. 162); and (3) *exhaustion,* or a collapse of the defensive capacity due to prolonged exposure to a noxious agent. If the third stage is reached, the organism experiences the physical damage that the noxious agent conveys, and of course this damage brings on pain and can result in death—depending upon the nature of the stressor (noxious agent).

Though Selye's researches began with a primary focus on strictly biophysical reactions such as infections, the adaptation of the eyes to light after leaving a darkened room (ibid., p. 80), and so forth, in time he found that psychological factors played an important role in precisely what the meaning of "stress" was to the phenomenal experience of the person. Stress can never be removed from the act of living. Only a dead organism is completely without stress. Life's excitements and challenges stress the physical organism, and as any athlete knows, the pain associated with excelling can be both positive and negative. Selye came to distinguish between *distress* and *eustress* (ibid., p. 74) The former is a negative phenomenal interpretation of stress, whereas the latter is a positive interpretation. Here is how Selye summed things up: "During both eustress and distress the body undergoes virtually the same nonspecific responses to the various positive or negative stimuli acting upon it. However, the fact that eustress causes much less damage than distress graphically demonstrates that it is 'how you take it' [phenomenally] that determines, ultimately, whether one can adapt successfully to change" (ibid., p. 74). We can readily add "challenge" and "threat" to the last sentence, because what the meaning of life's changes, challenges, and threats "is" depends in the final analysis on the person enacting them.

And so it is true that we find two people living identical *overt* lives of psychobiological stress—working hard, not sleeping enough, getting a marginal diet, pressed by deadlines and difficult decisions—but one develops ulcers and the other does not (Kobasa, 1979). Neither person may be a model of the ideal form of lifestyle, but one person views the "rat race" of life as a kind of challenging game to which he or she is committed and the other construes it phenomenally as a constant threat to personal security. One person is experiencing eustress much of the time, whereas the other is in a chronic state of distress. The distressed person cannot effect a state of *homeostasis* (keeping an even keel) but must resort to *heterostasis* (raising the level of defensive biological effort to carry on). The need to raise the stakes constantly in order to adjust to stress increases the chances that the stage of exhaustion will be reached in the GAS, resulting in some form of psychosomatic disorder as the body's natural defenses crumble.

## Psychosomatic Disorders as Adaptations

Psychosomatic disorders can threaten the life of a patient. They always mean some distortion or loss of function, or at the very least discomfort or disfigurement. How then can we call them adaptive? They can be adaptive in the same sense that disabling neuroses and psychoses can. If they begin by protecting the patient from something worse, then they begin as adaptations, no matter what their later course may be. In other words, psychosomatic disorders are maladaptive, but they at least begin by achieving something that the patient cannot achieve in other ways. We must always remember that the psychosomatic disorder, like the neurosis and the psychosis, is not something that a person thinks out consciously. It is something that happens to the person while he or she is under stress. The process of developing the disorder is an unconscious one; the patient does not know what is taking place. With this general orientation, we can approach psychosomatic disorders that, even though they are maladaptations, do perform certain functions. Some of these adaptive functions follow.

1. *A psychosomatic disorder puts an apparent or an actual physical illness in place of an intolerable current situation.* It makes a person physically sick instead of neurotic or psychotic. In most cultures today, a *physical illness* is honorable no matter how deplorable it may be, whereas a *neurotic illness* is looked upon as a weakness that is not honorable and a *psychosis* is called crazy. It is more dignified to suffer from a psychosomatic disorder, as long as the patient believes in the physical origin of his or her illness.

2. Although psychosomatic disorders often involve *primary anxiety*—the diffuse, regressive anxiety of a small child—this may be *easier to bear* than a secondary anxiety based upon conscious conflicts over childhood impulses, which a person cannot otherwise control and does not recognize. The end result may be a serious illness and even death, but the patient does not foresee this danger. The whole process is unconscious; its symptoms are those of a physical illness that seems as unavoidable as any other physical illness. A great many psychosomatic disorders are of mild or moderate degree, and do not lead to death.

3. *A psychosomatic disorder may protect a patient from developing a frank psychosis,* which is in itself frightening and may lead to a prisonlike confinement with loss of civil rights. This danger is known to every citizen, even to children, and although the processes leading to psychosis or psychosomatic disorder are unconscious, this does not mean that they lack some unconscious *choice* in the matter. Although there is a difference in opinion among experts as to the frequency with which the loss of psychosomatic symptoms is followed by psychosis, no one working in the field denies that there sometimes seems to be a close relationship between the two. For example, some patients with ulcerative colitis develop a paranoid psychosis when they improve, and others become psychotically depressed, as though the psychosomatic disorders and the psychoses were interchangeable (Grace, Wolf, & Wolff, 1951; West, 1961). This suggests caution in treating chronic psychosomatic disorders that do not threaten life, and prepares the therapist for the possibility that he or she may be called upon to treat psychotic trends as the patient recovers.

4. *Psychosomatic disorders give the patient the privileges of a sick person,* without lowering self-esteem or greatly restricting freedom. The *secondary gain,* as this is called, and the relationship of an unconsciously needed dependency upon a parent figure, the clinician, can bring valuable gratifications to a basically immature person. These gratifications should not be scorned. They sometimes protect a person from disabling neurotic or psychotic developments; and they often give meaningful interpersonal relationships to an otherwise empty life. It should be added that many emotionally immature, dependent men and women hide their personal wishes and needs from themselves as well

as from others, behind an energetic, independent façade. The wishes are still there, however, and they are still unsatisfied.

5. Finally, there remains to be considered the intensification of a physical illness by a psychosomatic disorder. The patient may use the *physical illness as a means of eliciting concern, care, and affection,* which he or she has needed all along but has not been able to obtain during the state of being physically well. This also should not be scorned. Life is objectively more difficult and less rewarding for some persons than for others, and subjectively it may seem bleak, even though objectively it is considered fortunate. The psychotherapeutic aim in treating psychosomatic disorders is to bring the wish to verbal expression, if this can be done skillfully and safely, so that, as a patient improves physically, there will be a psychodynamic maturation taking place as well. To give support and to permit independence during the early stage of therapy is usually the most important part of the treatment of psychosomatic disorders.

## Varieties of Psychosomatic Disorders

Psychosomatic disorder may involve the skin and any of the viscera in any of a number of different ways. It may complicate the course and affect the outcome of any physical illness. For this reason the psychiatrist or clinical psychologist, no matter how well versed he or she may be in medical and surgical problems, cannot expect to take over the work of the specialist, who is an expert in treating the particular physical illness from which the patient is suffering. Neither can the specialist in other fields expect to be able to carry out psychotherapy, except in relatively simple situations. Successful treatment of psychosomatic disorders depends upon the intelligent and willing cooperation of two therapists, each skilled in his or her own specialty. In what follows we shall discuss briefly seven of the systems most commonly involved in psychosomatic disorders.

### PSYCHOSOMATIC DISORDERS AND THE GASTROINTESTINAL TRACT

It is hardly surprising that psychosomatic disorders commonly involve the gastrointestinal tract. During the first year of postnatal life, as we pointed out in Chapter 2, most of a child's significant sources of pleasure, relief, and comfort, most of his or her sources of frustration and apparent anxiety, center around the mouth and feeding. In the beginning, most babies find delay in the feeding process intolerable. Their behavior, while they wait, looks like a desperate anxiety, which quickly vanishes when their mouth holds the nipple and they can suck. This frantic behavior gradually disappears as the infant learns to depend upon others to bring nourishment as needed. A *basic trust* must be framed or life would be intolerably anxiety-laden. We know also that *pleasure sucking,* unrelated to food intake, is a source of infantile gratification, which sometimes begins even before birth and often lasts for years after it.

Still more important than oral pleasure and oral frustration is the growth of oral dependence. At first, the infant seems not to differentiate between being hungry and needing love, between being fed lovingly and being loved. Nevertheless, it is through the feeding situation, with its sucking and swallowing and gastric comforting, that every infant makes his or her most important relationship with another person. It is through the mouth that the infant first incorporates part of the external world and learns the art of symbolic introjection. Before long, this differentiates into reactions to the one who feeds and loves the infant, as well as reactions to the feeding itself. It is also through the inevitable delays and frustrations during oral dependence that the early steps are taken in organizing an ego system. The child learns to look beyond his or her own body for sources of relief, pleasure, and comfort.

What is particularly relevant here is that early in life infants do not differentiate between their physiological functions and their earliest experiences of love and care. To some extent these remain undifferentiated, although distinguishable, in all adults. We all tend to equate *being asked to dinner* with *being loved,* or if love seems too strong a word, at least with *being accepted.* We never lose some pleasures of the mouth, of eating and drinking, or the healthy comfort of a satisfied stomach. We never wholly lose symbolic expressions of rejection and disgust that must also involve gastric action. The adult who develops gastric function as a psychosomatic disorder seems to be one whose regression under stress carries some of these reactions back to their infantile intensity and who uses them habitually in expressing personally sensed extremes of tension and anxiety.

*Peptic Ulcer.* Peptic ulcers occur most frequently in the stomach and duodenum. They are usually single and sharply demarcated from the normal or near-normal tissue that surrounds them. They may occur at any age, even in the newborn. Their direct cause is related to digestion of gastric or duodenal tissue by acid digestive juices. It cannot be taken for granted that every case of peptic ulcer is precipitated by emotional problems, but the ones that *are emotional in origin* present a formidable proportion (Baron, 1972). Anything that increases gastric acidity or gastric mobility may indirectly perpetuate a peptic ulcer. For example, people who work in high-stress jobs, such as physicians, business executives, or air traffic controllers, are found to have a higher percentage of ulcers than people in other forms of work (Cobb & Rose, 1973; Pflanz, 1971). There is no obvious "peptic ulcer personality" reflected in empirical studies of such patients versus normal controls (A. E. Phillips & Cay, 1972).

As a group, adults who develop peptic ulcers seem to be relatively stable. Traditional analytical explanations have stressed the fundamental dependency of peptic ulcer cases, even though the overt behavior of many such individuals is anything but that of a shrinking violet (Alexander, 1950). The popular image of the man with peptic ulcer is that of a successful business executive who works hard, drives himself, eats and drinks a great deal, and keeps a pill of some sort handy in case of trouble. Such a man would never be suspected of having imperious dependency needs—of wanting or needing to be taken care of. What is more important, such a man cannot allow himself even to become aware of his own dependency needs, let alone express them to others. To the world he presents the facade of the strong, successful achiever. To himself he appears as the image of the independent, powerful man who need depend upon no one else.

When it is studied psychodynamically, this facade often turns out to be overcompensatory, a strong expression of self-sufficiency that is basically a *reaction-formation* against powerful dependency needs. The man has built up a style of life that hides his strong dependency needs defensively, and he denies them even to himself. By means of this defense he remains unconscious of these needs. The mere suggestion of them would seem to him an insult. Whenever there is a threat to this life pattern, the man increases his strivings and feels more than ever the demand to be independent of everyone.

Such persons, whether actually executives or laborers, seem to develop peptic ulcers when an increase in dependency needs threatens to destroy their self-image. This may come from the loss, or even the threatened loss, of someone upon whom the patient is actually dependent or of the success upon which he has counted. The precipitating factor may be the loss of a mother, wife, or child; it may be marital discord or business failure, or even the stress of keeping a business or a marriage successful. It is believed that under such circumstances there is a regression to primary anxiety and that the anxiety over dependency is expressed by hypersecretion and overactivity in the stomach. It is probable that dependent personality tendencies alone do not result in ulcer formation during stress. Studies have shown that only those men who have high pepsinogen levels in combination with dependent personalities tend to develop ulcers during times of stress (Weiner et al., 1957). But the general outline of the analytical explanation remains the same. The unmet need for dependency and love activates mechanisms that are normal for an infant who cannot distinguish between hunger and love. These mechanisms require that someone provide food, or infantile love, which differentiates out of this need and its satisfaction during infancy. The physiological process whereby tissue damage results is readily understood in terms of Selye's GAS.

*Obesity.* Like peptic ulcer, obesity may be the result of many things, and among these many things must be counted strong irrational dependency needs. Obesity is frequently a psychosomatic disorder, and it can be a grave one. Chronic overweight is nearly always a result of overeating. Endocrine and metabolic disorders are seldom involved. Theoretically, the control of obesity should be an easy matter, a matter of controlling a person's food intake. In practice, the control of obesity is exceedingly difficult in those persons for whom food and eating have imperious unconscious meanings.

Such persons behave as if they were food addicts; they seem unable to control their excessive need for food. They go on a diet over and over again;

but as soon as they have lost weight they begin to overeat again, until they have gained back all that they had lost. A new kind of dieting may start the cycle all over again. For a time, weight is lost and the patient expresses enthusiasm and determination; but in the end obesity appears again, even though the patient knows that his or her life depends upon avoiding it.

Analytical studies of mothers of obese children found that often they could not provide their offspring with sincere mothering love, because of their own unmet needs to be dependent and loved (Bruch, 1957). They could, however, give their children food and conscientious care. The *giving of food* became a substitute for the *giving of love,* in the manner of primary processes, both in the mother and in the child. The child was left with an irrational craving for food because his or her cravings for love had never been met except at a primitive feeding level. In a study that reviewed case histories of eighty-four obese patients in psychoanalysis, it was found that the predominant themes of anxiety and/or depression were counterposed to the ingestion of food (Rand & Stunkard, 1978). In other words, lacking the basic sense of self-acceptance that satisfying mothering provides, these individuals seem to have sought to find a substitute for love in food. Even in adulthood, when they tried to refrain from taking in food, they became anxious and depressed. It is not likely that a lasting weight loss will be achieved in such cases until the individuals concerned have an understanding of the role that their oral needs play in their obesity.

*Ulcerative Colitis.* Ulcerative colitis is another serious gastrointestinal disorder in which, as in peptic ulcer, emotional experiences, tensions, and anxieties are generally accepted as playing important roles. Direct observation of the mucuous membrane of the colon while patients were experiencing conflicts over resentment and the desire to please revealed that it became congested and hyperactive. In such a state, the colon becomes fragile, so that minor traumata can produce hemorrhage and ulceration (Grace, Wolf, & Wolff, 1951).

Clinicians find that patients with ulcerative colitis present a façade of passivity, acquiescence, and blandness; but behind this outer shell there is anger and hostility. They tend not to be overtly aggressive but to show these feelings by being demanding, sensitive, brooding, and resentful of supposed personal slights. Their strong dependency needs (to be loved and accepted) are rivaled by angry feelings that stir up guilt and the fear that a loved person will reject them in retaliation for their hostile sensations. The mothers of these patients are often described as fostering an inordinate degree of dependency by their domination, but also as being fundamentally hostile toward their offspring.

The ulcerative colitis patient has, in development, compounded fixations at both the oral and especially the anal level of psychosexual development. During personality development, as we have seen in Chapter 2, the anal period is one in which children seek at the same time to *assert themselves* and to *control themselves.* Since bowel control is of central importance in this phase, the bowel can express giving and withholding in relation to parental figures.

There is pleasure in being dirty and pleasure in getting approval for being clean. The control can become stubborn and frustrating to others; the lack of control can take the form of an angry attack. This is a period full of ambivalence about a great many things, not the least of which is the struggle over *being good and yielding* or *being bad and withholding,* or of *being bad and soiling.* Children want to receive their mother's love, but they also tend to feel angry when constantly under the control of their parent. They develop a sense of guilt over their angry feelings toward their mother, and also fear retaliation for their "dirty" badness. There is always the threat of losing their mother's love.

An interesting case of a five-year-old boy in the literature reflects some of these dynamics (Bloom, 1955). He had his first attack of ulcerative colitis when he was three and a half years old, on the day when summer school ended and a maid to whom he was devoted left. He was tense and furious, but he dared not express his hostility. He had both oral and anal aggressive impulses and destructive fantasies in which people were represented as food and feces. The boy's mother, and most of the relatives in his environment, restrained their feelings and impulses in order to keep up a smooth social front. In them also there were primitive oral and anal destructive impulses, but they handled their own hostility by excessive self-control and encouraged harsh superego development. Because of such an ego-superego structure, it is reported, eight of the twelve members of this family developed psychosomatic, rather than psychotic, disorders. This interpretation is in line with a widely held view that psychosomatic disorder may be an alternative to psychotic disorder (T. Lidz & Rubenstein, 1959).

## THE RESPIRATORY SYSTEM

The respiratory system is involved in everyday emotional experience. There is the sigh of sadness, longing, and regret, the gasp of surprise, the cry of fear, and the wailing of grief. Crowds watching a tightrope walker hold their breath, and let it out audibly in relief when the act is finished. Mothers do the same when they watch a child pass through some danger of which he may not even be aware. One can often tell from a person's speech, from its pitch, rate, and rhythm, that he or she is emotionally disturbed.

The most primitive form in which emotionality is expressed by the respiratory system is the commonplace breath-holding spells of angry infants and small children. They express rage and frustration by crying and crying until they are literally blue in the face. Some infants even stop breathing completely and have convulsive movements because of the disturbed oxygen–carbon dioxide balance in the blood. Tense adults also *hyperventilate* in this fashion, particularly those who are aggressive, destructive, and prone to temper tantrums (Compernolle, Hoogdvin, & Joele, 1979). They breathe so that the *tidal air* does not reach the *alveolar air* of the lungs in such a way as to permit normal interchange of oxygen and carbon dioxide. Although they do not turn blue, as infants do, they experience dizziness, faintness, and sometimes "blacking out."

Patients are as a rule not aware that emotional disturbance is involved. They go to a physician for help because of the physical symptoms (Wittkower & White, 1959).

*Bronchial Asthma.* The most important of the psychosomatic disorders of respiration appears in the form of bronchial asthma. This involves constriction of the bronchioles, which results in wheezing, choking sensations, and gasping for breath. Some asthmatic patients are critically ill, and some are chronically disabled. Most of them experience remissions in which they seem quite well, and periods of attacks which can be severe.

It must not be supposed that all bronchial asthma is psychosomatic; in one study less than 50 percent of the asthmatics could be so classified (Rees, 1964). Some asthmatic patients follow a distinctly seasonal cycle that parallels such seasonal cycles in allergens as, for example, in ragweed and cottonwood. Even those who are more or less constantly asthmatic may be physiologically hypersensitive to pollens and molds that are always present in the air. Many of these can be desensitized by physiological means alone. Most experts today believe that there are several contributing factors to asthmatic attacks, including specific allergic sensitivity, autonomic nervous system susceptibility, an unusually responsive respiratory system, and life experiences which include conflicts that are no longer conscious (Dekker, Barendregt, & DeVries, 1961). The concurrence of different constellations in producing a psychosomatic disorder is exceptionally well illustrated in asthma. The following case shows this clearly, and it may be taken as representative of psychosomatic disorders in other systems as well.

Patricia M., a fourteen-year-old high school girl, was admitted to a general hospital because of severe attacks of bronchial asthma. The nurses reported that she entered the ward flanked by her frightened parents, the mother supporting her on one side and the father walking on the other side, carrying a syringe with adrenalin ready for instant use. This entrance was a dramatic representation of the attitudes that all three had developed during the four months of Patricia's asthmatic attacks. At home, the father, after work, had been devoting himself entirely to the task of diverting Patricia, so as to minimize her attacks. Actually, the attacks had increased in frequency and severity following his arrival at home, but neither the parents nor the child seemed to suspect that there might be some connection involved. By the time she was brought to the hospital her activities had been restricted to those of a person in imminent danger of collapse and sudden death.

Although a respiratory hypersensitivity to bacterial proteins was clearly demonstrated, it was obvious to everyone that the extreme anxiety of the child and her parents presented a major problem. At first, parental visits to the child, but not to the hospital, were limited. Both parents and the child received psychotherapy during the period of her desensitization to her specific allergens. Patricia's asthmatic attacks were treated competently and without anxiety on the part of the staff. When it was observed that she had an increase of attacks on "Protein Clinic" days, the allergist made arrangements to have her treated on the psychiatric ward, and the increase disappeared. Because of her long period of inactivity, it was necessary to schedule increasing activity until Patricia had regained the confidence that she had lost because of everyone's extreme anxiety. After four months, she was well enough to go home and resume a normal life. When asthmatic attacks then occurred, which they did at infrequent intervals, both the parents and the girl were able to handle the situation without alarm. Patricia was seen in office treatment for some time after discharge so that some of her personal problems could be worked through.

Both clinical and empirical evidence support the view that asthmatic individuals are caught in a severe conflict of emotional ambivalence concerning their parents (Alexander, 1950; Straker & Tamerin, 1974). There is a strong sense of dependency involved, but also much suppressed aggression. Indeed, it has been demonstrated empirically that asthmatic patients find it difficult to express hostility even when this emotion is called for in the circumstances facing the person (Mathe & Knapp, 1977). Some clinicians have interpreted the asthmatic attack as a *suppressed cry for help* from a mother figure, when the patient faces loss or separation. The assumption being made here is that the patient can express dependency only in an infantile manner. Asthmatic patients frequently report difficulty in crying and relief from the asthma when they have "learned to cry." Attacks in psychosomatic patients are also relieved sometimes by *confession,* if they have had conscious or unconscious feelings of guilt over their hostility and fears of losing the love they need. Patients who discover that they are accepted, in spite of real or fantasied "badness," often experience relief.

Some clinicians maintain that the dependency needs of asthmatic patients are inordinate because they were not met in childhood. Others feel that allergic children have been unusually sensitive, from birth on, so that they raise difficulties in early mother-child relationships and precipitate mutual frustration. Some of the mothers studied clinically had obviously not solved their own dependency conflicts. They often showed their ambivalence by first holding their child so close as almost to choke it and then pushing it away in a gesture of rejection. In these cases, the asthmatic attacks disappeared after the child was separated from the mother, so that the child's needs for love and protection were not in constant conflict with maternal demands for surrender and maternal rejection. This type of conflict, of course, is almost universal in small children, but in the asthmatic child it seems to be especially intense. *Early infection* may make the respiratory system chronically hypersensitive, so that conflict, frustration, and anxiety lead to profound regression without symbolic expression.

## CARDIOVASCULAR DISORDERS ON A PSYCHOSOMATIC BASIS

Like other psychosomatic disorders, cardiovascular disorders are related to the normal occurrences of everyday life. It is the intensity, the exaggeration, or the sustained character of the reaction that makes them pathological. The cardiovascular system is normally in constant flux, even while the body is at rest. It responds with changes in blood flow and blood pressure under conditions of physical exertion, tension, vigilance, and relaxation. Its shifts participate in all emotional experience and behavior. A man's heart beats faster, and his blood pressure may rise, when he feels joyous, angry, or afraid, or even when he feels hurried or pushes himself. He may flush because of the heat or because he is anxious or frightened. Palpitation and skipped beats are by no means unusual in healthy men and women.

As we have already seen, in the *anxiety reactions,* even the most ordinary cardiovascular changes—in heart action, blood pressure or distribution of the flow—may themselves arouse anxiety and become the focus of new fears. Thus we find persons frightened at the prospect of a heart attack and of impending death when they are in no such danger. Behind the symptoms there may be unexpressed anxiety, guilt, or rage. When a person becomes enraged and *expresses* it, he or she gains some discharge through violent action or a verbal assault. The difficulty in social group living is that violence in action or speech may be met with violence, or at least by anger and disapproval. We must include in such reactions to one's anger or hate the forces of repression within the person, and the threat such emotions may pose to the self-image of the person as a civilized and even perhaps a benevolent human being. It seems to be when a chronically hostile person suppresses anger that certain of the vascular concomitants of rage lead to psychosomatic disorders. We shall discuss two of the most common cardiovascular manifestations.

*Essential Hypertension and Heart Disease.* In about 75 or 80 percent of persons suffering from chronic high blood pressure no consistent organic etiology can be found. Their hypertension is called *essential,* which really means that it is of unknown etiology. The active participation of cardiovascular mechanisms in all emotional changes and in all situations of stress has focused attention upon this group as one involving psychosomatic factors. It has been pointed out that *stress discharge* implicates the same endocrine and autonomic mechanisms that mediate *diffuse arteriolar* and *peripheral blood vessel constriction.* The not unreasonable conclusion is then drawn that continued emotional stress stimulates pathophysiological activity that underlies the development of essential hypertension (B. Engel & Bickford, 1961; Kalis et al., 1961; Van der Valk, 1957).

While it is generally believed that constitutional, genetic, and early traumatic experiences are responsible for the development of essential hypertension, there is room for disagreement about the specific type of personality dynamic related to this disorder. Clinicians have noted that some patients with essential hypertension report that they used to have temper outbursts, but changed suddenly to strict self-control (Alexander, 1950). This appears to mean that they reacted to frustration with anger, which is a normal reaction, but *suppressed the expression* of it and probably repressed the feeling as well. This does not mean, however, that they erased all physiological traces of the unexpressed anger. If the demands and the critical attitudes of a man's superior infuriate him and make him feel inferior, they may make him drive himself on to *prove* that he is competent. If he submits to ill-treatment during the process, feeling more hostile all the time, he may stir up deep-seated conflicts involving childhood dependency and hostility. This may begin the controlled hostile aggression and the blood pressure changes.

In recent years a series of experiments have been conducted on two styles of behavior related in a positive/negative sense with heart disease. The description of these two types of individuals is reminiscent of what we have just mentioned about hypertense individuals, who need to prove themselves more competent than the next person. Coronary disease tends to be associated with a *Type A* behavioral style, which may be seen in persons who are impatient, aggressive, highly competitive, ambitious, and very desirous of being in control of almost every situation in which they participate (Friedman & Rosenman, 1974). On the other hand, coronary disease is less likely in a *Type B* behavioral style, which is more relaxed, realistic, and oriented to cooperation in many of life's situations. The pervasiveness of findings on Type A versus Type B behavior is impressive. In one study, over three thousand men were followed up for several years, and the incidence of coronary disease among the Type A subjects was six times as great among Type B men in the thirty-nine to forty-nine year age decade (Rosenman et al., 1966).

*Migraine.*  This is also an illness of unknown etiology which many ascribe to psychosomatic sources. In its most characteristic form it consists of a unilateral periodic headache, often with nausea and vomiting, and sometimes with diarrhea or constipation. An attack may be preceded, for hours or even days, by attacks of facial flushing or facial pallor; there are often signs of constriction in the arteries of the head, face, and eye-grounds just before an attack begins. Paresthesias, vertigo, and scintillating visual phenomena may provide a warning. Migraine is considered by many clinicians to be an epileptic equivalent; by others it is placed among the headaches without definite commitment (H. Wolff, 1963). Some researchers have described the migraine personality as perfectionistic, highly competitive, ambitious, orderly, and compulsive—which sounds a little like the description given above of Type A behavior. The hereditary basis of migraine has not been supported as an exclusive determinant, but in combination with environmental stress there does appear to be a role for constitutional predisposition (Bakal, 1975; Waters, 1971).

## RHEUMATOID ARTHRITIS

Rheumatoid arthritis is another common disorder of unknown etiology in which emotional stress is believed to play a part. Persons who develop rheumatoid arthritis are described as active, energetic achievers who do not express their feelings freely (Alexander, 1950). There are serious doubts as to what factors are involved in precipitating rheumatoid arthritis. Both an *increase in responsibility* and a *decrease in responsibility* have been reported. Such global phrases tell us little about the patient's experiences in either situation.

The parents of patients who develop rheumatoid arthritis are said to have been restrictive and sometimes overprotective, while not allowing their children to express anger through the usual channels when they became frustrated. The mother is usually described as a "cold" person who allows herself little emotional expression (Bloom & Whipple, 1959). The father is said to be passive and gentle, allowing the mother to exert domineering control over their offspring. The child who feels rebellious because of the mother's strict control is so dependent upon her love that he or she does not dare to express angry feelings. The guilt created by the child's own hostility adds an internal restricting pressure to the external restraint imposed by the mother.

## THE SKIN

The skin is a paradox and almost a miracle. It *separates* the organism from the surroundings, but it has unnumbered sensitive little sense organs which, together with the eyes, ears, nose and mouth, *connect* the organism with its surroundings. Taken as a unit, it is the most external of external organs; yet it originates from the same embryological layer as the brain, the *ectoderm,* and it functions in many ways like an internal organ. A massive network of small blood vessels grows into it that include *mesodermal* derivatives, and the skin has innumerable glands and smooth muscle elements that relate it directly to the viscera. The skin also grows hair, which on the face is the mark of the male and on the head is a distinctive aspect of the woman's femininity.

The skin is a major organ of body temperature control, of evaporation, excretion, and secretion. Its blood vessels, glands, and smooth muscles undergo all kinds of important changes that are not under conscious or preconscious control. They participate actively in the emotional components of experience and behavior. Early in life the skin is involved in need-satisfaction sequences that bring mother and child into a reciprocal relationship and help to establish the normal symbiotic mother-child union. Throughout life the skin has erotic functions as well as aggressive and hostile ones. It can as easily become the locus of injury as the source of comfort.

The skin shows some remarkable changes in less normal situations. When a person is greatly excited, ecstatic, or under hypnosis his or her skin may be insensitive to pain; it also may retain for a long time the mark of even a light scratch. It is not difficult to understand that the skin can react in all kinds of ways to all kinds of emotional disturbances. Eczema, urticaria, and the dermatoses have all been found to be related to emotional factors. The skin is the site of so many malfunctions and diseases that specialists devote their whole professional lives to its study and therapy. Considering its complex structure, its diverse and often conflicting functions, its immediate visibility to others and its narcissistic value, there can be no doubt that the skin plays an important part in psychosomatic disorders.

Clinicians have generally found that over half of the patients treated in dermatology clinics have psychological problems related to the skin lesions for which treatment is sought. Some allergic patients, who develop contact dermatitis whenever they are exposed to their specific allergen, also develop the same kind of lesion in a stress situation when the allergen is absent. The stress or tension appears to act as though it were the allergic substance itself.

Psychoanalytic interpretations of psychosomatic skin disorders have noted the compulsive nature of the scratching that accompanies them (Schur, 1955). Indeed, the scratching gives the impression of a regressive masturbatory action that reaches a crescendo and is followed by relief. Sometimes the scratching is so extreme that it produces tissue injury, chronic irritation, and pain. It then seems to serve self-punitive functions as well. Scratching is often associated with destructive impulses and fantasies in relation to other persons. It has been observed that the clawlike position of many patients' hands suggests that they are inhibiting the desire to scratch someone else. It may be the guilt over having such hostile impulses that leads to destructive self-scratching. Still other cases suggest a dynamic of exhibitionistic impulses and defenses against such promptings.

## HYPERTHYROIDISM

It has long been recognized clinically that psychological stress can precipitate hyperthyroidism and that anxiety, irritability, restless overactivity, and mood swings are among the most prominent symptoms. In this disorder the interaction between visceral functioning and psychological activity is especially clear. Excessive thyroid secretion increases anxiety, and the increased anxiety increases thyroid secretion, thus completing the vicious cycle.

People who suffer from hyperthyroidism usually appear to be responsible, active, sensitive and self-sufficient, but according to some experts this is a façade based upon defensive *reaction-formation.* The patient has adopted a style of life that denies personal dependency longings and the threats to his or her security early in life. A fear of loss through death seems to underlie many cases. This has sometimes been justified by the death of the mother when the patient was still a child. As part of an attempt to master the anxiety from frustrated dependency longings, the patient may identify with the lost person by assuming an *attitude* of self-reliance that has no other basis. Even in childhood, the hyperthyroidic person may assume responsibilities that are beyond his or her actual powers and suffer thereby under a constant sense of pressure.

According to the leading psychoanalytical theory of psychosomatic hyperthyroidism, the thyroid gland—which promotes growth in childhood—may again become preponderant under adult stress and resume its childhood functions as part of a general regression (Alexander, 1950; Alexander et al., 1961). Thus increased thyroid activity in adulthood represents something that, although appropriate in childhood, is now pathological in its effects. This is somewhat analogous to the undifferentiated, infantile mode of functioning ascribed to the stomach of those who develop peptic ulcers. The hyperthyroid adult overdoes the process of trying to be self-sufficient and mature. He or she fails in this attempt and actually regresses to a level at which thyroid hyperactivity was a normal part of growth acceleration.

Naturally, whether or not this is the mechanism underlying hyperthyroidism, and whether or not hereditary factors also need to be considered, are still matters of controversy. Until recently it was thought quite unlikely that the person could have *intentional* control over the functioning of bodily organs and/or glands. However, the findings on so-called biofeedback in human behavior demonstrate that people can in fact influence autonomic functions such as rate of heartbeat or the volume of blood vessel size (vasodilation/ constriction) in the forehead region (N. E. Miller et al., 1974; Friar & Beatty, 1976). The explanatory language of biofeedback suggests that a mechanical process is in operation, but actually the partial direction of such "automatic" bodily functions is *teleological.* The person "wills" the outcome, based on a knowledge of the ongoing heart rate, extent of vasoconstriction, and so forth. There is no demonstrable mechanism determining the willful intention brought into the procedure, nor is there a way of describing how this intention is brought to bear on bodily functioning. It just happens when the person sets his or her conscious mind to comply with instructions. If we now postulate unconscious willing of this nature, the *possibility* of activating glands intentionally can be entertained. We shall have more to say on biofeedback when we take up dynamics of psychosomatic disorders, below.

## DIABETES MELLITUS

Diabetes mellitus is another endocrine disorder with important emotional components; but the emotional etiology of the disturbance in glucose metabolism is questionable. In *normal persons,* fear or anxiety does result in changes in the blood-sugar level, but the changes are transient. Long-lasting or widely fluctuating changes in blood sugar are characteristic of *diabetic persons* who are exposed to emotional stress. The common stresses seem to be frustration of dependency needs and the reactivation of dependency needs through loss. It is reported that when a patient feels cared for, when the required attention is forthcoming, his or her blood-sugar levels return to normal limits, and they can then be controlled by a dietary regimen or the insulin level that was previously required. The dietary control of diabetes always involves food deprivation, and this may aggravate any conflict the patient has over dependency needs. A mother whose only expression of love is through feeding may find great difficulty in restricting her diabetic child's diet. Diabetic patients, whether children or adults, may feel deprived and unloved to such an extent that they eat what they should not, both to provide themselves with the symbol of love and to punish authority figures secretly. Whatever the etiological relationships, these factors should be kept in mind by those responsible for the care and treatment of diabetics.

## Dynamic and Developmental Background

Two questions are basic to the psychopathology of psychosomatic disorders, neither of which has been as yet answered to everyone's satisfaction. First, why does the patient react to stress with *primitive autonomic* and *vegetative changes at a physiological level?* Second, why is *one particular tissue, organ,* or *system* utilized by one patient and *some other one* by another patient?

### WHY DOES ANYONE GET A PSYCHOSOMATIC DISORDER?

The question of why anyone gets a psychosomatic disorder asks, in effect, why the patient does not react to stress with a neurosis or psychosis.

The *neurotic patient,* as we have seen, manages his or her otherwise intolerable tension and anxiety by means of a compromise, the product of which we call the *neurotic symptom.* This compromise includes the regressive reactivation of infantile material, some of which escapes repression. But the neurotic patient's defensive organization is relatively intact, so that his symptom is usually limited in scope.

In *psychotic patients,* the regression is deeper than in neurosis and is usually subtotal in extent. What we call the *psychotic symptom* is likewise an attempt at a compromise—for example, the delusion or the hallucination—but unlike the neurotic compromise it involves serious distortions of reality. This is because of the massive breakthrough of primary process material that the symptom attempts to include by reconstructing external reality.

The person with a *psychosomatic disorder* neither forms a neurotic compromise nor seriously distorts external reality. Instead he or she tries to discharge tensions and relieve anxiety through direct autonomous and visceral processes. How is this to be explained? A great many ingenious explanations have been offered by experts in this field (e.g., Grinker & Robbins, 1954; Jacobson, 1953a; Schur, 1955). To do justice to them and their authors would require a volume in itself. We shall have to be satisfied here with a small sampling of certain representative views.

One point on which there is some agreement is that psychosomatic disorders are deep regressions to an almost undifferentiated phase of ego development. This agreement rests upon the primitive physiological character of the psychosomatic reaction. With few exceptions, a working distinction can be made even between the *psychosomatic disorders* and such neuroses as *anxiety disorders* and *conversions.* The neuroses employ obvious fantasy and symbols in creating the neurotic symptom, whereas there is an apparent lack of such fantasy and symbolization in psychosomatic disorders. A differentiation is sometimes difficult to make with respect to anxiety disorders because of their diffuse character. A careful study of the patients themselves, however, brings out a great deal of unconscious symbolism in anxiety disorders. This is quite different from the lack or the paucity of symbolism in psychosomatic disorders.

As for conversion symptoms, they almost always use unconscious symbolization that involves sense organs or the skeletal musculature (paralyses, anesthesias, blindness, deafness, etc.). Their symbolization can usually be translated into relatively sophisticated verbal statements, which is not the case in psychosomatic disorders. We cannot expect a patient to exclude mixtures of the two methods of dealing with stress, of course, and this seems to happen when the symptoms overlap, such as in cases of *anorexia nervosa,* recurrent *vomiting,* and *pseudopregnancy.*

The *deep physiological regressions* characteristic of *psychosomatic disorders* have received many interpretations. Purely physiological hypotheses are widely used. Since the autonomic nervous system, the internal organs, and the skin are involved in a variety of different ways, many interpretations are confined to interrelationships between the central nervous system and the autonomic nervous system, including the latter's central nervous system centers.

As we noted above, within recent years there has been a rapid advance in our knowledge of the physiological functioning of bodily systems in terms of feedback, as well as new discoveries concerning the hypothalamus, the limbic system, and the reticular systems and a differentiation between the secretion of noradrenalin and epinephrin by the adrenal glands. What is encouraging about the modern interpretation of such findings is that no longer do we find the experts totally committed to a completely reductive explanation—to the exclusively material and efficient causation of yesteryear (see Chapter 1, p. 6). There is a growing recognition that interpersonal relationships within the social structure of human beings are an important aspect of the totally functioning psychophysiological organism. As Selye (1976, p. 409) has noted, this is a two-way street—with bodily changes affecting mental states and vice versa.

Biofeedback research has—knowingly or unknowingly—supported the view of a mental contribution to the ongoing processes of the body. Neal Miller (1978, p. 373) has noted that most people are poorly prepared to understand signals coming from one part of their body or another. A change in physical functioning might therefore have an unappreciated impact on the person's frame of mental outlook at any point in time. Psychosomatic manifestations of tension generated in the interpersonal sphere might be the reverse course of influence, whereby the individual may not be symbolizing a conflict so much as actually *behaving* in a conflicted manner. The clenched teeth of a person in a state of "inexpressible" rage may in time lead to pains in the jaw, headache, and generalized fatigue. By sensitizing the person to his or her bodily behavior we can make it possible for such new information to aid the person's ongoing life adjustment.

Researchers in this area of biofeedback use various electromechanical sensing devices to instruct the person in how to recognize heart rate, blood-pressure, GSR changes, vasodilation/constriction, and so on, with remarkable results. Once the person can sense a high or low heart rate it becomes possible to influence such changes "at will" (see our discussion above). Cardiac arrhythmia (B. Engel, 1973), hypertension (G. E. Schwartz, 1977), chronic anxiety (Raskin, Johnson, & Rodestvedt, 1973), migraine (Friar & Beatty, 1976), and certain gastrointestinal disorders (N. Miller, 1978) have been treated through conscious, intentional efforts to adjust to the biological signals being manufactured in the body. The control here is impressive. It has even been shown that subjects can regulate their blood pressure and heart rate *independently* of each other simply by intending that this come about, while practicing with the sensing devices attached (G. E. Schwartz, 1972).

The overwhelming importance of the internal psychic life of the human being, so different from anything found among other living organisms, and the intricately structured emotional interactions among human beings in a socially integrated society, cannot be slighted in dealing with the psychosomatic disorders, any more than can the physiological factors. We must always bear in mind the fact that, no matter how regressive a psychosomatic disorder may be, it occurs in an adult who has a lifetime of acquired experience and behavior built into his or her responsive equipment. As was true of the neuroses and psychoses, regression in psychosomatic disorders is never the same thing as a return to infancy. Infants do not have the background of a long life of secondary process experience, and very early in their life they show little differentiation in their emotional responses to frustration.

When a very young infant reacts to stress, he or she does so in a total way, using everything psychically available in discharging tension (Grinker, 1953). As time goes on, the infant *differentiates* the psychological or psychic from the physiological, and within the psychic systems makes those differentiations outlined in Chapter 2. Analysts maintain that when the adult psychosomatic patient regresses he or she loses the acquired reactions to the particular stress involved. In this sense, the patient suffers a *dedifferentiation* (Grinker & Robbins, 1954). The result is that he or she deals with excessive tension and anxiety in primitive ways. Hence, the psychosomatic disorders are interpreted as examples of deep regression with concurrent dedifferentiation to a *primitive visceral level,* at which emotional disturbances directly alter visceral functioning; if this alteration becomes chronic or recurrent, the result may be tissue or organ damage along the lines of Selye's GAS. The exact form of these primitive processes, which differs among different adults, is believed to have been determined by experiences during the first two years of life. They may then be used in meeting almost any form of adult stress, even though the psychosomatic response is wholly inappropriate in adulthood.

## "CHOICE" OF ORGAN OR SYSTEM

Why does one psychosomatic patient develop disturbances in one organ, system, or tissue, while another psychosomatic patient develops disturbances in another? Why, for example, does one emotionally disturbed person develop peptic ulcer, another essential hypertension, and a third a skin disorder? This is basically the same question as that of the "choice" of neurosis; and our answers are similar. We have some interesting leads but no definitive conclusions.

Some of the leads have already been mentioned in the preceding discussions of the various systems involved in psychosomatic disorder. There seems to be a preponderance of passive-dependent persons, who strive reactively to be self-sufficient, among patients with peptic ulcers, but some peptic ulcer patients feel angry and hostile inside. Bronchial asthma in some patients seems related to a cry for help or a need to confess to a mother figure, but it appears only in persons who are physiologically allergic. There is no reason to assume that every asthmatic patient belongs to this psychological group (Ittelson, Seidenberg, & Kutash, 1961).

In other words, we seem to be dealing with multiple factors in the "choice" of psychosomatic symptoms. Even among the most skeptical of experts there is a feeling that some as yet undiscovered relationship exists between constitution, personality type, infantile experiences, and some special organic involvement on the one hand, and the site of the psychosomatic disorder on the other (Kreitman, Pearce, & Ryle, 1966; Wittkower & Lipowski, 1966). No one has so far come up with a wholly satisfactory solution of the problem. Let us review briefly some of the attempts that have been made.

At one extreme are the hereditary, constitutional, and congenital sensitivity theories. No one doubts that newborns differ in their autonomic nervous system patterns and in their potentialities for vegetative response to stress. We pointed out in Chapter 2 that no two newborns are anatomically and physiologically identical, even identical twins. Such individual differences must include the internal organs, the skin, and the autonomic nervous system and its central nervous system representation. Even though newborns respond to stress with everything they have, there must be differences in their total patterns, both qualitatively and quantitatively.

The trouble with this kind of explanation is that it is too general, and so far it has been neither confirmed nor refuted. There seem to be familial tendencies to develop diabetes and essential hypertension, for example, quite apart from questions of psychosomatic disorder. As for peptic ulcer, it has been demonstrated among newborns, when longings for dependence and strivings for self-sufficiency obviously do not exist (Mirsky, 1953). Congenital differences in activity levels, sensitivity, and responsiveness have been found, but even these are not simple factors because they involve interaction with the mother. A mother begins to respond with her own characteristic behavior to her newborn infant from the very start. Her responses must be increasingly important factors in the situation as the infant begins to develop his or her first primitive discriminations. The hereditary, constitutional, and congenital sensitivity theories are really ways of saying, "The person was born that way." Obviously, this explanation cannot suffice for all that we know about psychopathological disorders.

Closely related to hereditary, constitutional, and congenital theories are those that try to explain the "choice" of psychosomatic disorder on the grounds of the *special weakness* or the *overuse* of a particular organ, tissue, or system. Some writers maintain that emotional disturbances injure an already inadequate, abnormal body part, one that has developed abnormally during intrauterine life or early infancy, or one that has been damaged by childhood infection, metabolic deficiency, or injury. Others point out that an originally normal body part might become the site of psychosomatic disorder because it has been a source of strength in early childhood and has therefore borne the brunt of emotional stress. Such hypotheses also can be neither confirmed nor refuted at present.

At the other extreme are *specificity theories,* which seek to account for the site of psychosomatic disorders in terms of the constellation of problems facing the adult patient and the specific pattern of his or her emotional response to the stress that these problems represent. No matter how diffuse the autonomic nervous system and the visceral responses may be, there are certainly marked differences in adult *experience* and *behavior* during fear, rage, and love. Moreover, there are marked individual differences in the *specific patterns* of fear, rage, and love among different adults. And among adults there are many who suppress their responses with the help of reaction-formation, so that while they experience at some level one kind of emotional expression, they also experience its opposite at another level.

Specificity theories seemed at first to be borne out by the detailed, prolonged study of individual patients. As more reports appeared and different investigators became interested in more and more kinds of psychosomatic disorder, the specificity theories as complete explanations came more and more into question, even among those who first proposed them (Mordkoff & Parsons, 1967). Some found their peptic ulcer patients to be passively dependent, for example, while others found them filled with rage, whether they longed for dependence or not. The complexity of emotional response in adults, the quick shifts from fear or passivity to fury and hostility, and the simultaneous presence of both dependent longings and hostile resentment over their frustrations, or even over having to be in a dependent position—all contribute to the inadequacy of the specificity theories to account for the facts now at our disposal (Buck & Hobbes, 1959).

A compromise between the extremes of congenital weakness and adult conflict has much to be said for it. This compromise begins with the observation that a young infant's emotional storms are not specific but seem to involve the whole organism at once. During the first two years of life, however, each child develops differentiations, within his or her emotional reactions as well as within behavioral expressions generally. This is normally one of an intimate mother-child relationship. The mother's reactions have to be considered as part of every interaction, and as important determinants of the child's emotional expression.

Even a child with normal emotional organization may suppress or distort his or her emotional discharge because of maternal anxiety, overconcern, indifference, or hostility. A child burdened from the moment of birth with general hyperactivity in emotional responsiveness, with an unusual degree of anxiety or fury, or with a specific tendency for one organ, one system, or one kind of tissue to take the burden of emotional expression, would be even more vulnerable to specific maternal reactions. During these first two years, as we saw in Chapter 2, oral dependent needs and later needs for self-assertion, which inevitably involve toilet-training crises, are of great intensity. The infant and very young child has little chance of finding relief in substitute expressions or activities that play so important a role in adult emotional control and channeling.

Dependency needs persist in everyone throughout life, as normal components of human love and human interdependence. So also do needs for self-assertion and independence, and the ability to be angry on occasion and express it. The capacities to be anxious, fearful, aggressive, trustful, and loving, under appropriate conditions, are likewise a normal aspect of human experience and behavior. The difficulty lies in achieving a good balance among these capacities and in releasing emotional expressions appropriately, within reasonable bounds.

We have several times called attention to the enormous enrichment of human life that comes from the ability to imagine, to plan, and to ruminate. We have said also that these telic human capacities expose the person to hazards that seem not to be the lot of other living organisms. A person can worry about dangers weeks or years before they come and about dangers that never come. A woman can become angry and resentful for weeks or months over something that she cannot express, or that she does express but still goes on generating a smoldering anger. She may not even realize at preconscious and conscious levels that she is angry, but her viscera go right on expressing the anger at unconscious levels. A man can remember and fantasy about past fears, past hates, past frustrations, and past guilt, ruminating over them and reviving as he does so all the visceral intensities that were part of the original experience. Only an organism reasoning "for the sake of" meanings (i.e., final causation) can be pictured behaving in this fashion.

The biological apparatus is therefore placed in a continuing state of activation, bearing up under a level of stress that is inappropriate because it is unnecessary. We have here a misuse and abuse of biological mechanisms designed to alert the organism, to put it on an emergency basis, or to prepare it to endure an unusual hardship by mobilizing its biological resources (Selye, 1976). The visceral systems that are involved in *long-lasting emotional expression* cannot be expected to function normally in performing their *nonemotional tasks.* The continually hyperactive, hypersecretory stomach, for example, is not nearly as good as a digestive organ as the stomach that increases its motility and secretion only during periods of hunger and the approach of food.

With more sophisticated theoretical constructions, and with further clinical studies carried out under controlled conditions, it may some day be possible to be more specific about psychosomatic disorders and to bring them under better therapeutic control. Biofeedback procedures are obviously very promising, and it is to be hoped that they will be underwritten by more properly teleological theories of mind in the future. Whether or not psychosomatic disorders can, as a group, be prevented in the future depends as much upon social and cultural factors as upon physiological ones, since individual modes of emotional experience and expression develop and differentiate within specific interpersonal relationships. A repressive social or familial milieu should result in more psychosomatic disorders than a freely expressive one.

## SUMMARY

Chapter 17 takes up *psychological factors affecting physical condition,* which is DSM-III terminology. We have employed the traditional term *psychosomatic* to describe these disorders. In a *psychosomatic disorder* the patient reacts to stress, tension, and anxiety with a direct physiological malfunction that may lead to irreversible organ or tissue damage. Unlike a neurotic disorder such as the conversion disorder, a psychosomatic illness does not typically involve symbolic expression of a conflict. There is no significant distortion of reality in the psychosomatic disorders. Psychosomatic illness stems from the fact that when the human body is exposed to stress that is internally or externally generated, there is a physiological alteration reflecting a "fight-or-flight" readiness that takes place.

Chapter 17 takes up Selye's *general adaptation syndrome* (GAS) in some detail. The GAS consists of three stages: *alarm reaction, resistance,* and *exhaustion.* Organisms reaching the third stage experience physical damage, resulting in pain and even death depending upon the nature of the stressor bringing on the alarm reaction. Selye was to find that psychological stress can trigger the GAS as well as physical stress (noxious agents) can. What is psychological *distress* (negative tension) for one person can prove to be *eustress* (positive tension) for another. The distressed person cannot effect a state of *homeostasis* (keeping an even keel) but must resort to *heterostasis* (increasing defensive biological efforts to carry on).

There are obvious adaptive features to the development of a psychosomatic disorder. The patient is able to substitute an actual physical illness for an intolerable psychological situation. To be sick is to be given an honorable excuse (secondary gain). Sometimes the illness protects the patient from developing a frank psychosis. Sometimes psychosomatic illness is added to the course of a strictly physical illness. It is important for the psychopathologist to seek expert assistance in the diagnosis and treatment of a disorder suspected to be psychosomatic.

Many psychosomatic disorders involve the *gastrointestinal tract*. Here we find the *peptic ulcer*, which occurs most frequently in the stomach and duodenum. The direct cause of such disorders is the digestion of gastric or duodenal tissue by acid digestive juices. Anything that increases gastric acidity or gastric mobility may indirectly perpetuate a peptic ulcer. Traditional analytical explanations of such patients have stressed an underlying dependency masked by assertive, independent-appearing behavior. The mechanism suggested here is *reaction-formation*. The ulcer is precipitated when an increase in dependency promptings threatens the person's conscious self-image.

Another gastrointestinal disorder is *obesity*. Analytical understanding of this craving to eat as an adult traces the pattern to a childhood in which maternal figures substituted the giving of food for the giving of love. The child was left with an irrational craving for food because his or her cravings for love had never been met except at a primitive feeding level. *Ulcerative colitis* is a serious gastrointestinal disorder in which the tissues of the colon become hyperactive as a result of chronic tension. The colon becomes fragile, so that minor traumata can produce hemorrhage and ulceration. Clinicians find that patients with ulcerative colitis present a façade of passivity, acquiescence, and blandness, but that behind this outer shell there is anger and hostility. The mothers of these patients are often described as fostering an inordinate degree of dependency by their domination, but also as being fundamentally hostile toward their offspring. The primary fixation point for the colitis patient is the anal level, with secondary fixations at the oral level.

The *respiratory* system is also important in psychosomatic illnesses. Emotion is readily expressed through alterations in breathing, so that tense individuals *hyperventilate*. The most important of the psychosomatic disorders of respiration appears in the form of *bronchial asthma*. This involves constriction of the bronchioles, which results in wheezing, a choking sensation, and gasping for breath. Research suggests that less than 50 percent of all cases of bronchial asthma are psychosomatic in origin. Traditional psychoanalytical explanations of the psychosomatic manifestations of asthma suggest that the patient is caught in a severe conflict of emotional ambivalence concerning his or her parents. There is a strong dependent attraction but also much hostility directed toward a parental figure. Some clinicians have interpreted the asthmatic attack as a suppressed cry for help from a mother figure, brought on when the patient faces loss or separation. The dependency is thus regressively manifested, in an infantile fashion.

Another systemic aspect of the body that is subject to psychosomatic illness is the *cardiovascular*. Once again, not all cardiovascular diseases are psychosomatic in origin. Along with changes in breathing, changes in heart rate and blood pressure are highly related to emotional expression. *Essential hypertension* refers to chronic high blood pressure in which no consistent organic etiology can be found. Some clinicians have found that psychosomatic patients with this disorder had previously released tension through temper outbursts but had changed suddenly to strict self-control. Sustained high levels of tension for any of a number of reasons have been found to be related to essential hypertension. *Coronary heart disease* has been linked to personality styles termed *Type A,* in which we observe people who are impatient, aggressive, highly competitive, ambitious, and very desirous of being in control of almost every situation. On the other hand, coronary disease is less likely in a *Type B* behavioral style, which is more relaxed, realistic, and oriented to cooperation in many of life's situations. In *migraine* due to psychosomatic involvement, the patient is likely to be described as perfectionistic, competitive, ambitious, orderly, and compulsive.

Various other forms of psychosomatic disorder are reviewed in Chapter 17. Once again, in all these examples we are stressing that not *every* person with the disorder is suffering from psychosomatic problems. Persons who develop *rheumatoid arthritis* have been described clinically as active, energetic achievers who do not express their feelings freely. The childhood background of such individuals probably includes a cold, emotionless mother and a passive, gentle father who allows the mother to dominate. *Skin rashes* of various types have been linked to psychosomatic problems in roughly half of the patients seen. The skin reflects the person's moods very directly, as in blushing and so forth. Psychodynamic factors are not difficult to find in such cases. Psychological stress has also been linked to certain endocrine disorders like *hyperthyroidism* and *diabetes mellitus.*

It seems clear that the person with a psychosomatic disorder neither forms a neurotic compromise nor seriously distorts reality as in the case of a psychotic. Instead he or she tries to discharge tensions and relieve anxiety through direct autonomic and visceral processes. Psychosomatic regression seems to be quite profound, to an almost undifferentiated phase of ego development. It is for this reason that the psychosomatic reaction is of such a primitive physiological character. In the case of a psychosomatic adult, rather than symbolizing a conflict in the manner of a conversion disorder, the person may actually be living out a conflict biologically. The clenched teeth of a person in a state of inexpressible rage may in time lead to pains in the jaw, headache, and generalized fatigue. Biofeedback research has lent support to such an interpretation.

Some analysts speak of a *dedifferentiation* in the personality system thanks to the deep regression of the psychosomatic patient. This reverses the usual course of *differentiation* in development, whereby the child learns to separate the physiological from the psychological aspects of experience. Hence, the psychosomatic disorders are interpreted as examples of deep regression with concurrent dedifferentiation to a *primitive visceral level,* at which emotional disturbances directly alter visceral functioning. If this alteration becomes chronic or recurrent, the result may be tissue or organ damage along the lines of Selye's GAS.

The final question taken up in Chapter 17 is why one patient selects "this" organ system and another "that" system through which to experience a psychosomatic disorder. Some theories stress a "special weakness" or "overuse" type of explanation. People break down at their biologically determined weakest "link" in the total body. Other so-called *specificity theories* try to account for the site of psychosomatic disorders in terms of the constellation of problems facing the adult patient and the specific pattern of his or her emotional response to the stress that these problems represent. Most experts believe that there is a mix of heredity, early life experience, and defensive pattern selected by the individual entering into the etiology of "a" psychosomatic symptom picture.

# 18

## *Organic Brain Syndromes and Mental Disorders*

The brain, even to a greater degree than most other organs, depends upon the maintenance of physiological equilibrium within a relatively narrow range if it is to operate effectively. Anything that seriously interferes with this equilibrium will reduce cerebral competence and may result in pathological behavior and experience. Among the common sources of disturbed equilibrium are marked changes in temperature, in water balance, and in the concentration of electrolytes in the brain, interference with the supply of oxygen and food materials, and interference with the removal of waste products from the brain. If the disturbance in the physiological equilibrium of the brain is sudden and severe — usually referred to as an *acute* disturbance — it may help precipitate one of the major organic brain syndromes. If, however, such a disturbance develops slowly — usually referred to as a *chronic* disturbance — it may be paralleled by some degree of compensatory adaptation, psychological as well as physiological. In this case there may be little impairment of cerebral function for a long time, even in some cases for a lifetime. Nevertheless, in many instances there comes a sudden halt to the compensatory adaptation, and the brain decompensates and precipitates an acute organic brain syndrome.

An *organic brain syndrome* is a recognizable pattern of symptoms which signify that there is brain involvement in the person's behavior without specifically indicating the nature of the illness or other causal agent. When the etiology of the organic brain syndrome is known, the pattern of symptoms is referred to as an *organic mental disorder*. In other words, the organic mental disorder diagnosis *specifies* the etiological factors that have brought about the clinical manifestation of an organic brain syndrome. For example, *senile dementia* (organic mental disorder of old age, due to atrophy of brain cells) can cause the elderly person so afflicted to become confused, suffer a memory loss, and eventually develop personality changes and a serious depression (all of which are symptoms of an organic brain syndrome). The DSM-III lists dozens of different organic mental disorders that can bring about a half-dozen or so common forms of organic brain syndromes. In Chapter 18 we shall review these major organic brain syndromes and point to some of the major organic mental disorders that have been shown to bring them about.

The interesting thing about organic brain syndromes is that not every person suffering from the same organic mental disorder experiences the same degree of loss in mental efficiency. The effectiveness of compensatory adaptation varies considerably from individual to individual under comparable circumstances, and even in the same person under different physiological and psychological stresses (L. Phillips & Zigler, 1961). In alcoholic intoxication, for example, if the dosage of alcohol is held constant, the same person will react differently when such conditions as food and water intake, work, rest, incentive, and social stimulation are varied. When all these conditions are controlled and the dosage held constant, it is still possible to demonstrate marked individual differences in susceptibility to alcoholic intoxication. As we shall see later, there is also wide diversity among different individuals, and in the same person under different conditions, when it comes to other forms of intoxication, to cardiovascular disturbances, head injury, brain disease, and brain deterioration.

Cerebral incompetence often develops gradually and progressively without an acute episode. Senile persons who develop the signs of cerebral incompetence mentioned above usually do so gradually, reflecting a progressive but undramatic decline in their adaptive capacity—until such point as an atrophy of the brain takes place (Cumming & Henry, 1961). But even here the picture is not clear, for when postmortem study of 104 patients ranging in age from sixty-five to ninety-four was done, there was *no* significant correlation between the amount of brain damage and clinical manifestations of an organic brain syndrome (Gal, 1959). In chronic disorders such as senile dementia, where there is a gradual loss in metabolic efficiency, it is no longer clear that the primary cause of the organic brain syndrome is biological (Terry & Wisniewski, 1974). On the other side of the coin, it is possible for human beings to have serious organic brain diseases that are misdiagnosed as functional (e.g., conversion) disorders (Geschwind, 1975; Malamud, 1975). The point seems to be that *both* organic and purely psychological factors always enter into the behavior of people, and hence we should never rely on a single explanation until every alternative is exhausted in the diagnostic process.

It is reassuring today to realize that there are many cases of head injury, brain infection, cerebral arteriosclerosis, and even senile deterioration in which the progress of cerebral incompetence may be halted or even reversed. Persons with brain damage are often able to adapt satisfactorily to life at home, or outside the home as a boarder, or even in an institution, provided that enough is expected of them to make full use of their potential but they are not exposed to more demand than they can meet. Studies combining such sensitive and understanding care with modern medications (e.g., Hydegine) have shown encouraging results in senile dementia (Gaitz, Varner, & Overall, 1977). Institutional life that is exclusively custodial and not planned well is usually very negative as regards prognosis for the person with brain damage. The lack of freedom and privacy, the monotony and boredom, the loss of friends, and the sense of having been deserted are enough in themselves to lead to an irreversible deterioration.

Today it is generally recognized that cerebral incompetence, unless it is sudden and severe or profound and inclusive, need not necessarily lead to outspoken psychopathology. When it does, there are usually other factors to be considered. On the one hand, brain injury, infection, or intoxication may help precipitate psychopathology that becomes chronic, or grows progressively worse, even though meanwhile there has been complete recovery from the cellular effects of the cerebral damage. On the other hand, severe neurotic or psychotic reactions may develop during senile deterioration, for example, and then clear up without a corresponding improvement in the senile picture (Stein, Vidich, & White, 1960).

It is also recognized today that many neurotic and psychotic reactions appearing in the wake of cerebral incompetence are not actually *organic mental disorders* but are the reactions of sick or injured persons to the fact or the consequences of being sick or injured. In this sense they are not fundamentally different from neurotic and psychotic reactions to illness or injury involving other parts of the body. Thus, for example, a person may develop an *anxiety disorder* to having broken his or her hand. Another may react with an *agitated depression* or with *mania* to attacks of dizziness and fainting, whether these attacks result from cardiac disease or from cerebral arteriosclerosis. A third may develop a *conversion disorder* following a head injury for the same reasons that he or she might have developed it following a back injury.

## The Organic Brain Syndromes

We shall now survey and provide examples of the major forms of organic brain syndromes. Once again, these are constellations of symptoms that can be seen to occur in more than one type of organic mental disorder. What they have in common is not their etiology but the fact that they are obviously being mediated by a dysfunction in the brain.

### DELIRIUM

*Delirium* refers to a *clouded state of consciousness* in which the person has difficulty sustaining attention to both external and internal stimuli, experiences sensory misperceptions, and has a disordered stream of thought. In its more acute manifestations, delirium is characterized by gross distortions of experience, defective memory, and both hallucinations and delusions. Delirious patients initially strike an observer as being restless, irritable, and confused. Their attention is difficult to get and to hold; they seem uncertain as to their whereabouts and the identity of persons and objects around them; their talk becomes rambling or groping, and they misspeak, slur, and mispronounce words. At night they sleep fitfully and awaken often with a start. They complain of weird and terrifying dreams and of dreamlike hypnagogic hallucinations when they shut their eyes. They begin to show obvious defects in recent memory and immediate recall, but their remote memory may at first be relatively little affected.

As the delirium progresses, increasing signs of confusion and disorientation appear. The patient now misidentifies persons and objects and grossly misinterprets what is going on in the surrounding environment. Tremors may appear, particularly in the fingers, tongue, and facial muscles of the patient. Ataxia (loss of muscle coordination) may develop, with marked reflexive alterations and a profusion of perspiration taking place. The patient then grows more and more restless and sleepless, hallucinating now with his or her eyes wide open, in the daytime as well as at night.

Sometimes delirious patients speak to others as though they were different people with different functions. Sometimes these patients listen and talk to hallucinated persons in hallucinated settings. Occasionally, they will get up and attempt to go out in response to imagined demands made upon them or to imagined threats made against them. Delirious patients often engage in confused, fragmentary activities that resemble their usual occupation or some habitual mode of entertainment. When interfered with or restrained, they may quiet down for a time, or they may respond with angry or frightened combative behavior, which is sometimes dangerous to the patient or to others.

The acute delirious syndrome may last a few hours or persist for days or weeks, and in exceptional cases for many months. It is not rare for a person in the midst of a delirium to clear up suddenly for a brief period and then lapse into as great confusion as ever. This transient clearing up is referred to as a *lucid interval.*

> An acutely delirious elderly man suddenly improved one afternoon and began asking for information as to where he was and what had happened to him. He conversed connectedly with the nurse and the physician, discussed persons and places of mutual interest, described accurately a previous visit to another division of the hospital, and appeared to understand his present situation. His speech was a little slow, there was some groping for words, and there were occasional long silences; but otherwise there was nothing unusual in his behavior. By evening, however, this man's talk was becoming less adequate, and by night he was again acutely delirious. His delirium had followed an arteriosclerotic cerebral accident or "stroke." He made a partial recovery after four months of delirium, but less than a year later death came as the result of a second cerebral accident.

Recovery from acute delirium may be a gradual affair, with progressive improvement in cerebral competence, or it may occur rapidly, following a deep sleep, as in many cases of febrile disease. If, on the other hand, the acutely incompetent brain becomes still more physiologically incompetent, the patient typically becomes less and less reactive. Noisy restlessness and insomnia give way to drowsiness and torpor, with occasional tossing about. Movements are slower, more aimless, and disjunctive. Speech becomes fragmentary, incoherent, and muttering. The patient may then become at first difficult to arouse and to keep aroused (*stupor*), and later on impossible to arouse (*coma*). In the moribund patient deepening stupor and coma are the usual preludes to death. The patient who recovers from a comatose state returns to normal as a rule by way of stupor. The stuporous patient, as he or she improves, sometimes passes through a delirious phase on the road to recovery.

When cerebral incompetence occurs suddenly, as in cases of head injury, cerebral hemorrhage, blood loss, massive infection, or overwhelming intoxication, the comatose state may be almost instantaneously induced. Persons recovering from abruptly induced coma sometimes also pass through a delirious syndrome, after first passing through a stuporous phase.

> A young adult woman who had sustained a severe head injury in an automobile accident spent several days in profound coma. Then as she improved, she became intermittently active enough to be called stuporous. Finally she developed a typical acute delirium that lasted several weeks. Marked defects in orientation and recall persisted throughout most of the delirious period, but the ultimate recovery was complete, with no defects that could be detected on clinical examination.

In acute delirium we see what happens to human behavior and experience when the body's chief organ of integration, the brain, suffers from an acute physiological disruption of function. We shall now discuss the overt manifestations of behavioral disorganization under four major categories: (1) *incoordination,* (2) *interpenetration,* (3) *fragmentation,* and (4) *overinclusion.* These dynamic factors in delirium are not to be thought of as mutually exclusive categories, but merely as four convenient ways of describing the same process. None of these manifestations of brain dysfunction are limited to delirium. It is only their combination with gross disorientation, memory defect, delusions, and hallucinations that is specific to delirium.

*Incoordination.* Incoordination of behavior results from the interference of disruptive tensions and movements that break up normal timing and harmony (*synergy*) of behavior. Unsteadiness and tremor destroy the precision of movements. Uncoordinated patients overreach, underreach, and misdirect their movements (Ferraro, 1959). If disorganization of behavior becomes severe, these patients can no longer stand, walk, or manipulate objects adequately. They may sway, stagger, misstep, fumble, and even lurch or fall to the ground. In speech and thinking there are decided incoordinations as well. Speech becomes slurred, disjointed, and unsteady. Patients mispronounce and misspeak. They may be unable to recall familiar words and names. They give signs that their thinking changes its normal pace, losing direction and becoming both undependable and unpredictable. Often it is the loss of coordinated speech and thinking that appears earliest and most disturbs the patient's sense of well-being.

*Interpenetration.* In interpenetration an intrusive movement, word, or thought appears inappropriately in some ongoing activity. In normal life many of the absurd actions performed by preoccupied persons are examples of interpenetration. A preoccupied man may go to a closet to get a jacket, only to find that he has put on his hat as though he were going out. The concept of interpenetration was originally formulated in relation to speech and thinking (Cameron, 1959a), and it is in talking and thinking that we encounter the most significant examples from everyday life. Freud's early and systematic account of slips of the tongue and pen (1901/1960a) includes the interpenetration of preconscious and conscious thought and action by products of unconscious themes. In delirium, as we shall see in a moment, the behavioral disorganization is compounded because of the invasion of preconscious and conscious processes by derivatives of unconscious primary processes.

*Fragmentation.* Fragmentation refers to the appearance of discontinuous and abortive behavior, to the sudden termination of a theme begun, often followed by a silence or by something quite unrelated. Surprise, shock, and the demands of competing stimulation under stress may fragment behavior in normal persons. In delirium and in severe schizophrenic regression we find the most dramatic examples of fragmentation, in which sometimes no two successive actions or thoughts seem related to one another. Fragmentation also appears in delirious states when activity and thinking become repetitive, perseverative, and marked by stereotypy. This phenomenon seems often to represent an unsuccessful attempt to control behavior by limiting it and by fixating on some one aspect of it. In somewhat the same way, frightened normal people sometimes stare at something, hang on to something, or repeat a meaningless action that may not be relevant to their anxiety but that nevertheless serves as an anchor in their sea of emotional turmoil. The delirious patient, who is usually frightened by the nightmarish experience with a world that seems to have lost its stability, may utilize repetition, perseveration, and stereotypy as his or her form of anchorage (Goldstein, 1939, 1948).

*Overinclusion.* Overinclusion represents a failure to limit the number and kind of simultaneous excitants to a relatively few coherent ones. The concept of *overinclusion* was originally developed in relation to schizophrenic thinking, and we have already defined it and given a generous sample of it in Chapter 14 (see p. 436). It has since then been extended to include perceptual and cognitive failure in other disorders (Payne, 1961). In delirium, overinclusion results not only from the invasion of preconscious and conscious organizations by primary processes and previously unconscious fantasy, but also from the loss of perceptual and cognitive structure, which the delirious brain cannot sustain. The latter defect gives rise to the gross disorientation that is specific for delirium but not for schizophrenia. The schizophrenic confuses fantasy and fact, mixes primary process material together, hallucinates, and has delusions; but in spite of all this the schizophrenic patient knows where he or she is and who the people are in the immediate environment. There may be a misidentification of strangers as someone known, but the schizophrenic does not typically suffer the utter confusion in relation to external reality that typifies acute delirium.

If we now supplement the overt manifestations of delirium, as just described, by a consideration of the delirious person's subjective experience, we can see at once that we are dealing with disturbances of cerebral competence. To the delirious patient, surroundings unaccountably lose their stability. Objects come and go unexpectedly. People seem to be doing things that are strange, inexplicable, inappropriate, and disconnected. People and things often appear distorted in weird ways that lie entirely outside the delirious person's previous experience with waking adult life. The gross disturbances in perception may destroy normal perspectives, proportions, and reality relationships in space and time. Little things may appear enormous and large things very small. Shapes and spatial organizations undergo all kinds of distortion. Sounds are misidentified, misunderstood, and located incorrectly. Skin sensations give rise to all kinds of delusions and hallucinations. Taste and smell may also be involved in strange ways. The gross disturbances in cognition, if these can be separated from perception, lead to all kinds of misinterpretation and misidentification. They render it impossible for the delirious patient to construct an intelligible whole out of his or her fragmented experience.

Acute delirium is sometimes compared to ordinary dreaming, in which the normal person is grossly disoriented, witnesses kaleidoscopic and often wholly unintelligible changes, experiences perceptual and cognitive distortions, and suffers from an invasion of his or her preconscious thinking by unconscious and primary process products. The comparison in some respects is apt. The sleeping person who is dreaming has regressed to a level of activity at which repression is weak. Denial, projection, and introjection may perform primitive defensive functions, primary process thinking rules, and ego or self boundaries dissolve. There is one great difference between delirium and the dream. This is that the normal person manages to dream by excluding most of his or her external stimulation, by entering into a state of perceptual isolation. The absence of nearly all external stimulation during sleep greatly simplifies the situation for the dreamer. Even a sleepwalker is much better organized with regard to this environment than an acutely delirious person.

Hallucinations and delusions may develop at first in acute delirium under conditions similar to those of ordinary dreaming. In fact, a delirium may be preceded by terrifying dreams. As cerebral incompetence increases, however, hallucinatory and delusional experiences begin to trouble the patient in the borderline state between waking and sleeping. The patient may be afraid to close his or her eyes for a period of time. Eventually, with growing instability of perceptual and cognitive structures, the boundaries between external and internal reality melt, and daydreams and previously unconscious fantasies mingle with the shifting, unstable perceptual and cognitive processes to form a confused and confusing mass of unintelligible experience.

*Freud at age eighty-two, perusing a page of manuscript from* Moses and Monotheism *after having successfully escaped from Nazi-occupied Austria. This photograph was taken in July 1938 in England.*

Delirious experience is nearly always frightening. The delirious person is typically apprehensive, insecure, and fearful. This is in part because of the loss of perceptual and cognitive stability, the loss of one's familiar world, with its familiar organization and its predictable happenings. We all depend upon the stability of our surroundings for our feelings of security. If we move to unfamiliar surroundings, where we do not know what to expect and cannot understand what is going on, we need all the cerebral competence we can muster to cope with the strange situation. The delirious person is like a normal person who has been dropped into a weird environment not only without warning but also without the cerebral competence to cope with it.

In addition to perceptual and cognitive instability, the delirious person must also cope with a wholesale eruption of previously unconscious fantasies, with an invasion by primary process thinking, and with the reconstructions of external reality that his or her delusions and hallucinations have manufactured. The specific fears, suspicions, fantasies, needs, and defenses appearing in a delirious picture belong, of course, to the specific personality organization of the individual patient. One patient may enact business concerns, while another may indulge in domestic preoccupations. Usually the patient's fears, fantasies, conflicts, wishes, and perplexities appear in more or less disconnected, dreamlike episodes. Occasionally, as we shall see, these episodes lead to psychopathology, which may outlast by weeks, months, or even years the signs of actual cerebral incompetence.

The memory deficits characteristic of acute delirium are of complex origin. Poor recall of recent events may be due to their having occurred during early phases of the delirium, when cerebral incompetence was already present. Memory deficits may also be a consequence of the fragmentation, discontinuity, and overinclusion in delirious perception and cognition. In addition, the delirious person experiences direct products of primary processes, which in themselves are extremely difficult for even the best-organized and most effective person to remember. Following their recovery, formerly delirious persons may be unable to fit many events that are only partially recalled into their now normal organizations; these events seem weird and unnatural, like the manifest dreams of normal persons. There are often islands of relatively good recall that probably correspond to periods of relatively high cerebral competence during the fluctuations of the delirium.

## DEMENTIA

Dementia refers to a *loss of intellectual abilities* of sufficient severity to interfere with social or occupational patterns of behavior. Memory, judgment, and abstract thought are all adversely affected. Chronic brain disorders are the result of relatively permanent, irreversible, diffuse brain damage. If the pathological process that underlies the brain damage is arrested, there will still remain a certain amount of brain defect. The rest of the brain will then have to function as best it can in relation to this residual damage. The residual defect may be so slight as to have little practical importance for the recovered patient. On the other hand, it may be so great as to interfere more or less permanently with normal orientation, memory, perception, cognition, and behavioral actions.

DSM-III emphasizes that dementia may be progressive, static, or remitting. Sometimes it is reversible when the underlying cause (organic mental disorder) is curable. We shall focus on the progressive form of dementia for didactic purposes. Most chronic brain diseases are progressive rather than stationary, and some of these diseases cause the patients to lead an almost vegetative existence. In the course of such progression there may develop a great deal of psychopathology, that is, pathology of activity and of experience, or there may develop very little psychopathology until the brain has undergone considerable destruction. In what follows we shall look at the course of progressive cerebral incompetence to get some conception of the various levels at which an arrested brain disorder may leave a patient stranded.

*Progressive Dementia.* Syndromes of progressive dementia are characterized by decreasing adaptiveness, increasing loss of memory and cognitive grasp, and increasing signs of cerebral pathology. These defects may develop slowly and insidiously, running a course of gradual decline over a period of years and sometimes of decades. Many cases that begin with a slow and insidious development are suddenly interrupted by a convulsion, after which the symptoms of cerebral incompetence are generally more pronounced and the decline more rapid. Still other cases have an abrupt onset with transient confusion, acute delirium, or a convulsion, followed by chronic progressive cerebral incompetence and usually punctuated by convulsive episodes. Temporary remissions are not unusual. These occasionally last a few months, and rarely, a few years. Regardless of the type of onset or the occurrence of remissions, the course of progressive dementia is downhill. Some patients reach an almost vegetative level of existence before they die, their behavior reduced to little more than a few stereotyped acts, with perhaps a phrase or two uttered entirely out of context.

> An aged patient did nothing but sit and rock all day, wetting and soiling herself and having to be fed, washed, dressed, and undressed as though she were a baby. No matter what was said to her, whether it was a kind greeting or a threat, she always replied, "Yes, darling," "Why, of course, darling," or "Certainly, darling."

In progressive dementia there is considerable variability in the order of appearance and the prominence of different symptoms, as well as in what changes are first noticed. *The first observed change is usually a memory defect or some confusion with regard to orientation.* The patient becomes increasingly forgetful. A previously competent man cannot remember where he has left or hidden personal belongings; he does not recall having met recent acquaintances before; he forgets engagements, whether they are recreational or in the line of duty. He tends to repeat himself, telling the same thing over and over to the same person and with the same detail. He cannot learn new procedures and he becomes easily confused in a new environment.

> A business executive in late middle life was first recognized as incompetent by his family when he could not find his way back to the hotel at an unfamiliar summer resort. Each day he would drive back from the beach and pass the hotel without recognizing it, in spite of the family's protests. He was a pleasant man and took the whole situation good-naturedly as a joke. The family, however, discussed his situation with his business associates and discovered that he had been showing poor judgment and defective memory for at least a year before this vacation. Following his retirement he had a brief delirious episode in which he suffered from delusions and hallucinations of a frightening character. For this he was hospitalized. He was able to leave the hospital for home after a few weeks of care and protection, but although he was still good-natured and cheerful, he had severe defects in memory and orientation. His prognosis was regarded as poor.

The loss in recent memory is often paralleled by a progressive change in character. Thus, a woman with a senile or arteriosclerotic brain may seem a "changed person," at first only to her close friends and relatives, but eventually to everyone. She may become careless of her appearance and react with indifference, anger, joviality, or tears to situations that would not have evoked these reactions before. She may show a degree of instability and unpredictability quite foreign to her habitual behavior. A person with progressive dementia may begin to exhibit striking ineptitude in business, social, or domestic matters, squandering or giving away property and dissipating earnings by glaringly injudicious spending.

> An unusually able, shrewd manufacturer suffered a stroke in late middle life which left him with muscular weakness on one side of his body. His previously well-controlled aggression now appeared in an attempt to force his industrial competitor to sell out to him at a price far above the market value of the rival concern. Only the ethical restraint of the competitor, who realized what the situation was, saved the patient and his family from financial ruin.

Some persons, before their cerebral incompetence is realized, lose the respect and affection of their friends and relatives by becoming entangled in a sexual liaison of an inexplicable character or by commiting a sex offense in relation to minors. An inability to include the probable consequences and implications of an act as controlling factors is often one of the most striking defects in progressive cerebral incompetence, whether the incompetence is of toxic, traumatic, infective, arteriosclerotic, or senile origin. A person may thus appear to be in good contact with the immediate environment while he or she is, at the same time, grossly defective with respect to past training and future probabilities. This involves, of course, the whole question of responsibility, legal and moral, in the person suffering from cerebral decline.

*Dynamic Background of Progressive Dementia.* The syndromes of slowly or relatively slowly developing progressive cerebral incompetence give examples of the gradual deterioration of the brain as an organ. The slowness of the pathological process when there is no stormy incident allows for some compensatory adaptation, physiological as well as psychological, which varies from person to person. The business executive who could not find his way back to a summer resort hotel is an example of fairly good adaptive compensation, since he had been carrying on well at home for at least a year after his defects were noticed in the more exacting situations in his business.

Because of the compensatory adaptation we do not see for a long time the overt manifestations of behavioral disorganization that characterize cerebral incompetence with an acute onset or with an acute episode. Thus incoordination, interpenetration, fragmentation, and overinclusion, so obvious in acute delirium, may not appear in chronically progressive cases until a low level of decline has been reached, unless of course the slow decline is interrupted by an acute attack. The most successful adaptations usually occur in persons who voluntarily limit the scope of their activities as they deteriorate and in those who remain good-natured and complacent. The aggressive, irritable person, like the manufacturer who suffered a stroke, is not likely to hide his or her defects for long.

Compensatory adaptation probably depends upon the physiological flexibility of cerebral function, upon the physiological youth of undamaged parts, and perhaps upon vicarious activities of undamaged areas that are little used in ordinary life. Since outspoken delusions and hallucinations do not occur for a long time, or do not occur at all, in slowly progressive cerebral incompetence, the major requirements for successful adaptation are *compensations* for the inevitable memory losses, for the inability to carry out new and complex tasks, and for the disturbances of orientation—all of which are interrelated. Memory losses may be concealed by circumlocution; something forgotten is referred to in a roundabout way. They are also overcome by getting other people to supply the forgotten link. Some persons use *confabulation*, that is, they substitute imaginary happenings ("lies") for the forgotten ones, a process closely related to delusion and to what younger people do when they find that they cannot explain their behavior or their attitudes. The dislike many aging persons show for new ways and new adventures is often sparked by their difficulties in orientation and in handling new and complex situations. *Conservatism* is one expression of this; *seclusion* is another. Both are defensive in function, and both may to a certain extent be necessary for the preservation of ego integration.

Ultimately progressive dementia leads, with few exceptions, to deterioration that cannot be compensated for. Progressively impaired retentivity and recall make a person less and less able to participate in the life around him or her. The person's interest flags with the decreasing span of attention and increasing sense of fatigue in just trying to keep up with experience. There is a tendency to fall back upon repetitive reminiscences because the flow of current events can no longer be kept up with. Remote memory at first suffers much less than recent memory, but eventually it also becomes hopelessly inadequate. The decreasing effectiveness of retentivity and recall isolates the person from what is going on in the immediate environment. It may also promote disorientation. Present happenings are relocated in the daily routines of the person's earlier years, which are still remembered and clung to at all costs.

> An institutionalized woman of eighty-three always gave her age as eighteen or nineteen. If questioned as to her whereabouts she would just say that she was resting awhile before going on home. Almost every evening on rounds she would ask if she could "stay in this hotel tonight," often adding that she had started out too late to get home before dark. She usually lamented, in a dignified way, her inability to help her father with the chores of closing the family business that evening. When asked her father's age, however, she often said, "Oh, he's been dead many years," apparently forgetting what she had said about helping him.

When a patient's recall of remote as well as of recent events grows fragmentary, when circumlocution fails and verbal confabulations no longer fill in the gaps, the continuity of his or her behavior virtually disappears. Certain relatively simple automatized sequences remain, such as walking, getting up and sitting or lying down, chewing, and sucking. Often regression revives some more or less infantile patterns. Increased emotional lability (*emotional incontinence*) is common. It varies from mere exaggeration and perseveration of normal emotional expression to inappropriate as well as uncontrollable laughing, crying, or shouting.

Disturbances of language and thinking are particularly detrimental. Normally we all depend upon these functions, not only for communication with others but also as points of reference in our own ongoing behavior. Their disturbance interferes with communication, thus further isolating and desocializing the patient who can no longer represent external, somatic, and internal reality in a meaningful way based upon secondary processes.

As the brain deteriorates as an organ, ego disintegration becomes inevitable. In the end, even though patients may avoid an acute delirium, their defensive functions deteriorate along with their adaptive ones, and they undergo an irreversible regression. Previously unconscious fantasies, conflicts, wishes, and impulses may come to the fore in undisguised forms, making the patient unpredictable and primitive. Why this kind of thing should happen early in some cases of progressive cerebral dementia and not in others we do not know.

## AMNESIC SYNDROME AND ORGANIC HALLUCINOSIS

Delirium and dementia are obviously among the most important forms of the organic brain syndromes, and their impact on the person's behavior is global. We move on now to a more specific or selective form of organic brain syndrome. Also, the clouding of consciousness typical of delirium is not to be seen in the syndromes we shall now consider. The first is an *amnesic syndrome,* in which the person's long-term or short-term memory is adversely affected even as his or her state of consciousness remains fairly normal (i.e., it is not clouded). Such a person cannot recall the essentials of a short paragraph of information after five minutes have passed. Nor can he or she retain long-term information such as birthplace, schooling, work history, major historical events, names of presidents, and so forth. However, as in cases we have discussed above, there is more ability to retain long-term than short-term information. Highly personal events occurring a decade or more before the examination may be recalled well (such as marriage, hospitalization, or the birth of a child). So-called immediate memory, as in repeating three or four numbers presented at one-second intervals, is *not* impaired in the amnesic syndrome.

In the *organic hallucinosis* form of organic brain syndrome there are persistent or recurrent hallucinations that occur in a normal state of consciousness (again, nonclouded); moreover, these hallucinations are attributable to a specific organic factor. When the etiological agent is a substance, the term *organic* is dropped and the name of the substance is substituted. For example, if the hallucinations are traceable to the ingestion of alcohol, the person would be diagnosed as suffering from *alcohol hallucinosis*. Different substances induce different types of hallucination; hallucinogens bring on visual forms and alcohol auditory forms of hallucinations. The affected individual may be aware that his or her hallucinations are not real, or there may be a delusional belief that the sights or sounds are real. Extended delusional systems are not typical of this disorder. The delusional belief is focused upon the content of the hallucination.

## ORGANIC AFFECTIVE, DELUSIONAL, AND PERSONALITY SYNDROMES

We continue now with organic brain syndromes reflecting a distinctive change in mood or personality but lacking in delirium or dementia. An *organic affective syndrome* obtains when a disturbance in mood resembling either a manic episode or a major depressive episode occurs because of a specifiable organic influence. The diagnosis is not made if there is a clouded consciousness (delirium) or significant loss of intellectual abilities (dementia). This disorder is frequently noted in toxic infections due to various drugs, as well as to endocrine diseases. It is the knowledge of a specific toxic cause or disease process that enables a differential diagnosis to be made vis à vis the affective disorders.

An *organic delusional syndrome* obtains when the person has delusions in a normal state of consciousness (nondelirious) that are due to a specific organic factor. If delirium or dementia are present this diagnosis is not made. It is also common for a delusion to appear in organic hallucinosis, but as we noted above, in this case the focus is on the hallucinated material. In organic delusional syndromes the most common form of delusion is persecutory. Clinicians have found that amphetamine abuse can cause a highly systematized paranoid delusion to be framed by the abuser. Some patients with cerebral lesions develop the delusion that a limb of their body is missing. Hallucinations may be present in the organic delusional syndrome, but they are not the predominant feature of the symptom picture. A dysphoric mood is common in this disorder.

As we have seen, there are personality changes in organic brain syndromes like delirium or dementia. However, when there is marked change in personality that does not fit into such diagnoses, DSM-III permits a unique diagnosis of *organic personality syndrome*. The main idea here is that the person undergoes noticeable changes in style of behavior following a brain injury or disease process. The changes noted are invariably in a negative direction. The person may no longer care about the consequences of his or her behavior, reflect poor social judgment, and "fly off the handle" at slight provocation. Sexual indiscretions may be engaged in by someone who to that point in life was completely and maturely proper. Another pattern is a loss of interest in hobbies and activities that were previously very attractive. Some experts believe that frontal-lobe damage results in such personality changes, although the temporal lobe is also implicated (Blumer & Benson, 1975; Hecaen & Albert, 1975). Not infrequently, suspiciousness and paranoid ideation predominate in an organic personality syndrome.

## INTOXICATION AND WITHDRAWAL

The final organic brain syndromes that we shall briefly mention refer specifically to aspects of drug ingestion. Thus, *intoxication* is an organic brain syndrome resulting in maladaptive behavior due to the recent use and presence in the body of a specific substance. Although the specific clinical picture is determined by the nature of the substance used (amphetamine, alcohol, marijuana, etc.), the most common changes involve *disturbances of perception, wakefulness, attention, thinking, judgment, emotional control, and psychomotor behavior.* DSM-III stresses the *maladaptive* aspects of intoxication. Hence, recreational use of a substance like alcohol, in which loquacity, euphoria, and slurred speech result is *not* a psychiatric form of intoxication unless the person reflects impaired judgment, interpersonal difficulties (fights, arguments), poor job performance, and a failure to meet responsibilities.

Finally, we must recognize that *withdrawal* is the development of a substance-specific syndrome following the cessation of or reduction of the intoxicating substance. We have already discussed withdrawal in some detail in Chapter 15, and shall not go over familiar ground. The main challenge in diagnosis is to avoid confounding withdrawal with other organic brain syndromes such as delirium, organic hallucinosis, or organic affective syndrome. We move next to a consideration of some of the major forms of organic mental disorders.

## Organic Mental Disorders

No one needs to be reminded that psychopathology sometimes develops in persons who at the time show signs of cerebral incompetence, as well as in persons whose brains appear to be functioning normally. What does deserve to be emphasized is that the mere presence of relative cerebral incompetence need not account for the presence of psychopathology. The clinician often finds that cerebral incompetence, although present, plays an insignificant part in the psychopathology. Patients in these cases do not differ significantly, either from the pattern of their reaction or in the ease with which they react, from patients exposed to similar stresses and strains who give no evidence of cerebral incompetence. When the consequences of brain disorder contribute significantly to psychopathology—that is, to neurotic and psychotic reactions, to psychosomatic disorders and personality changes—they may do so in one of several ways.

A person may develop pathological self-reactions to behavior resulting from his or her own cerebral incompetence. Thus, during an acute delirium a patient's delusional and hallucinatory experiences may arouse such intense anxiety and lead to so much ego disintegration that a schizophrenic disorganization occurs or a manic or depressive illness results, as we shall see in the section on acute intoxication.

Ego disintegration also contributes to the precipitation of psychopathology in acute and chronic progressive dementia. Suppose, for example, that an individual who for decades has been successfully dealing with serious conflicts and unacceptable impulses by means of repression and other defensive measures develops dementia. A significant reduction in cerebral competence is likely to result in failure of ego defenses and in the invasion of preconscious and conscious organizations by previously unconscious primary process material. The heightened tension and anxiety that follow such an invasion lead to psychopathology. The exact character of the psychopathology will correspond to the individual's dominant personality trends.

The point here is that we should not *reduce* the personality "to" the brain per se. The brain is not a "command central," which functions in strictly material- and efficient-cause fashion to bring about mental actions or personality patterns depending upon the cybernetic "working order" of its parts (see Chapter 1, p. 6). Modern research on the brain suggests that it is anything but a model of cybernetic parsimony. It is noteworthy that two of the leading experts on brain functioning in modern times—John C. Eccles and Wilder Penfield—have proposed theories of brain function in which a self or personal agent is postulated. Eccles points out that there are basically two kinds of neurons operational in the brain, one that forms excitatory synapses and one that forms inhibitory synapses (Popper & Eccles, 1977, p. 232). The corpus callosum has fibers joining brain halves that are in a mirror-image relationship with each other (ibid., p. 241; see also Sperry, 1977). The prefrontal lobes, often cited as important to higher brain functions, have been shown to be in a reciprocal relationship with the limbic system (Popper & Eccles, 1977, p. 349).

The fundamental organization of nerve fibers in the brain is modular, in which up to ten thousand nerve cells are locked together by mutual connectives. Each of these modules takes electrical power from its neighbor, given only the chance to be activated. Thus, Eccles states, "We think the nervous system always works by conflict—in this case by conflicts between each module and the adjacent modules" (ibid., p. 243). Finally, Eccles suggests that there is a two-way communication between certain modules of the brain and what he has termed the *self-conscious mind* (ibid., p. 285). Eccles therefore theorizes in a clearly teleological manner to suggest that there is in human behavior a selecting, evaluating, and judging capacity that is something *other than* and *irreducible to* "brain mechanics," as follows: "The self-conscious mind is always as it were working backwards and forwards, and we could even say that in all of its perceptual processes it is moulding or modifying the modular activities in the brain in order to get back from them what it wants [memories, etc.]" (p. 514).

Penfield's equally teleological theory (1975) holds that there are two brain mechanisms, a higher and a lower. The highest brain mechanism has direct contact with the temporal lobes and the prefrontal areas of the cerebral cortex. These areas evolved more recently than the older motor and sensory areas of the diencephalon. The older cortex has a cybernetic, computerlike quality about its functioning. This is where information gleaned from past life is most probably stored. But the interpretation given to such stored information as knowledge is framed by the higher brain mechanism, which is directed by a totally different energy source—the mind! The mind acts independently of the brain in the same way that a human programmer acts independently of the computer he or she uses to organize data and extract information from. The mind has no memory, relying instead on the computerlike brain. Summing up, Penfield says: "A man's mind, one might say, is the person. He walks about the world, depending always upon his private computer, which he programs continuously to suit his ever-changing purposes and interest" (ibid., p. 61).

Therefore, when we speak of brain disorder on the one hand and psycho-pathological aspects of behavior on the other, we are merely recognizing such modern theories of brain function as those of Eccles and Penfield. Some people develop an organic mental disorder because they—their "selves" or "persons"—cannot recognize and accept their diminished cerebral competence. It is this inability that leads patients to attempt things of which they are no longer capable, as in the case of the competitive manufacturer who had suffered a stroke, and to resist aggressively the limitations others attempt to impose upon them. One sees obvious examples in the irritable, self-assertive excitement of patients with cerebral intoxication or cerebral infection. The problem, however, is socially far more important and therapeutically more challenging in the maladaptations that develop among the millions of people whose cerebral incompetence progresses slowly. In aging persons, for example, an inability to recognize and accept their own decline in competence, when the decline is inexorable but slow, often culminates in psychopathology that is at least potentially preventable.

An important challenging problem is also presented by those persons who cannot accept their changed social status. Some of them recognize and accept their diminished adequacy, but they cannot adapt to their reduced security and prestige. They cannot adapt to the neglect and prejudices other people express or to the restrictions placed upon their range of opportunity and their interests. Persons whose abilities have declined because of cerebral intoxication, injury, infection, or deterioration need emotional acceptance and emotional support. They need the prestige and the social status to which they have been accustomed. But because they are inefficient and a social burden, we tend to neglect and depreciate persons with cerebral incompetence. By so doing we give them a standing invitation to develop psychopathology, which then further incapacitates them and makes them a still greater social burden.

In order to illustrate more specifically the precipitation of psychopathology in persons with cerebral incompetence we have selected four common and important organic mental disorders. (1) *Acute intoxication* will introduce us once more to the psychopathology of the delirious patient. (2) *Head injury* represents the physically traumatic basis of psychopathology. (3) *General paresis,* although less common and more treatable than it once was, is a typical cerebral infection. (4) *Senile* and *arteriosclerotic brain disorders* are not only common examples of slowly and usually undramatic progressive cerebral incompetence, but also illnesses that are certain to be of increasing importance as our aging population grows.

## PSYCHOPATHOLOGY IN ACUTE INTOXICATION

The most interesting direct consequence of acute intoxication is the acute delirium that we have already described. There is general agreement today that in delirium the exact character of the disorientation, the delusions, and the hallucinations cannot be predicted solely on the basis of the kind of toxic substance involved. The personality organization of the intoxicated person must always be considered. Certain hallucinogenic drugs produce perceptual and cognitive distortions that may be indistinguishable from those reported by schizophrenic patients. The important difference is that schizophrenic patients give no evidence of being intoxicated.

Studies of toxic psychotic reactions have shown that there is no specific relationship between a particular toxin and the character of the psychopathology appearing in the delirium (Levin, 1959; G. W. Robinson, 1956). The behavior and experience of patients having more than one delirious episode is characteristic for the individual and not for the intoxicating agent. Fear is expressed in the great majority of cases, but neither the presence nor the degree of fear bears any relationship to the nature of the intoxicating agent. Feelings of annoyance and persecution are also prevalent, but the level of this emotional disturbance and the content of the delusional material are not related to the specific intoxicating agent.

The *disorientation* in deliria is likewise on a personal basis, just as it is in ordinary dreaming. The delirious seaman in a shore hospital believes himself to be on shipboard or at the waterfront. The delirious actress believes that she is onstage, in contract negotiations, or rehearsing a new play. Even the most confused, weird disorientative behavior and experience are still the products of a patient's individual past and of his or her immediately present surroundings. The invasion by unconscious fantasies and primary process material is still an invasion from the patient's own unconscious.

Despite the claim that certain drugs are "mind expanding," the *delusional* and *hallucinatory reconstructions* in acute delirium are also specific for the individual patient and not for the toxic agent. Except for the gross disorientation and impaired retentivity, there is nothing about delirious delusions that is essentially different from any other delusion. The content is drawn from factors in the external and internal worlds as conceptualized by the individual patient. We shall cite cases below in which psychopathology in a delirium was strikingly similar to psychopathology in the same person at another time when there was no delirium.

There is a great deal of folklore about hallucinations in the *delirium tremens* of the alcoholic patient, to the effect that pink elephants, rodents, green monkeys, and spotted giraffes are commonly experienced in alcoholic delirium. A study of over one hundred patients with delirium tremens, however, showed that dogs, insects, and snakes are the commonest animal hallucinations, three groups that are also regarded by nonalcoholic persons as dangerous (Dynes, 1939). Only one individual in the study reported seeing a pink elephant and only one reported seeing rodents. The influence of the immediate environment is reflected in the fact that patients being treated by continuous baths tend to hallucinate fish and other sea creatures most often.

It is well known that schizophrenic reactions may be precipitated in acute deliria resulting from intoxication, infection, high fever, and debilitating disease. Of thirteen cases reported in one study of bromide delirium none had previously shown schizophrenic symptoms (Levin, 1959). Of these patients two were severely disoriented on admission, seven were seriously disoriented for time but only occasionally for place or person, and four showed only fleeting disorientation. In ten cases the duration varied from four days to seven and one-half weeks, and in the remaining three cases the duration was five, ten, and twelve months respectively.

We shall close this section by presenting two of our own cases that demonstrate that the psychopathology of delirium is specific for the *person* and not for the *toxin*. The first patient developed a manic attack in a bromide delirium and later developed another manic attack in a setting of marital discord uncomplicated by intoxication. The second patient suffered a manic attack during litigation that threatened to destroy her economic security; thirty years later she suffered another attack when she became disoriented following an operation for a cataract.

Beverly D., a married woman of thirty, was admitted to a psychiatric service in an acute delirium two weeks after she had undergone minor surgery. She had been apprehensive before the operation. On the first postoperative day she seemed so anxious that she was given small doses of morphine. This only alarmed her further. She thought she heard the attending surgeon saying that she had taken a turn for the worse. She spoke to her relatives of dying. On the fourth postoperative day bromide sedation was substituted for the morphine. Beverly continued to be apprehensive and irritable and thus was given bromide sedation for the next ten days. When she became combative she was tied down on the bed. She was soon acutely delirious.

When transferred to the psychiatric service Beverly was grossly disoriented and had obvious memory defects. She told of having delusional fears of being poisoned and dreamlike visual and auditory hallucinations. She was dehydrated on admission and had a bright red body rash. As soon as Beverly had received fluids and chlorides, restraint became unnecessary. She was free to move about the room and the adjacent ward. She remained fearful, confused, and easily stirred to resentment for another ten days. Although she still showed considerable fear, her talk became coherent, and then she began rhyming, punning, swearing, and showing flight of ideas. She was distractible, aggressively overactive, overtalkative, and erotic. This manic behavior persisted for three weeks after the delirious symptoms had disappeared (suggesting a change in diagnosis from delirium to an organic affective syndrome). After another month the patient was discharged.

Three years later Beverly was readmitted in a typical manic attack. Her behavior pathology in this attack closely resembled that in the first one, not only in her general behavior but also in most of the specific details. This time, however, there was no delirium in the picture. The precipitating situation was one of severe marital discord. The diagnosis was again changed to that of an affective disorder, manic episode. Recovery was complete after five months.

Irene T., a widow aged sixty-five, developed an acute delirium following a cataract operation. The delirium began with disorientation, most obvious at night, and was soon accompanied by visual and auditory hallucinations and poor recall. As time went on, Irene became noisy, talking loudly, singing, and occasionally shouting. Her speech became vulgar and profane. She rhymed, punned, and showed some flight of ideas.

On the psychiatric service, Irene was typically manic, except for her behavior at night—when she was disoriented and hallucinating—and whenever she was restrained or interfered with, when she developed fearful delusions and misidentifications. The manic excitement subsided as the delirium disappeared, but at a slower rate. There was no clinical evidence to justify a diagnosis of cerebral arteriosclerosis or senile deterioration.

Thirty years earlier, when Irene was thirty-five years old, she had suffered a manic attack with closely similar behavior. The precipitating situation at that time was a lawsuit that threatened to destroy her security. Irene's husband had died when she was thirty-three. The aim of the lawsuit was to prove that she was not really the wife of the dead man and to thereby deprive her of a large inheritance. She recovered from this illness just as she recovered from the one thirty years later. In one there was a delirious episode preceding the manic attack; in the other there was no delirium at all.

## PSYCHOPATHOLOGY IN HEAD INJURY

Head injury does not necessarily mean brain injury. But when it does, and the resulting cerebral incompetence is extreme, the patient may go quickly into coma or stupor. If the brain damage is serious and the person survives, he or she may pass from coma or stupor into a typical delirium. The highly disoriented state of the *Korsakoff syndrome* may follow, with memory defects and confabulation, before behavior returns to a more nearly adequate state (Brosin, 1959). None of these patterns of symptoms is unique to head injury, of course. The same syndromes are common in any severe cerebral incompetence, whether it occurs in intoxication, infection, or brain degeneration. Even the apparent sequence of phases, when it occurs, is no more than a succession of recognizable clinical syndromes that represent different degrees of adequacy in a recovering organism.

In most cases of head injury that result in immediate severe cerebral incompetence, that is, in which the patient becomes "unconscious," the initial improvement is rapid. Neither acute delirium nor the Korsakoff syndrome appears. Instead, there may be only transient periods of confusion, mild ataxia, dulling, and amnesia, events being forgotten that occurred before the brain injury as well as after it. The course of convalescence after brain injury is highly variable. It can seldom be predicted from a consideration of the apparent brain damage alone. There is even doubt that progressive deterioration can result from moderate trauma alone in an otherwise healthy brain.

Nothing has brought out more clearly the intricate interweaving of biological and social factors in psychopathology than the study of reactions to head injury. For a long time professional interest was directed mainly toward the problem of recognizing and treating the consequences of brain damage — convulsive attacks, deformities, emotional storms, and impaired performance. Whenever brain injury leaves such permanent residuals, a considerable degree of adaptiveness may be demanded of the patient having them. But whether or not these sequelae are present in a given case, there are still other aspects of head injury of equal importance, sometimes of greater importance, that deserve special consideration.

There are, for example, the reactions of the injured person to the accident, to the experience of having been hurt, helpless, frightened, in pain, comatose, forgetful, or confused. Injury to the head in our society is apt to be an object of greater concern than injury to an arm or leg. There is also the necessity for adapting oneself to minor residuals, in themselves perhaps unimportant, which often become the focus of anxiety, worry, and complaints of fatigue and which can lead to conversion reactions and chronic invalidism. Finally, there are primary and secondary gains, which we have already discussed in relation to other adjustment disorders. The modern trend in treatment is to ascribe chronic residual symptoms not only to neurophysiology and neuropathology but also to personality organization — to the patient's habitual attitudes, preferred defenses, and coping mechanisms and the level of social maturity he or she had achieved prior to the accident (Barker, et al., 1953).

In a study of the pre- and post-traumatic personalities of patients with head injuries it was found that the complaints made by these individuals were related to the clinical signs (Ruesch, Harris, & Bowman, 1945). Shortly following their accident, patients with evidence of brain damage in addition to head injury had more complaints than patients with head injury but no clear evidence of brain damage. When, however, all patients were studied later on, those with minor head injuries (and presumably little actual brain damage) had *more* residual complaints than the seriously injured patients. The longer these complaints persisted, the more diffuse they grew until an obvious post-traumatic syndrome occurred. Even headache was not specific to head injury; it was much more common in persons without clear neurological signs of brain damage than in persons with residual signs. Only a small number of patients without neurological signs show personality changes that can be ascribed to the head injury (e.g., develop an organic personality syndrome). The majority have had difficulties in interpersonal relationships *before* their accident. Persistence of complaints in these patients seems best understood as adaptive measures, comparable to neurotic reactions, through which tension and anxiety are reduced. It is the pretraumatic personality organization of the patient with head injury that seems to determine what the post-traumatic adaptation will be.

## PSYCHOPATHOLOGY IN GENERAL PARESIS

General paresis is an encephalitis, an inflammation of the brain that develops because of the presence in it of the spirochete of syphilis. Although the spirochete may be active throughout the cerebral cortex, it affects most intensely the frontal regions where, in cases that end fatally, the invading organism is most concentrated. The neurological signs of general paresis are less specific than this. All of them appear in other central nervous system disease in one combination or another. Among the most common paretic signs are the so-called *Argyll-Robertson pupil* (one that does not respond to light but does to accommodation of the eye for distance) and tremors of the fingers, tongue, eyelids, and facial muscles. Speech is slow and slurred. Writing is tremulous, often illegible, with letters omitted or transposed. There is muscular weakness (*paresis*), and there are often convulsive attacks and attacks of transient paralysis. In untreated cases the course is a downhill one, death coming within two or three years. The course is usually uneventful, but if the inflammatory process should flare up there may be an episode of nonspecific excitement in which the patient is sometimes violent.

Apart from the occasional episodic excitement, cases of general paresis show a clinical picture of relatively rapid progressive cerebral incompetence after an insidious onset and a gradual development of symptoms. The psycho-pathology that appears seems to be nonspecific. If there is an acute inflammatory episode it may lead to an excitement with expansive, aggressive, elated features. Otherwise the time-honored principle still holds that *the type of psychosis or psychoneurosis exhibited by the paretic patient is that which the individual would have developed at that time, provided that syphilis was absent, and any other adequate precipitating factor was present* (Schube, 1934). In other words, the brain made incompetent by this specific inflammatory and degenerative injury lowers the efficiency of adaptive and defensive systems. The paretic patient then reacts in accordance with preparetic personality tendencies, but without the checks and balances provided by whatever adaptive defensive structure that he or she has developed through the preparetic years. The following two case histories will illustrate this point:

Louis Z., aged forty-one, was a married carpenter with a small repair business. He was hospitalized because he had threatened to kill his competitors. His wife said that he had always been a jealous, insecure, suspicious man. Eight weeks before admission he seemed irritable, moody, and fatigued. Three weeks before admission he told his wife that competitors were stealing his tools and putting inferior ones in their place. When he found his "real" tools, he insisted that the alleged thieves had secretly returned them to make a fool of him. This kind of behavior, his wife said, was not at all out of character for him. When, however, Louis threatened to kill his supposed persecutors he was brought to the hospital. In addition to his delusions, he had tremors, a mild memory defect, and sluggish pupils. His cerebrospinal fluid was typical for general paresis. Under penicillin therapy his cerebrospinal fluid became normal. He was able then to return to work, athough he did not lose his suspicions.

Pierce B., a thirty-eight-year-old barber, had been a frugal, honest, hard-working man. He was generally considered in his home town to be a model citizen. Two years before he had to be hospitalized, he changed into an irritable, intolerant person with frequent angry outbursts. His business suffered because people did not want to confront him. A month before his admission to the hospital he became extremely irritable, forgetful, and undependable. At home he became violently angry over trivial things. He was restless, talkative, and excitable until finally he could not work, eat, or sleep as he had in the past. He was full of grandiose schemes, like a manic patient, and he boasted about his abilities, his achievements, and his possessions. When humored he could be led; but when contradicted or frustrated he became explosively angry, threatening members of his family.

On admission to a hospital Pierce was found to have slurred speech, tremors, pupils that reacted slightly to accommodation of the eyes for distance but not at all in response to light (Argyll-Robertson pupils), and paretic cerebrospinal fluid. His general excitement and his delusions were manic in character. He did not respond well to treatment, rapidly went downhill, and died within a year.

With the advent of penicillin therapy there was a dramatic decrease in the incidence of syphilis during the 1950s, but since that time there has been an alarming increase. It has been estimated that there may be as many as a half-million undetected and hence untreated cases of syphilis in the United States as a whole (Krugman & Ward, 1973). It is from such cases that eventual paresis is likely to develop. Hence, syphilis and its derivatives remain a serious health problem.

## PSYCHOPATHOLOGY IN SENILE AND ARTERIOSCLEROTIC BRAIN DEGENERATION

It is inevitable that the aging brain, as an organ, should undergo degenerative changes. If these changes affect the cerebrum gradually and diffusely the disorder is called *senile degeneration*. If the changes come suddenly, and are focal rather than diffuse, the condition is called *arteriosclerotic cerebral degeneration* (Rothschild, 1956). In the latter disorder those areas of the cerebrum supplied by diseased blood vessels will be more or less completely destroyed, while intervening cerebral areas, where the blood vessels are functioning adequately, will be fairly well preserved. As might be expected, many cases of cerebral degeneration show both kinds of anatomical change. Nevertheless, more or less pure cases of one or the other do occur, and even when the two are mixed there is usually a predominance of one process over the other.

The onset in senile cerebral degeneration is often so gradual and insidious that the progressive cerebral incompetence is not recognized until some particularly ineffectual performance calls attention to the change. If acute confusional or convulsive attacks occur at all in senile degeneration, they come late in the degenerative process or in response to a sudden emotional crisis. The business executive who could not find his way back to the unfamiliar hotel illustrates this kind of onset. The acute delirious episode from which he suffered after retirement was precipitated by a sudden fright, and he recovered from it without recovering full competence.

The onset in arteriosclerotic cerebral degeneration is usually sudden. It may be marked by an acute confusional episode or a convulsive attack. Neurological signs of focal damage are common. It occurs much more often in the fifties than the senile diffuse type, which usually appears in the sixties, seventies, or eighties. Sudden remissions followed by sudden declines are also more common. The industrialist who almost ruined himself financially illustrates this kind of onset.

The course is inevitably downhill in both types. Because senile degeneration is slow and gradual, it allows a person to adapt to the decline as it develops; this is particularly true if the surroundings support the patient. The sudden, stormy beginning in arteriosclerotic cerebral degeneration, with its confusional or convulsive attacks and the paralyses that so often accompany it, presents much more difficult adaptive problems. The patient's relatives and close associates are called upon to make sudden adaptations to the unexpected fluctuations. Otherwise the situations confronting patients in the two groups are more alike than dissimilar. Therefore, in the interest of simplicity and clarity of exposition, we shall confine further discussion mainly to the psychopathology that arises during senile cerebral degeneration, and treat arteriosclerotic cases as variants with their own special problems.

It has often been said that the ultimate prognosis in senile cerebral degeneration is hopeless. In the long run this is true. Nerve cells in the cerebrum disappear gradually with age. They cannot be replaced, and their progressive loss will finally incapacitate the aging person. The work of brain pathologists demonstrates, however, that factors other than cell destruction must be taken into account (Gal, 1959; Rothschild, 1956). Thus one finds relatively little cell loss in the cerebrum of many persons who have suffered a severe, senile decline before dying, while many whose cerebrum shows extensive cell destruction have suffered little or no senile decline.

What is true of general senile decline is also true of specific psychopathology arising in old age. If the environment is exceptionally favorable, and the aging person is stable and adaptable, there is every reason to expect that his or her adjustment will remain adequate until the brain is severely deteriorated. It seems clear that the brain, as an organ, has a great deal of reserve potentiality with which to compensate for nerve cell losses. A favorable environment allows the aging person to make full use of these potentialities. When, at last, he or she does suffer a decline, the patient may reach an almost vegetative level before any serious personal maladaptation appears. Such a course places the least burden upon society as well as upon the patient. It is the one least likely to call out resentment in others during the final decline, or remorse after it is over.

Typical senile or late senescent individuals, as their biosocial adequacy declines, do not find that the general conditions of their life improve or that they provide new rewards to replace old rewards that aging individuals no longer enjoy. On the contrary, for the great majority of aging men and women the increase in years brings only an increase in handicaps—biological, personal, social, and economic.

Psychosomatic disorders are common. The elderly have neither the strength nor the endurance of the young. Their visceral performance is often less effective and more easily disturbed than it was earlier in life. In the gastrointestinal system, and to a lesser degree in the cardiovascular and genitourinary systems, disturbances frequently appear that, although not in themselves a threat to continued health and life, are reacted to as if they were. Symptoms of gastrointestinal malfunction are common results of deficiencies and diseases in other systems, of general malnutrition, or of overexertion and lack of adequate sleep. All of these conditions appear more frequently in old age than in youth.

Once middle age has been reached, the older a person grows the more familiar he or she becomes with the incursions of personal illness and both illness and death among friends and associates. The accumulation of such incidents may make a person sensitive to signs of declining health when this is not actually the case. Most aging men and women in our culture have reason to feel neglected and in need of more attention, comfort, and affection than they receive. The frustrations and the unhappiness that are imposed upon the elderly by restrictive social conventions, economic dependence, and reduced biosocial adequacy do much to reinforce and to perpetuate such developments. If behavior pathology appears in a setting of senile decline it is likely to be the same as what would have developed if cerebral incompetence had been absent and any other adequate precipitating factor had been present (Birren, 1961; Stein, Vidich, & White, 1960).

Anxiety is a common symptom in the psychopathology of senile decline. Anxiety disorders in senile persons do not differ fundamentally from anxiety disorders at any other period of life. The same general factors precipitate them and perpetuate them. Only the details are peculiar to old age. The aged have many reasons for feeling insecure. Most of them become economically dependent upon the good will of others, sometimes upon the caprice of others. Unemployment compensation, the growth of local social welfare responsibility, and the establishment of federal social security benefits have done a great deal to ameliorate the anxious dependence of the aging person upon others, but they have not yet eliminated socioeconomic sources of anxiety. A great many persons who never actually become dependent live in constant dread that someday they will. The high probability of ultimate infirmity and the certainty of death are also important sources of persistent anxiety in aging persons. Helplessness and dependence are much more dreaded than death (Sands & Rothschild, 1952).

Guilt is also a common source of anxiety in aging persons. A decline in the adequacy of adaptive and defensive maneuvers often allows primary process material to emerge, hostile and erotic impulses to gain expression, and fantasies that have previously been kept unconscious to become preconscious and conscious. The consequence may be a return of the repressed, the revival of conflicts and ambitendencies previously controlled, and sometimes the appearance of unwise and impulsive behavior. The aging person may become involved in misconduct because his or her reactions to an immediate situation no longer include self-control in terms of future consequences. He or she may, on the other hand, develop guilt because of vengeful fantasies in relation to close relatives who seem to be domineering, belittling, or obstructing the person's every move. Sex conflicts and sex fantasies often play a part in the precipitation and perpetuation of guilt. Sometimes the lonely, unhappy senile person, like the adolescent, finds in sexual preoccupation and sexual gratification what cannot be achieved otherwise.

Obsessive-compulsive disorders appearing in senility often represent the regressive revival of a technique used earlier in life to cope with conflicts that have also been regressively revived. On the other hand, obsessive-compulsive reactions may develop for the first time in old age, as a response to newly increased insecurity, conflict, and anxiety. If an aging person finds the complexities of life more than he or she can manage, there may be a retrenchment and defensive reliance on stereotyped, perseverative, and ritualistic patterns of behavior. This is what any person would do, given only that he or she were having to confront situations that exceeded the usual level of challenge in life.

Psychotic disorders in senility have atypical features due in some measure to the unique problems of old age (A. C. Gibson, 1961; Rothschild, 1956). A relatively high incidence of paranoid reactions in hospitalized senile patients is due in part to the greater difficulty that relatives find in tolerating an aggressive, accusing, delusional senile person than a sad, self-reproachful one or a neurotic or psychosomatic person. Paranoia is also prompted by the confusion arising from serious impairment of hearing and sight, so that the aging person must fill in with imagination what has not been heard or seen clearly. We also know that in our society it is customary to belittle and restrict the aged, to deny them freedom of action and opportunity, and to meet their protests and their resentment with evasiveness or counteraggression. These are all optimal conditions for the development of paranoid symptoms in susceptible persons at any age.

It is generally accepted today that people approaching middle life and old age should begin to prepare for the inevitable physical changes that they will encounter (Lewis, 1956). In all aged populations the most important considerations are to keep these individuals in contact with others and to encourage active behavioral efforts at optimal capacity, which is usually considerably higher than the elderly realize due to the effects of lowered self-esteem. The universally recognized bad effects of retirement upon those persons who do not prepare themselves for the changes it brings about make it mandatory that a retiring person maintain an active life at whatever level his or her strength permits. It is the teleological factor of *looking forward to* some recurring (daily) activity—solitary or social, mental or physical, recreational or occupational, simple or complex—that seems to enrich life in the closing phase of the life cycle. Life can be lived "into tomorrow" when there is something to be looked forward to, even though the days ahead are not so many as they once were. Those who lose interest in such ongoing activities are most likely to slip rapidly into physical and psychological decline.

## SUMMARY

Chapter 18 deals with the *organic brain syndrome,* which is a recognizable pattern of symptoms that signify a brain involvement in the person's behavior without specifically indicating the nature of the illness or other causal agent. When the etiology of the organic brain syndrome is known, the pattern of symptoms is referred to as an *organic mental disorder.* Not everyone suffering from the same organic mental disorder experiences the same degree of loss in mental efficiency. It is also recognized today that many neurotic and psychotic reactions appearing in the wake of cerebral incompetence are not actually organic mental disorders, but are the reactions of sick or injured persons to the fact or the consequence of being sick or injured.

*Delirium* refers to a clouded state of consciousness in which the person has difficulty sustaining attention to both external and internal stimuli, experiences sensory misperceptions, and has a disordered stream of thought. The delirious patient appears restless, irritable, and confused. Hallucinations may appear in the clinical picture. Some patients experience a transient clearing up of the delirium, known as a *lucid interval.* If the disorder continues, the patient may move from noisy restlessness and insomnia to drowsiness and torpor. Movements may slow down, and in time the patient is difficult to arouse and keep aroused (*stupor*), and later on impossible to arouse (*coma*).

Chapter 18 next considers four major symptoms to be seen in acute delirium as well as in other forms of the organic brain syndrome. *Incoordination* of behavior can be seen, including overreach, underreach, tremor, stagger, fumble, slurred speech, and so forth. *Interpenetration* involves the intrusions of thoughts or actions that are appropriate in one context but appear in an unrelated or inappropriate context. Preconscious and conscious processes are invaded by unconscious derivatives. *Fragmentation* appears, in which discontinuous and abortive behavior occurs so that the person may abruptly stop doing something and look befuddled or simply remain silent. Fragmentation also appears in delirious states when activity and thinking become stereotyped, repetitive, and perseverative. It is as if the person seeks to control behavior by limiting it and fixating on some one aspect of it. Finally, we can note *overinclusion* taking place, in which the patient cannot limit the number and kind of simultaneous thought contents to a relatively few coherent ones (see Chapter 4).

Another form of organic brain syndrome is *dementia,* which refers to a loss of intellectual abilities that is severe enough to interfere with social or occupational patterns of behavior. Memory, judgment, and abstract thought are all adversely affected. Syndromes of *progressive dementia* are characterized by decreasing adaptiveness, increasing loss of memory and cognitive grasp, and increasing signs of cerebral pathology. The first observed change is usually a memory defect or some confusion with regard to orientation. The loss in recent memory is often paralleled by a progressive change in character. The progress of deterioration is very slow, so that incoordination, interpenetration, fragmentation, and overinclusion may not appear until a low level of decline has been reached. Ability to *compensate* for the slowly declining capacities may influence the rapidity of the diagnosis. Some patients *confabulate;* that is, they substitute imaginary happenings ("lies") for the forgotten ones. If the process is unchecked, and in senility this is often the case, the person's defensive functions deteriorate along with adaptive ones, and there is an irreversible regression to a vegetative state. We do not know why some people deteriorate to such an extent while others do not.

The *amnesic syndrome* is a more specific or selective form of organic brain syndrome, in which the person's long-term or short-term memory is adversely affected even as his or her state of consciousness remains fairly unclouded. In the *organic hallucinosis* form of organic brain syndrome persistent or recurrent hallucinations occur in a normal state of consciousness; moreover, these hallucinations are attributable to a specific organic factor. For example, if the hallucinations are traceable to the ingestion of alcohol, the person would be diagnosed as suffering from *alcohol hallucinosis.*

An *organic affective syndrome* obtains when a disturbance in mood resembling either a manic episode or a major depressive episode occurs because of a specifiable organic influence. An *organic delusional syndrome* obtains when the person has delusions in a normal state of consciousness (nondelirious) that are due to a specific organic factor (e.g., cerebral lesion). DSM-III presents a diagnostic category of *organic personality syndrome,* which can be used when the person undergoes noticeable changes in style of behavior following a brain injury or disease process. These changes are invariably in the negative direction, such as lack of personal hygiene, poor social judgment, and hair-trigger temper. *Intoxication* is an organic brain syndrome resulting in maladaptive behavior due to the recent ingestion of a specific substance. DSM-III stresses the maladaptive aspect of intoxication. Thus, this label would not be assigned as a psychiatric diagnosis for recreational uses of various drugs. When impaired judgment, interpersonal difficulties, and poor job performance relate to intoxication, the condition is considered to be of psychopathological proportions.

Chapter 18 takes up four major syndromes of *organic mental disorder.* The first is *acute intoxication,* in which we note individual differences based upon the psychodynamics of the person involved. The *disorientation* in deliria is reflective of personal experiences. Thus, the invasion by unconscious fantasies and primary process material is still an invasion from the patient's *own* unconscious. Despite the claim that certain drugs are "mind expanding," the *delusional* and *hallucinatory reconstructions* in acute delirium are specific for the individual patient and *not* for the toxic agent. In *delirium tremens,* dogs, insects, and snakes are the commonest animals hallucinated. Schizophrenic reactions may be precipitated in acute deliria resulting from intoxication.

A severe *head injury* can lead to coma or stupor. If the brain damage is serious, and the person survives, he or she may pass from coma or stupor into a typical delirium. The highly disoriented state of *Korsakoff syndrome* may follow, with memory defects and confabulation prominent before the patient returns to normal. *General paresis* is an encephalitis, an inflammation of the brain that develops because of the presence in it of the spirochete of syphilis. The frontal lobes are most seriously affected. Muscular weakness (*paresis*) and a pupil that does not respond to light but adapts to distance (*Argyll-Robertson pupil*) are prominent symptoms, along with tremors of the fingers, tongue, eyelids, and facial muscles. The type of psychosis or psychoneurosis exhibited by the paretic patient is that which the individual would have developed at the time, provided that syphilis was absent and any other adequate precipitating factor was present.

The final organic mental disorder taken up in Chapter 18 is *brain degeneration* due to *senility* or *arteriosclerosis.* It is inevitable that the aging brain, as an organ, should undergo degenerative changes. If these changes affect the cerebrum gradually and diffusely the disorder is called *senile degeneration.* If the changes come suddenly and are focal rather than diffuse, the disorder is diagnosed as *arteriosclerotic cerebral degeneration.* The onset in senile cerebral degeneration is often so gradual and insidious that the progressive cerebral incompetence is not recognized until some particularly ineffectual performance calls attention to the change. The onset in arteriosclerotic cerebral degeneration is usually sudden, marked by an acute confusional episode or a convulsive attack. Neurological signs of focal damage are common. The course of both disorders is usually downhill. Much depends upon environmental supports. A favorable environment allows the aging person in particular to make use of his or her declining potentials to good advantage. Anxiety and guilt typify the patient with brain deterioration. In the main, if such patients have something to look forward to each day their adjustment levels can be reasonably satisfactory.

# 19

## Freudian Psychoanalysis

### Some Background Considerations

Beginning in Chapter 19 and continuing through Chapter 20 we shall review the vast field of psychotherapy, placing less emphasis upon the somatic therapies relying on drugs, coma, or electric shock even as we recognize that these can prove to be valuable auxiliary treatments. Chapter 19 will be devoted exclusively to Freudian psychoanalysis. Chapter 20 will take up the somatic therapies and survey a number of nonanalytical approaches to the treatment of psychopathological behaviors.

*Definition. The term "psychotherapy" covers a wide range of treatment procedures whose common characteristic is that they deal with psychogenic illnesses by psychological means, rather than by the use of medicines and other somatic procedures.* The relationship between psychological and somatic treatments is not mutually exclusive. Medicines are often used to lessen a patient's anxiety when the level is so great as to interfere with psychotherapy. Medication is widely employed today to decrease suffering and disturbance in psychotic patients, making it possible to return such individuals to their home environment, where psychological changes have a better chance of taking hold. This is the modern trend in dealing with even severe mental illness—to return the patient to life outside the institution as soon as it is possible to arrange suitable living arrangements. Medication is an important aspect of this treatment philosophy.

It is helpful to distinguish between *insight* and *noninsight* forms of psychotherapy. Those theories of human behavior like Freud's, which begin from a teleological assumption, seek to understand mental disturbance introspectively, from the viewpoint of the conceptualizing human being. Since it is assumed that these conceptualizations act as phenomenal grounds "for the sake of which" (formal/final causation) behavior is enacted, insight is called for when the person is out of touch with the meaning of certain (i.e., unconscious) grounds (as per fuero claims; see p. 151). *Insight* may therefore be defined as *understanding the grounds for the sake of which one's unique life is being enacted.*

Therapies that are considered noninsight approaches place their emphasis on the extraspective, overt, observable behavior being enacted on the assumption that it carries forward *without* such intentional grounding. The person is not viewed as an agent of his or her behavior but as a mediator or conduit of earlier life "inputs" or "stimuli" that coalesce into an ongoing sequence of efficiently caused motions which eventuate in "outputs" or "responses" according to the principles of classical and/or operant conditioning (see Chapter 2, pp. 34-38, and Chapter 5, pp. 142-147). Therapy in this case involves the supposed manipulation of antecedent stimuli/inputs to bring about a more effective course of responses/outputs on the assumption that whatever insight may be taking place in the patient's verbalizations is irrelevant to the process of change.

Recall that in Chapter (pp. 154-158) we reviewed the three-stage compromise model of psychopathology. This was Freud's basic theory of illness, and as we now turn to his form of psychotherapy we are considering the other side of the coin—that is, his theory of cure. The clinical syndromes we have studied in Chapters 6 through 18 are merely variations on the common theme framed by the three-stage compromise model. How, then, do we go about rectifying things once a problem has developed over the life span of an individual? We will study Freud's theory of cure and the techniques he devised in an historical format, capturing his maturing thoughts on the nature and cure of psychopathological conditions.

## The Basic Theory of Cure in Psychoanalysis

### THE ROLE OF INSIGHT

As we have already suggested, Freudian psychoanalysis is an insight therapy. If one believes that a neurotic is suffering from certain meanings buried (repressed) deep in the unconscious, then the tactic of cure should be to provide the person with an understanding of these *unadmitted* meanings. We say "unadmitted" to stress the fact that unconscious meanings *are* known to the psyche at one level. These grounding meanings are even made known in the expressive behavioral style of the patient, in his or her dreams, paraplaxes, and freely associated ideas. Therapy is therefore pitched at providing such *insight* to the client. As Freud phrased it, "The principal point is that I should guess the secret [unadmitted meaning] and tell it to the patient straight out; and he is then as a rule obliged to abandon his rejection of it" (Breuer & Freud, 1955, p. 281).

The general steps in providing client insight include (1) determining which decision for the flight into illness was made and why; (2) assuring the patient that a different pathway in life is possible and worthwhile; and (3) stressing all the changes of a positive nature that have taken place in the patient's life since his or her act of primal repression occurred (Freud, 1916-17/1963b, p. 438).

Freud viewed insight therapy as something different from traditional medical therapies. A physical therapy that could remove symptoms of illness through the use of chemical agents (pills, drugs), he termed a *causal therapy* (meaning, of course, material and efficient causes were involved; see Chapter 1, p. 4). Freud did not claim that psychoanalysis was a causal therapy (ibid., p. 435-436). There are no chemical agents to give the patient in psychoanalysis, and so Freud said that he worked at symptom removal from a more distant point of origin (ibid., p. 436). Even if a chemical were someday discovered that could alter levels of libido and therefore make a truly causal therapy possible, Freud believed that psychoanalysis would have already clarified how it was that the libido became abnormally distributed (fixated, cathected, and so on) in the first place. A physical or causal therapy would *not* therefore invalidate his theory of illness and cure.

## The Fundamental Rule of Psychoanalysis: Free Association

To facilitate insight, Freud asked his clients to be as free and open in their dealings with him as was humanly possible. He was, of course, trying to relax the level of client censorship, loosening the grip of anticathexes (repressions). One day, a female patient criticized him for talking too much during the hour, asking questions of her, so Freud simply sat back in his chair and let her speak. He found that he could gain as much insight into her condition by letting her do all of the talking during the hour as he could gain through questioning her directly. The main factor of importance was that she say everything that occurred to her, no matter how irrelevant or silly it might appear to her conscious judgment. Thus, open verbal expression and complete honesty are the hallmarks of the *fundamental rule of psychoanalysis,* and the procedure flowing from this known as *free association* (Freud, 1913/1958h, p. 134).

The usual free-association procedure is to have the client report what comes to mind spontaneously, no matter how irrelevant or even foolish it may appear to common sense. A female client might say: "I don't know, for some stupid reason the idea of 'face cream' just popped into my mind. Now, I can see my face all covered with this cream when I close my eyes—just like when I give myself a facial. What has that to do with my problems?" The analyst need not answer at this point, merely recording what is freely associated and waiting until the full picture begins falling into place.

Gradually, the patient will probably drift off into a recollection of past life events, trailing back to childhood times (where the fueros continue to press their claims). If the client cannot get started during any one therapy session, the therapist may cue him or her by returning to material that has been mentioned earlier or possibly by taking an image or an idea from a dream or free association (like the face cream "mask") and asking the client to focus on this for a time to see what ideas or images occur next.

Although we refer to *free* association, the fact that Freud believed he could in time come to guess or discern his patient's repressed mental contents reflected his belief in *psychic determinism* (see our discussion of Freud's views on this matter in Chapter 5, p. 147). Incidental ideas like "face cream" were not irrelevant or chance affairs to Freud. As he said, "I cherished a high opinion of the strictness with which mental processes are determined, and I found it impossible to believe that an idea produced by a patient while his attention was on the stretch could be an arbitrary one and unrelated to the idea we were in search of" (Freud, 1909/1957a, p. 29). Freud said that he believed in chance only in the realm of external events; in the internal world of psychical events, he was an uncompromising determinist (Freud, 1901/1960a, p. 257). It is fundamental to the Freudian view that mental events press on to expression. The unconscious is said to have an " 'upward drive' and desires nothing better than to press forward across its settled frontiers into the ego and so to consciousness" (Freud, 1938/1964f, p. 179).

### RESISTANCE AND TRANSFERENCE

From the first, when he was using hypnotism, Freud noted that neurotics disliked having to look into themselves (Freud, 1892-99/1966c, p. 217). They tried in countless ways to end or at least alter the course of therapy, in hopes of retaining the status quo in their lives. According to Freud's later theory of defense, any neurotic person has two motives for beginning therapy—one to be cured and one to avoid being cured (discovered, uncovered) (Breuer & Freud, 1955, p. 268). He called these defensive efforts during therapy *resistance,* which in its broadest phrasing refers to *"whatever interrupts the progress of analytic work"* (Freud, 1900-01/1953b, p. 517). Literally anything the client does to disrupt or even detract from the validity of analysis is considered resistance, no matter how innocent it appears on the face of things. Asking for a change in the appointment hour is resistance. Telling the analyst a joke in which psychoanalysis is made to appear a hoax is resistance. In fact, even when the patient miraculously loses his or her presenting symptoms after a brief period of analysis, this "sudden cure" is resistance (Freud, 1916-17/1963b, p. 291). There can be a "flight into health" in order to avoid confronting (resisting) the details of the Oedipal repressions.

Freud had some interesting things to say about regression in resistance. Sometimes, in reaction to the frustration of being analyzed by the therapist, the ego of a patient regresses in hopes of re-creating a life period that was more pleasant than the present (Freud, 1909/1957a, p. 49). The analyst can actually see the psychosexual level at which fixation occurred being reflected in the nature of this resistance (Freud, 1892-99/1966c, p. 266). For example, a man with an anal personality might begin going into extreme detail (pedantism) on each freely associated memory, stalling, through his obsessiveness, any chance the therapist has to pull things together into a coherent picture. The resultant confusion of details acts as a smoke screen. A woman with an oral personality might regress to a state of childlike dependency and "yes doctor" the therapist, letting insightful comments go over her head by agreeing to everything the analyst says without *really* letting the insights register and thereby have an impact on her personal adjustment.

Another way in which the patient can resist is to change the nature of the relationship, from analyst-*analysand* (the latter is the person being analyzed) to one of father-son or father-daughter or two brothers or two lovers. Freud found that several of his female clients began relating to him in a most unprofessional and often amorous manner. They asked him questions about his personal life, what kinds of books he read, and what he did with his free time. If he gave in to any of these diversions by answering such questions, he found his therapeutic effectiveness declining. In one session a woman threw her arms around his neck in an erotic gesture, and as Freud later said, the "unexpected entrance of a servant relieved us from a painful discussion" (Freud, 1924/1959f, p. 27). Freud did not attribute these amorous feelings to his personal charm. He saw in these maneuvers the re-enactment of *earlier* paternal affections (Oedipal feelings for the father).

By projecting her lust from father to therapist, the patient achieved two results: (1) she could re-enact her past dynamic, thereby repeating attitudes and emotional displays from her fixation point (repetition compulsion) (Freud, 1916-17/1963b, p. 290); and (2) she could establish the possibility that therapy would have to be ended like a broken love affair, because how can the analyst—a married man, with many other patients to treat daily—return such love? (Freud, 1914/1958k, p. 167). Freud called this emotional involvement with the therapist *transference,* by which he meant "transference of feelings on to the person of the doctor, since we do not believe that the situation in the treatment could justify the development of such feelings" (Freud, 1916-17/1963b, p. 442). The female patient was *acting out* her repressed images and ideas, now coming to consciousness and diverted into sexual feelings for the therapist by way of a *father imago* (ibid.). An *imago* is someone we have known in the past, whose image acts like a prototype so that we can press it onto other people, turning someone in the present (therapist) into someone in the past (father). Considered in terms of libido theory, transference always involves cathecting the therapist with libido that has been withdrawn from the imago and then invested in the image of the therapist as a stand-in. The emotional feelings for the imago *then* follow as the patient re-enacts the earlier dynamic (that is, libido is *not* feeling, but feelings are generated in the repeated dynamic).

Thus, through use of the imago the patient can "replace some earlier person by the person of the physician" (Freud, 1901/1953c, p. 116). Re-enactments of this sort, in which present-day people are substituted for early people, go on all of the time in the neurotic's life as a result of the repetition compulsion (Freud, 1914/1958j, p. 101). A man or woman working on some job turns the "boss" into a father or mother imago and begins to act very strangely toward the person. As we have already indicated in citing the variety of relationships that can be attempted, the imagoes being projected onto the therapist by the client need not be *only* those of the parents. A brother, sister, or literally any figure of importance out of the client's past can serve as an imago projection (ibid., p. 100). The therapist often finds himself or herself a composite of *many* people (including both sexes!) over the course of psychoanalysis with a single client.

The feelings transferred onto the therapist are not always *positive* in tone, of course. As all psychoanalysts have found, it is virtually impossible for a patient to remain in a positive state of transference throughout his or her analysis (Freud, 1916-17/1963b, p. 441). This is due to the fact that the feelings (evaluations) generated by the dynamic interaction with imagoes are never one-way, but are always *ambivalent;* inevitably the therapist sees both sides to the feelings being expressed concerning an imago figure. In addition to this unrealistic factor, there is the course of therapy itself to consider. As the patient reveals more of his or her unconscious conflicts in the ongoing analysis, there is sure to be a sense of threat generated by this *uncovering process.* This threat invariably brings on resistance, which shows up as what Freud called *negative transference.*

Precisely when the negative transference will emerge is hard to say. Freud believed he could sense it beginning when a client's free associations began to fail (called *blocks*), or there were no dreams to report; any prolonged period of silence in the therapy hour suggested the possibility of negative transference. The analyst begins at this point to *interpret* the nature of these positive or negative transferences. To interpret is to find "hidden sense in something" (Freud, 1915-16/1963a, p. 87). In providing insight through analysis of the transference, the therapist is trying to *overcome the client's resistance.* This move on the therapist's part is all the more threatening, and hence it is not unusual for the patient to go through some very difficult therapy sessions at this point in the series, suffering high levels of neurotic anxiety at the challenge of having to face up to the *return of the repressed.* The therapist is present to assist the client, but this does not make it much easier, and the person of the therapist becomes a scapegoat for irritation and hostility.

It is therefore no surprise that, as time went by, Freud began to think of overcoming resistance as the most difficult and yet crucial aspect of psycho-therapy. He once defined psychoanalytic treatment as "a *re-education in overcoming internal resistances*" (Freud, 1904/1953d, p. 267). Clients can become quite hostile and abusive during this period of analysis. Freud summed up the hard work of analyzing resistance (negative transference) as follows:

> Resistance, which finally brings work to a halt, is nothing other than the child's past character, his degenerate character . . . . I dig it out by my work, it struggles; and what was to begin with such an excellent, honest fellow, becomes low, untruthful or defiant, and a malingerer—till I tell him so and thus make it possible to overcome this character. (Freud, 1892-99/1966c, p. 266)

Although it need not always proceed in step fashion—sometimes both sides of the ambivalence emerge in the early sessions—the usual course of transference is from a positive to a negative stage. Freud believed that successful therapy calls for a complete resolution of the transference phenomenon. The full implications of the transference onto the therapist must be made clear to the patient, who through insight gains an understanding of his or her dynamics. As Freud put it, "At the end of an analytic treatment the transference must itself be cleared away; and if success is then obtained or continues, it rests, not on suggestion, but on the achievement by its means of an overcoming of internal resistances, on the internal change that has been brought about in the patient" (Freud, 1916-17/1963b, p. 453).

Many former patients who leave their therapists during the stage of negative transference are highly critical of the procedure and give psycho-analysis an undeservedly bad name (Freud, 1932-36/1964b, p. 155). Even so, Freud did not favor avoiding such—what he took to be—necessities of the therapeutic procedure; he did not think it advisable to use the transference love to manipulate patients and thereby allow the hostile repressions to escape examination (Freud, 1914/1958k, p. 166).

The therapist must also be careful about forming a *countertransference,* which involves the unconscious motives that the therapist might have acted out in relations with the patient (Freud, 1910/1957c, pp. 144-145). If the therapist has not developed adequate insight into his or her own personality dynamics, then very possibly there will be a reversal of the usual procedure, in which the therapist uses the client as a "blank screen" on which to project imagoes. This is why Freud believed that a psychoanalyst should be analyzed before personally undertaking the role of therapist (Freud, 1932-36/1964b, p. 150). Indeed, as we shall see below, he even favored a kind of continuing, periodic psychoanalysis for therapists (as patients!) to keep them growing and in command of their mental and emotional faculties. A therapist who actually engages in sexual relations with a patient would not only be doing something that is professionally unethical, he or she would literally be bringing the client into what are *personal* neurotic dynamics. Therapy ends when there is such a turn of events, and indeed, clients can be made worse.

### FINAL THEORY OF CURE

Thus far we have been considering the general terminology that evolved in Freudian psychoanalytical treatment. His final formulation brought in libido as well (which we mentioned only in passing above) as fundamental to trans-ference. The final theory of cure may be summarized in six points.

1. The neurotic is a person with significant *primal repressions* (see Chapter 5, p. 135), including those surrounding the unresolved Oedipus complex. Due to the *repetition compulsion* (see Chapter 5, p. 121), the neurotic seeks in interpersonal relations to re-enact these Oedipal themes, trying to find that

sense of love that he or she never adequately repressed, substituted, or sublimated. Freud termed this seeking of love in relations with others a *libidinal anticipatory idea* (that is, looking forward in anticipation of recapturing the Oedipal cathexes by projecting the imago onto others) (Freud, 1912/1958c, p. 100). This libidinal-idea concept is, in effect, the *fuero* demand emanating from the person's early life (see p. 151). An unconscious demand of this type might be, "Won't you [the imago] give me your love and sexual commitment?" or "Maybe now I can smooth things over with you [the imago] and experience that love that was denied me earlier." These libidinal anticipatory ideas influence the neurotic's behavior in his or her everyday routine, bringing about those transferences onto others whom the person must deal with daily. It is this re-enactment with others that eventually drives the neurotic person into therapy, because all sorts of interpersonal problems arise as the acting-out process distorts normal social relations.

2. In therapy this same acting-out process occurs in the *transference* of feelings onto the therapist. There are three aspects to transference, two of which are positive and one negative. First, a neurotic person transfers affectionate, friendly feelings for the therapist *as a person*—a helper with the power and authority to cure a sickness or solve a problem. Second, there are the positive transferences of an erotic, sexually lustful nature that are actually intended for the imago. Third, there are the negative transferences of a hostile, death-wishing variety that are also aimed at the imago rather than the person of the therapist. Freud candidly admitted that it is on the basis of the first factor in transference that the relationship between patient and doctor is built and out of which the therapist gains a certain power of *suggestion* to influence the neurotic to change. But it is the neurotic who must do the hard work of facing up to the repressed meanings if therapy is to work. As Freud put it:

> We readily admit that the results of psycho-analysis rest upon suggestion; by suggestion, however, we must understand . . . the influencing of a person by means of the transference phenomena which are possible in his case. We take care of the patient's final independence by employing suggestion in order to get him to accomplish a piece of psychical work which has as its necessary result a permanent improvement in his psychical situation. (1912/1958c, p. 106)

3. Neuroses stem from a personal dynamic, and it is only the neurotic who can directly confront his or her own unconscious and try to end the lack of communication between the private realms of mind. Freud measured his success as a psychoanalyst according to the extent that he could remove amnesias dating from roughly the second to the fifth year of the patient's life, when the Oedipus complex was active (Freud, 1919/1955i, p. 183). Because it brings out the dynamics of such Oedipal fixations, Freud called transference the "true vehicle of therapeutic influence" (Freud, 1909/1957a, p. 51). We must also keep in mind that transference has its resistance components to hinder therapy, and that such duality is common to neurotics who are generally

ambivalent in behavior (Freud, 1912/1958c, pp. 106-107). Recall that every neurotic symptom means *at least* two things—the repressed plus the repressing wish!

4. As the neurotic patient moves through psychoanalysis, he or she develops an *artificial* or *transformed neurosis* within the four walls of the consulting room (Freud, 1916-17/1963b, p. 444). This is a miniature replica of the neurotic dynamics then being acted out in everyday life. It is prompted by the repetition-compulsion nature of the instincts, so that the neurotic cannot help but reflect the Oedipal dynamics in the therapeutic relationship. Freud occasionally referred to this miniature re-enactment as the *transference illness* (ibid., p. 454), a usage that has led to some confusion, because the artificial or transformed neurosis has since been called the *transference neurosis* by some of his followers. Actually, the latter phrase is better served for a distinction that Freud made between those mentally disturbed individuals who can profit from therapy and those who cannot.

5. Put in mental-energy (libidinal) terms, when we speak of positive or negative feelings being transferred to the therapist via imagoes, we are *also* saying that libidinal or hostile cathexes are taking place (eros and/or the death instinct are active; see Chapter 4, p. 122). This is another way of speaking about the libidinal anticipatory idea. Recall that feelings are generated bodily, but the imago and fuero dynamics occur *exclusively* in the psychic (mental) sphere. Shifting our emphasis to the energic type of explanation, we might say that psychoanalysis as a therapeutic method requires that the patient be able *in fact* to cathect objects. If an individual cannot cathect objects, he or she will be unable to develop a transformed neurosis within the transference relationship; how then can a psychoanalyst hope to provide such a client with insight? He or she cannot, really. The dynamic play staged by the acting out is needed in order to interpret for the client what is going on in his or her life.

Based on this capacity for cathexis to occur or not, Freud distinguished between those people who can profit from psychoanalysis and those who cannot. People, he said, suffer from two basic kinds of neuroses: (1) the *transference neuroses,* which include anxiety disorders, hysteria (somatoform disorders), and obsessive-compulsive disorders; and (2) the *narcissistic neuroses,* which include the schizophrenias and the more serious affective disorders like manic-depression. We recognize in the latter disorders the bulk of the psychotic disturbances, of course. The point Freud was making, however, is that any mental disorder taking on a narcissistic feature means that the individual has removed all libidinal cathexes from the external world and affixed them onto the imagined products of a pseudocommunity into which he or she relates without concern for what we all know as "reality." Recall from Chapter 5 (p. 158) that this disavowal of reality is a crucial aspect of the psychotic form of regression, in which there is no longer any effort made to connect with and hopefully readjust what has been amiss in that reality.

The woman who has regressed to the severe psychotic state of hebephrenia (see Chapter 14)—doing nothing all day long but making faces and giggling repeatedly, sucking her thumb, and soiling herself without concern—is no longer in libidinal contact with the outer world. She has built her dream world in her narcissistic neurosis (psychosis) and now lives completely within it as a baby, and no psychoanalyst can hope to break into her delusions as a significant part of her daily life (Freud, 1916-17/1963b, pp. 444-447). The man who goes through life with all kinds of physical symptoms, expecting to be worried over and cared for by others, *does* experience libidinal anticipatory ideas, meaning he *does* cathect others in his transference neurosis, and therefore he *would* be a proper candidate for psychoanalysis. Therapists could expect him to re-enact his dynamics in the transformed neurosis of the therapy hour. Using this fascinating replay of the Oedipal situation, said Freud, "we oblige him to transform his repetition into a memory," which is *insight* (ibid., p. 444).

Two comments should be made at this point. First, it must be appreciated that though Freud held out little hope for effective treatment of psychosis through psychoanalysis alone, this did not mean that he believed it was impossible either to study psychosis analytically or to experience an occasional cure through hard work on the part of the analyst. As we know, psychoanalysts have subsequently worked successfully with schizophrenic and manic-depressive patients. However, there is much failure in such efforts, and no one doubts that some cases of psychotic disturbance are literally hopeless. The contribution of organic factors to such cases is always kept in mind.

Second, we see in Freud's distinction between transference and narcissistic neuroses his basic emphasis on the importance of *interpersonal* relations in life, and how it is important to use libido both as a tool for building "ego strength" *and* as a vehicle through which we bind ourselves to others. Harking back to his theory of homosexuality (see Chapter 16), it is the fact that homosexuals are engaged in a highly narcissistic object choice that is seen by Freud to be the source of their abnormal adjustment pattern. We might say that the imagoes that homosexuals project onto (certain) others are *themselves*.

6. As a successful psychoanalysis is carried forward, the patient comes gradually to remove libido from object cathexes in the environment and from the (conversion) symptoms manifested in the body and to redirect this free libido onto the relationship with the therapist. This is why the therapist becomes so important to the client; he or she is now an object in which very much libido is invested. The therapist's tactic is to make this additional libido available to the conscious aspects of the client's ego and thereby to further the strengthening of the ego, thanks to its added quota of energy. How is this accomplished? By having the therapist support and encourage the client's ego to study its total personality (re-education). As the conscious portion of ego confronts the return of the repressed and finds it possible to live with what this all means, an increasing amount of the libido initially invested in the therapist returns to the control of the ego and strengthens it. A libidinal bond remains in the ambivalence of the patient's tie to the therapist, but now much more control in the relationship takes place on the side of the patient's ego. Narcissism is avoided even as a build-up of the ego takes place.

The therapist must watch out lest this reinvestment in the conscious ego become narcissistic. It may even begin in a slightly narcissistic fashion, but in time thanks to proper interpretations made by the therapist a growing sense of competence in interpersonal relations should result—both in the form of love ties and the aim-inhibited contacts of friendship with other human beings. It is also important to prevent a patient from forming additional repressions. When this happens the ego has to use libido to form anticathexes, and this simply wastes energies that could be better used in adapting to the external world. Gradually, the "ego is enlarged at the cost of the unconscious" (ibid., p. 455). The man who had before shrunk from people and regressed to states of physical self-concern now begins to meet others, to entertain and be entertained by them. He finds a woman companion and begins to mature into love relationships that until this time had been impossible due to the unproductive use of libido in the past. Assuming that this man also has a good idea of the role of transference in his change of behavior, we would consider his case to have reached a successful therapeutic outcome.

## Extent and Permanence of Cure

Experience with clients was in time to suggest that psychoanalysis was not a cure-all. In a paper entitled "Analysis Terminable and Interminable," written in 1937, a few years before his death, Freud made some rather limited claims for the effectiveness of psychoanalysis. He had found that only those instinctual conflicts that were *literally* being acted out in the transformed neurosis could be helped through providing insight of the dynamics involved (Freud, 1937/1964e, p. 231). If some *other* problem exists in the psyche but does not come alive in the therapy hour, then simply talking about it in *post hoc* fashion will not result in a cure.

Assume that a young man has authority problems in everyday life, projecting a father imago onto others. In therapy he acts out this problem with the therapist in the transformed neurosis. He at some point is literally alive with the hostility feelings he once had in relations with his father, projected now onto the therapist. The therapist waits for the right moment, and when these feelings are clearly active, makes an interpretation to the young man concerning his paternal dynamics. The resultant insight works, even though there may still be a degree of resistance to work through. But now, a related problem in this case might be this young man's inability to compete with other men. The therapist might include this fear of competition in the broader interpretation of the young man's personality conflicts. But since the young man has not brought this conflict into the transformed neurosis—for example, by awkwardly trying to compete with the therapist in the use of language, only to abruptly switch and ridicule all those who use "big words"—no interpretation made by the therapist based on past life competitions with other men will work. In order to *really understand* this personality dynamic, the young man has to be feeling in a competitive mood "right now," when the therapist makes the interpretation.

*Freud's study in his residence at Maresfield Gardens, London (1938-1939). Apparently his consulting-room furniture and study furniture were combined, for we see his armchair, couch, and desk furniture in a common grouping. A cluster of favorite antiquities from Freud's vast collection also adorns his desk.*

This phenomenon has come to be known as the difference between *intellectual* and *emotional understanding* in psychotherapy. It shows up in all insight approaches, in which the experienced therapist soon learns that intellectual insight is not enough. There has to be a fundamental feeling involved in the patient's understanding at the time insight is provided, or it will just not take hold. The feeling is in effect a reflection of the fact that the repetition compulsion is underway, that the person is indeed re-enacting a dynamic from out of the past, that a fuero claim is being advanced, and that the unconscious dynamic is ripe for interpretation!

Freud believed that a patient never brings *all* of his or her past conflicts into the transference relationship in one transformed neurosis (ibid., p. 233). Nor can the therapist artificially stimulate the appearance of these conflicts by using theatrical tricks, such as acting like a parent in order to bring out the patient's death wishes for this parent (ibid., pp. 232-233). Here again, fakery is less than useless to the curative process. The backbone of psychoanalysis remains truthfulness and genuineness. All the therapist can hope for is to end a psychoanalysis on the best terms possible. As Freud put it:

Our aim will not be to rub off every peculiarity of human character for the sake of a schematic "normality," nor yet to demand that the person who has been "thoroughly analysed" shall feel no passions and develop no internal conflicts. The business of the analysis is to secure the best possible psychological conditions for the functions of the ego; with that it has discharged its task. (ibid., p. 250)

Because of this likelihood that certain conflicts have not been experienced emotionally in the transformed neurosis, Freud advocated periodic reanalyses even for practicing psychoanalysts. He felt that a practitioner should go back into analysis every five years or so, as a kind of continuing prophylactic against the menace of countertransference (ibid., p. 249). This is why psychoanalyses never seem to end. They *do* end for one problem, but then begin again (in a sense) to consider another problem.

### Social Revision as Therapeutic

Freud was a "proper" man, and in no sense revolutionary. His hope for the future emphasized not sexual license, but a life based on the insights of science and the *rule of reason* (Freud, 1916-17/1963b, p. 435). People should not give themselves over to base emotions at every turn. In the final analysis, Freud's therapy is more *preventive* than anything else. If humankind is instructed by the insights of psychoanalysis—as a "student body" or a "patient" en masse— then just possibly it will no longer need to bring on those harmful repressions that it now bears up under. Oedipal conflicts need not be so severe, superegos need not be so rigid, and human understanding and mutual acceptance based on something more honest and true than even brotherly love can be brought about in human relations. A gradual revision in the social structure is clearly implied in Freud's writings (Freud, 1910/1957c, pp. 144-150). Sometimes, in removing repressions during analysis, a patient's life situation is actually made worse. The resulting frustration at having to give up a symptom picture that provided a secondary gain may lead the patient to act out against the society. Even so, said Freud:

The unhappiness that our work of enlightenment may cause will after all only affect some individuals. The change-over to a more realistic and creditable attitude on the part of society will not be bought too dearly by these sacrifices. But above all, all the energies which are to-day consumed in the production of neurotic symptoms serving the purposes of a world of phantasy isolated from reality, will, even if they cannot at once be put to uses in life, help to strengthen the clamour for the changes in our civilization through which alone we can look for the well-being of future generations. (ibid., pp. 150-151)

This is the ultimate therapeutic message of Freudian psychoanalysis. As is well known and freely admitted to, Freud was never a doctor "in the proper sense" (E. Jones, 1953, p. 28). He envisioned a form of therapy that transcended the individual and even an individual generation of human beings. By helping to bring about certain social revisions it was his hope that mental health for everyone could be promoted albeit not perfected.

## Therapeutic Techniques

### EVOLUTION OF THE RELATIONSHIP

Freud began his career as most neurologists of his day did, using various physical remedies for the treatment of mental illness, including sedatives, rest, massage, hydrotherapy (for example, baths or stimulating showers), diet control, and change of daily routine. Freud's clients were predominantly of the upper socioeconomic classes, and therefore he could send them off for a period of rest at a local resort spa (Ansbacher, 1959). Of course, in extremely disturbed (psychotic) cases, he hospitalized the patient. Freud gradually defined a new doctor-patient relationship as he evolved the psychoanalytical technique (Freud, 1910/1957c, p. 144).

Freud actually began his search for the pathognomic (repressed) memory through the technique of *hypnotic age* or *time regression.* The patient was asked to relax in a reclining or semireclining position on a sofa, and hypnosis was induced through the usual suggestions of drowsiness, falling off to sleep, and so forth. As he used this technique with more clients, Freud found that not all of them could be put into a sufficiently deep hypnotic state to bring about time regression. In fact, several could not be hypnotized at all. Freud recalled that Bernheim (one of the doctors he had studied with in France) could get subjects to remember what had gone on during a previous hypnotic trance by taking their heads in his hands and essentially ordering them (strong suggestion) to do so. When one day a difficult patient was not responding to the hypnosis instructions, Freud took her head in his hands, asked her to concentrate, and while applying slight pressure he confidently asserted that she *would* recall when her symptoms had begun. Sure enough, the patient remembered the pathognomic situation and obtained a certain cathartic release in reliving it (Freud, 1909/1957a, pp. 22-26).

Freud called this the *pressure technique,* and he used it successfully for several years, feeling that it had definite advantages over hypnosis because the client was conscious of the thought processes as he or she made the mental search. The therapist did not have to retrace these steps later after the client came out of hypnosis, when the added problem now arose of trying to remember what went on in the hypnotic trance. Freud had surpassed Bernheim! Even so, the focus of psychoanalysis was still on symptom removal during this period of its development. It was only a matter of time until Freud noted a strange and annoying tendency in the patients' efforts to recall the past while under hypnosis. He found them recalling all matter of trivia, apparently unrelated scraps of information that had no bearing on their neurotic symptoms. He did not dismiss these apparent irrelevances; instead, drawing on his assumption of psychic determinism (see Chapter 5, p. 148), he considered them to be *screen memories* or *screen associations* (Freud, 1901/1960a, p. 43).

These supposedly random memories were covering up a more deep-seated complex of memories clustering around the pathognomic situation in which the symptoms of neurosis took root. Freud began to question his clients about these screen memories, taking them even further back in time, until he hit upon the technique of free association. For a time, Freud used the pressure technique and free association in combination, but by 1905 he had stopped touching the client entirely (a dangerous procedure, considering the matter of transferences). Thus free association has emerged as the exclusive technique of the classic psychoanalyst.

## VIEW OF THERAPEUTIC CHANGE

Freud was aware of the historic relationship psychoanalysis had with hypnosis, and by way of this tie, the possible criticism that he had cured people exclusively through suggestion. He defined *suggestion* as uncritically accepting an idea implanted in one's mind by another (Freud, 1892/1966b, p. 83), but he did *not* accept that this is what went on during psychoanalysis. He felt that the id promptings that lay at the root of neurosis could not be so easily influenced, thanks to the countering influence of the superego and the compromise effected by the ego. The id, after all, is illogical and refuses to evaluate any of its anticipatory ideas realistically. The therapist can use a little suggestion because the client likes him or her as a person, but this kind of suggestion is directed to the ego and it might not help at all with the id! Freud loved to point out that anyone who works with clients in therapy soon learns that they do not swallow every idea the therapist offers them (Freud, 1914/1955f, pp. 51-52).

He also critically observed that those who use the concept of suggestion never say what it *is*. According to Freud, suggestion is based on sexual forces in operation between two people. Its power in therapy results from the childlike dependency—the re-enactment of an infantile relationship—on the person of the therapist as a stand-in for others. To understand the nature of suggestion we must first understand the nature of transference. Thus Freud's goal in therapy was to provide a certain type of relationship and thereby to learn something of the client's past history. He was not out to prove some obscure theoretical point in each case, and he observed, "The most successful cases are those in which one proceeds, as it were, without any purpose in view, allows oneself to be taken by surprise by any turn in them, and always meets them with an open mind, free from any presuppositions" (Freud, 1911/1958a, p. 114). Freud said that he refused emphatically to make a patient into his private property, to force his own ideals on the patient "and with the pride of a Creator to form him in our own image" (Freud, 1918/1955h, p. 164).

The point is: *a neurotic is not a free person.* He or she is locked into the past like a character in a play. The past forces the neurotic person to re-enact the unresolved Oedipus complex again and again. Thus, says Freud, "analysis sets the neurotic free from the chains of his sexuality" (Freud, 1922/1955o, p. 252).

## CLIENT PROGNOSIS AND TRIAL ANALYSIS

Freud once suggested (half jokingly) that the ideal client for psychoanalysis is a person suffering considerably from an inner conflict that he or she cannot solve alone. This person would therefore come to analysis literally begging for help (Freud, 1920/1955l, p. 150). Anything short of this ideal circumstance—which is probably never realized, we might add—detracts from the prognosis in a given case. If a man is forced into analysis by relatives, this is *not* a good prognostic sign. If a woman is using psychoanalysis as a way of getting back at her husband through making him pay for large doctor bills, this is *not* a good prognostic sign. As we know from our discussion of the narcissistic neurosis above, psychotic individuals are not good bets for psychoanalysis, nor are the mentally retarded, the brain-damaged, or the senile members of our society.

Children present a special difficulty, and in truth Freud was not much attracted to the role of the child therapist. His famous case of Little Hans (p. 197) (Freud, 1909/1955a) was based on the work of an intermediary therapist—the boy's father—who saw Freud privately and then carried the (sexual) interpretations to his five-year-old son in a most open and straightforward manner. In general, Freud thought it was best for the parent and child to enter therapy together. Children *externalize* their problems—acting out *in vivo*—and therefore it is not too helpful to search about in their internal psychic lives for solutions. The best bet is simply to try to improve the parent-child relationship in the ongoing present (Freud, 1932-36/1964b, p. 148).

When a therapist takes a patient, usually he or she is "buying a pig in a poke" (ibid., p. 155). Freud favored a trial period of diagnostic assessment of from a few weeks to a few (or even several) months during which the therapist can make the decisions so important to prognosis, such as whether a relationship can be formed, whether there is a narcissistic or a transference neurosis, and so on. This trial period is quite flexible, and when it is not extended, the reputation of psychoanalysis suffers because these rejected clients are considered failures by critics who do not understand or accept the principle of a trial analysis. Freud admitted that psychoanalysis takes a long time, in some cases several years, but he could see no other way of curing neurosis short of the superficial, suggestive cures that relied on manipulation and the authority of positive transference to suppress a symptom (ibid., p. 156).

## INTERPRETATION TECHNIQUES IN DREAMS AND PARAPRAXES

We have already reviewed the essentials of dream construction in Chapter 5 (see pp. 162-167), so we shall not go over old ground. Freud once said that he based the entire science of psychoanalysis on the foundation stone of dream interpretation (Freud, 1913/1955e, p. 170). As totally mental phenomena, dreams express a meaning, they say something, and though we think we do not know what their content is getting at, in the unconscious regions of mind *we know full well* (Freud, 1915-16/1963a, p. 101). While asleep, all of those fueros or anticipatory libidinal ideas that we cannot consciously express because of their repression by the ego and superego—which combined might be thought of as the censoring agency of the mind—are given expression. Of course, in order to get around the censorship, these ideas must be distorted in various ways so that their content is expressed through symbols that must be deciphered (manifest versus latent content, etc.). Since dreams always deal with our more important mental concerns, the interpretation of dreams provides the analyst with a *"royal road to a knowledge of the unconscious activities of the mind"* (Freud, 1900-01/1953b, p. 608). Freud gave the following rules of thumb for analyzing a dream:

1. Do not take the manifest content of a dream literally, because it never reflects the unconscious meaning intended.
2. Present various portions of the dream contents to the patient as a prompt for free association, and do not worry about how far this line of investigation takes you from the original dream story.
3. Never lead or suggest things about the dream to the client; wait until several dreams and/or free associations to dream contents suggest the direction to be taken in making interpretations (Freud, 1915-16/1963a, p. 114).

Freud made many practical hints for dream interpretation over the years. The following are examples of his insightful interpretations. Dreams produce logical connections by simultaneity in time, so that things happening together are probably seen by the dreamer as somehow related. When a cause-effect relationship is suggested, then the dream content is changed or distorted, as by a sudden shift in scene or the distortion of a face from one person into another's. Such "reactive" dream contents have been shown to be especially significant to the personality dynamics of the dreamer (Rychlak & Brams, 1963). The dreamer is unable to express *either/or* in a dream, but instead links such alternatives with an *and* so that opposites can be combined into single images or actions. Indeed, dreams are prime examples of all forms of dialectical-reasoning machinations (Freud, 1913/1955d).

Whenever there is a condensation of dream figures, one must always suspect that the dreamer sees a similarity, identity, or possession of common attributes between the figures. Thus, if a woman dreams of a canary, flitting about carrying out unusual acts, knowing that she views her mother in such a birdlike fashion—as delicate and inconsistent in behavior—encourages the psychoanalyst to believe that this dream expresses something about the mother.

A popular device used by the dreamer is dialectical *reversal,* or the turning into its opposite of some latent wish or image in the manifest content. For example, a businessman may recall dreaming that his competitor scored a major financial gain of some sort, and wonders why he should be having such unhappy dreams. All such devices Freud referred to as the *means of representation* in dreams (see Chapter 5 for other terms relating to dream construction) (Freud, 1900/1953a, p. 310).

In addition to the content of free associations and dreams, Freud found that he could gain insights into the motives of others through what he called *parapraxes,* or errors in behavior, "misactions" in which the person does something he or she is not (consciously) intending to do. When a man intends to say to his wife "please sit down" and says instead "please fall down," he is actually substituting the opposite of his intention—in this case, hostility for affection (Freud, 1901/1960a, p. 59). Here again, the censoring agency is circumvented for a fleeting moment when the person's attention is caught off guard. When the new bride writes a letter to her mother-in-law beginning with "Dead mother" instead of "Dear mother," the underlying hostility is made plain. Whether in spoken or written word, these are the notorious *Freudian slips* that tell us something of our unconscious wishes. The reason they are often humorous to uninvolved people observing us is that they know intuitively what our true feelings are (ibid., p. 94).

## SOME PROCEDURAL DETAILS

Our final discussion in Chapter 19 relates to certain procedural details that a practicing psychoanalyst must take into consideration. No one can learn to be a psychoanalyst simply through the study of written accounts. But the reader can get a more realistic "feel" for the role of psychoanalyst through a consideration of such practical matters.

Although such techniques have been altered considerably today by psychoanalysts, Freud had his patients lie on a sofa while he sat behind the head of the patient, out of direct sight (Freud, 1913/1958h, pp. 133-134). This position reflected the influence of his earlier hypnotic and pressure techniques, but Freud also believed that it was wise to eliminate possible misinterpretations of his facial expressions that the patient might make. In addition, he frankly admitted that he could not stand being stared at by other people for eight hours or more per day. He felt it advisable to tell the patient that therapy would take a long time—a year or more at the very least. His patients assumed a heavy burden in time commitment, for he met with them several times a week— anywhere from two or three to five or six sessions weekly. As therapy wore on, the number of sessions might well be reduced, depending on how well the client was progressing.

Another important burden to the client was financial. Freud stressed that analysts must treat money matters as frankly as they treat sensitive personal topics. Money can be a tool of resistance for the patient, who can use this excuse to terminate the contacts—particularly because the practice followed by Freud (and since by his followers) was to charge for *every* scheduled session, including those that a client missed (except under highly unusual circumstances). The only recourse, Freud thought, is simply to state things clearly to the client at the outset and then to carry on without any further embarrassment. As Freud summed it up, in any case "nothing in life is so expensive as illness—and stupidity" (ibid., p. 133).

Freud saw his patients for what has come to be known as the classic fifty-minute hour. He was not much attracted to taking notes during the hour, preferring to do this sort of record keeping between patient appointments and at the close of the day. In the very earliest—including the first—sessions, Freud would simply turn the lead in the conversation over to the patient as follows: "Before I can say anything to you I must know a great deal about you; please tell me what you know about yourself" (ibid., p. 134). Many of these early sessions undoubtedly were spent in going over details of the illness that had prompted the client to seek assistance. Gradually, they would turn their attention to dreams and other materials emerging in the free associations. Freud would begin instructing the client in the basics of psychoanalysis, even as early as the fifth or sixth session (Freud, 1909/1955b, p. 180), but he was decidedly opposed to the patient's independent reading and studying of psychoanalysis from books (Freud, 1912/1958d, pp. 119-120).

Freud advised his patients not to make important decisions—such as choosing a profession or selecting a marital partner—during the course of treatment (Freud, 1913/1958i, p. 153). His reason was to limit the patient's chances of making important errors in life decisions through the acting out of unconscious impulses during the transformed neurosis. This suggestion may appear inconsistent with Freud's desire to avoid living the patient's life, but he viewed this request to *delay* important decisions as something quite different from the making of decisions *for* the client. In the lesser of life's decisions, he definitely favored a hands-off policy for the therapist.

When he first began treating patients, Freud went quickly into an interpretation of their personality dynamics, but later in his career he cautioned against rushing the client. He favored having the therapist delay an interpretation until the client is "one step short" of making it himself or herself (ibid., pp. 140-141). Freud also dabbled in setting time limits to a therapy series—particularly since one of his followers, Otto Rank (1968) made this a major technique variation. He admitted that at times if a client is told that there will be only so many more sessions, this can act as a prompt to get around the client's resistance. But Freud felt that one has to use this time-setting technique sparingly, and his reference to it as a "blackmailing device" obviously suggests that Freud did not think highly of it in any case (Freud, 1937/1964e, p. 218). Freud said that analysis ends when the analyst and analysand mutually decide to stop seeing one another. From the therapist's point of view, two general conditions have to be met before an ending to therapy is called for:

First, that the patient shall no longer be suffering from his symptoms and shall have overcome his anxieties and his inhibitions; and secondly, that the analyst shall judge that so much repressed material has been made conscious, so much that was unintelligible has been explained, and so much internal resistance conquered, that there is no need to fear a repetition of the pathological processes concerned. (ibid., p. 219)

## Summary

The term *psychotherapy* covers a wide range of treatment procedures whose common characteristic is that they deal with psychogenic illnesses by psychological means, rather than by the use of medicines and other somatic procedures. In an *insight* form of psychotherapy the therapist seeks to assist a patient to understand the grounds for the sake of which he or she behaves in an abnormal fashion. *Noninsight* therapies claim that such understanding is irrelevant or impossible. Chapter 19 takes up Freudian *psychoanalysis,* which is an insight form of psychotherapy. Freud labeled noninsight, biological therapies as *causal* (i.e., efficiently causal) cures. Psychoanalysis is *not* a causal therapy. The "fundamental rule" of psychoanalysis is *free association,* by which is meant complete and honest disclosure of thoughts as they occur to consciousness no matter how silly or unusual they may appear to rational analysis. Actually, such associations are not "free" but determined psychically (i.e., via formal and final causality).

*Resistance* in psychoanalysis is anything that interrupts the progress of analytical work. The *analysand* (i.e., the person being therapized) may reflect a regression in the type of resistance put up to the analytical procedure. *Transference* of either a *positive* or a *negative* variety arises in the psychoanalytical procedure, due to the fact that patients project onto the person of the doctor certain imagoes from out of their past. The analysand thus *acts out* past fixations with a *father imago* or a *mother imago,* or both. Considered in terms of libido theory, transference always involves cathecting the therapist with libido that has been withdrawn from the imago and then invested in the image of the therapist as stand-in. Emotional feelings for the imago *then* follow (i.e., libido is *not* emotion per se). Transference is invariably *ambivalent* in nature, because both positive and negative attitudes, emotions, and so on, are being sent the therapist's way.

Negative transference is likely to be precipitated by the therapist's *interpretations,* which are aimed at providing the analysand with insight. To interpret is to find the hidden sense in some behavior, memory, or reverie. Psychoanalytical treatment is in large measure an effort on the part of the analyst to understand and then re-educate the analysand by way of overcoming the latter's resistances to insight. Therapists can form *countertransferences,* which refer to the unconscious motives that they have in relation to their patients. Therapists have imagoes to project as well, particularly if they have not developed sufficient personal insight. This is why it is so important to be analyzed as a psychoanalyst, and indeed Freud believed that analysts should be continually checking into their own dynamics through peer contacts.

Freud's final theory of cure emphasized the role of inadequate *primal repression,* with the resulting problems encountered in repression proper as Oedipal material came to consciousness. Due to the *repetition compulsion* the neurotic seeks to re-enact these Oedipal themes in interpersonal relations, forming *libidinal anticipatory ideas* that frame certain *fuero claims* on the personality system. The acting-out process in transference during psycho- analysis brings these fuero demands into the open thanks to interpretations made by the analyst. This process of interpretation relies upon a modicum of *suggestion,* but it is impossible to suggest just anything to the analysand. The therapist can suggest insights and changes, but the patient must find what really works in his or her case and achieve ultimate independence.

As therapy proceeds, the analysand develops an *artificial* or *transformed neurosis* within the four walls of the consulting room—another manifestation of the repetition compulsion. This miniature enactment of the patient's broader life pattern has also been referred to as the *transference illness,* and even— unfortunately!—as the *transference neurosis.* The latter usage is unfortunate because Freud also distinguished between *narcissistic* and *transformed neu- roses.* The former were considered unamenable to psychoanalysis because libido would not be sent anticipatorily into the person's life milieu, but narcissistically sent inward, into a pseudocommunity of delusional fantasy. The narcissistic neurotic (today we would say *psychotic*) is thus incapable of forming a transformed neurosis, which is the vehicle of cure because it is in providing interpretations during such acting out that the analyst succeeds in giving the analysand insight, which in turn leads to cure.

The libidinal explanation of cure is that the patient removes libido from the life situation, focuses this upon the therapist (leading to transference), and eventually recoups this libido in strengthening the ego as insight progresses. Caution must be taken lest this ego investment become narcissistic. In order for insight to work in psychoanalysis the analysand must be literally acting out some dynamic, with attendant emotional feelings, when the interpretation is made. All of the person's fixations (fuero claims) cannot be cured in one transformed neurosis. This is why psychoanalysis seems to go on interminably. In the long run, Freud can be viewed as much a social revisionist as a therapist of the individual person.

In working out his specific therapeutic technique, Freud began by using *hypnosis,* in age- or time-regression strategies. The *pressure technique* was then devised as an aid to help patients recall past life events even though they were not in a deep hypnotic trance. The *free-association* method followed, in which patients were allowed to say whatever came into their mind spontaneously. Freud found that the so-called trivia and unrelated scraps of information arising from free association were *screen memories* or *screen associations* akin to the manifest content of dreams. He began to see a pattern of meaning lying behind such screening devices. The typical practice in psychoanalysis is for a patient to enter upon a trial analysis period of several weeks. If at that time there is serious difficulty in forming a relationship, the therapy may be discontinued. Freud admitted that psychoanalysis takes a long time, in some cases several years, but he could see no other way of curing neurosis short of the superficial, suggestive cures that relied on manipulation and the authority of positive transference to suppress a symptom. He rejected the latter strategy completely.

# 20

## Biological and Behavioristic Therapies

There are far too many treatment procedures practiced today for coverage in a chapter or two of the present volume. Chapter 19 has taken a close look at Freudian psychoanalysis, which is an insight form of psychotherapy. To provide grounds for comparison, in the present chapter we shall survey two of the major *noninsight* approaches widely used in the treatment of both neurotic and psychotic disorders. We refer here to the *biological* and *behavioristic* therapies so widely used today. The reader is referred elsewhere for a broader consideration of insight approaches such as the nondirective, existentialistic, rational, familial, dramatic, dance, and many other forms of psychotherapy practiced today (see Abt & Stuart, 1982; Rychlak, 1981b). There is also a lively literature concerning the efficacy of psychotherapy, with both positive (Bergin & Lambert, 1978) and negative (Eysenck, 1952) evaluations rendered. Though we cannot hope to resolve this long-standing dispute over the findings on researches in psychotherapy, it is at least worth noting that statistical meta-analyses which blanket this vast literature in a systematic manner have generally concluded that psychotherapized patients are more likely to improve in adjustment than patients given a placebo manipulation or no therapy at all (Landman & Dawes, 1982; Smith & Glass, 1977).

### Biological Therapies

Biological therapies are interventions based upon the fairly reasonable assumption that body and mind are interrelated aspects of total human behavior. If the body is malfunctioning it is quite possible that this will adversely affect the mind. Hence, any biophysical process that can effect changes in those aspects of the human body relating to mental states must be taken as a potential source of cure. In some cases, this is a purely empirical "trial-and-error" effort based upon clinical oBservation. In other instances, there is a firm basis in laboratory findings, such as those concerning the biochemical studies in schizophrenia that we presented in Chapter 14 (see pp. 448-449).

## INSULIN COMA THERAPY

*Insulin coma therapy* was devised in 1933 by the Polish psychiatrist Manfred Sakel, who was trained in Vienna. Sakel first used this procedure for the treatment of excited states experienced by morphine addicts during their period of withdrawal. Based on success in this patient group, Sakel later extended this treatment to reducing excitement in a schizophrenic population. In 1936 Sakel brought his method of treatment to the United States, where it was initially hailed as a new cure for schizophrenia. This did not prove to be true, of course, but as an adjunct therapy insulin coma therapy has had its modicum of success, particularly with schizophrenic patients who are acutely ill and therefore among the best bets for recovery in any case.

Insulin is a hormone that regulates sugar metabolism in the body, and its administration results in hypoglycemia (deficiency of blood glucose). If this deficiency becomes pronounced, the patient slips into a coma with or without convulsions. Treatment with insulin coma usually consists of daily intramuscular injections of insulin, which are increased until the patient becomes comatose, that is, unresponsive to a point short of death. After an hour or more, the patient is given an injection of glucose to terminate the coma. A full series for any patient ordinarily involves a total of roughly fifty hours spent in a state of coma. Insulin therapy has steadily lost ground in recent times, but it is still occasionally used with patients in their twenties who have a stormy, sudden onset of schizophrenia and who have up until the time of their illness presented a fairly well-integrated personality (Kalinowski & Hippius, 1969; Noyes & Kolb, 1958). Once the patient is in good contact with reality, insight therapy or behavioral manipulations can be introduced into a total treatment program.

## ELECTROCONVULSIVE THERAPY

*Electroconvulsive therapy* (ECT) or, as it is sometimes called, *electric shock therapy* (EST) was to follow insulin coma therapy and become the biological treatment of choice in schizophrenia for a period of years following World War II. The "theory" on which it seems to have been based was the erroneous clinical observation that epileptics rarely suffered from schizophrenia. Since epileptics do suffer from convulsions, it seemed reasonable to induce a convulsion in a schizophrenic patient and thereby counteract the psychopathological process. In 1938 two Italian psychiatrists, Cerletti and Bini, perfected a method of attaching electrodes to the temple area of the skull. An electric current of approximately 160 volts was then passed from one side of the patient's head to the other for up to about one and one-half seconds.

When this occurs, the patient is rendered unconscious and manifests a marked tonic (extensor) seizure of the muscles, followed by a lengthy series of clonic (contractile) seizures. The procedure has been perfected with the introduction of muscle relaxants, so that patients no longer injure themselves during the gyrations of their seizures. Upon wakening, the patient has amnesia for the period immediately preceding shock administration. There is a period of confusion for an hour or so. Headaches are common and may be severe. The schedule of treatments vary, but usually three administrations per week are given during which the patient's mental state continues to be disoriented. In most cases, ECT is discontinued in four weeks (a total of twelve shocks). Impaired memory has been noted for weeks and even months following the ECT series (Squire, Slater, & Chase, 1975). However, assuming that the patient responds to the treatment, when the confusion, disorientation, and memory loss dissipates there is a noticeable improvement in his or her behavior.

Though ECT was initially heralded as a cure for schizophrenia, subsequent experience with the therapy revealed that it is most effective with psychotic depressions, particularly involutional melancholia (see Chapter 12, p. 381). It does not take effect in every instance, but quite often a patient given ECT recovers from depression in a matter of weeks or months rather than months or years. At that point, insight or behavioral therapies can be employed if they are in order. The leading modern theoretical account of why ECT may prove effective is that the electrical current somehow induces changes in the biochemistry of synapses in the cells of the brain (Fink, 1979). We are far from conclusively establishing the validity of this theory.

There have been interesting variations in the biological therapies. For example, in both insulin and electric shock applications a kind of limited use of the therapeutic vehicle has been attempted, resulting in some successes without the dramatic manifestation of coma or convulsion. Lower doses of insulin are given, resulting in a milder level of hypoglycemia, or less electrical voltage is sent through the patient's brain so that he or she does not actually lose consciousness and manifest the convulsive seizure. There is also a *unilateral* form of ECT in which, rather than sending electricity across the electrodes attached at the temple, a current is sent through only one of the brain's hemispheres, usually the nondominant one (e.g., in a right-handed person this would usually be the left cerebral hemisphere) (Squire & Slater, 1978). In this procedure a seizure is effected, but there is encouraging evidence that some of the distressing side effects such as memory impairment due to brain damage is reduced. It is the brain damage which results from ECT that has brought this technique under severe criticism (Brengelmann, 1959; Fink, 1977). Critics are likely to think of ECT as the therapy of last resort, and it is not nearly so widely used as it once was.

## PSYCHOSURGERY

Another controversial biological therapy is *psychosurgery,* a global term referring to various brain operations performed to relieve the symptoms of schizophrenia and depression. The most common operation has been lateral *transcranial prefrontal lobotomy,* but other procedures have included *transorbital lobotomy, topectomy, gyrectomy,* and *thalamotomy.* The psychosurgery procedure was introduced by the Portuguese neurologist Egas Moniz and subsequently perfected by others (e.g., W. Freeman & Watts, 1950). The essential theory underlying psychosurgery is that a deranged person is likely to be suffering from abnormal electrochemical brain activity—for example, obtaining excessive inputs in the frontal lobes, where higher thought processes are located, from lower brain centers such as the thalamus, where emotional reactions are patterned and transmitted.

Thus, in *prefrontal lobotomy* the surgeon enters the cranial cavity through a trephine (hole) in the temple region of the skull. Using a special surgical instrument, he or she then severs the nerve fibers connecting the frontal areas of the cerebral cortex and the thalamus. This procedure was eventually improved upon in *transorbital lobotomy.* In the latter procedure no trephine need be drilled in the skull, because the surgeon enters the cranial cavity through the eye socket. Once again, using a special surgical instrument, he or she can sever the critical cortical nerve pathways (Valenstein, 1973). Since brain tissue does not regenerate, psychosurgery renders the patient permanently brain damaged, and the attendant personality changes have brought psychosurgery under considerable criticism since its quite frequent application in the 1940s and 1950s (Gaylin, Meister, & Neville, 1975).

Though some of the early findings on psychosurgery were positive (see, e.g., Landis & Erlick, 1950), later findings of a more extensive nature suggested that only a small percentage of patients were able to return to a normal life outside of the institution following their operations (Barahal, 1958). The formerly agitated patient often did become tranquil and manageable, but there was also a dramatic change in personality so that the person appeared emotionally shallow, lost interest in life's more challenging activities, overate, and simply "existed" in a kind of mental vacuum. Observers sometimes referred to these patients as "zombies." Still other patients developed seizures following their operation. Psychosurgery is thus even more of a "therapy of last resort" than ECT. It is rarely used today, but estimates as late as 1973 suggest that about five hundred such operations were performed in the United States (Holden, 1973). In most cases it is the highly violent and self-destructive patient who has not responded to anything else for years and years who is selected for psychosurgery (Mark & Ervin, 1970).

## PHARMACOLOGICAL THERAPY

The biological therapy of choice in the present is, by far, the use of pharmacological agents or drugs. *Pharmacological therapy* or *chemotherapy* as it is often called has its roots in ancient practices in the treatment of the mentally ill through diet and various purgatives. But it is only through modern advances in the development of drugs applicable to the symptoms of psychopathology that we can now speak of a well-defined area of biological therapy. It is not our intention to go into great detail concerning these modern chemical agents, for undoubtedly there will be advances in their manufacture and development by the year. We shall simply survey the three major types of these agents, giving examples of the drugs concerned under the appropriate designation.

*Antianxiety Drugs.* Antianxiety drugs are depressants of the central nervous system, reducing arousal and relaxing muscular tension so that the person feels less tense and anxious. The *sedatives* fall into this category, with barbiturates (e.g., secobarbital; trade name: Seconal) a frequent drug of choice in the past. However, barbiturates are less likely to be prescribed today because they are highly addictive, and sudden withdrawal from the drug can result in the death of the patient (K. L. Jones, Shainburg, & Byer, 1973). More widely used today are the *minor tranquilizers,* which are less addicting and equally effective in the control of anxiety. Here we have such drugs as meprobamate (Equanil), diazepam (Valium), and chlordiazepoxide (Librium).

Antianxiety drugs are used as an adjunct treatment in cases of neurosis or psychosomatic disorders in which tension and anxiety are the predominant symptoms. They are not ordinarily used to treat the psychotic individual. Minor tranquilizers are widely prescribed to assist individuals through periods of emotional upheaval, and in recent years this wide usage has been criticized as excessive. As with all drugs, there are side effects to be considered. Patients feel sleepy and sometimes complain of dizziness and loss of coordination. Although less addicting than the barbiturates, the minor tranquilizers can become addictive, and withdrawal symptoms such as insomnia, vomiting, and tremor are not uncommon when the patient begins to stop using these drugs (Detre & Jarecki, 1971).

*Antidepressant Drugs.* In Chapter 12 (p. 380) we reviewed the catecholamine hypothesis, which suggested that depression is due to a *deficit* of the neurotransmitter *norepinephrine* at the synaptic connections of the brain's neural tissue. The antidepressant drugs we are now considering are thought to stimulate the production of norepinephrine and related neurotransmitters, although the research evidence is not yet conclusive (P. A. Berger, 1978). There are two subgroups of antidepressant drugs: (1) *tricyclic antidepressants,* which include imipramine (Tofranil) and amitriptyline hydrochloride (Elavil), and (2) *monoamine oxidase (MAO) inhibitors* like isocarboxazid (Marplan). The tricyclics are used more generally because they seem to have proven more effective and there are fewer side effects and dietary restrictions involved (Detre & Jarecki, 1971). The antidepressant drugs are sometimes referred to as "mood elevators" because they do appear to elevate the mood of the depressed person, sometimes in dramatic fashion. Of course, in a severely regressed, psychotic depression there is little success with antidepressants and at that point ECT is taken under advisement (see above).

*Antipsychotic Drugs.* Antipsychotic drugs are also referred to as the *major tranquilizers,* and they are recommended when the patient manifests symptoms of agitation, inappropriate emotional display, social withdrawal, and, of course, delusional and/or hallucinatory activity. They serve as more profound depressants of central nervous system arousal than the drugs mentioned above as minor tranquilizers. Also, recall from Chapter 14 (p. 449) that certain antipsychotic drugs may prove beneficial through blocking the reception of dopamine at the synaptic sites of the schizophrenic patient's central nervous system.

Among the most widely used antipsychotic drugs are chlorpromazine (Thorazine), trifluoperazine (Stelazine), and haloperidol (Haldol). These drugs have been shown to be effective in cases of acute schizophrenia (Cole, 1964; P. R. A. May, 1968), but the more chronically disabled schizophrenic patient does not respond quite so well (G. L. Paul, Tobias, & Holly, 1972). But the immense impact that the antipsychotic drugs have had on treatment of the severely mentally ill can hardly be denied. They have literally revolutionized institutionalized care of the severely mentally ill, making the modern trend toward care in the community possible.

Common criticisms of the antipsychotic drugs include the fact that they supposedly make the patient over into an emotionless automaton, second only to the patient who has been given psychosurgery (Honigfeld & Howard, 1973). Other side effects include convulsions, sensitivity to light, and various uncontrollable movements of the throat and tongue. There are countermeasures to such side effects, and recent developments in pharmacology suggest that the more serious side effects may be overcome (Kolata, 1979). Another criticism hinges on the fact that no real cure is attained in the use of antipsychotic drugs, and that often, when they are terminated the patient reverts to his or her former pattern of behavior (P. A. Berger, 1978). However, given that there is no other way in which to begin a therapeutic program with many schizophrenic patients, it seems only prudent to be thankful that the antipsychotic drugs do enable therapists to make contact with these patients and thereby to take an initial step in the direction of rectifying their psychopathological condition.

Other drugs do not fall neatly into the above three categories, but may be beneficial in the treatment of personal maladjustment. For example, the mineral salt *lithium carbonate* is sometimes prescribed for treatment of manic incidents in patients with affective disorders (Schou, 1976). Certain stimulants like *dexedrine* have been found to be useful in the paradoxical sense of calming down hyperactive children (Grinspoon & Singer, 1973). As with the other drugs we have discussed, there are frequent criticisms leveled against the use of such drugs for the side effects that they bring about, some of which can be damaging if not irreversible entirely. In line with the *biosocial* orientation of the present volume, we choose to look at drugs as only one side of the total picture in treatment, to be used with caution and on a restricted basis until such time as we can see it clear to begin a more dynamic examination of the patient's adjustment problems.

We next move to the noninsight therapies that have been developed in light of the laboratory experiments and theoretical explanations of behavioristic psychology.

## Behavioristic Therapies

We shall survey three of the most widely used behavioristic techniques of changing behavior. The first two, *systematic desensitization* and *implosive therapy,* rely upon classical (Pavlovian) conditioning theory to account for the changes that occur. The third, *behavior modification,* relies upon operant (Skinnerian) conditioning theory. It should be recalled that we have discussed factors relating to both classical and operant conditioning in Chapters 2 (pp. 34-38) and 5 (pp. 142-147). We shall want to return to the points made in these earlier discussions before terminating Chapter 20 (see below).

### SYSTEMATIC DESENSITIZATION

Systematic desensitization therapy was proposed by Joseph Wolpe, based upon Hull's learning theory (1952). Sherrington's concept of *reciprocal inhibition* (1947), and the practical steps in Jacobson's technique of *progressive relaxation* (1938). Hull had found that a kind of inhibition occurs in animal behavior when a response that has already been learned is opposed by a competing response. For example, an animal that had been conditioned to respond with anxiety to a given stimulus might find this anxiety response inhibited by the competing response of eating food in proximity to the feared stimulus (Wolpe, 1958, p. 28). In this experiment, Hull assumed that a *conditioned inhibition* of one response (anxiety) by an alternative response (eating) took place.

Wolpe wedded this notion of conditioned inhibition to Sherrington's concept of reciprocal inhibition, which referred to the fact that one spinal reflex can inhibit another stimulus (ibid., p. 29). Continuing in the vein of Hullian drive reduction theory, Wolpe therefore suggested, "When a response is inhibited by an incompatible response and if a major drive reduction follows, a significant amount of conditioned inhibition of the response will be developed" (ibid., p. 30).

The practical implication from all of this was that, if a therapist could first teach a patient to relax via Jacobson's technique and *then* get the patient to "respond" with relaxation in proximity to some anxiety-provoking stimulus, a *cure* through reciprocal inhibition might be effected. Rather than responding with fright to some "phobic stimulus," the patient could be conditioned into feeling quite relaxed in the presence of this stimulus (elevator, open street, high place, etc.). Wolpe was to put this program into effect, with good results, and the era of behavior therapy was underway (ibid., p. 139).

To carry out systematic desensitization we must first know the specific stimuli—invariably, social situations—that evoke the anxiety in a presumably efficient-cause fashion (see Chapter 1, p. 4). We learn this through a detailed interview of the patient, supplemented by personality-scale findings. In the case of free-floating anxiety, in which there has probably been a subtle form of anxiety snowballing over time, the specific stimuli may be hard to point out.

But usually the patient can name *some* situations that are more upsetting than others. He or she is able to rank order a series of life situations that are more or less upsetting, tension-provoking, frightening, and so forth. Let us assume that Dianne, a twenty-three-year-old public relations representative, has come to Wolpe with a claustrophobic fear of entering elevators. Her extreme fear upon entering an elevator makes her "go to pieces," and she is on the verge of quitting her promising work career due to this handicap because she simply has to take elevators in order to meet her clients.

After a detailed clinical interview and the administration of a paper-and-pencil personality scale, Wolpe finds that her anxiety pattern is not limited to elevators but extends to other situations as well. For example, Dianne is afraid of being engulfed by a crowd. She is ill at ease in automobiles and must keep a window wide open while driving. In fact, there are times when simply being in any room gives her the feeling that the walls are "closing in" on her. For many months she has been able to put up with a fear she recognizes as being irrational. But now she finds it almost impossible to enter an elevator, and her job future is severely threatened so she has come to Wolpe for help.

Once the total clinical picture is understood—not in any dynamic way, but simply as a syndrome of maladjustment—Wolpe sets about training Dianne how to relax. Jacobson (1938) had demonstrated that autonomic responses like pulse rate and blood pressure could be lowered through what he called *deep muscle relaxation.* In adapting these "progressive relaxation" exercises of Jacobson's to therapy, Wolpe found that roughly six interviews of thirty to fifty minutes each are required for the client to learn deep muscle relaxation. Dianne is instructed that in order to counteract her emotional anxiety, she must master this skill.

Wolpe might begin muscle-relaxation training by having Dianne grip the arm of her chair with one hand while leaving the other relaxed. Can she sense the difference between the tense hand and the one that is relaxed? Good, then she can proceed to other muscles of the body in this fashion. How limp can she make her arms feel if she places both hands in her lap and simply relaxes for a few minutes? From here, Wolpe may have Dianne work on the muscles of her shoulder and neck, for these are particularly important indicators of tension level (Wolpe, 1969, p. 103). Tenseness in the facial and tongue muscles are usually easy to identify as reflecting level of anxiety. Next, Dianne might be asked to focus on the larger muscles of the back, abdomen, and thorax before going to the muscles of her feet and legs. Through careful study and some practice at home between sessions, Dianne can acquire the skill of relaxing her muscles quite nicely in a half-dozen therapy contacts.

In some instances, Wolpe might prepare a patient for *hypnotism* at this point. Hypnosis is closely related to relaxation, of course. Wolpe's approach to hypnosis is strictly empirical; he uses it only when a subject seems especially prone to direction by suggestion and it has immediate benefit. Hypnosis is not essential for systematic desensitization to work, though Wolpe uses it in about 10 percent of his cases (ibid., p. 123).

The next step would involve constructing an *anxiety hierarchy,* which rank orders the degree of anxiety experienced by Dianne concerning the specific elevator phobia (later, other anxiety hierarchies could be devised for driving in automobiles, being in a crowded subway, and so forth). Anxiety hierarchies are usually arrayed as the case history is taken and as relaxation training is being carried out (ibid., p. 107). Wolpe's technique takes its name from the anxiety hierarchy, in that the patient is systematically desensitized to the anxiety-provoking stimuli contained therein. Dianne's anxiety hierarchy might look something like this, from greatest to least sense of anxiety:

1. When the doors of the elevator close above the street level during ascent.
2. Stepping on the elevator.
3. Feeling the elevator move.
4. When the doors of the elevator close at street level during initial entry.
5. Hearing that she has an assignment calling for an elevator ride.
6. Getting dressed the morning of her assignment with the elevator ride.
7. The night before she is going to take an elevator ride.
8. The afternoon of the day preceding her elevator ride.
9. Just thinking about being on an elevator at any time.
10. Seeing a picture of an elevator in the newspaper or on television.

Wolpe would know that this hierarchy reflects Dianne's rank ordering because in his clinical interview he would have proposed these situations and asked her to rate each according to what he terms a *sud* or *subjective unit of disturbance* (ibid., p. 28). This involves a 100-point scale, with the top score of 100 being the most extreme anxiety imaginable and the score of 0 representing absolute calm. Not all patients would give the same hierarchy of anxiety-provoking circumstances that Dianne gave, of course. Some might find the door closing at street level to be more frightening than the door closings above street level, whereas Dianne's anxiety seems to mount with each opportunity to "get off" the elevator that she is unable to take advantage of.

After Wolpe constructed a hierarchy for Dianne he would ask the young woman to begin relaxation exercises by imagining herself in the *least* frightening situation (seeing a picture of an elevator in a newspaper) and to make use of the muscle-relaxation training to reciprocally inhibit this lowest level of anxiety. Dianne would sit with her eyes closed, imagining she was looking at a picture of an elevator while she allowed her body to go limp in complete relaxation. She would continue doing so until she could imagine herself in this circumstance *without* anxiety. If she were a candidate for hypnotism, then Dianne would be doing the same thing while under a light trance with Wolpe giving her verbal instruction what it was that she should be imagining. A lifting of the finger signals Wolpe that Dianne is completely relaxed while imagining scene 10 of the anxiety hierarchy (0 suds). Usually, the patient is asked to relax for fifteen seconds before Wolpe verbally requests that a scene be brought to mind for five to ten seconds (ibid., p. 127). This brief enactment of a scene may be repeated several times. The more anxiety experienced by the client the shorter the scene presentation.

The number of scenes presented during a desensitization session also varies. In some cases only one or two exposures seems justified. In others, particularly in the advanced stages of therapy, as many as thirty to fifty presentations of five to seven seconds' duration each may be employed. Some patients can be moved up from one scene to another in the same session. Others require concentration on one scene per session. But the strategy remains the same, and that is to work the patient up the anxiety hierarchy until all ten scenes can be mentally contemplated without feeling anxiety. A desensitization session ordinarily can be completed in from fifteen to thirty minutes, and the length of therapy varies from as few as six to possibly one hundred or more sessions.

An interesting feature of this technique is that spacing of sessions does not seem to affect outcome. As a rule, clients are scheduled for two or three sessions per week, but even when sessions are massed on the same day (when for instance a client must travel long distances to therapy on a weekend) or carried on once monthly, positive results can be noted. Very little improvement occurs between sessions. Occasionally a client is so upset that it proves extremely difficult to achieve complete relaxation during the session. In such cases Wolpe has prescribed a sedating drug to be taken by the patient one hour before the interview (Wolpe, 1973, p. 182). It is also possible to reduce free-floating anxiety by having clients inhale various mixtures of carbon dioxide and oxygen (ibid.).

Occasionally a client is not a good subject for hypnotism or cannot imagine situations well enough for the usual procedure. In such cases the therapist may have to plan an anxiety hierarchy that can be desensitized *in vivo*. For example, airplane phobias can be worked out by systematically taking an individual closer to the airport and then onto a plane that can be rented and simply taxied about for a time, and so forth. Gradually, increasing approximations to flight might be engaged in on the airstrip, until an actual take-off and immediate return to earth is accomplished.

Wolpe's technique revolutionized the practice of psychotherapy in the 1960s and thereafter. Extensions and variations of the systematic desensitization tactic were to flower after Wolpe's initial efforts. For example, it was found that the precise rank ordering of an anxiety hierarchy is not essential, so that subjects might be given practice in the listed situations in any sequence with the same success rate. Though the principle of so-called *counterconditioning* (J. B. Watson & Rayner, 1920; see our discussion of "Little Albert" in Chapter 2, p. 37) had been known for decades, it was Wolpe's example that more than any other fostered the development of the noninsight or nondynamic psychotherapies of modern times. Whether or not systematic desensitization is free of telic considerations is another matter, one that we shall allude to later in this chapter.

## IMPLOSIVE THERAPY

Implosive therapy was introduced by Thomas G. Stampfl, who relied upon O. H. Mowrer's elaboration (1939) of Hullian theory to suggest that any reduction in anxiety could serve as a reinforcement. Thus, Mowrer demonstrated that rats would run across active electric grids in order to flee a compartment in which electricity had previously been administered but was no longer being delivered. The earlier experience of being shocked in this compartment motivated the rats to flee, even though they literally shocked themselves in the process because the only "way out" of the anxiety-provoking compartment was across an electrified grid. But the *reduction* in anxiety once out of the feared compartment served as a reinforcement of the "fleeing" behavior when the rat was next placed in the compartment (Mowrer, 1948). The only way in which to stop the rat from running again and again was to block the exit—the pathway across the electrified grid. Rapidly, the rats discontinued their running behavior as their anxiety in the compartment *extinguished.*

Stampfl, as Mowrer before him, reasoned that maladjusted people also continually punish themselves for something out of their past, when if they could somehow allow this residual anxiety to extinguish they would lose their pathognomic behaviors. An *implosion* is a bursting inwards, in contrast to the outward bursting of an explosion. Hence, *implosive therapy* implies that emotive reactions are erupting, but their expression is internal to the individual's fantasy life, that is, within his or her imagination. Emotion is displayed, but action is totally through imagery and talk about what is being imagined. In other words, *primary* reinforcements or punishments do not follow re-enactment of emotionally arousing scenes. Rather than relaxing Dianne up her anxiety hierarchy in the style of Wolpe's systematic desensitization, Stampfl might encourage this young woman to picture herself "running amok" in complete anxiety as she is trapped in the elevator for hours. If her fear is connected with a crashing elevator, he might encourage her to picture herself actually being killed in a wretched plunge of fifty floors to the crunching termination of life as the metal box within which she is encased breaks through the concrete floor below.

The core theory of illness on which implosive therapy rests is as follows: for any of a number of reasons—including all of the typically Freudian explanations that we have surveyed in the present volume—the individual has been emotionally conditioned (via autonomic nervous system) to some stimulus pattern in his or her environment (elevator). Whenever this stimulus (elevator) comes into view—through imagination, a dream, or actual experience—the person is gripped with a sense of mounting anxiety. As this level of anxiety increases, it acts as an additional signal of the horrible things that might happen. Stampfl thus essentially agrees with Freud's final formulation of anxiety in this sense, that it is a warning signal that a dangerous situation is about to develop in the person's life (see Chapter 5, p. 126).

Rather than permitting the anxiety state to reach complete expression, the individual has learned to do something that will lower the level of anxiety before it has a chance to take over his or her complete state of awareness. This something is what we know as either a host of defense mechanisms or the *symptoms* of a neurosis (Stampfl & Levis, 1968, p. 34). Such behaviors are aimed at avoiding the impending doom the autonomic responses suggest are about to take place ("I just know something terrible is going to happen to me"). Stampfl suggested that probably the most common defense mechanism is what Freud had called *repression* (ibid.). Neurotics have learned to forget what raises their anxiety level, and when this forgetting results in lowered anxiety, they find themselves in a state of continuing ignorance.

Symptoms, on the other hand, are simply the more dramatic and personally harmful extensions of this mechanism for reducing anxiety. Technically, Stampfl would refer to symptoms as *conditioned avoidance responses* (Stampfl & Levis, 1967b, p. 24). Dianne sees her feared stimulus of the elevator and is gripped with anxiety until a distance is put between herself and this feared object. Compulsive neurotics must wash their hands to counteract their horror of dirt. Obsessives must hum a lucky tune or repeat some magic formula that seems to calm them for a time. Hysterical tics and even paranoid delusions can all be learned methods of reducing anxiety promptings. Unlike Freud's explanation, there is no use made here of intentionality. A portion of the ego does not "inoculate" (see Chapter 4, p. 126) itself with anxiety so that a threatening item of knowledge is kept out of consciousness. Stampfl sticks closely with the efficient-cause style of explanation so typical of behaviorism. Hence, conditioned avoidance responses are *not* self-directed maneuverings of one side of the mind against the other. They are typical stimulus-response habits.

An interesting feature of Stampflian theory holds that the symptom may have symbolic ties to the origin of the neurosis (a problem that does not draw Wolpe's interest at all!). Thus, when the stimulus triggering a symptomatic reaction appears, a host of unknown or forgotten (repressed) thoughts, memories, and images are *redintegrated* (ibid.). To redintegrate is to reopen or re-enliven past cues of an anxiety-provoking nature (once again, in an automatic, nonintentional fashion!). This is the reason anxiety seems to snowball when the neurotic is placed in a threatening situation. Our claustrophobic, Dianne, is responding not only to the present cues but to other long-forgotten cues as well. When she begins to suffer anxiety in riding an elevator, her mounting fears are not only to the four walls of the elevator but *also* to the fact that these symbolize the four sides of her baby crib, in which she was often placed and emotionally neglected as an infant.

Stampfl properly recognizes that this teaches us something about neurotic symptoms. The reason they are retained in a behavioral repertoire is that they effectively offset the return to mind of a number of other even more painful stimuli. Dianne flees the elevator stimulus pattern with its four walls pressing in on her long before she begins to recall the more dynamic memories of a fear that she is being abandoned by her loved ones and buried alive in the blankets of her crib (symbolically equated now with a coffin). Hence, the level of anxiety experienced by an individual in any given situation is a rough measure of the *relevance* of this situation to his or her neurosis. Relevant situations redintegrate more anxiety than irrelevant situations. In effect, therefore, symptoms always tell us what the patient is avoiding (Stampfl, 1966, p. 14). This idea also meshes perfectly with Freudian views on symptomatology!

If neurotics are pressed to face up to the signals contained in their area of symptom formation and block their attempts to flee (repress, etc.), Stampfl notes that in time a series of meaningful cues will emerge to reveal more and more about what has provoked their neuroses in the first place. It is thus possible to distinguish between two types of cues in neurosis: first, the *symptom-contingent cues,* which might be something as simple as the sight of the elevator; and second, the *hypothesized conditioned aversive cues,* which relate to what we have been calling the symbolic (or dynamic) meaning tied to the neurosis. The former essentially redintegrate the latter (Stampfl & Levis, 1969).

The fascinating dynamics of symptom formation and redintegration can be demonstrated by reviewing one of Stampfl's earliest cases, concerning a young man—let us call him Daryl—who suffered from a compulsion to make certain his radio was turned off before going to sleep at night (Stampfl & Levis, 1966). Daryl came to Stampfl complaining that he found it necessary to check this fact as many as fifty times per night before he could doze off. Pulling out the electric plug did not help, and the symptom seemed to be getting worse. When asked what he felt might happen if the radio were left on, Daryl replied that he experienced a subjective feeling that something terrible or catastrophic would happen—possibly a fire that would consume him in flames. Rather than reassure him or teach him to relax while close to radios, Stampfl instructed Daryl to go to bed that night imagining that the radio was actually on or to turn it on so that he was certain it was alive with electricity. Then Daryl was to lie in bed and imagine that a spark from the radio produced a tiny flame that would get bigger and bigger until the room was filled with snapping, popping flames several feet tall, which would burn his bed and body to a cinder in a horribly painful manner! Stampfl encouraged Daryl to imagine this entire scene as vividly as possible and to experience fully the anxiety it provoked.

In the next therapy session Daryl reported that he had followed Stampfl's instructions, and though the image of the fire and his burning body was terrifying, he had found great relief from his compulsion immediately following the imaginary exercise. He was able to fall asleep without the recurring round of radio checks. Further, he told of an interesting thing that happened during the height of the imagined fire. He "heard" his father's voice calling to him over the roar of the flames. He had not mentioned his father up to this time, and Stampfl was to learn on further questioning that Daryl's father had been a stickler for security measures in the home. Such things as lights left on, dripping faucets, or running electrical appliances sent the father into a rage that almost always ended in a spanking for Daryl or one of his siblings. At the very least, the father would devote much time lecturing his children on the potentially dangerous consequences of such carelessness around the home.

Though Stampfl did not feel that insight into such factors was essential for a cure, he did accept the likelihood that a Freudian analysis of this family structure could well account for his patient's symptom. Daryl may have sensed a death wish on the part of his father; the father wanted his son dead but expressed it through an obsessive preoccupation with safety measures (reaction-formation). Even if this were the dynamic explanation, the practical factor that kept the symptom alive today was the fact that by checking his radio, Daryl could gain a sense of protective relief from mounting anxiety ("I will not die"). This reduction in anxiety sustained the abnormal pattern and *also* prevented a redintegration of the broader clinical dynamics (father hostility, rejection, the need to defend the self, the need to make the father guilty for his hostility by killing oneself in a fire, and so on).

By encouraging Daryl to experience his anxiety when no punishment resulted—a fire did not start—Stampfl found that the autonomic reactions quickly extinguished. After a few such practiced self-destructions, Daryl lost his radio compulsion completely. There was no warning sign to begin the compulsion at bedtime because permitting anxiety full expression interrupted the triggering mechanism. We are reminded here of Mowrer's blocking of the exit for his rats, enabling them to extinguish the ongoing anxiety drive because nothing punishing took place (the compartment's floor was no longer electrified and hence they were "safe"). It is this rapid *extinction* of the autonomically generated anxiety sensations that forms the basis of a cure in implosive therapy.

If Stampfl were to treat our imaginary patient, Dianne, he would begin with a careful study of her symptoms, trying as did Wolpe to get a clear picture of what frightens her and what does not. Once again, a hierarchy of anxiety-provoking stimuli is arranged, but more by the therapist than strict measurement in suds. Dianne would then be given some training in the framing of visual images, because Stampfl is hoping to bring her fear-provoking stimuli clearly to mind. This training usually takes only a portion of one session with the patient.

Now that Stampfl has some idea of what things frighten Dianne—including not only the elevator but other situations as well—he will array a hierarchy of such avoidant images in ranked order. The technical term for this ordering is the *avoidance serial cue hierarchy* (ASCH). The ASCH runs serially from the least to the most anxiety-provoking set of circumstances in the client's life (Stampfl & Levis, 1967a, p. 500). The patient need not be told about the particular steps of this hierarchy, since some highly upsetting scenes may be readied for presentation at its apex. For example, Stampfl may have discerned that Dianne's fear of elevators is tied to a fear of coffins, funeral parlors, or anything at all to do with death. He might, therefore, at some point in therapy, alter imagery induction and have Dianne crash to death in a plunging elevator, and then be "laid out" in a funeral parlor where people walk by her coffin and comment on her mangled appearance.

Once the ASCH is arrayed, the next step involves scene presentations with attendant anxiety. The main point the patient must understand is that in order to extinguish an emotion like anxiety, it must be experienced to the fullest. Hence, as implosive therapy begins, and Stampfl is verbally describing the least anxiety-provoking scene, Dianne is encouraged to picture it as clearly as possible, live through it fully, and let as much anxiety flow as possible (Stampfl & Levis, 1967b, p. 26). Focusing on the anxiety sensation per se is important, because at least part of the reason anxiety snowballs is that each succeeding wave of anxiety acts as a mounting secondary cue to further the extent of emotion being felt. Invariably, the anxiety sensations are found to coalesce with other emotions, such as hostility directed toward parental figures, and when such feelings emerge Stampfl encourages their expression as well (Stampfl & Levis, 1967a, p. 501).

Scenes are presented repeatedly, and their elaboration can take up to ten minutes (taking Dianne through a horrendous death on the elevator, and so on). The autonomic responsiveness of the patient (perspiration, breathing rate, and so on) dictates the success a particular scene is having in arousing anxiety, and each scene is presented until anxiety reduction is achieved. A unique feature of implosive therapy is the practice of having the client work through the scenes of his or her ASCH at home between sessions with the therapist. This form of homework speeds up the process of extinction. A similar technique had been used by the existential therapist Viktor Frankl (1960), who called it *paradoxical intention.* Thus, paradoxically, rather than intending to avoid having some symptom—such as an anxiety attack—the neurotic intends that it come about at predetermined times throughout the day (for example, 1 P.M., 3 P.M., and so on). In time, this psychological control over the symptom seems to permit the neurotic to willfully decide *not* to have the symptom. Implosive therapy has also spawned a number of so-called *flooding* therapies—that is, techniques that induce emotional release in a nonpunishing environment. Stampflian implosive therapy remains the finest example of these approaches.

## OPERANT CONDITIONING AS SHAPING BEHAVIOR

We move now from classical, Pavlovian conditioning to B. F. Skinner's construct of operant conditioning. Most behavioristic theorists accept the fact that there are two types of conditioning—classical and operant—but for the purist only one of these quite different types of explanation need suffice. Recall from Chapter 4 (p. 112) that classical conditioning is a drive reduction explanation, whereas in operant conditioning the claim is made that behavioral responses are emitted and then retained according to the *contingent reinforcements* that they create (see also Chapter 4, p. 113). Skinnerian responses "operate on" the environment to bring about reinforcing effects in the contingent circumstances that may be observed extraspectively. When the *base rate* emission of such responses is seen to rise, we speak of "positive" reinforcement and forgo any speculations as to whether or not a drive has been reduced in the process.

Most experts agree that Skinner (Skinner & Lindsley, 1954) actually coined the phrase *behavior therapy*. Subsequently, Robert I. Watson (1962) proposed the phrase *behavior modification,* which is often shortened to *behavior mod* today. Though they do not deny the occasional physiological-biological cause, by and large operant-behavior therapists believe that maladjustment is no different from any other behavior, once the learning principles that keep it going are understood. The psychotic individual's behavior, based on past environmental shaping, is now considered incorrect or inappropriate by the broader social culture. This usually leads to a loss of reinforcement, behavior under the control of aversive stimulation (punishments, negative reinforcements), or the complete rejection of external stimuli by the psychotic person in favor of an imagined dream world (delusions).

Social expectations then enter once again to damn the abnormal person as lazy, bad, crazy, or possessed by the devil, none of which helps in adjusting his or her operant level to life in a more realistic fashion. Once labeled as sick or a mental patient, the maladjusted person is effectively shaped into behaving in this very manner. The so-called secondary-gain features of mental illness are part of this *behavioral shaping,* but there is much more as well. The good patient is not troublesome but rather passive and willing to accept the direction and dependency-inducing manipulations of his or her caretakers.

The broadest phrasing of the operant therapist's theory of psychopathology is that two things have gone wrong: (1) adaptive behaviors have never been learned by the person, and (2) maladaptive behaviors *have* been learned. The problem facing the therapist is therefore to identify maladaptive behaviors in an individual's repertoire and *remove* them through operant techniques. At the same time, more adaptive responses should be shaped into the repertoire. There is little or no need for an extensive review of the client's past life, though the more information a therapist has concerning the maladaptive patterns, the easier it is to arrange a program of operant conditioning for the client. Though informal insights doubtless occur to the client, there is no attempt to make cure dependent on the extent of self-understanding that a client may have, because according to the operant theory, such "verbal reports" are themselves under the control of contingent reinforcements rather than being controlling agents in the ongoing course of behavior. We can consider operant shaping of behavior in terms of individual or group applications.

*Individual Treatment Cases.* Let us assume that Mr. and Mrs. Greenfield bring their eight-year-old son, Jimmy, to Dr. Thomas, a behavior therapist who specializes in Skinnerian behavior modification. The presenting complaint is that their son's verbal pattern has deteriorated terribly since he began attending school a few years ago. At present, Jimmy is virtually mute. He was held back in first grade for another year because of his inability to communicate. The Greenfields are at their wit's end, because up until the time of entering school Jimmy's speech was completely normal. Physical examinations and consultations with medical specialists have not helped. Dr. Thomas might spend several sessions reviewing the case history with the Greenfields and then, after careful planning, institute a program of operant conditioning.

First, he would ask the parents to take the pressure off Jimmy to speak, because all this does is attach aversive (punishing) cues to the speaking situation. Next, he would ask that Jimmy be brought in to see him over a series of half-hour to one-hour sessions. Having determined from the parents what Jimmy prefers in the way of sweets, Dr. Thomas would then have on hand in the therapy room (which might be equipped with several games, construction toys, and so forth) an ample supply of—let us say—chocolate candy (*reinforcers*). Now, therapy would begin.

At the outset of the first hour Dr. Thomas might or might not tell Jimmy something about what they hope to accomplish together. More than likely he would simply introduce the boy to the playroom and permit him to select any toy or game that struck his fancy as a means of passing the hour. If Jimmy seemed to want it, Dr. Thomas would enter into the play. At the first sign of vocalization—a throat clearing, a grunt, or possibly merely a movement of the lips—Dr. Thomas would slip Jimmy a chocolate—that is, the *contingent* reinforcer! With each following approximation to speech, Jimmy would obtain the desirable reinforcer of chocolate candy (this is called the *method of successive approximations*—see Skinner, 1974). The chocolate candy pieces are small, but they can be increased in number, particularly if Jimmy increases his vocal sounds or actually emits a word (two pieces of chocolate). After a very few such meetings (three or four), most children with Jimmy's problem will begin saying a few words to their therapist.

Dr. Thomas might change the nature of the reinforcement after a time. For example, he might work out some arrangement whereby, instead of chocolates, little plastic chips can be collected over the therapy hour, the amount based on the number of words and sentences emitted. At the end of the hour, these chips can be turned in for prizes, such as various model airplanes or picture books, which Mrs. Greenfield reports are among Jimmy's most prized possessions at home. Dr. Thomas may now instruct the Greenfields in how to operantly reinforce Jimmy's behavior *in vivo*—that is, in the life setting. Rather than showing concern—hence attention and thereby reinforcement—for muteness, Dr. Thomas instructs the parents to ignore Jimmy when mute (*removal of reinforcement*) but to make every reasonable show of attention when he does speak, grunt, or even move his lips (*shaping* through *successive approximations* to speech). In this way, the operant level of speech emission that has been raised slightly in the therapy session can be transferred to the life setting proper.

The final phase of therapy would then demand an environment in which reinforcement for speaking would be arranged for Jimmy. Friends who are supportive and nonthreatening should be brought into the home, with the same schedule of ignoring muteness and attending to speech efforts followed. Gradually, this circle of environmental manipulation can be extended. Dr.

Thomas may wish to speak to Jimmy's schoolteachers and to make recommendations along the above lines to them as well. Behavior therapists continually emphasize that there is no real evidence that *symptom substitution,* or the replacement of one disorder (such as muteness) with another (such as bedwetting), is likely to take place. Though such substitutions may occur, research evidence suggests that this is a relatively rare occurrence (Ullmann & Krasner, 1965). Hence, Skinner proposed that the claim that an underlying dynamic reason must be brought to light before lasting cures result is simply another one of those unfounded superstitions that therapists have accepted without proper follow-up on their clients.

It may be recalled from Chapter 5 (see p. 143) that Greenspoon's original experiment held out hope that adult individual therapy could be manipulated akin to the modification of Jimmy's speech problem. Greenspoon (1955) suggested that a therapist could, by ignoring a patient's negative verbal contents and reinforcing (*mmm-hmm*) positive contents, actually manipulate the verbal production of the client so that self-defeating, painful outputs would be less prevalent. As it turned out, such efforts to manipulate client statements have not been successful. The reasons why this is the case are related to the role of awareness in operant conditioning, and we shall put off further comment on this matter until the closing section of this chapter.

*Group Treatment: Token Economy.* In applying operant conditioning techniques to groups of people the behavior therapist designs a total program encompassing what is termed a *token economy* (see, e.g., Atthowe & Krasner, 1968). We shall consider such a total program designed to improve the behavioral performance of patients in a mental hospital. By designing an appropriate token, either circular or rectangular like the modern credit card, and enlisting the cooperation of the entire mental hospital staff or at least one or two large wards, operant conditioners can begin a designed program of behavioral manipulation and improvement. The first step involves determining the typical behavior of patients. Do they engage in ward activities, attend group functions, meet at scheduled times for meals, and so forth? What is the incidence of bed-wetting? Do patients take reasonable care of themselves, comb their hair, make their beds, and so forth? Do any patients take weekend leaves from the hospital? Naturally, the general rate of turnover—hospital discharge—would be a significant measure of overall efficiency as well.

Once these *base rates* are clearly measured, a therapist can begin operantly reinforcing all those behaviors he or she takes to be generally oriented toward personal adjustment both within and outside the hospital milieu. For example, each time patients make their beds, clean themselves, get through the night without bed-wetting, or show an interest in others they are given a token. The level of reinforcement can be varied by having differently colored tokens represent more or less value. A patient who wishes to watch television would have to hand over a token before this privilege would be made available. Tokens would be required in exchange for candy or cigarettes. The limitations on what should be reinforced and for how much is left entirely to the ingenuity of the therapists who supervise the program.

The therapist acts as a consultant. It is not necessary that he or she walk about the wards, administering tokens to the patients. Nurses and attendants do most of the actual operant conditioning (i.e., administer tokens following "positive" behavioral emissions). The therapist meets with the hospital staff regularly to point up various techniques for successively approximating normal behaviors in the patients. The staff is told to, when possible, ignore certain histrionics that the patients may manifest. Involved delusional and hallucinatory displays can be diminished if the staff avoids showing interest in such patient behavior. Whenever the patient behaves relatively normally, *that* is the time to express an interest in his or her behavior. Thus, it is not strictly the token reinforcers that influence in a token economy, but the outlook in general of the hospital staff.

Given this total commitment, it is not unusual to find that the more adaptive behaviors begin to rise, and the maladaptive behaviors decline. By zeroing in on both types of behaviors, and employing a time-sampling procedure, the behavior therapist can usually demonstrate with empirical data that the operant conditioning of patients *does* work. The question remains: Why does this as all behavioral techniques take hold in the behavior of human beings? This takes us to the closing section of this chapter.

## The Role of Teleology in Biological and Behavioristic Therapies

It is unfortunate that the distinction between insight and noninsight therapies makes it appear that there is no role for telic behavior under the latter designation. These designations, and the theories that prompted the distinction in the first place, bear the weight of historical differences and conflicts that are no longer profitable to the fields of psychiatry and psychology. We have tried in the present volume to maintain a consistent teleological perspective on human behavior even as we acknowledged the biological and sociocultural (*biosocial*) factors that enter into the self-images and life premises of human beings. Our teleological view is completely compatible with the biological therapies. The compatibility of our telic view with behavioristic techniques is a bit more complex and subtle.

Thus, a teleologist need not dismiss the importance of biological factors in human behavior. As every physician knows, people can become hypertense through an overingestion of sodium in their diet, leading in turn to a growing sense of emotional upheaval, from which may stem arguments with colleagues or loved ones, followed by feelings of resentment and even revenge. As human beings—teleological organisms!—we look for *reasons* in such exchanges, focusing upon the psychological (formal/final) causes to the exclusion of strictly biological factors that not only enter into many of these fractured interpersonal relations, but also represent the *major* (material/efficient) causes of them. We feel tense in relation to some incident in our lives, and wind this emotional sensation into our contacts with others—making up a meaning which would *not* be the case were it not for our purely biophysiological disbalance.

We have made use of the construct of *reaction sensitivity* in a predominantly psychological sense, but there is also the strictly physical sensitizing of the body to interpersonal stresses, challenges, and responsibilities. It is entirely likely that events that are purely psychological (interpersonal, fantasied, etc.) generate concomitant bodily tensions which can themselves become reaction sensitized to both external and internal cues. It is not difficult to picture strictly internal, biological feedback mechanisms that make anxiety tensions progressively worse (*reactively sensitized*) no matter how the person struggles to understand the *reasons* for this biological disruption. Biofeedback research suggests that a certain degree of psychological control over physical processes is possible (see Chapter 17, p. 534), but there are limits to such intentional manipulations of the body. In more unmanageable physical disruptions the biological therapies may prove beneficial to the organism. There may indeed be psychopathological disorders that, though generated psychologically, require a physical treatment if they are to be rectified. But this in no way detracts from the fundamentally teleological organism, behaving *for the sake of* certain psychological attitudes, wishes, and aspirations, who has managed to set this physical disorder underway in the first place. We should not change the image of humanity to suit our therapeutic vehicles.

Changing the image of humanity to suit the demands of the research laboratory is what we fear has taken place in the behavioristic approaches to behavioral description. There is a continuing effort by the behaviorists to describe behavior extraspectively, in efficient-cause fashion based upon conditioning principles in their so-called cognitive (information-processing) parallels, when in point of empirical fact the preponderant evidence—as we have seen in Chapters 2 (pp. 33-41) and 5 (pp. 142-147)—suggests that the human being is best captured introspectively, in final-cause fashion. We once thought that behavioristic conditioning procedures received little or no contribution from the person of the subject in the procedure, but the growing body of evidence on awareness belies this simplistic view. Subjects are seen to be active agents in the conditioning procedure, conceptualizing as best they can what has to happen in order for this laboratory phenomenon to take place and then *complying* with the experimental instructions to achieve this end, *or not*. It is clear that the same agency must occur in the psychotherapy or behavior modification context.

Thus, patients in a token economy know full well what is taking place, and they are opting to go along with the reward system, otherwise there would be no "modification" of their behavior to be observed. They are thus more conformers than controllees! Indeed, on one occasion, a group of prisoners threatened with a behavior modification regimen *blocked* its completion by taking the penal authorities to court (*Monitor*, 1974). It is clear in this case that a group of human beings, who reason "for the sake of" (final cause) certain assumptions about who they are and what their rights are in a society founded on telic principles ("given" assumptions), expressed those rights in a court of law dedicated to enforcing these just principles. In the discussion that followed this court action, a leading behavioral psychopathologist advocated giving some of the responsibility for running behavioral modification programs to the prisoners (patients, etc.) themselves (see Bandura's comments in *Monitor*, 1974, p. 4).

This has now become a common practice. Therapist and patient work out a behavior modification program, select the reinforcers, track the base rates, and then evaluate improvements together. Indeed, as Stampflian therapy readily demonstrates, it often happens that patients develop some informal dynamic hypothesis for why it was that their symptoms arose in the first place. All such combinations of what we would suggest is a telically behaving organism with a mechanistically conceived succession of events are taken in stride by the behavioristic therapist, just as the awareness findings have been taken in stride. That is, no alteration of the human image has ensued. Though both implosive therapy and systematic desensitization rely upon the person's capacity to judge, evaluate, rank order, imagine, and role play a sequence of make-believe occurrences, the fact that such "that-for-the-sake-of-which" (final-cause, telic) behaviors are *central* to their behavioristic manipulations has not dampened the mechanistic spirit of Stampflian or Wolpean therapists. Why? Surely therapeutic requirements do not demand this spirit. It is clear that the behavioristic therapist continues to embrace a mechanistic image of human behavior because this is what the traditions of the laboratory have called for since the advent of behaviorism (J. B. Watson, 1913). We are more in the realm of an ideology here than a properly scientific attitude based exclusively on evidence.

It was Freud's unique genius to have remained true to this teleological characterization of the human being, even as he threw his "ultra" scientific colleagues off the track in his quasi-mechanistic libido theory. But we are in a new age, where such subterfuge and guile are no longer needed. As teleologists, we must continually guard against conveying a machine model of human nature, knowing as we do that this model simply fails to meet either the clinical *or* the empirical facts of human behavior. Moreover, it is our feeling that a machine model of behavior is detrimental to mental health—at least in the sense of ascribing all problems in living to the breakdown of a machine, or to inadequate adjustments of a machinelike apparatus in which the person has no role to play except as a *responder* to initial inputs and then a mediator of later interactions. We prefer to think of the person as a *telosponder*—as behaving "for the sake of" premised meanings that are brought forward into behavior intentionally (see Rychlak, 1977, 1981a). Once we take this introspective approach to the study of behavior, we achieve a full, dynamic understanding of the person in all of his or her unique manifestations.

## SUMMARY

Chapter 20 begins with a consideration of the *biological therapies. Insulin coma therapy* involves an induced hypoglycemia through injection of insulin, which renders the patient comatose. After an hour or more the patient is given an injection of glucose to terminate the coma. In *electroconvulsive therapy* (ECT) or *electric shock therapy* (EST) an electric current of approximately 160 volts is passed from one side of the patient's head to the other for up to about one and one-half seconds. This electric shock renders the patient unconscious and also stimulates a seizure, which can be controlled through appropriate drugs. Sometimes insulin and ECT techniques are combined in the same patient. Theories accounting for the success of these therapies are either biological or emphasize the positive role of having to regroup one's sensibilities following the unconsciousness and confusion brought on by the coma and/or seizure.

*Psychosurgery* is a global term referring to various brain operations performed to relieve the symptoms of schizophrenia and depression. There are various techniques employed, the most common of which is *prefrontal lobotomy* or *transorbital lobotomy.* The essential point here is a severing of the nerve fibers connecting the frontal areas of the cerebral cortex and the thalamus. The rationale for this operation flows from the role that these brain centers play. As a lower brain center dealing with emotions, the thalamus is disengaged from the higher brain centers of the frontal lobes. Some rather pronounced personality changes occur in people who have been subjected to psychosurgery, including dullness, obesity, and emotional shallowness.

*Pharmacological therapy* or *chemotherapy* is concerned with administering to the patient various drugs that have been demonstrated experimentally to aid in symptom removal. Chapter 20 takes up three broad classifications of such drugs: *antianxiety drugs* (sedatives, barbiturates, minor tranquilizers such as Equanil, Valium, and Librium); *antidepressant drugs* (tricyclic type, MAO inhibitors); and the *antipsychotic drugs* (major tranquilizers like Thorazine, Stelazine, or Haldol). As with psychosurgery, there are side effects when taking these drugs, including convulsions, sensitivity to light, and various uncontrollable movements of the throat and tongue. Some variation on a medical-model explanation is usually advanced in support of chemotherapy. That is, it is assumed there are biochemical actions within the body that these various drugs act upon to effect behavioral improvements.

Chapter 20 next moves into a consideration of the major noninsight *behavioristic therapies* in use today. Joseph Wolpe's *systematic desensitization* is based upon the concept of *reciprocal inhibition,* as taken from Sherrington's biological theory and Hull's learning theory. Wolpe's nontelic theory of behavior has habits forming exclusively through contiguous stimulus-response relationships aligning over time, given only that a *drive* is in ascendance and the stimulus-response sequence in question reduces this drive level (drive reduction theory). The drive state that is most likely to be reduced when unhealthy habits are formed is *anxiety* (viewed in exclusively physical terms). A person will flee a threatening (stimulus) situation rather than confront it, leading thereby to anxiety reduction, stamping in the stimulus-response habit of flight. What the therapist must do to inhibit the fleeing response is to substitute another, incompatible response to the threatening stimulus. This is what reciprocal inhibition amounts to.

In his technique of systematic desensitization Wolpe first trains his patients in the art of *progressive relaxation* (taken from Jacobson). One cannot be both relaxed and anxious at the same time. He then has the patient rank order a series of disturbing (e.g., phobic) life situations, from most to least anxiety provoking. These situations are measured in *suds* (subjective units of disturbance) and then ordered into an *anxiety hierarchy*.

In the actual therapeutic contacts, the patient is asked to imagine the anxiety-provoking (stimulus) situation and then is encouraged to relax— reciprocally inhibiting the resulting anxiety response by making the relaxation response. Clients are begun at the lowest sud level (least anxiety provoking), and then taken gradually to the highest level of anxiety-provoking stimuli. Occasionally, *hypnotism* is used to enhance the realism of these imagined situations. Another term for the reciprocal inhibition technique is *counter-conditioning*.

The next behavioristic therapy taken up in Chapter 20 is Thomas G. Stampfl's *implosive therapy*. Stampfl based his therapy on Mowrer's learning theory. This view suggests that learning consists of (1) problem solving, mediated by the central nervous system and under voluntary control, and (2) conditioning, mediated by the autonomic nervous system and therefore not open to conscious influence. Emotional responses like anxiety, depression, love, hate, and so on are tied to conditioning processes. In the case of neurotic behavior, the person is viewed as having been conditioned to avoid problem solution through a pattern of behavior that reduces autonomic responses but does *not* permit problem solution to take place. Symptoms of neurosis are thus *conditioned avoidance responses*. Stampfl reasoned that if clients were to remain in place, confronting their feared expectations but *not* receiving punishment, though they would express much autonomically mediated emotion, they would quickly *extinguish* the contiguous relationship between the feared stimulus situation and the emotional (avoidant) response.

An *implosion* is a bursting inward. This describes what takes place when the patient is verbally encouraged by the therapist to imagine any of a number of fear-provoking or guilt-provoking life situations. In bringing forward his or her idea concerning what the patient fears, the implosive therapist may begin with *symptom-contingent cues* that are known to be causing the autonomic response, but in quick order move on to *hypothesized conditioned aversive cues* of even a fantastic variety (such as dying and going to hell). Patients often *redintegrate* (recall from the past) memories of relevant circumstances relating to the avoidance-provoking situation. Therapy proceeds through certain steps:

symptom study; training in neutral imagery; framing a hierarchy of avoidance images called the *avoidance serial cue hierarchy* (ASCH), which is based on the extent of fear the patient manifests; and then actual scene presentation and repetition to extinction.

The final behavioristic therapy taken up in Chapter 20 is B. F. Skinner's so-called *behavior modification* or *behavior mod.* According to Skinnerian theory, whether a behavior is abnormal or normal depends upon how it is *shaped* by the environment. The point is to remove or greatly reduce all maladaptive behavior from the person's operant level, and then shape the person's behavior in the desired "normal" direction through *contingent reinforcement.* A program of reinforcement is designed and carried out in which *base rates* of the target behaviors—that is, both the "abnormal" and the "desirable" behaviors—are first determined empirically. The undesirable, abnormal behaviors are simply ignored or extinguished through nonreinforcement, and the desirable behaviors are reinforced into the person's behavior through the *method of successive approximations.* The resultant *shaping* effects the cure. Whole groups of people in mental hospitals can be treated in this manner, by placing them on a *token economy* designed to contingently reinforce certain (healthy) behaviors and to extinguish other (unhealthy) behaviors through nonreinforcement. In general, *operant conditioning* has worked best in the nonverbal type of therapy. The highly verbal, insight therapies have not been shown to be amenable to operant manipulation.

# 21

## *Psychopathology and the Law*

In the first chapter of this volume (see p. 18) we noted that diagnosticians had to be concerned with a nosology because there were legal reasons for doing so. Courts often require that some such assessment be made. In this, the last chapter of the volume, we are going to take a closer look at the involvements of psychopathology and the Law.* Forensic psychiatry and psychology are growing fields, with concerns going far beyond those on which we shall focus in Chapter 21. But there has been a long-standing problem for the psychopathologist who is called on as an expert witness to assess a defendant's level of sanity or competency to stand trial in the first instance. The term *insanity* is a legal one, paralleling but far from being identical in meaning to the psychiatric conception of a *psychosis*. Precisely what a judgment of psychosis or mental illness has to do with the question of a person's legal sanity or lack of it is what we shall be considering in this chapter.

We have throughout this volume taken a teleological view of human behavior, based on the insights of Freudian theory. To a teleologist, who may believe that human beings *telospond* (see p. 616) or behave "for the sake of" intentions which they personally affirm, the question of *responsibility* for one's actions is not meaningless. Mechanists would find such questions meaningless, because how can an efficiently caused sequence of events be held "responsible" for anything? Despite the teleologist's openness to a consideration of responsibility, as we shall see below, some of the questions put to expert witnesses in the

---

*We shall use the term "Law" with the first letter capitalized to refer to the entire complex of jurisprudence, including the U.S. Constitution, lawyers, judges, and the various courts involved. We are getting at the collective opinion of all those human beings who frame our societal intentions and codify them in particular ways as individual "laws."

courtroom are extremely difficult if not impossible to answer. There is a theoretical gulf between what the court expects and what psychiatrists believe they can deliver. As a result, considerable tension is generated in the courtroom alliance of the legal and psychiatric professions. Of even greater interest to us as students of psychopathology is the fact that there is also an internally generated tension within psychiatry over the precise meaning of concepts like purpose, intention, and free will. Can modern psychiatric/psychological theory truly encompass these meanings?

We shall begin our analysis with a discussion of the conflicting views of the concept of responsibility in the Law and in psychiatry, move to an historical review of the insanity defense, and then take up the ramifications of the contrasting and conflicting viewpoints represented. Our focus will be primarily on the theory underlying legalistic and psychiatric understandings of the lawbreaker. In particular we shall want to see if there are any insights in Freudian theory that might help us to take a firmer stand on just what we consider personal responsibility to entail. We shall not be able to solve all of the problems, but we may be able to shed some light on the future considerations that an enlightened jurisprudence must take under advisement. Finally, we expect to demonstrate that a teleological approach to human behavior is not without merit, and indeed, anything to the contrary places one outside the expectations of one's society as embodied in its codified understandings of human behavior.

## Responsibility in Law and Psychiatry

Legal judgments are based on the assumption of human responsibility. The Law assumes that the normal human being can make choices among alternatives, evaluate the rightness or wrongness of an action, and direct his or her behavior accordingly. In other words, the Law presumes agency or free will. More correctly, the lawyers and judges who interpret and write our laws presume agency or free will. Justice Cardozo affirmed this presumption when he wrote in an opinion that the Law "is guided by a robust common sense which assumes the freedom of will as a working hypothesis" (quoted by Fingarette, 1972, p. 79). Other judges have put it as follows: "The basic behavioral concept of our social order is free will" (ibid., p. 81), and "The concept of 'belief in freedom of the human will and a consequent ability and duty of the normal individual to choose between good and evil' is a core concept that is universal and persistent in mature systems of law" (LaFave, 1978, p. 333). The legal concept of responsibility flows from this telic assumption, because it is held that "criminal responsibility is assessed when through 'free will' a man elects to do evil" (ibid.)

Now it is at this point that a psychiatrist's knowledge of psychopathology enters to confound him or her. Did not Freud (Rychlak, 1981b, pp. 266-267) say that people merely have an illusion of free will, due to their general lack of understanding of unconscious motivation? Psychiatrists tend to believe that the Law represents a simplistic and outmoded style of understanding and explanation in the realm of human behavior. Many psychiatrists believe that there is no such thing as a "free" choice in behavior—ever! Occasionally, we see prominent psychiatrists combining Freudian with what seems to be a reinforcement or conditioning explanation of the early "shaping" of behavior. Thus, Karl Menninger (1966) has stated: "Freud showed that men are extremely unequal in respect to endowment, discretion, equilibrium, self-control, aspiration, and intelligence—differences depending not only on inherited genes and brain-cell configurations but also on childhood *conditioning* [italics added] (p. 92). As we demonstrated in Chapters 4 (p. 123) and 5 (p. 147), Freud was anything but a reinforcement or conditioning theorist. Even so, we tend to see this notion of "conditioned" behavior entering into psychiatric objections to the legalistic assumption of free will (see, e.g., Glueck, 1962, pp. 7, 32).

To the psychiatrist, who is fully cognizant of unconscious factors in behavior, it seems highly simplistic to say that a person need necessarily opt for evil through an act of free will (ibid., p. 6). Though the psychiatrist may hold a patient "responsible" for meeting the therapeutic appointment on time and for paying his or her bills on time, it is likely that there will be an element of doubt concerning the actual "free choices" being carried on by the patient. Thus, Glueck argues that "an understandable psychologic definition of an individual's freedom of will is his particular capacity for conscious, purposive, controlled action when confronted with a series of alternatives" (ibid., pp. 11-12). Once things are defined this way, we can see that people differ in their *capacity* to make choices and hence must be judged accordingly. Speaking for what he assumes to be most practicing psychoanalysts, Hospers (1961) suggests that "a person's freedom is present *in inverse proportion to his neuroticism;* in other words, the more his acts are determined by a *malevolent* unconscious, the less free he is. Thus, they [psychoanalysts] would speak of *degrees* of freedom" (p. 473).

It seems clear that legal propositions are generalizations drawn "across the board" so as to frame a grounds on the basis of which a decision can be rendered. The lawyers and judges are saying, "People have by their natures a free will," and the psychiatrists are countering with, "Not in every case" or "Only to a degree." The Law is prepared to deal with mitigating factors, of course, which is why there are distinctions between first- and second-degree murder, manslaughter, and so forth. Invariably, such distinctions come down to the degree of intent (forethought, planning, etc.) involved in the act. Basically, the Law distinguishes between the offensive act per se and the person's mental state at the time of committing the deed in question. The offensive act is termed the *actus reus* and the state of mind that suggests that this wrongful deed was intentional is termed *mens rea.* Mens rea is thus a "guilty mind," suggesting criminal intent or wrongful purpose (Black, 1979, p. 34, p. 889).

If we hold someone blameworthy for his or her acts, and hence potentially guilty of some infraction of Law, then we speak of the person's *culpability*. This legal term has several aspects to it, all of which are teleological in significance. Thus, the person is more likely to be culpable if he or she has purposively or intentionally sought to do the offensive act. Knowing, or being consciously aware that a particular result is likely to occur from the actus reus, adds to culpability. Recklessness, or consciously being aware of the potential rise of injury from one's actions, also increases the culpability of a wrongful deed. Finally, excessive negligence in not being concerned with the potential risks as outcomes of one's actions can add to the culpability of the actus reus. It is therefore the alleged actus reus that brings the person as "defendant" before the court. The actions of the court that follow (trial, etc.) seek to determine (1) whether or not the defendant actually committed the alleged actus reus, and (2) if there was clear mens rea in the illegal action or if there were circumstances mitigating the culpability of the defendant.

The question of responsibility for personal actions takes us into the theoretical realm of determinism. To "determine" is to limit the number of alternatives that might take place, or to fix the direction that events will take. What really determines the person's behavior? Recall from Chapter 5 (p. 147) that we distinguished between four types of determinism based upon the causal meanings involved. In a *material-cause determinism* the limitation on what might occur would be due to some substantial essence that goes to make a thing up. In human behavior, we might say that a person born with inferior physical equipment is limited (determined) in the number and variety of behaviors that he or she might manifest. Mentally deficient people frequently have obvious genetic deficiencies. All such understandings of behavior rely heavily on a material-cause determinism.

*Efficient-cause determinism* in behavior would be epitomized by the stimulus-response and cognitive input-output theories of psychology (see Chapter 4, p. 123, and Chapter 5, p. 142). An antecedent stimulus cues, triggers, or impels a consequent response to occur in exactly the same way that the wind may blow a leaf about or the force of gravity draws a raindrop from the sky. What happens at any point in time is limited by what has gone before, quite without foresight or choice. All mechanistic theories rely upon efficient-cause determinism. A *formal-cause determinism* in behavior takes its influence from the delimitations of certain patterns. The mathematician derives a certain proof based upon the patterned assumptions made at the outset, as well as by the transformations of pattern and the tautological identification of patterns made possible in the working out of the logically necessary line of proof.

In quite another sphere, the program of a computer embraces a certain formal-cause pattern that determines precisely how the line of "reasoning" will be carried out as the computer organizes, analyzes, and presents data that have been given to it for analysis by the user. The computer has physical parts that move this analytical process along quite mechanically. As such, we can see material- and efficient-cause determinism taking place in the total action. But it is the formal-cause determination, the logical patterning of the program, that is ever primary in the working of the computer.

*Final-cause determinism* implies that the organism behaving or reasoning through (analyzing, examining, etc.) some line of information can fix (determine) the direction taken as a self-selecting (choosing) agent. In telosponding, or reasoning "for the sake of" a plan (formal-cause determinism), unlike the computer this *human* can challenge the import (meaning, intention, purpose) of the programlike assumptions made available in experience, modifying the course of his or her behavior accordingly. We noted in Chapter 5 (p. 148) that Freud's psychic determinism was underwritten by final-cause determinism. It is the—often unconscious—thought that directs the behavior of the individual, and this thought (cathected idea or image) is itself frequently a negotiated and compromised outcome of an internal struggle among different aspects of the total personality (id, ego, superego).

Can these four types of determinism shed any light on the controversy over the question of personal responsibility that we have seen arising between psychiatry and the Law? First of all, it seems clear that the Law functions pretty much as a formal-cause determination. That is, when we consider strictly the codified regulations and restrictions in our laws, we can see that they lay down or represent certain patterns of living (the legal) rather than others (the illegal). These regulations and restrictions "stand" as guideposts for a rational society. Many of these guideposts, such as those in civil law, require no examination of the offender in terms of mens rea. Even with the best of intentions, we may park our car in a restricted area of the city. We did not know that we were violating the law. Our ignorance of the law is no excuse. But in criminal proceedings, the question of intent (mens rea) is always raised.

Stepping back to view things in light of our causal meanings of determinism, we might suggest that codified prescriptions or laws function primarily on the basis of a formal-cause determinism. They stipulate a "right way" of doing things, punishing in greater or lesser degrees those who fail to conform to the stipulations. Of course, the human beings who framed the laws could be said to be under a final-cause determinism as well. Laws are the "thats" for the sake of which their framers intended that the society be organized. As is well known, the Constitution of the United States is constantly being reviewed to see whether some current practice meets with the intentions of the Founding Fathers as well as those who have since passed amendments to the original codification. Even so, once a law is framed and is capable of standing alone we can think of it as reflecting primarily a formal-cause determination of the affairs of people.

In recognizing the mens rea aspects of an illegal deed, the Law makes allowance for other kinds of determinism as well. Thus, a person who suffers an epileptic seizure while driving an automobile might injure or kill a pedestrian. So long as this epileptic person has been under proper medical care and is licensed to drive, the physical illness would be grounds for mitigating culpability.

In like fashion, a person with a brain tumor who concocts an inappropriate fear of someone and attacks this person in a deluded sense of self-defense would have mitigating factors when brought before the court. In both the epileptic and the brain-tumor examples we have a material-cause determinism at play. Indeed, it is this medical-model form of defense that seems to prove most convincing to judges and juries. A sickness that reflects itself in an abnormal EEG tracing or shows up as an image on the X-ray provides strong evidence for the defense.

When called as expert witnesses, psychopathologists can be found who take the entire gamut of determinisms under consideration. Psychiatrists can be classified along the lines of traditional, medical-model practitioners versus those who introduce more dynamic considerations into an examination of the defendant. Obviously, the resulting judgment concerning responsibility for an actus reus could differ markedly. Still other psychiatrists might combine both material- and efficient-cause considerations, suggesting that people have genetic "givens" but that their environment "molds" them within these parameters to make them behave as they do. No final-cause determinism need enter this account. Behavioristically oriented psychologists are especially committed to explanations in light of an efficient-cause determinism. Based on such mechanistic assumptions, it follows that punishment is itself some kind of miscarriage of justice. How can we punish people for behaviors that they never opted to perform in the first place? They never opted to do so because, though they may have thought they made choices, free will is an illusion (Immergluck, 1964; Lefcourt, 1973).

By basing its fundamental approach to judgment and punishment on the concept of free will, the Law opens the door to an even broader range of defense. That is, there are *functional* disorders and temporary derangements that a dynamic psychologist or psychiatrist can identify in evidence to support claims of innocence by the defendant. Functional disturbances of this sort do not show up on EEG tracings or X-ray slides. Note in this instance that we are completely in the realm of formal/final-cause determinisms. That is, though there may be underlying biological factors in the functional disturbance, at "this point in time" we are unable to identify them. Or we are introducing factors in addition to the purely biological (i.e., material/efficient-cause) determinations of the medical model.

If criminal cases were handled like civil infractions, then it would be a lot easier on all those who participate in a trial. The issue would be strictly focused on the actus reus. Did the person do the wrongful deed or not? Was the car parked in the no-parking zone? Did the defendant actually shoot and kill the victim? There is no problem of mens rea here, no question of free will or intentionality to consider. Some experts believe that judges merely make their jobs more difficult by confounding the legal decision they have to make with considerations of free will (Fingarette, 1972, p. 81). But judges seem to need this presumption in order to justify their decisions and the setting of punishment.

Finally, as if to complicate matters even further, dynamically oriented psychopathologists can also find themselves opposed to punishing people for behaviors that they are not *consciously* responsible for! Thus, though dynamic theorists in psychiatry and psychology may view the person as under psychic determination—a variant theory of final-cause determinism—they may be resistant to claims of free will in behavior (refer above) and hence argue that it is wrong to punish people for their *unconsciously* directed behaviors. Thus, dynamic and mechanistic theorists arrive at the same position concerning responsibility and punishment before the court. Actually, the Law has been struggling to work out a practical solution to this question of unconscious factors in behavior, and to understand all of the ramifications we shall next move to a consideration of the insanity defense and related matters.

## The Insanity Defense

*Insanity* is the technical term used in Law to signify that a defendant is not mentally responsible (Gifis, 1975, p. 106). This can refer to criminal responsibility or to the competency of an individual to stand trial in his or her own defense for any type of charge. Insanity also refers to an inability to conduct business and take care of one's personal affairs. Finally, this term can refer to a grounds for commitment to a mental institution. Insanity as a concept thus grows out of the concern reflected in the Law for mens rea in relation to an actus reus. There are three major grounds or *rules* in the insanity defense that have been followed in the Law: (1) the M'Naghten rule, (2) the Durham rule, and (3) the Model Penal Code Test of the American Law Institute (ALI rule). We shall consider each of these rules in turn, developing and enlarging upon the issues involved in the insanity defense as we move along.

*The M'Naghten Rule.* The M'Naghten rule dates from 1843, following an event that shocked the sensibilities of the British citizenry. Daniel M'Naghten was found innocent by reason of insanity in the killing of the secretary to the Tory Prime Minister, Sir Robert Peel. M'Naghten had developed the delusion that there was a Tory plot against him, and that he could somehow rectify the situation by killing Peel. He lay in wait for the passage of Peel's carriage, and when it appeared he shot the occupant. As it turned out, this proved to be Edward Drummond, private secretary to Peel. Due to the public outcry following the insanity decision, the House of Lords requested that the highest judges of England review the matter and present an explicit statement and explanation of the legal grounds for the acquittal by reason of insanity. Five questions were framed by the Lords, and the answers to these questions were appended to the report of the original case, so that they are taken as essentially part of the original decision (LaFave, 1978, p. 325).

It is helpful to consider these questions in turn, since they frame the entire issue of insanity before the Law in a way that often escapes psychopathologists, who come at things from a different perspective. The first question asked what

*Twenty Maresfield Gardens, London, Freud's residence in England, where at 3:00 a.m. on September 23, 1939, he succumbed following two injections of morphine (two centigrams each) administered by his personal physician, Max Schur. Freud and Schur had agreed on this euthanasic alternative early in their relationship, and it was Freud who decided when the end would come. Freud was eighty-three years old at his death.*

the law was concerning delusional actions, such as the one committed by M'Naghten. Can a person be held guilty of a delusional act like this? The essential answer given by the judges was as follows: "We are of the opinion that, notwithstanding the party accused did the act complained of [actus reus] with a view, under the influence of insane delusion, of redressing or revenging some supposed grievance or injury, or of producing some public benefit, he is nevertheless punishable according to the nature of the crime committed, if he knew at the time of committing such crime that he was acting contrary to . . . the law of the land" (ibid.). In other words, if M'Naghten knew at the time of the shooting that he was violating the law of the land, he was culpable even though delusional.

The second and third questions dealt with various aspects of the charge to the jury: On what grounds are they to decide the issue of legal insanity? The key phrasing in answering these questions was as follows: "To establish a defence on the ground of insanity, it must be clearly proved that, at the time of the committing of the act, the party accused was labouring under such a defect of reason, from disease of the mind, as not to know the nature and quality of the act he was doing; or, if he did know it, that he did not know he was doing what was wrong" (ibid., p. 326). This phraseology is what has come to be known as "the" M'Naghten rule or the "right/wrong" rule. Now, in 1843 there was no such thing as dynamic psychology. The British judges were undoubtedly thinking of "disease of the mind" in terms of the medical model. If M'Naghten had a brain tumor or related malfunction of the central nervous system that somehow destroyed his capacity to evaluate right from wrong *at the time of his actus reus,* then he would be considered innocent by reason of insanity.

A second aspect of the right/wrong assessment is that the defendant was to be judged according to his or her *conscious* intent. There was no real appreciation of the determinate influence of unconscious motivations in 1843. Hence, the judges summarized the situation for the jury as follows: "If the accused was conscious that the act was one which he ought not to do, and if that act was at the same time contrary to the law of the land, he is punishable; and the usual course therefore has been to leave the question to the jury, whether the party accused had a sufficient degree of reason to know that he was doing an act that was wrong" (ibid.). It is in this charge to the jury that we find the basis of calling expert witnesses for both the prosecution and the defense. The psychopathologist is to present evidence that must be evaluated by the jury, and it is the *jury* that makes the ultimate decision as to sanity or insanity. Of course, as things have turned out, the jury's reliance on the psychiatrist or psychologist is usually great. A recent study covering a ten-year period in one jurisdiction and involving 202 insanity pleas found that the court/jury disagreed with the forensic psychiatric report in only 7 percent of the cases. That is, if the forensic report diagnosed the defendant as psychotic, the court/jury concurred to this extent (93 percent) in the judgment of insanity (Steadman et al., 1983).

The fourth question put to the judges concerned whether simply by the fact of having a delusion the defendant is to be adjudged innocent of the charges. The answer is no. It depends upon the nature of the delusion: "For example, if under the influence of his delusion he supposes another man to be in the act of attempting to take away his life, and he kills that man, as he supposes, in self-defence, he would be exempt from punishment" (LaFave, 1978, p. 326). *Any* defendant who kills in self-defense has grounds for a decision of not guilty—sane or insane! But "if his delusion was that the deceased had inflicted a serious injury to his character and fortune, and he killed him in revenge for such supposed injury, he would be liable to punishment" (ibid.). In other words, a psychotic person whose delusional system reflects a known reason or intention for the actus reus that is contrary to law is still culpable. It is also obvious that in their phrase "defect of reason" (see above)—in addition to "disease of the mind"—the judges were holding open the possibility of a delusional person committing a crime who would not be mentally diseased but rather mentally deficient (retarded, simply erroneous, etc.). In time, the "defect-of-reason" phrase was frequently dropped from jury instructions, a practice which has probably facilitated the identification of "psychotic" (mentally diseased) with "insane."

The last question posed by the House of Lords asked whether an expert in mental disease who never saw the prisoner but who was present at the entire trial and heard all of the testimony could be asked his or her opinion as to the state of the prisoner's mind (mens rea) at the time of the commission of the alleged crime. The judges responded as follows: "We think the medical man, under the circumstances supposed, cannot in strictness be asked his opinion in the terms above stated, because each of those questions involves the determination of the truth of the facts deposed to, which it is for the jury to decide, and the questions are not mere questions upon a matter of science, in which case such evidence is admissible" (ibid. pp. 326-327). Here again, the judges wished to place the responsibility for a judgment in the hands of the jury and not have the psychopathologist do the work of the court. However, the judges also stated, "Where the facts are admitted or not disputed, and the question becomes substantially one of science only, it may be convenient to allow the question to be put in that general form, though the same cannot be insisted on as a matter of right" (ibid., p. 327).

Even though there was no dynamic psychology in the mid-nineteenth century, there was fairly immediate reaction to the M'Naghten rule as overly cognitive or "intellectual" in its assessment of the circumstances of mental illness. The psychopathologists of that era, who were theorizing based on biological reductionism (medical model), complained that anyone who dealt with the members of an insane asylum could readily establish that these patients usually knew the quality of their acts, and the rightness or wrongness of their acts, but that they could still not control themselves. In an opinion written in 1887, an Alabama court (Justice Somerville in *Parsons* v. *State;* see ibid., p. 327) held that this *power of self-control* must be taken into consideration. If, due to mental disease, the person "had so far lost the *power to choose* between the right and wrong [even though "knowing" this difference], and to avoid doing the act in question, as that his free agency was at the time destroyed" (ibid., p. 328), the defendant was to be judged free of legal responsibility. This decision came to be known as the *irresistible impulse* elaboration of the M'Naghten rule.

We now have three points to consider in following the M'Naghten rule: (1) Did the defendant know the nature and quality of his or her act? (2) Knowing the nature of the act, did the defendant know that it was wrong? This does not refer to what the person may "think" is the right or the wrong thing to do, but rather knowing what is prescribed by others as right and/or wrong. In other words, we would not excuse a defendant for stealing something from another based on an idiosyncratic belief in personal justice. The jury must assess the defendant in terms of a general standard of what is right and/or wrong, as embodied most generally in our laws. (3) Given that both (1) and (2) are answered in the affirmative, was the person capable of *resisting* his or her impulses to "do" a wrongful deed? The late nineteenth century was the era of widespread interest in and study of the hysterical disorders, whereby it was patently clear that the patient was essentially "taken over" by a power seeming to negate the will. Such disturbances did not always result in an actus reus, of course, although we have had dramatic examples of this sort of Jekyll and Hyde behavior in the context of crime—as when a murderer writes upon a mirror in the apartment of his latest victim, "Stop me before I kill again." There is obviously something going on here that must be taken into consideration. The question remains: Are such irresistible impulses due solely to material/efficient-cause determinism, or might they also reflect a formal/final-cause determinism as well?

We do not mean to give the impression that all courts in the United States accepted the irresistible impulse elaboration of the M'Naghten rule. Many did not, but the most widely followed principle has been the right/wrong feature of the M'Naghten rule. This has continued to frustrate psychopathologists who feel that there is a disregard reflected here for the more emotional features of behavior, features that ordinarily form the core of an irresistible impulse. Knowing right from wrong is hardly the only or even the proven "major" consideration in influencing the course of human behavior. Psychiatrists and psychologists have continued to find that disturbances in behavior relate as much to the control of impulses as to the disturbance in reasoning reflected in the "knowing" of anything. In time, a court was to take such factors of mental illness into consideration.

*The Durham Rule.* In 1954, Judge David Baselon, Chief Justice of the United States Court of Appeals in the District of Columbia, framed a decision that most leading psychiatrists favored. The key paragraph reads as follows:

> The rule we now hold . . . is simply that an accused is not criminally responsible if his unlawful act was the *product* [italics added] of mental disease or mental defect. We use "disease" in the sense of a condition which is considered capable of improving or deteriorating. We use "defect" in the sense of a condition which is not considered capable of either improving or deteriorating and which may be congenital, or the result of injury, or the residual effect of a physical or mental disease. (cited in Menninger, 1966, p. 115)

This decision, which extends the logic of irresistible impulse, was referred to as the "product" rule. In essence, it took the emphasis off the "right/wrong" decision of the actus reus and placed it more on the background factors of the defendant's life. Psychopathologists liked this instruction to the jury, because in this instance they did not have to answer a simple yes or no to the question, "Did the defendant know the difference between right and wrong at the time of his criminal act?" But note that the Durham rule permits the psychopathologist to frame *background* considerations in rendering a judgment as to the mental state of the defendant. It is up to the jury to decide whether these background considerations are of sufficient proportion to produce or cause the actus reus, but the emphasis has definitely shifted from the illegal act per se to the broader questions of a person's history of adjustment.

Though this shift in emphasis from the actus reus to the clinical history of the defendant suited the psychopathologists, it did not suit the minions of the court. The problem arises in the fact that the Law does not excuse a defendant simply because he or she has a life history of maladjustment. The Durham rule seemed to be suggesting that just as long as a mental illness could be proven in the case history, this itself excused the defendant from culpability. Subsequent decisions attempted to clarify the meaning of "product," identifying it with a "but for" causation—that is, but for the mental illness the actus reus would not have been committed (LaFave, 1978, p. 330). But the main problem of the product rule was that it seemed to be taking the decision-making role away from the jury and placing it on the expert witness (ibid., p. 331). With the advent of dynamic psychiatry and the "psychopathology of everyday life" (Freud, 1901/1960a), it seemed more likely than not that an insightful psychiatrist could make the case for the jury—recall the importance of the forensic report (refer above)—without a complete and satisfactory consideration of the Law.

In a return to the focus upon the actus reus, a 1967 decision in the very Washington court district that spawned the product rule *reversed* this decision and forbade experts from testifying to the so-called productivity issue altogether (LaFave, 1978, p. 331). At present the Durham rule is not used by any court in the United States (Arens, 1974, p. 304). Most courts have returned to the M'Naghten rule, but developments are occurring regularly, and one of the first to appear takes us to the last major rule that we shall consider.

*ALI Rule.* The American Law Institute (ALI) drafted a Model Penal Code Test in 1962 that is widely in use today. It is interesting to note that this test combines the considerations of emotional factors and control with the traditional considerations of a more cognitive nature. Thus, the ALI rule defines "mental disease or defect as an abnormal condition of the mind, and a condition which substantially (a) affects mental or emotional processes and (b) impairs behavioral controls" (LaFave, 1978, p. 335). Given this definition, the grounds for a judgment of no criminal responsibility for certain conduct (actus reus) results if "the defendant who, as a result of this mental condition, at the time of such conduct, either (i) lacks substantial capacity to appreciate that his conduct is wrongful, or (ii) lacks substantial capacity to conform his conduct to the law" (ibid.).

Note that the focus has returned to the actus reus, which is not viewed as a "product" of the mental illness—or more accurately, the relationship between the mental illness per se and the wrongful deed is not taken for granted. The ALI rule goes on to observe in this regard: "Exculpation is established not by mental disease alone but only if 'as a result' defendant lacks the substantial capacity required for responsibility. Presumably the mental disease of a kleptomaniac does not entail as a 'result' a lack of capacity to conform to the law prohibiting rape" (ibid.). There is also a "caveat paragraph" in the ALI rule designed to exclude the psychopathic personality from using this defense. In penal psychopathology, recidivism is often equated with psychopathy. Psychopaths thus continually run up against the legal restrictions of their community. The caveat paragraph of the ALI rule reads: "The terms 'mental disease or defect' do not include an abnormality manifested only by repeated criminal or otherwise anti-social conduct" (ibid., p. 336).

It is obvious that the effect of the ALI rule is to present us with the M'Naghten rule and irresistible impulse elaborations in new language. We are back to a focus on the actus reus per se rather than on the background factors that "produced" this behavior per se. This may appear to be a distinction without a difference to some psychopathologists, but the spirit of this revision is in line with keeping the jury—the representatives of the community!—attuned to the defendant's behavior that violated the law. The jury is not supposed to decide whether the defendant had a lifelong pattern of abnormal behavior. This is irrelevant except only insofar as it can be demonstrated that this lifelong pattern mitigated or excused the defendant's illegal behavior. Considerations of this sort (men rea) enter *all* criminal cases. The development of psychology and psychiatry, from strict reliance on the medical model (material/efficient-cause determinism) to the understanding of unconscious *intentions* (formal/final-cause determinism) has undoubtedly had its effect on the Law. The ALI rule seems to be trying to accommodate a more dynamic view of mental illness (although many lawyers believe that the M'Naghten rule can be interpreted as broadly).

Thus, in the phrase "lacks substantial capacity to appreciate that his conduct is wrongful" the ALI rule is making allowance for the fact that a psychotic defendant may "know" right from wrong, yet not really appreciate the meaningful significance of the actus reus. Here we have the psychotic person who tells us how he shot and killed his parents one afternoon, grinning throughout the account as if he were making a positive impression on his listeners. Precisely how the ALI rule functions in any one courtroom probably depends upon the jury's understanding of the key word "appreciate." Here is where the judge's instruction to the jury becomes crucial. Finally, it is only realistic to observe that in the exchanges between the prosecution and defense, precisely what "appreciation of wrongfulness" means may be convoluted into the familiar "knowledge of right from wrong" definition of the M'Naghten rule.

There are a few other considerations we should note regarding the sort of defense we are considering in this section. It is possible to be given *diminished-capacity* consideration in certain crimes. Sometimes, even though the defendant knew the nature and quality of his act (M'Naghten rule) or appreciated its wrongfulness (ALI rule), there are grounds for a reduced charge based on, for example, long-term intoxication, chronic insomnia, and so forth. This does not remove guilt, of course, but a first-degree murder charge might be reduced to a second-degree charge if this diminished-capacity defense is proven. We should also observe that children below the age of seven are never held criminally responsible for their acts. This is, in effect, a mens rea consideration. Children between the ages of seven and fourteen are presumed to be *not* criminally responsible. Someone fourteen years old can be treated as an adult if the jurisdiction makes this decision based upon the nature of the crime.

More frequent than the insanity defense is the consideration of a defendant's competency to stand trial. *Mental incompetence* is essentially defined as when "a defendant who as a result of mental disease or defect lacks capacity to understand the proceedings against him or to assist in his own defense" (LaFave, 1978, p. 314). A defendant's amnesia for the actus reus has not been held to be grounds for incompetency. In the typical case, the court appoints two psychiatrists who independently evaluate the accused. A competency hearing is then held, at which a decision is reached concerning competency. The accused has a right to an attorney at this competency hearing and can introduce testimony and evidence contradicting the medical reports. If the person is found incompetent, there is a commitment made to a mental hospital until such time as he or she has recovered. Difficulties arise here because in some cases this amounts to a life sentence without due process. Individuals have been detained for twenty years or more, a period exceeding the penalty they would have been given if found guilty for their actus reus. The due process considerations of the Sixth and Fourteenth Amendments to the U.S. Constitution have been invoked successfully to gain acquittal for such individuals. But if a defendant who had previously been adjudged incompetent to stand trial does recover in a reasonable period of time and advances to the courtroom for trial, he or she can still employ the insanity defense if such is indicated (Arens, 1974, p. 8). Competency thus refers to a person's *present* mental condition, whereas the insanity defense refers to the *past* state at the time of the actus reus.

## Contrasting Psychiatric Views of Punishment

The insanity defense is not widely used in the courts of the United States. Estimates range from less than 1 percent to as high as 3 percent of all cases seen in various jurisdictions. When a defendant and his or her lawyers opt for this defense, it means that they are prepared to accept a period of incarceration while therapy for the condition that excused the defendant is being conducted — assuming that they gain acquittal on the grounds of insanity! Not only do many defendants dislike the stigma of being called insane, but also many of them would prefer to be punished through prison incarceration rather than an indefinite stay in a "crazy house."

We noted above how the judgment of being incompetent to stand trial has occasionally resulted in a miscarriage of justice, in that the defendant is held for many years without really improving. This amounts to a prison sentence of sorts, and even a "life" sentence at that. A similar problem arises when a person has been acquitted of some crime based on the insanity defense. Just what should be done with these people? Some psychiatrists, such as Karl Menninger (1966, pp. 138-139), favor excluding members of their profession from the courtroom. Better to try the case on the basis of the actus reus, and then when convicted, refer the offender to a panel of psychiatric judges who will examine this person and submit reports regarding his or her potentialities, liabilities, and remedial possibilities. An indeterminate sentence would be taken for granted, with the focus decidedly on rehabilitation rather than punishment. Indeed, Menninger believes that punishment is fundamentally irrational behavior on the part of societal watchdogs (ibid., p. 113). Similar psychiatric opinions have termed punishment an archaic remnant of an earlier societal level, one that we should have moved beyond in the modern era (Diamond, 1968, p. 151).

There is a contrasting position on the nature of punishment. Rather than interpreting punishment as a means of rehabilitating the offender, or even as deterring others from following suit, this line of thought stresses the matter of group morale, and the fact that it would diminish if rule or law infractions were continually dismissed (Louch, 1965, p. 501). No patterned social order—as no "game" relying upon rules—can long sustain interest among the participants if the violators of its laws are repeatedly excused. The insanity defense seeks to provide an exception for rule violators of a certain type. But even here, the advantage gained need not be complete acquittal. The psychiatrist Lee Coleman (1980) argues in this vein when he observes: "Without punishment for crime, there *is* no crime. We cannot escape the fact that if we deem a law necessary, we must impose a punishment for breaking it" (p. 17).

Coleman believes that a defendant found not guilty by reason of insanity who is then hospitalized for an indefinite treatment period is being punished just as much as the offender who is sent to prison (ibid.). This is incarceration without the benefit of knowing when the loss of liberty will end. Studies have shown that the period of incarceration for mental patients is just as long as and sometimes longer than that for those persons found guilty of the same offense. Coleman would also like to remove psychiatrists from the courtroom, but he proposes a role for the post-trial psychiatrist different from that proposed by Menninger. Coleman believes that because psychiatrists cannot really answer the questions put to them concerning the various rules of insanity, it is better for the jury to focus on the actus reus (ibid., p. 18), which ordinarily provides the best evidence of what the person was about in any case (mens rea). No one should be excused from blame because of insanity per se: "Once it is recognized that no one is excused from blame, the next question is whether or not we want to make the moral choice to *alter* (but not forego) the punishment for those felt by the court to have been under the influence of a major mental 'disorder.' We could allow such a condition to be a mitigating factor in the setting of punishment" (ibid., p. 19). There should be specific sentences assigned for the crime involved (i.e., no indeterminate sentencing). Once incarcerated, a person with a mental disorder could then ask for and hopefully receive satisfactory therapy for the condition. When the sentence is up (including parole, etc.), the person would be released. If the prison officials want a longer stay, then commitment procedures would have to be initiated against the person, who would be defended by counsel as in any commitment proceeding for even the noncriminal. The aim here, of course, is to protect the rights of the offender as well as to keep the application of law uniformly in the hands of jurors, who should determine guilt or innocence and then leave the question of mental illness to the judge in considering mitigating factors, possibly leading to a reduced sentence, but not acquittal.

Basic to Coleman's argument is the thesis that psychiatrists can do no better than the layperson in "diagnosing" mental illness. He makes many of the criticisms that we have pointed to in Chapter 1 (pp. 17-19) concerning the unreliability of psychiatric diagnosis, adding that there is much fanciful terminology thrown about in the field of psychiatry that is just not proven, scientific knowledge. Although Menninger (1966) believes that he is a legitimate scientist, he too is opposed to the practice of diagnosing people—excepting only as globally "mentally ill" (p. 133). It is interesting to see two such opposed viewpoints agreeing on the single point of removing the psychiatrist from the courtroom. This removal seems highly problematic in light of the due process considerations and right to a jury trial prescribed in the U.S. Constitution.

That is, the finding of mental illness (or insanity) may have to be made by a jury rather than by psychiatrists who remain entirely outside the courtroom. As of the present writing a handful of states permit juries to render a decision of "guilty but mentally ill" rather than the more traditional decision of "not guilty by reason of insanity." It follows that juries require expert testimony on such matters if they are to arrive at a sound decision. There has been considerable "bad press" for the psychopathological expert witness in recent years. We frequently read in the newspaper that the psychiatrist for the defense did not agree with the decisions of the psychiatrist who took the stand for the prosecution. The average layperson wonders whether an impartial judgment of mental illness is possible in psychiatry or psychology. Despite such professional embarrassment—which is not unique to psychopathology, incidentally—it does not seem probable that psychiatrists or psychologists as expert witnesses will be excluded from the courtroom in the near future.

## Free Will and Freudian Psychology

We have now surveyed the main issues in the insanity defense, as well as related matters like the competency to stand trial. As we noted in the introduction to this chapter it is *fundamental* to Law that we think of the human being as an agent, capable of self-direction, choice, purpose, and intention. All such terms relate to what is known generally as the freedom of a person's will. We have also seen that psychopathologists are likely to take issue with this teleological assumption of the Law. Menninger (1966) said, "The most significant basic assumptions of modern psychiatry are actually in contradiction and opposition to many basic assumptions of the law" (p. 118). It is the view of the present text that this dour assessment need not hold. Our historical overview of the insanity defense suggests that there is considerable agreement between members of the legal profession and members of the psychiatric and psychological professions on the basic nature of the human person. Psychopathologists probably differ as much among themselves as they do interprofessionally.

But there is one realm in which Menninger's assessment may be completely correct. That is, if psychiatry and/or psychology base their arguments on exclusively material/efficient-cause determinism, thinking that this is the *only* proper form of explanation for a science of human behavior, then we would have a clear contradiction between the Law and psychopathology. Fingarette (1972) summarized this possibility very well: "The questions asked by the law in connection with *mens rea* are essentially teleological in character. They ask for accounts of human conduct in terms of the reasons a person had, his choices, his purposes, and, in short, the meaning of what he did. If psychiatry is at bottom a nonteleological science of energies, structures, causes and effects [i.e., efficient causes], and if questions of will make no sense psychiatrically, then there is indeed a profound logical gap between the answers psychiatry can give and the questions posed by the law" (p. 86).

We are back to the theoretical problems confronted by Freud throughout his career. Can it be shown that Freudian theory accommodates the legal assumption of a free will in human behavior? We believe that this is possible, although there will be some difficulties lying in the way of a complete rapprochement. First of all, let us remind ourselves that Freudian libido theory can in no way be considered an efficient-cause or material-cause determinism (see Chapter 4, p. 127). Recall also the dialectical formulations of Freud, dating from his initial speculations on the antithetical-ideas theory (see Chapter 4, p. 132). It is from this oppositional, contradictory, either-or kind of human thinking capacity that Freud derives his understanding of human freedom— freedom to restructure the world as we would have it, rather than as it literally might be. This world restructuring works from *both* the conscious and the unconscious direction. The id intentions seek to make hedonistic fantasy into reality, and the countering defensive intentions of the ego and superego place an ingenuine façade over the personality. We recognize in this collage of dialectical oppositionality the distinction between an unconscious and conscious psyche. Each side of the personality must be accommodated. Freud now employs this dynamic totality to comment on free will—or rather its *lack* in the personality structure—as follows:

> According to our analyses it is not necessary to dispute the right to the feeling of conviction of having a free will. If the distinction between conscious and unconscious motivation is taken into account, our feeling of conviction informs us that conscious motivation does not extend to all our motor decisions. . . . But what is thus left free by the one side receives its motivation from the other side, from the unconscious; and in this way determination in the psychical sphere is still carried out without any gap. (Freud, 1901/1960a, p. 236)

This quote is taken from *The Psychopathology of Everyday Life,* in which Freud was to demonstrate convincingly that the same dynamics to be seen in the neurotic individual are taking place in the behavior of the normal individual. Indeed, it is not always easy to draw this line between neurosis and normality. Recall from Chapter 5 (p. 148) that Freud was a *hard* determinist in the mental sphere, basing his position ultimately on a formal/final-cause determinism. He was more of a *soft* determinist (i.e., admitting some indeterminism) in the realm of material events, where chance occurrences can arise. So when he spoke here about what he sometimes referred to as the *illusion* of free will (Rychlak, 1981b, pp. 266-267), Freud was saying that what one side of the mind claims is a decision freely made is in fact the effect, outcome, compromise, conclusion, implication, wish, and so forth, of the *other* side of the mind. Freud was *not* saying that underlying efficient causes thrust the mind along as a mediating mechanism (efficient-cause determination à la "energies"). He *was* saying that mind is a determinate cause in the sequence of events—and should have added that it is a final cause of these events (final-cause determinism). This is why he had necessarily to make libido into an *intentional* conception, distorting thereby the classical meaning of an energic impulse (see Chapter 4, p. 127).

Freud's penchant for the dialectical tension of opposition is so obvious that we are justified in subsuming under this single conception a host of dichotomies such as the will versus counterwill, idea versus antithetical idea, conscious versus unconscious, and ego (superego) versus id. It seems clear that running through all of these bipolarities is the single message that Freud had for his medical colleagues—that is, that mind is more than just a one-sided, linear, unidirectional collation of singularities. Thinking one way we are always thinking the other, then the other, and another *ad infinitum.* Some of this convoluted and even perverted thinking goes on at a primitive level of mind, a level which is not constrained by the rules of demonstrative logic, a level which is totally inconsistent, arbitrary, and sophistical. Yet, *it wants to gain its ends* just as certainly as does the more proper side.

The Freudian claim is that before actions called behaviors occur there is a mental working through of intentions, many of which are in conflict, one with the other. Sometimes the total mind is aware of this conflict and sometimes it is not, but *always* a portion of the mind *is* cognizant of what these mental conflicts are all about. In most cases such conflictual intentions are managed without promoting too much confusion, but when they mount in number a person can pay the price in neurosis. The important thing then is to clarify for the individual in psychoanalysis (see Chapter 19) what is involved in his or her unconscious intentions. Hence, though certain portions of mind are often constrained to do things thanks to the direction (psychic determinism) of other portions of mind, when we consider the totality of mentation we always have a clear "that-for-the-sake-of-which" description of behavior taking form. And we also have it possible for the individual to *willfully* cause things to come about that might satisfy a preceding, preliminary intention—even a self-harmful intention.

But is this free will? Freud's answer seems to be no, because the conscious side of the mind is never free of the direction of the unconscious side. And yet the topographical identities of id, ego, and superego are surely free to "discuss" eventualities and come thereby to a compromise course of action in directing the total personality—as represented by the conscious portions of the ego. The compromise struck in this unconscious bargaining session is arrived at through a dialectical examination of, essentially, "do this" versus "don't do this" (i.e., "do that") until at some point there is a resolution (synthesis) into "let this be done." There is no mechanical or mathematical way in which to arrive at such compromises. In fact, even after a bargain has been struck the party that is set back in the psychic compromise can through guile circumvent the psychic determinism inflicted on consciousness and make its unique intentions known (via the parapraxes).

If free will relates *only* to consciousness, then most assuredly Freudian psychology can teach us nothing about this form of human behavior. But what if free will means "free from unidirectional control by the environment" or "free to concoct the premises (meanings) for the sake of which we will be determined?" A telosponding organism would have first to concoct or affirm a premise (free selection, choice, etc.) that in turn would psychically (willfully) determine what takes place in subsequent behavior. The question of awareness, of levels of consciousness, is left aside in this formulation. As we framed things in Chapter 5 (p. 149), awareness is akin to self-admission or self-acknowledgement. We may not wish to admit, acknowledge, or recognize "that" for the sake of which we are framing our behavior, but this does not mean we are "unfree" in this course of action taking place.

There would be no point to the insights provided by psychoanalysis if the person were really incapable of altering the premises (grounds, beliefs, etc.) for the sake of which he or she behaves. The entire strategy of psychoanalysis is teleological, even though its theory of cure is masked by the (quasi-)energic explanations of the libido theory (see Chapter 19, p. 583). Strange though it may appear, Freud's theory has a free-will conception functioning at *both* the conscious and unconscious levels. There is a uniformity in the way that mind works regardless of level of conscious awareness (see Chapter 5, pp. 148-150). This is what makes it so difficult to tell when a person is truly under unconscious direction, or when he or she is simply malingering. Both mental machinations are alike in their fundamental operation. If we take away the matter of awareness, we have a consistency in the way the mind works, and that "way" is in line with a free-will conception.

Unlike the cybernetic machine, which takes information that is "input" in a demonstrative, literal, unipolar fashion, the Freudian dialectical conception of mind has the person capable of reasoning to the opposite of inputs, and to the opposite of these opposites *ad infinitum,* arriving thereby at purely psychic constructions (wishes) that have little or no relation to the "input" per se. It is in this capacity to transcend the "is" and see the "is not," to turn back on the "given" and imagine the "possible," that Freud justified his mental mechanisms such as repression, sublimation, and reaction-formation. Though he disparaged the concept of dialectic as he understood it (Freud, 1932-36/1964b, pp. 545-546), there can be no doubt that it is the dialectical ploy that enabled him to capture the intricacies of human behavior in a way that has survived for generations despite setbacks in certain realms and a host of alternative formulations.

What is the Law to make of such *unconscious freedom of the will*? And are people who are motivated to break the law via unconscious choices receiving justice when we punish them for such infractions that are beyond their conscious free will? These are difficult questions to answer without reaching into broader theoretical considerations. First of all, it should be noted that in seeking to find grounds for incompetency, diminished capacity, and insanity, the Law is already providing room for mitigating circumstances that could just as well involve "unconscious free will" as any other theoretical explanation of why it is that people commit crimes. It makes no difference to strictly legal considerations whether a person commits an actus reus because of a brain disease, chronic intoxication, or some dynamic unconscious *decision* to do so in spite of defensive efforts at self-control (Freudian counterwill idea).

Just so long as modern psychiatry can assure the court that the conscious versus unconscious distinction is a legitimate mitigating circumstance, this is all that need matter. The defendant being moved by unconscious intentions would not necessarily be found innocent, of course. As we have seen, there is an array of possibilities in the kinds of judgments that might be rendered. But to argue, as psychiatrists now argue (refer above), that unconscious decisions remove psychiatry from the realm of telic explanation is unwarranted. As a fundamentally telic endeavor the Law represents what civilization aspires to become. The *strictly rule-governed expectations* for behavior known as "laws" may be thought of as "thats" for the sake of which the culture-society wishes to guide or direct its participants.

There are many reasons why any one person may violate such a codified "that." We have court proceedings so that we may determine the nature of guilt—if any—regarding such violations. As it is already predicated on teleology, there is no threat to the integrity of Law if we now point out that people are indeed telic organisms, but that sometimes the premises for the sake of which they behave are sufficiently removed from conscious examination that they lead to serious misbehaviors, and occasionally bizarre behaviors, without benefit of *conscious* self-determination. This is essentially what is meant by the so-called irresistible impulse. The "impulse" is not simply or even primarily an energic biological thrust of some type. It is often an obsession, an idea that builds into an emotional state in spite of the person's countermeasures. Indeed, it would be helpful to the defendant's case if it could be shown that he or she did indeed take steps to resist this unconscious prompting. Evidence of this sort would represent the "facts" of the case. If such existed, an analysis of the defendant's delusional system—along the lines first proposed by the British judges (see above, p. 628)—would also help establish his or her state of mind at the time of the crime.

In arguing as we do now, we place as much emphasis on the "defect-of-reason" phraseology that began with the M'Naghten rule as we do on the "mental-disease" phraseology. Not all defects of reason stem from innate mental inferiorities, tumors of the brain, or infections of the central nervous system. Some do issue from the dynamics of a lifelong series of misunderstandings, miscalculations, and erroneous intentions. The "lack-of-appreciation" phraseology in the ALI rule also supports this approach to the problem of establishing culpability. It clearly *does not* tie the defense down to a medical model. Therefore, it would be our view that the legal profession could readily accept the distinction between unconscious and conscious levels of free will (self-determination via telosponsivity). It is the professions of psychology and psychiatry that we have some concern about in this regard. There is a tendency in the latter professions to allow an outdated conception of Newtonian science to block needed theoretical reforms (Rychlak, 1977, 1981c). As Glueck (1962) said of his colleagues:

> Those psychiatrists who cling to a rigid [i.e., efficient-cause] determinism in the belief that the "demands of science" require this, are confusing cause-and-effect linkage once a train has been initiated, with capacity to intervene at the outset and at various stages in initiating or modifying a causative sequence. Such psychiatrists are behind the times. In recent years even physical science has rejected a rigid and inflexible [efficient] cause-and-effect determinism for a theory of "indeterminacy" or probability. (pp. 15-16)

If they are prepared to see this capacity to intervene as final-cause determinism, that is, to reason by way of dialectical oppositionality to alternatives, and redirect a course of behavioral events accordingly, then psychologists and psychiatrists can offer the Law of our land a theoretical conception of behavior that is consistent with its telic tenets. All we ask of the Law is that it appreciate our findings on free will—that is, that this form of telosponsive self-determination extends beyond simply conscious to an unconscious self-determination as well. We must never forget that the borderline between what is conscious and what is unconscious is framed around intentions, and especially those intentions that the person is *unwilling* to admit to himself or herself. This countermeasure—of removing items from potential awareness through repression, denial, compromise, and so forth—is clearly a *willful*, intentional act of a mind capable of free will! The loss of consciousness does *not* mean a loss of free will.

Turning to our second question, is it really "just" to hold people responsible for unconscious choices, decisions, intentions, and the like? Let us consider this question in the context of Freudian theory. The distinctive contribution of *The Psychopathology of Everyday Life* (Freud, 1901/1960a) is that it pointed out the influence of an unconscious agency in *every* form of behavior, normal as well as abnormal. If we are to disregard unconscious choices—cathexes, countercathexes, parapraxes, compromises, wishes, and so on—in the case of those individuals whom we term "normal," then on what grounds are we to place primary emphasis on such factors in those who are mentally ill? To be consistent, we would have to say that *no one* is responsible for his or her behavior, and therefore the very concept of punishment is inappropriate for human behavior. This is an interesting position, but it cannot be based upon the insights of psychoanalysis.

Why not? Well, assume a civilization were to abolish the concept of punishment. According to the tenets of psychoanalysis, this would have an eventual influence on the superegos of the citizens. As we noted, the mores and values of a civilization are embodied in the codified laws that it produces. A nonpunishing superego would mean that the ego would have to negotiate exclusively with the id in the eventual personality structures of the citizens of our imaginary civilization. One can only speculate on what sort of civilization this would be. Surely Freud's attitudes concerning human nature did not suggest that he thought such a personality system would have much chance for a satisfactory existence. Civilization was said by Freud (1929/1961i) to have two purposes: "namely to protect men against nature and to adjust their mutual relations" (p. 89).

The prohibitions against instinctive gratification that began as religious taboos were subsequently codified into the laws as a system of values: "Sublimation of instinct is an especially conspicuous feature of cultural development" (ibid., p. 96). In this cultural requirement, which involves repression of both sexual and aggressive impulses, we find the root source of the human being's dissatisfaction with culture (ibid., pp. 114-115). In a true sense, each person becomes an enemy of civilization, which is to say that each person would prefer to receive instinctual gratification. The aggressive instinctual promptings in human beings is an especially pronounced impediment to the advances of civilization (ibid., p. 121). Civilization is more on the side of eros, "whose purpose is to combine single human individuals, and after that families, then races, peoples and nations, into one great unity, the unity of mankind" (ibid., p. 122). At its very basis, the evolution of civilization reflects this fundamental struggle between eros and the death instinct, the "battle of the giants," as Freud put it (ibid.).

If we recall from the "origins-of-society" theory (Chapter 3, p. 73), it is clear that Freud tied the superego as "heir" to the Oedipal conflict to the origins of society. That is, taboos and prohibitions, which issued from the contractual arrangements made by the brothers following the patricide, were intrinsically related to superego formation. And as a completely "internal" facet of the personality—in contrast to the ego's "external" orientation—the superego "is also the expression of the most powerful impulses and most important libidinal vicissitudes of the id" (Freud, 1923/1961a, p. 36). In mastering the Oedipus complex through formation of a superego the personality system has actually placed itself under subjection of the id: "Whereas the ego is essentially the representative of the external world, of reality, the super-ego stands in contrast to it as the representative of the internal world, of the id" (ibid.).

This may strike us as inconsistent because we tend to think of the superego as a representative of the values of society, as the handmaiden of culture. But looked at more dynamically, it is clear that Freud's conception of the origin of the superego was as a defensive maneuver, as a compromise in which there is an "identification" with the now deceased aggressor (i.e., the father) so that not only is this aggressor made into a deity (origins of religion), and taboos set up to perpetuate this deity's will, but the expectations for punishment when these taboos are violated are part and parcel of this total process. This basic tie of superego to id is what makes harsh or excessive punishment possible:

> From the point of view of instinctual control, or morality, it may be said of the id that it is totally non-moral, of the ego that it strives to be moral, and of the superego that it can be super-moral and then become as cruel as only the id can be. It is remarkable that the more a man checks his aggressiveness towards the exterior the more severe—that is aggressive—he becomes in his ego ideal [superego]. . . . Even ordinary normal morality has a harsh restraining, cruelly prohibiting quality. It is from this, indeed, that the conception arises of a higher being who deals out punishment inexorably. (ibid., p. 54)

Now let us assume that there were no superego (ego-ideal) in the personality structure. First of all, this would imply that a completely different solution to the Oedipus complex would have to take place. We would obviously have some basic rewriting of the Freudian theory to accomplish. Furthermore, we would have to think of the ego as an aspect of the personality "striving" for morality or civility (as codified in laws) without the benefit of an internal stipulation of just what these concepts mean. Though it may be harsh and even cruel at times, the superego does at least represent a system of prohibitions affording the ego internal "thats" for the sake of which behavior can be intended. Freud expressed this in a more anthropomorphic form, as if the superego were watchdog to the actions of the ego: "The super-ego is an agency which has been inferred by us, and conscience is a function which we ascribe, among other functions, to that agency. This function consists in keeping a watch over the actions and intentions of the ego and judging them, in exercising a censorship. The sense of guilt, the harshness of the super-ego, is thus the same thing as the severity of conscience" (ibid., p. 136).

In essence, what we find here is the idea that the *standards* are carried by the superego, which in turn is an aspect of the ego structure that must counter and compromise id impulses even as these impulses are being somehow accommodated. The id is *the* primary structural factor of the personality. Freud was adamant in his opinion that even the ego is structurally nothing more than an extension of the id:

We have said that the ego is weak in comparison with the id, that it is its loyal servant, eager to carry out its orders and to fulfil its demands. We have no intention of withdrawing this statement. But on the other hand, this same ego is the better organised part of the id, with its face turned towards reality. We must not exaggerate the separation between the two of them too much, and we must not be surprised if the ego on its part can bring its influence to bear on the processes of the id. I believe the ego exercises this influence by putting into action the almost omnipotent pleasure-unpleasure principle by means of the signal of anxiety." (ibid., p. 93)

The dynamics of the ego, which "inoculates" itself across levels of unconscious-conscious quite by design (see Chapter 4, pp. 126-127) help to keep the id in check. And the sense of moral anxiety that the superego relies upon helps keep the ego in bounds as well. Thus, Freud had both the ego and superego taking root from the id, drawing libidinal and related energies from an id source, yet capable of dialectically countering the free expression of id impulses. It is difficult to imagine how anxiety might arise in the personality system without some sense of a prohibition backed up by punishment, that is, by the *unpleasure* Freud referred to. That is, though Freud may have personally disliked the excesses of a rigidly harsh superego, excesses which were often linked to sadistic tendencies in the person involved, he did not really believe that by removing superego prohibitions and absolving people of all punishment that a better world or higher civilization might result.

As the id itself is only too willing to punish sadistically, the Freudian dynamic requires a countering sense of anxiety over the possibility of punishment. This need not be corporeal, of course, but whatever it is that a civilization construes as punishment—incarceration, loss of property, restitution with penalty, fines, and so on—most assuredly aids in checking the free expression of id intentions. In the final analysis, human understanding through an exercise of reason is what Freud offered as antidote to the blind following of religious-like taboos (Freud, 1932-36/1964b, p. 151). But reason is itself framed by assumptive "thats" for the sake of which anything can be known. Freud identified his science of behavior with the fruits of reason (ibid.). But what his science teaches is that human behavior is not *only* reasoned or rational. And in its need for framing standards, as well as anxiety to oppose the forces of the irrational id impulses, the total character structure most certainly requires some form of "unpleasure," which in legal terms amounts to punishment.

We therefore conclude that punishment in some form is taken by psychoanalysis as an aspect of civilization, as the outcome of rules through which human beings seek to "adjust their mutual relations." Unconscious factors enter into the decisions of every citizen of a given culture, each of whom seeks to maximize pleasure and minimize unpleasure. Unfortunately, through what are clearly intentional maneuverings, some members of the culture arrive at such poor adjustments—not always due to their specific choices, but to which they eventually become a party—that they are unable to keep their unconscious (id) intentions in check, resulting in the distortions of reality we know of as mental illness. The Law makes allowances for such distorted behavior, whether stemming from physical or purely psychological determinations. Freudian psychology is no enemy to the Law, which it accepts in a spirit of realism as one aspect of the total human experience.

## SUMMARY

Chapter 21 takes up the complex problems associated with the role of the psychopathologist in the courtroom. Since laws are predicated on the assumption of *free will* among the populace expected to obey the Law, it follows that a psychopathologist who believes that people are nontelic organisms, moved by their biology or cultural shaping without agency, cannot in good conscience serve as an expert witness in the courtroom. The offensive act that brings a person before the bar of justice is termed the *actus reus.* The point of a trial is to determine whether the defendant actually committed the actus reus. In addition, in criminal cases the court seeks to assess whether there was *mens rea* ("guilty mind"), which amounts to the degree of intent (purpose) connected with the actus reus. *Culpability* refers to the blameworthiness of an act, which in turn would point to a judgment of guilt if a person has violated the Law.

In order to shed light on precisely what sort of determinism the Law is concerned with, Chapter 21 next reviews the four types that were first presented in Chapter 5: *material-cause, efficient-cause, formal-cause,* and *final-cause determinism.* All mechanistic theories rely upon efficient causation as the major mover of events. Freud's *psychic determinism* was underwritten by final-cause determinism. Laws stand as formal-cause patterns, as the "thats" for the sake of which their framers intended that the society be organized. Thus, we can introduce final-cause determinism to any consideration of the Law. *Expert witnesses* drawn from psychiatry or psychology run the gamut of determinisms in their theories of psychopathology. Problems arise when we begin to permit *functional* psychiatric disorders, based upon unconscious factors, to enter into our consideration of the culpability of a defendant brought before the bar of justice on a criminal charge.

Chapter 21 next takes up the *insanity defense* in light of the three major grounds or rules that have been followed by the courts. The *M'Naghten rule* is the oldest of the three, dating from 1843. The core idea of this line of defense is whether "at the time of the committing of the act [actus reus], the party accused was labouring under such a defect of reason, from disease of the mind, as not to know the nature and quality of the act he was doing; or, if he did know it, that he did not know he was doing what was wrong." Knowing the difference between "right and wrong" is thus the central thrust of the M'Naghten rule. In 1887, the *irresistible impulse* elaboration of the M'Naghten rule was introduced, which suggested that if a person's free agency was destroyed at the time of the crime, so that he or she had lost the power to choose between the right and wrong course of action—even if this course was known!—then culpability would be mitigated.

In 1954 the *Durham rule* was written into an opinion, suggesting that "an accused is not criminally responsible if his unlawful act was the product of mental disease or mental defect." This "product" rule was to cause much difficulty because it seemed to take the focus off the actus reus and gave too much authority to the testimony of the expert witness concerning factors in the early life of the defendant that might or might not be relevant. The Durham rule seemed to suggest that so long as a mental illness could be proven in the case history of the defendant, this itself excused the defendant from culpability in the case before the court. In 1967 the Durham rule was reversed, and at present it is not employed in any court in the United States.

The *American Law Institute (ALI) rule* was drafted in 1962, and states that a defendant with mental disease or an abnormal condition of mind who "(1) either lacks substantial capacity to appreciate that his conduct is wrongful, or (2) lacks substantial capacity to conform his conduct to law" may be adjudged less culpable or even innocent of a crime. This removes the actus reus as a "product" of mental illness. Many experts on the matter believe that the ALI rule is simply the M'Naghten rule and irresistible impulse elaboration in new language. The aim is to allow the jury to rule on mens rea, taking the defendant's general level of adjustment into consideration but focusing upon the criminal offense (actus reus) per se. The ALI rule does seem to take a more dynamic view of mental illness than is true of the traditional M'Naghten rule. In any case, these two rules are the main lines of defense allowed in courts today.

Chapter 21 next considers *diminished capacity* and *competence to stand trial,* judgments that take the same factors as the insanity defense into consideration in a slightly different context. There is some concern expressed over the practice of detaining people in mental hospitals as incompetent because sometimes this amounts to a long-term prison sentence without due process. Actually, few defendants take the insanity defense, with estimates ranging from less than 1 percent to as high as 3 percent of all cases presented before the court. Psychiatrists differ on the question of what to do with criminals who are also insane. Some believe in the indefinite sentence. Others believe that fixed sentences for crimes is the only solution. Many psychiatrists believe that there is no place for the psychiatrist as expert witness in the courtroom. The complex issue of punishment is next discussed, with attitudes both pro and con expressed by leading psychiatrists.

Chapter 21 closes with an extended discussion of free will and punishment from the perspective of Freudian theory. It is shown how Freud was a *soft* determinist in the realm of material events but a *hard* determinist in the realm of mind (psychic determinism). Although Freud once referred to free will as an illusion, he was speaking of the fact that what one side of mind (consciousness) considers a decision freely made is in fact the effect, outcome, compromise, conclusion, implication, wish, and so forth, of the *other* side of mind (unconscious). Freud never took the position of a biological reductionism into mechanism. Indeed, he made libido an *intentional* conception, distorting the traditional efficient-cause meaning of "energy" as used in the physical sciences. It is through dialectical machinations of the mind, in which id, ego, and superego negotiate to frame a compromised solution which is then enacted in behavior, that we trace the Freudian conception of free will. In other words, free will in psychoanalysis refers to *both* consciousness and unconsciousness. Once we remove the conscious/unconscious dichotomy we see that there is but one way that mind "works" in Freudian theory, and that way is according to final causation—that is, telic behavior encompassing free will.

The unconscious refers to the unavowed, the ideas that we humans would not believe yet we know full well that we do believe! Furthermore, unlike the cybernetic machine which takes information that is "input" in a demonstrative, literal, unipolar fashion, the Freudian dialectical conception of mind has the person capable of reasoning to the opposite of inputs, and to the opposite of these opposites *ad infinitum,* arriving thereby at purely psychic constructions (wishes) that have little or no relation to the "input" per se. Most of these dialectical machinations occur at the unconscious level. It is argued that the Law could readily accommodate its basic assumption of free will to include unconscious intentions of this type. By examining the person's defenses it would be possible to assign culpability at a full or somewhat mitigated level.

As for punishment in Freudian theory, it is germane to the development of personality as presently conceived that the mores of civilization have some influence on this process. A nonpunishing or nonexistent superego would mean that the ego would have to negotiate exclusively with the id in the eventual personality structures of the citizens of a society without punishment for infractions. At its very basis, the evolution of civilization reflects a fundamental struggle between eros and the death instinct. The id retains a great influence in the personality of the civilized human being, making itself known through both the ego and the superego. The superego in particular is framed as a defensive maneuver, in which there is an identification with an aggressor. A nonpunishing superego would mean that there would have been a completely different resolution to the Oedipal conflict than psychoanalysis now posits, based on the evolution of society (see Chapter 3).

Given that both the ego and the superego take root from the id but serve also to balance the id off against reality, it is difficult to imagine how anxiety might arise in a personality without some sense of prohibition backed up by unpleasure or "punishment." As the id itself is only too willing to punish sadistically (death instinct) the Freudian dynamic requires a countering sense of anxiety to be experienced by the conscious portion of the ego in order to avoid the mere "possibility" of the immense guilt that would be forthcoming if id intentions were made known without proper insight. We therefore conclude that punishment in some form is taken by psychoanalysis as an aspect of civilization, which is itself based upon evolutionary forces in which hostility played no small part.

# Glossary

*Abreaction:* Working over and reliving reactions that were not displayed earlier in life due to constraining environmental circumstances. This concept was used by Breuer and Freud to account for hysterical disorders. It makes reference to the mental aspects of this disorder. The emotional release during an abreactive experience is termed *catharsis*.

*Accommodation:* Piaget's concept suggesting that a newborn child can modify or somehow influence the "fit" or known relationship between a schema (such as reflexive sucking) and the world to which it is being applied. The child is not behaving mechanically, but is actively altering what is already known to the ongoing reality. *See also:* Assimilation.

*Acrophobia:* The irrational fear of heights. *See also:* Phobia.

*Acting out:* A phrase used to describe the fact that both normal and abnormal individuals enact unconscious dynamics in their everyday affairs. *See also:* Repetition compulsion.

*Actus reus:* An offensive act; the alleged act that brings a person before the court as defendant. *See also:* Mens rea.

*Acute intoxication:* An organic mental disorder typified by delirium, disorientation, and delusional and hallucinatory reconstructions (delirium tremens). *See also:* Organic mental disorder.

*Agent, agency:* The view holding that an identity factor enters into behavior, so that the individual may be said to direct (determine) his or her own behavior—at least to some extent. Agency theories are framed from the introspective perspective and rely on final-cause descriptive terminology. As such, they are teleologies. *See also:* Final cause; Introspective perspective; Teleology.

*Agitated depression:* A major depressive episode in which the patient becomes restless, tense, and overactive in expressing extreme apprehensiveness.

*Agoraphobia:* Traditionally, this has referred to an irrational fear of open spaces. However, DSM-III views this phobic disorder as occurring when there is a marked fear in the patient of being alone, or being in a public place where escape would be difficult in the case of a sudden incapacitation; this includes fear of crowded streets, bridges, stores, elevators, or a public conveyance. *See also:* Phobia.

*Aim-inhibition:* When an instinct is not seeking satisfaction, as during latency where there is little or no manifestation of sexual cathexes toward the cross-sex parent —and, by extension, to other members of the opposite sex in general. *See also:* Instinct.

*Algophobia:* The irrational fear of pain. *See also:* Phobia.

*ALI rule:* An insanity defense based upon the American Law Institute (ALI) Model Penal Code Test; this rule states that no judgment of criminal responsibility should be made if the defendant, due to a mental-emotional disease, with impaired behavioral controls, "(i) lacks substantial capacity to appreciate that his conduct is wrongful, or (ii) lacks substantial capacity to conform his conduct to law." *See also:* Durham rule; M'Naghten rule.

*Alternating personality:* A dissociative disorder in which two or more ego-superego organizations have become more or less completely separated in the same personality system. One such subpersonality dominates all conscious perception, thinking, and action for a time to the virtual exclusion of its rival. Then the other subpersonality takes over, with the alternation occurring as often as several times a day, or as seldom as once in several years. Each subpersonality has massive amnesia for the other. *See also:* Dissociative disorder; Double or multiple personality.

*Ambivalence:* Feeling both positive and negative toward some object, attitude, or style of behavior.

*Amnesic syndrome:* An organic brain syndrome typified by loss in long-term or short-term memory without a clouding of consciousness. If anything, long-term memory is retained better than short-term. *See also:* Delirium; Organic brain syndrome.

*Anal personality:* Adult character structure due to predominant fixations in anal level and characterized by parismony, petulance, and pedantry.

*Anal stage:* The second psychosexual stage in order of development, according to Freudian theory. The anus is the erogenous zone of importance. This is the period of toilet training, and hence frustrations and prohibitions enter the child's life. The basic outlook emanating from this stage is aggressive. *See also:* Anal personality.

*Anorexia nervosa:* A pathological loss of appetite as a manifestation of a conversion disorder. *See also:* Bulimia.

*Anthropomorphize:* To frame a theory in humanlike (teleological) description when it is wrong or at least questionable to do so.

*Anticathexis:* In effect, repression defined in libidinal terms. To anticathect (or "countercathect") is to oppose a fixing of libido onto objects, or to oppose the acting out that follows such cathecting, by pressing a countering measure of libido in the act of repression. *See also:* Cathexis; Libido; Repression.

*Antisocial personality disorder:* Known in times past as psychopathic inferiority, sociopathic personality, and semantic dementia, this disorder reflects a lifelong tendency to violate the legal sanctions of the culture within which the person lives. Behavior is typified by deceit, manipulation, self-indulgence, and a lack of consideration for the rights of others. Often these personality types become delinquents and criminals, but they can also remain out of jail by finding occupations that require their unconventional lifestyles. *See also:* Personality disorder.

*Antithetical idea:* The opposite of a person's affirmed intentions which can be enacted "against the will" of the person. This was a construct in Freud's very first theoretical explanation of the neurosis. It rests upon *dialectical* reasoning assumptions concerning the human being. *See also:* Counterwill; Dialectical reasoning.

*Anxiety attack:* An acute episode of emotional decompensation usually appearing in a setting of chronic anxiety, and exhibiting to an exaggerated degree the character-istics of normal fright. *See also:* Generalized anxiety disorder.

*Anxiety, castration:* An aspect of the Oedipal conflict in which the male offspring fears that his father will castrate him for lusting after his mother.

*Anxiety, clinical manifestation of:* A state of apprehension, without an apparent object, in which attempts are made to discharge internally generated tension and to reduce physiological discomfort through increased bodily activity.

*Anxiety disorder:* A clinical syndrome in which diffuse emotional tension and free anxiety clearly dominate the clinical picture, while other symptoms are merely incidental. *See also:* Anxiety, clinical manifestation of.

*Anxiety, Freudian theory of:* Interpreted as "transformed libido" by Freud for several years before crystallizing the definition as a "reaction to a situation of danger." This made anxiety a signal or instrumentality, and Freud further claimed that it could be induced by the unconscious portions of the ego "onto" the conscious portions of the ego—on the analogy of inoculation. Anxiety of this type would be *neurotic* (i.e., a fear of revealing the repressed contents). It is also possible to experience *realistic* anxiety (an objective threat) and *moral* anxiety (guilt). *See also:* Drive induction theory.

*Anxiety hierarchy:* A technique of rank ordering fear-provoking stimuli (situations) from greatest to least sense of anxiety. In systematic desensitization the patient is then made to relax while imagining these situations, beginning with the least anxiety provoking and extending to the most anxiety provoking. *See also:* System-atic desensitization.

*Arachnophobia:* An irrational fear of spiders. *See also:* Phobia.

*Archaic ego:* Some analysts refer to this as reflecting the earliest precursors of what eventually becomes the ego. The archaic ego and superego are disputed concepts in psychoanalysis. *See also:* Archaic superego.

*Archaic superego:* The remnant of some of the earliest attempts made by the infant to gain self-control. Remnants of this early effort remain in everyone throughout life. Some psychoanalysts object to this concept, reserving the term superego for post-Oedipal personality structures.

*Argyll-Robertson pupil:* A pupil that does not respond to light but does to accommo-dation for distance. This is a major symptom of general paresis. *See also:* General paresis.

*Arteriosclerotic cerebral degeneration:* An organic mental disorder caused by brain damage resulting from arteriosclerosis. The onset of this disorder is usually sudden, marked by an acute confusional episode or a convulsive attack. Neurological signs of focal damage are common. *See also:* Senile cerebral degeneration.

*Assimilation:* Piaget's concept suggesting that a newborn child can "take in" experience based upon certain reflexive schema, such as the sucking response. The process of sucking acts as a frame of reference through which the child learns about experience. *See also:* Accommodation.

*Attachment:* Bowlby's concept suggesting that all immature animals form an emotional bond or link to a mature animal. This bonding can be seen in the first year of life, as when a human infant is desirous of being in close proximity to a mothering figure. Attachments also occur to fathers. *See also:* Symbiosis.

*Autism:* A state of mind in which the person is detached from his or her surroundings on a regular basis, as if living in a dream world. The autistic person cannot be reached through the usual interpersonal avenues of verbal discourse or spontaneous demonstration.

*Autoerotism:* Gaining pleasure from the organ or bodily part (mouth, anus, penis) per se rather than from the object toward which that particular organ is biologically oriented to gain satisfaction. Infants who gain pleasure from sucking per se are reflecting autoerotic behavior. *See also:* Object-choice.

*Aviophobia:* An irrational fear of airplanes. *See also:* Phobia.

*Avoidance serial cue hierarchy (ASCH):* In implosive therapy, this is the hierarchy of fearful situations, running from the least to the most anxiety-provoking set of circumstances in the client's life. This hierarchy can also include completely fantastic situations, such as "after-life" confrontations with dieties. The therapist takes the client through these situations, encouraging anxiety expression which is followed by extinction thanks to the lack of punishment. *See also:* Implosive therapy.

*Avoidant personality disorder:* A maladaptive pattern in which the person is over-sensitive to the moods and evaluations of others and actively seeks to avoid social contact as a form of defense. This person would like to have social contact and verbalizes frustration and low self-esteem. *See also:* Personality disorder.

*Awareness, conscious vs. unconscious:* In Freudian theory, it is not proper to limit awareness to consciousness. The unconscious is actually more *aware* of things than the conscious aspect of mind. As a result, we must recognize that complex thoughts relating to reality as conceptualized by the person can go on at an unconscious level. *See also:* Free will.

*Awareness, of subjects in conditioning experiments:* The widespread findings which suggest that not unless a subject in a conditioning experiment knows the patterned relationship between the conditioned and unconditioned stimulus (classical conditioning) or between the operant response and the contingent reinforcer (operant conditioning), and *complies* thereby with what is intended by the experimental design, does "conditioning" occur. *See also:* Conditioning, classical; Conditioning, operant.

*Base rate:* In operant conditioning, the rate at which a target response is being emitted over a period of time. For example, how often per day does a child throw a temper tantrum? The average number of times per day over a week or two would represent the base rate. *See also:* Conditioning, operant.

*Behavior modification ("behavior mod"):* Also called behavior therapy, behavior modification refers to the use of classical and especially operant conditioning to effect changes in behavior. The undesirable behavior is extinguished and the desirable behavior is reinforced.

*Behavior therapy: See:* Behavior modification.

*Behavioral shaping:* A general term used by behavioral therapists to describe how people are controlled (via efficient causality) by their environment. *See also:* Efficient cause; Method of successive approximations.

*Biological naturalism:* A nativistic theory in which an effort is made to understand an organism without foreclosing on the style of causation that might be required to account for what is observed. The organism's biological, physiological, and other "innate" equipment is taken at face value with no effort to "reduce" it to presumed underlying material/efficient causes. *See also:* Biological reductionism; Nativism.

*Biological reductionism:* A nativistic theory in which it is held that the only kind of influence to be seen in behavior is of a material- and efficient-cause variety. All behavior must be understood as due to hereditary forces that make the person what he or she "is" regardless of environmental conditions. *See also:* Biological naturalism; Nativism; Reductionism.

*Bipolar disorder:* A syndrome that can reflect a full symptomatic picture of both manic and major depressive episodes, intermixed or rapidly alternating every few days. If the patient has a series of manic episodes without intervening depression the diagnosis of *bipolar disorder, manic* is assigned. If the patient is currently depressed, but has a history of a manic episode, the diagnosis would be *bipolar disorder, depressed.* If both manic and depressive mood swings occur daily or over several days, the diagnosis would be *bipolar disorder, mixed. See also:* Cyclothymic disorder; Major depressive episode; Major manic episode.

*Bipolarity:* The view that some meaningful relations or patterns are dual "by nature," as in the case of opposite meanings. Rather than two separate meanings united, opposites may be thought of as intrinsically bipolar so that "left" necessarily implies the existence of "right." We cannot understand one pole (left) without understanding the other (right). *See also:* Dialectical meaning.

*Bisexuality:* A viewpoint that Freud received from Fliess, in which it is held that both sexes have the biological/psychological characteristics of the other in reduced form. Freud used this concept to suggest positive and negative forms of the Oedipus complex. *See also:* Oedipus complex.

*Body language:* The symbolized manifestation of unconscious conflicts in disorders such as the somatoform (conversion) disorder. *See also:* Organ speech; Somatoform disorder.

*Borderline personality disorder:* A pattern of maladaptive behavior typified by significant instability of mood, inconsistent and unpredictable behavioral changes, and serious conflict in self-image or identity recognition. *See also:* Cyclothymic disorder; Personality disorder.

*Bronchial asthma:* A respiratory disorder in which there is constriction of the bronchioles, which results in wheezing, choking sensations, and gasping for breath. This disorder is often tied to psychosomatic dynamics. *See also:* Psychosomatic disorder.

*Brontophobia:* The irrational fear of thunder. *See also:* Phobia.

*Bulimia:* Excessive overeating as a manifestation of a conversion disorder. *See also:* Somatoform disorder.

*Castrating female:* A woman who seeks to compete and best men in various traditionally masculine realms of competition (business, sports, etc.) as a reflection of her unresolved Oedipus complex.

*Catecholamine hypothesis:* A hypothesis that depression is caused by a deficit of norepinephrine (a catecholamine substance), and that mania is the result of an oversupply of this neurotransmitter at the synaptic connections of the brain's neural tissues.

*Cathexis:* The fixing or entering of a psychic energy into the thought or image of a desired object. A man lusting after a woman cathects her visual image in his mind's eye. *See also:* Libido; Object-choice.

*Cause(s):* A concept originating with Aristotle to account for the nature of things and behaviors. There are four basic types of causes—material, efficient, formal, and final—and by using these meanings as universal models, we can better understand the common knowledge we have of everything in our experience, including the behavior of people. *See also:* Efficient cause; Final cause; Formal cause; Material cause.

*Censorship:* An early Freudian construct, supplanted by repression or the defensive effort to keep out of consciousness what is fully known by unconscious mentation. *See also:* Repression.

*Circular insanity: See:* Bipolar disorder.

*Clang associations:* When a patient's speech is characterized by words that rhyme, even though they may not present a coherent thought. It is as if the rhyming quality invades on the rationality of the line of reasoning. *See also:* Flight of ideas.

*Claustrophobia:* An irrational fear of closed spaces. *See also:* Phobia.

*Coitus interruptus:* An early theory of Freud's in which he suggested that hysterical symptoms were due to sexual noxa that had been generated in the patient's physical functioning during a time of sexual frustration.

*Competence, mental:* A legal judgment relating to the question of whether or not a person accused of some crime is capable of standing trial. Thus, mental *incompetence* is adjudged when "a defendant who as a result of mental disease or defect lacks capacity to understand the proceedings against him or to assist in his own defense."

*Compulsive personality disorder:* A maladaptive pattern typified by inflexibility, a cheerless outlook on life, inability to express warm and tender emotions, and a fanatic preoccupation with order, rules, organization, and efficiency. *See also:* Obsessive-compulsive disorder; Personality disorder.

*Condensation: See:* Dream condensation.

*Conditioned avoidance response:* A behavioristic interpretation of the "symptom" of psychopathological behavior. This comes down to a typical stimulus-response habit, in which the phobic person has been conditioned to fear the elevator stimulus quite without intention, design, or meaningful significance. The elevator stimulates the patient to avoid it as a response. *See also:* Symptom.

*Conditioning, classical (Pavlovian):* The observed fact that responses made to a "natural" stimulus can be transferred to a neutral stimulus. Thus, flashing a light (conditioned stimulus) before blowing food powder (unconditioned stimulus) into a dog's mouth can result in the dog's natural process of salivating to food (unconditioned response) to be triggered by the light (conditioned salivation response ensuing). *See also:* Conditioning, operant.

*Conditioning, operant (Skinnerian):* The observed fact that when a response is made that "operates" on the environment to produce a contingent circumstance which is reinforcing, the base rate of this operant response rises and continues at a higher emission rate. *See also:* Base rate; Conditioning, classical.

*Confabulation:* A device used by patients with organic brain syndromes, who in compensation for failing memory tell "lies" in order to substitute imaginary happenings for the forgotten circumstances.

*Conflict:* A severe form of frustration in which there are different ends, goals, wishes, and so forth, serving to block one another. *See also:* Frustration.

*Conscious, consciousness:* Defined by Freud as the sense organ for the apprehension of psychical qualities. *See also:* Preconscious; Unconscious.

*Constancy, principle of:* Introduced by Julius Robert Mayer and popularized as the conservation-of-energy principle by Helmholtz, this principle held that in any isolated (or closed) system, the sum of physical forces at play remains constant—that is, seeks a uniform level of distribution—so that if there is a mobilization of forces at one point there is an immediate and automatic mechanism brought into play that reduces this disparity in pressure point and re-establishes the balance.

*Conversion disorder:* According to DSM-III, a somaticizing patient who focuses on a *single* symptom through which secondary gain is achieved. This clinical syndrome used to be called *hysteria. See also:* Somatization disorder.

*Counterconditioning:* Another term for the process of reciprocal inhibition. *See:* Reciprocal inhibition.

*Countermeasures:* Conscious efforts to oppose the expression of unconscious wishes that are dimly perceived. In obsessions, the person may devise a conscious scheme of counting items in the environment to avoid dealing with the return of the repressed.

*Counterphobic behavior:* Doing precisely that behavior which is phobic in an effort to master it. This can be done in fantasy, play, or actual enactment as when a person fearful of heights forces himself or herself to climb a stepladder. *See also:* Phobia.

*Countertransference:* The unconscious feelings and attitudes projected onto the patient by the therapist. *See also:* Psychoanalysis; Transference.

*Counterwill:* Freud's earliest conception of mind, suggesting that with each intention framed there is a countering (negating, doubting, etc.) willful intention framed that might at some time be enacted. Hence, behavior *not* intended could be enacted. *See also:* Antithetical idea.

*Cue-producing response:* Dollard and Miller's theoretical assertion that former responses can work as cue-stimuli in the present. Cue-producing responses are therefore "mediators," assisting the ongoing process of behavior. *See also:* Mediation.

*Culpability:* In legal matters, the degree of blameworthiness assigned to an infraction of law. *See also:* Mens rea.

*Cyclothymic disorder:* A disorder bearing the symptoms of *both* depressive and manic syndromes, but to a lesser degree so the diagnosis of a bipolar disorder is not justified. *See also:* Bipolar disorder; Major depressive disorder; Major manic disorder.

*Death instinct: See:* Instinct, death.

*Decompensation:* A term used to describe the collapse of defenses and regression of the personality in general. The process "as a whole" is said to be underway as the person progressively loses control. This may occur slowly or come about suddenly.

*Dedifferentiation:* A loss in the distinction between the psychological and the physiological functioning of the total organism. This is viewed as concurrent with deep regression. For example, a person suffering a psychosomatic disorder has dedifferentiated and hence is not symbolizing the psychological in the physiological but simply confounding one with the other very directly. *See also:* Psychosomatic disorder.

*Defense hysteria:* Freud's psychodynamic explanation of the hysterical disorders, which he opposed to Breuer's biological explanation. *See also:* Hypnoid state.

*Delirium:* An organic brain syndrome typified by a clouded state of consciousness in which the person has difficulty sustaining attention to both external and internal stimuli, experiences sensory misperceptions, and has a disordered stream of thought. As the delirium progresses increasing signs of confusion and disorientation appear. There may be occasional lucid intervals, but relapses are likely.

*Delusion:* A fixed belief that persists even though social reality contradicts it. Delusions can be inconsistent or poorly systematized, or they can be internally consistent and thus highly systematized.

*Delusion of grandeur:* A false belief resting upon self-aggrandizement, boastfulness, pride, and self-assertiveness. Extravagant and impossible claims are made and plans drawn. This delusion is typical in manic disorders. *See also:* Major manic episode.

*Delusional paranoid jealousy:* A disproportionate level of jealousy in a patient with a paranoid disorder. The extremity of the reaction betrays the unconscious factors lying behind the delusional dynamics.

*Delusional reconstruction:* Another way of referring to restitution following psychotic regression. *See also:* Restitutive process.

*Dementia:* An organic brain syndrome typified by a loss of intellectual abilities of sufficient magnitude to interfere with social or occupational patterns of behavior. Memory, judgment, and abstract thought are all adversely affected. DSM-III notes that dementia may be progressive, static, or remitting. Sometimes it is reversible when the underlying cause (organic mental disorder) is curable. *See also:* Organic brain syndrome; Organic mental disorder.

*Dementia praecox:* A serious mental disorder occurring in a young person. This was Kraepelin's phrase for the syndrome that Bleuler later renamed "schizophrenia." DSM-III states that the symptoms of schizophrenia should be noted in the patient before the age of forty-five, so it is no longer simply "young" people who are judged capable of developing this disorder. *See also:* Kraepelinian nosology; Schizophrenic disorder.

*Denial:* Believed by many psychoanalysts to be a more primitive manifestation of repression, arising when the ego is not yet well formed in personality development and a clear sense of consciousness has not been attained. *See also:* Repression.

*Dependent personality disorder:* A maladaptive pattern in which the person gravitates to others in hopes that they will make his or her life decisions. Dependents assume a passive role in social contact and follow the lead of others uncritically. Although they have a good "front," there is an underlying sense of unhappiness in the outlook of dependent personalities. *See also:* Personality disorder.

*Depersonalization:* When due to an emotional shock the person feels that he or she is "not real." Reality is as a dream state in which other actors are doing things. It is not the person but others who are hearing, witnessing, or feeling what is going on. Normal individuals have this reaction but in extreme cases this results in a dissociative disorder. *See also:* Estrangement.

*Depressive episode: See:* Major depressive episode.

*Depressive stupor:* An extreme form of retarded depression in which literally all forms of spontaneous activity cease. *See also:* Retarded depression.

*Depth model:* Freud's initial partitioning of the psyche into conscious, unconscious, and preconscious levels. *See also:* Topographical model.

*Derivative(s):* A term used to describe the meaningful expression emanating from repressed contents, which come to be manifested in various aspects of conscious behavior.

*Detachment:* Bowlby's concept suggesting that when an infant who has become attached to a parent is denied contact with that parent for a prolonged period, there is a deterioration in the infant's behavior typified by emotional despair and environmental disinterest. *See also:* Attachment.

*Determine, determinism:* To set a limit on the number of alternatives that can be brought about in the course of events, including behavior. There are four types of determinism, based on the causal meanings. *See also:* Cause(s).

*Determinism, efficient-cause:* Limitations in alternatives based upon the impetus in events. For example, wind flow determines the course of a leaf falling from the branch of a tree, or the stimulus in stimulus-response theory impels the response. *See also:* Cause(s); Constancy, principle of; Determine; Efficient cause; Mechanism.

*Determinism, final-cause:* The reason, premise, hypothesis, assumption, and so on, for the sake of which an outcome is brought about. Final-cause determinisms may be seen in any intentional sequence of behavior, as when a person sets a goal and achieves it through willful effort. This form of determinism is to be seen in "free will" behavior. *See also:* Cause(s); Determine; Final cause; Free will; Intention.

*Determinism, formal-cause:* Limitations in alternatives based upon a patterning of some type. For example, the shape or outline of a certain cloud formation heralds the onset of a tornado in the distance, or a derivation of a mathematical proof is established by the equation of patterned numbers in tautological order. *See also:* Cause(s); Determine; Formal cause.

*Determinism, hard vs. soft:* Refers to the level of determinism accepted in a theory. The hard determinist believes that *everything* that occurs (e.g., in behavior) is 100 percent determined. The soft determinist believes that there is some modicum of indeterminism or "chance" in events, which are in the main determined.

*Determinism, material-cause:* Limitations in alternatives based upon the substance of which an object or person is constituted. For example, marble statues last longer than wooden statues and genetic deficiencies result in mental subnormality. *See also:* Cause(s); Determine; Material cause.

*Determinism, psychic:* The position held to by Freud on mentation, which is based upon formal/final-cause determinism and not upon material/efficient-cause determinism. *See also:* Determinism, final-cause; Determinism, formal-cause; Determinism, hard vs. soft.

*Diagnosis:* The process of delineating syndromes in hopes of arriving at a change in an abnormal pattern or cure of a disease process. *See also:* Syndrome.

*Dialectical alternatives and choice:* A recognition of the fact that for a dialectically reasoning organism, the possibilities that arise due to bipolarity constantly require that a choice be made regarding what premise to affirm. *See also:* Bipolarity; Dialectical meaning.

*Dialectical change:* Oppositional alternation of the pattern of precedent events, thereby affecting changes in meaning "for the sake of which" sequacious (logically necessary) events occur. *See also:* Dialectical meaning; Meaning; Telosponse.

*Dialectical meaning:* A way of describing meaning in which meaning relations are said to bear the characteristics of oppositionality, duality, relationality, contradiction, and arbitrariness. There is often a uniting of opposites or contradictions into a new totality, described most frequently as the synthesis of a thesis and an antithesis. *See also:* Bipolarity; Meaning.

*Dialectical reasoning:* Reasoning by way of arriving at beginning premises through an act of choice. Thus, an element of arbitrariness can be seen in the opening meaning affirmation based upon the fact that either a "given" idea or its "opposite" meaning or implication can be affirmed. *See also:* Dialectical alternatives and choice; Dialectical change; Dialectical meaning.

*Diminished capacity:* A legal term used when there are grounds for mitigating culpability due to certain behavioral irregularities such as amnesia or long-term chronic intoxication. Diminished capacity does not remove guilt, but can lead to a reduced sentence.

*Displacement:* A redirecting of some concern from one realm to another in life, as when a father takes out his hostility for his boss on his children. Dream themes can also reflect displacement in that a concern over personal competency might be displaced into a dream over whether one's children will be promoted in school.

*Dissociated personality:* A dissociative disorder in which an extreme depersonalization takes place so that there occur instances of (1) alternating personality or (2) double/multiple personality. *See also:* Alternating personality; Depersonalization; Dissociative disorder; Double or multiple personality.

*Dissociative disorder:* An abnormal pattern in which the person attempts to escape from excessive tension and anxiety by separating off some parts of personality function from the rest. DSM-III distinguishes four subsyndromes in this disorder: psychogenic amnesia, psychogenic fugue, multiple personality, and depersonalization. The text departs from these specific labels, but captures their meanings in related terminology.

*Dopamine hypothesis:* Dopamine is a catecholamine which acts as a neurotransmitter in the chemical transmission of nerve impulses. The dopamine hypothesis suggests that schizophrenia may be due to an excess of dopamine at the synaptic sites of the patient's central nervous system.

*Double-bind hypothesis:* A theoretical construct which traces schizophrenic behavior to a family setting in which parents convey two simultaneous messages to their offspring, one verbally and one in actual behavior. Problems arise from the fact that one of these messages contradicts the other. As a result, the offspring is never adept at assessing reality accurately.

*Double or multiple personality:* A dissociative disorder in which one comparatively mature and realistic ego-superego organization dominates other such subpersonalities nearly all the time. The latter subpersonalities are relatively circumscribed and sometimes incompetent organizations, but they do occasionally take over the personality as a whole (especially under hypnosis). Ordinarily, the dominant subpersonality is amnesic for the subordinate organizations. The order of emergence also dictates the direction of amnesia, so that the last subpersonality to emerge is knowledgeable of the others. *See also:* Alternating personality; Dissociative disorder.

*Dream:* "Thinking in pictures" encompassing a "picture puzzle" that misleads the dreamer concerning what meaning was actually being expressed in the dream. *See also:* Dream work; Manifest vs. latent dream content.

*Dream condensation:* The inclusion of more than one concern, person, activity, and so on, into a single dream image or action. We might dream about someone who combines features (looks, attitudes, etc.) of both our parents into a single "individual."

*Dream work:* Freud's phrase to describe the translation of a wish fulfillment or compromise of wish fulfillments into a dream theme. *See also:* Displacement; Dream; Dream condensation; Manifest vs. latent dream content; Overdetermination.

*Drive:* A personality construct based upon material and efficient causation which holds that before the person behaves there must be a biological pressure of some sort impelling the overt action. There are *primary* drives (hunger, thirst, sex, etc.) and *secondary* drives (power, wealth, etc.) postulated, with the latter based upon the former.

*Drive induction theory:* A theory, like Freud's motivational explanations, in which unconscious identities literally induce or bring about a heightened state of anxiety in the conscious aspects of the personality so that defensiveness may be increased.

Intentionality takes precedence here, much in contrast to traditional drive reduction theory. *See also:* Drive reduction theory.

*Drive reduction theory:* An explanation of behavior holding that not until a drive has been reduced will learning take place. Thus, personality style must be accounted for on the basis of satisfactions (drive reductions) for specific or generalized states of arousal or activation. *See also:* Drive.

*DSM-III:* The third edition of the *Diagnostic and Statistical Manual of Mental Disorders,* which is published by the American Psychiatric Association to standardize and provide proper criteria for the diagnosis of abnormal behavior. *See also:* ICD.

*Dualism:* A theory relying upon two realms of explanation, as in Freud's concepts of *psyche* (mind) and *soma* (body). *See also:* Monism; Psyche; Soma.

*Durham rule:* An insanity defense which holds that "an accused is not criminally responsible if his unlawful act is the *product* of mental illness or defect." This "product rule" is no longer in use. *See also:* ALI rule; M'Naghten rule.

*Dynamic:* In psychological theory, this term refers to a view of the interplay of forces in the mind, as a manifestation of purposeful intentions working concurrently or in mutual opposition.

*Dyspareunia:* A psychosexual dysfunction in which a woman suffers from pain during sexual intercourse. *See also:* Psychosexual dysfunction.

*Dysthymic disorder:* a mood disturbance in which tension and anxiety are expressed in the form of dejection and self-depreciation, somatic disturbance, and repetitive complaints of feeling inferior, hopeless, and worthless. The text employs the older name of *depressive neurosis* interchangeably with this designation. DSM-III classifies the dysthymic disorder with all of the other *affective disorders* that the text singles out, especially the distinction between a neurotic and a psychotic form of depression.

*Efficient cause:* Any concept used to account for the nature of things (including behavior) based on the impetus in a succession of events over time. Explanations of behavior based on energy pushes, gravity attractions, and the machinelike flow of motion are examples of efficient-cause theorizing. *See also:* Cause(s).

*Ego:* Freud referred to this as the better-organized portion of the id, meaning that this aspect of the personality seeks to take reality demands into consideration and to reason according to secondary process thought. The ego is active at all three levels of mind, but its conscious aspects are what we ordinarily think of as our identity ("I," "me," "myself," etc.). *See also:* Depth model; Id; Reality principle; Secondary process thinking; Superego.

*Ego alien:* A term used to describe the process of dissociation, in which the person separates aspects of his or her behavior in an effort to deny their existence. *See also:* Depersonalization; Dissociative disorder; Ego-dystonic behavior.

*Ego-dystonic behavior:* Behavior which is offensive or otherwise repugnant to the ego, but is enacted through compulsivity or in spite of a wish not to behave in this fashion. *See also:* Ego-syntonic behavior.

*Ego-ideal:* Synonymous with superego. *See:* Superego.

*Ego-identity:* Erikson's construct referring to the awareness by the person of a selfsameness and continuity to the ego's synthesizing methods and that these methods are effective in safeguarding the sameness and continuity of the person's meaning for others.

*Ego introjects:* A general term referring to the attitudes and behaviors taken over early in life from identifications with parents. These are seen as precursors of the superego in psychoanalytical writings. *See also:* Identification; Incorporation; Introjection.

*Ego-splitting:* A term used to describe the dissociative process observed in dissociated personalities, whereby the ego (and its superego aspects) divides into two or more autonomous parts.

*Ego-syntonic behavior:* Behavior that is acceptable to the ego, in line with its values, and welcomed as a reflection of the personality system. *See also:* Ego-dystonic behavior.

*Élan vital:* A general life force having telic properties. *See also:* Teleology.

*Electra complex:* Phrase used to describe the female Oedipus complex. *See also:* Oedipus complex.

*Electroconvulsive therapy (ECT):* Also termed electric shock therapy (EST), this is a biological therapy in which an electric current of approximately 160 volts is passed through the patient's head for up to one and one-half seconds. The result is an abrupt loss of consciousness and seizure of the muscles, although the latter can be mitigated through the use of relaxant drugs. Most ECT series involve approximately twelve shocks over a four-week period.

*End-pleasure:* The pleasure achieved from attaining an object as an end. For example, the interpersonal act of sexual copulation results in end-pleasure. *See also:* Fore-pleasure.

*Environmentalism:* A theory which holds that though nature provides the organism with certain crude capacities to behave, these capacities are developed and perfected only because of environmental stimulations and shapings. The latter manipulations are construed extraspectively, in efficient-cause fashion. *See also:* Efficient cause; Nativism.

*Erogenous (erotogenic) zone:* A region of the body through which a pleasurable experience can be had. Sometimes this pleasure comes directly from an activity like sucking; at other times it can come through a sense of mastery, as in the achievement of sphincter control in toilet training.

*Eros:* Also termed the life instinct, this innate process aims to enhance life and to keep it homeostatically balanced. Its energy is libido, and its opponent is the death instinct. Eros and the death instinct can fuse (fusion of instincts) and be reflected in the same behavioral act. *See also:* Instinct, death; Repetition compulsion.

*Erotic paranoid disorder:* A paranoid disorder in which the patient has the delusional belief that someone loves him or her but dares not make an open avowal because of other commitments or because of embarrassment.

*Essential hypertension:* Chronic high blood pressure for which no organic etiology can be identified. This disorder is often tied to psychosomatic dynamics. *See also:* Psychosomatic disorder.

*Estrangement:* When due to an emotional shock the person feels that everything looks strange and different; things seem unnatural, distant, indistinct, and foggy or too distinct and clear. This psychic state can be normal, but in extreme forms it results in a dissociative disorder. *See also:* Depersonalization.

*Eupsychian:* Maslow's term describing an idealized society in which self-actualized people would live. *See also:* Self-actualization.

*Exhibitionism:* A paraphiliac disorder in which the patient has the compulsion to display his or her sexual organs to persons of the opposite sex. This disorder is almost exclusively confined to men. DSM-III limits this diagnosis to cases in which no attempt is made to have sexual contact with the woman to whom exposure is directed. *See also:* Paraphilias.

*Extraspective perspective, of theory:* Framing theoretical explanations of things and/or events in the third person, from the convenience of an observer. Extraspective theory describes "that," or "it" rather than "I," or "me." *See also:* Introspective perspective, of theory.

*Factitious disorder:* A disorder which is not genuine, but merely apes mental or physical illness through voluntary albeit unconscious efforts on the part of the person involved.

*Fetishism:* A paraphiliac disorder in which the person uses inanimate objects (fetishes) as a repeatedly preferred or exclusive ingredient in sexual arousal and orgasmic release. The fetish takes on a symbolic power that becomes an essential ingredient in sexual arousal. *See also:* Paraphilias.

*Final cause:* Any concept used to account for the nature of things (including behavior) based on the assumption that there is a reason, end, or goal "for the sake of which" things exist or events are carried out. Explanations that rely on the person's intentions, aims, or aspirations are final-cause descriptions of behavior. *See also:* Cause(s); Teleology.

*Fixation:* In libido terms, a trapping or pocketing of libido during any given stage of psychosexual development. In fuero terms, a claim made against the total personality earlier in life being "called in" at the present. *See also:* Fuero; Libido; Psychosexual stages.

*Fixed idea:* Janet's concept accounting for the unusual behavior of hysterics—as if an idea had split off from the rest of mind and came to function alone. *See also:* Hypnoid state.

*Flight into illness:* The regressive symptom formation in neurosis, which solves a problem for the person concerned. This is also referred to as the "primary gain" of any neurosis. *See also:* Secondary gain.

*Flight of ideas:* Also termed "topical flight," this arises when the patient's thoughts run wildly from one topic to another with no transition and often the hint of irrationality. This symptom is most likely to be seen during a major manic episode.

*Flooding therapies:* Further developments in implosive therapy which rely upon the person's expression of emotional release in a nonpunishing environment. *See also:* Implosive therapy.

*Folie à Deux:* A form of paranoid disorder in which two persons share the same delusional beliefs. DSM-III refers to this as a "shared paranoid disorder." It is possible for there to be more than two persons entering into such a dynamic, in which case we could speak of a *folie à trois,* etc. *See also:* Paranoid disorder.

*Fore-pleasure:* Essentially autoerotic pleasure, obtained from an erogenous area per se. This pleasure is contrasted with end-pleasure. *See also:* End-pleasure.

*Formal cause:* Any concept used to account for the nature of things (including behavior) based on their patterned organization, shape, design, or order. Explanations of behavior emphasizing the style or type of behavioral pattern taken on are formal-cause descriptions. *See also:* Cause(s); Personality.

*Fragmentation:* A major overt manifestation of behavioral disorganization, seen particularly in organic brain syndromes. Fragmentation refers to the appearance of discontinuous and abortive behavior, to the interruption of a theme begun, or the theme's sudden termination, often followed by a silence or by something quite unrelated. *See also:* Organic brain syndrome.

*Free association:* The "fundamental rule" of psychoanalysis, in which the patient is instructed to say whatever comes to mind while relaxing on a couch or in a comfortable chair.

*Free will, freedom of the will:* The assumption that it is possible for a person to set or affirm the grounds for the sake of which he or she will be determined. The text relies upon the concept of dialectical reasoning to account for how it is possible for the person to behave according to free will in mentation. A telosponding organism is free to affirm a premise, selecting this from among alternatives (freedom), but once this premise is affirmed it is carried out sequaciously, that is, with logical necessity (willful behavior). The text suggests that there is both a conscious and an unconscious reflection of free will in the behavior of people. *See also:* Dialectical reasoning; Telosponse.

*Frigidity:* A psychosexual dysfunction in which a woman's sexual excitement is inhibited. *See also:* Impotence; Psychosexual dysfunction.

*Frustration:* In general terms, any blocking of an organism on the way to a goal. Barriers to satisfaction can be physical or psychological, so that some people continually frustrate themselves because of their low self-opinions.

*Fuero:* Strictly considered, an ancient Spanish law or decree made by a ruler that is given to a province for some reason and can at a later date be exercised or used. Hence, this is a claim on the head of state for privilege. The text uses this analogy drawn from Freud in the Fliess correspondence as a *nonenergic* understanding of fixation. A personal fuero is a claim made upon the total personality system for consideration, stemming from an earlier time (fixation point) and calling for some kind of action in the ever recurring present (repetition compulsion). *See also:* Fixation; Regression; Repetition compulsion.

*Fugue:* A dissociative disorder in which the person flees bodily from a life situation in an effort to forget it completely (massive amnesia). *See also:* Dissociative disorder; massive amnesia.

*Functional disorder:* A disturbance in personal adjustment which has no known organic or biological etiology. Psychogenic disorders fall into this category. *See also:* Organic disorder.

*Ganser syndrome:* A factitious disorder, also called pseudopsychosis, in which the person through unconscious promptings apes a mental illness, presenting a clinical picture that burlesques the genuine syndrome. *See also:* Factitious disorder.

*Gender identity:* Knowing privately what sex one belongs to, in the sense of "I am a man" or "I am a woman." This private experience is not always congruent with a person's anatomical sexual identity. *See also:* Gender identity disorder; Psychosexual disorder; Transsexualism.

*Gender identity disorder:* A disorder which comes about when a person's gender identity is incongruent with his or her anatomical sex. *See also:* Gender identity; Transsexualism.

*Gender role:* The overt behavior manifested by masculine and/or feminine individuals. Cultural standards define what these patterns of behavior will be like. Gender identity does not always follow the gender role assumed by a person. *See also:* Gender identity; Gender identity disorder.

*General paresis:* An organic mental disorder due to encephalitis, that is, an inflammation of the brain which develops because of the presence of syphilitic spirochete. Frontal lobe destruction is most evident. The patient reflects an Argyll-Robinson pupil, slowed and thickened speech, muscular weakness (paresis), and convulsive attacks. Mental decline depends upon the course of the disease and the personality of the patient. *See also:* Argyll-Robinson pupil; Organic mental disorder.

*Generalized adaptation syndrome (GAS):* Selye's concept of a triadic syndrome of defensive measures taken by the body in warding off any form of stress which the tissues and organ systems might be subjected to. The GAS consists of three stages: (1) alarm reaction, (2) resistance, and (3) exhaustion. *See also:* Local adaptation syndrome.

*Generalized anxiety disorder:* Formerly termed an "anxiety neurosis," this syndrome refers to a person suffering from unstructured fear so that he or she cannot point to what is bringing on a chronic anxiety that has lasted for a month or more.

*Grandiose paranoid disorder:* A paranoid disorder in which the patient believes that he or she is of noble birth, of wealthy background, exceptionally beautiful or powerful, a saint, a prophet, or a genius. Any grandiose premise of this sort may be taken and enacted. The major symptom is thus a *delusion of grandeur.*

*Guilt neurosis:* A phrase used by some psychopathologists to capture the fact that both obsessive-compulsives and dysthymic (neurotic-depressive) disorders have prominent expressions of guilt wound into their dynamics. *See also:* Dysthymic disorder; Obsessive-compulsive disorder.

*Hallucination:* A sensory experience leading the person to see, hear, feel, smell, and so forth, things that cannot be established as existing in objective or shared reality. *See also:* Delusion.

*Hematophobia:* The irrational fear of blood. *See also:* Phobia.

*Histrionic personality disorder:* Also known as the hysterical personality, this maladaptive style is typified by a lifelong flair for a dramatic, exhibitionistic, and egocentric behavioral pattern. These individuals are demanding, egocentric, and inconsiderate. Interpersonal relations are superficial and insincere. *See also:* Personality disorder.

*Homosexuality, ego-dystonic:* A pattern in which the person is sexually attracted to members of the same sex and finds this situation distressful. DSM-III allows this form of homosexuality to be considered abnormal so long as the distress is basic and not due to a fleeting recognition of the fact that the person "is" homosexual (i.e., homosexual panic reaction). *See also:* Homosexuality, ego-syntonic.

*Homosexuality, ego-syntonic:* A pattern in which the person is sexually attracted to members of the same sex and finds this perfectly natural. DSM-III considers ego-syntonic homosexuality to be a normal behavioral pattern. *See also:* Homosexuality, ego-dystonic.

*Hyperthyroidism:* A disorder in which there is an excessive secretion of thyroid, which makes the person feel hyperstimulated and anxious. This disorder is often tied to psychosomatic dynamics. *See also:* Psychosomatic disorder.

*Hypnoid state:* Breuer's construct based upon a medical model, in which it is suggested that hysteria arises because of an innate disposition to "split" one's psyche apart.

*Hypochondriasis:* A somatoform disorder typified by habitual preoccupation with a supposed disease or defect in an organ or body part which is actually functioning within normal limits, or by habitually exaggerated concern over organic or body parts which are defective or diseased. The varieties of body overconcern are endless.

*Hypomania:* A slight or reduced manic episode which appears to be a normal form of self-elation, but on closer contact can be seen to be abnormally excessive albeit short of psychotic proportions. *See also:* Major manic episode.

*Hypothesized conditioned aversive cues:* According to behavioristic theory, these are the cues that are not so apparent, and which may be redintegrated by symptom-contingent cues. In essence, these are the more symbolic or dynamic cues entering the symptom-picture, relating to the patient's unique fantasy life rather than to the direct, fear-producing stimulus. For example, if an elevator meant "mother's womb" to a claustrophobic, this would be an hypothesized conditioned aversive cue. *See also:* Redintegration; Symptom-contingent cues.

*Hysteria: See:* Conversion disorder.

*ICD:* The *International Classification of Diseases,* published by the World Health Organization to standardize and provide proper criteria for the diagnosis of abnormal behavior. *See also:* DSM-III.

*Id:* The fundamental hedonistic, logically inconsistent (i.e., dialectically manipulative) aspect of mind which Freud described as a chaos, a cauldron of seething excitations. The id is active only in the unconscious level of mind, functions according to the pleasure principle, and reasons by way of primary process thought. *See also:* Ego; Pleasure principle; Primary process thinking; Superego.

*Ideas of reference:* A symptom, prominent in paranoid disorders, in which the person relates things going on in the environment to himself or herself when there is no basis in fact for this belief. Overheard conversations all relate to the patient. Major political developments are shaped to somehow influence the patient. The pseudo-community is framed around such thoughts, with the patient as the focus of all that takes place. *See also:* Pseudocommunity.

*Identification:* The taking in or internalization of experience that results in the person's patterning his or her behavior, value system, and life attitudes on another individual. It is possible to identify out of fear as well as out of love. *See also:* Incorporation; Introjection

*Identity crisis:* Erikson's concept referring to the sense of aimlessness, role confusion, and diffusion that can be experienced by an adolescent.

*Imago:* An internal object carried by the individual in re-enacting an Oedipal dynamic (e.g., father, mother, some combination of both, etc.). Imago projections take place during psychotherapy, when the therapist becomes the "blank screen" onto which they are sent and "acted out" against. *See also:* Transference.

*Implosion:* A bursting inward as opposed to the outward bursting of an explosion. *See also:* Implosive therapy.

*Implosive therapy:* A behavioristic therapy in which patients are exposed to fear-provoking stimuli and actually encouraged to experience the anxiety "elicited" by these more or less realistic scenes. However, as no punishment (disaster, significant loss, etc.) takes place, the anxiety attached to the stimuli is said to extinguish. Thus, implosive therapy implies that emotive reactions are erupting, but their expression is internal to the person's fantasy life.

*Impotence:* A psychosexual dysfunction in which a man is unable to achieve penile erection. *See also:* Psychosexual dysfunction.

*Incoordination:* A major overt manifestation of behavioral disorganization, seen particularly in organic brain syndromes. Incoordination of behavior results from the interference of disruptive tensions and movements that break up normal timing and harmony (synergy) of behavior. The patient reflects unsteadiness and tremor, with a tendency to overreach, underreach, and misdirect his or her movements. *See also:* Organic brain syndrome.

*Incorporation:* The taking in of experience into the literal body, as when the child takes in mother's milk as a forerunner to introjection and identification. *See also:* Identification; Introjection.

*Insanity:* The technical term used in Law to signify that a defendant is not mentally responsible for the actus reus. The term also refers to an inability to conduct business and take care of one's personal affairs. Finally, this term can refer to grounds for commitment to a mental institution. *See also:* Actus reus; ALI rule; Durham rule; M'Naghten rule; Mens rea; Psychosis.

*Insight:* Understanding the grounds for the sake of which one's unique life is being enacted. It is invariably true that some of these grounds are framed at an unconscious level of mentation. The term *insight* refers to a level of understanding achieved through psychotherapeutic means. *See also:* Psychotherapy.

*Instinct:* In early Freudian theory, a bridge construct uniting body with mind. All instincts have a source in the body, a level of pressure (vicissitudes), an aim of satisfaction, and an object that will satisfy the instinct. Even so, it is the mental energy set loose by the instinct which "runs" the personality system. In later Freudian theory, an instinct was defined as an urge inherent in organic life to restore an earlier state of things which the living entity had to abandon under the pressure of external disturbing forces. *See also:* Repetition compulsion.

*Instinct, compound: See:* Instinct(s), primal.

*Instinct, death:* An instinct which aims to restore the final state of homeostatic quiescence—that is, death! It is essentially opposed to eros, the life instinct. Freud never named an energy of the death instinct although he alluded to such. *See also:* Eros; Repetition compulsion.

*Instinct(s), primal:* Underlying, basic instincts that enter into various combinations resulting in compound instincts.

*Instinct(s), self-preservative:* Also known as the ego instincts, these were early postulated as having the aim of preserving the individual "as a person." Later, self-preservation was seen as a special case of eros. *See also:* Eros; Instinct; Instinct(s), sexual.

*Instinct(s), sexual:* Also known as the object instincts, these were early postulated as having the aim of preserving the species. The energy of these instincts was libido. Subsequently, eros supplanted these instincts in Freudian theory. *See also:* Eros; Instinct; Libido; Instinct(s), self-preservative.

*Insulin coma therapy:* A biological therapy in which insulin is injected into the bloodstream of a patient, leading to hypoglycemia, which in turn induces a coma with or without convulsions. After an hour or more the patient is given an injection of glucose to terminate the coma. A full series of insulin therapy may involve fifty hours of such comatose reactions.

*Intention:* Behaving "for the sake of" or "because of" purposive meanings ("reasons") as encompassed in images, language terms, affections, emotions, and so on, all of which are encompassed as premises in the telic act of predication. When purpose and intention combine we have telosponsivity. Intention is as pure an expression of final causation as possible. *See also:* Final cause; Purpose; Telosponse.

*Internalization:* The clinical observation that behavioral adaptations following birth can effect permanent changes in the ongoing psychic processes of the human being. Thus, experience external to the psyche is "brought inward" from the bodily sphere or the physical environment and adapted to in some way, resulting in a permanent change in the ongoing mentation and overt behavior of the human organism. *See also:* Incorporation; Identification.

*Interpenetration:* A major overt manifestation of behavioral disorganization, seen particularly in organic brain syndromes. The patient is seen to allow an intrusive movement, word, or thought to appear inappropriately in some ongoing activity that actually belongs to some other activity. Some of this interpenetration involves unconscious material spilling over into ongoing conscious behavior. *See also:* Organic brain syndrome.

*Interpretation:* A technique employed in psychoanalysis which entails finding a hidden sense in some thought or action that the patient manifests. *See also:* Psychoanalysis.

*Intoxication:* An organic brain syndrome resulting in maladaptive behavior due to the recent ingestion of a specific substance. The most common signs of maladaption include disturbances of perception, wakefulness, attention, thinking, judgment, emotional control, and psychomotor behavior. *See also:* Organic brain syndrome.

*Introjection:* The taking in of experience in a *symbolic* form, enabling the child to identify with parents and other significant people during development. *See also:* Identification.

*Introspective perspective, of theory:* Framing theories of things and/or events in the first person, from the outlook of an identity acting within them. Introspective theory refers to "I" or "me" rather than to "that" or "it." *See also:* Extraspective perspective, of theory.

*Involutional melancholia:* An agitated depression occurring during the late midlife period, or early during the old-age period of the life cycle. This disorder is often attributed to the "change of life" (climacterium) phenomenon. DSM-III does not single this diagnosis out for separate consideration. *See also:* Agitated depression.

*Irresistible impulse:* An elaboration of the M'Naghten rule which permitted a judgment of innocence by reason of insanity if the defendant "had so far lost the *power to choose* between the right and wrong [even though "knowing" this difference], and to avoid the act in question, as that his free agency was at the time destroyed." *See also:* M'Naghten rule.

*Isolation:* Separating an idea from its emotional content. A soldier in battle may have to isolate in order to bring himself to actually kill another human being.

*Korsakoff syndrome:* An organic mental disorder due to head injury in which a patient becomes highly disoriented after regaining consciousness. Residual memory defects and confabulations are common. *See also:* Organic mental disorder.

*Kraepelinian nosology:* The classical scheme of diagnosis in neurosis and psychosis: (1) *neuroses:* hysteria, hypochondria, obsessive-compulsivity, neurasthenia, anxiety, and depressive reactions; (2) *psychoses:* dementia praecox or schizophrenia (including simple, paranoid, catatonic, and hebephrenic), and manic-depressive. *See also:* Diagnosis; Nosology; Syndrome.

*La belle indifférence:* The disinterest and lack of concern exhibited by somatoform (hysterical) patients over the loss of some significant sensory capacity (vision) or physical ability (use of an arm or limb).

*Latency:* The fifth period of psychosexual development in Freudian theory, falling between the phallic stage and the onset of adolescence via pubescence. The Oedipal conflict is repressed at this time, and the sexual instinct becomes aim-inhibited. Biological factors enter at the close of latency as secondary sexual characteristics herald the rejuvenation of sexuality. *See also:* Aim-inhibition.

*Libidinal anticipatory idea:* The wishful anticipations framed by a neurotic who is in the continual process of re-enacting (repetition compulsion) his or her unresolved Oedipal conflict. These libidinal anticipatory ideas form the basis for transference in psychoanalysis. *See also:* Libido; Split-level functioning; Transference.

*Libido:* The energy of the sexual instinct and/or eros (life instinct). Freud defined this variously as psychical desire, erotic tendencies, the motive force of sexual life, and sexual desire in its broadest sense. As such, the term has both psychological and strictly energic connotations. It is important to keep libido separate and distinct from emotions. Emotions are discharges in the somatic realm. Libido is energy in the psychic realm, energy which takes on intentional actions. Libido can be invested in the ego (narcissistic libido) or in other persons (object libido).

*Local adaptation syndrome (LAS):* Selye's concept of a defensive system in the physical body which comes into play at the region of an injury or infection. Inflammation at the point where microbes enter the body would be an example of the LAS. *See also:* General adaptation syndrome.

*Major depressive episode:* Also termed a psychotic depression, this syndrome refers to mood disorders in which dejection and self-depreciation reach delusional proportions.

*Major manic episode:* A major affective disorder typified by psychotic excitement, overactivity, and delusional elation or self-assertion without serious disorganization or disorientation. *See also:* Major depressive episode.

*Malingering:* Faking a psychopathological syndrome.

*Manic-depressive insanity: See:* Bipolar disorder.

*Manifest vs. latent dream content:* This Freudian distinction captures the defensive aspects of dreaming. The manifest content is the apparent, evident, overt story line of the dream. The latent content is the hidden meaning lying behind the manifest content.

*Marital schism:* A theoretical construct which traces schizophrenic behavior to a family setting in which parents are seen to undermine each other's values and actions. The result is that a child identifying with one or the other parent is immediately caught within a marital schism. *See also:* Marital skew.

*Marital skew:* A theoretical construct which traces schizophrenic behavior to a family setting in which one parent dominates a family by advancing eccentric ideas and/or bizarre behavioral patterns. Children of such families are made prone to schizophrenic behaviors. *See also:* Marital schism.

*Masochism:* A paraphiliac disorder in which the person obtains sexual pleasure from suffering injuries and indignities of various types. *See also:* Paraphilias; Sadism; Sadomasochism.

*Massive amnesia:* A dissociative disorder in which there is sweeping estrangement and/or depersonalization. There may be flight from the present environment. Personality alternatives may emerge in the same person. *See also:* Depersonalization; Estrangement.

*Material cause:* Any concept used to account for the nature of things (including behavior) that assumes that things are comprised of underlying, unchanging substances. Explanations of behavior based on genetic transmission or chemical elements are examples of material-cause description. *See also:* Cause(s); Medical model.

*McNaughten rule: See:* M'Naghten rule.

*Meaning:* A relational tie of one item to another, extending in time to form a concept within a host of interlacing relationships. Meanings relate ultimately to the purpose of a concept, and are therefore fundamentally telic in nature. *See also:* Purpose, Teleology.

*Mechanism:* An explanation of behavior based predominantly on efficient causality, with occasional use of material causality. In no case is a final/formal concept employed. Hence, mechanism is essentially the opposite of teleology. *See also:* Efficient cause; Material cause; Teleology.

*Mediation or mediation theory:* The assumption that mind works as a "middle term," as processing earlier stimuli (inputs) into responses (outputs) in an essentially efficient-cause manner. *See also:* Efficient cause.

*Medical model:* The traditional style of explanation used in medicine, which seeks to reduce overt behaviors to underlying biological mechanisms. As such, its tenets spring from heavy reliance on material and efficient causation.

*Mens rea:* A "guilty mind," suggesting that a person who violated the Law had a wrongful purpose or criminal intent to do so. *See also:* Actus reus; Culpability.

*Mentation:* A general term referring to the processes of thought, ideation, and so forth, whether at a conscious, preconscious, or unconcious level.

*Method of successive approximations:* A technique employed in behavior modification. Rather than trying to shape behavior directly the strategy here is to reinforce approximations to the target behavior, thereby gradually modifying a person's behavioral style. Each move in the shaping procedure brings the person closer to the desired outcome. *See also:* Behavioral shaping.

*Microphobia:* The irrational fear of germs. *See also:* Phobia.

*Midlife crisis:* A form of identity crisis precipitated in midlife, when the individual finally realizes that he or she will die without achieving the dreams of youth.

*Migraine:* A circulatory disorder in which the person suffers from a unilateral periodic headache, often with nausea and vomiting, and sometimes with diarrhea or constipation. This disorder is often tied to psychosomatic dynamics. *See also:* Psychosomatic disorder.

*M'Naghten rule:* Also spelled "McNaughten," this rule is an insanity defense which takes as grounds the presumed fact that "the party accused was laboring under such a defect of reason, from disease of mind, as not to know the nature and quality of the act he was doing; or, if he did know it, that he did not know he was doing what was wrong." *See also:* ALI rule; Durham rule; Mens rea.

*Monism:* A theory relying upon just one realm of explanation, as in biological reductionism. *See also:* Biological reductionism; Dualism.

*Mood congruent:* Refers to the case when a patient's delusion is consistent with his or her diagnosis. For example, a depressed person's delusion would reflect dejection and loss of world.

*Moral realism:* Piaget's concept suggesting that early in life children hold to moral precepts very literally, without grasping the grounding principles involved.

*Motivation:* That aspect of a personality theory which seeks to account for why the person is moved to behave as he or she does. All four causes can be used to account for the motivation of a personality dynamic. *See also:* Cause(s); Dynamic.

*Munchausen syndrome:* A long-term tendency for a person to seek medical attention for physical disorders, including actual operations, when there is no biological reason for doing so. The patient remains in good contact although he or she is difficult to manage while hospitalized because of a tendency to break the rules and regulations of the institution. This is a factitious disorder because the person is not simply malingering. *See also:* Factitious disorder; Malingering.

*Narcissism:* The taking of one's own body as love-object. The normal period of narcissism in development occurs as transitional, between autoerotism and object-choice. However, it is possible for fixations to occur at this level, and an adult person can therefore manifest narcissistic behaviors thanks to regression. *See also:* Autoerotism; Object-choice.

*Narcissistic neuroses:* These are disorders that Freud believed were unamenable to psychoanalytical therapy because of an incapacity to form cathectic ties to the therapist. The serious psychotic disturbances such as the schizophrenias and the major affective disorders would fall under this designation. It should be noted that psychoanalysts since Freud have successfully treated narcissistic neuroses. *See also:* Transference neuroses.

*Narcissistic personality disorder:* A maladaptive lifestyle typified by an exaggerated sense of self-importance, self-centeredness, and self-absorption without any appreciation of the impact which such attitudes and behaviors have on other people. Narcissists are usually fairly aggressive, placing demands on others for admiration, and in love relationships they expect to be adored. Power needs are evident. *See also:* Personality disorder.

*Narcissistic supplies:* A phrase used by some psychopathologists to refer to the self-indulgent needs expressed by certain abnormal individuals who constantly need reassurance, displays of love, excessive praise, and unequivocal esteem from others.

*Nativism, nativistic theory:* An account in which the theorist presumes that there are certain fundamental, innate processes and propensities which the organism brings to life and that, *beginning from birth* (or possibly *in utero*), carry forward in some way to influence the organism's learning and behavioral actions. These innate capacities are not themselves learned, but make human learning possible. There are two types of nativism: biological reductionism and biological naturalism. *See also:* Environmentalism; Biological naturalism; Biological reductionism.

*Natural science:* An approach to the description of things or events in a nontelic manner, by essentially reducing all formal- and final-cause explanations to underlying material- and efficient-cause explanations. In this sense, "natural" means "nonintentional." *See also:* Intention; Reductionism; Teleology.

*Neologism:* A "new word," as concocted by a patient in fantasy and expressed as if it communicated a meaning. But the word has no objective meaning and hence is not understood by a listener (i.e., the meaning is completely subjective).

*Neuroses, actual:* Disorders due to toxic causes and hence not treatable by psychoanalysis. Freud placed neurasthenia, anxiety, and hypochondria disorders here. Subsequently, psychoanalysts have treated the latter disorders successfully. *See also:* Neuroses, proper.

*Neuroses, proper (psychoneuroses proper):* A host of disorders that Freud considered related to the hysterias which were psychodynamic in origin and therefore treatable by psychoanalysis. *See also:* Neuroses, actual.

*Neurosis:* A psychiatric-psychological conception referring to abnormal behavior which is not necessarily debilitating but is clearly harmful to interpersonal relations and personal adjustment. Hallucinations and delusions are *not* observed in neurotic conditions. *See also:* Psychosis.

*Neurotic depression: See:* Dysthymic disorder.

*Nihilistic delusion:* A delusion that everything is coming to an end (life, the world, etc.), or that some terrible catastrophe is about to take place.

*Normal behavior:* In Freudian accounts, behavior that disavows reality as little as does neurosis, but indicates an effort to change reality when it is not suitable to the person concerned. However, unlike the psychotic, the normal person avoids fantasied alterations of reality in favor of a head-on, realistic approach to its change.

*Nosology:* The study and classification of diseases including behavioral disorders. *See also:* DSM-III; ICD.

*Nyctophobia:* The irrational fear of dark places. *See also:* Phobia.

*Obesity:* Significant overweight, which is often due to psychosomatic dynamics. *See also:* Psychosomatic disorder.

*Object:* That thing (person, food item, etc.) in regard to which an instinct is able to achieve its aim of satisfaction. *See also:* Autoerotism; Object-choice.

*Object-choice:* A more mature manifestation of instinctive gratification, in which rather than gaining autoerotic pleasure the individual orients an organ toward an object. *See also:* Autoerotism; Object.

*Obsessive-compulsive disorder:* Grouped within the family of the anxiety disorders in DSM-III, this syndrome consists of apparently useless but irresistible repetitious acts, words, or thoughts whose aim is to reduce tension and anxiety by: (1) indulging in something forbidden, (2) denying such indulgence or guarding against it, or (3) punishing oneself for having had the impulse to indulge. An *obsession* is an irresistible thought and a *compulsion* is an irresistible impulse to act out.

*Oceanic feeling:* The all-powerful sensations that it is postulated infants experience during gratification of the pleasure principle. Some psychoanalysts liken this to the effects of drugs on adults.

*Ocholophobia:* The irrational fear of crowds. *See also:* Phobia.

*Oedipus complex:* A family dynamic described by Freud in which the origins of society are re-enacted and in which the offspring ordinarily cathects the opposite-sex parent. All neurotics have poorly resolved Oedipal conflicts. A *positive* Oedipal dynamic involves lusting after the opposite-sex parent. A *negative* Oedipal dynamic involves lusting after the same-sex parent.

*Ontogeny recapitulates phylogeny:* Haeckel's biogenetic rule which Freud analogized to in framing the Oedipus complex. The rule suggests that organisms developing *in utero* re-enact the evolutionary history of their species. Freud extended this to include the history of society following birth in the Oedipal drama.

*Opposition, principle of:* The assumption which Jung based his conception of the psyche upon. Thus, everything in mind that is believed in, expressed, or known with certainty has its opposite implication carried immediately in the total psychic functioning of the person concerned.

*Oral personality:* Adult character structure due to predominant fixations in the oral level, and typified by passivity, gullibility, and receptivity.

*Oral stage:* The first psychosexual stage in Freudian theory of development, typified by "taking in" and exploration of the environment through sucking. The mouth is the erogenous zone of importance. The basic outlook emanating from this stage is passive, but a sadistic period has also been identified by psychoanalysts.

*Organ speech:* The fact that neurotic symptoms express a meaning, reflecting the wishes and compromises that led to their occurrence. *See also:* Symptom.

*Organic affective syndrome:* An organic brain syndrome in which there is a disturbance in mood resembling either a manic episode or a major depressive episode. The disorder arises from a specifiable organic influence. The diagnosis is not made if there is a clouded consciousness (delirium) or significant loss of intellectual abilities (dementia). *See also:* Delirium; Dementia; Organic brain syndrome.

*Organic brain syndrome:* A recognizable pattern of symptoms that signify a brain involvement in the person's behavior without specifically indicating the nature of the illness or the causal agent. *See also:* Organic mental disorder.

*Organic delusional syndrome:* An organic brain syndrome in which the person has delusions in a normal state of consciousness (unclouded) that are due to a specific organic factor. If delirium or dementia are present this diagnosis is not made. *See also:* Delirium; Dementia; Organic brain syndrome.

*Organic disorder:* A disturbance in personal adjustment due to a known etiology, such as hereditary brain damage or an infection to the central nervous system. *See also:* Functional disorder.

*Organic hallucinosis:* An organic brain syndrome typified by persistent or recurrent hallucinations that occur in a normal state of consciousness ("unclouded"). These hallucinations are attributable to a specific organic factor. When the etiological agent is a substance, the term *organic* is dropped and the name of the substance substituted. Thus, in *alcohol hallucinosis* the person is hallucinating due to heavy ingestion of alcohol. *See also:* Delirium; Organic brain syndrome.

*Organic mental disorder:* A diagnosis assigned when the specific etiological factors that have brought about an organic brain syndrome are known. DSM-III lists dozens of different organic mental disorders which can bring about a half-dozen or so common forms of organic brain syndromes. *See also:* Organic brain syndrome.

*Organic personality syndrome:* An outcome in which the person manifests significant changes in his or her behavioral style following brain injury or a disease process. These are invariably negative changes, such as shortened temper, poor social adjustment, and sexual indiscretions.

*Overdetermination:* When more than one wish fulfillment, intention, or purpose is expressed in a single dream, symptom, or behavioral manifestation. Sometimes these multiple reasons are contradictory.

*Overexclusion:* Excluding from cognition too many vital meanings so that the person loses touch with significant aspects of his or her bodily functioning, emotional feelings, and general behavioral actions. This is typical in the hysterias or somatoform disorders. *See also:* Overinclusion.

*Overinclusion:* Allowing too many factors to enter cognition, thereby leading to confusion and ineffective thought processes. This is typical of primary process thought as typified in the behavior of a regressed schizophrenic. *See also:* Overexclusion.

*Panic disorder:* Uncontrollable fear that prompts the person to headlong flight, loss of ego control, violent aggression, or suicide. The duration of panic may be brief, lasting a few hours or days, or it may persist for months, during which the level of panic fluctuates. *See also:* Generalized anxiety disorder.

*Paradoxical intention:* A therapeutic technique introduced by Victor Frankl in which the patient is asked to induce or "practice" his or her symptom at specific times during the day. In time, the control over the symptom enables the patient to discontinue it altogether.

*Paranoid disorder:* A psychopathological attempt to escape from the return of repressed ideations, and the anxiety/tension with which they are associated, through processes of denial and projection that result in more or less systematized delusions. In traditional psychoanalytical theory there is a link to be seen between paranoia and homosexuality. DSM-III recognizes an acute onset of this disorder, as well as a more insidious onset which is termed "paranoia." *See also:* Delusion; Projection; Return of the repressed.

*Paranoid personality disorder:* A maladaptive pattern typified by great suspiciousness and mistrust of others, hypersensitivity to criticism, and lack of spontaneous emotional expression. There is a profound lack of basic trust in the outlook of these individuals.

*Paraphilias:* A group of psychosexual disorders in which the person either carries out or in some cases merely fantasizes unusual acts, or utilizes atypical objects in order to become sexually aroused.

*Parapraxes:* The misactions and slips of the tongue which reveal unconscious intentions or wishes as they are 100 percent determined. *See also:* Determinism, psychic.

*Parataxic mode of experience:* H. S. Sullivan's concept of the second stage of cognitive development in which there develops some fragmentary understanding of unreality thanks in part to a beginning grasp of language. Autistic language terms are employed here, lacking in consensual validation and leading to parataxic distortion. *See also:* Prototaxic mode of experience; Syntaxic mode of experience.

*Passive-aggressive personality disorder:* A maladaptive pattern in which the overtly passive person expresses a covert aggression toward others. Negativistic, critical, resistive people with a veneer of soft-spoken passivity typify this lifestyle. Oral-sadistic behaviors are prominent. *See also:* Personality disorder.

*Peak experience:* Maslow's term to describe an exceedingly wonderful experience in the lives of people who are self-actualizing. Peak experiences submerge everything else in life by comparison. *See also:* Self-actualization.

*Pedophilia:* A paraphiliac disorder in which the person either fantasizes or actually engages in sexual relations with prepubertal children as a repeatedly preferred or exclusive method of achieving sexual excitement and release. DSM-III sets the arbitrary age disparity between the prepubertal child and the adult at ten years. *See also:* Paraphilias.

*Penis envy:* An aspect of the female Oedipal dynamic in which the little girl feels castrated and envious of the opposite sex.

*Peptic ulcer:* An ulcer that occurs most frequently in the stomach and duodenum, and is often due to psychosomatic dynamics. *See also:* Psychosomatic disorder.

*Periodic cycles:* Fliess's theory of physiological influences on human behavior. Psychopathology was viewed as a loss in synchrony of these biological fluctuations, as typified in the menstrual cycle, and so forth.

*Persecutory paranoid disorder:* A paranoid disorder in which the patient believes that someone or some group is purposively making his or her life miserable through various taunts, subversive acts, the spreading of untrue rumors, and actual physical attacks of one sort or another.

*Personality:* In its broadest phrasing, the style a course of behavior takes on. Considered by itself, personality is a formal-cause conception, but in bringing out theories of personality two or more causes are used. Freud considered personality or "character" to be the working out of conflicts and compromises among the id, superego, and ego, involving repressions, sublimations, and reaction-formations of instinctual pressures. *See also:* Cause(s); Formal cause.

*Personality development:* The transformation that takes place as a human being moves from being predominantly a biological organism to a biosocial person.

*Personality disorder:* Arises when some distortion of the personality develops early in life and persists as a person's style, as the characteristic way in which he or she copes with the environment and defends against real or imagined threats to personal competence and integrity.

*Phallic stage:* The fourth period of psychosexual development in which the pregenital penis or clitoris becomes the erogenous zone of importance. This is the period of the Oedipus complex. *See also:* Oedipus complex.

*Phantom limb:* A denial of body change, so that the patient insists that he or she can feel (pain, etc.) in a hand, foot, or some other aspect of a limb that has been amputated.

*Pharmacological therapy:* Also termed chemical therapy, this method of treatment relies upon the ingestion of various drugs that act upon the nervous systems of the body to counter the symptoms of various psychopathological conditions. These drugs can be classified as to the *antianxiety* type (sedatives, barbiturates, minor tranquilizers such as Equanil, Valium, Librium), the *antidepressants* (tricyclic type, MAO inhibitors), and the *antipsychotic* type (major tranquilizers like Thorazine, Stelazine, or Haldol).

*Phobia, phobic disorder:* A persistent and irrational fear of a specific object, activity, or situation that results in a compelling desire to avoid the dreaded object, activity, or situation. *See also:* Anxiety disorder.

*Pleasure principle:* The principle dominating id motivation in which everything mental is directed toward achieving immediate pleasure and avoiding immediate pain. *See also:* Reality principle.

*Preconscious, preconsciousness:* That realm of mind receiving contributions from both consciousness and unconsciousness, and in which repression or censorship is carried out. *See also:* Conscious; Unconscious.

*Pressure technique:* An early technique employed by Freud to suggest to patients in psychoanalysis that they could recall a pathognomic situation in their past. This was an offshoot of the hypnotic technique used earlier. Freud placed his hands on the patient's head and confidently asserted that the patient "would" recall the unhealthy life incident. In time, this technique gave way to free association. *See also:* Free association.

*Primary process thinking:* A primitive form of thinking in which the person expects immediate gratification and will hallucinate a desired object if it is not immediately forthcoming. *See also:* Secondary process thinking.

*Progressive relaxation:* A technique devised by Jacobson in which the person learns to bring his or her entire body into a state of deep muscle relaxation by degrees. This relaxation "response" is used to reciprocally inhibit anxiety in the behavioristic technique of systematic desensitization. *See also:* Systematic desensitization.

*Project for a Scientific Psychology:* Freud's solo effort to write a completely biological explanation of behavior. He never completed it and tried to have the manuscript destroyed when a draft surfaced decades after he had burned his own copy.

*Projection:* Attributing internal feelings, fantasies, attitudes, wishes, and fears to the external world. A woman projects her hatred of another person onto this person and thereby accuses the object of her projection of being "vicious."

*Prototaxic mode of experience:* H. S. Sullivan's concept describing the early period of psychic life, before language development, in which there is the "raw feel" of life with much subjective distortion (unreality).

*Prototype:* An early frame of reference, taken on by the personality system as a premising meaning and then brought forward so that the person comes to learn things in light of this assumptive understanding. *See also:* Telosponse.

*Pseudocommunity:* An imaginary community concocted by a patient in an effort to reconstruct reality. The behavior of real and imagined people is organized into some fantasied scenario that supports the particular delusional system of the patient in question. For example, the paranoid patient will have a complex of persons all in league against him. The patient is always the focus of his or her pseudocommunity.

*Psyche, psychic:* Refers essentially to the mind or mental events. In psychoanalysis, psyche is opposed to soma. *See also:* Dualism; Soma.

*Psychoanalysis:* A form of psychotherapy in which the insight gleaned follows Freudian (or Jungian, Adlerian, etc.) lines of explanation, and which employs certain techniques in the relationship between therapist and patient. The present volume focuses upon Freudian psychoanalysis, which Freud once defined as "a re-education in overcoming internal resistances" to the therapist's interpretations. *See also:* Psychotherapy.

*Psychogenic pain disorder:* A somatoform disorder typified by complaints of pain that cannot be related to physical causes and that give evidence of a psychological origin. It is the symbolic feature of the symptom picture which distinguishes this disorder from psychosomatic disorders. *See also:* Psychosomatic factors affecting physical condition.

*Psychogenic stupor:* A dissociative disorder which has regressed into apathy and inaction. Stuporous patients sit motionless, except for an occasional shift in position, or they lie with eyes closed as if in a deep coma, without overt responses. Few recall the stuporous episode, but those who have report that there is fantasy of a deeply regressive nature going on during the stupor. *See also:* Dissociative disorder; Trance state.

*Psychoneuroses proper: See:* Neuroses, proper.

*Psychopathology:* Study of the contributions which mental or psychological problems make to the emotional disturbances of behavior, disturbances which may be reflected in physical diseases (psychosomatic illness) or interpersonal relations.

*Psychosexual disorder:* A maladjustment in which, due to psychological factors in development, an individual finds it impossible to function sexually in ways that are indicated as normal for his or her sex.

*Psychosexual dysfunction:* A disorder in which a person's appetitive or psychophysiological changes that characterize the complete sexual cycle are somehow inhibited.

The diagnosis is not made if such changes are due to organic disease, or if the dysfunction is merely one aspect of a broader clinical picture (e.g., of a psychosexual disorder). *See also:* Psychosexual disorder.

*Psychosexual stages:* Periods in development dominated by certain erogenous zones, and appearing in the following order: oral, anal, urethral, phallic, latency, genital. *See also:* Erogenous zones.

*Psychosis:* A psycniatric-psychological conception referring to severe abnormal behavior in which delusions and hallucinations are to be expected. *See also:* Delusion; Hallucination; Insanity; Neurosis.

*Psychosomatic disorder:* A clinical syndrome in which the patient reacts to stress, tension, and anxiety with direct physiological malfunction, which may lead to irreversible organ or tissue damage. Unlike the conversion disorders, which symbolize an unconscious conflict and do not specifically damage bodily organs (except indirectly, through disuse), psychosomatic symptoms rarely take on symbolic functions and the physical damage is a direct result of the disturbance. *See also:* Conversion disorder; Somatic compliance.

*Psychosomatic factors affecting physical condition:* DSM-III terminology that replaces the older phrase of "psychosomatic disorder." The text retains the latter terminology. *See also:* Psychosomatic disorder.

*Psychosurgery:* A biological therapy such as prefrontal lobotomy or transorbital lobotomy, in which the aim is to surgically sever the nerve fibers connecting the frontal areas of the cerebral cortex and the thalamus. Emotional behavior is localized in the thalamus and the idea here is that a patient may be made more tranquil and manageable through the disconnection. This is a therapy of last resort, and is frequently criticized by psychopathologists.

*Psychotherapy:* Refers to a wide range of treatment procedures whose common characteristic is that they deal with psychogenic illnesses by psychological means, rather than by the use of medicines and other somatic procedures.

*Purpose:* The aim or point of a meaning. When this aim is incorporated as an intention by a telosponding organism telic behavior is taking place. A pencil has a purpose as a concept—a writing tool—but this purpose is not made manifest until a person intends that this purpose be brought about. *See also:* Intention; Teleological; Telosponse.

*Pyrophobia:* The irrational fear of fire. *See also:* Phobia.

*Rationalization:* Finding an acceptable or plausible reason for doing something rather than being aware of what the real motive was in doing the act. A person may rationalize by declaring he or she was "too ill" to perform well on a test, thereby justifying the reduced grade level.

*Reaction-formation:* Behaving in diametrically opposite ways to one's unconscious wishes and intentions. A mother who has rejected her child may at the same time "smother" the child with affection.

*Reaction sensitivity:* A readiness to react in the same emotional direction once a person has experienced an emotion in a given environmental context. Some of this increasing sensitivity is probably due to congenital influences. Certain people experience fear, anxiety, or defeat more intensely than others as biological organisms. But surely an aspect of such increasing sensitivity is due to the person's expectations. As such, telic considerations enter. Thus, there are both physical and psychological aspects of reaction sensitivity in human behavior.

*Reactive depression:* A depression that occurs in reaction to an objectively discernible life incident, such as the loss of a loved one. These depressions were typically called "neurotic depressions," or as DSM-III names them today, dysthymic disorders. *See also:* Dysthymic disorder; Retarded depression.

*Reality principle:* The principle dominating ego motivation, which though it does not abandon the intention of ultimately obtaining pleasure, demands and carries into effect the postponement of satisfaction, the abandonment of opportunities for gaining certain satisfactions, and the temporary toleration of unpleasure as a step in the long indirect road to pleasure. *See also:* Pleasure principle.

*Receptive orientation:* Fromm's concept of a passive-dependent personality, orally seeking the passive role in life rather than taking independent action. *See also:* Oral personality.

*Reciprocal inhibition:* The fact that one response to a stimulus can inhibit another response being made to the same stimulus. This principle is employed in systematic desensitization. *See also:* Systematic desensitization.

*Reconstruction, psychotic:* The restitutive efforts made by a psychotic person following regression, in which reality is delusionally framed along fantasied lines.

*Redintegration:* To re-enliven past cues in an automatic, nonintentional fashion. Often these are fear provoking in nature, so that by re-experiencing a fearful situation the person can actually recall more and more about it. This term is used by behavioristic therapists to describe the fact that in recalling fearful situations in imagination long forgotten aspects of these situations recur.

*Reductionism:* The philosophical assumption that we have rendered a better understanding of anything (including behavior) after we have broken down formal- and final-cause theoretical conceptions to underlying material- and efficient-cause theoretical conceptions. *See also:* Cause(s); Mechanism.

*Regression:* A return of the personality system to an earlier stage of development at which a fixation or partial fixation has taken place. A limited regression of only certain behavioral manifestations is termed *formal,* but when the entire personality returns to an infantile state this is termed *temporal* regression. A *topographical* regression is not so infantile, but does involve complete return to an earlier level *in toto. See also:* Fixation.

*Regression, from object-choice to narcissism:* Refers to a giving up of the more advanced stage of development in which objects are cathected in order to gain instinctive gratification by way of taking one's own body as an object. There is a turning away from external objects to a self-indulgent form of behavior. *See also:* Narcissism; Object-choice; Regression.

*Reinforcement:* A general term referring to the linkage formed between an antecedent event (usually interpreted as a stimulus) and a consequent event (usually interpreted as a response) based upon some principle of bonding such as drive reduction, contiguous association, and the like. Reinforcements "reinforce" the tie of the antecedent to the consequent. This can be done based on a *positive* or *negative* form of reinforcement. *See also:* Awareness, of subjects in conditioning experiments; Conditioning, classical; Conditioning, operant; Drive reduction theory.

*Repetition compulsion:* A concept Freud relied upon when he revised his instinct theory. By this Freud meant a compulsion in mind to repeat past events, underwriting this notion with a definition of the instinct as an urge inherent in organic life to restore an earlier state of things, a kind of homeostatic balance. *See also:* Instinct.

*Repression:* Countering of one cathexis by an anticathexis, or opposing the enactment of one intention by a countering intention. Repression is automatic, whereas suppression is a conscious effort to achieve the ends of repression. *Primal repression* takes place during the time of original conflict. *Repression proper* (or *after-repression*) is the continuing effort to hold things out of mind that follows. *See also:* Anticathexis; Denial.

*Resistance:* According to traditional analytical thinking, anything that interrupts the progress of psychoanalysis. Even when the patient "flees into health" to avoid confronting the threat of the uncovering process, this is considered resistance. *See also:* Psychoanalysis; Psychotherapy.

*Restitutive process, restitution:* The effort made by a psychotic person, following initial regression, to reconstruct reality in fantasy rather than adjusting to or changing reality as it is actually taking place.

*Retarded depression:* A major depressive episode which has an insidious onset, often without a specific initiating incident, and eventually encompasses delusions and hallucinations. These patients look stunned with grief, and tend to be motionless and silent for long periods. *See also:* Agitated depression; Major depressive episode; Reactive depression.

*Return of the repressed:* Typically, when following pubescence in the diphasic sexual development of human beings, there is a new surge of libido which begins to press unconscious material previously repressed toward consciousness. However, this phrase is often used generally to describe the situation following a frustration, at which point the person is most vulnerable to the return of previously repressed contents (fueros). *See also:* Fixation; Fuero.

*Reverting from object-choice to identification:* Occurs when the person relinquishes object-choice in favor of incorporating the values, attitudes, and behavioral patterns of some figure in his or her life sphere. As identification is more primitive than object-choice, this is invariably accompanied by regressive tendencies in the personality system. *See also:* Identification; Object-choice.

*Role representation:* The understanding that a person has of how to relate interpersonally. If this is unrealistic, there is a lifelong tendency to maladjustment as the person is entering into interpersonal relations based more on the distortions of fantasy than on cultural expectations.


*Sadism:* A paraphiliac disorder in which the person obtains sexual pleasure from inflicting pain, including psychological suffering and humiliation. *See also:* Masochism; Sadomasochism.

*Sadomasochism:* Obtaining erotic pleasure from inflicting pain (sadism) or receiving pain (masochism). Many analysts trace this dynamic to the early workings out of the relationship between the ego and superego functions, with the latter reflecting very primitive incorporations of parental pressures bordering on hostility as well as projections of hostility onto parental figures. *See also:* Masochism; Sadism.

*Scatter:* A term occasionally used to describe the verbal discontinuity in schizophrenic thinking and verbal expression. *See also:* Word salad.

*Schedule of reinforcement:* In operant conditioning this refers to the particular rate at which a subject will be reinforced for behavior that is emitted (e.g., every fifth response, or every ten seconds, etc.).

*Schizoaffective disorder:* A syndrome combining features of schizophrenia and a major

affective disorder. DSM-III does not classify this as a true schizophrenic disturbance. *See also:* Schizophrenic disorder.

*Schizoid personality disorder:* Essentially what is meant by "simple" schizophrenia.
This maladaptive pattern is typified by an inability to form social relationships
because of a lack of emotional stability and spontaneity. Autism may be in the
clinical picture. There is an appearance of mental retardation, but intelligence
testing proves otherwise. *See also:* Autism; Personality disorder; Schizophrenia,
simple type.

*Schizophrenia, ambulatory:* The view held to by certain psychopathologists that schizophrenia can be had in a mild form, so that the person affected can move about in
the world of normal individuals, behaving much like a schizotypal personality type.
*See also:* Schizophrenia, latent; Schizotypal personality disorder.

*Schizophrenia, catatonic type:* A schizophrenic disorder in which the patient may be
mute and motionless, as though in a stupor, or at the other extreme, in a completely
disorganized state of excitement. *See also:* Schizophrenic disorder.

*Schizophrenia, disorganized type: See:* Schizophrenia, hebephrenic type.

*Schizophrenia, hebephrenic type:* DSM-III refers to this as the *disorganized type* of the
schizophrenic disorder. Sometimes called the "silly psychosis," the major symptoms
include disorganized behavior in which there is much smiling, giggling, and laughter
that is produced by fantasy during regression. Speech is bizarre and incoherent.
Hallucinations are evident. *See also:* Schizophrenic disorder.

*Schizophrenia, latent:* The view held to by certain psychopathologists that schizophrenia can be latent in a personality system, in which neurotic symptoms are
enacted as a façade in order to cover up the deeper-seated psychotic disturbance.
Not all clinicians accept this view of the schizophrenic process.

*Schizophrenia, paranoid type:* The most prevalent form of schizophrenic disorder, in
which the patient is heavily delusional and hallucinatory with somewhat less
disorientation and disorganization than is seen in the other schizophrenic subtypes.
Delusions of persecution are prominent, but magical, mystical, and religious
delusions are also prominent. *See also:* Schizophrenic disorder.

*Schizophrenia, simple type:* A schizophrenic disorder characterized by a slow, insidious
onset and an undramatic downhill course. There are rarely delusions or hallucinations in the clinical picture. The person appears mentally retarded, but intelligence
tests discount this alternative. *See also:* Schizophrenic disorder.

*Schizophrenic disorder:* A regressive attempt to escape tension and anxiety by abandoning realistic interpersonal object relations and constructing delusions and hallucinations. DSM-III requires schizophrenic symptoms to appear before age forty-five in
order for this diagnosis to be assigned. There have been four subcategories
diagnosed in the "family" of the schizophrenias (formerly "dementia praecox"):
simple, paranoid, catatonic, and hebephrenic types. *See also:* Kraepelinian nosology.

*Schizophrenic spectrum:* A phrase used by some psychopathologists to refer to a
presumed range of schizophrenic disorders, traversing the classical Kraepelinian
diagnostic categories and carrying over to various mixed types, on to the schizophreniform manifestations and the schizothymic personality types.

*Schizophreniform:* A brief manifestation of schizophrenic symptoms lasting less than
six months. If such symptoms persist beyond six months, the convention adopted in
DSM-III allows for the assigning of a "schizophrenic disorder" diagnosis. *See also:*
Schizophrenic disorder.

*Schizothymic personality:* A person with schizophreniclike tendencies, such as difficulties in relating to the environment realistically, yet not really maladjusted sufficiently to be considered psychopathological.

*Schizotypal personality disorder:* A maladaptive pattern in which there are schizoid tendencies plus eccentricities in communication and odd behaviors suggesting that a thought disorder is underway in addition to the problems in interpersonal adjustment. *See also:* Personality disorder; Schizoid personality disorder.

*Screen memory:* A recollection of a patient in which the incident recalled hides or "screens" some other incident that is *not* being recalled. For example, a depressed patient may recall "stealing" some cookies from the household supply of sweets *instead* of recalling masturbating to a picture of her father.

*Secondary gain:* After the "primary gain" of flight into illness, neurotics often obtain a secondary gain in the fact that they are given allowances for being a "sick person." The neurotic can use his or her illness to curry sympathy, extract favors, or make excuses. *See also:* Flight into illness.

*Secondary process thinking:* A mature, reality-oriented thinking in which it is understood that compromises might have to be made and delays put up with before pleasurable gratification is achieved. *See also:* Primary process thinking.

*Seduction theory:* An early theory of Freud's in which he postulated that neurosis could be seen as the result of a too early stimulation of sexuality in young children.

*Self-actualization:* Maslow's term, based on a belief that higher or "metaneeds" are prompted in human behavior following the satisfaction of basic needs. *See also: Peak experience.*

*Self-conscious mind:* Eccles's concept of a selecting, evaluating, judging capacity that is something other than and irreducible to the mechanical functioning of the brain.

*Senile cerebral degeneration:* An organic mental disorder caused by the atrophy of brain cells in the aging process. The onset is gradual and insidious, often occurring initially as minor memory lapses and confusions, but progressing to serious levels of disorientation. *See also:* Arteriosclerotic cerebral degeneration.

*Sexual cycle:* DSM-III classifies disorders in psychosexual adjustment based upon the four stages in the sexual cycle: appetitive, excitement, orgasm, and resolution. *See also:* Psychosexual disorder.

*Shaping, of behavior:* The view held to by behaviorists that people are molded into behavioral patterns without benefit of agency. Behavioral shaping assumes that only material and/or efficient causes bring behavior about.

*Simple phobia:* According to DSM-III, this refers to any persistent, irrational fear or a compelling desire to avoid an object or situation not covered by the diagnoses of agoraphobia or social phobia. *See also:* Agoraphobia; Phobia; Social phobia.

*Social phobia:* According to DSM-III, this disorder is typified by the fear of being seen, assessed, or scrutinized by others whether in a group or in individual contact; this includes fears of eating in restaurants, using public lavatories, speaking before groups, or even having to write something in the presence of another person. *See also:* Phobia.

*Soma, somatic:* Refers to the body or physical being of an individual. In psychoanalysis, soma is opposed to psyche. *See also:* Dualism; Psyche.

*Somatic compliance:* The body part in a somatoform disorder which enters into the conversion of psychological conflicts into symbolic manifestation in the biological realm. Unconscious intentions bring on the symbolization, selecting a body organ or part which complies with what is being expressed. *See also:* Conversion disorder; Somatoform disorder.

*Somatization disorder:* According to DSM-III, these are long-term somatoform disorders beginning before the age of thirty and lasting with various levels of intensity. Complaints may refer to any bodily organ system and often move from one to another aspect of bodily functioning. *See also:* Conversion disorder.

*Somatoform disorder:* Formerly known as "conversion disorder," this syndrome involves transforming an unconscious conflict or linking it in some way to a bodily symptom that reduces or accounts for the anxiety by expressing the conflict symbolically. The symbolization is what distinguishes the somatoform disorder from the psychosomatic disorder. *See also:* Psychosomatic factors affecting physical condition.

*Somnambulism (sleepwalking):* A dreamlike dissociative state in which the person walks about with open eyes and carries out complex tasks before returning to bed. The behaviors carried out seem to be at the service of the dream being enacted. *See also:* Dissociative disorder.

*Somnambulistic attack:* Also referred to as the "hysterical convulsion" or "hysterical fit," this dissociative disorder involves loss of consciousness and enactment of a fantasy that is under repression. There is no memory of the attack. *See also:* Dissociative disorder.

*Specificity theory:* A theory that seeks to account for psychosomatic symptoms by examining the specific patterning of emotional expression in light of specific problems facing the person at the time of the disorder's appearance.

*Split imago:* A form of psychosexual dysfunction in which a man has idealized "good" women as somehow being above something so base as sexual passion, whereas "bad" women are sexually thrilling ("dirty"). The upshot is that such a man is unable to perform sexually with the "good" woman that he marries. The split is between the good versus bad images of womanhood.

*Split-level functioning:* Behavior at both an adult and an infantile level that is carried on during the same time period. Thus, unconscious conflicts can be worked over even as the person behaves perfectly appropriately in the consciously directed aspects of his or her behavior. *See also:* Libidinal anticipatory idea.

*Stimulus-response psychology:* An efficient-cause explanation of behavior, framed from the extraspective perspective and designed specifically to avoid final-cause explanations. *See also:* Efficient cause; Extraspective perspective, of theory; Final cause.

*Subjective Unit of Disturbance (SUD):* A 100-point scale, with the top score of 100 being the most extreme anxiety that a patient can imagine and 0 being the complete absence of anxiety. By verbalizing any number from 0 through 100 a patient in systematic desensitization can convey the level of anxiety being experienced at the moment. *See also:* Anxiety hierarchy; Systematic desensitization.

*Sublimation:* When both the object and the aim of an instinct are accomplished, and a higher ethical valuation occurs in the resulting behavior. When the artist disdains sexual activity and pours his resultant preoccupations and mental energies into his art, this reflects the mechanism of sublimation.

*Substance abuse:* Refers to the fact that a person can no longer get through the day without ingestion of some crucial substances such as alcohol or cocaine.

*Substance dependence:* Diagnosed when substance abuse extends to an actual physiological dependence on the crucial substance. The key symptoms here are tolerance and withdrawal. *See also:* Substance abuse; Tolerance; Withdrawal.

*Substance use disorder:* Diagnosed when a person takes a substance affecting the central nervous system on a regular basis, leading to undesirable developments in his or her experience.

*Substitute ego:* A term used by some psychoanalysts to refer to a parent (usually the mother) who acts in place of the infant's as yet poorly formulated ego to reassure the infant and thereby keep tension and anxiety from becoming excessive. The mothering person acts as a buffer to offset early traumatic reactions of this sort.

*Substitution:* Finding alternate objects in life, as when an unmarried woman dotes over her pet dog.

*Superego:* An aspect of the ego which frames what the ego "ought" to do as an *ego-ideal,* based upon the judgments of the values incorporated following resolution of the Oedipus complex, to which it is heir. Even so, the superego seeks to further id satisfactions albeit often combining self-punishment for such gratification. It is the ego which must ultimately meliorate between id and superego. *See also:* Ego; Id.

*Suppression: See:* Repression.

*Symbiosis:* A mutual tie of child to parent and parent to child, in which each gains from close relationship with the other. *See also:* Attachment.

*Symptom:* Particular manifestations of a disease, entering into the total picture or "syndrome." In Freudian accounts of psychopathological symptoms, these manifestations are always viewed as compromises and wish-fulfillments. Freud referred to a symptom as a "function" that has undergone some unusual change. Every symptom has both the repressed and repressing mental contents reflected in it. *See also:* Conditioned avoidance response; Syndrome.

*Symptom-contingent cues:* According to behavioristic theory, these are the cues that directly elicit the psychopathological behavior, such as the cue of an "elevator" which elicits anxiety in the claustrophobic patient. *See also:* Hypothesized conditioned aversive cues.

*Symptom substitution:* Replacing one symptom by another. The claim has been made that behavioral therapy merely takes away one symptom only to have another take its place. Behavioral therapists deny this charge, claiming there is no empirical evidence to support it. *See also:* Behavior modification.

*Syncretic cognition:* A concept of Piaget's which describes how very young children jumble cognitive concepts together into an ill-conceived whole so that the elements of knowledge are not properly related to each other in a more operational fashion.

*Syndrome:* A patterned collection of symptoms, sometimes thought of as "a" disease or abnormality.

*Syntaxic mode of experience:* H. S. Sullivan's concept of the third and highest level of cognitive development in which consensual validation of language is attained. *See also:* Parataxic mode of experience; Prototaxic mode of experience.

*Systematic desensitization:* A form of behavioristic therapy in which the patient is first taught to relax and then through imagining a hierarchy of fear-provoking stimuli is progressively desensitized to these stimuli by repeated relaxation while imagining that the stimuli are actually taking place when they are not. It is assumed that the relaxation reciprocally inhibits the anxiety that had formerly been evoked by the fearful stimuli.

*Tabula rasa:* A "smoothed tablet." The view that at birth the mind is without capacity for thought until experience "etches" some preliminary content upon the smoothed tablet. *See also:* Mediation.

*Taraxein hypothesis:* Taraxein is a ceruplasm that has been found in the blood of some schizophrenics. The hypothesis suggests that taraxein induces difficulties in the septal region of the brain which in turn bring on antibodies that adversely affect certain neurohumors. The result is bizarre behavior of the afflicted person, known as schizophrenia.

*Teleology, telic:* The view that events are predicated according to plan, design, or assumption—that is, based upon purposive meanings or reasons—and therefore directed to some intended end. Teleologies can be natural, deistic, or human in formulation.

*Telosponse:* A mental act in which the person takes on (predicates, premises) a meaningful item (image, language term, judgmental comparison, and so forth) relating to a referent acting as a purpose for the sake of which behavior is then intended. Telosponsive behavior is done "for the sake of" grounds (purposes, reasons, etc.) rather than "in response to." *See also:* Final cause; Intention; Purpose.

*Tic:* A seemingly useless, involuntary coordinate movement that keeps recurring intermittently. This is a symptom in the conversion disorder. *See also:* Conversion disorder.

*Token economy:* A form of behavior modification in which a group of patients (prisoners, etc.) is given reinforcers in the form of plastic tokens for accomplishing certain targeted behaviors. The tokens have economic value and can be spent for various goods or activities (e.g., magazines, a special movie, etc.). It has been shown that base rates for desirable behaviors (bed making, personal hygiene, etc.) can be raised among groups of individuals through use of this operant conditioning procedure. *See also:* Base rate; Behavior modification.

*Tolerance:* The ability of an addict's central nervous system to absorb the crucial substance at a dosage level formerly resulting in an effect, but now no longer resulting in the desired effect (i.e., the "high"). As the tolerance level increases, the addict must take more and more of the crucial substance to gain the desired effect. *See also:* Substance dependence; Withdrawal.

*Topographical model:* Freud's later modification of the psychic apparatus to include id, ego, and superego as dynamic identities which could interact within as well as across the levels of consciousness. *See also:* Depth model.

*Trance state (twilight state):* A dissociative disorder in which the person moves about in objective reality but is deeply immersed in regressive preoccupations that cannot be expressed in words or shared with others. The person may appear stunned. Most persons have no memory of this episode. *See also:* Dissociative disorder.

*Transference:* Placing onto the therapist positive and/or negative feelings and attitudes that are in fact aimed at important people from out of the patient's past (imagos). *See also:* Imago; Libidinal anticipatory idea.

*Transference neuroses:* The neurotic conditions that Freud believed were amenable to psychoanalytical treatment, based on the fact that such patients were capable of forming cathectic ties (i.e., transference) to the therapist. They include the anxiety disorders, hysterias (somatoform disorders) and obsessive-compulsive disorders. This phrases should not be confused with the "transformed neurosis." *See also:* Narcissistic neuroses; Transformed neurosis.

*Transformed neurosis:* Also known as the artificial neurosis, this refers to the neurotic acting out that occurs within the four walls of the consulting room in which a patient in psychoanalysis reveals his or her unconscious dynamics. It is through this transformed neurosis that the psychoanalyst effects his cures by way of interpretation and the overcoming of resistance. *See also:* Acting out; Insight; Psychoanalysis.

*Transsexualism:* A gender identity disorder in which the person believes that he or she has somehow been placed in the wrong physical body. These are not homosexual individuals, and care must be taken lest a person in homosexual panic seek a sex-change operation on the mistaken assumption of being a transsexual. DSM-III recommends that a period of at least two years must pass in which the person seriously wants to change physical sexual identity before a diagnosis of transsexualism be made.

*Transvestism:* One of the paraphilias, in which a person either gains sexual gratification or identification with the opposite sex as symbolized through the wearing of clothing designed for the opposite sex. DSM-III assigns this diagnosis *only* to men. Three out of four transvestites are heterosexual. There are degrees of cross-dressing, ranging from occasional solitary wearing of a few female undergarments to a completely feminine attire. *See also:* Paraphilias.

*Traumatic neurosis:* A dissociative disorder in which due to some trauma (e.g., automobile accident, battlefield fatigue) the person finds it difficult to get his or her thoughts straight and may even block out everything via amnesia. *See also:* Dissociative disorder; Massive amnesia.

*Type A behavior:* Behavior reflected in people who are impatient, aggressive, highly competitive, ambitious, and very desirous of being in control of almost every situation in which they find themselves. Type A individuals are prone to develop coronary disease. *See also:* Psychosomatic disorder; Type B behavior.

*Type B behavior:* Behavior reflected in people who are basically relaxed, realistic, and oriented to cooperation rather than competition in life. Type B individuals are *not* high risks for coronary disease. *See also:* Psychosomatic disorder; Type A behavior.

*Ulcerative colitis:* A serious gastrointestinal disorder in which hemorrhage and ulceration of the colon occur along with constipation and/or diarrhea. This disorder is often tied to psychosomatic dynamics. *See also:* Psychosomatic disorder.

*Unconscious, unconsciousness:* Freud defined the unconscious sphere of the psyche as the "true psychic reality," meaning that it was the fundamental aspect of mind. The unconscious realm of mind has its own wishful impulses, its own mode of expression, and its peculiar mental mechanisms that are not in force elsewhere. We always know more unconsciously than we admit or avow consciously. *See also:* Conscious; Preconscious.

*Undoing:* Unconsciously motivated behavior which attempts to rectify, cleanse, or set straight some fantasied misbehavior on the person's part. The misbehavior, of course, relates to re-enactments of Oedipal problems (repetition compulsions). Often, magical rituals are performed by the person, as in the obsessive-compulsive disorder. *See also:* Obsessive-compulsive disorder; Repetition compulsion.

*Urethral stage:* A brief period, occurring in the late anal period, which amounts to a third stage in psychosexual development. The urethra is the erogenous zone of importance. Feelings of self-worth center around competition, the ability to retain continence in urination, and so on.

*Vaginismus:* A psychosexual dysfunction in which a woman has involuntary spasms of the musculature of the outer third of the vagina that interfere with the male partner's penile penetration. *See also:* Psychosexual dysfunction.

*Vitalism:* A term dating from Galenic medicine denoting a belief in some kind of spiritual energy (*pneumata*) that permeates human organisms and influences bodily functioning over and above strictly physiological mechanisms. Galenic vitalism was based upon a deistic teleology, but today vitalism is used as an opprobrious allusion to human teleological theory in medicine and psychology. *See also:* Teleology.

*Voyeurism:* A paraphiliac disorder in which the person repeatedly achieves sexual excitement and obtains release by observing unsuspecting people, usually strangers, disrobe, perform sexually, or simply be naked. This is a disorder performed almost exclusively by men. *See also:* Paraphilias.

*Waxy flexibility:* A symptom occasionally seen in catatonic behavior in which the patient's limbs and body posture can be positioned, much as one shapes wax into various contours. In time, the patient will return to a normal posture. Modern medications have made it less likely that this symptom will be seen in the catatonic clinical picture.

*Withdrawal:* The feelings of illness experienced by an addict as the drug to which he or she is addicted is taken away. *See also:* Substance dependence; Tolerance.

*Word salad:* A series of words strung together by a psychotic patient that fail to communicate. The words may have dictionary meanings, but these meanings are not being conveyed in the "tossed together" (like a salad) form of this communication. Neologisms may also be tossed into the sequence to further confound things. *See also:* Neologism.

*Xenophobia:* The irrational fear of strangers. *See also:* Phobia.

*Zoöphilia:* A paraphiliac disorder in which the person either fantasizes or actually engages in sexual relations with a lower animal as a repeatedly preferred or exclusive method of gaining sexual release. *See also:* Paraphilias.

*Zoöphobia:* The irrational fear of "a" or all animals. *See also:* Phobia.

# References

Abel, G. G., Levis, D. J., & Clancy, D. (1970). Aversion therapy applied to taped sequences of deviant behavior in exhibitionism and other sexual deviations: A preliminary report. *Journal of Behavior Therapy and Experimental Psychiatry, 1,* 59-66.

Abraham, K. (1927). *Selected papers on psychoanalysis.* London: Hogarth Press.

Abraham, K. (1949). Notes on manic-depressive insanity. *Selected papers of Karl Abraham.* London: Hogarth Press.

Abravanel, E. (1967). Developmental changes in the inter-sensory patterning of space. *Proceedings of the 75th Annual Convention of the American Psychological Association, 2,* 161-162.

Abse, D. W. (1966). *Hysteria and related mental disorders.* Baltimore: Williams & Wilkins.

Abt, L. E., & Stuart, I. R. (Eds.). (1982). *The newer therapies: A sourcebook.* New York: Van Nostrand Reinhold.

Acosta, F. X. (1975). Etiology and treatment of homosexuality: A review. *Archives of Sexual Behavior, 4,* 9-29.

Adams, P. L. (1972). Family characteristics of obsessive children. *American Journal of Psychiatry, 128,* 1414-1417.

Adelson, J., & Doehrman, J. (1980). The psychodynamic approach to adolescence. In J. Adleson (Ed.), *Handbook of adolescent psychology.* New York: Wiley-Interscience.

Adler, A. (1964). *Problems of neurosis: A book of case histories* (Phillippe Mairet, Ed.). New York: Harper & Row. (a)

Adler, A. (1964). *Social interest: A challenge to mankind.* New York: Capricorn Books. (b)

Adler, A. (1968). *The practice and theory of individual psychology.* Totowa, NJ: Littlefield, Adams.

Ainsworth, M. D. S., & Bell, S. M. (1974). Mother-infant interaction and the development of competence. In K. Connolly & J. Bruner (Eds.), *The growth of competence.* London: Academic Press.

Akiskal, H. S., & McKinney, W. T. (1975). Overview of recent research in depression. *Archives of General Psychiatry, 32,* 285-305.

Alacron, R. D. (1973). Hysteria and hysterical personality: How come one without the other? *Psychiatric Quarterly, 47,* 258-275.

Alexander, F. (1930). The neurotic character. *International Journal of Psycho-Analysis, 11,* 292-313.

Alexander, F. (1950). *Psychosomatic medicine.* New York: W. W. Norton.

Alexander, F., Flagg, G. W., Foster, S., Clemens, T., & Blahd, W. (1961). Experimental studies of emotional stress: I. Hyperthyroidism. *Psychosomatic Medicine, 23,* 104-114.

Allport, G. W. (1961). *Pattern and growth in personality.* New York: Holt, Rinehart and Winston.

American Psychiatric Association. (1980). *Diagnostic and statistical manual of mental disorders* (3rd ed.). (*DSM-III*). Washington, DC: Author.

Ansbacher, H. L. (1959). The significance of the socio-economic status of the patients of Freud and of Adler. *American Journal of Psychotherapy, 13,* 376-382.

Anthony, E. J. (1957). An experimental approach to the psychopathology of childhood: Encopresis. *British Journal of Medical Psychology, 30,* 146-175.

Anthony, E. J. (1976). *Emotions and intelligence.* In V. P. Varma & L. Williams (Eds.), *Piaget, psychology and education.* London: Hodder & Stoughton.

Arens, R. (1974). *Insanity defense.* New York: Philosophical Library.

Arieti, S. (1955). *Interpretation of schizophrenia.* New York: Brunner.

Arieti, S. (1959). Manic-depressive psychosis. In S. Arieti (Ed.), *American handbook of psychiatry.* New York: Basic Books.

Arieti, S. (1961). A re-examination of the phobic symptom and of symbolization in psychopathology. *American Journal of Psychiatry, 118,* 106-110.

Aristotle (1952). *Physics.* In R. M. Hutchins (Ed.), *Great books of the Western world* (Vol. 8). Chicago: Encyclopaedia Britannica.

Atthowe, J. M., & Krasner, L. (1968). Preliminary report on the application of contingent reinforcement procedures (token economy) on a "chronic" psychiatric ward. *Journal of Abnormal Psychology, 73,* 37-43.

Ausubel, D. P. (1961). Causes and types of narcotic addiction: A psychosocial view. *Psychiatric Quarterly, 35,* 523-531.


Baastrup, P. C., & Schou, M. (1967). Lithium as a prophylactic agent against recurrent depressions and manic-depressive psychosis. *Archives of General Psychiatry, 16,* 162-172.

Bagley, C. (1973). Occupational class and symptoms of depression. *Social Science and Medicine, 7,* 327-340.

Bak, R. C. (1946). Masochism in paranoia. *Psychoanalytic Quarterly, 15,* 285-301.

Bakal, D. (1975). Headache: A biopsychological perspective. *Psychological Bulletin, 82,* 369-382.

Bandura, A. (1978). The self system in reciprocal determinism. *American Psychologist, 33,* 344-358.

Bandura, A., Grusec, J., & Menlove, F. L. (1967). Observational learning as a function of symbolization and incentive set. *Child Development, 37,* 499-506.

Barahal, H. S. (1958). 1000 prefrontal lobotomies: Five-to-ten-year follow-up study. *Psychiatric Quarterly, 32,* 653-678.

Barker, R., Wright, B., Meyerson, L., & Gonick, M. (1953). *Adjustment to physical handicap and illness* (2nd ed.). New York: Social Science Research Council.

Barnes, K. E. (1971). Preschool play norms: A replication. *Developmental Psychology, 5,* 99-103.

Baron, J. H. (1972). Aetiology. In C. Wastell (Ed.), *Chronic duodenal ulcer.* New York: Appleton-Century-Crofts.

Barrett, B. H. (1969). Behavior modification in the home: Parents adapt laboratory-developed tactics to bowel-train a five and one-half year-old. *Psychotherapy: Theory, Research, and Practice, 6,* 172-176.

Bartlett, F. (1932). *Remembering a study in experimental and social psychology.* Cambridge: Cambridge University Press.

Bartlett, F. (1958). *Thinking, an experimental and social study.* New York: Basic Books.

Bateson, G. (1959). Cultural problems posed by a study of schizophrenic process. In A. Auerback (Ed.), *Schizophrenia: An integrated approach.* New York: Ronald Press.

Bateson, G. (1960). Minimal requirements for a theory of schizophrenia. *Archives of General Psychiatry, 2,* 477-491.

Bateson, G. (1972). *Steps to an ecology of mind.* New York: Ballantine Books.

Bateson, G., Jackson, D. D., Haley, J., & Weaklund, J. (1956). Toward a theory of schizophrenia. *Behavioral Science, 1,* 251-264.

Baumrind, D. (1971). Current patterns of parental authority. *Developmental Psychology, 4,* 1-103.

Bayer, R. (1981). *Homosexuality and American psychiatry: The politics of diagnosis.* New York: Basic Books.

Beach, F. A. (1950). *Sexual behavior in animals and man.* Springfield, IL: Charles C. Thomas.

Beaumont, W. (1833). *Experiments and observations on the gastric juice and the physiology of digestion.* Pittsburgh: F. P. Allen.

Beck, A. T. (1967). *Depression: Clinical, experimental, and theoretical aspects.* New York: Harper & Row.

Beck, A. T. (1972). *Depression: Causes and treatment.* Philadelphia: University of Pennsylvania Press.

Beck, A. T., Ward, C. H., Mendelson, M., Mock, J. E., & Erbaugh, J. K. (1962). Reliability of psychiatric diagnoses. 2: A study of consistency of clinical judgments and ratings. *American Journal of Psychiatry, 119,* 351-357.

Becker, J. (1974). *Depression: Theory and research.* Washington, DC: Winston-Wiley.

Becker, J. (1977). *Affective disorders.* Morristown, NJ: General Learning Press.

Bell, A. P., & Weinberg, M. S. (1978). *Homosexualities: A study of diversity among men and women.* New York: Simon and Schuster.

Bell, A. P., Weinberg, M. S., & Kiefer-Hammersmith, S. (1981). *Sexual preference: Its development in men and women.* Bloomington: Indiana University Press.

Bem, S. L. (1975). Sex-role adaptability: One consequence of psychological androgyny. *Journal of Personality and Social Psychology, 31,* 634-643.

Bemis, K. M. (1978). Current approaches to the etiology and treatment of anorexia nervosa. *Psychological Bulletin, 85,* 593-617.

Bengston, V. L., & Starr, J. M. (1975). Contrast and consensus: A generation analysis of youth in the 1970s. In R. I Havighurst & P. H. Dreyer (Eds.), *Youth: The seventy-fourth yearbook of the National Society for the Study of Education.* Part 1. Chicago: University of Chicago Press.

Benjamin, H. (1967). Transvestism and transsexualism in the male and female. *Journal of Sex Research, 3,* 107-127.

Bentler, P. M. (1976). A typology of transsexualism: Gender identity theory and data. *Archives of Sexual Behavior, 5*, 567-584.

Bentler, P. M., & Prince, C. (1969). Personality characteristics of male transvestites. *Journal of Abnormal Psychology, 74*, 140-143.

Berg, W. K., & Berg, K. M. (1979). Psychophysiological development in infancy: State, sensory function, and attention. In J. D. Osofsky (Ed.), *Handbook for infant development.* New York: John Wiley & Sons.

Berger, A. (1965). A test of the double-bind hypothesis of schizophrenia. *Family Process, 4*, 198-205.

Berger, P. A. (1978). Medical treatment of mental illness. *Science, 200*, 974-981.

Bergin, A. E., & Lambert, M. J. (1978). The evaluation of therapeutic outcomes. In S. L. Garfield & A. E. Bergin (Eds.), *Handbook of psychotherapy and behavior change: An empirical analysis.* New York: John Wiley & Sons.

Berko, J. (1958). The child's learning of English morphology. *Word, 14*, 150-177.

Berlyne, D. E. (1958). The influence of the albedo and complexity of stimuli on visual fixation in the human infant. *British Journal of Psychology, 49*, 315-318.

Berrington, W., Liddell, D., & Foulds, G. (1956). A re-evaluation of the fugue. *Journal of Mental Science, 102*, 280-286.

Bianchi, G. N. (1973). Patterns of hypochondriasis: A principal components analysis. *British Journal of Psychiatry, 122*, 541-548.

Bieber, I. (1973). Homosexuality: An adaptive consequence of disorder in psychosexual development. *American Journal of Psychiatry, 130*, 1209-1211.

Bieber, I. (1976). A discussion of "Homosexuality: The ethical challenge." *Journal of Consulting and Clinical Psychology, 44*, 163-166.

Bieber, I., Dain, H. J., Dince, P. R., Drellich, M. G., Grand, H. G., Gundlach, R. H., Kremer, M. W., Rifkin, A. H., Wilbur, C. B., & Bieber, T. B. (1962). *Homosexuality: A psychoanalytic study.* New York: Random House, Vintage Books.

Biller, H. B., & Bahm, R. M. (1971). Father-absence, perceived maternal behavior, and masculinity of self-concept among junior-high-school boys. *Developmental Psychology, 4*, 178-181.

Bird, F. (1957). Feelings of unreality. *International Journal of Psycho-Analysis, 38*, 256-265.

Birk, L. (1974). Group psychotherapy for men who are homosexual. *Journal of Sex and Marital Therapy, 1*, 29-52.

Birnbaum, K. (1914). *Die psychopathischen verbrecker* (2nd ed.). Leipzig: Thieme.

Birns, B. (1965). Individual differences in human neonates' responses to stimulation. *Child Development, 36*, 249-256.

Birren, J. E. (Ed.). (1959). *Handbook of aging and the individual.* Chicago: University of Chicago Press.

Bixler, E. O., Kales, A., Soldatos, C. R., Kales, J. D., & Healey, S. (1979). Prevalence of sleep disorders in the Los Angeles metropolitan area. *American Journal of Psychiatry, 136*, 1257-1262.

Black, H. C. (1979). *Black's law dictionary* (5th ed.). (Contributing authors: J. R. Nolan, M. J. Connolly). St. Paul, MN: West.

Blair, A. W., & Burton, W. H. (1951). *Growth and development of the preadolescent.* New York: Appleton-Century-Crofts.

Blane, H. (1968). *The personality of the alcoholic.* New York: Harper & Row.

Blank, H. R. (1954). Depression, hypomania, and depersonalization. *Psychoanalytic Quarterly, 23*, 20-37.

Bleuler, E. (1922). Die probleme der Schizoidic und der Syntonie. *Zeitschrift fur die gesamte Neurologie und Psychiatrie, 78,* 373-388.

Bleuler, E. (1950). *Dementia praecox or the group of schizophrenias* (J. Zinkin, Trans.). New York: International Universities Press.

Bleuler, M. (1974). Offspring of schizophrenics. *Schizophrenia Bulletin, 8,* 93-107.

Bliss, E. L., & Branch, C. H. (1960). *Anorexia nervosa: Its history, psychology, and biology.* New York: Hoeber.

Bloch, H. S. (1969). Army clinical psychiatry in the combat zone—1967-1968. *The American Journal of Psychiatry, 126,* 289-298.

Bloom, G. E. (1955). Ulcerative colitis in a five-year-old boy. In G. Caplan (Ed.), *Emotional problems in early childhood.* New York: Basic Books.

Bloom, G. E., & Whipple, B. (1959). A method of studying emotional factors in children with rheumatoid arthritis. In L. Jessner & E. Pavenstedt (Eds.), *Dynamic psycho-pathology in childhood.* New York: Grune & Stratton.

Bloom, K. & Esposito, A. (1975). Social conditioning and its proper control procedures. *Journal of Experimental Child Psychology, 19,* 209-222.

Blos, P. (1962). *On adolescence.* New York: Free Press.

Blumer, D., & Benson, D. F. (1975). Personality changes with frontal and temporal lobe lesions. In D. F. Benson & D. Blumer (Eds.), *Psychiatric aspects of neurological disease.* New York: Grune & Stratton.

Boekelheide, P. D. (1978). Incest and the family physician. *Journal of Family Practice, 6,* 87-90.

Boring, E. G. (1950). *A history of experimental psychology* (2nd ed.). New York: Appleton-Century-Crofts.

Bowen, M. (1960). A family concept of schizophrenia. In D. D. Jackson (Ed.), *The etiology of schizophrenia.* New York: Basic Books.

Bowlby, J. (1969). *Attachment: Vol. I: Attachment and loss.* New York: Basic Books.

Braucht, G. N., Brakarsh, D., Follingstad, D., & Berry, K. L. (1973). Deviant drug use in adolescence: A review of psychological correlates. *Psychological Bulletin, 79,* 92-106.

Braungart, R. G. (1980). Youth movements. In J. Adleson (Ed.), *Handbook of adolescent psychology.* New York: John Wiley & Sons.

Brengelmann, J. C. (1959). *The effect of repeated electroshock on learning in depressives.* Munich: Springer.

Breuer, J., & Freud, S. (1955). *Studies on hysteria* [1893-1895]. In J. Strachey (Ed.), *The standard edition of the complete psychological works of Sigmund Freud* (Vol. II). London: Hogarth Press.

Brewer, W. F. (1974). There is no convincing evidence for operant or classical conditioning in adult humans. In W. B. Weimer & D. S. Palermo (Eds.), *Cognition and the symbolic processes.* Hillsdale, NJ: Lawrence Erlbaum.

Briscoe, C. W., Smith, J. B., Robins, E., Marten, S., & Gaskin, F. (1973). Divorce and psychiatric illness. *Archives of General Psychiatry, 29,* 119-125.

Broen, W. E., Jr. (1968). *Schizophrenia research and theory.* New York: Academic Press.

Bronfenbrenner, U., Devereux, C. E., Jr., Suci, G. J., & Rodgers, R. R. (1965). Adults and peers as sources of conformity and autonomy. Unpublished study, Cornell University, Dept. of Child Development and Family Relations.

Brosin, H. W. (1959). Psychiatric conditions following head injury. In S. Arieti (Ed.), *American handbook of psychiatry.* New York: Basic Books.

Brown, F. (1961). Depression and childhood bereavement. *Journal of Mental Science,* *107,* 754-777.

Brown, G. W. (1972). Life-events and psychiatric illness: Some thoughts on methodology and causality. *Journal of Psychosomatic Research, 16,* 311-320.

Brown, G. W., Birley, J. L. T., & Wing, J. K. (1972). Influence of family on the course of schizophrenic disorders: A replication. *British Journal of Psychiatry, 121,* 241-258.

Brown, J. L. (1964). States in newborn infants. *Merrill-Palmer Quarterly, 10,* 313-327.

Brown, R. (1973). *A first language: The early stages.* Cambridge: Harvard University Press.

Bruch, H. (1957). *The importance of overeating.* New York: W. W. Norton.

Bruner, J. S. (1961). The cognitive consequences of early sensory deprivation. In P. Solomon, P. E. Kubzansky, H. Leiderman, J. H. Mendelson, R. Trumbill, D. Wexler (Eds.), *Sensory deprivation: A symposium held at Harvard medical school.*

Buck, C., & Hobbs, G. E. (1959). The problem of specificity in psychosomatic illness. *Psychosomatic Research, 3,* 227-233.

Buckner, H. T. (1970). The transvestic career path. *Psychiatry, 33,* 381-389.

Bullard, D. M. (Ed.). (1959). *Psychoanalysis and psychotherapy.* Chicago: University of Chicago Press.

Bullard, D. M., Glaswer, H. H., Heagarty, M. C., & Pivchech, E. C. (1967). Failure to thrive in the neglected child. *American Journal of Orthopsychiatry, 37,* 680-690.

Bunney, W. E., Pert, A., Rosenblatt, J., Pert, C. G., & Gallaper, D. (1979). Mode of action of lithium: Some biological considerations. *Archives of General Psychiatry, 36,* 898-901.

Bursten, B. (1972). The manipulative personality. *Archives of General Psychiatry, 26,* 318-321.

Burton, R. V., Maccoby, F., & Allinsmith, W. (1961). Antecedents of resistance to temptations in four-year-old children. *Child Development, 32,* 689-710.

Burtt, E. A. (1955). *The metaphysical foundations of modern physical science* (rev. ed.). Garden City, NY: Doubleday.

Buss, A. H. (1961). *Psychology of aggression.* New York: John Wiley & Sons.

Bychowski, G. (1952). *Psychotherapy of psychosis.* New York: Grune & Stratton.

Bychowski, G. (1953). The problem of latent psychosis. *Journal of the American Psychoanalytic Association, 4,* 484-503.

Bychowski, G. (1956). General aspects and implications of introjection. *Psychoanalytic Quarterly, 25,* 530-548.

Bychowski, G. (1958). Struggle against introjects. *International Journal of Psycho-Analysis, 39,* 182-187.

Cameron, N. (1938). Reasoning, regression and communication in schizophrenics. *Psychological Monographs, 50* (Whole No. 221).

Cameron, N. (1939). Schizophrenic thinking in a problem-solving situation. *Journal of Mental Science, 85,* 1012-1035.

Cameron, N. (1942). The place of mania among the depressions from a biological standpoint. *Journal of Psychology, 14,* 181-195.

Cameron, N. (1943). The paranoid pseudocommunity. *American Journal of Sociology, 49,* 32-38.

Cameron, N. (1944). Experimental investigation of schizophrenic thinking. In J. Kasanin (Ed.), *Language and thought in schizophrenia.* Berkeley and Los Angeles: University of California Press. (a)

Cameron, N. (1944). Functional psychoses. In J. McV. Hunt (Ed.), *Personality and the behavior disorders*. New York: Ronald Press. (b)

Cameron, N. (1947). *The psychology of behavior disorders: A biosocial interpretation.* Boston: Houghton Mifflin.

Cameron, N. (1959). The geography of disordered reasoning. In S. J. Beck & H. B. Molish (Eds.), *Reflexes to intelligence*. Glencoe, IL: Free Press. (a)

Cameron, N. (1959). Paranoid conditions and paranoia. In S. Arieti (Ed.), *American handbook of psychiatry*. New York: Basic Books. (b)

Cameron, N. (1959). The paranoid pseudocommunity revisited. *American Journal of Sociology, 65,* 52-59. (c)

Cameron, N., & Magaret, A. (1951). *Behavior pathology*. Boston: Houghton Mifflin.

Cannon, W. B. (1932). *The wisdom of the body*. New York: W. W. Norton.

Cappell, H., & Pliner, P. (1973). Volitional control of marijuana intoxication: A study of the ability to "come down" on command. *Journal of Abnormal Psychology, 82,* 428-434.

Caprico, F. S. (1973). Fetishism. In A. Ellis & A. Abarbanel (Eds.), *Encyclopedia of sexual behavior*. New York: Jason Aronson.

Carlsson, A. (1978). Antipsychotic drugs, neurotransmitters, and schizophrenia. *American Journal of Psychiatry, 135,* 164-173.

Carns, D. E. (1973). Talking about sex: Notes on first coitus and the double standard. *Journal of Marriage and the Family, 35,* 677-688.

Carpenter, G. (1975). Mother's face and the newborn. In R. Lewin (Ed.), *Child alive*. New York: Doubleday.

Carr, A. T. (1971). Compulsive neurosis: Two physiological studies. *Bulletin of the British Psychological Society, 24,* 256-257.

Carson, T. P., & Adams, H. E. (1979). Affective disorders: Behavioral perspectives. In S. M. Turner, K. S. Calhoun, & H. E. Adams (Eds.), *Handbook of clinical behavior therapy*. New York: John Wiley & Sons.

Cary, G. L. (1972). The borderline condition: A structural-dynamic viewpoint. *Psychoanalytic Review, 59,* 33-54.

Cavanagh, P., & Davidson, M. (1977). The secondary circular reaction and response elicitation in the operant learning of six-month-old infants. *Developmental Psychology, 13,* 371-376.

Chapman, L. J., & Chapman, J. P. (1973). *Disordered thought in schizophrenia.* New York: Appleton-Century-Crofts.

Chessick, R. D. (1960). The pharmacogenic orgasm in the drug addict. *Archives of General Psychiatry, 3,* 545-555.

Chodoff, P. (1974). The diagnosis of hysteria: An overview. *American Journal of Psychiatry, 131,* 1073-1078.

Christoffel, H. (1956). Male genital exhibitionism. In S. Lorand & M. Galint (Eds.), *Perversions: Psychodynamics and therapy*. New York: Random House.

Churchill, W. (1967). *Homosexual behavior among males*. New York: Hawthorne Books.

Clark, T. R. (1975). Homosexuality and psychopathology in nonpatient males. *American Journal of Psychoanalysis, 35,* 163-168.

Clarke-Stewart, K. A. (1973). Interactions between mothers and their young children: Characteristics and consequences. *Monographs of the Society for Research in Child Development, 38* (6-7, Whole No. 153).

Cleckley, H. (1941). *The mask of sanity.* St. Louis: C. V. Mosby.

Clifton, R. (1974). Heart rate conditioning in the newborn infant. *Journal of Experimental Child Psychology, 13,* 43-57.

Cobb, S., & Rose, R. M. (1973). Hypertension, peptic ulcer, and diabetes in air traffic controllers. *Journal of the American Medical Association, 224,* 489-492.

Cohen, L. (1979). Our developing knowledge of infant perception and cognition. *American Psychologist, 34,* 894-899.

Cohen, L., & Salapatek, P. (Eds.). (1975). *Infant perception: From sensation to cognition.* Vol. 1: *Basic visual processes.* New York: Academic Press.

Cohen, M. (1954). An intensive study of twelve cases of manic-depressive psychosis. *Psychiatry, 17,* 103-137.

Cole, J. O. (1964). Phenothiazine treatment in acute schizophrenia: Effectiveness. *Archives of General Psychiatry, 10,* 246-261.

Coleman, J. C. (1974). *Relationship in adolescence.* London: Routledge and Kegan Paul.

Coleman, L. (1980). Psychiatry in criminal trials—Reflections of an abolitionist. *Prosecutor's Brief,* Jan.-Feb., 16-20.

Compernolle, T., Hoogduin, K., & Joele, L. (1979). Diagnosis and treatment of the hyperventilation syndrome. *Psychosomatics, 20,* 612-625.

Conger, J. J. (1975). Sexual attitudes and behavior of contemporary adolescents. In J. J. Conger (Ed.), *Contemporary issues in adolescent development.* New York: Harper & Row.

Conger, J. J. (1977). *Adolescence and youth: Psychological development in a changing world* (2nd ed.). New York: Harper & Row.

Copans, S. A. (1974). Human prenatal effects: Methodological problems and some suggested solutions. *Merrill-Palmer Quarterly, 20,* 43-52.

Cornwell, D., Hobbs, S., & Prytula, R. (1980). Little Albert rides again. *American Psychologist, 35,* 216-217.

Costanzo, P. R., & Shaw, M. E. (1966). Conformity as a function of the age level. *Child Development, 37,* 967-975.

Coyne, J. C. (1976). Toward an interactional description of depression. *Psychiatry, 39,* 14-27.

Crandall, V. J., & Preston, A. (1961). Verbally expressed needs and overt maternal behaviors. *Child Development, 32,* 261-270.

Cumming, E., & Henry, W. E. (1961). *Growing old.* New York: Basic Books.


Dare, C. (1976). Psycho-analytic theories. In M. Rutter & L. Hersov (Eds.), *Child psychiatry.* Oxford: Blackwell Publishers.

Davison, G. C. (1977). Homosexuality and the ethics of behavioral intervention: Paper 1—Homosexuality, the ethical challenge. *Journal of Homosexuality, 2,* 195-204.

Davitz, J. R. (1959). Fear, anxiety and the perception of others. *Journal of General Psychology, 61,* 169-173.

Dekker, E., Barendregt, J. T., & DeVries, K. (1961). Allergy and neurosis in asthma. In A. Jores & H. Freyberger (Eds.), *Advances in psychosomatic medicine.* New York: Basic Books.

Dement, W., & Kleitman, N. (1957). The relation of eye movements during sleep to dream activity: An objective method for the study of dreaming. *Journal of Experimental Psychology, 53,* 339-346.

Dempsey, G. M., Tsuang, M. R., Struss, A., & Dvoredsky-Wortman, A. (1975). Treatment of schizo-affective disorder. *Comprehensive Psychiatry, 16,* 55-59.

DeNike, L. D. (1964). The temporal relationship between awareness and performance in verbal conditioning. *Journal of Experimental Psychology, 68,* 521-529.

Detre, T. P., & Jarecki, H. G. (1971). *Modern psychiatric treatment.* Philadelphia: Lippincott.

Deur, J. I., & Parke, R. D. (1970). Effects of inconsistent punishment on aggression in children. *Developmental Psychology, 2,* 403-411.

Deutsch, F. (Ed.). (1959). *The mysterious leap from the unconscious to the conscious.* New York: International Universities Press.

Deutsch, H. (1932). Homosexuality in women. *International Journal of Psycho-Analysis, 14,* 34-56.

Deutsch, H. (1937). Absence of grief. *Psychoanalytic Quarterly, 6,* 12-22.

Deutsch, H. (1938). Folie à deux. *Psychoanalytic Quarterly, 7,* 307-322.

Diamond, B. L. (1968). The fallacy of the impartial expert. In R. C. Allen, E. Z. Ferster, & J. G. Rubin (Eds.), *Readings in law and psychiatry.* Baltimore: Johns Hopkins University Press.

Dion, K. K. (1973). Young children's stereotyping of facial attractiveness. *Developmental Psychology, 9,* 183-188.

Doerr, P., Kockott, G., Vogt, H. J., Pirke, K. M., & Dittmar, F. (1973). Plasma testosterone, estradiol, and semen analysis in male homosexuals. *Archives of General Psychiatry, 29,* 829-834.

Dollard, J., & Miller, N. E. (1950). *Personality and psychotherapy: An analysis in terms of learning, thinking, and culture.* New York: McGraw-Hill.

Douvan, E., & Adelson, J. (1966). *The adolescent experience.* New York: John Wiley & Sons.

Douvan, E., & Adelson, J. (1966). *The adolescent experience.* New York: John Wiley & Sons.

Dulany, D. E. (1962). The place of hypotheses and intentions: An analysis of verbal control in verbal conditioning. In C. W. Eriksen (Ed.), *Behavior and awareness: A symposium of research and interpretation.* Durham, NC: Duke University Press.

Dunbar, F. (1943). *Psychosomatic diagnosis.* New York: Hoeber.

Dunbar, F. (1946). *Emotions and bodily change* (3rd ed.). New York: Columbia University Press.

Durrett, N. E., & Davy, A. I. (1970). Racial awareness in young Mexican-American, Negro, and Anglo children. *Young Children, 26,* 16-24.

Dynes, J. (1939). Survey of alcoholic patients admitted to the Boston Psychopathic Hospital in 1937. *New England Medical Journal, 220,* 195-203.

Easton, K. (1959). An unusual case of fugue and orality. *Psychoanalytic Quarterly, 28,* 505-513.

Ekstein, R., Bryant, K., & Friedman, S. W. (1958). Childhood schizophrenia and allied conditions. In L. Bellak (Ed.), *Schizophrenia: A review of the syndrome.* New York: Logos Press.

Elkind, D., & Weiner, I. B. (1978). *Development of the child.* New York: John Wiley & Sons.

Engel, B. (1973). Clinical applications of operant conditioning techniques in the control of cardiac arrhythmias. *Seminar in Psychiatry, 5,* 433-438.

Engel, B., & Bickford, A. (1961). Response specificity: Stimulus-response and individual response specificity in essential hypertension. *Archives of General Psychiatry, 5,* 478-489.

Engel, M. (1959). The stability of the self-concept in adolescence. *Journal of Abnormal and Social Psychology, 58,* 211-215.

English, H. B., & English, A. C. (1958). *A comprehensive dictionary of psychological and psychoanalytical terms.* New York: Longmans, Green.

Erikson, E. H. (1963). *Childhood and society.* New York: W. W. Norton.

Erikson, E. H. (1968). *Identity: Youth and crisis.* New York: W. W. Norton.

Erikson, E. H. (1980). *Identity and the life cycle.* New York: W. W. Norton.

Eron, L. D., Huesmann, L. R., Lefkowitz, M. M., & Walder, L. O. (1974). How learning conditions in early childhood—including mass media—relate to aggression in late adolescence. *American Journal of Orthopsychiatry, 44,* 412-423.

Evans, R. B. (1970). Sixteen personality factor questionnaire scores of homosexual men. *Journal of Consulting and Clinical Psychology, 34,* 212-215.

Evans, R. B. (1972). Physical and biochemical characteristics of homosexual men. *Journal of Consulting and Clinical Psychology, 39,* 140-147.

Evans, R. I. (1968). *B. F. Skinner: The man and his ideas.* New York: E. P. Dutton.

Eysenck, H. J. (1952). The effects of psychotherapy: An evaluation. *Journal of Consulting Psychology, 16,* 319-324.


Fagan, J. F. (1973). Infants' delayed recognition memory and forgetting. *Journal of Experimental Child Psychology, 16,* 424-450.

Fairbairn, W. R. D. (1954). *An object-relations theory of personality.* New York: Basic Books.

Fantz, R. L. (1958). Pattern vision in young infants. *Psychological Record, 8,* 43-49.

Farber, I. E., Harlow, H. F., & West, L. J. (1956). Brainwashing, conditioning, and DDD (debility, dependency and dread). *Sociometry, 19,* 271-285.

Federn, P. (1947). Principles of psychotherapy in latent schizophrenia. *American Journal of Psychotherapy, 1,* 129-139.

Federn, P. (1951). *Ego psychology and the psychoses.* New York: Basic Books.

Feldman, M. P., MacCullough, M. J., Orford, J. F., & Mellor, V. (1969). The application of anticipatory avoidance learning to the treatment of homosexuality. *Acta Psychiatrica Scandinavica, 45,* 109-117.

Fenichel, O. (1945). *Psychoanalytic theory of neuroses.* New York: W. W. Norton.

Fenichel, O. (1953). The pregenital antecedents of the Oedipus complex. In *Collected papers* (Vol. 1). New York: W. W. Norton.

Ferraro, A. (1959). Presenile psychoses, senile psychoses and psychoses with cerebral arteriosclerosis. In S. Arieti (Ed.), *American handbook of psychiatry.* New York: Basic Books.

Fieve, R. R. (1975). *Moodswing: The third revolution in psychiatry.* New York: Bantam Books.

Fingarette, H. (1972). *The meaning of criminal insanity.* Berkeley and Los Angeles: University of California Press.

Fink, M. (1977). CNS sequellae of EST: Risks of therapy and their prophylaxis. In C.

Shagass & A. Friedhoff (Eds.), *Psychopathology and brain dysfunction.* New York: Raven Press.

Fink, M. (1979). *Convulsive therapy: Theory and practice.* New York: Raven Press.

Finney, J. C. (1961). Some maternal influences on children's personality and character. *Genetic Psychological Monographs, 63,* 199-278.

Fisher, C. (1945). Amnesic states in war neuroses: The psychogenesis of fugues. *Psychoanalytic Quarterly, 14,* 437-468.

Fisher, C. (1957). Construction of dreams and images. *Journal of the American Psychoanalytic Association, 5,* 5-60.

Fisher, S., & Cleveland, S. E. (1958). *Body image and personality.* New York: Van Nostrand.

Fontana, A. F. (1966). Family etiology of schizophrenia: Is a scientific methodology possible? *Psychological Bulletin, 66,* 214-227:

Ford, C. S., & Beach, F. A. (1951). *Patterns of sexual behavior.* New York: Harper & Bros.

Forgus, R. H., & DeWolfe, A. S. (1974). Coding of cognitive input in delusional patients. *Journal of Abnormal Psychology, 83,* 278-284.

Frank, V. E. (1959). *Man's search for meaning: An introduction to logotherapy.* New York: Washington Square Press.

Frankl, V. E. (1959). *Man's search for meaning: An introduction to logotherapy.* New York: Washington Square Press.

Freedman, B. J. (1974). The subjective experience of perceptual and cognitive disturbance in schizophrenia. *Archives of General Psychiatry, 30,* 333-340.

Freeman, T., Cameron, J. L., & McGhie, A. (1958). *Chronic schizophrenia.* New York: International Universities Press.

Freeman, W., & Watts, J. W. (1950). *Psychosurgery* (2nd ed.). Springfield, IL: Charles C. Thomas.

Freud, A. (1958). Adolescence. *The psychoanalytic study of the child* (Vol. 13). New York: International Universities Press.

Freud, S. *The standard edition of the complete psychological works of Sigmund Freud* (Ed. and Trans. by J. Strachey). London: Hogarth Press. 23 vols. (Note: Date of original writing at left, with the *standard edition* publication date following the volume number.)

1888-89  Preface to the translation of Bernheim's *suggestion.* In Vol. I, 1966. (a)

1892     A case of successful treatment by hypnotism. In Vol. I., 1966. (b)

1892-99  Extracts from the Fliess papers. In Vol. I, 1966. (c)

1893     On the psychical mechanism of hysterial phenomena: A lecture. In Vol. III, 1962. (a)

1894     The neuro-psychoses of defence. In Vol. III, 1962. (b)

1894     On the grounds for detaching a particular syndrome from neurasthenia under the description "anxiety neurosis." In Vol. III, 1962. (c)

1895     Project for a scientific psychology. In Vol. I, 1966. (d)

1896     Further remarks on the neuro-psychoses of defence. In Vol. III, 1962. (d)

1896     The aetiology of hysteria. In Vol. III, 1962. (e)

1900     *The interpretation of dreams* (First Part). In Vol. IV, 1953. (a)

1900-01  *The interpretation of dreams* (Second Part). In Vol. V, 1953. (b)

1901    *The psychopathology of everyday life.* In Vol. VI, 1960. (a)

1901    Fragment of an analysis of a case of hysteria. In Vol. VII, 1953. (c)

1904    On psychotherapy. In Vol. VII, 1953. (d)

1905    *Three essays on the theory of sexuality.* In Vol. VII, 1953. (e)

1905    My views on the part played by sexuality in the aetiology of the neuroses. In Vol. VII, 1953. (f)

1905    *Jokes and their relation to the unconscious.* In Vol. VIII, 1960. (b)

1906    Delusions and dreams in Jensen's Gradiva. In Vol. IX, 1959. (a)

1906    Psycho-analysis and the establishment of the facts in legal proceedings. In Vol. IX, 1959. (b)

1908    Character and anal erotism. In Vol. IX, 1959. (c)

1908    "Civilized" sexual morality and modern nervous illness. In Vol. IX, 1959. (d)

1908    Some general remarks on hysterical attacks. In Vol. IX, 1959. (e)

1909    Analysis of a phobia in a five-year-old boy. In Vol. X, 1955. (a)

1909    Notes upon a case of obsessional neurosis. In Vol. X, 1955. (b)

1909    *Five lectures on psycho-analysis.* In Vol. XI, 1957. (a)

1910    Leonardo Da Vinci and a memory of childhood. In Vol. XI, 1957. (b)

1910    The future prospects of psycho-analytic therapy. In Vol. XI, 1957. (c)

1910    A special type of choice of object made by men. In Vol. XI, 1957. (d)

1910    "Wild" psycho-analysis. In Vol. XI, 1957. (e)

1910    Letter to Dr. Friedrich S. Krauss on *Anthropophyteia.* In Vol. XI, 1957. (f)

1911    Psycho-analytic notes on an autobiographical account of a case of paranoia (dementia paranoides). In Vol. XII, 1958. (a)

1911    The handling of dream-interpretation in psycho-analysis. In Vol. XII, 1958. (b)

1912    The dynamics of transference. In Vol. XII, 1958. (c)

1912    Recommendations to physicians practicing psycho-analysis. In Vol. XII, 1958. (d)

1912    Types of onset of neurosis. In Vol. XII, 1958. (e)

1912    Contributions to a discussion on masturbation. In Vol. XII, 1958. (f)

1912    A note on the unconscious in psycho-analysis. In Vol. XII, 1958. (g)

1912-13 *Totem and taboo.* In Vol. XIII, 1955. (c)

1913    On beginning the treatment. In Vol. XII, 1958. (h)

1913    The theme of the three caskets. In Vol. XII, 1958. (i)

1913    Observations and examples from analytic practice. In Vol. XIII, 1955. (d)

1913    The claims of psycho-analysis to scientific interest. In Vol. XIII, 1955. (e)

1914    Papers on technique. In Vol. XII, 1958. (j)

1914    Observations on transference-love. In Vol. XII, 1958. (k)

1914    On the history of the psycho-analytic movement. In Vol. XIV, 1957. (g)

1914    On narcissism: An introduction. In Vol. XIV, 1957. (h)

1914    From the history of an infantile neurosis. In Vol. XVII, 1955. (f)

1915    Instincts and their vicissitudes. In Vol. XIV, 1957. (i)

1915    Repression. In Vol. XIV, 1957. (j)

1915    The unconscious. In Vol. XIV, 1957. (k)

1915    A metapsychological supplement to the theory of dreams. In Vol. XIV, 1957. (l)

1915    Mourning and melancholia. In Vol. XIV, 1957. (m)

1915    A case of paranoia running counter to psycho-analytic theory of the disease. Vol. XIV, 1957. (n)

1915    Thoughts for the times on war and death. In Vol. XIV, 1957. (o)

1915-16  *Introductory lectures on psycho-analysis* (Parts I and II). In Vol. XV, 1963. (a)

1916    Some character-types met with in psycho-analytic work. In Vol. XIV, 1957. (p)

1916-17  *Introductory lectures on psycho-analysis* (Part III). In Vol. XVI, 1963. (b)

1917    A difficulty in the path of psycho-analysis. In Vol. XVII, 1955. (g)

1918    Lines of advance in psycho-analytic therapy. In Vol. XVII, 1955. (h)

1919    "A child is being beaten." A contribution to the study of the origin of sexual perversions. In Vol. XVII, 1955. (i)

1919    Introduction to psycho-analysis and the war neuroses. In Vol. XVII, 1955. (j)

1920    *Beyond the pleasure principle.* In Vol. XVIII, 1955. (k)

1920    The psychogenesis of a case of homosexuality in a woman. In Vol. XVIII, 1955. (l)

1921    *Group psychology and the analysis of the ego.* In Vol. XVIII, 1955. (m)

1922    Some neurotic mechanisms in jealousy, paranoia and homosexuality. In Vol. XVIII, 1955. (n)

1922    Two encyclopedia articles. In Vol. XVIII, 1955. (o)

1923    *The ego and the id.* In Vol. XIX, 1961. (a)

1923    A short account of psycho-analysis. In Vol. XIX, 1961. (b)

1923    *New introductory lectures on psycho-analysis.* In Vol. XXII, 1964. (a)

1924    The dissolution of the Oedipus complex. In Vol. XIX, 1961. (c)

1924    The loss of reality in neurosis and psychosis. In Vol. XIX, 1961. (d)

1924    An autobiographical study. In Vol. XX, 1959. (f)

1925    Some additional notes on dream-interpretation as a whole. In Vol. XIX, 1961. (e)

1925    Some psychical consequences of the anatomical distinction between the sexes. In Vol. XIX, 1961. (f)

1926    *Inhibitions, symptoms and anxiety.* In Vol. XX, 1959. (g)

1927    Fetishism. In Vol. XXI, 1961. (g)

1927    Humour. In Vol. XXI, 1961. (h)

1929    *Civilization and its discontents.* In Vol. XXI, 1961. (i)

1931    Libidinal types. In Vol. XXI, 1961. (j)

1931    Female sexuality. In Vol. XXI, 1961. (k)

1932-36  *New introductory lectures on psycho-analysis.* In Vol. XXII, 1964. (b)

1932    Why war? In Vol. XXII, 1964. (c)

1936    A disturbance of memory on the Acropolis. In Vol. XXII, 1964. (d)

1937    Analysis terminable and interminable. In Vol. XXIII, 1964. (e)

1938    *An outline of psycho-analysis.* In Vol. XXIII, 1964. (f)

Freud, S. (1951). Letter to a grateful mother. *International Journal of Psycho-Analysis, 32,* 331.

Freud, S. (1954). *The origins of psycho-analysis, letters to Wilhelm Fliess, drafts and notes: 1887-1902.* New York: Basic Books.

Freud, S. (1974). *Cocaine papers* (R. B. Buck, Ed.). New York: Stonehill.

Freud, S. & Bullitt, W. C. (1967). *Thomas Woodrow Wilson: A psychological study.* Boston: Houghton Mifflin.

Freund, K., Langevin, R., Cibiri, S., & Sajac, L. (1973). Heterosexual aversion in homosexual males. *Archives of General Psychiatry, 122,* 168-169.

Friar, L. R., & Beatty, J. (1976). Migraine: Management by trained control of vaso-constriction. *Journal of Consulting and Clinical Psychology, 44,* 46-53.

Friedman, M., & Rosenman, R. H. (1974). *Type A behavior and your heart.* New York:

Alfred A. Knopf.

Fromm, E. (1947). *Man for himself.* New York: Rinehart.

Fromm-Reichmann, F. (1959). Intensive psychotherapy of manic-depressives. In D. M. Bullard (Ed.), *Psychoanalysis and psychotherapy.* Chicago: University of Chicago Press. (a)

Fromm-Reichmann, F. (1959). Psychoanalytic remarks on the clinical significance of hostility. In D. M. Bullard (Ed.), *Psychoanalysis and psychotherapy.* Chicago: University of Chicago Press. (b)

Gagnon, J. H. (1977). *Human sexualities.* Glenview, IL: Scott, Foresman.

Gaitz, C. M., Varner, R. V., & Overall, J. E. (1977). Pharmacotherapy for organic brain syndrome in late life: Evolution of an ergot derivative vs. placebo. *Archives of General Psychiatry, 34,* 839-845.

Gal, P. (1959). Mental disorders of advanced years. *Geriatrics, 14,* 224-228.

Gallup, G. (1977, October 9). Gallup youth survey. *Denver Post.*

Gartell, N. K., Loriaux, D. L., & Chase, T. N. (1977). Plasma testosterone in homosexual and heterosexual women. *American Journal of Psychiatry, 134,* 1117-1118.

Garvey, C. (1977). *Play.* Cambridge, MA: Harvard University Press.

Gaylin, W., Meister, J., & Neville, R. (Eds.). (1975). *Operating on the mind: The psychosurgery conflict.* New York: Basic Books.

Gebhard, P. H., Gagnon, J. H., Pomeroy, W. B., & Christerson, C. V. (1965). *Sex offenders.* New York: Harper & Row.

Geleerd, E. R., Hacker, F. J., & Rapaport, D. (1945). Contributions to the study of amnesia and allied states. *Psychoanalytic Quarterly, 14,* 199-220.

Gero, G. (1962). Sadism, masochism and aggression: Their role in symptom formation. *Psychoanalytic Quarterly, 31,* 31-42.

Gero, G., & Rubenfine, D. L. (1955). Obsessive thoughts. *Journal of the American Psychoanalytic Association, 3,* 222-243.

Geschwind, N. (1975). The borderland of neurology and psychiatry: Some common misconceptions. In D. F. Benson & D. Blumer (Eds.), *Psychiatric aspects of neurological disease.* New York: Grune & Stratton.

Gibson, A. C. (1961). Psychosis occurring in the senium: A review of an industrial population. *Journal of Mental Science, 107,* 921-925.

Gibson, R. W., Cohen, M. B., & Cohen, R. A. (1959). On the dynamics of the manic-depressive personality. *American Journal of Psychiatry, 115,* 1101-1107.

Gifford, S. (1960). Sleep, time and the early ego. *Journal of the American Psychoanalytic Association, 8,* 5-42.

Gifis, S. H. (1975). *Law dictionary.* Woodbury, NY: Barron's Educational Series.

Glueck, S. (1962). *Law and psychiatry.* Baltimore: Johns Hopkins University Press.

Gold, M., & Mann, D. (1972). Delinquency as defense. *American Journal of Orthopsychiatry, 42,* 463-479.

Goldstein, K. (1939). *The organism.* New York: American Book Co.

Goldstein, K. (1948). *Language and language disturbances.* New York: Grune & Stratton.

Gonsiorek, J. C. (1977). Psychological adjustment and homosexuality. *JSAS Catalog of Selected Documents in Psychology, 7,* 1-45.

Goodwin, D. W., Schulsinger, F., Moller, N., Hermansen, L., Winokur, G., & Guze,

S. B. (1974). Drinking problems in adopted and nonadopted sons of alcoholics. *Archives of General Psychiatry, 31,* 164-169.

Goodwin, F. (1974). On the biology of depression. In R. J. Friedman & M. M. Katz (Eds.), *The psychology of depression: Contemporary theory and research.* New York: John Wiley & Sons.

Gorsuch, R. L., & Butler, M. C. (1976). Initial drug abuse: A review of predisposing social psychological factors. *Psychological Bulletin, 83,* 120-137.

Gottesman, I. I., & Shields, J. (1972). *Schizophrenia and genetics.* New York: Academic Press.

Gottschalk, L. A., & Gleser, G. C. (1960). An analysis of the verbal content of suicidal notes. *British Journal of Medical Psychology, 33,* 195-204.

Gottschalk, L. A., Gleser, G. C., Magliocci, E. B., & D'Zmura, T. L. (1961). Further studies on the speech patterns of schizophrenic patients. *Journal of Nervous and Mental Disease, 132,* 101-113.

Grace, W. J., Wolf, S., & Wolff, H. G. (1951). *The human colon.* New York: Hoeber.

Gralnick, A. (1942). Folie à deux: The psychosis of association. *Psychiatric Quarterly, 16,* 230.

Green, A. H., Gaines, R. W., & Sandgrund, A. (1974). Child abuse: Pathological syndrome of family interaction. *American Journal of Psychiatry, 131,* 882-886.

Green, R. (1968). Childhood cross-gender identification. *Journal of Nervous and Mental Disease, 147,* 500-509.

Green, R., & Money, J. (Eds.). (1969). *Transsexualism and sex reassignment.* Baltimore: Johns Hopkins University Press.

Greenson, R. R. (1959). Phobia, anxiety and depression. *Journal of the American Psychoanalytic Association, 7,* 663-674.

Greenspoon, J. (1955). The reinforcing effect of two spoken sounds on the frequency of two responses. *American Journal of Psychology, 68,* 409-416.

Grimshaw, L. (1965). The outcome of obsessional disorder: A follow-up of one hundred cases. *British Journal of Psychiatry, 111,* 1051-1056.

Grinker, R. R. (1953). *Psychosomatic research.* New York: W. W. Norton.

Grinker, R. R., & Robbins, F. P. (1954). *Psychosomatic case book.* New York: Blakiston.

Grinker, R. R., & Spiegel, J. (1945). *Men under stress.* Philadelphia: Blakiston. (a)

Grinker, R. R., & Spiegel, J. (1945). *War neuroses.* Philadelphia: Blakiston. (b)

Grinspoon, L., & Singer, S. B. (1973). Amphetamines in the treatment of hyperactive children. *Harvard Educational Review, 43,* 515-555.

Guggenheim, F. G., & Babigian, H. M. (1974). Catatonic schizophrenia: Epidemiology and clinical course. *Journal of Nervous and Mental Disease, 158,* 291-305.

Guttman, O. (1965). The psychodynamics of a drug addict. *American Journal of Psychotherapy, 19,* 653-665.


Hackett, T. P. (1975). Encounters by women or children with exhibitionists. *Medical Aspects of Human Sexuality, 9,* 139-140.

Hadden, S. B. (1966). Treatment of male homosexuals in groups. *International Journal of Group Psychotherapy, 16,* 13-22.

Haertzen, C. A., Hill, H. E., & Belleville, R. E. (1963). Development of the Addiction Research Center Inventory (ARCI): Selection of items that are sensitive to the effects of various drugs. *Psychopharmacologia, 4,* 155-166.

Haith, M. M. (1980). *Rules that babies look by: The organization of newborn visual activity.* Hillsdale, NJ: Lawrence Erlbaum.

Halikas, J. A., & Rimmer, J. D. (1974). Predictors of multiple drug abuse. *Archives of General Psychiatry, 31,* 414-418.

Hamlin, R. M., & Lorr, M. (1971). Differentiation of normals, neurotics, paranoids, and nonparanoids. *Journal of Abnormal Psychology, 77,* 90-96.

Harlow, H. (1971). *Learning to love.* New York: Ballantine Books.

Harris, T. G. (1973). As far as heroin is concerned, the worst is over. *Psychology Today, 7,* 68-79.

Hartmann, H. (1958). *Ego psychology and the problem of adaptation.* New York: International Universities Press.

Hartmann, H. (1964). *Essays on ego psychology: Selected problems in psychoanalytic theory.* New York: International Universities Press.

Heath, R. G. (1960). A biological hypothesis on the etiology of schizophrenia. In D. D. Jackson (Ed.), *The etiology of schizophrenia.* New York: Basic Books.

Heath, R. G., Guschwan, A. F., & Coffey, J. W. (1970). Relation of taraxein to schizophrenia. *Diseases of the Nervous System, 31,* 391-395.

Heath, R. G., & Krupp, I. M. (1967). Schizophrenia as an immunologic disorder. *Archives of General Psychiatry, 16,* 1-33.

Hecaen, H., & Albert, M. L. (1975). Disorders of mental functioning related to frontal lobe pathology. In D. F. Benson & D. Blumer (Eds.), *Psychiatric aspects of neurological disease.* New York: Grune & Stratton.

Hefferline, R. F., & Keenan, B. (1963). Amplitude-induction gradient of a small-scale (covert) operant. *Journal of Experimental Analysis of Behavior, 6,* 307-315.

Hefferline, R. F., Keenan, B., & Harford, R. A. (1959). Escape and avoidance conditioning in human subjects without their observation of the response. *Science, 130,* 1338-1339.

Henrichsen, J. J., & Katahn, M. (1975). Recent trends and new developments in the treatment of homosexuality. *Psychotherapy: Theory, Research, and Practice, 12,* 83-92.

Heron, W. (1957). The pathology of boredom. *Scientific American, 196,* 52-56.

Herschkowitz, S., & Dickes, R. (1978). Suicide attempts in a female-to-male transsexual. *American Journal of Psychiatry, 135,* 368-369.

Hesselbach, C. F. (1962). Superego regression in paranoia. *Psychoanalytic Quarterly, 31,* 341-350.

Heston, L. L. (1966). Psychiatric disorders in foster-home reared children of schizophrenic mothers. *British Journal of Psychiatry, 112,* 819-825.

Hetherington, E. M. (1972). Effects of father-absence on personality development in adolescent daughters. *Developmental Psychology, 7,* 313-326.

Hicks, D. (1965). Imitation and retention of film mediated aggressive peer and adult models. *Journal of Personality and Social Psychology, 2,* 97-100.

Hilgard, E. R. (1977). *Divided consciousness: Multiple controls in human thought and action.* New York: Wiley-Interscience.

Hilgard, J. R., & Newman, M. F. (1961). Evidence for functional genesis in mental illness: Schizophrenia, depressive psychoses, and psychoneuroses. *Journal of Nervous and Mental Disease, 132,* 3-16.

Hodgson, R. J., & Rachman, S. (1972). The effects of contamination and washing in obsessional patients. *Behavioral Research and Therapy, 10,* 111-117.

Hoffer, W. (1950). Development of the body ego. *The psychoanalytic study of the child* (Vol. 5). New York: International Universities Press.

Hogan, D. R. (1978). The effectiveness of sex therapy: A review of the literature. In J. Lopiccolo & L. Lopiccolo (Eds.), *Handbook of sex therapy.* New York: Plenum.

Holden, C. (1973). Psychosurgery: Legitimate therapy or laundered lobotomy? *Science, 179,* 1109-1112.

Hollander, R. (1960). Compulsive swearing. *Psychiatric Quarterly, 34,* 599-622.

Hollingshead, A. B., & Redlich, F. C. (1958). *Social class and mental illness: A community study.* New York: John Wiley & Sons.

Honigfeld, G., & Howard, A. (1973). *Psychiatric drugs: A desk reference.* New York: Academic Press.

Hooker, E. A. (1957). The adjustment of the male overt homosexual. *Journal of Projective Techniques, 21,* 18-21.

Horney, K. (1925). The flight from womanhood. *International Journal of Psycho-Analysis, 7,* 324-339.

Horney, K. (1939). *New ways in psychoanalysis.* New York: W. W. Norton.

Horney, K. (1945). *Our inner conflicts.* New York: W. W. Norton.

Hospers, J. (1961). Free will and psychoanalysis. In H. Morris (Ed.), *Freedom and responsibility.* Stanford, CA: Stanford University Press.

Hraba, J., & Grant, G. (1970). Black is beautiful: A reexamination of racial preference and identification. *Journal of Personality and Social Psychology, 16,* 398-402.

Hull, C. L. (1943). *Principles of behavior.* New York: Appleton-Century-Crofts.

Hull, C. L. (1952). *A behavior system.* New Haven, CT: Yale University Press.

Hutt, C., & Bhavnani, R. (1972). Predictions from play. *Nature, 237,* 171-172.

Immergluck, L. (1964). Determinism-freedom in contemporary psychology. An ancient problem revisited. *American Psychologist, 19,* 270-281.

Isakower, O. (1938). A contribution to the pathopsychology of phenomena associated with falling asleep. *International Journal of Psycho-Analysis, 19,* 331-345.

Ittelson, W. H., Seidenberg, B., & Kutash, S. B. (1961). Some perceptual differences in somatizing and nonsomatizing neuropsychiatric patients. *Psychosomatic Medicine, 23,* 219-223.

Jacobs, T. (1975). Family interaction in disturbed and normal families: A methodological and substantive review. *Psychological Bulletin, 82,* 33-65.

Jacobson, E. (1938). *Progressive relaxation.* Chicago: University of Chicago Press.

Jacobson, E. (1953). The affects and their pleasure-unpleasure qualities in relation to the psychic discharge process. In R. M. Loewenstein (Ed.), *Drives, affects, behavior.* New York: International Universities Press. (a)

Jacobson, E. (1953). Contribution to the metapsychology of cyclothymic depression. In P. Greenacre (Ed.), *Affective disorders.* New York: International Universities Press. (b)

Jacobson, E. (1954). Contributions to the metapsychology of psychotic identification. *Journal of the American Psychoanalytic Association, 2,* 239-262.

Jacobson, E. (1957). Denial and repression. *Journal of the American Psychoanalytic Association, 5,* 61-92.

Jacobson, E. (1959). Depersonalization. *Journal of the American Psychoanalytic Association, 7,* 581-610.

James, W. (1952). *The principles of psychology.* In R. M. Hutchins (Ed.), *Great books of the Western world* (Vol. 53). Chicago: Encyclopaedia Britannica.

Janet, P. (1920). *The major symptoms of hysteria* (2nd ed.). New York: Macmillan.

Janis, I. (1958). *Psychological stress.* New York: John Wiley & Sons.

Jaques, E. (1965). Death and the mid-life crisis. *International Journal of Psycho-Analysis, 46,* 502-514.

Jenkins, R. L. (1968). The varieties of children's behavioral problems and family dynamics. *American Journal of Psychiatry, 124,* 1440-1445.

Jenner, F. A., Gjessing, L. R., Cox, J. R., Davies-Jones, A., & Hullin, R. P. (1967). A manic-depressive psychotic with a 48 hour cycle. *British Journal of Psychiatry, 113,* 859-910.

Jessor, S., & Jessor, R. (1975). Transition from virginity to non-virginity among youth: A social-psychological study over time. *Developmental Psychology, 11,* 473-484.

Jones, E. (1927). Early development of female homosexuality. *International Journal of Psycho-Analysis, 8,* 459-472.

Jones, E. (1938). *Papers on psychoanalysis.* London: Ballière, Tindall & Cox.

Jones, E. (1953). *The life and work of Sigmund Freud* (Vol. 1): *The formative years and the great discoveries, 1856-1900.* New York: Basic Books.

Jones, E. (1955). *The life and work of Sigmund Freud* (Vol. 2): *Years of maturity, 1901-1919.* New York: Basic Books.

Jones, K. L., Shainberg, L. W., & Byer, C. O. (1973). *Drugs and alcohol* (2nd ed.). New York: Harper & Row.

Jones, K. L., Shainberg, L. W., & Byer, C. O. (1977). *Sex and people.* New York: Harper & Row.

Josselson, R. (1980). Ego development in adolescence. In J. Adelson (Ed.), *Handbook of adolescent psychology.* New York: Wiley-Interscience.

Jucovy, M. E. (1976). Initiation fantasies and transvestism. *Journal of the American Psychoanalytic Association, 24,* 525-545.

Jung, C. G. (1961). *Freud and psychoanalysis.* In H. Read, M. Fordham, & G. Adler (Eds.), *The collected works of C. G. Jung* (Vol. 4). Bollingen Series XX. New York: Pantheon Books.

Jung, C. G. (1964). *Civilization in transition.* In H. Read, M. Fordham, & G. Adler (Eds.), *The collected works of C. G. Jung* (Vol. 10). Bollingen Series XX. New York: Pantheon Books.

Kadushin, A. (1967). Reversibility of trauma: A follow-up study of children adopted when older. *Social Work, 12,* 22-23.

Kadushin, L., & Kadushin, A. (1969). The ex-addict as a member of the therapeutic team. *Community Mental Health Journal, 5,* 386-393.

Kagan, J. (1967). The growth of the face schema: Theoretical significance and methodological issues. In J. Hellmuth (Ed.), *The exceptional infant* (Vol. I): *The normal infant.* New York: Bruner/Mazel.

Kahlbaum, K. L. (1882). *Uber syklisches Irresein, Irrenfreund.* Berlin: Springer.

Kalinowski, L. B., & Hippius, H. (1969). *Pharmacological convulsive and other somatic treatments in psychiatry.* New York: Grune & Stratton.

Kalis, B. L., Harris, R. E., Bennett, L. F., & Sokolow, M. (1961). Personality and life history factors in persons who are potentially hypertensive. *Journal of Nervous and Mental Disease, 132,* 457-468.

Kallmann, F. J. (1952). Twin and sibship study of overt male homosexuality. *American Journal of Human Genetics, 4,* 136-146.

Kallmann, F. J. (1953). *Heredity in health and mental disorder.* New York: W. W. Norton.

Kallmann, F. J. (1958). The use of genetics in psychiatry. *Journal of Mental Science, 104,* 542-549.

Kanfer, F. H., & Phillips, J. S. (1970). *Learning foundations of behavior therapy.* New York: John Wiley & Sons.

Kanfer, F. H., & Saslow, G. (1969). Behavioral diagnosis. In C. M. Franks (Ed.), *Behavior therapy: Appraisal and status.* New York: McGraw-Hill.

Kanner, L. (1943). Autistic disturbances of affective contact. *Nervous Child, 2,* 217-226.

Kanner, L. (1944). Early infantile autism. *Journal of Pediatrics, 25,* 211-217.

Kaplan, H. S. (1974). *The new sex therapy: Active treatment of sexual dysfunctions.* New York: Times Books, Quadrangle.

Karlen, A. (1971). *Sexuality and homosexuality.* New York: W. W. Norton.

Karlssom, J. D. (1968). Genealogic studies of schizophrenia. In D. Rosenthal & S. Kety (Eds.), *The transmission of schizophrenia.* New York: Pergamon Press.

Katan, M. (1953). Mania and the pleasure principle. In P. Greenacre (Ed.), *Affective disorders.* New York: International Universities Press.

Katchadourian, H. A., & Lunde, D. T. (1975). *Fundamentals of human sexuality* (2nd ed.). New York: Holt, Rinehart and Winston.

Kaufman, A., Baron, A., & Kopp, R. E. (1966). Some effects of instruction on human operant behavior. *Psychonomic Monograph Supplements, 1,* 243-250.

Kaufman, I., Frank, T., Heims, L., Herrick, J., Reiser, D., & Willer, L. (1960). Treatment implications of a new classification of parents of schizophrenic children. *American Journal of Psychiatry, 116,* 920-924.

Kelly, D. H., & Walters, C. J. S. (1968). The relationship between chemical diagnosis and anxiety, assessed by forearm blood flow and other measurements. *British Journal of Psychiatry, 112,* 789-798

Kelly, D. H., & Walters, C. J. S. (1969). The clinical and physiological relationship between anxiety and depression. *British Journal of Psychiatry, 115,* 401-406.

Kelly, G. A. (1955). *The psychology of personal constructs* (Vol. 1): *A theory of personality.* New York: W. W. Norton.

Kernberg, O. F. (1970). A psychoanalytic classification of character pathology. *Journal of the American Psychoanalytic Association, 18,* 800-822.

Kernberg, O. F. (1975). *Borderline conditions and pathological narcissism.* New York: Jason Aronson.

Kessen, W., Williams, E. J., & Williams, J. P. (1961). Selection and test of response measures in the study of the human newborn. *Child Development, 32,* 7-24.

Kestenberg, J. S. (1961). Menarche. In S. Lorand & H. I. Scheer (Eds.), *Adolescents.* New York: Hoeber.

Kety, S. S. (1967). Current biochemical approaches to schizophrenia. *New England Journal of Medicine, 276,* 325-331.

Kilpatrick, D. G., Sutker, P. B., & Smith, A. D. (1976). Deviant drug and alcohol use:

The role of anxiety, sensation seeking, and other personality variables. In M. Zuckerman & C. D. Spielberger (Eds.), *Emotions and anxiety: New concepts, methods and applications.* New York: John Wiley & Sons.

Kinsey, A. C., Pomeroy, W. B., & Martin, C. E. (1948). *Sexual behavior in the human male.* Philadelphia: W. B. Saunders.

Kinsey, A. C., Pomeroy, W. B., Martin, C. E., & Gebhard, P. H. (1953). *Sexual behavior in the human female.* Philadelphia: W. B. Saunders.

Klaf, S. F. (1961). Evidence of paranoid ideation in overt homosexuals. *Journal of Social Therapy, 7,* 48-51. (a)

Klaf, S. F. (1961). Female homosexuality and paranoid schizophrenia: Survey of seventy-five cases and controls. *Archives of General Psychiatry, 4,* 84-86. (b)

Klaf, S. F., & Hamilton, J. G. (1961). Schizophrenia: A hundred years ago and today. *Journal of Mental Science, 107,* 819-827.

Klein, M. (1948). *Contributions to psychoanalysis.* London: Hogarth Press.

Klein, M. (1950). A contribution to the psychogenesis of manic-depressive states. In M. Klein (Ed.), *Contributions to Psychoanalysis.* London: Hogarth Press.

Knight, R. A., Roff, J. D., Barnett, J., & Moss, J. L. (1979). Concurrent and predictive validity of thought disorder and affectivity: A 22-year follow-up of acute schizophrenics. *Journal of Abnormal Psychology, 88,* 1-12.

Knight, R. C., & Prout, C. T. (1951). A study of results in hospital treatment of drug addicts. *American Journal of Psychiatry, 108,* 303-308.

Knight, R. P. (1953). Borderline states. *Bulletin of the Menninger Clinic, 17,* 1-12.

Kobasa, S. C. (1979). Stressful life events, personality, and health: An inquiry into hardiness. *Journal of Personality and Social Psychology, 37,* 1-11.

Koch, J. L. (1891). *Die psychopathischen minderwertigkeiten.* Ravensburg: Maier.

Kohlberg, L. (1976). Moral stages and moralization: The cognitive-developmental approach. In T. Likona (Ed.), *Moral development and behavior.* New York: Holt, Rinehart, and Winston.

Kohn, P. M., Barnes, G. E., & Hoffman, F. M. (1979). Drug use history and experience seeking among adult male correctional inmates. *Journal of Consulting and Clinical Psychology, 47,* 708-715.

Kohut, H. (1966). Forms and transformations of narcissism. *Journal of the American Psychoanalytic Association, 14,* 243-272.

Kohut, H. (1971). *The analysis of the self.* New York: International Universities Press.

Kolata, G. B. (1979). Mental disorders: A new approach to treatment? *Science, 203,* 36-38.

Kotelchuck, M., Zelanzo, P., Kagan, J., & Spelke, E. (1975). Infant reaction to parental separations when left with familiar and unfamiliar adults. *Journal of Genetic Psychology, 126,* 255-262.

Kraepelin, E. (1919). *Dementia praecox and paraphrenia.* Edinburgh: Livingstone.

Kraepelin, E. (1921). *Manic-depressive insanity and paranoia.* Edinburgh: Livingstone.

Kreitman, N., Pearce, K. I., & Ryle, A. (1966). The relationship of psychiatric, psycho-somatic, and organic illness in a general practice. *British Journal of Psychiatry, 112,* 569-579.

Kretschmer, E. (1925). *Physique and character.* London: Kegan Paul.

Kringlen, E. (1967). *Heredity and environment in the functional psychosis: An epidemiological-clinical twin study.* Oslo: Universitsforlaget.

Kris, E. (1950). On preconscious mental processes. *Psychoanalytic Quarterly, 19,* 540-560.

Krugman, S., & Ward, R. (1973). *Infectious diseases of children and adults.* St. Louis: C. V. Mosby.

Lader, M. H. (1975). *The psychophysiology of mental illness.* London: Routledge & Kegan Paul.

Lader, M. H., & Sartorius, N. (1968). Anxiety in patients with hysterical conversion symptoms. *Journal of Neurology, Neurosurgery, and Psychiatry, 31,* 490-497.

Lader, M. H., & Wing, L. (1966). *Physiological measures, sedative drugs, and morbid anxiety.* London: Oxford University Press.

LaFave, W. R. (1978). *Modern criminal law: Cases, comments, and questions.* St. Paul, MN: West.

Laing, R. D. (1969). *The divided self.* New York: Pantheon Books.

Lamb, M. E. (1977). Father-infant and mother-infant interaction in the first year of life. *Child Development, 48,* 167-181.

Lamy, R. E. (1966). Social consequences of mental illness. *Journal of Consulting Psychology, 30,* 450-455.

Landesman-Dwyer, S., Keller, S. L., & Streissguth, A. P. (1977). Naturalistic observations of newborns: Effects of maternal alcohol intake. Paper presented at the Eighty-fifth Annual Convention of the American Psychological Association, San Francisco.

Landis, C., & Erlick, D. (1950). An analysis of the Proteus maze test as affected by psychosurgery. *American Journal of Psychology, 63,* 557-563.

Landman, J. T., & Dawes, R. M. (1982). Psychotherapy outcome: Smith and Glass' conclusions stand up under scrutiny. *American Psychologist, 37,* 504-516.

Langevin, R., Stanford, A., & Block, R. (1975). The effect of relaxation instructions on erotic arousal in homosexual and heterosexual males. *Behavior Therapy, 6,* 453-458.

Lansky, L. M., Crandall, V. J., Kagan, J., & Baker, C. T. (1961). Sex differences in aggression and its correlates in middle-class adolescents. *Child Development, 32,* 45-58.

Laskowitz, D. (1962). Wechsler-Bellevue performance of adolescent heroin addicts. *Journal of Psychological Studies, 13,* 49-59.

Laughlin, H. P. (1965). *The neurosis of clinical practice.* Philadelphia: W. B. Saunders.

Lazarus, R. S., & Launier, R. (1979). Stress-related transactions between person and environment. In L. A. Pervin & M. Lewis (Eds.), *Internal and external determinants of behavior.* New York: Plenum.

Lefcourt, H. M. (1973). The function of the illusions of control and freedom. *American Psychologist, 28,* 417-425.

Lehman, H. E. (1963). Phenomenology and pathology of addiction. *Comprehensive Psychiatry, 4,* 168-180.

Lemon, N., & Warren, N. (1974). Salience, centrality and self-relevance of traits in construing others. *British Journal of Social and Clinical Psychology, 13,* 119-124.

Leonard, C. V. (1974). Depression and suicidality. *Journal of Consulting and Clinical Psychology, 42,* 98-104.

Lerner, R. M., & Lerner, J. (1977). Effects of age, sex and physical attractiveness on child-peer relations, academic performance, and elementary school adjustment.

*Developmental Psychology, 13,* 585-590.

Levin, M. (1959). Toxic psychoses. In S. Arieti (Ed.), *American handbook of psychiatry.* New York: Basic Books.

Levit, E. E. (1972). A brief commentary on the "psychiatric breakthrough" with emphasis on the hematology of anxiety. In C. D. Spielberger (Ed.), *Anxiety: Current trends in theory and research* (Vol. I). New York: Academic Press.

Levy, S. M. (1976). Schizophrenic symptomatology: Reaction or strategy? A study of contextual antecedents. *Journal of Abnormal Psychology, 85,* 435-445.

Lewin, B. D. (1950). *The psychoanalysis of elation.* New York: W. W. Norton.

Lewin, B. D. (1952). Phobic symptoms and dream interpretation. *Psychoanalytic Quarterly, 21,* 295-322.

Lewin, B. D. (1954). Sleep, narcissistic neurosis and the analytic situation. *Psychoanalytic Quarterly, 23,* 487-510.

Lewin, B. D. (1959). Some psychoanalytic ideas applied to elation and depression. *American Journal of Psychiatry, 116,* 38-43.

Lewis, N. D. C. (1956). Mental hygiene in later maturity. In O. Kaplan (Ed.), *Mental disorders in later life* (2nd ed.). Stanford, CA: Stanford University Press.

Lichtenberg, J. D. (1959). Theoretical and practical considerations of the management of the manic phase of the manic-depressive psychosis. *Journal of Nervous and Mental Disorders, 129,* 243-281.

Lidz, R. W., & Lidz, T. (1949). The family environment of schizophrenic patients. *American Journal of Psychiatry, 106,* 332-345.

Lidz, T. (1959). General concepts of psychosomatic medicine. In S. Arieti (Ed.), *American handbook of psychiatry.* New York: Basic Books.

Lidz, T. (1978). Egocentric regression and the family setting of schizophrenic disorders. In L. C. Wynne, R. L. Cromwell, & S. Matthysee (Eds.), *The nature of schizophrenia: New approaches to research and treatment.* New York: John Wiley & Sons.

Lidz, T., Fleck, S., & Cornelison, A. R. (1965). *Schizophrenia and the family.* New York: International Universities Press.

Lidz, T., & Rubenstein, R. (1959). Psychology of gastrointestinal disorders. In S. Arieti (Ed.), *American handbook of psychiatry.* New York: Basic Books.

Liem, J. H. (1974). Effects of verbal communications of parents and children: A comparison of normal and schizophrenic families. *Journal of Consulting and Clinical Psychology, 42,* 438-450.

Lipsitt, L. P., Kaye, H., & Bosack, T. N. (1966). Enhancement of neonatal sucking through reinforcement. *Journal of Experimental Child Psychology, 4,* 163-168.

Littin, E. M., Giffin, M. E., & Johnson, A. M. (1956). Parental influence in unusual sexual behavior in children. *Psychoanalytic Quarterly, 25,* 37-55.

Loewald, H. W. (1962). Internalization, separation, mourning and the superego. *Psychoanalytic Quarterly, 31,* 483-504.

Lorand, S. (1930). Fetishism in statu nascendi. *International Journal of Psycho-Analysis, 11,* 419-427.

Lorenz, K. (1952). *King Solomon's ring.* London: Methuen.

Lorenz, K. (1957). The nature of instincts. In C. Schiller (Ed.), *Instinctive behavior.* New York: International Universities Press.

Lorenz, M. (1953). Language behavior in manic patients: An evaluative study. *Archives of Neurological Psychology, 69,* 14-26.

Lorenz, M., & Cobb, L. (1952). Language behavior in manic patients. *Archives of Neurological Psychology, 67,* 763-770.

Lothrop, W. W. (1961). A critical review of research on the conceptual thinking of schizophrenics. *Journal of Nervous and Mental Disease, 132,* 118-126.

Louch, A. R. (1965). Scientific discovery and legal change. *The Monist, 49,* 485-503.

Lucas, C. J., Sansbury, P., & Collins, J. G. (1962). A social and clinical study of delusions in schizophrenia. *Journal of Mental Science, 108,* 747-758.

Mächtlinger, V. J. (1976). Psychoanalytic theory: Pre-Oedipal and Oedipal phases with special reference to the father. In M. E. Lamb (Ed.), *The role of the father in child development.* New York: Wiley-Interscience.

MacKinnon, R. A., & Michels, R. (1971). *The psychiatric interview in clinical practice.* Philadelphia: W. B. Saunders.

Maddi, S. R. (1961). Affective tone during experimental regularity and change. *Journal of Abnormal and Social Psychology, 62,* 338-345.

Mahler, M. S. (1952). On childhood psychosis and schizophrenia. Autistic and symbiotic infantile psychosis. *The psychoanalytic study of the child* (Vol. 7). New York: International Universities Press.

Main, M. (1973). *Exploration, play and level of cognitive functioning as related to child-mother attachment.* Unpublished doctoral dissertation, Johns Hopkins University.

Malamud, N. (1975). Organic brain disease mistaken for psychiatric disorder: A clinico-pathologic study. In D. F. Benson & D. Blumer (Eds.), *Psychiatric aspects of neurological disease.* New York: Grune & Stratton.

Manosevitz, M. (1970). Early sexual behavior in adult homosexual and heterosexual males. *Journal of Abnormal Psychology, 76,* 396-402.

Marcia, J. E. (1980). Identity in adolescence. In J. Adelson (Ed.), *Handbook of adolescent psychology.* New York: Wiley-Interscience.

Mark, V. H., & Ervin, E. P. (1970). *Violence and the brain.* New York: Harper & Row.

Marks, I. M. (1977). Behavioral psychotherapy of adult neurosis. In S. L. Garfield & A. E. Bergin (Eds.), *Psychopathology: Experimental models.* San Francisco: W. H. Freeman.

Marks, I. M., & Gelder, M. G. (1966). Different onset ages in varieties of phobias. *American Journal of Psychiatry, 123,* 218-221.

Marlatt, G. A., Demming, B., & Reid, J. (1973). Loss of control drinking in alcoholics: An experimental analogue. *Journal of Abnormal Psychology, 81,* 233-241.

Marmor, J. (1971). Homosexuality in males. *Psychiatric Annals, 4,* 45-59.

Marmor, J. (1973). Homosexuality and cultural value systems. *American Journal of Psychiatry, 130,* 1208-1209.

Marquis, D. P. (1931). Can conditioned responses be established in the newborn infant? *Journal of Genetic Psychology, 39,* 479-492.

Marquis, J. N. (1970). Orgasmic reconditioning: Changing sexual object choice through controlling masturbation fantasies. *Journal of Behavior Therapy and Experimental Psychiatry, 1,* 263-272.

Marshall, W. L. (1973). The modification of sexual fantasies: A combined treatment approach to the reduction of deviant sexual behavior. *Behavior Research and Therapy, 11,* 557-564.

Martin, H. (1976). *The abused child.* Cambridge, MA: Ballinger.

Maslow, A. H. (1968). *Toward a psychology of being* (2nd ed.). Princeton: Van Nostrand.

Maslow, A. H. (1970). *Motivation and personality* (2nd ed.). New York: Harper.

Masters, W. H. & Johnson, V. E. (1966). *Human sexual response.* Boston: Little, Brown.

Masters, W. H., & Johnson, V. E. (1979). *Homosexuality in perspective.* Boston: Little, Brown.

Masterson, J. F. (1967). *The psychiatric dilemma of adolescence.* Boston: Little, Brown.

Mathe, A. A., & Knapp, P. H. (1977). Emotional and adrenal reactors to stress in bronchial asthma. *Psychosomatic Medicine, 33,* 323-327.

Maxmen, J. S., Silberfarb, P. M., & Ferrell, R. B. (1974). Anorexia nervosa: Practical initial management in a general hospital. *Journal of the American Medical Association, 229,* 801-803.

May, J. R. (1977). Psychophysiology of self-regulated phobic thoughts. *Behavior Therapy, 8,* 150-159.

May, P. R. A. (1968). *Treatment of schizophrenia: A comparative study of five treatment methods.* New York: Science House.

May, R. (1950). *The meaning of anxiety.* New York: Ronald Press.

Mayerson, P., & Lief, H. I. (1965). Psychotherapy of homosexuals: A follow-up study of nineteen cases. In J. Marmor (Ed.), *Sexual inversion.* New York: Basic Books.

McClelland, D., Davis, W., Kalin, R., & Wanner, E. (1972). *The drinking man.* New York: Free Press.

McGuire, W. (Ed.). (1974). *The Freud/Jung letters.* Bollingen Series XCIV. Princeton, NJ: Princeton University Press.

McNamee, H. B., Mellow, N. K., & Mendelson, J. H. (1968). Experimental analysis of drinking patterns of alcoholics: Concurrent psychiatric observations. *American Journal of Psychiatry, 124,* 1063-1069.

Meissner, W. W. (1978). *The paranoid process.* New York: Jason Aronson.

Mendels, J. (1970). *Concepts of depression.* New York: John Wiley & Sons.

Menninger, K. (1940). Character disorders. In J. F. Brown (Ed.), *The psychodynamics of abnormal behavior.* New York: McGraw-Hill.

Menninger, K. (1966). *The crime of punishment.* New York: Viking Press.

Meredith, H. V. (1975). Somatic changes during prenatal life. *Child Development, 46,* 603-610.

Miller, N. E. (1978). Biofeedback and visceral learning. *Annual Review of Psychology* (Vol. 29). Palo Alto, CA: Annual Reviews.

Miller, N. E., Barber, T. X, DiCara, L., Kamiya, J., Shapiro, D., & Stoyva, J. (Eds.). (1974). *Biofeedback and self-control.* Chicago: Aldine.

Miller, P. M. (1976). *Behavioral treatment of alcoholism.* New York: Pergamon Press.

Miller, P. Y., & Simon, W. (1980). The development of sexuality in adolescence. In J. Adelson (Ed.), *Handbook of adolescent psychology.* New York: John Wiley & Sons.

Millon, T. (1969). *Modern psychopathology: A biosocial approach to maladaptive learning and functioning.* Philadelphia: W. B. Saunders.

Millon, T. (1981). *Disorders of personality: DSM-III: Axis II.* New York: Wiley-Interscience.

Mirsky, I. H. (1953). Psychoanalysis and the biological sciences. In F. Alexander & H. Ross (Eds.), *Twenty years of psychoanalysis.* New York: W. W. Norton.

Mishler, E. G., & Waxler, N. E. (1968). *Interaction in families: An experimental study of family processes and schizophrenia.* New York: John Wiley & Sons.

*Monitor.* (1974, April). Vol. 5, No. 4. Washington, DC: American Psychological Association.

Monsour, K. J. (1961). School phobia in teachers. *American Journal of Orthopsychiatry, 31,* 347-355.

Moore, S. G. (1967). Correlates of peer acceptance in nursery school children. In W. W. Hartup & N. L. Smothergill (Eds.), *The young child.* Washington, DC: National Association for the Education of Young Children.

Mordkoff, A. M., & Parsons, O. A. (1967). The coronary personality: A critique. *Psychosomatic Medicine, 29,* 1-14.

Moriarty, D. M. (1961). Observations of the superego in a schizophrenic patient. *Psychoanalysis and Psychoanalytical Review, 48,* 3-18.

Morrison, J. R. (1973). Catatonia: Retarded and excited types. *Archives of General Psychiatry, 28,* 39-41.

Mowrer, O. H. (1939). A stimulus-response analysis of anxiety and its role as a reinforcing agent. *Psychological Review, 46,* 553-566.

Mowrer, O. H. (1948). Learning theory and the neurotic paradox. *American Journal of Orthopsychiatry, 18,* 571-610.

Mucha, T. F., & Reinhardt, R. F. (1970). Conversion reactions in student aviators. *American Journal of Psychiatry, 127,* 493-497.

Munjack, D. J., & Staples, F. R. (1977). Psychological characteristics of women with sexual inhibition (frigidity) in sex clinics. *Journal of Nervous and Mental Disease, 163,* 117-129.

Mussen, P. (1979). *The psychological development of the child* (3rd ed.). Englewood Cliffs, NJ: Prentice-Hall.


Nathan, P. E., Zare, N., Simpson, H. F., & Andberg, M. M. (1969). A systems analytic model of diagnosis: I. The diagnostic validity of abnormal psychomotor behavior. *Journal of Clinical Psychology, 25,* 3-9.

Neisser, U. (1967). *Cognitive psychology.* New York: Appleton-Century-Crofts.

Nelson, K. (1974). Concept, word, and sentence: Interrelations in acquisition and development. *Psychological Review, 81,* 267-285.

Newman, L. E., & Stoller, R. J. (1974). Nontranssexual men who seek sex reassignment. *American Journal of Psychiatry, 131,* 437-441.

Newsom, J. (1977). An intersubjective approach to the systematic description of mother-infant interaction. In H. R. Schaffer (Ed.), *Infant interaction.* London: Academic Press.

Noyes, A. P., & Kolb, L. C. (1958). *Modern clinical psychiatry* (5th ed.). Philadelphia: W. B. Saunders.

Nunberg, H., & Federn, E. (Eds.). (1962). *Minutes of the Vienna psycho-analytic society: 1906-1908* (Vol. I). New York: International Universities Press.


Offer, D., & Offer, J. F. (1975). *From teenage to young manhood.* New York: Basic Books.

Ostow, M. (1960). The psychic function of depression. *Psychoanalytic Quarterly, 29,* 355-394.

Page, M. M. (1972). Demand characteristics and the verbal operant conditioning experiment. *Journal of Personality and Social Psychology, 23,* 372-378.

Page, M. M. (1974). Demand characteristics and the classical conditioning of attitudes experiment. *Journal of Personality and Social Psychology, 30,* 468-476.

Papousek, H. (1967). Conditioning during early postnatal development. In Y. Brackbill & G. G. Thompson (Eds.), *Behavior in infancy and early childhood.* New York: Free Press. (a)

Papousek, H. (1967). Experimental studies of appetitional behavior in newborns and infants. In H. W. Stevenson, E. H. Hess, & H. L. Rheingold (Eds.), *Early behavior.* New York: John Wiley & Sons. (b)

Paul, G. L., Tobias, L. L., & Holly, B. L. (1972). Maintenance psychotropic drugs in the presence of active treatment programs. *Archives of General Psychiatry, 27,* 106-115.

Paul, W. (1981). Social and cultural evidence on homosexuality as a social issue. Paper presented at the Eighty-ninth Annual Convention of the American Psychological Association, Los Angeles.

Pavlov, I. P. (1927). *Conditioned reflexes.* (G. V. Anrap, Trans.). London: Oxford University Press.

Paykel, E. S. (1973). Life events and acute depression. In J. P. Scott & E. C. Senay (Eds.), *Separation and depression.* Washington, DC: American Association for the Advancement of Science.

Payne, R. W. (1961). Cognitive abnormalities. In H. J. Eysenck (Ed.), *Handbook of abnormal psychology.* New York: Basic Books.

Payne, R. W., Mattussek, P., & George, E. I. (1959). An experimental study of schizophrenic thought disorder. *Journal of Mental Science, 105,* 627-652.

Pemberton, D. A., & Benady, D. R. (1973). Consciously rejected children. *British Journal of Psychiatry, 123,* 575-578.

Penfield, W. (1975). *The mystery of the mind.* Princeton, NJ: Princeton University Press.

Pepitone, E. A. (1972). Comparison behavior in elementary school children. *American Educational Research Journal, 9,* 45-63.

Perry, J. C., & Klerman, G. L. (1978). The borderline patient. *Archives of General Psychiatry, 35,* 141-150.

Petersen, R. C. (Ed.). (1980). *Marijuana research findings: 1980.* NIDA Research Monograph 31. Washington, DC: U.S. Government Printing Office.

Peto, A. (1955). On the so-called "depersonalization." *International Journal of Psycho-Analysis, 36,* 375-378.

Pflanz, M. (1971). Epidemiological and sociocultural factors in the etiology of duodenal ulcers. *Advances in Psychosomatic Medicine, 6,* 121-151.

Phillips, A. E., & Cay, E. L. (1972). Psychiatric symptoms and personality traits in patients suffering from gastro-intestinal illness. *Journal of Psychosomatic Research, 16,* 47-51.

Phillips, L., & Zigler, E. (1961). Social competence: The action-thought parameter and vicariousness in normal and pathological behavior. *Journal of Abnormal and Social Psychology, 43,* 137-146.

Piaget, J. (1932). *Language and thought in the child* (M. Gabain, Trans.). London: Kegan Paul, Trench, Trubner.

Piaget, J. (1954). *The origins of intelligence in children.* New York: International Universities Press.

Piaget, J. (1956). *Construction of reality in the child.* New York: Basic Books.

Piaget, J. (1965). *The moral judgment of the child.* New York: Free Press.

Piaget, J. (1967). *Six psychological studies.* New York: Random House.

Piaget, J. (1970). *Structuralism.* New York: Harper & Row.

Piaget, J., & Inhelder, B. (1967). *The child's conception of space.* New York: W. W. Norton.

Pious, W. L. (1961). A hypothesis about the nature of schizophrenic behavior. In A. Burton (Ed.), *Psychotherapy of the psychoses.* New York: Basic Books.

Plato. (1952). *Gorgias.* In R. M. Hutchins (Ed.), *Great books of the Western world* (Vol. 7). Chicago: Encyclopaedia Britannica.

Pollak, J. M. (1979). Obsessive-compulsive personality: A review. *Psychological Bulletin, 86,* 225-241.

Pollitt, J. D. (1960). Natural history studies in mental illness: A discussion based on a pilot study of obsessional states. *Journal of Mental Science, 106,* 93-113.

Popper, K. R., & Eccles, J. C. (1977). *The self and its brain.* New York: Springer Verlag.

Prince, M. (1906). *Dissociation of a personality.* New York: Longmans, Green.

Professional Staff of the U.S.-U.K. Cross-National Project. (1974). The diagnosis and psychopathology of schizophrenia in New York and London. *Schizophrenia Bulletin, 11,* 80-102.

Pugatch, D. (1971). Manic-depressive psychosis. In P. Solomon & V. D. Patch (Eds.), *Handbook of psychiatry* (2nd ed.). Los Angeles: Lange Medical Publications.

Pulver, S. E., & Brunt, M. Y. (1961). Deflection of hostility in folie à deux. *Archives of General Psychiatry, 5,* 257-265.

Rachmann, S., & Costello, C. G. (1961). The aetiology and treatment of children's phobias: A review. *American Journal of Psychiatry, 118,* 97-105.

Rado, S. (1933). The psychoanalysis of pharmacothymia. *Psychiatric Quarterly, 2,* 1-23.

Rado, S. (1956). *Psychoanalysis of behavior.* New York: Grune & Stratton. (a)

Rado, S. (1956). Schizotypal organization: Preliminary report on a clinical study of schizophrenia. In S. Rado & G. E. Daniels (Eds.), *Changing concepts of psychoanalytic medicine.* New York: Grune & Stratton. (b)

Rado, S. (1959). Psychodynamics of depression from the etiologic point of view. *Psychosomatic Medicine, 13,* 51-61.

Rado, S. (1969). *Adaptational psychodynamics.* New York: Science House.

Rand, C., & Stunkard, A. J. (1978). Obesity and psychoanalysis. *American Journal of Psychiatry, 135,* 547-551.

Rangell, L. (1959). Nature of conversion. *Journal of the American Psychoanalytic Association, 7,* 632-662.

Rank, O. (1968). *Will therapy and truth and reality.* New York: Alfred A. Knopf.

Rapaport, D. (1942). *Emotions and memory.* Baltimore: Williams & Wilkins.

Rapaport, D., Gill, M. M., Schafer, R., & Holt, R. R. (1968). *Diagnostic psychological testing* (rev. ed.). New York: International Universities Press.

Raskin, M., Johnson, G., & Rodestvedt, J. W. (1973). Chronic anxiety treated by feedback induced muscle relaxation. *Archives of General Psychiatry, 23,* 263-267.

Rees, W. L. (1964). The importance of psychological, allergic, and infective factors in childhood asthma. *Journal of Psychosomatic Research, 7,* 253-262.

Reich, W. (1949). *Character analysis* (3rd ed.). New York: Farrar, Straus, & Giroux.

Research Task Force of the National Institute of Mental Health. (1975). *Research in the service of mental health.* DHEW Publication No. (ADM) 75-236. Washington, DC: U.S. Government Printing Office.

Ribble, M. A. (1944). Infantile experience in relation to personality development. In J. McV. Hunt (Ed.), *Personality and the behavior disorders* (Vol. 2). New York: Ronald Press.

Ringuette, E. L., & Kennedy, T. (1966). An experimental study of the double-bind hypothesis. *Journal of Abnormal Psychology, 71,* 136-142.

Ritvo, S., & Solnit, A. (1960). The relationship of early ego identifications to superego formation. *International Journal of Psycho-Analysis, 41,* 295-300.

Roback, H. B., McKee, E., Webb, W., Abramowitz, C. V., & Abramowitz, S. I. (1976). Psychopathology in female sex-change applicants and two help-seeking controls. *Journal of Abnormal Psychology, 85,* 430-432.

Robinson, G. W. (1956). The toxic delirious reactions of old age. In O. Kaplan (Ed.), *Mental disorders in later life* (2nd ed.). Stanford, CA: Stanford University Press.

Robinson, H., Kirk, R. G., Jr., Frye, R. F., & Robertson, J. R. (1972). A psychological study of patients with rheumatoid arthritis and other painful diseases. *Journal of Psychosomatic Research, 16,* 53-56.

Rochlin, G. R. (1953). The disorder of depression and elation. *Psychoanalytical Quarterly, 22,* 438-457.

Rochlin, G. R. (1959). The loss complex: A contribution to the etiology of depression. *Journal of the American Psychoanalytic Association, 7,* 299-316.

Rogers, C. R. (1951). *Client-centered therapy: Its current practice, implications, and theory.* Boston: Houghton Mifflin.

Rooth, G. (1973). Exhibitionism, sexual violence and paedophilia. *American Journal of Psychiatry, 122,* 705-710.

Rosenfeld, H. (1959). An investigation into the psychoanalytic theory of depression. *International Journal of Psycho-Analysis, 40,* 104-129.

Rosenhan, D. L. (1973). On being sane in insane places. *Science, 180,* 365-369.

Rosenman, R., Friedman, M., Strauss, R., Wurm, M., Jenkins, D., & Messinger, H. (1966). Coronary heart disease in the Western Collaborative Group Study: A follow-up experience of two years. *Journal of the American Medical Association, 195,* 86-92.

Rosenthal, D. (1970). *Genetic theory and abnormal behavior.* New York: McGraw-Hill.

Rosenthal, D. (1971). *Genetics of psychopathology.* New York: McGraw-Hill.

Rothschild, D. (1956). Senile psychoses and psychoses with cerebral arteriosclerosis. In O. Kaplan (Ed.), *Mental disorders in later life* (2nd ed.). Stanford, CA: Stanford University Press.

Rubin, K. H., Malone, T. L., & Hornug, M. (1976). Free play behaviors in middle and lower-class preschoolers: Parten and Piaget revisited. *Child Development, 47,* 414-419.

Ruesch, J., Harris, R., & Bowman, K. (1945). *Trauma of the central nervous system.* Baltimore: Williams & Wilkins.

Rutter, M., & Schopler, E. (Eds.) (1978). *Autism: A reappraisal of concepts and treatments.* New York: Plenum.

Rychlak, J. F. (1960). Recalled dream themes and personality. *Journal of Abnormal and Social Psychology, 60,* 140-143.

Rychlak, J. F. (1977). *The psychology of rigorous humanism.* New York: Wiley-Interscience.

Rychlak, J. F. (1981). Freud's confrontation with the telic mind. *Journal of the History of the Behavioral Sciences, 17,* 176-183. (a)

Rychlak, J. F. (1981). *Introduction to personality and psychotherapy: A theory-construction approach* (2nd ed.). Boston: Houghton Mifflin. (b)

Rychlak, J. F. (1981). *A philosophy of science for personality theory* (2nd ed). Malabar, FL: R. E. Krieger. (c)

Rychlak, J. F., & Brams, J. M. (1963). Personality dimensions in recalled dream content. *Journal of Projective Techniques, 27,* 226-234.

Rychlak, J. F., & Legerski, A. T. (1967). A socio-cultural theory of appropriate sexual role identification and level of personal adjustment. *Journal of Personality, 35,* 31-49.

Sadger, J. (1910). Analerotik und analcharakter. *Die Heilkunde, 4,* 11-20.

Saghir, M. T., & Robins, E. (1973). *Male & female homosexuality: A comprehensive investigation.* Baltimore: Williams & Wilkins.

Salmon, R., & Salmon, S. (1977). The causes of heroin addiction—A review of the literature (Part I). *The International Journal of the Addictions, 12,* 679-696.

Sameroff, A. J., & Cavanagh, P. J. (1979). Learning in infancy: A developmental perspective. In J. D. Osofsky (Ed.), *The handbook of infant development.* New York: John Wiley & Sons.

Sandler, A. M. (1975). Comments on the significance of Piaget's work for psychoanalysis. *International Review of Psycho-Analysis, 2,* 365-378.

Sandler, S. (1945). Somnambulism in the armed forces. *Mental Hygiene, 29,* 237-247.

Sands, S. L., & Rothschild, D. (1952). Socio-psychiatric foundations for a theory of the reactions to aging. *Journal of Nervous and Mental Disease, 116,* 233-239.

Sarbin, T. R., & Mancuso, J. C. (1980). *Schizophrenia: Medical diagnosis or moral verdict?* New York: Pergamon Press.

Sarnoff, I., & Corwin, S. M. (1959). Castration anxiety and the fear of death. *Journal of Personality, 27,* 374-385.

Sartorius, N., Shapiro, R., & Jablensky, A. (1974). The international pilot study of schizophrenia. *Schizophrenia Bulletin, 1,* 21-34.

Sarvis, M. A. (1962). Paranoid reactions: Perceptual distortion as an etiological agent. *Archives of General Psychiatry, 6,* 157-162.

Schaffer, H., & Emerson, P. (1964). Patterns of response to physical contact in early human development. *Journal of Child Psychology and Psychiatry, 5,* 1-13.

Schanche, D. A. (1974). The emotional aftermath of "the largest tornado ever." *Today's Health, 52,* 16-19.

Schildkraut, J. J. (1965). The catecholamine hypothesis of affective disorders: A review of supporting evidence. *American Journal of Psychiatry, 122,* 509-522.

Schmideberg, M. (1947). The treatment of psychopaths and borderline patients. *American Journal of Psychotherapy, 1,* 45-55.

Schneidman, E. S., & Farberow, N. L. (1970). A psychological approach to the study of suicide notes. In E. S. Schneidman, N. L. Farberow, & R. E. Litman (Eds.), *The psychology of suicide.* New York: Jason Aronson.

Schou, M. (1976). Advances in lithium therapy. In J. H. Masserman (Ed.), *Current psychiatric therapies* (Vol. 16). New York: Grune & Stratton.

Schreiber, F. R. (1973). *Sybil.* Chicago: Regnery Press.

Schube, P. (1934). Emotional states of general paresis. *American Journal of Psychiatry, 94,* 625-638.

Schur, M. (1955). Comments on the metapsychology of somatization. *The psychoanalytic study of the child* (Vol. 10). New York: International Universities Press.

Schur, M. (1972). *Freud: Living and dying.* New York: International Universities Press.

Schwartz, D. A. (1961). Some suggestions for a unitary formulation of the manic-depressive reactions. *Psychiatry, 24,* 238-245.

Schwartz, D. A. (1963). A re-view of the "paranoid" concept. *General Psychiatry, 8,* 349-361.

Schwartz, G. E. (1972). Voluntary control of human cardiovascular integration and differentiation through feedback and reward. *Science, 175,* 90-93.

Schwartz, G. E. (1977). Psychosomatic disorders and biofeedback: A psychobiological model of disregulation. In J. D. Maser & M. E. P. Seligman (Ed.), *Psychopathology: Experimental models.* San Francisco: W. H. Freeman.

Sears, R. R. (1961). Relation of early socialization experiences to aggression in middle childhood. *Journal of Abnormal and Social Psychology, 63,* 466-492.

Sears, R. R., Maccoby, E. E., & Lavin, H. (1957). *Patterns of child rearing.* Evanston, IL: Row, Peterson.

Seligman, M. E. P. (1970). On the generality of the laws of learning. *Psychological Review, 77,* 406-418.

Seligman, M. E. P. (1975). *Helplessness: On depression, development and death.* San Francisco: W. H. Freeman.

Selye, H. (1976). *The stress of life* (rev. ed.). New York: McGraw-Hill.

Shaw, M. E. (1974). Changes in sociometric choices following forced integration of an elementary school. *Journal of Social Issues, 29,* 143-157.

Sherrington, C. S. (1947). *The integrative action of the central nervous system.* Cambridge: Cambridge University Press.

Shields, J. (1967). The genetics of schizophrenia in historical context. In A. Coppen & A. Walk (Ed.), *Recent developments in schizophrenia.* Ashford, Kent: Headley Bros.

Shields, J. (1968). Summary of the genetic evidence. In D. Rosenthal & S. Kety (Eds.), *The transmission of schizophrenia.* New York: Pergamon Press.

Shimkunas, A. M. (1972). Demand for intimate self-disclosure and pathological verbalizations in schizophrenia. *Journal of Abnormal Psychology, 80,* 197-205.

Shopsin, B., Wilk, S., Sathananthan, G., Gershon, S., & Davis, K. (1974). Catecholamines and affective disorders revised: A critical assessment. *Journal of Nervous and Mental Disease, 158,* 369-377.

Siegel, M., Niswander, G. D., Sachs, J., & Stravros, D. (1959). Taraxein, fact or artifact? *American Journal of Psychiatry, 115,* 819-820.

Siegelman, M. (1974). Parental background of male homosexuals and heterosexuals. *Archives of Sexual Behavior, 3,* 31-38.

Simon, W., Berger, A. S., & Gagnon, J. S. (1972). Beyond anxiety and fantasy: The coital experiences of college youth. *Journal of Youth and Adolescence, 1,* 203-222.

Singer, J. L. (1977, August). Television, imaginative play and cognitive development: Some problems and possibilities. Paper presented at the Eighty-fifth Annual Convention of the American Psychological Association, San Francisco.

Skinner, B. F. (1971). *Beyond freedom and dignity.* New York: Alfred A. Knopf.

Skinner, B. F. (1974). *About behaviorism.* New York: Alfred A. Knopf.

Skinner, B. F., & Lindsley, O. R. (1954). Studies in behavior therapy, status reports II and III, Office of Naval Research Contract N5 ori-7662.

Slater, E., & Gilthero, E. (1965). A follow-up of patients diagnosed as suffering from hysteria. *Journal of Psychosomatic Research, 9,* 9-13.

Slater, E., & Shields, J. (1969). Genetical aspects of anxiety. In M. H. Lader (Ed.), *Studies of anxiety.* Ashford, Kent: Headley Bros.

Slavney, P. R., & McHugh, P. R. (1974). The hysterical personality. *Archives of General Psychiatry, 30,* 325-329.

Small, I. F., Small, J. G., Alig, V. B., & Moore, D. F. (1970). Passive-aggressive personality disorder: A search for a syndrome. *American Journal of Psychiatry, 126,* 973-983.

Smart, D. E., Beumont, P. J., & George, G. C. (1976). Some personality characteristics of patients with anorexia nervosa. *British Journal of Psychiatry, 128,* 57-60.

Smith, M. L., & Glass, G. V. (1977). Meta-analysis of psychotherapy outcome studies. *American Psychologist, 32,* 752-760.

Snyder, S. H. (1971). *Uses of marijuana.* New York: Oxford University Press.

Snyder, S. H. (1974). *Madness and the brain.* New York: McGraw-Hill.

Snyder, S. H. (1976). The dopamine hypothesis of schizophrenia. *American Journal of Psychiatry, 133,* 197-202.

Socarides, C. W. (1978). *Homosexuality.* New York: Jason Aronson. (a)

Socarides, C. W. (1978). The sexual deviations and the diagnostic manual. *American Journal of Psychotherapy, 32,* 414-426. (b)

Sojit, C. M. (1976). The double-bind hypothesis and the parents of schizophrenics. *Family Process, 10,* 53-74.

Solomon, P., Kubzansky, P. E., Leiderman, P. H., Mendelson, J. H., Trumbull, R., & Wexler, D. (Eds.). (1961). *Sensory deprivation: A symposium held at Harvard medical school.* Cambridge, MA: Harvard University Press.

Solomon, R. L. (1977). An opponent process theory of motivation: The affective dynamics of drug addiction. In J. D. Maswer & M. E. P. Seligman (Eds.), *Psychopathology: Experimental models.* San Francisco: W. H. Freeman.

Sontag, L. W. (1944). Differences in modifiability of fetal behavior and psychology. *Psychosomatic Medicine, 6,* 151-154.

Sorensen, R. C. (1973). *Adolescent sexuality in contemporary America: Personal values and sexual behavior, ages thirteen to nineteen.* New York: Harry N. Abrams.

Spark, R., White, R., & Connolly, R. B. (1980). Impotence is not always psychogenic. *Journal of the American Medical Association, 243,* 750-755.

Spengler, A. (1976). Sadomasochists and their subculture: Results of an empirical study. Paper presented at the Annual Meeting of the International Academy of Sex Research, Hamburg, Germany.

Sperry, R. W. (1977). Bridging science and values: A unifying view of mind and brain. *American Psychologist, 32,* 237-245.

Spielberger, C. D. (1972). Conceptual and methodological issues in anxiety research.

In C. D. Spielberger (Ed.), *Anxiety: Current trends in theory and research.* New York: Academic Press.

Spielberger, C. D., Berger, A., & Howard, K. (1963). Conditioning of verbal behavior as a function of awareness, need for social approval, and motivation to receive reinforcement. *Journal of Abnormal and Social Psychology, 67,* 241-246.

Spinetta, J. J., & Rigler, D. (1972). The child-abusing parent: A psychological review. *Psychological Bulletin, 77,* 296-304.

Spitz, R. (1957). *No and yes.* New York: International Universities Press.

Spitz, R. (1961). Some early prototypes of ego defenses. *Journal of the American Psychoanalytic Association, 9,* 626-651.

Spitzer, R. L. (1973). A proposal about homosexuality and the APA nomenclature: Homosexuality as an irregular form of sexual behavior and sexual disturbance as a psychiatric disorder. *American Journal of Psychiatry, 130,* 1214-1216.

Spitzer, R. L., & Fleiss, J. L. (1974). A reanalysis of the reliability of psychiatric diagnosis. *British Journal of Psychiatry, 125,* 341-347.

Squire, L. R., & Slater, P. C. (1978). Bilateral and unilateral ECT: Effects on verbal and nonverbal memory. *American Journal of Psychiatry, 135,* 1316-1320.

Squire, L. R., Slater, P. C., & Chase, P. M. (1975). Retrograde amnesia: Temporal gradient in very long-term memory following electroconvulsive therapy. *Science, 187,* 77-79.

Staffieri, J. R. (1967). A study of social stereotype of body image in children. *Journal of Personality and Social Psychology, 7,* 101-104.

Stampfl, T. G. (1966). Implosive therapy: The theory, the subhuman analogue, the strategy, and the technique. In S. G. Armitage (Ed.), *Behavior modification techniques in the treatment of emotional disorders.* Battle Creek, MI: Veterans Administration Publication.

Stampfl, T. G., & Levis, D. J. (1966). Implosive therapy. Unpublished manuscript.

Stampfl, T. G., & Levis, D. J. (1967). Essentials of implosive therapy: A learning-theory based psychodynamic behavioral therapy. *Journal of Abnormal Psychology, 72,* 496-503. (a)

Stampfl, T. G., & Levis, D. J. (1967). Phobic patients: Treatment with the learning theory approach of implosive therapy. *Voices, 3,* 23-27. (b)

Stampfl, T. G., & Levis, D. J. (1968). Implosive therapy—A behavioral therapy? *Behavioral Research and Therapy, 6,* 31-36.

Stampfl, T. G., & Levis, D. J. (1969). Learning theory: An aid to dynamic therapeutic practice. In L. D. Eron & R. Callahan (Eds.), *The relation of theory to practice in psychotherapy.* Chicago: Aldine.

Stamps, L. E., & Porges, S. W. (1975). Heart rate conditioning in newborn infants: Relationships among conditionability, heart rate variability, and sex. *Developmental Psychology, 11,* 424-431.

Steadman, H. J., Keitner, L., Braff, J., & Arvanites, T. M. (1983). Factors associated with a successful insanity plea. *American Journal of Psychiatry, 140,* 401-405.

Steffan, J. J., Nathan, P. E., & Taylor, H. A. (1974). Tension-reducing effects of alcohol: Further evidence and methodological considerations. *Journal of Abnormal Psychology, 83,* 542-547.

Stein, M. R., Vidich, A. J., & White, D. M. (Eds.). (1960). *Identity and anxiety.* Glencoe, IL: Free Press.

Stephens, R., & Levine, S. (1971). The street addict role: Implications for treatment. *Psychiatry, 34,* 351-357.

Stewart, M. A., & Gath, A. (1978). *Psychological disorders of children: A handbook for primary care physicians.* Baltimore: Williams & Wilkins.

Stoller, R. J. (1973). Criteria for psychiatric diagnosis. *American Journal of Psychiatry, 130,* 1207-1208.

Straker, N., & Tamerin, J. (1974). Aggression and childhood asthma: A study in a natural setting. *Journal of Psychosomatic Research, 18,* 131-135.

Strauss, M. S. (1978). *The abstraction and integration of prototypical information from perceptual categories by ten-month-old infants.* Unpublished doctoral dissertation, University of Illinois.

Sue, D. (1979). Erotic fantasies of college students during coitus. *Journal of Sex Research, 15,* 299-305.

Sullivan, H. S. (1953). *The interpersonal theory of psychiatry* (H. S. Perry & M. L. Gawell, Eds.). New York: W. W. Norton.

Sullivan, H. S. (1962). *Schizophrenia as a human process.* New York: W. W. Norton.

Sulloway, F. J. (1979). *Freud, biologist of the mind: Beyond the psychoanalytical legend.* New York: Basic Books.

Sutton-Smith, B., & Rosenberg, B. G. (1970). *The sibling.* New York: Holt.

Sviland, M. A. P. (1972). The heroin addict on methadone maintenance: His attitudes, resistance to psychotherapy, and identity problems. *Proceedings of the Eightieth Annual Convention of the American Psychological Association.* Washington, DC: American Psychological Association.

Swanson, D. W., Bohnert, P. J., & Smith, J. A. (1970). *The paranoid.* Boston: Little, Brown.

Szasz, T. S. (1967). *The myth of mental illness: Foundations for a theory of personal conduct.* New York: Hoeber and Harper.

Terry, R., & Wisniewski, H. (1974). Sans teeth, sans eyes, sans taste, sans everything. *Behavior Today, 5,* p. 84.

Thigpen, C. H., & Cleckley, H. (1951). *The three faces of Eve.* Kingsport, TN: Kingsport Press.

Thompson, N. L., McCandless, B. R., & Strickland, B. R. (1971). Personal adjustment of male and female homosexuals and heterosexuals. *Journal of Abnormal Psychology, 78,* 237-240.

Topping, G. G., & O'Connor, N. (1960). The response of chronic schizophrenics to incentives. *British Journal of Medical Psychology, 33,* 211-214.

Tsuang, M. T., Fowler, R. C., Cadoret, R. J., & Monnelly, E. (1974). Schizophrenia among first-degree relatives of paranoid and nonparanoid schizophrenics. *Comprehensive Psychiatry, 15,* 295-302.

Ullmann, L. P., & Krasner, L. (1965). *Case studies in behavior modification.* New York: Holt, Rinehart and Winston.

Valenstein, E. S. (1973). *Brain control.* New York: John Wiley & Sons.

Van der Valk, J. M. (1957). Blood pressure changes under emotional influences with hypertension and control subjects. *Journal of Psychosomatic Research, 2,* 134-145.

Van Kammen, D. P. (1977). Y-aminobutyric acid (gaba) and the dopamine hypothesis of schizophrenia. *American Journal of Psychiatry, 134,* 138-143.

Vener, A. M., & Stewart, C. S. (1974). Adolescent sexual behavior in middle America revisited: 1970-1973. *Journal of Marriage and the Family, 36,* 728-735.

Walters, R. H., & Parke, R. D. (1964). Influence of response consequences to a social model on resistance to deviation. *Journal of Experimental Child Psychology, 1,* 269-280.

Waring, M., & Ricks, D. F. (1965). Family patterns of children who became adult schizophrenics. *Journal of Nervous and Mental Disease, 140,* 351-364.

Waters, W. E. (1971). Migraine: Intelligence, social class and familial prevalence. *British Medical Journal, 2,* 77-78.

Watson, J. B. (1913). Psychology as the behaviorist views it. *Psychological Review, 20,* 158-177.

Watson, J. B. (1924). *Behaviorism.* New York: W. W. Norton.

Watson, J. B., & Rayner, R. (1920). Conditioned emotional reactions. *Journal of Experimental Psychology, 3,* 1-14.

Watson, R. I. (1962). The experimental tradition and clinical psychology. In A. J. Bachrach (Ed.), *Experimental foundations of clinical psychology.* New York: Basic Books.

Weiner, H. F., Thaler, M., Reiser, M. F., & Mirsky, I. A. (1957). Etiology of duodenal ulcer: 1. Relation of specific psychological characteristics to rate of gastric secretion (serum pepsinogen). *Psychosomatic Medicine, 19,* 1-10.

Weiss, J. M., Glazer, H. I., Pohorecky, L. A. (1975). Coping behavior and neurochemical changes: An alternative explanation for the original "learned helplessness" experiments. In G. Serban & A. Ling (Eds.), *Relevance of the animal model to the human.* New York: Plenum.

Weissman, M. M., Fox, K., & Klerman, G. L. (1973). Hostility and depression associated with suicide attempts. *American Journal of Psychiatry, 130,* 450-455.

Weissman, P. (1954). Ego and superego in obsessional character and neurosis. *Psychoanalytic Quarterly, 23,* 529-543.

Weissman, P. (1959). Characteristic superego identifications of obsessional neurosis. *Psychoanalytic Quarterly, 28,* 21-28.

Wenger, M. A. (1936). An investigation of conditioned responses in human infants. *University of Iowa Studies in Child Welfare, 12,* 1-90.

Wertheimer, M. (1961). Psychomotor coordination of auditory and visual space at birth. *Science, 134,* p. 1692.

West, R. (1961). The place and recognition of emotional factors in the etiology and treatment of chronic non-specific colitis. In J. A. Jores & H. Freyberger (Eds.), *Advances in psychosomatic medicine.* New York: Brunner.

Whitwell, J. (1936). *Historical notes on psychiatry.* London: Lewis.

Wickens, D. D., & Wickens, C. (1940). A study of conditioning in the neonate. *Journal of Experimental Psychology, 26,* 94-102.

Winkler, A., & Rasor, R. (1953). Psychiatric aspects of drug addiction. *American Journal of Medicine, 14,* 566-570.

Winokur, G., Clayton, P. J., & Reich, T. (1969). *Manic depressive illness.* St. Louis: C. V. Mosby.

Wittels, F. (1924). *Sigmund Freud: His personality, his teaching, and his school.* New York: Dodd, Mead.

Wittkower, E. D., Lipowski, Z. J. (1966). Recent developments in psychosomatic medicine. *Psychosomatic Medicine, 28,* 722-737.

Wittkower, E. D., & White, K. L. (1959). Psychophysiological aspects of respiratory disorder. In S. Arieti (Ed.), *American handbook of psychiatry.* New York: Basic Books.

Wohlberg, G. W., & Kornetsky, C. (1973). Sustained attention in remitted schizophrenics. *Archives of General Psychiatry, 28,* 533-537.

Wolberg, A. (1952). The "borderline patient." *American Journal of Psychotherapy, 6,* 694-701.

Wolf, E., Gedo, J., & Terman, D. (1972). On the adolescent process as a transformation of the self. *Journal of Youth and Adolescence, 1,* 257-272.

Wolf, S., & Wolff, H. G. (1943). *Human gastric function.* New York: Oxford University Press.

Wolff, H. (1963). *Headache and other head pain* (2nd ed.). New York: Oxford University Press.

Wolff, P. H. (1960). *The developmental psychologies of Jean Piaget and psychoanalysis.* New York: International Universities Press.

Wolpe, J. (1958). *Psychotherapy by reciprocal inhibition.* Stanford, CA: Stanford University Press.

Wolpe, J. (1969). *The practice of behavior therapy.* New York: Pergamon Press.

Wolpe, J. (1973). *The practice of behavior therapy* (2nd ed.). New York: Pergamon Press.

World Health Organization. (1978). *Mental disorders: Glossary and guide to their classification in accordance with the ninth revision of the International Classification of Diseases.* Geneva: Author.

Yalom, D. (1960). Aggression and forbiddenness in voyeurism. *Archives of General Psychiatry, 3,* 305-319.

Yankelovich, D. (1974). *The new morality: A profile of American youth in the 1970s.* New York: McGraw-Hill.

Zetzel, E. R. (1955). The concept of anxiety in relation to the development of psychoanalysis. *Journal of the American Psychoanalytic Association, 3,* 369-388.

Zigler, E., Levine, J., & Zigler, B. (1977). Premorbid social competence and paranoid-nonparanoid status in female schizophrenic patients. *Journal of Nervous and Mental Disease, 164,* 333-339.

Zigler, E., & Phillips, L. (1961). Psychiatric diagnosis: A critique. *Journal of Abnormal Psychology, 63,* 607-618.

Zilboorg, G. (1941). Ambulatory schizophrenia. *Psychiatry, 4,* 149-155.

Zung, W. W. K., & Green, R. L., Jr. (1974). Seasonal variations of suicide and depression. *General Psychiatry, 30,* 89-91.

# Name Index

Abel, G. G., 508
Abraham, K., 73, 363, 378, 466–468, 470
Abravanel, E., 53
Abse, D. W., 277
Abt, L. E., 596
Acosta, F. X., 493
Adams, H. E., 424
Adams, P. L., 226
Adelson, J., 88, 89, 92
Adler, A., 7, 69, 80, 97, 120, 130, 231, 466
Ainsworth, M. D. S., 45
Akiskal, H. S., 311, 381
Alacron, R. D., 249
Albert, M. L., 558
Alexander, F., 462, 519, 524, 529–531, 533
Allinsmith, W., 85
Allport, G. W., 99
Ansbacher, H. L., 587
Anthony, E. J., 49, 61
Arens, R., 631, 633
Arieti, S., 187, 325, 377, 436
Aristotle, 4, 5, 8, 25
Atkinson, R., 73
Atthowe, J. M., 613
Ausubel, D. P., 479, 480

Baastrup, P. C., 376
Babigian, H. M., 421
Bagley, C., 363
Bahm, R. M., 93
Bak, R. C., 335
Bakal, D., 531
Bandura, A., 34, 83, 616
Barahal, H. S., 599
Barendregt, J. T., 528
Barker, R., 565
Barnes, G. E., 478
Barnes, K. E., 82
Baron, A., 145

Baron, J. H., 524
Barrett, B. H., 61
Bartlett, F., 323
Baselon, D., 630
Bateson, G., 450
Baumrind, D., 86
Bayer, R., 492
Beach, F. A., 490, 491
Beatty, J., 534, 537
Beaumont, W., 519
Beck, A. T., 17, 363, 407
Becker, J., 376, 381
Bell, A. P., 493–495
Bell, S. M., 45
Belleville, R. E., 480
Bem, S. L., 77
Bemis, K. M., 242
Benady, D. R., 30
Bengston, V. L., 98
Benjamin, H., 504, 506
Benson, D. F., 558
Bentler, P. M., 507
Berg, K. M., 42
Berg, W. K., 42
Berger, A., 144, 450
Berger, A. S., 91
Berger, P. A., 600, 601
Bergin, A. E., 596
Berko, J., 61
Berlyne, D. E., 40
Bernays, M., 32
Bernheim, H., 587
Berrington, W., 277
Beumont, P. J., 244
Bezzola, D., 8
Bhavnani, R., 82
Bianchi, G. N., 255
Bickford, A., 530
Bieber, I., 494, 495, 501

Biller, H. B., 93
Bini, L., 597
Bird, F., 264
Birk, L., 493
Birley, J. L. T., 423
Birnbaum, K., 461
Birns, B., 42
Birren, J. E., 569
Bixler, E. O., 289
Black, H. C., 622
Blair, A. W., 87
Blane, H., 482
Blank, H. R., 291
Bleuler, E., 419, 438, 471, 472, 498
Bleuler, M., 256, 451
Bliss, E. L., 246
Bloch, H. S., 268, 275
Block, R., 493
Bloom, G. E., 527, 532
Bloom, K., 40
Blos, P., 88
Blumer, D., 558
Boekelheide, P. D., 507
Bohnert, P. J., 326, 351
Boring, E. G., 10
Bosack, T. N., 38
Bowen, M., 450
Bowlby, J., 44, 65, 66
Bowman, K., 565
Brams, J. M., 590
Branch, C. H., 246
Braucht, G. N., 478, 480, 481
Braungart, R. G., 94
Brengelmann, J. C., 598
Breuer, J., 10, 75, 104, 106, 116, 127, 128,
    131–133, 154, 166, 237, 238, 258,
    497, 575, 577
Brewer, W. F., 145
Brill, A. A., 313
Briscoe, C. W., 363
Broen, W. E., Jr., 450
Bronfenbrenner, U., 84
Brosin, H. W., 564
Brown, F., 374
Brown, G. W., 412, 423, 519
Brown, J. L., 42
Brown, R., 61
Bruch, H., 246, 526
Brücke, E., 10, 104, 124
Bruner, J. S., 56
Brunt, M. Y., 343
Bryant, K., 60
Buck, C., 539
Buckner, H. T., 506

Bullard, D. M., 29, 412
Bullitt, W. C., 123, 153
Bunney, W. E., 381
Bursten, B., 462
Burton, R. V., 85
Burton, W. H., 87
Burtt, E. A., 6
Buss, A. H., 360
Butler, M. C., 479
Bychowski, G., 327, 412, 472
Byer, C. O., 506, 600

Cameron, J. L., 412
Cameron, N., 57, 325, 379, 386, 402, 408,
    420, 434, 436, 441, 550
Cannon, W. B., 519
Cappell, H., 479
Caprico, F. S., 505
Cardoza, B. N., 621
Carlsson, A., 449
Carns, D. E., 90
Carpenter, G., 44
Carr, A. T., 204
Carson, T. P., 424
Cary, G. L., 464
Cavanagh, P. J., 36, 40
Cay, E. L., 524
Cerletti, H., 597
Chapman, J. P., 17, 434
Chapman, L. J., 17, 434
Charcot, J., 32, 251
Chase, P. M., 598
Chase, T. N., 491
Chessick, R. D., 482
Chodoff, P., 249
Christoffel, H., 508
Churchill, W., 494
Clancy, D., 508
Clark, T. R., 492
Clarke-Stewart, K. A., 45
Clayton, P. J., 407
Cleckley, H., 260, 279, 461
Cleveland, S. E., 246, 266
Clifton, R., 36
Cobb, L., 392
Cobb, S., 524
Coffey, J. W., 448
Cohen, L., 40, 53, 363, 374, 377
Cohen, M., 363, 374, 377, 393, 395, 401
Cohen, R. A., 401
Cole, J. O., 601
Coleman, J. C., 92, 93
Coleman, L., 634, 635
Collins, J. G., 54, 423

Compernolle, T., 527
Conger, J. J., 90, 91, 98
Connally, R. B., 512
Copans, S. A., 33
Cornelison, A. R., 449
Cornwell, D., 37
Corwin, S. M., 69
Costanzo, P. R., 92
Costello, C. G., 186
Coyne, J. C., 297
Crandall, V. J., 46
Cumming, E., 546

Dare, C., 47
Darwin, C., 73
Davidson, M., 40
Davison, G. C., 491
Davitz, J. R., 332
Davy, A. I., 84
Dawes, R. M., 596
Dekker, E., 528
Dement, W., 269
Demming, B., 478
Dempsey, G. M., 424
DeNike, L. D., 144
Detre, T. P., 600
Deur, J. I., 86
Deutsch, F., 254
Deutsch, H., 343, 396, 503
DeVries, K., 528
DeWolfe, A. S., 412
Diamond, B. L., 634
Dickes, R., 504
Dion, K. K., 83
Doehrman, J., 89
Doerr, P., 491
Dollard, J., 7, 8, 124, 126, 142
Douvan, E., 88, 89, 92
Drummond, E., 626
Dulany, D. E., 144
Dunbar, F., 518
Durrett, N. E., 84
Dynes, J., 563

Easton, K., 277
Eccles, J. C., 560, 561
Einstein, A., 114
Eitingon, M., 378
Ekstein, R., 60
Elkind, D., 325
Ellis, H., 120
Emerson, P., 42, 44
Engel, B., 530, 537
Engel, M., 90

English, A. C., 187
English, H. B., 187
Erikson, E. H., 14, 88, 94–97, 102, 103,
    170, 267, 292
Erlick, D., 599
Eron, L. D., 86
Ervin, E. P., 599
Esposito, A., 40
Evans, R. B., 491, 492
Evans, R. I., 113
Eysenck, H. J., 596

Fagan, J. F., 50
Fairbairn, W. R. D., 387
Fantz, R. L., 40
Farber, I. E., 344
Farberow, N. L., 357
Federn, E., 115, 158
Federn, P., 266, 472
Feldman, M. P., 493
Fenichel, O., 340, 458, 465, 466, 482, 503
Ferenczi, S., 313, 378, 498
Ferraro, A., 549
Ferrell, R. B., 244
Fieve, R. R., 407
Fingarette, H., 621, 625, 636
Fink, M., 598
Finney, J. C., 58, 343
Fisher, C., 181, 276
Fisher, S., 246, 266
Fleck, S., 449
Fleiss, J. L., 17
Fliess, W., 10–13, 26, 70, 74–76, 101, 104,
    121, 129, 154, 160, 496–500, 514
Fontana, A. F., 450
Forgus, R. H., 412
Foulds, G., 277
Fox, K., 357
Frankl, V. E., 344, 610
Freedman, B. J., 433
Freeman, T., 412
Freeman, W., 599
Freud, A., 87, 102, 442
Freud, S., 3, 4, 7–12, 14, 15, 25–27, 32–34,
    42, 43, 47, 49, 50, 57, 58, 63–65, 68–
    79, 81, 87, 88, 92, 95, 96, 99, 101,
    102, 104–140, 142, 143, 147–162,
    164–166, 168–170, 173, 184, 188–
    190, 197–199, 208, 209, 213, 221,
    223–225, 231, 233, 237, 238, 240,
    250, 251, 253, 254, 257, 258, 268,
    277, 282, 285, 312, 313, 319–321,
    324, 340, 341, 344, 345, 363, 374,
    378, 397, 402, 403, 406, 410, 412,

Freud (*cont.*)
    419, 439, 442, 458, 460, 462, 467,
    470, 482–484, 494–503, 506, 507,
    509, 510, 514, 516, 550, 552, 574–
    595, 606, 607, 616, 621, 622, 624,
    627, 631, 636–645
Freund, K., 493
Friar, L. R., 534, 537
Friedman, M., 531
Friedman, S. W., 60
Fromm, E., 466, 484
Fromm-Reichmann, F., 360, 361, 379

Gagnon, J. H., 504
Gagnon, J. S., 91
Gaines, R. W., 86
Gaitz, C. M., 546
Gal, P., 546, 568
Galileo, 5, 26
Gallup, G., 98
Gartell, N. K., 491
Garvey, C., 83
Gath, A., 412
Gaylin, W., 599
Gebhard, P. H., 506, 508, 509
Gedo, J., 88
Gelder, M. G., 186
Geleerd, E. R., 255, 261
George, E. I., 436
George, G. C., 244
Gero, G., 63, 211
Geschwind, N., 546
Gibson, A. C., 570
Gibson, R. W., 363, 374, 377, 401
Giffin, M. E., 226
Gifford, S., 41
Gifis, S. H., 626
Gilthero, E., 234, 249
Glass, G. V., 596
Glazer, H. I., 381
Gleser, G. C., 357
Glueck, S., 622, 640
Gold, M., 94
Goldstein, K., 550
Gonsiorek, J. C., 491, 494
Goodwin, D. W., 477
Goodwin, F., 407
Gorsuch, R. L., 479
Gottesman, I. I., 448
Gottschalk, L. A., 357, 434
Grace, W. J., 522, 526
Gralnick, A., 343
Grant, G., 84
Green, A. H., 86

Green, R., 504
Green, R. L., Jr., 357
Greenson, R. R., 186
Greenspoon, J., 143, 144, 613
Grimshaw, L., 204
Grinker, R. R., 172, 233, 268, 535, 537
Grinspoon, L., 601
Grusec, J., 83
Guggenheim, F. G., 421
Guschwan, A. F., 448
Guttman, O., 481

Hacker, F. J., 255, 261
Hackett, T. P., 508
Hadden, S. B., 493
Haeckel, E. H., 73, 101, 121
Haertzen, C. A., 480
Haith, M. M., 40, 53
Halikas, J. A., 479
Hamilton, J. G., 419
Hamlin, R. M., 441
Harford, R. A., 145
Harlow, H., 44, 344
Harris, R., 565
Harris, T. G., 478
Hartmann, H., 58, 66, 107
Heath, R. G., 448
Hacaen, H., 558
Hefferline, R. F., 145
Helmholtz, H., 10
Henrichsen, J. J., 493
Henry, W. E., 546
Heron, W., 56
Herschkowitz, S., 504
Hesselbach, C. F., 350
Heston, L. L., 448
Hetherington, E. M., 93
Hicks, D., 83
Hilgard, E. R., 149, 150
Hilgard, J. R., 358
Hill, H. E., 480
Hippius, H., 597
Hobbs, G. E., 539
Hobbs, S., 37
Hodgson, R. J., 204
Hoffer, W., 49
Hoffman, F. M., 478
Hogan, D. R., 512
Holden, C., 599
Hollander, R., 224
Hollingshead, A. B., 17
Holly, B. L., 601
Honigfeld, G., 601
Hoogduin, K., 527

Hooker, E. A., 492
Horney, K., 14, 69, 79–81, 96, 102, 170, 460, 465, 503
Hornug, M., 83
Hospers, J., 622
Howard, A., 601
Howard, K., 144
Hraba, J., 84
Hull, C. L., 7, 8, 112, 126, 313, 602, 617
Hutt, C., 82

Immergluck, L., 625
Isakower, O., 181, 427
Ittelson, W. H., 538

Jablensky, A., 423
Jacobs, T., 450
Jacobson, E., 268, 285, 327, 388, 438, 444, 464, 535, 602, 603, 618
James, W., 68
Janet, P., 133
Janis, I., 172, 285, 416, 518
Jaques, E., 16, 100, 384
Jarecki, H. G., 600
Jenkins, R. L., 60, 185
Jenner, F. A., 407
Jessor, R., 90, 91
Jessor, S., 90, 91
Joele, L., 527
Johnson, A. M., 226
Johnson, G., 537
Johnson, V. E., 493, 513
Jones, E., 137, 313, 378, 467, 482, 498, 503, 586
Jones, K. L., 506, 600
Josselson, R., 88
Jucovy, M. E., 507
Jung, C. G., 7–9, 12, 69, 73, 119, 120, 130–132, 282, 313, 341, 497, 498

Kadushin, A., 256, 451, 480
Kadushin, L., 480
Kagan, J., 40
Kahlbaum, K. L., 462
Kalinowski, L. B., 597
Kalis, B. L., 530
Kallmann, F. J., 358, 447, 448, 491
Kanfer, F. H., 17, 18
Kanner, L., 59, 412
Kaplan, H. S., 513
Karlen, A., 490, 492
Karlssom, J. D., 447
Katahn, M., 493
Katan, M., 397, 404

Katchadourian, H. A., 508, 509
Kaufman, A., 145
Kaufman, I., 450
Kaye, H., 38
Keenan, B., 145
Keller, S. L., 31
Kelly, D. H., 172, 175, 358
Kelly, G. A., 29
Kennedy, T., 450
Kernberg, O. F., 461, 464
Kessen, W., 41
Kestenberg, J. S., 89
Kety, S. S., 438, 448
Kiefer-Hammersmith, S., 493
Kilpatrick, D. G., 478
Kinsey, A. C., 90, 490, 510
Klaf, S. F., 328, 419
Klein, M., 374, 406
Kleitman, N., 269
Klerman, G. L., 307, 462
Knapp, P. H., 529
Knight, R. A., 412
Knight, R. C., 481
Knight, R. P., 463
Kobasa, S. C., 521
Koch, J. L., 461
Kohlberg, L., 97, 98, 103
Kohn, P. M., 478
Kohut, H., 88, 461
Kolata, G. B., 601
Kolb, L. C., 597
Koller, C., 482
Kopp, R. E., 145
Kornetsky, C., 412
Kotelchuck, M., 45
Kraepelin, E., 16, 17, 203, 402, 407, 419, 451, 462, 463, 471, 485
Krasner, L., 613
Kreitman, N., 538
Kretschmer, E., 471
Kringlen, E., 448
Kris, E., 225
Krugman, S., 567
Krupp, I. M., 448
Kutash, S. B., 538

Lader, M. H., 183, 251, 358
LaFave, W. R., 621, 626, 631, 633
Laing, R. D., 443, 450
Lamb, M. E., 45
Lambert, M. J., 596
La Metrie, J. O., 7
Lamy, R. E., 18
Landseman-Dwyer, S., 31

Landis, C., 599
Landman, J. T., 596
Langevin, R., 493
Lansky, L. M., 90
Laskowitz, D., 481
Laughlin, H. P., 311
Launier, R., 172
Lavin, H., 62
Lazarus, R. S., 172
Lefcourt, H. M., 625
Legerski, A. T., 77
Lehman, M. L., 482
Lemon, N., 267
Leonard, C. V., 357
Lerner, J., 84, 266
Lerner, R. M., 84, 266
Levin, M., 562, 563
Levine, J., 441
Levine, S., 481
Levis, D. J., 508, 607–610
Levit, E. E., 449
Levy, S. M., 435
Lewin, B. D., 187, 285, 401, 402, 404
Lewis, N. D. C., 570
Lichtenberg, J. D., 393
Liddell, D., 277
Lidz, R. W., 449
Lidz, T., 449, 518, 527
Lief, H. I., 493
Liem, J. H., 451
Liepmann, H. K., 8
Lincoln, A., 114
Lindsley, O. R., 611
Lipowski, Z. J., 538
Lipps, T., 150
Lipsitt, L. P., 38
Littin, E. M., 226
Loewald, H. W., 110
Lorand, S., 507
Lorenz, K., 186
Lorenz, M., 392
Loriaux, D. L., 491
Lorr, M., 441
Lothrop, W. W., 434
Louch, A. R., 634
Low, B., 122
Lucas, C. J., 54, 423
Lunde, D. T., 508, 509

Maccoby, E. E., 62,
Maccoby, F., 85
Mächtlinger, V. J., 71
MacKinnon, R. A., 465
Maddi, S. R., 323

Magaret, A., 379
Mahler, M. S., 60
Main, M., 46
Malamud, N., 546
Malone, T. L., 83
Mancuso, J. C., 15
Mann, D., 94
Manosevitz, M., 492
Marcia, J. E., 97, 98
Mark, V. H., 599
Marks, I. M., 186
Marlatt, G. A., 478
Marmor, J., 491, 494
Marquis, D. P., 35
Marquis, J. N., 501
Marshall, W. L., 501
Martin, C. E., 490
Martin, H., 86
Maslow, A. H., 114, 115, 139
Masters, W. H., 493, 513
Masterson, J. F., 88
Mathe, A. A., 529
Mattussek, P., 436
Maxmen, J. S., 244
May, J. R., 186
May, P. R. A., 601
May, R., 172
Mayer, J. R., 10
Mayerson, P., 493
McCandless, B. R., 492
McClelland, D., 480
McGhie, A., 412
McGuire, W., 8, 12, 130, 498
McHugh, P. R., 249
McKinney, W. T., 311, 381
McNamee, H. B., 479
Meissner, W. W., 326, 351
Meister, J., 599
Mellow, N. K., 479
Mendels, J., 371
Mendelson, J. H., 479
Menlove, F. L., 83
Menninger, K., 368, 470, 622, 630, 634–636
Meredith, H. V., 31
Meyer, E., 8
Michels, R., 465
Miller, N. E., 7, 8, 124, 126, 142, 534, 536, 537
Miller, P. M., 477
Miller, P. Y., 89
Millon, T., 461, 463, 464, 467
Mirsky, I. H., 538
Mishler, E. G., 451

M'Naghten, D., 626–628
Moniz, E., 599
Money, J., 504
Monsour, K. J., 186
Moore, S. G., 83
Mordkoff, A. M., 539
Moriarty, D. M., 447
Morrison, J. R., 421
Mowrer, O. H., 606, 609, 618
Mucha, T. F., 233, 251
Munjack, D. J., 513
Mussen, P., 40

Näche, P., 120
Nathan, P. E., 422, 438, 479
Neisser, U., 323
Nelson, K., 61
Neville, R., 599
Newman, L. E., 504
Newman, M. F., 358
Newsom, J., 46
Newton, I., 6
Noyes, A. P., 597
Nunberg, H., 115, 158

O'Connor, N., 412
Offer, D., 88
Offer, J. F., 88
Ostow, M., 363
Overall, J. E., 546

Page, M. M., 145
Papousek, H., 39, 50, 65
Parke, R. D., 83, 86
Parsons, O. A., 539
Paul, G. L., 601
Paul, W., 491
Pavlov, I. P., 18, 519
Paykel, E. S., 363
Payne, R. W., 436, 550
Pearce, K. I., 538
Peel, R., 626
Pemberton, D. A., 30
Penfield, W., 560, 561
Pepitone, E. A., 83
Perry, J. C., 462
Petersen, R. C., 477
Peto, A., 268
Pflanz, M., 524
Phillips, A. E., 524
Phillips, J. S., 18
Phillips, L., 17, 546
Piaget, J., 29, 39, 42, 48, 49, 52, 61, 65,
    81, 97, 98, 103, 204, 283, 284

Pious, W. L., 417
Plato, 5
Pliner, P., 479
Pohorecky, L. A., 381
Pollak, J. M., 62
Pollitt, J. D., 204, 226
Pomeroy, W. B., 490
Popper, K. R., 560
Porges, S. W., 36
Preston, A., 46
Prince, C., 507
Prince, M., 260, 279
Prout, C. T., 481
Prytula, R., 37
Pugatch, D., 407
Pulver, S. E., 343

Rachman, S. J., 186, 204
Rado, S., 361, 380, 465, 472, 482
Rand, C., 526
Rangell, L., 254
Rank, O., 160, 308, 378, 592
Rapaport, D., 255, 261, 279, 472
Raskin, M., 537
Rasor, R., 482
Rayner, R., 37, 605
Redlich, F. C., 17
Rees, W. L., 528
Reich, T., 407
Reich, W., 458, 460, 467, 469
Reid, J., 478
Reinhardt, R. F., 233, 251
Ribble, M. A., 29
Ricks, D. F., 450
Rigler, D., 226
Rimmer, J. D., 479
Ringuette, E. L., 450
Ritvo, S., 110
Roback, H. B., 504
Robbins, F. P., 535, 537
Robins, E., 491
Robinson, G. W., 562
Robinson, H., 519
Rochlin, G. R., 363, 375, 403
Rodestvedt, J. W., 537
Rogers, C. R., 17, 308
Roosevelt, E., 114
Rooth, G., 508
Rose, R. M., 524
Rosenberg, B. G., 83
Rosenfeld, M., 380
Rosenhan, D. L., 18
Rosenman, R. H., 531
Rosenthal, D., 381, 438, 448, 477, 491

Rothschild, D., 567–570
Rubenfine, D. L., 211
Rubenstein, R., 527
Rubin, K. H., 83
Ruesch, J., 565
Rutter, M., 60
Rychlak, J. F., 4–6, 8, 9, 41, 56, 77, 112,
    134, 323, 590, 596, 616, 621, 637, 640
Ryle, A., 538

Sachs, H., 378
Sadger, J., 467
Saghir, M. T., 491
Sakel, M., 597
Salapatek, P., 53
Salmon, R., 480
Salmon, S., 480
Sameroff, A. J., 36
Sandgrund, A., 86
Sandler, A. M., 49
Sandler, S., 269
Sands, S. L., 569
Sansbury, P., 54, 423
Sarbin, T. R., 15
Sarnoff, I., 69
Sartorius, N., 251, 423
Sarvis, M. A., 326, 351
Saslow, G., 17
Schaffer, H., 42, 44
Schanche, D. A., 275
Schildkraut, J. J., 381
Schmideberg, M., 463
Schneidman, E. S., 357
Schopenhauer, A., 131
Schopler, E., 60
Schou, M., 376, 601
Schreiber, F. R., 260, 279
Schube, P., 566
Schur, M., 74, 497, 533, 535, 627
Schwartz, D. A., 326, 351, 394, 401
Schwartz, G. E., 537
Sears, R. R., 62, 86
Seidenberg, B., 538
Seligman, M. E. P., 39, 172, 311
Seyle, H., 520, 521, 525, 536, 537, 540,
    541, 543
Shainberg, L. W., 506, 600
Shapiro, R., 423
Shaw, M. E., 84, 92
Sherrington, C. S., 602, 617
Shields, J., 183, 447, 448
Shimkunas, A. M., 435
Shopsin, B., 381
Siegel, M., 449

Siegelman, M., 494
Silberfarb, P. M., 244
Simon, W., 89, 91
Singer, J. L., 83
Singer, S. B., 601
Skinner, B. F., 7, 13, 34, 38, 106, 113,
    610–613, 619
Slater, E., 183, 234, 249
Slater, P. C., 598
Slavney, P. R., 249
Small, I. F., 469
Smart, D. E., 244
Smith, A. D., 478
Smith, J. A., 326, 351
Smith, M. L., 596
Snyder, S. H., 449, 476
Socarides, C. W., 490, 492, 493, 502
Socrates, 5
Sojit, C. M., 450
Solnit, A., 110
Solomon, P., 262, 283, 477
Somerville, O., 629
Sontag, L. W., 33
Sophocles, 69, 70
Sorensen, R. C., 91
Spark, R., 512
Spence, K., 7
Spengler, A., 510
Sperry, R. W., 51, 560
Spiegel, J., 172, 233, 268
Spielberger, C. D., 144, 173
Spinetta, J. J., 226
Spitz, R., 52
Spitzer, R. L., 17, 19, 491
Squire, L. R., 598
Staffieri, J. R., 83
Stampfl, T. G., 606–610, 618
Stamps, L. E., 36
Stanford, A., 493
Staples, F. R., 513
Starr, J. M., 98
Steadman, H. J., 628
Steffan, J. J., 479
Stein, M. R., 547, 569
Stephens, R., 481
Stevenson, R. L., 260
Stewart, C. S., 90
Stewart, M. A., 412
Stoller, R. J., 492, 504
Straker, N., 529
Strauss, M. S., 40
Streissguth, A. P., 31
Strickland, B. R., 492
Stuart, I. R., 596

Stunkard, A. J., 526
Sue, D., 510
Sullivan, H. S., 51, 55, 61, 66, 440
Sulloway, F. J., 11, 69
Sutker, P. B., 478
Sutton-Smith, B., 83
Sviland, M. A. P., 480, 481
Swanson, D. W., 326, 351
Sydenham, T., 7, 13
Szasz, T. S., 15

Tamerin, J., 529
Taylor, H. A., 479
Terman, D., 88
Terry, R., 546
Thigpen, C. H., 260, 279
Thompson, N. L., 492
Thorndike, E. L., 7, 8, 112
Tobias, L. L., 601
Tolman, E. C., 7
Topping, G. G., 412
Tsuang, M. T., 450

Ullmann, L. P., 613

Valenstein, E. S., 599
Van der Valk, J. M., 530
Van Kammen, D. P., 449
Varner, R. V., 546
Vener, A. M., 90
Vidich, A. J., 547, 569

Walters, C. J. S., 172, 175, 358
Walters, R. H., 83
Ward, R., 567
Waring, M., 450
Warren, N., 267
Waters, W. E., 531
Watson, J. B., 7, 13, 14, 35, 37, 112, 605,
    616
Watson, R. I., 611
Watts, J. W., 599
Waxler, N. E., 451

Weinberg, M. S., 493–495
Weiner, H. F., 525
Weiner, I. B., 325
Weiss, J. M., 381
Weissman, M. M., 357
Weissman, P., 223
Wenger, M. A., 35
Wertheimer, M., 53
West, L. J., 344
West, R., 522
Whipple, B., 532
White, D. M., 547, 569
White, K. L., 528
White, R., 512
Whitwell, J., 237
Wickens, C., 35
Wickens, D. D., 35
Williams, E. J., 41
Williams, J. P., 41
Willis, T., 420
Wilson, W., 123
Wing, J. K., 423
Wing, L., 183
Winkler, A., 482
Winokur, G., 407
Wisniewski, H., 546
Wittels, F., 238, 251
Wittkower, E. D., 528, 538
Wohlberg, G. W., 412
Wolberg, A., 463
Wolf, E., 88
Wolf, S., 519, 522, 526
Wolff, H. G., 519, 522, 526, 531
Wolff, P. H., 49
Wolpe, J., 602–606, 609, 617, 618

Yalom, D., 509
Yankelovich, D., 91, 98

Zetzel, E. R., 172
Zigler, B., 17, 441
Zigler, E., 441, 546
Zilboorg, G., 472
Zung, W. W. K., 357

# Subject Index

Abreaction
  as mental dissipation, 10
  as reliving mentally, 132
  early Breuer-Freud concept, 238
Accommodation
  Piagetian construct, 39
  and biological schemata, 42–43
  and incorporation, 54
  *see also* Assimilation
Acting out
  in paranoid disorder, 331
  in mania, 405
  in transference, 578
Actus reus
  definition of, 622
  *see also* Insanity; Mens rea
Adolescence
  discussion of, 87–94
  ego-ideals under development, 88
  turbulence during, 89–90
  sexual attitudes during, 90–91
  peer group in, 91–94
Adulthood
  discussion of, 99–101
Agency, agent
  and teleology, 5–6
  and introspective theory, 6
  denied in extraspective theory, 8
  in Freudian theory, 12, 68, 635
  *see also* Identity; Teleology
Agitated depression
  vs. neurotic depression, 299
  vs. retarded depression, 358
  discussion of, 359
American Law Institute (ALI) rule
  discussion of, 631–633
  definition of mental disease in, 631
  caveat paragraph in, 632

relation to M'Naghten rule, 632
  *see also* Durham rule; M'Naghten rule
Anal personality
  definition of, 62
Anal psychosexual phase (stage)
  definition of, 47
  in development, 60–63
Analysand
  definition of, 578
Anorexia nervosa
  loss of appetite, 243
Anthropomorphize, 2
Anticathexis
  as repression, 71
  synonymous with countercathexis, 71
  in the Oedipal dynamic, 119
  *see also* Countercathexis
Antisocial personality disorder
  definition of, 461
  as psychopathic personality, 461
  as semantic dementia, 461
  Oedipal aspects of, 462
  seeking of punishment, 462
  *see also* Personality disorder
Antithetical idea(s)
  in early Freudian theory, 132
  as precursor of internal dynamics, 312
  as conflicting wishes, 320
  *see also* Dialectic, dialectical
Anxiety
  as limited to ego consciousness, 125–126
  realistic, moral, neurotic, 126, 161–162
  final definition, as reaction to danger, 126, 161
  ego's self-inoculation with, 126, 161
  Freud's successive theories of, 158–162
  as transformed sexual tension, 159
  transformed libido, 160

Anxiety (*cont.*)
  fuero claims in, 160
  versus fear, 161
  social, 162
  as guilt, 162
  as significant to all neuroses, 170
  secondary, 171
  definition, neurotic, 172
  attack, 174
Anxiety disorder(s)
  in Kraepelinian nosology, 17
  definition of, 170–171
  generalized anxiety disorder, 173–178
  anxiety attack, 174
  panic disorder, 178–180
  symptom-formation in, 181–182
  phobic disorder, 185–198
  *see also* Anxiety
Archaic superego
  as pre-Oedipal superego, 223
  in obsessive-compulsivity, 223–224
  precursor of mature superego, 225
  in dysthymic disorder dynamics, 301
  in psychotic depression, 374
  *see also* Superego
Artificial neurosis
  *see* Transformed neurosis
Assimilation
  Piagetian construct, 39
  and biological schemata, 42–43
  and incorporation, 54
  *see also* Accommodation
Attachment
  Bowlby's construct, 44
Autistic child, 59
Autoerotism
  definition of, 63
  parallels to narcissism, 121
Autonomous ego functions
  adaptive and nondefensive, 58
Avoidant personality disorder
  definition of, 464
  phobias in, 465
  anal fixations in, 465
  *see also* Personality disorder
Awareness
  in conditioning experiments, 143–147
  conscious vs. unconscious, 148–149, 638

Basic trust
  Erikson, 96
Behavior modification
  as Skinnerian approach, 611

behavioral shaping in, 611
  individual treatment cases, 611–613
  method of successive approximations in, 612
  token economy, 613–614
Behaviorism
  concordance with medical model, 7
Behavioristic therapies
  major approaches in, 602–614
  role of teleology in, 614–616
Biofeedback
  in control of autonomic functions, 534, 536
  as intentional, 534
Biological naturalism
  as Freud's approach, 13–14
Biological reductionism
  *see* Reductionism
Biosocial
  as emphasis of book, 15
  aspects of development, 30
  aspects of mother-child relations, 42
  congenital and social sources of behavior, 321
  aspects of schizophrenia, 449
  in organic brain disorders, 546
  aspects of pharmacological therapy, 601
Bipolar disorder
  manic, depressed, mixed, 407
  bipolar vs. unipolar symptoms, 407
  use of lithium carbonate in, 407
  prodromal period in, 408
  *see also* Manic-depressive psychosis
Bisexuality
  and psychotherapy, 493
  in Fliess's theory, 496
Body image
  in somatoform disorders, 266
Body language
  as symbolical, 232
  *see also* Organ speech
Borderline personality disorder
  definition of, 462
  as cyclothymic personality, 452
  and schizoaffective disorder, 463
  broad fixation pattern in, 463
  *see also* Personality disorder
Brain functioning
  theories of, 560–561
  modular, 560
  conflict, 560
  teleological nature of, 560–561
British empiricism
  influence, on behaviorism, 7

Bronchial asthma
  definition of, 528
  suppressed aggression in, 529
  suppressed cry for help in, 529
  *see also* Psychosomatic disorder(s)
Bulimia
  overeating, 244


Case histories, in text
  generalized anxiety disorder, 176–178,
    184–185
  panic disorder, 179
  acrophobia, 190–192
  claustrophobia, 193–194
  agoraphobia, 195–196
  zoöphobia (Little Hans), 197–198
  obsessive-compulsivity, 203–204, 209–
    211
  obsessive-compulsive countermeasures,
    211–213
  obsessive-compulsive handwashing, 215–
    220
  obsessive doubt and rumination, 221
  somatoform disorder, 231–232
  somatization disorder, 234
  conversion disorder, 235–237
  mutism, 239–240
  tic, 241–242
  anorexia nervosa, 243–244
  bulimia, 244–245
  psychogenic pain disorder, 246–247
  hypochondriasis, 247–248
  symbolical symptom-formation, 252–254
  Anna O., 237–238
  dissociative disorder, 260–261
  object estrangement, 264–265
  somnambulism, 269–270
  somnambulistic attack, 271–272
  massive amnesia without fugue, 274–275
  massive amnesia with fugue, 276
  alternating personality, 278
  dysthymic disorder, 301–306
  persecutory paranoid disorder, 333–335
  delusional paranoid jealousy, 335–339
  agitated psychotic depression, 366–367
  retarded psychotic depression, 368–373
  manic episode, 396
  aggressive, self-assertive mania, 398–399
  elated manic reaction, 399–401
  bipolar disorder, 408
  schizophrenic disorder, 413–416
  schizophrenic disorder in adolescence,
    425
  schizophrenic disorder in young child-
    hood, 430
  schizophrenic scatter, 435
  schizophrenic mutism, 435
  overinclusion in schizophrenia, 436–437
  homosexuality, 488–489
  psychosomatic illness, 518
  bronchial asthma, 528–529
  delirium, 548–549
  progressive dementia, 554–556
  acute intoxication, 563–564
  general paresis, 566–567
Castrating female
  Horney's critique of, 80
Castration anxiety
  origins of, in Oedipal resolution, 73–74
Catecholamine hypothesis
  in major depressive episodes, 380–381
  norepinephrine and, 381
  in schizophrenia, 448
  *see also* Depressive episode; Schizo-
    phrenia
Catharsis
  physical release of emotion, 238
  *see also* Abreaction
Cathexis
  as a purposive wish, 4, 128
  as physical conception in *Project*, 11, 118
  occupying images of intended ends, 34
  forming of, in narcissistic neurosis, 582–
    583
  *see also* Libido
Cause, causation
  Aristotelian theory of, 4
Censorship
  early Freudian usage, 105
  as repression, 107
Chemotherapy
  *see* Pharmacological therapy
Childhood molestation theory, 155
Clang association(s)
  nature of, 393
  in manic disorder, 393
Cognition
  definition of, 50
Coitus interruptus, 154
Complex
  definition of, 70
Compromise(s)
  ego's role in forming, 109
  three-stage model of, in psychopathology,
    154–158, 575
  in phobias, 191
  *see also* Symptom(s)

Compulsion(s)
  definition, 204, 206
  see also Obsession; Obsessive-compulsive
    disorder
Compulsive personality disorder
  definition of, 466
  and the anal personality, 467
Condensation
  in dreams, 164
  in neologisms of schizophrenics, 434
Conditioning
  in infancy, 33–41
  classical or Pavlovian, 34–35, 112
  of Little Albert, 37
  operant or Skinnerian, 37–38, 113
  role of awareness in, 142–147
Consciousness
  Freud's definition of, 105
Constancy, principle of
  definition, 10
  Freud's struggles with, 115
  and principle of neuronic inertia, 116
  relation to pleasure principle, 117
  as a drive-reduction theory, 124
  see also Libido
Construe, construing
  versus shaping, 29
  via biological schemata, 42–43
Conversion
  definition of, 157
  in somatoform disorders, 231
Conversion disorder
  as single symptom somatoform disorder,
    235
  classic symptoms of, 235
  formerly "hysteria," 237
  childhood experiences and, 255–256
  see also Somatoform disorder(s)
Coronary heart disease
  type A vs. type B in, 531
  see also Psychosomatic disorder(s)
Countercathexis
  as opposing a wish, 4
Countertransference
  definition of, 580
  measures taken to counter, 586
  see also Transference
Counterwill
  in early Freudian theory, 131
  see also Antithetical idea(s)
Cue-producing response(s)
  definition of, 124
  in mediational theory, 124

when lacking, unconsciousness results,
    142
Culpability, legal
  definition of, 623
Cyclothymic disorder
  definition of, 394
  see also Bipolar disorder

Death instinct
  dynamics of, 120–123
  repetition compulsion and, 121
  Thanatos, Freud rejects, 122
  energy of, as mordido, 123
Decompensation
  sudden, in neurotic depression, 299
Defense mechanism(s)
  in early development, 58
  review of Freudian, 134–138
Delusion(s)
  definition of, 16, 324
  delusional vs. nondelusional thought, 324
  as effort to work out a cure, 351
  of self-depreciation, 360
  of expected punishment, 361
  of unreality and estrangement, 361
  nihilistic, 361–362
  somatic, 362
  of grandeur, 394
  in schizophrenia, 417–418
  as primary in paranoid schizophrenia, 422
  persecutory, 423
  see also Hallucination(s)
Dementia praecox
  in Kraepelinian nosology, 17
  vs. dementia senilis, 419
  discussion of, 419
  see also Schizophrenia
Denial
  as a primitive form of repression, 135,
    285
  in dissociative disorders, 286
  in paranoia, 346
  in mania, 394, 395, 404–405
  in schizophrenia, 444–445
Dependent personality disorder
  definition of, 465
  oral involvements in, 466
  and the receptive orientation, 466
  see also Personality disorder
Depersonalization
  as self-estrangement, 267
  in schizophrenia, 440

Depressive episode, major affective disorder
  definition of, 357–358
  delusions in, 360–362
  oral features of, 373–374
  "ego divided" in, 374
  recovery rate in, 376
  dependency, low self-esteem in, 377
  poor role taking, hostility in, 379
  oral traits and defenses, 380
  depressive superego, 380
  catecholamine hypothesis, 380–381
  involutional melancholia, 381–382
  childhood background in, 384–388
Depressive neurosis
  in Kraepelinian nosology, 17
  see also Dysthymic disorder
Detachment
  Bowlby's construct, 44
  see also Attachment
Determinism
  psychic, 147, 577
  material-cause, 147, 623
  efficient-cause, 147, 623
  formal-cause, 147, 623
  final-cause, 147, 624
  hard, 148
  soft, 148
  in legal deliberations, 624
  and irresistible impulse, 630
  in Freudian theory, 637
Development, developmental
  definition, 1
  personality, 30
  fetal, 31–32
  Freudian phases of, 47
  and "primacy" views of Freud, 49, 151
  versus regression, 57
  fixation in, 62
  Erikson's stages of, 96–97
  moral, 97–99
Diagnosis
  and moral judgment, 15
  problems of psychiatric, 15–19
  differential, neurosis vs. psychosis, 319–321
  variability in schizophrenia, 438
Dialectic, dialectical
  in opposing intentions, 4
  aspects of Freudian dynamics, 131–132, 149, 636
  aspects of reaction-formation, 137
  aspects of dreaming, 164
  in identification, 267

in alternating personality, 277
in ego-splitting, 283–284
clash, in dynamics of depression, 312
mood nuances and paranoia, 327
in homosexual-heterosexual substitution, 340
in manic dynamics, 395, 399, 400
in schizophrenic thinking, 436
divisioning, 437
in double-bind, 450
in dynamics of dreaming, 590–591
in free will, 636–638
in dynamics of punishment, 643
Diffusion
  vs. identity, Erikson, 97
Discrepancy hypothesis, 40
Displacement
  definition of, 136
  in dreaming, 164
  in obsessive-compulsivity, 208, 220–221
Dissociated personality
  most extreme form of depersonalization, 277
  alternating personality, 277–278
  double or multiple personality, 279
Dissociative disorder(s)
  formerly, hysteria, 261
  definition of, 262–263
  regression in, 282
  ego-splitting in, 283–284
Distance
  Adler's concept, 97
Distancing
  as removal via unreality, 263
Distantiation
  Erikson's concept, 97
  see also Distance
Dopamine hypothesis, 449
  see also Schizophrenia
Double-bind hypothesis
  as a dialectical dilemma, 450
  see also Dialectic; Schizophrenia
Dream(s), dreaming
  rapid eye movements in, 42, 269
  oral incorporation in, 54
  dreamer knows meaning of, 127
  encompass intentions, 128
  manifest vs. latent content, 162–163, 590–591
  condensation in, 164
  displacement in, 164
  symbol, as stable translation, 165
  day residues, 165

Dream(s), dreaming (*cont.*)
  wish fulfillment in, 165
  self-punishing wish, 166
  dream work, 166
  as a "picture puzzle," 166
  overdetermination in, 166
  as foundation stone of psychoanalysis,
    590
  rules of thumb, in analysis of, 590
  dialectical nature of, 590–591
Dreamlike dissociative states
  definition of, 268
  varieties of, 268–274
Drive(s), drive theory
  as motivator, 111
  employed in lieu of telic theory, 112
  reduction, 112, 126
  stimulus, 112
  secondary, 113
  and Freudian theory, 123–131
  induction, in Freudian view, 127
DSM-III, DSM-III viewpoint
  general format of, 19–25
  multiaxial system of classification in, 21–
    22
  on anxiety, 173
  on panic disorder, 180
  on phobias, 199–200
  on obsessive-compulsive disorders, 228
  on anorexia nervosa and bulimia, 242
  on dissociative disorder, 279–280
  on dysthymic disorder, 316
  on acute paranoid disorder, 330
  on folie à deux, 342
  on affective disorder, 356–357, 388
  on involutional melancholia, 382
  on bipolar disorder, 407
  on manic episode, major affective disor-
    der, 409
  on schizophrenia, 411, 412, 416
  vs. ICD-9, on schizophrenia, 418
  on schizoaffective disorder, 424
  on personality traits, 455
  on definition of aggression, 468
  substance abuse vs. dependence, 475,
    476–477
  on alcohol abuse, 476
  on homosexuality, 489–490
  on gender identity disorder, 503
  on transvestism, 506
  on pedophilia, 507
  on exhibitionism, 508
  on sadomasochism, 510
  on dementia, 553
  on organic personality syndrome, 558
Dualism
  in Freudian theory, 104
Durham rule
  discussion of, 630–631
  as "product" rule, 630
  reversal of, 631
  *see also* American Law Institute rule;
    M'Naghten rule
Dynamic theory
  Freud's definition of, 3–4
  employing final causes, 5
  role of unconscious in, 106
  clash and conflict in, 107
  source of Freud's, 131–134
  in phobic organization, 187
Dysthymic disorder
  definition of, 295, 296
  guilt in, 296
  precipitating factors, 297–299
  suicidal fantasies in, 299
  estrangement and depersonalization in,
    300
  self-depreciation in, 300
  anger in, 307
  as guilt neurosis, 307–308
  oral dependency in, 308
  narcissism in, 309
  and learned helplessness, 311

Eclectic, Eclecticism
  theory, 3
Efficient cause(s)
  definition of, 4
  as the S-R concept, 7
  in mediational theory, 124
  determinism, 147, 623
  *see also* Cause
Ego
  differentiated from the id, 58
  -introjects, 58
  cannot be located biologically, 105
  description of, 108–109
  as organized portion of id, 108
  effects compromises, 109
  introjects, 110
  use of reality principle, 108, 120
  as the sole seat of anxiety, 126
  inoculates itself with anxiety, 126, 161
  not really totally different from superego,
    109, 224

Ego (*cont.*)
  infantile, regressed, in depressions, 301, 374
  substitute, 349
  enlarged, in successful psychoanalysis, 584
Ego-dystonic
  definition of, 204
  in obsessive-compulsivity, 204
  in personality disorders, 456
  in homosexuality, 490
  *see also* Ego-syntonic
Ego-ideal
  *see* Superego
Ego-splitting
  in dissociative disorders, 283
Ego-syntonic
  definition of, 489
  in homosexuality, 489–490
  *see also* Ego-dystonic
Electra complex
  female Oedipus complex, 71
  *see also* Oedipus complex, conflict
Electric shock therapy (EST)
  *see* Electroconvulsive therapy
Electroconvulsive therapy (ECT)
  in psychotic depression, 371, 598
  description of, 597–598
  unilateral form of, 598
Emotion(s)
  versus libido, 124–125
  as a discharge of physical energy, 160
Environmentalism
  definition of, 12–13
Erogenous, erotogenic
  zones of the body, 47
  and autoerotic pleasure, 117
Eros
  *see* Life instinct
Essential hypertension
  and handling aggression, 530
  *see also* Psychosomatic disorder(s)
Estrangement
  definition of, 263
  object, 264
  somatic, 264, 265
  self-, 267
  in schizophrenia, 440
Eupsychian
  Maslow's construct, 115
Exclusion
  in normal behavior, 249, 280
  *see also* Overexclusion

Exhibitionism
  definition of, 508
  almost exclusively confined to men, 508
  castration anxiety and narcissism in, 509
  *see also* Paraphilias
Expert witness
  reason for having, 628
  psychiatrists incapable as, 635
Extraspective, theoretical slant
  definition of, 6
  in mediational theory, 124
  *see also* Introspective, theoretical slant

Factitious disorder
  definition of, 473
  as Ganser syndrome, 473
  as pseudopsychosis, 473
  as pseudodementia, 473
  as Munchausen syndrome, 473
  secondary gain in, 474
  vs. malingering, 474
  *see also* Malinger, malingering
Fetishism
  definition of, 505
  as substitute for human contact, 506
  *see also* Paraphilias
Final cause(s)
  definition of, 4–5
  determinism, 147, 624
  in behavioristic therapies, 615–616
  as a "telosponse," 616
  in legal deliberations, 624
  in Freudian determinism, 637
  *see also* Cause; Teleology; Telosponse
Fixation
  definition of, 62, 151
  in anxiety disorders, 180
  in mania, 402–404
  in borderline personality disorder, 463
  in avoidant personality disorder, 465
  in compulsive personality disorder, 467
  in substance use disorder, 483
  oral, in gastrointestinal disturbances, 524–526
  *see also* Development, developmental
Flight into illness
  in neurotic disorders, 158
  as primary gain, 233
  *see also* Primary gain
Flight of ideas
  definition of, 393
  in manic disorders, 393
  as topical flight, 397

Folie à deux
  as shared paranoid disorder, 342
  reversion from object-choice to identification, 343
Formal cause
  definition of, 4
  determinism, 147
  in meanings, 147
  as personality trait, 455, 623
  in legal deliberations, 624
  in Freudian determinism, 637
  *see also* Cause
Free association
  definition of, 576
  *see also* Psychoanalysis
Free will
  versus conditioning, 113–114
  presumption of, in Law, 621
  rejected in psychiatry, 622
  as an illusion, 625
  in Freudian theory, 635–638
  in unconscious realm of mind, 638–639
  *see also* Agency; Teleology
Freudian slip(s)
  *see* Parapraxes
Frigidity
  dynamics of, 513–514
Frustration(s)
  encountered in development, 158
Fuero(s)
  as a claim on the personality, 151
  versus libido terminology, 151
  in anxiety states, 160
  in anxiety disorders, 180
  in dynamics of conversion disorder, 254
  as derivatives, 285
  in dysthymic disorders, 301, 308
  in schizophrenia, 441
  anal, in paranoid tendencies, 470
  and insight, 575
  in free association, 576
  in acting out, 581
  in libidinal anticipatory idea, 582
  in psychoanalysis, 585
  *see also* Final cause; Formal cause; Telosponse
Functional disorder(s)
  lacking organic basis, 17

Gender identity disorder
  definition of, 503, 504
  lacking in castration anxiety, 504
  vs. homosexual panic, 504

Gender role
  definition of, 503
General adaptation syndrome
  vs. local adaptation syndrome, 520
  three stages of, 520
  distress vs. eustress in, 521
  homeostasis vs. heterostasis in, 521
Generativity
  Erikson's concept, 97
Genital psychosexual phase (stage)
  definition of, 47
  *see also* Development
Guilt
  nature of, 162
  in dysthymic disorders, 296
  unconscious, 300, 315

Halfway house(s)
  in drug rehabilitation, 479
Hallucination(s)
  definition of, 16
  as a created "reality," 56
  dynamics of, in schizophrenia, 418
  auditory most common form of, 423
  frequent in paranoid schizophrenia, 423
  common in schizoaffective disorder, 424
  *see also* Delusion(s)
Hedonism
  in Freudian instinct theory, 116
Histrionic personality disorder
  definition of, 458
  formerly hysterical personality disorder, 458
  as erotic libidinal type, 458
  and phallic personality, 459
  *see also* Personality disorder
Homosexuality
  as narcissistic disorder, 345
  as normal, DSM-III, 489
  ego-syntonic vs. ego-dystonic, 489–490
  biological arguments, 490
  sociocultural arguments, 491
  Gay Activist Alliance, 492
  Mattachine Society, 492
  Daughters of Bilitis, 492
  DSM-III vs. World Health Organization, 492
  personal adjustment arguments, 492–495
  family dynamic psychoanalysis, 494
  San Francisco study, 494–495
  Freud's views on, 495–500
  latent, in Freud-Fliess relationship, 496–499

Homosexuality (*cont.*)
  relation to paranoia, Freud, 498–499
  regression from object choice to narcis-
    sism in, 499
  as inversion, Freud, 499
  psychoanalytical dynamics of, 500–503
  idealization of penis in, 501
  castration anxiety in, 501
  female theory of, 502–503
  and aim-inhibition, 502
  role of fantasy in, 503
Humor
  Freudian view of, 403
  in mania, 403
Hypnosis
  in hysteria, Charcot, 251
  in early Freudian therapy, 587
  in systematic desensitization, 603
Hypochondriasis, hypochondria
  in Kraepelinian nosology, 17
  definition of, 247
Hysteria
  in Kraepelinian nosology, 16
  hypnoid state, Breuer, 133
  defense, Freud, 133
  as conversion disorder, 237
  history of, 237
  *see also* Dissociative disorder


ICD-9
  vs. DSM-III, 19
  nosological differences from DSM-III,
    418
  *see also* DSM-III
Id
  and primary-process thinking, 58
  description of, 107–108
Ideas of reference
  definition of, 340
  in paranoia, 340
  in psychotic depression, 360
  in paranoid schizophrenia, 423
  in schizotypal personality disorder, 472
Identification
  patterned on incorporation, 51
  as more primitive than object-choice, 64
  as reversion from object-choice, 64, 71,
    178, 327, 343, 344
  in superego formation, 71
  bisexuality in, 74–77
  with the aggressor in paranoia, 327
  in manic episode, 405
  in schizophrenia, 445

Identity
  personal, in Freudian theory, 11
  ego-, in Erikson's theory, 95, 267
  Erikson vs. Freud on ego-, 95
  vs. diffusion, Erikson, 95
  crisis, Erikson, 97
  vs. estrangement, 267
  loss of, in schizophrenia, 440
  loss of, in borderline personality disorder,
    464
  loss of, in schizotypal personality disor-
    der, 472
  *see also* Agency; Teleology
Imagery
  definition of, 50
Imago
  definition of, 386, 578
  in Oedipal dynamics, 462
  father, and transference, 578
  projection, in homosexuality, 583
  *see also* Psychoanalysis; Transference
Implosive therapy
  overview of, 606–610
  definition of implosion, 606
  conditioned avoidance responses, 607
  redintegrated images in, 607
  symptoms tell what person is avoiding,
    608
  symptom contingent cues in, 608
  hypothesized conditioned aversive cues
    in, 608
  extinction of anxiety in, 609
  avoidance serial cue hierarchy (ASCH),
    609
  and flooding therapies, 610
Impotence
  dynamics of, 512
  split imago in, 512
Inclusion
  in normal behavior, 249, 280
  *see also* Overinclusion
Incorporation
  definition of, 51
  as an active process, 54
Indefinite sentence(s)
  pro and con views on, 634
Insanity
  definition of, 626
  "guilty but mentally ill" decision, 635
  *see also* Mens rea; Responsibility
Insight
  definition of, 575, 579
  steps in providing, 575–576
  vs. noninsight therapy, 596

Instinct(s), instinct theory
  as bridge conception, 115–117
  aim, pressure, source, object, 116
  sexual, many such, 117, 119
  Freud's changing views on, 119–123
  primal, 119
  compound, 119
  self-preservative (ego-), 119
  object-, 119
  final definition of, 121
  life vs. death, 122
  fusion of, 122
  see also Libido
Insulin coma therapy
  description of, 597
  used with schizophrenics, 597
Intention(s)
  versus stimulus-response habit, 112–113
  in libido construct, 127–128, 637
  in wishes, 128
  in repression, 128
  in parapraxes, 128
  in mental illness, 129
  in conditioning experiments, 145
  in conversion symptoms, 231
  in exclusion and inclusion, 280
  in paranoid symptoms, 331
  unconscious form of, 441
  opposite, in double-bind, 450
  in drug abuse, 479
  in biofeedback research, 534
  as fundamental to legal decisions, 624
  in Freudian determinism, 637
  see also Final cause; Purpose; Teleology
Internalization
  as primitive introjection, 51, 255
Intoxication
  loss of functional boundaries in, 56
Introjection
  as symbolic internalization, 51, 55
  in schizophrenia, 445
  see also Identification; Incorporation
Introspective, theoretical slant
  definition of, 5–6
  Freud's proclivity for, 8
  see also Extraspective, theoretical slant
Involutional melancholia
  discussion of, 381–382
  see also Agitated depression
Irresistible impulse
  definition of, 629
  nature of determinism in, 630
  see also M'Naghten rule

Isolation
  definition of, 137
  in obsessive-compulsivity, 208

La belle indifférence
  patient attitude, 233
  dynamics of, 251
  see also Hysteria
Latency
  anticathexes in, 72
  discussion of, 81–87
  a time of separation between ego and id,
    81
  peer culture in, 83
  the school in, 84
  the church in, 84–85
  not without conflict, 85–86
Latent content
  in dreams, 162–163
  in mania, 405–406
  see also Dream(s); Manifest content
Libidinal anticipatory idea
  as framing intentions, 128
  as leading to frustrations, 184
  Freud's definition of, 581
  fuero demands in, 582
Libido
  as a reductive theoretical effort, 9
  as instrumental concept, 9
  not a physical construct, 34
  Freud's definitions of, 118
  as an élan vital, 120
  narcissistic, 121
  ego, 120
  object, 121
  not an emotion, 125
  has an intentional meaning, 127–128, 583
  as construct without methodological jus-
    tification, 129–130
  Freud and Jung disputed over, 130–131
  quantitative factors in, 150
  explanation versus fuero, 151
  see also Life instinct
Life instinct
  definition of, 122
  vs. death instinct, 122
  libido as energy of, 122–123
  active in transference, 582
  see also Death instinct; Libido
Little Hans, 197–198

Malinger, malingering
  versus somatoform disorder, 234

Malinger, malingering (*cont.*)
  vs. factitious disorder, 474
Manic attack
  dynamics of, 406
  *see also* Manic episode
Manic-depressive psychosis
  in Kraepelinian nosology, 17
  an ancient diagnosis, 401
  as circular insanity, 402
  oral features of, 402
  *see also* Bipolar disorder
Manic episode, major affective disorder
  definition of, 392
  as defense against psychotic depression,
    393
  oral aspects of, 402
  via fusion of ego and superego, 402
  *see also* Depressive episode
Manifest content
  in dreams, 162–163
  in mania, 406
  *see also* Dream(s); Latent content
Marital schism, 449
  *see also* Schizophrenia
Marital skew, 449
  *see also* Schizophrenia
Massive amnesia without fugue
  definition of, 274
  as traumatic neurosis, 275
Material cause(s)
  definition of, 4
  determinism, 147, 623
  *see also* Cause
Meaning(s)
  as formal-cause patterns, 147
  in conversion symptoms, 252
  and somatic compliance, 254
Mechanism
  in causal usage, 6
  J. Watson's definition of, 13
  and validity of infant conditioning, 34, 41
  efficient-cause determinism in, 148
Mediation, mediational theory
  versus agency, 34
  definition of, 123–124
  *see also* Mechanism
Medical model
  definition of, 7
  concordance with behaviorism, 7
  Freud's criticism of, 8
Mens rea
  definition of, 622
  *see also* Insanity

Mental incompetence
  legal definition of, 633
Metaneeds
  Maslowian theory, 114
Midlife crisis, 100
Migraine
  definition of, 531
  personality tendencies in, 531
  constitutional predisposition in, 531
  *see also* Psychosomatic disorder(s)
M'Naghten rule
  discussion of, 626–630
  as "right/wrong" rule, 628
  conscious intent in, 628
  as overly intellectual, 629
  irresistible impulse adaptation of, 629
  *see also* American Law Institute rule;
    Durham rule
Moral realism
  in theories of Piaget and Kohlberg, 98
Motivation
  definition of, 111
Munchausen syndrome
  *see* Factitious disorder
Mutism
  in schizophrenia, 435

Narcissism
  dynamics of, in development, 63
  reverting to, from object-choice, 63–64,
    309, 340, 344
  mythological precursor, 120–121
  and autoerotism, 121
  in homosexuality, 499
Narcissistic neurosis
  definition of, 582
  *see also* Transference neurosis
Narcissistic personality disorder
  definition of, 459
  growing in importance, 459
  poorly differentiated ego-superego, 460
  *see also* Personality disorder
Narcissistic supplies
  in dysthymic disorders, 311, 314
  in psychotic depression, 362
  *see also* Narcissism
Nativism
  definition of, 12
  *see also* Environmentalism
Natural science
  as antiteleological, 7
  *see also* Teleology

Naturalism
  see Biological naturalism
Neologism(s)
  made-up words, 421
  as condensations, 434
Neurasthenia
  in Kraepelinian nosology, 17
  as neurotic depression, 299
Neuronic inertia
  Freud-Breuer use of, 116
  in *Project,* 118
Neurosis
  definition of, 16
  vs. psychosis, 16
  actual vs. psychoneurosis proper, 77–78,
    155–156
  see also Psychosis
Norm(s)
  internalization of, 30–31
Normal, normalcy
  qualitative vs. quantitative views of, 15
  in adulthood, 100
  behavior, Freud's definition, 323
Nosology
  Kraepelinian, 16–17

Obesity
  dependency in, 525
  food equated with love, 526
  see also Psychosomatic disorder(s)
Object, object-choice
  as cathected ends, 34
  as attachment, 45
  mother's breast as, 48
  and superego formation, 59
  vs. narcissism, 63–64, 309, 340, 344
  vs. reverting to identification, 64, 71,
    178, 327, 343, 344, 500
  as tied to instinct, 116
  see also Cathexis
Object constancy
  correcting for perceptual distortion, 264
Obsession(s)
  definition of, 204, 206
  as compulsive thoughts, 206
  doubt, 220
Obsessive-compulsive disorder
  in Kraepelinian nosology, 17
  definition of, 203, 204, 206
  adaptive function of, 207
  relation to phobia, 208
  displacement in, 208
  isolation in, 208

  regression to anal level, 209
  countermeasures in, 211
  reaction-formation in, 213
  undoing in, 213
  ambivalence in, 219
  doubt and rumination, 220–222
  pre-Oedipal regression in, 222–227
  as not true "guilt" neurosis, 223
Oedipus complex, conflict
  the legend, 69–70
  male, 70–71
  female, 71–72
  primal father, 73
  and super-ego formation, 71, 74
  and origins of society, 73–74
  bisexuality and identification in, 74–77
  positive versus negative, 76
  poor resolution and neurosis, 77–78, 134,
    156
  and the role of punishment, 641–644
Ontogeny recapitulates phylogeny
  Haeckel's biogenetic law, 73
  Freud's use of in his theory, 73–74
Opposition, principle of
  Jung's theory, 131
  see also Dialectic
Oral psychosexual phase (stage)
  definition of, 47
  discussion of, 48–52
  dependency in, 48
  reality-testing in, 49
  anticipation in, 50
  internalization of experience in, 51
  denial in, 52
  projection in, 52
Organ speech
  in symptom manifestation, 157
  in somatoform disorders, 231
Organic affective syndrome
  definition of, 558
  see also Organic brain syndrome
Organic brain syndrome(s)
  definition of, 545
  delirium, 547–549
  lucid interval, 548
  incoordination, 549
  interpenetration, 550
  fragmentation, 550
  overinclusion, 550
  primary process thinking, 551
  dementia, 553–557
  compensation, 556
  confabulation, 556

Organic brain syndrome(s) *(cont.)*
  loss of memory, 556–557
  amnesic syndrome, 557
  organic hallucinosis, 557–558
  *see also* Organic mental disorder(s)
Organic mental disorder(s)
  definition of, 545
  brain functioning in, 560
  acute intoxication, 562–564
  head injury, 564–566
  Korsakoff syndrome, 564
  Argyll-Robertson pupil, 566
  general paresis, 566–567
  senility, 567
  arteriosclerotic brain degeneration, 567
  obsessive-compulsive symptoms in, 570
  *see also* Organic brain syndrome(s)
Overdetermination
  in dreams, 166
  in conversion symptoms, 252
Overexclusion
  definition of, 280
Overinclusion
  definition of, 280, 436
  in schizophrenic thought, 435–437
  in organic brain syndromes, 550
Overprotection
  maternal, 60

Paradoxical intention, 610
  *see also* Implosive therapy
Paranoia
  *see* Paranoid disorder
Paranoid disorder
  definition of, 322, 324
  delusional thinking in, 322
  varieties of, 325–326
  personality tendencies in, 326
  persecutory paranoid disorder, 326
  identification with aggressor in, 327
  and homosexuality, 328, 498–499
  reconstruction of reality in, 329–330
  acute, DSM-III, 330
  and "true" paranoiacs, 330
  delusional paranoid jealousy, 335
  erotic paranoid disorder, 340
  and narcissistic love projection, 340
  grandiose, 341–342
Paranoid personality disorder
  definition of, 469
  relation to homosexuality, 470
  anal-sadistic fueros in, 470

  usually intelligent, 470
  *see also* Personality disorder
Paraphilias
  definition of, 505
  varieties of, 505–511
Parapraxes
  nature of, 591
Parataxic mode
  Sullivanian construct, 55
  distortion of experience in, 61
Passive-aggressive personality disorder
  definition of, 467–468
  aggression vs. hostility, 467
  aggression vs. assertiveness, 468
  oral sadism in, 468
  *see also* Personality disorder(s)
Pathognomic situation
  Breuer-Freud concept, 238
Peak experience
  Maslow's construct, 114
Pedophilia
  definition of, 507
  pre-Oedipal fixations in, 507
  *see also* Paraphilias
Peeping
  *see* Voyeurism
Penis envy
  in female Oedipus complex, 71–72
  Horney's criticism of, 79
Peptic ulcer
  definition of, 524
  dependency in, 524
  reaction-formation in, 525
  *see also* Psychosomatic disorder(s)
Periodic cycles
  Fliess's theory of, 10, 74–77
  and Freud's instinct theory, 121
Personality
  as style of behavior, 1
  in psychopathology, 2
  transformations in, 30
  Erikson's definition of, 95
  in psychoanalytical view, 104
  as working out conflicts, Freud, 153
  trait, 455
  *see also* Agency; Identity; Teleology
Personality disorder(s)
  definition of, 455, 456
  vs. neuroses and psychoses, 457
  dramatic and erratic types of, 458–464
  anxious and fearful types of, 464–469
  eccentric and peculiar types of, 469–473
  *see also* Personality

Phallic psychosexual phase (stage)
definition of, 47
Phantom limb
denial of bodily change, 266
Pharmacological therapy
description of, 599–602
antianxiety drugs in, 600
antidepressant drugs in, 600
antipsychotic drugs in, 600–601
lithium carbonate in, 601
dexedrine in, 601
Phobia(s)
definition of, 185
disorder, definition, 187
overdetermination in, 187
symbolism in, 187, 192
Table 3: various phobias, 188
counterphobic measures, 198–199
comparison to anxiety disorder, 200–201
in avoidant personality disorder, 465
see also Anxiety disorder(s)
Pleasure principle
and immediate gratification, 50
and the id, 107
related to constancy principle, 117
not just thrill seeking, 118
see also Reality principle
Preconscious
definition of, 107
Pressure technique
early Freudian therapy technique, 587
see also Psychoanalysis
Primary gain
of illness, as convenient solution, 233,
319
see also Secondary gain
Primary process thought
and early experience, 58
in id functioning, 107
dialectical nature of, 164
in schizophrenia, 411, 433, 438
see also Secondary process thought
Project for a Scientific Psychology, "Project"
and Fliess's influence on Freud, 10
use of cathexis in, 11
telic aspects of, 11
as Freud's single "natural science" effort,
12
Projection
based on oral ejection, 52
definition of, 136–137
in dysthymic disorder, 312
in paranoia, 346

in schizophrenia, 444–445
see also Defense mechanism(s)
Promotion depression, 298
Prototaxic mode
Sullivanian construct, 51
Prototype
use of biological schemata as, 42–43
of psychosexual level, 153–154
Pseudocommunity
as reconstruction of reality, 332
in paranoia, 332–333
in mania, 395
Psychoanalysis
fundamental rule of, 576
two motives in, 577
definition of, Freud, 579
as uncovering process, 579
theory of cure in, 580–584
role of suggestion in, 581, 588
ego enlarged in successful, 584
interminable aspects of, 584–586
intellectual vs. emotional understanding
in, 585
evolution of relationship in, 587–588
trial period in, 589
dreams in, 589–591
parapraxes in, 591
termination of, 592
see also Psychotherapy
Psychogenic pain disorder
definition of, 246
Psychogenic stupor
definition of, 274
Psychological factors affecting physical condition
see Psychosomatic disorder(s)
Psychopathic personality
see Antisocial personality disorder
Psychopathology
definition of, 2
personality in, 2
quantitative vs. qualitative view of, 15,
320
Psychosexual disorder(s)
definition of, 487
sexual cycle in, 487
Psychosexual dysfunction(s)
definition of, 511
in the male, 512–513
in the female, 513–514
Psychosis
definition of, 16
vs. neurosis, 16
vs. insanity, 620

Psychosis (*cont.*)
  *see also* Insanity; Neurosis
Psychosomatic disorder(s)
  definition of, 517
  adaptive features of, 521–523
  unconscious choice in, 522
  gastrointestinal tract, 523–527
  respiratory system, 527–529
  cardiovascular, 529–531
  rheumatoid arthritis, 531–532
  the skin, 532–533
  hyperthyroidism, 533–534
  diabetes mellitus, 534
  dynamics of, 535–537
  "choice" of organ system in, 537–541
Psychosurgery
  description of, 598–599
  lateral transcranial prefrontal lobotomy,
    599
  transorbital lobotomy, 599
  topectomy, 599
  gyrectomy, 599
  thalamotomy, 599
  personality changes in, 599
Psychotherapy
  definition of, 574
  theory of cure in, 575
  insight vs. noninsight, 596
  research findings in, 596
  *see also* Psychoanalysis
Psychotic depression
  *see* Depressive episode; Major affective
    disorder
Punishment, legal
  as inappropriate, 625
  contrasting psychiatric views of, 633–635
  Freud's views on, 641–644
Purpose
  in dynamic theory, 4
  *see also* Intention; Teleology

Rape
  as sadistic crime, 510
Rationalization
  definition of, 137
Reaction sensitivity
  definition of, 183
  readiness to react, 321
  phenomenal basis of, 321
  in sexual dysfunction, 513
Reactive depression
  vs. retarded depression, 299
  *see also* Retarded depression

Reaction-formation
  definition of, 46, 137
  in mother-child relations, 46
  during anal phase of development, 61
  in obsessive-compulsivity, 213
  in manic episode, 405
  in peptic ulcer, 525
  *see also* Defense mechanism(s)
Reality, reality-testing
  as reality-*tasting* in infancy, 49
  vs. hallucinatory experience, 56
  disturbed, in schizophrenia, 439–440
Reality principle
  and frustration tolerance, 50
  ego functioning according to, 108, 120
  *see also* Pleasure principle
Reconstruction
  *see* Restitutive processes
Reductionism
  in causal usage, 6
  in medical model, 7
  in libido theory, 9
  biological, 13–14, 447–449
Regression
  in ego-deterioration, 57
  from object choice to narcissism, 63–64,
    499
  definition, 152
  topographical, 153
  temporal, 153
  formal, 153
  as flight into illness, 158
  in service of ego, 225, 254
  neurotic vs. psychotic, 309, 320
  in dysthymic disorder, 313–314
  normal, 320–321
  in manic episode, 404, 406
  deepest form of, in schizophrenia, 439,
    443
  ego-superego, in schizophrenia, 446–447
  in narcissistic neurosis, 582
  *see also* Defense mechanism(s)
Reinforcement
  in classical conditioning, 112
  positive, 112
  and drive-reduction, 112
  as reinforcer, 113
  *see also* Awareness; Conditioning
Repetition-compulsion
  based on Haeckel's principle, 121
  and Fliess's periodic cycles, 121
  in traumatic neuroses, 160
  in antisocial personality disorder, 462
  in psychoanalysis, 580

Repetition-compulsion (*cont.*)
  *see also* Ontogeny recapitulates
    phylogeny
Repression
  discussion of, 134–136
  vs. suppression, 135
  primal vs. "proper," 135, 156
  derivatives of, 135
  and denial, 135
  after-repression, 156
  return of repressed memories, 156, 320,
    348
  in paranoia, 345–346, 349–350
  in manic episode, 404
  in schizophrenia, 443–444
  primal, and psychoanalysis, 580
  *see also* Defense mechanism(s)
Resistance
  definition of, 577
  regression in, 577, 579
Responsibility
  legal, 621
  conscious vs. unconscious, 626
  insanity, as lack of under law, 626
Restitutive processes, restitution
  in psychosis, 291
  as reconstructing reality, 331
  pseudocommunity as, 332
  delusions in, 351
  in depressive episode, major affective dis-
    order, 371
  in schizophrenic symptoms, 417–418,
    440–441
  *see also* Regression
Retarded depression
  vs. reactive depression, 299
  as major affective disorder, 356
  vs. agitated depression, 358
  discussion of, 359
  as depressive stupor, 359

Sadomasochism
  anal aspects of, 62–63
  in obsessive-compulsive disorders, 224
  sadism in dysthymic disorders, 301
  in psychotic depression, 374
  as paraphiliac disorder, 510–511
  aspects of rape, 510
  psychoanalytical dynamics of, 510–511
  and identification with the aggressor, 511
Scatter
  definition of, 434
  *see also* Flight of ideas

Schizoaffective disorder
  definition of, 424
  *see also* Schizophrenia
Schizoid personality disorder
  definition of, 471
  as simple schizophrenia, 471
  as autistic personalities, 471
  *see also* Personality disorder; Schizotypal
    personality disorder
Schizophrenia, schizophrenic disorder
  childhood, 60, 412
  overlapping symptoms in, 411
  definition of, 417
  latent, 418
  borderline, 418
  undifferentiated, 419
  residual, 419
  Bleuler coined term, 419
  simple, 420
  hebephrenic or disorganized, 420–421
  catatonic, 421–422
  paranoid, 422–424
  mutism in, 435
  overinclusion in, 435–437
  developmental aspects of, 437–438
  one-third change subtype diagnosis, 438
  regression to primary narcissism in, 439
  wide dispersal of fixation points in, 442
  "active" disorder in, 446
  biological theories of, 447–449
  catecholamine hypothesis, 448
  taraxein, 448
  dopamine hypothesis, 449
  methylphenidate, 449
  phenothiazine drugs, 449
  family dynamics in, 449–451
  marital schism, 449
  marital skew, 449
  double-bind hypothesis, 450
Schizophrenia spectrum
  as a range of symptoms, 438
  biological aspects of, 447–448
  *see also* Schizophrenia
Schizophreniform disorder
  definition of, 416
  example of, 419
Schizothymic personality
  and the schizophrenic spectrum, 438
Schizotypal personality disorder
  definition of, 471
  as latent schizophrenia, 472
  as ambulatory schizophrenia, 472
  as preschizophrenia, 472

Schizotypal personality disorder (*cont.*)
  *see also* Personality disorder; Schizoid
    personality disorder
Screen memory
  defensive recall of trivia, 276
  as screen associations, 588
  in free association, 588
Secondary gain
  of illness, as advantages gained, 233, 319
  in factitious disorder, 474
  in psychosomatic disorder, 522
  *see also* Primary gain
Secondary process thought
  and early experience, 58
  in ego functioning, 108
  *see also* Primary process thought
Self, self-image
  disturbed in schizophrenia, 440
Sensory deprivation, 56
Sexual cycle
  four stages of, 487
Shape, shaping
  of behavior, versus construing, 29
  in operant conditioning, 39
  infant, not clearly established, 41
Social revision
  in Freudian outlook, 586–587
Somatic compliance
  in conversion disorder, 251
  and meaning, 254
Somatoform disorder(s)
  definition of, 233
  personality of patients with, 254
Somnambulism
  definition of, 268
  *see also* Dreamlike dissociative states
Somnambulistic attack
  definition of, 270
  *see also* Dreamlike dissociative states
Split-level functioning, 181
S-R psychology
  and efficient causality, 7
  *see also* Efficient cause(s)
Strangulated affect
  Breuer-Freud concept, 238
Sublimation
  definition of, 136
  *see also* Defense mechanism(s)
Substance abuse
  definition of, 476
  *see also* Substance use disorder(s)
Substance dependence
  definition of, 476

tolerance and withdrawal in, 476
  *see also* Substance use disorder(s)
Substance use disorder(s)
  definition of, 475
  abuse vs. dependence, 475–477
  puzzling aspects of, 477–480
  sensation seeking in, 478
  personality dynamics in, 480–483
  oceanic feeling in, 482
  primitive denial in, 482
  oral fixation in, 483
  *see also* Substance dependence
Substitution
  definition of, 136
  *see also* Defense mechanism(s)
Suggestion
  role of in psychoanalysis, 588
  definition of, 588
  Freud's views on, 588–589
Suicide
  in dysthymic disorder, 299
  rate of, and depression, 357
Superego
  differentiated from the ego, 58
  as heir of the Oedipal complex, 71
  male vs. female, in Freudian view, 72
  discussion of, 109–110
  synonymous with ego-ideal, 109
  relation to id, 641
  as defensively formed, 642
  role of, in punishment, 643–644
Suppression
  as defensive maneuver, 135
  *see also* Defense mechanism(s)
Symbiosis, symbiotic
  definition of, 45
  in mother-child relations, 45–46
  resolution of relationship, 59
  child, 59–60
Symptom(s)
  relation to syndrome, 14
  selection, Freud, 78
  source of, Freud, 132
  as compromises, 157, 320
  as wish-fulfillments, 157
  Freud's definition of, 157, 319–320
  organ speech in, 157
  as defenses in depression, 310–311
  neurotic, always means two things, 582
  reveal avoidant responses, Stampfl, 608
Syndrome(s)
  definition of, 14
  *see also* Symptom(s)

Syntaxic mode
  Sullivanian construct, 56
Systematic desensitization
  overview of, 602–605
  reciprocal inhibition and, 602
  progressive relaxation and, 602
  conditioned inhibition in, 602
  deep muscle relaxation in, 603
  anxiety hierarchy in, 604
  subjective unit of disturbance, 604
  use of hypnotism in, 604
  in vivo, 605
  counterconditioning in, 605

Taraxein, 448
  see also Schizophrenia
Teleology, telic
  definition of, 5
  in dynamic theories, 5
  rejected by natural science, 7
  in Freud's Project, 11
  in conditioning experiments, 37–38
  in infant behavior, 41
  in Freudian theory generally, 68, 75, 115,
    128–129, 251
  in precursors of obsessions and compul-
    sions, 205
  in splitting consciousness, 285
  in neurotic self-evaluation, 311
  in reaction sensitivity, 321
  in dynamics of antisocial personality, 462
  in factitious disorder, 473
  in substance use disorder, 481
  in psychosexual disorder, 488
  in general adaptation syndrome, 520
  via unconscious choice, 522
  in biofeedback experiment, 541
  in modern brain theories, 560
  in understanding behavior therapy, 614–
    616
  as basic to all legal systems, 621
  see also Agency; Identity; Intention; Pur-
    pose
Telosponse
  as a telic construct, 616, 620
  see also Teleology, telic
Third force
  as Maslow's view, 114
Tic(s)
  definition of, 240
  spasmodic torticollis, 241
Tolerance
  in drug use, 476
  see also Substance use disorder(s)

Topographical model
  in Freudian theory, 107
Trait
  of personality, 455
  see also Personality
Trance state
  definition of, 273
  see also Dreamlike dissociative states
Transference
  definition of, 578
  positive vs. negative, 579
  composite nature of, 579
  complete resolution of, 580
  three aspects of, 581
  as true vehicle of therapy, 581
  see also Psychoanalysis
Transference neurosis
  definition of, 582
  see also Narcissistic neurosis; Trans-
    formed neurosis
Transformed neurosis
  definition of, 582
  as transference illness, 582
  repetition-compulsive nature of, 582
  re-enactment of Oedipal situation in, 583
Transsexualism
  see Gender identity disorder
Transvestism
  definition of, 506
  confined largely to men, 506
  castration anxiety in, 507
  see also Paraphilias
Traumatic neurosis
  anxiety in, 160
  as massive amnesia without fugue, 275

Ulcerative colitis
  definition of, 526
  problems with aggression in, 526
  oral and anal fixations in, 526
  see also Psychosomatic disorder(s)
Unconscious
  definition of, 106
  instincts and drives never are, 124
  refers to ideas, 125
  intentions, 441, 626
  choice, 522
  willing, 534
  "upward drive" of, Freud, 577
  see also Consciousness
Undoing
  definition of, 213
  in obsessive-compulsivity, 215–219

Vicissitude
  definition of, 116
Vienna Psycho-Analytic Society, 115
Vitalism
  Brücke's rejection of, 10
  *see also* Teleology
Voyeurism
  definition of, 509
  Oedipal survivals in, 509
  *see also* Paraphilias

Wasting away
  in infancy, 29, 44
Waxy flexibility
  in catatonia, 422

*see also* Schizophrenia
Will
  in the use of libido, 9
  in Freud's first theory, 131
  in precipitating dissociative attacks, 272
  in the splitting of consciousness, 285
Withdrawal
  in drug use, 476
  *see also* Substance use disorder(s)
Word salad
  in schizophrenia, 421
  *see also* Neologism(s)

Zoöphilia, 507
  *see also* Paraphilias